ABC Etymological Dictionary of Old Chinese

ABC CHINESE DICTIONARY SERIES

Victor H. Mair, General Editor

The ABC Chinese Dictionary Series aims to provide a complete set of convenient and reliable reference tools for all those who need to deal with Chinese words and characters. A unique feature of the series is the adoption of a strict alphabetical order, the fastest and most user-friendly way to look up words in a Chinese dictionary. Most volumes contain graphically oriented indices to assist in finding characters whose pronunciation is not known. The ABC dictionaries and compilations rely on the best expertise available in China and North America and are based on the application of radically new strategies for the study of Sinitic languages and the Chinese writing system, including the first clear distinction between the etymology of the words, on the one hand, and the evolution of shapes, sounds, and meanings of characters, on the other. While aiming for conciseness and accuracy, series volumes also strive to apply the highest standards of lexicography in all respects, including compatibility with computer technology for information processing.

Other titles in the series

ABC Chinese-English Dictionary (desk reference and pocket editions)
Edited by John DeFrancis

ABC Dictionary of Chinese Proverbs
Edited by John S. Rohsenow

ABC Chinese-English Comprehensive Dictionary
Edited by John DeFrancis

A Handbook of 'Phags-pa Chinese
W. South Coblin

ABC Etymological Dictionary of Old Chinese

Axel Schuessler

University of Hawai'i Press
Honolulu

Printed in the United States of America
12 11 10 09 08 07 6 5 4 3 2

Library of Congress Cataloging-in-Publication data

Schuessler, Axel.
ABC etymological dictionary of old Chinese / Axel Schuessler
p. cm. — (ABC Chinese dictionary series)
Includes bibliographical references and index.
ISBN-13: 978-0-8248-2975-9 (cloth : alk. paper)
ISBN-10: 0-8248-2975-1 (cloth : alk. paper)
1. Chinese language—Etymology—Dictionaries—English I. Title. II. Series

PL1281.S38 2007
495.1'321—dc22 2005056872

University of Hawai'i Press books are printed on acid-free paper and meet the guidelines for permanence and durability of the Council on Library Resources.

Camera-ready copy prepared by the author.

Printed by IBT Global

CONTENTS

PREFACE

This etymological dictionary attempts to provide information on the origin of Old Chinese words, including possible word family relationships within Chinese and outside contacts.

When traditional Chinese scholars discuss "etymology" (*cíyuán* 詞源), they tend to debate the history and uses of Chinese characters and perhaps variant reading pronunciations, but not words. The present endeavor is an etymological dictionary which is concerned with the actual words of Old Chinese (OC), not with their graphic representations.

Pulleyblank (1991: 20) remarked that the compilation of a "proper etymological dictionary" of Chinese still lies in the future. In this sense, the future has not yet arrived and, for that matter, may never arrive, because many morphological mechanisms and morphemes are not understood. It is usually difficult to identify even the root or stem of a word, although this crucial question has been addressed by Sagart (1999). Often the best we can do is group words into word families (wf[s]) on the basis of phonological and semantic similarity.

A glance at an etymological dictionary for a well-studied and reasonably well-understood Indo-European language shows that even there, many, perhaps a majority, of the entries state outright that the etymology is "unknown" or "obscure" or the entry is qualified by such terms as "probably," "perhaps," "possibly," or "hardly." The history of Old Chinese is much less understood. Nevertheless, over the past decades our knowledge of Chinese and related Tibeto-Burman (TB) languages has progressed far enough that for many OC words some historical insights can be suggested. Frequently, different scholars have proposed competing etymologies; this work mentions some of these alternatives as long as they seem to hold some plausibility. As we gain more insights, one or another etymological suggestion may be confirmed or turn out to be untenable.

Of competing possible or plausible etymologies, the ones in this dictionary are justified by the phonological and morphological patterns and parameters set forth in the introductory chapters. Given the many open questions and multiple interpretations, fellow investigators will probably not find their favorite etymologies in these pages, as these are, of course, based on their particular reconstructions of Old Chinese and its etymological frameworks. To elucidate the history of a word, one looks for possible connections and relationships with other items. However, just as often, similar-looking words are not related. Sino-Tibetan (ST) proto-forms are generally not reconstructed because of many uncertainties. For example, it is obvious and virtually certain that *duǒ* 鬌 *tôiʔ 'hanging tuft of hair' is cognate to Written Burmese (WB) *twai*^{B} 'be pendant, hang', but we cannot tell if the ST source might have been *toi,*twai, *tol, *twal, or something else.

This work has been written also with the non-specialist, someone who is not familiar with Chinese linguistics, in mind. Therefore, conventional Chinese linguistic terms have on occasion been replaced with ones that are more easily interpreted by non-experts. For instance, the tones *píngshēng, shǎngshēng, qùshēng,* and *rùshēng* are identified by the letter symbols with which they are often marked in transcriptions, thus tone A, B, C, and D.

The lexical material on which this work is based is attested in Old Chinese texts from the Shang dynasty oracle bone inscriptions (ca. 1250–1050 BC) down through the Han period (ca.

200 BC–AD 200). In the compilation of this work, later items as well as modern dialect forms have been noted on occasion, and have been left in as gratuitous material; the reader who wishes for thematic purity can cross them out. Words for which there is no etymological information or hypothesis are generally not cited, as are, unfortunately, items overlooked or not recognized by this compiler. Occasionally tonal derivations are also ignored because they are often quite transparent, requiring no comment.

The present work has relied heavily on, and quotes accordingly, comprehensive works on languages of the area, including: Benedict 1972, *Sino-Tibetan Conspectus* (*STC*); N. C. Bodman 1980, *Chinese and Sino-Tibetan*; W. S. Coblin 1986, *A Sinologist's Handlist of Sino-Tibetan* (*HST*); I. Peiros and S. Starostin 1996, *A Comparative Vocabulary of Five Sino-Tibetan Languages* (*CVST*); J. A. Matisoff 2003, *Handbook of Proto-Tibeto-Burman*; R. Schafer 1974, *Introduction to Sino-Tibetan* (*IST*); Shī Xiàngdōng 2000, *Hànyǔ hé Zàngyǔ*; U. Unger, *Hao-ku*; Wáng Lì 1982, *Tóngyuán zìdiǎn*; Jenner and Pou 1980-1981, *A Lexicon of Khmer Morphology*; G. Diffloth 1984, *Dvaravati Old Mon*; and more detailed studies by many others. It is these informative sources which are quoted; reference is not systematically made to the scholar or work which should be credited with an etymology's origin, as these sources can be looked up in Jeon Kwang-jie 1996, *Etymological Studies of Sino-Tibetan Cognate Words*. This work has anticipated many an etymological proposal which, at the time unbeknownst to me, had already been made by others; may they claim credit who are entitled to it (I encountered many such in works by Gong Hwang-cherng and the dissertation of Barbara Geilich). A wealth of linguistic data from languages in Assam, SE Asia, and SW China has become available in recent years (e.g., Huáng Bùfán 1992, *A Tibeto-Burman Lexicon*). However, until these raw data are analyzed and protoforms or morphemic transcriptions developed, they are difficult to evaluate. They are therefore rarely quoted in this work. Reference is made not only to formal publications, but also to conference papers and personal communications, because these have provided many insightful or interesting suggestions relevant to the present endeavor.

A note on rhyme ~ rime. In the literature on Chinese linguistics, one often encounters the spelling 'rime' instead of 'rhyme' in reference to Chinese rime categories, rime tables, and the like. (A recent book is on Rime Tables, not Rhyme Tables.) This practice, started by Chao Yuen Ren in 1943, is followed here.

A note on the paragraphs starting with [E] (etymological connections). Is the connection with Sino-Tibetan or Tibeto-Burman languages, the relationship is genetic. With any other language family, we have to assume a loan relationship (also substrate or adstrate), the direction of borrowing is often not clear, although more material has apparently been absorbed by Proto-Chinese and Old Chinese than is customarily admitted.

The index of English glosses ('English Index') is hoped to be useful as a starting point for inquiries. But such an index has its limitations, because only a few words are selected, and because many vague definitions like 'ample' or 'brilliant' are not very instructive. Also, the index does not distinguish between homophones like wind vb. and wind n.

ACKNOWLEDGMENTS

This project has profited from conversations with, and suggestions and advice from, many scholars and friends, including the late P. K. Benedict, William Baxter III, Wolfgang Behr, W. South Coblin, Richard Cook, Gérard Diffloth, Barbara Geilich, Zev Handel, Gong Hwang-cherng, Victor Mair, Prapin Manomaivibool, James A. Matisoff, Martine Mazaudon, Boyd Michailovsky, Jerry and Stella Norman, Kathleen Nuzum, Martha Ratliff, Paula Roberts, Laurent Sagart, Jackson T.-S. Sun, Ken-ichi Takashima, Ulrich Unger, Anne Yue-Hashimoto, Zhu Ling, and many others. W. S. Coblin has kindly provided the forms for Early Ming and Yuan Mandarin, as well as his Han Dynasty transcriptional data, which have been taken into consideration for Later Han Chinese. James A. Matisoff has generously supported me by providing crucial books and material.

I am particularly grateful to an anonymous reader who made thoughtful suggestions and significant comments on a penultimate draft version. But the mistakes which are still in the following pages are this author's responsibility. Most of all, I wish to express my special gratitude and appreciation to Victor Mair for his encouragement and manifold generosity; it was he who arranged for the compilation of this work and secured financial support through grants from the Freeman Foundation and other sources.

ARRANGEMENT OF THE DICTIONARY

This etymological dictionary groups related words into word families (wf[s]), which are listed either under the most common member or under what appears to be the shortest and most basic word from which the others are thought to derive or to which they may be related. The head of a wf is not necessarily a common or well-known word. The reason for this arrangement is dictated by the etymological purpose of this work. Large wfs or somewhat speculative ones are broken up into smaller groups with cross-references.

The sections of the **Introduction** are not intended as a coherent narrative, but as a brief reference manual for the purpose of explaining and justifying the etymological groupings (word families, cognate sets) in the dictionary. The introduction presents morphological and phonological correspondence patterns so that readers may judge for themselves the degree of the plausibility of suggested etymological connections. Phonology and morphology are discussed together under the particular phoneme in question.

Dictionary entries make reference to these sections of the Introduction, preceded by the symbol § (e.g., "see §12.1").

Sample entry:

shuǐ 水 (świ^{B}) **LH** śui^{B}, S tśui^{B}, **OCM** *lhuiʔ, OCB *[l]huiʔ ?
'Water, river' [OB, Shi].
[T] *Sin Sukchu SR* ʂuj, ʂi (上), *PR* ʂi, *LR* ʂuj; *MGZY* shue (上) [ʂuɛ]; *ONW* śui
[D] PMin *tšui^{B}
[E] ST: TB *lwi(y) [*STC* no. 210] > JP *lui*^{33} 'to flow'.

FIRST LINE

pīnyīn transcription of Mandarin, followed by the Chinese character(s) *zì* 字. When no character exists (as is often the case with colloquial dialect forms) an empty box □ takes its place.

(...) Middle Chinese (MC) or Qièyùn system (QYS), ca. AD 600. See §12.1.

LH Later Han Chinese (also LHan) of the 1st and 2nd century AD. See §12.1.1. In the text, LHan is usually placed in brackets, thus [kɑ] = LHan kɑ unless otherwise identified.

S alternate Old South form of LHan, as revealed by later southern, usually Mǐn, dialects.

OCM Minimal Old Chinese form (starred items). See §12.1.2. For comparison, Baxter's OC (OCB) is ocasionally also supplied.

SECOND LINE

Gloss not a complete definition of a word. Glosses are mostly taken from, or are based on, Karlgren's *GSR*, Schuessler's *DEZ*, *Gǔdài Hànyǔ cídiǎn* 古代漢語詞典, edited by Chén Fùhuá 陳复華 (Beijing 1999), and the *Zhōngwén dàcídiǎn* 中文大辭典.

[...] in brackets, the **text** in which the CH word is first attested, e.g., [Shi] = occurs first in the text *Shījīng*, which implies that the word existed already by 600 BC or earlier. For abbreviations, see p. xvii ff.

THIRD LINE and subsequent lines

[<] shows the **morphological** derivation from its simplex.

[D] Chinese **dialect** forms; col. = colloquial form (bai 白), lit. = literary or reading form (wén 文). Dialects (actually Sinitic languages) are identified by location. See §12.1.3. Since many of them are not well known, the dialect affiliation is prefixed to the name of the location. These abbreviations are: G = Gàn, K = Kèjiā (Hakka), M = Mǐn, W = Wú, X = Xiāng, Y = Yuè (Cantonese), Mand. = Mandarin, P- = Proto-, as in PMin = Proto-Min, also CMin = Common Min.

[E] comments on **etymology**, especially foreign connections. When flush with the preceding gloss, it relates only to the preceding word; when flush with subentries (ꝏ allofams), it relates to the whole wf and its stem / root.

[N] introduces further **notes** or comments.

[T] **transcriptions** of the Chinese word; these are occasionally provided to show a word's later development (see §12.1):
Sin Sukchu or ***Sin S.*** (EMing = Early Ming period Chinese); *SR* 'standard reading,' *PR* 'popular reading,' *LR* 'left reading.'
MGZY = *Měnggǔ zìyùn* ('Phags-pa) of the Yuan (Mongol) period (1270–1308).
ONW(C) = Old Northwest Chinese from about AD 400, as interpreted by Coblin 1994. Occasionally Sui-Tang Chang'an (Coblin's STCA, ca. AD 640) and MTang (Middle Tang, ca. AD 775) forms are also added.

(...) the scholarly source, literature.

[...] the source of a foreign word without reference to etymological connection with Chinese. In the sample entry above, [STC...] indicates that the TB items are taken from Benedict's work, but he has not identified CH *shuǐ* as the cognate.

ꝏ 'cognate (to)' or '**allofam**' (fellow member in a word family).

<> 'related, cognate to' other languages, including ones from other language families, genetically or by loan; the direction of borrowing is not certain.

> 'developed into, becomes'.

< 'derives from an earlier form / from an earlier stage of a language'.

→ cross-reference to other dictionary entries. Less common pronunciations of a character can easily be located under a better-known cognate: thus *sì* 思 is not separately entered in the dictionary with a reference to → sī 思 because *sì* 思 can be found under its better-known simplex *sī* 思.

-> 'loaned to'.

<- 'borrowed from'.

SYMBOLS AND ABBREVIATIONS

□	no Chinese graph exists (for a dialect word)
ɜɛ	cognate, allofam, members of a wf within a language
<>	cognate(s), or loans between languages in either direction; separates forms cited from different language families
=	s. w. as = same word as
~	variant
>	develops into
<	derives from
[<]	introduces a morphological derivation, a derivative from
<-	borrowed from
->	loaned into
→	cross-reference
§	section / paragraph of the Introduction
a.	and
AA	Austroasiatic (languages)
AAS	Association for Asian Studies
abbr.	abbreviation(s)
acc. to	according to
AM	*Asia Major*
aux.	auxiliary (e.g., verb)
Běidà	Běijīng Dàxué: *Hànyǔ fāngyán cíhuì* 漢語方言詞匯
AN	Austronesian (languages)
BEFEO	*Bulletin de l'Ecole Française d'Extrême Orient*
BI	bronze inscriptions
BIHP	*Bulletin of the Institute of History and Philology* (Academia Sinica, Taiwan) (中央研究院, 歷史語言研究所集刊)
BMFEA	*Bulletin of the Museum of Far Eastern Antiquities*, Stockholm
BSLP	*Bulletin de la société linguistique de Paris*
BSOAS	*Bulletin of the School of Oriental and African Studies*, London
BTD	Han Buddhist Transcriptional Dialect (W. S. Coblin. ms)
BV	Bahing-Vayu languages (= Kiranti languages; Tibeto-Burman)
[C]	introduces comments on further cognates
CAAAL	*Computational Analysis of Asian and African Languages*
CH	Chinese
CDC	Common Dialectal Chinese (J. Norman's reconstruction)
CLAO	*Cahiers de Linguistique Asie Orientale*
cogn.	cognate
[D]	introduces Chinese dialect forms
DEZ	A. Schuessler, *A Dictionary of Early Zhou Chinese*
ditr.	ditransitive
E	east(ern); early
[E]	introduces etymological comments
EAC	Dobson, *Early Archaic Chinese*
EOC	Early Old Chinese, Shang and early Western Zhou
f. (ff.)	following page(s)
FY	(1) *Fāng yán* 方言 by Yáng Xióng 揚雄; (2) the modern journal *Fāngyán* 方言

G-	Gàn dialects
GSR	B. Karlgren, *Grammata serica recensa*
GY	Guǎng-yùn 廣韻: Yú Nǎi-yǒng 1974. *Hù zhù jiàozhèng Sòng běn Guǎng-yùn*
GYSX	Shěn Jiānshì 沈兼士. *Guǎngyùn shēngxì*
Hao-ku	Ulrich Unger, *Hao-ku. Sinologische Rundbriefe*
HCT	Li Fangkuei 1977, *A Handbook of Comparative Tai*
HJAS	*Harvard Journal of Asiatic Studies*
HK	Hong Kong
HOCP	William H. Baxter 1992, *Handbook of OC phonology*
HPTB	Matisoff 2003, *Handbook of Proto-Tibeto-Burman*
HST	W. South Coblin 1986, *A Sinologist's Handlist of Sino-Tibetan Lexical Comparisons*
ICSTLL	International Conference on Sino-Tibetan Languages and Linguistics
id.	idem (the same as above)
intr.	intransitive
IG	indo-germanisch ('Indo-European')
IST	R. Shafer, *Introduction to Sino-Tibetan*
J(.)	Journal
JA	*Journal Asiatique*
JAOS	*Journal of the American Oriental Society*
JAS	*Journal for Asian Studies*
JCL	*Journal of Chinese Linguistics*
JCLTA	*Journal of the Chinese Teachers' Language Association*
JDSW	*Jīngdiǎn shìwén* 經典釋文 by Lù Démíng 陸德明
JGWZ	Lǐ Xiàodìng 李孝定, *Jiǎgǔ wénzì jíshì* 甲骨文字集釋
JIES	*Journal of Indo-European Studies*
JP	Jǐng-pō 景頗 (a Tibeto-Burman language)
JR	rGya-rung = Jia-rong (a Tibeto-Burman language)
JWGL	Zhōu Fǎgō 周法高, *Jīnwén gǔlín (bǔ)* 金文詁林 (補)
K-	Kèjiā (Hakka) dialects
K.	Kachin (a Tibeto-Burman language close to or identical with Jing-po)
Kan.	Kanauri (a Tibeto-Burman language of the Himalayan branch)
KC	Kuki-Chin languages (Tibeto-Burman)
KN	Kuki-Chin-Naga languages (Tibeto-Burman)
KS	Kam-Sui languages
KT	Kam-Tai languages
LAC	Dobson, *Late Archaic Chinese*
LB	Lolo-Burmese languages (a Tibeto-Burman branch)
LB-M	Matisoff's reconstruction of LB
lg. (lgs.)	language(s)
LH, LHan	Later Han Chinese
LL	*Language and Linguistics* 語言暨語言學 (Academia Sinica, Taipei)
LOC	Later Old Chinese (Zhànguó)
LTBA	*Linguistics of the Tibeto-Burman Area*
Lush.	Lushai (a Tibeto-Burman language of the Kuki-Naga branch)
M-	Mǐn dialects
Mxx	Middle xx (e.g., MM = Middle Mon)
MC	Middle (or ancient) Chinese (ca. AD 600)
MGZY	*Měnggǔ zìyùn*
MK	Mon-Khmer languages

MKS	*Mon-Khmer Studies*
MM, MMon	Middle Mon (an Austroasiatic language)
MS	*Monumenta Serica*
MSOS	*Mitteilungen des Seminars für Orientalische Sprachen*
MY	Miao-Yao (Hmong-Mian) languages
MZYW	*Mínzú yǔwén* 民族語文
[N]	introduces further notes
n.	noun
Oxx	Old xx (e.g., OC = Old Chinese)
OB	Shang dynasty oracle bone inscriptions
OC	Old (or archaic) Chinese
OCB	Old Chinese, Baxter's reconstruction
OCM	Minimal Old Chinese, see §13.1
OE	*Oriens extremus*
OL	*Oceanic Linguistics*
OM	Old Mon (an Austroasiatic language)
ONW(C)	Old Northwest Chinese ca. AD 400 (W. S. Coblin, *Old Northwest Chinese*)
P	Proto
p. c.	personal communication
PCH	Proto-Chinese
perh.	perhaps
PLB	Proto-Lolo-Burmese (= 'Lolo-Burmese,' LB)
PMin	Proto-Min (J. Norman's reconstructions)
poss.	possibly
prob.	probably
PTai	Proto-Tai
PTib.	Proto-Tibetan
PVM	Proto-Viet-Mong languages
PWA	Proto-Western-Austronesian
PWMiao	Proto-Western-Miao
QY	*Qièyùn* 切韻
QY(S)	Qieyun system, i.e., MC (or 'ancient Chinese') reconstructions
S.	Siamese
Siam.	Siamese
Skt.	Sanskrit
Sōrui	Shima Kunio 島邦男, *Inkyo bokuji sōrui* 殷墟卜辭綜類
SSYP	*Sì shēng yùnpǔ* 四聲韻普 by Liáng Sēngbǎo
ST	Sino-Tibetan
STC	Paul K. Benedict, *Sino-Tibetan: A Conspectus*
SV	Sino-Vietnamese
sv.	stative verb
SW	Xǔ Shèn 許慎, *Shuōwén jiězì* 說文解字
SWJZGL	Dīng Fúbǎo 丁福保, *Shuōwén jiězì gǔlín* 說文解字詁林
s. w. as	same word as
[T]	introduces transcriptional forms
TB	Tibeto-Burman
TSR	James A. Matisoff, *The Loloish Tonal Split Revisited*
Tib.	Tibetan
tr.	transitive
vb.	verb

Viet.	Vietnamese
W	west(ern)
W-	Wú dialects
WB	Written Burmese
wf(s)	word family (families)
W(r)	Written-
WT	Written Tibetan
WTib.	Western Tibetan dialects
X-	Xiāng dialects
Y-	Yuè dialects (Cantonese)
YWYJ	*Yǔwén yánjiū* 語文研究
YYWZX	*Yǔyán wénzì xué* 語言文字學
Zang-Mian 1992	Huáng Bùfán 黃布凡 et al., *Zàng-Miǎnyǔ zú yǔyán cíhuì* 藏緬語族語言詞匯
ZGYW	*Zhōngguó yǔwén* 中國語文
ZM92	short for *Zang-Mian* 1992 (Beijing)
ZWDCD	*Zhōngwén dàcídiǎn* 中文大辭典

1

OLD CHINESE AND ETYMOLOGY

1.1 Chinese

Old Chinese (OC = 'archaic Chinese', *Shànggǔ Hànyǔ* 上古漢語) is the language of texts and documents from the beginning of writing, around 1250 BC, to the Hàn period. See §12.1.2 for the characteristics of the OC language as well as for its subsequent stages: Later Han Chinese (LH, LHan), ca. 2nd–3rd cent. AD; Old Northwest Chinese (ONW) of ca. AD 400; Middle Chinese (MC = 'ancient Chinese', *Zhōnggǔ Hànyǔ* 中古漢語) of about AD 600, which is widely quoted as a reference for historical phonological categories; and later transcriptions of Chinese. The different stages of written Chinese probably represent koines which are not necessarily descended from one another in a straight line (§1.3). Modern dialects (more properly Sinitic languages), including Mandarin, have evolved over centuries and millennia. The most archaic group of these languages is the Mǐn dialects, which had split off from the mainstream during the Qín and Hàn dynasties (§12.1.3).

1.1.1 Sources of Old Chinese

The earliest records of the Chinese language are the oracle bone inscriptions (OB) of the Shāng 商 dynasty from c. 1250–1050 BC. From the subsequent Western Zhōu 周 period (1050–770 BC) have survived not only hundreds of inscribed bronze vessels (BI), but also the older parts of the *Shījīng* 詩經 (*Book of Songs*), parts of the *Shūjīng* 書經 (*Book of Documents*), the old parts of the *Yìjīng* 易經 or *Zhōuyì* 周易 (*Book of Changes*), and the *Yì Zhōushū* 逸周書. Literary records gradually increase in volume and variety after the end of Western Zhōu with the beginning of the Spring and Autumn period (Chūnqiū 春秋 722–481 BC), the Warring States period (Zhànguó 戰國 403–221 BC), Qín 秦 (221–206 BC) and Hàn 漢 (206 BC–AD 220) dynasties. The literary sources are abbreviated as in Karlgren's *GSR* (see Appendix C). Complete information on all the early Chinese texts is conveniently available in Michael Loewe, ed. 1993.

1.2 Old Chinese and its linguistic neighbors

The eastern half of the China of today's political maps, including the provinces Yunnan, Sichuan, and Gansu, is, and has been, rich in linguistic diversity with several language families: Sino-Tibetan (ST) with its Sinitic (Chinese = CH) and Tibeto-Burman (TB) branches, Kam-Tai (KT), Miáo-Yáo (MY = Hmong-Mien), and Austroasiatic (AA). In adjacent areas are spoken Austronesian (AN) and Altaic languages; at one time the Indo-European (IE) Tocharians were China's western neighbors (Pulleyblank 1983; Norman 1983: 6ff).

No language lives in a hermetically sealed sphere. "Whatever their genetic affiliation, the languages of the East and SE Asia area have undergone massive convergence in all areas of their structure — phonological, grammatical, and semantic" (Matisoff *HPTB:* 7). Throughout the millennia, prehistoric and early historic "Chinese" had interacted with speakers of other languages. An expanding and magnetic state and civilization attracts and absorbs other populations and their languages; compare, for instance, the situation in early China with that of ancient Italy where Latin absorbed words and features from Central Italian IE languages. Thus

Latin has two words for 'red': *rufus* and *ruber.* The latter reflects the regular Latin development from IE, while *rufus* was absorbed from another Italic language.

Outside influences on the Chinese language have long been noted. M. Hashimoto (1976; 1984) draws attention to foreign substrate influence in the syllable structure and tone systems of modern Chinese dialects which agree with Tai and Miáo-Yáo languages in the south, while words become more polysyllabic and tones fewer in number as one moves northward in the direction of China's polysyllabic, atonal Altaic neighbors. The modern Yuè dialects have been shown to include a Tai substratum (Yue-Hashimoto 1976; R. Bauer 1987), Mǐn dialects an Austroasiatic (AA) one (Norman / Mei 1976; Norman 1983; Mei 1980). Mei Tsu-lin and J. Norman have collected AA loan words found in Old Chinese literature, while other items have long been thought to be of Miáo-Yáo and Tai origin (Bodman 1980). Therefore it should be no surprise that the vocabulary which we encounter in the earliest Old Chinese writing, the oracle bone and bronze inscriptions, includes many non-ST words.

Over the years, proposals have been made to connect Chinese genetically with other language families in the area, particularly (Kam-)Tai, Miáo-Yáo (Hmong-Mien), and even as far removed as Austronesian and Indo-European. Genetic relationship to language groups other than TB have, for the purposes of the present work, not yet been convincingly demonstrated, or are so remote and controversial as to be of little practical value for the understanding of Old Chinese. Shared linguistic features and vocabulary with languages other than TB are therefore treated here as borrowings in one direction or the other. Relationships and contacts with other languages will be treated briefly below.

1.2.1 *Chinese and Sino-Tibetan*

Chinese and Tibeto-Burman (TB) languages are descended from a hypothetical Sino-Tibetan (ST) proto-language (Benedict *STC*; Thurgood / LaPolla, eds. 2003; Matisoff *HPTB*; and others). TB proto-forms are reconstructed on the basis of languages which extend from Tibet in the west to Burma and SE China in the east. Among these, Tibetan and Burmese play a prominent role because they have long written traditions and are well documented; they are therefore extensively cited in the literature and convey, rightly or wrongly, the impression of particularly close historical ties to OC. (For a list of Chinese dialects and classification of TB and other languages, see Appendices A and B.)

ST languages agree in fundamental ways in their phonology, lexicon, and morphology. This dictionary includes numerous examples of the shared OC–TB (i.e., ST) lexical stock. OC and TB phonology and morphology will be compared and discussed throughout this introduction (§2–§12). The reader will get the impression that OC (at least as reconstructed within Baxter's framework) does not look very different from TB reconstructions and shares much of its morphology (prefixes, suffixes, etc.). Syntax is, however, quite varied among ST languages; thus in Chinese, the qualifier is placed before the qualified element whereas Written Tibetan, for example, reverses the order, e.g., OC *dà* ('great') *wáng* ('king') 'great king' vs. WT *rgyal-po č^hen-po* ('king / great'); WT agrees in this regard with many other East Asian languages. Nevertheless, given the agreement in the remaining three areas of phonology, lexicon, and morphology, this does not disprove a genetic relationship.

The cleavage of ST into a Sinitic and TB branch rests on a hypothetical ST vowel *ə which has been retained in OC, but has merged with ST *a in TB. There are occasional hints, however, that the TB proto-language might also have made this distinction (*STC* p. 183, n. 482). Innovations unique to CH do not establish a fundamental split in the ST family, they only distinguish the Sinitic branch from other TB branches and from languages like Lolo-Burmese or Tibetan. Such Sinitic diagnostic items include the split of syllables into high vs. low types (later reflected in the Qièyùn system's [MC] division III vs. I/IV; see §12.1); this looks like the split into lax vs. tense register in MK languages (Ferlus 1998). To some words which end in an open syllable in TB, and elsewhere, a final *-k is added, thus TB *(b)rya* vs. *bǎi* 百 OCM *brâk '100'. Universal PTB *(s)mrul ~ *(s)brul ≭ CH *huǐ* 虫虺 (xjwei[B]) *hm(r)uiʔ (< *hmrulʔ) already has been replaced on the OB by *shé* 蛇 (dźja) *m-lai as the common word for this creature.

1.2.2 Tibeto-Burman languages

TB languages are found today in some isolated pockets in SW China; the speakers are referred as *tǔ-jiā* 土家 'locals'. This shows that TB speakers lived in ancient times in the vicinity of the Xià and Shāng states. Especially the Qiāng 羌 neighbors of Shāng China to the west have probably been TB, as well as the Róng 戎 in Shanxi (Pulleyblank 1983: 416ff). Since Chinese absorbed loans from KT, MY, and MK languages, we can expect loans from TB also. These are difficult to detect, though, because they would probably look like ST cognates. A likely TB loan is the word for 'tea', *chá* 茶 (ḍa) *d-la; it likely goes back to the Loloish word *la 'leaf', unless the CH word was directly borrowed from an AA language, ultimately the source of the Loloish word.

1.2.3 Miáo-Yáo

Miáo-Yáo (苗瑤 MY = Hmong-Mien) languages form, for our purposes, their own language family, unrelated to Chinese and ST. The vocabulary of MY languages includes a large number of Chinese words, borrowed at different periods and from different dialects (notably Yuè), but also loans from TB (Benedict 1987) and AA (Forrest 1948; Haudricourt 1966).

Today, MY settlements are scattered over wide areas of southern China and Southeast Asia. It is suspected that the people in the ancient state of Chu spoke MY languages (Pulleyblank 1983: 423ff), among others, because words of MY origin show up in the text *Chǔcí* (Songs from the Chu area) of the Han period (Schuessler 2004).

A MY loan, for example, is *xiǎng* 饟餉 (śjaŋ[A/B/C]) *nhaŋʔ/h 'bring food to' (workers in the field), 'to eat', from MY: Anc. Miao *n̥on[C]* 'cooked rice, food', Yao: Biao Min *ṇaŋ[5]*, Mien (Chiang Rai dial.) *ṇhaaŋ[5]*, Dzao Men *nɔŋ[5]*.

1.2.4 Tai-Kadai, Kam-Tai

Kam-Tai languages (KT) are not related to Chinese and ST (Dài Qìngxià 1991). Massive lexical exchanges in both directions between Chinese and Tai, from OC to more recent dialects, have led some investigators to conclude otherwise. In the distant past, people speaking these languages likely lived in areas as far north as the Yangtze River basin. For example, the ruling family of the ancient state of Chǔ 楚 had the clan name *xióng* 熊 'bear', but in the Chu language the name was *mǐ* 芈, which is the KT word for 'bear'. Today, though, KT people live farther to the south in Guǎngxī, Guìzhōu, and southern Húnán (Pulleyblank 1983: 429ff).

There have been significant exchanges of vocabulary in both directions between MK (including Viet-Muong) and Tai languages; Lao especially has many loan words from its Vietnamese neighbor. Tai languages also have relatively recent Khmer loans, an earlier layer of loans from Mon, and loans from an even older Northern AA language that today is represented by Khmu and that the Tai must have overlain at some early date (Ferlus 1978:

13–14, n.22). Consequently, some alleged Chinese–Tai lexical sets turn out to be spurious, the Tai words being loans from Khmer or elsewhere. For example, Siamese *suan*^{A1} 'garden' has nothing to do with → *yuán* 園 *wan 'garden', but is borrowed from Khmer *swna* /sùuən/ 'care for, look after > flower / pleasure garden'. Or consider Tai *luaŋ* 'royal'; it reflects the Khmer word *luəŋ* 'king' and has no (direct?) connection with Chinese → huáng 皇 'august, royal'.

An example of a KT word in OC is *chán* 廛 *dran 'farm, farmyard', from Tai: Siamese *rɨan*^{A2} < *rɨan^{A}, Kam-Sui (PKS) *hraːn^{1} 'house'.

1.2.5 Austroasiatic

The Austroasiatic (AA) language family is unrelated to ST and Chinese. AA languages fall into two major groups: Munda (exclusively on the Indian subcontinent); and Mon-Khmer (MK) scattered over Assam, Southeast Asia, and SW China and includes the Mon language in Burma, and Khmer in Cambodia. As only MK languages could have left traces in China, the terms MK and AA are often synonymous here.

AA loans have been identified in TB languages such as Lepcha (Forrest 1948) and in languages in Assam such as the Tani group (J. Sun *LTBA* 16:2, 1993: 165); AA lexical material is also encountered in Lushai (in this dictionary), in the TB Kanauri-Almora language Raji (Sharma 1990, vol. III, part II: 170–228), as well as transparent Khasi loans in Mikir. MK influence in Old Chinese and ST has also received some attention (Shorto 1972; Ferlus 1998; *LTBA* 22:2, 1999: 1–20; Schuessler 2003; 2004; studies by Norman and Mei). Languages from at least two AA branches or layers have contributed to prehistoric and perhaps early historic Chinese: an early Viet-Muong language similar to Vietnamese (that may be called 'Viet-Yuè') (§1.2.6) and a language (or languages) in the Yellow River basin that shows affinities to the modern Khmer and Khmu branches of MK, and on occasion also to Mon (§1.2.7).

Purely historical and philological considerations also point to the prehistoric and early historic presence of AA in parts of northern China. The ancient Yí 夷 people, who lived in the east from the Shandong peninsula south to the Yangtze, were probably AA (Pulleyblank 1983: 440ff). The ancient Yuè 越 people in Zhèjiāng were certainly AA; the place Lángyé 琅琊 in Shandong was their traditional cultural center (*Yuè juè shū;* Eberhard 1968: 414ff).

Under the year 645 BC, the *Zuǒzhuàn* quotes a line from the famous *Yìjīng* where we find the AA word for 'blood', *huāng* 衁 *hmâŋ (PAA *mham or the like) substituted for the usual ST etymon *xuè* 血 (Mei 1980). The deliberations in which context this line is quoted and apparently understood by all participants took place north of the Yellow River in today's Shanxi. *Huāng* cannot have been a CH innovation, rather it must have been a survival from an earlier substrate language that was replaced by a ST layer, i.e., 'Chinese' as we know it.

When pursuing OC and TB / ST etyma down to their apparent roots, one often seems to hit AA bedrock, that is, a root shared with AA.

1.2.6 Vietnamese

In addition to the significant influx of Chinese loans from antiquity to more recent times, Vietnamese has incorporated a large contingent of Tai words (Maspero 1912: 115). A language close to Vietnamese was spoken in SE China as late as the Han period by the ancient Yuè 越粵 people (Yuè OC *wat, the 'Viet' in Vietnam); it left a residue of Viet-Yuè words in the modern Min dialects in Fújiàn province (see articles by Norman and Mei, also quoted in Schuessler 2004). Early Chinese commentators have stated that the words *zhá* 札 'epidemic' and *sōu* 獀 'dog' are from the ancient Yuè language (Pulleyblank 1983: 438f), but these might have come from "northern" AA instead (see §1.2.7); Han period scholars merely noted the similarity with the Yuè words of which they happened to be aware. Unlike the later Mǐn dialects, OC does not include many words that compel us to conclude that the source was specifically Viet-Yuè.

1.2.7 "Northern" Austroasiatic

An AA substrate ("AA-OC") contributed a significant number of AA words as well as fragments of AA morphology to prehistoric and subsequent CH (§2.6; §5.10). MK words gradually trickled from a substrate into mainstream ST-based OC over hundreds or thousands of years, so that layers and various MK sources can be discerned.

The earliest, prehistoric layer of AA items is already encountered in the language of the first written records, the OB (1250–1050 BC); OC borrowings from this remote past occasionally do not agree very closely with MK phonologically (though in a regular fashion). For example, *chú* 芻 *tshro 'hay' vs. PMonic *ksɔɔy (cf. below), *hǔ* 虎 *hlâʔ 'tiger' vs. PMK *klaʔ.

More "recent" items (found in BI, *Shījīng*, and then later texts) agree more closely with AA forms, e.g., *cuò*$_1$ 莝 *tshôih 'hay' vs. PMonic *ksɔɔy (cf. above), *jiāng* 江 *krôŋ 'river' vs. PMonic *krooŋ. Many such OC words appear to be very similar to Khmer. This does not mean that the MK substrate was Khmer, but only that Khmer happens to have preserved (and / or scholars happen to have provided) data that provide suggestive comparisons with OC, just as the great number of Tibetan – OC comparative sets reflect more on the availability of Tibetan data, but not necessarily on a close historic relationship.

1.2.8 Summary

The OC lexicon has many sources (Schuessler 2003). A few sample ST vs. non-ST words follow, to provide an impression (for details and explanations consult the dictionary entries):

Animals:

- ST words: 'ox' gāng 犅, 'dog' quǎn 犬, 'rhinoceros' xī 犀, 'horse' mǎ 馬, 'fowl' yàn 鴳 (quail), 'louse' shī 虱, 'muntjac' jǐ 麂
- Non-ST words: 'elephant' xiàng 象, 'dog' gǒu 狗, 'buffalo' sì 兕, 'chicken' jī 雞, 'tiger' hǔ 虎, 'pig' tuàn 彖, 'pig' shǐ 豕, 'small deer' zhì 廌

Body parts:

- ST: 'head' yuán 元, 'head' shǒu 首, 'eye' mù 目, 'hair' shān 髟, 'fem. breast' rǔ 乳, 'bitter / liver' xīn 辛, 'forehead' é 額, 'blood' xuè 血
- Non-ST: 'gall' dǎn 膽, 'forehead' sǎng 顙, 'blood' huāng 衁

Others:

- ST: 'root' běn 本, 'forest' lín 林, 'firewood' xīn 薪, 'house' jiā 家, 'temple' zōng 宗, 'day' rì 日, 'year' nián 年, 'breath' xī 息, 'eat / meal' cān 餐
- Non-ST: 'root' gēn 根, 'forest' lù 麓, 'palace' gōng 公宮, 'farm' chán 廛, 'temple' miào 廟, 'moon' (goddess) héng-é 姮娥, 'year' rěn 稔, 'breath' qì 氣, 'eat / meal' xiǎng 餉

Numerals and grammatical words generally are ST:

- 'two' èr 二, 'copula' wéi 惟, 'behind' hòu 後

Of uncertain provenance:

- 'Wood' mù 木, 'mountain' shān 山, 'flower' huā 花

1.3 Old Chinese dialects

Languages which are spread over large areas and mountainous terrain naturally develop regional varieties; stratified societies also exhibit differences in speech along class lines. The OC language of the Shang and Zhou period and subsequent Classical Chinese was a standardized written language without noticeable regional flavors. The Chinese script would have hidden differences in pronunciation that might have existed, just as today 日 'day' is read *rì* in Mandarin, *jɐt* in Cantonese.

Yet one catches a few glimpses of language variation within OC when comparing the *Shījīng* 詩經 rimes, the phonetic series and the later Middle Chinese (MC) as reflected in the *Qièyùn* 切韻 dictionary (AD 601) as well as modern dialects.

First, in the *Qièyùn* and modern dialects, as well as in the OC phonetic series there are certain words with the OC analogue rimes *-eŋ such as *míng* 名 'name' which had in the *Shījīng* the rime *-in. The ST rimes *-iŋ / *-ik became either *-eŋ / *-ek or *-in / *-it in OC; which way a word went depended presumably on the dialect. Thus we find for ST *-iŋ / *-ik the OC rime *-eŋ / *-ek: *míng* 名 'name', *míng* 鳴 'to sound', *mìng* 命 'order', *shēng* 生 'live'; but *xīn* 薪 'firewood', *jí* 堲 *tsit 'masonry'.

1-1	ST	Later South	QYS / MC	Shijing
not	--	--	*bə > bù 不	*bə > bù 不
not	*ma	***ma**	--	--
not have			*ma > wú 無	--
not have			--	*maŋʔ > wǎng 罔
name	*r-miŋ	*miaŋ	*meŋ > míng 名	***min** 名
dark	*miŋ		*mêŋ > míng 冥	*mêŋ > míng 冥
night	(MK maŋ)	***maŋ**	*mêŋ > míng 冥	*mêŋ > míng 冥
green	*C-seŋ	***tsʰaŋ**	*tshêŋ > qīng 青	*tshêŋ > qīng 青
green			*tshâŋ > cāng 滄	*tshâŋ > cāng 滄
mother	*mo		*môʔ > mǔ 母	***mə̂ʔ** > mǔ 母
go-between	MK dməj		*mə̂ > méi 媒	*mə̂ > méi 媒

Secondly, OC labial-initial syllables of the type *Pə and *Po merged into *Pə in the *Shījīng* dialect(s) and the phonetic series, but remained distinct in the *Qièyùn* and modern dialects (Baxter 1992); for example, we have the Mandarin readings *měi* 每 'each' vs. *mǔ* 母 'mother' (same phonetic, same *Shījīng* rime). Finally, a strain of OC must have retained ST *ma in the meaning 'not' because it is preserved in modern southern dialects, but does not exist in Shang and Western Zhou texts, apart from an occasional occurrence in classical texts. Table 1-1 illustrates these and additional differences within OC.

Choice of words in individual texts often shows particular preferences that may be due to dialects. For example, in the *Zuǒzhuàn* 左傳 we find the interrogative *xī* 奚 *gê 'how' instead of *hé* 何 *gâi. In some chapters of the *Shūjīng* 書經 the words for 'you' and 'your' are *rǔ* 汝 and *nǎi* 乃 respectively; in others, the word for both 'you' and 'your' is *ěr* 爾. Later texts replace words common in earlier ones, e.g., the OB, BI, and some parts of the *Shījīng* and

Shūjīng have the word *wǎng* 罔亡 *maŋʔ for 'not have, there is no'; only near the end of the Western Zhou period is it replaced by the familiar *wú* 無 *ma.

These and similar phenomena suggest a language that is far from uniform, but we cannot tell whether these are individual preferences, or class or regional distinctions, nor if the latter, from which regions.

1.3.1 Rural dialects

Additional phonological oddities in OC may also be the result of dialectal differences. MC and, by backward projection, OC, has multiple phonological correspondences for what one surmises ought to be a single OC phonological configuration. Words with rare and unusual features typically have meanings with a rustic or vulgar flavor. We will, therefore, for now call this strain (or strains) 'Rural' as opposed to 'Standard', i.e., literary OC.

The following phonological peculiarities may be identified as Rural:

(1) OC voiceless initials *r-, *l-, and *n- are normally reflected in MC coronal t^h-, *śj-*, and, in the case of *r-, in MC $ṭ^h$-, t^h- (§5.1). However, in a few words such a voiceless continuant has yielded MC *x-*, *xj-*, and its equivalents in modern dialects. This unexpected development to a guttural initial is found in words that relate to ordinary, especially rural, life; they include words for: beard, to face / toward, ribs (of a horse), to know, to vomit, to rear animals, stupid, to roar, tiger, pig (§5.6). To differentiate the two developments of voiceless initials, we will write OCM *lh-, *nh-, *rh- for MC t^h-, *śj-*, etc., but OCM *hn-, *hl-, *hr- when it is the aspiration that survives as MC *x-*. Of course, voiceless *hŋ-, *hm-, and *hw- regularly yield MC *x-*, thus any voiceless initial that shows up as *x-* in MC is written in OCM with the *h- preceding the sonorant.

(2) Standard OC and foreign initial *l- (> MC *ji-*), or *l in the initial, have in some words merged with *r- (> MC *l-*). This might be another Rural feature; examples in §7.3 include: salt, turtle, grain / to sow, bamboo. The *l = Rural OC *r equation is often encountered in loans from non-ST languages, e.g., eel, splint hat, barrier / bolt, descend, frost; or the confusion of laterals may be due to the late date of borrowing in either direction.

(3) Some non-ST words with initial *kl- have MC initial *t-* which may have been *tl- in OC. Such words include:

Carry dān 擔 [tɑm] 'to carry on the shoulder'
<> AA: Khmuʔ *klam* 'carry on the shoulder'

For more examples and comments, see §8.2.1.

(4) MC initial *ḍj-* and *ṭj-* stand in a few correspondence sets for a foreign initial *r*, or *r* in combination with labial or velar consonants (§7.1.4). The semantic range of such items conjures up a rural sphere: farm, pheasant, old man, to fall, bamboo, sickle, wrist, etc.

(5) Some modern southern dialects have in their colloquial layers the vowel *a* for standard *e*. This trend seems to be foreshadowed in some OC words which have the vowel *a* also for foreign *e* or *i*; see Table 1-1 above, and §11.1.3.

1.4 The study of Old Chinese etymology

A Chinese word may have one of several origins: (1) It can have been inherited from the hypothetical Sino-Tibetan proto-language when it has cognates among the related Tibeto-Burman languages. (2) It can be a loan from another language, or can have survived from an earlier substrate (Miáo-Yáo, Kam-Tai, Austroasiatic / Mon-Khmer). (3) It can be the result of internal innovation, i.e., word derivation by morphology, internal borrowing from dialects, or phonological change.

A word is usually assumed to be genetically related to another because of transparent or impressionistic phonological and semantic similarity. The range of sound alternations within an OC wf will be suggested throughout the introductory sections. Members of a wf, i.e., 'allofams' (Matisoff's term, alias 'cogeners') typically differ in tone, initial voicing (e.g., *kêns 'to see' ꭗ *gêns 'appear'), and / or the Middle Chinese division (*děng* 等, i.e., vocalism, e.g., MC *kâŋ* vs. *kjaŋ*; see §9.1). Occasionally, they also differ in the vowel, in initial consonant(s) or final consonant. Since much concerning ST and Chinese morphology is still not well understood, the terms 'wf' and 'allofam' are often fuzzy but conventional catch-all categories. For example, it seems obvious that the words *jiàn* 監 *krâms 'look at' and *lǎn* 覽 *râmʔ 'to see' are related, but what the difference in later tones and the presence / absence of an initial *k- might have entailed is so far a matter of speculation. On the other hand, we can confidently state that *zhì* 織 *təkh or *təks, literally 'something that has been woven', is a regular exopassive derivation from *zhī* 織 *tək 'to weave'. We consider both *jiàn* and *lǎn*, and *zhī* and *zhì* to be allofams in their respective word families.

1.4.1 *Approaches to word families and cognates*

Investigators have differed significantly over the range of sound alternations within a word family. Karlgren (1933) allows for a broad range: a word family could have a final of the type -K, -T, or -P, etc. in conjunction with the initial consonant type K-, T-, N-, or P-, etc. where T- includes any acute initial consonant, i.e., any which is not a guttural or labial. For instance, his wf with items 242–262 (1933: 69) has a root T-K and includes the following words (Karlgren's 'archaic Chinese', i.e., OC; in parentheses OCM):

> yáng 陽 *di̯aŋ (*laŋ) 'light' ꭗ zhāo 昭 *ȶi̯og (*tau) 'bright' ꭗ zhòu 晝 *ȶi̯ôg (*trukh) 'day time' ꭗ xīng 星 *sieŋ (*sêŋ) 'star'

In this proposed wf, the OC initials, as understood today (Baxter), are *l-, *t-, *s-; the vowels are *a, *au (OCB *-aw), *e, *u; the finals are *-ŋ, *-k, *-V (vowel). The TB cognate for *yáng* is *laŋ (e.g., WB *laŋ*^{B} 'be bright'), *zhòu* is clearly cognate to WT *gdugs* (< *g-duk-s*) 'midday, noon'. These two TB items are certainly not related. Therefore, Karlgren's phonological parameters are much too broad.

Cognates usually share the same rime and initial consonant type. However, in many instances an obvious cognate has a different final or rime, or initial variation outside the normal spectrum. LaPolla (see §6) has dedicated a study to ST rimes and finals. In order not to go off in all directions, investigators prefer to keep to a given rime and allow the initials to vary, or keep to one category of initials and then allow for variations in finals. Wáng Lì (1958: 542–545) provides examples for both approaches: same initial but different rimes (such as the negatives with initial *m-), and same rime but different initials (such as rime *-aŋ 'bright'). Or note a wf proposed by Pulleyblank (1973: 121) (traditional MC forms in parentheses): *róu* 柔 (ńźjəu) ꭗ *ruǎn* 耎 (ńźjwän^{B}) ꭗ *nuò* 懦 (ńźju, ńźjwän^{B}, nuân^{C}) ꭗ *ruò* 弱 (ńźjak), all meaning 'soft', but he has not included *rěn* 荏 (ńźjəm^{B}) 'soft'. Wáng Lì (1982) splits this particular group into one with a tendency toward final velars, and one with final dentals. Thus the set *rù* 茹 (ńźjwo^{B}) ꭗ *ruǎn* 耎 (ńźjwän^{B}) ꭗ *nèn, nùn* 嫩 (p. 571) is distinct from *róu* 柔 (ńźjəu) ꭗ *ruò* 弱 (ńźjak) ꭗ *ròu* 肉 (ńźjuk) 'meat, flesh' (p. 236). As long as we do not know more about OC morphology, we cannot tell if distinctions in this wf are due to morphological derivation, dialect interference, or to convergence in which the initial *n-* would be associated with 'soft', just as words with initial *gl-* typically suggest something 'gliding, glossy' in English (§2.9).

1.4.2 Approaches to etymology through the graph

The above approaches start with the OC word while the graph that writes it is of secondary concern. However, approaching etymology from the other end by emphatic reliance on the graph is fraught with the danger of misinterpretation or overinterpretation. This leads occasionally to "strained explanations of loangraph meanings as semantic extensions" (Qiu Xigui 2000: 287); it has been suggested, for example, that *lái* 來 'wheat' and *lái* 來 'to come' are the same word ('wheat' is the cereal that 'came' from abroad), but the two are unrelated. Boodberg (1937: 339–341) went so far as to suggest that even graphic elements that are nearly universally recognized as semantic and not phonetic play a phonological and etymological role; for example, he believes that graphs written with the element *zì* 自 derive from a root *BDZi ~ *BSI: *zì* 自 'self', *bí* 鼻 'nose', *xī* 息 'breathe'.

The traditional source for the interpretation of ancient graphs is Xǔ Shèn's *Shuōwén jiězì* (SW) of ca. AD 150. But this is explicitly a dictionary of graphs, not words; it often describes a graph, which is not the same as an etymological explanation. For example, the SW (and also *GSR* 1166c) explains *jiǎo* 烄 [kau^B] 'burn on a pyre of crossed logs' as cognate to *jiāo* 交 [kau] 'to cross'. But the definition 'burn on crossed logs' could well have been suggested by the graphic element 'to cross'; therefore the word may have had just the meaning 'to burn' and be related to relevant TB items, but not to 'to cross'. Xǔ Shèn also was unaware of the earlier forms of graphs as they are known today from the OB inscriptions; he was inadvertently misled by the graphic forms available at his time. Thus he explains the left element in the graph for *shè* 射 'to shoot' as *shēn* 身 'body'; the *shēn* element, however, goes back to the OB image of a bow with an arrow (Qiu Xigui 2000: 55f).

We study the phonetic series and composition of graphs with interest because they often offer etymological clues, but two words are not a priori assumed to be etymologically related just because they share a phonetic element. In the end, every one of the above approaches contributes to interesting discoveries.

1.4.3 Identification of cognates

Beside morphological patterns which are discussed throughout the introduction, the following considerations also help in the identification of etymological connections (see also §2.10). Matisoff's *Conclusion* to his *HPTB* (pp. 535–542) could be quotes here in full as well.

Semantic parallels strengthen the case for the identification of etymological relations. For example, since *jīng* 京 'capital city' also means 'mound, hill', it is likely that *qiū* 丘 'village, town' is also the same word as the homophone *qiū* 'mound, hill'. Settlements are often built on higher ground.

Cognates from related TB languages sometimes help identify connections within Chinese. For example, 'naked' *luǒ* 裸 *roiʔ, and *chéng* 程 *dreŋ are probably cognate to such forms as PTB *groy > WT *sgre-ba*, and WT *sgren-mo* 'naked', Lushai *ṭeen*^R 'bare', respectively. As the TB items derived from the same root, Chinese forms may have as well (*chéng* from PCH *(d)roi-ŋ ?).

On the other hand, the correct identification of cognates is sometimes impeded by one or another type of interference or obstacle, as follows.

Etymological investigation is hampered or helped by the *investigator's native language* and culture. A native speaker of Chinese would with little hesitation, and probably correctly, equate *yá* 芽 'sprout' with *yá* 牙 'tooth', while this connection might not be self-evident to speakers of European languages.

The *composition of a Chinese character* interferes occasionally with the semantic understanding of the word behind it (see also §1.4.2). *Yú* 餘 'leftover, rest' is usually thought to mean originally 'food leftovers' because it is written with the radical *shí* 'to eat'. Yet the radical may have been chosen because concrete food leftovers were easier to represent graphically than the abstraction 'remainder, rest'. Thus 'food leftovers' is merely one semantic extension of the word.

The Chinese writing system is not alphabetic, although a phonetic element in the majority of graphs provides some clue for a word's OC sound. But there is disagreement on some details of *OC reconstruction*, especially about the initial consonants. Depending on whose OC system one follows, one may arrive at startlingly different etymologies; for example, *wéi* 維 (MC *jiwi*) 'to be' is reconstructed *rəd by Li Fang Kuei who relates this then to WT *red-pa* 'to be', but reconstructed *wjij by Baxter, which turns out to be related to PTB *wəy 'to be'. Our investigations are based on Baxter (1992), many uncertain details notwithstanding.

Variant forms are common occurrences in *dialects*, i.e., *bái* 白 'colloquial' vs. wén 文 'literary' forms, such as Mandarin col. *tā* 他 'he, she, it' vs. lit. *tuō* 'other'. These are lexically two different words but historically one and the same etymon, no ablaut morphology derived one from the other. This phenomenon is so ubiquitous in China that one might expect this to have occurred already in ancient and archaic times.

Subjective judgment slips into etymological consideration easily because of the monosyllabic nature of the words (countless words have the syllable structure CV) and the often diffuse and fuzzy field of meanings that Chinese words and graphs have accumulated over millennia. Even when the meaning is specific or when the syllable structure is complex, it is occasionally difficult to decide what is related to what. Two illustrations:

(1) *Tóu* 頭 *dô 'head' agrees exactly with TB-PL *du 'head' (PLB *u = PTB, ST *o). But it agrees equally well with a MK etymon: note Khmer /dool/ 'head'; a MK final consonant is often lost in OC after a long vowel, hence the equation is also perfect. Which is related to Chinese? Are both CH and PL descended from MK?

(2) *Chǎn* 產 *srân or *srên 'to produce' strikes one as the obvious cognate of WT *srel-ba* 'to raise, bring up'. The Chinese word even has a counterpart with initial *m- in the word *miǎn* 娩 *mran 'give birth', thus forming a well-known ST pair *s- (transitive / causative) ~ *m- (intr.). But then Khmer has a word /sɑmraal/ (i.e., *s-m-raal) 'to give birth', derived from *rāla* /ríiəl/ 'to increase, ... distribute, propagate'. On the one hand, Chinese is closely related to Tibeto-Burman; on the other, Mon-Khmer provides a possible etymology for both OC words, i.e., a root from which the items in question could be derived, while there is no TB counterpart to *miǎn*. Is the Chinese wf ST or AA? Or do both Chinese and WT go back to the same area etymon?

1.4.4 The present approach

The present approach to OC etymology tends to diverge from most others in two respects.

First, linguistic givens tend to override graphic representations and their phonological impli- cations when the choice of a phonetic element in a graph is unusual in light of MC and other data. Phonological patterns and changes do normally follow their own immutable rules; but why over 3000 years ago a certain graphic element was chosen to write a certain word was up to the whim of a writer (see more in §12.1.2). Thus *zhuī* 隹 OCM *tui (*GSR* 575; OCB *tjuj) 'a bird' was selected to write 'to be' which could have been due to all kinds of mental processes and associations. MC *jiwi* points to OC *wi 'to be'; PTB *wəy (or *wi?) 'to be' confirms this. Thus the comparative method as well as MC point to OC *wi and nothing else, notwithstanding the initial *t- in the phonetic element.

Second, phonological identity, or variation supported by well-documented correspondence patterns (hence the introductory chapters), tend to override the expectation for identical meanings in comparative sets, as long as the semantic disparity has a plausible explanation. Thus → jí 疾 *dzit 'be sick' is the same word as *jí* 堲 *dzit 'detest; burn, torch'; both belong to a ST etymon *tsik (apparently 'to smolder') with the semantic range 'burn (in a smoldering fashion), angry, detest, be in rut, feverish, sick'. Conversely, Chinese *kǒu* 口 *khôʔ 'mouth' is not cognate to PTB *m-ka = WT k^ha 'mouth' because the vowel correspondence is highly unusual.

Our reliance on phonological correspondence patterns occasionally leads to the conclusion that words are related even though they look superficially quite different. *Zhì* 雉 MC $ḍi^B$, OCM *driʔ 'pheasant' is the direct and regular cognate of PTB *rik 'pheasant', because OC *-ʔ is one regular equivalent of PTB *-k, and MC *ḍ-* (OC *dr-) for foreign *r- also has compelling parallels.

We usually follow sinological traditions in setting up certain OCM forms. 'Dog' *quǎn* 犬 MC k^hiwen^B is thus OCM *khwə̂nʔ (similar to Karlgren). However, there is no old rime which might have indicated the exact OC vowel, but TB *kwi (not *kwa or the like) and the fact that MC *-ien* can just as well derive from OC *-in makes it almost certain that the word was really OCM *khwînʔ.

2
MORPHOLOGY AND WORD DERIVATION

Comments and discussions on morphology and morphemes are divided between this chapter, which provides a broad overview, and later chapters and sections, which deal with specific phonemes and morphemes.

2.1 Grammatical relations in Old Chinese

OC has *no inflectional morphology;* all morphology serves the purpose of deriving *new words* from stems or other words (Beard 1998: 44ff; Aronoff and Anshen 1998: 239). A word's grammatical role is determined (1) by its position and use in a sentence and (2) by its inherent word class.

2.1.1 Word order

OC word order is SVO (subject — verb — indirect object — direct object; the few exceptions have no bearing on etymology and do not concern us); the modifier stands before the modified element, as in English ('green grass', 'incredibly bright'). In OC and all Sinitic languages, as well as others in the area, any part of speech can be placed in front of the sentence as its topic. Thus the context (be it textual or cultural) requires that in the sentence *rì shí zhī* 日食之 (sun / eat / it), for example, *rì* 'sun' is not the subject but the topic so that the sentence means 'as for the sun, (something) ate it' (i.e., there was a solar eclipse).

2.1.2 Word class

OC word classes are morphologically unmarked. Their definition and demarcation has occasioned much debate because the categories have fuzzy edges. What may appear to be a noun can often behave like a verb, etc. However, some broad categories are generally recognized; they are determined by a word's meaning and typical place in a sentence. "Typical" usage is predictable by the word class — or vice versa. The word 'to see' is a transitive verb because it typically occupies the verbal position in a sentence followed by an object. Without an object, it has an intransitive or passive meaning given its implicit transitive nature. There are other ways of looking at classification. Thus Cikoski (*CAAAL* 8, 1978: 17ff; *CAAAL* 9, 1978: 133 ff) divides verbs into "ergative" and "neutral" (or "direct") which by and large seem to overlap with the conventional categories "transitive" and "intransitive" respectively.

The meaning of a word, even as reflected in the English gloss, usually implies its inherent word class, and therefore the latter is not explicitly remarked upon in this dictionary.

Here follow the broad word class categories:

Noun (n.)

— 'dog' is an obvious noun because it refers to a thing and typically functions as subject or object in a sentence. Abstract nouns form a subcategory; they frequently behave like verbs. When a noun functions as an intr. verb (ex. 1: *jūn* 'lord'), it means "to behave in a way that a noun typically behaves or is expected to behave"; a noun as a tr. verb (ex. 2: *hàn* 'drought') means "to treat the object like that noun" (Boltz *JAOS* 119.1, 1999: 222).

(1) *Jìn Líng gōng bù jūn* 晉靈公不君 (Jin / Ling / duke / not / ruler n.) 'Duke Ling of Jin does not behave like a ruler' (i.e., is expected to) [Zuo: Xuan 2, 4].

(2) *dì wéi hàn wǒ* 帝隹暵我 (god / to be / drought n. / us) 'God is the one who causes us drought' [OB, Hayashi 1.25.13].

Ditransitive verb (ditr.)

— Verbs for *give, receive, tell, show* typically have an indirect and / or a direct object, as their meanings imply. The word order is subj. – verb – indir. obj. – direct obj. (ex. 3: *yǔ* 'to give'); often, the order is subj. – verb – dir. obj. – *yú* 於 'preposition' + indir. obj. (ex. 4: *wèn* 'to ask about').

(3) *gōng yǔ zhī yì* 公與之邑 (duke / give / him [ind. obj.] / town [dir. obj.]) 'The Duke gave him towns' [Zuo: Xiang 27: 5].

(4) *wèn Kǒngzi yú Zǐlù* 問孔子於子路 (ask about / Confucius [dir. obj.] / prepos. / Zilu) 'he asked Zilu about Confucius' [Lunyu 7, 19].

Transitive verb (tr.)

— is followed by an obj. (exs. 5, 7). In a sentence without an obj., the latter is either implied, or the verb is used intransitively (ex. 8: *tīng* 'listen'), or the verb is passive when followed by the agent in a prepositional phrase (ex. 6: *jiàn* 'see, visit').

(5) *Mèng-zǐ jiàn Liáng Huì wáng* 孟子見梁惠王 (Mengzi / see, visit / Liang / Hui / king) 'Mengzi (saw) paid a visit to King Hui of Liang' [Meng 1A, 1].

(6) *tō rì jiàn yú wáng* 他日見於王 (other / day / see / prep. / king) 'Another day, he was (seen) received by the king' [Meng 2B, 4].

(7) *tìng mìng* 聽命 (listen to / order) 'They (listened to) received an order' [Zuo: Xiang 8, 4].

(8) *shì zhě jiàn, bù tìng* 侍者諫不聽 (attendants / part. / remonstrate / not / listen) 'His attendants remonstrated (with him); he did not listen' [Zuo: Xiang 7, 10].

Causative and putative uses are rare with a transitive verb. The tr. vb. *yì* 衣 *ʔəih 'to wear' (ex. 9) is used as causative in ex. 10:

(9) *yì yī* / *ʔəih *ʔəi 衣衣 (wear / clothes) 'They wore clothes' [Yi Zhouzhu 37, 9].

(10) *zài yì zhī tì* 載衣之裼 (then / to dress / them [ind. obj.] / wrappers [dir. obj.]) 'Then they dressed them [the babies] in wrappers' [Shi 189, 9].

Intransitive verb (intr.)

— fills a verbal position without an object (ex. 14: *sǐ* 'to die' intr., and *zhǎng* intr. used as an adjective). But intransitive verbs can take oblique objects such as 'the place to/at', for example (some examples are taken from Gabelentz):

(11) *sǐ zhī* 死之 'to die for it' (the city) [Zuo: Xuan 13, 5].

(12) *sǐ fú rén suǒ* 死夫人所 'to die in the palace of the princess' [Hanfei 4,14b].

(13) *rù dà shì* 入大室 'enter the main hall' [frequently found in BI].

When an intr. verb is followed by a direct obj., the meaning is causative (ex. 15: *zhǎng*) or putative (ex. 17).

(14) *zhǎng zǐ sǐ yān* 長子死焉 (grow intr. / son / to die intr. / there) 'My eldest son died there' [Meng 1A, 5].

(15) *zhǎng wǒ yù wǒ* 長我育我 (grow intr. / me / raise tr. / me) '(My mother) let me grow up and raised me' [Shi 202, 4].

Stative verb (sv.)

— functions like an intr. verb (ex. 16: *cháng*), or modifies a noun (*zhǎng* in ex. 14). These often correspond to English adjectives and numerals. When a sv. is followed by an obj., the meaning is usually either caus. (ex. 15) or put. (ex. 17 *yuǎn*); however, the verb can also behave like a regular intr. or tr. verb: Gabelentz (p. 333) lists verbs that include *hòu* 後 'be after, behind' > tr.vb. 'to follow behind', > caus. (factitive) 'to place behind'.

(16) *dào zǔ ér cháng* 道阻而長 (road / be difficult / part. / be long sv.) 'the road is difficult and long' [Shi 129, 1].

(17) *bù yuǎn qiān lǐ ér lái* 不遠千里而來 (not / be far sv. / thousand / miles / part. / come) 'You have not considered a thousand miles too far to come' [Meng 1A, 1].

Copula or link verb
— 'to be', 'to be not', 'be like', etc. The word order is A - vb. - B.

(18) *yú wéi xiǎo zǐ* 予惟小子 (I / to be / small / child) 'I am a young person' [Shu 27, 9].

(19) *dì wéi hàn wǒ* 帝隹暵我 (god / to be / drought n. / us) 'God is (the one) who causes us drought' [OB, Hayashi 1.25.13].

(20) *bái mǎ fēi mǎ* 白馬非馬 (white / horse / to be not / horse) 'A white horse is not a horse' [Gongsun Longzi 2].

Particle (part.)
— 'not' (see *bù* 不 'not' in examples above), interrogative particle *ma* 嗎, etc.

2.1.3 Derivation and word class

A word can belong to up to four different grammatical / lexical layers. Let us consider the sv. *cháng* 長 'be long' in this sentence:

(1) ... *yǐ cháng wǒ wáng guó* ...以長我王國 (thereby / be long / I, my / king / state)
'... thereby (make long, lengthen) perpetuate my, the king's, state' [Shujing 39, 24].

(a) *Syntactically, cháng* fills the position of a **transitive** verb, i.e., it is followed by an object.
(b) *Grammatically, cháng*'s function is **causative** because it is an intr. sv. with an object.
(c) *Lexically,* the word *cháng* 'be long' belongs to the **stative verb** class (sv.).
(d) *Etymologically, cháng* is an **endopassive** derivation from *zhāng* 張 'to stretch' (see §4.1.1–2 for definitions).

The usages and properties (a) to (c) are usually unmarked in OC, whereas morphology applies only to word derivation (d). However, these different levels often coalesce and are irrelevant in practice. In §2.1.2 ex. 5, *jiàn* 見 tr. 'to see, visit' is a transitive verb on all levels; since it is not a derivation, the etymological level does not apply. *Xiàn* 現 with a MC voiced initial is said to be the intransitive of *jiàn*; however, *xiàn* is not the grammatical intr. as in 'the eyes are seeing' (which would be expressed by word order as in *mù jiàn* 目見), but it is a new endopassive word 'to appear' (§4.6) as in

(2) *zhāo mù xiàn* 朝暮見 (morning / evening / to appear intr.) '(the official) appeared mornings and evenings' [Mengzi 2B, 6].

In IE languages, where derivation usually effects a change in word class or grammatical properties, we find also instances where word class has no connection with its derivational morpheme. The English word 'a painting' belongs to the word class noun, although it is etymologically an inflectional verb form as in 'be painting' (Beard 1998: 60).

2.2 Types of derivations and allofams

The morphemic and / or phonemic distinctions within a wf can have several types of explanations in ST languages:

(1) Distinction based on identifiable, meaningful morphemes or morphological processes, e.g., *zhì* 織 *təkh < *təks 'what is woven' is derived from *zhī* < *tək 'to weave' with a passive-forming suffix *-s (tone C); or WT *skor-ba* 'to surround' < *'*k^h*or-ba* 'to turn round' with the transitive s-prefix; or endopassive voicing of the initial in *xiàn* 現 *gêns 'to appear' < *jiàn* 見 *kêns 'to see' (§4.6). Here we may include the fusion of two known words, e.g., *fēi* 非 *pəi 'it is not' < *bù* 不 *pə 'not' + *wéi* 惟 *wi 'to be'; or WT *sbrul* 'snake' < *ša* 'flesh' + PTB *b/mrul (but *s-* is already a prefix for all practical purposes).

(2) Distinction due to morphophonemic change whose function is (so far) not understood, such as the final *-k in *zhī* 隻 *tek 'single' ꭗ *zhǐ* 只 *teʔ 'only'; or WT k^h*a* 'bitter' ꭗ k^h*ag* 'difficult'; or 'hundred' *bǎi* 百 *prâk vs. PTB *brya; or the *b-* in WT *bse* 'rhinoceros'.

(3) The cause for the differentiations in wfs may lie outside of CH and belong to the parent language; in unrelated languages, they have been introduced from the outside with the loan / substrate word. For example, *xiāng* 纕 *snaŋ 'belt, sash' < MK: Khmer *cnaŋ* 'rope, belt' derives from Khmer *caŋ* 'to bind, tie'. Here the *n* in the OC initial represents a MK nominalizing infix which is unknown in ST and OC; the initial *s- in *xiāng* is not an OC / ST prefix, even though it looks like one.

(4) Distinction due to dialect divergence, including that between colloquial vs. literary styles. Thus (colloquial) Mandarin *tā* 他 'he, she, it' is the same etymon as the literary word *tuō* 'the other'.

(5) The reasons for the distinctions are as yet unknown; allofamic relationships can be due to any or all the above, plus others, for example (MC after the graph):

	qiáng	強	(gjaŋ)	'be strong'
ꭗ	qiǎng	彊	(gjaŋ^B)	'make an effort, compel'
ꭗ	qíng	勍	(gjɐŋ)	'strong, powerful'
ꭗ	jìng	勁	(kjäŋ^C)	'strong'
ꭗ	háng	行	(ɣâŋ)	'strong, vigorous'
ꭗ	gěng	梗	(kɐŋ^B)	'strong'

Additional kinds of changes which are often encountered in wfs are alternations in the MC divisions, especially div. III vs. others (§9); and 'vowel change', sometimes called 'Ablaut' (§11.1.2).

Since OC morphological processes have so far been difficult to understand, word family relationships have been the best one could offer (Karlgren, Wáng Lì). The present work will attempt to bring more precision to the study of etymology by suggesting, when possible, morphological explanations for allofams. This is the purpose of this and the subsequent introductory chapters.

2.3 Sino-Tibetan morphology

2.3.1 The nature of Sino-Tibetan affixation

Affixes in TB languages and OC are prefixes, or pre-initials, and suffixes. There are no infixes in the Austroasiatic or Austronesian sense, but for possible exceptions, see §2.7 and §7.5. Affixes are attached to a root or a stem, which is often another word. We assume here that a ST / OC root can have a shape ranging from a simple CV (even V?) to a complex CCVC (*tu, [*fia?], *sri, *kruk) (Sagart 1999 has a simpler theory). The difference between stem and root is often not obvious or is nonexistent, thus *tuŋ may look like a root in CH, but comparisons with

TB may show it to be a stem belonging to *tu. Since every root can serve as a stem, we will generally use this latter term.

Most of the affixes in OC also have counterparts in TB languages; they are therefore of ST heritage. Most are unproductive in OC.

The term 'pre-initial' is used for 'prefix' by some when the morpheme has no discernible meaning, even though it may have a function. Thus WT *s-* is a transitive prefix; the meaning of the WT prefix or 'pre-initial' *g-* in *gsum* 'three' is not clear, but it still has a function in word derivation (*gsum* vs. *sum*); the *b-* in WT *bse* 'rhinoceros' has no discernible function, although it is phonologically treated as a prefix. We will use the term 'prefix' because many a 'pre-initial' may well be an as yet unidentified 'prefix' in the stricter sense; after all, 'prefix' literally means something (anything) 'attached in front' of a word (Yves Duhoux, *JIES* 26, 1998: 5). At least some prefixes in area languages may have started as full words in compounds, but have over time been simplified. Thus the TB 'animal prefix' *s-* derives from *ša 'flesh', and *m-* from *mi* 'human being'; or note MK: Khmu *klɲaʔ* 'resin', where the prefix *kl-* is short for the word *kɔ̆l* 'tree'.

TB prefixes tend to fall away in compounds, e.g., WT *gsum* 'three' and *bču* 'ten', but *sum-ču* 'thirty'; *sñiŋ* 'heart', but *ñiŋ-kʰu* 'heart, spirit'; or Mikir *-piʝo* (*p-ja) 'bee', but *ʝò-hōj* 'wasp' (Grüßner 1978: 36; for many examples from Jingpo [JP], see Dai Qingxia / Wu Hede 1995). Since these pre-initials are removable, they may vary from language to language and branch to branch, thus 'five' is *l-ŋa in WT, but *b-ŋa in other branches of TB. We should not expect a given prefix to have existed in every branch of ST. In this work we assume that they were not present in OC unless there is evidence to the contrary within Chinese. For example, in PTB *m-sin 'liver': we cannot tell if there ever was a pre-initial in the CH cognate *xīn* 辛 *sin 'bitter', and therefore we must assume that there was none; the meaning 'bitter' would, in fact, speak against the 'human' m-prefix.

2.3.2 Sino-Tibetan morphemes

Most OC morphemes are ST because they also occur in TB languages. Unger (*Hao-ku* 20–21, 1983) has identified over 200 OC items with MC tone C (final *-s/-h) which show similarity with the PTB suffix *-s (§4.2.1). A few examples may illustrate the survival of ST morphological distinctions in OC by providing two or three parallel cognate forms from OC, WT, WB, or Lushai. In Tables 2-1 to 2-5 we note a ST suffix *-s (OC *-s / *-h) with a past / passive meaning (ex. 2-1; §4.4); the same suffix in 2-5 (there OC *-h, Lushai *-ʔ < -h) with a transitive

2-1	Form 1	Form 2
OC	zhī 織 *tək 'weave'	zhì 織 *təkh 'what is woven, cloth'
WT	'tʰag < *ɴtak 'weave'	tʰags < *taks pf. 'woven, cloth'

2-2	Form 1	Form 2
OC	zhǐ 只 *teʔ 'only'	zhī 隻 *tek 'one, single'
WT	--	gčig 'one'
WB	tʰiᴮ < TB *te (?) 'single'	tac < *tik < TB *tek (dek?) 'one'

2-3	Form 1	Form 2
OC	kǔ 苦 *khâʔ 'bitter, difficult'	--
WT	k^ha 'bitter'	k^hag 'difficult'
WB	$k^h a^B$ 'bitter'	k^hak 'difficult'

2-4	Form 1	Form 2
OC	shí 食 *m-lək 'eat'	sì 食 *s-ləkh caus. 'to feed'
TB	*m-ljak 'to lick, eat'	*s-ljak caus. 'to feed'

2-5	Form 1	Form 2	Form 3
OC	cí 慈 *dzə 'loving'	zì 孳字 *dzəh 'breed'	zǐ 子 *tsəʔ 'child'
WT	mdza'-ba 'to love'	--	ts^ha-bo < *tsa 'grandchild'
WB	ca^A 'have tender regard for'	--	sa^B 'son, offspring'
Lush.		*faʔ/h 'feed baby'	*faaʔ 'child'

connotation (§4.3); a ST final *-k of unknown function (ex. 2-2, 2-3); a ST causative s-prefix, and perhaps also an m-prefix (ex. 2-4; §5.2; 8.1.3); and a morphological role of voicing of initial consonants (ex. 2-5; §4.6).

2.4 Morphemes in Old Chinese

2.4.1 Historical layers of morphemes in Old Chinese

Derivational morphemes or their traces in OC and MC belong to one of three identifiable historical layers:

(1) The oldest, and unproductive, morphemes have survived in words inherited from the ST parent language; these morphemes are typically part of words that have direct TB cognates, e.g., prefixes such as introvert *m- and extrovert *s- (§8.1.4; Table 2-4 above).

(2) A middle layer belongs to Proto-Chinese (PCH); it is represented by segmental morphemes of ST origin, which were, however, not any more productive in OC. Since this layer has hardly any TB cognate words with these ST morphemes, the OC words in question cannot have been inherited from ST; they must have been produced between ST and OC, i.e., PCH.

(3) The youngest layer was still productive or at least transparent in OC; the source of its morphological features (later reflected in MC tones and voicing) was also ST. This system requires a more detailed discussion (see Chapter §4).

2.4.2 Suffixes in Old Chinese

Segmental suffixes, that is, those which can still be identified as MC phonemes, are indistinguishable from final consonants which belong to a stem; they can be identified only on etymological grounds. These suffixes were productive no longer in OC; they belong to the PCH or ST layer. For more details, see §6. Here we will draw attention to a few of them to illustrate their survival in OC.

Suffix -n (1)
marks nouns, either as derivation from another word, or redundantly attached to a noun. E.g., *jīn* 津 'a ford' is a noun derived from *jì* 濟 'to ford'. The ST root *kwi (> PTB *kwi) 'dog' is obviously nominal, yet Chinese adds this nominal *-n*, thus *quǎn* 犬. Suffix *-n* is a ST inheritance because it is also found sporadically in TB languages, e.g., WT *rkun* 'thief' < *rku* 'to steal'. However, this ST suffix must have been productive only during some phase of Proto-Chinese because there are hardly any OC – TB cognate sets with this suffix: OC has no final *-n* counterpart to WT *rkun*; conversely, *quǎn* occurs only in CH, i.e., there are no final *-n* forms in TB. Furthermore, suffix *-n* in *jīn* has been attached to an AA stem (§6.4.3).

Suffix -n (2)
stands for the third person pronoun after certain auxiliary verbs (prepositions), thus *yān* 焉 'at it' < *yú* 於 + *-n* 'be at'; *yú zhī* 於之 'at it' is ungrammatical and does not occur in OC. This suffix is a PCH innovation, perhaps the result of a fusion of the preposition with a pronoun with initial *n-*. Several non-ST languages in the area have such pronouns, and one occurs also in Mandarin (*nà* 那), though not in OC (§6.4.5).

Suffix -ŋ
derives a terminative word from a simplex. This is a ST / PCH morpheme, e.g., *wáng* 亡 *maŋ 'to lose' (< 'get to not have') < *wú* 無 *ma 'not have' (§6.5.1).

Suffix -t
is a ST morpheme, productive in Proto-Chinese, which typically marks natural objects; it is often found redundantly attached to nouns, e.g., *xuè* 血 *hwît 'blood', *yuè* 月 *ŋot 'moon' (§6.2.1).

Suffix -k
forms distributives, a Proto-Chinese innovation: *mò* 莫 *mâk 'none, no one' < *wú* 無 *ma 'there is no' (§6.1.2).

2.4.3 Sino-Tibetan prefixes in Old Chinese

The most conspicuous among ST prefixes in OC are *s- and *m-. The ST and PCH s-prefix is reflected in MC in several ways, including these three (for additional details, see §5).

(a) MC *s-* < OC *s-, MC ṣ- < *sr- from a PCH s-prefix or preinitial, it occurs before OC sonorant initials, most typically *n-, *ŋ-, and *r- (as MC ṣ-) (§5.2.1)
(b) MC *zj-* before OC *l-, *j- and *w- (§8.1.2)
(c) MC voiceless consonants from OC voiceless sonorants (see §5.1)

Three functions of the ST s-prefix can be identified:

Prefix s- (1)
creates *causatives* (§4.3.1; §8.1.2):

Feed   sì 食 (zjɨ[C]) *s-ləkh 'to feed' < caus. of shí 食 (dźjək) *m-lək 'to eat'

Prefix s- (2)
forms *iteratives* (§5.2.3):

Seven   qī 七 *tshit < *snhit ? 'seven', lit. 'two again'
<> PTB *snis 'seven' < ST *nis 'two'

Prefix s- (3)
marks common *nouns* (§5.2.4):

Fire huǒ 火 (huâi^B) *hməiʔ < ST *smey, OTib. *sme* 'fire'

Louse shī 虱 (ṣjɛt) *srit < ST *srik 'louse', PTB *s-rik (*s- is not the 'animal prefix' in this word, at least not in OC; see §5.2.4).

MC *zj-* and initial voicelessness often have direct cognates with s-prefix in TB languages. Words with these initials, therefore, include material directly inherited from ST and belong to the oldest morphological layer in CH. However, words with MC initial *s-* (from earlier s-prefix) hardly ever have TB counterparts. Therefore, the ST *s- was still a productive morpheme in PCH which explains (a) its occurrence in uniquely CH words, and (b) its survival as MC *s-* because its meaning remained transparent. For example:

Lose sàŋ 喪 *smaŋh 'to lose, destroy' < wáng 亡 *maŋ 'to lose'

This OC *sâŋh < *smaŋs with the survival of initial *s-* seems to be a more recent, more transparent causative creation than

Neglect huāng 荒 *hmaŋ 'neglect, reject' < wáng 亡 *maŋ 'to lose'.

New PCH nouns with the MC *s-* include

Frost shuāng 霜 *sraŋ 'hoarfrost' < liáng 涼 *raŋ 'cold'.

ST *s- is well attested in WT and other TB languages as a causative, directional or intensive marker (*STC* 105–108; Sun Hongkai *LTBA* 22:1, 1999: 183–199) and has been identified as such in OC (among others Mei 1985: 334–343; 1989; Baxter / Sagart 1998: 53). In WT the s-prefix changes intr. verbs into tr. ones, e.g., *'gyur-ba* 'change, become' intr. > *sgyur-ba* 'cause to change, transform' tr. (Beyer 1992: 116). This function includes the formation of verbs from nouns, e.g., JP *mjiŋ*^{33} 'name' > *ʃə*^{31}*-mjiŋ*^{31} 'to name' (more JP examples in Dai / Wu 1995: 95). Later in PCH and OC, causatives were formed with the exoactive tone C (§4.3), and eventually in OC and later, simply by word order (§2.1.2).

It has been suggested that causativity and intensive / iterative are two aspects of one original morpheme as, for example, in Indo-European languages where both are expressed by the same suffix *-éyo- (W. Lehmann 1993: 168), as in Greek words ending in *-éō* like 'make tremble' (Palmer 1980: 266), or Vedic Indic *patáyati* 'flies about' vs. *pātáyati* 'causes to fly' (A. MacDonell 1916: 195), with the Skt. iterative / causative morpheme *-ya-*. However, for practical purposes, the two functions are distinct in CH.

Prefix *m-
is a ST morpheme which tends to mark introvert / intr. verbs, which contrast with ST *s- for causative / extrovert verbs (Matisoff *LTBA* 15:1, 1992). It survives in the rare initial MC *dźj-* (LH ź-) from earlier *m-l-. This m-prefix, apparently already unproductive in PCH, is very old because in OC we usually observe direct TB cognates with this morpheme, even in contrasting pairs (see above; §2.3.2, Table 2-4; §8.1.4).

2.4.4 Infixation

OC and ST had no infixation. An exception may be OC medial *r which derives causative verbs (§7.5), e.g., *chù* 黜 [ṭʰut] *-rut 'to expel' < *chū* 出 [tśʰut] 'to come out'. It is not certain whether this *r was an infix or prefix. If the source was ST, it may be related to the r-prefix as found in WT; alternatively, some MK languages have a causative r-infix. Since *chū* was prob.

OCM *k-hlut, it is difficult to imagine what a cluster with *r might have sounded like.

2.5 Parallel roots and stems

A difficulty in TB and ST historical linguistics and reconstruction is the frequent existence of two or more stems or words with similar meaning and similar phonological shape (examples below). They are difficult to reconcile by known phonological or morphological processes, even though they look like members of a wf. This is also the case in other language families in the area, including MK about which Shorto (1973: 375) observes: "... it is noticeable that within the general range of meanings encountered in each of the three series [i.e., word families that he discusses] there is only limited agreement between the specific meanings assigned to a given variant or derivate in different languages. This implies a marked tendency to semantic shift in phonaesthetic series, a tendency which would itself help to explain the retention of variants as distinct lexemes in individual languages."

Pending further insights, we will assume parallel roots and stems for ST (Shorto's variants and derivates) and individual branches and languages to account for the occurrence of not quite homophonous stems which are distributed rather erratically over CH and TB languages (Matisoff 1978, esp. p. 21). Since CH has often inherited these parallels from the ST parent language, their etymology cannot be uncovered within OC. As in MK, parallel stems often differ in vowels (a ~ e/i), in the presence or absence of medial *r, or both. Examples include (also in §11.1.2–3; throughout Matisoff 1978):

ST *sriŋ 'live' (→ shēng$_2$ 生) ~ ST *siŋ 'alive, green' (→ qīng$_1$ 青)
~ ST *sraŋ 'live' (WB hraŋ) ~ ST *saŋ 'alive, green' (→ cāng$_3$ 蒼)
ST *saŋ 'clear' (WT saŋ) ~ ST *seŋ 'clear' (→ qīng$_2$ 清)
OC ān$_1$ 安*ʔân 'calm' ~ OC yàn$_1$ 宴燕 *ʔêns 'be at ease'
ST *(r)wa 'rain' (→ yǔ$_3$ 雨) ~ ST *(r)we 'rain' (→ yǔn$_2$ 隕殞霣)
ST *ka 'solid' (→ gù$_1$ 固) ~ ST *kar 'solid' (→ gù$_1$ 固)
ST *traŋ (?) 'stretch' (→ zhāng$_1$ 張) ~ WT t^haŋ 'id.'
WB *kruik 'meet with' ~ WT k^hug-pa ~ k^hugs-pa 'to find, get'
JP kruʔ^{55} < kruk^{55} 'to sprout' ~ JP kuʔ^{55} < kuk^{55} 'id.'
JP kroʔ^{55} < krok^{55} 'to hatch' ~ kòu 鷇 *khôkh 'chick' (→ gǔ$_{14}$ 穀)
OC chù$_4$ 畜 *hruk, *rhuk 'nourish' ~ jú$_5$ 鞠 *kuk 'nourish'
OC chǔ$_3$ 處 *k-hlaʔ 'dwell' ~ jū$_2$ 居 *kah 'id.'
ST *lap(s) 'foliage, generation' (→ yè$_4$ 葉) ~ WT rabs 'lineage'
ST *l(j)am 'blaze' (→ yán$_2$ 炎) ~ ST *wam 'blaze' (→ yán$_3$ 炎)

These variants cannot be the result of early ST dialectal evolution, because they do not correspond in a systematic way to later branches of ST; also, on occasion, both are found in the same language, frequently CH. We may speculate that Ur-ST complex sound clusters might have been responsible, thus ST *sriŋ vs. *k-sriŋ ? > *sring vs. *k-siŋ; or ST *lwam ? > *lam ~ *wam. Eventually, simple explanations may be found.

2.5.1 Parallel stems of 'swell'

Parallel stems can be quite numerous and present a picture of meaning / stem distributions that looks rather boundless and chaotic. However, considering the overall semantic field of a parallel stem (related or not) can sometimes clarify CH and ST etymologies and even

2-6	*bo	*bu	*bur or *bru	*bun
swell	WT 'bo-ba 'to swell, sprout' WB p^{h}o^{B} 'swollen' WB p^{h}u^{B} 'to swell, bud' WB pu 'bulge in middle'	Lush. puk^{L} 'swollen'	WT 'bur-ba 'prominent, bud, unfold' Chep. pyur- 'bulge, swell' ? WB p^{h}rui^{B} 'fat, swell' AA-Khm bura /pur/ 'swell up'	fèn 墳 *bəns 'swell' Lushai ti^{L}-puun^{H} 'increase' (water) AA-Khmer būna / puun/ 'to amass, accumulate, heap'
protrude, prominent	Lushai poʔ^{L} 'protrude' WB p^{h}u^{C} 'protuberance'		WT 'bur-ba 'rise, be prominent, bud, unfold' WB pru^{B} 'protuberate'	
bloom, bud	WT 'bo-ba 'to swell, sprout' WB ə-p^{h}u^{B} 'bud, swell...'	WT 'bu-ba, 'bus 'open' (flower) JP pu^{55} ' to bloom, bud' [illegible] pu^{33} 'flower'	WT 'bur-ba 'rise, be prominent, bud, unfold'	fén 蕡 *bən 'well-set' (fruit)
head	JP bo^{33} 'head'	WT dbu' 'head'		fén 墳 *bən 'big (head), horned'
hill, mountain	WT spo 'summit' WT 'bog 'small hillock'	fù 阜 *buʔ 'big, hill'		fén 墳 *bən 'mound, big'
assemble, plenty	póu 裒 *bô 'assemble, all' WB po^{B} 'plenti-ful, numerous'			
big / stout	pēi 垺 *phə̂ 'large'	fù 阜 *buʔ 'big'	? WB p^{h}rui^{B} 'fat, swell up'	fén 墳 *bən 'big, mound'

uncover connections that would not be obvious if one attempted to study a putative ST root in isolation, or study the lexicon of only a single language. For illustration, let us consider the complex of stems 'Swell' in some detail (Tables 2-6, 2-7; see also → chù$_{1}$ 觸 for additional illustration and considerations). We will not complicate the picture with too many AA data, like Khmer /bòok/ 'swelling mass', *pora* /baaor/ 'swell up, rise, bulge', /pur/ 'to swell up, overflow', /-pul/ 'to swell', /-puul/ 'mass, heap, pile', /-puuk/ 'mass, mound, group', etc.

Representative data about 'Swell' in the two tables list distinct ST stems or roots in the columns, while the rows represent similar meanings. The latter are randomly distributed over similar-looking roots and stems (labial stop initial, vowel *o* or *u*, without or with final nasal or *-r): *bo, bu, bur, bun* ('Swell' Table 2-6), *poŋ, puŋ, pom, pum* ('Swell' Table 2-7). (This list is not exhaustive.) Each of the eight stems (four in each table) means, in at least one language, 'to swell, swollen', or a transparent semantic derivative of 'swell' ('bubble', 'thigh'). The overall stem / meaning distribution shows, for example, that JP *bum*^{31} 'hill', JP *bum*^{55} 'swell', and CH *péng* 芃 *bə̂m 'luxuriant' belong to the same stem and are genetically related in spite of their rather different meanings, whereas JP *p*^{h}*um*^{31} 'lie down' is outside the semantic range and unrelated. Conversely, CH *fù* 阜 'big hill' probably is not cognate JP *bum* 'hill', etc. across the table in another column. Looking at this distribution from another angle: for 'hill' CH used the stems *poŋ and *bu, JP *pum; 'protrude': JP *poŋ, Lushai and WB *po, WT and WB *bur ~ *pru; 'assemble, amass': JP *poŋ, Lushai *puŋ, WB *pum, OCM *bo.

2-7	*poŋ	*puŋ	*pom	*pum
swell	Lush. pɔɔŋR 'swollen' WT 'pʰoŋs 'buttocks' WB pʰoŋ 'bubble'	NNaga *pu:ŋ 'swelling > breast, flower' Lushai puŋᴴ 'increase, assemble' AA-Khmer puṅa /puŋ/ 'bulge, swell'	Lushai puamᴴ 'to swell'	JP bum[55] 'swell'
bloom, bud	WT 'boŋs-ba 'roundness'	NNaga *pu:ŋ 'swelling > breast, flower'		Lushai pumF 'filled out' (as fruit)
luxuriant, abundant	fēng 丰 *pʰoŋ 'densely growing' běng 菶 *pôŋ? 'luxuriant'	fēng 豐 *pʰuŋ 'abundant' WB pruiŋᴮ 'full, abundant'	fán 蕃繁 *ban 'luxuriant'	péng 芃 *bôm 'luxuriant'
big ‖ numerous	féng 逢摓 *boŋ 'great'			WT 'bum '100,000'
heap, amass, assemble	JP pʰoŋ[31] 'amass' WT boŋ 'volume, bulk'	JP pʰuŋ[33] 'crowd, herd' WT pʰuŋ-po 'heap' Lushai vuŋᴴ 'heap, mound' Lushai puŋᴴ 'increase, assemble'		LB *bum[1] 'to divide, pile, heap' WB pum 'heap up, amass' Chep. bumh- 'double up'
protrude ‖ fat, stout	JP boŋ[33] 'protrude'		WT sbom-pa 'stout' JP bom[31] 'fat'	JP pʰum[33] 'fat, big'
hill, mountain	fēng 封 *poŋ 'mound'			JP bum[31] 'hill' Chep. bum ' id.'

2.6 Austroasiatic morphology in Old Chinese

Austroasiatic (AA), or rather Mon-Khmer languages (MK), have contributed to PCH linguistic development by providing a substrate (or rather "adstrate") vocabulary and with it fragments of MK morphology. These phonemes / morphemes have no identifiable meaning within the OC / ST frame of reference, but a MK connection can occasionally provide an explanation for the bewildering and odd array of sound variations within the OC word family.

2.6.1 Austroasiatic infixes in Old Chinese

The nominalizing n-infix (or *-mn-*) is common in MK languages. Several words which in OC had an initial *n, or an initial cluster with *n, are such MK nominal derivatives where the OC nasal represents the original MK infix. Such words include:

Year — rěn 稔 (ńźjəmᴮ) *nəm? 'year'
<- MK: PMonic *cnaam 'year', Khmer *cnam*, PVM *c-n-əm 'year', PNBahnaric *hanăm*, etc. The AA word is probably derived from the root 'to (trans-) plant'.

Peg — ruì 枘 (ńźjwäiᶜ) *nots 'peg, pin, tenon'
<- MK: Khmer *tnota* /tnaaot/ 'impaling pole, skewer, spit' < *ṭota* /daaot/ 'to impale, run into...'

Familiarity — nì 昵 (ṇjet) *nrit (?) or C-nit (?) 'familiarity', (a ruler's) 'favorite', 'lady's clothes closest to the body' 衵
<- MK: Khmer *jaṃnita* /cumnit/ (i.e., etymologically *ɟ-mn-it*) 'nearness, closeness, proximity, familiarity with, intimacy' < *jita* /cit/ 'to be near to, to be close' → jí$_7$ 即 (MC?) *tsit 'to approach'

Belt — xiāng 纕 (sjaŋ) *snaŋ 'belt, sash, horse's belly-band'
<- MK: Khmer *caṃṇaṅa* /camnɑɑŋ/ (etymologically *c-mn-aaŋ*) 'a tie, band, strap, bond' < *caṅa* /cɑɑŋ/ (OKhmer /cɔɔŋ/) 'to tie, knot, secure, attach by tying or knotting'

Wedge — xiè 楔 (siet) *sêt (from *snet?) 'wedge, piece of wood between the teeth of a corpse'
<- MK: Khmer *sniata* /snìiət/ 'peg, pin, ... wedge' < *siata* /sìiət/ 'to stick into, insert, stop or block up, plug'. The choice of the OC phonetic is not clear, perhaps mental association with *niè* 齧 'gnaw'.

Oar, rudder — ráo 橈 (ńźjäu) [ńau] *n(i)au 'oar' [Chuci]
<- MK: Khmer *thnaol* 'punting pole' < *daol* 'to punt'

A MK agentive m-infix survives in these OC words:

Male animal — mǔ 牡 *mûʔ (< *C-muʔ ?) 'male' (animal: steer, etc.)
<- MK: OKhmer *jmol* /cmo̤o̤l/ 'male of animals' is derived from a root meaning 'to hollow out, groove, perforate' > 'to plant' (with a planting stick with which one pokes into the soil).

Go-between — méi 媒 (muậi) *mə̂ 'marriage go-between, match-maker'
<- Khmer *dhmāya* /tmíiəj/ 'agent, representative' > 'marriage go-between' from a root 'to support, represent'

2.6.2 Austroasiatic word families in Old Chinese

Besides OC words with nasal initials, there are many other unanalyzable words in OC, some of which can be explained as fragments of MK word families. An example will serve: derivations from the AA root that occurs in Khmer as *dəj 'carry, bear' (Khmer *-əj* often corresponds to OC *ə). While the morphological and semantic connections between the various forms are recoverable in Khmer, none has an internal OC etymological explanation; they are all isolates. Hence AA seems to be the source, OC the recipient:

*də, *tə — OKhmer *-dai ~ -dāya* /-dəj ~ -daaj/ 'to bear, support' > OKhmer *dnāy* /dnaaj/ 'retainer, king's servant' (-> Tai *thanaaj* 'attorney, representative')
-> OC dài 戴 (tậi^{C}) *tə̂h 'to carry on the head, bear, support'

*d-m-ə — Khmer with agentive m-infix: *dhmāya* /tmíiəj/ 'agent, representative' > 'marriage go-between'
-> méi 媒 (muậi) *mə̂ 'marriage go-between, match-maker' 媒, (divine match-maker:) 'god of fecundity' 禖. OC reinterpreted the *m- as the root initial, as did Khmer in the next word:

*g/k-mə — Khmer *ghmāya* /kmíiəj/ 'marriage broker', by alteration of the (root-) initial from /tmíiəj/ above

-> gāo-méi 高禖 *kâu-mə̂, jiāo-méi 郊禖 [kau-mə] (ceremony for the divine match-maker:) 'a fecundity rite'

*p-də OKhmer /pdəj/ 'burden' > 'pregnancy'
-> pēi 胚 (pʰuậi) *phə̂ 'one month pregnant'

Morpheme substitution (or morpheme-calquing) seems to have taken place in one word where a MK causative p-prefix has been replaced by its ST counterpart *s-:

shǐ 使 (ṣɨ^B) [ṣəʔ] *srəʔ 'to send, employ, cause' < *s+rəʔ (ST s-causative)
= AA: OKhmer *pre* /prəə/ 'to send' (on an errand or commission), 'to order, assign, appoint, delegate, use, employ' < *p + rə (Khmer p-causative).

Calquing presupposes a familiarity with the donor language and its grammar; otherwise it is not possible to recognize and replace individual morphemes (H. H. Hock 1986: 399f). This implies bilingualism in prehistoric times in parts of the Yellow River basin, the cultural and political hub of the prehistoric Xià dynasty and its successor, the Shāng.

2.7 Expressives, reduplication

Expressives "are sentence adverbials that describe noises, colors, light patterns, shapes, movements, sensations, emotions, aesthetic feelings and so on" (Diffloth *Encyclopedia Britannica*, 5th ed. 1974–97, vol. 22: 701). Expressives are based on sound symbolism or "synaesthesia" (Shorto, Diffloth) and are therefore phonologically unstable with irregular developments. In Kam-Tai languages and sporadically in Chinese, animal names and other nouns can also take on an expressive shape (see 2c and 2e below).

Expressives are frequently encountered in the Early OC text *Shījīng* with its popular songs. They can take these types of phonological shapes:

(1) The ST s-prefix forms intensives / iteratives (§5.2.3).

(2) Reduplication (examples are taken from Baxter / Sagart 1998: 64ff):
(a) complete reduplication as in *guān-guān* 關關 OCM *krôn-krôn 'cry of the ospreys';
(b) partial reduplication involving the finals only (*diéyùn* 疊韻, riming), e.g., *yǎo-tiǎo* 窈窕 [ʔeu^B-deu^B] *ʔiûʔ-liûʔ 'elegant, beautiful'; this example belongs to a specialized version of this type (next item c):
(c) Repetition of the rime with initial *r- > MC *l-* (Sagart 1999: 111–120 'infix'), or *l- > MC ji- or d-, e.g., Mand. *zhāng-láng* 蟑螂 'cockroach',
kǎn-tàn 坎窞 [kʰəm^B-dəm^B] *khə̂mʔ-lə̂mʔ ? 'pit',
hàn-dàn 菡萏 [gəm^B-dəm^B] *gə̂mʔ-lə̂mʔ 'kind of waterlily';
(d) partial reduplication, involving only the initial (*shuāngshēng* 雙聲, alliteration), e.g., *cēncī* 參差 [tṣʰəm-tṣʰa] *tshrə̂m-tshrâi 'uneven, irregular';
(e) partial reduplication involving only the vowels as in a chiming expression; the alternations are typically between *e / *o or *i / *u, e.g., *zhǎnzhuǎn* 輾轉 *trenʔ-tronʔ 'toss and turn', or *xīshuài* 蟋蟀 *srit-srut 'cricket'.

Type (c) is also common in Tai; Li Fang Kuei (1977: 93) quotes Siamese *ma-lai*^A2 'damage, destroy'; because this word is probably borrowed from a Chinese form (note → huī$_6$ 墮隳 *hmai 'destroy') the /l/ is here an 'infix'. Historically, such forms probably originated as a type of reduplication where the first syllable is reduced to a vowel, and the rime is repeated with an initial *l-*. Siamese words like *mɛɛŋ* ~ *ma-lɛɛŋ*^A2 'insect', and *met* ~ *let* ~ *ma-let*^D2S 'grain' are ambiguous because the first syllable is also an animal / plant prefix. Aslian (AA) languages also have an l-infix for lower creatures. This shows that such forms do not always derive from earlier consonant clusters by 'dimidiation', but reflect bisyllabic forms.

Sagart (1999: 118ff) has concluded that in some Mǐn and Jìn dialects, bisyllabic reduplicative forms with the meanings intensive / durative / distributive are formed with the second syllable starting with /l/, similar to the Tai forms, as in Fúzhōu *tsing*[55] 'to stare' > *tsi*[31]*-ling*[55] 'stare fixedly'. This dialectal /l/ may be the continuation of an earlier OC *r-infix (div. II) (Sagart ibid.); note the OC word for 'to stare': *chēng* 瞠 MC ṭʰɐŋ < *thraŋ. This implies that in expressive words, the OC cluster with *r > div. II either was, or is descended from, a bisyllabic form.

2.8 Non-morphological word formation

2.8.1 Re-analysis

Sinitic languages (commonly "dialects") sometimes have word forms that are not the phonological analogues of standard Mandarin or MC forms. These near homophones are not the result of phonological change, but of re-etymologizing, either occasioned by taboo considerations or by folk etymology. For example:

Cantonese *jit*[12]*-tʰɐu*[45/31] 熱頭 'sun' is re-etymologized as 'the hot one' < MC *ńźjät* 熱 'hot' instead of MC *ńźjit* 日 'sun';

Mǐn, e.g., Xiàmén *tʰɔ*[31] 涂 'earth' = MC *duo*[A2] 'plaster, mud' is re-etymologizing of the analogue of Mand. *tǔ* 土 = MC *tʰuo*[B1] 'earth';

gùshì 故事 'story' has in southern dialects been re-analyzed as the Mand. equivalent of *gǔshì* 古事 'old affair', e.g., M-Fúzhōu *ku*[31/44]*-løy*[242];

qiān 鉛 'lead' n. < *kʰ-* for MC *jiwän* has been re-etymologized in most Mand. and Wú dialects as connected with 'hard, strong' *qiān* 堅 = MC *kʰăn*;

qiānbǐ 鉛筆 'pencil' is called in some dialects, such as Wǔhàn and Jiàn'ōu, the Mand. equivalent of *yángbǐ* 洋筆 lit. 'western / foreign pen', which may perhaps be an apt re-etymologizing of the original MC *jiwän* 'lead' (as in K-Méixiàn *ian*[11]*-pit*[11]);

jìng 鏡 MC *kjɐŋ*[C] 'mirror' (< 'the bright one') is perh. a late OC derivation from *liáng* 亮 MC *ljaŋ* 'light' n., re-etymologization of the earlier *jiàn* 鑑 MC *kam*[C] 'mirror';

niǎo 鳥 'bird' < MC *tieu*[B]*:* the initial may have been changed to /n/ because of Kam-Tai substrate forms for 'bird' like *nok*[D2]*S*. In fact, *niǎo* agrees with regular correspondence patterns in Kam-Tai.

An example from OC / PCH is the following:

Thumb   mǔ 拇 [mo[B]] *mô? 'thumb, big toe'
<> PL *C-ma[3] 'thumb'

The OC counterpart to PTB *a should be *a or *ə; the CH cognate should have been *měi* [mə[B]] *mə̂?. Due to paronomastic attraction to *mǔ* 'mother', the CH word had become a homophone of the latter. Perhaps the PL form and PTB *ma 'mother' are related ('mother of fingers/toes').

2.8.2 Backformation, re-cutting

A phoneme can be subtracted or lost due to back formation or re-cutting. This is also the result of re-analysis of the word (H. H. Hock 1986: 200f.). Examples of morphological re-analysis occur sporadically in many languages, for instance, English 'an adder' is a mis-analyzed 'a nadder'. Illustrative TB examples are the words for 'dog' and 'eight': 'dog' PTB *kwi, but Lushai *ui*^{R} 'dog' where the initial *k-* seems to have been dropped as an assumed prefix. The segments of ST *prjat ~ *pret (or *b instead of *p), including later epenthetic ones, are treated variously as part of the root or as a prefix in the different languages:

*prjat ~ *pret	> TGTM *prat	
	> OC *pret ~ *priat 八	> MC pǎt > Mand. bā 八
*p-hret	> WB *hrac*	
*b-ret	> Kanauri *re*, Lushai *riat*	
*br-jat	> WT *brgyad*	> Tib. dialects > *gjat > *ɟet*

A few OC words may be the result of such re-cutting, the best examples of which are the tone A derivations (§3.1).

Re-analysis may possibly explain the difference in OC initials between *tǐ* 體 [tʰei^{B}] *hrîʔ or *hrə̂iʔ 'body, form, shape' and *shēng* 生 [ʂɐŋ] *srêŋ 'to be alive, be born'. Both words probably belong to ST *sri 'to be'. In *shēng*, the initial *s- was understood as the causative prefix, although it happens to belong to the ST stem; in *tǐ*, no causative meaning was apparent, hence it developed regularly by devoicing from what was taken to be the root initial *r- (§5.2). But for an alternative explanation, see → tǐ 體.

2.8.3 *Metathesis*

In a few items, ST words with initial consonant clusters underwent a metathesis of the post-initial consonant and the following vowel (CCV > CVC). Benedict (*LTBA* 16:2, 1993: 121) calls these 'split cognates'. This is the result of a sesquisyllabic form (Matisoff's term) with a vowel between prefix and initial consonant which subsequently became the main vowel with loss of the now final vowel (CCV = CVCV > CVC). A case in point is

Five	PTB *b-ŋaʔ 'five' (variant of *l-ŋa) > Lushai *paŋa* > *poŋ*.

Here the intermediate sesquisyllabic stage of a form is attested. Such a form is not found in the few other cases; they all involve a putative ST *r or *m pre-initial:

To steal	PTB *r-ku, WT *rku-ba* 'to steal', WB *kʰui*^{B} vs. Lushai *ruk* (or variant of *rɔk* ?)
Sell	PTB *r-ŋa 'to sell' vs. WB *roŋ*^{B} 'to sell'
Control	ST *m-ŋa 'to drive, control', WT *mŋa'-ba* 'might, dominion', *yù* 御 *ŋah 'drive a chariot, direct' vs. WB *moŋ*^{B} 'threaten, drive away' ⋇ *ə-moŋ*^{B} 'driving'
Smell	ST *m-nəm ?, PTB *m-nam 'to smell', WT *mnam-pa* 'smell of' vs. *wén* 聞 *mən 'to smell'; in this stem the final dental nasal *-n* also could have been the result of labial dissimilation.

Some of the words with medial OC *r may also be the result of this process (§6.1; §7.7.3).

2.8.4 *Convergence*

Occasionally two etyma have coalesced in OC into one word or word family. This can even involve items from different language families (CH has attached the final *-k):

sè 色 (ṣjək) [ṣɨk, S ṣək] *srək (< sər-k)

(1) 'color, color of face, appearance, countenance' < ST: Lushai *saar*^{H} < *saar* 'prismatic colors' ж *saar*^{R} / *sarh*^{R} 'healthy looking, rosy, ruddy'

(2) 'good looks / charms of women, sexual pleasures' < AA: Khmer /srèek/ 'thirst or lust after' < /réek/ 'enjoy oneself'

Convergence is often the result of a semantic shift from one word to another. E.g., *rěn* 稔 [ńim^B] *nəmʔ 'year' < AA 'year' (no implication of 'harvest') has eventually also acquired the meaning 'harvest' under the influence of the nearly homophonous *nián* 年 [nen] *nîn 'harvest > year' of ST origin.

2.9 Meaning and sound

Occasionally, certain meanings are associated with certain sounds. These are phonesthemic (or 'phonaesthetic') phenomena, e.g. English sl- is suggestive in words like slide, slither, slip, slim, etc. Similar groups of OC words make the superficial, but often erroneous, impression of being somehow genetically related. Words that signify movement with an abrupt endpoint often end in *-k (§6.1). Words with the meaning 'shutting, closing', which also implies an endpoint, tend to end in final *-p. Words that imply 'keeping in a closed mouth' tend to end in a final *-m, such as 'keeping in the mouth' > 'resent' etc., savoring something in the mouth such as 'drink, sweet, salty, insipid'; 'keeping closed' extends to notions of 'hidden, dark, black'. The same and similar notions — 'dark, black, covered, blind, stupid' — tend to start with the stem initial *m-. Roots and stems meaning 'round, turn, return' have an initial *w- not only in Chinese, but generally in the languages of the area, including MK (Shorto 1973); such words do, of course, not end abruptly in a stop consonant, but trail off in a final nasal or lateral, hence such meanings are expressed with roots like *waŋ, *wal, and *war + variants with other vowels (see the dictionary under the letters H, W, Y). Anything to do with the tongue tends to have initial *l-, such as 'tongue, lick, sweet'; anything involving breathiness tends to have an aspirated initial consonant, as do notions of 'hollow, empty' (§5.8.5 to §5.8.6). Guttural sounds as in 'mute, strangle' and the like tend to start with glottal stop *ʔ- (examples can be gleaned from letters E and Y in the dictionary). Words for 'soft, subtle, flexible', including 'flesh; female breast' start with *n- (§1.4.1; dictionary N, R).

Some animal names or sounds are onomatopoetic: 'chicken' *ki (PKra) ~ *jī* 雞 *kê (OCM) ~ *(r)ka (PVM); 'chicken' in some TB languages, e.g., Lushai *ʔaar;* or 'crow' *wū-yā* 烏鴉 *ʔa; *māo* 貓 'cat' is universal; *niú* 牛 *ŋwə 'cow'; *fèi* 吠 < ST *baus 'to bark'.

2.10 Semantic extension

The unknown is metaphorically expressed by something known; the abstract is usually derived from the concrete: 'shake' > 'fear'; 'keep in the mouth' > 'dissatisfied, resentment'; 'rise' > 'anger'; 'cold' > 'grieved'; 'thick' > 'generous'; 'white' > 'understand'; 'black' > 'evil'; 'get the better of' > 'be able'; 'carry, bear' > 'endure'; 'heart' > 'mind'; 'gall' > 'courage'; 'sun' > 'day'. Metaphors become new words. Chinese shares many metaphors with other languages, including English.

Occasionally, the semantic leap of a suspected extension is difficult to follow; note the ST notion 'hear' > 'ask'. A few verbs with the meanings 'to think, to say' or other abstractions are apparently semantic extensions of verbs 'to be, to do, to act, to go'. Something similar is observed in many languages, such as Engl. *the saying went like this: "..."*, or *he went on and on.* In TB languages: WT *byed-pa*, *byas* 'to make, fabricate, do' > *žes byas-pa* 'thus said, so called' (i.e., marks direct discourse); WT *mč*^{h}*i-ba* 'to come, go' > 'to say' (marks direct discourse); Lushai *ti*^{L} / *tiʔ*^{L} < *tiiʔ* / *tiʔ* 'to do, perform, act, work; act towards; say; to think, consider, feel, wish'; Mandarin Chinese → wéi$_3$ 為 'do, act' in the phrase *yǐwéi* 以為 'to consider..., to think' (lit. 'take something to be, take something for'). These considerations make an etymological link between the following pairs likely:

fēi 非 is not > be wrong
shì 是 is, this > be right
yòu 右 right side > to honor, appreciate 佑
zǔo 左 left side > to disapprove
miè 蔑 will not / cannot > despise
fú 弗 cannot, will not > resist
sī 司 to act, manage > to think 思
wéi 唯惟 to be > to think 惟
huì 惠 should be > be kind

Formally, *wèi* 謂 *wə(t)s 'to tell, call' seems to fit the "irrealis" pattern (§6.2.2), looking like a derivation from *yǒu* 有 *wəʔ 'there is, have', but it is not clear if there is an etymological connection and how the semantic leap came about.

3

MIDDLE CHINESE TONES AND THEIR OLD CHINESE EQUIVALENTS

MC and LHan had three tones: tone A (*píngshēng* 平聲 = 'even' or 'level' tone), tone B (*shǎngshēng* 上聲 = 'rising' tone), and tone C (*qùshēng* 去聲 = 'falling' or 'departing' tone), and, according to traditional Chinese phonological analysis, tone D (*rùshēng* 入聲 = 'entering' tone) for words which end in a stop consonant (p, t, k), i.e., this short-stopped syllable type was toneless. These tonal categories are projected back to OC where tone A is thought to have been an open syllable or one ending in a nasal, tone B marked a syllable with a glottal stop in the final (or a glottolized syllable), and tone C a syllable with final *-s / *-h. Tones A and D are usually left unmarked as this causes no ambiguity. OC probably had no "tones" in the later sense but instead segmental phonemes. Nevertheless, we will here apply the term 'tone' also to OC in the sense of "later tonal category" for the sake of clarity and to sidestep arguments about their OC phonetic nature. Because MC tones are projected back to identical ones in LHan, subsequently examples will often be cited in simpler LHan forms.

All three tones can belong either to a root or stem, or play some morphological role. The most common morphological tones are B *shǎngshēng* and C *qùshēng*, which together with initial voicing form a derivational system which marks direction and diathesis (§4). The contrast between allofams in the three different tones is exemplified by the following paradigm, where the form in tone A is the simplex, the derivation in tone B is endoactive (§4.5), and the derivation in tone C is exopassive (§4.4) (LHan after the graph):

zhī 之 tśə, *tə	'to go, proceed'
zhǐ 止 tśə^B, *təʔ	'foot' (< 'that which is doing the going')
zhì 志 tśə^C, *təh	'goal, purpose' (< 'what is being proceeded to')

3.1 Middle Chinese tone A (*píngshēng* 平聲)

Tone A ('even' or 'level' tone) reflects OC open syllables or ones with a nasal coda; they are assumed to be the basic unmarkd type and usually go back to equivalent ST forms, e.g., *qiū* 丘 [k^{h}u^A] *khwə 'village' ⪤ Lushai *k^{h}ua^H* < *k^{h}ua*. However, individual languages, including CH, frequently have attached final consonants to open ST stems, e.g., *bǎi* 百 [pak] *prâk 'hundred' vs. WT *brgya*, WB *ə-ra^A*.

The rare tone A 'derivations' are *nouns* from stems that have an inherent tone B, tone C, or a final stop consonant. The original mechanism may have been re-analysis (§2.8).

Rain yǔ 雨 [wɑ^B] 'rain' > yú 雩 [wɑ^A] 'sacrifice with prayer for rain'

'Rain' *yǔ* is a widely attested ST word; it can be set up as ST *waʔ (with final glottal stop) on the strength of Kuki-Chin and Chepang forms in addition to MC. This rules out the possibility that 'rain' is a tone B derivation from 'sacrifice for rain', which would also be semantically implausible. However, elsewhere tone B can be a morpheme which creates or marks endoactive verbs or words (§4.5); 'to rain' fits this pattern, so that tone B may have been felt to be this morpheme rather than part of the root. 'Sacrifice for rain' was then created as a back formation by removal of the alleged suffix tone B.

Additional tone A derivations include the following items (LH forms after the character):

Slave	xì 繫	ge^C	'to be bound'
	> xī 奚	ge	'slave, captive'
Wine-master	jiǔ 酒	$tsiu^B$	'wine'
	> qiú 酋	dziu	'wine-master'
Writing slip	biǎn 扁	$pian^B$	'narrow'
	> piān 篇	p^hian	'writing slip'
Tally	fù 附	buo^C	'to adjoin'
	> fú 符	buo	'a tally'
Side by side	bìng 並	$beŋ^B$	'side by side'
	> pián 駢	ben	'two (horses) side by side'
Corpse	shǐ 矢	$śi^B$	'to display'
	> shī 尸	śi	'corpse, personator of a dead'

In 'Corpse' the derivation process could also have been the reverse. In a few cognate sets, tone A may be the result of loss of a final consonant, as in:

Bones hé 核 [gɛk] 'kernel fruit' ~ hái 骸 [gɛɨ] 'bones, skeleton'.

Hé is a ST etymon: WT *rag* 'fruit stone, bead', Mikir *rak* 'fruit stone'; therefore *hé* was the original form from which *hái* was derived.

3.2 Middle Chinese tone B (*shǎngshēng* 上聲): phonology

MC tone B probably derives from an OC *-ʔ. In some modern dialects tone B ends with glottal constriction (Branner 2000: 119) — note Mǐn-Sōngyáng *puɲʔ* ('measure for books' *běn* 本; Branner 2000: 344). Glottal stop after nasal codas is also shown by variants like *xǐ* 洗 [sei^B] ~ [sen^B] 'to wash', as well as *Shījīng* rimes such as *-anʔ / *-aʔ (Shi 301), *-uŋʔ / *-uʔ (Shi 264,7); some rimes confirm that the phoneme in question was a stop consonant: *-ap / *-amʔ (Shi 265,3) and *-et / *-enʔ (Shi 265,5). The glottal feature can, however, appear elsewhere, e.g., in the middle of a syllable (Sagart 1999: 132, n. 1: Xiàoyì dialect in Shānxī).

Tone B seems to be a weakened variant of final *-k* in some words (§3.2.2).

*3.2.1 Tone B from Sino-Tibetan *-ʔ*

Tone B can be part of the root. In some words it goes back to the ST level because some OC open syllable words with tone B correspond to Kuki-Chin and Chepang words, which are also reconstructible with a final glottal stop (Chepang still has final *-ʔ*). The first several items in the list below are taken from Ostapirat (*LTBA* 21:1, 1998: 238f) with WB and LHan forms added. The agreement in final *-ʔ is particularly persuasive because the first seven items have been selected without Chinese in mind. Tiddim and Lushai tones sometimes split according to vowel length or timbre (hence Lushai tones F(alling), R(ising), L(ow) < *-ʔ); the corresponding Tiddim Chin tone is 1; LHan forms follow the graph:

Gloss	Tiddim	Lushai	Chepang	LHan		
Bird	$va:^1$	va^F	waʔ	yǔ	羽	wa^B
Child	$ta:^1$	fa^F < faaʔ	coʔ	zǐ	子	$tsiə^B$
Water	$tu:i^1$	tui^R	tiʔ	tǐ	涕	$t^hei^{B/C}$

Tail	mei¹	meiᴿ	meʔ	wěi 尾 muiᴮ
Fire	mei¹	meiᴿ	hmeʔ	huǒ 火 huaiᴮ
Bitter	xaː¹	kʰaᴸ / kʰakᶠ	kháʔ	kǔ 苦 kʰɑᴮ
Rain	guaʔ⁴	ruaʔᴸ	waʔ	yǔ 雨 wɑᴮ
To plant	tuʔ⁴	tuʔᴸ		shù 樹 dźoᴮ <*doʔ
Blood	siː¹	tʰiᴿ	wəiʔ	suǐ 髓 syɑiᴮ ~ sɨoiᴮ
Eat		fakᶠ		jǔ 咀 dziɑᴮ chew
Nine		kuaᴿ < kuaʔ		jiǔ 九 *kwəʔ
Itch		zaᴿ / zatᴸ		yǎng 癢 jɑŋᴮ

A few correspondences where CH has tone A stand out as exceptions. They include:

Gloss	Tiddim	Lushai	Chepang	LHan
Fish	ŋaː¹	ŋhaᴿ	ŋaʔ	yú 魚 ŋɨɑ

CH tone B < *-ʔ also corresponds to *-ʔ in some AA words, which could be more than coincidence (LHan in square brackets or after the graph):

Tiger	hǔ 虎 [hɑᴮ] *hlâʔ 'tiger' <- PMK *klaʔ
Drum	gǔ 鼓 [kɑᴮ] *klâʔ 'drum' <> PWa *kloʔ 'bronze-drum'
Carry on the back	fù 負 [buᴮ] *bəʔ 'id.' <> PMK *tɓaʔ, Khmu *bɔʔ*, PWa *bɔʔ
Eat	jǔ 咀 [dziɑᴮ] *dzaʔ 'chew' <> PMK *cyaʔ 'eat' (also in TB)

*3.2.2 Tone B for Tibeto-Burman final *-k*

Some Chinese tone B words correspond not to TB *-ʔ, but to TB final *-k. There is clearly a system, although it is not yet understood (LH readings):

Drip, leak	WB cak	WT 'dzag	jù 沮 dziɑᴮ
Speak	WB hŋak 'bird'	WT sŋag	yǔ 語 ŋɨɑᴮ
War	WB -mak	WT dmag	wǔ 武 muɑᴮ
Under	WB ok	WT 'og	hòu 後 goᴮ
Turbid	WB nok		nǎo 惱 nɑuᴮ
Brain	WB hnok		nǎo 腦 nɑuᴮ
Warm	WB uik		yù 嫗 ʔɨoᴮ/ᶜ
Pheasant	WB rac < *rik	WT sreg-pa	zhì 雉 ḍiᴮ < *driʔ

Baxter (1992: 182) suggests that *-ʔ could have been added to stop finals (e.g., *-k + *-ʔ > *-ʔ), but the interchange *-k ~ *-ʔ may also have other causes; therefore we hesitate to set up clusters like *-kʔ.

The same correspondences are encountered in Tai and AA loans (one way or the other; LH after the graph):

Cover	Siam. *pokᴰ¹S* < *p- 'to cover, book cover' bǎo 保 [pouᴮ] *pûʔ 'preserve, protect'
Fall down	Siam. *tokᴰ¹S* < *t- 'fall down' dǎo 倒 [tɑuᴮ] *tâuʔ 'turn over, fall'
Mortar	Siam. *kʰrokᴰ²S* 'mortar' jiù 臼 [guᴮ] *guʔ 'mortar'

Pig	PMonic *cliik 'pig' shǐ 豕 [śe^{B}] *lheʔ ? 'pig'
Down, below	Khmer *gra'ka* /grɑk/ 'to be low' xià 下 [ga^{B}] *grâʔ 'down, below'
Drip	Khmer *sra'ka* /srɑk/ 'drip' xǔ 湑 [ṣɑ(^{B})] *sraʔ 'to drip'

However, TB final *-k for a Chinese open syllable does also occur, an often cited example, though of debatable etymology, is 'pig': *bā* 豝 [pa] < *pra ? ⋇ PTB *pak, but see §6.9.

*3.2.3 ST *-ʔ in closed syllables*

TB final *-ʔ and *-s in closed syllables (i.e., those ending in a nasal or lateral) have no systematic tonal correspondence in Chinese. The following cognate sets are typical:

Gloss	Tiddim	Chepang	LHan < OCM
To steal	gu:¹ < -ʔ	kuʔ	kù 寇 kʰo^{C} < *khôh
Thin	pa:¹ < -ʔ	beʔ	bó 薄 bɑk < *bâk
Give		bəyʔ	bì 畀 pis < *pis
Go around	Lush. *veelʔ		wéi 韋 wui^{A}

Where tone B does occur in OC *-nʔ (appearing identical with ST *-nʔ, *-rʔ, and *-lʔ), it is perhaps a CH innovation, as in 'gums' where tone B marks body parts (§3.3.1).

Gums	Lush. *-hniiʔ	PTB *rnil	shěn 矧 śin^{B}

WB has a final stop in some words which elsewhere end in a nasal. Chepang and Kuki-Chin languages suggest that the reason may be a PTB final *-Nʔ. CH, which has tone A, has eliminated the suspected ST final glottal stop, as expected (KC = Kuki-Chin; Chep. = Chepang; LHan). But it remains to be seen if there is really a system (Matisoff n. 12 in Ostapirat *LTBA* 21:1,1998: 243; *HPTB:* 516–525).

Tree	WB sac	KC *siŋʔ	Chep. siŋʔ	xīn	薪	sin^{A}
Dream	WB mak	KC *maŋʔ	Chep. maŋʔ	mèng	夢	muŋ$^{A/C}$
New	WB sac			xīn	新	sin^{A}
Year	WB hnac			nián	年	nen^{A}
Heart	WB hnac			? rén	仁	ńin^{A}
Strife	WB cac			zhēng	爭	tṣɛŋ^{A}

3.2.4 Tone B for foreign final -ŋ

In a few common words, Chinese has tone B for TB final *-ŋ. (For the reverse phenomenon, see §6.5.2.) This probably is related to the little understood incompatibility of tone B with OC finals *-əŋ and *-uŋ (i.e., OCM *-ə̂ŋʔ is rare, has either dropped the final nasal or shifted to final -əm^{B} or -ən^{B}; *-ûŋʔ does not occur at all; tone B occurs freely in rime *-oŋ). Generally, the final consonants preempted the ST *-ʔ (see above), but in a few common words *-ʔ seems to have prevailed. Where we do find MC tone B for PTB *-ʔ with nasal finals, the CH nasals are innovations, as in 'dog' (§6.4.3), 'itch' (§6.5.1), and 'far' (§6.5.2), or they are exceptions that require further investigation; by a curious coincidence, WT has almost no cognates. (Chep. = Chepang, Tid. = KC-Tiddim Chin):

You	WB naŋ^C Chep. naŋ Tid. *naŋʔ	WT –	rǔ 汝 nɑ^B
You	WB ñañ^B Chep. niŋ 'you' pl.	WT –	ěr 爾 ńe^B
Horse	WB mraŋ^B	WT rmaŋ	mǎ 馬 ma^B
To love	WB maŋ^A	WT –	wǔ 憮 muɑ^B
Contradict	WB ŋraŋ^B	WT –	yǔ 禦 ŋɨɑ^B
Post, column	WB tuiŋ^A	WT –	zhù 柱 ḍo^B
To beat	WB oŋ^A	WT –	ōu 毆 ʔo^B

Grammatical words often develop irregularly in individual languages; 'you' is typical: Tiddim Chin and OC agree in a final *-ʔ, while Chepang has a plain final.

Chinese has no final *-ŋ, as we see in some comparative sets with Tai and Miao-Yao (Li Fang Kuei 1976):

Shore pǔ 浦 LH [p^{h}ɑ^B] *phâʔ 'river bank'
<> PKS *pwaŋ^B 'bank, shore'

Mend bǔ 補 [pɑ^B] *pâʔ 'to mend, repair, assist'
<> S. *pɔɔŋ^{C1}* < *p- 'to protect, cover up'

Drum gǔ 鼓 [kɑ^B] *kâʔ < *klaʔ 'drum' <> PTai *klɔŋ^{A1} 'drum'

Stomach dù 肚 [dɑ^B] *dâʔ 'stomach'
<> PT *duɔŋ^C 'stomach'; PKS (E,Y) *loŋ 'a belly'

Handful bǎ 把 [pa^B] *prâʔ ? 'a handful'
<> PMY *phwaŋ^{2B} 'a handful'

Lady fù 婦 [bu^B] *bəʔ 'lady, daughter-in-law'
<> PMY *bwaŋ < *Nb- 'daughter-in-law'

One exceptional set has MC tone A, not B:

Wife and children nú 孥 [nɑ] *nâ 'wife and children'
<> Tai: S. *nɔɔŋ^{C2}* < *n- 'younger sibling', PKS *noŋ^C 'id.', but note also Tai: S. *naa^{C2}* < *n- 'mother's younger sibling'

3.3 Tone B as morpheme

Tone B does not always belong to the root (§3.2.1–3), it is also a derivational morpheme. Tone B derivations are not as common as those in tone C. The most common morphological role of tone B is to derive endoactive words (i.e., introvert and active) from a stem or simplex (§4.5).

3.3.1 Tone B (1): terms for body parts and humans

Tone B is encountered frequently in names for body parts (Unger *Hao-ku* 36, 1990: 47f; Zhengzhang Shangfang 1995: 280, in Sagart 1999: 134). It may have spread from endoactive derivatives like *hàn* 頷 'jaw', *zhǐ* 指 'finger', and *zhǐ* 止 'foot' (§4.5.1) to other body parts. Thus, *shǒu* 首 'head', *shǒu* 手 'hand', *chǐ* 齒 'tooth', *shěn* 矧 'gums', etc., may have been felt to be also 'things that do' something.

A conspicuously large number of words that refer to persons or kinship also have tone B as noted by Unger, Zhengzhang Shangfang (op. cit.): *nǚ* 女 [ṇia^B] 'woman', *mǔ* 母 [mo^B] 'mother', *bǐ* 妣 'deceased mother', *fù* 婦 [bwu^B] 'woman', *zǐ* 姊 [tsi^B] 'elder sister', *jiě* 姐 'elder sister', *fù* 父 [bwo^B] 'father', *jiù* 舅 [gu^B] 'uncle'. Tone B must be a CH inovation because there is no correlation with TB equivalents. We may speculate that the tone had spread from words like *zǐ* 子 [tsiə^B] 'son', *zǔ* 祖 [tsa^B] 'ancestor', *dì* 弟 [dei^B] 'younger brother' (§4.5.1) to similar terms.

Tone B in this category is the more striking, as words that refer to social status or profession are mostly in other tones: *wáng* 王 'king', *jūn* 君 'lord', *hóu* 侯 'lord', *nán* 男 'baron, male', *gōng* 公 'duke, uncle', *jiàng* 匠 'carpenter', *nóng* 農 'farmer'.

3.3.2 Tone B (2): coverbs and particles

Tone B derives some coverbs from other verbs:

Not have	mǐ 靡 [mɨai^B] *maiʔ 'not have, there is no' < wú 無 [mua] *ma 'not, no'
Not have	wǎng 罔 [muaŋ^B] *maŋʔ 'there is no, not have' < wáng 亡 [muaŋ] *maŋ 'disappear'
Able	kě 可 [k^{h}ai^B] *khâiʔ 'to bear, can, be able' < ? hé 何 [gai^B] *gâi 'to carry' (here tone B may belong to the stem)

Other coverbs in tone B are *gǎn* 敢 'dare' (<> PTB *hwam), *kěn* 肯 'approve', *yǐ* 以 'take, with', perhaps also *wǎng* 往 'go to' < *yú* 于 'to go'. However, the tone probably belongs to the stem, in light of other grammatical words in other tones: *yòng* 用 'use, with', *wéi* 為 'to do', *wéi* 惟 'to be', *yú* 於于 'be in, at'.

Tone B in final particles may be prosodic: *yě* 也 sentence final particle serving as copula, *yǐ* 矣 final particle, *zhě* 者 a phrase final particle.

3.3.3 Tone B (3): independent pronouns

Graham (1973) has sorted the many OC pronouns into 'neutral', 'non-adjunctive', 'adjunctive-possessive' and 'demonstrative', which we will call here 'independent' forms (Dobson *LAC*: 138: 'pregnant'), 'dependent' (Dobson: 'determinant' form), and 'possessive'; the 'demonstratives' behave mostly like independent pronouns. In the following tabulation, the earliest attested forms [OB, BI, Shi] have LHan forms shown in bold type (after the graph).

Independent form	Dependent form	Possessive form
wǒ 我 **ŋai^B** 'I, we'	wú 吾 ŋa 'I, my'	
yú 予 ja^B ? 'I, me'	yú 余 **ja** 'I, my'	yí 台 jə 'my'
rǔ 汝 **ńa^B** 'you'		nǎi 乃 **nə^B** 'your'
ěr 爾 **ńe^B** 'you'		ér 而 ńə 'you, your'
shì 是 dźe^B 'this'		
bǐ 彼 pɨai^B 'that'	fú 夫 bua 'that'	
cǐ 此 ts^{h}ie^B 'this'		
(qú 渠佢 gɨa 'he, she' — late word)		qí 其 gɨə 'his, her'

Our terminology is borrowed from Pacific languages (AN) such as Lenak (Lynch 1998: 103f) where the *independent* form stands alone as the answer to a question just as in OC

("Who did it?" — "*Wǒ* 我 ", not "*Wú* 吾"), and is also the form used for the object pronoun; when used in other positions (e.g., subject, possessive) the independent pronoun is used only for emphasis, just as in OC. The *dependent* form, e.g., *wú* 吾 'I, my' belongs to a following predicate as subject, or to a noun as a possessive. *Wú* cannot stand alone or at the end of a sentence, hence *wǒ* has to take over as object pronoun.

Independent forms are marked with tone B (*-ʔ), whose abrupt final glottal stop may have started out as a feature marking the end of a phrase or utterance. Some independent pronouns have in addition the diphthong *-ai; some end in *-e. Matisoff (1995: 74) suggests that the final *-i is a palatal suffix. In Tai languages interrogative / indefinite pronouns end in *-ay* (or *-ɨ*) (Gedney 1976: 72); there may be a connection with OC forms in *-i.

The marked independent forms in *-i / *-ʔ are the ones that have survived in modern dialects (*wǒ, rǔ, ěr, bǐ, cǐ, shì, hé, shéi*).

The other forms, and also the interrogatives, have tone A, i.e., open syllables probably with a long vowel which indicates incompletion of the utterance and the expectation of a following element or answer (suggested earlier by Kennedy; see Graham 1973). In addition to this independent / dependent distinction, a few pronouns have a proclitic possessive form in tone A with the vowel ə. In the words *rǔ* 'your' and *nǎi* 'your', tone B belongs to the root.

Independent forms of interrogative pronouns have final *-i, but with tone A:

Independent form	Dependent form
hé 何 [gɑi] 'what'	hú 胡 [gɑ] 'what'
	xī 奚 [ge] 'what, how' (Pulleyblank 1995: 95)
shuí 誰 [dźui] *dui 'who'	(cf. chóu 疇 [ḍu] 'who')

The demonstratives behave largely as independent pronouns: *shí* 時 [dźə] 'this' (independent); *zhī* 之 [tśə] 'obj. pr.: him, her...' (should be independent); *zhī* 之 [tśə] 'possessive particle'; *zī* 茲 [tsiə] 'this'; in early literature also *qí* 其 [gɨə] 'he, she, it'. Since the independents *shì, cǐ,* and *bǐ* occur later, they may be derivations from *shí, zī,* and *fú* respectively (cf. Pulleyblank 1995: 165).

There are more pronouns in addition to the ones cited. No text uses all the forms, most use only a small selection; different texts use the same pronoun in different ways (summary in Pulleyblank 1995: 76ff). The above system probably also combines forms from different periods and regions. Dependent pronouns are often implied and thus omitted.

Independent *wǒ*, *rǔ*, and *ěr* appear in the earliest texts and are of ST descent. Therefore the final *-i in *wǒ*, and *-ʔ in *rǔ* and *nǎi* are not Chinese innovations, whereas most of the other independent pronouns, which occur for the most part in later texts, have no direct TB counterparts. We may speculate that in PCH or early OC *-ʔ / *-i / *-iʔ has spread from the old items to other pronouns and has thus eventually become a mark of "independent" status.

3.4 Middle Chinese tone C (*qùshēng* 去聲): phonology

Tone C ('departing / falling tone') from ST *-s is the most common derivational device in OC as well as in TB (*HPTB:* 466ff). It is believed to have once been a *-s suffix (discussion in Baxter 1992). Since some of the dental finals, which are usually reconstructed as OC *-ts, seem to have had only a simple OC *-s, tone C must have been of a different nature after open vowels and velar finals than after dentals, so we write *-h after the former and *-s after the latter. These two are allophones:

-ah -akh -aŋh -aih -auh etc.
-as ats -ans -ams (PCH -aps had already merged with -ats in OC.)

We can speculate that the original difference between root final tone C < *-s and derivational tone C goes back to morpheme juncture and vowel length, thus root final *-s is found in a closed and short syllable as in

dà 大 PCH *das > OCM *dâs (OCB *dats).

but where *-s has been attached as the morpheme to an open, long syllable, the development was possibly

bù 布 PCH *paa + s > *paas > OCM *pâh (OCB *pas).

OC tone C often corresponds to a final stop consonant in other languages. This supports the assumption of an early final consonant cluster in the OC forms, but not necessarily in all instances:

Taste wèi 味 LH [mus] *məts <> PMonic *[ʔ]məp 'good tasting'
Lungs fèi 肺 [puɑs] *pats <> TB-PL *(ʃ-)pap^{L}.
Dark mèi 昧 [məs] *mə̂ts 'dusk, be dark, blindly' <> PKS *muut 'blind'
To angle diào 釣 [teu^{C}] *tiâukh 'to angle, fish' <> Tai: S. *tok*^{DI} 'to angle'

Occasionally, tone C is not a morpheme but seems to belong to the stem (Downer 1959: 263):

To see jiàn 見 [ken^{C}] 'to see, visit' >< xiàn 現見 [gen^{C}] 'to appear, show up'.

3.5 Tone C: later OC general purpose morpheme

Tone C has been prolific in word derivation in OC (*-s / *-h) (§4.2). For early OC, two tone C morphemes must be distinguished: one forms transitive / causative verbs and words (§4.3), the other forms passive words (§4.4). This system will be discussed in detail in §4. Because tone C marked both passive and transitive / causative in early OC (down to ca. 700 BC), it was well on its way to becoming a weakly marked general purpose derivational morpheme in EOC, but it became ubiquitous later. In EOC, tone C nouns were passive ('to mount' > 'what is mounted' > 'carriage') (§4.4) or exoactive (§4.3). In later Zhou Chinese (by Chūnqiū times and later), it also formed nouns that were endoactive (§4.5), e.g., *cóng* 從 [dzioŋ] 'to follow' > *zòng* 從 [dzioŋ^{C}] 'follower' [Shi 104] (i.e., the one who actively does the following, not the one who is passively followed, or makes someone else follow) (Downer 1959: 262). Thus tone C superseded tone B, the earlier marker of active voice, which ceased to be productive.

Not surprisingly, in early literature we already find derivations with tone C whose function and meaning are no longer obvious, as in:

To use yóng 庸 [joŋ *loŋ 'to use, employ, need' [Shi, BI]
> yòng 用 [joŋ^{C}] *loŋh 'to use' [OB, Shi]

The tone C form of this set is the one that has survived as the ordinary word for 'to use', and this trend toward tone C is common (Unger *Hao-ku* 20, 1983: 165). Eventually, lexica and commentaries record several sets of tone C / non-C words with identical meanings (Unger, ibid.: 157).

This universal morpheme can of course be divided into numerous subclasses (Downer 1959). A few subgroups of this general category with clearly identifiable semantic *foci* include:

Formation of *adverbs* (Downer 1959: 289), e.g., *yǒu* 有 'to have' ⋈ *yòu* 又 'moreover'; *sān* 三 'three' ⋈ *sàn* 三 'thrice'.

A late category (text examples are from *Zhōulǐ, Lǐjì* and from texts shortly before Han) consists of nouns derived from "gradable adjectives" (Baxter and Sagart 1998: 55), e.g., *cháng* 長 [ḍaŋ] 'long' > *zhàng* 長 [ḍaŋh] 'length'. Unger (*Hao-ku* 21, 1983: 177f), supplies WT parallels, e.g., WT *zab* 'deep' > *zabs* 'depth'. In these derivations, tone C had acquired the endoactive meaning which in EOC is expressed by tone B. Nouns in final *-s are common in TB (*HPTB:* 466ff).

Tone C forms are occasionally used in compounds, as *guān* 觀 'to see' ⋈ *guàn-tái* 觀臺 'observation tower' (Downer 1959: 289).

4

TONES B, C, AND VOICING: DIRECTION AND DIATHESIS

Because MC tones and phonemes at issue are projected back to identical ones in LHan, subsequently examples will often be cited in simpler LHan forms.

4.1 Direction and diathesis

A dichotomy in direction and causativity is well recognized in Chinese (e.g., Mei 1980; Takashima 1996: 446) and also in Tibeto-Burman languages (*STC:* 105); note introvert – extrovert / causative pairs like 'to hear' – 'to ask' in both CH and TB languages (Matisoff *D. of Lahu*: 726f; J. Sun *LTBA* 16.2, 1993: 152). These are therefore already Sino-Tibetan categories; furthermore, CH and TB languages share the two ST morphemes that mark this distinction: the s-prefix (Table 4-1) and the s-suffix (Table 4-2).

4-1	m-prefix - introvert	s-prefix - extrovert-causative
To eat, lick	OC *m-lək > shí 食 'to eat' TB *m-lyak 'to lick'	PCH *s-lək-s > sì 食 'to feed' TB *s-lyak 'make / let lick, feed'

4-2	simplex - introvert	s-suffix - extrovert-causative
Limbu	tʰuŋ- 'to drink'	tʰuŋs- 'give to drink'
OC / PCH	*ʔəmʔ > yǐn 飲 'to drink'	*ʔəm-s > yìn 飲 'give to drink'
OC / PCH	*m-lək > shí 食 *m-lək 'to eat'	*s-lək-s > sì 食 'give to eat, feed'

Historically, three phenomena have partially or completely coalesced in OC: (1) *semantic* introvert / extrovert; (2) *grammatical* transitivity distinctions; (3) *grammatical* active / passive distinctions. The result of these partial mergers is the intersecting pattern of **endoactive / exoactive / endopassive / exopassive** derivational categories (Table 4-3). These terms apply to morphologically marked *derivational* categories of new words; in the OC language, they are independent of grammatical / syntactic behavior and word class; see §2.1.3 (Beard 1998: 44ff). This system constitutes the 'youngest' morphological layer which was still productive or at least transparent in OC.

Introvert and *extrovert* (endo- / exo-) are semantic categories that are readily apparent from a word's meaning. In *introvert* words, the action is directed toward the subject, or happens to or within the subject (to buy, to watch, to grow); in *extrovert* words the action originates in or with the subject and is directed out and away to a necessarily external object (to sell, to show). Introvert verbs often tend to be intransitive, extrovert verbs transitive or causative. Transitive words like 'to buy' were originally perhaps purely introvert, while 'to sell' was purely extrovert. 'To grow' was intransitive or 'middle voice', whereas 'to sow' (derived from 'seeds' n.) was grammatically transitive / causative. The extrovert and valence increasing categories overlap to a large extent: 'to sow' is extrovert beside being transitive ('sow seeds'); and 'to sell' is ditransitive beside being extrovert; *zhǎng* 長 'to grow' is introvert beside being intransitive.

These two concepts overlap completely in words that imply 'giving', as in 'to drink' (introvert, transitive) > 'give someone something to drink' (extrovert, ditransitive, i.e., valence increasing), see Table 4-2. Thus direction and transitivity have merged in OC.

Furthermore, the active / passive distinction has been added to the mix. *Active* and *passive* agree with familiar IE (incl. English, Latin) grammatical concepts. The agent of an active verb is its subject: 'he is growing', 'he is buying something'. In a sentence with a *passive* verb (form), the object of the active counterpart becomes the subject of the passive; the agent (tr. subject) is placed in a prepositional phrase ('he heard this' > passive 'this was heard by him').

The terms 'endoactive' (Japanese *jidōshi* 自動詞, also 'intransitive') and 'exoactive' (*tadōshi* 他動詞, also 'transitive') describe pairs of introvert / extrovert verbs in Japanese grammar (Lewin 1990: 118f.; Shibatani 1990: 115; also Takashima 1996), for example:

naru 'to become' intr.	*nasu* 'to form' tr.
yurumu 'to become loose' intr.	*yurumeru* 'to loosen' tr.

Though nearly identical with the familiar 'intransitive' and 'transitive', the Japanese endoactive category includes verbs that can take an object, therefore the term 'intransitive' is not appropriate, e.g., *kado-wo deru* 'walk out the door' ('door' is the obj. in Japanese). The terms have already been used for Chinese (Sagart 1999: 133) where endoactive (introvert) verbs also can be tr. like *mǎi* 'to buy (something)'. Exoactive verbs are the extrovert, transitive / causative counterparts (*mài* 'sell something to someone').

'Endoactive' is similar to the 'middle voice' of some IE languages: the action was conceived as operating in or on the subject; in the exoactive, the verbal action was directed outwards from the subject (L. R. Palmer, *The Latin Language*, 1987: 262). H. H. Hock (1986: 347) provides the example 'to grow' intr. for one of the specific uses of the IE middle voice; note CH *zhǎng* 長 'to grow' as illustration for endoactive derivation (§4.1.1).

In accordance with this system, we add the terms 'endopassive' and 'exopassive'. In exopassive derivations, the agent (i.e., an external, 'exo-' element) is still available as in a typical passive sentence: 'it was heard by him' < 'he heard it'. Endopassive fits the definition of stative verbs: "... refer to a resultant state without any indication of an agent" (Sadler and Spencer 1998: 223); the endoactive verb *cháng* 長 'be long' *is* a stative verb ('be in a state of being stretched < be stretched').

We could have used the familiar labels 'middle' for 'endoactive', 'active' or 'causative' for 'exoactive', 'passive' for 'exopassive'. However, the IE middle voice drifts toward the passive, whereas the CH category remains active. Furthermore, IE languages make no clearly marked introvert – extrovert distinction. In the end, the labels endo- / exo- and active / passive describe quite well the nature of the CH categories. They also allow us to reserve the endo- / exo- terminology for word derivation, and continue to use 'active' and 'passive' for grammatical relationships.

These categories apply to *derivations* from a stem or other word, i.e., words fall into one of the four categories only when compared with their simplex. Many words have MC tone B, like *zhǎng* 長 (tjaŋ^{B}) 'to grow' where the tone marks the word as endoactive because it contrasts with, and is derived from, the simplex *zhāng* 張 (tjaŋ) 'to stretch'. But *huǒ* 火 (xuâ^{B}) 'fire' is underived; tone B marks nothing. Although underived words do not belong to such a category, one may occasionally feel that a word inherently does, as *sǐ* 死 'to die' with its typical endoactive meaning (see §4.5). Or *wén* 聞 'to hear (something)' tr. could be seen as inherently introvert. But these words are morphologically unmarked and their categorization would in many cases be arbitrary and add nothing to our understanding.

4.1.1 *Direction and diathesis in Old Chinese*

The OC morphological changes which mark direction and diathesis have left traces in later MC tones and voicing of the initial consonant of a word; the tones, possibly also voicing, go back to earlier segmental affixes in OC or PCH. The morphemes are

(1) Tone C (1) (MC *qùshēng* 去聲 < *-s/-h) — **exoactive**: extrovert, often valence increasing ('to hear' tr. > 'ask someone about something' ditr.) (§4.3);

(2) Tone C (2) (MC *qùshēng* 去聲 < *-s/-h) — **exopassive**, i.e., passive of exoactive / transitive words, agent available ('be heard by someone') (§4.4);

(3) Tone B (MC *shǎngshēng* 上聲 < *-ʔ) — **endoactive**: introvert, active, often valence decreasing ('to grow' intr. < 'to stretch' tr.) (§4.5);

(4) Voicing of the initial consonant — **endopassive**: introvert, passive, often valence decreasing, no agent available ('be long' sv. < 'to stretch') (§4.6).

Table 4-3 provides a synopsis of this OC system (LHan forms follow the graphs). Discussions of the individual categories follow below (§4.2–§4.6).

4-3	endo- (introvert)	exo- (extrovert) - Tone C (§4.2)
-active	*endoactive* – Tone B (§4.5) mǎi 買 mɛ^{B} 'to buy' tr. yǐn 飲 ʔim^{B} 'to drink' tr. zhǎng 長 ṭaŋ^{B} 'to grow' intr.	*exoactive* – Tone C (§4.3) mài 賣 mɛ^{C} 'to sell' ditr. yìn 飲 ʔim^{C} 'to give to drink' ditr. wèn 問 mun^{C} 'to ask about' ditr.
-passive	*endopassive* – Voiced initial (§4.6) cháng 長 ḍaŋ 'be long' sv. xiàn 現 gen^{C} 'to appear' intr.	*exopassive* – Tone C (§4.4) wèn 聞 mun^{C} 'be heard about, famous' intr.
simplex	zhāng 張 ṭaŋ 'to stretch' tr. jiàn 見 ken^{C} 'to see' tr.	wén 聞 mun 'to hear about' tr.

Sentence illustrations for most of the above words: *zhǎng, cháng* §2.1.2 ex.14–16; §2.1.3 ex. 1; §4.6; *wén, wèn* §4.3; §4.4; *jiàn, xiàn* §2.1.2 ex. 5–6; §2.1.3 ex. 2; *yìn* §4.3.

In addition to the merger of categories, the system had further been obfuscated not only by the use of its morphemic devices (tones, voicing) outside this system (see *huǒ* 'fire' above), but also by the disconnect between original grammatical categories, the eventual derivational categories, and word classes (§2.1.3). For analytical and descriptive purposes, we here discuss diathesis and valence in traditional grammatical terms. Once the original morphology of a derived word has thus been identified, we can observe how it has developed a life of its own.

Tone C derives passive words (exopassive) from active transitive words; but as already mentioned, the OC meanings and classifications do not always reveal the morphology involved. For example, from the verb *zhī* 織 *tək 'to weave' (tr.) is derived the word 'textiles' *zhì* 織 *təkh < *təks; *təkh is here analyzed as an exopassive derivation from *tək because it is literally 'something that has been woven by someone' (not active: 'something / someone that is doing the weaving'). The OC language had settled on this derivation as a noun and not as the passive verb of the simplex. Word classes like 'noun' are unmarked in CH, hence tone C does not make a noun out of a verb, as is often maintained. From *liǎng* 兩 *raŋʔ 'a pair' n. is derived *liàng* 輛 *raŋh 'carriage' n. which is a thing with two wheels that literally 'have been paired' (not active: 'are doing the pairing'). From *wēi* 威 'to scare, frighten' is derived the exopassive tone C form *wèi* 畏, as in 'I am scared by him'; however, this underlyingly passive *wèi* is actually a new active tr. verb in its own right, as in 'I fear him'; note that the meaning and word order are the same in both interpretations: 'I am scared by him' = 'I fear him'. (For sentence illustrations, see §4.4.1.) From *dēng* 登 *tə̂ŋ 'to rise, ascend' is derived the endoactive *děng* 等 *tə̂ŋʔ 'step of stairs', which literally 'are the ones that are doing the ascending' (not passive: 'which have been ascended'). This present analysis reduces the functions of tone C to one or two (exoactive / exopassive), whereas countless derivational categories need to be postulated if we try to understand tone C as changing word classification (nouns to verbs, verbs to nouns, intr. to tr. and so on; see Downer 1959).

Tense and aspect are not expressed morphologically in CH, but in exopassive derivations a perfective aspect and / or past tense is often implied by the meaning: textiles are obviously things that have been woven, a work that has been completed in the past; same with 'carriage'. Endoactives usually are tense neutral (i.e., the tense is implied by the context, as in 'stairs' above). However, by convention the meaning of certain endoactive derivations can also be past and / or perfect. Thus *zhǎng* intr. 'to grow' can have any tense required by the context, but when used as an adjective or noun, it implies completed aspect, thus *zhǎng* 'grown-up, eldest, elder' (see §2.1.2 ex. 14 for illustration). From *cú* 徂殂 *dzâ 'to go away, pass away, die' is derived endoactive *zǔ* 祖 *tsâʔ 'deceased grandfather, ancestor', lit. 'one who has passed away' (perfective, active, not passive).

4.2 Tone C (*qùshēng* 去聲): two morphological functions

For OC we must assume two distinct morphemes *-s (here *-s / *-h; see §3.4), both of ST provenance, both extrovert: (1) 'exoactive', i.e., extrovert and transitive, and (2) 'exopassive'. Note, for example, the two meanings of *wèn* and *shàn* (text illustrations for *wén* are offered in §4.3; §4.4):

wén [mun]	聞 'to hear about' tr. (simplex)
> wèn [mun^C]	(1) 問 'to ask about, inquire' tr. (exoactive)
	(2) 聞 'be heard about, renowned' intr. (exopassive)
shàn [dźian^B]	善 'be good at' tr. (simplex)
> shàn [dźian^C]	(1) 繕 'repair, put in order' tr. (exoactive)
	(2) 膳 ('be done well':) 'cooked food' n. (exopassive)

Over time, the meanings of tone C had converged until by late Zhou it had become a general purpose device to derive any kind of word from another; see §3.5.

Theoretically, the two functions of tone C could derive from a single ST morpheme *-s (Schuessler 1985). There are parallels for this double duty in other languages, e.g., the Korean suffix *-ita* added to *pota* 'to see' > *poita* (a) passive 'to be seen', (b) caus. 'to show' (Dixon 2000: 31). Ho-Min Sohn (1999: 367) suggests that the Korean "passive suffixes have developed from causative suffixes via functional shift." This could also have been the Chinese development (note §4.1.1 'Fear' above). Also the Japanese suffix *-eru* serves a dual function: it makes exoactives out of endoactives (no suffix), and endoactives out of suffixless exoactives (Lewin 1990: 119; Shibatani 1990: 115), for example:

yurumu 'become loose' (endoactive) > *yurum*-eru 'to loosen' tr. (exoactive)
kak-eru 'to be missing' (endoactive) < *kaku* 'to miss, do without' tr. (exoactive)

The same dual function is encountered in Ainu where the suffix *-ke* makes intr. verbs out of transitives and vice versa (Shibatani 1990: 44). Below, §4.4.1 provides a further comment in favor of a single origin.

4.2.1 *The Sino-Tibetan sources of tone C*

The exopassive morpheme MC tone C < PCH *-s (OC *-s / -h) is related to the TB s-suffix, which in WT forms the past tense, perhaps including the completed aspect of verbs (Beyer 1992: 261), often with a passive connotation in transitive verbs; these derivations can then become nouns; see §2.3.2 Table 2-1 for an example. In Lushai the second verb form (or "modification of the root") creates passives by adding a suffix *-ʔ < -h < -s* (J. H. Lorrain 1940: xiii; *HPTB:* 468ff). The modification form is used also as a 'subjunctive' (J. H. Lorrain 1940: xiii) which, as Geilich (1994: 169–170) points out, corresponds to the IE (Greek, Sanskrit) middle voice (do something for one's own benefit); also in Dulong / Rawang, the suffix *-shi* is a reflexive / middle-marking (LaPolla 2000: 288; also *STC*: 98 'middle voice'; Michailovsky 1985: 369). For additional functions of this suffix in TB languages, see Huang Bufan *LTBA* 19:1, 1996: 29–42; *HPTB:* 439ff; 465ff).

The exoactive function of tone C is also inherited from ST. In some TB languages the second form (*-s) forms transitives / causatives (*HPTB:* 472ff), for example, in Lushai (J. H. Lorrain 1940: xiii): *puŋ*^{H} intr. 'to assemble' ⪤ *pun*^{L} < *puŋs* tr. 'to call together'; *zaal*^{H} < *jaal* 'to lie down, recline' ⪤ *zalʔ*^{L} < *jalʔ/h* 'lay on the back' (a similar function in Hakha Lai: David Peterson, in Thurgood and LaPolla 2003: 418). Other TB languages have a causative final *-s* (Qiang: Sun Hongkai *MZYW* 1998.6: 3–4); we have cited above an example from Limbu: *tʰuŋ-* 'to drink' > caus. *tʰuŋs-* 'give to drink' (§4.1, Table 4-2).

Although these two distinct functions may go back to a single ST morpheme, as in other languages (above §4.2), there is also the possibility that the final *-s in OC, Lushai, and others had two sources, one a past / passive *-s*, one a transitivizing *-t*, as found in the WT present tense final *-d* (note *byed-pa < bya-t* 'to do', fut. *bya* [Beyer 1992: 175; Michailovsky 1985: 368ff]), *-t > -s* after final consonants as in *'debs-pa* (< ɴ*dap-t*), *btab, gtab, tʰob* 'to throw' (Coblin 1976). A final dental stop also occurs in Dulong / Rawang (LaPolla 2000: 308); in JP (Dai Qingxia / Xu Xijian 1992: 78f), and in Himalayan languages.

Be that as it may, for practical purposes we assume two distinct functions for tone C.

4.3 Tone C (1): exoactive derivation

Exoactive (MC tone C [1] < *-s/-h). The agent of an exoactive *-s / *-h verb is the subject whose action is directed outward toward an object that often affects an indirect object. Exoactive appears to be the result of a partial coalescence of a suffix for extroversion (sell tr. < buy tr.; see §4.3.1), and one for increasing valence, i.e., noun > verb, verb intr. > tr.; verb intr. or tr. > ditrtansitive / causative / putative (to sow < seed; see §4.3.2); often the introvert counterpart has the endoactive tone B (§4.5). A paradigmatic example is 'drink' (LHan forms follow the graph):

Drink	yǐn 飲	ʔɨm^{B} tr. 'to drink something'
	> yìn 飲	ʔɨm^{C} ditr. 'to give / offer someone something to drink'

Text illustrations for yìn; often only the indirect object (person, animal) is mentioned:

(1) *yìn xiāng rén jiǔ* 飲鄉人酒 (offer drink / country / people / wine) '(Nan Kuai) offered wine to drink to his country's people' [Zuo: Zhao 12.8].

(2) *hé yìn sì zhī* 曷飲食之 (what / give drink / give eat / him) 'what shall I give him for drink and food?' [Shijing 123.1].

'To ask' *wèn* is an outward directed action which is derived from a directionally neutral (or perhaps inherently introvert) verb 'to hear' *wén* (ex. 3). As a ditransitive verb, it can take a direct object (ex. 4) or an indir. obj. (5).

(3) *wǒ wén qí shēng* 我聞其聲 (I / hear / his / voice) 'I hear his voice' [Shi 199, 3].

(4) *wèn qí bìng* 問其病 (ask about / his / affliction [dir. obj.]) 'he asked [him] about his affliction' (dir. obj.) [Zuo: Xuan 2, 4].

(5) *wèn Zhòng Ní* 問仲尼 (ask / Confucius [ind. obj.]) 'He asked Confucius'. [Zhuang 6, 75].

This 'recent' exoactive s-/h-suffix was occasionally added to an old verb which already had the (unproductive) ST causative s-prefix; 'to feed' (also in §2.3.2 Table 2-4) prob. had acquired tone C in order to fit the pattern of exoactive verbs like 'to drink' above.

Feed	sì 食	LH ziə^{C}, *s-ləkh 'to feed'
		< caus. of shí 食 (dźjək) [źək] *m-lək 'to eat'
Lose	sàŋ 喪	sɑŋ^{C}, *smâŋh 'to lose, destroy'
		< wáng 亡 [muɑŋ] *maŋ 'to lose'

4.3.1 Tone C: exoactive — extrovert, ditransitive

These derivations also tend to be causative. 'To drink' and 'to feed' have just been cited. See also *yì* 衣 'to wear' used as a ditransitive verb in §2.1.2 (ex. 9; 10). A few more examples:

Sell	mǎi 買	mɛ^{B} 'to buy'
	> mài 賣	mɛ^{C} 'to sell' < 'to give someone something to buy'
Give	shòu 受	dźu^{B} 'receive, accept'
	> shòu 授	dźu^{C} 'to give' ditr.
Show	shì 視	gi^{B} 'to look at'
	> shì 示	gi^{C} 'to show' ditr. < 'make someone look at'
Teach	xué 學	gɔk, *gruk 'to learn'
	> xiào 斆	gau^{C}, *grukh 'to teach'
Ask	wén 聞	mun 'to hear about' tr.
	> wèn 問	mun^{C} 'to ask about something', 'ask someone' tr.
Wife	qī 妻	tsʰei 'consort, wife'
	> qì 妻	tsʰei^{C} 'give a wife to', 'give as a wife' tr.

Often, the added argument of a ditransitive verb is an indirect object which typically is a beneficiary. This indirect object is the essence of tone C, while in many sentences a direct object is only implied, as in 'give someone to drink' with no specification of the thing involved (direct object). In a way, tone C replaces a thing by a person. For example, (LHan after the graph):

Listen	tīng 聽	tʰeŋ 'to listen'
	> tìng 聽	tʰeŋ^{C} 'to listen to, obey'

Reply	dá 答	təp 'respond to'
	> duì 對	tuəs, *tə̂ps < *tûps 'to reply' (to a person)
Tell	yǔ 語	ŋɨa^{B} 'to speak'
	> yù 語	ŋɨa^{C} 'to tell someone'
Overturn	fù 覆	p^{h}uk, *phuk 'to overturn, overthrow' tr.
	> fù 覆	p^{h}u^{C}, *phukh 'to overspread, provide cover for someone'
Aid	yòu 右	wu^{B}, wu^{C} 'right (side), be to the right'
	> yòu 右佑	wu^{C} tr. 'to aid, support, assist someone'
Before	xiān 先	sen 'to go in front, ahead, before, former'
	> xiàn 先	sen^{C} (1) tr. 'to walk before' (in order to protect) > 'take care of someone, attend'; (2) caus. 'to put first'
After	hòu 後	go^{B} or ɣo^{B} 'be behind, after', 'to follow'
	> hòu 後	go^{C} or ɣo^{C} (1) tr. 'be behind someone, attend, support'; (2) caus. 'to put after'
Attend	shì 恃	dźə^{B} 'to depend on'
	> shì 侍	dźə^{C} 'to wait upon someone, attend'
Woman	nyǔ 女	ṇɑ^{B} 'woman, wife' n.
	> nyù 女	ṇɑ^{C} 'give (as) a wife' tr.
Take a wife	qǔ 取	k^{h}ɨo^{B} 'to take' tr.
	> qù 娶	k^{h}ɨo^{C} 'to take a wife'

In this last example, we might have expected that tone C makes the derivation *qù* extrovert, whereas it is still introvert ('take', not 'give'). However, the key was apparently the person as indir. object. After all, the meanings of derivations are by their very nature unpredictable.

4.3.2 Tone C: exoactive — transitive, causative / putative

When applied to nouns or stative verbs, tone C effects an increase in *transitivity* (valence), while extroversion is more coincidental (LHan after the graph):

Sow	zhǒng 種	tśoŋ^{B} 'seeds, cereals' n.
	> zhòng 種	tśoŋ^{C} 'to sow' tr.
Hit center	zhōng 中	ṭuŋ 'be in the middle, middle, inside'
	> zhòng 中	ṭuŋ^{C} 'hit the center, hit, attain'
Repair	shàn 善	dźan^{B} 'be good (at)' tr. (intr.)
	> shàn 繕	dźan^{C} caus. (make good:) 'repair, put in order' tr.
Love	hǎo 好	hou^{B} 'be good' sv.
	> hào 好	hou^{C} put. (consider / treat someone as good:) 'to love' tr.
Hate	è 惡	ʔɑk, *ʔâk 'be evil' sv.
	> wù 惡	ʔɑ^{C}, *ʔâkh put. (treat as bad:) 'to hate'
Far	yuǎn 遠	wɑn^{B} 'far away, distant' sv.
	> yuàn 遠	wɑn^{C} put. (treat as far away:) 'keep at a distance'

4.3.3 Residue

There remains the inevitable residue where the exact function of tone C is not obvious: perhaps 'Lose' follows the pattern of 'feed' (§2.3.2).

Below	xià 下	ga^B 'to descend, down, below'
	> xià 下	ga^C tr. 'descend, fall'

4.4 Tone C (2): exopassive derivation

Exopassive (MC tone C [2] < *-s/-h) is the passive of a transitive or exoactive word. As in *passives*, incl. endopassive, the subject is the object of the exoactive / transitive counterpart; in contrast to *introvert* endopassive, exopassive is extrovert in the sense that there is an explicit or implied outside agent which acts on the subject. Usually, passive agrees in meaning with Western languages, although in OC we are dealing with word derivation, not grammar (ex. 2); an exopassive derivation is often a noun, literally meaning "the thing that has been verb-ed" (as opposed to endoactive where the noun is "the thing that is doing the verb-ing"). Exopassive is the counterpart to exoactive. Contrast the simplex ex. 1 with the exopassive ex. 2; the passive is still in the extrovert column because the former (outside) subject is still available in the prepositional *yú* phrase as agent, i.e., there is still 'the outside' which hears the sound.

(1) *wǒ wén qí shēng* 我聞其聲 (I / hear / his / voice) 'I hear his voice' [Shi 199, 3].

(2) *shēng wèn yú wài* 聲聞于外 (sound / be heard [passive] / preposition / outside) '(The instruments') sound is heard outside' [Shi 229, 5].

In this sentence, the passive verb *wèn* looks like a grammatical form as if OC still had inflection. But an inflectional suffix *-s should change other verbs in a predictable way as well, which is not the case in OC. Furthermore, in OC grammar, passives are regularly created from active verbs by word order alone (§2.1.2, ex. 6). However, example (2) does suggest an earlier inflectional origin of the morpheme. More passives:

Renowned	wén 聞	mun 'to hear about' (simplex)
	> wèn 聞	mun^C 'be heard about, renowned, fame'
Grasped	zhí 執	tśip, *təp 'to hold, grasp'
	> zhì 摯	tśi^C, *təps 'be grasped, seized'
Exhausted	jìn 盡	dzin^B 'exhaust' > jìn 燼 dzin^C 'be exhausted, destroyed'
Put down	xià 下	ga^B 'descend, below' [Shijing]
	> xià 下	ga^C 'be put down'
Back n.	běi 北	pək, *pə̂k 'north'
	> bèi 背	pə^C, *pə̂kh 'what is turned north (passive): the back'
Measured	duò 度	dɑk ,*dâk 'to measure, plan'
	> dù 度	dɑ^C, *dâkh 'be measured' > 'to regulate'

Naturally, such an exopassive derivation can occasionally be a noun (see 'cloth' and 'carriage' in §4.1.1), for example:

Inside	nà 納 *nə̂p < *nûp 'to bring into'
	> nèi 內 *nə̂ts < *nûps 'what is entered > inside'
Purpose	zhī 之 *tə 'to go' > zhì 志 *təh 'what is gone to > goal, purpose'

4.4.1 Exopassive as a transitive verb

An exopassive can become a new active verb, for example:

Fear	wēi 威	ʔui 'to overawe, terrorize', i.e., 'frighten someone' tr.
	> wèi 畏	ʔui^{C} 'to fear' tr., 'be afraid' intr. < 'be made frightened'

Text illustrations:

(1) *fǒu zé wēi zhī* 否則威之 (not / then / frighten, overawe / them) '... if not, then one overawes them' [Shu 5, 14].

(2) *wèi tiān zhī wēi* 畏天之威 (to fear / Heaven / -'s / frighten, scariness) 'May we fear Heaven's majesty' [Shi 272].

The tr. verb *wēi* 威 'to scare' turns passive with tone C *wèi* 畏 "I am scared [of Heaven]"; but *wèi* is actually a new transitive verb 'to fear', thus "I fear Heaven". What remains of the passive is the switch in the direction of the action, i.e., the new subject is still the object of the simplex 'to scare'. This is similar to what has been observed in Kuki-Chin languages. In Tiddim and Lushai the second verb form can itself become a new transitive verb (Geilich 1994: 170). An example from Lushai:

kaŋ^{R} < kaaŋʔ 'be off the ground, lifted off one's feet'
kaan^{L} < kaans 2nd form: subjunctive: 'lift off oneself'; passive 'be lifted off'
= kaan^{L} < kaans tr. 'to lift up, raise'

That the passive form of a verb can flip over into a new transitive verb could therefore be an old ST phenomenon; it also may speak in favor of a single origin of the two functions of tone C. Other examples (LHan after the graph):

Yield	ráng 攘	ńaŋ 'to remove, steal something'
	> ràng 讓	ńaŋ^{C} 'to remove oneself' > 'yield to someone'
Leave	qǔ 去	k^{h}ɨa^{B} 'put away, eliminate'
	> qù 去	k^{h}ɨa^{C} 'to remove oneself' > 'leave'
Mirror	jiān 監	kam 'to observe'
	> jiàn 監	kam^{C} 'to observe oneself: to mirror; a mirror'

4.5 Tone B (*shǎngshēng* 上聲): endoactive derivation

Endoactive (MC tone B < *-ʔ) is active, i.e., the agent is the subject as in an exoactive word; the derivation is also introvert, i.e., the action takes place in the subject or is directed toward the subject. Sometimes, valence is decreased, but introvert forms can also be tr. verbs (endoactive 'to buy something' tr.). Again, it seems that two earlier phenomena have coalesced, one valence decreasing, one introvert; both are the opposite of the exoactive tone C (§4.3). An introvert meaning is obvious in 'to buy / receive something'. In *zhǎng* 'to grow' intr. (ex. 2), the action takes place in the subj., no outside agent acts on it; this contrasts with the tr. simplex *zhāng* 'to stretch something' (ex. 1) where the direction from the subj. outward affects the obj.:

(1) *zhāng wǒ gōng* 張我弓 (stretch / our / bows) 'we drew our bows' [Shi 180, 4].

(2) *shēng ér zhǎng, zhǎng ér dà* 生而長長而大 (give birth / particle / to grow / to grow / part. / big) '(the living things) ... are born and grow, they grow and become big...' [Lüshi chunqiu 3, 5].

The endoactive verb *zhǎng* (intr.) can, of course, be used causatively (§2.1.2 ex. 15) and as an adjective (§2.1.2 ex. 14).

Grow	zhāng 張	ṭaŋ	'stretch'
	> zhǎng 長	ṭaŋ^{B}	'to grow tall'
Above	shàng 上	dźaŋ^{C}	'above'
	> shàng 上	dźaŋ^{B}	'to rise'
Face	miàn 面	mian^{C}	'the face'
	> miǎn 偭	mian^{B}	'to turn from'
High	áng 卬	ŋaŋ	'be high'
	> yǎng 仰	ŋɨaŋ^{B}	'look up'
Lift	yáng 揚	jaŋ	'to lift, raise'
	> ? yǎng 養	jaŋ^{B}	'nourish, raise, support'

Often the exoactive word has an introvert counterpart which in many pairs has tone B. This tone could be a CH innovation because of the inherent introvert meaning of the word, and in order to create morphologically marked introvert / extrovert pairs (LHan after the graph):

Sell	mǎi 買	mɛ^{B} 'to buy'
	> mài 賣	mɛ^{C} 'to sell' < 'to give someone something to buy'
Give	shòu 受	dźu^{B} 'receive, accept'
	> shòu 授	dźu^{C} 'to give' < 'to give someone something'
Show	shì 視	gi^{B} 'to look at'
	> shì 示	gi^{C} 'to show' < 'make someone look at something'
Good at	shàn 善	dźan^{B}, *danʔ 'be good (at)' tr. (intr.)
	> shàn 繕	dźan^{C}, *dans caus. (make good) 'repair, put in order' tr.
Good	hǎo 好	hou^{B} 'be good' sv.
	> hào 好	hou^{C} put. (consider / treat someone as good) 'to love' tr.

In addition, note 'to drink' in §4.3.

Tone B may have been added to some intr. verbs because of their implicit endoactive nature so that it came to mark change of state:

To die	sǐ 死	si^{B}	'to die' <> PTB *si (not *siʔ) 'to die'
Change	gǎi 改	kə^{B}	'to change'
Rise	qǐ 起	k^{h}ɨə^{B}	'to rise'
Sit	zuò 坐	dzuai^{B}	'to sit'
Dwell	chǔ 處	tś^{h}a^{B}	'to dwell' <> PTB *gla

Many words remain in which the role of tone B is not clear, for example:

Expand	shī 施	śai 'to expand, spread out, expose'
	> shǐ 弛	śai^{B} 'to extend, spread'
Offer	zhēng 烝	tśɨŋ 'to offer (gift, sacrifice)'
	> zhěng 氶	tśɨŋ^{B} 'lift, save, help'

Tone B had ceased to be productive probably by the end of the Western Zhou period (ca. 770 BC); from that time on, tone C replaced it as the universal morpheme for marking any kind of derivation (§3.5). Thus we find that derivations like *jì* 騎 'rider' (active; not: 'what is being ridden') occur with increasing frequency.

4.5.1 Tone B: endoactive nouns

Many endoactive tone B derivates are *nouns* meaning "the thing / person which does the verb-ing." Some of the following items are not minimal pairs, but the key semantic aspect of tone B is apparent (LHan after the graph):

Offspring	ST *tsə	'to come forth' (at birth)
	> zǐ 子	tsiə^{B} 'offspring, child', lit. 'who has come forth'
Jaw	hán 含	gəm 'hold in mouth'
	> hàn 頷	gəm^{B} 'jaw' ('that which holds in the m.')
Foot	zhī 之	tśə 'to go, proceed'
	> zhǐ 止	tśə^{B} 'foot' ('that which is doing the going')
Bottom	dī 低	tei 'to lower'
	> dǐ 氐	tei^{B} 'bottom' ('that which is low')
Stair	dēng 登	təŋ 'rise, ascend'
	> děng 等	təŋ^{B} 'step of stairs' ('that which rises')
Category	dāng 當	tɑŋ 'be equal of, rank'
	> dǎng 黨	tɑŋ^{B} 'category, party' ('equal in rank')
Brother	dì 第	dei^{C} 'order, sequel'
	> dì 弟	dei^{B} 'younger brother'
Dry	gān 乾	kɑn 'dry' > hàn 旱 gɑn^{B} 'dry, drought'
Low ground	bēi 卑	pie 'be low, humble'
	> bì 埤	bie^{B} 'low ground' 埤; 'female slave' 婢
A turn	zài 再	tsə^{C} 'twice, again and again'
	> zǎi 載	tsə^{B} 'a turn, a year' ('that which comes again')

In addition, see *zǔ* 祖 'ancestor' in §4.1.1.

In the following sets, it is not apparent which word is derived from which:

Way	dào 導	dou^{C} 'to bring along, conduct'
	}{ dào 道	dou^{B} 'way' ('that which does the conducting, leading')
Ladle	zhù 注	tśo^{C}, ṭo^{C} 'to conduct water, to pour'
	}{ zhǔ 斗	tśo^{B} 'ladle' ('that which does the pouring')

4.6 Voicing of the initial consonant: endopassive derivation

Endopassive (MC voicing). Voicing of the initial consonant derives an 'endopassive' word from a simplex. Endopassives are: (a) introvert (not extrovert); (b) passive in the sense that the subject of the endopassive word was the object of the simplex, whereas in endoactive words, the subject is the same as that of the former simplex; (c) unlike exopassives, the hypothetical subject of the simplex is grammatically and semantically not available (§4.1.1). In fact, a definition of a stative verb agrees well with 'endopassive': "Stative verbs refer to a resultant state without any indication of an agent" (Sadler and Spencer 1998: 223). The difference between exopassive and endopassive is that in the former, the agent (subject of the active verb) is still available in a prepositional phrase or in context, whereas no former subject or agent is available or even implied in the latter. Thus in 'to be long' sv. an agent who might have done the stretching, the 'making long', never existed (ex. 2).

(1) *zhāng wǒ gōng* 張我弓 (stretch / our / bows) 'we drew our bows' [Shi 180, 4].

(2) *dào zǔ ér cháng* 道阻而長 (road / difficult / part. / be long) 'the road is difficult and long' [Shi 129, 1].

A hypothetical endopassive of ex. 1 張弓 'draw the bows' might be *gōng cháng* 弓長 'the bows are (drawn:) long'.

Morphological voicing of the initial consonant is a common ST phenomenon which is encountered in OC and many TB languages, e.g., WT *'debs-pa* < *N-deps*, past *btab*, future *gtab*, imperative *t*^{h}*ob* 'to throw'. Voicing has the function of changing transitive to intransitive, or marking a verb as intr.; WT *'dzag-pa* 'to trickle' × *'ts*^{h}*ag-pa* 'to cause to trickle' (Beyer 1992: 163; 258f). Thus there is not necessarily a connection between voicing, intransitivization, and the WT prefix *'a-čhung* which is transcribed as *'x* as in *'dzag*; the letter was probably used as a diacritic to mark prenasalized consonants, as in modern Tibetan dialects it corresponds to a nasal (Coblin, *LTBA* 25:2, 2002: 169–184). Pulleyblank (*JCL* 1, 1973: 114) holds an OC prefix *ɦ- (later amended to some kind of *a-) responsible for intransitive voicing, Baxter and others a prefix *N-. We will leave the prefix question open and consider these initials to have been simple voiced ones in OC as in MC.

The first few examples are in fact sv. in OC (LHan after the graph):

Long	zhāng 張	ṭaŋ 'make long, stretch'
	> cháng 長	ḍaŋ 'be long' sv.
Divide	bié 別	pɨat 'to divide, separate'
	> bié 別	bɨat 'be different' sv.
Between	jiā 夾	kεp 'be on both sides, press between'
	> xiá 狹	gεp 'be narrow' sv.
Loosen	jiě 解	kε^{B} 'to loosen'
	> xiè 解	gε^{B} 'be slack, idle, careless' sv.

In OC, sv. is a well-defined word class whose members can freely function as adjectives. Many endopassive verbs are, however, intr. and even tr., but they still agree more or less with the above definition of a 'stative verb'.

See	jiàn 見	ken^{C} 'to see, visit'
	> xiàn 現	gen^{C} 'to appear' intr. (get oneself seen)
Descend	jiàng 降	kɔŋ^{C} 'to descend'
	> xiáng 降	gɔŋ 'to submit' intr. (get oneself down)
Go into water	jiān 熸	tsiam 'extinguish' (= put water on a fire)
	> qián 潛	dziam 'go into water, wade' (get oneself into w.)
Mix	jiāo 交	kau 'to cross, mix with, exchange'
	> yiáo 殽	gau 'mixed, confused' (get mixed)
Burn	jiāo 焦	tsiau 'to roast, burn'
	> qiáu 樵	dziau 'firewood, to burn' intr. (get to burn itself)

Attach	zhǔ 屬	tśok 'to attach, apply'
	> shǔ 屬	dźok 'be connected, attached to' (get to be attached)
Apply	zhuó 著	ṭɑk 'to place, put, apply'
	> zhuó 著	ḍɑk 'to come in contact with' (be placed)
Set	zhì 置	ṭə^{C} 'to set, place'
	> zhí 值	ḍə^{C} 'hold upright, a pole' (got set and held)
Half	bàn 半	pɑn^{C} 'half'
	> pàn 畔	bɑn^{C} 'separate from, rebel'

The endopassive nature of the following two examples is not obvious. Yet 'to imitate, follow an example' and 'to learn' are introvert processes and can be felt to be passive. The choice of endopassive voicing may be due to the inappropriate extrovert flavor of the exopassive.

Set example	jiào 教	kau^{C} 'teach, set an example'
	> xiào 效傚	gau^{C} 'imitate, follow (an example)'
Get insight	jué 覺	kɔk 'to wake up' intr., 'get insight'
	> xué 學	gɔk 'to learn'

Two derivations behave exopassively because the subject of the simplex is presumably available:

Destroy	bài 敗	pas 'to ruin, destroy'
	> bài 敗	bas 'to go to ruin, be defeated'
Ruin	huài 壞	kuɛi^{C} 'to destroy, ruin'
	> huài 壞	guɛi^{C} 'to be ruined'

4.6.1 Residue

This residue may constitute a subclass of verbs that are derived from nouns (Baxter and Sagart 1998: 47 with additional examples). The meaning of some items implies introversion (LHan after the graph):

Back	bèi 背	pə^{C} 'the back'
	> bèi 背	bə^{C} 'turn the back on' (introvert)
Morning	zhāo 朝	ṭɑu 'morning'
	> cháo 朝潮	ḍɑu 'go to court, morning tide' (introvert)
Shore	bīn 濱	pin 'shore, bank'
	> pín 頻	bin 'river bank, be on the edge, close to'
Dike	dī 隄	te 'bank, dike'
	> tí 提	de 'to raise, to take up' (tr.)
Pole	zhí, dé 樴	tśɨk 'a pole'
	> zhí 植	dźɨk 'to plant, raise, establish' (tr.)
Finger	zhǐ 指	ki^{B} 'to point to, finger'
	>< shì 視	gi^{B} / gi^{C} 'to see, look' / 'to show'

5
INITIAL CONSONANTS

Because MC initial consonants and other phonemes are projected back to (nearly) identical ones in LHan, subsequently examples will often be cited in simpler LHan forms.

Most of the OC – TB or foreign initial consonant equations are straightforward: *m-* = *m-*, *p* ~ p^h ~ *b* = *p-* ~ p^h*-* ~ *b-*, etc. For unusual correspondences with laterals and semivowels, see §7–§10. Voiced initials are discussed in other contexts:

morphological voicing of the initial (endopassive), see §4.6;
MC initial *d-* from OC *d- and *l-, see §8.1.1;
MC initial *zj-* from OC *s-l- (§8.1.2), *s-j- (§9.4), and *s-w- (§10.1.2);
MC initial *dźj-* (LHan *ź-*), the rare initials, from OC *m-l-, see §8.1.3;
MC initial *źj-* (LHan *dź-*), the common initial from OC *d-, but also from *j-, see §9.3;
and on the initials in *GSR* 413 至, see §8.1.5.

5.1 Devoiced initials

Some voiceless initials are discussed in connection with *r- (§7.1.2; 7.1.4) and OC *l- (§8.2.1).

Devoicing of sonorants is common within ST wfs and in OC. Many of the following MC initials reflect an earlier voiceless sonorant; examples can be found in §5.2.2 to §5.6.

MC t^h- from *lh-, *nh-, rarely from *rh-.
MC *śj-* from *lh, *nh-, *hj-(?); MC *śj-* never represents OC *sj-!
MC *x-* from *hŋ, *hŋ, *hw, also *h-; rarely from acute initials (§1.3.1; §5.6).
MC $ṭ^h$- occasionally from *rh-, otherwise from *thr- (§7.1.2).
MC *tśhj-* occasionally from *k-hl- (§5.9.3), otherwise from *th-.

Other languages indicate that the loss of consonants like *s-, *k-, *p-, *ʔ- were the cause of OC voicelessness, by first devoicing the following sonorant, then disappearing. Devoiced initials co-occur in phonetic series with the voiced counterparts *l-, *-n, *-r, *m-, *ŋ-, *w-. Because they do not mix in phonetic series with other types of consonants like *s-*, *k-*, *t-*, we must assume devoiced sonorants already for pre-literate Chinese, i.e., at least 1250 BC; thus 'fire' → huǒ 火 has never been anything but *hmə̂iʔ in OC (never *smə̂iʔ). The prefix / pre-initial which had caused voicelessness must have disappeared by that time.

Words from all sources, ST, KT, MY, and AA participated in this devoicing in PCH. Because several solid ST etymologies are in this list (including *huǒ* 'fire'), the items in the present section represent the normal PCH / OC development from ST clusters and must reflect an early layer in PCH. Many of the words with OC voiceless continuants have foreign counterparts with discrete clusters. If Chinese was the donor of such words, then the exchange would have taken place at a very early age indeed. Less dramatic would be the assumption that PCH had absorbed foreign vocabulary during its expansion which then underwent the regular PCH process of cluster simplification.

*5.1.1 Devoicing of ST initial *z-> MC s-*

MC *zj-* reflects an original s-prefix in the combinations *s-l- (§8.1.2), *s-j- (§9.4), and *s-w- (§10.1.2). But the voiced ST root initial *z- is devoiced in OC to *s-, for example:

Small — ST *zi: xì 細 (siei^{C}) [se^{C}] *sêh or [sei^{C}] *sîh 'thin, small' <> PTB *ziy > West Tib. *zi* 'very small'; WB *se*^{B} 'small, fine'; Kachin *zi* 'small'

To act, do — ST *zə: sī 司 (sɨ) [siə] *sə 'be in charge, manage' <> WT *mdzad-pa* (< *m-za-t*) 'to do, act' ⋈ *bzo* 'work, labor'

Sleep — ST *k-zim: qǐn 寢 [ts^{h}im^{B}] 'sleep' <> WT *gzim-pa* 'sleep' (§5.9.1)

5.2 Sino-Tibetan *s-prefix

The ST and PCH s-prefix is reflected in several MC initials:

(1) MC *s-* < OC *s-, and MC ṣ- from *sr-, from a PCH s-prefix, it occurs mostly before the initials *n-, *ŋ-, and *r-, occasionally also in front of others; see §5.2.1.
(2) MC *zj-* before OC *l-, *j-, and *w-; see §8.1.2.
(3) MC voiceless sonorants in OC; see §5.2.2–3; §5.6.
(4) Perhaps MC dental affricates *ts-*, etc. from earlier *s* + stop consonant; see §5.7.

The s-prefix is of ST origin. It survives in OC as a non-productive morpheme which once formed causatives (Mei 1985: 334–343; 1989; Baxter and Sagart 1998: 53) (§5.2.1 and §5.2.2), iteratives (§5.2.3), and common nouns (§5.2.4). See §2.4.3 for the history of this prefix.

5.2.1 Causative s-prefix > Middle Chinese s-

In some MC forms which have preserved *s-, the original causative / transitive function is still detectable (LHan after the graph):

Lose — sàŋ 喪 — saŋ^{C}, *smaŋh 'to lose, destroy' < wáng 亡 [muaŋ] *maŋ 'to lose'

Revive — sū 蘇 — sa, *sŋa 'to revive' < wù 悟寤 [ŋa^{C}] *ŋâh 'to awake'

Fear — sū 蘇 — sa, *sŋâ 'to tremble, fear' ⋈ wù 遻 [ŋa^{C}] *ŋâkh 'unexpectedly come across'

Tremble — suǒ 索 — sak, *sŋâk 'tremble, fear' < è 愕噩 [ŋak] *ŋâk 'scared, tremble, fear'

Entice — xù 訹 — sut, *sjut, ? 'to entice' is prob. a caus. of *yòu* 誘 'to entice' (under → shù$_{4}$ 述術鉥) (?)

Expel — xiāng 襄 — siaŋ, *snaŋ 'to remove, expel' < ráng 攘穰 [ńaŋ] *naŋ 'to remove, steal'

5.2.2 Causative s-prefix > MC voiceless initial

As already suggested, the voiceless initial consonant represents an early layer in which a ST or PCH causative *s- has been lost after devoicing the following sonorant:

Neglect — huāng 荒 — huaŋ, *hmaŋ 'neglect, reject' < wáng 亡 [muaŋ] *maŋ 'lose'

Let go — shī 失 — śit, *lhit tr. 'to lose, fail, neglect, let go, err' < yì 佚逸 [jit] *lit intr. 'to escape, retire'

Transport — shū 輸 — śo, *lho (or *hjo ?) 'to transport, transmit' < yú 踰逾 [jo] *lo or *jo ? 'pass over'

Injure shāng 傷 śaŋ, *lhaŋ 'to injure, hurt', tr. or caus. of
< yáng 痒 [jaŋ] *laŋ 'be sick'

In at least one word, an s-causative has been added to the already devoiced initial (§5.9.2):

Let go yì 繹 [śak] ~ [jak] *lak 'unfold, unravel'
> devoicing caus.: shì 釋 [śak] *lhak 'unloose, put away, let go'
> s-suffix caus.: shè 赦 [śa^{C}] *lhakh 'let go, liberate, pardon'
> s-prefix caus.: cì 赤 [ts^{h}iak] *s-lhak ? 'to expel'

Some causative derivations with s-prefix have in addition tone C which also marks causative (exoactive; §4.3).

5.2.3 Iterative s-prefix > MC s-, ṣ-, voiceless initial

PCH *s- forms iteratives and intensives. While 'intensive' is often a subjective perception, iterative can readily be identified when it refers to repeated action or movement. Some examples of iteratives follow; the first item is particularly illuminating:

Flicker shǎn 閃 LH [śam^{B}] *lham? ('flicker') 'to twinkle, time of a short glance, moment'. 'Flicker' is a repetitive phenomenon.
< derived from yán 炎 [jam] *lam 'to flame, blaze, burn'

Drip shān 潸 [ṣa/ɛn(^{B})] *srâ/ên(ʔ) 'be flowing (of tears)'
< lián 連聯 [lian] *ran or *ren ? 'to join, in a row, go one after another, be dripping or running'

Sprinkle sǎ 灑 [ṣe$^{B/C}$], [ṣai$^{B/C}$] 'to sprinkle'

Count shǔ 數 [ṣo^{B}] *sroʔ 'to calculate, count' involves repeated mental moves

Generation shì 世 [śas] *lhats < *-ps 'generation, epoch'
< yè 葉 [jap] *lap 'foliage' – 'generation' implies repetition

Instruct huì 誨 [huə^{C}] *hmə̂h 'to instruct'
<> PL *s-ma^{2} 'to teach', WB *hma^{A}* 'give instructions, order' — teaching involves repetition

Comb shū 梳 [ṣa] *sra 'comb'
<> TB *hryat 'to comb': KN-Lai *hriat / hriaʔ* 'to comb', WT *(g)šad-pa* < *g-rhyat 'to comb'

Brush shuā 刷 [ṣuat] ~ [ṣot] *srot 'scrape clear, brush'

Lick tiǎn 舔 [t^{h}em^{B}] *lhîmʔ ? 'to lick'
<> TB *(s-)lyam — licking involves a repetitive motion

Taste tiē 呫 [t^{h}iep] *nhêp 'to taste'
<> WT *sñab-pa* 'to taste, savor' — tasting is similar to licking, implying repetitive motion

Snore hōu 齁 [ho] *hŋô 'to snore'
<> WT *ŋur-ba* 'to grunt' ⋇ *sŋur-ba* 'to snore' — 'snore' typically involves repetition as opposed to 'grunt'

Annoy xù 頊 [hɨok] *hŋok 'disconcerted'
<> WT *sŋog-pa, bsŋogs* 'to vex, annoy' — involves repeated instances

Wash — shì 釋 [śak] *lhak 'to put into water, moisten, wash (rice)' — washing involves repetitive movements <> KS *s-lak 'to wash clothes'

Signal — huī 麾 [hyɑi] *hmai 'signal flag, to signal'

Wink — xuè 罗 [hyɑt] *hmat or *hmet 'to wink at, give signal with the eyes' <> WB *hmit* 'to wink'

Headband — xǐ 縰 [ṣe]*sre 'band wound round the hair' < lí 纚 [lie] *re 'a rope'

Sieve — shāi, shī 篩 [ṣi], [ṣɛi] 'a sieve, sifter, strainer', post-Han

Strain — shū 釃 (ṣjwo^{A}) [ṣɑ^{B}] 'to strain (spirits) < lü 濾 liɑ^{C} 'to drip', post-Han

Suck — shù 欶 [ṣɔk] *srôk or *C-sôk 'suck, inhale'

In some words, the iterative *s- means repetition, 'again':

Seven — qī 七 OCM *tshit < *snhit ? 'seven', lit. 'two again' <> TB *snis 'seven' < ST *nis 'two'

New moon — shuò 朔 *sŋrâk ? 'new moon', lit. 'go toward (the full moon) again' < nì 逆 *ŋrak 'go to meet, go toward'

Year — suì 歲 *swats 'year' < perh. yuè 越 *wat 'pass over', lit. 'pass over again' or 'start the circle again'

The following are perhaps intensive (no obvious repetition):

Blaze — shàn 煽 LH [śan^{C}] *nhans 'blaze' × rán 然 [ńan] *nan 'burn'

Black — hēi 黑 [hək] *hmə̂k 'black' <> WT *smag* 'dark, darkness'

Evil — tè 慝 [tʰək] *nhə̂k 'evil, wrong' <> WT *nag* 'black', *gnag* 'black, evil' × *snag* 'ink'; LB *(s)nak 'black' — extreme phenomena tend to be expressed with redundant intensives

Cut off — tī 剔 鬄 [tʰek] *lhêk 'to cut off, cut to pieces'

Many words remain in which no obvious meaning is associated with the initial *s- or devoicing; some items have connections outside ST, and therefore the OC feature in question may reflect a foreign morphological process (note *xiāng* 纕 'belt' in §5.12.3):

Bestow — shě 舍 [sa^{B}] *lhaʔ 'to let off, bestow, grant' <> MMon *salah* 'to give away, disburse', LMon 'give up, free' — causative?

To rest — shè 舍 [śa^{C}] *lhah < *lhwah 'to rest in, stop' ~ shuì 說 [śuas] ~ [śos] *lho(t)s (*lhwa(t)s ?) 'rest over night' <> KS *s-lwa^{B} 'to rest'

*5.2.4 Nouns with *s- > MC s-, voiceless initial*

A ST *s- / devoicing is also conspicuous in nouns, but the function / meaning of the *s- is not clear. We may speculate that nouns with iterative meaning, such as 'Fire', 'Comb', 'Brush', 'Sieve' (in §5.2.3) served as a paradigm. Dai and Wu (1995: 99) include examples from JP, e.g., *si^{33}* 'to die' > *tʃə^{33}-si^{33}* 'a dead person' (LHan after the graph):

Archery hall	xiè 榭	zia^C, *s-lakh 'archery hall' (initial as in §8.1.2)
Beard	xū 須鬚	sio, *sno 'beard' <> PTB *sno(w) ~ *sno(t) 'mouth, vessel'
Frost	shuāng 霜	ṣɑŋ, *sraŋ 'hoarfrost' < liáng 涼 *raŋ 'cold'
Bean	shú 菽	śuk, *nhuk 'bean' <> PLB-M *(s-)nok 'bean' > WB *nok*
Fire	huǒ 火	huɑi^B, *hmə̂iʔ 'fire' <> PTB *mey, OTib. *smye*; PL *C-mi^2 'fire'
Louse	shī 虱	ṣit, *srit < ST *srik 'louse' <> PTB *s-rik
Scorpion	chài 蠆	ṭ^{h}as, *rhâts 'scorpion' < *lì* 厲 lias, *rats 'sharp'

In 'Louse' and 'Scorpion', the *s- looks like the common TB and SE Asian "animal prefix." However, it occurs rarely with animals in OC; furthermore an equivalent to the word PTB *sya 'animal, meat', the source of the *s-, does not exist in Chinese, therefore the initial in these creatures is probably also this ST nominal prefix.

5.3 Devoicing and PTB *r-

Voicelessness corresponds in some CH words to PTB *r- which can also show up as OC medial *-r- (Shī Xiàngdōng 2000: 208–210) (§7.4):

Grasp	shè 攝	śap, *nhep 'to grasp, gather up' <> WT *rñab-rñab-pa* 'to seize or snatch together'
Gums	shěn 矧	śin^B, *nhinʔ 'the gums' <> PTB *s-nil > WT *rñil* ~ *sñil* 'gums'
Peaceful	tuǒ 妥	t^{h}oi^B, *nhôiʔ 'peaceful' <> WT *rnal* 'to rest' ⪤ *mnal* 'to sleep'

In light of the frequent PTB (WT) *r- ~ *s- doublets, however, we suspect that the cause of OC devoicing was *s- as in other instances (not *r-):

Sky	WT *rmu ~ smu ~ dmu*
To desire	WT *rkam-pa ~ skam-pa*
Gums	WT *rñil ~ sñil*
Excrement	WT *rkyag-pa ~ skyag-pa*
To pull / throw down	WT *rñil-ba ~ sñil-ba*
Body hair	PTB *(r-)mul ~ *(s-)mul
Sleep	PTB *(r-)miy ~ *(s-)miy

The vacillation between pre-initial *r- and *s- is particularly common with nasal root initial words. The cognates below ('Shame', 'Long-necked') demonstrate, first, that this uncertainty is also found within Chinese, and second, that OC medial *-r- often derives from an earlier prefix or pre-initial *r-, not from an 'infix' *-r- which is typologically unlikely in TB languages and therefore probably also unlikely in OC (but see §7.5):

Shame	xiū 羞	[siu] *snu 'shame' ⪤ niǔ 忸 [ṇuk] *nruk < *r-nuk 'ashamed'
Long-necked	qiān 顅	[k^{h}en] ~ [kan] *khên ~ *kren < *h/s-ken ~ *r-ken 'long-necked'

All things considered, OC medial *-r- derives from earlier *r-, even where TB cognates have initial *s-*; and OC aspiration / voicelessness / *s- derives from earlier pre-initial *s-, even where TB cognates have pre-initial *r-*.

When the initial consonant is a stop or affricate, pre-initial *r- and *s- show up as aspiration in MC; see §5.8 below.

5.4 ST and PCH *k-

Voicelessness in an OC initial can correspond to ST or foreign *k- (TB *d-*, *g-*) in the initial configuration. The TB prefixes *d-* and *g-* can also correspond to OC medial *-r- (§7.4).

Hull vb. chōng 舂 LH śoŋ, *lhoŋ 'to hull grain with a pestle'
<> S. *klooŋ 'to hull rice'

Excrement shǐ 屎 śi^B, *lhiʔ 'excrement, dung'
<> PTB *k-liy 'excrement', Kanauri *kli*, PL *ʔ/k(l)e^2, WB *k^{h}ye^B*

Swallow tūn 吞 t^{h}ən 'to swallow'
<> PT *kl-: S. *klɨɨn^{A1}* 'to swallow', Ahom *k(l)en*

Evil tè 慝 t^{h}ək, *hnə̂k 'evil, wrong'
<> WT *nag* 'black', *gnag* 'black, wicket' ж *snag* 'ink'

Covet tān 貪 t^{h}əm, *rhə̂m 'be covetous' ж lán 婪 ləm, *g-rəm ? 'covetous'
<> PTB *d-rum > WT *drum-pa* 'to desire', WB *krum* 'to pine'

House shì 室 śit, *lhit ? 'house, hall'
<> WT *gži* 'ground, residence, abode' ж *gžis* 'native place'

Shore hǔ 滸 hɑ^B, *hŋâʔ 'river bank' <> WT *dŋo* 'shore, bank'

Sagart (Baxter and Sagart 1998: 47–51) has proposed that initial *k- functions in some words as a prefix that forms *nouns;* it also occurs with clan names. His examples include:

Potter's wheel jūn 鈞 LH kwin 'potter's wheel' < yún 匀 [win] 'even, uniform'

Ghost guǐ 鬼 kui^B 'ghost' < wēi 威 [ʔui] 'overawe, terrorize'

Country guó 國 kuək 'country' < yù 域 [wɨk] 'boundary, region'

Additional examples may include → qiào 竅 'hole'; → qīn 衾 'a blanket'; → gōu 溝 'drain, irrigation canal'.

This morpheme is not ST. Perhaps AA was the source; note that Khmer has a prefix *k-* which forms nouns (Jenner and Pou 1982: xxxix–xl); or note PVM *k-veːl 'village' < *veːl 'to return' (Ferlus).

5.5 Other sources of devoicing

Other sources of devoicing involve non-ST words where the function, if any, is outside the OC system.

Pour táo 洮 LH t^{h}ɑu, *lhâu 'to pour water, wash'
<> PMiao *ʔleu^{2A} 'to pour'

Iron tiě 鐵 t^{h}et, *lhît or *lhêt 'iron'
<> Tai: S. *lek^{D1}S* < *hl- 'iron', PKS *k^{h}lit^7

Food xiǎng 餉 śɑŋ($^{B/C}$), *hnaŋʔ/h 'bring food to'
<> MY: Anc. Miao *n̥on^C* (Wang Fushi) 'cooked rice, food', Yao: Biao Min *n̥aŋ^5*, Mien (Chiang Rai dial.) *n̥haaŋ^5*

Blood huāng 衁 huɑŋ, *hmâŋ <> AA: e.g., Bahnaric *maham 'blood' where the *h* belongs to the root

Even among ST items, the reason for devoicing is not always clear (loss of *p-?), as in

Straight tǐng 挺 t^{h}eŋ^B, *lhêŋʔ 'straight' <> PTB *bleŋ ~ *pleŋ 'straight'

5.6 MC initial x- from voiceless acute initials

MC initial *x*- from voiceless acute initials in OCM *hr-, *hl-, *hn- is rare; it seems to have its origin in the popular / rural sphere; see §1.3.1.

In the standard dialect, voiceless *l- and *n- are reflected in MC coronal *t^h-*, *śj*-, and, in the case of *r-, in MC *ṭ^h-*, *t^h-* (§7.1.2). To differentiate the two types of voiceless initials, we will write OCM *lh-, *nh-, *rh- for MC *t^h-*, *śj*-, etc., but OCM *hn-, *hl-, *hr- when it is the aspiration that survives as MC *x*-. Of course, voiceless *hm- and *hŋ- regularly yield Middle Chinese *x*-.

MC *x*- < foreign *hn-

Beard huì 顪喙 LH hyɑi^C, *huats 'beard of chin' < Tai: S. *nuat^{DIL}* <*hn- 'beard'

MC *x*- < OC / foreign *hr-

Ribs, sides xiē 脅 hɨap, *hrap ? 'sides of body, ribs' (earliest occurrence in *Shijing* with reference to horse's trappings)
<> TB: JP *kə^{31}-rep^{31}* 'rib', Kanauri *hrip, WT *rtsib < rhyip*

To rear chù 畜 ṭ^{h}uk, huk, *rhuk ~ *hruk ? 'to rear' (livestock)
※ chù 畜 [ṭ^{h}u^C, hu^C] *rhukh ~ *hrukh ? 'domestic animal'

Scare hè 嚇 hak, ha^C, *hrak(h) 'to scare'
<> PTB *krak ~ *grak 'to fear' > WT *skrag-pa* 'afraid'

Vomit xuè, hù 嗀 (xåk, xuk) *h(r)ok 'vomit' <> PTai *r̭uak^{D2} 'vomit'

Know xiǎo 曉 heu^B, *hiâuʔ 'clear, understand, know'
<> KT: PTai *ruo^{C2} 'to know', PKS *h-ro^C 'to know (how)'

Sound symbolic and deprecatory terms seem to belong to this vulgar stratum:

Babble xiāo-xiāo 嘐嘐 (xau) *hru 'magniloquent' (i.e., talk big without knowing anything). The phonetic suggests an OC *r in the initial.

Roar xiǎn 闞 (xăm^B, xam^B), and hǎn (xâm^B) *hramʔ 'roaring' of a tiger. This is an area word which is also found in TB and AA as *gram, etc.

Stupid zhuàng, hòng 戇 (xuŋ^C, ṭåŋ^C) *hoŋh ~ *troŋh 'stupid'. It is an AA substrate word — note PMon *trɔɔʔ 'foolish, insane'.

MC x- < OC / foreign *hl- / *C-l-:

Tiger hǔ 虎 [hɑ^B] *hlâʔ 'tiger' < PAA *kalaʔ. The graph is phonetic in chǔ 處 OC *k-hlaʔ 'place'; a "Standard" form *lha(k) 'tiger' survived as a "dialect" variant

Pig xǐ 狶 [hɨ(^{B})] *həi(ʔ) < *hləi(ʔ) ? 'swine' (said to be a Chǔ dialect word).
※ shǐ 豕 [śe^B] or [śɑi^B] ?, *lheʔ ? (*lhaiʔ ?) 'pig' < AA: PMonic *cliik

5.7 MC affricates from *s + stop consonant

In some words, dental affricates are sometimes thought to have resulted through metathesis from OC or PCH s + stop consonant, as suggested by possible WT cognates (Bodman 1969):

Soak — jìn 浸 [tsim^C] *tsəms 'to soak, overflow' <> WT *stim-pa, bstims* 'to enter, penetrate, be absorbed' ≭ caus. of *t^{h}im-pa* 'disappear, being absorbed'. See also → qīn 侵

Grasp — xié 挾 [tsep, kiep, kap] 'grasp', the reading *tsep* from PCH *sk-?

In a few words with dental affricate initials, an original s + stop consonant cluster agrees with identified meanings of the s-prefix; the following words are iteratives (§5.2.3):

Add — zēng 曾增 [tsəŋ] *tsə̂ŋ 'to add' > 'to double, to rise high' 曾; 'increase, numerous' 增 appears to be a derivation from < dēng 登 [təŋ] *tə̂ŋ 'to rise, ascend, mount, raise'

Twist — jī 績 [tsek] *tsek < **s-kek? 'to twist, spin' appears to be a derivate from < xì 係繫 [ke^C] *kêh 'to bind, tie up, attach'

This metathesis is rare, though. Several often cited examples have alternative explanations. 'Carpenter' → jiàng 匠 [dziaŋ^C] is supposed to be cognate to WT *sbyoŋ-pa, sbyaŋs* 'to train, exercise, practice', but the CH word has a better etymology, q.v. The same goes for *cóng* 叢 (under → jù 聚) and the words written with the phonetic → zú 卒 (also under → zāo 遭) which Bodman had associated with WT words with initial *st-*, etc. (cited under → tún 屯窀). This throws some doubt on the metathesis theory.

5.8 Aspirated initial consonants

Only one out of six MC words with velar and labial initials has an aspirated surd stop. Many other MC aspirated words probably had complex OC or ST initials which were not necessarily aspirated; others fall into certain semantic categories which OC apparently marked with aspiration. Therefore aspirated stops and affricates are not of ST origin, but are CH innovations.

Several different sources of MC aspirated initial consonants can be distinguished:

(1) Aspiration due to loss of pre-initial (§5.8.1)
(2) Initial MC *ts^h-* from OC or PCH *k-s- and *s-ʔ- (§5.9.1–2)
(3) Initial MC *tś^{h}j-* from OC *k-hl- (§5.9.3)
(4) Sound-symbolic aspiration (§5.8.5–§5.8.6)
(5) For sources of MC initial *t^h-*, see §5.1)

As expected, there remains a residue where aspiration defies explanation; it includes common words like → kǔ 苦 [k^{h}ɑ^B] 'bitter'. In light of the secondary nature of most aspiration, words like *kǔ* may perhaps go back to an original *C+h* cluster that is known from Mon-Khmer languages.

5.8.1 MC aspiration: loss of ST pre-initial

Some Middle Chinese aspirated words correspond to TB (and / or WT) initials with *s-* or *r-* prefix, also to Lolo-Burmese *ʔ-. This is parallel to devoicing (§5.2–3), although it is only a trend (Sino-Tibetan prefixes are volatile and change from language to language).

Cliff — kàn 磡 LH k^{h}əm^C, *khə̂ms 'cliff, bank, step' <> PTB *r-ka[:]m id.

Dig	kū 窟	k^huət, *khût 'dig in the ground, cave, hole' <> PTB: *r-ko-t 'dig'
Rob	kòu 寇	k^ho^C, *khôh 'to rob, robber' <> PTB *r-kuw > WT *rku-ba* 'to steal'
Girdle	xié, qiè 絜	get, k^het, *gêt, 'khêt 'girdle' <> WT *rked-pa* 'the waist, loins, the middle'
Body	qū 軀	k^hɨo, *kho 'body, person' <> PTB *(s-)kuw > WT *sku* id.
Leather	kuò 鞹	k^huɑk, *khwâk 'leather' <> WT *skog-pa* ~ *kog-pa* 'shell, peel, rind'
Send	qiǎn 遣	k^hian^B, *khenʔ 'to send to, send away' <> WT *skyel-ba* 'to send'
Get rid	qǔ 去	k^hɨɑ^B, *khaʔ 'get rid, eliminate' <> *skyag-pa, bskyags* 'to lay out, expend' ж *skyag* ~ *rkyag* 'dirt, excrement' (unless this ex. belongs to §5.8.5)
Dismember	pò 膊	p^hɑk, *phâk 'dismember' <> PLB *pak ~ *ʔpak > Lahu *phâʔ* 'unfasten, dismantle'

5.8.2 *MC aspiration: causative*

In some words, the aspiration may perform the same causative function as *s- and devoicing (§5.2.1–2) and may in fact be the trace of a lost s-prefix. The aspiration existed already in OC because *qiāng* 將 (ts^hjaŋ) 'to beg' (→ jiāng 將) writes 'tinkle' in *Shījīng* 274 which must likely have been simply *tshaŋ, not *s-tsaŋ. Aspiration also forms causatives in TB languages, e.g., Tiddim Chin: *kâŋ* 'to rise' > *k^hâŋ* 'to raise' (Geilich 1994: 171).

Bright	qiāo 皢	LH k^heu, *khiâu 'bleached white (of bones)' (i.e., 'made white') ж jiǎo 皎 [keu^B] *kiâuʔ 'bright'
Half	pàn 判片	p^hɑn^C, *p^hâns 'to cleave, divide' (i.e., 'make half') ж bàn 半 [pɑn^C] *pâns 'half'
Overturn	fù 覆	p^huk, *phuk 'to overturn, overthrow / repeatedly' caus./iter. ж fù 複 [puk] *puk 'double, lined' (garment) ж fù 復 [buk] *buk 'to come back, return, restore'

5.8.3 *MC aspiration: iterative*

Words that suggest repetitive motion are often aspirated, which parallels the iterative / intensive function of the s-prefix and devoicing (§5.2.3).

Gnaw	kěn 齦	k^hən^B OCM *khənʔ 'to gnaw'
Strike	kò 叩	k^ho$^{B/C}$, *khôʔ/h 'to strike, attack'
Cut open	kū 刳	k^huɑ^C, *khwâh 'cut open, cut to pieces' ж huá 華 [ɣua] *grwâ 'to cleave'
Pass over	kuà 跨	k^hua^C, *khrwâh 'to step over, pass over'
Stride	kuǐ 跬	k^hye^B, *khweʔ 'a stride'
Notches	qì 契	k^hes, *khêts 'script notches'
Cut through	qiè 鍥	k^het, *khêt 'to cut, cut through'
Splinter	quē 缺	k^huet, k^hyat, *khwet 'to break, splinter'

Disperse	pī	披	pʰɨai, *phai 'divide, disperse'
Break	pò	破	pʰɑi^{C}, *phâih 'to break (into pieces)'
Brush off	fú	拂	pʰut, *phut 'to brush off, shake off' (iterative)
			< fú 茀 [put] *put 'clear away (dense vegetation)'
Pull off	tiāo	條	tʰeu, *lhiû 'pull leaves off branches' (iterative)
			< tiáo 條 [deu] *liû 'branch, to be extending (branches)'

5.8.4 *MC aspiration: auxiliary verbs*

Some auxiliary verbs are aspirated (LHan follows the graph):

Endure	kān	勘	kʰəm, *khə̂m 'to endure, equal to'
			< hán 含 [ɣəm] *gə̂m 'have [hold] in the mouth'
Able	kě	可	kʰɑi^{B}, *khâiʔ 'to bear, can, be able'
			< hè$_1$ 何荷 [gɑi^{B}] *gâiʔ 'to carry'
Able	kè	克	kʰək, *khə̂k 'be capable, able, can, conquer, vanquish'
Willing	kěn	肯	kʰəŋ^{B}, *khə̂ŋʔ 'be willing'

5.8.5 *Aspiration: outward and / or forceful motion*

Words that connote breathing, exhaling, an emphatic outward gesture or forceful motion such as 'spitting', 'ejecting', 'motion away', 'hewing', 'hitting', 'beating' tend to be aspirated. This is a sound-symbolic feature in CH although the origin may have been s-intensives:

Lungs	fèi	肺	LH pʰuɑs, *phas (< *phos ?) 'lungs'
Breathe	chōu	犨	tśʰu 'sound of an ox breathing'
Sigh	xì	愾	hɨs. kʰəs 'sigh'
Breath	qì	氣	kʰɨs 'breath'
			ж kài 愾 [kʰəs] 'be angry'
Anger	fèn	忿	pʰun$^{B/C}$ 'anger, angry'
			< bēn 賁 [pən] 'be ardent, brave'
Stench	chòu	臭	tśʰu^{C} 'smell, stench'
Spit	fèn	噴	pʰun(^{C}) 'spit out'
Spit	tǔ	吐	tʰɑ$^{B/C}$ 'spit'
Spit	kā, kè	喀	kʰak 'spit out, vomit'
Cough	ké	欬	kʰə^{C} 'cough'
Weep	qì	泣	kʰɨəp 'weep'
Weep	kū	哭	kʰok 'weep, howl'
Throw away	qì	棄	kʰɨs 'throw away, abandon'
Leave	qù	去	kʰɨɑ^{C} 'go away, leave' (unless this belongs to §5.8.1)

An extension of forceful action include the following words:

Kill	kān$_3$	戡	kʰəm 'to kill, execute'
Cut, chop	kǎn$_2$	砍	kʰəm^{B} 'to chop (wood, a tree), decapitate'
Cut, engrave	kè$_2$	刻	kʰək 'to cut, injure, engrave, intense'
Attack	kòu	扣叩	kʰo$^{B/C}$ 'to strike, attack'
Stab	kuī	刲	kʰue 'to stab, slaughter'

5.8.6 Aspiration: hollow, empty

Words that imply 'hollow, empty' are typically aspirated, again for sound-symbolic effect. The first example illustrates this meaning quite clearly where aspiration derives the word 'vault' from one which does not imply 'hollow':

Vault	qiōng 穹	LH k^{h}uŋ 'vault' < gōng 弓 [kuŋ] 'bow'
Pit	kǎn 坎	k^{h}əm^B 'pit'
Pit	kēng 坑	k^{h}aŋ 'a pit (hole)'
Empty	kōng 空	k^{h}oŋ 'hollow, empty'
Hollow	kǒng 孔	k^{h}oŋ^B 'hollow'
Mouth	kǒu 口	k^{h}o^B 'mouth'
Hole	kuǎn 窾	k^{h}uɑn^B 'hole' < PTB kwar?
Basket	kuāng 匡	k^{h}yɑŋ^C 'square basket'
Crotch	kuí 奎	k^{h}ye 'crotch'
Hollow	què 殼	k^{h}ɔk 'hollow shell, hollow'
Hole	qiào 竅	k^{h}eu^C 'hole, opening'
Husk	kāng 糠	k^{h}ɑŋ 'husk of grain'
Hollow	pàng □	in Min dialects: PMin *p^{h}aŋ^C ~ *p^{h}oŋ^C

A more recent echo of this tendency is perhaps the irregular surd aspiration of *tàn* 窞 (dậm^B) [dəm^B] *lə̂m? 'pit' (where Mand. *dàn* is expected).

5.8.7 Aspiration in foreign words

Some foreign words have aspirated initials in CH; perhaps OC perceived aspiration where phonemically the donor language had none. (The aspiration can also be due to loss of a foreign post-initial phoneme; see §5.9.4.)

Spear fish	chuō 擉 (tṣ^{h}åk) [tṣ^{h}ɔk] *tshrôk 'to spear' (fish) <> AA: Khmer *cūka* /cɔ̀ok/ 'lift with tool...' ⋈ *cpūka* /cbɔ̀ok/ (archaic) 'trident for lifting fish'
Pick out	chāi 差 (tṣ^{h}ai, tṣ^{h}ăi) [tṣ^{h}ai] (or [tṣ^{h}ɛ] ?, *tshrâi ? 'to pick (an animal) out of (a herd, etc.), select' <> AA: Khmer /sral/ 'to take the pick of, select'

5.9 Aspiration from PCH consonant clusters

*5.9.1 MC ts^h- from *k-s- and *s-ʔ-*

In some words, MC initial *ts^h-* corresponds to a ST cluster *k-s- (WT *gs-*) (LHan readings follow the graph):

Triad	cān 參	ts^{h}əm < PCH *k-səm 'a triad, three' <> WT *gsum* (< ST *k-sum) 'three'
	⋈ sān 三	sɑm, *sə̂m 'three' <> ⋈ WT *sum* 'three' in composition
Clear	qīng 清	ts^{h}eŋ < PCH *k-seŋ 'clear' (water, sound) <> WT *gseŋ-po* 'clear' (sound) ⋈ *seŋ-po* ~ *bseŋ-po* 'clear'
Granary	cāng 倉	ts^{h}ɑŋ < PCH *k-saŋ 'granary' <> WT *gsaŋ-ba* 'to hide'
Eat	cān 餐	ts^{h}ɑn < ST *k-dzan 'eat' <> WT *gzan-pa* 'to eat'

Sleep — qǐn 寢 — ts^{h}im^B < ST *k-zimʔ 'sleep' <> WT *gzim-pa* 'sleep'

Hay — chú 芻 — tṣ^{h}o < PCH *k-sroʔ 'hay, cut hay'
<> AA-PMon *ksɔɔj 'hay', Wa *sɔh 'cut grass'

Wife — qī 妻 — ts^{h}ei < PCH *k-səi 'wife'
<> AA: Khmer *ksai 'wife'; PWMiao *ntshai^D 'daughter, wife'

Additional cases may include cāng 倉 (→ cáng 藏).
The phonetic series *GSR* 613 possibly still supports a cluster *k-s- for OC:

qiān 僉 [ts^{h}iam] *k-sa/em? 'all' is phonetic in *jiǎn*檢 [kɨam^B] 'accumulate'.

In a few words that start with MC *ts^h-*, the source might have been PCH *s + ʔ-; see, for example, → cǎn 噆, → chā$_3$ 臿; → qì$_7$ 葺.

5.9.2 MC ts^h- from s + voiceless sonorant

A few words with MC initial *ts^h-* probably had a PCH n-like initial: *qī* 七 [ts^{h}it] 'seven' (<> PTB *snis), and *qiān* 千 [ts^{h}en] 'thousand' (*rén* 人 [ńin] is said to be phonetic). Perhaps the original pre-initial *s-* in *snis was lost in regular fashion after devoicing the initial nasal, but then reattached in this common word, especially since the iterative meaning 'again' (§5.2.3) was still apparent ('seven' = 'two again').

In the following sets, a causative s-prefix was apparently put in front of OC *lh- which resulted in MC *ts^h-* ('Expel' has already been cited in §5.2.2 as 'Let go'):

Expel — cì 赤 [ts^{h}iak] *s-lhak ? 'to expel' < shì 釋 [śiak] *lhak 'put away, do away, let go' (see → yì$_{35}$ 繹)

Hurt — qiāng 㺊 [ts^{h}iaŋ] *s-lhaŋ 'to hurt' < lhaŋ + s-prefix caus.

Additional cases may include → cāng$_2$ 滄 'cold'.

*5.9.3 MC tś^{h}j- from OC clusters *k-hl-*

A few MC *tś^{h}j-* words derive from the rare OC clusters *k-hl-. When these words were committed to writing, the initial still contained a velar *k-, because most of these words are found in phonetic series with velar initials beside evidence for OC *l-. Thus, MC *tś^{h}j-* in such words was not a variant of *śj-* (OC voiceless *lh-), but of a different nature. Except for the first item 'carriage', all are of ST stock, yet if Baxter and Sagart (1998) are correct, even 'carriage' would be a ST etymon which could allow us to generalize that this kind of cluster is restricted to ST items.

Carriage — chē 車 [tś^{h}a] ~ [kɨɑ] *k-hla ~ *ka 'carriage'

Separate — chǐ 誃 [tś^{h}ɑi^B] *k-hlaiʔ 'to separate' <> PL *C-klay$^{A/C}$ 'to separate'

Come out — chū 出 [tś^{h}ut] *k-hlut 'to come out'
<> JP^l*lot*^{31}-*lam*^{33} 'outlet', Trung *klot* 'come out'

Dwell — chǔ 處 [tś^{h}ɑ^B] *k-hlaʔ 'to dwell' ~ jū 居 [kɨɑ] *ka 'to dwell'
<> PTB *gla ꞏꞏ WT *gda'-ba* locative verb, 'to be there'; TGTM *gla

River — chuān 川 [tś^{h}on] *k-hlun 'river' <> PTB *klu:ŋ 'river'

5.9.4 MC aspiration from other types of PCH initial clusters
In a few words, aspiration seems to have been caused by loss of a post-initial consonant; note also 'To polish' and 'Booty' in §5.10.1.

Blanket	qīn$_3$ 衾 [kʰɨm] *khəm 'blanket' < *k- + *ʔəm 'cover' yīn$_5$ 陰 'cover' (k- forms concrete nouns §5.4)
Slant	qīng 傾頃 [kʰyeŋ] *khweŋ 'be slanting' <> AA-PMon *kʔiəŋ / *kʔeeŋ 'to lean, be slanted'
Pregnant	pēi 胚 [pʰə] *phə̂ 'one month pregnant' <> AA: OKhmer /pdəj/ 'burden > pregnancy'

5.10 Reflexes of Mon-Khmer affricates in Chinese
MK languages have typically one set of affricate consonants which are transcribed *c, j, ch,* and *jh* following Indic conventions. Two sets, one sibilant (*ts, dz*), one perhaps palatal (*tš, dž*), can be reconstructed for PMK (Ferlus *MKS* 7, 1978: 1–38). This may explain the multiple correspondences with OC, but this issue requires further study. Since OC had only dental affricates, these had to be substituted for the foreign palatals.

5.10.1 MK c, j = MC affricates

To ford	jì 濟 [tsei^C] *tsîh or *tsə̂ih 'to ford, cross' <> AA: Mon inscr. *cnis* [cnøs] > *cnih* 'a ghat, place of access to river..., landing place' < *cis* [cøs] 'to go down, descend'
To polish	cuō 磋 [tsʰɑi] *tshâi 'to rub, polish' < AA: Khmer /cnaj/ 'to cut (gems), to polish'
Booty	jié 捷 [dziap] *dzap 'victory, booty' ⋈ qiè 妾 [tsʰiap] *tshap 'slave woman, concubine' < AA: Khmer, OKhmer *cā'pa* /cap/ 'to grasp..., seize, catch, take or seize by conquest' ⋈ *caṃṇā'pa* /cɑmnap/ 'detainee, prisoner, hostage'; Pearic *čap²* 'to catch' -> Tai: S. *čiap⁴* 'to plunder, rob, steal'
About to	jiāng 將 [tsiɑŋ] *tsaŋ 'be on the point of, about to, intend to, going to' < AA: OKhmer *caṅ* /cɔŋ/, Khmer *ca'ṅa* /cɑŋ/ 'to want, desire, hope for, be willing to, about to, on the point of'

5.10.2 MK c, j = MC retroflex affricates
The reason for MC retroflexion (OC *-r-) in some correspondence sets is not clear. The AA substrate language might have had a complex initial; or, what later had become a MC supradental affricate was somehow acoustically close to what was heard. Most of these words are late (i.e., mid to late Zhou, and Han).

Spear fish	chuō 擉 (tʂʰåk) [tʂʰɔk] *tshrôk 'to spear (fish)' < AA: Khmer *cūka* /còok/ 'lift with tool...' ⋈ *cpūka* [cbòok] (archaic) 'trident for lifting fish'
Dog	sōu 獀 (GY ʂjəu) [ʂu] < AA: PVM *ʔa-cɔːʔ

Pestilence zhá 札 (tṣɛt) 'to die prematurely, pestilence'
< AA: PVM *k-ceːt, PMK *kcət 'to die'

To dry shài, shì 曬 (ṣie^{C}) [ṣe^{C}] *sreh 'to dry something in the sun'
<> AA: PMonic *cay 'to spread in the sun to dry'

Cut off zhǎn 斬 (tṣăm^{B}) [tṣam^{B}] *tsrê/âmʔ ? 'to cut off, cut down'
< AA: PVM *cɛm^{B} 'to chop', Khmer *cam* or *cram* 'to hack'

5.10.3 MK cr-, jr- = MC retroflex affricates

A hoe chú 鉏 (dẓjwo) *dzra 'a hoe' < AA: Khmer *rā'sa* /roəh/ 'to scrape, rake, hoe, harrow' ⪤ OKhmer /crās/ 'to scrape or brush against'

Thorns chǔ 楚 (tṣhjwo^{B}) *tshraʔ 'thorny bush / tree'
< AA: PMonic *jrlaaʔ 'thorn, thorny bamboo', Khmu' [cərlaʔ], Semai [jərlaaʔ]

High chóng 崇 (dẓjuŋ) *dzruŋ 'to pile on, pile high, high (of a mountain)'
< AA: Khmer /croŋ/ 'to raise up, re-establish...' ⪤ *crūṅa* /cròoŋ/ 'be upright...'

Needle zān 簪 (tsậm, tṣjəm) *tsrəm 'hairpin'
< AN-PCham *jurŭm 'needle'; AA-PNBahn. *jarŭm*; TB-Lepcha *ryŭm*

Select chāi 差 (tṣʰai, tṣʰăi) *tshrâi 'to pick out, select'
< AA: Khmer /sral/ 'to take the pick of, select'

Tilt zè 仄昃 (tṣjək) *tsrək 'be slanting' > 'sun going down, afternoon'
< AA: OKhmer *jre* /crée/ 'to tilt, slope, decline, (of sun) go down, set' (for final *-k, see §6.1.1)

Quiver zé 笮 (tṣɐk) *tsrâk 'a quiver'
< AA: Khmer /crɑɑk/ 'insert, introduce, shove into...'

*5.10.4 MK c, j = MC tśj-, ṭj-, etc. from OC *t(r)j-*

These initial correspondences are rare and therefore uncertain, but they could be understood if the OC words had a medial *i (*j), so that OC *ti- / *tj- may have come close to the AA sound. A post-initial palatal almost certainly was inherent in graphs with the element 周, and variants in 'Look at' suggest an original *-iam ~ *-em (rather than *-am) (§11.3.2).

Look at zhān 占瞻 (tśjäm) OCB 占 *tjem, 瞻 *tjam 'to look at'
⪤ chān 佔覘 (ṭʰjäm) *thram or *threm ? 'to look, observe'
< AA: OKhmer /cam/ 'to watch over, watch for, keep in mind'

Aid zhōu 周 (tśjəu) *tu or *tiu 'to help, relieve, succor'
< AA: Khmer *jwya* /cúuəj/ 'to aid, help, succor, rescue, save' (for loss of final *-j*, see §6.9)

Circle chóu 綢 (ḍjəu) *dru 'to be wrapped round, bind round, nightgown' 裯
< AA: Khmer *jwta* /cúuət/ 'to encircle or wrap (the head) in a length of cloth'; and / or Tai: S. *diw*^{3} 'strips of rattan or bamboo bent in a circle to which ribs of a cage are fastened'

Tree	zhū 株 (tju) *tro or *trio ? 'tree trunk' < ? AA: PMonic *chuuʔ 'wood'; in Mon also 'tree'

5.10.5 MK c, j = velar initials k, g

For reasons not yet understood, an AA affricate shows up as a velar in CH, but this is rare and therefore suspect. This is reminiscent of Viet-Muong where *d-* and *gi-* have merged, but much later (Maspero 1912: 69). This phenomenon may perhaps explain 'Companion' below.

Dog	gǒu 狗 (kəu^B) *kôʔ < *kloʔ 'dog' < ultimately AA: PMon *clur, Mon *klə, WMon *cluiw, kluiw* [kløw]
Bird	qín 禽擒 (gjəm) *gəm ? 'game bird, bird, fowl' < AA: PVM *-ciːm 'bird', PMon *kɲciəm 'bird'
Companion	chóu 儔 (ḍjəu) *dru ? 'mate, companion, category, equal' ~ qiú 仇 (gjəu) *gu 'mate, companion, antagonist'

5.11 MC ʔ- from foreign kl-type clusters

A few comparanda show a MC glottal stop initial *ʔ-* where Tai or other languages have initial *l-*, but the rimes and meanings agree so closely that usually a relationship is assumed. The nature of the hypothetical common initial remains uncertain; one could assume an OC configuration *ʔl- (an *l in the OC initial in *wèng* 'jar' is possible because its phonetic is *kloŋ 公). Unger (*Hao-ku* 33, 1986) suggests an initial ʔa-prefix forming nouns, as in:

Jar	wèng 瓮	LH ʔoŋ^C, *ʔôŋh 'jar' <> PL *ʔ-loŋ 'pot' <> Tai: S. *luŋ^{C2}* < *l- 'vessel'
House	wū 屋	ʔok, *ʔôk 'roof, house' <> Tai: Po'ai *luk^{D2}S* < *dl- 'room'
Sprout	yāng 秧	ʔɨɑŋ, 'sprout, rice shoot' <> WT *ljaŋ-ba* < *ly- 'shoots, sprouts'
Waist	yāo 腰	ʔiau, *ʔiau 'waist' <> PMiao *qlau^B 'waist, lower back'
Eagle	yīng 鷹	ʔɨŋ, *ʔəŋ 'eagle, falcon' <> PMK *knleeŋ 'hawk'
Middle	yāng 央	has, however, a Chinese etymology and is therefore unrelated to PTai *klaŋ^{A1} 'middle'.

5.12 Nasal initials

5.12.1 ŋ(w)- ~ nw-

Some words with initial nasals show *ŋ(w)- ~ *nw- variation already on the ST level. Perhaps an earlier *ŋw- had changed to *nw- in some languages, something that is observed also later, as in Sino-Tibetan *ŋwə 'cow' > WB *nwa*, 牛 OC *ŋuə > Mandarin *niú*. Tables 5-1 and 5-2 illustrate parallel stems (§2.5) of 'hungry', 'cow', 'lean', and 'to rest' (in addition, see also → ruò 爇 'hot').

5-1	Hungry	Hungry	Cow, buffalo	Cow, buffalo
OC	*nûiʔ (*niûk) → něi 餒	*ŋâih → è 餓		*ŋwə → niú 牛
ST	*nw(ə)i	*ŋai		*ŋwə
WB		ŋat	nwa	
JP		ŋ̇jo^{31}		ŋa^{33} > wă^{33}-
Lush		ŋhei^{H}		
WT	(gñog-pa)		? nor	? ba < ŋ-wa

5-2	Lean over	Lean over	To rest	To rest, gentle
OC		*ŋâi → é 俄	*nhôiʔ/ *snui → suī 綏	*ŋôih /*ŋuâih → wò 臥
TB	*hnwai	*ŋai	C-nwal/r	ŋwal > ŋoi
WB	hnwai^{B}	ŋai^{C}		ŋwe^{C}
LB, PL	*ʔnwe			
JP		ŋaʔ^{31}		ŋui^{31} slow
Lush		ŋer^{L} < ŋerh		ŋɔi / *ŋɔiʔ/h
WT	sñe-ba		r-nal ⋇ m-nal ñal-ba, mñel-ba	ŋal-ba

5.12.2 Chinese m- for TB and foreign b-

Among ST languages and also others in the area, root initial *m-* and *b-* do occasionally interchange, especially after a prefix or when followed by a lateral (see also *HPTB:* 133); CH has initial *m-*, WT initial *b-:*

Fly (n.) méng 虻 (mɐŋ) [maŋ] *mrâŋ 'gadfly' vs. WT *sbraŋ* (< *s-mraŋ ?) 'a fly'

Snake huǐ 虫虺 (xjwei^{B}) [hui^{B}] *hmuiʔ
<> PTB *b-ru:l > WT *sbrul*; vs. PLB *m-r-wiy^{1} > WB *mrwe* 'snake', KN *m-ruul

Herdsman mù 牧 (mjuk) [muk] *mək 'pasture, herdsman, to tend (animals)'
<> WT *'brog-pa* < *ɴbrok* 'summer pasture, solitude, wilderness, nomad'

To buy mǎi 買 (maɨ^{B}) [mɛ^{B}] *mrêʔ 'to buy'
<> PTB *b-rey (> WT *rje-ba* < *ɴ-rje* ?) 'to barter', Garo *bre*, Dimasa *barai* 'to buy', vs. JP *ma^{31}-ri^{33}* 'to buy'

Ransom shú 贖 (dźjwok) [źok] *m-lok ? 'to ransom'
vs. WT *blu-ba, blus* 'to buy off, ransom'

Shaman wū 巫 (mju) [muɑ] *ma 'shaman, spirit medium, magician'
vs. WT *'ba-po* < *ɴba* 'shaman(ess)'

Sort wù 物 (mjuət) [mut] *mət 'class, sort, things', PTB *mruw
vs. WT *'bru* < *ɴbru* 'grain, seed'

Ten thousand wàn 萬 (mjän 3) [mɨɑn^{C}] *m(r)ans (< *C-mom ?) 'ten thousand'
vs. WT *'bum* < *ɴbum* 'hundred thousand'

To wipe, wash mì 滵 (mjiet 4) [mit] *mit 'to wipe a vessel', JP *myit*^{55} 'wash (the face)'
vs. WT *'p^{h}yid-pa* 'to wipe, blot out', Lushai *p^{h}iʔ* < *p^{h}is* 'wash (the face)'

Temple miào 廟 (mjäu^{C} 3) [mɨɑu^{C}] *m(r)auh 'ancestral temple'
vs. PMY *prau^{2} < *br- 'house'

Deceive wǎng 罔 (mjwaŋ^{B}) [muɑŋ^{B}] *maŋʔ 'to deceive, confusion, to outwit, wits'
vs. Tai: S. *p^{h}raaŋ^{A2}* < *br- 'to deceive, cheat'

Also southern dialects have initial *m*- in a few words for a labial stop consonant elsewhere; see → bāo$_3$ 剝, → bò$_3$ 擘; there is at least one parallel with velar initials: → yǎo$_2$ 咬.

5.12.3 Austroasiatic nasal infix

An AA nominalizing n-infix after affricates would result in an inadmissible OC cluster of the type *tsn- which is reduced to a canonical *sn-.

Belt, sash *xiāng* 纕 (sjaŋ) [siɑŋ] *snaŋ 'belt, sash, horse's belly-band'
< AA: Khmer *caṃṇaṅa* /camnaaŋ/ 'a tie, band, strap, bond' < nominal n-infix derivative of *caṅa* /caaŋ/ 'to tie, knot, secure, attach by tying or knotting'

In such a MK initial consonant cluster, one element can be considered the root initial, the other a prefix or infix. Thus the Khmer root *-sapa* /-saap/ 'to cover, protect' yields with n-infix *snapa* /snaap/ 'shroud', but derived from this is *napa* /nɔɔp/ 'mat in which one wraps oneself for protection...', as if the root initial were *n*-, and *s*- a prefix (Jenner and Pou 1982: 358). Like some AA languages, OC occasionally sheds the original root initial, leaving the nasal infix as the word initial. For examples, see §2.6.

6
FINAL CONSONANTS

Because MC final consonants, tones, and other phonemes are projected back to identical ones in LHan, subsequently examples will often be cited in simpler LHan forms.

To account for variations in final consonants in ST cognate sets and within wfs, such as *wú* ~ *wǎng* 'not have', *bǎi* '100' < *brak ~ PTB *brya, we can, according to LaPolla (*BIHP* 65.1, 1994: 131–173), either (1) reconstruct a very complex proto-language using phonetic symbols (for example, final *-g as done by Karlgren and Li Fang Kuei, e.g., MC *kâk : kuo* < OC *kâk : *kâg), or (2) use non-phonemic symbols (-H, -X), or (3) reconstruct a simple system which allows for a certain amount of variation (ibid. p. 142), e.g., MC *kâk : kuo* < OC *kâk : *kâ. With LaPolla (and others, like Pulleyblank, Baxter, Sagart), we assume the third possibility because it provides on balance simple explanations, and is in agreement with the typology of the languages in the area.

6.1 Final *-k

Some ST / PCH words in final *-iŋ, *-ik have shifted to OC *-in, *-it, see §6.4.1.

Some words with final *-k* have a variant in tone B (OC *-ʔ):

Arrive	gé 格 LH [kak] *krâk 'arrive' ж jiǎ 假 [ka^B] *krâʔ 'arrive'
Let go	shì 釋 [śak] *hlak 'put away, let go' ж shě 舍捨 [śa^B] *hlaʔ 'to let off, set aside, let go'
You	ruò 若 [ńɑk] *nak 'you' ж rú 如 [ńɑ^B] *naʔ 'you'

The form in *-ʔ is perhaps a weakened form in 'Arrive', 'Let go', and 'Lame' below (see §6.2 for parallels with *-t; Baxter and Sagart 1998: 60; for ST exs. see §3.2.2). Thus the final *-k* would be part of the stem. On the other hand, in 'You' the final*-k must be secondary.

However, items like 'Shrivel' and 'Shame' (below) have an open vowel variant which suggests that final *-k* is not only an OC addition in these words (k-extension § 6.1.1), but possibly also in 'Lame' ('Let go' represents probably two different etyma). Occasionally, a final *-k* is also added to words in TB languages, as in WT *k^ha*, WB *k^ha^B* 'bitter' ж WT *k^hag*, WB *k^hak* 'difficult' (*HPTB:* 479f). In some items, the phenomenon is reversed where CH has an open syllable for TB and foreign final *-k* or *-t*; see §6.9. A few examples:

Hundred	bǎi 百 LH [pak], OCM *prâk 'hundred' <> WT *brgya* < *brja 'hundred'
Shrivel	sù 肅 [siuk] *siuk 'shrivel' ж xiū 修 [siu] *siu ? 'shrink'
Shame	niǔ 忸 [ṇuk] *nruk < *r-nuk 'ashamed' < xiū 羞 [siu] *snu 'shame'

When the base form ended in a diphthong, the latter was leveled before the final consonant, thus *–ai + k > *-ek:

Change	yì 易 [jek] *lek (< *lai-k) 'to change' <> PTB *lay 'change'
Lame	bì 躄 [piek] *pek (< *pai-k) 'to walk lame' < bǒ 跛 [pɑi^B] *pâiʔ (< *pai-k) 'to walk lame'
Oblique	pì 僻 [p^{h}iek] *phek < pō 頗坡 [p^{h}ai] *phâi

Labor yì 役 [wek] *wek (< *wai-k) 'to labor, serve'
< wéi 為 [wɑi] *wai 'make, do'

Diphthong levelling does not always take place, though; perhaps a PCH final *-l was the source of the OC *-i:

Cut trees zé 柞 (tṣɐk) [tṣak] *tsrâk 'clear away (trees)'
⋇ chá 槎 (dẓa(B)) [dẓai] *dzrâi 'cut trees'

The final *-r of a Sino-Tibetan root is metathesized in OC (sometimes resulting in open syllables; see §7.7.3):

White bái 白 [bak] *brâk (< *bar-k) 'be white' <> PTB *pwa:r

Vein mài 脈 [mɛk] *mrêk ? (< *mər-k?) 'vein' <> Lushai *marH* < *mar* 'pulse'

Color sè 色 [ṣɨk] *srək (< *sər-k) 'color, countenance'
<> Lushai *saarH* < *saar* 'prismatic colors, ruddy, healthy looking'

Sometimes, foreign final *-r has no CH equivalent in div. III syllables:

Pierce cì 刺 [tsʰieC, tsʰiek] *tshek(h) 'pierce, stab'
<> WT *gzer-ba* 'to bore into', *gzer* 'nail'

Metathesis also occurs in TB: WT: *bar* 'interstice, intermediate space' ⋇ WT *pʰrag* < *par-k* 'intermediate space, interstice'; *smar-ba* 'to speak', pf. *smras* ⋇ *smraŋ* 'word' (Geilich 1994: 67); Lepcha *mlem* 'face' < *mel-m*, from PTB *mel 'face' with the common Lepcha m-suffix.

6.1.1 k-extension

So far, no perceptible function or meaning has been identified for this velar suffix (except for items in §6.1.2 below) which is also encountered in TB (*HPTB:* 479ff). This addition may for the time being be referred to as 'k-extension'. Yet in some words the final k-sound seems to symbolize an abrupt end (as in notions 'stab', 'split', 'whack'), which implies a singular event. In Table 6-1 all the items in the second column (final *-k*) mean 'split, cleave' (something accomplished with a single blow, or a sequence of individual blows), whereas the non-k stems tend to have a more general meaning. One can rip open a victim or split a melon only once, but one can open a door many times. From this is perhaps derived the semantic narrowing that is often observed, as in *cuò* 錯厝 [tsʰɑk] *tshâk 'whetstone, grindstone' < *cuō* 磋 [tsʰɑi] *tshâi 'rub, polish' (in general, not necessarily with a stone); WT *kʰag* 'difficult' < *kʰa* 'bitter'. This morpheme might possibly be related to the WT suffix *-kʰa* as in *ser-ka* 'cleft' (Beyer 1992: 133). This narrowed or singular meaning may also explain the specific word *zhī* 隻 *tek 'single, one' <> WT *gčig* 'one', vs. the more general *zhǐ* 只 *teʔ 'only' <> PLB *day² ⋇ *tí* 'only'. The final *-k* in CH *bǎi* 百 *prâk 'hundred', vs. PTB *prya, possibly plays the same role

6-1

-V	-k
zhā 奓 *trâi 'to open (door)'	zhé 磔 *trâk 'rip open (victim)'
chǐ 拸 *rhaiʔ 'cleave' WT hral-ba 'to rend, tear up'	chè 坼 *thrâk < *thra(i)-k 'split'
pò 破 *phâih 'break'	pī 劈 *phêk < *phâi-k 'split'

if the word is felt to refer to a single numerical unit, i.e., '*one* hundred' 一百. However, occasionally there seems to be little difference in meaning, for example, JP $p^{h}jai^{33}$ 'break' × $p^{h}je?$ < $p^{h}jek$ 'break'. Other languages also have a final *-k* in this semantic range; Gedney (1976: 72) draws attention to words in Tai with final *-εεk* which imply separation, for instance.

6.1.2 Suffix -k: distributive

A k-suffix forms distributives or partitives as Pulleyblank (1973: 122; 1995: 134f) calls them; they refer to one of a set. These words include → shú 孰, → ruò 若, → zé$_1$ 則, and

None	mò 莫 [mɑk] *mâk 'none, nothing' < wú 無 [muɑ] *ma 'there is no'
Someone	huò 或 [ɣuək] *wə̂k 'someone' < yǒu 有 [wu^B] *wə? 'there is'
Each	gè 各 [kɑk] *klâk 'each' < ? jǔ 舉 [kɨɑ^B] 'all'

This distributive suffix may possibly be the same "singular event" final *-k* (§6.1.1) hence *mò* 莫 *mâk, lit. 'there is no single one', 'one by one, there is no', etc.

6.2 Final -t

Some ST / PCH words in final *-iŋ, *-ik have shifted to OC *-in, *-it; see §6.4.1.

A final *-n, *-t, or *-s is sometimes added to open syllable words, also in TB (*HPTB:* 439ff; 457–465); however, *-t is not nearly as common as final *-k. The first two items suggest that occasionally final *-? (> tone B) is a weakened form of the final consonant, but the last set ('Bend', no final *-?) casts doubt on that (for a parallel, see §6.1.1 above):

C. square	kuò 栝 [kuɑt] *kwât or *kôt 'carpenter's square' × jǔ 矩 [kyɑ^B] *kwa? 'carpenter's square'
Filth	gǔ 淈 [kuət, guət] *kût 'dirt, to sully' × gòu 垢 [ko^B] *kô? 'filth' <> WT *bsgo-ba* 'to soil, stain'
Bend	qū 屈 [kʰut] *khut 'to bend, subdue' × gōu 句鉤 [ko] *kô 'hook, curved'
Discern	chá 察 [tʂʰat] *tshrât 'to examine, discern' × chā 差 [tʂʰai] *tshrâi ? 'divergence, difference'
To end	zú 卒 [tsut] *tsut 'to finish, end, die' × qiú 酋 [dziu] *dzu 'to end (one's life naturally)'
Say, said	yuē 曰 [wɑt] *wat 'say(s) / said: "...", lit. 'he went: "..."' × yú 于 [wɑ] *wa 'to go to'

6.2.1 Nouns with final -t

OC (> MC) final *-t can be a suffix that creates or marks nouns (Benedict *LTBA* 14.2, 1991: 149ff; *HPTB:* 454ff), typically ones that refer to natural objects or conditions; excluded are human beings and living creatures in general (Unger *Hao-ku* 39, 1992). This restriction indicates an earlier morphological role for final *-t (probably also in 'Square' and 'Filth' above).

Moon	yuè 月 [ŋyɑt] *ŋwat 'moon' <> WT *ŋo(s)* 'half moon'

Tongue — shé 舌 [źat] *m-lat or *m-let ‘tongue’
< shì 舐 [źe^{B}] *m-leʔ ‘to lick’ <> PTB *m-le ‘tongue’

Tip — mò 末 [mɑt] ‘tip, end’ (the thing that comes to nothing?)
< wú 無 [muɑ] ‘not have, there is no’

Sort — wù 物 (mjuət) [mut] ‘class, sort, things’
<> PTB *mruw (*STC* no. 150): WT *’bru* < *ɴbru* ‘grain, seed’

Group — zú 卒 [tsuət] *tsût ‘group (of men), soldier’
< zāo 遭 [tsou] *tsû ‘meet, encounter’, allofams mean ‘assemble’, etc.

Tears — lèi 淚 [lius] ‘tears’
< liú 流 [liu] ’to flow’

After the OC front vowel *i, OC > MC *-t* can also derive from PCH *-k (§6.4.1), but words like ‘Sun’, ‘Blood’, and ‘House’ agree with this semantic category and therefore had original final *-t:

Sun — rì 日 [ńit] *nit ‘sun, day’ <> PTB *nyiy

Blood — xuě 血 [huet] *hwît ‘blood’ <> PTB *s-hwiy ‘blood’

House — shì 室 [śit] *lhit (?) ‘house’
<> WT *gži* ‘foundation, abode’, Lepcha *lí* ‘house’

This nominalizing t-suffix is of ST provenance, but since there are not many OC – TB cognate sets with this morpheme, it can only have been productive between the ST and OC stages, i.e., in PCH — something that can be observed with other ST morphemes (§2.4.2–3). The ST origin of the t-suffix is established by its survival in TB languages (Benedict *LTBA* 14:2, 1991: 149–153; *STC* p. 101–102; *HPTB:* 454ff), most transparently in WT where it has the same range of meanings as in CH, although abstract nouns predominate (Geilich 1994: 10–48 has an exhaustive collection):

ltad-mo ‘play, the watching’ < lta-ba ‘to see, watch’
nad ‘illness’ < na-ba ‘be ill’
šid(-ma) ‘funeral meal’ < ’č^{h}i-ba, ši ‘to die’
drod ‘heat’ < ’dro-ba ‘be hot’
lčid ‘weight’ < lči-ba ‘heavy’
rgyud ‘cord, string’ < rgyu-ba ‘to run’

6-2	*-t: modal	*-(t)s: irrealis or future
bù 不 *pə 'not'	fú 弗 *pət 'cannot, will not > resist'	
(wú) 毋 *mə 'don't!'	wù 勿 *mət 'do not want to!' etc.	wèi 未 *mə(t)s 'not yet'
wú 無 *ma 'there is no, not have'	mò 末 *mât (if...) 'not' miè 蔑 *mêt (if...) 'not > despise'	
wéi 惟 *wi 'to be > think'		huì 惠 *wî(t)s 'should be > be kind'
yǒu 有 *wəʔ 'there is, have'		? wèi 謂 *wə(t)s 'tell, call'

*6.2.2 Final *-t, *(t)s with grammatical words*

Final *-t forms “aspectual” (Pulleyblank) or “modal” (Dobson) words, *-(t)s forms an ‘irrealis’ (or perh. ‘future’) counterpart to certain grammatical words; see Table 6-2. For the semantic extension of some of these grammatical words, see §2.10.

6.2.3 Final -t = foreign final -s

In some words OC *-t corresponds to foreign final *-s;* in the word for ‘seven’ many TB languages also show this correspondence (*HPTB:* 441f; 477ff). It is also possible that in these sets the finals derive from an original *-ts. Unger (*Hao-ku* 39, 1992: 88) has collected a dozen such sets; a few examples follow.

Finish	bì 畢 [pit] *pit ‘to finish, complete’ <> Lushai *peiʔ*^{L} < *peis* ‘id.’
Seven	qī 七 [tsʰit] *tshit < *snhit ? ‘seven’ <> PTB *snis > Himalayish *snis; PLB *snit > PBurm *ʔnit > WB *kʰu-hnac*; JP *sə*^{31}*-nit*^{31}; Trung *snit*
Knee	fú 韍芾 ~ bì 韠 [put] ~ [pit] *put ~ *pit ‘knee cover’ <> PTB *put > WT *pus-mo* ~ *pis-mo*

6.3 Final -s

Final *-s occurs in TB as part of a root as well as a suffix (*HPTB:* 431ff; 477ff). Hypothetical final *-s in OCM has the same MC outcome as OCM *-ts (§3.4). Although words and their respective phonetic series are commonly reconstructed across the board as OC *-ts (Baxter et al.), phonetic series seem to fall into two groups, one of which consists of words exclusively in tone C. We suspect that words in such series ended in simple OCM *-s, which was not a suffix or morpheme (like tone C), but belonged to the root, for example:

Great	dà, dài 大 (dâi^{C}) [dɑs, dɑ^{C}] *dâs ‘big, great’ ⪤ tài 太泰 (tʰâi^{C}) [tʰɑs] *thâs ‘very big, excessive’

Yet OCM *-s on rare occasions is added to a root, but it is not clear if this is a variant of ordinary tone C derivations, or if it had some other function:

Arrive	dài 迨 (dậi^{B}) [də^{B}] *lə̂ʔ ‘arrive’ ⪤ dài 逮 (dậi^{C}, i^{C}) [dəs, jis] *lə̂(t)s, *lə(t)s ‘come’
Come	lái 來 (lậi) [lə] *rə̂ʔ/k < *C-rəʔ or *C-rək ‘come’ ⪤ lì 莅 (lji^{C}) [lis] *rə(t)s ? ‘arrive’ ⪤ lì 戾 (liei^{C}) [les] prob. *rə̂(t)s ‘arrive’

6.4 Final -n

Final *-ŋ* has merged with *-n* after high vowels. Final *-n* can also be a morpheme.

6.4.1 Final -in / -it

ST / PCH *-it / *-in and *-iŋ / *-ik have coalesced in some ST languages with final *-in / *-it (for TB, see *HPTB:* 527ff). In Chinese, however, ST and PCH rimes *-iŋ, *-ik have apparently shifted in two directions in OC:

(1) PCH *-iŋ, *-ik > OC *-in, *-it:

Wood — xīn 薪 [sin] *sin 'firewood'
<> PTB *siŋ > WT *šiŋ* 'tree, wood', PLB *sik ~ *siŋ

Year — nián 年 [nen] *nîn 'harvest, crop, year'
<> PTB *s-niŋ 'year' > WT *na-niŋ* 'last year', JP *niŋ*^{33}, WB *ə-hnik*

Louse — shī 虱 [ṣit] *srit 'louse'
<> PTB *s-rik > WT *šig < hrjik* 'louse', Bunan *śrig*, Lushai *hrik*^{L}

Additional examples include → tián 田 'field',→ jí 堲 'masonry', → jié 結 'to tie'.

(2) PCH *-iŋ,*-ik > OC *-eŋ, *ek
In many words, ST and foreign finals *-iŋ / *-ik have merged with *-eŋ, *-ek. In addition, a few phonetic series combine words in OC *-in / *-it with ones in *-əŋ / *-ək. This indicates that the rimes *-iŋ / *-ik may still have been distinct in OC (Baxter 1992). Here follow examples with OC *e, for earlier *i.

Sound — míng 鳴 [mieŋ] *mreŋ, OCB *mrjeŋ 'to sound, to call'
<> WB *mrañ < mriŋ* 'to sound'; Mikir *marèŋ < m-riŋ* 'make noise, cry', Lushai *riŋ*^{H} / *rin*^{F} 'be loud'

Dark — míng 冥 [meŋ(^{B})] *mêŋ 'be dark, night'
<> WB *mañ*^{B} ~ *mai*^{B} < *miŋ*^{B} 'dark, black'

Birth, live — shēng 生 [ṣɛŋ] *srêŋ 'be born, live'
<> PTB *s-riŋ (*śriŋ) > Kanauri *sriŋ* 'to live, alive'

Drip — dī 滴 [tek] *têk 'to drip, drop'
<> WT: *gtig(s)-pa ~ 'tʰig-pa, tʰigs* 'to drop, drip'

Calculate — lì 歷曆 [lek] *rêk 'to add up, a number, calculate'
<> WB *re < ri* 'to count', Kanauri *ri*, WT *rtsi-ba < rhji < rhi*

(3) Some words have OC *-in ~ *-eŋ doublets, presumably from foreign *-iŋ / PCH *-iŋ. In such words, *Shījīng* rimes require a final *-in, but the same words have MC rimes which go back to OC *-eŋ. Some doublets have survived into MC and later (e.g., 'Dazzle' below). The phonological condition for this vacillation is not clear; OC dialect differences may have been responsible (Baxter 1992; note 'To pity' below).

Name — míng 名 [mieŋ] *meŋ ~ *min 'name'
<> PTB *r-miŋ > WT *miŋ*, Jiarong *termi*, PLB *ʔ-miŋ$^{1/3}$

Order — mìng 命 [mieŋ^{C}] *meŋh ~ *min 'to order'

Rain — líng 零霝 [leŋ] *rêŋ ~ *rîn

Distant — jiǒng 泂迥 [ɣweŋ^{B}] *wêŋʔ 'distant' ⋈ xuán 洵 [hwen] *hwîn 'far away'

Dazzle — yíng 熒 [ɣweŋ] *wêŋ 'the light' (of a lamp, fire) 熒 > 'glow-worm' 螢 > 'dazzle, confuse, delude' 熒
~ xuàn 眩 [ɣwen(^{C})] *wîn(s) 'troubled sight, delude, deceive'
~ xuàn 炫 [ɣ(w)en^{C}] *wîns 'bright, dazzle, show off'

To pity — lián 憐 (lien) [len] *rîn 'to pity'
~ líng 怜 (lieŋ) [leŋ ?] 'id.'
~ líng 悽 (ljəŋ) [lɨŋ] a Han period dialect variant

*6.4.2 Final *-un from *-uŋ*

Parallel to the above (§6.4.1), PCH rime *-uŋ has merged with OC *-un (*-ən after labials); however, in a few words the rime has survived as OC *-uŋ, especially in QYS div. III. Thus the distribution of OC *-uŋ (冬 category) is limited; in later div. I, there is no syllable with grave initial (K-, P-), only one syllable *tuŋ 冬. We find, however, some etyma with *-un ~ *-oŋ doublets, sporadically also after non-high vowels, including:

Mosquito	wén 蚊 [mun] *mən < *mun ‘mosquito’
	~ mĕng 蠓 [moŋ] *môŋ ‘midge, mosquito’
Deceive	wăng 罔 [muɑŋ^{B}] ⋈ màn 謾 [mɑ/an(^{C}), mɨan]
Reckless	wàng 妄 [muɑŋ^{C}] ⋈ màn 謾 [mɑn^{C}]
Goose	yàn$_{2}$ 雁 [ŋan^{C}] <> WT ŋaŋ ‘goose’, but see dictionary entries

Although OC has final *-n for TB final *-ŋ in some words with back vowels (Bodman 1980: 81–83), the problem remains that in some words WB / TB *-ŋ* may be secondary, CH final *-n* primary. Curiously, all these WB cognates have tone B (breathy):

Stream	chuān 川 *k-hlun ‘stream’	WB k^{h}joŋ^{B}
Boat	chuán 船 *m-lon ‘boat’	WB loŋ^{B}
Change	biàn 變 *pron ‘to change’	WB proŋ^{B} ‘change place’
Tumult	luàn 亂 *rôn ‘tumult’	WB bjoŋ^{B} ~ broŋ^{B} ‘tumultuous’
Soft	ruăn 軟 *nonʔ ‘soft’	WB hñaŋ^{B} ‘soft, gentle, quiet’
Short	duăn 短 *tônʔ ‘short’	WB toŋ^{B} ‘short, as garment’
Shield	dùn, shùn 盾 *dunʔ ‘shield’	WB duiŋ^{B}
Divide	fēn 分 *pən ‘divide’	WB puiŋ^{B}
Flee	bēn 奔 *pə̂n ‘to run, flee’	PTB *ploŋ ‘flee, run’
Burn	fén 焚 *bən ‘to burn’	PTB *ploŋ ‘burn’

6.4.3 Nominalizing suffix -n

A ST suffix *-n has survived in some TB languages where it forms nouns (*STC* p. 99 ff; *HPTB*: 439ff; 443–453), most conspicuously in WT, e.g., *rkun-ma* ‘thief’ < *rku-ba* ‘to steal’, *gčin* ‘urine’ < *gči-ba* ‘urinate’ (Beyer 1992: 117; Geilich 1994: 26 ff.); there are also traces of this suffix in other TB languages (Michailovsky 1985: 369). It occurs also in Chinese where it is often attached redundantly to nouns, but in some instances derives nouns from other words (as already suspected by Sagart 1999: 135f). The final *-n was once productive in PCH as there are no cognate sets that share this ST morpheme with TB (except ‘Chisel’ below); see also §2.4.2. Benedict (*STC*: n. 284, 428–429) believes it to form collectives; however, it seems to form or mark nouns in general.

Ford	jīn 津 LH [tsin] OCM *tsin ‘a ford’ n. (< *tsəi-n)
	< jì 濟 [tsei^{C}] *tsə̂ih ‘to ford, to cross’ vb.
Wrist	wàn 腕 [ʔuɑn^{C}] *ʔôns or *ʔwâns ‘wrist’
	< yū 迂紆 [ʔyɑ] *ʔwa ‘to bend’
Speech	yán 言 [ŋɨɑn] *ŋan ‘to speak, speech’
	< yǔ 語 [ŋɨɑ^{B}] *ŋaʔ ‘to speak’
Guest	bīn 賓 [pin] *pin ‘a gift, present > to present a gift > guest’
	< bì 畀 [pis] *pis or *pits ‘to give’ <> WB *pe^{B}* ‘give’

Worm — yuān 蜎肙 [ʔuen] *ʔwên (< *ʔuâi-n) 'small worm, bending, crawling (as a caterpillar)'
< wēi 逶 (ʔjwie 3) [ʔyɑi] *ʔuai or *ʔoi ? 'tortuous movement'

Heir — yìn 胤 [jin^C] *ləns 'successor, heir, posterity'
< yí 貽詒 [jə] *lə 'to transmit, bequeath, hand down'

Suffix *-n is occasionally added to existing nouns, rather than creating new ones:

People — mín 民 LH [min] *min 'people' <> PTB *mi 'person, man'

Dog — quǎn 犬 [k^{h}uen^B] *khwîn? 'dog'
<> ST *kwi 'dog': PTB *kwiy > PTib. *ki* > WT *k^{h}yi*

Monkey — yuán 猿 [wɑn] *wan 'monkey' <> PL *C-lwaj, JP *woi*, *we* 'monkey'

Bowl — wǎn 碗 [ʔuɑn^B] *ʔôn? 'a bowl' < ōu 甌 [ʔo] *ʔô 'a bowl'

Hammer — duàn 鍛 [tuɑn^C] *tôns 'hammer'
<> PTB *tow > WT *mt^{h}o-ba* ~ *'t^{h}o-ba* < ɴ*to* 'large hammer', WB t^hu^C 'to hammer' ⋇ tu^A 'a hammer'

Chisel — juān 鐫 [tsyɑn] *tson 'chisel, sharp point'
<> WT *mts^{h}on* 'any pointed instrument, forefinger', JP *dźu* 'thorn, prick, WB ts^hu^B 'to sting'

Fat — juǎn 臇 [tsyɑn^B] *tson? 'fat' <> WT *tsho-ba* 'be fat', WB $tshu^A$ 'be fat'

Bank of river — àn 岸 [ŋɑn^C] *ŋâns 'river bank'
< hǔ 滸 [hɑ^B] *hŋâ? 'river bank' <> WT *dŋo* 'bank, side'

Egg — luǎn 卵 [luɑn^B] *C-rôn? 'egg' <> West Tib. *sro-ma* 'nit'

Goose — yàn 雁 [ŋan^C] *ŋrâns? 'domestic goose' < é 鵝 [ŋɑi] *ŋâi 'goose' (but see above and in the dictionary)

Date — chén 辰 [dźɨn] *dən 'date, point in time, season'
< shí 時 [dźə] *də 'time, season'

6.4.4 Final -n with verbs

The role of final *-n* in verbs is not clear, but among the items are many stative or descriptive verbs; this is reminiscent of WT where verbs in *-n* are typically adjectival (Geilich 1994: 40–50). In some wfs, the *-n* ~ open final variation may indicate an earlier final *-l or *-r.

Weak — ruǎn 耎 [ńuɑn^B] *non? 'soft, weak'
< nuò 懦 [ńo] *no 'weak, timid'

Lovely — wǎn 婉 [ʔyɑn^B] *ʔon? (< *ʔau-n? ?) 'be lovely'
< yāo 妖 [ʔɨɑu] *ʔau 'be delicate, slender, beautiful, charming'

Quarrel — nuán 奻 [ṇuan(^{C})] *nrâun(s) 'to quarrel'
< nǎo 撓 [ṇau^B] *nrâu? 'to trouble, disturb'

Thick — dūn 敦 [tuən] *tûn 'be solid, thick' <> WB t^hu^A 'thick'

To drip — luán 欒 [luɑn] *rôn 'dripping (of water)'
< lòu 漏 [lo^C] *ro(k)h 'to leak'

To wither	yuàn 苑 [ʔyɑn^B] *ʔonʔ 'to wither' < wēi 萎 [ʔyɑi ~ ʔɨoi] *ʔoi or *ʔuai ? 'to wither'

6.4.5 Pronominal final -n

Suffixed to coverbs (prepositions), *-n* takes the place of the pronoun *zhī* 之 (him, her, it) which never follows a coverb (Pulleyblank 1995: 10; 56):

yān 焉 'in / at... it' < 於 yú 'be in / at...'
yuán 爰 'in / at... it' < 于 yú 'be in / at...'
rán 然 'like it' < 如 rú 'be like'

The source of this final -n is not certain. It could perhaps be of ST origin; note WT *-na* 'locative suffix', Lushai verbal suffix *-na* 'the place where, with what, whom'. Alternatively it could have been reduced from a widespread AA 3rd person / demonstrative pronoun *na (see under → nà 那).

6.5 Final -ŋ

The interrelationship between final *-ŋ* and tone B has been observed in §3.2.4; it also alternates with final *-n* in §6.4.1.

6.5.1 Final -ŋ as a morpheme: terminative

A ST suffix *-ŋ long ago formed *terminative verbs / words* that imply an action with an endpoint, a goal. The term 'terminative' is borrowed from IE, e.g., Skt. *gáchhati* 'he arrives' (< *gm̥-sk-) from PIE *gam 'to go' (Lehmann 1993: 168f). This meaning is still obvious in the first two sets below: 'there is no' > terminative 'disappear'; 'above' > 'rise, raise'; and in the item 'to go' where *yú* is the general term, *wǎng* always means 'go / come to a place'. 'Live' is a full verb with the terminative meaning 'to give birth, live' which is derived from a ST stem 'to be'.

Disappear	wáng 亡 LH [muɑŋ] OCM *maŋ 'to disappear' < wú 無 [muɑ] *ma 'there is no'
Rise	yáng 揚 [jɑŋ] *laŋ 'to rise, raise' <> WT: *laŋ-ba* 'to rise, arise' ⋈ *ldaŋ-ba* 'get up' < WT *bla* 'above'
Become warm	xiǒng 煦 (xjwoŋ^B) [hɨoŋ^B] *hoŋʔ 'become warm' (of the rising sun) < xǔ 煦 (xju$^{B/C}$) [hɨo$^{B/C}$] *hoʔ/h 'to warm' (with breath or air)
Go to	wǎng 往 [wɑŋ^B] *waŋʔ 'to go to, gone, past' <> PTB *waŋ > WT *'oŋ-ba* 'to come'; WB *waŋ* 'to enter, go or come in' < yú 于 [wɑ] *wa 'go to, in, at, on, to' <> PTB *wa, *(s-)wa 'go, come'
Live	shēng 生 [ṣɛŋ] *srêŋ 'to live, be alive' > ('cause to live') 'give birth' <> PTB *sriŋ 'live, alive' < PTB *sri 'to be, exist'; but see → shēng$_2$ 生
Center	yāng 央 [ʔɨɑŋ] *ʔaŋ 'hit the center, reach the middle' (< 'get to be in it') < yú 於 [ʔɨɑ] *ʔa 'be in, at, on'

6.5.2 Final -ŋ and open syllables

Often, allofams in *-ŋ do not seem to be terminatives. In ST languages, open syllable words alternate with some ending in a final consonant, including final *-ŋ* with or without semantic distinction. Perhaps tone B is associated with this feature (§3.2.4):

Itch	yǎng 癢 [jɑŋ^{B}] *jaŋʔ ? 'to itch' <> WT *g-ya-ba* 'to itch', WB *ya^{B}* 'itch'
Far	jiōng 泂 [ɣueŋ^{B}] *wêŋʔ 'distant' <> PLB *wiy > WB *we^{B}* 'far'
Meet	yíng 迎 [ŋɨɑŋ] *ŋaŋ 'to meet' (< 'going against someone to meet him') ≍ yà 御迓 [ŋa^{C}] *ŋrâh 'to meet, receive' <> PTB *ŋra > WB *ŋra^{B}* 'meet, encounter'
Bend	wǎng 枉 [ʔyɑŋ^{B}] *ʔwaŋʔ 'bent, crooked' ≍ yū 迂紆 [ʔyɑ] *ʔwa 'to bend, deflect'
Pool	wāng 汪 [ʔuɑŋ] *ʔwâŋ 'pool' ≍ wū 汙洿 [ʔɑ] *ʔwa 'pool'
Deceive	wǎng 罔 [muɑŋ^{B}] *maŋʔ 'to deceive' ≍ wū 誣 [muɑ] *ma 'to deceive'
Square	kuāng 筐 [k^{h}yɑŋ] *khwaŋ 'square basket' ≍ jǔ 矩 [kyɑ^{B}] *kwaʔ 'carpenter's square'

6.6 Final stop consonant ~ nasal

Final stop consonants occasionally alternate with nasals in Chinese as well as in TB wfs (*HPTB:* 516–526). The origin and meaning of this change has not yet been determined (Karlgren 1949: 92ff; Baxter and Sagart 1998: 60). Examples include:

Wide	guǎng 廣 [kuɑŋ^{B}] 'wide' ≍ kuò 廓 kuɑk 'large, extravagant'
Watch	jiān 監 [kam] *krâm 'to see, look at, inspect' <> WB *krap* 'superintend, watch over and direct'
Wood	xīn 薪 [sin] *sin 'firewood' <> PLB *sik ~ *siŋ 'tree, wood' > WB *sac*

6.7 Dissimilation with labial finals -p / -m

In CH and area languages, words that refer to a closing / closed mouth or opening, also the notion 'full ~ round', tend to end in a labial consonant. Rare instances of a final labial appearing as a possible morphological variation to a stem probably have their origin in this sound-symbolic tendency. For example, Geilich (1994: 70–73) draws attention to a few TB words where a final *-m* might have been an addition, including WT *mnam-pa* 'to smell' (something done with the mouth closed) ≍ *sna* 'nose', *'bru-ma* 'swelling, tumor' ≍ *sbrum-pa* 'pregnant'; see also Table 2-7 under §2.5.1 for a possible CH relict. Yet in CH, cases of this type are so rare and of ST heritage, that for practical purposes, we will here not count labial finals among the morphemes.

Because of labial dissimilation, rimes *-op / -om, -up / -um* are phonotactically impossible in MC and probably also in OC (hence no such forms in OCM), although Baxter reconstructs such finals in some words. The dissimilation affects the vowel (§11.10.2) so that *rù* 入 MC *ńźjəp* 'enter' descends from ST *nup (WT *nub*) via *nuəp* > OC *nəp; or *sān* 三 'three' ST *sum (PTB *sum) > OC *sə̂m via *suəm*.

Perhaps in a few instances, the earlier back vowel was preserved, but the final consonant has dissimilated instead. All these words have the ST vowel *u. There are very few sporadic suspects for this dissimilation, such as

Turn over fù 覆 [p^{h}uk] *phuk 'to overturn' <> WT *spub-pa* 'to turn over'

Warm sūn 飧 [suən] *sûn or *slun ? 'cooked rice, warm meal'
?～ xín 尋燂 *s-ləm 'to heat (food)' <> PTB *slum 'to heat'

To end zhōng 終 [tśuŋ] *tuŋ 'to end'
? <> WB *tum*^{C} 'be ended (season)', JP *t*^{h}*um*^{31} 'be ended', Lai *t*^{h}*um* 'be ended' ⋇ *džə-t*^{h}*um* 'end something'

Double chóng 重 [ḍoŋ] *droŋ 'double, accumulate'
<> WB *cum* 'double, form a pair'

To descend jiàng 降 [kɔŋ] *krûŋ 'to descend, send down'
? <> TB-Lai *trùm / trúm* 'descend' ⋇ *t*^{h}*rúm / t*^{h}*rumʔ* 'to put down'

Yet these examples and the idea of such dissimilation may be spurious. Although *-um* ~ *-uŋ* variation is observed in TB (e.g., *[s-]luŋ ~ *s-lum 'heart / liver' — Matisoff 1978: 203–205), the above examples have possible alternate etymologies. Labial initial and final consonants are incompatible in most environments, however, hence the final labial is dissimilated:

Blood huāng 衁 [huɑŋ] *hmâŋ 'blood'
< AA: PNorth Bahnaric *maham, PMnong *mham

Tray mǐn 皿 [mɨaŋ^{B}] *maŋʔ ? 'vessel, dish, bowl'
< AA: Viet. *mâm*, PVM *ʔbəm^{A} 'food tray'

Ten thousand wàn 萬 [muɑn^{C}] *mans < *mons? 'ten thousand'
<> WT *'bum* < *ɴbum* 'hundred thousand'

Ice bīng 冰 [pɨŋ] *prəŋ ? 'ice' <> PTB *pam 'snow' > Jiarong *ta-rpam* 'ice'

Burry bèng 堋 (pəŋ^{C}) [pəŋ^{C}] *pə̂ŋh 'put the coffin into the ground, bury'
<> ? WT *'bum* 'tomb, sepulcher', Lushai *p*^{h}*uum*^{H} 'to bury'

Gush fú 沸 [put] *pət (< *put) 'be gushing, rushing (as spring, water, wind)'
<> PTB *brup ~ *prup 'gush forth'

6.8 OC final -i

Matisoff (1995: 35–91; *HPTB:* 482–489) has proposed a TB palatal diminutive suffix *-i. In OC, this morpheme marks the independent pronouns (§3.3.3). It also appears in *mǐ* 靡 [miɑi^{B}] 'have not, there is no' < *wú* 無 [muɑ] 'not' (§3.3.2). Otherwise, final *-i occurs in variation with simple vowels or with *-n; see Table 6-3.

6-3	-V	-Vi	-Vn
Wither (1)		wēi 萎 *ʔoi	yuàn 苑 *ʔons
Wither (2)	yū 菸 *ʔa		yān 蔫 *ʔan
Bend (1)	yǎo 夭 *ʔauʔ	wěi 委 *ʔoiʔ	yuǎn 宛 *ʔwanʔ
Bend (2)	yū 迂紆 *ʔwa		wàn 腕 *ʔwâns yuān 冤 *ʔwan
To lean		yī 依 *ʔəi	yīn 因 *ʔin
Luxuriant leaves		yǐ 猗 *ʔaiʔ	wǎn 苑 *ʔonʔ

6.9 Absence of final consonant after long vowel

A Chinese open syllable, often with tone A, for a foreign syllable ending in a final consonant, has several supporting examples. The reason might be loss of coda after a foreign long vowel, something also observed in other languages (Benedict *LTBA* 5.1, 1979: 6):

Ploughed fields — chóu 疇 (ḍjəu) *dru <> Tai: S. *t*^{h}*ɯak*^{D2} < *dɯɯak*

Hold, grasp — chí 持 (ḍɨ) *drə <> Tai: S. *t*^{h}*əək* < *dəək*

Boat — zhōu 舟 *tu <> AA: Khmer *du:k*

Male animal — mǔ 牡 *mû? or *C-mu? 'male (animal)'
<> OKhmer *jmol* /cmọọl/ 'male, of animals'

Each — měi 每 *mə̂? 'each, every' <> Khmer /mooj/; PMon *muə̯* 'one'

Helmet — móu 鍪 *mu 'helmet' <> TB-WT *rmog* 'helmet'
<> AA: Khmer *mùək* 'hat', Biat *mo:k*, PEKatuic *muak (<- Khmer?);
Khmer -> Tai: S. *muak*^{D1} < *hm- 'hat, cap'

Branch — méi 枚 *mə̂i 'branch' <> AA: OKhmer *mēk* /mɛɛk/ 'branch'

Sad — sāo 騷 *sû 'sad, worried, grief'
< AA: OKhmer *sok* /sook/ 'sorrow, affliction, pain, grief, be sad'

Pig — shǐ 豕 (śje^{B}) *lhe? ? (*lhai? ?) 'pig'
<> AA: PMonic *cliik, Mon *klot, kloik* 'pig', PWa *lik 'pig'

For contrast, compare items with MK short vowels:

Polish — cuō 磋 (ts^{h}â) [ts^{h}ɑi] *tshâi 'to rub, polish'
<> AA: Khmer /cnaj/ 'to cut (gems), to polish'

Tree trunk — gēn 根 (kən) *kə̂n 'root, trunk' <> AA: PVM *kəl 'tree (trunk)' (short vowel), PMon *t[l]gəl 'stump (of tree, mushroom, tooth)'

Stop, block — sài, sāi, sè 塞 (sək) *sə̂k 'to stop up, block'
<> AA-Khmer *suka* /sok/ 'to stop up, block, cram...'

Shelter — sù 宿 (sjuk) *suk 'pass the night'<> AA: OKhmer /sruk/ Proto-Khmer 'shelter, settlement, homeland' ⋇ Khmer *jruka* /cruk/ 'shelter, refuge, asylum' < derivatives of /ruk/ 'go down into, take shelter'

Occasionally, the coda was retained in OC even after a long vowel:

To spear fish — chuō 擉 (tṣ^{h}åk) *tshrôk 'to spear (fish)'
< AA: Khmer *cūka* /còok/ 'lift with tool...' ⋇ *cpūka* /cbòok/ (archaic) 'trident for lifting fish'. For the CH retroflex initial, see §5.10.2.

Retention of a coda after a long vowel seems to indicate a late layer of borrowing; compare
cuò$_{2}$ 莝 (ts[^{h}]uâ^{C}) *tshôih 'hay, fodder', mid- to late Zhou word from AA *ksooy; MC ts^{h}- for foreign *ks- is common, especially in late words; vs.
chú$_{4}$ 芻 (tṣ^{h}ju) *tshro 'hay, fodder' on Shang OB from the same AA *ksooy; very old is also OC *r with foreign pre-initial *g- or *k-.

Residue may include → bā$_{5}$ 豝 *prâ ? 'wild pig'; → fū$_{9}$ 膚 *pa 'human skin'.

7

OLD CHINESE AND FOREIGN *R

Many different MC / LHan reflexes are believed to derive from OC *r: initial *l*-; retroflex consonants; QYS div. II and *chóngniǔ* div. III vocalism; final *-n* or *-i*; or no trace at all. Because MC initial and final consonants and other phonemes are projected back to (nearly) identical ones in LHan, subsequently examples will often be cited in simpler LHan forms.

7.1 OC *r as reflected in MC initial consonants

7.1.1 MC initial l-

MC / LHan initial *l*- < OC *r- frequently alternates with velars, but with other initials also, in phonetic series as well as wfs. It typically corresponds to foreign *r*- in the initial. However, the foreign equivalents usually have an initial cluster, therefore Baxter (1992: 200f) suggests that MC *l*- derives from a cluster *C-r-. Among the examples he cites are 'Indigo' and 'Stand' below. In the jod-less div. I/IV (§9.1.1), indications for a lost pre-initial are so frequent with MC *l*- that this division's vocalism may have been caused by this loss. We therefore tend to write OCM *g-r- or *C-r- > MC *l*- and so on when there is some indication of what has disappeared (LHan after the graph):

MC / LHan initial *l*-:

Stand	lì 立	lip, *g-rəp 'to stand' <> PTB *krap 'to stand'
Indigo	lán 藍	lɑm, *râm < *g-ram 'indigo' <> Thai *khraam* < PTai *gr-
Barrier	lán 闌	lɑn, *rân < *g-ran 'barrier, to protect'
	≍ xián 閑	gɛn, *grên 'barrier, bar'
Orchid	lán 蘭	lɑn, *rân< *g-ran 'orchid'
	≍ jiān 蕑	kan, *krân 'orchid'
To train	liàn 湅	len^{C}, *rêns < *g-rens 'to train'
	≍ xián 閑	gɛn, *grân 'to restrain, train'
Refine	liàn 湅練	len^{C}, *rêns < *g-rens 'to purify' 練 > 'refine (metal)' 鍊
	≍ xiàn 僩	gɛn^{B}, *grênʔ 'be beautiful, refined'
Lotus fruit	lián 蓮	len, *rên < *g-ren 'lotus fruit'
	≍ jiān 蕑	kɛn, *krên 'lotus fruit'
Lazy	lǎn 懶	lɑn^{B} 'lazy'
	≍ xián 閑	gɛn, *grên 'leisure'
Accumulate	liǎn 斂	liam$^{B/C}$, *ramʔ/s 'gather, accumulate'
	≍ jiǎn 檢	kɨam^{B}, *kamʔ 'accumulate'
To see	lǎn 覽	lɑm^{B}, *râmʔ < *g-ramʔ 'to see'
	≍ jiān 監	kam, *krâm 'to see, look at, inspect'
Overflow	làn 濫	lɑm^{C}, *râms < *g-rams 'overflow, put into water'
	≍ hàn 濫	gɑm^{C}, *gâms 'bathtub'

Burn	liào 燎	leu^{C}, *riâuh < *g-riauh 'to burn, torch'
	⋙ jiǎo 烄	kau^{B}, *kr(i)âuʔ 'burn on a pyre of crossed logs'

In some words, MC initial *lj-* may reflect a ST pre-initial *r-; see §9.2.1; §10.1.3.

*7.1.2 OC voiceless *r-*

OC voiceless *r is rare, is reflected in MC / LHan t^h- and ṭ^h-. Cases include → tǐ 體 'body' and 'Sorpion' in §5.2.4.

MC / LHan initial *l-* (< OC *r-) corresponds to *s-* in some northern Min dialect words, which points to an earlier voiceless initial (Mei, Tsu-lin, and J. Norman, 1971). How this voiceless lateral would be different from other voiceless laterals (> MC t^h- etc.) is not clear.

7.1.3 MC retroflex initials

MC / LHan retroflex initials *ṭ(^{h}), ḍ, ṇ, tṣ(^{h}), dẓ, ṣ* correspond to foreign ones with an *r* in the initial, for example:

Extend — zhāng 張 [ṭaŋ] *traŋ 'make long, stretch, extend, draw (a bow)'
<> WT *'dren-ba, draŋ(s)* 'to draw', PLB *raŋ 'draw, pull'

Louse — shī 虱 [ṣit] *srit < *srik 'louse'
<> PTB *s-rik > WT *šig* < *hrjik 'louse', Bunan *śrig*

Live — shēng 生 [ṣɛŋ] *srêŋ <> PTB *sriŋ 'live'

Often, retroflex initials correspond to WT / TB dental initials with a prefix *g-, r-*. The OC phoneme sequence is unknown; Gong Hwang-cherng (2002, vol 2: 167–172) writes OC *rt- in such words. For the sake of consistency, OCM assumes only medial *-r- in such configurations.

Unfold — zhǎn 展 [ṭan^{B}] *tranʔ 'unfold, open'
<> WT *rdal-ba, brdal* 'to spread, unfold, extend over'

For MC / LHan retroflex initials in words with MK connections, see §5.10.2–3.

7.1.4 MC initial ḍj- and ṭj-

MC initial *ḍj-* and *ṭj-* (LHan *ḍ-* and *ṭ-*) stand in a few correspondence sets for a foreign initial *r-*, or *r* in a more complex initial where we would expect OC *r- or *kr-, *pr- (as in §7.2).

MC *ḍj-* = foreign *r:

Pheasant — zhì 雉 [ḍi^{B}] *driʔ 'pheasant'
< ST: WB *rac* < *rik 'id.', WT *sreg-pa* 'partridge'

Old man — zhàng 丈 [ḍaŋ^{B}] *draŋʔ 'old man'
< ST: PTB *źraŋ (or rather *ryaŋ ?) > WT *žaŋ* 'chief, uncle', WB *ə-hraŋ* 'master, lord', Kuki *r(j)aŋ ~ *traŋ 'father's sister's husband'

Ramie — zhù 苧紵 [ḍa^{B}] 'ramie, cloth / rope woven of ramie'
? < ST: WT *ras* 'cotton cloth'

Lamb — zhù 羜 [ḍa^{B}] 'lamb' ? < ST: WT *ra* 'goat', Kanauri *la*

To fall — zhuì 墜 (ḍwi^{C}) [ḍus] *drus 'to fall down'
< MK: OKhmer *ruḥ* /ruh/ 'to fall, drop' ⋙ *jruḥ* /cruh/ 'to fall, drop'

Farm chán 廛 [ḍan] *dran 'farm, farmyard'
< KT: Tai S. *rɨan*^{A2}, PKS *hra:n^{1} 'house'

Call zhào 召 [ḍɑu^{C}] *drauh 'to call, summon'
? < Tai: S. *rɨak*^{A2} 'summon, call'

MC *ṭj-* / LHan *ṭ-* = foreign or dialectal *Cr-*:

Pig zhū 豬 [ṭɑ] *tra 'pig' ⋊ jiā 豭 [ka] *krâ 'boar, pig'

Sickle zhì 銍 [ṭit] *trit 'sickle, cut with a sickle' <> WT *gri* 'knife', WB *kre*^{B} 'copper', JP *mə*^{31}*-gri*^{33} 'brass', Lushai *hrei*^{L} < *hreih* 'axe, hatchet'

Wrist zhǒu 肘 [ṭu^{B}] *truʔ 'wrist, elbow' (< 'bend') <> WB *krui*^{C} 'bow down, stoop'

Bamboo zhú 竹 [ṭuk] *truk 'bamboo'
<> Tai: S. *tɔɔk*^{DIL} < *prɔɔk, PKS *t^{h}ruk 'bamboo strip'

Morning zhāo 朝 [ṭɑu] *trau 'morning' <> Tai: S. *p*^{h}*rau*^{A2} < *br- 'morning'

Know zhī 知 [ṭe] *tre 'to know, understand'
? <> Lushai *hria*^{R} / *hre*^{H} / *hriat*^{F} 'to know'

Doublets MC / LHan l- (< *r-) and retroflex stops are also found within Chinese:

Provisions liáng 糧 [liɑŋ] *raŋ 'grain, provisions'
⋊ zhāng 粻 [ṭɑŋ] *traŋ 'provisions'

Mound lǒng 壟隴 [lioŋ^{B}] *roŋʔ 'mound'
⋊ zhǒng 冢塚 [ṭoŋ^{B}] *troŋʔ 'mound'

7.1.5 MC dẓ- = foreign r-

Non-ST initial *r-* corresponds occasionally to MC / LHan *dẓ-* (< *dzr-).

Shape zhuàng 狀 [dẓɑŋ^{C}] *dzraŋh 'form, shape' <> Tai: S. *raaŋ*^{B2} 'form, shape' < AA: Khmer *rāṅa* [ríiəŋ] 'body build, form, figure, shape'

Category chái 儕 [dẓɛi] *dzrî or *dzrəi 'class, category, equals'
<> Tai: S. *raai*^{A2} 'set, category, list'

Nest cháo 巢 [dẓau' *dzrâu <> PMY *rau^{2} 'nest'

A shed zhàn 棧 [dẓan^{B}] *dzrânʔ ? 'a shed made of intertwined branches'
<> Tai: S. *raan*^{C2} 'machan, booth, stall, shop'

7.2 MC div. II, *chóngniǔ* div. III, and OC medial *-r-

Many cognate sets support the hypothesis that an OC medial *r is responsible for QYS division II vocalism and LHan equivalents (Bodman 1985). Baxter (1992) suggests that certain *chóngniǔ* div. III syllables also had a medial *r, but as with div. II, not all such MC words correspond to words with foreign medial *r* (see §7.4). For div. II in general, see §9.1.4.

Div. II syllables correspond not only to foreign medial *r syllables, but also to syllables that have a final *-r*, a pre-initial *r-*, as well as pre-initials like *d-* or *g-*, medial *-l-*, or no medial at all; some MC syllables may represent archaisms; some foreign words with medial *r* have MC counterparts in div. I/IV or III (no OC *r is assumed there). Why there is a multitude of correspondences is at present only a matter of speculation.

*7.2.1 Foreign medial *r*

MC div. II and certain *chóngniǔ* div. III ('3/3') vocalism (and LHan equivalents) reflect an OC medial *-r-; this is supported by foreign cognates and loans.

Add jiā 加 [kai] *krâi 'to add to, apply'
<> WT *bkral-ba* 'to impose, place upon (tax)'

Shell jiǎ 甲 [kap] *krâp 'shell, nail, armor'
<> WT *k^{h}rab* 'shield, fish scales'

River jiāng 江 [kɔŋ] *krôŋ 'river' <> PMonic *krooŋ, Bahnar *kroŋ* 'river'

Horn jiǎo 角 [kɔk] *krôk 'horn' <> PTB *kru(w) > WB *k^{h}yui, k^{h}rui* 'horn'

Eight bā 八 [pɛt] *priât or *prêt 'eight'
<> WT *brgyad* < *bryat; TGTM *^{3}pret; Lush *pà-riát*

Hundred bǎi 百 [pak] *prâk 'hundred' <> PTB *r-ya > WT *brgya* < *br-ya

Divide bān 班 [pan] *prân 'divide, distribute'
<> WT *'p^{h}ral-ba* 'to separate, part'

Womb bāo 胞 [p^{h}ɔu] *prû, *p^{h}rû 'womb' <> WT *'p^{h}ru-ma/-ba* 'uterus'

Stool jǐ 几 [kɨ^B] *kriʔ 'stool, small table'
<> TB: WT *k^{h}ri* 'seat, throne, chair, frame'

Hungry jī 飢 [kɨ] *kri or *krəi ? 'be hungry, starve' <> TB: WT *bkres* 'id.'

7.2.2 Div. II = archaism

See §9.1.4 on div. II syllables which have resulted from a post-OC shift from div. III. In some syllables div. II vocalism may be due to retention of an earlier vocalic timbre, i.e., they represent an archaism:

Afraid pà 怕 (p^{h}a^C) 'to be afraid' [(Tang) Han Yu]
~ pù 怖 [p^{h}ɑ^C] *p^{h}âh 'to fear' [Zhuangzi]

Crow yā 鴉 [ʔa] *ʔa 'crow, raven' ~ wū 烏 [ʔɑ] *ʔa 'crow, raven'

In 'crow', the vocalism may instead (or also) be due to interference from the development of the OC rime *-ak (§9.1.4).

7.3 MC l- (OC *r-) = foreign l

In a few words, foreign initial *l- (> MC *ji-* / LHan *j-*), or *l in the initial, shows a reflex of OC *r-; this may be a Rural feature (§1.3.1).

To sow jià 稼 [ka^C] *krâh 'grain, to sow' <> KT: PTai *kla^{C1} 'young rice plant', Saek *tlaa^3* > *traa^3* 'rice seedlings', PKS *kla^3 'rice seedling'

Salt lǔ 鹵 [lɑ^B] *râʔ 'rock salt' <> PTB *s-la 'salt' > Miri *əlo*, PKaren *hla

Bamboo lù 簬 [lɑ^C] *râh < *g-rah 'a kind of bamboo'
<> Tai: S. *k^{h}laa^{C2}* < *gl- 'bamboo' <> AA-Bahnar *pəle*, Viet. *le* 'bamboo'

Turtle liè 獵 [liap] *r(i)ap ? 'a kind of turtle'
<> PTB *lip / *lep 'turtle' > WB *lip*, Khami *lip*, Mru *lip* 'tortoise'

Descend jiàng 降 [kɔŋ] *krûŋ 'to descend'
<> Tai: S. *loŋ*^{A2} < *dl- 'to descend'; but see also §6.7.

In some of the above words, the correspondence may be due to the late date (Han >) of borrowing in either direction; note in addition:

Eel lái 鯠 [lə > lɑi] *rə̂ 'a kind of eel' [Han period EY] <> Tai: S. *lai*^{A1} (WSiam *hlai*) 'id.' Tai final *-ai* agrees with LHan and later *-ai*, but not with OC *-ə.

Splint hat lì 笠 [lip] *rəp 'splint hat'
<> Tai: Wuming *klop*^{D1S} < *kl- 'bamboo hat'

Barrier guān 關 [kuan] *krôn ? 'bar, barrier, frontier'
<> PTai *klɔn^{A1} 'rafter, latch on door'

Frost jiāo 膠 [kɔu(B)] *krû(?) 'frost' [Chuci] <> PWMiao *klau^{7} 'ice, snow'. First appearance in Chuci points to late (Han period) loan.

7.4 OC medial *r and TB prefixes

Some foreign, especially TB, items have pre-initial *g-*, *d-*, *r-*, *s-*, or no pre-initial / prefix, where a medial *r (> MC division II) is postulated for OC. These same TB prefixes also seem to be responsible for devoicing in some OC words (§5.3). Here is no reason to assume anything other than ST or PCH pre-initial *r-, thus ST *d- / *g- > PCH *r-; for ST / TB *s- = OC *r-, see §5.3. We cannot be sure where in the OC syllable the *r was; by default we must assume that it was a medial, indistinguishable from other medial *-r-. Shī Xiàngdōng (2000: 208ff) has collected cognate sets which include some of the following (the words belong to MC div. II or 3/3 [and LHan equivalents]):

Scold mà 罵 [ma^{B}] *mrâʔ 'to scold' <> WT *dmod-pa* 'curse' < root *ma 'below'

Crowd méng 氓 [maŋ] *mrâŋ <> WT *dmaŋs* 'common people, crowd'

Crab xiè 蟹 [ɣai^{B}] *grêʔ 'crab' <> PTB *d-ka:y 'id.'

Poor pín 貧 [bɨn] *brən? 'be poor' <> WT *dbul* 'id.'

Day zhòu 晝 [ṭu^{C}] *trukh 'day time' <> WT *gdugs* 'midday, noon'

Latrine cè 廁 [tṣʰɔ^{C}] *tshrəkh ? 'latrine' <> WT *gči(d)-pa* 'to urinate'

Kill shā 殺 [ṣɛt] *srât 'to kill'
<> PTB *g-sat 'to kill' > WT *gsod-pa, bsad*, PL *C-sat

Muntjac jǐ 麂 [kɨ^{B}] *kriʔ 'muntjac' <> PTB *d-kiy 'barking deer'

Unfold zhǎn 展 [ṭɑn^{B}] *tranʔ 'unfold, open'
<> WT *rdal-ba, brdal* 'to spread, unfold, extend over'

Bamboo bā 笆 (ba^{B}, pa) 'kind of bamboo' <> WT *spa ~ sba* 'cane'; Lushai *rua*^{55} (*rɔ*^{53}) (< *r-wa) 'a kind of bamboo'
ж bā 笆(pa) 'bamboo hedge or fence' <> KN *rpa: Kom *ra-pe*, Tširu *ra-pa*

Disturb náo 撓 [ṇau^{B}] *nrâuʔ 'to trouble, disturb'
<> WT *sñog-pa* 'to trouble, rub; troubled, thick, turbid, dirty'

Stair jiē 階 [kɛi] *krə̂i 'steps, stairs, ladder' ? <> WT *skas-ka, skad* 'ladder'

7.5 OC medial *-r- as a morpheme: causative

OC *r in the initial (> MC div. II, ṭ- etc.) forms *causatives* (Pulleyblank 1962: 125; Sagart 1999: 111). As there is occasional vacillation between pre-initial *r and *s in TB and OC (§5.3), this *r may be a manifestation of the same morpheme which usually shows up as causative *s-. Originally it may have been a prefix as Pulleyblank points out (§2.4.4), and as a case in §5.3 suggests. On the other hand, MK languages like Khmer have an iterative / causative r-infix (Jenner and Pou 1982: xlix). This OC *r morpheme implies an out / away motion.

Transmit zhì 至 [tśi^C] *tis 'to arrive' > caus. zhì 致 [ṭi^C] *tris 'to transmit'

Expel chū 出 [tśʰut] *thut 'go out' > caus. chù 黜 [ṭʰut] *thrut 'to expel'

Drive out bìng 屏 [bieŋ^C] *beŋh 'to eliminate'
> caus. bèng 迸 [pɛŋ^C] *preŋh 'to drive out'

Additional words include → chú 除 'eliminate'; bá 拔 'uproot' (under → bá 犮).

7.6 Residue

7.6.1 Foreign medial -r- = no trace in MC

Occasionally, foreign *-r-* leaves no trace in MC /LHan (i.e., the word is not in div. II, but in div. I/IV or III), even though the medial belonged probably to the earlier root. One reason for this is the lack of *chóngniǔ* doublets (< OC *-r- vs. no *-r-) in many MC rime categories. Baxter writes such forms *k(r)jəm, etc.

Prohibit jìn 禁 [kɨm^C] 'to prohibit' <> WT *kʰrims* 'rule, right, law'

Orange jú 橘 [kuit] 'orange' <> Khmer *krōč* 'citrus fruit'

Stable gǔ 牿 [kouk] 'pen, stable' <> PLB *krok 'pen'

*7.6.2 OC medial *r = no r in foreign word*

The opposite also occurs: OC medial *-r- (as suggested by MC divisions) corresponds to a simple foreign initial:

Decrease jiǎn 減 [kɛm^B] *krêm? 'decrease, abridge, moderate'
<> Lushai *kaam* 'to decrease'

Pig bā 豝 [pa] *prâ 'wild pig' ? <> WT *pʰag* 'pig'

Here, OC *r may reflect some earlier pre-initial which has not been preserved in related languages. Alternatively, these sets may be spurious. At least 'pig' has an alternative etymology.

7.7 Foreign final -r in OC / MC

7.7.1 MC -n = foreign -r

CH *-n* for foreign *-r* is the most common and widely noted correspondence. This is parallel to foreign final *-l* (§8.3). Two examples may suffice here.

Separate pàn 畔 [bɑn^C] *bâns 'bank between fields, separate from'
<> WT *bar* 'interstice, intermediate space', NNaga *pʰar* 'divide'

To fear dàn 憚 [dɑn^C] *dâns 'to fear, dislike' <> WT *'dar-ba* tremble'

7.7.2 MC div. II or 3/3 + n = final -r elsewhere

Some CH words have final *-n* in conjunction with div. II vocalism (< *-r-).

Between	jiān 間閒 [kɛn] *krên 'to be in the middle, interstice' <> Lushai *in*^{L}*-kaar*^{H} 'the space, interval'
Board	bǎn 板 [pan^{B}] *prânʔ 'board, plank' <> WT *'p*^{h}*ar* 'small plank'
Blossom	bàn 瓣 [bɛn^{C}] *brê/âns 'petals of a flower' <> WT *'bar-ba* 'to blossom'
Fowl	yàn 鴳鷃 [ʔan^{C}] *ʔrâns 'a quail-like bird' <> Lushai *ʔaar*^{H} 'fowl'
Strong	jiàn 健 (gjän 3) [gɨan] *gran ? 'strong' <> WT *gar-ba* 'strong'

7.7.3 MC div. II = final -r elsewhere (metathesis)

Some CH words have no final *-n* and only MC div. II / LHan equivalents (< OC *medial *r) as the result of a metathesis (metathesis with the addition of a consonant after final *-r; see §6.1).

House	jiā 家 [ka] *krâ 'house' <> WT *mk*^{h}*ar* 'house, castle'
Borrow	jiǎ 假 [ka^{B}] *krâʔ 'to borrow' <> WT *kar-skjin* 'a loan'
Price	jià 賈價 [ka^{C}] *krâh 'price' <> Lushai *k*^{h}*aar* 'to buy the whole, buy in large quantities'
Wrap	bāo 包 [pɔu] *prû 'to wrap, bundle' <> WT *'p*^{h}*ur-ba* 'to wrap up, envelop'
Satiated	bǎo 飽 [pɔu^{B}] *prûʔ 'to eat to the full, satisfied' <> Lushai *puar* 'having eaten enough'
Step over	kuà 跨 [k^{h}ua^{C}] *khwrâh 'to step over, pass over' <> Lushai *kaar*^{F} 'to step, pace, stride', WT *gar* 'dance'

*7.7.4 MC final -i for foreign *-r*

A few common words with TB final *-r have OC final *-i instead; this is parallel to foreign final *-l* (§8.3).

To sow	bò 播譒 [pɑi^{C}] *pâih 'to spread, sow, publish' <> PTB *b^{w}âr > WT *'bor-ba* 'to throw, cast', Bahing *war* 'throw away', Chepang *wa:r* 'sow', Mikir *wár* 'throw'
Exhausted	duǒ, tuō, tuò 痑 [tɑi^{C}, t^{h}ɑi] *tâih 'exhausted, sick (of horses)' <> WT *ldar-ba* 'weary, tired, faint'
To fly	fēi 飛 [pui] *pəi 'to fly' <> PTB *pur ~ *pir > WT *'p*^{h}*ur-ba*
Ant	yǐ 蟻 [ŋɨai^{B}] *ŋaiʔ 'ant' <> KN-Lai *hŋeʔr* 'ant'

7.7.5 Foreign final r = open syllable

Open syllables in OC *-o (= LHan -o) may in some instances be the result of the metathesis of the kind observed in §7.7.3, because the final LHan *o* has no MC div. II equivalent which might otherwise indicate an earlier medial *r (Baxter writes such forms OCB *k(r)o, etc.). The vowel *i preempts, of course, a final *i (< *r), as does perhaps *e.

To present	gòu 購 [ko^{C}] *kôh 'to present, give' <> WT *skur-ba* 'to send, transmit, give'
Throat	hóu 喉 [go] *gô 'throat' <> WT: *mgul(-pa)* ~ *'gul* 'neck, throat'~ *mgur* 'throat, neck, voice'
Snore	hōu 齁 (xəu) 'to snore' [JY] <> WT *ŋur-ba* 'to grunt' ɜɛ *sŋur-ba* 'to snore'
Ant	fú蜉 [bu] *bu 'large ant, ephemera' <> WT *sbur* 'ant'
To cleave	sī 斯 [sie] *se 'cleave, lop off' <> WT *ser-ka* 'cleft, split'
Bare	tú 徒 [dɑ] *dâ 'bare, naked, only' ɜɛ tǎn 袒襢 [dɑn^{B}] *dânʔ 'to bare (to the waist)' <> WT *star-ba* 'to clean, polish', *t^her* 'bald, bare'

8

OLD CHINESE AND FOREIGN *L

Middle Chinese initial *ji-* / LHan *j-* derives often from OC *l-, but also corresponds to OC *j- (§9) and OC *wi- (§10). This initial MC *ji-* < OC *l- alternates in phonetic series with MC *d-*, *tʰ-*, *śj-*, *ḍj-* as well as *ṭʰj-* (see §12.1.2 Table 12-1). In one type of initial consonant cluster, MC *t-* is also associated with *l (§8.2.1). LHan initials are practically the same as in MC, therefore often the simpler LHan forms will be provided as illustrations. OC L-like initials are:

MC ji-	< OC *l-; also *j-, *w- (in *wi and *we)
MC d-	< OC *l- div. I/IV (§8.1.1); also *d- div. I/IV
MC ḍj-	< OC *dr- < *ʔl- (Baxter *rl-); also *dr- (§12.1.2 Table 12-2)
MC dźj-	< OC *m-l- (§8.1.3)
MC zj-	< OC *s-l- (§8.1.2); also *s-j-, *s-w- (§9.4; §10.1.2)
MC śj-	< OC *lh- (§5.2.2–3); also *hj- ?
MC tʰ-	< OC *lh- div. I/IV (§5.2.2–3); also *rh-, *th- div. I/IV
MC tśʰj-	< OC *k-lh- (§5.9.3); also *th-
MC ṭʰj-	< OC *rh- < *ʔlh- ?; also *rh- (§12.1.2 Table 12-2)
MC t-	< OC *t- div. I/IV < *tl- (?); also *t- (§8.2.1)

Since foreign initial consonant clusters with a medial *l* have numerous equivalents in MC and OC, the many examples in the various parts of this introduction should not lead to the erroneous conclusion that *l occurs particularly frequently in OC.

8.1 OC initial *l-

8.1.1 MC d- and ḍj-, ṭʰj- from OC L-series

MC *d-* has two OC sources: (1) OC *d- from T-like phonetic series; (2) OC *l- in later div.I/IV from an OC L-like initial or cluster with *l- (Bodman 1985: 163f); §12.1.2 Table 12-2 shows how the T- type and L-type phonetic series are distinguished. The L-type *d* corresponds usually to foreign clusters with *l*, such as *gl-*, *bl-*, *kl-*, etc. (Baxter 1992: 232f).

The *d-* < L-type has two distinct voiceless counterparts: the Tl-type yields MC / LHan *t-* < OC *tl- (? < *kl-) (§8.2.1); and the voiceless sonorants *tʰ-/śj-* < *lh- (§5.2.2–3). While the MC *t-* < Tl-type is restricted to non-ST words, initial MC *d-* < L-type comprises words from all sources, including ST. Therefore, this latter type represents the earliest layer in PCH.

Tl-type words are found mostly in phonetic series with dental stop initials; therefore, the OC dental stop feature must have been more prominent than the lateral. But the voiced *d-* < L-type category occurs only in OC L- series, which means that an L-like feature was the prominent one in this initial configuration. Examples of MC *d-* from OC L-like initials are:

Wave dài 汏 [dɑiᶜ] OCM *dâ(t)s or *lâ(t)s 'wave' <> WT *rlabs* 'wave'

Rice dào 稻 [douᴮ] *lâuʔ 'rice, paddy' <> PMY *nblauᴬ

Lightning diàn 電 [denᶜ] *lîn 'lightning' <> PYao *(ʔ)liŋ 'lightning'

Stumble dié 跌 [det] *lît 'to stumble'
<> TB: TGTM *ple:ᴮ, PKaren *ʔble² 'slippery'

Leaf dié 牒 [dep] *lêp 'tablet' 牒 <>WT *ldeb* 'leaf, sheet'

Moss tái 苔 [də] *lə̂ 'moss' <> PTai *glai^{A2} 'moss'

Peach táo 桃 [dɑu] *lâu, OCB *g-law 'peach' <> PMY *glaau^{3A} 'peach'

MC *ḍj-* and the rare initial *ṭʰj-* from OC L-series will for our purposes be symbolized by OCM *d-l- and *th-l-, as in *chí* 池 (ḍje) [ḍiɑi] *d-lai 'pond', *chàng* 暢 (ṭʰjaŋ^{C}) [ṭʰiɑŋ^{C}] *t-hlaŋh 'spread out'. Baxter sets up OCB *rl- > MC *ḍj-*. There is no MC *ḍj-* from an L-series in rimes *-ak; in *GSR* 790 we find *ḍ-* II instead (otherwise always from OC *dr-), as in *zé* 澤 (ḍak) [ḍak] *d-lak ? 'marsh'. The unexpected vocalism (MC *a*, not *ja*) is parallel to the vowel in div. III in this rime where we find in the QYS *shí* 石 (źjäk) [dźak] *dak 'stone' instead of the expected MC *źjak;* Min dialects have preserved the expected vowel: PMin *džiɔk < LHan *dźak* (not *dźak*). This shows that MC ḍak can also come from an L-like series; and that the phenomenon is a Han period dialect feature.

*8.1.2 MC zj- from PCH *s- before initial *l, *j, *w*

MC *zj-* / LHan *zi-* goes back to an OC cluster whose initial element was *s-, as we can see from association with both MC *ji-* and MC *s-* in phonetic series. This MC initial corresponds to the TB s-prefix and reflects the ST causative / iterative *s-. Other manifestations of the ST s-prefix are found under §5.2.2–3.

Repeat xí 習 [zip] *s-ləp 'to do repeatedly, repeat'
<> WT *slob-pa, slabs* 'to learn, teach' ⋇ *slobs* 'exercise, practice'

Feed sì 食 [ziə^{C}] *s-ləkh 'to give food to, feed'
<> PTB *s-lyak 'to feed an animal'
< shí 食 [źɨk] *m-lək 'to eat' ⋇ PTB *m-lyak 'lick'

Warm up xín 尋爓 [zim] *s-ləm 'to warm up'
<> PLB *s-lum > WB *hlum*^{C} 'heat again, warm over', JP *ʃa*^{31}*-lum*^{33} 'to heat, warm (food)'; from ST *lum 'warm': WB *lum* 'warm'

Warm xián 燅 [ziam] *s-lam 'to heat, warm' ⋇ yán 炎 [jɑm] 'burn'
<> WT *slam-pa* 'to parch'

*8.1.3 MC dźj- (LHan ź-) from OC *ml-*

Karlgren's rare MC palatal initial *dź'i̯-* contrasts with the common *źi̯-* / LHan *dź-*. Some scholars have considered this QY distinction artificial, but it is confirmed by the early Tang commentator Yán Shīgǔ 顏師古 (581–645) who kept these two voiced palatals distinct in his language (Coblin 1991: 19–21). This rare palatal corresponds systematically to Norman's PMin softened stop initial, whereas QYS initial *źj-* occurs with PMin softened as well as regular affricates. Norman believes that the softened stops reflect an earlier pre-nasal, and other languages support this (MC in parentheses); we will write OC *m-l- (also *m-d-?) for this initial:

Tongue shé 舌(dźjät) [źet] *m-let 'tongue'
<> PY *byet^{6}, PM *nplai^{6}; Proto-Western Min *Ndžiɑt 'tongue'

Lick shì 舐 (dźje^{B}) [źe^{B}] *m-leʔ 'to lick' <> PTB *m-lay 'tongue'

Eat shí 食 (dźjək) [źɨk] 'to eat'
<> PTB *m-lyak 'to lick': Lepcha *lyak* 'to taste, eat'

Suck shǔn 吮 (dźjuen^{B}) [źun^{B}] *m-lunʔ ? 'to suck'
<> PTB *mlyuw 'swallow' > Kanauri *myun, WB *myui* (inscr. *mlyui*), JP *mə^{31}-yuʔ^{31}*

Glutinous shú 秫 (dźjuet) [źut] 'glutinous millet'
<> PMY *nblut 'glutinous, sticky'

Boat chuán 船 (dźjwän) [źuan] *m-lun 'boat'
<> PTB *(m-)loŋ: KN *m-lauŋ 'canoe'

Ransom shú 贖 (d)źjwok) [źok] *m-luk ? 'to ransom'
ƷƸ yù 賣 (jiuk) [juk] *luk 'to sell'
<> WT *blu-ba, blus* 'to buy off, ransom' ƷƸ *blud-pa* 'release, ransom'; the WT forms can theoretically derive from earlier *mlu(t)

These cognate sets indicate that words with this initial have been directly inherited from ST or another language. In TB, the prefix *m* is often associated with words for body parts and body functions (*IST:* 32; Unger *Hao-ku* 31, 1985 collect and discuss WT words with *m-). In the word for 'smell, hear' → wén 聞 [mun] < PCH *mən, the initial *m* may also represent this ST prefix.

The OC phonetic nature of this pre-initial is not certain. However, not only do TB cognates point to *m-, but also a phonetic loan in which *shéng* 繩 (dźjəŋ) [źɨŋ] *m-ləŋ 'string, cord' is written with the phonetic *mǐn* 黽 (mɛŋ^{B}) *mrəŋʔ 'toad' (Schuessler "Thoughts on Old Chinese Initials," ICSTLL, Hawai'i 1989; Sagart 1999: 79ff). Sagart offers a doublet that provides further evidence:

Lay hands on mén 捫 (muən) [mən] *mlun ? 'to lay hands on'
ƷƸ shùn 揗 (dźjuen$^{B/C}$, zjuen) [źun$^{B/C}$, ziun] *m-lunʔ/s, *s-lun 'to lay hands on'

*8.1.4 ST *m- ~ *s-*

ST *m- ~ *s- prefixes marking introvert / extrovert pairs can be assumed for ST because they occur not only in TB (Matisoff), but also as unproductive relics in OC (§2.4.3); 'Lay hands on' above is an additional example.

Eat shí 食 (dźjək) [źɨk] *m-lək 'to eat'
<> PTB *m-lyak 'to lick': Lepcha *lyak* 'to taste, eat'
ƷƸ sì 食 [ziə^{C}] *s-ləkh 'to give food to, feed' <> PTB *s-lyak 'to feed'

Agree shùn 順 (dźjuen^{C}) [źun^{C} > źuin^{C}] *m-luns 'to follow, agree'
ƷƸ xún 循馴 (zjuen) [ziun > zuin] *s-lun 'to follow, obey, be docile'

Follow shù 述術鉥 (dźjuet) [źut > źuit] *m-lut ? 'to follow, proceed, pass on'
ƷƸ xù 訹 (sjuet) [sut > suit] *sut < slut ? 'to entice'

*8.1.5 Pre-initial *m- in GSR 413* 至

Indirect hints of the survival of this ST *m- can also be detected in the phonetic series *GSR* 413 至 which includes words whose TB cognates have an m-prefix; almost all words in this series have TB cognates (Matisoff 1995: 52). Since this series mixes OC *l- and *t- initials and also has the puzzling MC reflex of OC *t for TB cognates in *l-, it is perhaps the initial *m- which some key words shared. 'Leech' shows that the voiceless *m-lh- configuration possibly yielded MC *tśj-* (unaspirated):

413a zhì 至 [tśis] *tits 'to arrive'
<> WT *mčʰi-ba, mčʰis* 'to come, go, say': from ST *m-ti(t)s

(413) zhì 蛭 [tśit] PCH *m-lhit (?) 'water leech'
<> KN *m-hliit 'water leech'

413n dié 垤 [det] *lît 'anthill' <> KN *m-hliŋ/t 'ant'

413o zhí 姪 [det, ḍet] *lît, *d-lit ? 'nephew'
<> PTB *b-ləy 'nephew, grandchild', OBurm. *mliy* 'grandchild'

413j shì 室 [śis] *lhits 'house'
<> PTB *m-lei 'earth' ≭ WT *gžis-ka < g-lyis* 'native place'

413d zhì 致 [ṭis] *trits 'to transmit', caus. of 413a zhì 至

413e zhì 輊 [ṭis] *r-lhits ? 'heavy'
<> PTB *s-ləy 'heavy' (*r* ~ *s* do alternate within ST cognate sets (§5.3)

8.2 Other initial clusters with l

For a possible 'infix' -l-, see §2.7.

8.2.1 MC t- from foreign clusters with l

With few exceptions, all Chinese words in this section belong to the "jod-less" QYS div. I/IV (§9.1), which suggests that one source of the QYS div. I/IV is loss of an OC medial *l. Hardly any of the foreign words are ST. These words may have been absorbed in PCH after the regular sound changes which had yielded voiceless sonorants (§5.2.2–3) had run their course. The phonological change from *kl- to *t- may have come about in one of at least two different ways, one exemplified by KT: PTai *klɔŋ^{A1} > Saek *tlɔɔŋ^{A1} > trɔɔŋ^{A1}* 'drum', or PVM *kleːŋ > Viet. *trên* 'rise'; the other development as seen in MK: PNB *klàm 'liver', but Wa-Lawa-Bulang *kətɔm. The initial *t-* words might possibly have been filtered through an intermediary that affected this change, while those in section §8.2.2 have not. Some Tai and TB words seem to have run through the same 'filter'. Foreign *Cl- = MC *t-* < OC *tl- (?):

Red dān 丹 [tɑn] *tân< *tlan 'be red, vermilion' <> PKS *h-lan^{C} 'red'

Carry dān 擔 [tɑm] *tâm < *tlam 'to carry on the shoulder'
<> AA: Khmuʔ *klam* 'carry on the shoulder'

Gall dǎn 膽 [tɑm^{B}] *tâmʔ < *tlamʔ 'gall' <> AA: PNB *klàm 'liver'

Fall down diān 顛 [ten] *tîn < *tlin 'fall down' <> Miao *gliŋ* 'to fall'

Many duō 多 [tɑi] *tâi < *tlai 'many' <> PTai *hlai^{A1} 'many', Hlai *ɬaai^{1}*

Rain dōng 涷 [toŋ$^{A/C}$] *tôŋ < *tloŋ 'violent rain'
<> PM *(ʔ)nuŋ (Downer 1982), PY *bluŋ^{6} (Purnell) 'rain'

Rainbow dì-dōng 螮蝀 [tes-toŋ] *-tôŋ < *-tloŋ ? 'rainbow'
~ hóng 虹 [goŋ] *gôŋ < *gloŋ
~ jiàng 虹 [kɔŋ^{C}] *krôŋh 'rainbow'

8.2.2 MC div. I/IV from foreign clusters with l

Foreign *Cl- becomes QYS div. I/IV vocalism and LHan equivalents, from OC clusters with *l, for example:

Sweet gān 甘 [kɑm] *kâm < *klam 'be sweet' <> PTB *klum 'sweet'

Purple gàn 紺 [kəm^{C}] *kə̂ms < *kləms 'be purple'
<> PT *kləm^{B} 'dark red, purple, dark, black'

Announce gào 告 [kou^{C}, kouk] *kûk(h) < *kluk(h) 'to announce, inform'
<> Tai: S. *klaau*^{B1} < *kl- 'to say, declare'

Palace gōng 公 [koŋ] *kôŋ < *kloŋ 'palace' <> Mon *gloŋ* 'citadel, palace'

Dog gǒu 狗 [ko^{B}] *kôʔ < *kloʔ 'dog' > PMY *klu^{2} (Purnell), WMon *kluiw*

Drum gǔ 鼓 [kɑ^{B}] *kâʔ < *klaʔ 'drum' <> PTai *klɔŋ^{A1} 'drum'

QYS div. III does not often correspond to foreign clusters with *l, therefore we suspect some irregular development similar to the traceless loss of medial *r (§7.6.2):

Wind n. fēng 風 [puoŋ] OCB *p(r)jɨ/um 'wind'
<> Tai: S. *lom*^{A2} < *dlu̯om^{A2} 'wind', PKS *hlwum^{1}

Level píng 平 [bieŋ] *beŋ 'be level, even' <> PTB *pleŋ 'flat surface'

High sōng 崧嵩 [siuŋ] *suŋ 'high'
<> PMonic *slooŋ 'be high up, high', LitMon *sluŋ* 'be high'

8.3 ST and foreign final -l in OC

In the majority of words ST final *-l has become final *-n* in Chinese, but a significant number has final *-i* instead; see Table 8-1 on the next page. There we notice that in some TB languages like WB and Mikir, TB final *-l* has become *-i* (WB *-e*); in others, like JP, it has become *-n*. Perhaps two different strains of ST have converged in PCH — one close to SE Asian languages like Lushai, one closer to WT — because cognates of OC final *-i are weighted toward Lushai, cognates in final *-n toward WT. (Final OC *-i: 60% of cognates are WT, 80% Lushai, 20% have only a WT cognate, 30% only a Lushai cognate; final OC *-n: 76% have WT cognates, 41% Lushai, a little over 50% have only WT cognates, only 18% have a Lushai connection.) Even the OC initial *m- in the word for 'snake' huǐ 虫 *hmuiʔ is closer to WB *mrwe* than to WT *sbrul* (*m-* vs. *b-*; §5.12.2). Alternatively, the words in OC *-i tend to have an oblique tone, or a TB cognate with the corresponding final *-ʔ or *-h < *-s, while MC tone B in those with final *-n may be Chinese innovations (shěn 矧 [śin^{B}] 'gums' as body part; *-n* a suffix in běn 本 'root', etc.). This needs further study.

8-1

Gloss	Mand.	OC *-n	OC *-i	WT	Lushai	WB
cover, wear	bèi 被		*baiʔ/h		*beelʔ	
wriggle	wēi 委		*ʔoi / ʔuai		*vaiʔ	
feed animal	wèi 餧		*ʔuih		*vulʔ/s	(kywe^{B})
snake	huǐ 虫		*hməiʔ	sbrul	*ruul	mrwe
hang	chuí 垂		*d(j)oi	'ǰol	*tsualʔ	
hair	méi 眉	?ɜɛ	*məi ?	(smin)	*hmuulʔ	mwe^{B}
play, joke	xì 戲		*haih	'k^{h}yal	*k^{h}aals	
pass over	guò 過	? ɜɛ	*kôih	rgal	(*kai/kais)	kai^{B} 'exceed'
load, carry	hè 何		*gâiʔ	bkal		
add	jiā 加		*krâi	bkral		
silver	yín 銀	*ŋrən		dŋul		ŋwe
dust	chén 塵	*drən		rdul		
poor	pín 貧	*brən		dbul		
all, herd	qún 群	*kun		mkul		
ashes, coal	tàn 炭	*thân		t^{h}al		
sorcery	huàn 幻	*grôn		rol		
unfold	zhǎn 展	*tranʔ		rdal		
produce	chǎn 產	*srâ/ênʔ		srel		
kidney, liver	gān 肝	*kân		mk^{h}al	*kalʔ/s	
resist	hàn 扞	*kân		kal, rgol	*kalʔ/s	kan repel
root	běn 本	*pânʔ		pul	*buulʔ	
gums	shěn 矧	*hninʔ		r/sñil	(hni)	
shield	dùn 盾	*m-dûnʔ ?		rtul	Chep. d^{h}əl	duiŋ^{B}
face	miàn 面	*men		TB *hmel	*hmeel	
circle	yuán 員	*wan			*valʔ/s	
lie down	yǎn 偃	*ʔanʔ			*jaal	
sleep	mián 眠	*mên		TB *myel		

9

INITIAL AND MEDIAL J AND THE MIDDLE CHINESE DIVISIONS (等)

9.1 The MC divisions and medial j

The Song Dynasty rime tables, which interpret the *Qièyùn*, divide syllables within a traditional rime category into four "divisions" or "grades" (*těng* 等). Karlgren's MC div. III is characterized by a medial jod glide (*-i̯-* =Li Fang Kuei's *-j-*), div. I and IV are jod-less (IV has a vocalic medial *i* in Karlgren's system), and II contrasts with I/IV in having a vowel of a more centered timbre which resulted from loss of OC medial *-r-. Thus the QYS divisions within a traditional MC set are:

I	kâŋ (no MC medial)	LH kɑŋ	< OCM *kâŋ
II	kɐŋ (no MC medial)	LH kaŋ	< OCM *krâŋ
III	kjaŋ (MC medial-j-)	LH kɨɑŋ	< OCM *kaŋ
IV	kieŋ (MC medial-i-)	LH keŋ	< OCM *kêŋ

With some initial consonants the distribution is restricted; e.g., MC *t-* occurs only in div. I/IV syllables, MC *tś-* only in div. III syllables; div. II syllables permit only a retroflex *ṭ-*.

Some rime categories have two sets of MC div. III rimes after grave initials (velars and labials): one so-called *chóngniǔ* 重紐 div. III (here labeled 3/3), and one *chóngniǔ* div. IV (here 3/4) (Baxter 1992). For most 3/3-type syllables Baxter reconstructs also a medial *-r- similar to div. II. Since OCM does not project the medial *j* of div. III (including 3/3 and 3/4) back into OC, it marks the non-jod div. I/IV and II with a circumflex accent over the vowel, as seen in the illustrations. Thus the traditional rime category OCM *əi ~ *-i can include all these "divisions" (Mand. after the graph; graphs in parentheses do not correspond completely with the hypothetical MC form):

Div.	MC	LHan	OCM
I	muậi	məi	< *mə̂i 枚 méi
II	pɛi	pɛi	< *prə̂i (排 pái)
III	mjwei	mui	< *məi 微 wéi
3/3	mji 3	mɨ	< *mri 眉 méi
3/4	pji 4	pi	< *pi (匕 bǐ)
IV	miei	mei	< *mî 迷 mí

Some MC rime categories distinguish two rimes within div. III with slightly different vowel timbres, which seems to reflect the same distinction as that between div. III and 3/3 (Baxter). For example, the rimes in *-aŋ / *-eŋ fall within the *chóngniǔ* pattern:

I	kâŋ	< OCM *kâŋ 剛 gāng	IV	kieŋ	< OCM *kêŋ 經 jīng
II	kɐŋ	< OCM *krâŋ 庚 gēng	II	kɛŋ	< OCM *krêŋ 耕 gēng
III	kjaŋ	< OCM *kaŋ 彊 jiāng	3/4	kjäŋ	< OCM *keŋ (勁 jìng)
3/3	kjɐŋ	< OCM *kraŋ 京 jīng	3/3	kjɐŋ	< OCM *kreŋ 荊 jīng

The MC homophones *kjɐŋ* / LHan kɨɑŋ are differentiated in OC (*kraŋ and *kreŋ) on the basis of phonetic series and rimes. (MC kjäŋ corresponds to LHan kɨeŋ; MC kɛŋ = LHan kɛŋ.)

9.1.1 Sources of div. I/IV

Internal logic as well as comparative data suggest that OC never had Karlgren's ubiquitous medial *j* in div. III words — it is unlikely that more than half of all words in an actual language had a medial palatal glide (Pulleyblank 1973; see Norman 1994 for a summary of the various theories). So far, there is no consensus on the OC sources of the MC divisions. We leave the question open, but follow Norman in assuming an OC plain syllable (without *-j-*) for most later div. III, and mark the later div. I/IV syllables with a circumflex accent (Pulleyblank distinguishes them with grave and acute accents on the vowels).

We have already suspected two causes for the emergence of I/IV-type syllables:

(1) Loss of a (voiced?) pre-initial (see §7.1.1).

(2) Loss of a medial *-l- (see §8.2).

(3) Thirdly, an unmarked open syllabel (in QYS div. III) becomes a div. I syllable when the distributive suffix *-k is attached (§6.1.2).

(4) Finally, some modern colloquial words gravitate toward the analogue of MC div. I/IV syllables, while the traditional, literary counterparts reflect div. III:

fú 弗 (pjuət) div. III 'not'	vs. Mand. bù 不 (puət) 'not'
ěr 爾 (ńźjie^{B}) 'you'	vs. Mand. nǐ 你 < ni 'you'
xī 噏 (xjəp) 'to drink'	vs. Mand. hē 喝 < xəp 'to drink'
zǐ 子 (tsɨ^{B}) 'son, child'	vs. southern dialects zǎi 崽 < tsə^{B} 'son, child'
ér 兒 (ńźjie) < *ŋe 'child'	vs. southern dialects yá 伢 < ŋa 'child, boy'

9.1.2 Div. III vs. I/IV in word families

Alternations MC div. I/IV ~ III are regularly encountered in wfs (e.g., Baxter and Sagart 1998: 61). No meaning has been convincingly identified for these distinctions. Examples:

Solid	dūn 敦惇 (tuən, div. I) [tuən] 'be solid > earnest, generous'
	ж zhūn 肫 (tśjuen, div. III) [tśun ~ tśuin] 'sincere, diligent'
Inside	nèi 内 (nəp I) [nəp] 'inside' ж rù 入 (ńźjəp III) [ńip] *nəp 'to enter'

9.1.3 "Pure" div. IV

In "pure" div. IV words (i.e., not *chóng-niŭ* div. 4/4) with back vowels, the medial -i- must have been primary, i.e., part of the root, and not a secondary development from front vowels as in *kêŋ > MC *kieŋ*. However, Kam-Tai languages have occasionally no medial palatal where Chinese cognates have medial div. IV *i:

To fish	diào 釣 [teu^{C}] *tiâukh 'to angle, fish with hook and line'
	<> Tai: S. *tok*^{DI} 'to angle, fish with hook and line'
Fade	diāo 凋 [teu] *tiû 'to fade' <> Tai S. *tok* 'become faded' (color)

9.1.4 Sources of MC div. II

MC div. II vocalism (*a, ɐ, ă, å, ộ* in Karlgren's system) is set up for LHan as *a, ɛ, ɔ* (contrasting with div. I *a, e, o*). The OC source was medial *-r- and possibly also other configurations (§7.2). However, not all div. II syllables necessarily go back to OC medial *-r-; the cause could perhaps also have been archaism (§7.2.2) or prefixes (§7.4).

In the OC rime categories *-ak, *-ek, *-e, *-ok, and *-auk, the expected precursors of MC div. III have partially shifted to the later MC div. II after acute initials, and possibly also after

*ʔ- and *w-. For example, the nasal counterpart to *-ak, the rime *-aŋ, has the same LHan vowel *a* in both div. I and III syllables (LHan *kaŋ* and *kɨaŋ*); this is indicated by the PMin forms which presuppose a back *a*, not Karlgren's MC *a*, e.g., PMin *kiũ* (< *kjaŋ*) for the conventional MC *kjaŋ*. In the rime *-ak, the vowel has been raised, resulting in MC rimes *-jäk* III, *-ɐk* II. Min forms again have the expected back vowel, i.e., LHan *-(i)ak*. Since the Min dialects probably separated from the rest of CH during the Han period, we can set up for LHan the anticipated back vowel forms; it was mainstream and / or northern-central Chinese that innovated this front shift. Table 9-1 illustrates the situation. Parentheses indicate unique or exceptional forms. The survival of forms with back *ak* is apparently due to dialect interference, or to incomplete shifting. (Simpler LHan forms instead of MC.)

9-1

OCM *-aŋ Div. I	*-aŋ Div. III	*-aŋ Div. II	*-ak Div. I	*-ak Div. III	*-ak >II or III
kaŋ 剛	kɨaŋ 疆	kaŋ 行	kak 各	(kɨak 卻)	kak 客 II
paŋ 旁	puaŋ 方	paŋ 祊	pak 博	(buak 縛)	pak 百 II
tsaŋ 藏	tsiaŋ 將		tsak 作	PMin *tsiak (tsiak 鵲)	tsiak 籍 III
	ziaŋ 象			PMin *ziak	ziak 席 III
ʔaŋ 盎	ʔɨaŋ 央		ʔak 惡	---> ?	ʔak 啞 II
	waŋ 王			---> ?	wak 獲 II
	ṭaŋ 張	(ṭaŋ 瞠)		--->	ṭak 宅 II
	tṣaŋ 莊			tṣak 斮	tṣak 稓 II
	tśaŋ 章			PMin *tśak	tśak 石 III
	ńaŋ 讓			ńak 若	

After the initials *ṭ* and *tś*, the shift was complete; after *ts* and *tṣ* one or a few words did not participate in this change. Thus *zé*$_3$ 擇 (ḍɐk II) LHan *ḍak* was OCM *d-lak and not the expected *drak. The same applies to corresponding syllables with the other vowels, as pointed out above. The situation after *ʔ-* and *w-* is not clear: MC *ʔak* II might go back to either OC *ʔak, or to *ʔrak; or MC *ɣwɛk*, LHan *wak*, to OCM *wak or *wrak.

This shift has bled into OC syllables in open vowel *-a, probably via tone C words like *takh > MC *tśia*^{C} (not *tśjwo*^{C}). Thus OCM *taʔ 者 becomes MC *tśja*^{B}, not *tśjwo*^{B}; and 'crow' OCM *ʔa has a doublet MC *ʔa 鴉 beside the expected *ʔjwo* 烏.

9.2 Initial j- in OC

MC *ji-* corresponds occasionally to TB and foreign initial *j- and therefore probably to OC *j-, but it is difficult to distinguish a putative OC initial *l- > MC *ji-* from OC *j- > MC *ji-*. As to ST medial *j, it seems almost always to correspond to MC div. III, but there are exceptions. Therefore, it is possible that in PCH the ST medial *j was redistributed or lost.

An OCM *j- is likely in certain environments. In a few phonetic series and wfs MC *ji-* and *tsj-* co-occur. There, MC *ji-* seems to derive from OCM *j-, not *l-. In two etyma, some TB languages have the initial *ny. OC *ts- and PTB *ny-, which are in variation with MC *ji-*, are highlighted in bold letters:

Wine — jiǔ 酒 (tsjəu^{B}) [tsu^{B}] ***tsiu(?)** 'wine';
< ST: PTB *yu(w) 'wine'
phonetic is *yǒu* 酉 (jiəu^{B}) [ju^{B}] *ju?

To decay — yǒu 脜 (jiəu(^{B})) [ju(^{B})] *ju? 'to rot, decay'
< ST *(z-)ju: PTB *zya:w ~ *zyu(w) 'to rot, decay, digest', WT *'ǰu-ba, bžus, bžu* (< *N-ju*) 'to digest, melt'

Footprint — jī 跡 (tsjäk) [tsiek] ***tsiak** 'footprint, track'
~ jī 蹟 (tsjäk) [tsiek] *tsek 'footprint, track'
< ST *(C-)jak: Limbu *yok*^{2} 'trace, track',
but Lushai **hniak^{H}** 'footprint, hoof-mark';
phonetic is *yì* 亦 = 腋 (jiäk) [jak] *jak 'armpit'
< ST: TB-Mru *yak* 'armpit', Lushai *zak*^{L} (< *jak*)

Night — yè 夜 (jia^{C}) [ja^{C}] *jah, later jak(h) 'night'
< ST *(-)ja: PTB *ya? 'night'
but WB **ña^{C}** 'evening', JP *na?*^{55} < **nak^{55}** 'evening';
phonetic is *yì* 亦 = 腋 (jiäk) [jak] *jak 'armpit'
< ST: TB-Mru *yak* 'armpit', Lushai *zak*^{L} (< *jak*)

Rodent 1 — qūn 㕙 (ts^{h}juən, tsjuən^{C}) [ts(^{h})(i)un] ***tsiun** 'hare, marmot'
< ST: PTB *yu(w) ~ *yun > JP *yu*^{55} ~ *yun*^{33} 'rat, mouse', WB *yun* 'rabbit';
phonetic is *yǔn* 允 (jiuen^{B}) [jun^{B}] *jun?

Rodent 2 — yòu 鼬 (jiəu^{C}) [ju^{C}] *juh 'weasel'
< ST: PTB *yu > Chepang *yu?* 'animal, rodent', Mru *yu* 'weasel'

*9.2.1 MC initial j- ~ l- from OC *r-j-*

MC initial *j-* derives from OC *j- where MC has initial *l-* ~ *ji-* doublets. Some of these MC *ji-* initial words have phonetic series or comparative contacts with *r- (Baxter 1992: 200f). The ST pre-initial *r- was lost before or during early OC, therefore MC *ji-* is not a reflex of an OC initial *r, but only of a stem initial *j. Here *r-* was treated as a pre-initial in PCH and later lost, with occasional doublets in MC *lj-*. An interesting example for a lost pre-initial *r- is

Salt — yán 鹽 (jiäm) 'salt' which is alone in a *xiéshēng* series with initials like OC *r- > MC *l-* and *kr- > MC *k-* div. II. The WT cognate is *rgyam* 'salt' < *r-yam* (when in such configurations *r-* was felt to be a pre-initial, an epenthetic *-g-* emerged; otherwise *ry- > WT *ž-*).

The placement of *yán* in a (k)r-series suggests that the pre-initial *r- was still there in early OC. If *yán* exemplifies the Chinese fate of ST *r-j-, then further items are revealed by doublets and / or TB cognates:

Wander — yóu 游 (jiəu) *ju < *r-ju 'to flow, roam about'
<> WT *rgyu-ba* < *r-yu* 'to walk, move, wander, range' ꭗ *rgyun* 'the flow, current'; CH variant with survival of initial *r- is
ꭗ liú 流 (ljəu) *r(i)u 'to flow, float'

Beautiful	yàn 豔 (jiäm^C) *jamh < *r-jamh 'beautiful' <> Tai: S. *riam*^B2 'beautiful'
Fluid	yè 液 (jiäk) *jak 'fluid' <> PTB *rjak 'grease, juice'
Pass over	yú 踰逾 (jiu) *lo or *jo 'to leap or pass over, transgress' <> WT *rgyud-pa* < *r-yut 'to pass over, traverse'
Sharp	yǎn 剡 (jiäm^B) *jam? < *r-jam? ? 'sharp, pierce' <> PTB *(s-)rjam 'sharp': Kuki-Chin *(s-)rjam: Lush *hriam* 'sharp' ⋇ lián 磏/鐮 (ljäm) *rjam 'sharp, keen (of soldier/sickle)'
Rope	yù 繘 (jiuet) *jut 'well-rope', also MC kjuet <> WT *rgyud* < *r-yut* 'string, cord'; again, CH has a doublet that preserves the initial r-: ⋇ lǜ 率 (ljuet) *r(i)ut (the graph seems to represent a rope) 'edge, border, leather strap, rope'
Follow	yù 遹 (jiuet) *jut 'following, then' ⋇ lǜ律 (ljuet) *r(i)ut 'follow a model'
Cure	yào 藥 (jiak) *jauk 'to cure' ⋇ liào 樂 (ljäu^C) *riaukh 'to cure'
Drag	yú 臾 (jiu) *jo 'to pull, drag' ⋇ lǘ 婁 (lju) *r(i)o 'to drag, trail'

A parallel loss of pre-initial *r- occurred before OC *w- (§10.1.3). A CH doublet with pre-initial *s- before *j- may be → xī 夕 [ziak] *s-jak 'evening' vs. → xī 昔 [siak] *s(j)ak 'formerly, yesterday'.

9.3 MC źj- (LHan dź-) from ST initial *j-

MC initial *źj-* (normally from LHan *dź-* < OC *d-) is in some words a reflex of ST *j- (PTB *y-), perhaps via some kind of PCH *dj- combination where the dental may be secondary. In the phonetic series, OCM *d(j) < **d(j)- seems to have merged with OCM *dj- < **C-j-. These words are likely to have had OC initial *dj- or the like, not *d-, but OC *d- and *dj- (both MC *źj-*) are difficult to disentangle. Certain phonetic series include words with earlier *j-, among them *GSR* 31 垂, 725 尚, 726 上, 1096 酉, 1120 勺.

To sleep	shuì 睡 (źwie^C) [dźuai^C, dźoi^C] 'sleep' <> WT *yur-ba* 'to slumber' ⋇ *g-yur* 'sleep'
Hang down	chuí 垂 (źwie) [dźuai ~ dźoi] 'to let hang down' <> PTB *dzywal > WT *'jol-ba* 'to hang down' ⋇ PTB *yol: WT *yol-ba* 'curtain'
Ladle	zhuó 汋 (tśjak, źjak, jiak) [tśauk, dźauk, jauk] <> PTB *s-kyok 'ladle' > WT *skyogs-pa* 'scoop, ladle', WB *yok* 'ladle'
Above	shàng 上 (źjaŋ^C) [dźaŋ^C] 'above' <> ST *ya 'above', WT *ya* ⋇ shàng 尚 (źjaŋ^C) [dźaŋ^C] 'upwards'
Garment	cháng 常 (źjaŋ) [dźaŋ] 'lower garment' <> WT *g-yaŋ* 'animal skin clothing'
Still	cháng 常 (źjaŋ) [dźaŋ] 'perpetuate, still' <> WT *yaŋ* 'again, still, once more'

To taste — cháng 嘗 (źjaŋ) [dźɑŋ] 'to taste, try'
<> PTB *m-yaŋ: Chepang *yaŋ-sā* 'to taste (sample food)', WT *myoŋ-ba, myaŋs / myoŋ* 'to taste, enjoy'. However, WB *mrañ*^{B} 'to taste, try by taste'.

The initial is apparently devoiced (MC *tśj-*) in a few words (see also 'Ladle' above):

Locust — zhōng 螽 (tśjuŋ) [tśuŋ] *t(j)uŋ < *C-juŋ ? <> WB: *kjuiŋ*^{B} ~ *gjuiŋ*^{B} 'locust'

Multitude — zhòng 眾 (tśjuŋ^C) [tśuŋ^C] *t(j)uŋh < *C-juŋh ? 'numerous, all, the multitude'
<> WT *yoŋs* 'all, whole' (incl. of people)

The difficulty in pinning down OC J-series is illustrated by *yáng* 昜 and *yáng* 羊, both MC *jiaŋ*. The former is clearly an L-series, we suspect that the latter is a J-series. However, it includes the words *yáng* 羊 MC *jiaŋ* 'sheep' and *yǎng* 養 MC *jiaŋ*^{B} 'to raise, nourish' whose Tai counterparts are S. *liaŋ*^{A2} *-pʰaa*^{A1} 'goat, antelope' (related ?) and S. *liaŋ*^{C2} 'feed, nourish' (almost certainly a loan) respectively. Tai has both *l-* and *-i-* in the initial.

9.4 MC zj- with OC *j-

MC *zj-* derives from OC *s-l- (§8.1.2), *s-j-, and *s-w- (§10.1.2). An example for *s-j-:

Evening — xī 夕 (zjäk) [ziak] *s-jak 'evening'
<> PTB *s-ryak > Lep. *ayak* 'day' (i.e., 24 hrs.) JP *yaʔ*^{55} < *yak*^{55} 'day', Limbu *ya:kt-* 'to stay' (especially overnight).

In at least two words, this initial seems to represent a foreign palatal as a PCH voiced (?) dental sibilant + palatal glide; it may have been closest to the foreign sound.

Elephant — xiàng 象 [ziɑŋ^B] *s-jaŋʔ ? or *zjaŋʔ / *ziaŋʔ ? 'elephant'
<> PTai *ǰaŋ^C, MK-PMonic *ciiŋ, WB *chaŋ*^{A}, Lepcha *tyaŋ-mo* 'elephant'

Buffalo — sì 兕 [ziʔ] *s-jəiʔ ? or *zjəiʔ / *ziəiʔ ? 'wild water buffalo'
<> NTai *ǰɨə$^{A/C}$ or *ǰɨa^A 'buffalo'

10

INITIAL AND MEDIAL *W

10.1 Initial *w-

MC *jw-* (div. III) goes back to LHan and OC *w- (Karlgren's *gi̯w-, Li F. *jwi-*). ST *w- is preserved in many TB languages; in WT it has disappeared completely. Examples for the survival of ST *w- in CH are numerous (see dictionary part under W), for example:

To go yú 于 (jwo) [wɑ] *wa 'to go' <> PTB *wa 'to go, come'

The high front vowel *i causes a MC div. IV ji- reflex:

To be wéi 惟 (jiwi IV), OCM *wi (and not *lui or the like)

The ST initial *wj- survives as MC initial *ji-* < OC *j- (pre-initial *w- was apparently lost):

Also yì 亦 (jiäk) [jak] *jak 'also' < *wiak ? <> Lushai *vek*^{R} < *vek* 'again'

*10.1.1 Loss of *w*

An OC or PCH *w- has apparently been preempted by back vowels (there is no syllable with MC *jw-* reconstructable as *wo, *wu, *wau). After the loss of *w- the high onset syllable (§12.1.1) can only result in MC initial *ji-* IVsince there is no *ji-* III (except *jw-*). Hence with back vowels, a syllable of the type MC *jiəu* can derive from PCH *ju, *lu, as well as *wu. Cases of MC *ji-* IV from *w- are in *GSR* 1095; see → yòu$_7$ 褎, → xiù$_1$ 秀, yǒu 莠 (under→ yún$_4$ 耘), also → yōu$_5$ 櫌耰.

*10.1.2 MC zw- < OC *s-w-*

MC *zjw-* goes back to OC *s-w-; this is parallel to §8.1.2 and §9.4.

Advance suì 遂 (zwi^{C}) [zus > zuis] *s-wis 'to advance, accomplish, achieve'
<> "Kamarupan" *s-yuy ~ *m-yuy 'to follow', Kuki-Naga *jwi 'follow'

Ear of grain suì 穗穟 (zwi^{C}) [zuis] *s-wis 'ear of grain'
<> Lushai *vui*^{L} */vuiʔ*^{L} < *vuis* 'to ear (of grain, grass)', Kuki-Chin *vui

10.1.3 Loss of pre-initial r-

Foreign pre-initial *r-* was lost before OC *w-; this is parallel to *r-j-, see §9.2.1; an additional item is perh. → huì$_8$ 彙 and → huì$_9$ 彙.

Monkey wèi 蜼 [wi^{C} ~ lui^{B}] *wih ~ *ruiʔ (< *r-wiʔ) 'monkey'
<> Wa-Lawa-Bulang *rəyol 'white-handed gibbon'

A fly wèi 蠵 (jwi^{C}) *wuih ? 'gadfly'
<> AA: PAA *ruwaj > PVM *ruəy^{A} 'a fly'

10.2 Medial *-w-

10.2.1 Loss of ST and foreign medial -w- in Chinese

ST and foreign medial *-w- (or *-u-*, *-o-*) has no counterpart in Chinese except after velar initials (*kw-, etc.; §10.2.3), and perhaps in OC rimes with final *-n, *-t, and *-i. This medial has apparently not survived in WT (§12.9). Thus phonological correspondences between Chinese words without medial *w and foreign words with *w are regular.

Bear — mǐ 芈 [mie^{B}] *meʔ 'Bear, the clan name of the rulers of the state of Chǔ'
<> KT: PKS *muːi^{1}-fi, PTai *hm-: S. *mii*^{A1}, Po-ai *muui*^{A1} 'a bear'

Female — pìn 牝 [bi^{B}, bin^{B}] 'female of animals' <> PTB *pwi(y) 'female'

Laugh — ér 唲 [ńe] *ne 'forced laugh' <> PTB *m-nwi(y) 'to laugh'

Easy — yì 易 [je^{C}] *lekh 'be easy, at ease' <> PTB *lway 'easy'

Brother — dì 弟 [dei^{B}] OCB *dəjʔ < *dujʔ ? 'younger brother'
<> PTB *doy 'younger brother'

Tears — tì 涕 [tʰei$^{B/C}$] 'tears, mucus from nose' <> PTB *ti or PTB *tuy 'water'

Mud — ní 泥 [nei] *nəiʔ 'mud, mire' <> TB: KN-Lai *noy* 'muddy (of water)'

To spit — tǔ 吐 (tʰuo^{B}, tʰuo^{C}) [tʰɑ^{B}] *thâʔ 'to spit out'
< ST *twa > PTB *(m-/s-)twa 'spit'

Measure — dù 度 (duo^{C}) [dɑ^{C}] *dâkh 'a measure (of length), rule'
< ST *dwa / *twa: WB *tʰwa* 'measure with a span', WB *twak* 'cipher, reckon', Mru *twak* 'consider'

To rest — shè 舍 [śa^{C}] 'to rest in, stop' <> PKS *s-lwa^{B} 'to rest'

Village (1) — lǐ 里 [liə^{B}] *rəʔ 'village'
<> PTB *r-wa > WB *rwa* 'town, village' < ST *rwə

*10.2.2 Chinese doublets with and without medial *w*

Medial *w or rounding was lost by MC or even OC, especially before front vowels, even in environments in which rounding is phonotactically permissible:

yān 蔫 — *ʔan 'to wither' ≍ yuàn 苑 *ʔuans 'to wither'
yū 菸 — *ʔa 'to wither' ≍ wēi 萎 *ʔuai 'id.'
yǐ 猗 — *ʔaiʔ 'luxuriant leaves' ≍ wǎn 苑 *ʔuanʔ 'rich foliage, umbrageous'
qīng 傾 — [kʰieŋ ~ kʰwieŋ] 'incline'
xì 信 — [sin^{C}] ~ xún 洵 [suin] 'true' (< *swin)
rè 熱 — *net or *ŋet 'hot' ~ ruò 爇 *n/ŋwetʔ *n/ŋiotʔ 'hot'

In one instance, a text (*Huainanzi*) writes *rén* 仁 [nin] for *rùn* 潤 [ńun > ńuin] (*ZWDCD*).

*10.2.3 ST *-wə in OC*

ST *-wə has later merged with either *u or *a, except in reconstructed OC forms and sporadically in TB languages.

Village — qiū 丘 [kʰu] *khwə 'village, district' < ST *k(h)wə
<> TB-Phön *kəwa*, Lushai *kʰua*^{H} 'village'

Nine — jiǔ 九 [ku^{B}] OCB *kʷjuʔ, OCM *kuʔ ~ *kwəʔ 'nine' < ST *kuʔ ~ *kwəʔ:
<> Lushai *kua*^{R} < *kuaʔ

Cow — niú 牛 [ŋu (or ŋɨu)] *ŋwə 'bovine, ox, cow' < ST *ŋwə
<> TB *ŋwa > WB *nwa*^{B} 'bull, cow'; JP *ŋa*^{33}, *wǎ*^{33}-; Nung *ŋwa* ~ *ŋa* ~ *nwa*

11

OLD CHINESE VOWELS AND THEIR FOREIGN COUNTERPARTS

In this section examples for vocalic correspondences are arranged by OC vowels:

11.1	*a	11.7	Variations between *ə ~ *əi ~ *i ~ *e
11.2	*ə	11.8	OC and ST *u and *o
11.3	*e	11.9	*o
11.4	*-ai	11.10	*u
11.5	*i	11.11	*-au, *-auk
11.6	*-əi, *-ui		

OC and TB phonemes agree rather closely, but consistent correspondence involving *e, *ə, and *i, and especially *o and *u within TB and ST, is often elusive. See §12 for the vowels of individual TB languages.

Vowel alternations do occasionally occur within OC wfs. For this present work we shall keep wfs and words with different vowels separate, unless we have some compelling cases such as near-homonyms with minimal phonological contrast.

For the rare inversion of elements in a diphthong, see the comments under → něi 餒 'hungry' and → shuāi 衰 'diminish'.

Vowel length was not distinguished in OC as far as we can tell. Length distinctions in some modern dialects are either a concomitant feature of tone, or have secondarily emerged as in Cantonese; there vowel length correlates regularly with MC segmental features and pro- bably has emerged due to Tai substrate influence. Since CH dialects, OC rimes and phonetic series have no unambiguous traces of length distinctions, we will not assume them for OC. Han Buddhist transcriptions confirm this for the Han period, where any type of CH syllable indiscriminately renders both Indic long or short vowels; the exception is the strict avoidance of open tone-B syllables for Indic long vowels; hence these syllables were markedly shorter (final glottal stop) than tone-A (and C?) syllables; this is still the case in some modern dia- lects. But these are tone-related length distinctions. AA and Kam-Tai substrate words with apparently long vowels lose the final consonant in OC, which indicates that PCH did not have closed syllables with long vowels (§6.9).

11.1 OC *a

OC *a descends from ST *a = PTB *a (LHan forms in brackets):

Five	wǔ 五 [ŋɑ^B] *ŋâʔ 'five' <> PTB *-ŋa(ʔ) > WT *lŋa*; WB *ŋa^B*
Not (have)	wú 無 [muɑ] *ma 'not have' <> PTB *ma > WT *ma*, WB *ma^C* 'not'
Concede	ràng 讓 [ńɑŋ^C] *naŋh 'concede, yield' <> PTB *naŋ > WT *gnaŋ, gnaŋs* 'to concede'; WB *hnaŋ^B* 'to give'

*11.1.1 WT o for PTB *a*

ST = PTB *a = OC *a (as well as ST / OC *ə = PTB *a) shows up occasionally as WT *o* (see also §12.9 [3]):

Hair	shān 髟 [ṣam] *srâm 'long hair' <> PTB *(C-)sam > WT *ʔag-tsʰom* 'beard of the chin', WB *tsʰam* 'head hair', PL *ʔ-tsam[1]
To hear	WT *tʰos* <> Proto-Himalayish *tʰas

*11.1.2 OC *a ~ *ə variations*

With Baxter we assume six vowels for OCM. A wf is usually restricted to only one OC vowel. Obvious cases of vowel alternations within a wf are not often encountered; therefore, a pair like 'speak' below may represent non-morphological variants of some sort.

Speak	tán 談 [dɑm] *dâm 'to speak' <> WT *gdam-pa* 'to advise, give council' ꭗ tán 譚 [dəm] *də̂m 'to speak'
Islet	zhǔ 渚 [tśɑᴮ] *taʔ 'islet' ~ zhǐ 沚 [tśəᴮ] *təʔ. Note also chí 坻 [ḍi] 'islet' [Shi], and zhōu 洲 [tśu] 'island in a river'
Lean on	yǐ 倚 [ʔɨɑiᴮ] *ʔaiʔ 'to lean against, pull aside, rely upon' ꭗ yī 依 [ʔɨi] *ʔəi 'to lean on, rely on, depend on'
Ant	yǐ 蟻 [ŋɨaiᴮ] *ŋaiʔ 'ant' ~ yǐ 螘 [ŋɨiᴮ] *ŋəiʔ 'ant' <> KN-Lai *hŋeʔr-tee* 'ant' (*tee* is diminutive 'small')
Sinew	jīn 筋 (kjən) [kɨn] *kən vs. jiàn 腱 (kjɐn, gjɐnᶜ) [kɨɑn, gɨɑnᶜ] *kan, gans

*11.1.3 OC *a alternating with *-e / *-i*

In some cognate sets, *a alternates with *e / *i, both within OC and in sets with foreign items. On one hand, this may reflect parallel stems (§2.5); on the other, it is reminiscent of later dialect variation where some southern dialects occasionally have *a* for standard *e*. Examples of *a* ~ *e* variations within CH:

Black	lú 壚盧玈 [lɑ] 'black and hard soil, black' ꭗ lí 驪 [le] 'black horse'
Beam	lǘ 梠 [liɑ] 'beam supporting rafters' ꭗ lì 欐 [leᶜ] 'a beam'
Son-in-law	xù 婿 'son-in-law': (sjwoᶜ) Mand. xù (phonet. ɕyᶜ), G-Nánchāng ɕyᴬ ~ (sieiᶜ): Coll. Shazhou *siei* (*si*?). W-Wēnzhōu *seiᶜ*, K-Méixiàn *sɛᶜ*, Y-Guǎngzhōu *ʃaiᶜ²*, M-Xiàmén col. *saiᶜ*, lit. *seᶜ*
Good	liáng 良 *raŋ 'be good' ~ líng 令 *reŋ 'be good'
Cold	liáng 涼 *raŋ ꭗ lěng 冷 *reŋʔ
Green	qīng 青 [tsʰeŋ] *tshêŋ 'green, blue' ꭗ cāng 蒼 [tsʰɑŋ] 'green, azure' <> PMin *tsʰaŋ 'raw'

Examples of *a* ~ *e* variations with outside connections:

Chicken	jī 雞 [ke] 'chicken' <> MK-PVM *r-ka: 'id.'

Rain	líng 零霝 [leŋ] *rêŋ ~ *rîn 'rain' <> TB-JP *raŋ*^{31}*-ga*^{31} 'violent rain'
Turtle	liè 獵 [liap] *rap (or *riap ?) 'a kind of turtle' <> PTB *lip / *lep 'turtle' > WB, Khami, Mru *lip* 'tortoise'
Ribs, sides	xiē 脅 [hɨap] *hrap (or *hriap ?) 'sides of body, ribs' <> TB: JP *kə*^{31}*-rep*^{31} 'rib', Kanauri *hrip, WT *rtsib < rhjip*
Also	yì 亦 [jak] *jak(or *[w]iak?) <> ST *wjak ? > TB-Lushai *ve*^{L} *< veʔ/h* 'also' ⋈ *vek*^{R} *< vek* 'again, over again'

In addition, ST wfs with such variant forms include (all dictionary entries →) *kēng* 脛 'leg', *xiāng* 香 'fragrance', *shēng* 生 'alive', *qīng* 清 'clear', *gāng* 剛鋼 'hard', *hé* 涸 'dry up', *yè* 葉 'leaf, flat'.

Some words have OC *a for foreign *i (as in 'Ribs' above); this is especially the case involving MK, specifically PMonic items with *i. Such a vocalic shift has parallels elsewhere, as, for example, in Angami Naga: PTB *g-ni 'two' > Angami *kennā*, *si 'die' > *sā-*, *mi 'man' > *mā*, *ni 'sun' > *nā-ki, ne-ki* (Hutton 1921: 296f).

Elephant	xiàng 象 [ziɑŋ^{B}] *s-jaŋ or *ziaŋʔ 'elephant' <> MK: PMonic *ciiŋ, PSemai *ciigŋ, but other languages have *a
To plow	jí 耤 [dziak] *dzak 'to cultivate, sacred field' <> PMK *jiik, OM *jik* 'to harrow, break up for planting, to cultivate'; Khmer /cì:k/ 'to dig, dig over'
Fear	pù 怖 [pʰɑ^{C}] *phâh 'to fear' <> PMon *phiic 'be afraid'
Earth	tǔ 土 [tʰɑ^{B}] *thâʔ 'land, soil' ? <> MK-PMon *tiiʔ 'soil, earth', PWa *kətɛʔ — This etymology is not certain.
Rat	shǔ 鼠 [śɑ^{B} ~ tśʰɑ^{B}] *nhaʔ 'rat, mouse' ? <> MK-PMon *kniiʔ 'rat, mouse', PNBahnaric *kane 'rat' — But see dictionary for alternative etymologies.

*11.1.4 Variants *-a ~ *-ai*

Variants *-a ~ *-ai are rare, and they may be due to the Han period phonetic change of OC *-ai to *-a so that graphs which wrote OC *-ai could now be used for LHan *-ɑ* and vice versa:

Drip	lǜ 濾 [liɑ^{C}] *rah 'to drip', post-Han ⋈ lí 離 [liɑi] *rai 'to droop, drip'

*11.1.5 Variants *-a ~ *o*

This rare vocalic variation may simply be the result of a late graphic substitution when LHan *a* and *o* may have merged in some dialect:

Lay hands on	fǔ 撫 [pʰuɑ^{B}] *phâʔ 'lay hands on' ~ fǔ 拊 [pʰuo^{B}] *phôʔ 'lay hands on'
To grasp	jù 據 [kɨɑ^{C}] *kah 'to grasp' ~ jū 拘 [kɨo] *ko 'to grasp'

11.2 OC *ə

OC *ə is projected back to ST; in TB it has merged with *a. For additional examples, see §10.2.3.

Son — zǐ 子 [tsiə^{B}] *tsəʔ 'child, son'
<> PTB *tsaʔ > WT *ts^{h}a-bo* 'grandchild'; PBurm. *tsa^{B} 'child'

Ear — ěr 耳 [ńə^{B}] *nəʔ 'ear'
<> PTB *r-na > WT *rna-ba* 'ear', PL *(C-)na^{2} 'ear'

Weave — zhī 織 [tśɨk] *tək 'to weave' <> WT *'t^{h}ag-pa* 'to weave'

Eat, lick — shí 食 [źɨk] *m-lək 'to eat'
<> PTB *m-lyak > PLB *m-lyak 'to lick'; WT *lǰags* < *ɴlyak* 'tongue'; JP *mə^{31}-ta^{55}*; Lepcha *lyak* 'taste, try', WB *lyak*, Lushai *liak^{F} / liaʔ^{L}*

Forest — lín 林 [lim] *rəm 'forest'
<> ST *rəm: TB-NNaga *C-ram 'forest', Lushai *ram^{H}* 'forest, jungle, country'

Stand — lì 立 [lip] *rəp or *C-rəp 'to stand'
<> ST *rjəp: PTB *g-ryap > PLB *ʔrap 'stand', WB *rap*, Mikir *arǰàp* < *rjap^{l}*

Weep — qì 泣 [k^{h}ɨp] *khəp ? 'to weep'
<> ST *krəp: PTB *krap > WT *k^{h}rab-k^{h}rab* 'a weeper', Kanauri *krap* 'to weep', JP *k^{h}rap^{31}*

*11.2.1 OC *ə in unstressed syllables*

In some unstressed forms of grammatical words, the vowel is reduced to *ə (§3.3.3):

ér 而	(ńźɨ)	*nə	'-like, -ly'	< rú 如	(ńźjwo)	*na	'be like'
ér 而	(ńźɨ)	*nə	'your'	< rǔ 汝	(ńźjwo^{B})	*naʔ	'you'
nǎi 乃	(nậi^{B})	*nəʔ	'your'	< rǔ 汝	(ńźjwo^{B})	*naʔ	'you'
yí 台	(jiɨ)	*lə	'I, we'	< yú 予余	(jiwo)	*la	'I, we'
qí 其	(gjɨ)	*gə	'this, his'	< qú 渠	(gjwo)	*ga	'he'

*11.2.2 OC *-ə = PTB *i*

In a few etyma, OC *ə (> MC div. III, LHan -iə) corresponds to PTB *i:

Latrine — cè 廁 [tṣ^{h}ə^{C}] *tshrəkh ? 'latrine'
<> PTB *ts(y)i 'urinate > WT *gči(d)-pa*

Yak — lí 犛 [liə] *rə 'yak' <> WT *'bri-mo* 'domesticated female yak'

Cut, write — lǐ 理 [liə^{B}] *rəʔ 'cut jade according to its veins'
<> PTB *riy > Lushai *ri^{R} < riʔ* 'boundary, frontier, limit, line of demarcation', WT *'bri-ba, bris* 'to draw, write' ꭗ *ris* 'figure', WB *re^{B}* 'write, delineate, paint', Mru *pri* 'to scratch'

Container — guǐ 簋 [kwɨə^{B}] *-əʔ, OCB *k^{w}rjuʔ 'name of a ritual vessel'
<> PLB *k^{w}iy^{1} 'receptacle, container'

For additional variations between *ə, *i, and *e, see §11.7. For OC *ə = PTB *u, see §11.10.5.

11.3 OC *e

Usually, OC *e corresponds to PTB and foreign *e(y):

Buy mǎi 買 [mɛ^{B}] *mrêʔ 'to buy'
<> ST *mrey ~ *brey: PTB *b-rey, WT *rje-ba* (< ɴ-*rye* ?) 'to barter', JP *ma*^{31}-*ri*^{33} 'to buy'

Straight tǐng 挺 [tʰeŋ^{B}] *hlêŋʔ 'straight'
<> PTB *pleŋ 'straight' ж *bleŋ 'straight'

Sleet xiàn 霰 [sen^{C}] *sêns 'sleet' <> WT *ser-ba* 'hail', JP *sin*^{33} 'hail'

Additional examples include (all entries →) *xī* 析 'to cleave', *píng* 平 'level', *biǎn* 扁 'flat and thin', *jiàn* 見 'to see', *shì* 舐 'to lick', *ěr* 邇 'near'.

Vowel breaking before dental finals has led to the new MC head vowel *a* / *ä*, thus MC *-jiän* < *en (in div. III and 3/4 from OC *-en, not *-ên which became later *-(i)en)*. This is parallel to *o; see §11.9. It is a universal development in northern and written Chinese as in:

Face miàn 面 (mjiän^{C} 4) [mian^{C}] *mens 'face' <> PTB *s-mel > Lushai *hmeel*^{H}

Send qiǎn 遣 (kʰjiän^{B} 4) [kʰian^{B}] *khenʔ 'to send' <> WT *skyel-ba* 'to send'

*11.3.1 OC *e in open syllables*

In open syllables, OC *-e corresponds often to PTB and foreign *-ay (*-aj, *-ai):

Only zhǐ 只 [tśe^{B}] *teʔ 'only'
<> PLB *day^{2} ж tí 'only' > WB *tʰi*^{B} 'single, alone', JP *tai*^{33} 'single'

Child ér 兒 [ńi] *ŋe 'child' <> JP *ʔŋai*^{33} 'baby', Mru *ŋia* 'child'

Young ní 倪 [ŋe] *ŋê 'young and weak' <> WB *ŋai* 'small, little, inferior'

God dì 帝 [de^{C}] *dêh 'god'
<> WT *tʰe* 'celestial gods', JP *mə*^{31}-*tai*^{33} 'god of the sky'

Spleen pí 脾 [bie] *be 'spleen, bile'
<> PTB *r-pay: JP *pāi*, but Angami Naga *ú-prì*, Mikir *pli-ha* < *-i

This shì 是 [dźe^{B}] *deʔ 'this is, this'
<> PTB *day > WT *de* 'that'; JP *n*^{55}-*deʔ*^{55} 'this, there', Kachin *dai*

Deer zhì , zhài 廌 [ḍɛ^{B} ?] *drêʔ 'a kind of deer'
<> WB *darai* 'hog deer' <> MK: OMon *draay* 'hog deer'

Crab xiè 蟹 [gɛ^{B}] *grêʔ ? 'crab'
<> PTB *d-kaːy > Mikir *čehē* 'crab', Lushai *ai*^{R} 'id.', Tangkhul *khai* 'fish'

ST *-əj, *-ej, and *-aj have merged in many TB languages, including WT (-e). When only CH and WT forms are available, the original ST vowel or diphthong is impossible to recover, as in *zhī* 禔 [tśe] *te 'peace, happiness' <> WT bde-ba 'happy'.

*11.3.2 OC *-e = foreign ia / ja*

In closed syllables, foreign *-ja -(*-ya-, *-ia-) corresponds to monophthongized OC *e. This is similar to PTB *i ~ *ya variations (*HPTB:* 506–508).

Light adj. qīng 輕 (k^{h}jäŋ) [k^{h}ieŋ] *kheŋ 'light' (weight)
< ST: PTB *r-ya:ŋ ~ *gya:ŋ

Flame tiǎn 炶 [t^{h}em$^{B/C}$] *lhêmʔ/s 'brightness of fire' 火光:
<> WT *lčam-me-ba < hlyam* 'variegated, shining, dazzling', PL *ʔ-lam[1] 'flame', WB *ə-lhyam* 'coruscation of flame'

Taste tiē 呫 [t^{h}ep] *nhêp 'to taste' <> WT *sñab-pa* 'to taste, savor'

Hold xié 挾 [gep] *gêp ? 'grasp, hold'
<> WT *k^{h}yab-pa* 'embrace, comprise' ⪤ *skyob-pa, bskyabs* 'protect, preserve'

Plait biān 編 [pen] *pên 'to weave'
<> PTB *pyar ~ *byar > Bahing *p^{h}jer* 'to sew'; Lushai *p^{h}iar^{H}* 'to knit, plait', WT *'byor-ba ~ 'byar-ba* 'stick to, adhere to' ⪤ *sbyor-ba, sbyar* 'to affix, attach, join, connect'

Iron tiě 鐵 [t^{h}et] *lhît or *lhêt 'iron'
<> WT *lčags < hlyaks* 'iron'<> Tai: S. *lek^{D1S}* < *hl- 'iron', PKS *k^{h}lit^{7}; PVM *khăc 'iron'

Pinch shè 攝 [śap] *nhep 'pinch between'
<> PTB *C-nyap > WT *rñab-rñab-pa* 'to seize or snatch together', PLB *(s-)nyap > WB *ñap* 'be pinched' ⪤ *hñap* 'to squeeze'

Single zhī 隻 [tśek] *tek? 'single'
<> PTB (*tyik ~) *tyak > (PLB *C-tik 'one' > WB *tac*, WT *gčig* 'one'); JR *kətiag*, Bumthang *t(h)ek*, Cuona Monpa *t^{h}eʔ^{54}*

Further cases of leveling are → jì$_{21}$ 蹟 *tsek 'footprint', and → jí$_{15}$ 蹐 *tsek 'walk ...'. An earlier configuration *-ja- (*-ya-,*-ia-) may explain the OC doublets jì 跡 *ts(i)ak 'footprint', and → jí$_{16}$ 踖 *ts(i)ak 'walk...', respectively. Also → xié$_{1}$ 挾協.

*11.3.3 OC *e from *ai*

OC *e can be the result of leveling when a consonant is attached to *-ai (§6.1):

Easy yì 易 [je^{C}] *lekh 'easy, at ease'
<> PTB *lway 'easy' > WB *lwai* 'easy, yielding'

Diphthong leveling may have been responsible for rare OC *-e ~ *-ai variations:

Catch in net lì 麗 [le^{C}] 'to get caught / fasten (fishes in a net), attach'
⪤ lí 離 [liɑi] 'to fasten in a net, get caught in a net (fishes), tangled'

Rope lí 纚 [le] 'a rope' ⪤ lí 縭 [liɑi] 'scarf'

*11.3.4 OC *-e for foreign *i*

Some words with ST and foreign rimes *-iŋ / *-ik have merged with OC *-in, *-it; others with *-eŋ, *-ek; see §6.4.1. Also with non-velar finals, we encounter items where foreign *i was lowered to *e in OC (due to the labial in the ST initial?):

Laugh ér 唲 [ńe] *ne 'forced laugh'
<> PTB *m-nwi(y) 'to laugh' > Lushai *nui^{H} / nuiʔ^{L}*

Hip bì 髀 [beᴮ, pieᴮ] *bêʔ, *peʔ 'thighbone'
<> WT *dpyi* 'hip, hipbone', Lushai *pʰeiᴸ* 'foot, leg'

Destroy miè 蔑 [met] *mêt 'to destroy' (but see alternative etymology)
<> PTB *mit > Abor-Miri *mit* 'destroy', Lushai *mitᴸ / miʔᴸ* 'to go out, die out, be extinguished'

*11.3.5 OC *e ~ *o*

OC *e ~ *o in reduplications of the 'ding dong' type have been discussed by Baxter (1992: 501f) (§2.7). Perhaps such alternations can occur also in wfs:

Ulcer yōng 癰 [ʔɨoŋ] *ʔoŋ 'ulcer' ≭ yǐng 癭 [ʔieŋᴮ] *ʔeŋʔ 'tumor'

11.4 OC *-ai

OC *-ai has several sources: (1) ST *-ai (but see §11.3.1), (2) ST *-al (§8.3), (3) other rare correspondences, including *-ar (§7.7.4). See §11.1.4 for *-a ~ *-ai variants.

Change yí 移 [jɑi] *lai 'to change, alter'
<> PTB *la:y 'change, exchange' > WB *laiᴮ*

Necessary yì 義 [ŋɨɑiᶜ] *ŋaih 'be right, righteous, proper'
<> PTB *ŋa:y > KN-Lushai *ŋaiᴴ / ŋaiʔᴸ < ŋais* 'necessary, customary'

Come yí 儀 [ŋɨɑi] *ŋai 'to come' <> TB: JP *ŋai³³* 'to come, arrive'

Lame bǒ 跛 [pɑiᴮ] *pâiʔ 'to walk lame'
<> PTB *pay ≭ *bay 'lame, limp, oblique' > WB *pʰai* 'go aside'

Winnow bò 播簸 [pɑiᶜ] *pâih 'to winnow'
<> PTB *pʷa:y 'chaff, scatter' > PL *pway² 'chaff'

OC *-ai may also correspond to a different TB diphthong (note also 'Ant' in §11.1.2):

Hungry è 餓 [ŋɑiᶜ] *ŋâih 'hungry, starve'
<> Lushai *ŋheiᴴ* 'to go without', WB *ŋat* 'thirsty, hungry'

11.5 OC *-i

ST *-i can be assumed for words that have *i in both TB (*i, *-əy – *HPTB:* 185ff) and OC. Where the word is placed in QY *chóngniǔ* div. 3/3, we may assume with Baxter an earlier medial *r. Some ST words in *-iŋ, *-ik have merged in OC with *-in, -*it; see §6.4.1.

Die sǐ 死 [siᴮ] *siʔ 'to die'
<> PTB *siy 'to die' > WT *'čʰi-ba < ɴsi, ši*; PL *ʃe²; WB *se*

This yī 伊 [ʔi] *ʔi 'this', CH dialects 'he'
<> TB-Lushai *ʔiᴸ* 'this, that', Chepang *ʔiʔ* 'he'

Stool jǐ 几机 [kɨᴮ] *kriʔ ? 'stool, small table'
<> WT *kʰri* 'seat, chair, throne, couch'

Ear of grain suì 穗 [zuis] *s-wis 'ear of grain'
<> Lushai *vuiᴸ /vuiʔᴸ < vuis* 'to ear (as grain, grass)'

Two èr 二 [ńis] *nis 'two'
<> PTB *g-nis > WT *gñis*, Lushai *hniʔ*^{L} < *hnis*, PLB *nit ~ *ni ~ *ʔnit

Ten shí 十 (źjəp) [dźip] *gip <> ST *gip: PTB *gip > WB *kyip*, Mikir *kep* < *kip*

Blood xuě 血 [huet] *hwît 'blood'
<> PTB *s-hywəy 'blood' > Magari *hju* < *hwi*, Chepang *wi*, Kanauri *śui*; PL *suj^{2}, WB *swe*^{B}

Tears tì 涕 [tʰei^{B}, tʰei^{C}] *thîʔ/h or *thəiʔ/h 'tears'
<> PTB *ti, *tui 'water' > WT *mčʰi-ma* 'a tear', Kanauri *ti 'water'

Kindness lián 憐 [len] *rîn 'to pity, pitiful'
<> WT *drin* < *ɴrin* 'kindness, favor, grace'; WB *rañ*^{B}- 'love'

Sweet tián 甜 [dem] *lîm 'sweet'
<> PTB *lim > WT *žim-pa* 'sweet scented or tasting', Manang *lim* 'sweet'

Additional examples include (all dictionary entries →) *shǐ* 屎 'excrement', *rì* 日 'sun', *yī* 一 'one', *xīn* 辛 'bitter', *shěn* 矧 'the gums', *qī* 七 'seven', *jǐ* 麂 'muntjac', *xǐ* 洗洒 'to wash', *lǐn* 稟廩 'rations', *niē* 捻 'to pinch'.

*11.5.1 ST *i ~ *u variations*

In TB languages fluctuation between the high vowels *i* and *u* is common in closed syllables, especially when in contact with a labial consonant (*HPTB:* 493–505). For example:

Hair	PTB *mil ~ *mul
Knee	WT *pis-mo* ~ *pus-mo*
Cane	WT *smyig-ma* ~ *smyug-ma*
To fly	PTB *pir ~ *pur
Go down	PTB *nip ~ *nup
Sleep	PTB *(y)ip ~ *yup
Wipe	PTB *sit ~ *sut
Shelter	Lushai *uup*^{F} ~ WT *skyibs* < *s-ʔips

This is a ST phenomenon, because CH also has these variations:

Headrest zhěn 枕 [tśim^{B}] *kimʔ <> PTB *kum 'block, headrest'

Believe xìn 信 [sin^{C}] *sins 'believe, trust, need'
⋇ xún 恂洵 [sun] > [suin] *sun ? 'sincere, believe'

This variation also occurs in other language families, e.g., AA-Mon *kmun* ~ *kmin* 'ruler'.

In addition to phonological reasons, OC i/u vowel alternations occur in reduplications (Baxter and Sagart 1998) (§2.7).

*11.5.2 OC *i for AA *a*

In some words of AA origin, OC has the vowel *i for PAA *ja (cf. *e from *ja §11.3.2):

Person rén 人 *nin <> ? PMK *ɲah 'person, people'

Glue ní 昵 *nrit <> ? MK: Khmu *klɲaʔ* (i.e., *kl-ɲaʔ*) 'resin'

11.6 OC *-əi, *-ui

OC *-əi corresponds to PTB *-ey and *-ay (from ST < *-əj). This distinction is preserved in Kuki-Naga languages. Occasionally, the OC counterpart is *-ai (note 'Ant' below) or *-e.

Fire — huǒ 火 [huɑi^B] *hmə̂iʔ 'fire'
<> PTB *(s-)mey > OTib. *smye*; PLB *ʔmey², Lushai *mei^R < meiʔ*

Tail — wěi 尾 [mui^B] *məiʔ 'tail'
<> PTB *r-may > PL *ʔ-mri², WB *mri^B*; KN-Aimol *rəmai*; Lushai *mei^R < meiʔ*

Ant — yǐ 蟻 [ŋɨɑi^B] *ŋaiʔ 'ant' ~ yǐ 螘 [ŋɨi^B] *ŋəiʔ 'ant'
<> PTB: KN-Lai *hŋeʔr-tee* 'ant' (*tee* 'small')

Rhinoceros — xī 犀 [sei] *sə̂i 'rhinoceros'
<> WT *bse* (< *-ay* < *-əy ?) 'rhinoceros' ? ⋈ Kuki-Naga *k-say, Lushai *saai^H* 'elephant'

OC *-ui (as opposed to *-wi) may go back to ST *-uj, *-ul, et al. (see §8.3). For variations between *əi, *i, and *e, see §11.7.

11.7 Variations between *ə ~ *əi ~ *i ~ *e

In OC and within ST wfs, the vowels *ə ~ *əi ~ *i ~ *e fluctuate without an apparent system, especially with dental finals. For additional variations between *ə and *i, see §11.2.2. These fluctuations are parallel to back vowel behavior; see §11.8. Similar fluctuations are also known from TB (*HPTB:* 509–512).

*11.7.1 OC *-əi ~ *-i*

OC rimes in *-əi and *-i have merged in LHan and MC, except after grave initials where they remained distinct, thus *bǐ* 比 [pi^B] < OC *piʔ (MC div. *chóngniǔ* 4/4) vs. *fěi* 匪 [pui^B] < *pəiʔ (MC div. III). In his reconstructions, Baxter (following previous scholarship) distinguishes OCB *-ij from OCB *-əj after acute initials according to *Shījīng* rimes and phonetic series, yet many irregular and undetermined rimes remain; OCB *-əj rime predominates, and among the *-əj words are items which according to ST and AA relations should be expected to have OCB *-ij = OCM *-i. Within CH there are also doublets; see 'hungry' → $jī_2$ 飢. Furthermore, div. IV and div. III syllables are segregated into their own phonetic series as if *-əi and *-i already began to converge and sort themselves out in OC on the basis of the feature which gave rise to the MC divisions. Thus, in div. IV OCB *-ij and *-əj (OCM *-i, *-əi) can both correspond to foreign *-i as well as foreign *-əj.

OC rime *-i has its regular counterpart in PTB *i (§11.5). However, occasionally WT *e* also corresponds to OC *i. The reason is unclear, but theoretically a ST diphthong like *ei (= Lushai *ei) might have been responsible; note 'Know' below:

Enjoy — shì 嗜 [gi^C] *gih 'enjoy' (food)
<> WT *dgyes-pa* 'rejoice' ⋈ *dge-ba* 'happiness, virtue'; palatalization implies an OC *i (not *əi)

Hungry — jī 飢 (ki 3) [kɨ] *kri 'be hungry, starve, hunger, famine'
<> WT *bkres* 'be hungry', JP *kyet^31* 'hungry'; the phonetic series implies OC *i (not *əi)

Know xī 悉 [sit] *sit 'to know, comprehend'
<> PTB *syey 'know' > WT *šes-pa*, Vayu *ses*; Lushai *tʰei*ᴸ / *tʰeiʔ*ᴸ

*11.7.2 OC *ə ~ *e, *i in closed syllables*

The same variations pertain to syllables with dental finals. According to phonetic series and rimes, we find OC *-i- ~ *-ə- ~ *-e- variants which are homophones in MC div. III, e.g., *zhì* 疐 (ṭiC) *trits ~ *zhì* 躓 (ṭiC) *trəts 'slip / stumble'; or *hé* 翮 (ɣɛk) *grêk 'root of a feather'~ 翱 (ɣɛk) *grə̂k 'wing, feather'; *jiè* 界 (kăiC) [kɛs] *krê(t)s 'boundary, limit' vs. *jiè* 届 (kăiC) [kɛs] *krə̂(t)s 'to end up, arrive, end, limit'; *shí* 寔 *dək or *djək (?) 'really' < ST: PLB *dyak 'truly, very', Lushai takᴸ 'real, true' vs. *shí* 實 (dźjet) *m-dit (?) 'really'. According to

11-1	TB, WT	Chinese	MC div. III	OC
WT	srel 'to rear'	chǎn 產 'produce'	(ṣănB)	*srâ/ênʔ
Lush	*hmeel 'face'	miàn 面 'face'	(mjiänC 4)	*mens
WT	skyel-ba 'send'	qiǎn 遣 'send'	(kʰjiänB 4)	*khenʔ
Lush	belF < beelʔ 'put on garment'	bèi 被 'put on clothes'	(bjieB/C 3)	*baiʔ/h
WT	'dred-pa 'slip'	zhì 疐 'slip' zhì 躓 'stumble'	(ṭiC) (ṭiC)	*trits *trəts
WT	šes 'know'	xī 悉 'know'	(sjet)	*sit or *sət
WT	bden 'true'	zhēn 真 'true'	(tśjen)	*tin
WT	žed-pa < *rjet 'fear'	lì 慄 'careful'	(ljet)	*rit
WT	mčʰin 'liver'	xīn 辛 'bitter'	(sjen)	*sin
Lush	kʰirʔᴸ < *kʰirh 'to tie'	jǐn 緊 'bind tight'	(kjienB 4)	*kinʔ
TB	*r/sñil 'gums'	shěn 矧 'gums'	(śjenB)	*nhinʔ

11-2	TB, WT	Chinese	MC div. IV, 3/4	OC
WT	m-kyen 'know'	jiàn 見 'see'	(kienC)	*kêns
WT	ser 'hail' < *swer	xiàn 霰 'sleet'	(sienC)	*sêns
TB	*peːr 'flat'	biǎn 扁 'flat'	(pienB)	*pênʔ
Lush	beelH 'pot'	biān 籩 'food vessel'	(pien)	*pên
WT	gser 'gold'	xiǎn 毨銑 'glossy, polished metal'	(sienB)	*sə̂nʔ
TB	*myel 'sleep'	mián 瞑眠 'sleep'	(mien)	*mə̂n or *mîn
WT	bsel 'escort'	xiān 先 'go in front'	(sien)	*sə̂n
WT	bsil 'wash'	xǐ 洗洒 'wash'	(sienB, sieiB)	*sə̂iʔ ~ *sə̂nʔ
WT	mtʰil 'bottom'	dǐ 氐底 'bottom'	(tieiB)	*tîʔ

GSR 457 Karlgren believed that *mín* 民 (mjen) 'people' had two readings: OCM *min and *mən. This word, as well as *xǐ* 洗 *sə̂iʔ / *sə̂nʔ 'to wash' and *quǎn* 犬 *khwə̂nʔ 'dog', have TB cognates with indisputable *i, which also should be expected to be the source of the vowels in MC *mjen, siei*^{B}, *k*^{h}*iwen*^{B}. Hence OC *ə in words with dental finals (including diphthong *-əi) corresponds regularly (though unsystematically) to foreign *ə as well as *i. Table 11-1 (MC div. III syllables) and Table 11-2 (MC div. IV syllables) show correspondence sets with ST final dentals, including earlier *-l and *-r.

11.8 OC and ST *u and *o

PTB *u and *o usually correspond to OC *u and *o, but not in a systematic way, so that either of the two can be expected to correspond "regularly" to any in other languages. For the situation in TB, see *STC:* 66; *HPTB:* 178ff. The rime *-uŋ is rare in OC, and it does not exist after grave initials (K-, P-) in MC div. I. The fate of this rime is parallel to PCH *-iŋ, as it may have converged with *-oŋ or *-un (§6.4.2). Within OC we also find doublets *o ~ *u:

Soft, weak	rú 懦臑 [ńo] *no ~ róu 柔[ńu] *nu
Bushy (hair)	róng 茸 [ńoŋ] *noŋ ~ róng 茙 [ńuŋ] *nuŋ
To bend	qū 曲 [kʰɨok] *kok ~ jú 鞠鞫 [kuk] *kuk <> PTB *kuk
To hatch	fú 孚桴 [pʰuo] *pho 'to hatch' ~ fù 伏 [bu^{C}] *bəkh or *bukh 'to hatch' <> Tai: S. *vak*^{D2} 'to hatch'
Incubate	yù, yǔ 嫗 [ʔɨo^{B}] *ʔoʔ 'to sit on eggs, incubate' (of birds) ~ yòu 蓲 [ʔu^{C}] 'to brood, hatch (eggs)' (old dialect word)

Where TB lgs. and OC have a simple vowel, Lushai occasionally has a diphthong *-ua*:

Pop	bǔ 卜 [pok] *pôk 'cracking' <> PLB *ɴpuk ~ *ʔpuk 'explode, pop', Lushai *puak*^{F} / *puaʔ*^{L} 'to explode, burst, pop'
Satiated	bǎo 飽 [pɔu^{B}] *prûʔ 'eat to the full, satisfied' <> Lushai *puar*^{H} 'having eaten enough'
Full grown	Lushai *puam*^{H} 'be full grown (but not ripe) of fruit, to swell' ⋈ *pum*^{F} < *pumʔ* 'be filled out (as fruit)'

11.9 OC *o

PTB and foreign *o (and *-ow) typically corresponds to OC *o; a few samples:

Stitch	zhuó, zhuì 綴 [[ṭuɑt, ṭuɑs^{C}~ ṭot, ṭos^{C}] *trot(s) 'to sew, stitch, connect' <> WT *gtod-pa, btod-pa* 'tie up, stake' ⋈ *rtod-pa* 'to tether'
Behind	hòu 後 [go^{B} or ɦo^{B}] *ɦôʔ 'behind, after' <> PTB *ok > WT *'og* (not *ʔog*); PLB *ʔok > WB *ok* (i.e., *ʔok*)
Hull grain	chōng 舂 [śoŋ] *hloŋ 'to hull grain with a pestle' <> Tai: S. *klooŋ 'hull rice'
Move	sōu, sǒu 搜 [so^{B}] *sô(ʔ) 'to move' <> PTB *m-sow > Dimasa *masau*, Lushai *tʰo*^{R} / *tʰɔʔ*^{L}, Lakher *pətʰeu*, Khami *əntʰau*, Ao Naga *meso* 'arise, awake'

Vowel breaking before dental finals has led to a new MC / LHan head vowel *a*, thus MC *-uan* < *on; this is parallel to *e (§11.3) and *u (§11.10.3). This is a universal development in northern and written Chinese, although southern dialects seems to have preserved the original OC vowels. In syllables with labial initial consonants and with dental or labial finals, labial dissimilation has led to the loss of rounding or the rounded element, so that ST *o > OC / MC *a, e.g., ST *pom > *puam > OC *pam, or ST *poi > *puai > OC *pai; see Table 11-3. '3/3' refers to the *chóngniǔ* doublet in the rime tables, with Baxter's OCB medial *r.

11-3 Theoretical developments

PCH	MC div. 1	MC div. 3/3	MC div. 3
*pon/t	> *pân: [pɑn] (puân)	> *pran: [pɨan] (pjän 3)	> *pan: [puɑn] (pjwan)
*poi	> *pâi: [pɑi] (puâi)		> *pai: [pɨe] (pje 3)
*pom	> *pâm: [pɑm] (pâm)		> *pam: [pɨam] (pjam)

*11.9.1 OC *o corresponding to ST *-u > PTB *-u*

In many words, especially those with open syllables, PTB *u corresponds to OC *o. Furthermore, the distribution of OC *-uŋ is limited; among the relatively few syllables with that final, there is none in div. I that starts with a velar; the final must have shifted elsewhere (see §6.4.2; §11.10.4 *gōng* 弓 'Bow').

Rob kòu 寇 [kʰoᶜ] *khôh 'to rob, robber'
<> PTB *r-kuw > WT *rku-ba* 'to steal', Kachin *ləku*, NNaga *C/V-kəːw, WB *kʰuiᴮ* < *C-kuiᴮ

Body qū 軀 [kʰɨo] *kho 'body, person'
<> PTB *(s-)kuw > WT *sku*, WB *kui* 'body (of an animal)'

Cough sòu 嗽 [soᶜ] *sôh 'to cough'
<> PTB *su(w) > Magari *su*, Garo, Dimasa *gu-su*, WT *sud-pa* 'cough'

Additional examples include → jū 駒 'colt', → qū 驅 'to drive (animals), gallop', → rǔ 乳 'nipple', → shǔ 樹 'to plant, place upright', → zhù 柱 'pillar'.

OC *-o in closed syllables has no systematic correspondence in other languages:

Cage lóng 籠 [loŋ(ᴮ)] *rôŋ(?) 'bird cage, basket'
<> WB *khruiŋᶜ* 'cage for birds'

Mound fēng 封 [puoŋ] *poŋ 'mound, tumulus, raise a mound'
<> WT *pʰuŋ-po* 'heap' ⋈ *spuŋ* 'a heap', *spuŋ-pa* 'to heap', Rawang *póŋ* 'heap'

Sharp point fēng 鋒蜂峰 [pʰuoŋ] *phoŋ 'sharp point (of weapon, insect)'
<> WT *buŋ-ba* 'bee'

Mound zhǒng 冢塚 [ṭoŋᴮ] *troŋ? 'a mound, peak'
<> WT *rduŋ* 'small mound, hillock', WB *toŋ* 'hill, mountain'

Torch zhú 燭 [tśok] *tok 'torch'
<> PLB *duk 'blazing' ⋈ *ʔduk 'kindle, set on fire' > WB *tok* 'blaze, shine'; WT *dugs-pa* 'to light, kindle'; Lushai *dukᴸ* 'glowing with heat'

Custom sú 俗 [ziok] *s-lok 'rustic, vulgar, custom, popular usage'
<> WT *lugs* 'custom, way, manner'

Inferior liè 劣 [lyat] *rot 'inferior'
<> PTB *ryut > JP *yut*^{31} 'become worse (illness)', WB *yut* < *rut* 'inferior, mean' ꭗ *hrut* 'put down'

Vomit yuē 噦 [ʔyɑt] *ʔwat or *ʔot 'sount of vomiting'
<> TB-PLB *ut (not *ʔut) 'to belch'

Additional examples with final *-ŋ include → yōng 癰 'ulcer', → yōng 邕 'city moat', → gōng 工功攻 'work'.

*11.9.2 OC *-o ~ *-au*

OC *-o ~ *-au variation is exceptional:

Scoop out yú 揄[jo, do^B] *lo ~ *lôʔ 'to scoop out (as a mortar)'
~ yóu ~ yǎo 舀 [ju, jau^B] *lu ~ *lauʔ 'to scoop hulled grain from a mortar'

Monkey yù 禺 [ŋɨo^C] *ŋoh 'monkey'
<> PTB: *ŋa:w 'ape' > Lushai *ŋau*^{H} 'grey monkey'

*11.9.3 OC *o / *u for foreign *a?*

In a few common words, OC appears to have the vowel *o or *u for PTB or foreign *a. (§11.1.5 mentions possible instances within CH.) Such rare correspondences may be chance similarities. Thus *yóu* 猶 [ju] *ju (?) 'to laugh' is probably unrelated to PTB *r-ya 'to laugh' > WT *gža-ba* 'to sport, joke, play' because the TB form agrees in a regular way with → chěn, chī 䟢 'laugh'. CH *kǒu* 口 *kʰoʔ 'mouth' is not related to TB *kʰa 'id.', etc. In the following, the ST root was perhaps *kwal with the medial *w lost in WT (?):

Pass over guò 過 [kuɑi^C ~ koi^C] *kôih 'to pass, transgress'
<> WT *rgal-ba, brgal* 'to pass over, travel through, ford', Lushai *kai*^{H} / *kai*^{L} 'to cross over' ? ꭗ *kal*^{H} 'walk, travel, pass by', WB *kai*^{B} 'exceed'

11.10 OC *u

OC *u usually corresponds to ST and foreign *-u; however, above, in §11.9.1, it has been noted that many OC words have *o for PTB *u. In some words, a suspected ST or foreign rime *-uŋ has shifted to OCM *-un; see §6.4.2.

Day zhòu 晝 [ṭu^C] *trukh 'time of daylight, day' <> WT *gdugs* 'noon'

Womb bāo 胞 [pɔu, pʰɔu] *prû, *phrû 'womb'
<> WT *pʰru-ma* ~ *'pʰru-ma/-ba* 'uterus, placenta'

Nine jiǔ 九 [ku^B] OCB *kʷjuʔ 'nine'
<> PTB *d-kuw > WT *dgu*; WB *kui*^{B}; PL *go^2; Lushai *kua*^{R}

Suck, swallow shǔn 吮 [źun^B] *m-lunʔ 'to suck'
<> PTB *mlyun > Kanauri *myun 'to swallow'

Grandchild sūn 孫 [suən] *sûn 'grandchild'
<> PTB *śu(w) > Mikir, Meithei, Dimasa, etc.; *su*, JP *ʃu*^{51} 'grandchild'

Additional examples include (all dictionary entries →): *zhōu* 粥鬻 'rice gruel', *bāo* 包 'to wrap, bundle', *páo* 匏 'gourd', *bǎo* 寶 'be precious', *mào* 冒 'to see', *yòu* 誘 'to entice', *yōu* 呦 'cry of deer', *yóu* 游遊 'float', *yòu* 鼬 'weasel', *tún* 純 'tie together', *tún* 臀 'buttock', *zūn* 尊 'to honor', *tū* 突 'to dig through', *chóng* 蟲虫 'insect, worm', *zhōng* 螽 'locust'.

*11.10.1 OC *-u for PTB and foreign *-o*

In some etyma, it may well be TB that changed *u to *o; WB does this regularly:

Awake	jué 覺 [kɔk] *krûk 'to awake' <> PTB *grok ~ *krok > WT *dkrog-pa* = *skrog-pa* 'to stir, churn, rouse'; PLB *krok 'be afraid' > WB *krok* ⪤ PLB *ʔkrok 'frighten'
Come out	chū 出 [tśʰut] *k-lhut 'to come out' <> JP *lot*^{31}*-lam*^{33} 'outlet', Trung *klot* 'come out', KN-Chinbok *hlɔt* 'id.'
Dig	kū 窟 [kʰuət] *khût 'dig in the ground, underground' <> PTB *r-ko-t > WT *rkod-pa* 'excavate, dig' ⪤ *rko-ba* 'to dig'
Sunrise	tūn 暾 [tʰuən] *thûn 'the rising sun' <> WT *'tʰon-pa, tʰon* 'to come out, go out', Monpa Cuona *tɕʰuŋ*^{53}, Motuo *tʰoŋ* 'to come out (sun)', WB *pɔ-tʰon*^{B} 'come out (e.g., the sun)'
Temple	zōng 宗 [tsouŋ] *tsûŋ 'ancestral temple, ancestral, lineage' <> WT *rdzoŋ(s)* 'castle, fortress', WB *(ə-)cʰoŋ* 'a building'
Bean	shú 菽 [śuk] *nhuk 'bean' <> PLB *(s-)nok 'bean' > WB *nok*, JP *noʔ*^{31}*-* 'red bean'
Morning	sù 夙 [siuk] *suk 'early morning, early, soon' <> PLB *C-sok ~ *V-sok 'morning, morrow'
Six	liù 六 [liuk] *C-ruk 'six' <> PTB *d-ruk 'six' > WT *drug*, JP *kruʔ*^{55}; Lushai *pa*^{L}*-ruk*^{L}; WB *kʰrok*

11.10.2 Labial dissimilation

Labial dissimilation in PCH and OC is responsible for gaps in the system where we should expect *u, which must have dissimilated to *ə. Labial dissimilation which affects the final consonant has been suggested in §6.7. See Table 11-4 for the uneven distribution of such syllables.

Several types of labial dissimilation had taken place in OC and later (as seen through MC), which have affected the vowels. With final *-m / *-p the back vowels *o, *u were unrounded which resulted in *a (< *o via *ua; see §11.9) and *ə (< *u via *uə).

Three	sān 三 [sɑm] *sə̂m 'three' <> ST *sum: WT *sum* 'three (in compositions)'; JP *mə*^{31}*-sum*^{33}, WB *sum*^{C}
Inhale	xī 吸 [hip] *hŋəp 'to inhale' <> ST *Cŋup: TB-WT *rŋub-pa*, *brŋubs* 'to draw in (air), breathe'
Sweet	gān 甘 (kâm) [kɑm] *kâm < *klam (prob. < *kluam < *klom) <> PTB *klum 'sweet'

However, in many OC words in final *-əm / *-əp the vowel *ə is original; see §11.2.

11.10.3 *Labial dissimilation before dental finals*

Between labial initial and dental final (including *-ui), earlier *u and *ə had apparently merged — in div. I *pûn merged with *pôn, in div. III *pən merged with *pun, hence MC *puən* [pən] vs. *pjuən* [pun]; we conservatively assume for OCM syllables *pən only (Table 11-4).

Root	běn 本 [pən^B] *bə̂nʔ 'root, stem' <> PTB *bul ~ *pul 'root, beginning, cause, origin, source'
Burst forth	pó浡 [bət] *bə̂t 'burst forth (as plants, fountain)' <> WT *'bu-ba, 'bus* 'to open, unfold (flower)'
Poor	pín 貧 [bɨn] OCB *brjən 'poor' <> WT *dbul* 'poor'
Tail	wěi 尾 (mjwei^B) [mui^B] *məiʔ <> PTB *r-may
Branch	méi 枚 (muậi) [məi] *mə̂i <> AA: Khmer *meek*

11.10.4 *Labial dissimilation with open / velar final syllables*

The OC syllables of the type *pə, *pək have merged with *pu, *puk in what corresponds to MC div. III; this is parallel to dental finals (above). In div. I, *pə̂ and *pû were kept distinct, and *pûk does not occur at all; see Table 11-4 (Sagart 1999: 58ff). The *Shījīng* rimes distinguish between *pə and *pu (div. III), but both become MC *pjəu*, and *pək and *puk (div. III) both become MC *pjuk*. Words with the phonetic as in 福 consistently rime with *-ək, words with the phonetic as in 復 consistently rime with *-uk. Likewise, 孚桴 蜉 rime always with *-u, and 伏服負婦 rime always with *-ə. Thus *Shījīng* rimes allow us to sort out these words for OC. The problem for ST comparisons is, however, that words with both 福 and 復 as phonetic derived from etyma with ST *-uk. Also 'carry on the back' has in many languages the equivalent of OC *ə, while PTB *buw suggests, of course, an *u for *fù* 負 contrary to its *Shījīng* rimes.

OC syllable type *puŋ does not occur at all (in none of the MC div. — apart from one or two doublets). As in rimes *puk ~ *pək, MC div. III *mjuŋ* resulted from *məŋ. In *Shījīng,* 弓 (kjuŋ) rimes consistently as *kwəŋ in spite of its ST origin *kuŋ which is a behavior parallel to 負 and 福. The issue remains unclear.

Lie down	fú 伏服 [buk] *bək 'to lie down' <> TB-Lushai *bɔk^L / bɔʔ^L* 'to lie down, recline'
To hatch	fù 伏 [bu^C] *bəkh 'to hatch' ~ fú 孚桴 (p^{h}ju) [p^{h}uo] *pho 'to hatch' <> Tai: S. *vak^{D2}* 'to hatch'
Woman	fù 婦 [bu^B] *bəʔ 'woman, wife' <> Yao *bwaaŋ^4 < nb-* 'daughter-in-law' <> Tai *baa^A 'wife'
Back	běi 北 [pək] *pə̂k 'north' ꭗ bèi 背 [bə^C] *bə̂kh 'to carry on the back' <> PTB *ba(k) > WT *'ba-ba* 'to bring, carry', JP *baʔ^{31}* (< *bak*) 'carry (child on back)', Lushai *pua^L / puak^F* 'carrying on the back as a child' <> PTai *baa^A: S. *p^{h}aa^{A2}* <> MK-Bahn. *bʌʔ , Katuic *baʔ* 'carry (on the back)', PPal. *bɔ, Khmu *bɔʔ,* PWa *bɔʔ 'carry child on back'

Benefit fú 福 [puk] *pək 'benefit, good fortune' <> WT p^h*yug-pa* 'rich' ⋈ p^h*yugs* 'cattle'

Ant fú 蜉 [bu] *bu 'large ant, ephemeria' <> WT *sbur* 'ant'

11-4 (for §11.10.3)

PCH	MC div. 1	MC div. 3/3	MC div. 3
*pə	[pə] (puậi) 培	[piə] (pji 3) 丕	[pu] (pjəu) 婦 also < *pu
*pək	[pək] (pək) 北	[pik] (pjək) 逼	[puk] (pjuk) 福 also < *puk
*pəŋ	[pəŋ] (pəŋ) 堋	[piŋ] (pjəŋ) 冰	[muŋ] (mjuŋ) 夢
*pən/t	[pən] (puən) ?	[pin] (pjen 3) ?	[pun] (pjwən) 聞 also < *pun
*pəi	[pəi] (puậi) 枚	[pii] (pji 3) 悲	[pui] (pjwei) 尾 also < *pui
*pəm	[pəm] (buŋ) 芃 ?	[pim] (pjəm) 品	[pum] (pjuŋ) 風
*pu	[pou] (pâu) 保		[pu] (pjəu) 孚 also < *pə
*puk *kuk	-- [kouk] (kuok) 告		[puk] (pjuk) 復 also < *pək [kuk] (kjuk) 菊
*puŋ *kuŋ	-- -- ?		[puŋ] (pjuŋ] 豐 [kuŋ] (kjuŋ) 宫
*pun/t	[pən] (puən) 本	[pin] (pjen 3) 貧	[pun] (pjwən) 文 also < *pən/t
*pui	[pəi] (puậi)	[pii] (pji 3)	[pui] (pjwei) 虫 also < *pui
*pum	?		?
*po	[po] (pəu) 母		[puo] (pju) 付
*pok	[pok] (puk) 卜		--
*poŋ	[poŋ] (puŋ) 蒙		[puoŋ] (pjwoŋ) 蜂

Comments on Table 11-4: PCH are hypothetical syllables, with vowels based on TB cognates; the CH (LHan, MC) forms are those that theoretically could derive from PCH. Gaps in the distribution are left blank or indicated by hyphens (–); the CH characters exemplify only the rime — the initials do not necessarily agree with the hypothetical PCH.

11.10.5 Exceptional correspondences

We have noted above that OC *-ə (> MC *-ɨ* div. III) seems to correspond in a few words to WT and PTB *i; similarly, OC *ə̂ (> MC div. I *-ậi*) occasionally = WT *u* or *o*. Instances are rare, the reason for this irregularity is not clear, and these may even be chance similarities or a matter of borrowing:

Able néng 能 [nəŋ] *nə̂ 'be capable, have ability, can' <> WT *nus-pa* 'be able'

Manner tài 態 [tʰəᶜ] *nhə̂h 'apparition, bearing, manner' <> WT *mtʰu* (< *m-nhu* ?) 'ability, power'

Cup bēi 杯 [pə] *pə̂ 'cup' <> WT *pʰor-pa* 'bowl, dish, cup' (late word)

Unusual variations ə ~ *u* are encountered, also within MC:

Sincere kěn 懇狠 (kʰənᴮ) [kʰənᴮ] *khə̂nʔ vs. kǔn 悃 (kʰuənᴮ) [kʰuənᴮ] *khûnʔ

To swallow tūn 呑 (tʰən) Sin Sukchu PR *t'ən*; MGZY *thʰin* (平) [t'ən] vs. Sin Sukchu SR *t'un* (平)

11.11 OC *-au, *-auk

This rime corresponds to PTB and foreign *au; in languages without diphthongs it corresponds to *o*, as in WT:

Float piāo 飄 [pʰiau] *phiau 'to float (in the air)' <> PTB *pyaw > WT *'pʰyo-ba* 'swim, soar, float'

Fat, grease sāo 膘 [sɑu] *sâu 'fat of swine or dog' <> PTB *sa:w > Lushai *tʰau*ᴸ 'fat, grease', JP *sau*³³

Sickle zhāo, jiāo 釗鉊 [keu, tśau < kiau] *kiau 'to cut' 釗, 'a big sickle' 鉊 <> Tai: Lao *kiau*ᴮ¹ 'to reap, sickle', S. *kiau*ᴮ¹ 'to cut with a sickle'

Additional examples include (all entries→) *máo* 毛 'hair, fur', *sāo* 鱢 'putrid smell', *yáo* 搖 'to shake, be agitated', *nǎo* 撓 'to trouble, disturb'.

The OC rime *-au has a closed syllable (*rùshēng*) counterpart. This goes counter to the system, which allows only short vowels in stopped syllables. But for now 'music', for example, will be written *yuè* 樂 (ŋåk) [ŋɔk] *ŋrâuk; perhaps it was phonetically leveled to *ŋrɔ̂k, just as *-aik became *-ek.

12
TRANSLITERATIONS OF FREQUENTLY QUOTED LANGUAGES

This chapter deals with frequently cited languages; they are, in alphabetical order: 12.1 Chinese, 12.2 Jingpo, 12.3 Lushai, 12.4 Mikir, 12.5 Tai, 12.6 Tibeto-Burman, 12.7 Tiddim Chin, 12.8 Written Burmese, 12.9 Written Tibetan.

This work draws mostly on languages that are reasonably well studied and understood, with extensive lexica and recorded tones, when applicable. TB languages which are cited in addition to the above include: Lepcha, Kanauri, Tamang-Gurung-Thakali-Manangba (TGTM), PTani (= Abor-Miri-Dafla), Chepang, as well as Proto-Lolo-Burmese ([P]LB) and Northern Naga (NNaga). Furthermore, Austroasiatic (AA) / Mon-Khmer (MK) languages — Proto-Viet-Muong (PVM), Khmer, and Proto-Monic (PMon). Miao-Yao (MY = Hmong-Mien) is cited according to either Purnell or Wáng Fúshì. Kam-Tai (KT) languages that are often cited include Proto-Tai (PTai) and Kam-Sui (KS).

Forms are usually cited in the spelling of their source. Occasionally, graphic changes have been made: *ɟ* or *ǰ* for *j* to make sure it is not confused with IPA *j*; IPA *j* for *y*; *č* for *c* to rule out confusion with ts; aspiration as in k^h- for *k'*- or *kh*-.

Tones are noted in the numerical system (55 high level, 11 low level, etc.); in some cases, these numbers are placed in front of the syllable, not after it, for example, in TGTM and in some CH dialects when also the tonal category is noted. In Sinitic (CH "dialects"), Tai and Miao-Yao, tone categories are assigned the letters ABCD. In some TB languages, tones are indicated by superscript letters: H = high tone, L = low tone, R = rising tone, F = falling tone, and M = mid tone.

12.1 Chinese (CH)

Mandarin, Middle Chinese (MC), Later Han Chinese (LHan or LH), and Minimal Old Chinese (OCM) are provided on the first line of every entry. After the symbol [T] follow early transcriptions of the word (see below); thereafter are [D] dialect forms (see §12.1.3). The [T] and [D] items are cited as sample illustrations for later (post-Han) developments. Varieties and reconstructions of Chinese are transcribed or written as follows:

Mandarin (Mand.) = *pīnyīn* 拼音

Middle Chinese (MC) from ca. AD 600 as reconstructed by Karlgren (1957) and amended by Li Fang Kuei (1971), is placed in parentheses. MC is based on the rime dictionary *Qièyùn*, hence it is also referred to as the Qièyùn system (QYS). Often, the Mandarin word is phonologically not the direct descendent of the MC form. Tones are indicated in superscript letters: *píngshēng* 平 A (usually unmarked), *shǎngshēng* 上 B (= Karlgren 'x:', Pulleyblank 'x/'); *qùshēng* 去 C (=Karlgren 'x-', Pulleyblank 'x\'), *rùshēng* 入 D (usually unmarked). Thus the entries here write, for example, MC *kiei*, $kiei^B$, $kiei^C$, *kiet*. The letter scheme has been adopted from modern dialect studies.

The nature and validity of MC has been much debated (recently by Coblin and Norman 1995; Pulleyblank 1998). MC forms are widely quoted, even by critics, for reference and identification of traditional phonological categories. MC (= QYS) does not reflect a natural language, as many scholars emphasize; for example, MC has three medial palatal glides: *-j-*,

-ji-, -i-; no known Sinitic language makes such distinctions. The LHan forms provide a transliteration which is probably closer to some actual language.

Later transcriptional forms follow the symbol [T], but only for illustration and when available.

Early Ming (EMing) and Yuan (Mongol) period Chinese has kindly been provided by S. Coblin. Early Ming has been recorded by the Korean Sin Sukchu (ca. AD 1475), SR = 'Standard reading', PR = 'Popular reading', LR = 'Left reading' (i.e., an additional pronunciation noted by a different author); the transcription of the source is provided, followed by the phonological interpretation in [IPA], as worked out by Coblin. Tones are indicated in CH characters: 平上去入 (ABCD). A word's different readings, recorded by the Koreans, reflect a split into a standard and a popular idiom.

Yuan (Mongol) period Chinese (1270–1308) is recorded in 'Phags-pa: **MGZY** (*Měnggǔ zìyùn*), followed by the phonological interpretation in [IPA], as worked out by Coblin. Tones are indicated in CH characters as above.

Old Northwest Chinese (ONW[C]) from about AD 400 as interpreted in Coblin 1994b. The transcriptions do not indicate tone. Occasionally Sui-Tang Chang'an (Coblin's 'STCA', ca. AD 640) and MTang (Middle Tang, ca. AD 775) forms are also provided.

12.1.1 Later Han Chinese

Later Han Chinese (LHan, LH) (Schuessler 2006) is suggested to reflect a language of the first and second centuries AD. It is based on modern dialect evidence (including Mǐn), Old Northwest Chinese (ONW, ONWC; Coblin 1991a; 1994b), Wei-Jin rimes (Ting 1975) and Buddhist transcriptional data form the Han period (Coblin 1982; 1993), as well as the *Quèyùn*. In this introduction, these forms are placed in brackets unless otherwise identified, thus [kɑ] = LH *ka*. Tones are marked as in MC. LHan is about 400 to 500 years older and is simpler than MC.

LHan follows the transcriptional conventions used for CH dialects; thereby it has shed the graphic complexities of MC; the components of diphthongs and triphthongs are represented by vowels, not semi-volwels (thus *au, ai, iau*). LHan has the following peculiarities:

(1) Like MC and CH dialects, it has *no consonant clusters.*

(2) Rimes which derive from those reconstructed earlier as OC *-d or *-ts with tone C still had a *final *-s* in LHan (*dà* 大 LH *das*).

(3) Universal *vowel bending* (or "warping") has resulted from a distinction between high vocalic onset syllables vs. low vocalic onset syllables (Schuessler 2006). In high syllables, the later MC div. III, the vocalic onset of a vowel is bent up as in OCM *ka > *kəa* > LHan *kɨa* 居; OCM *saŋ > *səaŋ* > LH *siaŋ* 相; OCM *ma > *moɑ* > LH *mua* 無. In low syllables, the later MC div. I/IV types, the vocalic onset is bent down, thus OCM *sî > LH *sei* (> MC *siei*) 西; OCM *pû > LH *pou* (> MC *pâu*) 寶; OCM *mə̂ > LH *mə* > *mɑə* > MC *muậi* 每. A high vowel in a high syllable cannot bend any higher, it remains unchanged: OCM *si > LH *si*, > MC *si* 死; OCM *ku > LH *ku* > later *kiu* 九 > MC kjəu. Equally, the low vowel *a* cannot bend lower; it remains unchanged in LHan: OCM *ka > LH *ka* (> MC *kuo*) 古.

Initial velar consonants eventually palatalized under the influence of the immediately following high vowel *i*, even a secondary one (perhaps phonetically *j*), thus OCM *ke > LH *kie* > MC *tśjie* 支. For reasons that are not yet clear, this palatalization of velars did not occur in all rimes (e.g., *jí* 吉 MC *kjet* < OCM *kit), nor with initial aspirated k^h-, nor with voiced *g*- in tone A (Did aspiration block palatalization?) (Schuessler *JCL* 24–2, 1996: 197-211).

The cause of this warping is a matter of speculation; see §12.1.2.

(4) LHan seemes to have preserved, at least in open syllables, OC segmental features which later resulted in MC tones, thus LHan *kaa, kaʔ, kah*; however, for the sake of consistency we will use the tone letters instead, hence LHan *ka*, ka^B, ka^C.

Table 12-1 provides some LHan sample forms for OC rimes *-a and *-aŋ. LHan syllable types are distributed over *Qièyùn* divisions (columns); the initials in the rows are LHan. The top row lists the rimes, L-a is a low-onset syllable with rime *-a* = QYS div. I, H-a a high onset syllable, etc. Shaded fields block out initial / final combinations that are phonotactically impossible.

12-1

	L-ɑ I	H-ɑ III	H-a III	a II	L-ɑŋ I	H-ɑŋ III	H-aŋ III	aŋ II
t	tɑ 土				tɑŋ 當			
l	lɑ 魯	liɑ 旅			lɑŋ 浪	liɑŋ 涼		
ts	tsɑ 祖	tsiɑ 沮	tsia 且		tsɑŋ 藏	tsiɑŋ 將		
s	sɑ 素	siɑ 胥			sɑŋ 桑	siɑŋ 相		
p	pɑ 布	puɑ 父		pa 巴	pɑŋ 旁	puɑŋ 方	pɨaŋ 柄	paŋ 烹
k	kɑ 古	kɨɑ 居	kia 車	ka 家	kɑŋ 剛	kɨɑŋ 疆	kɨaŋ 京	kaŋ 行
w		wɑ 雨				wɑŋ 王	wɨaŋ 永	
ṭ		ṭɑ 豬				ṭɑŋ 張		ṭaŋ 瞠
tṣ		tṣɑ 初		tṣa 抯		tṣɑŋ 莊		
ṣ		ṣɑ 所				ṣɑŋ 霜		
tś		tśɑ 處	tśa 者			tśɑŋ 昌		
ś		śɑ 書	śa 舍			śɑŋ 傷		
j		jɑ 與	ja 野			jɑŋ 羊		

12.1.2 Minimal Old Chinese (OCM)

Transcription of Minimal OC (OCM) is based on Baxter 1992 (OCB), but it errs on the side of simplicity because we try to account, as far as possible, for features which enjoy broader agreement among investigators, thus OCM *t- where some now suggest *ql- or the like. OCM seems to bring out etymological connections better than other systems. Two points need to be stressed: (1) OCM does not imply or preclude that other OC reconstructions are invalid; OCM restricts itself to those features which are knowable, as far as possible, without recourse to speculations and etymologizations. (2) The nature of the etymological relationship between many words remains unaffected by the MC system or OC reconstruction applied.

Crucial for the recovery of OC is the phonetic element with which a word is written, and its interpretation. Graphs with the same phonetic form a "phonetic series" or *xié-shēng* 諧聲 series. Karlgren and Li Fang Kuei rigidly adhered to a "*xie-sheng* principle" of their strict definition which advanced the understanding of OC in their time. But a graph whose phonological interpretation is difficult to reconcile with its phonetic element has led to rather complex reconstructions based on ingenious theories. Although such reconstructions may turn out to be correct, we will here take a step back and transcribe an OC form in a simple way which is compatible with MC and overall Chinese phonological structure, because phonological evolution is expected to be regular; but the reason for the selection of one phonetic element or graph over another can be at the whim of a writer (Qiú Xīguī 2000: 269, quoting Zhèng Xuǎn to that effect). The selection of graphic elements can be on a sliding scale from purely phonetic (as in *jū* 居 *ka 'dwell', phonetic *gǔ* 古 *kâʔ 'old') to semantic (e.g., *jiān* 尖 'pointed': graph for 'small' on top of 'big'). Many graphic choices fall between these ends. The original graph for *xiān* 僊 LH *sian* 'an immortal' has been replaced by the simplified 仙 with *shān* 山 LH *ṣan* 'mountain'; though phonetically close, the simplified graph was probably created and attained currency because immortals were thought to live as recluses in the mountains. In the graph *wèi* 位 MC *jwei*^{C} *w(r)ə(t)s 'position, seat', *lì* 立 MC *ljəp* *rəp 'to stand' (<> PTB *k-rap 'to stand') is often believed to be phonetic, and hence cognate to *wèi*. Yet *lì* would be a prime candidate for a semantic element in a graph for 'position'; hence *wèi* and *lì*, which are phonetically quite different anyway, are not likely to be related. Given these considerations, we will occasionally leave the phonological discrepancy of the phonetic elements an open question.

As far as possible, we will not base OCM forms on etymological considerations. For example, *nèi* 內 MC *nuậi*^{C} 'inside' is written with the phonetic element *rù* 入 MC *ńźjəp* 'enter'; *rù* was apparently OCM *nup, while *nèi* was *nûts. There is not rime and other evidence to suggest that *nèi* had a labial final in OC (*nups). The phonetic *rù* for *nèi* is explained by the transparent etymological relationship beside some similarity in sound. Thus *nèi* was probably *nûps in PCH, but not in OCM. Similarly, we mechanically take MC div. II and retroflex initials back to OCM medial *-r-, even when comparative data suggest that there was no medial. We may reconstitute a phoneme for OC using the comparative method even though CH writing has no trace of it, as in *huǒ* 'fire' and *huǐ* 'snake'. We reconstitute an OC *hm- initial because (1) these words are certainly related to PTB *smey and *(s-)b/m-rul; (2) by default: the graphic elements are unique, they don't belong to a phonetic series which could otherwise have indicated an *m-; and (3) in such cognate sets, every indication is that MC *x*- invariably corresponds to a foreign *sm-*, *hm-*, *km-*, and the like. Therefore, OCM *hmə̂iʔ 'fire' and *hməiʔ (< *hmuiʔ) 'snake'.

OCM differs from Baxter's (OCB) in some ways:

(1) For Baxter's 1992 *ɨ we write *ə, as he does in his recent work.

(2) It is widely believed now that Karlgren's MC div. III yods (medial *-j-*) did not exist in OC (Baxter, Pulleyblank, J. Norman, and others); see §9.1.

(3) For the later tone C (*qùshēng*) Baxter and most investigators add a final *-s to the OC syllable, where Li Fang Kuei used the symbol *-h. We suspect that some words in final OCB *-ts actually had only *-s (see §3.4); consequently *-s cannot be used for tone C with open syllables, therefore we use the symbol *-h, also after velar finals. Thus, OCB *njits, here *nis or *ni(t)s; OCB *njis, here *nih; OCB *tjəks, here *təkh.

(4) We will ignore the finer, more debatable points of Baxter's and others' systems; thus we will retain final *-an where Baxter and Starostin suggest *-ar (though they may well be right).

(5) As in dialect descriptions, all elements in diphthongs are written as vowels, thus *-ai*,

-au, -iu, -iau. A palatal medial thus shows up as *-i-*, not *-j-*. However, after velar initials, the rounded medial is written *w* because the combination represents labiovelars: *kwi, kwaŋ* (for $k^{w}i$, $k^{w}aŋ$), hence *kwi^{B} (k^{w}i^{B}) 癸 vs. *kui^{B} (kuj^{B}) 鬼. When the coda is a dental *-n/t* or *-i*, PCH and OC *o* (as in *-on/t, -oi*) have broken to *-uan/t* and *-uai* in at least some Han dialects and later standard Chinese. This makes the OC origin of a syllable like MC *kuân* ambiguous — it could derive from either *kwan (k^{w}an) or *kon. Baxter has tried to sort these out. When in doubt, we write *kwan/t, *kwai.

12-2 (for item [6])

MC	GSR OC	*R-series	*T-series	*L -series	*J-series	*N-series
t I	t	--	t^ 單	tl^		
t^{h} I	t‘	rh^ 體	th^ 土	lh^ 兔		nh^ 歎
d I	d‘	--	d^ 圖	l^ 途		
n I	n					n^ 奴
ńźj III	ńi̯					n 如
tśj III	ȶi̯	--	t 戰	--	tj, kj 勺	
tś^{h}j III	ȶ‘i̯	--	th 幝	k-hl- 出		
źj III	ȡi̯	--	d 善	--	dj 上	
dźj III	ȡ‘i̯ (rare)	--	m-d ? 晨	m-l 食		
ji- IV	gi̯, di̯, bi̯, zi̯			l 易	j 夜	
śj III	śi̯	--	--	lh 屎	hj ? 聲	nh 菽
s I	s			sl^ 錫		sn^
sj III	si̯			sl 賜		sn 襄
zj III	dzi̯	--	--	s-l 習	s-j 夕	
ţj III	ti̯	--	tr 張	--	--	
ţ^{h}j III	t‘i̯	rh 寵	thr 悵	t-hl 暢		nhr 丑
ḍj III	d‘i̯		dr 長	d-l 場		
ṇj III						nr 女
ṣ II/III	ṣ	sr 史				
l I	l	r^ 禮				
lj III	li̯	r 立				
x- I	x	(hr^)		(hl^ 虎)		(hn^)
xj III	xi̯	(hr)		(hl)		(hn)

Notes for Tables 12-2 and 12-3:
• These tables list relevant MC initials in the left column, Karlgren's *GSR* system for OC in the second, in the rest OCM initial types as reflected in phonetic series (exceptional combinations in parentheses).
• The circumflex after an OC initial indicates later MC div. I/ IV vocalism (no *j*).
• A hyphen distinguishes a pre-initial (or prefix) from an otherwise identical one; e.g., some MC ḍj- are consistently found in L-series (*d-l-), others in T-series (*dr-), hence the ones in L-series cannot have been very prominent dental stops; indeed, the element may have been something quite different, such as a *g, hence perhaps PCH *gl > ḍj.

12-3 (for item [6])

MC	GSR OC	*W-series	*NG-series	*M-series	*N-series	*L-series
N I			ŋ^ 五	m^ 莫	n^ 奴	
Nj III			ŋ 禦	m 無	n 如	
s / sw I	s- / sw		sŋ^ 愬	sm^ 喪	sn^	sl^ 錫
sj / sjw III	si̯ / si̯w	sw 宣			sn 襄	sl 崧
zj / zjw III	dzi̯ / dzi̯w	s-w 檖				s-l 習
ɣw I	gw	w^ 魂				
jw III	gi̯w	w 雲				
x / xw I	x / xw	hw^ 血	hŋ^ 滸	hm^ 荒	hn^ 嫨	hl^ 虎
xj / xjw III	xi̯ / xi̯w	hw 熏	hŋ 許	hm 虺		

(6) OCM consonants and consonant clusters agree with what is conservatively assumed within Baxter's overall framework. Many MC dental and related initials, as well as *x*-, have several OC sources (Yakhontov, Pulleyblank, Li Fang Kuei, Baxter), depending on the OC phonetic series. The different types of phonetic series are presented and compared in Tables 12-2 and 12-3. The distinction between a possible OC J-series and L-series is somewhat elusive, but the tables include suspected MC equivalents.

(7) OCB sets up six vowels: *a, ə, e, i, o, u,* plus diphthongs *aw, aj,* etc., which correspond roughly to Karlgren's *a/o, ə, e, ər, u, ô, og/k, ar/â.*

(8) OCM rimes are as below (OCB writes *-aw for *-au, *-aj for *-ai, etc.; for tone C see item (3) above; a tone-C form is added in the first row for illustration):

a	a(k)h, ak	aŋ, aŋh	/	ai, aih	at, as	an, ans	/	ap	am, ams
ə	ək	əŋ	/	əi	ət, əs	ən	/	əp	əm
e	ek	eŋ	/	–	et, es	en	/	ep	em
i	–	–	/	(i)	it, is	in	/	ip	im
o	ok	oŋ	/	oi	ot, os	on			
u	uk	uŋ	/	ui	ut, us	un			
au	auk								

(9) The following list compares Karlgren's OC in *GSR* with OCM final consonants and rimes; div. I/IV syllables are cited for each rime category:

GSR *-o, *-ag = OCM *-a; except some GSR *-ag in MC tone C
= OCM *-akh (Baxter *-aks), i.e. MC tone C

GSR *-âk, *-âŋ	= OCM *-ak, *-aŋ
GSR *-u, *-ug	= OCM *-o, except some *-u(g) with MC tone C
	= OCM *-okh (Baxter *-oks), i.e. MC tone C
GSR *-uk, *-uŋ	= OCM *-ok, *-oŋ
GSR *-ôg	= OCM *-u, except some *ôg with MC tone C
	= OCM *-ukh (Baxter *-uks), i.e. MC tone C
GSR *-ôk, -ôŋ	= OCM *-uk, *-uŋ
GSR *-og	= OCM *-au (Baxter *-aw); except some *-og with MC tone C
	= OCM *-aukh (Baxter *-awks), i.e. MC tone C
GSR *-ok	= OCM *-auk (Baxter *-awk)
GSR *-eg	= OCM *-e; except some *-eg with MC tone C
	= OCM *-ekh (Baxter *-eks), i.e. MC tone C
GSR *-ek, *eŋ	= OCM *-ek, *-eŋ
GSR *-â, *-âr	= OCM *-ai
GSR *-uâ, *-uâr	= OCM *-oi, except after gutturals also *Kwai; not after labials
GSR *-ât, *-âd, -ân	= OCM *-at, *-a(t)s (Baxter *-ats, and similarly passim), *-an
GSR *-uât, *-uâd, *-uân	= OCM *-ot, *-o(t)s, *-on, except after gutturals also *Kwat etc.; not after labials
GSR *iat, *-ian	= OCM *-et, *-en
GSR *-ət, *-əd, *-ən	= OCM *-ət, *-ə(t)s, *-ən, also after gutturals *Kwət etc.
GSR *-uət, *-uəd, *-uən	= OCM *-ut, *-u(t)s, *-un, after gutturals also *Kwət etc.; not after labials
GSR *-ər	= OCM *-əi or *-i
GSR *-uər	= OCM *-ui; rarely after gutturals also *Kwi; not after labials
GSR *-et, *-en	= OCM *-it, *-in
GSR *-âp, *-âm	= OCM *-ap, *-am
GSR *-iap,*-iam	= OCM *-ep, *-em
GSR *-əp, *-əm	= OCM *-əp or *-əm
GSR *-iəp, *-iəm	= OCM *-ip, *-im

12.1.3 Chinese dialects (= Sinitic languages)

Forms from modern Chinese dialects, or "Sinitic languages," are occasionally provided to illustrate later developments of a word; they are cited following their sources. Dialect forms are referred to by their location (town, village, county); they are here prefixed with a letter that indicates the major group to which a dialect belongs: G = Gàn 贛 (including the city Nánchāng 南昌); K = Kèjiā 客家(Hakka, incl. Méixiàn 梅縣); M = Mǐn 閩 (incl. Xiàmén 夏門 = Amoy, Fúzhōu福州); Mand. = Mandarin; W = Wú 吳 (incl. Shànghǎi 上海, Sūzhōu 蘇州); X = Xiāng 湘 (incl. Chángshā 長沙); Y = Yuè 粵 (Cantonese, incl. Canton = Guǎngzhōu 廣州). Mǐn dialects are of particular interest because of forms which are not the analogues of the QYS of MC. Mǐn dialects apparently split off from the rest of the language, starting with the Qin and Han dynasties (second, even third centuries BC). PMin = Proto-Min = CMin = Common Min are Norman's earlier reconstructions, sometimes with slight amendments, notably: Norman's "softened initials" are marked with a breve, thus *ğ-* or *d̮z-*; his voiceless continuants are marked with a dot, not an 'h', thus *l̥*-, *m̊*-; OCM *h in the initials is reserved for other MC reflexes.

12.2 Jingpo (JP) (= Kachin)

Jingpo is quoted in the phonetic interpretation of Xú Xījiān, Dài Qìngxià, except: *ă* in pre-syllables is replaced by *ə*; *g, b, d* for *k, t, p* in lax syllables; nasals and resonants in tense syllables start with *ʔ-* (*HPTB:* 114f); *r* for *ʒ*; aspiration ʰ. Kachin, the same language as JP, is spelled as in the sources that cite forms from Hanson 1906, or as provided by informants.

In JP, TB medial *r and *l occasionally become *y* after a nasal: *mr- / *ml- > my-. Occasionally, *l > r; thus there exist two forms of the PTB etymon *mlyu[n/k]:

(1) JP mə^{31}-run^{31} 'suck' <> Kanauri *myun 'to swallow', shǔn 吮 [źiun^{B}] *m-ljunʔ ? 'to suck'

(2) JP mə^{31}-yuʔ^{31} < *m-yuk 'throat, swallow' <> Lushai zu^{11} / zuuk^{53} < juʔ/h / juuk 'to drink', PLB *myuk ~ *myuw

PTB *ry- > JP *ts-*, *dź-* (Dai /Xu 1992 96f, 75):

JP mə^{31}-tsat^{55} < m-rjat 'eight'	<> WT brgyad < b-rjat, Lushai pa^{L}-riatF
JP tsa^{33} < rja^{33} 'hundred'	<> WT brgya < b-rja
JP tsap^{55} < rjap 'stand'	<> Mikir arǰap^{L} < rjap^{L}
JP tsiʔ^{55} < rjik 'head louse'	<> Chepang srəyk, Lushai hrik^{11} < hrik

In a few common words, PTB *l corresponds to JP *t* (when preceded by a prefix? See also *HPTB:* 52): JP *ʃiŋ^{31}-teʔ^{55}* 'to shoot' (< *sm-lhek* ? <> → shí 射); JP *ta^{33}* 'month', *ʃə^{33}-ta^{33}* 'moon' < PTB *sla; *mə^{31}-taʔ^{55}* 'lick' < PTB *mlyak (→ shí 食) 'lick'; JP lə^{31}-taʔ^{55} < PTB *lak 'hand' (*HPTB:* 51). JP occasionally lacks TB medial *y: mə^{31}-taʔ^{55}* < PTB *mlyak (→ shí 食), *naʔ* 'night' < PTB *ya.

12.3 Lushai

Lushai (TB - Kuki-Naga [KN] - Kuki-Chin [KC]): some of Lorrain's transcriptions have been replaced by IPA symbols: his *aw* by *ɔ*, final *-h* by *-ʔ*, *ch, chh* are simplified to *č, čʰ* (the symbol x̌ has been added to avoid ambiguities; Weidert 1975 writes *ts-* and *tsh-*), long vowels are doubled (*ʔaar*), and tones are added (a copy of the dictionary with tones marked has been kindly provided by J. A. Matisoff): low tone x^{L}, rising tone x^{R}, high tone x^{H}, falling tone x^{F}; see below for more on tones.

In open syllables and those ending in *-ʔ* (Lorrain's *-h*) these vowels and diphthongs occur:

a, ai, au
ɔ (Lorrain's aw), ɔi (Lorrain's awi), ui, o, u, ua, iu
e, ei̯, i, iai

In closed syllables we find:

aC	eC	iC	iaC
	ɔC	uC	uaC

In wfs vowels interchange with each other, e.g., *puam^{H}* 'be full grown (but not ripe), to swell (of fruit)' ⋊ *pum^{F}* < *pumʔ* 'be filled out (as fruit)'.

A closed syllable can end in a consonant *k, ŋ, t, n, p, m, l, r, ʔ*. These correspond usually to their counterparts in other TB languages: *-ʔ* is derived (1) from *-h* which in turn derives from final *-s*; (2) a final *-ʔ* < *-ʔ* can be reconstructed on the basis of tones (Ostapirat 1998). Lushai has occcasionally *-k* for WT *-t* (*STC* p. 101–102).

The initial consonants are the same as in TB, in addition and including *z-* < *j-, *h-*, *v-*, *ʔ-*.

PTB *s- and *z- have become t^h- in Lushai and related languages, also as s-prefixes: Ukhrul *thărik* 'pheasant' < *s-rik*, Mikir *the-rák* 'shy' < *s-rak*, hence Lushai t^h*la* 'moon' < *s-la* or k^h*la*. In some words, Lushai has apparently unaspirated *t* for PTB *z-, occasionally also for *s-. Weidert (1987: 286) cites Lushai (L.) *tuʔ* 'to plant' for Tamang *'su'-*. Also:

L. tee^R / teet^F 'to be small': ST *zi: xì 細 (siei^C) [se^C (or sei^C)], *sîh or *sêh 'thin, small'; PTB *ziy > West Tib. zi 'very small'; WB se^B 'small, fine'; Kachin zi 'small'

L. teei^L < teeis 'myself, thyself...': ST *si or *zi: sī 私 (si^B) [si^B] *siʔ 'private, egotistic'

L. tu... 'who': ? PTB *su: WT su 'who'

L. tu^F 'grandchild': ST *su ? PTB *su(w) 'grandchild'

L. tuuk^F 'early morning': sù 夙 [siuk] *suk 'early morning'; PLB *C-sok ~ *V-sok 'morning, morrow'

L. tin^R 'nail, claw': WT sen-mo 'finger- or toe-nail'

TB medial *r* and *l* are lost in the configurations of some initials; otherwise TB clusters with *r* and *l* show up as *ṭ-*, $ṭ^h$- and *tl-*, t^hl-.

Lushai has preserved TB final laterals *-r* and *-l*; however, in some words *-l has been replaced by *-i* as in many other languages (loans from elsewhere?):

'face'	hmel^H	vs.	hmai^R	PTB *s-mel; cf. Tiddim mai
'pass over'	–		kai	WT rgal
'gums'	–		hni	PTB *s/r-nil

But regular:

'kidney'	kal^R		PTB *kal
'snake'	ruul	–	PTB *s-b-rul

Reconstructed Lushai final *-ʔ shows some correlation with Chepang and OC final *-ʔ (MC tone B); Lushai *-h correlates with *-s (Ostirapat *LTBA* 21:1, 1998); ambiguous finals (short vowels ending in -ʔ low tone) are symbolized by *-H (Lushai form first, after the graph is the LHan Chinese form):

ai^R < aiʔ 'crab', PTB *d-ka:y <> xiè 蟹gɛ^B
tui^R < tuiʔ 'water' <> tì 涕tʰei$^{B/C}$ 'tears'
hlai^R < hlaiʔ 'to flay, to skin, split', Chep kləyh-sa <> chǐ, chí 誃 tśʰiɑi^B, ḍɑi 'to separate'
bai^R < baiʔ 'walk lame' <> bǒ 跛pɑi^B 'walk lame'
in^L-hnai^R < hnaiʔ 'near' <> ěr 邇 ńe^B
pa^F < paaʔ 'father' <> fù 父 buɑ^B
sa^H-khi^L < saa-khiH 'barking deer' <> OCjǐ 麂 kɨ^B 'muntjac'
hrui^R < hruiʔ 'a creeper, cane, rope, cord, string' <> lěi 櫐 lui^B 'creepers, liana'
kʰaar^R < khaarʔ 'to buy in large quantities' <> gǔ 賈 kɑ^B 'to sell, buy'
kʰaar^R < khaarʔ 'dam or weir, roughly constructed of leafy bows or bamboo lattice-work (sometimes used for catching fish)' <> hù / gǔ 滬 / 罟 gɑ^B / kɑ^B 'weir, fish stakes for catching fish / net'
peer^L / perʔ^L < peerʔ / perh 'flat and wide', PTB *pe:r <> biǎn 扁 pen^B 'flat and thin'
bel^F < beelʔ ? 'to cause to or make wear, put on (garment, load , plaster...)' <> bèi 被 bɨɑi$^{B/C}$ 'to cover, incl. putting on clothes'
kalʔ^L < kalH 'to wrench, plait, lock' <> jiàn 楗 gɨɑn^B 'door bar, bolt'

k^{h}el^{F} < kheelʔ 'eat the outside of a thing, gnaw off' <> kěn 齦k^{h}ən^{B} 'gnaw'
sil^{R} < silʔ 'wash' <> xǐ 洗洒sei^{C} 'wash'

However, in many cognate sets the finals *-ʔ and *-h/s (LHan -^{B} and -^{C}) do not agree:

pi^{H} < pii 'grandmother' <> bǐ 妣pi^{B}, pi^{C} 'deceased mother, ancestress' (here a CH addition)
ʔi^{L} < ʔiH 'this' <> yī 伊 ʔi 'this'
hri:^{F} < hriiʔ ? 'evil spirit that causes sickness' <> chī 魑离螭ṭ^{h}iai 'mountain demon'

Lushai, like Tani and some other languages, has occasionally initial r- for PTB *l-:

KN *rit > Lushai rit^{L} / riʔ^{L} < rit / rih 'be heavy' <> PTB *s-ləy 'heavy' > WT lči-ba < lhyi; Kanauri li-ko 'heavy', Lepcha lí, lím, PL *C-li^{2} > WB le^{B}
riŋ <> PTB *liŋ 'field', but Kanauri also riŋ

Lushai has borrowed many words from MK languages, e.g., Lushai *ŋho^{L}* 'tusk'; note PVM *ŋà, also in CH → yá$_{1}$ 牙.

12.4 Mikir

Mikir final consonants, including *-y (< -l), -r*, can occur with any of the five vowels *a, e, i, o, u;* there is no *-iy* ; in open syllables, TB final *-a* has shifted to *-o*. Before final *-m*, TB *a* has shifted to *e* ~ *i* (*STC*:70).

Although it appears that any final consonant can follow any vowel, the distribution is uneven: -iC and -uC are not as common as -eC and -oC. Words inherited from TB have merged -iC with -eC and -uC with -oC, with only few exceptions.

TB initial *s-* shows up as Mikir *s-* or *th-* (as in Lushai), perhaps also as *č(h)-*.

Mikir has three tones (Grüßner's tone accents): á high tone, here rendered symbolically as x^{H}; ā level, here x^{M}; à low, here x^{L}.

12.5 Tai

Tai languages are cited per Li Fang Kuei's publications, Siamese occasionally according to McFarland. Tai tones are marked A1 (voiceless initial), A2 (voiced initial), and so on: B, C, D. Note that in loans Tai tone B corresponds to Chinese tone C and vice versa.

In some words, Tai has initial or medial *l* for OC initial or medial *r*; see §7.3. Occasionally, Tai has two forms with different vowels where Chinese has only one form:

S. *k^{h}lai^{1} < gl-* 'to untwist, unroll, disentangle ~ *k^{h}li^{3} < gli* 'to unfold, unfurl'
<> jiě 解 [kɛ^{B}] *krêʔ
PTai *g-: S. *k^{h}ɛɛp^{D2} < g-* 'narrow' ~ *k^{h}aap < g-* 'narrow'
<> xiá 狹 (ɣăp) [gɛp] *grêp 'narrow'
S. *kɔɔk < gɔɔk* 'pen, enclosure' ~ *kuk^{6} < g-* 'prison'
<> gù 牿 (kuok) [kouk] *kûk 'pen, stable'

Some Tai (Siamese) syllables are indicative of a foreign origin of a word (Gedney *CAAAL* 6, 1976: 65 ff). Siamese vowels inherited from PTai are CeC, CoC, CɛɛC, CɔɔC from *e, *o and *ee, *oo respectively. Innovative vowels are CeeC, CooC, and CɛC, CɔC. Final *ʔ* found in some Tai words is not historical, thus S. *thɔʔ^{2}* 'rabbit' must be a CH loan.

12.6 Tibeto-Burman (TB)

See Matisoff *Handbook of Proto-Tibeto-Burman* and *STC* for details. Final consonants are: k, p, t, ŋ, m, n, s, r, l, (y, w).

TB initial consonants within each set below alternate within wfs and between languages, just as in Chinese:

k ~ g	ŋ ~ hŋ	r ~ hr
p ~ b	m ~ hm	w ~ hw
t ~ d	n ~ hn	l ~ hl
s ~ z ~ ts ~ dz		y ~ hy

TB has preserved *z- (based on WT) which has merged with *s- in OC. The palatal affricates in ST daughter languages are thought to derive from *ty-, *dy- with either primary or secondary *y*. The working premise here assumes the following ST proto-vowels: *i, u, e, ə, o, a* (*ə has been preserved only in CH). The precise correlation of many TB diphthongs with OC still needs to be worked out.

12.7 Tiddim Chin

Tiddim Chin is a Kuki-Chin language that is close to Lushai. Tones are as follows:

low rising	= 1 = R	
level	= 2 = M	
high falling	= 3 = F	
low (falling)	= 3 (4)	= L (only in checked short syllables)

12.8 Written Burmese (WB)

WB follows the conventions used in the publications of Benedict and Matisoff. Affricates are rendered as c, c^h; however, here tones are marked by letters: A unmarked, B for breathy tone (â = a^B), C for creaky tone (a' = a^C).

The distribution of finals in WB is not symmetrical:

a	wa	o	u	ui	wai	i	e	we
ak	wak	ok		uik		ac		
aŋ	waŋ	oŋ		uiŋ		añ		
at	wat		ut			it		
an	wan		un			in		
ap	wap		up			ip		
am	wam		um			im		

12.9 Written Tibetan (WT)

The transcription is self-explanatory, except the coronals are *ts, ts^h, dz, s, z,* and *č, $č^h$, ǰ, ñ, š, ž* where the diacritics are added to avoid confusion with other transcriptions in which *c* may stand for *ts*; *'a-$č^h$uŋ* is written with an apostrophe (§4.6; Coblin 2002), *ʔa-$č^h$en* (glottal stop) with the IPA symbol *ʔ*. The vowels are *a, e, i, o, u;* there are no diphthongs.

Consonants:
k, k^h, g, ŋ, ʔ, 'x (*'a-čhung*)
č, $č^h$, ǰ, ñ, š, ž
t, t^h, d, n
ts, ts^h, dz, s, z
p, p^h, b, m
r, l, y (w rare, secondary?)

Some WT peculiarities:

(1) Voiced Pre-Tibetan *l* and *r* develop an epenthetic *d* after *'a-čʰuŋ*: N-*lag* > *ldag*, N-*ro* > *'dro* (Li Fang Kuei 1959).

Voiceless TB or Pre-Tibetan *l* and *r* develop an epenthetic *t: lhuŋ* pf. of *ltuŋ* < N-*lhuŋ*; *ltam* 'speech' <> Mikir *lam*.

The medial palatal glide *y* becomes devoiced when preceded by a voiceless consonant: *lče* 'tongue' < *lhçe* < *lhje* < *lhe*. The letter / sound combination *rǰi* and *rči* does not exist in WT; the affricates are instead de-palatalized, thus *rtsib* < *rhçip* < *rhjip* < *rhip* 'ribs'.

(2) Initial *y*- derives sometimes from vocalic ingress, also after loss of *w-; note the doublets *'og* ~ *yog* 'below', *'oŋ* ~ *yoŋ* 'to come' < *waŋ*; Chepang *wəyʔ* ~ *huy* 'blood', Magari *hyu* < *hwi*, Vayu *vi* ⋈ WT *yi* in *yi(d)-dam* 'oath' ⋈ *yid* 'sould, mind' (*STC* no. 222). Accordingly, WT *yur-ma* 'the act of weeding' is cognate to *yún* 耘 (jwən) [wun] *wən 'to weed' < ST *wur. In light of these equations, it is possible to connect *yǒu* 有 *wəʔ 'have' ⋈ WT *yod-pa* 'be, have' < ST *wəC; *yòu* 右 *wəh 'right' (side) ⋈ WT *g-yas* 'id.' < *wəs*; *yǒu* 友 *wəʔ 'friend, companion' ⋈ WT *ya* 'associate, companion, assistant' < ST *wə; *yóu* 尤 *wə 'guilt, fault, blame' ⋈ WT *yus* 'blame, charge' < ST *wu; *guǎng* 廣 *kwâŋʔ 'broad, wide', Lushai *vaaŋ*^{F} < *vaaŋʔ* 'be large, extensive' ⋈ WT *yaŋ* 'wide, broad, large' < ST *(C-)waŋʔ.

(3) Some WT words have the vowel *o* where all other languages consistently have *a* or its equivalent, from both ST *a and *ə (§11.1.1). *STC* reconstructs in such words PTB *â, others assume an earlier *wa. Here we treat this provisionally as a WT innovation: *lo* 'year' < *lop* (PTB *lap 'leaves, foliage'), *tsʰom* 'hair' <> PTB *tsam.

(4) TB and ST final *-op* lose the final consonant, thus resulting in an open syllable in WT, e.g., *lo* 'year', *lo-ma* 'leaf' = West Tib. *lob(-ma)* < *lop* (PTB *lap 'leaves, foliage'); *glo-ba* 'side' < *glop* (cf. TB words of similar shape for 'lungs'), *'ǰo-ba* 'to milk' < PTB *dzop 'to suck, to milk'. Words which belong to a verbal paradigm keep the final *-b: slob-pa, bslabs* 'to learn'.

(5) WT has a few words with initial *dr*- (without the usual prefix) where other TB languages have *kr*- (*gr*-); it seems that in these words WT *d*- itself is historically a prefix: WT *dr*- in *drug* 'six', *drub* 'to sew', *dri-ma* 'dirt, filth, excrement', *drum* 'to long, desire', *drel* 'mule', *dro* 'warm', *dom* 'bear', and perhaps *d*- in *du-ba* 'smoke' (*C-wu ?); compare WB *kʰrok* 'six', *kʰjup* < *kʰr*- 'sew', *kre*^{B} 'dirty', *ə-kʰje*^{B} 'dirt', *kʰrum* 'pine away', and the widely encountered form *ku* (*kʰu*, etc.) for 'smoke'.

In addition, WT *dr*- probably reflects earlier *dr-: WT *'dren-ba, draŋ(s)* 'to draw, drag, pull, draw tight (a rope)', PLB *raŋ 'draw, pull, drag'; cognates might be JP *kren*^{33} 'to tighten (a rope)', WB *kraŋ*^{C} 'tense, tight'.

(6) WT occasionally has initial *r*- for other languages' initial *l*-; see, for example, → *zhù* 羜 (ḍjwoᴮ) 'lamb', → *zhù* 苧紵 (ḍjwoᴮ) 'ramie', *yì* 裔 'posterity' (under *yè* 葉).

(7) Earlier medial *-w- is lost in WT (see also §10.2):

Dog	WT kʰyi < kʰi < PTB *kwi → quǎn 犬
To rest	WT ŋal-ba < ST *ŋwal → wò 臥 [ŋuɑiᶜ] *ŋôih or *ŋuâih
To rest	WT rnal-ba < ST *nwal → suī 綏 [sui] *snui
Tense	WT nar-mo < ST *nwar ('tensed'?:) 'oblong'

APPENDIX A
LANGUAGES AND LANGUAGE FAMILIES IN EAST ASIA

Since prehistoric times, Chinese has interacted with the ancestors of TB, MY, KT, and AA languages. There has also been (indirect?) contact with AN, IE, and others. Therefore, languages from several families will be cited throughout this dictionary. The TB languages are usually the best documented and most extensively researched ones.

(A) **Sino-Tibetan** (ST)
Together with the Tibeto-Burman (TB) branch, Chinese forms the Sino-Tibetan language family, with which it shares its oldest stratum of lexical items and morphology.

(1) *Chinese*
The Chinese (or Sinitic) branch has today evolved into seven major "dialect" groups, actually "Sinitic languages," which began to diverge during the Han period (ca. 200 BC and after), but most dialects can be traced back to the more recent Tang Dynasty (ca. 600–900) (Norman 1988: ch. 8–9).

Proto-Chinese (PCH), i.e., pre-literate Chinese >

> Old Chinese (OC) from the beginning of writing during the late Shang dynasty about 1250 BC down to the Han period (206 BC-AD 220); OC is sometimes subdivided into Early Zhou Chinese (EZC), Early Archaic Chinese, Late Archaic Chinese.

OC > Old Southern dialect > oldest stratum of modern southern dialects (all south of the Yangtze River), represented especially in Mǐn 閩 (in Fújiàn 福建 incl. Amoy = Xiàmén 夏門, Fúzhōu 福州, Cháozhōu 潮州, Cháoyáng 潮陽, Jiàn'ōu 建甌, Jiànyáng 建陽), but has also left traces in Wú 吳 (incl. Shànghǎi 上海, Wēnzhōu 溫州, Sūzhōu 蘇州); Gàn 贛 (incl. Nánchāng 南昌); Xiāng 湘 (incl. Chángshā 長沙); Kèjiā 客家 (= Hakka, incl. Méixiàn 梅縣); Yuè 粵 ("Cantonese" in Guǎngdōng 廣東 and Guǎngxī 廣西, incl. Guǎngzhōu 廣州, Táishān 台山, Zhōngshān 中山).

> Middle Chinese (MC, QYS) ("ancient Chinese," ca. AD 600)
MC > northern dial. > modern Mandarin dialects;
> southern dialects: Wú, Gàn, Xiāng, Kèjiā (Hakka), Yuè; Mǐn (especially literary layer)

(2) *Tibeto-Burman* (TB)
The classification of some TB languages is still a matter of debate. The following selective list is based on Shafer (IST), Benedict (STC), Matisoff, ed. 1995: 183f, Burling 2003: 169ff, as well as various specialized studies. Scholars combine the following branches, groups, subgroups, and isolates in different ways. The languages below are only those frequently mentioned in the dictionary.

> Tibetan: Old Tibetan, Written Tibetan (WT) > Tib. dialects (in Tibet, SE China, Himalayas): Amdo (NE), Kham (E), Central Tibetan (Lhasa, Ngari); Western Tibetan dialects (WTib.): Balti, Purik, Ladak (Leh), Zangskar; Dzongkha (Bhutan), Sherpa (Nepal).

> West Himalayish: Kanauri (Kanauri in NW India), incl. Almora, Bunan, Chitkuli, Lahuli, Thebor, Manchati, Spilo
> Ts(h)angla-Takpa: Cuona Monpa (or Takpa), Motuo Monpa (Tsangla, Cangluo) (NE India, China)
> Tamang-Gurung-Thakali-Manangba (TGTM, in Nepal)
> Bahing-Vayu (= Kiranti, in Nepal): Vayu (Hayu), Bahing, Limbu
> Chepang (Nepal)
> Bodo-Garo (BG, Baric) (NE India)
> Northern Naga = Konyak (NE India)
> Jingpo (JP ~ Kachin, in SW China, N Burma, Assam)
> Kuki-Chin (KC, in NW India, SE Asia): Lushai (Lush., Mizo), Lai, Lakher, Old Kuki lgs., Khami, Pangkua, Tiddim Chin, Siyin; Thado, Anal, Rankhol (= Mishmi) (NE India, Burma)
> Naga: Ao, Angami, Zeme, Tangkhul (= Mishmi) (NE India)
> Mikir (= Mishmi) (NE India)
> Lepcha (= Rong) (Sikkim)
> Limbu (Nepal)
> Meitei (Manipuri) (= Mishmi) (NE India)
> Tani (Abor-Miri-Dafla) (= Mishmi) (NE India), also Adi
> Idu-Digaru / Taraon-Miju / Kaman (= Mishmi) (NE India)
> Dulong (= Trung), Rawang; Nung
> Lolo-Burmese (LB, in SE China, NW Laos, N Thailand, N Burma), Written Burmese (WB, in Burma), Atsi (Zaiwa), Achang (Yunnan, Burma); Lolo lgs. (= Yi, in SW China, SE Asia), incl. Lahu, Lisu, Akha
> Other: Mru; Tangut; Qiang (SE China); Gyarong (= rGyal-rung, JR) (SE China)
> Karen (in Burma)

(B) **Kadai** languages
See Edmondson 1988, including proposals for classification (p. 180).

Kadai
> Kam-Tai (KT)
> Kam, Sui, Mak, Saek (in S and SE China)
> Tai lgs. (in SE China, SE Asia, Assam): Siamese (S., in Thailand) [Li Fangkuei]
> Proto-Kra (Ostapirat): Gelao, Lachi, Laha (Laqua), Paha, Pubiao, Buyang
> Other: Li (Hlai), Be (on Hainan)

(C) **Miao-Yao** (MY = Hmong-Mien)
> Miao (= Hmong, in S and SE China, SE Asia)
> Yao (= Mien, in S and SE China, SE Asia)

(D) **Austroasiatic** (AA) languages are today distributed from central India to Vietnam and even SW China. They must have extended all the way to SE China in prehistoric and early historic times because the word 'Jiāng' in 'Yangtze River' is the AA word for 'river'. For description and classification, see Diffloth 1974.

Austroasiatic [Pinnow]
> (1) Muṇḍā family: incl. Santhālī, Khaṛiā, Sora (mostly in E India)

> (2) Mon-Khmer (MK) family:
- > Khasian branch: Khasi (NE India)
- > Palaunic branch, incl. Palaung, Wa (Burma and across the border in China)
- > Khmuic branch, incl. Khmu (Vietnam, Laos, Cambodia)
- > Pakanic branch (S China)
- > Vietic branch, incl. Viet-Muong, Vietnamese, Muong
- > Katuic branch (Vietnam, Laos)
- > Bahnaric branch (Vietnam, Laos, Cambodia)
- > Pearic branch (Thailand, Cambodia)
- > Khmeric branch, incl. Khmer (Cambodia), Old Khmer
- > Monic branch, incl. Mon, Old Mon, Nyah Kur (Burma, Thailand)
- > Aslian branch (Thailand, but mostly the Malay peninsula): incl. Semai, Jah Hut
- > Nicobarese branch (Nicobar Islands, India)

Other language families with little contact with Chinese:

Austronesian (AN)
Altaic, incl. Mongolian, Turkic, Manchu
Indo-European (IE), especially Tokharian A and B (in China: Sinkiang Province), Indo-Iranian

APPENDIX B

ALPHABETIC LIST OF FREQUENTLY CITED LANGUAGES

Following a language, the author of publication(s) which served as a source for lexical and other material is indicated. Alternatively, sources are cited under the dictionary entries. Major sources are: *STC, HPTB, IST, HST*; for Chinese dialects, they are publications by Běijīng Dàxué and professional journals, especially *Fāngyán.*

AA = Austroasiatic
Adi (Abor-Miri-Dafla, Tani) / TB—J. Sun
Ahom / Tai
A-li = Ngari
Almora / Western Himalaya / TB—Sharma
Amdo / Tibetan / TB
Amoy = Xiàmén 夏門 / Mǐn 閩 / Chinese
AN = Austronesian
Angami / KN / TB
Aslian / MK / AA—G. Benjamin
Austroasiatic (AA)—Pinnow 1959
Austronesian (AN)—Dempwolff 1938; Sagart 1993
Bahing / Bahing-Vayu (BV) / TB
Bahnar / MK / AA—K. D. Smith
Balti / Tibetan / TB
Barish = Bodo
Bawm / KN / TB—Löffler 1985
Be / Kadai—Hansell 1988
BG = Bodo-Garo
Bo'ai (Boai, Po-ai) / Tai—Li F.
Bodo-Garo (BG), Proto-Bodo, Proto-Koch / TB—Burling 1959
Bumthang / Tibetan / TB—Michailovski
Bunan / Kanauri / TB
Burmese, Written Burmese (WB) / TB—Benedict 1940
BV = Bahing-Vayu / TB
Cantonese = Yuè
Chángshā 長沙 / Xiāng 湘 / Chinese
Cháoyáng 潮陽 / Mǐn / Chinese
Cháozhōu 潮州 / Mǐn / Chinese
Chepang / BV / TB—Caughley
Chinese / ST
Chitkuli / Kanauri / TB
Chrau / MK
Fúzhōu 福州 / Mǐn / Chinese
Gàn 贛 / Chinese
Garo / Bodo-Garo / TB—Burling
Gloskad / Tibetan / TB
Guǎngzhōu 廣州 = Cantonese / Yue / Chinese
Gurung / TGTM / TB—Mazaudon
Gyarung = Jiarong (rGyalrung = JR)
Hakka = Kèjiā 客家 / Chinese
Hlai = Li / Kadai—Matisoff 1988; Thurgood 1991
Hmong-Mien = Miao-Yao
Indo-European (IE)—Pokorny 1959; Buck 1949
Indonesian / AN
Jah Hut /MK / Aslian / AA
Jiarong (rGyalrung = JR) / TB
Jingpo (JP) / TB—Xú Xī-jiān et al. 1983; Dai Qingxia and Xú Xī-jiān 1992
JP = Jingpo
JR = Jiarong
Kachin ~ Jingpo
Kadai (KD)
Kam-Sui (KS) / Kadai—Edmondson and Yang 1988; Thurgood 1988
Kamarupan / TB languages of Assam
Kanauri / TB—Sharma 1989–1992
Karen / TB—*STC*; Burling; Solnit
KD = Kadai
Kèjiā 客家 = Hakka / Chinese
Khami lgs. / KN / TB—Löffler 1960
Khams / Tibetan / TB
Kharia / Munda / AA—Pinnow 1959
Khasi / MK / AA
Khmer / MK / AA—Jenner and Pou; Jacob
Khmu / MK / AA
Khumi lgs. / KN / TB—Löffler 1960
KN = Kuki-Chin-Naga / TB
KS = Kam-Sui / Kam-Tai / Kadai
KT = Kam-Tai / Kadai
Kuki-Chin / KN / TB—Ono Toru 1965; Shafer 1952 (see Old Kuki = OKuki)
Ladakh / Tibetan / TB
Lahuli / Kanauri / TB

Lai / KN / TB—*LTBA* 20:1 (1997) and 21:1 (1998), various authors
Lakher / KN / TB—R. A. Lorrain 1949
LB = Lolo-Burmese
Leh / Ladakh / Tibetan / TB
Lepcha / TB—Mainwaring 1898
Limbu / Bahing-Vayu / TB—Michailovsky
Lolo-Burmese (LB) / TB—Matisoff 1972; Bradley 1979
Longzhou / Tai—Li Fang Kuei
Lushai / KN / TB—J. H. Lorrain 1940; Hillard 1975; Solnit 1978; Weidert
Malay / AN
Manangba / TGTM / TB—Mazaudon
Manchati / Kanauri / TB
Mandarin (Mand.) / Chinese
Méixiàn 梅縣 / Kèjiā / Chinese
Miao-Yao (MY = Hmong-Mian)—Purnell 1970; *LTBA* 10:2 (1987); Wang Fushi (WFS) 1995
Middle Chinese (MC = *Qieyun* system QYS)—Karlgren; Li Fang-kuei
Mien = Yao / MY
Mikir / TB—Grüßner 1978
Mǐn 閩 / Chinese
MK = Mon-Khmer / AA
Mon / MK / AA—Shorto 1971; Diffloth 1984
Mon-Khmer (MK) / AA
Monpa / TB—Sun Hongkai 1980
Mru / TB—Löffler 1966
Munda / AA
Muong / Viet-Muong / MK
Naga / KN / TB—Shafer 1950, 1953
Nánchāng 南昌 / Gàn 贛 / Chinese
Ngari = Mnga-ris, A-li / Tibetan / TB
Nocte / NNaga / TB
Northern Naga / TB —French
Nung / TB
Nyah Kur / MK / Monic / AA—Diffloth 1984
Old Chinese (OC)—Karlgren 1957; Baxter 1992; Schuessler 1987; Unger 1989
Old Kuki (OKuki) / KN / TB—Shafer 1952
Old Tibetan (OTib.) / TB—Li and Coblin 1987
Paang(khua) / KN / TB—Löffler 1985
Palaung / MK / AA—Diffloth
Pear, Pearic / MK / AA—Headley 1977, 1978
Proto-Kra / Kadai—Ostapirat 2000
Proto-Min / Chinese—Norman
Proto-Monic / MK / AA—Diffloth 1984
Purik / Tibetan / TB
Rawang / Nungish / TB
Rgyarung = Jiarong (rGyalrung = JR)
S. = Siamese
Semai / Aslian / MK / AA
Sherpa / Tibetan / TB
Siamese / Tai / KT
Sino-Tibetan (ST)—Benedict 1972; Bodman 1980; Coblin 1986; LaPolla 1994; Peiros and Starostin 1996; R. Shafer 1974
Sino-Vietnamese
Siyin Chin / KC / TB—Stern
Spilo Kanauri / Kanauri / TB—Bodman
ST = Sino-Tibetan
Stieng / MK
SV = Sino-Vietnamese
Tai / Kam-Tai—Li Fang-kuei 1976, 1977; Manomaivibool 1975
Táishān 台山 / Yue / Chinese
Tamang-Gurung-Thakali-Manangba (TGTM) / TB—Mazaudon
Tani (= Abor-Miri-Dafla) / TB—J. Sun
Tankhul / KN / TB
TB = Tibeto-Burman
TGTM = Tamang-Gurung-Thakali-Manangba
Thakali / TGTM / TB—Mazaudon
Tibetan, Written Tibetan (WT) / TB—Jaeschke; Beyer 1992
Tibeto-Burman (TB)—*STC*; *HPTB*; *IST*, *HST*; Huang Bufan 1992; Anon., *Zang-Mian...* 1991
Tiddim Chin / KN / TB—Ostapirat 1998; Henderson
Vayu = Hayu / Bahing-Vayu (BV) / TB
Viet-Muong / MK / AA—Ferlus 1991/1997; Thompson 1976
Wa / MK / AA—Diffloth 1980
WB = Written Burmese / LB / TB
Wēnzhōu (Wenzh) 溫州 / Wu / Chinese
WT = Written Tibetan / TB
Wú 吳 / Chinese
Wuming / Tai—Li Fang Kuei
Xiàmén 夏門 = Amoy / Mǐn / Chinese
Xiāng 湘 / Chinese
Yuè 粵 / Chinese
Zangskar / Tibetan / TB
Zhangzhung / Himalayish / TB
Zhōngshān 中山 / Yuè and Kèjiā / Chinese

APPENDIX C

TEXT SOURCES FOR EARLIEST OCCURRENCES

The text source of a word's earliest occurrences is taken from *GSR*, although on occasion this needed revision, as suggested by Pan Wuyun 1997. This abbreviated reference to a text is found in brackets. The list below indicates the period from which a text comes, but most texts are of a heterogeneous nature and stem from different periods; therefore the periods provided are only a rough approximation. More information on many of the Han and pre-Han texts can be found in Michael Loewe, ed., *Early Chinese Texts, a Bibliographical Guide*, 1993.

Periods:	Shāng	–1050 BC
	Western Zhōu	1050–770 BC
	Chūnqiū	772–481 BC
	Zhànguó	481 or 403–221 BC
	Qín	221–206 BC
	Hàn	206 BC–AD 220
	Former Han	206 BC–AD 8
	Later Han	AD 25–220

[BI] bronze inscriptions (金文) of the Western Zhou period (ca. 1050–770 BC)
[Chu(ci)] Chǔcí 楚辭 (Former Han)
[Chun(qiu)] Chūnqiū春秋(Qunqiu)
[Duan] Duàn Yùcái 段玉裁 (1735–1815), commentator of the *SW*
[EY] Eryǎ 爾雅 (Han) — commentator Guō Pú
[FY] Fāngyán 方言 by Yáng Xióng 揚雄 (Han 53 BC–AD 18) — commentator Guō Pú
[Gongyang] Gōngyáng zhuàn 公羊傳 (Zhanguo)
[Guan] Guǎnzǐ 管子 (Zhanguo)
[Guliang] Gǔliáng zhuàn 穀梁傳(Han)
[Guoce] see Zhanguo(ce) (Zhanguo)
[Guoyu] Guóyǔ 國語 (Zhanguo)
[GY] Guǎngyùn 廣韻 (rime dictionary, 1011, ed. Chén Péngnián)
[Hanfei] Hánfēizǐ 韓非子(Han)
[Hanshu] Hànshū
[Hou Hanshu] Hòu Hànshū
[Huainan] Huáinánzǐ 淮南子 (Han)
[JDSW] Jīngdiǎn shìwén 經典釋文 by Lù Démíng 陸德明 (556–627)
[JY] Jíyùn 集韻 (rime dictionary by Dīng Dù 990–1053)
[Lao] Lǎozǐ 老子, Dàodé jīng 道德經 (Zhanguo)
[Li] Lǐjì 禮記 (Han) — commentator Zhèng Xuán
[Lie] Lièzǐ 列子 (Han)
[Lun(yu)] Lùnyǔ 論語 (Zhanguo) — commentator Zhèng Xuán
[Lü] Lǚshì chūnqiū 呂氏春秋 (Qin- Han)
[Meng] Mèngzǐ 孟子 (Zhanguo)
[Mo] Mòzǐ 墨子 (Zhanguo)
[Mu (tianzi)] Mù tiānzǐ zhuàn 穆天子傳 (ca. 350 BC)
[OB] oracle bone inscriptions (jiǎgǔwén 甲骨文) of the Shang period (ca. 1250–1050 BC)

[QY]	Qièyùn 切韻 (AD 601) by Lù Fǎyán (rime dictionary)
[Shanhai]	Shānhǎijīng 山海經 (Han) — commentator Guō Pú
[Shi]	Shījīng 詩經 (ca. 1050–600 BC) — commentator Zhèng Xuán Guófēng: the latest section Xiǎoyǎ: from Western Zhou court Dàyǎ: early Zhou, Western Zhou Zhōu sòng: Western Zhou Lǔ sòng: rather late, 7th cent. BC Shāng sòng: rather late, 7th cent. BC
[Shiji]	Sīmǎ Qiān 司馬遷, Shǐjì 史記
[Shiming]	Shì míng 釋名 by Liú Xī 劉熙 (Eastern Han, ca. AD 200)
[Shu]	Shūjīng 書經, Shāngshū 尚書 (Western Zhou, Zhanguo, Qin) — commentator Zhèng Xuán
[SM]	Shìmíng 釋名 see [Shiming]
[SW]	Shuōwén jiězì 説文解字, completed AD 100, presented AD 121 (Xǔ Shèn 許慎, ca. 55–ca. 149) — commentator Duàn Yùcái
[Xun]	Xúnzǐ 荀子 (Zhanguo)
[Yi]	Yìjīng 易經 (Western Zhou and later additions and commentaries) — commentator Zhèng Xuán
[YJ]	Yùnjìng 韻鏡 (Song period rime table)
[Yili]	Yílǐ 儀禮 (Zhanguo, Han) — commentator Zhèng Xuán
[Yi Zhou]	Yì Zhōushū 逸周書 (Western Zhou and later)
[Yùpiān]	dictionary, ca. 6th cent. AD
[Zhanguo]	Zhànguócè 戰國策 (Zhanguo, Han)
[Zhouli]	Zhōulǐ 周禮 (Zhanguo, Han) — commentator Zhèng Xuán
[Zhuang]	Zhuāngzǐ 莊子 (Zhanguo, Former Han)
[Zuo]	Zuǒzhuàn 左傳 (Zhanguo or Han)

COMMENTATORS:

Duàn Yùcái 段玉裁 (1735–1815), commentator for *SW*
Guō Pú 郭璞 (276–342), commentator for *FY*, *EY*, Shānhǎijīng
Lù Démíng 陸德明 (556–627) *Jīngdiǎn shìwén* 經典釋文
Zhèng Xuán 鄭玄 (Eastern / Later Han 127–200), commentator for *Zhōulǐ, Yílǐ, Lǐjì, Shījīng, Shūjīng, Lùnyǔ*

REFERENCES

Note: This bibliographical list does not include items, usually periodical articles, which are mentioned only once or a few times; full references are provided where they are cited, but for the sake of brevity, without the title. They can still be traced with the other information. This list includes only works cited, not those that also have been consulted.

Anon. 1991. *Zàng-Miǎnyǔ yǔyīn hé cíhuì* 藏緬語語音詞彙. Beijing.

Aronoff, Mark, and Frank Anshen. 1998. Morphology and the Lexicon: Lexicalization and Productivity. In Spencer and Zwicky, 237–247.

Bauer, Robert. 1987. "In search of Austro-Tai strata in Southern Chinese dialects." *CAAAL* 28: 53–65.

Baxter, William H. 1977. *Old Chinese origins of the Middle Chinese chóngniǔ Doublets: A study using multiple character readings*. Ph. D. diss., Cornell Univ.

———. 1992. *A handbook of Old Chinese phonology*. Berlin, New York.

Baxter, William H., and Laurent Sagart. 1998. Word formation in Old Chinese. In Packard 1998, 35–76.

Beard, Robert. 1998. Derivation. In: Spencer and Zwicky 1998, 44-65.

Benedict, Paul K. (compiler ca. 1940). "Rhyming Dictionary of Written Burmese." *LTBA* 3:1.

———. 1972. *Sino-Tibetan. A Conspectus*. London.

———. 1975. *Austro-Thai, Language and Culture. With a Glossary of Roots*. New Haven.

———. 1976a. "Sino-Tibetan: Another Look." *JAOS* 96:2: 167–197.

———. 1976b. "Austro-Thai and Austroasiatic." *Mon-Khmer Studies* 1: 1–36.

———. 1979. "Four forays into Karen linguistic history." *LTBA* 5:1: 1–35.

———. 1986. "Archaic Chinese initials." *Wang Li Memorial Volume*: 25–71.

———. 1987. "Early MY/TB loan relationships." *LTBA* 10:2: 12–21.

———. 1988. Kadai linguistics: the rules of engagement. In Edmondson and Solnit, 323–340.

———. 1995. Proto-Tibeto-Burman / Proto-Sino-Tibetan *-i suffix. In Nishi, Matisoff, Nagano, eds., *New Horizons in Tibeto-Burman Morphosyntax*, 31–34. Osaka.

Benjamin, Geoffrey. 1976. Austroasiatic subgroupings and prehistory in the Malay peninsula. In Jenner et al., 69–123.

Beyer, Stephan V. 1992. *The classical Tibetan language*. Albany, NY.

Blench, Roger, and Matthew Spriggs, eds. 1997–1999. *Archeology and Language*. 4 vols. London and New York.

Bodde, Derk. 1975. *Festivals in Classical China*. Princeton.

Bodman, Nicholas C. 1969. "Tibetan *sdud* 'folds of garment', the character 卒, and the *st- hypothesis." *BIHP* 39: 327–345.

———. 1980. Chinese and Sino-Tibetan; evidence towards establishing the nature of their relationship. In Frans van Coetsem and Linda R. Waugh, *Contributions to historical linguistics*, 34–199. Leiden.

Boltz, William G. 1994. *The origin and early development of the Chinese writing system*. New Haven, CT.

Boodberg, Peter A. 1937. "Some proleptical remarks on the evolution of archaic Chinese." *HJAS* 2: 329–372.

Bradley, David. 1979. *Proto-Loloish*. Scandinavian Inst. of Asian Studies Monograph Series 39. London and Malmö.

Branner, David Prager. 1995. "A Gutyan Jongbao dialect notebook." *The Yuen Ren Society: Treasury of Chinese Dialect Data* I: 243–338.

———. 2000. *Problems in Comparative Chinese Dialectology. The Classification of Miin and Hakka*. Berlin, NewYork.

Branner, David Prager, ed. 2006. *The Chinese Rime Tables.* Amsterdam.

Buck, Carl Darling. 1949. *A Dictionary of Selected Synonyms in the Principal Indo-European Languages.* Chicago.

Burling, Robbins. 1959. "Proto-Bodo." *Language* 35:3.

———. 1961. *A Garo Grammar.* Puna: Indian Linguistics Monograph Series 2.

Caughley, Ross C. 1972. *A vocabulary of the Chepang language.* Kirtipur, Nepal.

———. 2000. *Dictionary of Chepang.* Pacific Linguistics. Canberra.

Chang, Kwang-chih. 1976. *Early Chinese Civilization. Anthropological Perspectives.* Cambridge, Mass.

Chao Yuen Ren. 1968. *A Grammar of Spoken Chinese.* Berkeley, CA

Chén Fùhuá 陳复華, ed. 1999. *Gǔdài Hànyǔ cídiǎn* 古代漢語詞典. Beijing.

Chén Zhāngtài 陳章太 and Lǐ Rúlóng 李如龍. 1991. *Mǐnyǔ yánjiù* 閩語研究. Beijing.

Chén Zhōng-mǐn. "The common origin of diminutives in southern Chinese dialects and Southeast Asian languages." *LTBA* 22:2: 21–47.

Coblin, W. South. 1976. "Notes on Tibetan verbal morphology." *TP* 62: 1-3: 45–70.

———. 1982. Notes on the dialect of the Han Buddhist transcriptions. In: *Proceedings of the International Conference on Sinology*, Taipei.

———. 1983. *A Handbook of Eastern Han Sound Glosses.* Hong Kong.

———. 1986. *A Sinologist's Handlist of Sino-Tibetan Lexical Comparisons.* Nettetal.

———. 1991a. *Studies in Old Northwest Chinese.* JCL Monograph 4.

———. 1991b. "Thoughts on dentilabialization in the Tang-time dialect of Shazhou." *TP* 77: 88–107.

———. 1993. "BTD revisited: a reconsideration of the Han Buddhist Transcriptional Dialect." *BIHP* 63:4: 867–943.

———. 1994a. "Remarks on some early Buddhist transcriptional data from Northwest China." *MS* 42: 151–169.

———. 1994b. *A compendium of phonetics in Northwest Chinese.* JCL Monograph 7.

———. 2002. "On certain functions of 'a-chung in early Tibetan transcriptional texts." *LTBA* 25:2: 169–184.

———. n.d. *Beyond BTD: An excursion in Han phonology.* Ms.

Dài Qìngxià 戴慶廈. 1991. "On the affiliation of the Kadai (Zhuang-Dong) group: indications from the nature of the relationship between TB and Chinese." *Kadai. Discussions in Kadai and SE Asian Linguistics* III: 51–63 (Coordinator Jerold A. Edmundson).

Dài Qìngxià 戴慶廈, Xú Xījiān 徐悉艱, et al. 1992. *Jǐngpōyǔ yǔfǎ* 景頗語語法 (*A grammar of Kachin*). Beijing.

Dài Qìngxià 戴慶廈 and Wu Hede. 1995. Jinghpo Prefixes: Their Classification, Origins, and Implications for General Morphology. In Nishi, Matisoff, Nagano, eds., 93–131.

Das, Sarat Chandra. 1902. *Tibetan-English Dictionary.* Calcutta.

Demiéville, Paul. 1950. "Archaïsmes de prononciation en chinois vulgaire." *TP* 40: 1–59.

Dempwolff, Otto. 1938. *Vergleichende Lautlehre des austronesischen Wortschatzes.* Vol. 3: *Austronesisches Wörterverzeichnis.* Berlin.

Diffloth, Gérard. 1974–97. Austroasiatic Languages. In *Encyclopedia Britannica,* 5th ed., vol. 22: 701ff.

———. "Mon-Khmer initial palatals and 'substratumized' Austro-Tahai." *Mon-Khmer Studies* 5: 39–57.

———. 1980. "The Wa Languages." *LTBA* 5:2.

———. 1984. *The Dvaravati Old Mon Language and Nyah Kur.* Chulalongkorn.

———. n.d. (1992?). *Wa-Lawa-Bulang Etymologies.* Ms.

Dīng Fúbǎo 丁福保. *Shuōwén jiězì gǔlín* 說文解字詁林

Dixon, R.M.W., and Alexandra Y. Aikhenvald, eds. 2000. *Changing Valency. Case studies in transitivity.* Cambridge, UK.

Dobson, W.A.C.H. 1959. *Late Archaic Chinese.* Toronto.

———. 1962. *Early Archaic Chinese.* Toronto.

Douglas, Carstairs. 1873. *Chinese-English Dictionary of the Vernacular or Spoken Language of Amoy...* Supplement by Thomas Barclay. London.

Downer, G. B. 1959. "Derivation by tone-change in classical Chinese." *BSOAS* 22: 258–290.

———. 1973. "Strata of Chinese loanwords in the Mien dialect of Yao." *AM* 18: 1–33.

———. 1982. "Problems in the reconstruction of Proto-Miao-Yao." Paper presented at the ICSTLL, Beijing.

Driem, George van. 1995. Black Mountain conjugational morphology... In Nishi, Matisoff, Nagano, eds., *New Horizons in Tibeto-Burman Morphosyntax*: 229–259. Osaka.

Eberhard, Wolfram. 1942. *Lokalkulturen im alten China.* 2 vols. Leiden and Peking.

———. 1967. *Guilt and sin in traditional China.* Taipei.

———. 1968. *The local cultures of South and East China.* Leiden.

———. 1983. *Lexikon chinesischer Symbole.* Cologne.

Edmondson, Jerold A., and David B. Solnit. 1988. *Comparative Kadai: Linguistic studies beyond Tai.* Arlington, TX.

Edmondson, Jerold A., and Yang Quan. 1988. Word-initial preconsonants and the history of Kam-Sui resonant initials and tones. In Edmondson and Solnit, 143–166.

Egerod, Søren. 1976. "Benedict's Austro-Thai hypothesis and the traditional views on Sino-Thai relationship." *CAAAL* 6: 51–63.

Egerod, Søren, and Else Glahn, eds. 1959. *Studia serica Bernhard Karlgren dedicata: Studies Dedicated to Bernhard Karlgren on his 70th Birthday*, Oct. 5, 1959. Copenhagen.

Embleton, Sheila, John E. Joseph, Hans-Josef Niederehe, eds. 1999. The emergence of the modern language sciences. *Studies on the Transition from Historical-comparative to Structural Linguistics in Honour of E. F. Koerner.* 2 vols. Amsterdam.

Emmerich, Reinhard, and Hans Stumpfeldt, eds. 2002. *Und folge nun dem, was mein Herz begehrt. Festschrift für Ulrich Unger zum 70. Geburtstag.* Hamburger Sinologische Schriften 8. Hamburg.

Erkes, Eduard. 1956. *Chinesische Grammatik. Nachtrag zur Chinesischen Grammatik von G. v. d. Gabelentz.* Berlin.

Ferlus, Michel. 1978. "Reconstruction de /TS/ et /Tš/ en Mon-Khmer." *Mon-Khmer Studies* 7: 1–38.

———. 1988. Les langues austroasiatiques. In Revel, 81–96.

———. 1991/1997. "Vocalisme du Proto Viet-Muong." ICSTLL (Bangkok).

———. 1998. "Du chinois archaïque au chinois ancien: monosyllabisation et formation des syllables *tendu/lâche.*" ICSTLL (Lund).

Forrest, R. A. D. 1948. *The Chinese Language.* Third ed. 1973. London.

French, Walter. 1983. *Northern Naga: a TB Mesolanguage.* Ph.D. diss., City University of NY.

Gabelentz, Georg von der. 1881. *Chinesische Grammatik.* Leipzig.

Gedney, William. 1976. "On the Thai evidence for Austro-Thai." *CAAAL* 6: 65–81.

———. *William Gedney's "The Saek language. Glossary, texts, translations."* Thomas John Hudak, ed. U. of Michigan.

Georg, Stephan. 1996. *Marphatan Thakali.* Munich.

Giles, Herbert. A. 1892. *A Chinese-English Dictionary.* Shanghai.

Geilich, Barbara. [1993] 1994. *Nasal-Suffigierung. Eine Studie zur vergleichenden Morphologie der indo-chinesischen Sprachen.* Münster i.W.

Gong, Hwang-cherng. 1995. The system of finals in Sino-Tibetan. In W. Wang, ed., *Ancestry*, 41–92. Gong 2002, vol. 2: 79–124.

———. 1999. Cóng Hàn-Zàng yǔ de bǐjiào kàn shànggǔ Hànyǔ de cítóu wèntí 從漢藏語的比校看上古漢語的辭頭問題. In Gong 2002, vol. 2: 125–160.
———. 2002a. *Xīxià yǔwén yánjiū lùnwénjí* 西夏語文研究論文集. Academia Sinica, Language and Linguistics Monograph III, vol. 1. Taipei.
———. 2002b vol. 2. *Hàn-Zàngyǔ yánjiū lùn wénjí* 漢藏語研究論文集. Academia Sinica, Language and Linguistics Monograph III, vol. 2. Taipei.
Graham, A. C. 1973. "The Terminations of the Archaic Chinese Pronouns." *BSOAS* 36:2: 293–298.
Granet, Marcel. 1948. *La civilisation chinoise. La vie publique et la vie privée.* Paris.
Gregerson, Kenneth J. 1976. "Vietnamese hoi and ngã tones and Mon-Khmer -h finals." *Mon-Khmer Studies* 5: 76–83.
Grüßner, Karl-Heinz. 1978. *Arleng alam, die Sprache der Mikir.* Wiesbaden.
Hansell, Mark. 1988. The relation of Be to Tai: evidence from tones and initials. In Edmondson and Solnit, 239–287.
Hanson, O. 1906. *A Dictionary of the Kachin Language.* Rangoon.
Harbsmeier, Christoph. 1981. *Aspects of Classical Chinese Syntax.* Scandinavian Institute of Asian Studies Monograph Series no. 45.
Hashimoto, Mantaro. 1976a. The agrarian and the pastoral diffusion of languages. In Hashimoto, ed., *Genetic relationships, diffusion, and Typological Similarities of East and SE Asian Languages,* Papers for the 1st Japan-US Joint Seminar on East and SE Asian Linguistics, 1–14. Tokyo.
———. 1976b. "Origin of the East Asian linguistic structure—Latitudinal transitions and longitudinal development." *CAAAL* 22: 35–41.
Haudricourt, André G. 1950 (1947–50). "Introduction à la phonologie historique des langues Miao-Yao." *BEFEO* 44: 555–576.
———. 1966. The limits and connections of Austroasiatic in the Northeast. In Norman H. Zide, ed., *Studies in Comparative Austroasiatic Linguistics.* London.
Haudricourt, André, and David Strecker. 1991. "Hmong-Mien (Miao-Yao) Loans in Chinese." *TP* 77: 4–5: 335–342.
Headley, Robert, K. 1977. "A Pearic vocabulary." *Mon-Khmer Studies* 5: 69–149.
———. 1978. "An English-Pearic Vocabulary." *Mon-Khmer Studies* 7: 61–94.
Henderson, Eugénie J. A. 1965. *Tiddim Chin. A descriptive analysis of two texts.* London.
Hillard, Edward. 1975. "On a phonological regularity in Lushei verbal alternation." ICSTLL.
Ho Dah-an (Hé Dà-ān) 何大安. 1993. "Linguistic layers of the Wu dialect during the Six Dynasties." *BIHP* 64:4: 867–875.
Hock, Hans Heinrich. 1988. *Principles of Historical Linguistics.* Berlin, New York, Amsterdam.
Hoffmann, Helmut. 1950. *Quellen zur tibetischen Bon-Religion.* Wiesbaden.
———. 1979. *Tibet. A Handbook.* Bloomington, Indiana.
Huáng Bùfán 黃布凡, ed. 1992. *Zàng-Miǎnyǔ zú yǔyán cíhuì* 藏緬語族語言詞匯 (A Tibeto-Burman Lexicon). Beijing.
Huffman, Franklin E. 1975. "An examination of lexical correspondences between Vietnamese and some Austroasiatic languages." ICSTLL.
Hutton, J. J. 1921/1969. *The Angami Nagas. With some notes on neighboring tribes.* London.
Jacob, Judith. 1974. *A Concise Cambodian – English Dictionary.* London.
Jaeschke, H. A. 1881, 1958. *A Tibetan-English Dictionary.* London.
Jenner, Philip N., et al. 1976. *Austroasiatic Studies.*
Jenner, Philip N., and Saveros Pou. 1980–1981. A Lexicon of Khmer morphology. *Mon-Khmer Studies* 9-10.

Jeon, Kwang-jie 全廣鎮. 1996. *Hàn-Zàngyǔ tóngyuáncí zōngtàn* 漢藏語同源詞綜探 (Etymological Studies of Sino-Tibetan Cognate Words). Taipei.

Karlgren, Bernhard. 1933. "Word families in Chinese." *BMFEA* 5: 9–120.

———. 1949. *The Chinese language*. New York.

———. 1956. "Cognate words in the Chinese phonetic series." *BMFEA* 28: 1–18.

———. 1957. *Grammata serica recensa*. Stockholm.

Keightley, David N. 1969. *Public Work in Ancient China: A Study of Forced Labor in the Shang and Western Zhou*. Ph. D. diss., Columbia University.

Keightley, David N., ed. 1983. *The Origins of Chinese Civilization*. Berkeley, L.A.

Kluge, Friedrich. 1989. *Etymologisches Wörterbuch der deutschen Sprache*. 22nd ed. Berlin, New York.

Kuiper, F.B.J. 1966. The sources of Nahali vocabulary. In Zide, 57–81.

LaPolla, Randy J. 1994. "Variable finals in Proto-Sino-Tibetan." *BIHP* 65:1: 131–173.

———. 2000. Valency-changing derivations in Dulong/Rawang. In Dixon and Aikhenvald, 282–311.

Lau, Ulrich. 1999. *Quellenstudien zur Landvergabe und Bodenübertragung in der westlichen Zhou-Dynastie (1045?–771 v. Chr.)*. MS Monograph Series XLI.

Laufer, Berthold. 1916. "Loan-words in Tibetan." *TP* 17: 403–552.

———. 1919. *Sino-Iranica: Chinese contributions to the history of civilization in ancient Iran*. Field Museum of Natural History, Publ. 201, Anthropological Series, vol. 15, no. 3. Chicago.

Lehmann, Winfred P. 1993. *Theoretical Bases of Indo-European Linguistics*. London and New York.

Levin, Beth, and Malka Rappaport Hovav. 1998. Morphology and lexical semantics. In: Spencer and Zwicky, 248–271.

Levy, Annick. 1988. Les languages thai. In Revel, 47–80.

Lewin, Bruno. 1990. *Abriss der japanischen Grammatik*. 3rd ed. Wiesbaden.

Lewitz, Saveros. 1976a. Note on words for male and female in Old Khmer and Modern Khmer. In Jenner et al., 761–771.

———. 1976b. The infix /-b-/ in Khmer. In Jenner et al., 741–760.

Li Fang Kuei (Lǐ Fāng-guì) 李方桂. 1959. Tibetan glo-ba'-'dring. In Egerod and Glahn: 55–59.

———. 1971. "Shànggǔ yīn yánjiù 上古音研究 (Studies on Archaic Chinese phonology)." *Tsing Hua Journal of Chinese Studies* n.s. 9: 1–61.

———. 1976. "Sino-Tai." *CAAAL* 3: 39–48.

———. 1977. *A Handbook of Comparative Tai*. Honolulu.

Li Fang Kuei and W. South Coblin. 1987. *A study of the old Tibetan inscriptions*. Taipei.

Lǐ Xiào-dìng 李孝定. 1965. *Jiǎgǔwén zì jíshì* 甲骨文字 集釋. Taipei.

Li Xu-lian. 1997. "The word rainbow in Zhuang language and word *didong* in ancient Chinese." *MZYW* 3: 41–42.

Liáng Sēngbǎo 梁僧寶. 1925. *Sì shēng yùnpǔ* 四聲韻譜. Taipei [reprint].

Loewe, Michael, ed. 1993. *Early Chinese Texts. A Bibliographical Guide*. Berkeley.

Löffler, Lorenz. 1960. "Khami / Khumi Vakabulare." *Anthropos* 55: 505–557.

———. 1966. "The contribution of Mru to Sino-Tibetan linguistics." *ZDMG* 116:1: 118–159.

———. 1985. A preliminary report on the Paangkhua languages. In Thurgood et al., eds., 279–286.

Lorrain, J. Herbert. 1940. *Dictionary of the Lushai language*. Calcutta.

Lorrain, Reginald Arthur. 1951. *Grammar and dictionary of the Lakher or Mara language*. Gauhati.

Lù Démíng 陸德明 (556–627). *Jīngdiǎn shìwén* 經典釋文.

Luó Chángpéi 羅常培, and Zhōu Zǔmó 周祖謨. 1958. *Hàn Wèi Jìn nán běi cháo yùnbù yǎnbiàn yánjiù* 漢魏晉南北朝韻部演變研究. Peking.

Luó Yǒngxiàn. 2000. "From 'Head' to 'Toes': Sino-Tai lexical correspondances in body part terms." *JCL* 28:1: 67–99.

Lynch, John. 1998. *Pacific languages. An Introduction*. Honolulu.

MacDonell, Arthur A. 1916. *A Vedic Grammar for Students*. London.

MacIver, D. 1926. *A Chinese–English Dictionary, Hakka Dialect*. Shanghai.

Mahdi, Waruno. 1994a. "Some Austronesian maverick protoforms with culture-historical implications" I. *OL* 33:1: 167–229.

———. 1994b. "Some Austronesian maverick protoforms with culture-historical implications" II. *OL* 33:2: 431–490.

———. 1999. The dispersal of Austronesian boat forms in the Indian ocean. In Blench and Spriggs, vol. III, 144–179.

Mainwaring, G. B., and Albert Grünwedel. 1898. *Dictionary of the Lepcha Language*. Berlin.

Manomaivibool, Prapin. 1975. *A study of Sino-Thai lexical correspondances*. PH.D. diss., University of Washington.

Maspero, Henri. 1912. "Études sur la phonétique historique de la langue annamite." *BEFEO* 12: 1-126.

———. 1924. "Légendes mythologiques dans le chou king." *JA* 204: 1–100.

Matisoff, James A. 1970. "Glottal dissimilation and Lahu high-rising tone." *JAOS* 90:1: 13–44.

———. 1972. *The Loloish Tonal Split Revisited*. Berkeley.

———. 1974. "The tones of Jinghpaw and Lolo-Burmese: common origins vs. independent development." *Acta Linguistica Hafniensia* 15:2: 153–212.

———. 1978. *Variational Semantics in Tibeto-Burman: the "Organic" Approach to Linguistic Comparison*. Philadelphia.

———. 1985a. Out on a limb: hand, arm, and wing in ST. In Thurgood and Matisoff, 421–450.

———. 1985b. "God and the Sino-Tibetan copula with some good news concerning selected Tibeto-Burman rhymes." *Journal of Asian and African Studies*, no. 29.

———. 1988a. Universal semantics and allofamic identification: two Sino-Tibetan case-studies: straight/flat/full and property/livestock/talent. In A. Sato, ed., *Languages and History in East Asia: Festschrift for Tatsuo Nishida on the occasion of his 60th birthday*, 3–14. Kyoto.

———. 1988b. *The dictionary of Lahu*. University of California Publications in Linguistics 111. Berkeley and Los Angeles.

———. 1988c. Proto-Hlai initials and tones: a first approximation. In Edmondson and Solnit, 289–321.

———. 1992. "Following the marrow: two parallel Sino-Tibetan etymologies." *LTBA* 15:1: 159–177.

———. 1995. Sino-Tibetan Palatal Suffixes Revisited. In Nishi, Matisoff, Nagano, eds., 35–91.

———. 1997a. *Sino-Tibetan numeral systems: prefixes, protoforms and problems*. Pacific Linguistics. Canberra.

———. 1997b. Primary and secondary laryngeal initials in TB. In Anne O. Yue and Mitsuaki Endo, *In memory of Mantaro J. Hashimoto*, 29–50. Tokyo.

———. 1999. "On 'Sino-Bodic' and other symptoms of Neosubgroupitis." 32nd ICSTLL.

———. 2000. "An extrusional approach to *p-/w- variation in Sino-Tibetan." *Language and Linguistics* 1:2: 135–186.

———. 2002. *Zài lùn Yíyǔ zhī de shēngdiào yǎnbiàn* 再論彝語支的聲調衍變. Taipei. (translation and update of *The Loloish Tonal Split Revisited*.

———. 2003. *Handbook of Proto-Tibeto-Burman: a system and philosophy of Sino-Tibetan Reconstruction*. Berkeley and Los Angeles.

Matisoff, James A., general editor. 1995. *Languages and dialects of Tibeto-Burman*. STEDT monograph series no. 2. Sino-Tibetan Etymological Dictionary and Thesaurus Project. Berkeley.

Mattos, Gilbert L. 1971. "Tonal 'anomalies' in the Kuo Feng odes." *Tsing Hua Journal of Chinese Studies*, n.s IX, nos. 1 and 2: 306–324.

Mazaudon, Martine. 1973. *Phonologie tamang* (Népal). Marseille.

———. 1985. Proto-TB as a two-tone lg.? Some evidence from Proto-Tamang and Proto-Karen. In Thurgood et al., 201–229.

———. 1996. "An outline of the historical phonology of the dialects of Nar-Phu (Nepal)." *LTBA* 19:1: 103–114.

Mazaudon, M., and B. Michailovsky. 1986. "Syllabicity and suprasegmentals: the Dzongkha monosyllabic noun." ICSTLL.

———. 1992. "Preliminary notes on the languages of the Bumthang group." ICSTLL.

McCoy, John, and Timothy Light, eds. 1986. *Contributions to Sino-Tibetan Studies*. (Nicholas Bodman Festschrift). Leiden.

McFarland, George Bradley. 1944. *Thai-English Dictionary*. [Reprint Stanford U. Press].

Méi, Tsŭ-Lín 梅祖麟. 1980. "Chinese and the languages of Southeast Asia." Assoc. for Asian Studies Conference, Chicago.

———. 1985. Some examples of prenasals and *s-nasals in Sino-Tibetan. Thurgood et al., eds.

Mei, Tsu-Lin, and J. Norman. 1971. "Cl- > s- in some Northern Min dialects." *Tsing Hua Journal of Chinese Studies* 9: 96–105.

Michailovsky, Boyd. 1985. Tibeto-Burman dental suffixes: evidence from Limbu (Nepal). Thurgood et al., eds., 363–375.

———. 2002. *Limbu-English Dictionary*. Kathmandu.

Miyake, Marc H. 1997. Pre-Sino-Korean and Pre-Sino-Japanese: reexamining an old problem from a modern perspective. In *Japanese/Korean Linguistics* vol. 6: 179–211 (ed. Ho-min Sohn and John Haig. Stanford: Center for the Study of Language and Information).

Nakajima, Motoki. 1979. *A comparative lexicon of Fukien dialects*. Tokyo.

Namkung, Ju, ed. 1996. *Phonological inventories of Tibeto-Burman languages*. STEDT monograph series no. 3. Sino-Tibetan Etymolological Dictionary and Thesaurus Project. Berkeley.

Needham, Joseph. 1954 ff. *Science and Civilization in China*. Cambridge, UK.

Nishi, Yoshio, James A. Matisoff, Nagano Yasuhiko. 1995. *New Horizons in Tibeto-Burman Morphosyntax*. Senri Ethnological Studies No. 41. Osaka.

Norman, Jerry. 1979. "Chronological strata in the Min dialects." *FY* 4: 268–274.

———. 1983. "Some ancient Chinese dialect words in Min dialects." *FY* 3: 202–211.

———. 1984. "Three Min etymologies." *CLAO* 13:2: 175–189.

———. 1985. A note on the origin of the Chinese duodenary cycle. In Thurgood, Matisoff, Bradley, 85–89.

———. 1986. The origin of the Proto-Min softened stops. In McCoy and Light, eds., 375–384.

———. 1988. *Chinese*. Cambridge, UK.

———. 1994. "Pharyngealization in early Chinese." *JAOS* 114: 397–408.

Norman, Jerry, and W. South Coblin. 1995. "A new approach to Chinese historical linguistics." *JAOS* 115: 576–584.

Norman, Jerry, and Mei Tsu-Lin. 1976. "The Austroasiatics in ancient south China: some lexical evidence." *MS* 32: 274–301.

Noss, Richard B. 1964. *Thai reference grammar*. Washington D.C.

Ono, Tōru. 1965. "The reconstruction of Proto-Kuki-Chin I: initials." *Gengo Kenkyū* 47: 8–20.

Ostapirat, Weera. 1998. "Tiddim Chin tones in historical perspective." *LTBA* 21:1: 235–248.
———. 2000. "Proto-Kra." *LTBA* 23:1.
Palmer, Leonhard R. 1980. *The Greek Language*. Norman, Oklahoma.
Pān Wù-yún 潘悟云. 1987. "Yuènányǔ zhōng de shànggǔ Hànyǔ jiècí céng 越南語中的上古漢語借辭層 (A layer of OC loan words in Vietnamese)." *YYWZX* 3: 38–47.
———. 2000. *Hànyǔ lìshǐ yīnyùnxué* 漢語歷史音韻學. Shanghai.
Pān Wù-yún et al., transl. 1997. *Hànwén diǎn* 漢文典. (Translation and improvement of Karlgren, *GSR*, with *pinyin* and stroke index.) Shanghai.
Peiros, Ilia. 1996. *Katuic comparative dictionary*. Pacific Linguistics, series C-132, Canberra.
Peiros, Ilia, and Sergej Starostin. 1996. *A comparative vocabulary of five Sino-Tibetan languages*. 6 vols. Melbourne.
Pinault, George-Jean, Klaus T. Schmidt, Werner Winter, eds. 1997. *Tocharian and Indo-European Studies*, vol. 7. Copenhagen.
Pinnow, Heinz-Jürgen. 1959. *Versuch einer historischen Lautlehre der Kharia-Sprache*. Wiesbaden.
———. 1965. Personal pronouns in the Austroasiatic languages: a historical study. In G. B. Milner and E. Henderson, eds., *Indo-Pacific linguistic studies*. Pt. I: *Historical linguistics*, 3–42. Amsterdam.
Pokorny, Julius. 1959. *Indogermanisches etymologisches Wörterbuch*. 2 vols. Tübingen and Basel.
Pulleyblank, E. G. 1962. "The consonantal system of Old Chinese." *AM* 9: 58–144, 206–265.
———. 1963. "An interpretation of the vowel systems of Old Chinese and Written Burmese." *AM* 10: 200–221.
———. 1973. "Some new hypotheses concerning word families in Chinese." *JCL* 1:1: 111–125.
———. 1983. The Chinese and their neighbors in prehistoric and early historic times. In Keightley, ed., 411–466.
———. 1991. *Lexicon of reconstructed pronunciation in Early Middle Chinese, Late MC, and Early Mandarin*. Vancouver B. C.
———. 1995a. The historical and prehistorical relationships of Chinese. In W. Wang, *Ancestry*, 145–194.
———. 1995b. *Outline of Classical Chinese Grammar*. Vancouver B. C.
———. 1998. "Qieyun and Yunjing: The essential foundation for Chinese historical linguistics." *JAOS* 118:2: 200–216.
Purnell, Herbert. 1970. *Toward a reconstruction of Proto-Miao-Yao*. Ph.D. diss., Cornell University.
Qiú Xīguī 裘錫圭. 2000. *Chinese writing*. Berkeley, CA. [*Wénzìxué gàiyào* 文字學概要, Beijing 1988; rev. Taibei 1994.] Translated by G. Mattos and J. Norman.
Revel, Nicole. 1988. *Le riz en Asie du sud-est. Atlas du vocabulaire de la plante*. Paris.
Rosemont, Henry. 1991. *Chinese texts and philosophical contexts: essays dedicated to A. C. Graham*. La Salle, Ill.
Sadler, Louisa, and Andrew Spencer. 1998. Morphology and argument structure. In Spencer and Zwicky, 206–236.
Sagart, Laurent. 1993a. *Les dialectes gan. Études sur la phonologie et le lexique d'un groupe de dialectes chinois*. Paris.
———. 1993b. "Chinese and Austronesian: evidence for a genetic relationship." *JCL* 21:1: 1–63.
———. 1995. "Chinese 'buy' and 'sell' and the direction of borrowings between Chinese and Miao-Yao." *TP* 81, 4-5: 328–342.
———. 1999. *The roots of Old Chinese*. Amsterdam and Philadelphia.

Schuessler, Axel. 1985. The function of *qusheng* in Early Zhou Chinese. In Thurgood, Matisoff, Bradley, eds.
———. 1987. *A dictionary of Early Zhou Chinese.* Honolulu.
———. 2002. Tenues aspiratae im Altchinesischen. In Emmerich and Stumpfeldt 2002, 155–164.
———. 2003. "Multiple Origins of the OC Lexicon." *JCL* 31:1: 1–71.
———. 2004. "Austroasiatic languages in early China: fragments of their lexicon and morphology in Old Chinese." ICSTLL (Lund).
———. 2006. The Qièyùn System 'Divisions' as a Result of Vowel Warping. In Branner, ed., 83–96.
Serruys, Paul L.-M. 1974. "Studies in the language of the Shang oracle inscriptions." *TB* 60: 12–120.
———. 1982. "Towards a grammar of the language of the Shang bone inscriptions." Proceedings of the International Sinological Conference, Academia Sinica, Taipei.
Shafer, Robert. 1950. "The Naga branches of Kukish. Vocalism." *Rocznik Orientalistyczny* 16: 467–530.
———. 1952. "Phonetik der Alt-Kuki-Mundarten." *ZDMG* 102: 262–279.
———. 1953. "Classification of the northernmost Naga languages." *Journal of the Bihar Research Society* 39:3: 225–264.
———. 1974. *Introduction to Sino-Tibetan.* Wiesbaden.
Sharma, D. D. 1989, 1992. *Studies in Tibeto-Himalayan Languages* II: *Tribal languages of Himachal Pradesh.* Part I 1989, Part II 1992. New Delhi.
———. 1989, 1990. *Studies in Tibeto-Himalayan Languages* III: *Tibeto-Himalayan Languages of Uttarakhand.* Part I 1989, Part II 1990. New Delhi.
Shaughnessy, Edward L. 1991. *Sources of Western Zhou History. Inscribed Bronze Vessels.* Berkeley, CA.
———. 1997. *I Ching, the Classic of Changes.* New York.
Shěn Jiān-shì 沈兼士. 1944. *Guǎngyùn shēngxì* 廣韻聲系.
Shī Xiàngdōng 施向東. 2000. *Hànyǔ hé Zàngyǔ tóngyuán tǐxì de bǐjiào yánjiù* 漢語和藏語同源體系的比較研究. Beijing.
Shibatani, Masayoshi. 1990. *The Languages of Japan.* Cambridge.
Shima Kunio 島邦男. 1971. *Inkyo bokuji sōrui* 殷墟卜辭綜類. Tokyo.
Shorto, H. L. 1971. *A dictionary of the Mon inscriptions from the sixth to the sixteenth centuries.* London.
———. 1972 (?). "Mon-Khmer contact words in Sino-Tibetan." Ms.
———. 1973. "Three Mon-Khmer Word Families." *BSOAS* 36:2: 374–381.
———. 1976a. The vocalism of Proto-Mon-Khmer. In Jenner, 1041–1067.
———. 1976b. "In defense of Austric." *CAAAL* 6: 95–104.
Sidwell, Paul J. 2000. *Proto-South-Bahnaric.* Pacific Linguistics. Canberra.
Smith, Kenneth D. 1972. *A phonological reconstruction of Proto-North-Bahnaric.* Santa Ana, CA.
Solnit, David B. "Proto-Tibeto-Burman *r in Tiddim Chin and Lushai." ICSTLL.
Spencer, Andrew, and Arnold Zwicky, eds. 1998. *A Handbook of Morphology.* Oxford.
Stadler, Louisa, and Andrew Spencer. 1998. Morphology and argument structure. In Spencer and Zwicky, eds., 206–236.
Starostin, Sergai. 1995. Old Chinese vocabulary: a historical perspective. In William S-Y. Wang, JCL Monograph 8, 225–251.
Strecker, David. 1989. "Sino-Mien evidence for Old and Middle Chinese phonology." First NE Conference on Chinese Linguistics, Columbus, Ohio.
Sùn, Hóngkāi 孫宏開. 1980. *Ménbā, Luòbā, Dengrén de yǔyán* 門巴珞巴...人的語言. Beijing.

Takashima, Ken-ichi. 1996. Language and Palaeography. In Gary F. Arbuckle, ed., *Studies in Early Chinese Civilization: Religion, Society, Language and Palaeography.* Vol. 1: Text; vol. 2: Tables and Notes. Kansai Gaidai Univ. Publ.

Ting Pang-hsin. 1975. *Chinese Phonology of the Wei-Chin Period: Reconstruction of the Finals as Reflected in Poetry.* Taipei.

Thomas, Dorothy. 1976. *A phonological reconstruction of Proto-East-Katuic.* SIL, Univ. of North Dakota Session, working papers vol. 20.

Thompson, Laurence C. 1976. Proto-Viet-Muong Phonology. In Jenner et al., 1113–1204.

Thompson, Laurence G. 1996. *Chinese Religion.* Belmont.

Thurgood, Graham. 1988. Notes on the reconstruction of Proto-Kam-Sui. In Edmondson and Solnit, 179–218.

———. 1994. "Tai-Kadai and Austronesian: the nature of the historical relationship." *OL* 33:2: 345–368.

———. 1999. "A comment on Gedney's proposal for another series of voiced initials in proto-Tai." Ms.

Thurgood, Graham, and Randy LaPolla, eds. 2003. *The Sino-Tibetan Languages*. London and New York.

Thurgood, Graham, James A. Matisoff, David Bradley, eds. 1985. *Linguistics of the Sino-Tibetan area: the state of the art.* Canberra. (Paul Benedict Festschrift).

Unger, Ulrich. 1982-1995. *Hao-ku. Sinologische Rundbriefe.* Nos. 1–51. Münster.

———. 1989. *Glossar des Klassischen Chinesisch.* Wiesbaden.

Vovin, Alexander. 1999. Once again on the reading of the Old Korean 尸. In Embleton et al., eds., vol. 2: 289–300.

Wáng Fúshì 王輔世. 1979. Miáoyǔ fāngyán shēng-yùn mǔ bǐjiào 苗語方言聲韻母比校. Beijing.

Wáng Fúshì 王輔世, and Máo Zōng-wǔ 毛宗武. 1995. *Miáo-Yáo gǔyīn gòunǐ* 苗瑤語古音構擬. Beijing.

Wáng Lì 王力. 1958. *Hànyǔ shǐgǎo* 漢語史搞. Beijing.

———. 王力. 1982. *Tóngyuán zìdiǎn* 同源字典. Beijing.

Wang, William S-Y., ed. 1995. *The Ancestry of Chinese.* JCL Monograph 8.

Wang, William S-Y. 1995. *The Ancestry of Chinese: Retrospect and Prospect.* In W. Wang, ed., I–XI.

Weidert, Alfons. 1975. *Componential Analysis of Lushai Phonology.* Amsterdam.

———. 1987. *Tibeto-Burman Tonology.* Amsterdam and Philadelphia.

Williams, C.A.S. 1932. *Outline of Chinese Symbolism and Art Motives.* Shanghai.

Wolfenden, Stuart N. 1929. *Outlines of Tibeto-Burman Linguistic Morphology.* London.

Xǔ Shèn 許慎. ca. 149. *Shuōwén jiězì* 説 文 解 字 (SW); see Dīng Fúbǎo.

Xú Xījiān 徐悉艱 et al., eds. 1983. *Jinghpo miwa ga ginsi chyum* 景漢辭典. Yùnnán.

Yáng Xióng 揚雄 (Han period). *Fāng yán* 方言. Cited edition: Fāngyán jiàojiān fù tóngjiǎn 方言校箋附通檢 Index du Fang yen, text établi par [Zhou Zumo], Centre franco-chinois d'études sinologiques.

Yú Nǎi-yǒng 余迺永. 1974. *Hù zhù jiàozhèng Sòng běn Guǎng-yùn* 互註校正宋本廣韻. Taipei.

Yue-Hashimoto, Oi-kan. 1976. "Substratum in Southern Chinese—the Thai connection." *CAAAL* 6: 1–9.

Zhōngwén dàcídiǎn 中文大辭典 (*Encyclopedic dictionary of the Chinese language*). 1973. Taipei.

Zhōu Fǎgāo 周法高. 1972. "Shànggǔ Hànyǔ hé Hàn-Zàngyǔ 上古漢語和漢藏語." *Journal of the Institute of Chinese Studies of the Chinese Univ.. of Hong Kong* 5: 159–244.

Zide, Norman H., ed. 1966. *Studies in Comparative Austroasiatic Linguistics.* London.

A

ā 阿 (ʔâ) *ONW* ʔɑ

A vernacular prefix added to kinship terms, personal names and personal pronouns, e.g. Mand. *ā-mǔ* 阿母 'mother' [Han texts], *ā-nú* 阿奴 'younger brother', *ā-shuí* 阿誰 'who', *ā-nǐ* 阿你 'you' (Norman 1988: 113); Yuè-Guǎngzhōu *a*^{33}*-ma*^{55} (*ʔa*^{C1}*-ma*^{A1}) 阿媽 'mother, mama', *a*^{33}*-ma*^{21} (*ʔa*^{C1}*-ma*^{A2}) 阿嫲 'grandmother'.

~ **yú** 於 (ʔjwo) **LH** ʔɨɑ, **OCM** *ʔa

Occurs already in *Zuǒzhuàn* prefixed to the Chǔ dialect word for → hǔ$_1$ 虎 'tiger'. Unger (*Hao-ku* 33, 1986) suggests that certain words with MC initial *ʔ-* might be the result of a fusion of this prefix with the following stem (§5.11).

[E] ST: PTB *ʔa- is a prefix for kinship terms, body parts or nouns in general, depending on the language (*STC:* 121–123), e.g., WB *ə-tʰaŋ* 'thought' < *tʰaŋ* 'think', *ə-pʰui*^{B} 'grandfather'; WT *ʔa-kʰu* 'uncle, husband'.

ā-nú 阿奴 (ʔâ-nuo) *ONW* ʔɑ-no

'Younger brother' [Jìn Dyn.] (Norman 1988: 113).

[E] For phonological and semantic reasons, this word is prob. not related to *rú* 孺 *no 'child' (under → rú$_4$ 懦臑 'weak'), nor to → rǔ$_3$ 乳 'milk'. It may be connected to PTB *na:w (*STC* no. 271): Lushai *nau*^{H} < *nau* 'child, younger brother or sister, younger cousin', etc., JP *kə*^{31}*-nau*^{33} 'younger brother / sister', WT *nu-bo* 'man's younger brother'. The putative OC final *-a cannot be reconciled with PTB *-a:w, though; perh. the CH word has been re-etymologized, or only committed to writing after *a > MC *o*.

āi 哀 (ʔậi) **LH** ʔəi, **OCM** *ʔə̂i, OCB *ʔəj

'To pity' [Shi] is prob. a sound-symbolic word.

ái 崖涯睚 → **yá**$_3$, **ái** 崖涯睚

ǎi 藹 → **è**$_8$ 遏閼

ài$_1$ 艾 (ŋâi^C) **LH** ŋɑs, **OCM** *ŋâ(t)s

'White-haired, old' [Shi], possibly related to TB items under → yuè$_1$ 月 'moon', but the vowels do not agree.

[T] *Sin Sukchu SR* ŋaj (去); *MGZY* ŋay (去) [ŋaj]

ài$_2$ 愛 (ʔậi^C) **LH** ʔəs, **OCM** *ʔə̂ts, OCB *ʔəts — [D] PMin *ʔuəi^C

'To love, to grudge' [Shi] > Mand. 'to like, be fond of'.

[T] *Sin Sukchu SR* ʔaj (去); *MGZY* 'ay (去) [ʔaj]; *ONW* ʔɑi^C

[E] ST: TB-PKaren *ʔai (Matisoff *BSOAS* 63.3, 2000: 364).

ài$_3$ 僾 (ʔậi^C) **LH** ʔəs, **OCM** *ʔə̂ts, OCB *ʔəts

'To lose one's breath' [Shi] is a sound-symbolic word (§2.9)

ài$_4$ 薆 → **yī**$_5$ 翳

ài$_5$ 礙 (ŋậi^C) **LH** ŋə^C, **OCM** *ŋə̂kh

'Obstruct, hinder' [Lie].

[T] *Sin Sukchu SR* ŋaj (去); *MGZY* ngay (去) [ŋaj]; *ONW* ŋɑi^C

[E] ? ST: WT *'geg(s)-pa, bkag, dgag* 'to hinder, prohibit, shut' ⋈ *'gag* 'obstruction, stoppage' (Bodman 1980: 72); PLB *ʔgak 'obstruct, block up'. TB voiced stops do occasionally correspond to Chinese initial nasals (§5.12.2). Alternatively, WT could be compared with → gù$_1$ 固. CH *ài* may be related to → yí$_{13}$ 疑 'hesitate'.

ān$_1$ 安 (ʔân) **LH** ʔɑn, **OCM** *ʔân, OCB *ʔan
'Be calm, peaceful, still, steady, take one's leisure' [BI, Shi].
[T] *Sin Sukchu SR* ʔɔn (平); *PR* ʔan; *LR* ʔan; *MGZY* 'an (平) [ʔan]; *ONW* ʔɑn.

⋈ **àn** 按 (ʔân^C) **LH** ʔɑn^C, **OCM** *ʔâns
'To push down with the hand' [SW], 'to stop, repress' [Shi], 'lay hand on, seize' [Xun]; 'stool, tray' 案 [Zhouli].
[<] exoactive of *ān* (§4.3), lit. 'cause to be settled, calmed'.

[C] Boltz (1994: 95ff) includes additional words which are written with this phonetic (*GSR* 146), such as → ān$_3$ 鞍. A parallel stem (§2.5) is → yàn$_1$ 宴燕 (Wáng Lì 1982: 543). → yǎn$_5$ 偃 is prob. a different etymon.

ān$_2$ 安 interrogative particle → **wū$_5$** 惡

ān$_3$ 鞍 (ʔân) **LH** ʔɑn, **OCM** *ʔân
'Saddle' [Guanzi] is cognate to → ān$_1$ 安 acc. to Boltz (1994: 95f), lit. 'seat'. Following the *Shìmíng*, Pulleyblank has suggested a connection with **è** 頞 (ʔat) 'bridge of the nose' [Meng] (Boltz 1994: 98).

ān$_4$ 喑 (ʔậm) **LH** ʔəm, **OCM** *ʔə̂m
'Dumb, silent' [Mo].

⋈ **ǎn** 唵 (ʔậm^B) **LH** ʔəm^B, **OCM** *ʔə̂mʔ
'Hold in the mouth, put in the mouth' [GY].
[T] *ONW* ʔɑm.
[<] endoactive of *ān* 喑 (§4.5).

⋈ **yìn** 喑 (ʔjəm^C) **LH** ʔɨm^C, **OCM** *ʔəms
'Pent up' [Zhuang].
[<] exopass. of *ān* 喑 (§4.4), lit. 'be held back in the mouth', but the role of MC div. III is not clear (§9.1.2).

[E] ST *ʔum: PTB *um 'hold in the mouth' (*STC:* 181) > WT *ʔum* 'a kiss' (cf. *ʔu* ~ *ʔo* 'a kiss'); Lepcha *ŭm* 'receive into the mouth without swallowing', Mikir *om* 'mouthful', Nung *im* 'mouthful' (*HST*: 95). Perh. also connected with PTB *(m-)u:m (*STC:* 181 n. 479). → cǎn 噆 is perh. a derivation.

ǎn$_1$ 唵 → **ān$_4$** 喑

ǎn$_2$ 晻 → **yǎn$_{10}$** 黶

àn$_1$ 犴 → **yǔ$_7$** 圉圄

àn$_2$ 岸 (ŋân^C) **LH** ŋɑn^C, **OCM** *ŋâns, OCB *ŋans
'River bank' [Shi].
[T] *Sin Sukchu SR* ŋɔn (去); *PR* ʔan; *LR* ʔan; *MGZY* ngan (去) [ŋan]; *ONW* ŋɑn

⋈ **hàn** 厂 (xân^C) **LH** hɑn^C, **OCM** *hŋâns
'Cliff' [BI, SW], 'high river bank' [Liù shū běnyì 六書本義].

⋈ **hǔ** 滸 (xuo^B) **LH** hɑ^B, **OCM** *hŋâʔ
'River bank' [Shi].

[<] These are all nouns derived from the stem *ŋaʔ 'oppose, resist' (→ yù$_{17}$ 禦), i.e. 'the thing that resists the river's flow, keeps the river in its bed'. The voiceless initial in *hàn* and *hǔ* denotes a noun referring to a natural object (§5.2.4), the final *-n in *hàn* and *àn*

marks nouns in general (§6.4.3). The role, if any, of tone C is not clear. For an overview of similar and related words, see under → yà$_2$ 御迓訝.
[E] ST: WT *dŋo* 'shore, bank'.

àn$_3$ 黯 (ʔậm^B) **LH** ʔəm^B, **OCM** *ʔə̂mʔ — **[T]** *ONW* ʔɑm^B
'A deep black' [SW].
※ **àn** 暗闇 (ʔậm^C) **LH** ʔəm^C, **OCM** *ʔə̂ms
'Be dark' 暗 [Guoyu]; 闇 (also read QY ʔậm^B) [Li] > Mand. 'dim, gloomy'.
[T] *Sin S. SR* ʔam (去); *PR* ʔan; *MGZY* 'am (去) [ʔam], *ONW* ʔɑm^C.
[<] perh. exoactive of *àn* 黯 (§4.3), here noun > verb.
[C] A probable allofam is → yīn$_5$ 陰 (so Wáng Lì 1982: 602).

áng$_1$ 卬昂 'high' → **yǎng$_1$** 仰

áng$_2$ 卬 'I' → **wú$_2$** 吾

àng 盎 (ʔâŋ^C) **LH** ʔɑŋ^C, **OCM** *ʔâŋh
'(A small-mouthed, large-bellied) earthen jar (for fetching water)' [Lunheng] > 'obese, swollen' [Zhuang]; later 盎 'basin, tureen' (which is large-mouthed).
[E] AA: Khmer *'āṅa* /ʔaaŋ/ 'a type of large, wide-mouthed earthen jar, cistern, tank'.
[C] There are (near) synonyms with different vowels: → wèng 瓮甕罋 *ʔôŋh, and yīng 罌 *ʔrêŋ (under → yǐng$_2$ 癭).

áo$_1$ 鼇 → **yuán$_1$** 元

áo$_2$ 嗷 (ŋâu) **LH** ŋɑu, **OCM** *ŋâu
'To cry, clamor' [Shi].
[E] Perh. cognate to PTB *ŋuw > WT *ŋu-ba* 'to weep, roar', WB *ŋui* 'cry, weep', PL *ŋo^1 'cry' (*HST*: 60). This identification is somewhat doubtful as the vowels and the meanings are not very close.

áo$_3$ 熬 (ŋâu) **LH** ŋɑu, **OCM** *ŋâu, OCB *ngaw
'To fry' [Zhouli], 'roast' [Li].
[E] ST *ŋau: PTB *r-ŋaw (*STC* no. 270) > WT *rŋod-pa, brŋos* 'to parch, roast, fry'; Chepang *ŋāw*; Mikir *arŋu* 'roast, fry'; JP *gə^{31}-ŋau^{33}* 'fry' (*STC*: 193; also Bodman 1980: 78).

ào$_1$ 澳隩 (ʔâu^C) **LH** ʔou^C, **OCM** *ʔûkh
'Inside' (of a realm) [Shi], 'bay, cove' was acc. to Guō Pú (ca. AD 300), a Jiāngnán (southern) word.
[T] *Sin Sukchu SR* ʔaw (去); *MGZY* 'aw (去) [ʔaw]; *ONW* ʔɑu
[D] This word is still used in Mǐn dialects: Fúzhōu *o^{C1}-t^{h}au^{A2}*, Xiàmén *u^{C1}*
[E] AA: Viet *ao* 'pool, pond', WrMon *'o, o* 'cove, small bay' (Norman 1983: 205).

ào$_2$ 傲 (ngâu^C) **LH** ŋɑu^C, **OCM** *ŋâuh
'Proud, arrogant' [Shu]. Etymology not clear.
[T] *Sin S. SR* ŋaw (去); *PR* aw; *LR* aw; *MGZY* ngaw (去) [ŋaw]

B

bā$_1$ 八 (pǎt) **LH** pɛt, **OCM** *prêt
'Eight' [OB, Shi].
[T] *MTang* pär, *ONW* pät — **[D]** PMin *pet, K-Méixiàn *pat*
[E] ST *priat ~ *pret: PTB *b-r-yat (*STC* no. 163) > WT *brgyad* (< *bryat); TGTM *^{3}pret, Kanauri *re; PLB *ʔrit or *ʔryat > WB *hrac*; Lushai *pa*^{L}*-riat*^{F} (Bodman 1980: 73); Bahing *ja*, Thulung *jet*; JP *mə*^{31}*-tsat*^{55} < *m-rjat*. CH -> Tai: PT *p-: S. *pɛɛt*^{DlL} is obviously a CH loan (otherwise we should find an /r/ in the Tai initial).

bā$_2$ 巴 (pa) **LH** pa, **OCM** *prâ
'Python' [SW, Shanhaijing].
[T] *Sin Sukchu SR* pa (平); *MGZY*: ba (平) [pa]); *ONW* pä
[E] ? Kam-Tai: note Lao *ŋuu*^{A4} *kǎbaa*^{A3} 'a kind of viper: Agkistrodon' (*ŋuu* 'snake', *kǎ-* perh. animal prefix) (James Chamberlain *ICSTLL* 1981). AA-PNB *qbǎyh 'snake'.

bā$_3$ 笆 (ba^B, pa)
'A kind of bamboo from southwest China' [GY].
[E] The word's place of origin (SW China) and late appearance suggest that it is a loan from a TB language: PTB *pa [*STC* no. 44; Matisoff *LL* 1.2, 2000: 140] > WT *spa* ~ *sba* 'cane'; WB *wa*^{B} 'bamboo'; JP *kə*^{55}*-wa*^{55}, *wə*^{31} 'bamboo', Lushai *rua*^{H} *(rɔ*^{F}*)* (< *r-wa) 'a kind of bamboo' (*HST:* 38).

ꭗ **bā** 笆 (pa)
'Bamboo hedge or fence' [GY].
[E] PTB: *rpa: Kom *ra-pe*, Tširu *ra-pa* 'fence' (Kuki lgs.) [Shafer: *IST* 29].

bā$_4$ 疤 (pa) **LH** pa ?
'Scar' [JY].
[E] ? ST: Perh. related to WT *'bar-'bar* 'uneven, rough, pock-marked' (Unger *Hao-ku* 35, 1986: 36).

bā$_5$ 豝 (pa) **LH** pa, **OCM** *prâ
'Wild pig, pig' [Shi].
[E] *Bā* is assumed to be a ST word related to PTB *p^{w}ak > WT *p*^{h}*ag*; PLB *wak > WB *wak;* JP *waʔ*^{31} 'pig' (*STC* no. 43; Matisoff *LL* 1.2, 2000: 157f). But the OC and TB forms are phonologically not very close. OC medial *r corresponds also to a TB pre-initial, but TB forms for 'pig' do not have one, therefore one needs to assume some kind of CH innovation which led to medial *r. An OC open syllable corresponding to TB final *-k* is not common (§6.9). Alternatively, MK-Wa-Lawa-Bulang *bras 'wild boar' is semantically and phonologically close to the OC form. CH -> Miao languages *npa*^{4}, *npua*^{4} 'pig' (Strecker *LTBA* 10.2, 1987: 51: Benedict, Wáng Fúshì).

bā$_6$ 胈 → **fǎ**$_3$ 髮

bá$_1$ 犮 (buât) **LH** bɑt, **OCM** *bât
'To expel' (a person) [Zhouli].

ꭗ **bèi** 拔, **pèi** 沛 (buâi^C) **LH** bɑs, **OCM** *bâts, OCB *bots
'Uprooted' 沛 [Shi], 'thinned out' (trees) 拔 [Shi], 'uprooted' figuratively of a person 沛 [Lunyu].
[<] exopass. of *bá* 犮 *bât (§4.4).

⋈ **bá** 拔 (bǎt) **LH** bat, **OCM** *brât
'To pull up, uproot, be uprooted' [Yi, Shu].
[<] r-caus. of *bá* 犮 *bât (§7.5), lit. 'cause to be uprooted'.
[E] ST: Lushai $pɔt^L$ / $pɔʔ^L$ 'to pull, pull up, out'; cf. WT 'bog(s)-pa, bog 'be uprooted'.
[C] Allofams may include → fā 發 and → fèi$_6$ 廢 'cast aside' (if derived from *fā*).

bá$_2$ 茇 (puât) **LH** pɑt, **OCM** *pât
'Roots of grass' [Huainan, SW]. *SW* considers this word related to → fā 發 'lift up / out' and → fá$_2$ 伐 'to plow' as the plow exposes the roots of the grass. An allofam may be → bá$_3$ 茇 'to camp', and *bá* 跋 'foot, base'.
[E] Etymology not clear. Comparanda may include TB-JP *(n^{31}-/$niŋ^{31}$-) pot^{31}* 'root; origin'; or TB-Chepang *plu-* 'fall out, come out' (from roots – hair, grass).

⋈ **bá** 跋 (buât) **LH** bɑt, **OCM** *bât
'To trample on (with feet), trudge' [Shi], 'foot, base' (of a torch) [Li]; 'the end of an arrow' [Shi]. The basic meaning is 'foot, base'.

bá$_3$ 茇 (buât) **LH** bɑt, **OCM** *bât, OCB *bat
'To camp on grassland' [Shi, Zuo]. Commentators to *SW* derive this word from → bá$_2$ 茇 'roots of grass' which they gloss simply as 'grass'.

bá$_4$ 拔 → **bá$_1$** 犮

bá$_5$ 跋 → **bá$_2$** 茇

bá$_6$ 耙杷 → **pá$_2$**, **bá** 耙杷

bǎ 把 (pa^B) **LH** pa^B, **OCM** *prâʔ
'A handful' [Guoyu], 'grasp' [Meng].
[T] *Sin Sukchu SR* pa (上); *MGZY:* suppl. ba (上) [pa])
[E] ST: WT *spar-ba* 'the grasping hand, paw, claw, a handful' (Unger *Hao-ku* 35, 1986: 36). Matisoff (2000: 155f) connects this word with PTB *r-pa-k 'palm / sole and leaf'. For the r-metathesis, see §7.7.3.
This word may be related to → pá$_2$, bá 耙杷 'rake'. Given its TB cognates, it is prob. not related to → fú$_3$ 扶 'breadth of two fingers'. Wáng Lì (1982: 173) relates this wf to → bǐng$_2$ 秉 'grasp'.

bà$_1$ 垻 (pa^C)
'Flat valley'. This word from SW China is a Tai loan: S. paa^{B1} < *pa^B 'meadow' (Li F. 1976: 46; Mei Tsu-lin, *AAS* 1980).

bà$_2$ 罷 ($baɨ^B$) **LH** $bɛ^B$ or bai^B ?, **OCM** *brâiʔ or *brêʔ ?
'To stop, cease' (work etc.) tr. [Lun]. Prob. not related to → bì$_{25}$ 畢.
[T] *Sin Sukchu SR* ba (去); *MGZY* pay (上) [baj]
[E] ST: WB pri^B < pre^B 'be done, completed' (*CVST* 1: 59).

bà$_3$ 霸 → **bó$_1$** 伯

bà-bà 爸 'Father, dad', Mand. col. for → fù$_1$ 父.

bái$_1$ 白 (bɐk) **LH** bak, **OCM** *brâk
'Be white' [OB, BI, Shi] always has been a basic color term (Baxter *JCLTA* 19, 1983), also applied to silver.
[T] *Sin Sukchu SR* bəj (入); *LR* bəjʔ; *MGZY* pay (入) [baj]; *ONW* bĕk
[N] The graph represents an acorn, note the element 白 in the original graphs for → lè

樂 = *lì* 櫟 'oak' and *zào* 皂 'acorn'. It is not clear why the graph has been selected for 'white'. (Unger *Hao-ku* 29, 1984).

[E] ST: Most plausibly, *bái* is a CH k-extension (§6.1) of the ST root *bar 'white' and thus cognate to → pó$_3$ 皤 'white' (so Wáng Lì 1982: 292), hence OC < *bar-k: PTB *pwa:r > Lushai *vaar*^{H} 'be white', PKaren *ʔ(b)wa 'white' (Matisoff *LL* 1.2, 2000: 145).

Tai: S. *pʰɨak* < *p^hr/l- ? 'white, albino' (Li F. 1976: 44) may be a CH loan. <> AA 'silver' may be related: Nyah Kur pra̲k, PVM *prak.

Alternatively, note this area word for 'white' without medial r which is, however, difficult to reconcile with MC: PMK (PAA) *ɓɔ:k, SBahn. *bɔ:k 'white'; PTB *bok (?): S. Kuki *bok* 'white', Garo *gibok* ~ *gipok*, Dimasa *g-pʰuk.

[C] Possible cognates are → bó$_1$ 伯 'elder'; → bó$_2$ 帛; → pò$_4$ 魄, → pò$_5$ 霸魄.

bái$_2$ 白

[D] Min: Fúzhōu *paiʔ*^{7}, Amoy *bat*^{7} 'to know', borrowed from AA: Viet *biết* 'to know, recognize', also PMY *pˡai^{1A} 'to know' (Norman / Mei 1976: 298).

bǎi$_1$ 百 (pɐk) **LH** pak, **OCM** *prâk

'Hundred' [BI, Shi]. The OB graph is similar to, but not identical with, → bái$_1$ 白 'white' (Unger *Hao-ku* 29, 1984).

[T] *Sin S. SR* pəj (入), *LR* pəjʔ; *MGZY* bay (入) [paj]; *ONW* pëk.

[E] ST *(p)rya: PTB *r-ya (*STC* no. 164) > WT *brgya* < *br-ya;* Kanauri *rā;* PLB *hrya, WB *əra* (inscriptional *rya*), Lushai *za*^{L}*-bi*^{R} < *jaʔ/h*, Paangkhua *razáa* < *rya*. For the final *-k*, see §6.1. CH -> PTai *p-: Lóngzhōu *paak*^{DIL} is obviously a CH loan (otherwise we should expect an *r* in the initial and almost certainly an open syllable).

bǎi$_2$ 捭 (baɨ^B) **LH** bɛ^B, **OCM** *brêʔ

'To open' [Guiguzi].

[E] ST *prai: WB *prai*^{B} 'to gape, expand, flare' ⋈ *pʰrai*^{B} 'to pull open, make gap'; Chepang *pre-ʔak-sa* 'to separate' (intr.).

A derivation is → bò$_3$ 擘 (pɛk). Possibly related to → zhā 奓 *trai 'to open'. For an overview of similar items, see the table under → pí$_7$ 罷疲. For a listing of similar words and possible allofams, see → lí$_{10}$ 離.

bài$_1$ 敗 (pai^C) **LH** pas, **OCM** *prâts

'To ruin, destroy' [Shi].

[T] *Sin Sukchu SR* pai, bai (去); *MGZY* bay, pay (去) [paj ~ bɑj]

⋈ **bài** 敗 (bai^C) **LH** bas, **OCM** *brâts, OCB *ɦprats

'To go to ruin, defeat' [OB, Shi].

[<] endopass. of *bài* 敗 (pai^C) (§4.6).

[E] Etymology not certain, but Tai: S. *prap*^{4} 'to subdue, conquer' is the same etymon and indicates a PCH form *praps > OCM *prâts. (The phonetic → bèi$_2$ 貝 is also connected to foreign *-p*.) The direction of borrowing is undetermined, yet Tai is prob. not the ultimate source of CH. More likely, the etymon is a 'medial r' causative derivation (§7.5) with the addition of the redundant exoactive final *-s (§4.3). AA is the most likely source of OC: OMon *pop* /pop/ 'to give way to', Khmer *-pap* /-bɑɑp/ 'be beaten, subdued, routed' ⋈ *paṁpapa* /bɑmbɑɑp/ 'to crush' (opposition), 'break down' (resistance). (Note that MK has a causative r-infix.) <> ST: WT *'brab-pa* 'to beat, scourge (e.g. with thorns), scatter' (e.g. grain for offering) is semantically somewhat removed.

Alternatively, *bài* may be derived from → fèi$_6$ 廢 'reject, fall'; however, fèi$_6$ 廢 ⋈ fá 乏 = WT *bab* 'fall down' is semantically different from *bài* 敗 = AA *pap* 'be beaten', hence we consider these two distinct wfs. Acc. to Wáng Lì (1982: 500) an allofam is → $bì_{10}$ 敝弊斃 'worn out'. Pulleyblank (1962: 215) relates this wf to → $pí_7$ 罷疲. See → $fèi_6$ 廢 for additional comments.

$bài_2$ 拜 (pǎi^C) **LH** pas, **OCM** *prâts, OCB *prots
'To bend or put together' (the hands in salute), 'to salute' [BI, Shi]. Etymology not clear.

$bài_3$ 粺 (baɨ^C) **LH** bɛ^C, **OCM** *brêh, OCB *bres
'Fine rice' [Shi].
[E] This etymon is close to → $lì_{21}$ 糲 *ras 'coarse grain' and its possible cognates, both hail perh. from the same foreign source. This word *bài* and → $mǐ_1$ 米 'rice' can on occasion be connected with the same foreign comparandum. The following items look similar to *bài*: AA-Kharia *pɛʔ*, Khmer *paj* < **paih*, *pih 'rice', PNB *pʰe 'husked rice'. Note also TB-Mru *rai* 'a species of rice', Lushai *ṭai^F* < *traih* (< *-s) 'species of early rice' [Löffler 1966: 132]; the Lushai word has also been associated with WT *kʰre* 'millet' (Sagart ms 2002: 8).

$bān_1$ 班 (pan) **LH** pan, **OCM** *prân
'To distribute' [BI, Shu] > 'spread out, scatter' [Zuo] > 'to arrange, classify' [Meng].
[T] *Sin Sukchu SR* pan (平); *MGZY* ban (平) [pan]
[E] ? ST *pral: WT *'pʰral-ba* 'to separate, part' ⋈ *'bral-ba* 'be separated, lose', WB *pra^B* 'be divided into several parts, various', JP *pə^{31}-ran^{31}* 'be separate, sort out' (for JP allofams, see → lí 離). In *HST:* 65, the WT item is associated with → $bàn_2$, biàn 釆, and with → $bàn_1$ 半 by Bodman (1980: 147), while Karlgren (1933: 92f) combines all of these into one wf (no. 26–37). <> AA has an alternative comparandum which is semantically closer to OC, even the initial *p- could represent an AA trans. / caus. prefix: Khmer *rāla* /ríiəl/ intr. 'to spread, extend, distribute' ⋈ *brāla* /príiəl/ tr. 'to spread'.

A cognate is prob. *(C-)ral → $lí_{10}$ 離 *rai with the occasional ST *-l > OC *-i shift (§8.3). → $bān_2$ 斑 is perh. the same word. For an overview of similar items, see $lí_{10}$ 離 and Table P-1 under → $pī_3$ 披.

$bān_2$ 斑 (pan) **LH** pan, **OCM** *prân
'Variegated' [Li] may either be the s. w. as → $bān_1$ 班 'scatter'; or may be a derivation from → $bó_9$ 駁 'mixed colors'. In this case, OCM *prân would derive from earlier *pron.

$bān_3$ 搬 (puân) **LH** pɑn — **[D]** CDC *pon^1*
'To move, transport', a post-classical word.
[T] *Sin Sukchu SR* pwɔn (平), *PR* pɔn, *LR* pɔn; cf. 般 *MGZY* bon (平) [pɔn]

$bǎn_1$ 板版 (pan^B) **LH** pan^B, **OCM** *prânʔ
'Board, plank' [Shi].
[E] ST *par: WT *'pʰar* 'a panel, small plank' (Bodman 1980: 145; *HST:* 45). CH -> PTai *p-: S. *pɛɛn^{C1}*. For the OC medial *r, see §6.1.

$bǎn_2$ 昄 (pan^B, ban^B) **LH** pan^B, ban^B, **OCM** *prânʔ, *brânʔ ?
'Great' (of demeanor, domain, god) [Shi].
[E] ? ST: WT *'pʰar-ba* 'raised, elevated' (Bodman 1980: 145; *HST:* 88). For the OC medial *r, see §6.1.

bàn$_1$ 半 (puân^C) **LH** pɑn^C, **OCM** *pâns

'Half' [Yi].

[T] *Sin Sukchu SR* pwɔn (去), *PR* pɔn, *LR* pɔn; *MGZY* bon (去) [pɔn]; *ONW* pɑn

꙳ **pàn** 判片泮 (p^{h}uân^C) **LH** p^{h}ɑn^C, **OCM** *p^{h}âns

'To cleave' [Zhouli], 'divide' 判 [Zuo]; 'one half, one of two parts' 片 [Zhuang] > semi-circular pool, shore' 泮 [Shi], and additional specialized meanings based on 'half'.

[<] exoactive of *bàn* (§4.3), perh. caus. aspiration (§5.8.2).

꙳ **pàn** 畔 (buân^C) **LH** bɑn^C, **OCM** *bâns — **[T]** *ONW* bɑn

'Bank between fields, separate from' [Zuo], 'to separate from, rebel' [Lunyu].

[<] endopass. of *bàn* (§4.6), lit. 'be separated from'.

[E] ST *par: WT *bar* 'interstice, intermediate space, middle, mean' (*HST:* 109) ꙳ WT *p^{h}rag < par-k* 'intermediate space, interstice, interval' (§6.1); NNaga *p^{h}ar* 'divide' [French 1983: 183]. JP *ban* 'division, part', Bodo *pan* 'share, part' may belong here which *CVST* I: 4f relates to → fēn$_1$ 分, however. Li F. (1976: 41) also relates Tai: S. *pan^{A1}* < *p- 'to divide into shares' to *fēn*. For alternative connections, see → bān$_1$ 班.

bàn$_2$, **biàn** 釆 (bǎn^C, bjän^C 3) [Shiwen] **LH** bɛn^C, bɨan^C, **OCM** *brens

'Discriminate, distinguish' [Shu].

[<] exopass. of *biàn* 辨辯 below (§4.3), lit. '(cause to) be divided'.

꙳ **bàn** 瓣 (bǎn^C), **LH** bɛn^C

'Sections of a fruit' [SW].

[<] exopass. of *biàn* 辨辯 below (§4.3), lit. 'what is divided'. → bàn$_4$ 瓣 'petals' is perh. the s. w.

꙳ **biàn** 辨辯 (bjän^B 3) **LH** bɨan^B, **OCM** *brenʔ ?

'Divide' [Zhouli], 'distinguish, discriminate' 辨 [Lunyu] (also MC *bǎn^C*), 辯 [Yi], 'dispute' [Meng].

[T] *Sin Sukchu SR* bjen (上); *MGZY* pen (上) [bɛn]; *ONW* ban

[E] ? ST: This wf may belong to TB-Lushai *p^{h}el^H* 'to split, cut in halves' (medial *r* does not occur in Lushai after labial initials), and / or to *pral > → bān$_1$ 班 (§2.5).

bàn$_3$ 辦 (bǎn^C) **LH** bɛn^C, **OCM** *brêns

'To deal with, handle, manage' [BI, Zuo].

[T] *Sin Sukchu SR* ban (去); *MGZY* pan (去) [ban]

[E] ST *brel: WT *brel-ba* 'be employed, busy, engaged' (Bodman 1980: 163).

bàn$_4$ 瓣 (bǎn^C) (**LH** bɛn^C ?)

'Petals of a flower' is a late word [14th cent. AD]. The MC reading applies to the meaning 'sections of a fruit' (under → bàn$_2$, biàn 釆). In the QYS, the rimes *-an* and *-ǎn* seem to have been confused on occasion; therefore *-ǎn* could also go back to *-rân.

[E] 'Petals' is possibly the same word as *bàn* 瓣 'section of fruit' (under → bàn$_2$, biàn 釆). Alternatively, it could be the same etymon as → pā 葩 'flowers, blossoms' and prob. related to 'burn' → fán$_5$ 燔, note the WT word *me-t^{h}og* 'flower', lit. 'fire-top'.

bāng 邦 (påŋ) **LH** pɔŋ, **OCM** *prôŋ

'Country' [Shi], possibly the same etymon as → fēng$_1$ 封 (Wáng Lì 1982: 388).

[T] *Sin Sukchu SR* paŋ (平); *MGZY* bang (平) [paŋ]

bǎng$_1$ 榜 (pwâŋ^B) **LH** pɑŋ^B, **OCM** *pâŋʔ — **[T]** *ONW* pɑŋ

'Board' [Jinshu].

[E] ST: WT *spaŋ* 'board, plank' (Unger *Hao-ku* 36, 1990: 48). Superficially, this word looks like a doublet of → bǎn$_1$ 板版. The graph also writes a word QYS *pɐŋ*^{C}, LH *paŋ*^{C} 'oar' [Chuci].

bǎng$_2$ 膀 → **bó$_4$** 膊

bàng$_1$ 棒 (båŋ^B) **LH** bɔŋ^B, **OCM** *brôŋʔ
'Club, stick' [Post-Han: Weishu].
[E] <> Tai: S. *p^{h}lɔɔŋ*^{A2} < *b- 'club, cudgel' (Manomaivibool 1975).

bàng$_2$ 旁傍 → **páng** 旁傍

bàng$_3$ 艕, **huáng** 艎 → **fāng$_2$** 方

bāo$_1$ 包 (pau) **LH** pɔu, **OCM** *prû
'To wrap, bundle' [Shu], 'contain' [Zuo].
[T] *Sin Sukchu SR* paw (平); *MGZY* baw (平) [paw]
[E] ST: WT *'p^{h}ur-ba* 'to wrap up, envelop' (Unger *Hao-ku* 35, 1986: 36), perh. also Lepcha *prók* ~ *prek* 'wrap up' [Bodman *ICSTLL* 1987: 21]. For the r-metathesis, see §7.7.3. This word is often thought to be cognate to → bào$_1$ 抱 'carry in arms', but the TB cognates cast doubt on this.

bāo$_2$ 胞 (pau, p^{h}au) **LH** p(^{h})ɔu, **OCM** *p(h)rû — **[T]** *ONW* p^{h}äu
'Womb' [Zhuang].
[E] ST: WT *p^{h}ru-ma* ~ *'p^{h}ru-ma/-ba* 'uterus, placenta' (Bodman 1980: 142; *HST:* 161); Löffler (*ZDMG* 116.1, 1966: 152) adds Mru *bur* 'menstruation'. Acc. to Karlgren (1956: 5) this is the s. w. as → bāo$_1$ 包 'wrap', but this is doubtful in light of TB cognates which distinguish these two items. Löffler relates 'womb' to → páo 匏 'gourd'.

bāo$_3$ 剝 (påk) **LH** pɔk, **OCM** *prôk.
'To cut up, peel, pluck' [Shi].
[D] Guǎngzhōu *mɐk*^{7} 'to peel' (Sagart 1999: 80), Zhōngshān *mɔk*^{55} 'to undress'.
[E] <> Tai: S. *pɔɔk*^{D1} 'to peel', but also PTai *dlɔɔk : S. *lɔɔk*^{D2} 'to skin, peel' ⋈ *plɔɔk*^{D1} 'an encasement, slipcover, sheath' (Manomaivibool 1975: 120). This word is considered to be related to → lù$_1$ 彔 'carve', but 'carve' and 'peel' are rather different activities.

bǎo$_1$ 保 (pâu^B) **LH** pou^B, **OCM** *pûʔ
'To take care of' (a baby by wrapping it in swaddling cloth) [Meng], (people) [Shu]; 'preserve, protect, maintain' [Shi].
[T] *Sin Sukchu SR* paw (上); *MGZY* baw (上) [paw]

= **bǎo$_1$** 葆 (pâu^B) **LH** pou^B, **OCM** *pûʔ
(What protects, shields:) 'secure' (residence, land) 葆 [Shu]; 'fort, stronghold' 保 [Li]; 'cover' for a chariot 葆 [Lun Heng].

= **bǎo$_1$** 褓 (pâu^B) **LH** pou^B, **OCM** *pûʔ
'The cloth' (in which children are carried on the back) [Lüshih], 'swaddling cloth' [Liezi], used in the expression *qiǎng bǎo* 繈 or 襁褓 (*qiǎng*, MC *kjaŋ*^{B}, 'string, cord', here prob. 'strap'); apparently *bǎo* refers to the protective swaddling cloth, not to the notion of carrying a baby on the back.

[E] Etymology not certain. Following Táng Lán, Qiu Xigui (2000: 212f) interprets an OB form of the graph as well as an occurrence in *Shūjīng* 17,10 as 'to carry (a baby) on the back', thence 'take care of' etc.; *bǎo* would then be the OC cognate of the TB items under → fù$_{11}$ 負. However, in no textual occurrence, incl. *Shūjīng*, has *bǎo* the unequivocal meaning 'carry on the back'. Alternatively, this could be the s. w. as → bǎo₃ 寶 'precious' used in a putative sense, lit. 'consider something precious', and then act accordingly.

It is not clear if / how → bāo₁ 包 'wrap, contain', and WT *pʰru-ma* 'fortified camp, palace, fort' (*HST:* 164) may be related.

bǎo₂ 飽 (pauᴮ) **LH** pɔuᴮ, **OCM** *prûʔ
'To eat to the full, satiated' [Shi].
[T] *Sin Sukchu SR* paw (上); *MGZY* baw (上) [paw]; *ONW* päu
[E] Prob. area word: TB-Lushai *puarᴴ* < *puar* 'having eaten enough' (Unger *Hao-ku* 35, 1986: 36), Chepang *bʰorʔ-* 'eat in plenty, feed generously', perh. connected with AA-Khmer /póor/ 'to fill, be full, brim full, swollen'. For the r-metathesis, see §7.7.3.

bǎo₃ 寶 (pâuᴮ) **LH** pouᴮ, **OCM** *pûʔ
'Be precious, treasure' [BI, Shi].
[T] *Sin S. SR* paw (上); *MGZY* baw, ba'o (上) [paw]; *ONW* pɑu
[E] ST *pu: PTB *puw (*STC* no. 41) > WB *ə-pʰuiᴮ* ~ *ə-bʰuiᴮ* 'price', JP *pʰu³³* 'be of value, expensive' (*HST:* 155), Lushai *puᴴ* < *pʰuu* 'be worthy, deserving'. *CVST* 1: 63 adds WT *spus* 'goods, merchandise'. → bǎo₁ 保 could be the same word. Sagart (1999: 58) considers *bǎo* possibly related to *fù* 富 (under → fú₁₉ 福).

bào₁ 抱 (bâuᴮ) **LH** bouᴮ, **OCM** *bûʔ — **[D]** PMin *bʰâuᴮ² ~ *bâuᴮ²
'Carry in the arms' [Shi].
[T] *Sin Sukchu SR* baw (上); *MGZY* paw (上) [baw]
[E] This is perh. related to WB *puik* 'hold in arms, hug', and / or to AA-Khmer /pɔɔ/ and /pɔɔr/ 'hold or carry in the arm(s)'. Note also → bāo₁ 包 'wrap'. -> PMiao *buoᶜ.

bào₂ 報 (pâuᶜ) **LH** pouᶜ, **OCM** *pûh
'To repay, requite, reward, respond, announce' [Shi], 'report'.
= Prob. **bào** 報 'to plait, interweave' (i.e. 'return the thread') [Shi] > 'tie, wrap' [Li].
[E] This is prob. an allofam of → fù₁₂ 復 'return, reply, report' (so Wáng Lì 1982: 244; Sagart 1999: 58). <> Tai: S. *bɔk⁴* 'to tell, say, inform'.

bào₃ 豹 → **bó₉** 駁

bēi₁ 卑 (pjie 4) **LH** pie, **OCM** *pe — **[T]** *ONW* pie
'Be low, humble' [Shi], opposite of 'high' [Zuo].
ꭗ **bì** 埤庳婢 (bjieᴮ 4) **LH** bieᴮ, **OCM** *beʔ
(a) 'Be low' [Zuo], 'be short' 庳 [Zhouli].
(b) 'Low ground' 埤 [Guoyu]; 'female slave, servant' 婢 [Li].
[<] endoactive (§4.5.1) 'what / who is low'. A possible allofam is → bì₂₀ 嬖.

bēi₂, bī 陂 (pje 3) **LH** pɨai, **OCM** *pai
'Slope, bank, dike' [Shi, Shu], 'slanting' [Yi]. Prob. not related to → pǔ₁ 浦.
ꭗ **bì** 陂 (pjeᶜ 3) **LH** pɨaiᶜ, **OCM** *paih
'Be slanting, oblique' 陂 [Shu, Yi]; 'one-sided words, insincere' 詖 (also MC *pje*) [Meng].
[<] perh. exoactive, i.e. a verb derived from the noun *bēi, bī* 陂.
ꭗ **pō** 頗坡 (pʰuâ) **LH** pʰɑi, **OCM** *phâi — **[T]** *ONW* pʰɑ
'Oblique, slanting' [Chuci], 'partial, perverse' 頗 [Shu]; 'slope, bank' 坡.
[D] Y-Guǎngzhōu *pʰɔᴬ¹*, Táishān *puɔᴬ¹*; K-Méixiàn *pɔᴬ¹*
[E] <> Tai: S. *pʰlay²* (McFarland: 550) 'leaning, sloping'; MC div. I may indicate an OC medial *l* (§8.2).

※ **pì** 僻 (p^hjiäk 4) **LH** p^hiek, **OCM** *phek (< *phai-k)
'Oblique' [Chuci] > 'depraved, perverse' [Shu], 'despise' [Zuo].
[<] k-extension of the root *pai 'slanting, oblique' (§6.1).

※ **bì** 避 (bjie^C 4) **LH** bie^C, **OCM** *bekh (< *bai-ks)
'Avoid' [Shi, Meng], 'go away' [Guoyu].
[T] *Sin Sukchu SR* bi (去); *MGZY* pi (去) [bi]
[E] ST: Lushai *pai^R < paiʔ* 'out of a straight line, oblique'. Allofams are → bǒ 跛 'walk lame', → piān 偏 'oblique', perh. → $bō_1$ 波 'wave'.

$bēi_3$ 杯桮 (puậi) **LH** pə, **OCM** *pə̂ — **[T]** *ONW* pɑi
'Cup' 杯 [Li], 桮 [Meng].
[E] ST: WT *p^hor-pa* 'bowl, dish, cup' (Unger *Hao-ku* 35, 1986: 33).

$bēi_4$ 悲 (pji 3) **LH** pɨi, **OCM** *prəi, OCB *prjəj
'Be unhappy, pained' [Shi]; 'to pity' [Shiji]; 'long for, miss' [Hanshu]. Etymology not clear.
[T] *Sin Sukchu SR* pi (平); PR pəj; *MGZY* bue (平) [puɛ]

běi 北 → **$fù_{11}$** 負

$bèi_2$ 貝 (puâi^C) **LH** pɑs, **OCM** *pâts < *pops ?
'Cowry shell' [BI, Shi].
[T] *Sin Sukchu SR* puj (去), *PR* pəj, *LR* pəj; *MGZY* bay (去) [paj]
[E] ? ST *pop: Chepang *bop* 'snail', JP *lə^{55}-pop^{55}* 'snail' (Bodman 1980: 136). However, note the curious AA words: PMK *ɓa(a)y > Khasi *sbâi* 'cowry, shell, money', Khmer *pùuy* 'obsolete small coin' (Shorto 1972).

$bèi_3$ 否 (bji^B 3) **LH** bɨə^B, **OCM** *brəʔ ?
'Fill up, obstruct' (a hole) [Yi].

※ **bì** 愎 (bjək) **LH** bɨk, **OCM** *brək ?
'Resist, obstinate' [Zuo].

[E] ? ST: WT *'ba* 'hole' (*CVST* 1: 92). (But WB *p^ha* 'patch up, close a hole by patching' belongs to → $bǔ_2$ 補.)

$bèi_4$ 倍 (buậi^B) **LH** bə^B, **OCM** *bə̂ʔ — **[T]** *ONW* bɑi
'Double' [Shi].
[<] perh. endoactive of *péi* 陪培 (§4.5).

※ **péi** 陪培 (buậi) **LH** bə, **OCM** *bə̂
'To augment, double' [Zuo], 'accompany, associate, support' 陪 [Shi]; 'accumulate, add to' 培 [Zhuang].
[T] *Sin S. SR* buj (平); *PR* bəj; *MGZY* pue (平) [buɛ]; *ONW* bɑi

※ **póu** 裒 (bəu) **LH** bu ?, **OCM** *bu !
'To collect, assemble, be together' [Shi]. Given the dialectal differences in vowels after labial initials in the *Shījīng* and later, this word may be a variant of the stem *bə with *-u due to similarity with the complex 'swell' → $fù_8$ 阜.

[E] ? ST: WT *'p^har-ma* 'double, manifold' (Unger *Hao-ku* 35, 1986: 33), Lepcha *bǎr* [bər], Adi *par-* 'increase' [Bodman *ICSTLL* 1987: 7]. → $fù_7$ 阜 'big mound' is a different etymon.

$bèi_5$ 備 (bji^C 3) **LH** bɨə^C, **OCM** *brə(k)h ?, OCB *brjəks
'Ready, complete, perfect' [Shi], 'prepare, provide' [Zuo].
[T] *Sin Sukchu SR* bi (去), *LR* bi; *MGZY* pue (去) [buɛ]
[E] Area etymon: TB-WB *praŋ* 'prepare, put in order, correct'; JP *p^hraʔ^{31} < p^hrak^{31}* 'to

complete'. MK: Mon *preŋ* 'to have prepared, prepare, arrange'. Tai: S. p^hrak^{D2} < *b-* 'prepare, ready' (Manomaivibool 1975: 207). For the final consonants, see §6.6.

bèi$_6$ 被 (bje$^{B/C}$ 3) **LH** bɨai$^{B/C}$, **OCM** *baiʔ/h
'To cover', incl. putting on clothes, also figuratively [Shi], 'be covered, to wear' [Zuo], 'outside garment' [Yili].
[T] *Sin Sukchu SR* bi (上去), *LR* bi; *MGZY* pue (上去) [buɛ]; *MTang* bi, *ONW* be

ж **pī** 被 (p^{h}je 3) **LH** p^{h}ɨai, **OCM** *phai
'Cover oneself with' [Zuo] < caus. ? (§5.8.2).

ж **pì** 被 (p^{h}je^C 3) **LH** p^{h}ɨai^C, **OCM** *phaih
'A cloak' [Zuo] < general derivation (§3.5).

[E] ST: Lushai *bel^F* < *beelʔ* tr. 'to make wear, put on' (garment, load, plaster...). Following *Shìmíng*, Wáng Lì (1982: 446) relates → pí$_1$ 皮 'skin, hide' to this root.

bèi$_7$ 拔, **pèi** 沛 → **bá$_1$** 犮

bèi$_8$ 婢 → **bēi$_1$** 卑

bèi$_9$ 背 → **fù$_{11}$** 負

bēn$_1$ 奔 (puən) **LH** pən, **OCM** *pə̂n, OCB *pun, *Shījīng* *pûn < *plun
'To run, flee' [BI, Shi], 'to hasten' (奔命 'hasten to carry out an order' [Zuo]), frequently in the BI *bēn-zǒu* 奔走 'to run and hurry while serving someone > to busy oneself for'.
[E] ST: PTB *ploŋ (*STC* no. 140): JP $p^hroŋ^{33}$ 'flee, run away', Mikir *arploŋ* < *r-ploŋ* 'run' ж *iŋploŋ* < *m-ploŋ* 'run, gallop', Lahu *phɔ* 'flee', perh. also WB *hroŋ* 'flee' [Matisoff]. For the difference in final nasals, see §6.4.2.

bēn$_2$ 賁 (puən) **LH** pən, **OCM** *pə̂n
'Be ardent, brave' [BI, Shu], 'ardent' 奔 [Shi].
[E] ST: Lushai *p^huur^R* < *p^huurʔ* 'zealous, eager, earnest, enthusiastic'. Some of the words under → fén$_4$ 墳 probably belong here.

běn 本 (puən^B) **LH** pən^B, **OCM** *pə̂nʔ
'Root, stem' [Shi] > 'origin, fundament' [Zuo]; measure for books [Nanbaichao], the origin of this latter meaning is not clear (Norman 1988: 116).
[T] *Sin Sukchu SR* pun (上); *PR* pən; *LR* pən; *MGZY* bun (上) [pun]; *ONW* pon
[E] CH -> Tai-Wuming *pløn^{C1}* 'volume' (Bodman 1980: 108). If indeed the Wuming *-l-* should go back to OC, then the final *-n* in *běn* would not be the result of the sound change ST *-l > OC *-n, but be the PCH nominal n-suffix attached to *pul (§6.4.3).
ST *pul: PTB *bul ~ *pul > Lushai *bul^R* < *buulʔ* 'beginning, origin, base, stump, lower part' ? ж *buul^L* / *bulʔ^L* (< *buulh* / *bulʔ/h*) 'be broken off, lopped off' (as extremity, limb, shoot), NNaga *pul* 'tree' [French 1983: 177], Garo *bol* 'root, stump', Moshang *puul* 'root'; JP p^hun^{55} 'tree, wood' (*STC:* 166; *HST:* 127), perh. also WT *sbun* ~ *spun* 'stalk of a plant' (*CVST* 1: 14). This word may be cognate to a root → fēn$_1$ 分 'cut off, cut in two' (hence 'tree stump, tree trunk...').

bèn 笨 (puən^C)
'Be stupid', a post-Han word which may, however, be old (such words are not common in classical texts) and cognate to WT *blun-pa* 'dull, stupid'.

bēng$_1$ 伻 → **pēng** 伻

bēng$_2$ 崩 (pəŋ) **LH** pəŋ, **OCM** *pə̂ŋ. — **[T]** *ONW* pəŋ. — **[D]** PMin *p̌-: Jiànyáng *vaiŋ^9*
'Mountain slide; to collapse, die (of a prominent person)' [Shi]. PMin *p̌- derives perh.

from a prenasalized initial, note Yao *baaŋ¹* (< *nb-) 'collapse, fall over' (Norman 1986: 382).

[E] Etymology not certain, but note TB-Chepang *bəŋh-* 'to slip, slide' (earth, rock) ※ *bəŋh-* n. 'rock or earth slide, landslide'. Chepang *bom-* 'fall down' ※ WT *'pʰam-pa, pʰam* 'be beaten, conquered' (Bodman 1980: 119) is unrelated.

bēng₃ 綳 → **péng₂** 朋 'string'

běng 菶 → **péng₄** 蓬

bèng₁ 迸 → **bìng₃** 屏

bèng₂ 榜 → **bǎng₁** 榜

bèng₃ 堋 (pəŋ^C) **LH** pəŋ^C, **OCM** *pə̂ŋh

'To put the coffin into the ground, bury' [Zuo]. The word is not related to → biǎn₅ 窆.

[E] Prob. AA: OKhmer *pāṅ* /ɓaŋ/ 'to cover, hide, bury'. -> Tai *pɔɔŋ^C1* < *p- 'to protect, cover up' (not related to → bǔ₂ 補, as Li F. 1976: 40 suggests).

bī₁ 屄 (pjie 4) < *pe, *pet

'Vulva', a late word which could, however, be old since such items are not mentioned in classical texts.

[D] Mǐn: Amoy *tsi^A1-pai^A2*; with final consonant Kèjiā: Dōngguān *³³tsi^A1-²²pet^D1* 支北. Yuè dialects have *⁵⁵hɐi^A1* (Guǎngzhōu) which is a Tai loan (Benedict *LTBA* 5.1, 1979), but apparently also found in some TB languages: Limbu *hira* 'vagina', Tangkhul Naga *hai*.

[E] ST *bet ?, PTB *b(y)et (*HPTB:* 375): PLB *b(y)et^L 'vulva', Kanauri *pʰɛːts;* also Tamang and Baro *pi-si* [Benedict *LTBA* 5.1, 1979: 30; *LTBA* 14.1: 143-6; R. Bauer *LTBA* 14.1: 147–165]. Benedict [*LTBA* 14.2, 1991: 151] derives this etymon from a root 'hidden', WT *sbed-pa, sbas, sba* 'to hide, conceal', but a WT root with *a* as in *sba* normally does not correspond to one with vowel *e / i* in Chinese; see also → bì₁₂ 蔽.

[<] Derived from 'to open' (see → pì 闢, → pī₃ 披), final *-t marks nouns of naturally occurring objects (§6.2.1), hence lit. 'opening'. Syn. → zhì₆ 膣.

bī₂ 偪逼 (pjək) **LH** pɨk, **OCM** *prək ?, OCB *prjək — [T] *ONW* pik

'To crowd together, encroach upon, near to' [Zuo, Meng]; 'to urge, press, close' 逼 [Meng, Zuo].

[E] Prob. ST: TB-Lushai *pik^L* 'be thick, dense, impenetrable, overcrowded, overgrown'. Alternatively, Baxter (1992: 473) relates this item to → lì₁ 力.

bí 鼻 (bjiet 4) Tang period: col. Shāzhōu *bir, *bit

'Nose'.

[D] Mand. *bízǐ* 鼻子. This form in final *-t is found in modern central and northern dialects as well as in the medieval Shāzhōu dialects in the NW, e.g. Gàn *pʰit^D*, Línchuān *pʰit^D2*. Acc. to Baxter (1992: 319) this word may reflect an early loss of final *-s (in *-ts, *-ks) which seems to have occurred in the northwest area; or it may reflect a dialectal change from earlier *-s to *-t (Pulleyblank *JAOS* 118.2, 1998: 204f).

[E] Perh. cognate to WT *sbrid-pa* 'to sneeze' (*HST:* 113), but CH has no trace of an *r*. Given the lack of potential cognates in related languages, one might speculate that this is a CH innovation related to 'to open' (cf. → pì 闢, → pī₃ 披), hence lit. 'openings'; but the vowels would not agree very closely.

※ **bì** 鼻 (bi^C 4) **LH** bis, **OCM** *bi(t)s

'Nose' [OB, Meng].

[T] *Sin Sukchu SR* bi (去); *MGZY* pi (去) [bi]; *ONW* bii
[D] This tone C variant is found in ONW, Sui-Tang Cháng'ān, MC, and in modern southern dialects: Min *b^{h}i^{C}: Jiàn'ōu *p^{h}i^{C2}*, Fúzhōu *p^{h}ei^{C}*, Xiàmén *p^{h}ĩ^{C2}*; Kèjiā: Méixiàn *p^{h}i^{C1}* (Norman 1988: 223).

ꭗ **bì** 鼻 (bi^{C} 4)
'To smell' in Kèjiā and Mǐn: PMin *bi^{C}: Jiàn'ōu pi^{C2}, Xiàmén p^{h}i^{C2} < *b^{h}i^{C}.

bǐ$_{1}$ 比 (pi^{B} 4) **LH** pi^{B}, **OCM** *piʔ
'To be associating' [Shi], 'equal, similar' [Li], 'compare' [Zuo]. Possibly → pì$_{5}$ 譬 'example' could be related.
[T] *Sin Sukchu SR* pi (上), *PR* pəj, *LR* pi; *MGZY* bi (上) [pi]; *MTang* pɨ, *ONW* pii
[<] endoactive of *bì* 比 *pih (§4.5).

ꭗ **bì** 比 (pi^{C} 4) **LH** pi^{C}, **OCM** *pih
'To put together, match, assemble' [Shi].
[<] exoactive of *bǐ* 比 (§4.3). The readings of this and the next item are from *Jīngdiǎn shìwén*.

ꭗ **bì** 比 (bi^{C} 4) **LH** bi^{C}, **OCM** *bih, OCB *bjijs
'To join' [Shu], 'go together with' [Shi], 'follow' [Lun], 'close together, successive' [Li].

ꭗ **pín** 頻 (bjien 4) **LH** bin, **OCM** *bin
'Several together' [Guoyu], 'close to' [BI] (Geilich 1994: 125).
[E] ST: Lepcha *bín* 'follow closely, belong to, be with, be next to' (ibid.); WT *p^{h}yi* 'behind, after' ꭗ *p^{h}yi-ma* 'later, subsequently' ꭗ *p^{h}yid* 'after, following' ꭗ *p^{h}yin* 'later, afterward'. WT homophones which are mentioned under → bīn$_{2}$ 濱 could possibly belong to this root instead ('behind' > 'outside'?).

bǐ$_{2}$ 妣 (pi$^{B/C}$ 4) **LH** pi^{B}, pi^{C}, **OCM** *piʔ, pih, OCB *pjijʔ
'Deceased mother, ancestress' [OB, Shi].
[E] ST *pi: PTB *pəy or *piy > WT *ʔa-p^{h}yi, p^{h}yi-mo* 'grandmother', Kanauri *a-pi*, WB *ə-p^{h}e^{B}* 'great grandfather' ꭗ *ə-phe^{B}-ma^{C}* 'great grandmother' (*STC* no. 36); Lushai *pi^{H}* '(great-) grandmother' (Matisoff *LL* 1.2, 2000: 172).

bǐ$_{3}$ 秕 (pi^{B} 4) **LH** pi^{B}, **OCM** *piʔ
'Unripe grain, chaff' [Zuo], 'petty' [Zhuang].
[E] ? ST *pi: Lushai *pi^{H}* < *pii* 'short and small for one's age, stunted growth'.

bǐ$_{4}$ 疕 (p^{h}ji^{B} 3, p^{h}je^{B} 3, pji^{B} 3) **LH** p^{h}ɨ^{B}, p^{h}ɨe^{B}, **OCM** *p(h)əiʔ ?, *phaiʔ ?
'Sore on the head' [Zhouli].
[E] ? ST: WB *ə-p^{h}e^{B}* 'scab over' (head) (*CVST* 1: 101).

bǐ$_{5}$ 彼 → **fú$_{1}$** 夫 pronoun

bǐ$_{6}$ 筆 (pjet 3) **LH** pɨt, **OCM** *prut, OCB *prjut
'Writing brush' [Li].
[T] *Sin Sukchu SR* pi (入); *MGZY* bue (入) [puɛ]; *ONW* pit
[N] Baxter (1992: 280) reconstructs the OCB form on the basis of div. III *chóngniǔ* vocalism and the phonetic series which implies *-ut.
[E] *SW* (*Shuōwén jiězì gǔlín*: 1271) says that *bǐ* is a word from the region of Qín 秦 (NW), and that in Chǔ 楚 the word is *yù* 聿 (jiuet) *ONW* iuit (?), in Wú 吳: *bù-lǜ* 不律 (pjəu-ljuet) ONW *pu-luit*, and in Yān 燕 (NE) *fú* 弗 (pjuət) ONW *put* (discussed by Sagart *ICSTLL* 1990: 7). The word has been borrowed by Middle Korean (*pwut*), Old Japanese (*pude*), and Viet. (*bút*) (pre-Sino-Viet.) (Miyake 1997: 189, 192). All these data point to an initial cluster *pr- or *pl- and an OC rime *-ut. If derived

from → lǐ$_4$ 理里 (ljɨ^B) 'lines' ⋈ WT *'bri-ba, bris* 'to draw, write' as is sometimes proposed, one needs to assume the loss of a PCH medial *w in the latter items. Benedict compares *bǐ* with PAN *bulut 'fiber' (*STC* p. 178f). WT *bir* 'writing brush' is a MC loan (MC final *-t* > WT -r).

Baxter's OC form can be related to TB ones which are mentioned under → shuā 刷. Perh. → fú$_9$ 拂 'to brush off' may belong here. For an overview of similar etyma, see the Table S-2 under → shuā 刷.

bǐ$_7$ 鄙 (pji^B 3) **LH** pɨə^B, **OCM** *prəʔ ?
'Border, outskirts' [Zuo] > 'rustic, common' [Lun] > ('consider rustic, common':) 'to despise' [Shu]; 'district, border town' [Li, Zhouli]. Possibly related to TB items under → bīn$_2$ 濱.

bǐ$_8$ 俾 (pjie^B 4) **LH** pie^B, **OCM** *peʔ
'To make / let someone do something, cause, direct, provide' [Shi, Shu].
[T] *Sin S. SR* pi (上), *PR* pəj; *MGZY* bi (上) [pi]; *ONW* *pie
[E] Etymology not clear, although it brings to mind the MK causative prefix p-.

bì$_1$ 比 → **bǐ$_1$** 比

bì$_2$ 枇 (bi^C 4)
'A fine comb' [GY].
[E] Perh. ST: WB *p^{h}ri^B* ~ *p^{h}i^B* 'to comb, brush', but MC points to an OC form without medial *r.

bì$_3$ 必 (pjiet 4) **LH** pit, **OCM** *pit
'Be necessary, must' [BI, Shi]. — **[E]** Etymology not clear.
[T] *Sin Sukchu SR* pi (入); *MGZY* bi (入) [pi]

bì$_4$ 泌 (pji^C 3) **LH** pɨs, **OCM** *prits ?
'Bubble up' (as water from a spring) [Shi] is a vocalic variant of → fèi$_4$ 沸 (§11.5.1).

bì$_5$ 柲 (pjet, pji^C 3) **LH** pɨt, pɨs, **OCM** *prit(s) (?)
'Lath tied to bow for keeping it in shape' [OB, Yili].
[E] Perh. ST: Chepang *pit-* 'grip' (as with pincers, tongs, legs), 'hold between knees or under the arm'. Perh. related to → fēi$_3$ 扉.

bì$_6$ 挒 'beat' → **pì$_4$** 擗

bì$_7$ 閟 → **bì$_{23}$** 閉

bì$_8$ 畀 (pi^C 4) **LH** pis, **OCM** *pis, OCB *pjits — **[T]** *Sui-Tang* pɨ, *ONW* pii
'To give' [Shi].
[D] (MC pi^B) is common in Yuè dialects: Guǎngzhōu *pei^{BI}*, Táishān *i^{BI}* < *pi^B*, Téngxiàn *ʔbi^{BI}*.
[E] ST *pi(s): PTB *pəy (*STC* no. 427) > Chepang *bəyʔ-sa* 'to give', Lepcha *byi* ⋈ *byi-n* 'to give'; LB: WB *pe^B* ⋈ *p^{h}it* 'invite, offer to give', Atsi *pjí*, Lahu *pî*. PLB *bek 'give, bestow', Miri *bi*; Lushai *pe^L* / *peek^F* < *peeh (< pes)* / *peek* 'to give, offer'.
[C] A derivation is → bīn$_1$ 賓 'guest'.

bì$_9$ 鼻 → **bí** 鼻

bì$_{10}$ 敝弊斃 (bjiäi^C 4) **LH** bies, **OCM** *be(t)s
'Worn out' [Shi], 'damage, ruin' 敝 [Zuo]; 'to fall down, die, destroy' [Zuo] > caus. 'kill' 斃 [Li]; 'fall' [Guoyu], 'bring down, stop' 弊 [Zhouli].
[T] *Sin Sukchu SR* bi (去); *MGZY* pi (去) [bi]; *ONW* biei

[C] Allofam is → pí$_7$ 疲罷 'exhausted' (Pulleyblank 1962: 215), hence bì: *be(t)s < *bai-(t)s. See → fèi$_6$ 廢 for additional comments.
[E] ST: Lushai *pʰuai*^{H} < *pʰuai* 'be worn, worn out, frayed', JP *pʰje*^{31} 'to ruin'.

bì$_{11}$ 弊斃 → **bì$_{10}$** 敝弊斃

bì$_{12}$ 蔽 (pjiäi^C 4) **LH** pies, **OCM** *pe(t)s — **[T]** *ONW* piei^C
'To screen, keep in ignorance, deceive' [Zuo]. There may be a connection with Lushai *palʔ*^{L} < **palh* 'to miss, not know'; or alternatively with → píng$_6$ 屏軿 'screen'. Unger (presentation in Rome Sept. 6, 2001) relates *bì* to WT *sbed-pa, sbas* 'to conceal' (see also → bī$_1$ 屄).

bì$_{13}$ 詖 → **bēi$_2$**, **bī** 陂

bì$_{14}$ 陂 → **bēi$_2$**, **bī** 陂

bì$_{15}$ 辟 (pjiäk 4) **LH** piek, **OCM** *pek, OCB *pjek — **[T]** *ONW* piek
'Sovereign, ruler, governing official, the authorities' [BI, Shi].
×× **bì** 辟 (bjäk) **LH** biek, **OCM** *bek
'Corrective measures, punishment' [Shi], 'regulate, arrange' [Meng].

bì$_{16}$ 辟 'inner coffin' → **mì$_7$** 冪冥

bì$_{17}$ 臂 (pjie^C 4) **LH** pie^C, **OCM** *pekh or *peh ?
'Arm' [Liji].
[E] ST: Lepcha *a-ká pek*, Limbu *phuk-bek* 'forearm' (Matisoff 1985a: 429).

bì$_{18}$ 避 → **bēi$_2$**, **bī** 陂

bì$_{19}$ 躄 → **bǒ$_0$** 跛

bì$_{20}$ 嬖 (piei^C) **LH** pe^C, **OCM** *pêkh — **[T]** *ONW* pėi
'Favorite person' [Meng], 'favorite concubine' 嬖 [Mo]; → pián$_1$-bì 便嬖 'male and female servants' [Meng].
[E] KT: PKS *ɓjaak 'woman, girl'; PT *ʔb-: Boai *bik*^{D1} 'girl'.
Note *bèi* 婢 (bjie^B) OCM *beʔ 'female slave, servant' [Li] which is a derivation from → bēi$_1$ 卑 'low', perhaps a re-etymologization of *bì*.

bì$_{21}$ 埤庳婢 → **bēi$_1$** 卑

bì$_{22}$ 髀 (biei^B, pjie^B, pji^B) **LH** be^B, pie^B, **OCM** *bêʔ, *peʔ
'Thighbone' [Li].
[D] Yuè dial. 'thigh', e.g. Guǎngzhōu *tai*^{22}*-pei*^{35} 大髀 'thigh' (R. Bauer *LTBA* 10.1, 1987: 169ff).
[E] ST: WT *dpyi* 'hip, hipbone' (*CVST* I: 2). This etymon could be related to Lushai *pʰei*^{L} 'foot, leg' [Weidert 1987: 204] (so *CVST*), but see → féi$_2$ 腓.

bì$_{23}$ 閉 (piei^C, piet) **LH** pes, pet, **OCM** *pît(s) — **[T]** *ONW* pėi
'To shut, obstruct' [Shu].
×× **bì** 閟 (pji^C 3), **LH** pɨs, **OCM** *prits ?
'To close, shut' [Shi].
[E] Area etymon: TB-PL *pi^2 'to close', Mru *pit* 'shut, close' (Löffler 1966: 141). <> AA-OKhmer *pit* /ɓit/ 'to shut, close'.

bì$_{24}$ 畢 (pjiet 4) **LH** pit, **OCM** *pit
'Wooden fork' [Shi, Li], 'fork' (a constellation) [Shi], (fork with net:) 'hand-net' for catching birds [OB, Shi], 罼 [Guoyu]. This is probably the s. w. as → bì$_{26}$ 篳

'interlaced branches, wattle'. Perh. related to **bò** 䌟 (bɛk) *brek 'net for catching birds' [SW].

[E] Etymology not certain, possibly related to TB-Lushai p^hiir^L < p^hiir 'double, forked, twin'. But Lushai could be related to → pǐ₁ 匹 'pair' instead.

bì₂₅ 畢 (pjiet 4) **LH** pit, **OCM** *pit — [T] *MTang* pir < pɨr, *ONW* piit
'To finish, complete' [Xun] > 'completely, all' [Shu].
[T] *Sin Sukchu SR* pi (入); *MGZY* bi (入) [pi]; *MTang* pir < pɨr, *ONW* piit
[E] ST: Lushai *peiʔ*ᴸ < *peih* < *-s 'to finish, complete'; WT *dpyis pʰyin-pa* 'to come to the last, arrive at the end' (*pʰyin-pa* 'to go, come'). Prob. not related to → bà₂ 罷 'finish'.

bì₂₆ 篳 (pjiet 4) **LH** pit, **OCM** *pit
'Fence, hedge' [SW], 'wicker door' (made with interlaced branches) [Zuo, Li]; 篳路 'fuel cart' (Giles) or 'wooden cart' (Legge) [Zuo]. The association with with → bì₂₄ 畢 'wooden fork, hand-net' (which is prob. the s. w.) and with PLB *pyik 'thicket, jungle' (Bodman 1980: 158; *HST:* 148), is closer than Karglren's (1933: 94) association with → fú₁₁ 茀 'screen, cover'.

bì₂₇ 彃 (pjiet 4) **LH** pit, **OCM** *pit
'To shoot at' [Chuci]. — Etymology not clear.

bì₂₈ 韠 'knee cover' → **fú₁₄** 韍芾

bì₂₉ 愎 → **bèi₃** 否 'obstruct'

biān₁ 編 (pien) **LH** pen, **OCM** *pên — [T] *ONW* pėn
'To weave' [Li].

※ **biàn** 辮 (pienᶜ) **LH** penᶜ, **OCM** *pêns
'Braid, plait' [Hànshū].
[<] exopass. of *biān* (§4.4), lit. 'what has been woven'.

[E] ST: PTB *pyar ~ *byar (*STC* no. 178) > WT *'byor-ba* ~ *'byar-ba* 'stick to, adhere to' ※ *sbyor-ba, sbyar* 'to affix, attach, join, connect'; Bahing *pʰjer* 'to sew'; Lushai *pʰiar*ᴴ < *pʰiar* 'to knit, plait' (Bodman 1980: 173; *HST:* 119); PLB *pan² 'to braid, plait' (Matisoff *D. of Lahu:* 903).

biān₂ 猵 (pien) **LH** pen, **OCM** *pên — [T] *ONW* pėn
'Otter' [Huainan]. *CVST* 1: 100 relates this word to WB *pʰyam* 'otter' (for the vowel see §11.3.2, for the final see §6.7).

biān₃-fú 蝙蝠 (pien-pjuk) **LH** pen-puk
'Bat' (animal) [SW].
[E] ST *p/bək (?): PTB *baːk [*STC* no. 325]: Lushai *baak*ᴿ, Garo *do-bak* (*do* 'bird') 'bat' (*HST:* 39), Mikir *plàk-wúk* ~ *-plàk-bat.*

biān₄ 邊 (pien) **LH** pen, **OCM** *pên
'Side, periphery' [BI, Zuo], 'lean against' [Liji]. Probably cognate to → piān₁ 偏 'side'.
[T] *Sin Sukchu SR* pjen (平); *MGZY* bÿan (平) [pjɛn]; *ONW* pėn

biān₅ 籩 (pien) **LH** pen, **OCM** *pên
'A vessel of clay or wood for serving food' [Shi].
[E] ST *pel: Lushai *beel*ᴴ 'pot, utensil, vessel'.

biǎn₁ 扁 (pienᴮ) **LH** penᴮ, **OCM** *pênʔ
'Flat and thin' [Shi].

[E] ST *per: PTB *pe:r 'flat' [*STC* no. 340] > Lushai *peer*^{L} / *per?*^{L} (? ⋇ *p*^{h}*ei*^{H} 'level, flat, horizontal'); NNaga *pwe:r* 'thin' [French 1983: 222].

⋇ **biǎn** 褊 (pjiän^B 4) **LH** pian^B, **OCM** *pen?
'Narrow' [Shi].
[T] *MGZY* by̆an (上) [pjɛn]

⋇ **piān** 篇 (p^{h}jiän 4) **LH** p^{h}ian, **OCM** *phen
'Writing slip' [Guoce].
[<] Tone A nominalization (§3.1).

biǎn$_2$ 扁 (pien^B) **LH** pen^B, **OCM** *pên?
'A circumscription, population district' [Heguan].
[E] ST: Lushai *bial*^{H} < *bial* 'a circle, province, circuit; be round, include'. Prob. not related to → biàn$_7$ 遍 'all'.

biǎn$_3$ 褊 → **biǎn$_1$** 扁

biǎn$_4$ 貶 (pjäm^B 3, pjɐm^B) **LH** pɨam^B, **OCM** *pam?, OCB *prjem?
'To diminish, weaken' [Shi], Mand. 'demote, reduce, depreciate'.
[E] ST: OTib. *'p*^{h}*am-ba, p*^{h}*am* 'to be diminished, reduced, found wanting, of lesser quality' (WT 'be beaten, conquered') (*HST:* 63). Note PTai *p^{h}l/r-: S. *p*^{h}*ɔɔm*^{A1} 'lean'. A possible allofam may be → fèi$_6$ 廢 (so Karlgren 1956: 18).

biǎn$_5$ 窆 (pjäm^C 3, pəŋ^C) **LH** pɨam^C, **OCM** *pams < *poms ?
'To lower a coffin into the grave, bury' [Li]. The word is not related to → bèng 堋.
[E] ST: WT *'bum* 'tomb, sepulcher', Lushai *p*^{h}*uum*^{H} 'to bury, inter' (*CVST* 1: 7).

biàn$_1$ 弁 (bjän^C 3) **LH** bɨan^C, **OCM** *brans, OCB *brjons
'A cap' (symbol of manhood?) [Shi]. Wáng Lì (1982: 582) relates this word to → miǎn$_3$ 冕 [mɨan^B] 'ceremonial cap'.

biàn$_2$ 弁 'to fly' → **fān$_1$** 弁拚翻

biàn$_3$ 便 (bjiän^C 4) **LH** bien^C, **OCM** *bens — [T] *ONW* bian
'Convenient' [Li], 'comfortable' [Chuci]. — [E] Etymology not clear.

biàn$_4$ 變 (pjän^C 3) **LH** pɨan^C, **OCM** *prans, OCB *prjons
'To change' [BI, Shu].
[T] *Sin Sukchu SR* pjen (去); MGZY by̆an (去) [pjɛn]; *ONW* pan
[E] <> Tai: S. *plian*^{B1} < **pl-* 'to change'. Baxter (1992: 365) thinks it likely that this word is cognate to → luàn 亂 OCB *C-rons 'disorder'. It is perh. related to WT *sprul-ba* ⋇ *'p*^{h}*rul-ba* 'juggle, appear, change, transform' (Shī Xiàngdōng 2000: 200).

biàn$_5$ 辨 辯 → **bàn$_2$**, **biàn** 釆

biàn$_6$ 辮 → **biān$_1$** 編

biàn$_7$ 遍 (pien^C) **LH** pen^C, **OCM** *pêns — [T] *ONW* pėn
'All together, everywhere, comprehensive' [Shi].
[E] ? ST: Lushai *p*^{h}*iar*^{R} < *p*^{h}*iar?* (< *-?*) 'all, entirely, completely, the whole lot'. Prob. not related to → biǎn$_2$ 扁 'circumscription'.

biāo$_1$ 髟 (pjieu 4, pjiäu 4) **LH** piu, piau, **OCM** *piu or *piau
'Long hair' [Han time]. The graph also writes → shān$_2$ 髟.
[E] <> PMiao *preu^{2A}, PYao *py^{l}ei^1 'hair'.

biāo$_2$ 熛 (pjiäu 4) **LH** piau, **OCM** *piau
'Leaping flames' [Lü].

[E] <> Tai: S. *pleeu*^{A1} < *pl- 'flame' (Bodman 1980: 168). <> MK: Pearic *phlaw* ~ *phlew* 'fire'.

biāo$_3$ 標 (pjiäu(C) 4) **LH** piau(C), **OCM** *piauh
'Branch' [Zhuang].

※ **piāo** 剽 (p^{h}jiäu, pjiäu^B 4) **LH** p^{h}iau, piau^B, **OCM** *phiau, *piau?
'Tip, end' [Zhuang].

bié 別 (pjät 3) **LH** pɨat, **OCM** *prat, OCB *prjet
'To divide, separate' [Zhouli].
[T] *Sin Sukchu SR* pje, bje (入); *MGZY* bÿa (入) [pjɛ]; *ONW* pat

※ **bié** 別 (bjät 3) **LH** bɨat, **OCM** *brat, OCB *brjet
'Be different' [Li].
[<] endopass. of *bié* 別 (pjät 3) (§4.6) (Baxter / Sagart 1998: 46). This word is prob. cogn. to → liè$_1$ 列.

[E] ST: PLB *brat 'split, crack' > WB *prat* 'be cut in two' [Matisoff *D. of Lahu* 836].

bīn$_1$ 賓 (pjien 4) **LH** pin, **OCM** *pin, OCB *pjin
'A gift, present' [BI]; 'to present a gift' [BI] > 'guest' [BI, Shi] > 'ancestral spirits' (as guests at a sacrifice) [OB, Shu].
[T] *Sin Sukchu SR* pin (平); *MGZY* bin (平) [pin]; *ONW* *piin
[<] n-nominalization from → bì$_8$ 畀 'give' < ST *pi, lit. 'gift, gift-giver'.
[E] ST *pi 'give', see → bì$_8$ 畀; some TB items are close to OC: WT *sbyin-pa* 'to give, bestow; gift'; WB *phit* 'invite, offer to give, invite to take'.

※ **bìn** 賓殯 (pjien^C 4) **LH** pin^C, **OCM** *pins
'To receive as a guest, treat as a guest' 賓 (which involves presentation of gifts) [OB, Shi]; 殯 SW: "put the dead in a coffin to be taken out and buried where the ancestral spirits ('guests') meet him", i.e. lit. 'to have (the dead) treated like a guest (by the ancestral spirits)' > 'to put the body in a coffin' [Li], 'convey a coffin' [Zuo] (Wáng Lì 1982: 541).
[<] exoactive of *bīn* 賓 (pjien 4) (§4.3).

※ **pín** 嬪 (bjien 4) **LH** bin, **OCM** *bin
'To become a bride, wife' [Shi].
[<] endopass. of *bīn* 賓 (pjien 4), lit. 'be received like a guest' (§4.6).

bīn$_2$ 濱 (pjien 4) **LH** pin, **OCM** *pin
'Shore, bank' [Shu].

※ **pín** 頻 (bjien 4) **LH** bin, **OCM** *bin
'Be on the edge, urgent; river bank' [Shi]; → fén$_5$ 墳濆 may be a vocalic variant.
[<] perh. endopass., i.e. a sv derived from *bīn* (§4.6) ?

[E] This is a SE Asian etymon: AN-PMal.-Pol. *te(m)biŋ 'bank, shore' (Thurgood 1999:10); MK-PMonic *t[r]mɓaɲ 'rim, edge, lips'. It is not clear if or how possible TB comparanda may be connected: TB-Lepcha *bí* 'edge, border', *lyaŋ bí* 'utmost limit of a place'. WT *p^{h}yi* 'outside' (including the notion 'at the outer edge' as in *p^{h}yi žiŋ* 'the field outside') ※ *p^{h}yin* 'outside' could perh. belong to the Lepcha word, unless the WT items are part of → bǐ$_1$ 比 ('behind' > 'outside'?).

bǐn 稟 → **lǐn$_2$** 稟廩

bìn$_1$ 賓 → **bīn$_1$** 賓

bìn$_2$ 殯 → **bīn$_1$** 賓

bìn$_3$ 髕臏 (bjien^B 4) **LH** bin^B, **OCM** *binʔ
'Kneecap, shin, tibia' [Da Da Lliji, Hanfei].
[E] ST: TB-Nung *bɛ^{31}-p^{h}in^{55}* 'knee'.
[C] Karlgren (1933: 94) relates the CH word to → fú$_{14}$ 韍芾 'leggings, cover'. Partial synonyms are → bì$_{22}$ 髀 'thighbone'; → féi$_2$ 腓 'calf of leg'.

bīng$_1$ 兵 (pjɐŋ) **LH** pɨaŋ, **OCM** *praŋ, OCB *prjaŋ
'Weapon' [BI, Shi] > 'soldier' [Zhouli]. This may possibly be related to → bǐng$_2$ 秉 (handled instrument?).
[T] *Sin Sukchu SR* piŋ (平); *MGZY* bing (平) [piŋ]; *ONW* peŋ

bīng$_2$ 冰 (pjəŋ) **LH** pɨŋ, **OCM** *prəŋ ?, OCB *prjəŋ — **[T]** *ONW* piŋ
'Ice' [Shi].
[E] Perh. related to PTB *pam > Tangkhul Naga *p^{h}am* 'snow', Kanauri *pom* 'snow', Jiarong *ta-rpam* 'ice' (*CVST* 1: 64). Alternatively, Baxter (1992: 273) considers this cogn. to the following, he reconstructs *bīng* with initial *pr-:
⋇ **líng** 凌 (ljəŋ) **LH** lɨŋ, **OCM** *rəŋ, OCB *b-rjəŋ — **[T]** *ONW* liŋ
'Ice' [Shi].
[E] If the connection between OCB prjəŋ and *b-rjəŋ is correct, then this wf could have come from AA, although the meanings are not very compelling: Khmer *preṅa* /preŋ/ 'to become hard, solid' < *-reṅa* /-réeŋ/ 'to dry up' [Jenner / Pou 1982: 269; 523] (there are many vocalic and other variants of this etymon). The unusual initial alternation *p* ~ *r* also speaks for a non-ST origin. OC *ə = Khmer /e/ has parallels.

bǐng$_1$ 炳昺邴 (bjɐŋ^B) **LH** bɨaŋ^B, **OCM** *braŋʔ, OCB *brjaŋʔ
'Bright' 炳 [Yi]; 'happy, bright' 邴 [Zhuang].
[E] Belongs prob. to an AA wf, see under → liàng$_0$ 亮. Unger (*Hao-ku* 34, 1986) reconstructs OC *pl(j)aŋʔ and considers this word part of the wf under → yáng$_9$ 陽, as well as related to Tai: S. *plaŋ^{A1}* 'bright'.

bǐng$_2$ 秉 (pjɐŋ^B) **LH** pɨaŋ^B, **OCM** *praŋʔ ? — **[T]** *ONW* peŋ
'To grasp, hold in the hand' [BI, Shi].
⋇ **bìng** 柄 (pjɐŋ^C) **LH** pɨaŋ^C, **OCM** *praŋh ? — **[D]** PMin *paŋ^C.
'A handle' (of ax, flag) [Shi].
[<] exopass. of *bǐng*, lit. 'what is grasped, held' (§4.4).
[E] ? ST: Lushai *beŋ^H* 'ear, eye (of a needle), handle (of a cup), loops', or Lushai *liaŋ^H* 'handle' (of a pot); however vocalic and semantic agreement is not close. Alternatively, Unger (*Hao-ku* 34, 1986) relates this word to WT *len-ba (loŋ-pa, -pa), bloŋs, blaŋ, loŋ(s)* 'to take, grab'. Wáng Lì (1982: 173) relates this wf to → bǎ 把 'handful'. Perh. → bīng$_1$ 兵 is related.

bǐng$_3$ 怲 → **bìng$_5$** 病

bìng$_1$ 并 → **bìng$_2$** 並併

bìng$_2$ 並併 (bieŋ^B) **LH** beŋ^B, **OCM** *bêŋʔ
'Side by side' 並 [OB, Shi], 併 [Li]; 'next to each other' 並 [Shi]. The meaning 'together, even, also' has tone C (Downer 1959: 289).
[T] *Sin Sukchu SR* piŋ (去); *MGZY* bing (去) [piŋ]; *ONW* bėŋ
⋇ **bìng** 并 (pjäŋ[^{C}]) **LH** pieŋ(^{C}), **OCM** *peŋ(h)
'Combine two' (things) [Zhouli], 'all together' [Shi], 'likewise' [Shu].

⋈ **pián** 駢 (bien) **LH** ben, **OCM** *bên
'Two side by side, double' [Zhuang], 'two sticking together' [Zuo] > 'horse side by side with another' [Zuo] (also read MC *bieŋ*).

[E] ? ST: Chepang *bʰiŋ-* 'be close together (as object, friends), double up', but cf. → bǐ₁ 比. A similar TB etymon may be related, but the medial *r is unexplained, the items could possibly belong to → lián₁ 連聯 instead: Chepang *breŋʔ-* 'be close together, side by side', WB *hrañ* ~ *hyañ* (< *hriŋ* or *hreŋ*) 'put together side by side' ⋈ *ə-hrañ* 'a pair', Lushai *ţʰiaŋᴴ / ţʰianᴸ* 'side by side (only of two), in a pair'. However, Lepcha *byer, byăr* 'be in juxtaposition' ⋈ *byek* 'interval of time / space' may belong to WT *bar* 'intermediate'.

bìng₃ 屏 (pjäŋᴮ/ᶜ) **LH** pieŋᶜ, **OCM** *peŋh
'To remove' [Zuo], 'retire' [Li] (cognate to → píng₆ 屏軿 'screen' acc. to Karlgren 1956: 16).

⋈ **bìng** 偋 (bjäŋᶜ) **LH** bieŋᶜ, **OCM** *beŋh
'Eliminate' [Xun] (cognate to píng acc. to Karlgren *GSR* 824g; Wáng Lì 1982: 339).

⋈ **bèng** 迸 (pɛŋᶜ) **LH** pɛŋᶜ, **OCM** *prêŋh
'To drive out, relegate' [Meng].
[<] r-causative (§7.5).

bìng₄ 偋 → **bìng₃** 屏

bìng₅ 病 (bjɐŋᶜ) **LH** bɨaŋᶜ, **OCM** *braŋh ? — **[T]** *ONW* beŋ
'Be ill, suffer, sickness, disease' [Shu].
[D] PMin *baŋᶜ > Fúzhōu *paŋᶜ²*, Amoy *pĩᶜ²*

⋈ **bǐng** 怲 (pjɐŋᴮ/ᶜ) **LH** pɨaŋᴮ/ᶜ, **OCM** *praŋʔ/h ?, OCB *prjaŋs
'Be full of grief' [Shi] (Karlgren 1956: 10).

[E] This wf may belong with → bǐng₁ 炳昺邴 with the basic meaning 'warm, hot'. Also, a possible connection with *shāng* 傷 (under → yáng₄ 痒瘍) has been suggested.

bō₁ 波 (puâ) **LH** pɑi, **OCM** *pâi, OCB *paj
'A wave' [Shi], 'be shaken as on waves' [Zhuang].
[T] *Sin Sukchu SR* pwɔ (平); *MGZY* bwo (平) [pwɔ]; *ONW* pɑ
[E] This word may belong to the root *paj 'slanted, not level' → bēi₂, bī 陂 (so Huáng Jīn-guì, Shěn Xí-róng *YYWZX* 1987.8: 44), but prob. not to → bò₁ 播簸 'winnow' (as suggested by Wáng Lì 1982: 444).
Note WT *dba' (-kloŋ)* 'wave', but the vowels do not match (we should expect WT *dbe*).

bō₂ 鉢 (puât) **LH** pɑt — **[T]** *ONW* pɑt
'Alms bowl', also written with radical 金 [GY], or with an altogether different graph which acc. to *GY*, quoting the commentator Yán Shīgǔ 顏師古, occurs first in *Hànshū*. *Bō* derives from Skt. *pātra* which also has been loaned into Middle Korean (*pali*) and Old Japanese (*pati*) (Miyake 1997: 186).

bō₃ 剝 → **bāo₃** 剝

bó₁ 伯 (pɐk) **LH** pak, **OCM** *prâk
'Be the eldest' (as father, brother, sister) [Shi], 'elder, lord, clan head' [Shi], a feudal title ('earl, count') [BI], measure word for persons above commoners [BI]; later and in Mand. 'father's elder brother, uncle', in dialects also 'father', as in Gàn-Wǔníng *paʔᴰ¹* (~ *paᴬ¹*).
[T] *Sin S. SR* pəj (入), *LR* pəjʔ; *MGZY* bay (入) [paj]; *ONW* pĕk

⋈ **bà** 霸 (paᶜ) **LH** paᶜ, **OCM** *prâkh
'Take the lead, have hegemony' [Lunyu] (Wáng Lì 1982: 291).

[<] exoactive / trans. of *bó* (§4.3.2).

[E] ? Area word: TB-Mru *rak*, Kukish *prak* 'eldest brother' (Löffler 1966: 140); LB-Lahu *phâ* 'god, lord' <- Siam. *pʰráʔ* <- Khmer [Matisoff *D. Lahu:* 883]. Since Kuki-Chin languages have incorporated MK loans, this etymon may ultimately be AA. Among alternative proposals is derivation from → $bái_1$ 白 'white', hence *bó* 'the white-haired one' (so Karlgren 1956: 10), note the semantics of → $pó_3$ 皤 'white > white-haired' – but this is prob. a folk etymology.

$bó_2$ 帛 (bɐk) **LH** bak, **OCM** *brâk

'Silk material' [BI, Shu] is prob. the same word as → $bái_1$ 白 'white'.

$bó_3$ 癶 → **fā** 發

$bó_4$ 膊 (pâk) **LH** pɑk, **OCM** *pâk — **[T]** *ONW* pɑk

'Shoulder blade' 胉 [JY]; 拍 [Zhouli; *GYSX*, JY; *GSR* 782m].

[D] Mand. 'shoulder' 膊; 髆 (*GYSX:* 478; *GSR* 771l; also Pulleyblank MC). This form QYS *pâk* survives in Yuè dialects: Guǎngzhōu $pɔk^{D1}$-$t^hɐu^{A2}$ 膊頭. The following are variants or dictionary readings.

ꭗ **pò** 膊 (pʰâk) **LH** pʰɑk, **OCM** *phâk

'Shoulder blade', variant of the above: 胉 [Yili; *GYSX* 415; JY; *GSR* 782q], 膊 [SW, *GYSX*: 478; *GSR* 771l].

ꭗ **pò** 胉 (pɐk) **LH** pak, **OCM** *prâk

'Shoulder blade' [JY acc. to *ZWDCD* 7: 1002].

[E] Area word: PTB *p(r)ak ꭗ *r-pak (Matisoff 1999: 6): WT *pʰrag* < *prak* 'shoulder', JP $gə^{31}$-$p^haʔ^{31}$ < *pʰak*. Alternatively MK: PMon *pnah 'shoulder'. Possibly, the uncertainty in MC could be due to multiple sources for this word: MC *pɐk* < *prak would match Tib., MC *pâk* MK. It is not clear how Tai: S. baa^{B1} (PTai *ʔbaa^B) 'shoulder', Be via^{33} and WB pa^C-$khuṁ^B$ 'shoulders' relate to the CH items.

[C] A cognate may be *bǎng* 膀 'upper arms', which is a late word.

$bó_5$ 薄 (bâk) **LH** bɑk, **OCM** *bâk

'Thin' [Shi].

[T] *Sin S. SR* baw (入), *LR* bawʔ; *MGZY* paw (入) [baw]; *ONW* bɑk

[D] PMin *b̯ok

[E] ST: PTB *ba (actually *baʔ ?) 'thin' (*HPTB:* 24) > PLB *pa² (~ *ʔpya¹ ?) 'thin, flat' (Matisoff 1970: *JAOS* 90.1: 39) or *ba² (Thurgood *CAAAL* 13, 1980: 212) > WB pa^B; JP p^ha^{31} 'thin', Garo *ba* [Matisoff 1974 no. 206; *STC* no. 25]; Tiddim Chin paa^1 < *paːʔ*, Chepang *beʔ* < *baʔ* [Weidert 1987: 26; Ostapirat *LTBA* 21.1, 1998: 238]; WB *pak* 'shallow dish'. The following items are borrowed from some ST source: PKS *waːŋ¹ 'thin'; Yao *piaʔ*.

$bó_6$ 薄 礴 → **$fù_{15}$** 縛

$bó_7$ 鎛 (pâk) **LH** pɑk, **OCM** *pâk

'A hoe' [Shi] may be of MK provenance: PMonic *ɓɔk 'to hoe, clear land' ꭗ *c(l)-m-ɓɔk 'a hoe, spade', in Yuè dial. like Táishān $pɔŋ^{35/A1}$.

$bó_8$ 博 → **$bù_3$** 布

$bó_9$ 駁 (påk) **LH** pɔk, **OCM** *prâuk, OCB *pra/ewk

'Horse with mixed (brown and white) colors, mixed' [Shi].

[E] ST: WB *prok* 'be speckled, spotted' ꭗ *ə-prok* 'decoration' (-> MK-MidMon /əprɔk/ 'variegated color, surface decoration'), Mikir *pʰròk* 'speckled' (Bodman 1980: 142;

HST: 138), JP *prúʔ* [Matisoff *TSR* no. 360], Mru *preu* 'of mixed color' [Löffler 1966: 135]. A cognate may be → bān$_2$ 斑 'variegated'.

bào 豹 (pau^C) **LH** pau^C, **OCM** *prâukh

'Leopard' [Shi], lit. 'the spotted one'; **[<]** exopass. of *bó* 駁 *prauk (§4.4).

bó$_{10}$ 踣 (bək, pʰəu^C) **LH** bək, pʰo^C, **OCM** *bə̂k, *phôkh ?

'To overthrow, lay prostrate' [Zuo] is prob. cognate to the wf → fú$_4$ 伏服.

bó$_{11}$ 坲 (buət) **LH** bət, **OCM** *bə̂t

'Powdery' (soil) [Zhouli].

[E] ST *put: WB *pʰut* 'dust', Lushai *pʰut^L* 'flowery, powdery'; *CVST* 1: 8 adds these words to → fú$_8$ 怫 'gust of wind'.

bó$_{12}$ 勃 (buət) **LH** bət, **OCM** *bə̂t

'Sudden' [Zhuang, Lunyu].

[E] ST: Lushai *pʰuut^H* 'suddenly, on a sudden'. This word may be related to → fú$_8$ 怫 'gust of wind'.

bó$_{13}$ 脖 (buət)

'Navel' [GY], usually 'neck'. Benedict (*LTBA* 5.1, 1979) relates this late word to WT *dbus* 'middle, center'. Alternatively, this could be an AA word: PMonic *p[r/n]us 'navel, center, axis of wheel'.

bǒ 跛 (puâ^B) **LH** pɑi^B, **OCM** *pâiʔ — **[T]** *ONW* pɑ

'To walk lame' [Yi].

[D] Some southern dialects preserve the OC rime: Y-Fóshān *pɐi^{A1}*; PMin *pai^B.

⋈ **bì** 躄 (pjiäk 4) **LH** piek, **OCM** *pek

'To walk lame' [Li].

[<] either a derivation with an additional final *-k (*pai-k) (§6.1), or the result of an OC *-ʔ ~ *-k alternation.

[E] ST: PTB *pay ⋈ *bay 'lame, limp, oblique' ⋈ *bay 'left' (side) (Matisoff 1995a: 42; *LL* 1.2, 2000: 153) > WB *pʰai* 'go aside, put aside' ⋈ *pʰai^B* 'go aside, get out of the way' ⋈ *pai* 'put aside, away, reject' ⋈ *bʰai* 'left side', Lushai *bai^R* < *baʔ* 'walk lame'. This is prob. an allofam of → bēi$_2$, bī 陂 'slanting'.

bò$_1$ 播簸 (puâ^C) **LH** pɑi^C, **OCM** *pâih

'To winnow' 播 [Zhuang], 'shake' 播 [Lunyu].

[D] In most dialects, the verb 'to winnow' and the n. 'winnowing pan' are homophones: Y-Guǎngzhōu *pɔ^{C1}*; K-Dōngguān *pɔi^C* n., vb. But a few dialects make a distinction where the tone C reading is reserved for the noun: Mand. *bò* 簸; PMin *puɑi^C.

⋈ **bǒ** 簸 (puâ^B) **LH** pɑi^B, **OCM** *pâiʔ

'To winnow' [Shi] is in some dialects a reading for the verb: Mand. *bǒ*, K-Meix *pa:^{B}* 'to winnow'. This is prob. also the OC reading for the verb 簸 in *Shījīng*.

[E] ST: PTB *pʷa:y 'chaff, scatter' > PL *pway^2 'chaff' > WB *phwai^B* 'husk, chaff' [Matisoff *LL* 1.2, 2000: 143] (Bodman 1980: 138), Lushai *vai^H* 'husks of grain'. This etymon is prob. distinct from → bò$_2$ 播譒 as TB cognates suggest.

bò$_2$ 播譒 (puâ^C) **LH** pɑi^C, **OCM** *pâih

'To spread, sow, publish' 播 [Shi]; 'to promulgate' 譒 [SW: Shu].

[E] ST: PTB *bʷâr (*STC:* 174 n. 463; n. 460) > WT *'bor-ba* 'to throw, cast', Bahing *war* 'throw away', Chepang *wa:r* 'sow', Mikir *wár* 'throw' (*STC:* 172, 174; 191). Prob. an area word: MK-PVM: Uý-lô *wâr^4*, Lâm-la *vay^2* 'to sow', some languages have a form *kway*, Mĩ-so'n *pay^2;* Viet -> Tai: S. *hwan^1* (Maspero 1912: 71, 73). OC -> Tai:

PT *ʔb-: S. bɛɛ^{A1} 'extend, spread'. But S. *prai*^{1} 'to sow, scatter' seems to be unrelated. This etymon is prob. distinct from → bò$_1$ 播簸.

bò$_3$ 擘 (pɛk) **LH** pɛk, **OCM** *prêk
'To cleave, split' 擘 [Li]; 'crack, burst' 薜 [Zhouli]; 'tear apart, cleave' 捭 [Li].
[D] Southern dialects have initial *m-*: Y-Guǎngzhōu *ma:k*^{7} 'to break', G-Nánchāng *miɛ*^{3}, Kèjiā *mak*^{7} 'to open, break' (Sagart 1999: 80-81). This etymon is also found in KT: PKS *hma:k^{7} 'to split, chop'.
[E] Area word: TB-Chepang *prek-* 'cleave, divide down center'. <> KT (OC loan?) PKS *pra:k^{7}-ti 'break, tear'; PT *pr-: S *tɛɛk*^{DIL}, Lóngzhōu *p*^{h}*eek*, Boai *teek*. <> ? AA: Khmer (without medial *r): *pēka* /baaɛk/, OKhmer *pek* /ɓɛɛk/ 'to break, burst, split'.
Perh. related to → bǎi$_2$ 捭 *breʔ 'to open'. For an overview of similar items, see → lí$_{10}$ 離 and Table P-1 under → pī$_3$ 披.

bò$_4$ 繴 (bɛk) 'net for catching birds' → **bì$_{24}$** 畢

bò$_5$ 薜 → **bò$_3$** 擘

bò$_6$ 捭 → **bò$_3$** 擘

bū$_1$ 逋 (puo) **LH** pɑ, **OCM** *pâ
'To escape, run away, abscond' [Shu]. Benedict (*LTBA* 14.2, 1991: 152) relates this word to WT *sbed-pa, sbas, sba* 'to hide, conceal' ⋈ *'ba-bo* 'hole, cave, cavern', Kiranti *bha* 'anus', Mikir *iŋbò* < *m-ba*^{A} 'lose, get lost'(see also → bī$_1$ 屄).

bū$_2$, bù 餔 → **bù$_5$** 哺

bǔ$_1$ 卜 (puk) **LH** pok, **OCM** *pôk, OCB *pok — **[T]** *ONW* pok
('Cracking' of a bone or tortoise shell in fire, go 'pop':) 'To divine by oracle bone' [OB, Shi].
[E] ST: PLB *ɴpök^{H} ~ *ʔpök^{H} ~ *ʔbök^{L} 'explode, pop' [Matisoff 2002 no. 108] > WB *pok* 'go off' (as gun) ⋈ *p*^{h}*ok* 'to fire' (a gun), Lushai *puak*^{F} / *puaʔ*^{L} 'to explode, burst, pop', Mru *pok* 'to burst', JP *p*^{h}*ok*^{55} 'to hit', *boʔ*^{31} < *bok*^{31} 'erupt, burst out', Lepcha *bu* 'to burst' (vessel), crack, split'.

bǔ$_2$ 補 (puo^{B}) **LH** pɑ^{B}, **OCM** *pâʔ or *mpâʔ (*mpaʔ) — **[T]** *MTang* pu < po, *ONW* po
'To mend, repair, assist' [Shi].
[D] PMin *p̌uo^{B} 'to mend': Jiànyáng *vio*^{3} derives perh. from a pre-nasalized initial (for the medial *i* in Jiànyáng, compare W-Wēnzhōu *pəu*^{45}), note Yao *bia*^{3} (< *nb-), PMY *npa^{2} (Downer 1982) 'to patch, repair' (Norman 1986: 382).
[E] Area word: TB-WB *p*^{h}*a* 'mend, patch', Nung *əp*^{h}*a* 'adhere' (Matisoff *LL* 1.2, 2000: 163), JP *pa*^{31} 'be mended'. <> MK: PVM *k-pa:ʔ 'to repair, sew' [Ferlus], Khmer /pah/ (i.e. prob. = paʔ) 'to patch, mend, fix'. <> Tai-S. *paʔ*^{D1} and *poo*^{6} 'mend' is a loan. But Tai *pɔɔŋ*^{C1} < *p- 'to protect, cover up' (Li F. 1976: 40) is not related, see → bèng 塴.
[C] Perh. connected with → fú$_2$ 扶 'assist'.

bù$_1$ 不 (pjəu$^{B/C}$) **LH** pu, **OCM** *pə, OCB *pjə — **[T]** *ONW* pu
'Not' [OB, Shi]. The irreg. Mand. reading in *b-* (no dentilabial *f-*) belongs to the popular stratum, the regular development from QYS and OC is represented by *fǒu* 否 below. Although *bù* is the normal negative in literary Chinese from the OB down, it is now confined to Mand. dialects. In the OB, negatives with initial *p- negate actions which are beyond the control of living persons (Takashima 1996: 365ff).

= **fǒu** 否 (pjəu^{B}) etc., same word as above

'Not, be wrong' [OB, BI, Shi], same word as above. This is the expected Mand. reading of the negative 不 based on QY pjəu(^{B}/^{C}).

[T] *Sin Sukchu SR* fəw (上); *MGZY* Hwuw (上) [fuw]

ꭗ **fú** 弗 (pjwət) **LH** put, **OCM** *pət

(1) 'Cannot, do not want to, not' [OB, Shu] (*DEZC* p. 48; §6.2.2), later also 'resist'.

(2) 'Not (verb) him / her / it' [Shu], fusion of *bù* with the obj. pronoun *zhī* 之.

[T] *MTang* pfur, *ONW* put. — The later forms for *bù* 不 in final *-t* really reflect this word: *Sin Sukchu SR* pu (入); *MGZY* bu (入) [pu].

[E] <> Tai: S. *bɔ(ɔ)*^{B1} < *ʔb- 'not', Saek boo^{B1} 'negative, no'.

[C] Allofams: → fēi$_1$ 非, → fěi$_1$ 匪棐.

bù$_2$ 布 (puo^{C}) **LH** pɑ^{C}, **OCM** *pâh

'Cloth' [BI, Shi].

[T] *Sin Sukchu SR* pu (去); *MGZY* bu (去) [pu]; *ONW* po

[D] Min *pio^{C} (from *po*^{C} via *pəo*^{C}? This is the regular form up the coast in Wēnzhōu).

[E] *Bù* is often thought to be the s. w. as 'spread out' (→ bù$_3$ 布). More likely, it is an AA word. A Han dyn. variant borrowed from the (AA) 'Mán and Yí barbarians' on the middle Yangtze River is *jià-bù* 幏布 < QYS *ka(*^{C}*)-puo*^{C} 'cotton, cotton cloth' [SW, Hòu Hànshū]. A later loan (ca. 430 AD) is *gǔ-bèi* 古貝 *ONW* ko^{B}-pɛi^{C} < -pɑs (Baxter, 1989: Early China Conference, Chicago).

AA forms: *k-rn-paːs, e.g., Khmer *krabaah*, Bahnar *ko'paih* (< -s), PVM *k-paːs (Ferlus), Chrau *paih* (< -s), Khasi *kṇp*^{h}*aːt*. <> Tai: S. *p*^{h}*aa*^{C1} < *p^{h}- 'cloth' (Li F. 1976: 46). From AA into -> Skt. *kārpāsaṁ* 'cotton, cotton cloth', -> Greek *kárpasos*.

In turn, *bù* may have been loaned into Middle Korean *pwoy* 'hemp cloth' (Miyake 1997: 188).

bù$_3$ 布 (puo^{C}) **LH** pɑ^{C}, **OCM** *pâh — **[T]** *ONW* po

'To spread out' (a mat) [Li], 'display, announce, disperse' [Zuo]. → bù$_2$ 布 'cloth' is often thought to be the same word.

[D] PMin *pyo^{C} 'set out' (rice seedlings).

[<] exoactive of a root *PA(?) (§4.3).

[E] ST: Lushai *p*^{h}*aʔ*^{L} (< *phah*) 'to spread' (as cloth), 'place flat on the ground'. CH -> Tai: S. *pu*^{l} 'to spread out, lay or stretch out (carpet)'.

ꭗ **bó** 博 (pâk) **LH** pɑk, **OCM** *pâk — **[T]** *ONW* pɑk

'Be wide' [BI, Shi].

[<] k-extension (§6.1) of a root *PA(?).

[T] *Sin Sukchu SR* paw (入), *LR* pawʔ; *MGZY* baw (入) [paw]

ꭗ **pǔ** 溥 (p^{h}uo^{B}) **LH** p^{h}ɑ^{B}, **OCM** *phâʔ

'Be vast, wide' (of mandate, injury, walls, plain) [Shi].

ꭗ **fū** 尃敷鋪 (p^{h}ju) **LH** p^{h}uɑ, **OCM** *pha — **[T]** *ONW* p^{h}uo

'To spread out, extensively' 尃 [Yi], 鋪 [Shi] (鋪 also read QY *p*^{h}*uo*); 'to spread out, widely, extensively, arrange, set forth, publish' 敷 [Shi].

[<] caus. aspiration of *fǔ* 甫 'large' (§5.8.2).

ꭗ **fǔ** 甫 (pju^{B}) **LH** puɑ^{B}, **OCM** *paʔ

'Large' (of a field) [Shi].

[<] endoactive of a root *PA(?).

bù$_4$ 步 (buo^{C}) **LH** bɑ^{C}, **OCM** *bâh

'To walk, step (stride of two legs), course' [OB, Shi].

[T] *Sin S. SR* bu (去); *MGZY* pu (去) [bu]; *MTang* bu < bo, *ONW* bo

[D] PMin *b̯-: Jiànyáng *vo*⁶ 'to step, stride' derives perh. from a prenasalized initial, note Yao *bia*⁶ (< *nb-) 'step, stride' (Norman 1986: 382).

[E] ST: Mru *pak* 'go, walk', Lushai *vaak*^{F} / *vaʔ*^{L} 'to go, walk' [Löffler 1966: 146].

bù$_5$ 哺 (buo^C) **LH** bɑ^C, **OCM** *bâh

'Have food in the mouth' [Zhuang].

[D] This is the Mǐn word for 'to chew': PMin *bo^C, but Jiàn'ōu *piɔ*^{44} (prob. from *bo^C via *bəo*^{C}).

[<] endopass. of *bū* 餔 pɑ 'to eat' (§4.6).

⁑ **bū** 餔 (puo) **LH** pɑ, **OCM** *pâ

'To eat' [Meng], 'meal in the afternoon' [Lü].

⁑ **bù** 餔 (puo^C) **LH** pɑ^C, **OCM** *pâh

'To give to eat' [JY] (Unger *Hao-ku* 35, 1986: 34).

[<] exoactive / caus. of *bū* 餔 'to eat'.

[E] ST: PTB *wa (or *pa) 'bite, chew' (*STC* no. 424; *CVST* I: 119; Weidert 1987: 138) > WB *wa*^{B} 'to chew', JP *gə*^{31}-*wa*^{55} 'to bite'.

It is not clear if / how the following may be connected: TB-Lushai *baar*^{H} 'to stuff food into one's own mouth' ⁑ *barʔ* 'to stuff food into the mouth of another' (tones?) (Unger *Hao-ku* 35, 1986: 34). Note also Tiddim Chin *ba:k*^{F} / *baʔ*^{L} 'to feed forcibly (from *baarh* ?); and MK-Khmer *p̈ana* / -pɑɑn/ 'to feed by introducing premasticated or other food into the mouth of (infant, chick, etc.). -> Tai /pɔ̂ɔn/.

bù$_6$ 部 'hillock' → **fù**$_7$ 阜

C

cái₁ 才材財 (dzậi) **LH** dzə, **OCM** *dzə̂
'Be well endowed' [Shi], '(innate) ability' 才 [Zuo]; 'material, talent' 材 [Shu]; 'value' 財 [BI, Shu].
[T] *Sin S. SR* dzaj (平); *MGZY* tsay (平) [dzaj]; *ONW* dzɑi (dzɛi ?)
[E] Etymology not certain. Matisoff (1995: 42f) proposes cognation with PTB *(t)sa:y ⋈ *(d)za:y 'property, livestock, talent', but see → zī₇ 資.
Most likely, this word is derived from ST *tsə 'come forth' (as child, seedling, → zǐ₁ 子); for the semantic connection between 'birth' and 'natural characteristic / endowments', compare → shēng₂ 生 'give birth, live' ⋈ → xìng₂ 性姓 'what is inborn: one's inner nature; one's name'. Thus a WT cognate of *cái* is prob. *mtsʰan* 'name' ⋈ *mtsʰan(-ma)* 'shape and peculiar characteristics of separate parts of the body; genitals; mark, token, symptom' (with the nominalizing n-suffix §6.4.3).

cái₂ 才纔 (dzậi) **LH** dzə, **OCM** *dzə̂ — **[T]** *ONW* dzɑi (dzɛi ?)
'Only when / at (time)' (German 'erst') [Hou Hanshu]. Matisoff (1995: 74f) suggests that this is cogn. to TB-Lahu *šā* and *šē* 'inchoative particle'.

cǎi₁ 采 (tsʰậiᴮ) **LH** tsʰəᴮ, **OCM** *tshə̂ʔ
'To gather, pluck' [Shi].
⋈ **cài** 菜采 (tsʰậiᶜ) **LH** tsʰəᶜ, **OCM** *tsʰə̂h
'Vegetables, edible plants' 菜 [Shi] > 'appanage' 采 [Shu].
[T] *Sin Sukchu SR* ts'aj (去); *MGZY* tshay (去) [ts'aj]; *ONW* tsʰɑi
[<] exopass. of *cǎi*, lit. 'what is gathered, plucked' (§4.4).
[E] Etymology not certain. Perh. from ST *tsə: WT *btsa* 'fruit', *btsas* 'harvest, to reap' (*CVST* 4: 17); PLB *tsyakᴴ 'to pluck'. To the same stem may belong → cái₁ 才材財 and → zǐ₁ 子. Alternatively, note WT *tsʰod-ma* 'vegetable', the vocalic correspondence would be parallel to → cǎi₂ 采 'color' (see §12.9[3]).

cǎi₂ 采 (tsʰậiᴮ) **LH** tsʰəᴮ, **OCM** *tshə̂ʔ
'Color, pigment, be colorful' [Shi].
[E] ST: WT *tsʰos* 'paint, dye, to color'. The vowel correspondence is prob. ST *ə > OC *ə, > PTB *a > WT *o* (see §12.9[3]).

cài 菜采 → **cǎi₁** 采

cān₁ 參 → **sān** 三

cān₂ 餐 → **jǔ₁** 咀

cán 蠶 (dzậm) **LH** dzəm, **OCM** *dzə̂m
'Silkworm' [Shi].
[T] *Sin Sukchu SR* dzam (平), *PR* dzan; *MGZY* tsam (平) [dzam]
[E] Bodman (1980: 58) relates this word to WT *sdom* 'spider'. Perh. cogn. to → jiàn₁₂ 蔪 'entwine'.

cǎn 噆 (tsʰậmᴮ) **LH** tsʰəmᴮ, **OCM** *tshə̂mʔ < *s-ʔə̂mʔ ? (§5.9.1) — **[T]** *ONW* tsʰɑm
'Have in the mouth' tr. (have a taste in the mouth) [Huainan] is perh. derived from *ǎn*

唵 'hold in the mouth' (under → ān$_4$ 喑) with the transitivising s-prefix (§5.9.2). Karlgren (1956: 18) relates this word to → zá 噆 'bite'.

càn 燦粲 (tsʰânC) **LH** tsʰɑnC, **OCM** *tshâns
'Shiny, beautiful' 粲 [Shi], 燦 [Chunqiu fanlu].
[E] Perh. a ST word, it could either be related to WT *mtsʰar-ba* 'bright, shining, beautiful' (so *HST:* 49); or, acc. to Unger (*Hao-ku* 35, 1986: 30) to WT *gsal-ba* 'be clear, distinct, bright'. Since MC *tsʰ-* = WT *gs-* (§5.9.1), Unger's suggestion seems on balance preferable.

cāng$_1$ 倉 'granary' → **cáng** 藏

cāng$_2$ 滄 (tṣʰjaŋC, tsʰâŋ) **LH** tṣʰɑŋ(C), **OCM** *tshraŋ(h)
'Cold' [Yi Zhoushu].
[<] prob. intensive aspiration of → liáng$_3$ 涼 'cold': s + hraŋ (§5.9.2).
[D] LH *tṣʰaŋ* is an old Wú dialect word in *Shìshuō xīnyǔ;* it is still used in Mǐn dialects: Fúzhōu *tsʰeiŋCI*, Xiàmén *tsʰinCI*, Jiànyáng *tʰoiŋCI* 'cold (of weather)' (Norman 1983: 207). Unrelated to → qìng$_1$ 凊 'cold'.

cāng$_3$ 蒼 (tsʰâŋ) **LH** tsʰɑŋ, **OCM** *tshâŋ < *k-sâŋ ?
'Green, azure, blue' [Shi]. This may be an old dialect variant of → qīng$_1$ 青 (Baxter, *JCLTA* 19, 1983), note Mǐn *tsʰaŋ* for *qīng* 青 and its use for 'sky, heaven' in the ancient Yuè area (later Mǐn) of the Han period [Yuè juè shū].
In the form *cāng-láng* 蒼浪 / 狼 / 筤 (tsʰâŋ-lâŋ) the initial *l-* is the reduplicative syllable onset (§2.7).
[E] ST *saŋ: Garo *tʰaŋ* < *saŋ* 'live' ⋈ *gatʰaŋ* < *k-saŋ* 'green', Dimasa *gatʰaŋ* 'alive, living, green, unripe'. This stem is parallel to ST *siŋ, see → qīng$_1$ 青.

cáng 藏 (dzâŋ) **LH** dzɑŋ, **OCM** *dzâŋ, OCB *ɦtsʰaŋ
'To conceal, store' [Shi].
[T] *Sin Sukchu* S dzaŋ (平); *MGZY* tsang (平) [dzaŋ]; *ONW* dzɑŋ
⋈ **zàng** 藏臟 (dzâŋC) **LH** dzɑŋC, **OCM** *dzâŋh
(1) 'A treasure' 藏 [Shi] > 'intestines' 臟 [Zhouli]. For a semantic parallel see under → fù$_3$ 付.
[E] ST: WT *'dzaŋs-pa* 'to hoard wealth'.
[<] *dzaŋ + pass. s/h-suffix (§4.4), lit. 'what is being stored'.
(2) 'Storehouse' [Zuo] (Downer 1959: 275).
[<] *dzaŋ + general purpose s/h-suffix (§3.5) (lit. 'what does the storing').
⋈ **cāng** 倉 (tsʰâŋ) **LH** tsʰɑŋ, **OCM** *tshâŋ < *k-sâŋ ?, OCB *tshaŋ
'Granary' [Shi].
[T] *Sin Sukchu SR* ts'aŋ (平); *MGZY* tshang (平) [ts'aŋ]
[E] ST: WT *gsaŋ-ba* 'secret, conceal' (*HST:* 57), WT *'tsʰaŋ-ba* 'to press into, stuff inside' ⋈ *mtsʰaŋ* 'evil hidden in a person's heart'. Perh. → zàng$_1$ 葬 is related.

cáo 曹 → **zāo$_2$** 遭

cǎo$_1$ 草 (tsʰâuB) **LH** tsʰouB, **OCM** *tshûʔ
'Grass, small plant' [Shi].
[T] Sin S *SR* ts'aw (上); *MGZY* tshaw (上) [ts'aw]; *ONW* tsʰɑu
[E] Etymology not clear. Perh. related to WT *rtswa* 'grass, plant'; Balti, Purik *rtswa, stwa* (Jaeschke: 437a) confirm the medial *w*. The WT word could be reconciled with CH if analyzed as *rtsu-a with the a-suffix which is also found in *tʰa-ga-pa* 'weaver' < *tag-a. Alternatively, this could be another version of the AA word under → chú$_4$ 芻.

cǎo$_2$ 操 (tsʰâu^B) **LH** tsʰɑu^B, **OCM** *tshâuʔ — **[T]** *ONW* tsʰɑu
'To grasp' [Li], 'to handle' [Zuo].
⋈ **cào** 操 (tsʰâu^C) **LH** tsʰɑu^C, **OCM** *tshâuh
'Principles, purpose' [Meng].
[<] exopass. of *cǎo* 操 (tsʰâu^B) (§4.4), lit. 'what is grasped'.

cào 造 → **zào**$_2$ 造

cè$_1$ 側 (tṣjək) **LH** tṣɨk, **OCM** *tsrək
'Be going to the side, be slanting, deviating' > 'side' [Shi].
= **zè** 仄昃 (tṣjək) **LH** tṣɨk, **OCM** *tsrək
'Be slanting, oblique' 仄 [Zhouli] > 'sun going down, afternoon' 昃 [OB, Shu].
[E] AA: OKhmer *jre* /crée/ 'to turn down, tilt, slope, decline, (of sun) go down, set', acc. to Jenner / Pou (1982: 268) a derivative of OKhmer *re /ree ~ rəə/ 'move, stir, change course', from this root is also derived the Khmer (and OC) wf under → lǐ$_6$ 理. For the CH final *-k*, see §6.1.1.

cè$_2$ 測惻畟 (tṣʰjək) **LH** tṣʰɨk, **OCM** *tshrək
'To fathom, measure' depth 測 [Shi]; 'to pity, be pained' 惻 [Yijing, Meng]; 'deep (or sharp?) cutting' of a plow 畟畟 [Shi] (also QY tṣjək).
[T] *Sin Sukchu SR* tṣ'əj (入); *MGZY* chʰiy (入) [tṣ'əj]; *ONW* tṣhik

cè$_3$ 廁 (tṣʰɨ^C) **LH** tṣʰə^C, **OCM** *tshrəkh ?
'Latrine' [Zuo].
[T] *Sin Sukchu SR* tṣ'ʅ (去); *LR* tṣ'ʅ; *MGZY* chʰi (去) [tṣ'ʅ]
[E] ST: PTB *ts(y)i 'urinate' > WT *gči(d)-pa* 'to urinate' ⋈ *gčin* 'urine'; WB *tsʰi^B* 'urine', NN *C-chi 'urine', Chepang *cʰyuʔ* 'urine' [Weidert 1987: 27]. For the OC medial *r, see §7.4; the vowel correspondence is unusual, see §11.2.2.

cè$_4$ 冊策筴 (tṣʰɛk) **LH** tṣʰɛk, **OCM** *tshrêk — **[T]** *ONW* tṣʰëk
('Bamboo slips':) 'to document, write down' (on bamboo slips) [OB, BI, Shu] > n. 'document' [BI], 策 [Zuo], 'book' in M-Xiàmén lit. *tsʰik^{DI}*, col. *tsʰeʔ^{DI}*; 'Achilea stalks used for divination' (the radical implies bamboo 筴). Sagart (1999: 214) suggests a possible further connection with → jī$_9$ 積 'collect, accumulate'. OTib. *gtsigs* 'document, official text, decree' is perh. a CH loan.

cè$_5$ 籍 (tṣʰɐk) **LH** tṣʰak, **OCM** *tshrâk
'To spear' (fish) 籍 [Zhouli], 'a kind of lance' 矠 [SW].
[E] This is prob. a vocalic variant of the synonym → chuō 擉 (tṣʰåk) [tṣʰɔk] *tshrok, prompted by AA-OKhmer *cāk* /cak/ 'to pierce, stab, jab...'. Alternatively, the 'kind of lance' could represent the AA item Khmer /cak/, and 'spear fish' was a semantic extension in analogy to *chuō*. For the CH retroflex initial, see §5.10.3. Another syn. is → zé$_6$ 矠.

cēn 參 → **chán**$_2$ 漸

céng 層 → **zēng** 曾增

chā$_1$ 叉 (tṣʰai, tṣʰa) **LH** tṣʰɛ or tṣʰai, **OCM** *tshrê or *tshrâi
'A fork' [SW].
[T] *Sin Sukchu SR* tṣ'a (平); *ONW* tṣʰä
⋈ **chà** 杈 (tṣʰai^C) **LH** tṣʰɛ^C, **OCM** *tshrêh
'Forked branch of a tree' (used for spearing fish) [SW, Zhuang]. Duan Yucai says that *yā-chà* 椏杈 is an eastern Yangtze dialect word for 'branch' (Wáng Lì 1982: 440).

[E] ? AA: The reference to the eastern end of the Yangtze River, once inhabited by AA, may support an AA connection: Khmer *cēka* /chaaɛk/ 'to be divided, split, cleft, forked, bifurcated....' This AA etymon may also be represented in → xī$_4$ 析 'split'. For the absence of final *-k* in CH, see §6.9. Alternatively, *chā* may be the s. w. as → chā$_2$ 差 'divergence' (< 'branch off'), but see there.

The *SW* glosses the graph *chā* 叉 as 'crossing hands', thereby implying a basic meaning 'branches crossing each other'; this suggests a connection with → cuò$_4$ 錯 'crossing, mixing', also TB-JP *gə^{31}-tʃai^{55}* 'intersect'.

chā$_2$ 差 (tṣʰa) **LH** tṣʰai, **OCM** *tshrâi
'Divergence, difference, distinction' [Shu], 'mistake' [Xun] (cf. → cuò$_5$ 錯 'mistake').
[T] *Sin Sukchu SR* tṣ'a (平); *ONW* tṣʰä (~ tṣʰëi)

⋇ **cī** 差 (tṣʰjie) **LH** tṣʰɑi, **OCM** *tshrai
'Uneven, irregular' [SW] (Karlgren 1956: 16)

⋇ **cī-chí** 差池 (tṣʰjie-ḍjie) **LH** tṣʰɑi-ḍɑi, **OCM** *tshrai-drai or *-d-lai ?
'Graduated, of different length' [Shi].
[<] Prob. a reduplicated form where the second syllable has the *l ~ *r onset (§2.7).

[E] The etymology is not clear, perh. the s. w. as → chā$_1$ 叉 'fork', lit. 'branch off' > 'diverge', but the semantic field of this wf points in a different direction ('graduated'). Or perh. AA: Khmer *cāya* /caaj/ 'give out, scatter, disperse' ⋇ OKhmer /cŋaaj/ 'be separated, apart, far away, be different'. Or ST: WT *sre-ba* 'to mix with, mingle'.

[C] Allofams are perh. → chá$_3$ 察 'examine', and → cuō$_3$, chī 齹 'uneven teeth'.

chā$_3$ 臿 (tṣʰăp) **LH** tṣʰɛp, **OCM** *tshrêp or *tshrə̂p < *s-ʔrəp ? (§5.9.1), OCB *tshrjop
'To husk (grain) with a mortar and pestle' 臿 [SW], 'to insert' 插 [Guoce].
[T] *Sin Sukchu* 插 *SR* tṣ'a (入)

⋇ **cuì**, **chuì** 竄 (tsʰjuäi^C) **LH** tsʰyɑs ~ tsʰios, OCB *tshjots < *-ops?
'Pound wheat' (with mortar and pestle) (Duàn Yùcái; Baxter 1992: 548).

[<] prob. an s-prefix iterative derivation from → yā$_3$ 壓 'press down', hence < PCH *s-ʔrəp (§5.9.1), even though the MC vowels do not agree (ă vs. a < OC *rə vs. *ra?).

[E] Alternatively, it may be related to PLB *kyap ~ *tsap 'stick into, insert', WB *kyap* 'put into and twirl about...', Akha *tsaw^{HS}* 'pierce, stab'; but the initials are difficult to reconcile.

chá$_1$ 茶 (ḍa) **LH** ḍa, **OCM** *d-lâ
'Tea' [Han period].
[T] *Sin Sukchu SR* dẓa (平); *ONW* dä
[E] Sagart (1999: 188) suggests that *chá* is a loan from Loloish (TB) *la 'leaf, tea', PLB *s-la 'leaf / tea' (*HPTB:* 48), as tea may have originated in Sìchuān (Lolo area); this word has wider distribution, also in Zhuang (Tai) *la^4* means 'tea', the ultimate source is PAA *sla 'leaf'. Alternatively, Qiu Xigui (2000: 326) considers 'tea' with its bitter leaves a semantic extension of *tú* 荼 *lâ 'name of a bitter plant' (*Sonchus oleraceus*).

chá$_2$ 槎 (dẓa[^{B}]) **LH** dẓai, **OCM** *dzrâi
'Cut trees' [Guoyu].

⋇ **zé** 柞 (tṣɐk) **LH** tṣak, **OCM** *tsrâk
'Clear away (trees and bushes)' [Shi].

⋇ **zhuó** 斮 (tṣjak) **LH** tṣɑk, **OCM** *tsrak
'Cut off' [Gongyang].

[E] Possibly AA in light of *zé* 'clear away trees and bushes' (to make room for settlements): OKhmer *sre* /srɛɛ/ 'wet or irrigated rice field', perh. originally 'land cleared for cultivation' (Jenner / Pou 1982: 271). An allofam is perh. → chái₁ 柴 'firewood'.

chá₃ 察 (tṣʰat) **LH** tṣʰat, **OCM** *tshrât
'To examine' [Shu], 'discern' [Li] is either derived from → chā₂ 差 'distinction', or from → chāi 差 'choose, select'; 'examine, discern' is the process of sorting out differences, selecting.
[T] *Sin Sukchu SR* tʂ'a (入)

chà₁ 刹 (tṣʰat) **LH** tṣʰat — **[T]** *ONW* tṣʰät
'A Buddhist temple', borrowed from Skt. *kṣetra* 'field, place, seat, sphere of activity'; Middle Korean *tyel* and Old Japanese *tera* 'temple' derive perh. from the CH word (Miyake 1997: 189).

chà₂ 杈 → **chā₁** 叉

chāi 差 (tṣʰai, tṣʰăi) **LH** tṣʰɛ (or tṣʰai ?) **OCM** *tshrê (or *tshrâi ?)
'To pick out, select' (e.g. pick horses out of a herd) [Shi].
[E] Prob. AA: Khmer /sral/ 'to take the pick of, select'. Or semantically less likely, this may be the s. w. as → chā₂ 差. Allofam is perh. → chá₃ 察 'examine'.

chái₁ 柴 (dẓai) **LH** dẓɛ, **OCM** *dzrê
'Firewood' [Li] > 'burnt offering' [BI, Shu].
[T] *Sin Sukchu SR* dʐaj (平); *MGZY* cay (平) [dʐaj]
[D] The graph 柴 writes a Mǐn synonym, see under → jiāo₆ 焦.
[E] *Chái* is perh. related to → chá₂ 槎 'cut trees'; OC rimes *-ai and *-e are occasionally confused in wfs. Perh. from AA: OKhmer *jhe* 'wood'. Note also PHlai *tsʰai¹ 'tree' [Matisoff 1988c no. 293] (CH loan?).

chái₂ 儕 (dẓăi) **LH** dẓɛi, **OCM** *dzrî or *dzrəi
'Class, category, equals' [Zuo], occurs also in Tai: S. *raai*^{A2} 'set, category, list' (Manomaivibool 1975: 156). For the initials, see §7.1.5. Perh. connected with → qí₁₅ 齊 'be equal' (so Karlgren 1956: 16).

chái₃ 儕 (dẓăi)
The graph is used to write the Mǐn dial. word for 'many': PMin *dzeᶜ > Yǒngān *tse*^{C1}, Jiànyáng *lai*^{C2}, Fúzhōu *sa*^{C2}, Amoy *tsue*^{C2}. Yue Hashimoto (*CAAAL* 6, 1976: 1) relates this word to Tai: Zhuang (Lóngzhōu) *la:i*^{A1} 'many' < PTai *hlai^{A1}. The Tai word is related to → duō 多.

chài 蠆 (tʰaiᶜ) **LH** ṭʰas, **OCM** *rhâts
'Scorpion' [Shi]. The phonetic wàn₃ 萬 which writes words like → mài₅ 邁勱 *mra(t)s 'walk' suggests that the OC initial was *rh- rather than a dental stop.
[<] *Chài* is derived from → lì₁₅ 厲 'sharp' with the nominalizing ST s- / aspiration (§5.2.4); it may also be a connected with **zhé** 蜇 (tjät) LH ṭiat, *trat 'to sting' [Liezi].

chān₁ 佔覘 → **zhān₂** 占瞻

chān₂ 梴 → **yán₅** 延筵

chán₁ 儃 (źjän) **LH** dźian, **OCM** *dan
'Irresolute' [Chuci] is perh. cognate to the wf → chǎn₂ 嘽幝繟 'slow'.

chán₂ 漸 (dẓam) **LH** dẓam, **OCM** *dzrâm
'Be craggy' (of rocks on a mountain) [Shi].

⪤ **chán, zhàn** 儳 (dẓam, dẓăm^{B}) **LH** dẓam, dẓɛm^{B}, **OCM** *dzrâm, *dzrə̂mʔ
'Uneven, unequal, disorder' [Zuo].

⪤ **chàn, zhàn** 儳 (tṣʰam^{C}, dẓăm^{C}) **LH** tṣʰam^{C}, dẓɛm^{C}, **OCM** *tshrâms, *dzrə̂ms
'Mixed, disparate' [Li].
[<] perh. exopass. of *chán* (§4.4).

⪤ **cēn** 參 (tṣʰjəm) **LH** tṣʰəm, **OCM** *tsʰrəm
'Uneven, of varying length' (flowers) [Shi].

[E] AA: Khmer /krɔ́əm/ 'be rough, uneven, bumpy, rugged, rocky' ⪤ /crɔ́əm/ 'move around, restless, in motion, agitated...' ⪤ /prɔ́əm/ 'to move (around), stirred up, excited'. AA -> TB-WB *kram^{B}* 'rough, coarse, violent'. Khmer /krɔ́əm/ 'rocky' shows that → kān$_{3}$ 嵁 *khrə̂m 'rocky' is an AA allofam.

chán$_{3}$ 廛 (ḍjän) **LH** ḍan, **OCM** *dran
'Farm, farmyard' [Shi]
[E] KT: S. *rɨan^{A2}* < *rɨan^{A} 'house'; PKS *hraːn^{1} 'house'; PHlai *rʔuun^{1} 'house'. For the initials, see §7.1.4.

chán$_{4}$ 纏 (ḍjän[^{C}]) **LH** ḍan(^{C}), **OCM** *dran(s)
'To bind, wind' [Lie].

⪤ **dàn** 繵 (tân^{C}, dân^{B}) **LH** tɑn^{C}, dɑn^{B}, **OCM** *tâns, *dânʔ
'A belt or wrapping cord' [Shiji].

[E] ST: WT *star-ba* 'tie, fasten' ⪤ *dar* 'silk, piece of cloth, scarf' (*HST:* 43).

chán$_{5}$, zhàn 儳 → **chán$_{2}$** 漸

chán$_{6}$, zhàn 鑱 → **zhǎn$_{2}$** 斬

chán$_{7}$ 讒 → **zhǎn$_{2}$** 斬

chǎn$_{1}$ 闡 (tśʰjän^{B}) **LH** tśʰan^{B}, **OCM** *thanʔ
'To open up, make clear, explain' 闡 [Yi] is perh. the s. w. as → chǎn$_{2}$ 嘽幝繟.

chǎn$_{2}$ 嘽幝繟 (tśʰjän^{B}) **LH** tśʰan^{B}, **OCM** *thanʔ
'Slow, drawn-out, easygoing' 嘽 [Li]; 'slow' 幝 [Shi]; 'indulgent, generous' 繟 [Lao]. Perh. → chǎn$_{1}$ 闡 'explain' is the s. w.

⪤ ? **shàn** 禪 (źjän^{C}) **LH** dźan^{C}, **OCM** *dans
'Relinquish, cede, hand over' [Meng] (< 'be generous').

[C] Allofam is perh. → tǎn$_{3}$ 儃坦 'at ease'; → chán$_{1}$ 儃 'irresolute'.

chǎn$_{3}$ 產 (ṣăn^{B}) **LH** ṣɛn^{B}, **OCM** *srânʔ or *srênʔ (?), OCB *sŋrjanʔ
'To breed, bear' [Zuo], 'produce' [Li], 'product, livelihood' [Meng].
[T] *Sin Sukchu SR* tʂ'an (上); *MGZY* shan (上) [ṣan]; *ONW* ṣän
[E] ST: WT *srel-ba* 'to bring up, rear' (Bodman 1980: 143; *HST* p. 40). The MK-Khmer synonym /samraal/ is phonologically also compatible with this word (see → miǎn$_{2}$ 娩).

chàn, zhàn 儳 → **chán$_{2}$** 漸

chāng 昌 (tśʰjaŋ) **LH** tśʰɑŋ, **OCM** *k-hlaŋ or *thaŋ ? — **[T]** *ONW* tśʰaŋ
'Splendid, prosperous' [Shi] is perh. related to → yáng$_{9}$ 陽暘 in which case this word might go back to earlier *k-hlaŋ. This would be supported by PVM *hlaŋ^{B} 'bright'. Note the phonetic parallelism with → chàng$_{1}$ 唱倡.

cháng$_{1}$ 常 (źjaŋ) **LH** dźɑŋ, **OCM** *daŋ, actually *djaŋ ?
'Lower garment' [SW 8: 3410].

= **cháng** 裳 (źjaŋ) **LH** dźɑŋ, **OCM** *daŋ, actually *djaŋ ?
'Lower garment, skirt' [Shi].
[E] Bodman (1980: 80) compares this word to WT *g-yaŋ* 'animal skin clothing'. For the initials see §9.3.

cháng₂ 常 (źjaŋ) **LH** dźɑŋ, **OCM** *daŋ, actually *djaŋ ?
'To perpetuate, have or be forever' [BI, Shi].
[T] *Sin Sukchu SR* dʐjaŋ (平); *MGZY* zhang (平) [ʐaŋ]; *MTang* źaŋ, *ONW* dźaŋ
⋈ **shàng** 尚 (źjaŋC) **LH** dźɑŋC, **OCM** *daŋh, actually *djaŋh ?
'To continue, still, consider to continue, hope for' [BI, Shi].
[T] *Sin Sukchu SR* ʐjaŋ (去); *MGZY* zhang (去) [ʐaŋ]; *MTang* źaŋ, *ONW* dźaŋ
[E] ST *jaŋ: Acc. to Bodman (1980: 79) related to WT *yaŋ* 'again, still, once more'. For the initials see §9.3. WT *yaŋ* may possibly belong to → yòu₁ 又 instead, however.

cháng₃-é 常娥 → **é₂** 娥

cháng₄ 嘗 (źjaŋ) **LH** dźɑŋ, **OCM** *daŋ, actually *djaŋ ?
'To taste' [Shi] > 'try' (doing something) [Zhuang].
[D] PMin *d̯žioŋ points to earlier *m-d(j)aŋ
[E] ST *m-jaŋ: PTB *m-yaŋ : Chepang *yaŋ-sā* 'to taste' (sample food), WT *myoŋ-ba, myaŋs / myoŋ* 'to taste, enjoy, experience' (Bodman 1980: 80), from < PTib. *m-yaŋ. However, WB *mrañ^B* 'to taste, try by tasting' suggests that the ST initial might have been more complex. For the initials see §9.3.

cháng₅ 場 (ḍjaŋ) **LH** ḍɑŋ, **OCM** *d-laŋ (or *draŋ ?)
'Vegetable garden, a (pounded) threshing area' [Shi 154, 7 etc.]; this word also means 'meadow' (in the mountains) [BI] (related?).
[E] Etymology not certain, perh. ST: WT *ra-ba* 'enclosure, fence, wall, yard, courtyard, pen', and related to → zhù₁, chú 宁 [ḍɨɑ(B)]; for the initials see §7.1.4, for the finals see §6.5.2. The basic meaning would then be an 'enclosed area or yard'. Shī Xiàngdōng (2000: 32) relates *cháng* to WT *tʰaŋ* 'high plain', but see → chǎng 敞.

cháng₆ 腸 (ḍjaŋ) **LH** ḍɑŋ, **OCM** *d-laŋ
'Intestines' [Shi].
[T] *MTang* ḍaŋ, *ONW* daŋ — **[D]** PMin *dɔŋ
[E] ST: WT *loŋ-ka* 'intestines, entrails, guts', Chepang *yoŋ-kliʔ ~ lyoŋ-ki* (Matisoff, *BSOAS* 63.3, 2000: 364); perh. also PTB *yaŋ 'guts' (Matisoff 1978: 216). OC or TB ? -> PMY: *gl- (Solnit acc. to Strecker 1989: 28): PY *klaaŋ²* 'intestines' (Bodman 1980: 112). WT *gžaŋ* (< *gryaŋ? *glyaŋ?) 'anus' prob. belongs to → gāng₆ 肛 'lower intestines, anus'.

cháng₇ 長 → **zhāng₁** 張

chǎng 敞 (tśʰjaŋB) **LH** tśʰɑŋB, **OCM** *thaŋ?
'High, level land, spacious' [Han time].
[E] ST: WT *tʰaŋ* 'a plain' (*HST:* 119).

chàng₁ 唱倡 (tśʰjaŋC) **LH** tśʰɑŋC, **OCM** *k-hlaŋh ? — **[T]** *ONW* tśʰaŋ
'To lead in singing, intone' 倡 [Shi] > 'to take the lead' (generally) [Guoyu, Hou Hanshu].
[E] ST: WB *ə-kʰraŋ^B, ə-kʰyaŋ^B* 'a kind of song' (< *khlaŋB?); perh. also Proto-Bodo *ləʔŋ 'to sing' [Burling 1959: 443]. Parallelism with the phonetic element → chāng 昌 strengthens the OC reconstruction and ST etymology.

chàng$_2$ 鬯 (ṭ^{h}jaŋ^C) **LH** ṭ^{h}ɑŋ^C, **OCM** *thraŋh or *rhaŋh ?
'Wine, spirits' [BI, Shi].
[E] ST: WT *č^{h}aŋ* (< *C-hrjaŋ* ?) 'fermented liquor, beer, wine' (*HST:* 160).

chāo$_1$ 超 → **tiáo** 跳

chāo$_2$ 剿勦 (tṣ^{h}au) **LH** tṣ^{h}au, **OCM** *tshrâu
'To snatch' [Li] is prob. related to Tai: S. *chok^{D1}* 'id.' (Manomaivibool 1975: 156).
ꭗ **cuàn** 篡 (tṣ^{h}wan^C) **LH** tṣ^{h}uan^C, **OCM** *tshrôns (< *tshrâu-ns)
'To seize, take by force' (a throne) [Meng].
[C] An allofam may be → zhuā 抓 'grasp', but the OC vowels differ.

cháo$_1$ 朝潮 → **zhāo$_4$** 朝

cháo$_2$ 巢 (dẓau) **LH** dẓau, **OCM** *dzrâu
'Nest' [Shi], 'make a nest' [Zuo].
[T] *Sin Sukchu SR* dẓaw (平); *MGZY* caw (平) [dẓaw]
[E] Related to PMY *rau^2 'nest' (Downer ICSTLL 1982, Beijing); PHlai *rʔuak^7 'nest'. For the initials, see §7.1.5. This word is perh. cognate to → zhuā 抓 'grasp', hence *cháo* was originally a 'perch', but the OC vowels do not agree.

chē 車 (tś^{h}ja) **LH** tś^{h}a, **OCM** *k-hla
'Chariot' [OB, BI, Shi] > 'wheel' as in *fǎng-chē* 紡車 'spinning wheel'.
[T] *Sin Sukchu SR* tṣ'je (平); *MGZY* chÿa (平) [tṣ'jɛ]; *ONW* tś^{h}a
[D] PMin *tš^{h}ia; in some southern dialects 'to mill', e.g. Y-Guǎngzhōu *ts^{h}ɛ^{53}-mɐi^{13}* 車米 'mill rice'.
[E] Horse and chariot were introduced into China around 1200 BC from the West (Shaughnessy *HJAS* 48, 1988: 189-237). Therefore, this word is prob. a loan, apparently from an IE language (V. Mair, *EC* 15, 1990: 45ff; Robert Bauer, *Sino-Platonic Papers* 47, 1994): Toch. A *kukäl*, Tocharian B *kokale*, note Greek *kýkla* or *kýkloi* ('wheels':) 'wagon' [Pokorny *IG etym. Wörterbuch* I: 640]; an older variant survives in Northern Mand. *gū-lū* 'wheel' (so Bauer). Alternatively, acc. to Baxter / Sagart (1998: 48) *chē* is a derivation by k-prefix from → yú$_{11}$ 舁轝 'lift up' (§5.4); note the WT semantic parallel *t^{h}eg-pa* 'vehicle, carriage, riding beast' < id. 'to lift, raise, hold, support'.
~ **jū** 車 (kjwo) **LH** kɨɑ, **OCM** *ka — **[T]** *ONW* kio ? > kø
'Chariot' (a piece in a chess game), lit. for 'carriage' (as in Tang poetry: Branner *T'ang Studies* 17, 2000: 44). For a similar phonological doublet, note → chǔ$_3$ 處 ~ jū$_2$ 居. Different readings of 車 are discussed by Baxter (1992: 480; 862 n. 356). *Shìmíng* states that the reading in MC *-jwo* is the older one; this is prob. based on a scribal error in a *Shījīng* version (Baxter 1992: 360; 480). On the other hand, Baxter points out that therefore the reading MC *kjwo* may be a lexicographical ghost, while a reading MC *k^{h}jwo* mentioned in *JDSW* seems closer to MC *tś^{h}ja* with its aspiration. However, MC *kjwo* has enjoyed to this day general currency while MC *k^{h}jwo* is unknown apart from this sound gloss.
[C] Possible allofam → kù$_1$ 庫.

chè$_1$ 坼 → **chǐ$_1$** 拸

chè$_2$ 徹撤 (ḍjät, ṭ^{h}jät) **LH** ḍat, ṭ^{h}at, **OCM** *drat, *thrat, OCB *thrjet — **[T]** *ONW* t^{h}at
'To remove, take away, clear away' 徹 [BI, Shi], 撤 [Lunyu].
[<] r-causative of *shì* 逝 (§7.5) (Sagart 1999: 111). This word looks like a derivation from → chú$_2$ 除 [ḍiɑ] 'remove' with a t-suffix (§6.2.2). However, the phonetic of 徹

撤 implies a T-like initial consonant whereas the phonetic of 除 implies an L-like initial (§12.1.2).

ꭗ **zhì** 滯 (ḍjäi^C) **LH** ḍas, **OCM** *drats
'To discard, left over' [Shi] (Sagart 1999: 111).
[<] r-causative of *shì* 逝 (źjäi^C) (§7.5) with exoactive / extrovert tone C (§4.3.1).

ꭗ **shì** 逝 (źjäi^C) **LH** dźas, **OCM** *dats, OCB *djats
'Go away, pass on, come to the point that' [Shi]; a Han period dialect word for 'to marry' (of a woman) in Qín and Jìn [FY 1, 14].

ꭗ ? **shì** 適 (śjäk, tśjäk) **LH** tśek, **OCM** *tek ?, OCB *stjek — **[T]** *ONW* śek
'To go to' [Shi]; 'to marry' (of a woman), a Han period dialect word in Sòng and Lǔ [FY 1, 14]. Acc. to the phonetic series, *shì* has a T-like initial. There is an occasional interchange of final *-k* and *-t*, note that *chè* prob. also had the vowel *e (OCB).

chè₃ 徹 → **zhé₃** 哲

chè₄ 澈 → **zhé₄** 晢

chēn 琛 (ṭʰjəm) **LH** ṭʰim, **OCM** *-rim ?
'A precious object' [Shi].
[T] *Sin Sukchu SR* tʂ'im (平), *PR*, *LR* tʂ'in; *MGZY* chim (平) [tʂ'im]
[E] <> Tai: S. *ta-nim* 'jewel' (Unger *Hao-ku* 47, 1995: 141).

chén₁ 臣 → **shì₁₇** 視

chén₂ 沈 (ḍjəm) **LH** ḍim, **OCM** *d-ləm
'To sink' [Shi], 'submerged' [Guoce], 'submerge' something as a sacrifice [OB] > 'put poison in liquid' [Zhouli]; 'deep' [Zhuang] (~ *Chuci* → zhàn₁ 湛 [ḍɛm^B] *drə̂m? 'deep'). Acc. to Downer (1959: 282), the intr. 'to sink' is read in tone A, while the causative 'to drown, immerse' [Zuo] is read in tone C acc. to ancient commentators.
[T] *Sin Sukchu SR* dʐim (平), *PR*, *LR* dʐin; *MGZY* chim (平) [dʐim]; *ONW* dim
[<] derived from → yín₃ 淫 *ləm; the OC initial may have been *rl- as Baxter suggests; note the Khmer form below.

ꭗ **zhèn** 酖鴆 (ḍjəm^C) **LH** ḍim^C, **OCM** *d-ləms
'Poisoned wine' 酖 [Zuo]; 'to poison' 鴆 [Guoyu] (Karlgren *GSR* 656f).
[<] exopass. of *chén* 沈 'put poison in liquid' (§4.4).

[E] Area etymon: PMK *ləəm (Shorto 1976: 103), Khmer *ralāṃ* /rloəm/ 'be soaked, drenched, drowned'. Katuic *[s/c]əlim, *[t/d]əlɨm 'to sink'. PMonic *[_]ləm 'to immerse something' > OMon *tulum* 'to drown' (oneself) , Mon *kəla̤əm, Nyah Kur *chələ̤m; Mon *tanim* 'be inundated', Mon *tinlum* 'to sink' [Diffloth 1984: 221]. <> TB: Chepang: *klyum-* 'submerge, be hidden' ꭗ *klyum?-* 'bury, submerge, cover'.

[C] Allofams are prob. → yín₃ 淫, and perh. → chěn₂ 瀋沈 'a liquid', → hán₄ 涵, → zhàn₁ 湛. Similar looking word in final *-m* include: → dān 耽湛, → jiān 熸, → jiān 漸瀸湛, → lín 淋霖, → shēn₃ 深, → zhān₂ 沾霑, → zhēn₂ 斟, → rǎn 染.

Languages in the area have similar words, but they are difficult to match with potential OC relations:

AA: PNBahn. *krăm, PSBahn. *kəram 'sink'.
AA: Khmer /srə̀m/ 'to sink slowly into water, drop slowly out of sight'.
AA: PMonic *hoom 'to take a bath' ꭗ caus. *p-hoom 'bathe, wash'; PVM *tʰăm^B 'bathe' [Thompson], perh. PSBahn. *ʔum 'bathe'.
KT: Saek *ram^A2* 'be wet' (ꭗ ram^A1 'black'); PKS *ʔram¹ 'sink'.
Tai *čʰum^B1* 'wet', *čum^B1* 'soak, immerse'; Lóngzhōu *tum^A2* 'wet'.

TB: WT *tʰim-pa* 'disappear, being absorbed, evaporate, be melted, to sink' (e.g. into unconsciousness) ⋈ *stim-pa, bstims* 'to enter, penetrate, be absorbed'.
TB: Chepang *ɟyomʔ-* 'to sink in, be pressed down'.

chén$_3$ 辰 (źjen) **LH** dźɨn, **OCM** *dən
The 5th of the Earthly Branches, identified with the dragon [OB]; cf. **shèn** 蜃 (źjen^C) 'some kind of dragon' [Hànshū, Tiānwén zhì].
[T] *Sin S. SR* ʐin (平), *LR* dʐin; *MGZY* zhin (平) [ʐin]; *ONW* dźin
[E] Acc. to Norman (1985: 88) an AA loan: Viet. *trăn*, WrMon *klan* 'python'.

chén$_4$ 辰 'season' → **chén$_5$** 晨辰; 'time' → **zhī$_1$** 之

chén$_5$ 晨辰 (źjen) **LH** dźɨn, **OCM** *dən (晨 also MC dźjen, LH źɨn, OCM *m-dən?)
Time when life begins to stir: (1) 'early morning' 晨晨 [OB, BI, Shu; SW 1149].
(2) 'Start of the growing / agricultural season in the 3rd month; heavenly bodies that mark that time' 農晨辰 [SW 2991; 6629]; 'heavenly body' 辰 [Shu]. 辰 converges with 辰 'time' (under → zhī$_2$ 之).
[<] endopass. of *zhèn* 振震, lit. 'stir oneself' (§4.6). The meaning 'morning' may have been influenced by MK: Mon *tmin, tmiin* 'morning' (*m* can be an infix).

chén$_6$ 塵 (ḍjen) **LH** ḍɨn, **OCM** *drən — **[T]** *ONW* din
'Dust' [Shi].
[E] ST: WT *rdul* 'dust' (*HST:* 68).

chén$_7$ 陳 (ḍjen) **LH** ḍɨn, **OCM** *drən
'Set forth, set out, spread out, arrange, marshal, display' [Shi], 'diffuse, give' [Zuo].

⋈ **zhèn** 陳 (ḍjen^C) **LH** ḍɨn^C, **OCM** *drəns
'Battle array' [Lunyu].
[<] exopass. of *chén* 陳 (ḍjen) (§4.4), lit. 'what is arranged', thence 'line up in battle order' [Zuo] (Downer 1959: 286).

chěn$_1$, **chī** 䫖 (ṭʰjen^B, ṭʰi) **LH** ṭʰɨn^B, ṭʰɨ, **OCM** *thrənʔ, *thrəi
'To laugh' [Zhuang].
[E] ST *C-rə(-C): Lushai *ṭhen^R* 'smile'; perh. also related to PTB *rya-t 'laugh' (*STC* no. 202): WT *gža-ba* < *g-rya* 'sport, joke, play', Kanauri-Bunan *sred*, WB *rai* 'laugh'. For the initial, see §7.1.4.

chěn$_2$ 瀋沈 (tśʰjəm^B) **LH** tśʰim^B, **OCM** *k-hləmʔ
'A liquid' 瀋 [Zuo]; 'juice' 沈 [Li].
[<] nominalizing k-prefix derivation from the stem of → yín$_3$ 淫 'soak'; see → chén$_2$ 沈 for wider connections. Alternative: possibly related to Tai S. *nam^C* < *nl/r- 'water, liquid' (so Unger *Hao-ku* 47, 1995: 140), but the initials are difficult to reconcile.

chēng$_1$ 赬 (ṭʰjäŋ) **LH** ṭʰeŋ, **OCM** *hreŋ
'Red' [Shi], 赪 [Yili] as the color of a bream's tail or that of blushing, also glossed as 'deep red' (Giles), hence *chēng* referred originally perh. to the intensive red of certain types of exposed (naked) skin color.
[<] possibly an intensive derivation of → chéng$_5$ 裎 *dreŋ 'naked' (§5.8.3) (cf. Karlgren 1933: 69); then the Tai items would be CH loans.
[E] <> Tai: S. *dɛɛŋ^{A1}* < *ʔdl/riɛŋ 'red', Saek *riiŋ^1* < *ṛiiŋ^{A1}* 'be red', Be *liŋ^{13}* 'purple'; PMiao *ʔl_N^A 'red'. Prob. not related to PTB *kyeŋ (*STC* no. 162; *HST:* p.123).

chēng$_2$ 稱 (tśʰjəŋ) **LH** tśʰɨŋ, **OCM** *thəŋ — **[T]** *ONW* tśʰiŋ
'To weigh' [Li].

[E] This may either belong to the wf → chéng₂ 丞承 'lift'; or be of MK origin: Khmer *thlɤŋ* 'to weigh' (because of the medial *l*, the Khmer word cannot be a CH loan).

chēng₃ 瞠 (ṭʰɐŋ) **LH** ṭʰaŋ, **OCM** *thrâŋ
'To stare at' [Zhuang] also is found in Tai: S. *tʰlɨŋ* (WrSiam *tʰa-lɨŋ*) 'a fierce stare, to stare hard at' (Manomaivibool 1975: 154).

chéng₁ 成盛城 (źjäŋ) **LH** dźeŋ < gieŋ ?, **OCM** *geŋ ?
'To complete, achieve, build' 成 [BI, Shi]; 'put' (in receptacle), 'load, pack' [BI, Shi], 'a vessel full' 盛 [Meng]; (filled-in earth, stamped earth:) 'city wall' [Shi] > 'city' 城 [Zuo].
[T] *Sin Sukchu SR* dʐiŋ (平); *MGZY* zhing (平) [ʐiŋ]; *ONW* dźeŋ
[D] PMin *d̯žiaŋ 成 'percent'; PMin *žiaŋ 'town'.
ꭗ **shèng** 盛 (źjäŋ^C) **LH** dźeŋ^C < gieŋ^C ?, **OCM** *geŋh ?
'Abundant, highest degree' [Zhuang, Li].
[T] *Sin Sukchu SR* ʐiŋ (去); *MGZY* zhing (去) [ʐiŋ]; *ONW* dźeŋ
[<] exopass. of *chéng₁* 'be filled' (§4.4).
[E] Prob. not related to → yíng₂ 盈嬴 'full'. More likely, Bodman (1980: 160) relates 城 to WT *gyaŋ, gyeŋ* 'pisé, stamped earth, wall' ꭗ *rgyaŋ* 'wall' ꭗ *'geŋs-pa, bkaŋ* 'to fill, to fulfill' ꭗ *skoŋ-ba, bskaŋs* 'to fulfill'. For the vowels, see §11.3.2; for the initials §12.1.1 (3). The initial is confirmed by PWa which borrowed this word as *kɨŋ 'town, village'.

chéng₂ 丞承 (źjəŋ) **LH** dźɨŋ, **OCM** *dəŋ
'To lift, hold up, present, receive' [BI, Shi].
[T] *Sin Sukchu SR* dʐiŋ (平); *MGZY* zhing (平) [ʐiŋ]; *ONW* dźiŋ
ꭗ **chēng** 稱 (tśʰjəŋ) **LH** tśʰɨŋ, **OCM** *thəŋ — [T] *ONW* tśʰiŋ
'To lift, raise, set forth, display' [OB, BI, Shu]. 'To weigh' → chēng₂ 稱.
ꭗ **chèng** 稱 (tśʰjəŋ^C) **LH** tśʰɨŋ^C, **OCM** *thəŋh
'To appreciate, equal to, corresponding' [Shi] > 'capable of' [Li].
[<] exopass. of *chēng* 稱 (tśʰjəŋ), lit. 'be lifted to (a level)' (§4.4).
ꭗ **zhēng** 烝 (tśjəŋ) **LH** tśɨŋ, **OCM** *təŋ — [T] *ONW* tśiŋ
'To offer (gift, sacrifice)' [Shi]
ꭗ **zhěng** 拯 (tśjəŋ^B) **LH** tśɨŋ^B, **OCM** *təŋ?
'Lift' [Yi], 'save, help' [Zuo].
[E] This wf is prob. related to → dēng₁ 登. There is a similar wf, but with initial *l-: → chéng₃ 乘. *HST:* 104 relates this wf to WT *greŋ-ba* 'rise, stand up', but the WT medial *-r-* should be expected to have a MC counterpart.

chéng₃ 乘 (dźjəŋ) **LH** źɨŋ, **OCM** *m-ləŋ
'To mount, ascend, ride, drive' [Shi].
ꭗ **shèng** 乘 (dźjəŋ^C) **LH** źɨŋ^C, **OCM** *m-ləŋh
'Chariot, team of four horses' [Shi].
[<] exopass. of *chéng* 乘 (dźjəŋ), lit. 'what is mounted' (§4.4).
ꭗ **shēng** 升昇 (śjəŋ) **LH** śɨŋ, **OCM** *lhəŋ
'To mount, rise, raise' [BI, Shi] > 'to present' [Li].
[T] *Sin Sukchu SR* ʂiŋ (平); *MGZY* shing (平) [ʂiŋ]; *ONW* śiŋ
[<] perhaps caus. of *chéng* 乘 (dźjəŋ) (§5.2.2). Bodman (1980: 185) considers this word a doublet of → xīng₆ 興.
[C] See also → téng₂ 騰; → shèng₆ 勝 is perh. cognate.

chéng$_4$ 棖 (ḍɐŋ) **LH** ḍaŋ, **OCM** *drâŋ
'Door posts' [Li], 'serve as a stay or support to' [Zhouli].
[E] <> Tai: S. *soŋ*^{A2} (WrSiam. *drŋ*) (Manomaivibool 1975: 153). Or TB-Lepcha *tă-raŋ* 'upright beam in house' (Bodman p. c.).

chéng$_5$ 裎 (ḍjäŋ) **LH** ḍeŋ, **OCM** *dreŋ
'Naked' [Meng].
[E] This is prob. related to TB-Mikir *-reŋ*^{L} *angse*^{H} 'naked', WT *sgren-mo* 'naked' (WT *rjen* 'naked' is a dialectal backform: Beyer 1992: 146), JP *krin*^{31} 'naked', Lushai *ṭeen*^{R} 'be bare' (as a hillside) (Unger *Hao-ku* 38, 1992: 82). This word could ultimately belong to → luǒ$_2$ 裸, all based on a ST root *roi; see Table L-1 'Naked, red' for an overview of related and similar etyma. A derivation is → chēng$_1$ 赬 'red' (so Karlgren 1933: 69) as 'naked' is associated with 'red'.

chéng$_6$ 澄 (ḍjəŋ, ḍɐŋ) **LH** ḍɨŋ, ḍaŋ, **OCM** *drəŋ
'Limpid, clear' [Li].
[E] <> Tai: S. *rɨaŋ*^{A2} 'limpid, clear' (Manomaivibool 1975: 152).

chéng$_7$ 徵懲 (ḍjəŋ) **LH** ḍɨŋ, **OCM** *drəŋ
'Suppress' 徵 [Yi]; 'correct with harsh measures, repress' [Shu], 'warn' 懲 [Zuo]. This word may be connected with → líng$_7$ 陵冷凌 'oppress'.

chéng$_8$ 塍 → **tián$_1$** 田

chéng$_9$ 酲 → **dǐng$_1$** 酊

chī$_1$ 吃 (kjət) **LH** kɨt ?
'To stutter' [SW, Hanshu]. — **[E]** Etymology not clear.

chī$_2$ 吃 **[T]** *Sin Sukchu SR* k'i (入), *LR* tʂ'iʔ; *MGZY* khi (入) [k'i]
'To eat' [Xīnshū 新書, spurious?], has been since the 18th cent. the ordinary Mand. word for 'to eat' [Kāngxī zìdiǎn, Hóng Lóu Mèng] (*Sino-Platonic Papers* 98, Jan. 2000: 75ff). Phonetically the MC form does not agree with Mand., nor does the alleged older variant graph → chī$_3$ 喫. Etymology therefore unknown, perhaps it is the same word as 'stutter' ('eat one's sounds'?) (Norman 1988: 76, n. 6).

chī$_3$ 喫 (kʰiek) **[T]** *MTang* kʰɨk, *ONW* kʰėk
'To eat' 喫 [ONW, Yupian], said to be a variant graph for chī$_2$ 吃, etymology unknown; neither 喫 nor 吃 can be connected with Mand. *chī* phonetically (Norman 1988: 76, n. 6).

chī$_4$ 魑离螭 (ṭʰje) **LH** ṭʰai, **OCM** *rhai
'Mountain demon' 离 [SW], 魑 [Zuo], 螭 [Lü] occurs in texts only in the compound *chī-mèi* 魑魅; *chī* has been extensively discussed by Carr (*LTBA* 13.2: 136ff).
[E] ST: WT *'dre* < *ɴdre* 'goblin, demon, evil spirit' ⋇ *gre-bo / -mo* 'species of demon'; KN *t/s-rai [*IST*: 23]: Tangkhul *rai*^{H} 'unclean spirit', Bodo *ráj* 'devil'. This is distinct from WT *sri*, Lushai *hri*^{F} 'evil spirit which causes sickness'. Note also PKS *la:i^{4} 'devil, ghost' which may be a CH loan because of the initial *l-.

chī$_5$ 颸 → **sī$_6$, chī** 颸

chī$_6$ 絺 → **zhǐ$_9$** 黹

chī$_7$ 䟴 'laugh' → **chěn$_1$, chī** 䟴

chí$_1$ 池 (ḍje) **LH** ḍai, **OCM** *d-lai — **[T]** *Sui-Tang* ḍi < di, *ONW* de
'Pool, pond' [Shi] is perh. a ST word, note Lushai *dil^R* 'lake, pond, tank, pool', or Lushai *li^H* < *li* 'deep pool'.

chí$_2$ 坻墀 (ḍi) **LH** ḍi, **OCM** *dri
'Islet' 坻 [Shi] is the s. w. as 'raised path from gate to the wall of a palace' 墀 [Hanfei] acc. to Baxter (1992: 463f).

chí$_3$ 蚳 (ḍi) **LH** ḍi, **OCM** *dri
'Ant eggs' [Li] may possibly be connected with → dié$_1$ 垤 'anthill'.

chí$_4$ 漦 (dẓɨ, ljɨ) **LH** dẓə, **OCM** *dzrə
'Spittle of a dragon' [Guoyu]. *STC* (171 n. 457) relates this word to PTB *m-tśril 'spittle', but the rimes do not agree.

chí$_5$-chú 踟躕 (ḍje-ḍju) **LH** ḍe-ḍo, **OCM** *dre-dro
'Walk hesitatingly', or perh. 'pacing up and down' [Shi], Mand. 'hesitate, waver'.
[E] <> Tai: S. *rii^{A2}-rɔɔ^{A2}* 'walk hesitatingly, undecided' (Manomaivibool 1975: 152f); for the initials, see §7.1.4.

chǐ$_1$ 扡 (ṭ^{h}je^B) **LH** ṭ^{h}ai^B, **OCM** *rhaiʔ — **[T]** *ONW* t^{h}e
'To cleave, separate, take away' [OB, Zhuang].
[E] ST: WT *ral* 'rent, cleft' ⋇ *ral-ba* 'torn' (clothes) ⋇ *'dral-ba, dral / ral* 'to rip up, tear to pieces' ⋇ *hral-ba* 'to rent, tear up' ⋇ *sgral-ba* 'to cut to pieces'.

⋇ **zhì** 杝扡 (ṭ^{h}je^B, ḍje^B) **LH** ṭ^{h}ai^B, ḍai^B, **OCM** *rhaiʔ, *draiʔ
'To cleave wood following fibers' [Shi].

⋇ **chǐ, yǐ** 胣 (ṭ^{h}jie^B, jie^B) **LH** ṭ^{h}ai^B, jai, **OCM** *rhaiʔ, *laiʔ — **[T]** *ONW* t^{h}e, ie
'To disembowel' [OB Bingb. 7.1 Period I; Zhuang].

⋇ **chè** 坼 (ṭ^{h}ɐk) **LH** ṭ^{h}ak, **OCM** *thrâk
'To split, rent' [Shi], 'fissure' [Zhouli] occurs also in Tai: S. *hak^{D1}S* < *t^{h}r- 'to be broken' (stick) (Li F. 1976: 44). Prob. not related to → pò$_1$ 破.
[<] final *-k* form of *chǐ$_1$* 扡 (ṭ^{h}je^B) (§6.1.1).

[C] This wf may be related to → chǐ$_2$, chí 誃. For an overview of similar items, see Table P-1 under → pī$_3$ 披. For similar words and possible allofams, see → lí$_{10}$ 離.

chǐ$_2$, chí 誃 (tś^{h}je^B, ḍje) **LH** tś^{h}ai^B, ḍai, **OCM** *k-hlaiʔ, *d-lai — **[T]** *ONW* tś^{h}e, de
'To separate' [Guoce].

The original graph 多 shows two separate pieces of meat, hence 'separate', although the conventional interpretation of the graph is '2 pieces of meat' = 'many'. Since 多 occurs already in the earliest OB, but only as a loan for → duō 'many, all', the donor word 'cleave, separate' must already have existed at the beginning of writing.
[E] ST: PL *C-klay$^{1/3}$ 'to separate'; Chepang *kləyh-sa* 'to break' (as sticks), Lushai *hlai^R* 'to flay, to skin, split' (as cane).
[C] A cognate is perh. → tā 他 'other'. This word may belong to → chǐ$_1$ 扡 (ṭ^{h}jie^B) and to → chǐ$_3$ 侈哆移 'be wide, extend'; perh. also connected with Tai S. *sa^4-laai^2* 'to be split, cracked'.

For an overview of similar items, see Table P-1 under → pī$_3$ 披. For a listing of similar words and possible allofams, see → lí$_{10}$ 離.

chǐ$_3$ 侈哆移 (tś^{h}je^B) **LH** tś^{h}ai^B, **OCM** *k-hlaiʔ — **[T]** *MTang* tś^{h}i, *ONW* tś^{h}e
'Great' [Shi], 'extravagant, overbearing' 侈 [Zuo]; 'large' 哆 [Shi] (also read QY tś^{h}ja^B); 'enlarge' 移 [Li]; 'be wide, extend' [Guoyu].

[E] ST: OBurm *klai* [*IST*: 342], WB *kyai* 'wide, broad' ⋈ *kyai^B* 'wide apart' ⋈ *k^hyai^B* ~ *k^hrai^C* 'make wide apart, be diffused' ⋈ *k^hyai^C* 'wide, spread out'. *HST:* 139 relates 'wide, extend' 㢋 to WT *gčal-ba* 'to spread, lay out'. WT *č^he-ba, č^hen-po* 'great' < *te (*HST:* 88) seems to be a different etymon. *Chǐ₃* may be the s. w. as → chǐ₁ 拸 'to 'separate'.

⋈ Perh. **chì** 斥 (tśʰjäk) **LH** tśʰak, **OCM** *k-hlak
'Spread, grow numerous' [Zuo] < final *-k* form of chǐ 侈哆移 (tśʰjieᴮ) (§6.1).

⋈ **shǐ** 弛 (śjeᴮ) **LH** śɑiᴮ, **OCM** *lhaiʔ
'To extend' [Li], 'spread' [Shi].

⋈ **shī** 施 (śje) **LH** śɑi, **OCM** *lhai
'To expand' [Yi], 'spread out, expose' [Guoyu].
[T] *Sin S. SR* ʂi (平), *PR, LR* ʂʅ; *MGZY* shʰi (平) [ʂʅ]; *ONW* śe

[C] This wf may be part of a larger group, see → lí₁₀ 離.

chǐ₄, yǐ 胣 → **chǐ₁** 拸

chǐ₅ 恥 (ṭʰɨᴮ) **LH** ṭʰəᴮ, **OCM** *nhrəʔ ?, OCB *hnrjəʔ — **[T]** *MTang* tśʰi, *ONW* tʰiə
'Shame' [Shi], 'disgrace' [Zuo]. Pulleyblank (1973: 121) relates *chǐ* to words meaning 'shame' with initial *n- and different rimes, see → xiū₃ 羞. Psychologists tend to associate 'guilt' with auditory admonition (Eberhard 1967: 12), therefore → ěr₁ 耳 'ear' in the graph could possibly play not just a semantic role, but *chǐ* may even be cognate to 'ear'. For the *r in the OC initial, note the *r- prefix in TB words for 'ear'; MC *ṭʰj-* can derive from a complex initial nasal cluster.

chǐ₆ 齒 (tśʰɨᴮ) **LH** tśʰəᴮ, **OCM** *thəʔ or *khiəʔ ?
'Tooth (any kind), tusk' [OB, Shi] (Norman / Mei 1976: 289–292).
[T] *Sin Sukchu SR* tʂ'i (上); *PR, LR* tʂ'ʅ; *MGZY* chi (上) [tʂ'i]; *MTang* tśʰi, *ONW* tśʰə
[D] PMin *kʰiᴮ¹ ~ tʃʰɨᴮ¹
[E] The etymology is not clear; *chǐ* is not related to WT *mč^he-ba* 'canine tooth', see → diān₃ 顚 'eyetooth', but may be the same word as PMin *kʰiᴮ 'tooth'. An AA etymon for 'tooth' looks vaguely similar: e.g. Khmer *khnae* 'tusk, spur' (Shorto 1971: 85), Mon inscr. *gnis > gnih* 'eyetooth, canine' (AA medial *n* often disappears in CH).

chì₁ 斥 (tśʰjäk) **LH** tśʰak, **OCM** *k-lhak
'Salty soil' [Shu] is perh. connected to → xì₄ 潟 (sjäk) [siak] 'salty soil' and may belong to → gǔ₁₅ 鹽 and → lǔ₁ 鹵.

chì₂ 斥 → **chǐ₃** 侈哆移

chì₃ 赤 (tśʰjäk) **LH** tśʰak, **OCM** *k-hlak, OCB *KHjAk — **[T]** *ONW* tśʰek
'Red' [BI, Shi] is from earliest times the basic term for 'red' (Baxter *JCLTA* 1983), rivaled only by → zhū₁ 朱. The OC initial is suggested by *hl- in the phon. series.
<> Tai: S. *tʰiak^{D1}* 'red' may be a pre- or early-Han loan.
[D] PMin *tsʰiak
[E] Etymology not clear. The phonetic series implies an OC L-like initial, also the graph 赤 writes a word 'expel' with incontrovertible OC *l- (→ shě₂ 舍捨). There are no TB comparanda with a close phonological fit; one could cite WT *k^hrag* 'blood' (*HST:* 123) which is here associated with → hè₄ 赫; or PTB *tsyak = *tśak 'red' (cognate acc. to *STC* no. 184; p. 168 n. 452), Lushai *čak* 'red', as well as the TB items under → hè₄ 赫 'red' with which it may possibly be connected.

Perh. the following word may be related; like *chì₃*, it had apparently a complex initial cluster in OC.

ⱺ **shì** 奭 (śjäk, xjək) **LH** śak ? or śek ? or hɨk ?, **OCM** *lhak, *hək ?
'Red' [Shi]. — **[D]** Amoy *tsʰioʔA1*

chì₄ 翅, **shì** 翨 (śje^C) **LH** śe^C, **OCM** *lheh ? ~ **jì** 翨 (kjie^C 4) **LH** kie, **OCM** *ke ?
'Wing' 翅 [Guoce], 翨 [Zhouli]. Mand, *chì* has irregular aspiration.
[T] *Sin Sukchu SR* tʂ'ʅ, ʂi (去), *PR* ʂʅ, *LR* tʂ'ʅ; *MGZY* shi (去) [ʂi]; *MTang* śi, kie (?)
[N] Two words for 'wing' have been applied to two graphs 翨 and 翅: (1) *chì* < *lheh. (2) *jì* < *ke — a semantic extension of → zhī₄ 支肢 'limb' > 'wing'; MC tone C is prob. an analogy to *chì;* unpalatalized MC kjie^C 4 betrays a southern dialect origin; Mǐn *kʰek may be related. The graph 翅 must have been intended for *ke (the phonetic is 支 *ke), 翨 for *lheh. However, by convention, MC kjie^C is an alternate reading for 翨, while both shì 翨 = chì 翅 write original *lheh.

chì₅ 飭 → **lì₁** 力

chì₆ 饎饌 (tśʰɨ^C) **LH** kʰiə^C or tśʰə^C, **OCM** *khjəʔ ?, OCB *KHjəʔ(s)
'Cooked sacrificial millet' 饎 [Shi], 饌 [Zhouli]. The phonetic series imply an OC initial *j-, hence the word may be related to WT *yos* 'slightly roasted corn' (mostly barley or wheat). Baxter a. Sagart (1998: 52) relate *chì* to → qǐ₃ 芑.

chōng₁ 沖 (ḍjuŋ) **LH** ḍuŋ, **OCM** *druŋ
'Be young, weak' (of a person) [Shu].
[E] ST: WT *čʰuŋ-ba* 'small, young'.

chōng₂ 沖 (ḍjuŋ) **LH** ḍuŋ, **OCM** *druŋ
'Empty' [Lao] looks similar to WT *stoŋ-pa* 'empty'.

chōng₃ 舂 (śjwoŋ) **LH** śoŋ, **OCM** *lhoŋ
'To hull grain with a pestle' [Shi], 'beating stick for beating time in music' [Zhouli]; 'to beat' 摏 [Zuo].
[E] KT: S. *klooŋ 'hull rice' (*STC:* 178 n. 472), Kam-Sui *tyuŋ^B, which in turn is perh. ultimately related to AA: Kharia *du'ruŋ* 'to pound' (rice), Munda *ruṭuŋ* 'to husk grain' (in a husking machine). TB forms seem phonetically closer to → chuáng₂ 橦.

chōng₄ 衝 (tśʰjwoŋ) **LH** tśʰoŋ, **OCM** *thoŋ
'To pierce' (a person to kill him) [Guoce]. A syn. and cognate is → dòng₁ 洞.
[E] ? ST: Perh. related to WT *mduŋ* 'lance, spear, sting of insect' (*CVST* 2: 15).

chōng₅ 衝 → **chuáng₂** 撞

chóng₁ 蟲虫 (ḍjuŋ) **LH** ḍuŋ, **OCM** *druŋ ?
'Insect, worm' [Shi].
[T] *Sin Sukchu SR* dʐjuŋ (平), *PR* dʐuŋ; *MGZY* cÿung (平) [dʐjuŋ]
[E] ST: Bodo-Garo *dyuŋ 'insect, reptile' > Geman Deng *klauŋ⁵⁵*, or Garo *dźoŋʔ* (Joseph / Burling *LTBA* 24.2, 2001: 45), Dimasa *yuŋ < dyuŋ* (*HPTB:* 310; *HST:* 98).

chóng₂ 蟲 'hot' → **róng₄** 融

chóng₃ 重 → **zhòng₁** 重

chóng₄ 崇 → **lóng₁** 隆

chòng 揰 → **chuáng₂** 揰

chōu₁ 抽 (ṭʰjəu) **LH** ṭʰu, **OCM** *t-hliu ? — **[T]** *MTang* ṭʰeu < ṭʰu, *ONW* tʰu
'Take out, pull out, remove' (e.g. draw weapons, remove thorns from a branch) [Shi]. MC *ṭʰj-* is occasionally found in words with OC L-like initial.

[E] ? ST: TB-Chepang *klu-* 'pull out' (hair) ⋇ *glu-* 'pull out (larger) weeds, cultivate crop' ⋇ *blu-* 'remove, root out'. <> Tai: S. *tʰa-lok*^{D1} 'to pull up' (Manomaivibool 1975: 150) confirms the OC *l-, even though the Tai final stop is unexplained; note that Tai usually has no medial *i* to correspond to the CH element (§9.1.3).

Alternatively, the CH word may be connected with the following TB items instead: Chepang *hlyut-* 'strip off' (skin) ⋇ *hlyu* 'peel off' (skin) ⋇ *hlyun* 'undress, peel'; WT *šu-ba, (b)šus* 'to take off' (clothes), 'strip off' (leaves, skin), 'to skin, pare' ⋇ *šun* 'bark, rind, peel, skin'. This item enjoys a wider distribution: Tai-S. *lut*^{D1S} < *hl- 'to slip off, come off'; Yao *hlút* 'to slip off'.

[D] Mǐn words seem to be connected with this last foreign set: col. Amoy *lut*^{D1} (< *hlut?) 'to slip out of place' ⋇ *tʰut*^{D2} (< *dʰut) 'be dislocated' may derive from Tai, see above.

[C] This etymon is close to → tuō$_3$ 脱.

chōu$_2$, liáo 瘳 (ṭʰjəu, lieu) **LH** ṭʰu, leu, **OCM** *rhiu, *riû
'To improve, get cured, recover' [OB, BI, Shi], 'harm' [Guoyu] is prob. cognate to → liào$_3$ 療藥.

chōu$_3$ 犨 (tśʰjəu) **LH** tśʰu, **OCM** *thu
'Sound of an ox breathing' [SW].
[E] ST: The basic meaning of this etymon is 'breathe in': WB *huik* 'pant, be out of breath'; it is not clear if or how WB *hru* 'breathe, draw into the nose, mouth' ⋇ *hruik* 'draw into lungs with protracted effort' are related.

⋇ **chòu** 臭 (tśʰjəu^C) **LH** tśʰu^C, **OCM** *k-huh
'Strong smell' [Shi], 'foul' [Shu] > Mand. also 'stinking, disgusting'.
[T] *Sin Sukchu SR* tʂ'iw (去); *MGZY* chiw (去) [tʂ'iw]; *MTang* tśʰeu < tśʰu, *ONW* tśʰu
[D] M-Xiàmén lit. *tsʰiu*^{C1}, col. *tsʰao*^{C1}, Fúzhōu *tsʰau*^{C}

⋇ **xiù** 嗅 (xjəu^C) **LH** hu^C, **OCM** *huh
'To smell, inhale' [Lun] > Mand. 'smell, scent, sniff'. CH -> PTai *xiəu^{A1} 'to smell bad, putrid'.
[T] *MTang* hiu > heu; *ONW* hu — [D] M-Xiàmén lit. *hiu*^{C1} 'bad smelling'.

[C] An allofam is perh. → chǒu$_2$ 醜.

chóu$_1$ 酬 → **chóu$_3$** 儔

chóu$_2$ 愁 → **sāo$_3$** 騷

chóu$_3$ 儔 (ḍjəu) **LH** ḍu, **OCM** *dru
('Counterpart':) 'mate, companion' [Shu], ('equal items':) 'class, category' [Shu], 'equal' [Guiguzi]. Syn. **qiú** 仇 (gjəu) 'mate, companion, antagonist' [Shi].
[E] ST: WT *do* 'two, a pair, a couple, an equal, match, companion, mate' ⋇ *dod* 'an equivalent', WB *tu* 'be like, similar' (*CVST* 2: 14). On the other hand, note PWMiao A *ntrau*^{6} 'husband, lover'.

⋇ **chóu** 讎 (źjəu) **LH** dźu, **OCM** *du — [T] *MTang* źeu < dźu, *ONW* dźu
('To counter':) 'to pay back, reply, opponent, enemy' [Shi]; 'pledge with wine a second time' 酬 [Shi], 'requite' 醻 [Shu], 'recompense with gifts' 酬 [Zuo].
[E] ST: Lushai *do*^{H} 'be at enmity with, be hostile', *do*^{H} 'to counter contributions...'; but Lushai 'be at enmity with' may equally well belong to → dòu$_6$ 鬥 'quarrel'.

⋇ **chún** 淳 (źjuen) **LH** dźuin, **OCM** *dun
'A pair' [Zuo]
[<] n-nominalization of *chóu* 讎 *du (§6.4.3)

chóu$_4$ 綢 → **zhōu**$_3$ 周

chóu$_5$ 裯 → **zhōu**$_3$ 周

chóu$_6$ 疇 (ḍjəu) **LH** ḍu, **OCM** *dru
'Plowed field' [Zuo].
[T] *Sin Sukchu SR* dʐiw (平); *MGZY* ciw (平) [dʐiw]
[E] Manomaivibool (1975: 150–153) discusses the possibility of a connection with Tai: S. *tʰiak*^{D2} < *d- 'plowed field', but phonologically the forms are difficult to reconcile; see also → zhái 宅.

chóu$_7$ 疇 'who' → **shéi, shuí** 誰

chǒu$_1$ 丑 (ṭʰjəu^B) **LH** ṭʰu^B, **OCM** *thruʔ or *rhuʔ ?, OCB *hnrjuʔ
Cyclical sign for 'ox' [OB].
[E] MK (Mei 1980; Norman 1985: 87): PVM *c-luː > *kluː / tluː* 'buffalo' > Viet. *trâu* [ṭəw], PMon *j(-)ləw 'bovine, buffalo, ox', OMon *jlow* 'cattle, ox, bull', Mon *klɛ̤ə̤. The meaning 'ox' has been obsolete since the beginning of writing, but → láo$_1$ 牢 'calf' may belong to the same root. For the *l > *r shift, see §7.3. 丑 is the original graph for 'claw, finger' → niǔ$_1$ 狃丑.

chǒu$_2$ 醜 (tśʰjəu^B) **LH** tśʰu^B, **OCM** *k-huʔ ?
'Ugly, evil' [Shi] > 'to hate' [Zuo]. Acc. to Lau (1999: 53), this word is cognate to chòu 臭 'foul' (under → chōu$_3$ 犨), also in its meaning 'multitude (of enemies)' [Shi] (then originally 'the disgusting ones') > 'category, class' [Li] > 'of the same kind' [Meng].

⋇ **xiǔ** 朽 (xjəu^B) **LH** hu^B, **OCM** *huʔ ?
'To rot, decay' [Shi] > Mand. also 'aged, senile'.

chòu 臭 → **chōu**$_3$ 犨

chū$_1$ 出 (tśʰjuet) **LH** tśʰuit, **OCM** *k-hlut
'To come out' (of a place) [OB, Shi].
[T] *Sin Sukchu SR* tʂ'y (入); *MGZY* chÿu (入) [tʂ'y]; *MTang* tśʰur < tśʰuir, *ONW* tśʰuit
[D] PMin *tšʰuit > Xiàmén *tsʰut*^{D1}
[E] ST: JP *lot*^{31}*-lam*^{33} 'outlet', Trung *klɔ̆t* 'come out' (Zhengzhang Shangfang in Pan Wuyun 2000: 148); KN-Chinbok *hlɔt* 'come out'.

⋇ **chū, chuì** 出 (tśʰwi^C) **LH** tśʰuis, **OCM** *k-hluts
'To bring out, send out, take out' [Shi].
[<] exoactive of *chū* 出 (tśʰjuet) (§4.3).

⋇ **chù** 黜 (ṭʰjuet) **LH** ṭʰuit, **OCM** *r-hlut?
'To expel, degrade, expurgate' [Shu].
[D] M-Xiàmén lit. *tut*^{D1}, col. *lut*^{D1}
[<] r-caus. of *chū* 出 (§7.5) (Pulleyblank 1973: 118).
[C] Perh. → chūn 春 'spring' is related.

chū$_2$ 出 (tśʰjuet) **LH** tśʰuit — **[T]** *ONW* tśʰuit
'Nephew, sister's son' [EY] is related to PTB *tu ~ *du 'nephew' (*STC:* 158). A word with initial *t- could prob. be written in late Zhou with a graph with an earlier cluster *kl- (→ chū$_2$ 出). Sagart 1999: 167f derives this word from → chū$_1$ 出 'come out' in the sense of 'be born' which would be parallel to → shēng$_3$ 甥 'nephew'.

chū$_3$ 初 (tʂʰjwo) **LH** tʂʰɑ, **OCM** * tshra
'Be first, begin, beginning' [BI, Shi].

[T] *Sin Sukchu SR* tʂ'u (平); *MGZY* chu (平) [tʂ'u]; *MTang* tʂʰy, *ONW* tʂʰø < tʂʰo
[D] M-Xiàmén lit. *tsʰɔ*^{A1}, col. *tsʰue*^{A1}

ⅹ **chuàng** 創 (tʂʰjaŋ^C) **LH** tʂʰɑŋ^C, **OCM** *tshraŋh — [T] *ONW* tʂʰaŋ
'To start work' [Shi], 'commence, create' [Lunyu] (Pulleyblank 1962: 233).
[<] terminative of *chū* 初 *tshra (§6.5.1).

chú$_1$ 宁 → **zhù$_1$**, **chú** 宁

chú$_2$ 除 (ḍjwo) **LH** ḍɑ, **OCM** *d-la
'To remove, clear out' tr. [Zuo, Hanshu].
[T] *Sin S. SR* dẓy (平); *MGZY* cÿu (平) [dẓy]; *MTang* ḍy < ḍø; *ONW* dø < dio (?)
[D] M-Xiàmén lit. *du*^{A2}
[<] r-caus. of *shū* 抒 (dźjwo^B) (§7.5).

ⅹ **zhù** 除 (ḍjwo^C) **LH** ḍɑ^C, **OCM** *d-lah
'To be removed, pass away' [Shi].
[<] exopass. of *chú* 除 (ḍjwo) (§4.4).

ⅹ **shū** 抒 (dźjwo^B) **LH** źɑ^B, **OCM** *m-laʔ
'To eliminate' [Zuo].

[E] ? Perh. an area etymon, but the initials do not agree (OC *l- vs. foreign *d-): TB-WT *'dag-pa* 'clear away, remove' (*HST:* 124). <> AA: Khmer *ṭaka* /daɑk/ 'to pull or wrench out, uproot' ⅹ *raṭaka* /rdaɑk/ 'be pulled or torn out... removed'. Alternatively, cognation with WB *hra*^{B} 'remove out of the way' is phonologically also possible. The AA forms may be closer to OC because of the r-affix and the loss of final consonant after long vowel (§6.9). A derivation with t-suffix may be → chè$_2$ 徹撤 'remove', but that is doubtful.

chú$_3$ 鋤耡 (dẓjwo) **LH** dẓɑ, **OCM** *dzra (耡 also MC dẓjwo^C)
'A hoe' 鋤 [Chuci]; 'to hoe together, cooperate in cultivating public land' 耡 [Zhouli].
[D] 'Hoe': W-Kāihuà *zɑ*^{A2}; M-Xiàmén *ti*^{A1}, Cháozhōu *tɯ*^{A1}, Fúzhōu *tʰy*^{C2}, Jiàn'ōu *tʰy*^{C2} (the stop initials does not agree with the QYS; a similar case is → shāi, shī 篩).
[E] Perh. MK: OKhmer /crās/ 'to scrape / brush against' ⅹ *caṃrās* 'to rake, hoe' ⅹ *rā'sa* /roəh/ 'to rake, hoe, harrow'. For loss of foreign final consonant, see §6.9.
[C] → zhù$_{12}$ 助 is almost certainly a semantic generalization of 耡 (*GSR* 46o').

chú$_4$ 芻 (tʂʰju) **LH** tʂʰo, **OCM** *tshro — [T] *ONW* tʂʰuo
'Hay' (for fodder or fuel) [OB, BI, Shi], 'grass cutter' [OB, Shi]; 'to cut' tr. (grass, firewood) [Lüshi chunqiu, SW, Mand.]; factitive: 'to feed hay to' [Lüshi chunqiu].
[E] AA: PMon *ksɔɔy 'useless fiber, hay', Mon *chuẹ 'grass, weed, hay', PWa *sɔh 'cut grass'. For the absence of final *-y in CH see §6.9.
[C] Allofams → zōu$_2$ 騶 'groom'; → cuò$_2$ 莝 'hay'.

chú$_5$ 雛 (dẓju) **LH** dẓo, **OCM** *dzro
'Chicken, young of animals' [Liji]. — Etymology not clear.
[T] *Sin Sukchu SR* dẓu (平); *MGZY* cu (平) [dẓu]

chú$_6$ 躕 → **chí$_5$-chú** 踟躕

chú$_7$ 儲 → **zhǔ$_6$** 貯褚

chǔ$_1$ 杵 (tśʰjwo^B) **LH** tśʰɑ^B, **OCM** *thaʔ ?
'Pestle' [Yi].
[D] CDC *chu*^{B1}; M-Xiàmén (lit.) *tsʰu*^{B1}
[E] Etymology not clear. The right part in the graph, if phonetic, may indicate a complex OC initial with an *ŋ-like element. The word is reminiscent of MK-PMonic *gnri:ʔ, Nyah-Kur *ŋri̤:ʔ* 'pestle' (for the vowels, see §11.1.3).

chǔ$_2$ 楚 (tʂhjwo^B) **LH** tʂʰɑ^B, **OCM** *tshraʔ
'Thorny bush / tree' [Shi].
[T] *Sin Sukchu SR* tʂ'u (上); *MGZY* chu (上) [tʂ'u]; CDC chu^{B1}; *ONW* tʂʰo > tʂʰø
[E] AA: PMonic *jrlaaʔ 'thorn, thorny bamboo' (added to names of thorny plants), Khmu' /cərlaʔ/, Semai /jərlaaʔ/ [Diffloth 1984: 80]. The complex AA initial needed of course to be simplified in CH, apparently by elimination of the medial *l*.

Table C-1 'Knock, push, touch' (for → chù$_1$ 觸)

	*tok/ŋ, *to	*tuk, *tu	*trok, *truk/ŋ	*ts(j)- or *tj-
knock against	chù 觸 *tʰok knock against WT tʰogs-pa knock against Lush. tɔɔk^H knock (against)	WB tuik strike against JP tʰu^{55} push WB tui^B push, butt, shove against	WT rdug-pa strike against	WB cʰoŋ^C thrust, push, butt, stamp KNaga *tsjuk knock against
beat, strike	Mikir tòk- to strike JP tʰoŋ^{31} kick	dǎo 擣 *tûʔ beat, pound WB tʰui^B thrust, stab, strike	zhuó 椓 *trôk strike zhú 築 *truk beat, stamp earth chuáng 撞 *drôŋ(h) strike WT rduŋ-ba beat, strike	Lushai čʰu^H / čʰut^L to strike (with rod), pound, stamp Mikir chòk beat WB cʰoŋ^C thrust, push, butt, stamp
stamp, pound			zhú 築 *truk beat, stamp earth	Lushai čʰu^H / čʰut^L to strike (with rod), pound, stamp WB cʰoŋ^C thrust, push, butt, stamp
cut, hack	zhuó 斫 *tauk ? to cut, hack JP doʔ^{31} < tok^{31} cut off JP tok^{55} cut to pieces LB Ntök ~ *ʔtòk hack away at	zhù 祝 *tuk cut off Lushai tukL cut, chop shū 殊 *do cut off, kill, die JP tʰu^{33} cut	zhuó 斲 *trôk chop zhǔ 斸 *trok cut Mikir artòk < r-tòk chop off	WT 'tsʰog-pa to hew, chop
peck, beak	zhòu 咮 *toh beak LB *tok peck		zhuó 啄 *trô(k)h peck up zhòu 咮 *truh beak	Lushai ču^L / čuk^L to bite (as snake), peck WT mčʰu lips, beak

Comment on the table: The distribution of meanings over the different stems appears random, yet many stems tend (!) to have a semantic focus:

ST *tok	'knock against' → chù$_1$ 觸
(PTB *tsok	'beat, chop': Mikir chòk 'beat', WT 'tsʰog-pa 'hew, chop')
ST *truk	'strike against' → zhú$_5$ 築
ST *tro/uŋ	'strike' → chuáng$_2$ 撞
ST *tu	'push, beat' → dǎo$_3$ 擣
ST *do	'cut' → shū$_1$ 殊
ST *tu(k)	'cut': → zhù$_{11}$ 祝
ST *tauk ?	'cut, hack' → zhuó$_4$ 斫
ST *trok	'cut off' → zhǔ$_7$ 斸
	> 'peck, beak' → zhǔ$_7$ 斸
(PTB *ts/ju(k)	'strike': Lushai ču^H / čut^L 'strike, pound, stamp'
	> 'peck, beak': Lushai *ču^L / čuk^L* 'to bite (as snake), peck', WT *mčʰu* 'lips, beak')

The TB stems with affricate initial(s) in the last column are genetically separate from the others, although they share their field of meaning. As to the many stems with initial *t-, the semantic leap from 'accidentally knock against' to 'chop to pieces' is considerable, but these meanings still are within this particular semantic range. Given the plethora of stems, it seems that at least two originally unrelated roots, one meaning 'knock, push', the other 'cut' have converged, probably already beginning on the ST level, and then later in individual languages resulting in this chaotic distribution. The sound symbolic nature of the stems has probably contributed to the transfer of meaning from one stem to another. These sound-symbolic items are also found in other language families, eg. AA-Khmer /dok/ 'to beat, pound'.

---

chǔ$_3$ 處 (tś^{h}jwo^B) **LH** tś^{h}ɑ^B, **OCM** *k-hlaʔ

'To stay, keep still, dwell' [BI, Shi].

ꭗ **chù** 處 (tś^{h}jwo^C) **LH** tś^{h}ɑ^C, **OCM** *k-hlah

'A place'.

[T] *Sin S. SR* tʂ'y (去); *MGZY* chÿu (去) [tʂ'y]; *ONW* tś^{h}ø < tś^{h}o

[E] ST: TB: WT *gda'-ba* 'to be, be there' (locative vb.) ꭗ WT *gdan* 'seat': 'a bolster, a place of residence, situation, rank', Mikir *kedō* 'to dwell'; with the original l-initial in TGTM *gla:$^{A/B}$ 'place' (Mazaudon 1996 *LTBA* 19.1: 107); Lushai *tla^H* / *tlat^L* 'to be, exist, live, remain'; Pwo Karen (Kyonbyaw) *lân* 'place' (Kato A. 1995 *LTBA* 18.1: 68).

[C] → jū$_2$ 居 which is prob. a variant.

chù$_1$ 觸 (tś^{h}jwok) **LH** tś^{h}ok, **OCM** *t^{h}ok — **[T]** *ONW* tś^{h}uok

'To butt' [Yi], 'knock against' [Zuo].

[D] Mǐn Xiàmén lit. *ts^{h}iok^{D1}*, col. *ts^{h}ik^{D1}*

[E] ST *tok WT *t^{h}ogs-pa* 'to strike, stumble, run against', Lushai *tɔɔk^H* 'to knock (against)', Mikir *tòk-* 'to strike, beat'.

TB parallel stem with initial affricate are: Mikir *chòk* 'beat, hit, strike' (*STC:* 53), WT *'ts^{h}ogs-pa* 'to hew, chop', note also Kuki-Naga *tsjuk 'knock against'. Further cognates and / or parallel stems are listed in Table C-1.

chù$_2$ 絀 (tjuet) **LH** ṭuit, **OCM** *trut

'Bend' [Xun]. The word belongs to a root *tru from which is also derived → zhǒu$_1$ 肘 'wrist, elbow'.

[E] ST: WB *krui^C* 'bow down, stoop'. Bodman (1969: 337) relates this word to WT *'dud-pa, dud / btud* 'to bend down, incline'.

chù$_3$ 黜 → **chū$_1$** 出

chù$_4$, xù 畜 (ṭ^{h}juk, xjuk) **LH** ṭ^{h}uk, huk, **OCM** *rhuk, *huk

'To rear, to nourish, cherish' (animals) (also 慉 [Shi]) > 'support' [Shi].

[T] *Sin Sukchu SR* tʂ'y (入), *PR* tʂ'uʔ; *MTang* ṭ^{h}uk, *ONW* t^{h}uk

ꭗ **chù, xù** 畜 (ṭ^{h}jəu^C, xjəu^C) **LH** ṭ^{h}u^C, hu^C, **OCM** *rhukh, *hukh

'Domestic animal' [Zuo; EY 19] (tone C reading: Downer 1959: 276).

[T] *Sin Sukchu SR* xy (入); *MGZY* hÿu (入) [xy]

[<] exopass. of *chù, xù* 畜 (§4.4), lit. 'what is being / has been raised'.

[E] Etymology not clear, but prob. ST: PTB *hu 'rear, raise, nourish': PLB *hu^3, Abor-Miri *u*, Qiang (Mawo) *χu* [*HPTB:* 58]. Perh. related to → hǎo 好. Alternative affiliation: ST: JP *kruʔ^{55} < kruk^{55}* 'to sprout', *k^{h}ruŋ^{33}* 'be alive', WT *'k^{h}ruŋ-ba* 'be born, come up, to sprout' (*HPTB:* 285). See Table C-2 for synonyms.

Zhengzhang relates WT *lug* 'sheep' to this word (Sagart 1999: 195), this would be parallel to → yáng$_1$ 羊 'sheep' ? ꭗ yǎng$_2$ 養 'raise'; however, WT *lug* is prob. related to → dú$_6$ 犢.

Table C-2 'Birth, sprout, nourish'

	*lu(k)	*k(r)ok / -ŋ	*kuk	*kruŋ / -k
OC	yù 育毓鬻 *luk give birth, nourish yù 谷 *lok nourish	gǔ 㝅 *kôk baby, alive gòu 彀 *kôkh suckle kòu 鷇 *khôkh newborn chick	jú 鞠 *kuk suckle, nourish	chù 畜 *(r)huk rear, nourish
WT		(? srog life)		'kʰruŋ-ba be born, come up, sprout
JP	lu³¹ give birth	kroʔ⁵⁵ < krok⁵⁵ to hatch	kuʔ⁵⁵ < kuk⁵⁵ to sprout <~>	kruʔ⁵⁵ < kruk⁵⁵ to sprout
WB		kyoŋᴮ feed / tend cattle	ə-kuik sprout from a seed	

Table C-2 shows a web of stems (§2.5) which have blended into each other, stems with / without medial -r- and perh. also -l-, and with the vowels *o ~ *u. ST *lu(k) is unrelated to the other stems, unless we assume an OC *kl-cluster in *gǔ* etc. Most of the CH stems have eventually converged in the meaning 'nourish', except that *gǔ* 'nourish' is perh. a semantic extension of the homophonous but unrelated etymon → gǔ₁₃ 穀 'cereal'. The voiceless initial in CH *chù* is prob. due to a pre-initial.

---

chuān₁ 川 (tśʰjwän) **LH** tśʰuan, **OCM** *k-hlun
'River' [BI, Shi].
[E] Area word: PTB *klu:ŋ (*STC* no. 127) > WT *kluŋ* 'river'; Kachin *kruŋ* 'valley, dale', OBurm. *kʰloŋ* [*IST*: 353], WB *kʰyuiŋᴮ* 'stream'; perh. also Lushai *luaŋᴴ / luanᴸ < luaŋ / luanh (< luaŋs)* 'to flow' (water, river) (so Unger *Hao-ku* 50, 1995: 156). This etymon may ultimately be connected with → jiāng₁ 江 (*kruŋ ~ *kluŋ?). Like OC, MK-PWa has both forms for 'river': *klɔŋ 'river' and *krɔŋ 'large river, sea'. *STC* (p. 131f, n. 129) suggests that the WT root may be separate from the AA one, and considers it to be a variant of *shuǐ* 水 'water, river'. <> Tai: S. *kʰlɔɔŋᴬ²* 'canal' is unrelated, see → táng₁ 唐.

chuān₂ 穿 (tśʰjwän) **LH** tśʰuan, **OCM** *thon
'To bore through' [Shi].
[T] *Sin S. SR* tʂ'yen (平); *MGZY* chwÿan (平) [tʂ'yɛn]; *ONW* tśʰuan
[E] ST: WT *rtol-ba* 'to bore, pierce, perforate'.

⋙ **duān** 耑端 (tuân) **LH** tuɑn, **OCM** *tôn — **[T]** *ONW* tuɑn
'Tip, end, point' 耑 [Zhouli], 端 [Li]; 'beginning, first, symptom' 端 [Meng]; 'to bore' 鍴 [Fangyan].
[E] ST: WT *rdol-ba, brtol* 'to come out, break out, sprout' (*HST*: 117).

chuán₁ 船 (dźjwän) **LH** źuan, **OCM** *m-lon
'Boat' [Mo].
[T] *Sin Sukchu SR* dʐyen (平); *MGZY* cwÿan (平) [dʐyɛn]
[D] PMin *d̥žiun ~ *d̥žion
[N] The word appears in texts later than → zhōu₁ 舟 and seems to replace it by Han times (Huáng Jīnguì, Shěn Xíróng *YYWZX* 1987.8: 41–44). *FY* says that (ST) *chuán* is the word for 'boat' in western China, and (AA) *zhōu* and *háng* are the words common in central and eastern China. PMin *d̥ž- suggests a prenasalized initial. Graphic variants are written with 工 or 公 which are, however, not phonetic, i.e. a word like GY *xiāng* is spurious (Huáng Jin-guì, Shěn Xí-róng). There are more words which have a final *-n* in CH, but *-ŋ* in TB and other languages (§6.4.2).

[E] Area etymon of AA origin (Luce acc. to Weidert 1987: 129; Shorto 1972: 15). ST-PTB *m-loŋ (*HPTB:* 294) > WB *loŋ*^{B} 'canoe, long boat', also WB *hluiŋ* 'excavate, a niche'; Lushai *lɔŋ*^{L} 'boat' ⋈ *lɔŋ*^{F} 'to take out the heart' (of a tree), S. Khami *mlauŋ*, N. Khami *p*^{h}*lauŋ*, Kyaw *mlauŋ*. OC agrees closely with the Kuki-Chin forms *mloŋ; Mikir *telòŋ*. <> PMK *lu(u) ~ *l(u)əŋ 'to hollow out' (Shorto 1972: 15) > OMon *dluŋ* 'boat' ⋈ MidMon /kəmløŋ/ 'to hollow out', Khmer /luŋ/ 'make a hole / pit / cavity, dig, excavate, bore, hollow out', Bahn.-Sre *(daa) törluŋ* 'to hollow out' (Shorto 1971: 31), PSBahn. *pəluŋ 'canoe', PWa *ʔlɔŋ 'coffin', Lawa U *lo:ŋ* 'boat', Viet. *xuồng* [sɯə̀ŋ]. Related to this root are apparently words for 'inside' (< from 'hollowed out'): PVM *k-lɔ:ŋ 'inside' [Ferlus] > SViet. *trăwŋ*, PSBahn. *kəlu:ŋ 'middle', OKhmer *kaṃluŋ* /kənluŋ/ 'interior space, inside', Katuic *kəlho:ŋ 'inside', Khmuʔ *kluaŋ*. These items are prob. not connected with → zhōng$_1$ 中 'middle'.

From Southern Mǐn forms like *tsuŋ*^{55} is derived Malay *jong*, Java *ǰong* 'junk' (Zhāng Yǒng-yán *YYWZX* 1989.9: 94).

A semantic parallel (and cognate?) is → yú$_{14}$ 俞 OC *lo 'scoop out, make hollow, canoe', see there for further items. Syn. → fāng$_2$ 方; → háng$_4$ 航杭; → zhōu$_1$ 舟.

chuán$_2$ 傳 → **zhuǎn$_1$** 轉

chuáng$_1$ 床 (dẓjaŋ) **LH** dẓɑŋ, **OCM** *dzraŋ — **[T]** *ONW* dẓaŋ (?)

'Bed' [Shi]. Perh. cognate to AA-Khmer /rɔɔŋ/ 'to hold upright, support from below', and / or OMon *joṅ* /ɟɔŋ/ 'couch, bed' (a CH loan?). For the initials, see §7.1.5.

chuáng$_2$ 撞 (ḍåŋ) **LH** ḍɔŋ, **OCM** *drôŋ

'To strike' [Li].

⋈ **zhuàng, chòng** 撞 (ḍåŋ^C) **LH** ḍɔŋ^C, **OCM** *drôŋh

'To strike' [Li]. Unger (*Hao-ku* 20, 1983, 169) draws attention to the possible morphological parallel with WT where *brduŋs* is the pf. to *rduŋ* (pres.) above.

[T] *Sin S. SR* tʂaŋ (去), *PR, LR* tʂwaŋ; *MGZY* cwang (去) [dẓwaŋ]

⋈ **chōng** 衝 (tśʰjwoŋ) **LH** tśʰoŋ, **OCM** *thoŋ

'Assault engine, knocker' [Shi].

[E] ST: WT *rduŋ-ba, brduŋs* 'to beat, hammer, break to pieces, thrash, pound'; WB *t*^{h}*oŋ*^{B} 'pound' (vb?), JP *t*^{h}*oŋ*^{31} 'kick' (*HST:* 40).

This group is not related to → chōng$_3$ 舂 *lhoŋ. For ST cognate and / or parallel stems see Table C-1 under → chù$_1$ 觸.

chuàng 創 → **chū$_3$** 初

chuī$_1$ 吹 (tśʰjwe) **LH** tśʰuai, **OCM** *thoi or *k-hloi ?

'To blow, play a wind instrument' tr. 吹 [Shi]; 'to blow' (into a stove to get the fire going) > 'to heat, cook' 炊 [Gongyangzhuan], 'to steam' (rice) 炊 [Jìnshū 晉書].

[T] *Sin Sukchu SR* tʂ'uj (平); *MGZY* chue (平) [tʂ'uɛ]; *ONW* tśʰue

⋈ **chuì** 吹 (tśʰjwe^C) **LH** tśʰuai^C, **OCM** *thoih or *k-hloih ?

'Musical concert' [Liji].

[E] Perh. shared with AA: Khmer *khloy* n. 'flute'. CH aspiration is associated with exhaling §5.8.5.

chuī$_2$ 衰 → **shuāi** 衰

chuí$_1$ 垂 (źwie) **LH** dźuai, **OCM** *doi < *djoi

'To droop' (as wings of a bird; reins) [BI, Shi], 'sag, hang down' (as clouds from the sky) [Zhuang], 'let hang down' (sashes etc.) [Shi].

= Perh. **chuí** 陲 (so Wáng Lì 1982: 440).

('Drooping = ?) 'far end' (of a place): (of a hall) [Shi], 'border, frontier' [Zuo].

× **zhuì** 硾 (ḍwie^{C}) **LH** ḍuai^{C}, **OCM** *droih

'Press down, crush' [Lü].

[<] r-caus. (§7.5) of *chuí* (Pulleyblank 1962: 215), + exoact. / caus. tone C (§4.3).

[E] ST and area etymon. ST *(d)jol ?: PTB *dzywal (*STC* no. 242) > WT *'jol-ba* 'to hang down, dangle' (cow's udder; tail etc.) × *gžol-ba* 'train, trail, retinue' (including: as in robe with a train etc.) (Pulleyblank 1962: 215), *g-yol* 'curtain'; Lushai *fual^{R}* 'sag, hang low' (e.g. coat). <> AA: Khmer *yola* /jóol/ 'to hang, swing, dangle', *-yāla* /-jíiəl/ 'to hang down', also *yāra* /jíiər/ 'to hang down, dangle...'. MK -> Tai: S. *yoy^{5}* 'to hang down' (McFarland: 668), PTai *hɔi^{C1} 'to hang down, suspend'.

Alternative affiliation: WT *g-yur-ba* 'to droop, hang or sink down' (Bodman 1980: 80).

[C] Perh. related to → shuì$_1$ 睡, → duǒ$_2$ 朵, → wěi$_2$ 委, → ruǐ 縈惢.

chuí$_2$ 甀 (ḍwie[^{C}]) **LH** ḍuai(^{C}), **OCM** *droi(h) ?

'Pot, jar' [Lie]. Perhaps related is the ancient Chángshā dialect word for 'pot, jar' *duò* 瓿 (duâ^{B}) [GY]. — **[E]** ? ST: WT *yol-go, yol-ma* 'earthenware, crockery'.

chūn 春 (tśʰjuen) **LH** tśʰuin, **OCM** *thun

(The season when growth begins:) 'Spring' [Shi], 'spring–summer' [OB].

[T] *MTang* tśʰun, *ONW* tśʰuin — **[D]** PMin *tšʰuin

× **zhūn** 屯 (tjuen) **LH** ṭuin, **OCM** *trun — or:

~ **tún** 芚 (duən) **LH** duən, **OCM** *dûn

'To begin to grow' (of plants in spring) 屯 [Yijing], 芚 [Fǎyán].

[E] Cf. MK-Khmer /doh/ to grow, sprout'; or → chuān$_2$ 穿. **[C]** Perh. × → chǔn 蠢.

chún$_1$ 脣漘 (dźjuen) **LH** źuin, **OCM** *m-dun ?

'Lip' [Zuo] > 'banks' (of a river) 漘 [Shi]; the basic meaning was apparently 'edge, rim' (Wáng Lì 1982: 517).

[T] *Sin Sukchu SR* ʐyn (平), *PR* dʐyn; *MGZY* cÿun (平) [dʐyn]

[E] Etymology not clear. The most likely cognate is TB-Lepcha *a-dul* 'lips, edge of a vessel' (Geilich 1994: 272). Mikir *iŋtùr* < *mtùr* 'lip' is perh. a loan from MK-Khasi: *ʃṇtur* 'mouth'. *STC* (158 n. 428) associates *chún* with WT *mčʰu* 'lip, beak of birds' (but see under → zhǔ$_7$ 斸), *HST:* 39 connects WT with *zhòu* 啄咮 'beak' (→ zhǔ$_7$ 斸).

chún$_2$ 淳 (źjuen) **LH** dźuin, **OCM** *dun

'To flow' [Zhuang], 'to soak' [Guoyu] > (? 'soaked land':) 'salty and poor land' [Zuo].

× **zhūn** 淳 (tśjuen) **LH** tśuin, **OCM** *tun

'To moisten' [Zhouli], 'moist, fat' [Li].

chún$_3$ 淳 'a pair' → **chóu$_3$** 儔

chún$_4$ 醇 → **dūn$_1$** 敦惇

chǔn 蠢惷 (tśʰjuen^{B}) **LH** tśʰuin^{B}, **OCM** *thun?

'Be wriggling, moving, swarming' (of insects > people) 蠢 [Shi] > 'agitated' 惷 [SW: Zuo]. Boltz (*JAOS* 99.3, 1979: 436) relates → chūn 春 'spring' to this wf.

[T] *Sin Sukchu SR* tʂ'yn (上); *MGZY* (蠢) chÿun (上) [tʂ'yn]; *ONW* tśʰuin

× **dūn** 蜳 (tuən) **LH** tuən, **OCM** *tûn

'Be agitated, anxious' [Zhuang].

× **tún** 忳 (duən) **LH** duən, **OCM** *dûn

'Be sorrowful, anxious' [Chuci].

chuō 擉 (tṣʰåk) **LH** tṣʰɔk, **OCM** *tshrôk
'To spear' (fish) [Zhuang].
[E] AA: Khmer *cūka* /còok/ 'lift with tool...' ⋈ *cpūka* /cbòok/ (archaic:) 'trident for lifting fish', perh. also PWa *cɔk 'to catch' (fish by hand). For the CH retroflex initial, see §5.10.3. Synonyms / variants are → cè₅ 簎, → zé₆ 矠.

chuò₁ 逴 'distant' → **zhuō₂** 桌

chuò₂ 啜歠 (tśʰjwät) **LH** tśʰuat, **OCM** *thot ?
'To taste, eat' 啜 [Li], 'to drink' 歠 [Li].
[D] This is the word for 'to drink' in some southern dialects: 啜 K-Méixiàn *tsʰɔt¹¹*, M-Fúzhōu *tsʰuɔʔ⁴³*, Jiàn'ōu *tsʰyɛ³⁴*, Xiàmén *tsʰeʔ³²*.
[E] The TB words under → zá 噆 may possibly belong here.

cī 雌 (tsʰje) **LH** tsʰie, **OCM** *tshe
'Female' of birds, game [Shi], in modern dialects also of other animals, e.g., Wú-Sūzhōu *ts'ʅ⁴⁴-ȵiɤ²⁴/²¹* 雌牛 'cow'; opposite *xióng* 雄 'male'. — Etymology not clear.

cí₁ 茨 (dzi) **LH** dzi, **OCM** *dzəi or *dzi
'To pile up, thatch' [Shi]. *CVST* (4: 6) relates this word to Lushai *čiʔᴸ* 'to thatch, put on a roof'.

cí₂ 胔 (dzje, tsʰje) **LH** dzie, tsʰie, **OCM** *dze, *tshe
'Small intestines' [GY].
[E] <> PTai *saiᶜ¹ 'intestines' (Luo 2000: 86f). This word is distinct from → zì₃ 胔.

cí₃ 慈 → **zǐ₁** 子

cí₄ 疵 → **zǐ₅** 訾

cí₅ 辭詞 (zi) **LH** ziə, **OCM** *s-lə — [T] *Sin S. SR* zʅ (平), *LR* zʅ; *MGZY* zʰi (平) [zʅ]
'Word, speech, excuse, pleading' 辭 [BI, SW, Shu], 'word, expression' 詞 [Hanfei].
[E] ST *s-lə: WT *zla-ba, zlas* 'to say, tell, express' (*CVST* 3: 1). The similarity with Mand. [tsʰʅ], and Karlgren's OC *-g, have led to the erroneous identification with WT *tsʰig* 'word'.

cǐ₁ 此 (tsʰjeᴮ) **LH** tsʰieᴮ, **OCM** *tsheʔ
'This (here)' [Shi] is an independent pronoun (§3.3.3) (Pulleyblank 1995: 86). The phonetic series of *cǐ* is inconclusive concerning the OC rime, Karlgren assumes *-ar (i.e., OCM *-ai), but cognation with *sī* (next) suggests OC final *-e.
[T] *Sin Sukchu SR* ts'ʅ (上); *MGZY* tshʰi (上) [ts'ʅ]; *ONW* tsʰe

⋈ **sī** 斯 (sje) **LH** sie, **OCM** *se
'This' [Shi, but especially *Lúnyǔ* and *Lǐjì*: *Tángōng* where *sī* replaces the usual *cǐ*] (Pulleyblank 1995: 88).

cǐ₂ 跐 → **jí₁₅** 蹐

cì₁ 次佽 (tsʰiᶜ) **LH** tsʰiᶜ or tsʰis, **OCM** *tshis/h < *s-nhis ?
'Be second, next following' [Shi], 'to arrange in order, order, sequel' 次 [Zuo]; 'well arranged, convenient' 佽 [Shi].
[T] *Sin Sukchu SR* ts'ʅ (去); *MGZY* tshʰi (去) [ts'ʅ]; *ONW* tsʰi
[E] Since acc. to SW, → èr₁ 二 'two' is phonetic in *cì*, Pulleyblank (1962: 133) derives *cì* from *èr* and postulates an OC cluster of the type s + n- (see comment under → qī₁ 七 'seven'; §5.9.2).

cì$_2$ 朿 (tsʰjeC) **LH** tsʰieC, **OCM** *tshekh
'Thorn' [SW].
[<] This late (i.e. Han period) word is derived from *cì* 刺 [tsʰiek] by the general derivation tone C (§3.5).

ꭗ **cì** 刺 (tsʰjeC, tsʰjäk) **LH** tsʰieC, **OCM** *tshekh
'To criticize' [Shi], 'attack, satirize' [Zuo]; 'to kill' [Zuo].
[T] *Sin Sukchu SR* ts'ɿ (去); *MGZY* tshʰi (去) [ts'ɿ]
[<] exopass. / exoact. derivation of *cì* 刺 (tsʰjäk) (§4.3-4), lit. 'cause to be stabbed'. Downer (1959: 284) reserves the tone D form LH *tsʰiek* for the meaning 'stab'.

ꭗ **cì** 刺 (tsʰjäk) **LH** tsʰieC, tsʰiek, **OCM** *tshek(h)
'Pierce, stab' [Meng].

[E] ST: WT *tsʰer-ma* 'thorn, thorn bush' ꭗ *gzer-ba* 'to bore into' ꭗ *gzer* 'nail'. MC initial *tsʰ-* can regularly derive from ST *k-s-, *k-z- (§5.9.1); for the loss of final *r in OC, see §7.7.5. Khmer *jera* /céer/ 'to blame, criticize, scold' which cannot be a CH loan on phonological grounds, suggests that 'stab' and 'criticize' are seperate etyma which have converged in OC. A similar sound symbolic item is also found in MK: OKhmer *cāk* /cak/ 'to pierce, stab, prick' (or CH loan?).

cì$_3$ 赤 'expel' → **yì$_{35}$** 繹

cì$_4$ 賜錫 (sjeC) **LH** sieC, **OCM** *sekh < *slekh
'To give, to present with' [BI, Shi], 'bring' (tribute) 錫; 'be given, be presented with' 賜 [Lunyu]. *Xí* 錫 is simply a loan graph for *cì* (Qiu Xigui 2000: 399f).
[T] *Sin Sukchu SR* *sɿ* (去); *MGZY* *sʰi* (去) [sɿ]
[<] This word could be a final *-k form (§6.1) of → shī$_9$ 施 'give'. Sagart (1999: 71) relates this word to *yì* 易 'change' (under → yí$_8$ 移), hence lit. 'exchange'.

cōng 蔥 (tsʰuŋ) **LH** tsʰoŋ, **OCM** *tshôŋ
'Onion' [BI, Shi].
[E] ST: WT *btsoŋ* 'onion' (*HST:* 114); Mru *choŋ* (Löffler 1966: 142).

cóng$_1$ 從 (dzjwoŋ) **LH** dzioŋ, **OCM** *dzoŋ
'Go along with, follow' [OB, BI, Shi].
[T] *Sin Sukchu SR* dzjuŋ (平), *PR*, *LR* dzuŋ; *MGZY* tsÿung (平) [dzjuŋ]; *ONW* dzuoŋ

ꭗ **zòng** 從 (dzjwoŋC) **LH** dzioŋC, **OCM** *dzoŋh
'Follower' [Shi 104]; *zòng mǔ* 'mother's sisters' [Liji], *zòng dì* 'cousins' [Zuo] (Downer 1959: 290).
[<] LOC general derivation (§3.5).

[E] Etymology not certain. Perh. related to WT *rdzoŋ-ba, (b)rdzaŋ(s)* 'to send, expedite, dismiss' ꭗ *rdzoŋ(s)* 'act of accompanying, escorting'. Tib. *a* usually does not correspond to a Chinese back vowel. An alternative association could be with WT *stoŋs-pa* 'to accompany'; or perh. with → sòng$_1$ 送 (suŋC) 'to escort, follow after, go along'.

cóng 叢 → **jù$_7$** 聚

cǒu-mǎ 趨馬 → **zōu** 騶

cú 徂殂 → **zǔ** 祖

cù 促 → **sù$_6$** 速

cuàn 篡 → **chāo$_2$** 剿勦

cuī$_1$ 崔 (dzuậi) **LH** dzuəi, **OCM** *dzûi, OCB *dzuj (< *Sduj?)
'Be craggy, craggy height' *cuī-cuī* 崔崔 [Shi 101, 1], *cuī-wéi* 崔嵬 [Shi 201, 3]. Acc. to Baxter (1992: 231) *cuī* is perh. related to:

⪤ **duì** 陮 (duậi^B) **LH** duəi^B, **OCM** *dûiʔ, OCB *dujʔ
'High, precipitous' [SW].

⪤ **cuǐ** 漼 (ts^{h}uậi^B) **LH** ts^{h}uəi^B, **OCM** *tshûiʔ
'Deep' (of an abyss) [Shi 197, 4].

cuī$_2$ 催 → **tuī** 推

cuī$_3$ 摧 → **tuī** 推; → **cuò**$_2$ 莝

cuǐ 漼 → **cuī**$_1$ 崔

cuì$_1$ 淬 (ts^{h}uậi^C) **LH** ts^{h}uəs, **OCM** *ts^{h}ûts
'To dip into a fluid' 淬 [Guoce], 'plunge' (a red-hot sword blade into water to harden it) [Hanshu], 'to dye' [Yili], person getting 'soaked' by dew [Huainan].

⪤ **cuì** 翠 (ts^{h}wi^C) **LH** ts^{h}uis, **OCM** *ts^{h}uts
'Kingfisher' [Zuo] praised for its brilliant turquoise feathers. The bird is noted for diving into water to seize a fish.

[C] → zuì$_1$ 醉 belongs perh. to the same root.

cuì$_2$ 啐 → **zuì**$_1$ 醉

cuì$_3$ 萃 → **zāo**$_2$ 遭

cuì$_4$ 翠 → **cuì** 淬

cuì$_5$ 瘁悴 → **zú**$_1$ 卒

cuì$_6$, **chuì** 竁 → **chā**$_3$ 臿

cún 存 (dzuən) **LH** dzən !, **OCM** *dzə̂n, OCB *dzən (1992: 431) — **[T]** *ONW* dzon
'Be among, exist' [Shi] < 'be in there', is possibly a demonstrative *-n derivation from → zài$_1$ 在 *dzəʔ (Pulleyblank, ICSTLL 1998: 11).

cǔn 忖 → **cùn** 寸

cùn 寸 (ts^{h}uən^C) **LH** ts^{h}uən^C, **OCM** *tshûns
'Thumb' [Gongyang], 'inch' [Meng].
[T] *Sin Sukchu SR* ts'un (去); *MGZY* tshun (去) [ts'un]; *ONW* ts^{h}on
[<] general derivation (noun) of *cǔn* 忖 (§3.5).

⪤ **cǔn** 忖 (ts^{h}uən^B) **LH** ts^{h}uən^B, **OCM** *tshûnʔ
'To measure, consider' [Shi].

cuō$_1$ 磋 (ts^{h}â) **LH** ts^{h}ɑi, **OCM** *tshâi
'To rub, polish' [Shi] (e.g. ivory). A derivation is → cuò$_3$ 錯厝 'grindstone'.
[E] AA: Khmer /cnaj/ 'to cut' (gems), 'to polish'. And / or related to Lushai c^hai^R (Lorr. chhai) 'caress, fondle' (Baxter acc. to Matisoff 1995a: 42).

cuō$_2$ 撮 (ts^{h}uât) **LH** ts^{h}uɑt, **OCM** *tshôt
'To pinch with the fingers, a pinch full' [Li].
[E] ST: PLB *tswat ⪤ caus. *ʔtswat 'to pluck' (as a fowl, stringed instrument): WB c^hwat [Matisoff *TSR*: 39].

cuō$_3$, **chī** 齹 (ts^{h}â, dzâ) 'uneven teeth' [SW] is related to → chā$_2$ 差 'divergent'.

cuó 鹺 (dzâ) **LH** dzɑi, **OCM** *dzâi

'Salt' [Li]

[E] ST: PTB *tsa (*STC* no. 214) > WT *tsʰwa* (i.e. *tsʰa*) 'salt', Kanauri *tsa*; PL *(t)sa², WB *cʰa^B* (*HST:* 128). The OC rime does not agree with TB, perh. when the *Lǐjì*'s late Zhou / Han passage was written, the word had already lost its final OC *-i.

cuǒ₁ 脞 → **suǒ₅** 瑣

cuǒ₂ 硰 → **suǒ₅** 瑣

cuò₁ 剉 → **cuò₂** 莝

cuò₂ 莝 (tsʰuâC, tsuâC) **LH** ts(ʰ)uɑiC, **OCM** *tshôih

'Hay' 剉 [Wú-Yuè chūnqiū], 'cut hay' tr. 莝 [SW, Shiji]; factitive: 'to feed hay to' (horses) 摧 [Shijing].

[E] AA: PMon *ksɔɔy 'useless fibre, hay', Mon *chue̯ 'grass, weed, hay', PWa *sɔh 'cut grass' (for the initials, see §5.9.1). This is the same etymon as → chú₄ 芻 'hay' which had entered OC very early (Shang dynasty OB), while *cuò* is a later variant.

cuò₃ 錯厝 (tsʰâk) **LH** tsʰɑk, **OCM** *tshâk — **[T]** *ONW* tsʰɑk

'Whetstone, grindstone' 錯 [Shi], 厝 [SW] is a k-extension (§6.1.1) of → cuō₁ 磋 'rub, polish'.

cuò₄ 錯 (tsʰâk) **LH** tsʰɑk, **OCM** *tshâk

'Crossing, mixed, ornate' [Shi], 'alternating' [Li].

[T] *Sin Sukchu SR* ts'aw (入), *LR* ts'aw?; *MGZY* tshaw (入) [ts'aw]; *ONW* tsʰɑk

≋ **zuò** 酢醋 (dzâk) **LH** dzɑk, **OCM** *dzâk

'To present and drink a cup in response to the pledge cup' [Shi] (醋 [Yili]), 'a matching libation' [Shu], 'to reward' [Shi].

≋ **zuò** 祚胙 (dzuoC) **LH** dzɑC, **OCM** *dzâkh

'To reward, sacrificial meat and wine' [Zuo] > 'to give prosperity' > 'confer a fief' 胙 [Guoyu] > 'blessings' 祚 [Shi].

[E] ? ST: Chepang *caʔ-* 'be mixed' (colors, kinds).

[C] An allofam is → jiè₇ 借 'to borrow, lend'. Since SW glosses → chā₁ 叉 as 'crossing hands', these wfs may be related.

cuò₅ 錯 (tsʰâk) **LH** tsʰɑk

'Mistake' [Baopuzi].

[E] Etymology not certain. Perh. the s. w. as → cuò₄ 錯, hence lit. 'a mix-up'. Alternatively, note perh. AA: Khmer *khcoḥ* /kcaoh/ 'have a flaw, be defective, be wrong, mistaken, in error...' ≋ OKhmer /cak/ 'pierce, stab...'.

cuò₆ 措 → **zuò₃** 作

D

dā$_1$ 耷 → **zhé**$_1$ 耴

dā$_2$ 搭 (tập) **LH** tәp, **OCM** *tȃp
'To attach, fix' [JY]. — **[E]** ST: WB *tap* 'put in, fix' (*HST:* 38).

dā$_3$ 搭 (tập) **LH** tәp, **OCM** *tȃp
'To hit, strike' [GY]. — **[E]** ST: WT *tʰab-pa* 'to fight, quarrel' (*HST:* 94).

dá$_1$ 達 (dât) **LH** dɑt, **OCM** *dât
'To break through, come out, sprout, prosper, reach to, be born' [OB, BI, Shi].
[T] *Sin Sukchu SR* da (入); *ONW* dɑt
[E] ST: PLB *dat 'alive, to be' [Matisoff 1972: 30] (*HST:* 48); Lushai *dɔɔt*^{F} / *dɔʔ*^{L} 'to pierce, stick in, sprout up'. Perh. also connected to MK-Mon *das* 'be, become'.

dá$_2$ 答 (tập) **LH** tәp, **OCM** *tȃp < *tûp
'To respond' [Shi, Shu].
[T] *Sin Sukchu SR* ta (入); *ONW* tɑp

⋈ **duì** 對 (tuậi^C) **LH** tuәs, **OCM** *tûts < *tûps
'To reply (to a person), answer'.
[<] exoactive of *dá* 答 (tập) (§4.3).
[T] *Sin Sukchu SR* tuj (去); *MGZY* due (去) [tuɛ]; *ONW* tuɑi

[E] ST: Prob. WT *'tʰub-pa* 'get the better of, be able to stand or bear, be a match for' (so Bodman 1980: 117) ⋈ *gtub-pa* 'be able' (*HST:* 80). Other suggestions: *HST:* 37 relates this word to WT *'debs-pa, btab* 'cast, throw, respond'; Matisoff (1995: 44) to → dí$_3$ 敵 'opponent, enemy'; Unger (*Hao-ku* 21, 1983: 183) with reservations to WT *tʰab(s)* in *kʰyim-tʰab(s)* 'husband, wife' (however, the QY back vowel in *duì* does not normally correspond to WT *a*). CH -> Tai: S. *tɔp*^{4} 'to reply, answer'.

dá$_3$ 荅 (tập) **LH** tәp, **OCM** *tȃp, OCB *k-lup
'Small bean, pulse' [SW, Zhouli].
[E] PMY *dәp 'bean' (Bodman acc. to *STC:* 195; Sagart 1999: 187).

dǎ 打 (tɐŋ^B) *Sin Sukchu SR* tiŋ (上), *LR* ta
'To beat, hit' [Weishu, Liangshu; GY] is a post-classical word. It seems to occur also in PMon: *dah* 'hit' (CH loan?).

dà, dài 大 (dâi^C) **LH** dɑs, dɑ^C, **OCM** *dâs, OCB *lāts
[T] *Sin S. SR* daj (去), *PR, LR* da; *MGZY* tay (去) [daj]; *Sui-Tang* dɑ(i)^C, *ONW* dɑC
[D] PMin *dɑi^C; Y-Guǎngzhōu *tai*^{C2}, Táishān *ai*^{C}; K-Méixiàn *tʰa*^{C}
'Be big, great' [OB, Shi]. The diphthong reading *dài* is traditionally viewed as the correct one, or as the literary one. However, already in Han times we find the reading *da*^{C}, Sui-Tang has both *da*^{C} and *dai*^{C} which agrees with the modern pronunciations *dà* and *dài* (Coblin *TP* 1994: 156ff).

⋈ **tài** 太泰 (tʰâi^C) **LH** tʰɑs, **OCM** *tʰâs, OCB *hlāts — **[T]** *ONW* tʰɑC
'Be too great, very great, excessive', in titles 'grand-' [Shi]. It is not clear if *tài* 'name of the west wind' [OB, Shi] is related.

[E] There are no unambiguous outside cognates. Perh. ST: PTB *tay 'big' (Matisoff 1995a: 53) > WT *mtʰe-bo* 'thumb', Nung *tʰɛ* 'big, large, great', Mikir *tʰè, ketʰè* 'id.'; WB *tay* 'very'; Abor-Miri *ta* 'large'. The TB forms do not have a final *-s, though, but have a final *-y which "indicates emergent quality in stative vbs.," acc. to Matisoff. The TB word has also been associated with → duō 多 (Baxter acc. to Matisoff 1995a: 44), but a different etymology for the latter seems preferable. Possibly, what has resulted in CH *dà* and *duō* has elsewhere converged (*HST:* 42).

dài₁ 代 (dậiᶜ) **LH** dəh, **OCM** *lə̂kh
'Substitute, take the place of, supercede' [Shu] > 'generation' [Shi], 'dynasty' [Lunyu]. The fundamental notion of this wf is perh. 'switch things around', → tè₁ 貣 may also belong to this wf.
[T] *Sin Sukchu SR* daj (去); *MGZY* tay (去) [daj]; *ONW* dɑi

ꕤ **tè** 忒 (tʰək) **LH** tʰək, **OCM** *lhə̂k
'Change, alter, deceive, err' [BI, Shi].

ꕤ **dài** 詒 (dậiᴮ) **LH** dəᴮ, **OCM** *lə̂ʔ
'Deceive' [Li].
See → dài₉ 戴 for an AA parallel.

dài₂, tè 貸 → **tè₁** 貣

dài₃ 汏 (dâiᶜ) **LH** dɑs, from earlier *lâts ?
'Wave' [Chuci], a late OC word, apparently from a southern dialect. The older syn. is → bō₁ 波.
[E] ST: WT *rlabs* 'wave' (Bodman 1980: 52).

dài₄ 迨 (dậiᴮ) **LH** dəᴮ, **OCM** *lə̂ʔ
'Arrive, come to that, at the time that, when' [Shi].
[E] ST: PTB *la: PLB *la, WB la 'come, reach in degree'. The ST level had apparently already doublets *lə ~ *rə (→ lái₁ 來) 'arrive'.

dài₅ 詒 → **dài₁** 代

dài₆ 待 'wait' → **děng₁** 等

dài₇ 帶 (tâiᶜ) **LH** tɑs, **OCM** *tâs
'Belt, sash' [Shi], 'string' [Zuo].
[T] *Sin Sukchu SR* taj (去); *MGZY* day (去) [taj]; *ONW* tɑC
[E] ST with the basic meaning 'circumference, circumscription': PTB *m/s-ta:y (*HPTB:* 210), PLB *n-day³: Lahu *de* 'belt of land between the high rain-forest and the plains, expanse of terrain', WT *sde* 'part, portion (of a country); province, district, territory', Lushai *tai*ᴿ 'waist' (Matisoff 1995a: 43).

dài₈ 逮 (dậiᶜ, iᶜ) **LH** dəs, jis, **OCM** *lə̂ts, *ləts
'To come to, reach to' [Shi].
[E] Baxter (1992) reconstructs OCB *(g-)ləps and relates *dài* to → tà₂ 遝沓. Sagart (1999: 127) relates it to *lì* 莅 'arrive' (under → lái₁ 來). Alternatively, this could be an AA substrate word: Lave *leć*, Sre *lot*, Stieng *luh* 'to come'; AA -> TB-Lepcha *lat* 'to come, reach' (Forrest *JAOS* 82, 1962: 333–334). Or AA: Riang *laic*, Palaung *hlae:x*, Bahnar *klech* 'to reach'.

dài₉ 戴 (tậiᶜ) **LH** təᶜ, **OCM** *tə̂h
'To bear, support' [Zuo], 'carry on the head' [Meng].
[E] AA: (OKhmer *-dai ~ *-dāya /-dəj ~ -daaj/ 'to bear, support' >) OKhmer *dnāy* /dnaaj/ 'retainer, king's servant'. AA -> Tai *thanaaj* 'attorney, representative'; Khmer /pdaaj/ 'to support / base oneself on, rely on' ꕤ Khmer *tāṅa* /taaŋ/ 'to take the place

of, replace, substitute, represent'. The semantic development of the Khmer etymon is parallel to the CH word → dài₁ 代 *lə̂kh with OC initial *l (if our interpretation of OC is correct), rather than *t- which is suggested by Khmer.

The word belongs to an AA wf which includes → méi₆ 媒禖 'marriage go-between' and → pēi₁ 肧 'pregnant'.

dān₁ 丹 (tân) **LH** tɑn, **OCM** *tân (< *tlan ?), OCB *tān — **[T]** *ONW* tɑn
'Be red, vermilion, cinnabar' [Shi] has in antiquity been a mineral from the ancient southern states Bā (Yúnnán) and Yuè (Zhèjiāng) [SW].

ꭗ **gān** 矸 (kân) in dān-gān 丹矸 **LH** tɑn-kɑn, **OCM** *tân-kân < *tlan-klan?
'丹砂 vermilion ore' [Xun], 'ore' [JY] may be a variant of *dān*, both could theoretically derive from an original foreign *klan, see below.

ꭗ **zhān** 旃 (tśjän) **LH** tśan, **OCM** *tan — **[T]** *ONW* tśan
'A red flag' [Shi, Shiming] (Wáng Lì 1982: 563).

[E] KT: PKS *h-lan^C 'red' (Edmondson / Yang). The OC initial and *t- ~ *k- doublets indicate that OC has borrowed this item. Perh. → tǎn₁ 袒襢 'bare' is related, as skin color tends to be associated with 'red', but see there. Alternatively, *HPTB:* 177 suggests ST *tja-n (*tya-n) 'red'.

dān₂ 單 (tân) **LH** tɑn, **OCM** *tân
'Single, unit' [Shi], 'single, simple' [Li]; 'unlined garment' 襌 [Li].
[T] *Sin Sukchu SR* tan (平); *MGZY* dan (平) [tan]; *ONW* tɑn — **[D]** CDC *tan¹*

ꭗ **dàn** 但 (dân^B) **LH** dɑn^B
'Only' [Chǔci].
[T] *Sin Sukchu SR* dan (上); *MGZY* tan (上去) [dan]

[E] ST *twar ? : PTB *t(w)ar > WT *tʰor-bu* 'single, separate' (Matisoff 1995a: 80); or ST *day ~ *tay 'single' (Matisoff 1997a: 21). Pulleyblank (in Rosemont 1991: 31) connects *dàn* with → tǎn₁ 袒襢 'bare'.

dān₃ 癉 (tân^B, tâ^C) **LH** tɑn^B, tɑi^C **OCM** *tânʔ, tâih
'Disease, suffering, distress' 癉 [Shi], 亶 (dǎn) [Li].

ꭗ **dān** 殫 (tân) **LH** tɑn, **OCM** *tân — **[T]** *MGZY* dan (平) [tan]
'Exhaust' [Zhuang].

ꭗ **dàn** 旦 (tân^C) **LH** tɑn^C, **OCM** *tâns
'Painful' 旦 [Shi].

ꭗ **tān** 嘽 (tʰân) **LH** tʰɑn, **OCM** *thân
'Exhausted, fagged out' [Shi].

ꭗ **duǒ, tuō, tuò** 瘏 (tâ^C, tʰâ[n]) **LH** tɑi^C, tʰɑi, tʰɑn, **OCM** *tâih, *thâi/n
'Exhausted, sick' (horses) [SW: Shi], 'toiled, exhausted' 憚 (QY *tâ^C* only) [Shi].
[E] ST *-dar: WT *ldar-ba* 'weary, tired, faint' (*HST:* 159); Chepang *dyarh-* 'discomfit, sudden pain...'

dān₄ 殫 → **dān₃** 癉

dān₅ 耽湛 (tậm) **LH** təm, **OCM** *tə̂m — **[T]** *ONW* təm
'Abandon oneself (in pleasure)' 耽 [Shi]; 'to be sunk in, steeped in (pleasure), rejoice' 湛 [Shi].
[E] Area word: AA: PVM *tăm^B 'to drown, sink' [Thompson]; Wa-Lawa-Bulang *ntɤm 'soak rice'. AA -> Tai: S. *dam* < *ʔd- 'to dive' ꭗ *dam^B* 'to sink down deeply, to a great depth' (Unger *Hao-ku* 36, 1990: 58), *tuam³* 'be submerged, overwhelmed'. *Dān* is usually thought to be cognate to → chén₂ 沈 (Wáng Lì 1982: 607).

OCM *tə̂m can also derive from a hypothetical *tləm in which case there may be a TB connection instead, but the meanings do not agree closely: Lushai *liam*[R] < *liam?* 'to overflow, disappear', WB *hlyam*[B] 'be brimming full' ⋈ *hlyam* 'run over, overflow'; WT *ltam-pa, gtam-pa* 'full' ⋈ *ltem-pa* 'full, overflowing'. <> PTai *tl-: S. *tem*[A1] 'full'.

dān$_6$ 擔 (tâm) **LH** tɑm, **OCM** *tâm < *tlam — **[T]** *ONW* tɑm.
'To carry on the shoulder' [Guoce].
[D] PMin *t̬ɑm 'to carry'; acc. to Norman (1986: 382) the Northern Min 'softened initial' *t̬- points to OC prenasalization which is supported by Yao *daam*[1] < *nd-, PMY *ntam[1] 'to carry'.

⋈ **dàn** 擔 (tâm[C]) **LH** tɑm[C], **OCM** *tâms < *tlams — **[D]** PMin *tɑm[C] 'a load'
'Burden' [Zuo].
[<] *tam + pass. s/h-suffix (§4.4), lit. 'what is carried'.

[E] Area word whose source is prob. AA: Khmu? *klam* 'carry on the shoulder', PWa *klɐm (for the initial correspondence, see §8.2.1).

An alternative form with initial *t, which agrees with later OC, is widespread: Khmer *dāṃ* /toəm/ 'to bear' ⋈ *drāṃ* /troəm/ 'to support patiently' [Jenner / Pou 1982: xlix]. <> Yao *daam*[1] < *nd-, PMY *ntam[1] 'to carry'. <> TB: WB *tʰam*[B] 'to carry on the shoulder' (Bodman 1980: 112), JP *tʰam*[55] 'carry', Dulong *atɑm*. <> MK: Khmer *drāṃ* -> Kam-Tai: PT *tʰr-: S. *haam*[A1] 'two or more people carry' (Li F. 1976: 45), Saek *raam*[2] (< hr-?) 'two or more carry'.

dǎn$_1$ 扰 (tə̣m[B]) **LH** təm[B], **OCM** *tə̂m?
'To beat, pierce' [Lie] is perh. related to Tai: PTai *t-: S. *tam*[A1] 'to pound', esp. in a mortar (Li, *HCT:* 98).

dǎn$_2$ 膽 (tâm[B]) **LH** tɑm[B], **OCM** *tâm? < *tlam?
'Gall' [Xun].
[E] AA: PNBahn. *klàm 'liver', PVM *lɔːm, Katuic *luɑm (for the initial correspondence, see §8.2.1). As in the case of → dān$_6$ 擔, there is an alternative form with initial *t-: PPalaunic *kəntɔːm 'liver' (unique to Palaunic).

dǎn$_3$ 亶 (tân[B]) **LH** tɑn[B], **OCM** *tân?
'Sincerity, truth' [Shi].

⋈ **dàn-dàn** 旦旦 (tân[C]) **LH** tɑn[C], **OCM** *tâns
'Be done in a sincere manner, sincere' [Shi].

dǎn$_4$ 亶 → **dān$_3$** 癉

dàn$_1$ 旦 (tân[C]) **LH** tɑn[C], **OCM** *tâns
'The time of sunrise, dawn, morning, bright' [OB, BO, Shi]. This word is not related to 'red' → dān$_1$ 丹 as the TB cognate shows.
[E] ST: Chepang *dar?-do* (place) 'of sunrise, in east'.

dàn$_2$ 旦 'painful' → **dān$_3$** 癉

dàn$_3$-dàn 旦旦 → **dǎn$_3$** 亶

dàn$_4$ 但 → **dān$_2$** 單

dàn$_5$ 啖啗 (dậm[B]) **LH** dəm[B], **OCM** *lə̂m?
'Eat, swallow' 啗 [Guoyu]; 'devour' [Xun]; 'keep in the mouth' 嘾 [QY: Zhuang].
[E] <> Tai: S. *dɨɨm*[B1] < *?d- 'to swallow'.
[C] Perh. this is related to *hàn* 頷 (under → hán$_1$ 含函) (so Bodman 1980: 110), and perh. to → xián$_{11}$ 銜.

dàn$_6$ 淡 (dâm$^{B/C}$) **LH** dɑm$^{B/C}$, **OCM** *lâmʔ/s
'Insipid' [Li]. Geilich connects *dàn* with items under → tián$_4$ 恬 'calm'.
[D] Y-Guǎngzhōu *t^hɑːm^B*. PMin *t̂siam^B 'insipid' is prob. unrelated.

dàn$_7$ 憚 (dân^C) **LH** dɑn^C, **OCM** *dâns
'To fear, dislike' [Shi].
[<] exopass. of *tán* 彈 (dân), lit. 'be shaken'.

ꕢ **tán** 彈 (dân) **LH** dɑn, **OCM** *dân — **[T]** *ONW* dɑn — **[D]** CDC *dan^2*
'Shake' [Zhouli].

ꕢ **zhàn** 戰顫 (tśjän^C) **LH** tśan^C, **OCM** *tans
'To tremble (with cold)' 顫 [GY], 'be trembling, afraid' 戰 [Shi]; this is the s. w. as → zhàn$_2$ 戰 'war'.

[E] ST: WT *'dar-ba* 'tremble, shudder, shiver with fear or cold' ꕢ *sdar-ma* 'trembling' (*HST:* 152) ꕢ *dar-bu* 'throbbing'. Also PMK *gtar 'shiver, tremble' (Shorto 1976: 1047).

dàn$_8$ 彈 'bow' → **tán$_5$** 彈

dàn$_9$ 繵 → **chán$_4$** 纏

dàn$_{10}$ 窞 → **tàn$_2$** 窞

dàn$_{11}$ 澶 → **chǎn$_2$** 嘽幝繟

dàn$_{12}$ 誕 → **yán$_5$** 延筵

dàn$_{13}$ 憺澹 → **tián$_4$** 恬

dāng$_1$ 當 (tâŋ) **LH** tɑŋ, **OCM** *tâŋ — **[T]** *ONW* tɑŋ
'Have the value of, be equal of, rank, to face, vis-à-vis' [Zuo], 'match, capable' [Meng].

ꕢ **dàng** 當 (tâŋ^C) **LH** tɑŋ^C, **OCM** *tâŋh
'Right, ought' [Meng], 'suitable' [Zuo].
[T] *Sin Sukchu SR* taŋ (平); *MGZY* dang (平) [taŋ]
[<] exopass. of *dāng* 當 *taŋ (§4.4), lit. 'what is being matched'.

ꕢ **dǎng** 黨 (tâŋ^B) **LH** tɑŋ^B, **OCM** *tâŋʔ
'Class, category' [Lunyu] > 'party' [Zuo] > 'partisan, partial' [Shu].
[<] endoactive of *dāng* 當 *tâŋ (§4.5.1), lit. 'that which is equal in rank'.

[E] ? ST: Perh. related to WT *daŋ* '(together) with, and'.

dāng$_2$ 鐺 → **dǐng$_3$** 鼎

dǎng$_1$ 黨 (tâŋ^B) **LH** tɑŋ^B, **OCM** *tâŋʔ
'To know' [FY 1.1] is a Han period Chǔ dialect word. Two possible etymologies: (1) This may be compared to PTB *m-taŋ > WB *t^haŋ* 'visible' ꕢ *ə-t^haŋ* 'thought', WT *mt^hoŋ-ba* 'to see, perceive, know, understand', Kanauri *taŋ* 'to see'. (2) A southern dialect form of *dǒng* 懂 'understand' with the typical shift to *a* (J. Norman).

dǎng$_2$ 黨 'class, party' → **dāng$_1$** 當

dàng$_1$ 愓盪 (dâŋ^B, t^hâŋ^B) **LH** dɑŋ^B, t^hɑŋ^B
'To drop, submerge' means 'to fall' (of rain) in Mǐn and adjacent Wú dialects: Fúzhōu *tɛuŋ^{C2}* in *touŋ^{53}-ŋy^{31}* 'to rain' 㨢雨, Shùnchāng *t^hõ^{B2}* (Lǐ Róng *FY* 1992.2: 112–114).

dàng$_2$ 盪 → **tāng$_2$** 湯

dàng$_3$ 蕩 'move' → **dòng$_2$** 動

dāo 刀 (tâu) **LH** tau, **OCM** *tâu — **[T]** *ONW* tau
'Knife' [OB, Shi].
[E] ? Area word or CH loan: TB-Karen *ʔdo 'knife', JP n^{31}-do^{31} 'short knife', Viet. *daw* 'sword', Stieng *taaw*, etc., a common word for 'sword' in MK languages [Huffman 1975: 14].

dǎo$_1$ 倒 (tâu$^{B/C}$) **LH** tau$^{B/C}$, **OCM** *tâuʔ/h
'To turn over, invert' [Shi], 'contrary' [Hanfei], also 'to pour' (from a pot) occurs also in TB-JP du^{55} 'to pour' (from a pot), PVM *toh 'to pour', prob. a CH loan. <> Tai: S. tok^{D1S} 'to fall down' (Li F. 1976: 41); for the final consonant, see §3.2.2.

dǎo$_2$ 島 (tâu^B) **LH** tou^B, **OCM** *tûʔ
'Ocean island' [Shu] is reminiscent of Mon *tkoʔ* 'island', but prob. unrelated (we should expect a CH aspirated initial t^h-, see §5.9.4).

dǎo$_3$ 擣 (tâu^B) **LH** tou^B, **OCM** *tûʔ
'To pound' (as rice) [Li], still used in southern dialects, e.g. Yuè-Táishān au^{55}-$^m bai^{55}$ 搗米; 'to beat' [Hanshu].
[E] ST *tu: JP t^hu^{55} 'push', WB tui^B 'push, butt, shove against' ⋇ t^hui^B 'thrust, stab, strike'. A TB parallel stem is Lushai $č^hu^H$ / $č^hut^L$ 'to strike' (with rod), 'pound, stamp, knock, tap'. For ST cognate and / or parallel stems, see the table under → chù$_1$ 觸 for an overview.

dǎo$_4$ 禱 → **zhù$_{10}$** 祝

dào$_1$ 到 (tâu^C) **LH** tau^C, **OCM** *tâuh
'To arrive' [Shi].
[E] Perh. ST, yet the TB rime is different from OC: WT *gtug-pa* 'to reach, to touch' (e.g. putting the forehead against the breast of an image) ⋇ t^h*ug-pa* 'to reach, arrive at, come to, meet, touch'; WB *tuiŋ* 'to arrive, reach, attain', JP du^{31} 'arrive'. However, these TB items could just as well belong to → zhǔ$_8$ 屬.

dào$_2$ 道 (dâu^B) **LH** dou^B, **OCM** *lûʔ
'Road, way, method' [BI, Shi].
[T] *Sin Sukchu SR* daw (上去); *MGZY* taw (上) [daw]; *ONW* dau
[<] either an endoactive noun 'the thing which is doing the conducting' (§4.5.1) derived from the following word, or the latter is a LOC general tone C derivation from 'way' (§3.5):

⋇ **dào** 道導 (dâu^C) **LH** dou^C, **OCM** *lûh
'To go along, bring along, conduct' 道 [Zuo], 導 [Meng] > 'explain' [Li] > 'talk about' 道 [Lao, Meng]. The Han period dialect of Eastern Qi has the words **yù** 裕 [jo^C] *lokh and **yóu** 猷 [ju] *lu or *ju (?) 'road' [FY 3.23] which may be related.

[E] Pulleyblank (1973: 120) believes that *dào* 'talk' is cognate to → tán$_2$ 談. Gong Hwang-cherng (1995: 61) presents parallels which suggest a pattern of OC *ᵊm > *u. 道 is shared with Yao *klǎu^B* 'road' (Haudricourt 1950: 559; but Downer 1982 *kau^2).

dào$_3$ 盜 → see under **yú** 愉

dào$_4$ 稻 (dâu^B) **LH** dou^B, **OCM** *lûʔ
'Unhusked rice' [Shi].
[D] PMin *tiu^{B2} 紬 (corresponds to QYS *ḍjəu^C* [JY], LH *ḍuh*) may possibly be a variant (Norman, p.c.).
[E] Etymology is not certain. The word could belong to the wf → yóu$_4$ 油 'overflow'

(i.e. the notion of a flooded rice field). More likely, it is an area word (rice culture originated in the south): PMY *nblau^A (Bodman 1980: 112). The relationship with similar-looking MK words is ambiguous, we find PVM *ʔa-lɔːʔ 'unhusked rice', Viet. *lúa* 'paddy' [Ferlus], but Khmuic *lɔʔ 'glutinous rice' (Ferlus 31st ICSTLL, 1998: 90) whose meaning seems to connect the MK etymon with → nuò₄ 糯.

dé₁ 得 (tək) **LH** tək, **OCM** *tə̂k
'To get' [BI, Shi].
[T] *Sin Sukchu SR* təj (入), *LR* təjʔ; *MGZY* dʰiy (入) [təj]; *ONW* tək
[D] *Dé* is Mand. col., Gānsù *dei* (Demiéville 1950: 52); *dé* is sometimes thought to be an allofam of → dé₂ 德 'virtue'.
[E] Based on his theories on OC phonology, Pulleyblank (*EC* 16, 1991: 50) believes that *dé* and → dé₂ 德 are cognate to WT *tʰub-pa* 'be able, cope with', but see → dá₂ 荅.

dé₂ 德 (tək) **LH** tək, **OCM** *tə̂k — **[T]** *ONW* tək
'Moral force, virtue, character' (A. Waley) [BI, Shi], 'quality, nature' [Zuo].
[E] Based on his theories on OC phonology, Pulleyblank (*EC* 16, 1991: 50) believes that *dé* and → dé₁ 得 are cognate to WT *tʰub* 'a mighty one, having power', but see → néng₂ 能.
[C] An allofam is perh. → zhí₂ 直 'straight'.

de₃ 的
'genitive particle' in Mand., appears for the first time in a Song document (Coblin p. c.) and later in an inscription of 1238 (Mei Tsu-Lin *BIHP* 59.1, 1988). It is thought to be a col. archaism of the classical 'genitive particle' → zhī₁ 之.

dēng₁ 登 (təŋ) **LH** təŋ, **OCM** *tə̂ŋ — **[T]** *ONW* təŋ
'To rise, ascend, mount, raise' [Shi, Shu], 'to ripen' [Meng]; 'ritual vessel with high foot' [Yili], 'high foot' 鐙 [Li] is perh. the s. w. as → dēng₂ 燈 'lamp'. Wáng Lì (1982: 253) and Matisoff (*BSOAS* 63.3, 2000: 363) add → zhì₁₅ 陟 to this wf.

ꭗ **dèng** 隥 (təŋ^C) **LH** təŋ^C, **OCM** *tə̂ŋh
'A rising slope' [Mu Tianzi].

ꭗ **děng** 等 (təŋ^B) **LH** təŋ^B, **OCM** *tə̂ŋʔ
'Step of stairs' [Lunyu] > 'degree', [Yi], 'rank' [Zuo], 'classify' [Zhouli].
[T] *Sin Sukchu SR* təjŋ (上), *PR*, *LR* təŋ; *MGZY* dʰing (上) [təŋ]; *ONW* təŋ
[<] endoactive of *dēng* (§4.5.1).

[C] Additional allofams are perh. → zēng 曾增憎橧, → chéng₂ 丞承, also → téng₂ 騰.

dēng₂ 燈 (təŋ) **LH** təŋ, **OCM** *tə̂ŋ
'Lamp' 鐙 [Chǔci].
[E] Etymology not clear. Perh. the same word as *dēng* 鐙 'vessel with high legs', under → dēng₁ 登 'rise'. The relationship with 'candle' in MK languages, if any, is not clear (CH loan? MK loan ?): Viet *dèn* (North), *dèŋ* (South), Khmer *tiən*, Mon *nañ* (Huffman 1975). Khmer ? -> Tai: Saek *thian^A2* < *d-* 'candle'.

děng₁ 等 (təŋ^B) **LH** təŋ^B, **OCM** *tə̂ŋʔ
'To wait', a medieval northern dialect word, prob. related to the following (so Wáng Lì 1982: 90):

ꭗ **dài** 待 (dậi^B) **LH** də^B, **OCM** *də̂ʔ (< *də̂ŋʔ ?)
'To wait, treat, behave' [Lunyu]. For the final, see §3.2.4. Karlgren (1956: 17) adds this word to *shì* 侍 'wait upon' (under → shì₁₅ 恃).

děng₂ 等 'steps, category' → **dēng₁** 登 'rise'

dī₁ 低 (tiei) **LH** tei, **OCM** *tî

'To lower' [Zhuang].

[T] *Sin Sukchu SR* tjej (平), *PR* ti; *MGZY* di (平) [ti]; *ONW* tėi

⋇ **dǐ** 氐底 (tieiᴮ) **LH** teiᴮ, **OCM** *tîʔ — **[D]** PMin *tieᴮ

'Base, foundation, root' 氐 [Shi]; 'bottom' 底 [Lie]; 'root, base' 柢 (also tiei[ᶜ]) [Laozi].

[<] endoactive of *dī* 低 (tiei) (§4.5.1).

[E] ST: WT *mtʰil*, OTib. *tʰild < m-tild* 'bottom, floor, lower part' (*HST:* 47), Tamang *³ti:* 'below'.

dī₂ 滴 (tiek) **LH** tek, **OCM** *têk

'To drip, drop' [Wenxuan, GY].

[E] ST: This onomatopoetic root is shared with WT: *gtig(s)-pa ~ 'tʰig-pa, tʰigs* 'to drop, drip' ⋇ *'tʰig-pa, btigs* 'cause to fall in drops' ⋇ *tʰigs-pa* 'a drop' (*STC:* 180), JP *theʔ³¹ < tʰek³¹* 'dropping, dripping'.

dī₃ 堤隄 → **tí₁** 提堤題

dí₁ 狄 (diek) **LH** dek, **OCM** *dêk

'Low servant' [Shu], could either be derived from the name of a northern tribe; or, more likely, be AA: PMonic *ɗiik 'slave, temple slave', PNBahn. *qdĭč 'slave', PSBahn. *dəc 'slave, servant'.

dí₂-dī 狄鞮 (diek-diei) **LH** dek-de, **OCM** *dêk-dê

'Translators, interpreters' [Lüshi], later simply *dī* 鞮 'to translate' [Chenshu]. This may possibly contain a foreign loanword, note Turkic *til > til* 'tongue, language' (Behr 2000). However, Behr prefers to consider *dí* OC *lek an allofam of *shì* 釋 'to translate' (under → yì₃₅ 繹).

dí₃ 敵 (diek) **LH** dek, **OCM** *dêk

'Enemy, opponent, enmity' [BI, Shu].

[E] ST: PTB *m-ta:y (*tayʔ): JP *tai³¹* 'avenge, retaliate', *mə³¹-tai³¹* 'vengeance', Lushai *taiᴿ < taiʔ* 'be at enmity with one another, have a grudge against'. For *-k, see §6.1.

dí₄ 蹢 → **tí₄** 蹄

dí₅ 翟 → **zhuó₁₁** 濯

dí₆ 糴 (diek) **LH** dek < deuk, **OCM** *liâuk ?

'To buy grain' [Zuo].

[D] M-Xiàmén *tiaʔᴰ²*, Y-Guǎngzhōu *tɛk* (Lin et al. *YYWZX* 1996.2: 113ff)

⋇ **tiào** 糶 (tʰieuᶜ) **LH** tʰeuᶜ < tʰeuᶜ, **OCM** *lhiâukh ?

'To sell grain' [Mo; SW 2680].

[D] M-Xiàmén *tʰioᶜ¹*, Y-Guǎngzhōu *tʰiuᶜ*, K-Méixiàn *tʰiauᶜ*

[<] caus. aspiration (§5.8.2) + exoactive (§4.3) of *dí* 糴 (diek).

[E] This etymon is reminiscent of → yù₂₃ 賣 'sell'. Synonyms are → gǔ₁₁ 賈; → mǎi 買; → shòu₂ 售.

dí₇ 滌 (diek) **LH** dek < deuk, **OCM** *liûk, OCB *liwk

'To clean, clean out, denuded' [Shi], 'wash' [Li], 'to clarify' (spirits) [Zhouli] (Wáng Lì 1982: 302). The etymology is not clear. It could be either a derivation from → yóu₁₀ 滺油 *liu 'flow', or be related to → zhuó₁₁ 濯 *d-lauk 'be clean' (but the OC rimes do not agree).

dí$_8$ 笛篴 → **yuè$_{10}$** 籥

dí$_9$ 滌 → **diāo$_1$** 凋

dǐ$_1$ 氐底 → **dī$_1$** 低

dǐ$_2$ 底 (tiei^B) *ONW* tėi, *Sui-Tang Chang'an* tɨi^B
writes the col. genitive particle (→ zhī$_1$ 之 of classical texts); starting in Song and Yuan documents it is written → de$_3$ 的.

dǐ$_3$ 抵 'push away' → **jǐ$_5$** 擠

dì$_1$ 地 (di^C) **LH** di^C, **OCM** *lâih ?, OCB *lrjajs (?)
'Earth, ground' [Shi]. The QYS reading is unique and puzzling.
[T] *Sin S. SR* djej (去), *PR*, *LR* di; *MGZY* ti (去) [di]; *ONW* dii
[E] Etymology not certain. Since the OC initial was L-like, it may be compared with PTB *ml̥iy 'earth' (*STC* no. 152) > WB *mre* 'earth, ground', Mikir *mili* 'bare ground', Nung *məli* 'ground, mountain'. However, this TB etymon rather seems to belong to → shì$_{13}$ 室 'house'. On the other hand, there are AA words which resemble Chinese: Munda *ɔte* 'field, land', Khmer *ṭi* 'earth, soil', Mon *ṭi* 'land, earth', PSBahn. *(nə)təh 'earth'. Neither of these possibilities agrees phonologically with OC; perhaps these two etyma have converged.

dì$_2$ 弟 (diei^B) **LH** dei^B, **OCM** *dîʔ or *də̂iʔ, OCB *dəjʔ < *dujʔ ?
'Younger brother' 弟 [Shi]; 'younger secondary wife' 娣 [Shi] (also LH *dei^C*).
[T] *Sin S. SR* djej (上), *PR*, *LR* di; *MGZY* ti (上) [di]; *ONW* dėi
[D] PMin *die^B
[<] endoactive of *dì* 第 'order, sequel', lit. 'the person who is following in sequence' (§3.3.1).
[E] ST *dwi: PTB *doy 'younger brother' (*STC* no. 309; *HST:* 49) > WB *t^{h}we^B* 'be youngest', JP *šədói* 'last born child'; also found in Mon *deʔ* 'younger sibling' (<- TB?).

ⅹ **dì** 弟 (diei^C) **LH** dei^C, **OCM** *dîh or *də̂ih
'Respectful toward elder brothers, fraternal' 弟悌 (Mand. tì) [Meng].
[<] either exoactive (§4.3) or late OC general tone (§3.5) of *dì* 弟 (diei^B).

ⅹ **dì** 第 (diei^C) **LH** dei^C, **OCM** *dîh or *də̂ih — **[T]** *ONW* dėi
'Order, sequel' [Zuo]. Karlgren (1956: 14) connects this word with → tī$_1$ 梯 'ladder'.

dì$_3$ 睇 (diei^C, t^{h}iei) **LH** dei^C, t^{h}ei, **OCM** *də̂ih, *t^{h}ə̂i
'To look at from the side / askance, glance at' [Li]
[E] ST: Chepang *d^{h}əy-* 'concentrate, look at' (esp. when aiming), 'be watchful, alert' ⅹ *d^{h}es-* 'see clearly, sight clearly' (when aiming).

dì$_4$ 帝 (tiei^C) **LH** te^C, **OCM** *têkh
'God, ancestor, honorific for deceased fathers' [OB, Shi] (Eno *EC* 15, 1990: 1–26).
[T] *Sin Sukchu SR* ti (去), *PR*, *LR* ti; *MGZY* di (去) [ti]; *ONW* tėi

ⅹ **dì** 禘 (diei^C) **LH** de^C, **OCM** *dêkh
'A kind of great sacrifice' [OB, Zuo].

[E] ST: WT *t^{h}e* 'celestial gods' of the Bon religion (*HST:* 164), JP *mə^{31}-tai^{33}* 'god of the sky'.

dì$_5$ 疐 (tiei^C) **LH** tes, **OCM** *tîts
'Stem of a fruit' [Li].

ⅹ **dié** 瓞 (diet) **LH** det, **OCM** *dît
'(Gourd) stem' [Shi] (Sagart 1999: 91).

dì$_6$-dōng 蝃蝀 → **hóng$_1$** 虹

dì$_7$ 的 → **zhuó$_3$** 灼

dì$_8$ 踶 (diei^C) **LH** de^C, **OCM** *dêh
'To kick' [Zhuang] is prob. cognate to → tí$_4$ 蹄 'hoof' (so *HST:* 100).
[E] ST: WT *rdeg*, PLB *tek^H 'kick' (*HST:* 100), Garo *ga-tek*, Tangkhul Naga *kəkət^{h}ək*.

dì$_9$ 釱 軑 → **zhī$_8$** 桎

diān$_1$ 顛巔 (tien) **LH** ten (< tein), **OCM** *tîn — **[T]** *MTang* tian < tɨan, *ONW* tėn
'Top of head' 顛 [Shi]; 'top (of a mountain), forehead' 巔 [Shi].

ꭗ **dǐng** 頂 (tieŋ^B) **LH** teŋ^B, **OCM** *têŋʔ
'Top of the head' [Yi].
[<] endoactive of *diān* 顛巔 (tien) (§4.5). The rime *-eŋ may be due to paronomastic attraction to AA → dìng$_2$ 定顁 'forehead'.

ꭗ **tiān** 天 (t^{h}ien) **LH** t^{h}en (< t^{h}ein), **OCM** *thîn
'To brand' (the forehead) [Yi].
[<] caus. aspiration of *diān* 顛巔 (tien) (§5.8.2).

[E] ST: WT *steŋ* 'above' (Shafer, *IST*: 65; Unger *Hao-ku* 36, 1990: 48), JP *puŋ^{33}-diŋ^{33}* 'zenith, top, top of the head' (ꭗ dǐng: *STC:* 180); Zemi (Naga) *tiŋ* 'sky', Lushai *pa^L-t^{h}ian^H* 'god' (lit. 'father above') ꭗ *tiaŋ^H / tian^L* 'to pile up, pile on top of another' [French 1983: 157; 374]. Prob. → tiān$_1$ 天 'sky, heaven' belongs to this wf. In light of the simple T-initial in TB and prob. also OC, this wf is not related to → diān$_2$ 顛傎 (the same graph can be used for a stem *tin as well as *tlin).

diān$_2$ 顛傎 (tien) **LH** ten (< tein), **OCM** *tîn < *tlin — **[T]** *MTang* tian < tɨan, *ONW* tėn
'To topple, fall down, be overthrown' 顛 [Shi], 傎 [Guliang].
[E] Area word: TB-WB *lañ^B* ~ *lai^B* < *lin/ŋ* 'fall'; Miao *gliŋ* 'to fall'. This etymon is prob. not related to the wf → diān$_1$ 顛巔 'top of the head' whose initial is a simple dental stop in ST. For inital CH *t-* = foreign *gl-*, see §8.2.1.

diān$_3$ 齻 (tien) **LH** ten (< tein), **OCM** *tîn
'Eyetooth' [Yili].
[E] ST *tjw(a)i 'eyetooth': PLB *dzway (*HPTB:* 31) > WB *cwai*, WT *mč^{h}e-ba* (Tib. *tswe > *tse* > *tsye* > *č^{h}e*); *diān* has the nominal n-suffix (§6.4.3); for loss of ST medial *w, see §10.2.1.

diǎn$_1$ 典 (tien^B) **LH** ten^B, **OCM** *tənʔ
'To vouch for, guarantee' [Jīnshǐ] is perh. cognate to WT *sten-pa* 'to keep, adhere to, depend on' (Unger *Hao-ku* 36, 1990: 50). This may be the s. w. as → diǎn$_2$ 典.

diǎn$_2$ 典 (tien^B) **LH** ten^B, **OCM** *tənʔ — **[T]** *MTang* tian < tɨan, *ONW* tėn
'To direct, rule, norm, constant' [Shi, Shu], 'document' [OB] has been compared to WT *brtan-pa* 'firm, steadfast' ꭗ *gtan* 'constant, enduring' (*HST:* 79). This may be the s. w. as → diǎn$_1$ 典.

diàn$_1$ 田甸 → **tián$_1$** 田

diàn$_2$ 殿 (dien^C) **LH** den^C, **OCM** *dəns
'Buttock' [GY], a variant of → tún$_6$ 臀.
[E] ST: JP *šətīn* 'buttocks' (Matisoff *LTBA* 17.2, 1994: 138).

ꭗ **diàn** 殿 (tien^C) **LH** ten^C, **OCM** *təns
'The rear' (of an army) [Zuo] > 'to protect' [Shi].

diàn$_3$ 電 (dien^C) **LH** den^C (< dein^C), **OCM** *lîns
'Lightning' [Shi].
[E] ST or area word: PYao *(ʔ)liŋ 'lightning' (Benedict 1976: 97); TB-Chepang *pliŋh-ʔo* 'lightning' ⋈ *pliŋh-sa* 'flicker' (of fire).

diàn$_4$ 窴 → **tián**$_2$ 填顛

diàn$_5$ 簟 → **tán**$_1$ 覃

diāo$_1$ 凋 (tieu) **LH** teu, **OCM** *tiû
'To wither, fade, fall' [Guoce]

⋈ **dí** 菽 (diek) **LH** dek < deuk, **OCM** *diûk
'Dried up, wizened' [SW: Shijing] is prob. related to Tai: S. *tok^{D1}* 'to become faded (color)'. For the MC medial *-i-*, see §9.1.3.

diāo$_2$ 彫雕 (tieu) **LH** teu, **OCM** *tiû
'To engrave, carve > injure' 雕 [BI, Shu], 彫 [Zhuang, Zuo].
[E] Etymology not clear. *CVST* (2: 130) relates this word to WB *tʰui^B* 'engrave, write, stab'.
CH ? -> Tai: S. *tieu^C* (McFarland 1944: 367: *dtiew^3*), Saek *diiw^3* 'whittled sticks' (for shaking to tell fortunes) (§9.1.3)..

diào 釣 (tieu^C) **LH** teu^C, **OCM** *tiâukh
'To angle, fish with hook and line' [Shi] is related to Tai: S. *tok^{D1}* 'to angle, fish with hook and line'. For the phonological differences, see §9.1.3; §3.4.

dié$_1$ 垤 (diet) **LH** det (< deit), **OCM** *lît or *dît
'Anthill' [Shi] > 'mound' [Meng] (*GSR* 413o).
[E] ST: KN *m-hliŋ (but note Sabeu *pa̯-lait*) 'ant' [*IST*: 27]. TB cognates to words in *GSR* 413 have pre-initial *m- (§8.1.5). This may possibly be the s. w. as → dié$_2$ 咥 'bite', and / or also be connected with → chí$_3$ 蚳 'ant eggs'.

dié$_2$ 咥 (diet) **LH** det (< deit), **OCM** *lît or *dît
'To bite' [Yi] (a tiger a person) from which could be derived → zhì$_2$ 蛭 'water leech'. This could either be the s. w. as → dié$_1$ 垤 'anthill'; or be related to AA-Khmer *dica* /dic/ 'sting, bite, prick' (of insects, reptiles, plants). A syn. is → shì$_{23}$ 噬 .

dié$_3$ 跌 (diet) **LH** det (< deit), **OCM** *lît
'To stumble' [Xun].
[T] *ONW* dėt
[D] PMin *buɑt 'stumble' is possibly related in light of the TB cognates.
[E] ST: PTB *ble 'to slip' (*STC* no. 141; *HPTB:* 203f), TGTM *ple:^B 'slippery'; PKaren *pʰle^3 ~ *ʔble^2 'id.' (*STC:* 139 n. 375), JP *gə^{31}-pʰrai^{55}* 'to slip', Digaro *ble* 'slippery'; Mikir *-iŋlìt* < *m-lìt* 'be slippery'; WT *'byid-pa* 'to slip' < *mlit* ?, Lepcha *flut* ~ *flit* 'to slip from' ⋈ *plut* 'let slip' [Bodman ICSTLL 1987: 21]. Lushai has a possible cognate (medial *l* does not occur after labial stops): *pʰet^L* / *pʰeʔ^L* < *pʰeʔ/h* 'to trip up, slip away', also *pial^R* < *pialʔ* 'to slip' may be connected. <> This etymon is also found in Tai: S. *pʰlaat^{D2L}* < *blat 'to slip and fall', Dioi *śwat^1* [Maspero 1912: 86]. *HST:* 140 associates this word with WT *ldig-pa* 'to fall and sink through'.
[C] It is not clear if *dié* is connected with → yì$_{13}$ 泆溢. This word is apparently distinct from, and parallel to, the syn. → zhì$_{16}$ 疐 *tri(t)s; see Table D-1 for an overview.

Table D-1 To slip, slippery, trip

	*blai slip(pery)	*ble/it slip	*C-re/it
OC		dié 跌 *lît stumble, slip	zhì 疐 *trits to slip, trip
WT		'byid-pa to slip	'dred-pa to slip, slide
Other		Lepcha flut slip	Kanauri *bret
TGTM	*ple:ᴮ		
Digaro	ble slippery		
JP	gă³¹-pʰrai⁵⁵ to slip		
Lushai		pʰetᴸ / pʰeʔᴸ < pʰeʔ to trip, slip/h	
Mikir		-iŋlìt < *m-lìt slippery	
PKaren	*pʰle³ ~ ʔble²		

dié$_4$ 迭 → **yì**$_{13}$ 泆溢

dié$_5$ 胅 → **dì**$_5$ 疐

dié$_6$ 輒 (tiep) **LH** tep, **OCM** *têp
'Paralyzed, unable to move' [Zhuang].

ꭗ **tiē** 貼 (tʰiep)
'To stick to, glue to' [GY].

ꭗ **niè** 踂 (ṇjäp) **LH** ṇap, **OCM** *nrap or *nrep ?
'Legs sticking together, unable to walk' [Guliang], a Chǔ dialect word. The Chǔ connection and the n-initial which looks like the survival of an AA n-infix suggest a non-ST origin.

[E] ST or area word: TB-PLB *ʔtap 'adhere, stick to', Lushai *depᴸ / deʔᴸ* 'to be close to, close against, adjacent, adjoin, touch' ꭗ? *deep*ᴿ 'copulate with'. Perh. connected with AA-Khmer *jā'pa* /coəp/, OKhmer /ɟap/ 'to touch... stick, cling, adhere, be stuck, held fast...'

dié$_7$ 牒 (diep) **LH** dep, **OCM** *lêp — **[T]** *ONW* dėp
'Tablet' 牒 [Zuo]; in some Han period northern dialects 'board' [FY 5,36].
[E] ST: PTB *lyap (*STC* no. 212) > WT *ldeb* 'leaf, sheet', JP *gə³¹-lep³¹* 'flat', Lushai *dep*ᶠ 'flat' (not filled out like a pod).
CH -> Tai: S. *tʰɛɛpᴰ¹ᴸ 'classifier for long, flat, narrow objects'.

= **dié** 褶疊
'Double, lined' 褶 (garment) [Li] (*GY* reads this graph also MC *zjəp* and *źjəp*), 'double, accumulate' [Shuijingzhu].
[E] ST: WT *ldeb-pa* 'to bend round, double down' ꭗ *ltab-pa, bltabs* < ɴ*l̥ap* 'to fold', *ldab-pa* < ɴ*lap* 'to do again, repeat'; Mru *klep* 'fold up', Lushai *tʰlepᴸ / tʰleʔᴸ* 'to fold (up), bend over' [Löffler 1966: 122].

[N] These two words have distinctly different meanings and TB cognates, perh. two different words have converged phonologically in OC. Furthermore, this etymon is a syn. of → zhé$_7$ 摺, but the roots are different (*Clep ~ *Cliap vs. *tap); perh. some of the WT items *(ldab, ltab)* are a conflation of the two roots.

[C] 'Butterfly' → $hú_6$-dié 胡蝶 may belong to this wf, but see there. Allofams are perh. → $yè_4$ 葉, → $xiè_4$ 屧; → $xí_2$ 習.

$dié_8$ 褶疊 → **dié** 牒

$dié_9$ 蹀 → **$liè_5$** 躐

dīng 丁 (tieŋ) **LH** teŋ, **OCM** *têŋ
'To beat, strike' [Shi].

ж **dǐng** 打 (tieŋ^B, tɐŋ^B), **LH** têŋ^B, tâŋ^B ?
'To beat, strike' [GY].

[E] ST: Lushai *deŋ^H / den* 'to throw, strike, hit'.

$dǐng_1$ 酊 (tieŋ^B) **LH** teŋ^B
'Dead drunk' [Jin shu, GY].

ж **chéng** 酲 (ḍjäŋ, ṭʰjäŋ) **LH** ḍeŋ, ṭʰeŋ, **OCM** *d-leŋ, *t-hleŋ
'Dead drunk' [Shi].

$dǐng_2$ 頂 → **$diān_1$** 顛巔

$dǐng_3$ 鼎 (tieŋ^B) **LH** teŋ^B, **OCM** *têŋʔ
A three- or four-legged 'tripod, cauldron' [BI, Shi]. A large one is called → $nài_4$ 鼐.
[T] *Sin Sukchu SR* tiŋ (上); *MGZY* ding (上) [tiŋ]; *ONW* teŋ
[D] The south has preserved the original meaning 'cooking pot, pan': Old South *tâŋ^A* 鐺 [San-guo zhi] (Ho Dah-an, *BIHP* 1993: 869), but PMin *tiaŋ^B with medial *-i-* is from a later stratum: Jiànyáng *tiaŋ^B*, Fúzhōu *tiaŋ^B*, Xiàmén *tiã^B* (Norman 1988: 231).
[E] Most likely, this old area word is related to TB-Mru *teŋ* 'sacrificial tripod' (Löffler *ZDMG* 116.1, 1966: 141), AA-Wa-Lawa-Bulang *dɐŋ, *(n-)dɑŋ 'cooking pot' (or are these CH loans?). Alternatively, Benedict (*STC:* 178 n. 472; 1976: 98) connects this word with PT and PKS *gliaŋ^A 'tripod', perh. related to AA-Wa-Lawa-Bulang *klɐŋ 'basin', PPalaung (AA) *geŋ* 'tripod'; note also PTai *giŋ^A 'tripod'. But these last forms present phonological difficulties.

$dìng_1$ 定 → **$tíng_1$** 亭

$dìng_2$ 定頷 (tieŋ^C) **LH** teŋ^C, **OCM** *têŋh < *tleŋh ?
'Forehead' 定 [Shi 11, 2], 頷 [Erya2, 146]. *$Dìng_1$* 定 is an OC T-series (§12.1.2); however, this type of initial with QYS div. I/IV can also correspond to an earlier *tl- from a foreign cluster with medial *-l-* (OCM *tleŋh, see §8.2.1).
[E] Most likely AA: Mon *tneŋ* 'forehead', PVM *tlañ^B 'forehead' [Thompson], *k-le:ɲ > *kle:ŋ / tle:ŋ* 'top, upstream' ж *le:ɲ* 'to rise' (sun) [Ferlus]; Bahnaric *kliâŋ 'forehead' [Gregerson 1976: 389]; Pearic *kliŋ²*. Wa-Lawa-Bulang *k/sṇtɑŋ 'forehead'; ж PAA *kleŋ 'top'. Alternatively, a connection with → $diān_1$ 顛巔 'top of the head' could also be possible. The source of Kadai *C-dəŋ^A 'forehead' is not clear (CH?).
Syn. → $tí_1$ 提堤題, *é* 額 and *yán* 顏 (both under → $yà_2$ 御迓訝), → $sǎng_0$ 顙, → $yáng_8$ 揚錫.

$dìng_3$ 町 (dieŋ^B) **LH** deŋ^B, **OCM** *dêŋʔ
'Small boundary banks between fields' [Zuo] is perh. a variant or cognate of → $zhěn_3$ 畛 (so Lau 1999: 342). Furthermore (or alternatively), *dìng* could originally have referred to a trampled path, hence cognate to **tǐng-tuǎn** 町畽 (tʰieŋ^B-tʰuân^B) *thêŋʔ-thônʔ 'be trampled down (fields)' [Shi] (so Karlgren *GSR* 833g). Finally, there may be a connection with → $tí_1$ 提堤題 'raise'.

$dìng_4$ 鋌 → **$tǐng_3$** 梃

dōng₁ 冬 (tuoŋ) **LH** touŋ, **OCM** *tûŋ — **[T]** *ONW* tauŋ
'Winter' [Shi], in some Mǐn dialects 'harvest', what is harvested in the 10th month (winter). Wáng Lì (1982: 608) related this word to → zhōng$_4$ 終 'terminate'.

dōng$_2$ 東 (tuŋ) **LH** toŋ, **OCM** *tôŋ
'East' [OB, Shi]. The OB graph shows some object (but not the sun) in a tree.
[T] *Sin Sukchu SR* tuŋ (平); *MGZY* dung (平) [tuŋ]; *ONW* toŋ
[E] ? ST: Chepang *t^{h}oŋ-* 'lighten, be bright, bright' (esp. sky) ≭ *toŋh* 'awake time' (as opposed to dream time). Perh. related to, or influenced by, → tūn$_2$ 暾 'rising sun'; see there for TB and AA connections. After back vowels OC finals *-ŋ and *-n are occasionally confused, see §6.4.2.

dōng$_3$ 涷 (tuŋ$^{A/C}$) **LH** toŋ, **OCM** *tôŋ < *tloŋ ?
'Violent rain' [Chǔci].
[E] MY: The source of this word is apparently a form similar to Yao *bluŋ^6 'rain'; Wáng FS has PYao < PMY *mblɒəŋ^6, but almost all individual Yao languages have a back vowel: *blŭŋ^6, bjŭŋ^6, bŭŋ^6* (Huáng Shù-xiān *YYYJ* 1989.2: 113, see also Wáng FS 1995: 126). Perh. ultimately related to the AA etymon under → píng$_4$ 萍 'rain master'; note a back vowel form PEKatuic *piloŏŋ 'sky', perh. also Kharia tɔ-bluŋ 'above' [Pinnow 1959: 405]. PYao is prob. related to PMiao *noŋ^C. MY back vowels tend to correspond to other languages' front vowels and vice versa. The word is marked as a MY loan in CH because it first surfaces in the late Zhanguo / early Han text *Chǔcí* (songs from the southern state of Chǔ, a MY area), it has a narrower specialized meaning in CH, it is rare in CH while it is the common word for 'rain' in MY; and finally it lacks a CH etymology. For *t- < *Cl-, see §8.2.1. For syn. and semantics, see → fēn$_2$ 雰氛.

dòng$_1$ 洞 (duŋ^C) **LH** doŋ^C, **OCM** *dôŋh — **[T]** *ONW* doŋ
'To pierce' (chest with an arrow) [Shiji, Hanshu], 'a hole' [GY].
(1) 'To pierce' ≭ → chōng$_4$ 衝.
(2) 'excavate, hole'.
[E] ST: PTB *dwa:ŋ 'pit, hole' (*STC* no. 169; p. 22) > PLB *dwaŋ^2, WB *twaŋ^B* 'hole, pit' ≭ *t^{h}waŋ^B* 'make a hole into, scoop out', Tiddim Chin *wa:ŋ* 'hole, make a hole', WT *doŋ* 'deep hole, pit, ditch'.

dòng$_2$ 動 (duŋ^B) **LH** doŋ^B, **OCM** *dôŋ?
'To move, set in motion, shake' [Shu].
[T] *Sin Sukchu SR* duŋ (上); *MGZY* tung (上) [duŋ]; *ONW* doŋ
[E] Wáng Lì (1982: 357) believes that *dàng* 蕩 (dâŋ^B) *Sin Sukchu SR* daŋ (上); *MGZY* tang (上) [daŋ] 'to move, shake' [Shu, Zuo, etc., Guangya] is related. Downer 1959: 288 reads 'be moved emotionally' [Lunyu] in tone C.

dòng$_3$ 挏 Fúzhōu 'to rain' → **dàng$_1$** 湯盪

dōu 都 → **duō** 多

dǒu 斗 → **zhù$_5$** 注

dòu$_1$ 豆 → **tóu$_3$** 頭

dòu$_2$ 豆 (dəu^C) **LH** do^C, *dôh
'A round vessel' [BI, Shi] on a stem for serving meat dishes (K. C. Chang 1976: 128) which originated in the prehistoric eastern Lóngshān culture.
[T] *Sin Sukchu SR* dəw (去); *MGZY* t^{h}iw (去) [dəw]

[C] Perh. related to → tóu$_3$ 頭 'head', and dòu$_3$ 荳 'soybean'.

dòu$_3$ 荳 (dəu^C) **LH** do^C
'Soybean'.
[E] Etymology not certain, prob. area word: PTB *tu-ŋ 'bean' (LaPolla 1994: 171); AA-PSBahn. *tu:h, PNBahn. *tòh 'bean'. Unger (*Hao-ku* 24, 1984) raises the possibility that this is the same word as 'a round vessel' → dòu$_2$ 豆 and is derived from → tóu$_3$ 頭 (dəu) 'head'. *STC:* 195 draws attention to similarity with PMY *dop and → dá$_3$ 荅 (tập) 'a kind of pulse'.

dòu$_4$ 逗 → **zhú$_4$** 躅

dòu$_5$ 脰 (dəu^C) **LH** do^C, **OCM** *dôh
'Neck' [Zuo].
[D] An old Qí dial. word (acc. to Hé Xiū ca. 180 AD); it is still used in Mǐn dialects: Fúzhōu *tau^{C2}-kauk^{D1}*, Jiànyáng *lo^{C2}* (Norman 1983: 207).
[E] ST: PTB *tuk ⋇ *du(k) 'neck, head' (*STC* no. 392; Matisoff 1978: 64f): JP *duʔ^{31}* 'neck', Garo *gitok*, Mikir *tśethok*, Lepcha *tŭk-tok* 'neck'. See also → dú$_8$-lóu 髑髏.

dòu$_6$ 鬥 (təu^C) **LH** to^C, **OCM** *tôh — **[T]** *ONW* tou
'Quarrel, rangle' [SW], 鬪 [Lunyu].
[E] ST: PTB *daw (*STC* no. 267) > WB *do^B* 'resent an insinuation, interfere in a quarrel', Lushai *do^H* 'be at enmity with'. The TB words could possibly belong to → chóu$_3$ 儔 instead; WT *sdo-ba* 'to risk, venture, bid defiance' could be cognate unless it belongs to → dǔ$_3$ 賭 (tuo^B). Perh. also related to *zhuó* 椓 'to beat, strike' (under → zhǔ$_7$ 斸) (Sagart 1999: 113).

dòu$_7$ 鬪 'come in contact' → **zhù$_7$** 注 'touch'

dòu$_8$ 竇 → **yú$_{19}$** 窬俞

dú$_1$ 毒 (duok) **LH** douk, **OCM** *dûk — **[T]** *ONW* douk
'Poison' n. [Shi].
[D] Yuè *tuk^{D2}*, Kèjia *t^{h}uk^{D2}*, M-Fúzhōu *tøik^{D2}*

⋇ **dù** 毒 (dâu^C) **LH** dou^C < *dûkh
'To poison' vb., occurs only in Yuè, Kèjiā and Mǐn dialects (Norman 1988: 213):
[D] Yuè *tou^{C2}*, Kèjiā *t^{h}eu^{C1}*; M-Fúzhōu *t^{h}au^{C1}*

[E] ST *duk: PTB *duk ~ *tuk (*STC* no. 472) > WT *dug, gdug-pa* 'poison'; PLB *dok: WB *ə-tok* 'poison' ⋇ *ʔdok 'be poisoned' ⋇ *ɴdok 'poisoned, as an arrow' (*HST:* 120), JP *tuk^{55}* 'poison'.

dú$_2$ 毒 'nourish' → **chù$_4$, xù** 畜

dú$_3$ 瀆 (duk) **LH** dok, **OCM** *lôk
'Canal, ditch, drain' 瀆 [Lunyu]; 'abortion' 殰 [Li]; 'sully' [Li], 'insult' 瀆 [Zuo]. *CVST* 3: 33 relates *dú* 'abortion' to WT *rlug(s)-pa* 'to purge, abortion'. Perh. this is the s. w. as → dú$_4$ 櫝韣 'container'.

dú$_4$ 櫝韣 (duk) **LH** dok, **OCM** *lôk
(Any hollowed object > container:) 'box, case' 匵 [Lunyu]; 'coffer' [Lunyu], 'coffin' 櫝 [Zuo]; 'quiver' 韣 [Yili]. This belongs to the wf → yú$_{14}$ 俞. It may be the s. w. as → dú$_3$ 瀆 'drain'.

dú$_5$ 讀 (duk) **LH** dok, **OCM** *lôk ?
'Say / read aloud' [Shi] > 'read' [Lunyu].

[T] *Sin Sukchu SR* du (入); *MGZY* tu (入) [du]; *ONW* dok

[E] Perh. related to WT *klog-pa, (b)klags* 'to read', but the vowels do not match (WT *a* vs. OC *o*); acc. to Sagart (1999: 209), the WT word is a loan because 'read' is a derived meaning in Chinese.

dú₆ 犢 (duk) **LH** dok, **OCM** *lôk ? — [T] *ONW dok*

'Calf' [Li].

[E] Etymology not certain. (1) It could be a ST word: Kanauri *luk* 'calf', WT *lug* 'sheep', *lu-gu* 'lamb, calf', TGTM *g-luk 'sheep'. (2) Boodberg (1937: 359) suggests cognation with WT *pʰrug* 'calf' (not likely). (3) Alternatively, it could be a loan from Altaic acc. to Norman (1988: 18): Mongol *tuɣul*, Manchu *tukšan*, Evenki *tukučən* 'calf', Lamut *tu-* ~ *tuɣu-* 'to give birth to a calf'. (4) It could be related to → chù₄, xù 畜. *Dú* may be connected with:

⋈ **yú** 羭 (jiu) **LH** jo, **OCM** *lo

'Sheep' [Lie] (*HST:* 131).

dú₇ 獨 (duk) **LH** dok, **OCM** *dôk

'To be alone, alone' [Shi]. Acc. to *FY* 79, 111, this was a Han period 'southern Chǔ' dialect word for 'one', note also M-Fúzhōu *sioʔ⁸* (corresponding to QYS *źjwok* < *dok) 'one' which may be related (Norman *FY* 1983.3: 208).

dú₈-lóu 髑髏 (duk-ləu) **LH** dok-lo, **OCM** *dôk-rô

'Skull' [Zhuang, GY]. Li Fang Kuei (1976: 44) who relates this word to Tai: S. *(kra-) duuk^DIL* < *-ʔdl/ruok (actually *ʔluok ?), considers this a reduplication from a hypothetical OC *dlug. This bisyllabic word appears in more variants:

⋈ **tóu-lú** 頭顱 (dəu-luo) **LH** do-lɑ, **OCM** *dô-râ

'Skull' [Guoce]. This form is reminiscent of Lushai *lu^F-ro^H* 'skull' (lit. 'dried head') and *lu^F-ruʔ^L* 'skull' (lit. 'head-bone'), just as in CH the first syllable is 'head'.

⋈ **dú-lú** 頓顱 (dâk-luo) **LH** dɑk-lɑ > dɔk-lɔ

'Skull' [SW, GY], today in Shānxī 'forehead'. This late form seems to be the s. w. as *dú-lóu* above, but committed to writing when OC *a had become more back like *ɑ or *o. An additional MC variant is *ṭɐk-* / *ṭʰɐk-* [GY] which seems close to KS words for 'bone': *tla:k⁷ (Thurgood) or *k-la:k^D (Edmondson/Yang); yet these latter have entered Chinese as → gé₅ 骼 'bone'.

[E] These variants are partially composed of syllables meaning 'head' (*tóu*) of ST stock (Loloish languages have cognates in compound words for 'head': Matisoff 1978: 64). *Dú* 髑 is a ST item which is prob. related to → dòu₅ 脰 'neck': PTB *du(k) 'neck, skull' > Abor-Miri *a-tuk*, Atong *dək-əm*, Kaike *tʰoppā* (< *tʰok-pa*) 'head' (ibid. p. 65). One may speculate that the second syllable is related to *lóu* 婁 [lo] with a hypothetical meaning 'empty' or 'dried', hence lit. 'dried head' as in Lushai. More likely, though, the second part is a reduplication syllable starting with *r/*l (§2.7). Similar-looking items include → lú₄ 顱; AA-Khmer *rɔliə* 'shell, skull' (from earlier *rɔ-la:* ?).

dú₉-lú 頓顱 → **dú₈-lóu** 髑髏

dǔ₁ 篤 (tuok) **LH** touk, **OCM** *tûk

'Firm, solid, thick' [Shi].

[T] *Sin Sukchu SR* tu (入); *MGZY* du (入) [tu]

[E] ST: WT *'tʰug-pa* ~ *mtʰug-pa* 'thick' ⋈ *stug(s)-pa* 'thickness' (*STC* no. 356; *HST:* 148), WB *tʰuik-tʰuik* 'thickly'. CH has allofams with final *-n*, see → dūn₁ 敦惇.

dǔ₂ 睹 (tuo^B) **LH** tɑ^B, **OCM** *tâʔ — **[T]** *ONW* to
'To see' [Li], 覩 [Meng].
[E] ST: LaPolla (1994: 164) compares *dǔ* to PTB *ta 'to see' > WT *lta-ba* 'to look', JP *mə³¹-ta³¹* 'to see'. *Dǔ* has also been compared to PTai *traa^A 'eye' (so Unger *Hao-ku* 36, 1990: 45).

dǔ₃ 賭 (tuo^B) **LH** tɑ^B
'To gamble, bet' [GY]. Acc. to Norman (1986: 382) the Northern Min 'softened initial' *t̬- points to OC prenasalization which is supported by Yao *dou³ < nd-*. This word is also found in other languages: Tai: S. *tʰaa^C2* < *d- 'to challenge, dare' (Li 1976: 40). Unger (*Hao-ku* 36, 1990: 50) proposes cognation with WT *sdo-ba* 'to risk, hazard, venture', but see → dòu₆ 鬥 (dəu^C).

dù₁ 度 (duo^C) **LH** dɑ^C, **OCM** *dâkh — **[T]** *ONW* do
'A measure (of length), rule' [Shi], 'limits, bounds' [Zuo]; 'an instrument to measure length' [Shiji], 'law, regulation' [Xun].
[<] exopass. of *duó* 度 (dâk), lit. 'what is measured' (§4.4, also §3.5).

ӿ **duó** 度 (dâk) **LH** dɑk, **OCM** *dâk
'To measure, calculate, consider, plan' [Shi], 'a measure of width' [Meng].
[T] *Sin Sukchu SR* daw (入); *MGZY* taw (入) [daw]

ӿ **tú** 圖 (duo) **LH** dɑ, **OCM** *dâ
'To plan, consider' (e.g. the weight of something) [Shi, Shu] > 'a plan, a map' [BI, Shu]; 'calculate, expect' [Lun]; 'law, regulation' [Chǔci].
[T] *Sin Sukchu SR* du (平); *MGZY* tu (平) [du]

[E] ST *dwa / *twa: PTB *m-twa 'hand-span' [HPTB: 64], WB *tʰwa* 'measure with a span', *twak* 'cipher, reckon' ӿ *ə-twak* 'account, reckoning'; Mru *twak* 'consider' < Arakanese? [Löffler 1966: 121]; WT *mtʰo* 'a span' [*HPTB:* 167]. It is not clear if AA-PMon *cɗaaʔ* 'hand-span,unit of length' (i.e. distance of outstretched hand as measure), Bahn. *ʃɤda* (Pinnow 1959: 318) is related. For the lack of a CH medial *-w-*, see §10.2.1.

dù₂ 渡 (duo^C) **LH** dɑ^C, **OCM** *dâkh
'To ford' [Guoce].
[E] ST: WT *'da-ba, das* 'to pass over' (*HST:* 116). *Dù* occurs also in Tai *daa^B: S. *tʰaa^B2* 'wharf, landing', but 'river' in most other Tai lgs. (Li Fang Kuei 1976: 40). The semantic connection of 'ford' with 'river' has perh. a parallel, see → hé₄ 河. The virtual phonological identity of the Tai form with late OC (Chinese tone C = Tai tone B), as well as the restriction of this word to the Tai branch of the KT family suggest a Chinese loan. The AA syn. is → jì₁₅ 濟.

dù₃ 肚 (duo^B) **LH** dɑ^B, **OCM** *dâʔ
'Stomach' [late word].

ӿ **dù** 肚 (tuo^B) **LH** tɑ^B, **OCM** *tâʔ
'Animal stomach used as food'.

[E] Etymology not clear, either (1) ST: WT *lto-ba* 'belly, stomach'; and / or Tai: S. *tʰɔɔŋ^C2* < *d- 'stomach' (Li F. 1976: 40); PKS *loŋ^A 'belly' (Edmondson / Yang), MC tone B corresponds in several other words to foreign *-ŋ* (§3.2.4). Or (2) ST: TB with final nominal *-n*: WT *don*, Bunan, Almora *dan* 'belly' [*IST:* 140].

duān₁ 耑端 'tip, to bore' → **chuān₂** 穿

duān₂ 剬 → **duàn₁** 斷

duǎn 短 (tuânB) **LH** tuɑnB, S toiB, **OCM** *tônʔ
'Short' [Shu].
[T] *Sin Sukchu SR* twɔn (平); *MGZY* don (平) [tɔn]; *ONW* tuɑn
[D] PMin *toiB (Bodman 1980: 77)
[E] Prob. related to → duàn₁ 斷 'to cut'. TB has several comparanda: (1) Lushai *tɔiR* < *tɔiʔ* 'be short', WB *tui* 'short'. (2) NNaga *tʰuar 'short'. (3) WB *toŋB* 'short' (as garment). Perh. PMin has preserved an original ST etymon, while elsewhere the word has been reinterpreted as 'cut off'.

duàn₁ 斷 (tuânB, tuânC) **LH** duɑnB/C, **OCM** *tônʔ/s, OCB *tonʔ/s
'To cut off, decide, resolute' 斷 [Shi, Shu]; 'slice of dried and spiced meat' (*tuânC* only) [Zuo]. Karlgren (1956: 9) relates the latter to **duàn** 段 (duânC) 'torn to pieces' [Guan].

⋈ **duàn** 斷 (duânB) **LH** duɑnB, **OCM** *dônʔ, OCB *fitonʔ
'To cut off, decide, resolute'.

⋈ **duān** 剬 (tuân, tśjwänB) **LH** tuɑn, tśuanB ~ -on, **OCM** *tôn, *tonʔ
'To cut' [Guoce].

duàn₂ 段 → **duàn₁** 斷

duàn₃ 鍛 (tuânC) **LH** tuɑnC, **OCM** *tôns
'Hammer, to hammer' [Shi], 'strike' [Zhuang].
[E] ST: PTB *tow (*STC* no. 317) > WT *tʰo-ba* ~ *mtʰo-ba* 'hammer' (large), JP *tʰu³¹* 'to pound, husk', WB *tu* 'hammer'. CH has added the nominal n-suffix (§6.4.3).

duī 堆 (tuậi) **LH** tuəi, **OCM** *tûi
'Mound' [Chuci].
[E] The first textual appearance in *Chǔcí* suggests a foreign word. It seems to be related to PTai *ʔdl/rɔiA: S. *dɔɔiA1* 'mountain', Saek *rɔɔyA1*, PMY *glaɨD 'mountain'; or alternatively to MK: MMon *duiw* 'hill, hilltop'. A connection with → tún₁ 屯 'hill' is also possible, foreign items cited there could apply equally well to *duī*.

duì₁ 碓 (tuậiC) **LH** tuəiC, **OCM** *tûih
'Pestle' [first attested for the Han period: *Wú Yuè chūnqiū*, *Hànshū*, *SW*, *Fāngyán*].
[E] MY: PY *tui 'pestle'; the initial was not *kl- or *gl- as has been suggested in the past (M. Ratliff, p. c.).

⋈ **chuí** 槌 (ḍjwi) **LH** ḍui, **OCM** *drui
'Pestle' [SW].

duì₂ 兑 'glad' → **yú₁₇** 愉

duì₃ 兑 'opening' → **yú₁₉** 窬俞

duì₄ 奪 'narrow passage' → **yú₁₉** 窬俞

duì₅ 陮 'high' → **cuī₁** 崔

duì₆ 對 → **dá₂** 答

duì₇ 隊 (duậiC) **LH** duəs, **OCM** *dûs
'Troops' [Zuo].
[E] Etymology not clear. Sagart (1999: 85) relates *duì* to *yù* 遹 'follow' (under → suì₂ 遂), hence lit. 'followers'. Alternatively, the word could be related to → tún₂ 屯窀 and the TB items there. Or if OCM was *dûts < dûps, perh. related to AA: Khmer *dāba* /toəp/ 'armed forces, troops, army'.

dūn₁ 敦惇 (tuən) **LH** tuən, **OCM** *tûn — **[T]** *ONW* ton
'Be solid, thick' [Li] > 'earnest, generous' [Zuo] (in *Shūjīng* also *zhūn* 惇 LH *tśun*) > put. 'consider thick, weighty' [Shu].

ꕤ **tún** 窀 (duən) **LH** duən, **OCM** *dûn
'Thick' (as darkness in a grave) [Zuo] (also *zhūn* / LH *ṭun* or *ṭuin*).

ꕤ **chún** 醇 (źjuen) **LH** dźuin, **OCM** *dun
'Generous' [Lao]; 'ample' 淳 [Guoyu].

ꕤ **zhūn** 肫 (tśjuen) **LH** tśuin, **OCM** *tun
'Sincere, diligent' [Li].

[E] ST: Chepang *dunh-* 'be dense, closely spaced'; PTB *tow 'thick' (*STC* no. 319) > PL *tu¹, WB *tu^C* 'thickness' ꕤ *thu* 'thick, dense'.

[C] A cognate is → dǔ₁ 篤.

dūn₂ 蜳 → **chǔn** 蠢惷

dùn₁, shǔn 盾楯 (duən^B, dźjuen^B) **LH** źuin^B, **OCM** *m-lunʔ
'Shield' 盾 [Shi], 楯 [Zuo]. WB *duiŋ^B* 'shield' may be a CH loan since the OC and PTB initials are difficult to reconcile; also the relationship to Chepang *dhəl* 'shield' is not clear.

dùn₂ 頓 (tuən^C) **LH** tuən^C, **OCM** *tûns
'Worn, dull, blunt' [Zuo], 'exhaust' [Zuo], 'to ruin' [Guoyu].
[T] *Sin Sukchu SR* tun (去); *MGZY* dun (去) [tun]; *ONW* ton

ꕤ **dùn** 鈍 (duən^C) **LH** duən^C, **OCM** *dûns
'Dull, blunt' [Guoyu].

ꕤ **dùn** 沌 (duən, duən^B) **LH** duən(^B)
'Confused, stupid' [Lao].

[E] ST: *HST*: 67–68 relates this word to WT *rtul-po* 'dull, blunt' and adds WT *dul-ba* 'soft, mild, tame' ꕤ *'dul-ba, btul* 'to tame, conquer, subdue'; Chepang *dyulh-* 'be blunt, worn' (edge of tool). Other languages have similar-looking words which are unrelated, though: PTB-LB *dum² 'blunt' (Thurgood *CAAAL* 13, 1980: 212) > WB *tum^B*; PYao *bl_n_ 'dull, blunt'; AA-PSBahn. *lu:n 'dull, blunt'.

dùn₃ 頓 'hill' → **tún₁** 屯

dùn₄ 遯遁 (duən^B/C) **LH** duən^B/C, **OCM** *dûnʔ/s
'To withdraw, escape' 遁 [Shi], 遯 [Shu] > 'evasive' 遁 [Meng]. This word may lit. mean 'turn to the back' and thus be cognate to → tún₆ 臀 'buttock'.

duō 多 (tâ) **LH** tai, **OCM** *tâi < *tlai
'There are many, have many, all the...' [OB, BI, Shi]. For the initial, see §8.2.1. For an explanation of the graph, see → chǐ₂, chí 誃.
[T] *Sin Sukchu SR* tɔ (平), *LR* tɔ, twɔ; *MGZY* do (平) [tɔ]; *ONW* tɑ
[D] Y-Guǎngzhōu *⁵⁵tɔ^A1*, K-Méixiàn *tɔ^A1*, PMin *tɑi^A1
[E] KT: PTai *hlai^A1 'many', PHlai *ɬʔooi¹ '(how) many' (Thurgood 1991: 38; Baxter and Sagart 1998: 53); the Tai item is also suggested to be the source of the Mǐn word for 'many', see → chái₃ 儕. Others connect *dūo* with the TB items under → dà 大.

ꕤ **zhū** 諸 (tśjwo) **LH** tśɑ, **OCM** *ta — **[T]** *MTang* tśy, *ONW* tśø < tśo
'Many, all', forms plurals, especially for persons to whom respect is due [BI, Shi]. Graham (1973: 294ff) considers *zhū* a dependent ('non-adjunctive') pronoun. *Zhū* replaced earlier OB *duō* 多 in this sense, e.g. OB *duō yǐn* 多尹 'all the administrators' [OB Yib. 867] > 諸尹 [BI]. In BI both *duō* and *zhū* occur. Subsequently in

Shījīng, *duō* is rare in the sense 'all', *zhū* becomes the norm: *zhū hóu* 諸侯 'all the feudal lords' [Shi 6, 34]. Therefore, it is conceivable that *zhū* had branched off from *duō* 多 (tâ) *tlai in the sense 'all' as the pre-nominal proclitic with the loss of the final *-i in *tlai 多 in this position, hence *tlai winʔ 多尹 > *tla winʔ > *ta winʔ (Baxter acc. to Matisoff 1995a: 54). Alternatively, Karlgren (1956: 17) connects *zhū* with the wf → zhǔ$_6$ 貯褚 'collect'.

ⲻ **dōu** 都 'all', which is the Mand. col. form of *zhū*.

ⲻ **shù** 庶 (śjwo^C) **LH** śɑ^C, **OCM** *lha(k)h < *thla(k)h ?
'Be many, abundant' [Shi], adj. 'the many, all' [BI, Shi], syn. of *zhū* and *duō*: in *Shūjīng* occurs *shù yǐn* 庶尹, for example. Thus 'all the administrators' can be *duō yǐn* 多尹, *zhū yǐn* 諸尹 or *shù yǐn* 庶尹. Given the OC phonological similarity of these three words, it is therefore likely that *shù* is cognate to *duō*; the initial can be explained as a devoiced *lh- (§5.5) after loss of the *t- which was felt to be some sort of pre-initial.

duó$_1$ 度 → **dù$_1$** 度

duó$_2$ 奪 → **tōu$_2$** 偷

duó$_3$-lú 頊顱 → **dú$_8$-lóu** 髑髏

duó$_4$ 掇 (tuât, tjwat) **LH** tuɑt, ṭuɑt, **OCM** *trot (or *tôt ?)
'To pick, gather' [Shi], etymology is not clear, but note → luō 捋.

duó$_5$ 澤 (dâk) **LH** dɑk, **OCM** *lâk
A Wú dialect word for 'ice' [JY] is a loan from PMiao *qlak* 'ice' [Wáng FS].

duǒ$_1$ 朵 (tuâ^B) **LH** tuɑi^B
The second syllable in the modern word for → ěr$_1$ 耳 'ear': Mand. *ěr-duǒ* 耳朵; Y-Táishān ^{33}*ŋgi*$^{A1\text{-}55}$*tuɔi*^{B1}; K-Cónghuà ^{21}*ȵi*$^{B\text{-}35}$*tiɔ*^{A2}. This is perh. related to the word **tuǒ** 橢 (tʰuâ^B) 'oblong, oval' [Chuci]. It is also reminiscent of an AA word for 'ear': PSBahn. *toːr, PMon *ktɔɔr.
[T] *Sin S. SR* tɔ (上), *LR* tɔ, twɔ; *MGZY* dwo (上) [twɔ]; *ONW* tuɑ^B

duǒ$_2$, chuí 鬌 (tuâ^B, duâ^B, ḍwie) **LH** tuɑi^B etc., **OCM** *tôiʔ or *dôiʔ
'Hanging tuft of hair' [Li].

ⲻ **duǒ** 朵 (tuâ^B) **LH** tuɑi^B, **OCM** *tôiʔ
'Hang on a tree' [SW, GY].

[E] ST: WB *twai^C* 'hang suspensively' ⲻ *twai^B* 'be pendant, hang' [*HPTB*: 215].

[C] Perh. related to → chuí$_1$ 垂 *doi 'droop'.

duǒ$_3$, chuí 鬌 → **chuí$_1$** 垂

duò$_1$ → **zhì$_7$** 阤, 陊

duò$_2$ 憚 'exhausted' → **dān$_3$** 癉

duò$_3$ 舵 (dâ^B) **LH** dɑi^B, **OCM** *lâiʔ
'Rudder' 舵 [GY], 柁 [Shiming].
[D] Y-Guǎngzhōu ^{21}*tʰɔ*^{A2}, K-Méixiàn *tʰɔ*^{B2}; PMin *dâi^B
[E] Area word: Tai: S. *tʰaai*^{C2} < *d- 'sternpost'; Viet. *lai* (Pān Wùyún 1987: 29).

duò$_4$ 剁 (tuâ^C) **LH** tuɑi^C, **OCM** *tôih
'To chop, cut' [GY]. In some dialects, this graph is used for the syn. *zhuó* 斲 (under → zhǔ$_7$ 斸). Perh. related to WB *tʰwa* 'mince with a knife' (Benedict 1976: 181).

E

é$_1$ 俄 (ŋâ) **LH** ŋɑi, **OCM** *ŋâi — **[T]** *ONW* ŋɑ

'Slanting' [Shi].

[D] Y-Guǎngzhōu *ŋɔ*^{A2}; M-Xiàmén *go*^{A2}

[E] ST has *ŋ(w)aj ~ *nwaj parallel stems (§2.5; §5.12.1) for this etymon:

(1) *ŋaj > 俄 OCM *ŋâi, WB *ŋai*^{C} 'to lean, be inclined to one side' (Matisoff 1995a: 85) ⋈ *hŋai*^{C} 'incline, set on one side', JP *ŋaʔ*^{31} < *ŋak* 'slanted', perh. WT *sñe-ba* (< *s-ŋye* < *s-ŋe* ?) 'to lean against, rest on, lie down', but WT can phonologically also be connected with the parallel stem:

(2) *C-nwaj > PLB *ʔnwe 'lean over (and fall)' (Matisoff 1970, *JAOS* 90.1: 39), WB *hnwai*^{B} 'lean sideways, incline'. It is not clear if or how Lushai *ŋer*^{L} < *ŋerh* 'be tilted, leaning' (with final *-r*) is connected with the TB items.

CH -> Tai: S. *ŋia*^{B} 'lean to one side' (Unger *Hao-ku* 36, 1990: 52).

é$_2$ 娥 in **héng-é** 姮娥 (ɣəŋ-ŋâ), **LH** gəŋ-ŋɑi, **OCM** *gə̂ŋ-ŋâi

Name of the moon goddess [Huainan, Hou Hanshu], later *cháng-é* 常娥 because the Hàn emperor Wéndì's personal name was Héng (180–164 BC). For the legends and variant forms, see Maspero 1924: 14ff.

[E] Prob. area etymon: PTai *hŋai^{A1} 'moonlight', S. *ɗian*^{A1}*-ŋaai*^{A1} 'full moon', Po-ai *looŋ^{B2}-haai^{A1} 'moonlight' (acc. to Gedney *CAAAL* 6, 1976: 70, *ŋaai*^{A1} originally meant 'to lie face up', perh. connected with AA: Khmer /ŋə́əj/ 'to raise or hold up the head'). <> Note also TB-Tamang ^{3}*ŋia* 'full moon'. The semantic extension 'to face' > 'moon' is parallel to → wàng$_4$ 望.

[C] The first syllable may be related to → gèng$_1$ 恒 'waxing' (of the moon).

é$_3$ 鵝 (ŋâ) **LH** ŋɑi, **OCM** *ŋâi

'Goose' [Meng]. Prob. related to → yàn$_2$ 雁 'wild goose', may have ended in a PCH final *-l or *-r.

[T] *Sin S. SR* ŋɔ (平), *PR* ɔ; *LR* ɔ, ŋɔ; *MGZY* ngo (平) [NO]

[D] Y-Guǎngzhōu ^{21}*ŋɔ*^{A2}; Ke-Méixiàn *ŋɔ*^{A2}, PMin *ŋiɑ, Xiàmén *giɑ*^{A2}

é$_4$ 訛吪 (ŋuâ) **LH** ŋuɑi, **OCM** *ŋôi

'To move, act, change' 訛 [Shu], 吪 [Shi]. → é$_7$ 訛 may be the same word.

⋈ **huò** 貨 (xuâ^C) **LH** huɑi^C, **OCM** *hŋôih — **[T]** *ONW* huɑ

'Property, goods, riches, wares' [Shu].

[<] trans. / caus. devoicing (§5.2.2) + exoactive of *é* 訛吪 *ŋroi (§4.3.2), lit. 'what is being exchanged', or 'made to be exchanged'.

⋈ **huà** 化 (xwa^C) **LH** huai^C, **OCM** *hŋrôih

'To transform, change' [Shu], e.g. from a fish into a bird [Zhuang], people through education [Liji], raw food through cooking (fire) [Liji].

[T] *Sin Sukchu SR* xwa (去); *MGZY* hwa (去) [xwa]; *ONW* huä

[<] this looks like *é* 訛吪 with triple causative markings: devoicing (§5.2.2) + s/h-suffix (§4.3.2) + *r- 'infix' (§7.5).

[E] Bodman (1980: 60) relates this word to TB: Kanauri *skwal* 'to change' ⋈ Khaling *k*^{h}*waal* 'to shift, move'; but the phonology of the initials is not clear.

※ **wǎ** 瓦 (ŋwa^B) **LH** ŋuai^B, **OCM** *ŋrôiʔ
'An earthenware utensil' [Shi, SW] > 'tiles (of a roof)' [Zhuang] (Wáng Lì 1958: 568).
[T] *Sin Sukchu SR ŋwa* (上), *PR, LR wa; MGZY xwa* (上) [ɦwa]
[<] perh. derived from *huà* through elimination of caus. devoicing and addition of endoactive tone B (§4.5.1), lit. 'what has transformed' (i.e. chemically through fire; note *huà* meaning: transform raw victuals into cooked food through fire).

é₅ 詻 → **yà₂** 御迓訝

é₆ 額 'forehead' → **yà₂** 御迓訝

é₇ 訛 (ŋuâ) **LH** ŋuɑi, **OCM** *ŋôi
'False' [Shi].

※ **wèi** 僞 (ŋjwie^C) **LH** ŋyɑi^C, **OCM** *ŋoih
'False, deceive, cheat' [Shi].
[E] This word is commonly considered cognate to → wéi₃ 為 'make' (Karlgren 1956: 18). But phonologically *wèi* is closer to *é*. The phonetic *wéi* was prob. selected for semantic reasons, supported by the rime.

[E] ST ?: WT *rŋod-pa, brŋos* 'to deceive, seduce', but the rimes do not agree. This wf may belong to → é₄ 訛吪 'change'.

è₁ 厄軛 (ʔɛk) **LH** ʔɛk, **OCM** *ʔrêk or *ʔek — **[T]** *ONW* ʔëk
'Yoke ring' 厄 [Shi], 軛 [Yili] > 'straits, difficulties' 厄軛 [Meng], 隘 [Zhuang].

※ **è, ài** 隘阨 (ʔaɨ^C) **LH** ʔai^C, **OCM** *ʔrêkh or *ʔekh
'Be narrow' (of a lane) [Shi], 'defile, narrow pass' 隘阨 [Zuo] > 'straits, difficulties' 阨 [Meng] (also MC *ʔɛk*), 隘 [Zhuang].
[<] exopass. of *è* 厄軛 *ʔrêk, lit. 'being put in straits' (§4.3.2).

[C] A derivation is → gè₄ 鬲 'yoke'. Perhaps cognate to → yì₁₈ 嗌 'strangle, throat'.

è₂ 啞 → **yǎ₁** 啞

è₃ 惡 (ʔâk) **LH** ʔɑk, **OCM** *ʔâk
'Evil, evildoer' [Shi], 'bad, ugly' > 'wrong, fault' [Zuo].
[T] *Sin S. SR* ʔaw (入), *LR* ʔawʔ; *MGZY* 'aw (入) [ʔaw]; *ONW* ʔɑk

※ **wù** 惡 (ʔuo^C) **LH** ʔɑ^C, **OCM** *ʔâkh
'To hate' [Shi], 'dislike, abominate' [Mo — Harbsmeier 1981: 40].
[T] *Sin Sukchu SR* ʔu (去); *MGZY* 'u (去) [ʔu]
[<] exoactive / putative of *è* 惡 (ʔâk) (§4.3).

[E] ST: WT *ʔag-po* 'bad' (*HST*: 38). It occurs also in PTai *j-: S. *jaak^{D2L}* 'difficult, bad', in NTai *ʔj-. Karlgren (1956: 13) connects → yà₁ 亞 'second, inferior' to this wf.

è₄ 咢 (ŋâk) **LH** ŋɑk, **OCM** *ŋâk
'To beat the drum' [Shi].
[<] ST: WT *rŋa* 'drum' (Bodman 1980: 127), Tamang *³ŋa:*.

è₅ 鱷 (ŋâk) **LH** ŋɑk, **OCM** *ŋâk
'Aquatic reptile' [SW], 'saltwater crocodile'.
[E] Etymological possibilities are discussed by Carr (*LTBA* 13.2, 1990: 132ff); *è* has been related to words for 'fear' (→ è₆ 愕 鄂噩), and to → è₄ 咢 'beat the drum' because some drums had crocodile / alligator skins. Note also PTai *ŋɨek (Li F.; but Chamberlain *ŋwak) 'mythological sea monster, dragon'; *è* is distinct from → tuó₃ 鼉 'alligator'.

è$_6$ 愕鄂噩 (ŋâk) **LH** ŋɑk, **OCM** *ŋâk
'Scared' 愕 [Guoce]; 'tremble, fear' 噩 [Li]; (perh. 'startling':) 'suddenly' 鄂 [Shi], 'unexpectedly come across' 遌 [Chuci].
[D] M-Xiàmén *giaʔ*^{D2}, lit. *gok*^{D2}

ⱺ **wù** 遻 (ŋuo^C) **LH** ŋɑ^C, **OCM** *ŋâkh
'Unexpectedly come across' [Zhuang].

ⱺ **sū** 蘇 (suo) **LH** sɑ, **OCM** *sŋâ — **[T]** *ONW* so
'To tremble, fear' [Yi]. This looks like a doublet of suǒ 索.

ⱺ **suǒ** 索 (sâk) **LH** sɑk, **OCM** *sŋâk — **[T]** *ONW* sɑk
'Tremble, fear' [Yi].

[E] ST: WB *ŋraŋ-* ~ *ñaŋ-* 'have a settled dread'; WT *sŋaŋ-ba* 'be afraid, out of breath'.
Syn. →hè$_5$ 赫; → yà$_2$ 御迓訝.

è$_7$ 顎 (ŋâk) **LH** ŋɑk
Mand. 'jaw, palate' [GY].
[E] Area word: PTai *ŋɨak, PKS *ŋɨak. <> TB-WB *ŋak* 'gills' (Peiros and Starostin *CAAAL* 22, 1984: 123).

è$_8$ 遏閼 (ʔât) **LH** ʔɑt, **OCM** *ʔât
'To suppress, repress' 遏 [Shi], 'obstruct, stop' 閼 [Zhuang].

ⱺ **ǎi** 藹 (ʔâi^C) **LH** ʔɑs, **OCM** *ʔâts
('Be stopped up, accumulated'?:) 'be thronged, in a great crowd' [Shi], 'rich' (clouds) [Guanzi].
[<] exopass. of *è* 遏閼 (ʔât) (§4.4).

è$_9$ 頞 → **ān**$_3$ 鞍

è$_{10}$ 餓 (ŋâ^C) **LH** ŋɑi^C, **OCM** *ŋâih — **[T]** *ONW* ŋɑ
'Hungry, starve' [Meng]
[E] ST: Lushai *ŋhei*^{H} 'to fast, go without' (food, medicine) (*CVST* 5: 137), WB *ŋat* 'thirsty, hungry', also JP *ŋ̇jo*^{31} 'hungry', although the vowels do not agree. A ST parallel root (§2.5) has initial *n(w)- (*ŋaj ~ *nw(ə)i, see → něi 餒), see §5.12.1.

è$_{11}$ 枿櫱蘖 → **niè**$_{10}$ 蘖

ér$_1$ 而 (ńźɨ) **LH** ńə, **OCM** *nə — **[T]** *ONW* ńə
'Whiskers' of an animal [Zhouli].
[E] This word may be a cognate of → xū$_4$ 須鬚 'beard' (Pulleyblank *EC* 16, 1991: 43). After labial initials, there has been some dialectal confusion of OC *-o (母) and *-ə (每) in the *Shījīng*, and this looks like a similar case which is strengthened by *ér*'s use as a phonetic element in words with *-o (需) and *-on (耎). Alternatively, *ér* could perh. be related to PTB *(r-)ney or *-nəy 'hair' (of head) (*STC* no. 292) > Gyarung *rni* 'head hair', Garo *kʰəni*, Nung *(t)əni*. In either scenario the vowel correspondences are problematic, though.
[C] Allofam: → sāi 思 (sɨ, sậi) 'bearded' or 'white-haired' [Zuo] (Pulleyblank).

ér$_2$ 而 (ńźɨ) **LH** ńə, **OCM** *nə
A common particle which links verbs (Norman 1988: 122), a resumptive emphatic particle [Shi] which originated perh. as an unstressed variant of → rú$_1$ 如 'be like' (Pulleyblank 1995: 148) with the basic meaning '-like, -ly' (§11.2.1).
[T] *Sin S. SR* ri (平), *PR*, *LR* rɿ; *MGZY* Zhi (平) [ri]; *ONW* ńə
[E] ST: This particle *ér* is possibly shared with WT: *ni* an emphatic marker for nouns

and nominal phrases (*HST*: 71); however, WT has no equivalent of *rú* from which *ni* might have been derived.

ér₃ 而 'your' → **ěr₅** 爾

ér₄ 兒 (ńźie) **LH** ńe, **OCM** *ŋe, OCB *ŋje
'Child, baby' [Shi] as young human being in general (Sagart 1999: 164).
[T] *Sin S. SR* ri (平), *PR*, *LR* rɿ; *MGZY* Zhi (平) [ri]; *ONW* ńe
[E] Use as a diminutive suffix developed somewhat later than → zǐ₁ 子, was widespread by the Tang dyn. (Norman 1988: 114). In Mǐn and other southern dialects, this suffix has almost disappeared except perh. for traces in nasalization and in 'irreg.' tones (Chen Zhongmin 1999, on the diminutives in Mǐn dialects, *JCL* monograph 14). Acc. to Chao (1968: 46) the Mand. suffix *ér* has 3 sources: (1) *lǐ* 裡 'therein' (e.g. *zài zhèr* 'here'); (2) *rì* 日 'day' (e.g. *jīnr* 'today'); (3) *ér* 兒. Syn. → zǐ₁ 子.

⋈ **yá** 伢
[D] This is a div. I (j-less) southern dialect form (§9.1.1): Hénán 'child'; Yuè ^{53}*ŋA:*^{A1} 'baby' (Yue Hashimoto *Phonology of Cantonese* 1972: 322), Chángshā *ŋa* 'boy'. Also, the unique Kèjiā words for 'son' mentioned under → zǐ₁ 子 may have developed from an OC form. Southern dial. have additional words for 'son': K-Méixiàn *lai*^{C}, Huái *nai*^{C} (same etymon as ér 兒?).
[E] Area word: TB: JP *ʔŋai*^{33}, *tʃə*^{33}*-ʔŋai*^{33} 'baby', Mru *ŋia* 'child' (Löffler 1966: 146). AA: PSBahn. *ŋe 'baby', Khmer *ṅā* /ŋíiə/ ~ /ŋaa/ 'be tender, delicate, lovable', dialectal *kūna ṅā:* 'baby' (*kūna* 'child'); OMon *ṅāk* /ŋaik/ 'baby', *kwon ŋaak* 'young child' (*kwon* 'child'). Note also PMY *ŋau² 'child', but TB-Lushai also has a similar word.

⋈ **ní** 倪 (ŋiei) **LH** ŋe, **OCM** *ŋê — **[T]** *ONW* ŋėi
'Young and weak' [Meng] (Karlgren 1956: 16).
[E] Area word: WB *ŋai* 'small, little, inferior'. Weidert (1987: 191) suggests PTB *ŋa:l ~ *ŋa:r. Possible allofam is → ní₅ 麑麛 'fawn'.

ér₅ 唲 (ńźie) **LH** ńe, **OCM** *ne — **[T]** *ONW* ńe
'Forced laugh' [Chuci], 'prattle' (of children) [Xun].

⋈ **rú-ér** 嚅唲, 儒兒 (ńźju-ńźie) **LH** ńo-ńe
'Forced laugh, strong laughter' [Chuci] is a reduplicated form.
[E] ST: PTB *m-nwi(y) 'to laugh' [*STC* no. 191], KN *m-nui [*IST*: 25] > Lushai *nui*^{H} / *nuiʔ*^{L}, Bodo, Dimasa *mini*, JP *mə*^{31}*-ni*^{33} 'to laugh' (*HST*: 102). A ST medial *-w-* does not survive in Chinese after acute initials (§10.2).

ěr₁ 耳 (ńźɨ^{B}) **LH** ńə^{B}, **OCM** *nəʔ
'Ear' [OB, Shi] > 'to hear' [Hanfei]; > (a pair of) 'handles' (on a vessel etc.) [Zhouli].
[T] *Sin S. SR* ri (上), *PR*, *LR* rɿ; *MGZY* Zhi (上) [ri]; *ONW* ńə^{B}
[D] *JY* says that in Hédōng and Guānzhōng the word is pronounced *rěng* (ńźjəŋ^{B}), and Sagart (1999: 61) points to Northern Min forms in final *-ŋ*: Jiànyáng *noiŋ* etc. Colloquial southern CH dialect forms reflect what appears to be a different word with initial *ŋ-: Y-Táishān ^{33}*ŋgi*^{A1}*-*^{55}*tuɔi*^{B1}; M-Fúzhōu *ŋei*^{C2}, Jiēyáng *hĩ*^{B2}, Amoy *hi*^{C2}*-a*^{B}; these may be the result of the AA substrate, the AA word for 'ear' has initial *ŋ-*.
Mand. *ěr-dǒu* 耳朵. See also → duǒ₁ 朵, → jí₃ 吉.

⋈ **èr** 衈珥 (ńźɨ^{C}) **LH** ńə^{C}, **OCM** *nəh
'To cut a tuft from the ear of a sacrificial animal' 衈 [Li], 'cut the ear' (of game) 珥 [Zhouli]; 'pendant covering the ear' 珥 [Lie], 'guard of sword' 珥 [Chuci].

[<] prob. LOC general tone C derivation.

[E] ST: (1) PTB *r-na 'ear / hear' (*STC* p. 113 no. 453) > WT *rna-ba* 'ear'; Ang. Naga *rəńə* < *r-na* 'listen'; Rengma N. *na* 'hear'; PL *(C-)na² 'ear', *ʔ-na¹ 'to listen'; WB *na^B* 'ear', *na* 'listen'; JP *na^33* 'ear', *na^31* 'listen'. (2) PTB *g-na 'ear / hear' > Tangkhul *kʰəna* 'ear', Rengma N. *əkʰəna* 'ear', Mikir *-nò*, Garo *kʰna* 'hear'; WT *gna'-mi* ~ *gña'-mi* 'witness' ⋈ *ña-ma* 'a hearer' ⋈ *sñan* 'ear' resp. A possible allofam is → chǐ₅ 恥 'shame'.

TB has the same root *na for both 'ear' and 'nose'. That we are dealing here with the same etymon is supported by parallelism with → wén₃ 聞 'to smell' and 'to hear'.

ěr₂ 耳 'female' → **lǐ₂-ěr** 李耳

ěr₃ 餌 (ńźɨ^C) **LH** ńə^C, **OCM** *nəh ? — **[T]** *ONW* ńə
'Sinew' [Li]. — **[E]** ST *njə: WT: *ña* 'tendon, sinew'.

ěr₄ 爾 (ńźje^B) **LH** ńe^B, **OCM** *neʔ, OCB *njəjʔ — **[T]** *ONW* ńe
A suffix forming adverbs '-wise' (< '-like') [Shu] (*DEZC*: 147), derived from → rú₁ 如 with the suffix *-i* (Matisoff 1995a: 77); e.g. *shì-ěr* 適爾 ('happening-wise':) 'by chance'. See → rú₁ 如 for allofams.

ěr₅ 爾 (ńźje^B) **LH** ńe^B, **OCM** *neʔ, OCB *njəjʔ
'You, your' [BI, Shi].
[T] *Sin Sukchu SR* ri (上), *PR* rɿ; *MGZY* Zhi (上) [ri]; *ONW* ńe
[D] This is an independent pronoun (§3.3.3); it survives in most modern dialects in its col. form → nǐ₁ 你.

⋈ **ér₃** 而 (ńźɨ) **LH** ńə, **OCM** *nə — **[T]** *ONW* ńə
'You, your' [Shi]. This is the possessive derivative of ěr, not → rǔ₂ 汝 'you', because otherwise MC should have tone B, like *nǎi* 乃 'your' (§3.3.3).

[E] ST: TB-Chepang *ni* 'you' ⋈ *niŋ* 'you' (plural), WB *ñañ^B*; Tangut *ni^B* 'you' (sing., pl.) [Keping, *CAAAL* 11, 1979: 14]. This is a parallel stem of ST *na 'you' (→ rǔ 汝); Maring (Tangkhul-Kuki) (*naŋ* ~) *nai* 'thou' [Benedict 1995: 32] is prob. a derivation from the latter (PTB *na). In spite of the parallelism with *wǒ* 我 *ŋâiʔ (under → wú₂ 吾), the OC vowel *-e in *ěr* is not a leveled diphthong *-ai.

ěr₆ 爾 'that' → **nà₃** 那

ěr₇ 邇 (ńźie^B) **LH** ńe^B, **OCM** *neʔ, OCB *njəjʔ
'Near' [Shi].
[E] ST: PTB *s-ney (*STC* no. 291 *HPTB*: 215) > WT *ñe-ba* 'near' ⋈ *sñen-pa* 'come near'; JP *ni^31*, PLB *nay², PL *b-ni^55, WB *ni^B* < *ne^B* (Bodman 1980: 130; *HST*: 111); ⋈ PTB *s-na:y (*HPTB*: 215) > Lushai *in^L-hnai^R* < *hnaiʔ* 'near, close'.

⋈ **xiè** 褻 (sjät) **LH** siat, **OCM** *snat or *snet ?
'Be close, familiar' (people) [BI, Shi] > 'disrespectful' [Shu], 'ordinary' [Li], 'garment next to body' [Shi]. The last meaning may have been transferred from *nì* 昵衵 (under → jí₇ 即).
[E] ST: WT *sñed* 'about, near' (after round sums).

[C] CH has two distinct etyma for 'near', (1) ST *ne (ěr 邇), (2) PAA *tsit (→ jí₇ 即) > (ts-n-it >) nit (→ nì₂ 昵, → nì₄ 衵). Additional syn. → ní₁ 尼 'near', → nì₉ 暱.

èr₁ 二 (ńźi^C) **LH** ńis or ńi^C, **OCM** *nis or *nih
'Two' [OB]. The word rimes with *-t* in Yáng Xióng's (Later Han) dialect (Coblin *JCL* 11.2 1984: 10), hence OCM *-s (or *-ts, but not *-h).
[T] *Sin S. SR* ri (去), *PR, LR* rɿ; *MGZY* Zhi (去) [ri]; *ONW* ńi^C

[D] PMin *dzi^C ~ *ni^C; Y-Guǎngzhōu ²²*ji*^C2, Liánshān *ŋi*²¹⁴
[E] ST: PTB *g-nis > WT gñis; Kan, Chepang *nis, TGTM *⁴ni:; Jiarong *kĕnĕs;* PLB *nit ~ *ni ~ *ʔnit 'two' > WB *hnac < s-nik;* Lushai *hniʔ^L < hnis* [Matisoff 1997a: 67] (*STC* no. 4). <> PTai: *ńji^B2 is a CH loan, it occurs only in compounds; the native Tai word for 'two' is *sooŋ (Benedict 1976: 170).
[C] Perh. → cì₁ 次佽 and / or → réng 仍 are derivations.

èr₂ 衈珥 → **ěr** 耳

èr₃ 餌 (ńźɨ^C) **LH** ńə^C, **OCM** *nəh — [T] *ONW* ńə^C
'Cake' [Chuci], 'meat and rice dumpling' [Li], 'bait' [Zhuang]; *JY* also reads MC *ńźɨ^B* vb. 'to bait'? (Unger *Hao-ku* 36, 1990: 55).
[E] Area word: Khmer *nùy* 'bait' (for the absence of medial *u/w* in OC, see §10.2.1). <> PTai: *hň-: S. *jɨa^B1* 'bait'.

F

fā 發 (pjwɐt) **LH** puɑt, **OCM** *pat, OCB *pjat

'To start out, go out, come forth, sprout, issue, offspring' [Shi], 'to shoot' (an arrow) [Shi]; Mand. 'send out, deliver'.

[T] *Sin Sukchu SR* fwa (入), *PR*, *LR* faʔ; *MTang* pfar < pfuar, *ONW* puat

[D] M-Xiàmén col. *puʔ*^{Dl}, lit. *huat*^{Dl}

[E] Area word 'go out > eject', in TB lgs. 'vomit', in AA and AN 'to shoot'. TB: PLB *C-pat 'vomit', WB *pʰat*, JP *n*^{31}*-pʰat*^{31} (*HST:* 130); PVM *ɓah 'to vomit' [Ferlus] seems to have a TB origin. <> AA: Mon *pnoh* 'bow' ꭗ *poh* 'to shoot with a pellet-bow'.

A derivation is perh. → fèi$_6$ 廢 'cast aside' (Karlgren 1956: 11). Allofams are possibly → fá$_2$ 伐 'to plow', → fá$_4$ 伐蕟 'praise', → bá$_1$ 犮 'expel'.

fá$_1$ 發 'plow' → **fá$_2$** 伐

fá$_2$ 伐 (bjwɐt) **LH** buɑt, **OCM** *bat

'To plow, furrow' 坺 [Guoyu]; 'earth thrown up by a plowed furrow' 伐 [Zhouli]. Perh. the s. w. as → fá$_3$ 伐罰 which includes the notions of 'chop, hack', as the earliest form of 'plowing' was hacking with a hoe.

ꭗ **fá** 發 (pjwɐt) **LH** puɑt, **OCM** *pat

'To plow' (fields) tr. [Shi] is cognate or may simply be a graphic loan for LH *buɑt.*

[E] Commentators, incl. *SW*, consider this etymon to be the s. w. as → fā 發 'come out', hence 'lift out / up' (earth). Alternatively, it may possibly be related to → fá$_3$ 伐罰 'cut off, hew out' (Qiu Xigui 2000: 294); and / or to → bá$_2$ 茇 'roots of grass' and id. 'to camp'.

fá$_3$ 伐罰 (bjwɐt) **LH** buɑt, **OCM** *bat

'To cut off, chop off, beat, attack' 伐 [OB, BI, Shi] > 'to punish, fine' 罰 [BI, Shu]; 伐 also means 'to cut' as in: to cut (i.e., make) an axhandle, spokes, etc. [Shi] (Qiu Xigui 2000: 294). → fá$_2$ 伐 may be the same word.

[T] *MTang* bvar < bvuar, *ONW* buat

fá$_4$ 伐蕟 (bjwɐt) **LH** buɑt, **OCM** *bat

'Merit, boast' 伐 [Lunyu]; 'to praise' (a person) tr. 蕟 [BI]. This word is perh. cognate to → fā 發 'come out, start out' (i.e. < 'make stand out'?).

fá$_5$ 筏 (bjwɐt) **LH** buɑt, **OCM** *bat

'Large bamboo raft' [GY], a Han-period dialect word in the Qín-Jìn area [FY], 'ocean-going ship' [SW]. Perh. related to → fú$_{16}$ 浮 (Unger *Hao-ku* 39, 1992).

fá$_6$ 乏 'lack, neglect' → **fèi$_6$** 廢

fǎ$_1$ 法 'law, pattern' → **fán$_4$** 凡 'general'

fǎ$_2$ 法 'disregard' → **fèi$_6$** 廢

fǎ$_3$ 髮 (pjwɐt) **LH** puɑt, **OCM** *pat, OCB *pjot

'Head hair' [Shi, BI].

ꭗ **bā** 胈 (puât) **LH** pɑt, **OCM** *pât

'Small hairs on body' [Zhuang] is perh. cognate, or belongs to → bá$_2$ 茇.

[E] ? ST: WT *p^hud* 'hair-knot, tuft of hair' and possibly also *spu* 'hair' (Unger *Hao-ku* 39, 1992: 88). Alternatively, the etymon may be the same as → fā 發 'come out, sprout'.

fān₁ 弁拚翻 (pʰjwɐn) **LH** pʰuɑn, **OCM** *phan
'To fly, fly up' [Shi].

⋈ **fān-fān** 幡幡 (pʰjwɐn-p.)
('To be fluttering':) 'be waving about, changeable, versatile, frivolous' [Shi]. In *Shījīng*, the word is written with 弁 as phonetic loan: OCB *brjans (QY bjän^C 3); Baxter's OC medial *-r- is interesting in light of TB.

[E] ST: WB *p^hran^C* 'spread out, expand, spread wings' ⋈ *pran^C* 'expanded, spread out, be level'; JP *p^hyan^55* 'spread the wings, to open' (as the fist)' (< Burm.?) (*CVST* I: 1–2). It is not certain if and how the following is related: PTB *byer (*STC:* 83 n. 249) > Bahing *byer*, Abor-Miri *ber*, Trung *biel* 'to fly'. This word is not related to → fèn₄ 奮, → fēi₄ 飛.

fān₂ 帆 (bjwɐm) **LH** buɑm, **OCM** *bam
'Sail' [Han time].

~ **péng** 篷 (buŋ) 'sail' [San'guo yanyi] (post-classical).
[T] *Sin Sukchu SR* buŋ (平); *MGZY* pung (平) [buŋ]
[D] PMin *bʰoŋ seems to be a variant.

[E] *Fān* is believed to be cognate to → fēng₇ 風 'wind' (so Karlgren *GSR* 625a). WB *ə-p^hum* 'a sail' is cognate or a CH loan.

fān₃ 藩 (pjwɐn) **LH** puɑn, **OCM** *pan
'Hedge, screen' [Shi].

⋈ **fán** 樊 (bjwɐn) **LH** buɑn, **OCM** *ban
'Fence, hedge' [Shi] (Wáng Lì 1982: 581).

[E] ST: Lepcha *tuk-pól* 'hedge, fence' ⋈ *pól* 'magic circle', Lushai *pal^H* 'hedge, fence' (Unger *Hao-ku* 35, 1986: 31). Perh. also connected with → fán₇ 蕃繁 'luxuriant'.

fán₄ 凡 (bjwɐm) **LH** buɑm, **OCM** *bam (from earlier *bam or *bom)
'General(ly)' [Zuo], 'common' [Meng], 'every, all' [Shi]; 'general rule, pattern' [Xun] (Harbsmeier 1981: 153).
[T] *Sin Sukchu SR* vam (平) *PR* van; *MGZY* Hwam (平) [vam]; *MTang* bvuam < buam, *ONW* bam
[E] ST: Lushai *pum^H* 'whole, all, everywhere'; WB *pum* 'form, model, pattern'. This word is usually thought related to Tai: S. *p^hrɔɔm^C2* 'together' (under → xián₃ 咸), but this is doubtful in light of the likely TB cognates without medial *r.

⋈ **fǎ** 法灋 (pjwɐp) **LH** puɑp, **OCM** *pap
'Law, model' [Shu]. CH -> PTai *ʔb-: S. *bɛɛp^D1* 'pattern'.
[T] *Sin Sukchu SR* fa (入); *ONW* pap > puap

[E] ST: WT *byibs* < *bibs* 'shape, figure, form' (Simon, W. *MSOS* 32, 1929: 241). Alternatively, Yú Mǐn (1989: 20, see Jeon 1996: 103) related the CH word to WT *babs* 'shape, form, appearance'.

Cognation of *fǎ* with *fán* is suggested by the semantic range of the former. For the vocalic differences, note the common ST *-im/p ~ *-um/p alternations (§11.5.1). OC and TB can be reconciled if we assume furthermore the common *u ~ *o variations (§11.5.1).

fán₅ 燔 (bjwɐn) **LH** buɑn, **OCM** *ban, OCB *bjan
'To burn, roast' [Shi].
[E] ST: PTB *bar ~ *par (*STC* no. 220) > WT *'bar-ba* 'to burn, catch fire, beam, radiate, to begin to bloom, blossom' ⋈ *sbar-ba* ~ *sbor-ba* 'light, kindle', Kanauri *bar* 'burn', Miri *par* 'light (fire)'; WB *pa^B* 'to shine' (*HST:* 50), JP *wan^31* 'fire, lamp'.

Matisoff (1997: 44f; *LL* 1.2, 2000: 144ff) sets up a large ST wf that includes also → huī$_2$ 燀輝暉.

The TB semantic field suggests that → bàn$_4$ 瓣 'petals of a flower' and → pā 葩 'flowers, blossoms' are the same etymon, but that → fén$_3$ 焚 is unrelated.

fán$_6$ 蹯 (bjwɐn) **LH** buɑn, **OCM** *ban
'Paw' [Zuo].
[E] ST: WT *sbal* 'soft muscles or parts of inner hand or paw'; Jaeschke p. 404 says this word is perh. the same as *sbal-pa* 'frog' (Unger *Hao-ku* 35, 1986: 30).

fán$_7$ 蕃繁 (bjwɐn) **LH** buɑn, **OCM** *ban
'Luxuriant (growth), be numerous, to prosper, rich' 蕃 [Shi]; 'abundant, numerous' 繁 [Shi].
[E] ST *pom ? For wider relations and parallel stems, see §2.5.1. Unger (*Hao-ku* 35, 1986: 30) suggests a relationship with WT *dpal* 'glory, splendor, magnificence, abundance'. Perh. also related to fān$_3$ 藩 'hedge'. <> PTai *b- : S. p^huun^{A2} 'increase, flourishing'.

fǎn 反 (pjwɐn^B) **LH** puɑn^B, **OCM** *panʔ
'To turn, return, turn around, turn against' [BI, Shi] > 'rebel' [BI] > 'on the contrary, however' [BI, Shi].
[T] *Sin Sukchu SR* fwan (上), *PR* fan; *MGZY* h(w)an (上) [fan]

⪤ **fàn** 販 (pjwɐn^C) **LH** puɑn^C, **OCM** *pans
'To trade' [Zhouli].
[<] exoactive of *fǎn* 反 (§4.3).

⪤ **fān** 番幡 (p^{h}jwɐn) **LH** p^{h}uɑn, **OCM** *phan
'A turn, a time' 番 [Lie], 'turn, change' 幡 [Meng].
[<] iterative of *fǎn* 反 (§5.8.3).

[E] ST: WT *p^{h}ar* 'interest' (on money), 'exchange', Lepcha *far* 'price' ⪤ *par* 'buy' (*CVST* 1: 69). *Fǎn* is prob. cognate to → pán$_1$ 般 'turn around'.

fàn$_1$ 氾汎泛 (p^{h}jwɐm^C) **LH** p^{h}uɑm^C, **OCM** *phams
'To overflow, inundate' [Meng]; 'float, drift, glide, ride' (in a boat) 汎 (also MC *bjuŋ*) [Shi]; 'to float' 泛 [Zhuang].
[E] ST: WT *'byam-pa* < *ɴbyam* 'to flow over, be diffused' (Bodman 1980: 118).

⪤ **fàn** 氾 (bjwɐm^C) **LH** buɑm^C, **OCM** *bams
'To be thrown out, float about' [Chuci], 'disperse' [Zuo].
[<] endopass. of *fàn* 氾汎泛 (§4.6).

⪤ **fàn** 犯 (bjwɐm^B) **LH** buɑm^B, **OCM** *bamʔ
'To pass over' [Zhouli] > 'offend against, oppose' [Lunyu]. Formally, fàn 氾 looks like a derivation from this word; however, the root's basic meaning is 'float, overflow'; therefore it may be a different etymon.

fàn$_2$ 犯 → **fàn$_1$** 氾汎泛

fàn$_3$ 飯 (bjwɐn^C) **LH** buɑn^C, **OCM** *bans
'Cooked rice or millet' [Li], a late OC word.
[T] *Sin Sukchu SR* vwan (去), *PR*, *LR* van; *MGZY* H(w)an (去) [van]; *ONW* buan
[D] PMin *bɔn^{C2} 'dry cooked rice'
[<] exopass. of *fán* 飯 (bjwɐn) (§4.4).

⪤ **fán** 飯 (bjwɐn) **LH** buɑn, **OCM** *ban
'To eat' [Liji] (Downer 1959: 273).

[E] <> AA: PMonic *pooŋ 'cooked rice', *piaŋ* ~ *pieŋ* in South Bahnaric [Ferlus 1988: 88]. This stem could possibly be connected with *bū* 餔 [pɑ] *pâ 'to eat' (under → bù$_5$ 哺), but the Lushai cognate there speaks against this.

fāng$_1$ 方 (pjwaŋ) **LH** puɑŋ, **OCM** *paŋ

'Square, a regular thing, side, region' [BI, Shi], 'country' [OB, Shi].

[T] *Sin S. SR* faŋ (平); *MGZY* Hwang (平) [faŋ]; *MTang* pfuaŋ, *ONW* puaŋ < paŋ

[E] Tai: S. *buaŋ^3* 'side, direction'. Prob. related to → páng 旁傍.

fāng$_2$ 方 (pjwaŋ) **LH** puɑŋ, **OCM** *paŋ

'Two boats lashed side by side' [SW] > vb. tr. 'to lash (boats chuán 船 / zhōu 舟) together' in order to cross a river [Zhuang], 'to cross (a river) by raft' [Shi].

ж **fǎng** 舫 (pjwaŋ^C, pwâŋ^C) **LH** puɑŋ^C, **OCM** *paŋh

'Boat' [Li]; bàng 艕 (pwâŋ^C) an old Wú dialect word for 'boat' [Yupian].

= **bàng** 艕 (pwâŋ^C) and **huáng** 艎 (ɣwâŋ)

'Ancient Wú words for boat' [Yupian] are variants acc. to Mahdi 1994: 456.

[E] The meaning 'raft' seems to derive naturally from → fāng$_1$ 方 'square' (Egerod *CAAAL* 6, 1976: 58). Yet a boat is not necessarily square, and the special reading *pwâŋ^C* also sets this word apart from 'square'.

This etymon is an area word for 'raft': TB-WB *p^{h}oŋ, b^{h}oŋ* 'raft, float', Kachin *p^{h}oŋ* id., perh. also Mikir *-p^{h}án* 'raft'. <> Tai: S. *p^{h}uaŋ^{B2}* < *b- 'pontoon, raft'. <> The ultimate source is AA and AN: AA-Mon *kɓaŋ* 'seagoing vessel, ship'; PAN *qaBaŋ 'boat' (Blust; Peiros and Starostin *CAAAL* 22, 1984: 125; Mahdi 1999: 147f). To the same AA word belongs → háng$_4$ 航杭.

fāng$_3$ 方 (pjwaŋ) **LH** puɑŋ, **OCM** *paŋ

'Just now' [Shi], 'to begin' [Shi?] is an allofam of → fǔ$_7$ 甫 (Pulleyblank 1962: 233).

[E] The meaning 'to begin' may belong to a different ST etymon: PTB *praŋ: Mikir *a-p^{h}raŋ* 'first, before' ж *praŋ* 'dawn', JP *p^{h}aŋ^{33}* 'begin', NNaga *praŋ 'begin' [French 1983: 222]; Garo *p^{h}riŋ*, Dimasa *p^{h}oroŋ* 'morning' (*STC* no. 332). However, TB words for 'morning' may instead belong to → shuǎng$_1$ 爽 'dawn'.

ж **fǔ$_7$** 甫 (pju^B) **LH** puɑ^B, **OCM** *paʔ

'To begin' [Zhouli] (Pulleyblank 1962: 233).

fāng$_4$ 方 (pjwaŋ) **LH** puɑŋ, **OCM** *paŋ

'Method' [Lunyu, Shiji], 'law, norm, standard' [Xun]. This may be the s. w. as fāng$_1$ 方.

ж **fǎng** 放 (pjwaŋ^B) **LH** puɑŋ^B, **OCM** *paŋʔ

'To imitate, conform to' [Liji, Zhouli].

[E] Etymology not certain, perh. ST: WT *byaŋ-ba* 'skill, experience' ж *sbyoŋ-pa, sbyaŋs* 'to train, exercise, study, learn, practice' (*HST:* 143). Alternatively, the items may belong to AA: Khmer *brāṅa* /príiəŋ/ 'to represent the shape of, to sketch, design...' < *rāṅa* /ríiəŋ/ 'body build, form, shape, figure' (Jenner / Pou 1982: 233); if related, this group seems to belong to an AA wf which includes → zhuàng$_1$ 狀 'form, shape'. 'Law, norm, standard', etc., is a common semantic extension of 'form, shape, pattern', cf. *fǎ* 法 (→ fán$_4$ 凡).

fāng$_5$ 芳 (p^{h}jwaŋ) **LH** p^{h}uɑŋ, **OCM** *phaŋ

'Fragrant' [Chuci] is perh. related to → xiāng$_2$ 香 'fragrance' (Pulleyblank 1962: 140).

fáng$_1$ 坊防 (bjwaŋ) **LH** buɑŋ, **OCM** *baŋ

'A dike' 坊 [Li]; 'embankment, dike' 防 [Shi] > 'to stop up, block up' (river, peoples' talk) [Zuo, Guoyu].

[T] *Sin Sukchu SR* vaŋ (平); *MGZY* h(w)ang (平) [vaŋ]; *ONW* buaŋ < baŋ

[E] Etymology not clear, it could be the s. w. as → fáng$_2$ 房 'room' (i.e. 'walled in'?), or related to PKS *pwaŋ^B 'bank, shore' (under → pǔ$_1$ 浦).

fáng$_2$ 房 (bjwaŋ) **LH** buɑŋ, **OCM** *baŋ
'A room' 房 [Shi].
[T] *Sin Sukchu SR* vaŋ (平); *MGZY* h(w)ang (平) [vaŋ]; *ONW* buaŋ < baŋ
[E] Etymology not certain, prob. ST: WT *baŋ-ba* 'storeroom, storehouse'; WB *waŋ^B* 'fence' (Bodman 1980: 177; *HST:* 72); alternatively WT *braŋ* 'dwelling, house' in *p^{h}o-braŋ, braŋ-k^{h}aŋ*.

fǎng$_1$ 紡 (p^{h}jwaŋ^B) **LH** p^{h}uɑŋ^B, **OCM** *phaŋʔ
'To spin, twist' [Zuo], 'to tie' [Guoyu].
[T] *MTang* pfhuaŋ (?), *ONW* p^{h}uaŋ < p^{h}aŋ
[E] ST: PTB *p^{w}aŋ [*STC* no. 48; Matisoff *LL* 1.2, 2000: 161] > WT *p^{h}aŋ* 'spindle', WB *waŋ^C* 'to spin' ⋈ *ə-waŋ* 'spindleful of thread' (*HST:* 138), NNaga *ʔ-paŋ 'spindle' [French 1983: 178].

fǎng$_2$ 訪 (p^{h}jwaŋ^C) **LH** p^{h}uɑŋ^C, **OCM** *phaŋh
'To inquire, scrutinize, consult' [Shi].
⋈ **pìng** 聘 (p^{h}jäŋ^C), **LH** p^{h}ieŋ^C, **OCM** *pheŋh
'To inquire' [Shi] is identical with *fǎng* in OC except for the vowel (§11.1.3).

fǎng$_3$ 放 → **fāng$_4$** 方

fàng 放 (pjwaŋ^C) **LH** puɑŋ^C, **OCM** *paŋh
'To put away, neglect, banish' [Shu].
[T] *Sin Sukchu SR* faŋ (去); *MGZY* Hwang (去) [faŋ]; *MTang* pfhuaŋ (?), *ONW* p^{h}uaŋ < p^{h}aŋ
[E] Area word: WT *'p^{h}en-pa, 'p^{h}aŋs* 'to fling, throw, cast' (*HST:* 106). <> AA-OKhmer *paṅ* /ɓɔŋ/ 'to throw, cast, fling'. The connection with Tai is not clear: S. *ploŋ^{A1}* < *pl- 'to lay down, relinquish' (Li F. 1976: 45).

fēi$_1$ 非 (pjwei) **LH** pui, **OCM** *pəi (prob. < *pui)
'It is not, to be not' [OB, BI, Shi, Shu].
[T] *Sin Sukchu SR* fi (平), *LR* fi; *MGZY* h(w)i (平) [fi]; *ONW* pui
[E] Fēi is a fusion of → bù$_1$ wéi 不維 which is still found in the OB for the later *fēi*: QY pjəu-jiwi 4, *pə-wi. *Fēi* is rare in *Shījīng* where → fěi$_1$ 匪棐 is used instead.
= **fēi$_2$** 非 (pjwei) **LH** pui, **OCM** *pəi
'Be wrong' [Shi], (vs. *shì* 是 'right') [Meng], 'mistake' [Meng], 'violate, go counter' [Lun]. Since this is a regular semantic extension of *fēi$_1$* (§2.10), cognation with WT *p^{h}yar-k^{h}a* 'blame, affront, insult' (so *HST:* 162) is unlikely.
⋈ **fěi** 誹 (pjwei[^{C}]) **LH** pui(^{C}), **OCM** *pəi(h)
'To condemn, disapprove, slander' [Zhuang].
[<] exoact. / tr. of *fēi* (§4.3.2).

fēi$_2$ 非 'wrong' → **fēi$_1$** 非

fēi$_3$ 扉 (pjwei) **LH** pui, **OCM** *pəi
'Symmetrical leaves of a door' [Zhuang]; basic meaning: a symmetrical contraption.
⋈ **fěi** 棐 (pjwei^B) **LH** pui^B, **OCM** *pəiʔ
'Wooden frame to prevent warping of a bow' [Xun] > 'strengthen, assist, help' [Shu]. (Boltz *JAOS* 120.2, 2000: 220).

fēi$_4$ 飛 (pjwei) **LH** pui, **OCM** *pəi (prob. < *pui) — **[T]** *ONW* pui — **[D]** PMin *pye
'To fly' [Shi].
[E] Area word: PTB *pur ~ *pir (*STC* no. 398) > WT *'p*^{h}*ur-ba* 'to fly'; Nung *əp*^{h}*r* 'to shake' (cloth), *k*^{h}*oŋ-p*^{h}*r* 'moth'. <> AA: PVM *pər 'to fly' [Ferlus]; PMonic *par, Munda *apir* 'to fly'; Wa-Lawa-Bulang *pɤr, PNBahn. *păr.
For ST *-r > OC *-i, see §7.7.4; *fēi* is prob. related to → fēn$_6$ 翂 'to fly'. However, → fān$_1$ 弁拚翻 'to fly' and → fǒu$_1$ 不 (pjəu^B) 'to soar' are unrelated. Boltz relates this word, which is also written 蜚, to the wf → fēi$_3$ 扉 (*JAOS* 120.2, 2000: 220).

féi$_1$ 肥 (bjwei) **LH** bui, **OCM** *bəi — **[D]** PMin *byi.
'Fat, rich, fertile' [Shi].
[T] *Sin Sukchu SR* vi (平), *LR* vi; *MGZY* H(w)i (平) [vi]; *ONW* bui
[E] <> Perh. related to Tai *bii^A 'fat' (CH loan?).

féi$_2$ 腓 (bjwei) **LH** bui, **OCM** *bəi
'Calf of leg, leg; follow on foot' [Shi, Yi].
[E] ST: PKC *pey 'leg' [*HPTB:* 205] > Lushai *p*^{h}*ei*^{L} 'foot, leg, lower leg' (*CVST* I: 2), KN-Khami *p*^{h}*ai* 'calf of leg' (Löffler 1966: 148); WT *byin-pa* 'calf of the leg' (*HST:* 102). Geilich (1994: 52) relates 'calf' furthermore to → féi$_1$ 肥 'fat'. Similar items in the area are Tai: Saek *blii*^{A1} 'calf of leg'; PNBahn. *poyh 'calf of leg'.

fěi$_1$ 匪棐 (pjwei^B) **LH** pui^B, **OCM** *pəiʔ —**[T]** *ONW* pui^B
'It is not, to be not' replaces → fēi$_1$ 非 in *Shījīng* (匪) and *Shūjīng* (棐).

fěi$_2$ 棐 'wooden frame' → **fēi**$_3$ 扉

fěi$_3$ 誹 → **fēi**$_2$ 非

fěi$_4$ 朏 (p^{h}jwei^B, p^{h}uət) **LH** p^{h}ui^B, p^{h}ət, **OCM** *phəiʔ, *phôt (*phuiʔ, *phut < *phlut ?)
'New light of the moon' [Shu, SW], 'third day of the new moon' [Hanshu].
[E] Perh. AA: Khmer [/pluut/ >] /punluut/ 'to enlarge, augment', lit. 'cause to appear, get larger, grow' < /luut/ 'to sprout, get taller / longer, grow' [Jenner / Pou 1982: 315].

fèi$_1$ 吠 (bjwɐi^C) **LH** buɑs, **OCM** *ba(t)s < *bos ?, OCB *bjots
'To bark' [Shi]. — **[T]** *ONW* bei — **[D]** PMin *b̭ui^C
[E] ST: KN-Lushai *bauʔ < baus* 'to bark' is a direct cognate and shows the CH word to have a sound-symbolic origin (ST *baus ?).

fèi$_2$ 芾 'knee covers' → **fú**$_{14}$ 韍芾

fèi$_3$ 肺 (p^{h}jwɐi^C) **LH** p^{h}uɑs, **OCM** *phats < *phats or *phots from earlier *s-pot/ps ?
'Lungs' [Shi]. CH aspiration is symbolic for breathing §5.8.5.
[T] *ONW* p^{h}ei > p^{h}uei
[E] The OC form is close to items found in various languages in the area, but the exact relationships are elusive due to the uncertainty of the PCH form and the sound-symbolic nature of the word: AA-PVM *p-soːs > p-hoːc > poːc / p^{h}oːc 'lungs'. <> Tai: S. *pɔɔt*^{DIL} < *pɨɔt 'lung' (Li F. 1976: 43) ⋇ S. *p*^{h}*ɔɔt*^{DI} 'breathe, inhale' (Manomaivibool 1975: 124). Matisoff (1978: 113ff) sets up, among others, a ST form *p-(r-)wap: PL *(ʃ-)pap^L; Chepang *pop* (Bodman 1980: 115), which has the same final as WT *glo-ba* < *glop* 'lungs, side'; TMTG *glwap$^{2/1}$ 'lung'.

fèi$_4$ 沸 (pjwəi^C) **LH** pus, **OCM** *pəts (prob. < *puts)
'To bubble up' (water) [Shi]. The Northern Min 'softened initial' *pyi^C may point to OC prenasalization which is supported by the Yao word *bwei*^{5} < *nb-*, PMY *npwei^{1C} (Norman 1986: 382).

[E] ST: JP *prut*[31] 'to boil'; perh. also Lepcha *brut* ~ *brit* 'erupt' (of large pustules) [Bodman ICSTLL 1987: 14].

Allofam → fú₁₃ 沸 (Bodman 1985: 150). → bì₄ 泌 (pji^C 3) 'bubble up' (as water from a spring) [Shi] looks like a vocalic variant (§11.5.1).

fèi₅ 疿 (pjwei^C) *ONW* pui^C (LH pus)
'Pimples, an eruption' [late word].
[E] ST: WT *'bos* 'boil, bump, tumor' (Unger *Hao-ku* 39, 1992) ⋈ *'bo-ba, bos* 'to swell, rise, sprout', Lepcha *put* 'erupt' (of small pustules) [Bodman ICSTLL 1987: 14]; WB *pʰu^B* 'bud, swell into protuberance' ⋈ *ə-pʰu^C* 'protuberance, boil'; Lushai *puk^L* < *puk* 'be enlarged, swollen', JP *a-pʰùt* 'measles' [Bodman ibid.]. <> Tai: S. *pʰot^DI* 'prickly heat'. For similar etyma, see §2.5.1.

fèi₆ 廢 (pjwɐi^C) **LH** puɑs, **OCM** *pats
'To remove, reject, disregard, neglect, fail' [Shi], 'to fall' [Zuo] > 'to expel noxious influences, purify' 祓 [Zuo]. This word is hardly derived from → fā 發 (so Karlgren 1956: 11), but is certainly related to

⋈ **fá** 乏 (bjwɐp) **LH** buɑp, **OCM** *bap
'To lack' [Zuo], 'exhaust' [Meng], 'neglect, disregard' [Zhuang] (Yú Mǐn 1948: 44). In BI, the character fǎ 法 (pjwɐp) [puɑp] *pap also occurs in the meaning 'neglect, disregard' (Baxter 1992: 350) where it prob. stands for the present fá 乏.
[T] *MTang* bvuap, *ONW* buap < bap

[E] ST: WT *'bab-pa, babs* 'to move downward, fall down' ⋈ *'bebs-p, pʰab* 'to throw down, cast down' (Bodman 1980: 49). <> Tai: S. *bap*⁴ 'weak, exhausted, worn out'.

This wf and → bài₁ 敗 'destroy', → pí₇ 罷疲 'exhausted', → bì₁₀ 敝弊斃 'worn out' with the stems *pap(s), *pal ~ *pai(ts) are phonetically and semantically similar and flow into each other, note the partial synonymity of *fá* 'exhausted' with *pí* (Pulleyblank 1962: 215, and Wáng Lì (1982: 500), consider some or all of them cognates). Lushai *paiʔ^L* < *pais* 'to throw away, discard, annul' where final *-s could derive from *-s, *-ts or *-ps, is synonymous with *fèi*, but formally similar to → bì₁₀ 敝弊斃 *be(t)s < *bai(t)s. → bài₁ 敗 looks like a possible derivation from this wf, and the AA comparanda cited there may also be connected with it. TB-JP *prai*[33] 'be effaced, settled and forgotten (feud), healed' (old sore), WB *prai* 'be wasted, become weak' [Matisoff 1974: 161] also may belong to one of these stems. Additional allofams may be → biǎn 貶 (so Karlgren 1956: 18); → bá₁ 犮.

fēn₁ 分 (pjuən) **LH** pun, **OCM** *pən (prob. < *pun)
'To divide, separate' [BI, Shu]. The graph shows a thing cut in two with a knife. Acc. to Downer (1959: 284) commentators to the *Zuǒzhuàn* read the word in tone C when meaning 'distribute, give relief' (exoactive §4.3).
[T] *Sin Sukchu SR* fun (平), *PR* fən; *MGZY* H(w)un (平) [fun ?]; *ONW* pun

⋈ **fèn** 分 (bjuən^C) **LH** bun^C, **OCM** *bəns — [T] *ONW* bun
'A part' [Zuo], 'share' [Liji].
[<] exopass. of *fēn* 分 'divide' (§4.4)

[E] ST *pun: JP *pʰun*[55] 'part' (unit of weight) ⋈ *pʰun*[33] 'part' (monetary unit), Lushai *buŋ^H* / *bun^L* 'to cut, break or divide into two or more pieces for'; WB *puiŋ^B* 'divide, sever' ⋈ *ə-puiŋ^B* 'division, part' (there is no final *-uin* in WB [the counterpart of PTB *-un], therefore the final may have shifted in this and a few other etyma to *-uiŋ* [< PTB *-uŋ], see §6.4.2). The word → běn 本 'tree stump / trunk' may be cognate.

Some TB words in final *-l are sometimes associated with *fēn*: Lushai *pual^H* 'lot, share, portion'. WT *'bul-ba, pʰul* 'to give' something to someone of higher rank, 'represent, report, offering, gift' is semantically somewhat distant but could also belong to this wf. Some foreign items under → bàn₁ 半 are sometimes associated with the present etymon.

fēn₂ 雰氛 (phjuən) **LH** pʰun, **OCM** *phən, OCB *phjən

'Mist' [Yupian; GY], 'hoarfrost' 雰 [Chuci] > 'inauspicious vapors' (as evil omen) 氛 [GY 112].

⋡ **fēn, fén** 氛 (bjuən) **LH** bun, **OCM** *bən

'Ominous vapors or clouds in the sky' (inauspicious in the *Zuǒzhuàn* passages) [Zuo, Xiang 27, 5; Zhao 15, 2; SW 211]; 'auspicious vapors' [GY 110]; the *GY* assigns different meanings to MC *bjuən* and *pʰjuən* (above) which may be a later attempt to differentiate the two.

⋡ **fēn** 饙 (pjuən) **LH** pun, **OCM** *pən

'To steam food' [BI, Shi] perh. belongs to this wf.

[E] Prob. several distinct etyma have coalesced in this wf *fēn* and in → fěn 粉 'flour', but the various sources are phonologically and semantically ambiguous and difficult to disentangle, as words of the shape LH *pun* and their possible outside relations have meanings ranging from sky - weather - clouds - mist - snow - hoarfrost to flour - dust. Any foreign syllable pə/un, *pə/ur, pə/ul*, as well as *pan/r/l* could correspond to LH *pun*.

(1) PMY *mpan^C [Wáng FS; Downer 1982 *ɴpəːn^3] 'snow', PY *ɴbwon^5 [Purnell] 'cloud, snow'. MY 'snow' occurs in *Chǔcí*, while CH 'mist' agrees with Yao 'cloud'. Sagart (ICSTLL 1994: 7) relates this word to → fēn₄ 紛 'mixed' and argues that the MY word is likely to have been borrowed from CH.

(2) Tai: S. *bon^{A1}* < PTai *ʔb- 'sky, above', Saek *bɯn^{A1}* 'sky, weather', PKS *ɓun^1 'sky'; Benedict (in Edmondson / Solnit 1988: 329f) suggests wider connections with AN.

(3) TB-Lushai *vaan^L* (*v-* corresponds to labial stops in other lgs.) 'sky, heaven'.

(4) PTB *s-p^{w}a(l) 'frost, snow' > WT *ba-mo* 'snow', Amdo *wal*, Dulong *tɯ^{31}-wǎn^{53}* 'snow' etc. [Matisoff LL 1.2, 2000: 147].

(5) TB-Lushai *vuur^H* 'hoarfrost, ice, snow'.

(6) TB-PKiranti *pʰùl* 'flour', WB *pʰun* 'dust' (*CVST* 1: 7), *n^{31}-bun^{55}* 'dust'; perh. also WT *spun-pa* ~ *sbur-ma* 'chaff, husks', but *spun* is prob. cognate to *bud-* etc. 'to blow', *spur-* to *spur-ba* 'make fly up'. <> PVM *buːlʔ 'dust' may also be related, then also Tai: S. *mon^{B1}* 'dusty', Saek *mul^{A2}* 'dust'.

(7) → fěn 粉 'peeled (rice), flour', PMY *mpan^B 'flour'. Haudricourt / Strecker (*TP* 77, 1991: 339) believe that the CH word is a loan from PMY *mpan^B 'flour', Sagart (ICSTLL 1994: 7) argues the opposite.

For the close semantic relationship between 'sky' (item 2) and 'cloud, mist' (item 1) see → wù₁₂ 霧. The *Shìmíng* (*Shì tiān*) compares *fēn* 雰 'hoarfrost' to → fěn 粉 'flour', the two MY words (item 1 and item 7) would parallel the CH forms.

fēn₃ 雰 'mixed' → **fēn₄** 紛

fēn₄ 紛 (pʰjuən) **LH** pʰun, **OCM** *phən

'Be mixed', i.e. patterns on cloth [Shi], 'manifold' [Yi], 'confused' [Zuo]. Sagart (ICSTLL 1994: 7) relates this word to → fēn₂ 雰氛 'mist'.

\> **fēn-fēn** 雰雰 (pʰjuən-p-) **LH** etc. same as above

'Be mixed' (of rain and snow) [Shi], 'be disorderly' 棼棼 [Shu] (Wáng Lì 1982: 524f who adds → wěn 紊 'tangled').

[E] ST *pol (?) : Lushai *pɔɔl^H* 'to associate with, keep company with, have sexual intercourse; group, party, herd' ⋡ *pɔlʔ^L* 'to mix, mingle, together' (*CVST* 1: 62).

fēn$_5$ 芬 (pʰjuən) **LH** pʰun, **OCM** *phən, OCB *phjən
'Be fragrant' [Shi] is perh. cognate to WT *spod* 'spice' ⋈ *spos* 'perfume'.

fēn$_6$ 翂 (pjuən) **LH** pun, **OCM** *pən
'To fly, soar' [Zhuang].

⋈ **fèn** 奮 (pjuənC) **LH** punC, **OCM** *pəns
'Wing' [SW], 'to spread the wings, fly up' [Duàn Yùcái]. *Fèn* 'wing' is a late tone C derivation from *fēn* (§3.5).

[E] ST: PTB *pir ~ *pur, related is → fēi$_4$ 飛 'fly' (see there for TB cognates). Prob. loaned to Tai: S. *bin*^{A1} < PT *ʔb-.

[C] This etymon is unrelated to → fān$_1$ 弁拚翻 'to fly', → fǒu$_1$ 不 'soar'.

fēn$_7$ 饙 → **fēn$_2$** 雰氛

fén$_1$ 氛 → **fēn$_2$** 雰氛

fén$_2$ 羒 → **fén$_4$** 墳

fén$_3$ 焚 (bjuən) **LH** bun, **OCM** *bən (prob. < *bun)
'To burn' intr., tr. (carriages, things) [OB, Shi].
[T] *Sin Sukchu SR* vun (平), *PR* vən; *MGZY* h(w)un (平) [vun]
[E] ST: PTB *ploŋ (*STC* no. 139) > Kachin *proŋ*^{33} 'to be burnt' (as a house), Mikir *pʰloŋ* 'burn the dead, cremation'; Lhota *ˡruŋ* 'burn', Mishmi *lâuŋ* (Weidert 1987: 309). TB indicates that → fán$_5$ 燔 is distinct from this etymon. For the difference in finals, see §6.4.2.

fén$_4$ 墳 (bjuən) **LH** bun, **OCM** *bən — **[T]** *MTang* bvun, *ONW* bun
'Big (head, drum), big-horned' > 'greatness' 墳 [Shi], 'big drum' 鼖 [Shu]; 'well-set (fruit)' 蕡 [Shi]; 'ram' 羒 [SW], 'sheep-shaped demon' 羵 [Guoyu]; 'tumulus' 墳 [Li]; in most modern dialects 'a grave'. 'Raised bank, bank of a river' → fén$_5$ 墳濆 may be the same word, unless it is a vocalic variant of pín 頻 'river bank, edge' (so Wáng Lì 1982: 541) of the *bin ~ bun* type alternations (see under → bīn$_2$ 濱; §11.5.1).

⋈ **fèn** 墳憤 (bjuənB) **LH** bunB, **OCM** *bənʔ
'Swell up' 墳 [Zuo] > 'full of annoyance' 憤 [Guoyu], 'full of dissatisfied eagerness' [Lunyu] > 'ardor' 憤 [Zuo]. Some of the meanings may belong to → bēn$_2$ 賁 'ardent'.
[T] *Sin Sukchu SR* vun (上), *PR* vən; *MGZY* H(w)un (上) [vun]
[<] endoactive of *fén* (§4.5).

⋈ **fèn** 忿 (pʰjuənB/C) **LH** pʰunB/C, **OCM** *phənʔ/s
'Anger, angry' [Zuo]. This word may belong to → bēn$_2$ 賁 'ardent' instead.
[<] intensive of *fèn* ? (§5.8.3). CH aspiration is associated with forceful outward gesture §5.8.5.

[E] Area etymon: Lushai *ti*^{L}*-puun*^{H} 'to increase' (as water, wound). <> OKhmer *vva(n)i*, Khmer *būna* /puun/ 'to amass, accumulate, to heap, stack, pile'. For wider relations see §2.5.1.

fén$_5$ 墳濆 (bjuən) **LH** bun, **OCM** *bən — **[T]** *MTang* bvun, *ONW* bun
'Raised bank, bank of a river' 墳濆 [Shi] may be a vocalic variant of *pín* 頻 'river bank, edge' (so Wáng Lì 1982: 541) of the *bin ~ bun* type (see under → bīn$_2$ 濱; §11.5.1).
[E] ST: Lepcha *bun-rí* 'an edging, frame, border', this etymon is parallel to → bīn$_2$ 濱.

fén$_6$ 鼖 → **fén$_4$** 墳

fén₇ 蕡 → **fén₄** 墳

fén₈ 豶 → **fén₄** 墳

fén₉ 濆 → **fén₄** 墳

fěn 粉 (pjuən^B) **LH** pun^B, **OCM** *pənʔ
'Peeled (rice)' [Shu], 'flour' [Li].
[E] There are several possible etymologies (see → fēn₂ 雰氛 for additional considerations): (1) ST *pul: TB-PKiranti *pʰùl* 'flour', WB *pʰun* 'dust' etc., see → fēn₂ 雰氛 item (6). — (2) Haudricourt / Strecker (*TP* 77, 1991: 339) believe that the CH word is a loan from PMY *mpan^B 'flour'; Sagart (ICSTLL 1994: 7) argues the opposite. Both in MY and CH 'flour' and → fēn₂ 雰氛 'mist, hoarfrost' may be cognate.

fèn₁ 扮 (bjuən(^B) 'grasp, join hands' → **fèng₁** 奉

fèn₂ 秎 (bjuən^C) **LH** bun^C, **OCM** *bəns
'Cut grain put in sheaves' [Guan] is perh. a ST word: Lushai *pɔɔl^H* 'straw'.

fèn₃ 糞 (pjuən^C) **LH** pun^C, **OCM** *pəns — **[D]** PMin *piun^C
'Dung, manure' [Zuo].
[T] *Sin Sukchu SR* vun (去), *PR*, *LR* vən; *MGZY* H(w)un (去) [vun ?]
[E] ST: WT *brun* 'dung, excrement' (*HST:* 68), Mru *prün* 'manure, filth' (Löffler 1966: 144).

fèn₄ 奮 (pjuən^C) **LH** pun^C, **OCM** *pəns
'Start up, rush up, exert' [Shi, Shu] could be related to either → fén₄ 墳 (< 'swell') or to → fèn₄ 奮 'fly up'.

fèn₅ 奮 → **fēn₆** 翂

fèn₆ 憤 → **fén₄** 墳

fēng₁ 丰 → **péng₄** 蓬

fēng₂ 封 (pjwoŋ) **LH** puoŋ, **OCM** *poŋ
'Mound, tumulus, raise a mound' [Yi], 'altar' [Shu], 'earth up (a plant)' [Guoyu], 'wall, bank of field' [Zuo], 'boundary embankment, fief' [BI, Shi].
[D] M-Xiàmén lit. *hoŋ^A1*, col. *paŋ^A1*
[E] Area etymon: WT *pʰuŋ-po* 'heap' ⋈ *spuŋ* 'a heap', *spuŋ-pa* 'to heap' (*HST:* 110); Lepcha *a-pŭŋ* [apəŋ], Rawang *póŋ* 'heap' [Bodman ICSTLL 1987: 11]. Lushai *puŋ^H* / *pun^L* 'increase, assemble' ⋈ *vuuŋ^H* / *vuun^L* 'to swell, swollen' ⋈ *vuuŋ^R* 'a heap, a mound'; NNaga *puːŋ basically means 'swelling' > 'breast, flower' [French 1983: 490]; Chepang *bʰuŋh-* 'be burst or peak in activity (flowering, sleep soundly...)'. <> AA-Khmer *boṅa* /póoŋ/ 'knobby protuberance on either side of elephant's head' ⋈ *saṃboṅa* /sɑmpóoŋ/ 'be swollen'. → bāng₁ 邦 'country' may be the same etymon. For wider relations see §2.5.1.

fēng₃ 犎 (pjwoŋ) **LH** puoŋ, **OCM** *poŋ
'Kind of wild humped bovine' [GY].
[E] ST: WT *'broŋ* 'wild yak' (Boodberg 1937: 359), WB *proŋ* 'buffalo'. Alternatively, Eberhard (1968: 59) thinks that this and similar words, incl. → fēng₂ 封, are all related and fundamentally mean 'hump'.

fēng$_4$ 鋒蜂 (pʰjwoŋ) **LH** pʰuoŋ, **OCM** *phoŋ
'Sharp point (of weapon, insect)' 鋒 [Shi] > 'bee, wasp' [Guanzi, SW] > 'wasp-stung' 蜂 [Shi]. Perh. → fēng$_5$ 峰 is the s. w.
[T] *Sin Sukchu SR* fuŋ (平); *MGZY* hwung (平) [fuŋ]
[D] M-Xiàmén lit. *hoŋ^{A1}*, col. pʰɑŋ^{A1} 蜂
[E] ST: WT *buŋ-ba* 'bee' (*HST:* 40).

⋈ **féng** 縫 (bjwoŋ) **LH** buoŋ, **OCM** *boŋ
'To sew' [Shi].
[T] *Sin Sukchu SR* vuŋ (平); *MGZY* Hwung (平) [vuŋ]; *ONW* buoŋ
[D] M-Xiàmén lit. *hoŋ^{A2}*, col. *paŋ^{A2}*

⋈ **fèng** 縫 (bjwoŋ^C) **LH** buoŋ^C, **OCM** *boŋh
'A seam' [Shi].
[D] M-Xiàmén lit. *hoŋ^{C2}*, col. *pʰaŋ^{C2}*
[<] exopass. of *féng*, lit. 'what is sewn' (§4.4).

fēng$_5$ 峰 (pʰjwoŋ) **LH** pʰuoŋ, **OCM** *phoŋ
'Mountain peak' 峰 [SW] may be the s. w. as → fēng$_4$ 鋒蜂 'sharp point', but AA-Khmer /kpuŋ/ 'summit, peak' which, if not a CH loan, suggests a separate MK origin.

fēng$_6$ 豐 (pʰjuŋ) **LH** pʰuŋ, **OCM** *phuŋ
'Be abundant' [Shi]. For wider relations see §2.5.1.

fēng$_7$ 風 (pjuŋ) **LH** puəm, **OCM** *pəm, OCB *p(r)jə/um
'Wind, air, tune' [Shi]. Dèng Xiǎo-huā 鄧曉花 (*YYWZX* 1994.9: 142) suggests that the word *fēi-lián* 飛廉, glossed 疾風 'ill wind' in *Shǐjì*, is actually a dialect variant of *fēng*.
[T] *Sin Sukchu SR* fuŋ (平); *MGZY* hwung (平) [fuŋ]; *MTang* pfuŋ, *ONW* puŋ
[D] PMin *piɔŋ

⋈ **fèng** 諷 (pjuŋ^C) **LH** puəm^C **OCM** *pəms
'To chant, recite' [Zhouli].
[<] exoactive of *fēng* 風 (§4.3).

⋈ **féng** 渢 (bjuŋ) **LH** buəm, **OCM** *pəm
'Easy-flowing' (sound) [Zuo].
[<] endopass. of *fēng* 風 (§4.6).

[E] 'Wind' *fēng* is thought to be connected with Tai: S. *lom^{A2}* < *dluom^{A2} 'wind', PKS *hlwum[1] (Benedict 1976: 99); a 12th cent. Korean word for 'wind' is read *pallam* (Zhāng Xīngyà *YWYJ* 1996.4: 9) which also suggests a possible medial *l in a proto-form. The AA-Wa-Lawa-Bulang word *p-hom 'air' is closer to OC, but may be a loan. TB languages have a word with final velar as in MC: KN *m-puŋ 'air, wind' [*IST*: 27]. → fān$_2$ 帆 'sail' is prob. cognate.

fēng$_8$ 楓 (pjuŋ) **LH** puəm, **OCM** *pəm — **[D]** PMin *pĭɔŋ
'A kind of maple, *Liquidambar formosana*' [Chuci].

féng$_1$ 逢夆 (bjwoŋ) **LH** buoŋ, **OCM** *boŋ — **[T]** *ONW* buoŋ
'To meet with (calamities etc.)' (< 'be hit by'?); 'knock against' 夆 [SW] (also QYS *pʰjwoŋ*). A Mandarin colloquial variant is prob. → pèng 碰.

féng$_2$ 逢摓 (bjwoŋ) **LH** buoŋ, **OCM** *boŋ — **[T]** *ONW* buoŋ
'Great' (of descendants) 逢 [Shi], 摓 [Zhuang]. For wider relations see §2.5.1.

féng$_3$ 縫 → **fēng**$_4$ 鋒蜂

féng$_4$ 渢 → **fēng**$_7$ 風

fèng$_1$ 奉 (bjwoŋ^B, p^{h}jwoŋ^B) **LH** buoŋ^B, p^{h}uoŋ^B, **OCM** *boŋʔ, phoŋʔ < PCH *-uŋ.
'To hold in two hands, hold up, present' [Shi], 'receive' [Shi, Zuo]; 'grasp with both hands' (MC *p^{h}jwoŋ^B* only) 捀 [Zhuang]. Downer (1959: 284) reads 'to present' [Zuo] in tone C which agrees with its exoactive / ditransitive function (§4.3), 'receive' tone B agrees with the endoactive function.
[T] *Sin Sukchu SR* fuŋ (上), *LR* vuŋ; *MGZY* Hwung (上) [vuŋ]; *ONW* buoŋ
[D] MXiàmén (lit.) *hoŋ^{C2}*

× **fèng** 俸 (bjwoŋ^C) **LH** buoŋ^C, **OCM** *boŋh
(What is received:) 'salary' [Guoce].
[<] exopass. of *fèng* 奉 (§4.4).

[E] Bodman (1980: 165) compares this to WT *'broŋ* 'wait upon, serve'; alternatively, note Chepang *puŋ* n. 'present'. A possible variant may be *fèn$_1$* 扮 (bjuən[B]) 'grasp, join hands' [Guoce].

fèng$_2$ 諷 → **fēng**$_7$ 風

fèng$_3$ 鳳 (bjuŋ^C) **LH** puəm^C, **OCM** *pəms — **[D]** M-Xiàmén (lit.) *hoŋ^{C2}*
'Phoenix' 鳳凰 [Shi].
[E] This word has been related to → fēng$_7$ 風 'wind', and by Wáng Lì (1982: 318) to péng 鵬 (bəŋ) 'a fabulous great bird, roc' [Zhuang].

fǒu$_1$ 不 (pjəu^B) **LH** pu^B, **OCM** *pəʔ
'To soar' [Lü, SW] is a late word (Lü ca. 239 BC), but the original OB graph has been interpreted as a soaring bird (so *SW*; Karlgren *GSR* no. 999a) in which case the word would be very old. *Fǒu* is perh. cognate to → fēn$_6$ 翂 'to soar'. WT semantics suggest possible cognation with **pī** (p^{h}jɨ), LH p^{h}ɨə, *phrə ? 'grand' [BI].
[E] ST: WT *'p^{h}ag-pa* 'to rise, raise, soar up' (to heaven) > 'exalted, distinguished' (for the final consonants, see §3.2.2).

fǒu$_2$ 否 → **bù**$_1$ 不

(**fu**$_1$) □ A Min dial word for 'scum, froth'.
Fúzhōu *p^{h}uoʔ^8*, Fúān *p^{h}ut^{D2}*, Amoy *p^{h}eʔ^{D2}*, is from a MK substrate: Viet. *bọt* 'scum, bubbles, froth' (Norman / Mei 1976: 298). There may also be a connection with TB-Lushai *p^{h}uul^H* 'scum, foam'.

fū$_2$ 夫 (pju) **LH** puɑ, **OCM** *pa
'Man, husband'; suffix for men of various occupations, e.g. *nóng-fū* 農夫 'farmer, farm laborer' (to be distinguished from *nóng-fù* 農父 'minister of agriculture', see → fù$_1$ 父); measure word for ordinary and low ranking people [BI, Shi].
[T] *Sin Sukchu SR* fu (平); *MGZY* Hwu (平) [fu]; *MTang* pfu < pfuo, *ONW* puo
[E] ST: PTB *pa (*STC:* 174 n. 463: *(p)wa; Matisoff *LL* 1.2, 2000: 153ff) > WT suffix *-pa* for nouns, especially male concepts as opposed to female ones. JP *wa^{33}* 'man' (male), 'male', Lushai *paa^L* 'male person'. This word prob. belongs to the same root as → fù$_1$ 父 'father' (so Matisoff op. cit.).

fū$_3$ 鈇 → **fǔ**$_1$ 斧

fū$_4$ 尃敷鋪 → **bù**$_3$ 布

fū$_5$ 柎 → **fú**$_{16}$ 浮

fú$_1$ 夫 (bju) **LH** bua (or pua ?), **OCM** *ba or *pa ?

'That' [Shi, Zuo]. Pulleyblank (1995: 165) suggests that the earlier initial might have been *p- since *bǐ* 彼 is derived from *fú*; the reading *fú* OC *ba 'introductory particle' (Graham *BSOAS* 35, 1: 85–110) may have been applied to the rare word *fú* 'that'.

[E] ST: PL *m-ba¹, WT *pʰa* 'beyond, onward' (*HST:* 147).

ꕤ **bǐ** 彼 (pje^B 3) **LH** pɨai^B, **OCM** *paiʔ < *paʔi (i.e. pa+i) ?

'There, that' [Shi], independent form (§3.3.3).

[T] *Sin Sukchu SR* pi (上); *MGZY* bue (上) [puɛ]; *ONW* pe

fú$_2$ 扶 (bju) **LH** bua, **OCM** *ba — **[T]** *MTang* bvu < bvuo, *ONW* buo — **[D]** PMin *bʰio.

'To support, assist' [Lunyu].

ꕤ **fù** 傅 (pju^C) **LH** pua^C, **OCM** *pah

'Assistant' [Shi]; 'teacher, instruct' [Zuo].

ꕤ **fù** 賻 (bju^C) **LH** bua^C, **OCM** *bah

'Money contribution to the cost of burying' [Zuo] (Wáng Lì 1982: 175).

ꕤ **fǔ** 輔 (bju^B) **LH** bua^B, **OCM** *baʔ

'To help, support' [Shi] > 'poles on the outside of car wheels for stabilization' [Shi] > 'bones of upper jaw, cheeks' [Yi].

[E] Perh. AA: OKhmer *vnāk* /βnak/ 'support, prop, stay, agent, official'. <> Tai: S. *pʰaa^{A2}* < *b- 'to take along' (Li F. 1976: 41). Perh. cognate to → bǔ$_2$ 補.

fú$_3$ 扶 (pju) **LH** pua, **OCM** *pa

'Breadth of four fingers' [Li].

[E] ST: PTB *pa (*STC:* 174 n. 463 *pwa) > Nung *ur-pʰa* 'palm of hand', WB *bʰa-wa^B* ~ *pʰa-wa^B* 'palm, sole'. <> Occurs also in PKS *pʰwa^C 'palm' of hand (*HST:* 115). <> Note also PAA *palaj 'palm of hand': PMK *pla[ai]k. Given its TB cognates, it is prob. not related to → bǎ 把 'a handful'.

fú$_4$ 伏服 (bjuk) **LH** buk, **OCM** *bək, OCB *bjək

'To lie down, put down, suppress' 伏 [Shi]; 'to submit' 服 [BI, Shi, Shu].

[T] *Sin Sukchu SR* vu (入); *MGZY* hwu (入) [vu]; *MTang* bvuk, *ONW* buk

[E] ST: TB-Lushai *bɔk^L* / *bɔʔ^L* 'to lie down, recline' (as animals, or on stomach like animals or humans).

ꕤ **fù** 伏 (bjəu^C) **LH** bu^C, **OCM** *bəkh

'To hatch' [Li] is an allofam of *fú* (so Karlgren 1956: 12). It is still current in Mǐn: Fúzhōu *pou^{C2}*, Xiàmén *pu^{C2}*. This word has several variants: *fú* 孚桴 (pʰju) [pʰuo] *pho 'to hatch' [Dadai Liji]; *bào* 菢 (bâu^C) [GY]. The word also occurs Tai: S. *vak^{D2}* 'to hatch' (Manomaivibool 1975: 129).

[<] exoactive / transitive of *fú* 伏服 (bjuk) (§4.3).

[E] ST: Chepang *bhyuk-sa* 'to hatch'.

[C] Possible allofams: → fù$_{14}$ 蝮 'snake', → bó$_{10}$ 踣 'prostrate', perh. also → pá$_2$ 爬 'crawl'.

fú$_5$ 芾 → **fú**$_{14}$ 韍芾

fú$_6$ 符 → **fù**$_3$ 付

fú$_7$ 弗 'not' → **bù**$_1$ 不

fú$_8$ 弗 (pjuət) **LH** put, **OCM** *pət, OCB *pjut

'Gust of wind' [Shi].

[E] A sound-symbolic area word: ST: WT *'bud-pa, bus* 'to blow' intr. ꕤ *'bud-pa, pʰus, dbu* 'to blow' tr. ꕤ *bud* 'cloud of dust' ꕤ *sbud-pa* 'bellows'. <> PMK *puut 'to blow'

(Shorto 1976: 102). The Tai word S. p^hat^{D2} (PT *b-) may be a CH loan because of the vowel (from CH *ə). Many TB languages have initial *m-* in words for 'blow' as WB *hmut* 'blow with the mouth'; but these items seem to be unrelated and derived from 'mouth', see → wěn$_1$ 吻. *CVST* 1: 8 adds words for 'dust' which may be related to the WT etyma: WB *p^hut* 'dust', Lushai p^hut^L 'flowery, powdery'.

fú$_9$ 拂 (pʰjuət) **LH** pʰut, **OCM** *phət
'To brush off, shake off' [Li, Zuo]. CH aspiration is associated with forceful motion §5.8.5.
[E] The etymology is not certain: (1) *fú* may be an area word: PYao *pʰwot 'sweep, clear away'. It is not clear if and how these are related to Tai: S. $pat^{D1}S$ < *p- 'to wipe off, brush off' (Li F. 1976: 43); PKS *phjit[7] (i?) 'to sweep'; IN *pat'pat'* 'to shake, clear' (Benedict AT: 403). <> AA-Wa-Lawa-Bulang *(n)-pʰɔs 'to brush off' comes closest to OC semantically and phonologically. (2) It could be related to → fú$_{10}$ 茀 'eliminate'. (3) It could be a ST item from a root *prut 'to brush'; OC *phut could theoretically derive from earlier *sprut (aspiration from loss of causative *s, medial r hardly ever occurs after aspirated initials), see Table S-2 under → shuā 刷 for an overview. Finally, this word may be connected with → bǐ$_6$ 筆 'writing brush'.

fú$_{10}$ 茀 (pjuət) **LH** put, **OCM** *pət
'To eliminate, clear away' (dense vegetation) [Shi].
[E] ? ST: WT *'bud-pa, p^hud, dbud* 'remove' (clothing), 'take away, tear out' ≍ *p^hud-pa* 'lay aside, put away' (*HST:* 123); Lushai p^huul^L 'be denuded of forest, open tract of country', but the final consonants differ.

fú$_{11}$ 茀 (pjuət) **LH** put, **OCM** *pət
'Screen, cover' for a chariot [Shi]. This may be the s. w. as → fú$_{14}$ 韍芾 'apron, knee cover'.

fú$_{12}$ 茀 → **fú$_{15}$** 黻芾

fú$_{13}$ 沸 (pjuət) **LH** put, **OCM** *pət — **[T]** *ONW* put
'Be gushing, rushing' (as spring, water, wind) [Shi].
[E] ST: PTB *brup ~ *prup (*STC* no. 151) 'to gush forth': WT *'brup-pa* 'cause to overflow, gush, spout forth' (Bodman 1985: 150), JP $'p^hrup^{31}$ 'to squirt' (as water from mouth). It is not clear if and how the following may be related: Kachin *bɔp* 'foam, froth' (= swelling water), Rawang (Nung) *thi bɔp* 'bubble' (*thi* 'water') (*STC:* 20 n. 72). Matisoff links this etymon to TB words for 'calf of leg' etc. For the difference in final consonants, see §6.7.

This word may be related to → fèi$_4$ 沸 'bubble up' (Bodman 1985: 150), but the final consonants of the respective TB cognates differ (-p vs. -t).

fú$_{14}$ 韍芾 (pjuət) **LH** put, **OCM** *pət < *put
'Ceremonial apron' as knee cover, 'knee cover' 芾 [Shi], 韍 [Li].
~ **bì** 韠 (pjiet 4) **LH** pit, **OCM** *pit
'Ceremonial apron' as knee cover, 'knee cover' [Shi].
[E] ST: PTB *put > WT *pus-mo ~ pis-mo* 'knee' (*STC:* 181; *HPTB:* 368), Purik *puksmo*, Amdo *pig-mo < PTib *pu(t)s-mo ~ *puks-mo (from *puts ?), *pi(t)s-mo (Beyer 1992: 33); Nung *p^haŋ-p^hit* 'knee', *ur-p^hut* 'elbow'; JP p^hut^{31} 'to kneel', $lə^{31}$-p^hut^{31} 'knee'. Bodman (1980: 116) connects the CH word to WT *p^hub* 'shield'.

The basic meaning could be 'vertical cover' (> 'screen, knee cover, knee'), then the word would be the same etymon as → fú$_{11}$ 茀 'screen, cover' and perhaps → fú$_{15}$ 黻茀 'emblem-adorned'. Perh. also related to → bìn$_3$ 髕臏 'kneecap'.

Partial syn. are → bì$_{22}$ 髀 'thighbone'; not related to → féi$_2$ 腓 'calf of leg'.

fú$_{15}$ 黻茀 (pjuət) **LH** put, **OCM** *pət

'Emblem-adorned' 黻 [Shi]; 'head ornament' 茀 [Yi] is either cognate to WT *spud-pa* 'to decorate' ⋇ *spus* 'goodness, beauty'; or it may be the s. w. as → fú$_{14}$ 韍芾 'apron, knee cover' and → fú$_{11}$ 茀 'screen, cover'.

fú$_{16}$ 浮 (bjəu) **LH** bu, **OCM** *bu, OCB *b(r)ju

'To float' [Shi].

[T] *Sin Sukchu SR* vəw (平); *MGZY* Hwow (平) [vɔw]; *MTang* bvu, *ONW* bu

[D] M-Xiàmén, Fúzhōu p^hu^{A2}

[E] Acc. to Norman (1986: 382) the Northern Mǐn 'softened initial' *b̯- points to OC prenasalization which is supported by Yao *bjou*^{2} < *nb-.

⋇ **fú** 桴泭 (p^hju) **LH** p^huo, **OCM** *pho

'Small bamboo raft' 桴 [Lunyu, GY], 泭 [Guoyu] (Mand. *fū*).

~ **fū** 柎 (pju) **LH** puo, **OCM** *po

'A raft' 柎 [Guanzi, FY].

[E] Note Lepcha *să-pó* 'raft', perh. also Lushai *puum*^{L} (Unger; *HST:* 80).

⋇ **fú** 桴 (bju^B, bəu^B) **LH** buo^B, bo^B, **OCM** *boʔ, *bôʔ

'Board on which body lies in coffin' [Zuo]. Languages in the area often associate 'coffin' with 'boat'; both started out in prehistoric times as hollowed trees. A possible allofam is → fá$_5$ 筏.

fú$_{17}$ 蜉 (bjəu) **LH** bu, **OCM** *bu

'Large ant, ephemeria' [Shi].

~ **fú-yóu** 蜉蝣 (bjəu-jiəu) **LH** bu-ju, **OCM** *bu-ju

'Large (winged) ant, ephemeria' [Shi].

~ **pí-fú** 蚍蜉 (bi 4-bjəu) **LH** bi-bu, **OCM** *bi-bu

'Large ant' [GY].

[E] ST: WT *sbur* 'ant' (Unger *Hao-ku* 35, 1986: 33).

fú$_{18}$ 桴 → **fú$_{16}$** 浮

fú$_{19}$ 福 (pjuk) **LH** puk, **OCM** *pək, OCB *pjək

'Benefit, good fortune' [OB, BI, Shi].

[T] *Sin Sukchu SR* fu (入), *PR, LR* fu; *MGZY* Hwu (入) [fu]; *MTang* pfuk, *ONW* puk

⋇ **fù** 富 (pjəu^C) **LH** pu^C, **OCM** *pəkh — [T] *MTang* pfu, *ONW* pu

'Be rich, wealthy' [BI, Shi].

[E] ST: WT *p^{h}yug-pa* 'rich' ⋇ *p^{h}yugs* 'cattle' (Bodman 1980: 49), but the vowels do not agree (§11.10.4). Sagart (1999: 58) considers → bǎo$_3$ 寶 'precious' to be a likely cognate.

fú$_{20}$ 蝠 → **biān$_3$-fú** 蝙蝠

fú$_{21}$ 匐 → **pá$_1$** 爬

fǔ$_1$ 斧 (pju^B) **LH** puɑ^B, **OCM** *paʔ

'Ax' [Shi].

[T] *Sin Sukchu SR* fu (上); *MGZY* Hwu (上) [fu]; *MTang* pfu < pfuo, *ONW* puo

[D] PMin *puo^B

⋇ **fū** 鈇 (pju) **LH** puɑ

'Ax' [Li].

[E] ST: PTB *r-pa > JP $niŋ^{31}$-wa^{33} ~ n^{31}-wa^{33}, $wə^{33}$- 'ax'; Garo *rua* (*STC:* 174 n. 463; n. 78; no. 441; Matisoff *LL* 1.2, 2000: 137).

fǔ$_2$ 府 → **fù**$_3$ 付

fǔ$_3$ 腑 → **fù**$_3$ 付

fǔ$_4$ 腐 (pju^B) **LH** puo^B, **OCM** *poʔ
'Rotten, putrid' [Li] is prob. cognate to Lepcha *por, pór* 'to spoil, smell' (Unger *Hao-ku* 35, 1986: 34).

fǔ$_5$ 甫 (pju^B) **LH** $puɑ^B$, **OCM** *paʔ
An honorific suffix attached to names of high-ranking men, marks also respected persons engaged in a certain activity, e.g. *cóng-fǔ* 從父 (= 甫) 'followers' (of a respected clan) [BI, Shi]. This suffix is written → fù$_1$ 父 in the BI and seems to be a variant or cognate of same. Some TB languages have parallel developments where the cognate PTB *-pa is a nominalizing suffix, e.g. WT *t^ha-ga-pa* (< *tak-a-pa) 'weaver' from *t^hag-pa* 'to weave' [LaPolla, *LTBA* 17.1, 1994: 77].

fǔ$_6$ 甫 → **bù**$_3$ 布

fǔ$_7$ 甫 'begin' →**fāng**$_3$ 方

fǔ$_8$ 輔 → **fú**$_2$ 扶

fǔ$_9$ 膚 (pju) **LH** puɑ, **OCM** *pa
'Human skin' > 'skin' figuratively [Shi].
[E] This word is usually considered cognate to PTB *s-pak > WT *-lpags* 'skin' (Bodman 1980: 132; *HST:* 134), and to Tai-S. *plɨak^{DIL}* < *pl- 'husk, bark' (Li F. 1976: 41), also AA-PSBahn. *pəloːk 'skin'. However, the WT word may instead be related to **pò** 霩 (p^hâk) *phlak 'hide soaked in rain' [SW], which, however, could be just a dictionary word (the *SW* definition looks like a description of the graph, implying that its real etymology and meaning was a matter of speculation for Xǔ Shèn). Note also **luò** 鞈, LH *lak* 'raw skin, hide' [Lü] which may be connected.

fǔ$_{10}$ 撫 (p^hju^B) **LH** $p^huɑ^B$, **OCM** *phaʔ
'To accommodate oneself to, follow, manage, handle' [BI, Shi, Shu], 'lay hands on' [Li], 'pacify, stabilize' [Zuo]. Wáng Lì (1982: 176) relates this wf to → mù$_6$ 慕 'love' (unlikely).
~ **fǔ** 拊 (p^hju^B) **LH** p^huo^B, **OCM** *phoʔ
'Lay hands on, comfort, handle, strike (musical instrument)' [Shi, Shu].
[E] These two nearly identical items were homophones at least by ONW. They are prob. cognates (so Wáng Lì 1982: 176), if not even just phonological or graphical variants of the same word. Perh. an AA substrate word: AA-Wa-Lawa-Bulang *pac 'to caress'.

fù$_1$ 父 (bju^B) **LH** $buɑ^B$, **OCM** *baʔ
'Father, male relative of the father's generation: uncle' [BI, Shi].
[T] *Sin Sukchu SR* fu (上); *MGZY* hwu (上) [vu]; *MTang* bvu < bvuo, *ONW* buo
[N] Mand. *bà-bà* 爸爸 may be the col. version. As suffix *fù* has the same function as → fǔ$_5$ 甫 (prob. cognate), e.g. *nóng-fù* 農父 'minister of agriculture' (to be distinguished from *nóng-fū* 農夫 'farmer, farm laborer', see → fū$_2$ 夫); or the suffix *fù* may simply be intended to write *fǔ*, especially in the BI. → fū$_2$ 夫 may be from the same root.
[E] ST: a common onomatopoetic word 'father': PTB *pa (*STC:* 174 n. 463) > WT *p^ha*, WB *ə-bha^C, ə-pha^C;* JP *w<u>a</u>^{51};* Lushai *pa^F < paaʔ*. <> PTai *b-: S. *p^hɔɔ^{B2}* 'father'.

fù$_2$ 伏 → **fú**$_4$ 伏服

fù$_3$ 付 (pju^C) **LH** puo^C, **OCM** *poh — **[T]** *MTang* pfu < pfuo, *ONW* puo
'To hand over, give' [BI, Shu].
[<] exoactive of *fǔ* 府 (pju^B) 'accumulate' (§4.3).

ж **fǔ** 府 (pju^B) **LH** puo^B, **OCM** *poʔ
'Storehouse' > 'repository' [Zhouli], 'treasury' [Lunyu], 'magazine' 府 [Zuo] > 'the bowels' 腑 [Huainanzi]; 'accumulate' 府 [Shu] (Karlgren 1956: 6). *GY* says 腑 is the s. w. as fǔ 府, Wáng Lì (1982: 200) points to the semantic parallel *zàng* 藏 (dzâŋ^C) 'storehouse' > 臟 'intestines' (under → cáng 藏). However, 腑 may be a separate word, belonging to → fù$_4$ 胕.

ж **fú** 符 (bju) **LH** buo, **OCM** *bo
'A tally' [Zhouli]; Mand. 'symbol, to tally'.
[<] tone A nominalization derived from *fù* 附坿 below (§3.1).

ж **fù** 附坿 (bju^C) **LH** buo^C, **OCM** *boh
'To adjoin, stick to' 附 [Shi]; 'adjoin a dead person in a ceremony' [Zuo], 'bury two together' 祔 [Li]; 'additional horse' 駙 [Hanfei]; 'to add to, increase' 坿 [Lü] > 'lean on' [Yi].
[<] perh. endopass. of *fù* 付 (pju^C) (§4.6).

fù$_4$ 胕 (bju^C) **LH** buo^C, **OCM** *boh
'Intestines' [Han time].
= Perh. **fù** 蚹 (bju^C) **LH** buo^C, **OCM** *boh
'Scales under the stomach of a snake' [Zhuang].
[E] ST and area word: PTB *(s-)pu ж *(s-)bu 'belly, stomach' (Matisoff *LL* 1.2, 2000: 165). On the other hand, this word may belong to → fù$_3$ 付 (note 腑 'bowels'). Perh. related to → fù$_{13}$ 腹.

fù$_5$ 蚹 → **fù**$_4$ 胕

fù$_6$ 附坿祔駙 → **fù**$_3$ 付

fù$_7$ 阜 (bjəu^B) **LH** bu^B, **OCM** *buʔ, OCB *b(r)juʔ — **[T]** *MTang* bvu, *ONW* bu
'Big mound, earthen hill' [Shi]; prob. = 'be big and fat, ample' → fù$_8$ 阜.

~ **pǒu** 培, **bù** 部 (bəu^B) **LH** bo^B, **OCM** *bôʔ
'Hillock' 部 [Zuo]; 'mound' 培 [Guoyu]. In the Han period, *pǒu* was a dialect word for → fén$_4$ 墳 in the Qín-Jìn area [FY 13, 154].
[E] <> Tai: PTai *bu̯o^{A2}, Po'ai *poo^{A1}* < *p- 'mountain'.

ж **bù-lóu** 部婁 (bəu^B-ləu^B) **LH** bo^B-lo^B
'Small hill' [Zuo]; JP *po^{55}-lo^{55}* 'small hill' looks like a CH loan.

~ **fù-lóu** 附婁 (bju^C-ləu^B) **LH** buo^C-lo^B [SW].
The MC initial *l-* in the binomes above introduces reduplicative syllables and therefore does not necessarily indicate an OC initial consonant cluster.

[E] Prob. the same etymon as → fù$_8$ 阜. For wider relations see §2.5.1. This group prob. does not belong to the wf. → bèi$_4$ 倍 'double' (so Wáng Lì 1982: 103), although in a AA-Khmer parallel, the notion 'swelling mass, heap, mound, add on' are expressed by the same stem /bòok/ 'swelling mass', *baṃnūka* /pumnuuk/ 'heap, pile, stack, rick' < *-būka* /-puuk/ 'mass, mound, group'. AA -> TB-Lepcha *bok* 'to heap up' (Forrest *JAOS* 82, 1962: 334); Proto-Koch *bok 'to swell' [Burling 1959: 444].

If not connected with → fù$_8$ 阜, then perh. cognate to AA: PSBahn. *buəj 'hilltop'. For CH tone B for foreign -k, see §3.2.2.

fù$_8$ 阜 (bjəu^B) **LH** bu^B, **OCM** *buʔ, OCB *b(r)juʔ
'Be big and fat, ample' [Shi], prob. = fù$_7$ 阜 'big mound'.

ꕢ **pēi** 垺 (p^{h}ju, p^{h}jəu, p^{h}uậi) **LH** p^{h}io, p^{h}u, p^{h}ə, **OCM** *pho, *phu, *phə̂ ?
'Large', abstract as in 'largest thing possible' [Zhuang].

[E] ST: WB *p^{h}u^C* 'to swell' ꕢ *pu* 'to bulge', WT *'bo-ba, 'bos* 'to swell (up), rise, sprout', perh. also JP *pu^{55}* 'to bloom, bud', WT *'bu-ba, 'bus* 'to open, unfold' (flower) (*CVST* 1: 88). Also, note AA-Khmer *pora* /baaor/ 'to swell up, rise, bulge'; or PMK *pooʔ 'to swell' (Shorto 1976: 1063). Prob. the same etymon as → fù$_7$ 阜. For wider relations see §2.5.1.

fù$_9$ 婦 (bjəu^B) **LH** bu^B < buə^B, **OCM** *bəʔ, OCB *bjəʔ
'Woman, wife' [OB, BI, Shi].
[T] *Sin Sukchu SR* vu (去), vẅ (上), *LR* vu (去); *MGZY* Hwow (上) [vɔw]; *MTang* bvu, *ONW* bu
[D] M-Xiàmén *pu^{C2}*. Acc. to Norman (1986: 382) the Northen Mǐn 'softened initial' *b̬- points to OC prenasalization which is supported by Yao *bwaaŋ^4* < *nb- 'daughter-in-law'.
[E] Two outside connections are possible: (1) Tai *baa^A 'wife', Tianbao *paa^{A2}* < *b- which acc. to Li (HCT: 66) is a northern Tai word (hence a CH loan?). (2) Alternatively, traceable back to AA: Kharia *bui* 'girl', Munda *bui* 'vocative of address to little girls', Mon *mbuiy* 'female onomastic prefix', note also Aslian forms (Malay Penins.) like *mabɛh, baboʔ* etc. 'woman'. For the lack of final -j in CH, see §6.9.

fù$_{10}$ 賦 (pju^C) **LH** puɑ^C, **OCM** *pah
'To give, contribute > contributions, taxes' [BI, Shi, Shu] has been compared to WT *dpya* 'tax, duty, tribute'.

fù$_{11}$ 負 (bjəu^B) **LH** bu^B < buə^B, **OCM** *bəʔ, OCB *ɦpjə(k)ʔ — **[T]** *MTang* bvu, *ONW* bu
'To carry on the back, support' [BI, Shi].
[E] The OC and TB words cited in this wf belong to a well-established MK wf (Shorto 1972) and are encountered widely in the area: PMK *tɓaʔ: Bahn. *bʌʔ, Katuic *baʔ* 'carry (on the back)'; PPal. *bɔ, Khmu *bɔʔ*, PWa *bɔʔ 'carry child on back' (Shorto 1972). MK -> ST *bə, PTB *ba (*HPTB:* 24): WT *'ba-ba* 'to bring, carry'. MK -> TB-NNaga *baʔ > *ba^B 'carry on the back', Nung *ba* 'carry' (on shoulder). MK -> PTai *baa^A: S. *p^{h}aa^{A2}*.
Even though the OC vowel / rime was clearly *-ə (not *-u), *fù* could also, or instead, be connected with a synonymous etymon *bu or *bwə, because after labials earlier *u and *ə may have merged on occasion in OC (§11.10.4), unless the above TB items belong to → bǎo$_1$ 保 instead. PTB *buw or *bəw 'carry on back or shoulder' (*STC* no. 28; p. 22; *HPTB:* 199; *HST:* 52; Weidert 1987: 138) > Chepang *buy-* 'carry on back' ꕢ *bus-* 'carry on back'; Mikir, Meitei *pu*; Lepcha *bŭ* 'bear, carry, burden, load'; PLB *buw^2 [Matisoff *D. of Lahu:* 827] > WB *pui^B* 'bear on the back', Lushai *pua / pɔ / puak* (tone?) 'carry on the back' (as a child) , prob. also Lushai *pu^H / put^L* 'carry on the shoulder', *p^{h}ur^H* 'carry a load on the back, to bear'; Lepcha *buk* 'back, wrong side'.

ꕢ **bèi** 背 (buậi^C) **LH** bə^C, **OCM** *bə̂kh (or *bə̂ʔh ?) — **[T]** *ONW* bɑi
(1) 'To carry on the back' [post-Han] (Baxter 1992: 182).
(2) 'Turn the back to / on' [Shi], 偝 [Li]; 'turn the back on, obstinate' 倍 [Li].
[<] endopass. of *bèi* 背 [pəh] (§4.6).

[E] Northern PMK *tɓaʔ-s (Shorto 1972): Palaung *bər* 'to carry on tumpline', Riang-Lang ˥*bəs* 'carry on the head'.

ʂ **bèi** 背 (puậi^C^) **LH** pə^C^, **OCM** *pə̂kh
'The back' [Shi 300,4], 'back quarters' [Shi 62, 4].
[T] *Sin S. SR* puj (去); *PR* pəj; *LR* pəj; *MGZY* bue (去) [puɛ]
[<] exopass. of *běi* 北 [pək], lit. 'what is turned back' (§4.4).

ʂ **běi** 北 (pək) **LH** pək, **OCM** *pə̂k
'Turn the back to, retreat' [Zuo] > 'north' [BI, Shi] (what the back is turned to when facing south').
[T] *Sin S. SR* pəj (入), *LR* pəʔ; *MGZY* bue (入) [puɛ]; *ONW* pək
[E] PMK *[d]ɓak: Mon *həbɛk* 'wear around neck', et al.; Khmer *pèək* 'to put on, wear, hang up, bestride', Khmu *bak* 'to mount, ride, bestride', Viet. *vác* 'carry over the shoulder'. <> PTB *bak (*STC* no. 26) > JP *baʔ^31^ (< bak)* 'carry' (child on back).

fù$_{12}$ 復 (bjuk) **LH** buk, **OCM** *buk, OCB *b(r)juk
'To come back, return, restore' [BI, Shi], 'reply' [Zuo], 'report' [Lunyu].
[T] *Sin Sukchu SR* vu (入); *MGZY* hwu (入) [vu]; *MTang* bvuk, *ONW* buk

ʂ **fù** 復 (bjəu^C^) **LH** bu^C^, **OCM** *bukh
'Repeatedly, again' [BI, Shi], 'to repeat' [Meng], 'again' [Lunyu] is an adverbial derivation (Downer 1959: 289) (§3.5).

ʂ **fù** 複 (pjuk) **LH** puk, **OCM** *puk
'Double, lined' (garment) [Li].

ʂ **fù** 覆 (p^h^juk) **LH** p^h^uk, **OCM** *phuk
'To overturn, violate, ruin' [Shi], 'repeatedly' [Meng], 'overthrow' [Zuo] > 'on the contrary' [Shi].
[<] an aspiration causative / iterative form of *puk 'double', hence lit. 'make something double over' (§5.8.2–3).
[E] ST: WT *spub-pa* (pf. *spubs*) 'to turn over' (on the labial final, see §6.7).

ʂ **fù** 覆 (p^h^jəu^C^) **LH** p^h^u^C^, **OCM** *phukh — [T] *MTang* pfu, *ONW* p^h^u
'Overspread, cover' (as birds do to protect someone) [Shi], 'protect' [Shu]
[<] exoactive of *fù* 覆 (p^h^juk) (§4.3).

[E] ST: PTB *m-pup 'turn over, search for [*HPTB:* 369], WT *'bubs* 'put on a roof'; PL *pup 'turn over, search for' [Matisoff *TSR:* 32]. Perh. PLB *ʔpok 'time, occasion' is connected. For the difference in TB and CH finals, see §6.7. Probable allofam → bào$_2$ 報.

fù$_{13}$ 腹 (pjuk) **LH** puk, **OCM** *puk — [D] PMin *pok.
'Cave' 復 [SW], 'belly' 腹 [BI, Shi].
[E] ST: PTB *pu:k ~ *buk [*STC* no. 358] > WT *p^h^ug-pa* 'cavern' ʂ *p^h^ug(s)* 'innermost part' ʂ *bug-pa* 'hole' ʂ *sbug(s)* 'hollow, cavity' ʂ *p^h^ig-pa* 'make a hole'; Garo *bi-bik* 'bowels'; Lushai *puuk^F^* 'cave'; Ao Naga *tapok* 'cave' ʂ *tepok* 'belly'; WB *wam^B^-puik* 'outside of belly' ʂ *puik* 'pregnancy' (Bodman 1980: 177; Matisoff 1978: 124ff; *LL* 1.2, 2000: 164); Proto-Bodo *bi(?)-buk 'guts' [Burling 1959: 441]. A variant is prob. PTB *pik 'cavern / hole > belly > guts': Mikir *p^h^ek* 'bowels', WT *p^h^ig-pa* (~ *p^h^ug-pa*) 'make hole, pierce' [Matisoff *LL* 1.2, 2000: 164f]. Perh. related to → fù$_4$ 胕. This etymon is also found in AA: Khasi *kpoh*; Khmer *boḥ* /póh/ 'cavity, internal organ, stomach'. AA -> TB-Lepcha *bak* 'belly' (Forrest *JAOS* 82, 1962: 333).

fù$_{14}$ 蝮 (p^h^juk) **LH** p^h^uk, **OCM** *phuk
'A kind of snake' [Shanhaijing, Chuci], Guō Pú says fù-huǐ 蝮虫 'a snake with upturned snout'. This may be cognate to → fú$_4$ 伏服 'to lie down, lie on the stomach

(as animals)', as in some cultures the snake is associated with the notion of 'walking on the stomach'. Alternatively, *fù* may be connected to PTB *bu 'insect, snake'.

fù$_{15}$ 縛 (bjwak) **LH** buɑk, **OCM** *bak

'To bind, wrap, roll, bonds' [Zuo]. The MC div. III syllable of this type is unique (labial initial, rime -jak).

[T] *MTang* bvuak, *ONW* buak < bak

[D] PMin *buk > Amoy *bak^{D2}*, Fúzhōu *puoʔ^{D2}*, Jiànyáng *po^{D2}* 'to tie'.

[E] AA: Khmer *pā'ka* /pak/ 'to enlace, entwine, embroider' ⋈ /bɑmnak/ 'enlacing, stitching together'; Mon /pa̤k/, WrMon *buik* 'to put round lower half of the body', Semai /bək/, Temiar /bəg/ 'to bind'. The PMin form is closer to Tai than to MC. Alternatively, note S. *p^{h}uuk^{D1}* < *bl-/br- 'to bind, tie' (Manomaivibool 1975: 128).

The AA semantic range suggests that the following word is prob. related:

⋈ **bó** 薄 礴 (bâk) **LH** bɑk, **OCM** *bâk

'Trees with interlaced branches' 薄 [Chuci], 'trellis' [Liji]; 'sit with legs crossed under body' 礴 [Zhuang].

fù$_{16}$ 傅賻 → **fú$_2$** 扶

fù$_{17}$ 富 → **fú$_{19}$** 福

G

gāi 陔 (kâi) **LH** kə, **OCM** *kə̂
'Steps, stair' [Shi].
[E] ? ST: Perh. the cognate of the TB word for 'stairs, ladder' as represented in WB *hle-ka*^{B} 'stairs, ladder' (*hle* 'ladder'), JP *lə*^{33}-*ka*^{33} 'steps'. WT *skras, skas-ka, skad* 'ladder' may belong either here, or perh. to → jiē$_{3}$ 階 because of the medial *r.

gǎi 改 (kâi^{C}) **LH** kə^{B}, **OCM** *kə̂ʔ < *kləʔ
'To change' [Shi].
[T] *Sin Sukchu SR* kaj (上); *MGZY* gay (上) [kaj]; *ONW* kɑi
[C] Wáng Lì (1982: 81) considers *gǎi* an allofam of → gé$_{1}$ 革 and → gēng$_{1}$ 更.

gài 蓋 → **hé$_{8}$** 盇蓋

gān$_{1}$ 干 (kân) **LH** kɑn, **OCM** *kân — **[T]** *ONW* kɑn
'A shield' [Shi], 'knock against, violate' [Zuo]. → gān$_{2}$ 干 may be the s. w.
ж **hàn** 扞閈 (ɣân^{C}) **LH** gɑn^{C}, **OCM** *gâns
'Protect, guard' [Shu], 'ward off' 扞 [Li]; 'gate' 閈 [BI, Zuo].
[E] ST: WT *'gal-ba* 'to oppose, transgress, violate'; WB *ka* 'a shield, to ward off' (Bodman 1980: 137; *HST:* 157); Lushai *in*^{L}-*kalʔ*^{L} < -*kalʔ/h* 'to withstand, oppose' ж *kalʔ*^{L} 'to withstand, oppose, to cross'. CH -> Tai: S. *kan*^{1} 'to prevent, keep out'. <> Perh. an area etymon, note MK: Khmer /k(a)ar/ 'to defend, protect, guard, to shield, screen'.

gān$_{2}$ 干 (kân) **LH** kɑn, **OCM** *kân
'Riverbank' [Shi].
[E] The etymology is not certain. The graph might simply have stood for the word → àn$_{2}$ 岸 'river bank'. Or *gān* may be a variant of → kǎn$_{6}$ 顑 with aberrant final. Finally, it could be the same word as → gān$_{1}$ 干 in the sense that a bank is a protection against the water; a semantic parallel is found in the wf → yà$_{2}$ 御迓訝.

gān$_{3}$ 干 'pole' → **gān$_{4}$** 竿

gān$_{4}$ 竿 (kân) **LH** kɑn, **OCM** *kân
'A bamboo pole, rod' (for fishing etc.) 竿 [Shi], 'flag pole' (of slender bamboo) 干 [Shi]; 'bamboo slip' (for writing) 竿 [Zhuang]. This is apparently not a carrying pole, cf. → hè$_{1}$ 何荷.
ж **gǎn** 簳 (kân^{B}) **LH** kɑn^{B}, **OCM** *kânʔ
'Slender bamboo' [Lie]; 'straw of grain' 稈 [Zuo]; 'shaft of arrow' 笴 [Zhouli].
[E] <> Perh. PMY *nqaan^{2A} 'thatch grass'; Tai: S. *kan*^{5} 'twig, stem, stalk'.
~ **gě** 笴 (kâ^{B}, kân^{B}) **LH** kɑi^{B}, kɑn^{B}, **OCM** *kâiʔ, *kânʔ
'Shaft of an arrow' [Zhouli].
ж **gè** 箇個 (kâ^{C}) **LH** kɑi^{C}, **OCM** *kâih
'Bamboo stalk' > 'piece, item' [Xun] > classifier for every category of noun (Norman 1988: 115).
[T] *Sin Sukchu SR* kɔ (去), *LR* kɔ; *MGZY* go (去) [kɔ]; *ONW* kɑ
[D] Y-Táishān *kuɔi*^{C1}, Kāipíng *kuai*^{C1}; K-Méixiàn ^{55}*kɛ*^{C}; PMin *kɑi^{C}
[N] Contrary to what the phonetic suggests, the OC rime was *-ai, not *-a; perh. the graph became convention by the time OC *kai had become *kâ* in some dialect.

[E] <> PTai *kai^{B1}: Lóngzhōu *kaai^{B1}* 'noun classifier, piece', Saek *k^{h}al^4* (< *gal^A*) > *k^{h}an^4* 'classifier for spoons, pencils, saws'. It also has been borrowed by Korean from an OC stratum (prob. Han): New Korean *kay* (Miyake 1997: 186); Sino-Jap. *ka* is from MC.

ⅹ **gān** 干 (kân) **LH** kan, **OCM** *kân — [T] *ONW* kan
'Piece, item' [Li].

[E] Perh. ST: WT *mk^{h}ar-ba* ~ *'k^{h}ar-ba* (< *m-kar* ~ *N-kar*) 'staff, stick' (*HST:* 141), but the semantics are ambiguous, and OC *-i for foreign *-r is rare (§7.7.4).

gān$_5$ 肝 (kân) **LH** kan, **OCM** *kân — [D] PMin *kan^{A1}
'Liver' [Li]

[E] Etymology not certain. Perh. derivation from → kǔ 苦 'bitter', semantically parallel to → xīn$_2$ 辛 (*STC:* 158 n. 428), note TB: Garo *bi-ka* 'liver'; however, a liver is not noted for being unusually bitter. On the other hand, *gān* may correspond to PTB *m-kal 'kidneys' (*STC* no. 12): WT *mk^{h}al-ma*, Lushai *kal^R* < *kalʔ*, Chepang *gəl*. The TB etymon blends into words for 'lower back' (→ hè$_1$ 何荷).

gān$_6$ 矸 (kân) in *dān-gān* 丹矸 = '丹砂 'vermilion ore', see → dān$_1$ 丹 'vermilion'.

gān$_7$ 甘 (kâm) **LH** kam, **OCM** *kâm < *klam (prob. < *kluam < *klom)
'Be sweet' [Shi]. For the possible medial *-l-, see §8.2.2.

[T] *Sin S. SR* kam (平), *PR* kan; *MGZY* gam (平) [kam]; *ONW* kam

[E] The homophone **gān** 柑 'Mandarin orange' [Hanshu] may be the same etymon (Wáng Lì 1982: 623), but because of its southern origin, 'orange' may instead be connected with AA, note PNB *qŋam 'sweet'.

ⅹ **hān** 酣 (ɣâm) **LH** gam, **OCM** *gâm < *glam
'Be tipsy, drunk' [Shu]; Mand. 'drink to one's heart's content > fully, heartily'.
[<] endopass. of *gān* 甘 (§4.6).

[E] ST: PTB *klum 'sweet' [*STC:* 75 n. 231]: Lushai *t^{h}lum^H*; Lepcha *a-klyam* < *a-klyim* 'sweet' (Geilich 1994: 262). Possibly connected with → tián$_4$ 甜 *lîm 'sweet' (*-um* ~ *-im* variation (§11.5.1), difference in pre-initials).

gān$_8$ 柑 → **gān$_7$** 甘

gān$_9$ 乾 (kân) **LH** kan, **OCM** *kân
'Dry' (of food; plants dried by drought) [Shi].

[T] *Sin Sukchu SR* kɔn (平), *PR*, *LR* kan; *MGZY* gan (平) [kan]; *ONW* kan

ⅹ **hàn** 旱 (ɣân^B) **LH** gan^B, **OCM** *gânʔ
'Dry, drought' [Shi].

[E] ST *kar or *kan: WB *k^{h}an^B* 'dry up'; JP *kan^{31}* 'solidify, dry up'; Atsi *kʔan* 'dry up' (*STC:* 166 n. 444), perh. also Chepang *garʔ-* 'bask, warm oneself in the sun'. For related and similar items, see under → gù$_1$ 固 (including Table G-1) and → jiān$_2$ 堅 (including Table J-1). Karlgren (1956: 13) relates these items to → qián$_4$ 乾 'heavenly'.

gǎn$_1$ 趕
'Pursue, overtake', a recent word not found in *Guǎngyùn, Jíyùn*, etymology unknown (Norman 1988: 76 n.2).

gǎn$_2$ 稈 → **gān$_4$** 竿

gǎn$_3$ 敢 (kâm^B) **LH** kam^B, **OCM** *kâmʔ (< kwam ?)
'Dare, take the liberty, presume' [BI, Shi].

[T] *Sin Sukchu SR* kam (上), *PR* kan; *MGZY* gam (上) [kam]; *ONW* kam

[E] ST *k-wam: PTB *hwam (*STC* no. 216) 'to dare': Lushai *huam*^{H}, WB *wam*^{C}, JP *wam*^{33} 'dare'; perh. also WT *'gam-pa* 'to try'. TB and OC can be reconciled if we assume an original *kwam > OC *kâm (labial dissimilation, *STC:* 168 n. 449), but ~ *k-wam > PTB *hwam (devoicing of the initial with loss of voiceless pre-initial). If or how Viet. *dám* (< *y-*), Tai: S. *h-yam*^{2} 'dare' [Maspero 1912: 69] are connected is not clear.

gǎn$_{4}$ 感 (kậm^{B}) **LH** kəm^{B}, **OCM** *kə̂mʔ
'To sense, feel, touch' [Shi], 'move' (heart) [Lüshi]. — **[E]** Etymology not clear.
[T] *Sin Sukchu SR* kam (上), *PR* kan; *MGZY* gam (上) [kam]; *ONW* kɑm

gǎn$_{5}$ 笴 → **gān**$_{4}$ 竿

gǎn$_{6}$ 簳 → **gān**$_{4}$ 竿

gàn$_{1}$ 幹 (kân^{C}) **LH** kɑn^{C}, **OCM** *kâns
'Stem, framework, skeleton' [Zuo]; 'posts in a framework' [Shu]; 'support or occupations' (for citizens) [BI, Shu].
[T] *Sin Sukchu SR* kɔn (去), *PR*, *LR* kan; *MGZY* gan (去) [kan]

⋇ **hàn** 翰 (ɣân^{C}) **LH** gɑn^{C}, **OCM** *gân^{A} !, OCB *gans
'To support' (figuratively) [Shi]. OC tone A indicated by *Shījīng* rimes.

[E] Etymology not certain. This stem could be related to → hè$_{1}$ 何荷 'carry', → kē$_{1}$ 柯 'handle', or → gān$_{4}$ 竿 'bamboo rod'.

gàn$_{2}$ 紺 (kậm^{C}) **LH** kəm^{C}, **OCM** *kə̂ms < *kləms
'Purple' [Lun].
[E] Area word: PTai *kləm^{B1} 'dark red, purple, dark, black' [Li 1977: 221–222] (Geilich 1994: 262); PAN *kelam 'dark' [Thurgood 1994: 358]. See → tǎn$_{5}$ 黮 for further items.

gāng$_{1}$ 亢 (kâŋ) **LH** kɑŋ, **OCM** *kâŋ < *klaŋ ?
'Neck' [SW].
[C] Derivations are perh. → xiàng$_{4}$ 項 'neck', → háng$_{3}$ 頏 'stretch the neck'. This word prob. does not belong to → jǐng$_{2}$ 頸 (so Wáng Lì 1982: 321), unless *gāng* is a vocalic variant of the latter.
[E] ? ST: TB-Lolo lgs. 'neck', also of vases etc.: *khàŋ-láŋ* 'neck' (Akha), Lahu *qɔ̄*, WB *k*^{h}*oŋ*^{B} 'head' [Matisoff *D. of Lahu:* 253]. <> PMY *kla:ŋ^{A} 'neck, throat'.

gāng$_{2}$ 岡 (kâŋ) **LH** kɑŋ, **OCM** *kâŋ
'Ridge' [BI, Shi].
[E] ST: PL *kaŋ 'mountain', WB *k*^{h}*aŋ*^{A} 'roof, strip of high ground'; WT *sgaŋ* 'hill, spur' (*HST:* 94), JP *ləkāŋ* 'ridge connecting two hills' [Matisoff 1974: 167], NNaga *C-kooŋ 'hill'. This may be an area word, note AA-PSBahn. *təka:ŋ ~ *rəka:ŋ 'roof beams'.

gāng$_{3}$ 綱 (kâŋ) **LH** kɑŋ, **OCM** *kâŋ
'Guiding rope (of a net)' [Shu].
[T] *Sin Sukchu SR* kaŋ (平); *MGZY* gang (平) [kaŋ]
[E] Etymology not clear. Possibly related to → qiǎng$_{1}$ 繈襁 'string'; or be cognate to → qiáng 強彊 'strong'; not related to → jīng$_{4}$ 經 'pass through'.

gāng$_{4}$ 剛鋼 (kâŋ) **LH** kɑŋ, **OCM** *kâŋ — **[T]** *ONW* kɑŋ
'Hard, firm' 剛 [Shi] > 'steel' 鋼 [Lie].
[<] terminative (§6.5.1) of → gù$_{1}$ 固 *kah, lit. 'having become solid, hard'.

⋇ **qiǎng** 彊 (gjaŋ[B]) **LH** gɨaŋ[B], **OCM** *gaŋ?
'Hard (soil)' [Zhouli].
[E] ST root *ka (→ gù$_1$ 固): WT *gaŋs* 'ice' (terminative: < 'having become hard' of snow, water), Lushai *kʰaŋ*[F] 'congealed, solidified'. For related and similar items, see → gù$_1$ 固 (including Table G-1) and → jiān$_2$ 堅 (including Table J-1). Perh. the wf → qiáng 強彊 'strong' belongs here as well.

gāng$_5$ 犅 (kâŋ) **LH** kɑŋ, **OCM** *kâŋ < *klaŋ ? — **[T]** *ONW* kɑŋ
'Bull, stud' [BI, Shi].
[E] ST: PTB *-laŋ with animal prefix *s- or *k-: Mru *klaŋ* 'male', Lushai *tlaŋ* 'male' (i.e. *tlaŋ*[R]*-vaal*[H] 'young man'?) [Löffler 1966: 120]; Mikir *chè-lóŋ* 'buffalo', WT *glaŋ* 'ox' (Boodberg 1937: 363), *glaŋ-po-čʰe* ('big buffalo':) 'elephant'. The meaning *glaŋ* 'elephant' must have been secondary because this animal is not indigenous in Tibet and only known through texts and stories relating to India. The WT word is not related to → xiàng$_5$ 象 'elephant'. For the OCM initial *kl-, see §8.2.2.

gāng$_6$ 肛 (kåŋ, xåŋ)
'Lower intestines, anus' [GY, JY] is perh. related to TB-WT *gžaŋ* (< *gryaŋ? *glyaŋ?) 'anus' (Unger *Hao-ku* 50, 1995: 157); see also → cháng$_6$ 腸.

gǎng 港 → **jiāng$_1$** 江

gāo$_1$ 高 (kâu) **LH** kɑu, **OCM** *kâu
'High' [OB, BI, Shi]. See → yuán$_1$ 元 for possible TB cognates.
[T] *Sin Sukchu SR* kaw (平); *MGZY* gaw (平) [kaw]; *ONW* kɑu

⋇ **gāo** 高 (kâu[C]) **LH** kɑu[C], **OCM** *kâuh
'Height' [Lù Démíng: Zuo, Yin] (Unger *Hao-ku* 21, 1983: 183).

[C] Likely allofams are under → qiáo$_1$ 喬, perh. also → hào$_3$ 浩 'vast, rising'.

gāo$_2$-méi 高禖 → **méi$_6$** 媒禖

gāo$_3$ 膏 (kâu[C]) **LH** kɑu(C), **OCM** *kâu(h)
'Grease, ointment' [Shi], 'fat' (of animals, persons) [Zuo]> 'to fatten' (e.g. millet shoots) [Shi], 'fertile, rich' [Guoyu]; > 'be glossy' [Shi]. SW says that → zhī$_{10}$ 脂 'grease, fat' belongs to animals with horns, *gāo* 膏 to animals without horns (e.g. pigs). Downer (1959: 278) reserves tone C reading MC *kâu*[C] for verbal usages.

gāo$_4$ 羔 (kâu) **LH** kɑu, **OCM** *kâu
'Lamb' [Shi], *gāo* has the general meaning 'small, of an animal' in an ancient dialect (Wáng Lì 1982: 182f.); it is prob. not related to → gǒu 狗 'dog'.

gāo$_5$ 櫜 (kâu) **LH** kou, **OCM** *kû < *klu ?
'Bow case (of tiger hide)' [BI, Shi].

~ Perh. **tāo** 弢 (tʰâu) **LH** tʰou, **OCM** *lhû ?
'Bow case' [Zuo]. These two words could be reconciled if we assume that MC *tʰ-* derives from OCM *lh- rather than *th-, and the div. I vocalism of *gāo* is due to an earlier medial *-l- (§8.2.2). Such variants may indicate a foreign loan.

gǎo$_1$ 暠 (kâu[B]) **LH** kɑu[B], **OCM** *kâu?
'White, brilliant' 暠 [Meng]; 'plain white silk' 縞 [Shi].
[E] This is prob. the same word as *gǎo* 皓皋 (kâu[B]) (under → hào$_2$ 皓), although the reason for the difference in OC rimes is not clear. <> Tai: S. *kʰau*[A1] 'white, clear, pale'.

This item is prob. not related to **hè** 翯 (xåk, ɣåk) 'rich white colors of birds', perh.

rather 'glistening' [Shi], because the initials MC *x-* and *k-* do not normally occur in the same wf. However, → hè₂ 鶴 'crane, glistening white' may be related.

gǎo₂ 皓皋 → **hào₂** (皓)

gǎo₃ 稿 → **kǎo₃** 藁槁

gǎo₄ 縞 → **gǎo₁** 杲

gào 告 (kuok, kâu^C) **LH** kouk, kou^C, **OCM** *kûk(h) < *kluk(h) — **[T]** *ONW* kau
'To tell, report, announce, inform' [BI, Shi]. Downer (1959: 286) reserves the tone D form LH *kouk* for the meaning 'to tell' (superiors).

※ **gào** 誥 (kâu^C) **LH** kou^C, **OCM** *kûkh < *klukh
'Announcement, make an announcement' (to inferiors) [BI, Shi, Shu].
[<] exoactive of *gào* 告 (kuok, kâu^C) (§4.3.1), i.e. 'announce something to someone'.

[E] <> KT: S. *klaau^B1* < *kl- 'to say, declare' (Li 1976: 46); S. *lau^B2* 'to tell, recount' ※ *lau^A2* 'concise statement' are unrelated to *klaau^B1* (Gedney 1976: 72).

gē₁ 戈 (kuâ) **LH** kuɑi, **OCM** *kuâi
'Dagger-ax' [BI, Shi].
[E] Perh. area word: TB-WB *kʰwan* 'long-handled chisel' (Peiros / Starostin *CAAAL* 22, 1984: 125) <- Tai: S. *kʰwan^A1* 'an ax, hatchet' (used in a compound meaning long-handled battle-ax) <- AT *gwal ~ qwal* (Egerod *CAAAL* 6, 1976: 56). Possibly related to **huà** 絓 (ɣwa^B) 'thrust', and **huá** 划 (ɣwa) 'to punt' [Lü].

gē₂ 歌 (kâ) **LH** kɑi, **OCM** *kâi
'Song' [Shi].
[T] *Sin Sukchu SR* kɔ (平), *LR* kɔ; *MGZY* go (平) [kɔ]; *ONW* kɑ
[D] Y-Guǎngzhōu *kɔ^A1*, Ke-Méixiàn *kɔ^A1*; PMin *kɑi
[E] ? ST: Perh. related to Lushai *kai^L / kaiʔ^L < kai / kaih* 'to play' (a fiddle etc.), perh. also TGTM *^Bgwai 'song', Chepang *keʔ-* 'sing well', JP *kʰai^31* 'tell' (a story). It is not clear if or how PVM *tkal > *tkalʔ > Viet. *gáy* 'to crow' (of a rooster) [Ferlus] may be connected.

gē₃ 割 (kât) **LH** kɑt, **OCM** *kât
'To cut' [Zuo], 'destroy, injure' [Shu].
[T] *Sin Sukchu SR* kɔ (入); *MGZY* go (入) [kɔ] — **[D]** PMin *k̯ɑt

※ **hài** 害 (ɣâi^C) **LH** gɑs, **OCM** *gâts, OCB *ɦgat(s) — **[T]** *ONW* ɣɑC
'To harm, injure, harm, injury' [BI, Shi].

※ **jiè** 犗 (kai^C) **LH** kas, **OCM** *krâts
'To castrate' [Zhuang] is added by Karlgren (1956: 12).
[<] perh. r-caus. of *gē* 割 (kât) (§7.5).

[E] ST and area word: PTB *(s-)kat 'cut' (LaPolla 1994: 166), and / or WT *'gas-pa* 'to split, break'. <> PTai *kat : Lóngzhōu *kaat^D1L* 'to cut' may be CH loans. <> MK: NViet. *kắt*; Khmer *kat* [Huffman 1975: 16], PSBahn. *kat 'to chop, cut'.

gē₄ 胳 (kâk) **LH** kɑk, **OCM** *kâk < *klak
'Armpit' [Li, Shiwen] > 'armpit seam' 袼 [Li].
[E] MK: PMon *knlak, LitMon *knak*, Khmer *kliək* 'armpit'. The syn. → yì₄ 腋亦掖 is prob. a different etymon.

gē₅ 牁 → **kē₁** 柯

gé₁ 革 (kɛk) **LH** kɛk, **OCM** *krə̂k
'To change' [Shi]. Karlgren (*GSR* 931a) implies that this is the s. w. as 'a hide' [Shi]

which is the other meaning of this graph. Wáng Lì (1982: 81) considers *gé* an allofam of → gǎi 改 and gēng$_1$ 更 (kɐŋ) *kraŋ 'change'.

gé$_2$ 隔 (kɛk) **LH** kɛk, **OCM** *krêk —**[T]** *ONW* këk
'To separate' [Guanzi].
=**gé** 膈 (kɛk) **LH** kɛk, **OCM** *krêk
'Membrane'. Unger (*Hao-ku* 51, 1995) suggests that *mò* 膜 (mâk) 'membrane' which he sets up as OC *mrāk is a morphological variant of this word. Alternatively, *gé* may be a variant of, or the same etymon as → gé$_1$ 革 (kɛk) 'hide, skin', although the OC rimes are different (*-ək vs. *-ek).

gé$_3$ 格 (kɐk) **LH** kak, **OCM** *krâk
'(Clothes) rack' [Tang] is perh. a cognate or variant of **jià** 架 (ka^C) '(clothes) rack' [Jinshu] (so LaPolla 1994: 141). See also → gè$_2$ 格.

gé$_4$ 格 (kɐk) **LH** kak, **OCM** *krâk
'To come, go to, arrive' [OB, BI, Shu], originally written 各.
[T] *Sin Sukchu SR* kaw (入); *MGZY* gyay (入) [kjaj]
~**jiǎ** 假 (ka^B) **LH** ka^B, **OCM** *krâʔ —**[T]** *ONW* kä
'To come, go to' [Shi]. Because *jiǎ* is not a rime word in *Shījīng*, it is difficult to decide whether this character wrote a variant of *gé* or simply was borrowed for it.
[E] ? ST: Perh. cognate to WT *'gro-ba* 'to walk, go, travel' (which could derive from either *ɴgra or *ɴgro) ⋇ *'gro-ba-po* 'traveler' ⋇ *'gron-pa* 'to go, travel' ⋇ *gron-k^{h}aŋ* 'inn' ⋇ *mgron* 'guest' [Geilich 1994: 19f]. For the vocalic discrepancy, see §12.9 (3). Acc. to Baxter (1992: 329), → lù$_5$ 路 (*g-rak) could be related to the above; also → kè$_3$ 客 'guest', → lǚ$_2$ 旅 'travel, lodge', → xíng$_1$ 行 (root *kraŋ) 'to go'.

gé$_5$ 骼 (kɐk) **LH** kak, **OCM** *krâk
'Bones' [Liji 6/10 = Couvr. I: 338]
⋇ **gé** 骼 (kɐk, k^{h}ɐk, kâk) **LH** k(^{h})ak, kɑk, **OCM** *k(h)râk, *kâk < *klak
'Haunch' of victim [Yili] is prob. the same word as 'bones'.
[E] <> KT: PKS *k-la:k^D (Edmondson / Yang 1988: 157), *tla:k^{D1} (Thurgood 1988: 210) 'bone'. See also → dú$_8$-lóu 髑髏.

gé$_6$ 觡 (kɐk) **LH** kak, **OCM** *krâk
'Deer's horn' [Li]. Benedict (1976: 174) compares this word with PTB *rwâ ~ *rwâk ~ *rwâŋ 'horn' (→ gōng$_9$ 觥). He mentions Dzorgai (Thochu) *rak* 'horn', but we should expect a MC medial *w*.

gé$_7$ 閣 → **gè$_1$** 各

gé$_8$ 閤蛤 → **hé$_5$** 合

gě$_1$ 笴 → **gān$_4$** 竿

gě$_2$ 哿 → **jiā$_2$** 嘉

gè$_1$ 各 (kâk) **LH** kɑk, **OCM** *kâk
'Each' [Shi]. 各 is the original graph for → gé$_4$ 格 'go, come'; depicting two feet. *Gé* 閣 'one over the other' is perh. the s. w.
[T] *Sin Sukchu SR* kaw (入), *LR* kawʔ, kɔʔ; *MGZY* gaw (入) [kaw]; *ONW* kɑk
[<] perh. derived from *jǔ* 舉 with the distributive suffix *-k (so Pulleyblank 1973: 122); see §6.1.2.

※ **jǔ** 舉 (kjwo^B) **LH** kɨɑʔ, **OCM** *kaʔ
'All' [Zuo].
[E] ST: PLB *ka^1 'all' (*HPTB:* 163).

gè$_2$ 格 (kâk) **LH** kɑk, **OCM** *kâk — [T] *ONW* kɑk
'Tree branch' [Nan-Bei chao], but the word may be much older because the graph, which was apparently originally intended to write 'branch' ('wood' radical), occurs already in Zhou texts.
[E] ST: PTB *ka:k (*STC* no. 327) > PLB *ʔkak 'fork (of a tree), branch', WB ə-*k^{h}ak* 'branch of a tree', Lushai *kaak^L* (Lorrain), *kak^F* (Weidert 1975: 17) 'fork' (of a tree), 'be forked', Kachin *k^{h}aʔ^{31}* 'be parted, separated'.

gè$_3$ 箇個 → **gān$_4$** 竿

gè$_4$ 鬲 (kɛk) **LH** kɛk, **OCM** *krêk
'Yoke' [Zhouli] is prob. a nominal k-prefix derivation from → è$_1$ 厄軛 (§5.4).

gè$_5$ 搹 (kat, kăt) **LH** kat, kɛt, **OCM** *krêt
'To scrape' [SW].
[E] ST: TB: Lepcha *hrit* 'to comb', PLB *kret 'scrape' [Matisoff 1972: 48] > WB *k^{h}rac* 'to scrape', Kachin *k^{h}rèt* 'rasp, grate' (*HST:* 129). Tai: S. *k^{h}raat^{D2}* < *g- 'to scrape, rake' ※ *kraat^{D1}* 'metal scraper or grater'.
[C] Allofams are perh.: → qì 㓞 'skillful engraving', → qì$_2$ 契. Connection with → jié$_{10}$ 櫛 is doubtful.

gēn 根 (kən) **LH** kən, **OCM** *kôn — [D] PMin *kyn > Amoy *kun^{A1}*, Fúzhōu *kyŋ^{A1}*
'Root, trunk' [Zuo].
[T] *Sin Sukchu SR* kən (平); *MGZY* g^{h}in (平) [kən]; *ONW* kən
[E] AA: PVM *kəl 'tree' (trunk) [Ferlus], PMon *t[l]gəl 'stump' (of tree, mushroom, tooth), Khmer *găl* 'tree trunk' [Maspero 1912: 21]. MK -> PTai *g-: S. *khoon^{A2}* 'base of tree, stump' (irreg. tones, 'perch' in some Tai dialects).

gèn 艮 → **hèn** 恨

gēng$_1$ 更 (kɐŋ) **LH** kaŋ, **OCM** *krâŋ
'To change' [Zuo]. Perh. this is the s. w. as → gēng$_3$ 賡. Wáng Lì (1982: 81) relates *gēng* to → gǎi 改.
[T] *Sin Sukchu SR* kəjŋ (平), *PR* kəŋ ~ kiŋ, *LR* kiŋ; *MGZY* gÿing (平) [kjiŋ]; *ONW* këŋ
※ **gèng** 更 (kɐŋ^C) **LH** kaŋ^C, **OCM** *krâŋh
'Again, still' [Zuo].
[<] adverb from *gēng* 更 (kɐŋ) 'change' (§5.C.4.1) (Downer 1959: 289).

gēng$_2$ 埂 'pit, hole' → **kēng$_1$** 坑阬

gēng$_3$ 賡 (kɐŋ[C]) **LH** kaŋ(C), **OCM** *krâŋ(h)
'To continue, succeed' [Shu]; 'take over (duties etc.)' 更 [BI]. This is perh. the same word as → gēng$_1$ 更 'change'.

gēng$_4$ 庚 'road' → **xíng$_1$** 行

gēng$_5$ 耕 (kɛŋ) **LH** kɛŋ, **OCM** *krêŋ
'To plow' [Shi].
[T] *Sin Sukchu SR* kəjŋ (平), *PR* kiŋ ~ kəŋ; *MGZY* gÿing (平) [kjiŋ]
[E] *CVST* 2: 67 connects this word with Lushai *hreŋ^F* 'to clear for cultivation'.

gěng₁ 耿 (kɛŋ^B) **LH** kɛŋ^B, **OCM** *krêŋ?
'Be brilliant' (e.g. glory) [BI, Shu], 'wide awake' [Shi].
[E] ST: WB *krañ* < *kriŋ* 'clear, bright'.

gěng₂ 梗 'strong' → **qiáng₀** 強彊

gěng₃ 哽鯁 → **héng₂** 衡

gèng₁ 恆 (kəŋ^C) **LH** kəŋ^C, **OCM** *kə̂ŋh — **[T]** *Sin Sukchu SR* kəjŋ (去), *PR* kiŋ (去)
'To wax, increase' (of moon, plants spreading) [Shi].
[E] Etymology not clear, but this word has some resemblance to → gēng₁ 更 *kraŋh 'change', and / or to MK-PVM *k-raːŋ? 'month', Pearic *kaːŋ* ~ *kɔːŋ* 'moon'.

gèng₂ 堩 → **táng₁** 唐

gōng₁ 工功攻 (kuŋ) **LH** koŋ, **OCM** *kôŋ
'Work, artisan' 工 [BI, Shi] > 'achievement, merit' 功 [BI, Shu]; 'to work, apply oneself' > 'attack' 攻 [BI, Shi] (also MC *kuoŋ*).
[T] *Sin Sukchu SR* kuŋ (平); *MGZY* gung (平) [kuŋ]; *ONW* koŋ

ⵣ **sī-kōng** 司空 (sɨ-kʰuŋ) **LH** -kʰoŋ, **OCM** *-khôŋ
'Supervisor of artisans' [Shi], a (later?) variant of 司工 [BI] (unless the graph 工 was here intended for *khoŋ).

[E] ? Area word: TB-WB *kiuŋ^B* 'employ, order, commission'. Cf. AA-OMon *kloñ* /kloɲ/ 'to work', 'work as a cultivator' ⵣ *klon* /klon/ 'to have charge of cultivation'.
[C] Perh. → gòng₂ 貢 may be related.

gōng₂ 弓 (kjuŋ) **LH** kuŋ, **OCM** *kwəŋ, OCB *kʷjəŋ — **[T]** *ONW* kuŋ
'A bow' (for shooting) [OB, BI, Shi]. Foreign comparanda imply OC *kuŋ. The OC form *kwəŋ is proved by *Shījīng* rimes and may represent a particular OC dialect in which *u became centralized (Sagart 1999: 58).
[D] PMin *kioŋ; K-Méixiàn *⁴⁴tʰiɛn-⁴⁴kiuŋ^A1* 天弓 'rainbow'; PMin *kyŋ.
[E] PMK *k[o]ŋ (Shorto 1972) > NViet. *kǎwŋ* 'curved', Khmer /koŋ/ 'to bend, arch, curved, be bent (back)', Pear *kouŋ* 'curved' [Huffman ICSTLL 1975: 13], Khasi *pyrkhuŋ* 'to bend, arch'. MK -> Tai: S. *koŋ⁴* 'to arch, bend (bow)'. MK -> PTB *kuːŋ^A/^B (*STC* no. 359) > WB *kuiŋ^A* 'hang over in a curve'; note also PTB *ku[ː]m 'arched, vaulted' (*STC* p. 75 n. 321). <> The following are related acc. to *HPTB:* 310, but unrelated acc. to Shorto 1972: TB-WB *ə-kʰuiŋ^A* 'stalk, branch', *ə-kʰuiŋ^B* 'large branch, bough of tree', *kuiŋ^A* 'hang over in a curve'; JP *kuŋ³¹* 'branch'; Lep. *kuŋ* 'tree', Lushai *kuuŋ^F* 'plant, tree' (*STC:* 182 n. 479).
[C] Derivations are → qiōng₀ 穹 'vault, hole', → gōng₇ 肱 'arm'.

gōng₃ 躬 (kjuŋ) **LH** kuŋ, **OCM** *kuŋ — **[T]** *ONW* kuŋ
'Body, person, self' [Shi].
[E] ST: PTB *guŋ > PLB *guŋ¹ 'body' > WB *ə-koŋ* 'body, animal body', Rawang *guŋ* 'body, animal, self' (*STC:* 182 n. 479; *HST:* 46), JP *goŋ³¹*.

gōng₄ 公 (kuŋ) **LH** koŋ, **OCM** kôŋ < *kloŋ
(Male of older generation, higher rank to whom respect is due:) 'Father' [Lie; Hanshu], 'father's brother, uncle' [Hanshu]; 'clan head' [BI, Shi], a high feudal title ('prince', 'duke') [Meng]; 'male' of animals as in *gōng jī* 公雞 'rooster'.
[T] *Sin Sukchu SR* kuŋ (平); *MGZY* gung (平) [kuŋ]; *ONW* koŋ
[D] PMin *koŋ 'male'; Xiàmén *kaŋ^A1* 'grandfather'
[E] <> Tai: S. *luŋ^A2* < *l- 'parent's elder brother, uncle'. The difference in the OC and Tai initials may be explained by a MK origin: Khmer /looŋ/ 'chief' ⵣ /klooŋ/

'dignitary higher than /looŋ/' [Jenner / Pou 1982: xl]. <> WT *kʰoŋ ~ goŋ* 'a final syllable in names of important persons such as ministers and government officials' (*HST:* 96) may be a Chinese loan.

gōng $_5$ 公 (kuŋ) **LH** koŋ, **OCM** *kôŋ
'Impartial, fair' [Lunyu], 'public' [Shi].
ꭗ **húng** 鴻 (ɣuŋ), **LH** goŋ, **OCM** *gôŋ
'Equal, symmetrical' [Zhouli].
[E] ST: WT *(d)guŋ* 'middle' is prob. cognate considering the semantic association of 'middle' with 'balance' (note *zhōng* 中 'middle, proper, right').

gōng $_6$ 公 'palace' → **gōng** $_8$ 宫

gōng $_7$ 肱 (kwəŋ) **LH** kuəŋ, **OCM** *kwə̂ŋ
'Arm, upper arm' [Shi], *gǔ gōng* 股肱 'legs and arms' (metaphor for a ruler's ministers).
ꭗ **gōng** 軦 (kwəŋ, kʰwəŋ) **LH** kuəŋ, kʰuəŋ, **OCM** *k(h)wə̂ŋ
'Armrest' on a carriage [BI, Shi].
[E] 'Armrest' implies arms bent at the elbow, the arm is bow-shaped, therefore this etymon which has apparently no outside cognate is prob. derived from → gōng$_2$ 弓 'bow'.

gōng $_8$ 宫 (kjuŋ) **LH** kuŋ, **OCM** *kuŋ — **[T]** *ONW* kuŋ
'Palace, mansion' [BI, Shi], 'temple' [Shi 300, 1]. (Meanings discussed by Shaughnessy 1991: 199–201).
[E] *HST:* 98 relates the CH word to WT *kʰoŋ-pa* 'inside', *STC* (p. 182 n. 479) and Bodman (1980: 124) to PTB *k-yim ~ *k-yum 'house' (*STC* no. 53; *HPTB:* 504; for the difference in finals, see §6.7); but see next:
~ **gōng** 公 (kuŋ) **LH** koŋ, **OCM** *kôŋ < *kloŋ — **[T]** *ONW* koŋ
'Palace' [Shi 298, 1].
[E] Area word: MK: Mon *gloŋ* 'citadel, palace', Khmer *khluəŋ* 'treasury, storehouse' [Shorto 1971: 88]. MK -> Tai: S. *kluaŋ*^{A1} 'house, abode of a prince(ss)'.

gōng $_9$ 觥 (kwɐŋ) **LH** kuaŋ, **OCM** *kwrâŋ — **[T]** *ONW* (kuëŋ)
'Drinking vessel' of buffalo horn [Shi].
[E] PMY *krɔŋ^A 'horn' <- PTB (*kruŋ^A ~) *k-rwaŋ^A (Benedict *LTBA* 10.2, 1987: 17), PTB *ruŋ ~ *rwaŋ 'horn' (*STC* no. 85): Tsangla *wa-roŋ* 'horn' (of *wa* bovine); Chepang *roŋʔ* 'horn of animal'; PTani *rəŋ 'horn', Garo, Dimasa *groŋ* 'horn', Lep. *aróŋ*, Vayu, Bahing *ruŋ* (*CVST* V: 160), JP *ruŋ*^{33}- 'horn', also *koŋ*^{33} 'tusk'; Ge-man Deng *kɹăŋ*^{35}. This word belongs to the same root *(k-)ru ~ *(k-)rwa as → jiǎo$_5$ 角 'horn'. Shorto 1972 considers an AA origin likely: PMK *draŋ.

gōng $_{10}$ 恭龔 (kjwoŋ) **LH** kɨoŋ, **OCM** *kroŋ
'To respect' 恭 [Shi], 'sincerely respectful' 龔 (also MC *kuŋ, kuoŋ*) [BI, Han period] may be related to → gòng$_1$ 共 (i.e. < 'respectfully joining hands'?), and / or to → kǒng$_2$ 恐 'fear'.

gōng $_{11}$ 供 → **gòng** $_1$ 共

gōng $_{12}$ 軦 → **gōng** $_7$ 肱

gǒng 拱拲 → **gòng** $_1$ 共

gòng $_1$ 共 (gjwoŋ^C) **LH** gɨoŋ^C, **OCM** *goŋh — **[T]** *ONW* guoŋ
'All together' [Shu].

ꭗ **gǒng** 共拱拲 (kjwoŋ[B]) **LH** kɨoŋ[B], **OCM** *koŋʔ
'To join the hands' 共 [Yili], 拱 [Lunyu], 'hold round with both hands' 拱 [Zuo]; 'manacles' 拲 [Zhouli] (also MC *kjwok*). Note also AA: OMon *kloŋ* 'to join in salutation' (hands) (loan?).

ꭗ **gōng** 供 (kjwoŋ[C]) **LH** kɨoŋ(C), **OCM** *koŋ(h)
'To furnish, provide, carry out' [Shi] (< 'hand over with both hands'?).
[T] *Sin Sukchu SR* kjuŋ (平), *PR* kuŋ; *MGZY* gÿung (平) [kjuŋ]

[E] Etymology not clear. An OC medial *r should be assumed if related to → $gōng_{10}$ 恭龔. *CVST* 5: 57 relates this word to Western Tib. *'kʰyoŋ-ba, kʰyoŋs* 'to bring', WB *kuiŋ* 'take hold of, apply hand'. An allofam may perh. be → $gòng_2$ 貢.

$gòng_2$ 貢 (kuŋ[C]) **LH** koŋ[C], **OCM** *kôŋh — **[T]** *ONW* koŋ[C]
'Tribute, present' n. [Shu], 'to present' [Zuo] may perh. be related to either → $gōng_1$ 工功攻 or → $gòng_1$ 共. Unger (*Hao-ku* 50, 1995) connects the word with Lepcha *klóŋ* 'to grant'.

$gōu_1$ 句鉤枸區 (kəu) **LH** ko, **OCM** *kô
'Crooked' 區 [Li] > 'hook' [Shi], 'to hook' 鉤 [Zuo], 'hook, curved' 句 [Li] > 'crooked wood' 枸 [Xun].

ꭗ **jū** 痀 (kju) **LH** kɨo, **OCM** *ko
'Crooked spine' [Zhuang].

ꭗ **qú** 朐軥 (gju) **LH** gɨo, **OCM** *go
'Bent part of slice of meat' 朐 [Li]; 'curved exterior part of yoke' 軥 [Zuo].
The following is, however, not (directly) related:

ꭗ? **yǔ** 傴 (ʔju[B]) **LH** ʔɨo[B], **OCM** *ʔoʔ
'Bend the body' [Zuo], 'humpback' [Li].

[E] ST: WT *dgu-ba* 'to bend' ꭗ *dgur* 'something bent'; OC *-o can be derived from ST *u or *o. Syn. and likely cognate is → $qū_1$ 曲, perh. also to → $quán_3$ 卷拳 and / or → $quán_4$ 踡, → $qū_2$ 屈, → $jú_6$ 鞠鞫 'bend'. This wf is perh. also related to → $lóu_2$ 僂. Syn. → $yū_1$ 迂紆; → $hú_8$ 弧.

$gōu_2$ 溝 (kəu) **LH** ko, **OCM** *kô ?
'Drain, irrigation canal' [Lun], 'moat' [Li]. The QYS final -*əu* has no div. II counterpart; therefore the rime may represent both OC *-o and *-ro.
[<] possibly k-prefix noun of → $lòu_1$ 漏 'to leak' (§5.4).

$gōu_3$ 篝 → **$gòu_3$** 冓

gǒu 狗 (kəu[B]) **LH** ko[B], **OCM** *kôʔ < *kloʔ
'Dog' [Meng], 'puppy dog, cub of bear or tiger' [Erya] (also written with other radicals).
[D] PMin *k̯əu[B]
[E] Wáng Lì (1982: 182f) believes that the following are variants of this word (doubtful):
(1) → $jū_7$ 駒 (kju) 'young horse'. (2) hǒu 犺 (xəu[B]) 'calf' is a dialectal variant for *gǒu*, acc. to Guō Pú. (3) → $gāo_4$ 羔 is an ancient NE dialect word for *gǒu* 'young of dog, bear, tiger' which suggest that *gāo* 'lamb' is the same etymon.

More likely, *gǒu* is a loan or substrate word from PMY *klu² [Purnell] 'dog' which in turn is AA: PMon *clur, Mon *klə, WrMon *cluiw, kluiw* [kløw] (Haudricourt 1966; Norman / Mei 1976: 279–280; Norman 1988: 17), perh. also Bahnar *kŏ* 'dog' (K. Smith *LTBA* 2.1 [n.d.]: 7). For the initials, see §8.2.2. Some Himalayish forms, e.g. TB-

Bahing *k'li* 'dog' (*STC* no. 159) may derive from the same root of presumably wide prehistoric distribution.

Acc. to W. Eberhard (1968: 43–50), the dog plays a significant role in Yáo mythology. Customs in the ancient state of Zhèng 鄭 in Hénán (adjacent to the Shāng and Zhōu dynasty heartland) suggest to Eberhard that their inhabitants belonged originally to the Yáo culture (ibid. p. 36).

gòu₁ 垢 (kəu^B) **LH** ko^B, **OCM** *kôʔ — **[T]** *MTang* kəu, *ONW* kou
'Filth' [Shi].
[E] ? ST: WT *bsgo-ba* 'to soil, stain, defile, infect' (Unger *Hao-ku* 36, 1990: 50). See also → gòu₂ 詬.

ⵥ **gǔ** 淈 (kuət, ɣuət) **LH** kuət, guət, **OCM** *kût, *gût
'Dirt, to sully' [Chuci]. For the final *-t, see §6.2.1.

[E] This wf may be related with WB *kyu^C* 'filthy, dirty, foul', all words from a ST stem *klo-?

gòu₂ 詬 (xəu^C, kʰəu^C, kəu^B) **LH** ho^C, kʰo^C, ko^B, **OCM** *(k)hôh, kôʔ
'Disgrace, insult, revile' [Zuo].
[E] ST: WT *'kʰu-ba* 'insult, offend' (*HST:* 98). Unger (*Hao-ku* 36, 1990: 50) considers this to be the s. w. as → gòu₁ 垢 (kəu^B) 'filth'.

gòu₃ 冓 (kəu^C) **LH** ko^C, **OCM** *kôh
This root means basically 'interlacery, trelliswork' (Karlgren *GSR* 109): *zhōng-gòu* 中冓 'inner chamber'; 'to fabricate, build' 構 [Shu]. The original graph *gòu* 冓 shows apparently a wicker fish trap.

ⵥ **gōu** 篝 (kəu) **LH** ko, **OCM** *kô
'Bamboo cage' [Chuci].

[E] ? ST: JP *ku³¹* 'bed, furniture' (i.e. wooden frame).

[C] Possible allofams (Karlgren *GSR* 109) are → gòu₅ 購 'to present'; → gòu₄ 遘覯姤 'come across'. The word → hù₃ 互梐 is similar to this wf, but its vowel is different; possible TB cognates also indicate that *hù* is a separate root.

gòu₄ 遘覯姤 (kəu^C) **LH** ko^C, **OCM** *kôh
'To come across, meet with' 覯 [Shi]; 'meet with' 遘 [Shi]; 'to cross, join (weapons)' 搆 [Meng]; 'come in conflict with' 構 [Shi]; 'second marriage, favor' 姤 [Yi]. This may be the s. w. as → gòu₃ 冓 (so Karlgren), q.v. for possible allofams.
[E] ST: PTB *gow (*STC* no. 318) > WB *ku^B* 'cross over, transfer', JP *gau³³* 'pass over'; possibly also JP *koʔ⁵⁵* 'to ford', WT *kʰug-pa* ~ *kʰugs-pa* 'to find, get, earn' (i.e. 'come across') (*HST:* 72). WB *kruik 'meet with', Chepang *krus-sa* 'to meet', WT *'kʰrug-pa* 'fight, disturb' represent perh. parallel stems. Note that MC is ambiguous as to the presence or absence of OC medial *-r-. Karlgren (*GSR* 109) believes that all words with this phonetic are cognate, basically meaning 'intertwine, interlace'.

gòu₅ 購 (kəu^C) **LH** ko^C, **OCM** *kôh
'To present, give' [Guoce] is perh. cognate to WT *skur-ba* 'to send, transmit, give', WB *ku^B* 'cross over, transfer' may belong to → gòu₃ 冓.

gòu₆ 彀 → **gǔ₁₄** 穀

gū₁ 姑 (kuo) **LH** kɑ, **OCM** *kâ
'Father's sister, husband's mother' [Shi, Liji], 'wife's sister' [Liji] (Wáng Lì 1958: 569; K. C. Chang 1976: 89). Etymology not clear.

gū $_2$ 酤 → **gǔ** $_{11}$ 賈

gū $_3$ 孤 → **guǎ** 寡

gū $_4$ 罛 (kuo) **LH** kuɑ, **OCM** *kuâ

'Net' [Shi].

[E] ST: WB k^hwa^C 'kind of net' ⋈ PTB *kwan ~ *gwan 'casting net' (*STC:* 158 n. 428), WT *rkon* 'net'. It is prob. unrelated to *gǔ* 罟 'net' (under → hù$_3$ 互梐).

gū $_5$ 軱 → **hú** $_8$ 弧

gǔ $_1$ 古 (kuo^B) **LH** kɑ^B, **OCM** *kâʔ

'Antiquity, of old' [OB, BI, Shi].

[T] *Sin Sukchu SR* ku (上); *MGZY* gu (上) [ku]; *ONW* ko

⋈ **gù** 故 (kuo^C) **LH** kɑ^C, **OCM** *kâh

'An old one' [Shi].

[E] ST: PTB *r-ga 'old' (*STC* no. 445) > WT *rga-ba* 'be old, aged'; JP *ləga* 'old'. Boltz (OE 35, 1992: 36ff) relates *gǔ* to a wf 'hard, durable' which includes → gù$_1$ 固 'secure, strong', but WT cognates suggest that these etyma have separate ST origins. Boltz also includes → kǔ 苦 'duress, suffer', et al.

[C] Shī Xiàngdōng (2000: 120) adds **hú** 胡 LH *ga* or *ɣa* 'advanced in years' [Zhoushu].

gǔ $_2$**-bèi** 古貝 → **bù** $_2$ 布

gǔ $_3$ 牯 (kuo^B) *ONW* ko — [D] PMin *k̂o^B

'Male of bovine, steer' [Yupian, GY], a post-classical word. Prob. not cognate to → gǔ$_7$ 羖 'ram'.

[E] AA: Mod. Khmer *kloḥ* 'male, virile' ⋈ *kamloḥ* 'young man'; Chrau 'male' ⋈ *si-klo* 'husband'; Bahnar *klo* 'male', Stieng *klau, klo* 'male' ⋈ *sarlau* 'husband', Sre *klau* 'man, male'. Also the Yuè dialect word *lau* 'boy' may ultimately go back to this MK etymon.

gǔ $_4$ 罟 → **hù** $_3$ 互梐

gǔ $_5$ 谷 (kuk) **LH** kok, **OCM** *klôk

'Valley' [Shi].

⋈ **yù** 谷 (juk) **LH** jok, **OCM** *lok

'Valley' [EY, GY].

[E] ST or area word: TB-WT *luŋ-pa* 'valley, WB $k^hyoŋ$ 'valley', JP $kruŋ^{33}$ 'valley'. <> Tai: S. $k^hlɔɔŋ^{A2}$, Kam $loŋ^{A1}$, <> AA-Wa *roŋ* (TB loan?) (collected in Dǒng Wéiguāng et al. *CAAAL* 22, 1984: 119f); some TB words have final -k: Mikir *arlók* < *r-lók* 'valley'. But PTB *grok (*STC* no. 122) > WT *grog-po* 'deep deil, ravine', WB k^hyok 'chasm, gulf' is prob. to be kept separate.

gǔ $_6$ 股 (kuo^B) **LH** kɑ^B, **OCM** *kâʔ

'Thigh, leg' [Shi]

[E] KT: Tai: S. k^haa^{A1} < *k^h- 'leg, thigh' (Li F. 1976: 44), PKS *kwa^1 'leg'. The Tai word is prob. not related to → qiāo$_1$ 骹 (k^{h}au) 'foot'.

gǔ $_7$ 羖 (kuo^B) **LH** kɑ^B, **OCM** *kâʔ

'Ram' [Shi].

[E] Wáng Lì (1982: 126) relates this word to → gǔ$_3$ 牯 'male of bovine, steer', as well as to the wf → jiā$_8$ 豭 'boar', therefore gǔ 羖 meant originally 'male animal'. However, *jiā* and *gǔ* differ in MC vowel and tone, therefore *gǔ* prob. means basically 'ram' and is cognate to → jié$_4$ 羯 'ram'.

gǔ $_8$ 骨 (kuət) **LH** kuət, **OCM** *kût
'Bone' [OB].
[T] *Sin Sukchu SR* ku (入); *MGZY* gu (入) [ku]; *ONW* kot
[D] PMin *kot
[E] Outside relations are not obvious; *gǔ* is usually compared to PTB *rus 'bone': WT *rus*, Lushai *ruʔ* (< *rus*), Khami lgs. (Kuki-Chin) *hrut, Rengmitca *kh(r)u*, Areng *haw* (prob. from voiceless *hr-) (Löffler *Anthropos* 55, 1960: 547); Lepcha *a-hrăt* 'bone'; Karen *k(h)rut* (*STC:* 155 n. 419). But we could be more confident about these associations if there were a trace of an OC medial *r. WT *rus* 'clan', see → lèi$_2$ 類.

gǔ $_9$ 鼓 (kuo^B) **LH** kɑ^B, **OCM** *kâʔ < *klaʔ — **[D]** PMin *ko^B.
'The drum, to drum, strike (a musical instrument)' [BI, Shi]; 'musician > blind man' 瞽 [Shi] (Karlgren 1956: 4).
[E] Area word: PTai *klɔŋ^{A1} 'drum' (Li F. 1976: 40), Saek *tlɔɔŋ^{A1}*, PHlai *laŋ^1, MK-PWa *kloʔ 'bronze-drum'. For the finals, see §3.2.4.

gǔ $_{10}$ 瞽 → **gǔ** $_9$ 鼓

gǔ $_{11}$ 賈 (kuo^B) **LH** kɑ^B, **OCM** *kâʔ
'To sell' [Shi 264, 4], 'to buy' [Zuo] > 'merchant' [Shu 35, 5; Zuo].
⋇ **gū** 酤 (kuo[^{C}]) **LH** kɑ(^{C}), **OCM** *kâ(h)
'To buy' (wine) [Shi 165, 6].
[E] This word could be a cognate or variant of *gǔ* above, but the same graph also writes a word **hù** (ɣuo^B) 'overnight wine' [Shi 302, 2] with which it may be related since *gū* means 'buy wine'. Karlgren (*GSR* 49b') has assigned readings to meanings as given above, yet traditional commentaries and dictionaries don't agree which reading, *gū* or *hù*, goes with which meaning.
[C] Perh. cognate to → jià$_4$ 賈價. Syn. → dí$_6$ 糴; → mǎi 買; → shòu$_2$ 售; → yù$_{23}$ 賣.

gǔ $_{12}$, **zhuó** 穀 (kuok, tśjak) **LH** kouk ~ kiauk ?, **OCM** *kâuk ? ~ *kiauk ?
'Husk of grain' [Lü, GY]. *GY* also has a reading *zhuó* (tśjak).
[E] ST: PTB *kok (*STC* no. 342) > PLB *ʔkuk ~ *ʔguk 'outer covering, bark, skin' > WB *ə-kʰok*; WT *skog-pa ~ kog-pa* 'shell, peel, rind' ⋇ *'gog-pa, bkog* 'to tear away, take away, peel, rob' ⋇ *gog-pa* 'to scale off' (Bodman 1980: 128); Lushai *kʰok* 'peel off' (*STC:* 74). The CH distinction between → kuò$_4$ 鞹 *khwak 'leather' (< 'skin'?) and *gǔ* *kûk 'husk' is difficult to correlate with TB comparanda.

gǔ $_{13}$ 穀 (kuk) **LH** kok, **OCM** *kôk — **[T]** *ONW* kok
'Grain, cereal' [Shi] > 'emoluments' [Shi]; perh. 'auspicious, good' [Shi] is a semantic extension, lit. 'nourishing, supportive'. Not related to → gǔ$_{14}$ 穀.
[E] AA or area word: PVM *rkoʔ 'husked rice' [Ferlus 1988: 87], Khmu /rŋkŏʔ/, Khasi *khaw*, Palaung *rəkaw*. AA -> TB: JP *n^{33}-ku^{33}* 'rice', Monpa *kʰu* 'rice' (*HST:* 87). AA -> Tai: *kau^3, Yay (Dioi) *gau^4, S. *kʰau^3* 'rice, grain' [Levy 1988: 64; Ferlus *MKS* 7, 1978: 13f]. <> TB-WB *kok* 'rice plant'.

gǔ $_{14}$ 穀 (kuk) **LH** kok, **OCM** *kôk — **[T]** *ONW* kok
'Baby' [Xun], lit. 'a suckler'.
⋇ **gòu** 穀 (kəu^C [GY]) **LH** ko^C, **OCM** *kôkh
'To suckle' [Zuo], a Chǔ dialect word. Yán Shīgǔ [GY] also reads this graph *nəu$^{B/C}$*, prob. inspired by the standard word → rǔ$_3$ 乳. Pulleyblank (in Keightley 1983: 427) has EMC *kowk, kowʔ.*

ꭗ **kòu** 鷇 (k^hau^C) **LH** k^ho^C, **OCM** *khôkh
'Newborn nestling' [Zhuang], i.e. a 'baby bird'.
[E] ST: JP *kroʔ⁵⁵ < krok⁵⁵* 'to hatch', prob. a parallel stem, see Table C-2 (under → $chù_4$, xù 畜) for similar-looking words.

$gǔ_{15}$ 盬 (kuo^B) **LH** ka^B, **OCM** *kâʔ
'Salt' [Zhouli], 'salty marsh' [Zuo].
[E] PTai *klɨo^{A1} 'salt' (Li 1976: 45), Saek *tlua^{A1} > trua^{A1}*. Acc. to Li F., *gǔ* is possibly connected with → $lǔ_1$ 鹵 (luo^B) 'salty', which is supported by modern forms like Jin dialectal kəʔ^{D2}-lou^C (Zhāng Xīng-yà *YWYJ* 1996.4: 10). Possible variants or allofams are → $chì_1$ 斥, → $xì_4$ 潟.

$gǔ_{16}$ 蠱 (kuo^B) **LH** ka^B, **OCM** *kâʔ
'A poison which serves as a magic charm' [OB, Yi, Zuo]. *SW* and *Zhōulǐ* say it is an animal in the stomach. Eberhard (1968: 149–153) says: People south of the Yangtze prepare *gǔ* by putting into a pot five poisonous vermin, such as a centipede, a snake, etc., which devour each other; the one left is crushed and made into a medicine which is used as a magic charm (e.g. love charm; evil magic to obtain subservient spirits, and the like). — Etymology not clear.

$gǔ_{17}$ 淈 → **$gòu_1$** 垢

$gù_1$ 固 (kuo^C) **LH** ka^C, **OCM** *kâh
'Be solid, secure, sure' [Shi].
[T] *Sin Sukchu SR* ku (去); *MGZY* gu (去) [ku]; *ONW* ko

= **gù** 錮 (kuo^C) **LH** ka^C, **OCM** *kâh
'To pour metal into cracks, caulk' [Hanshu] > 'block, debar, keep in check' (Boltz *OE* 35, 1992: 37) [Zuo], a kind of 'stopper' used in metal casting [SW].

ꭗ **hù** 冱 ($ɣuo^C$) **LH** ga^C, **OCM** *gâh
'To shut in, stop up' (by freezing) [Zuo], 'to freeze' [Zhuang].

[C] Boltz (op. cit.) adds among others of the following: → $kū_1$ 枯 'wither', → $hú_1$ 胡 'dewlap', → $gù_2$ 固錮 'persistent', → $hù_2$ 怙 'rely on', → $gǔ_1$ 古 'old'; → $gù_3$ 故 'reason'.
[E] Several parallel or synonymous stems have partially converged and are difficult to disentangle, unless they should all be prolific variants and derivations from one ST source (for an overview see Table G-1 (A) below; Table J-1 (B) under → $jiān_2$ 堅). As often, MK words are also mixed into this wf complex, but the nature and history of their connection with OC and TB is not certain:

KA (1) 'solid, hard'
$gù_1$ 固 (kuo^C) [ka^C] *kâh 'solid' and cognates above
WT *kʰa-ba* 'snow'

KA-K or KAK (1a)
Limbu *kʰakt-* 'to harden, freeze, solidify'
MK-Khmer /kaak/ 'become hard and solid; harden, solidify, congeal, coagulate' ꭗ /skaak/ (of grain and the like:) 'have become hard and dry, dry up or out' > 'turn out to be futile...'

KA-NG or *KANG (1b)
→ $gāng_4$ 剛鋼 (kâŋ) [kaŋ] *kâŋ 'hard, firm'
WT *gaŋs* 'ice' (terminative: < 'having become hard' of snow, water)
Lushai *kʰaŋ^F* 'congealed, solidified'

MK: Khmer /-kaŋ/ 'hard, stiff', OKhmer *gaṅ* /gɔŋ/, OMon *goṅ* /gɔŋ/ 'be hard, stiff, firm, durable...'

KL/YAK ? 'freeze'

PTB *m/s-glak (*HPTB:* 325)
LB-Lahu kâʔ 'cold'
WT *'k^h^yag(s)-pa* 'freeze, coagulate'

KAR (1) 'solid, hard'

WT *gar-bu* 'solid' (not hollow) ⋈ *gar-ba* 'strong' (e.g. of beer) ⋈ *gar-mo* 'thick' (soup)
Lushai $k^h aar^R$ 'to congeal, crust over, frozen over'
MK-PWa *kɐr 'strong' (object) <- TB?

KAR-NG (1a)

WT *mk^h^raŋ-ba* 'hard' ⋈ *k^h^raŋ(-t^h^aŋ)* 'hard'
Lepcha *króŋ* 'hard'

KA (2) 'dry'

→ kū 枯 (kʰuo) [kʰɑ] *khâ 'withered, dried'
MK: Khmer /khah/ 'to dry up or out, dry until hard, wither'

KA-K (2a)

→ $hé_7$ 涸 (ɣâk) [gɑk] *gâk 'dry up'

KA-NG (2b)

Lushai $kaŋ^R$ / kan^L 'to be exposed to the full rays of the sun, be sunny' ⋈ $kaŋ^F$ 'to dry up, evaporate, run dry' (water, river, spring)

KA-T (2c)

→ $kě_2$ 渴 (kʰât) [kʰɑt] *khât 'be thirsty'

KAR (2) 'dry'

Chepang *garʔ-* 'bask, warm oneself in the sun'

KAR-K (2a)

hè 垎 (ɣɐk) [gak] *grâk 'water drying off land' (under → $hé_7$ 涸) 'dry'
PLB *ʔkrak 'dry'

KAR-NG (2b)

Lushai $ṭaŋ^R$ / $ṭan^L$ 'dry, dried'

KAR-T (2c)

→ $jié_5$ 渴 (gjät 3) [gɨat] *grat 'to dry up' (pool, swamp)

KAN 'dry' is prob. the same stem as KAR (2) since KAN is found only in languages with the shift *-r > *-n*.

→ $gān_9$ 乾 (kân) [kɑn] *kân 'dry'
WB $k^h an^B$ 'dry up'
JP kan^{31} 'solidify, dry up'

KIN 'solid, firm'

→ $jiān_2$ 堅 (kien) [ken] *kîn 'firm, solid, strong'
WB *kyañ* 'feeling of numbness'
JP *kyin* 'stiff, aching'
Lushai $k^h iŋ^F$ < *k^h^iŋʔ* dry out (get hard, of ouside of meat etc.)

(K-) RENG / K 'hard'

→ $yìng_3$ 硬 (ŋɛŋ^C^) 'hard' (but the hypothetical OC vowel might have been *ə)
JP $greŋ^{31}$ 'hard'; WT *reŋs-pa* 'solid' (not liquid), *mk^h^regs-pa* 'hard, firm' (snow)
MK-Mon *kriŋ (krɔŋ)* 'stiff, hard', Khm *rɯŋ*, Mon *krɔŋ* (original vowel?)
MK ? -> PTai *kʰlɛŋ^A1^ 'solid, hard'

Table G-1 Hard, congeal, dry (A) for gù₁ 固

	*ka	*ka-ŋ > *kaŋ	*kar > *kan	*kar-ŋ/k > *kraŋ/k	*ka-k
OC	gù 固 *kâh solid hù 沍 *gâh freeze	gāng 剛鋼 *kâŋ hard	gān 乾 *kân dry	hè 垎 *grâk water drying off land	hé 涸 *gâk dry up
WT	k^ha-ba snow	gaŋs ice	gar-ba strong, gar-bu hard	mk^{h}raŋ hard	'k^{h}yag-pa freeze
Limbu					k^{h}akt- harden, freeze, solidify
Lushai	k^{h}aŋF congealed, solidified		k^{h}aarR < k^{h}aarʔ to congeal	ṭaŋR dried	
JP	ga^{55} earth, place		kan be dried up		
LB				*ʔkrak dry	
WB			k^{h}an^B dry up		

The e/i-vowel variants can be found in Table J-1 under → jiān₂ 堅.

gù₂ 固錮 (kuo^C) **LH** kɑ^C, **OCM** *kâh — **[T]** *ONW* ko
'Persistent' (Boltz *OE* 35, 1992: 37) 固 [Meng]; 'chronic' (disease) 錮 [Li] is perh. the s. w. as → gù₁ 固 'solid, secure' (so Boltz).

gù₃ 故 (kuo^C) **LH** kɑ^C, **OCM** *kâh
'Reason, cause' [BI, Shi].
[E] Etymology not certain, *gù* may be the same word as → gù₁ 固 'be solid, secure, sure'; or may be derived from → gǔ₁ 古 'antiquity', hence lit. 'thing or person of former times' (Pulleyblank, Proceedings of the 2nd Int. Conf. on Sinology, Acad. Sin. Taipei 1989: 10).

gù₄ 故 'old' → **gǔ₁** 古

gù₅ 錮 → **gù₁** 固

gù₆ 牿 (kuok) **LH** kouk, **OCM** *kûk
(Perh. 'restrainer' >) 'Pen, stable' [Yi, Shu], 'manacle, handcuffs' [Yi].
[E] ST: PLB *krok 'jail; pen, enclosure for animals' [Matisoff *TSR* no. 16] (*HST*: 116). <> Tai: S. *kɔɔk < gɔɔk* 'pen, enclosure', *kuk⁶* 'prison'.

gù₇ 雇 (kuo^C) **LH** kɑ^C, **OCM** *kâh
'To hire' [Hànshū].
[T] *Sin Sukchu SR* ku (去); *MGZY* gu (去) [ku]
[E] ST: WB *ə-k^{h}a^C* 'pay for services, wages'. It is prob. an allofam of → jiǎ₃ 假 'borrow'.

gù₈ 顧 (kuo^C) **LH** kɑ^C ?, **OCM** *kâʔ !
'To turn the head to, look at, regard, look after, take care of' [Shi, Shu]. OC Tone B is indicated by *Shījīng* rimes (Mattos 1971: 309).

⫘ **gù** 顧 (kuo^C) **LH** kɑ^C, **OCM** *kâh
'A sight' n. [Shi].
[<] exopass. (§4.4) of the above, lit. 'what is seen'.

guā 1 瓜 (kwa) **LH** kua, **OCM** *kwrâ
'Melon' [Shi]. — Etymology not clear.
[T] *Sin Sukchu SR* kwa (平); *MGZY* gwa (平) [kwa]; *ONW* kuä

guā 2 蝸 → **wō, guā, luó** 蝸

guā 3 刮 (kwat) **LH** kuat, **OCM** *krôt
'To scrape' [Zhouli], 'polish' [Li].
[T] *Sin Sukchu SR* kwa (入); *MGZY* gwa (入) [kwa] — **[D]** PMin *kuot
[C] A cognate is prob. → shuā 刷; see there for an overview of similar and related etyma. Prob. not related to → luō 捋 'scrape off'.

guǎ 寡 (kwa^B) **LH** kua^B, **OCM** *kwrâʔ
'Be single, alone, unique' [Shu], 'orphan, alone' [Lunyu]. <> Tai: Wuming *kla*^C2 < *gl- 'orphan' (Li 1976: 46) is prob. a CH loan from around the Han period (*r > l).

⫘ **guān** 鰥 (kwăn) **LH** kuɛn, **OCM** *kwrə̂n, OCB *kʷrən
'Bachelor, widower' [BI, Shi] (Unger *Hao-ku* 33, 1986).
[<] n-nominalization of *guǎ* (§6.4.5).
[E] ST: WT *dgon-pa* 'solitary place, desert, wilderness, hermitage' (n-nominalization) ⫘ *sgos* 'private, individual'. OC *-r- can reflect different foreign elements in the initial (§7.4), therefore WT is the exact counterpart of OC, except that the WT noun refers to a place, the OC noun to a person.

⫘ **gū** 孤 (kuo) **LH** kuɑ, **OCM** *kwâ
'Be solitary, alone' [Shu].

⫘ **jǔ-jǔ** 踽踽 (kju^B) **LH** kyɑ^B, **OCM** *kwaʔ
(To walk) 'solitary, forlorn' adv. [Shi].

guà 挂 (kwai^C) **LH** kuɛ^C, **OCM** *kwrêh or *kwêh
'To suspend, hang' [Yili].
[E] ST: PTB *k(w)a:y 'hang' (*HPTB:* 214) > Tiddim *ka:i* 'be suspended' ⫘ *xa:i* 'hang something up', Lushai *kʰai* 'suspend'. This etymon is reminiscent of MK-PMonic *wak 'to hang' (sth. to a nail) ⫘ *k-wak 'to hook and pull, hang sth. by its hook' (tr.) [Diffloth 1984: 167], but MK is phonologically rather distant. Prob. → xuán 4 縣懸 and → qìng 3 磬 are related.

guài 1 怪 (kwăi^C) **LH** kuɛ^C ?, **OCM** *kwrə̂h ? — **[T]** *ONW* kuëi
'Strange, unusual, extraordinary' [Shu]. It seems that this word actually had the same OC rime as → guī 2 傀瑰; they may be mere variants.

guài 2 夬 → **jué** 2 決

guān 1 官倌 (kuân) **LH** kuɑn, **OCM** *kôn ?
'Office, magistrate, official' [BI, Shu] is prob. the s. w. as → guān 2 倌 'servant'.
[T] *Sin Sukchu SR* kwɔn (平); *MGZY* gon (平) [kɔn]; *ONW* kuɑn
[D] CDC *kuon*[1]

⫘ **guān** 管 (kuân) **LH** kuɑn, **OCM** *kôn ? — **[T]** *ONW* kuɑn
'To manage' [BI], 'take care of' [Li].

guān 2 倌 (kuân) **LH** kuɑn, **OCM** *kôn ? — **[T]** *ONW* kuɑn
'Servant, groom' (also MC *kwan*^C) [Shi].

⋇ **guàn** 貫 (kuân[C]) **LH** kuɑn(C), **OCM** *kôn(s) — **[D]** PMin *kuot
'To serve' [Shi].
[<] exoactive of guān 倌 (kuân) (§4.3.2).
[E] ST *kol > WT *kʰol-po* 'servant, vassal' ⋇ *'kʰol-ba, bkol* 'make someone a servant, use as a servant' (Bodman 1980: 137; *HST:* 131); PL *C-kjwan id.

guān₃ 棺 (kuân) **LH** kuɑn, **OCM** *kwân or *kôn
'Coffin' [Zuo].
⋇ **guàn** 棺 (kuânC) **LH** kuɑnC, **OCM** *kwâns or *kôns ?
'To (be) put into a coffin' [Zuo, Li] (Downer 1959: 278).
[<] exopass. of the above (§4.4).
[E] ST, area word: TB-Lushai *kuaŋH* 'coffin, trough, groove', Kukish *r-kuaŋ 'coffin, boat' [*IST:* 47], perh. also WB *kʰoŋB* 'trough, canoe', yet see → kōng 空 'empty' to which all these etyma may belong. Coffins and boats used to be hollowed tree trunks, hence some languages have the same word for both. For the discrepancy in final nasals see §6.4.2.

guān₄ 冠 (kuân) **LH** kuɑn, **OCM** *kôn, OCB *kon — **[T]** *ONW* kuɑn
'A cap' [Shi].
⋇ **guàn** 冠 (kuânC) **LH** kuɑnC, **OCM** *kôns, OCB *kons
'To put on a cap' (manhood ceremony) [Zuo, Li].
[<] exopass. (§4.4), lit. '(make someone to) be capped'.
[E] ST: PTB *gwa ~ *kwa:n (*STC* no. 160) > WT *bgo-ba, bgos* 'clothes, put on clothes' ⋇ *gos* 'dress' ⋇ *gon-pa* 'to put on, dress' ⋇ *skon-pa, bskon* 'to put on clothes', Nung *gwa ~ ga* 'to dress' intr. Alternatively, Unger (*Hao-ku* 36, 1990: 48) relates the WT words to **gǔn** 袞 (kuənB) 'royal robe' [Shi].

guān₅ 關 (kwan) **LH** kuan, **OCM** *krôn, OCB *kron
'Bar' [Lao], 'barrier, frontier' [Shi]. Note the syn. → jiàn₄ 楗, → xián₆ 閑.
[T] *Sin Sukchu SR* kwan (平), *LR* kwɔn; *MGZY* gwan (平) [kwan]; *ONW* kuän
[D] CDC *kuan¹*
[E] <> PTai *klɔnA1 'rafter, latch on door'.

guān₆ 鰥 → **guǎ** 寡

guān₇ 觀 (kuân) **LH** kuɑn, **OCM** *kôn
'To watch, look at, observe' (e.g. the ocean, progress) [Shi].
[T] *Sin Sukchu SR* kwɔn (平); *MGZY* gon (平) [kɔn]; *ONW* kuɑn
⋇ **guàn** 觀 (kuânC) **LH** kuɑnC, **OCM** *kôns — **[T]** *ONW* kuɑn
(1) 'To cause to see, show' [Zhouli].
[<] exoactive / caus. of *guān* 觀 (kuân) (§4.3.2).
(2) 'Aspect, scene' [Guan].
[<] exopass. of *guān* 觀 (kuân), lit. 'what is looked at' (§4.4); in *guàn tái* 觀臺 'look-out tower' [Zuo]; tone C occurs because the word is part of a compound (Downer 1959: 289).
[E] This stem *kon is derived from the root under → hóu₁ 侯. Often the form in final *-n* seems to have the same meaning as the base form.

guǎn 痯 → **juàn** 倦

guàn₁ 丱 (kwan) **LH** kuanC, **OCM** *krôns, OCB *krons
'Tuft of hair' [Shi].
[E] AA: Mon *klòn* 'crest, tuft', has been proposed with some hesitation by Bodman (1985: 157); for the medials see §7.3.

guàn$_2$ 涫 (kuânC) **LH** kuanC, **OCM** *kwâns or *kôns
'To bubble' [Xun] (*HST:* 49).
[E] ST *kol > WT *'khol-ba, khol* 'to boil' ⋇ *skol-ba* 'to cause to boil' (Bodman 1980: 137; *HST:* 49). Unger (*Hao-ku* 36, 1990: 50) relates the WT words to *gǔn* 混 (kuənB) 'to bubble, boil'; Y-Guǎngzhōu *kuɐn35 sœy35* 滾水 'hot water' may be related.

guàn$_3$ 貫 (kuân[C]) **LH** kuan(C), **OCM** *kôns, OCB *kons
'To pierce' (flesh, hand, foot, ear with a sharp object) [Zuo] > 'go through the center' [Shi], 'to string' [Li] > 'tightly bound together' > 'be intimate with' [Shi].
⋇ **guǎn** 管 (kuânB) **LH** kuanB, **OCM** *kwânʔ or *kônʔ
'To connect, comprise' [Liji].
[<] endoactive (§4.5).
[E] Together with → kuǎn 窾 'hole', this etymon belongs to a ST root *kwar.

guàn$_4$ 貫摜慣 (kuanC) **LH** kuanC, **OCM** *krôns
'Familiar with, used to' 貫 [Meng], 摜慣 [SW: Zuo] > 'custom, usage' 串 [Shi].
[E] Although this word is assumed to be related to → guàn$_3$ 貫 'bound together' (hence > 'familiar'), it prob. is a different etymon which is derived from the same ST root *-rol as WT *srol* 'usage, custom, habit', JP *a31-ron31* (*CVST* 2: 91).

guàn$_5$ 盥 (kuânB, kuânC) **LH** kuanB, kuanC, **OCM** *kwânʔ/s or *kônʔ/s
'To wash the hands' intr. [Shu].
⋇ **huàn** 浣 (ɣuânB) **LH** guanC, **OCM** *gwâns or *gôns
'To wash clothes' [Guan] (Wáng Lì 1982: 553).
[E] ST: KN-Lai *khoʔl* 'to clean' (with water) [*LTBA* 20.2: 79], 'to bathe' [*LTBA* 21.1: 49]. Possibly the same etymon as → guàn$_6$ 灌 'pour libation'.

guàn$_6$ 灌 (kuânC) **LH** kuanC, **OCM** *kwâns or *kôns
'To pour out; libation' 祼 [Shi], 灌 [Lun]; 'drink' (wine) [Liji]; 'flow into' (rivers) [Zhuang], 'to water, irrigate' [Hou Hanshu].
[E] ST: Chepang *khur*, Boro *kur* 'to scrape', Mikir *hòr* 'to ladle out', Ao *2a2kɯn* 'to scoop', Rongmei *n-xûan* 'to scratch' (Weidert 1987: 19). <> PTai *guon 'to ladle' (water) [Luo Yongxian *MKS* 27, 1997: 273]. Possibly the same etymon as → guàn$_5$ 盥 'wash'.

guāng$_1$ 光 (kwâŋ) **LH** kuaŋ, **OCM** *kwâŋ
'Be bright, glorious' [BI, Shi, Shu].
[T] *Sin Sukchu SR* kwaŋ (平); *MGZY* gwang (平) [kwaŋ]; *ONW* kuaŋ
⋇ **kuàng** 曠 (khwâŋC) **LH** khuaŋC, **OCM** *khwâŋh
'Bright' [Zhuang].
[C] An additional allofam is → huáng$_2$ 煌 'brilliant'.

guāng$_2$ 光 'extensive' → **guǎng$_2$** 廣

guǎng$_1$, wàng 迋 'fear' → **jù$_5$** 懼

guǎng$_2$ 廣 (kwâŋB) **LH** kuaŋB, **OCM** *kwâŋʔ
'Be extensive, wide, broad, vast' [BI, Shi].
[T] *Sin Sukchu SR* kwaŋ (上); *MGZY* gwang (上) [kwaŋ]; *ONW* kuaŋ
⋇ **guāng** 光 (kwâŋ) **LH** kuaŋ, **OCM** *kwâŋ
'Be extensive' [Shi, Shu]; the *Shījīng* rime indicates tone A, hence it is perh. not a graphic loan for *guàng* 廣 (kuâŋC) 'fully, extensively' (so Karlgren *GSR* 707a). Karlgren (1956: 14) adds:

⫘ **kuàng** 曠 ($k^hwâŋ^C$) **LH** $k^huaŋ^C$, **OCM** *khwâŋh — **[T]** *ONW* $k^huaŋ$
'Be vacant, desolate, neglect' [Shi, Shu].

⫘ **kuō** 擴 ($k^hwâk$) **LH** k^huak, **OCM** *khwâk
'To extend' [Meng].

⫘ **huáng** 潢 (ɣwâŋ) **LH** guaŋ, **OCM** *gwâŋ
'Great, vast' [Xun].

[E] Etymology not certain, CH may be related either to TB or Tai, or both (involving some loan relationship): ST: Lushai *vaaŋ*^{F} < *vaaŋʔ* 'be large, extensive' ⫘ *vaŋ*^{R} < *vaŋʔ* 'breadth, width, broad, wide', WT *yaŋ* 'wide, broad, large' (for the WT initial, see §12.9 [2]). <> Tai: S. *kwaaŋ*^{C1} is a derivation by k-prefix from S. *waaŋ*^{C1} 'unimpeded' (Noss 1964: 49). Baxter / Sagart (1998: 60) relate this wf to → kuān 寬 'wide'; perh. ultimately related to the root *wa under → kuàng$_1$ 況.

guī$_1$ 規 (kjwie) **LH** kye, **OCM** *kwe
'Circle' [Li] > 'a compass' [Meng] > 'regulate, admonish' [Zuo] > 'rule, law' [Li].
[T] *Sin Sukchu SR* kuj (平); *MGZY* gÿue (平) [kyɛ]
[<] perh. derived from *wê with the nominalizing k-prefix (§5.4).

⫘ **xí** 觿 (ɣiwei) **LH** ɣue, **OCM** *wê ?
'Length of the circumference of a wheel' 巂 [Li]; 'vapor round the sun' 鑴 [Zhouli] (also MC *xjwie*). This root prob. underlies → yíng$_4$ 營 et al.

[E] Etymology not certain, but note TB-Chepang *gweʔ* 'circular in shape' ⫘ *kweʔ* 'hook, fishhook'; PTB *koy 'bend round, be curved, coil, etc.' (*STC* no. 307).

guī$_2$ 傀瑰 (kuậi) **LH** kuəi, **OCM** *kûi
'Extraordinary' 傀 [Zhouli], 瓌 [Zhuang], 'rare, marvelous' 瑰 (Mandarin) > 'a kind of precious stone' 瑰 [Shi]. It seems that this word actually had the same OC rime as → guài$_1$ 怪 'strange, extraordinary'; they may be mere variants.

guī$_3$ 歸 (kjwei) **LH** kui, **OCM** *kwəi, OCB *k^wjəj — **[T]** *ONW* kui
'To return' (to a place where one belongs) intr. [BI, Shi] > tr. 'to return' > 'bring home' (a wife), 'give into marriage' [Shi]. Although the morphological role of the initial *k-* is not clear (but a k-prefix does occur, see §5.4), *guī* is prob. derived from → huí 回; see there for an overview of synonyms. Note the semantic parallelism with MK: PVM *veːl 'return' ⫘ *k-veːl 'village' (i.e. where one belongs) [Ferlus]. *Guī* is often related to WT *'k^{h}or* 'turn, return', but see the comment under → huí 回.

guī$_4$ 龜 (kjwi) **LH** ku ~ kuɨ, **OCM** *kwrə, OCB *kwrə
'Tortoise, turtle' [OB]. Southern dialects and Han rimes indicate doublets LH ku and kuiə (Luo / Zhou 1958).
[E] AA: PMonic *dwii ?, Nyah Kur 'freshwater soft-shelled tortoise'; Mon *kwiʔ* 'freshwater turtle' [Diffloth 1984: 76]; PWMiao *ki^A 'turtle'; cf. Min dial. → xī$_{16}$ 蠵 may be a variant.

guǐ$_1$ 鬼 ($kjwəi^B$) **LH** kui^B, **OCM** *kuiʔ
'Spirit, ghost' [OB, Shi]; originally: the ghost of a deceased who has returned to haunt (terrorize) the living (E. Childs-Johnson *EC* 20, 1995: 79ff).
[T] *Sin Sukchu SR* kuj (上); *MGZY* gue (上) [kuɛ]; *ONW* kui — **[D]** PMin *kyi^B
[E] Two etymologies have been proposed: (1) Derived from → wēi$_4$ 威 'to overawe, terrorize' (Childs-Johnson) with k-nominalization (§5.4; Baxter / Sagart 1998: 48; 59), and endoactive tone B, lit. 'the thing which is doing the overawing' (§4.5.1). (2) Or related to → guī$_3$ 歸 'return' (*SW;* Carr *CAAAL* 24, 1985: 61).

guǐ$_{2}$ 匭 → **guǐ**$_{3}$ 簋, → **kuì**$_{1}$ 匱

guǐ$_{3}$ 簋 (kjwi^{B} 3) **LH** kuɨ^{B}, **OCM** *kwrəʔ, OCB *kʷrjuʔ
Name of a bronze ritual vessel, a 'tureen' (Shaughnessy) [OB, BI, Shi], originally prob. some kind of basket or bamboo container.
[E] Possibly ST: TB-PLB *kʷiy^{1} 'receptacle, container' > Lahu *phɨ*, in some languages 'nest' [Matisoff *D. of Lahu:* 917]. CH ? -> Tai: S. *kuay* 'basket'. The name and shape of this vessel is reminiscent of 'turtle' → guī$_{4}$ 龜 LH *kuɨ*. The homophone guǐ 匭 'box, chest' [Shu] is prob. unrelated (under → kuì$_{1}$ 匱; however, acc. to *SW*, 匭 it is also the old graph for 簋).

guì$_{1}$ 貴 (kjwei^{C}) **LH** kuis, **OCM** *kus, OCB *kjuts
'Precious' [Yi], 'dear, expensive, eminent' [Zuo].
[T] *Sin Sukchu SR* kuj (去); *MGZY* gue (去) [kuɛ]; *ONW* kui
[D] PMin *kyi^{C}
[E] ST: WT *gus-po* 'costly, expensive' ɜɛ *gus-pa* 'respect, reverence' (*HST:* 121) ɜɛ *dkon* 'valuable'.

guì$_{2}$ 跪 (gjwie^{B}, kʰjwie^{B}) **LH** gyai^{B}, kʰ-, **OCM** *goiʔ, *khoiʔ
'To kneel' [Zuo], 'foot' [Xun] is perh. connected with PVM *t-ku:lʔ 'knee'.

guì$_{3}$ 會禬 → **huì**$_{1}$ 會

guì$_{4}$ 撅 'lift' → **kōu** 摳

gǔn$_{1}$ 緄 (kuən^{B}) **LH** kuən^{B}, **OCM** *kûnʔ
'A cord' [Shi].

ɜɛ **kǔn** 稛 (kʰuən^{B}) **LH** kʰuən^{B}, **OCM** *kʰûnʔ
'To bind, string together' [Guoyu].
[<] perh. causative aspiration (§5.8.2).

gǔn$_{2}$ 混 → **guàn**$_{2}$ 涫

gǔn$_{3}$ 袞 → **guān**$_{4}$ 冠

guō$_{1}$ 活 → **huó**$_{2}$ 活

guō$_{2}$ 鍋 (kuâ) **LH** kuɑi, **OCM** *kwâi or *kôi
'Earthenware cooking pot' [SW]
[E] Area word: AA-PWa *kʔol 'cooking pot, pan', AN-Malay *kuali* 'cooking pot, pan' (Bodman 1980: 137).

guó 國 (kwək) **LH** kuək, **OCM** *kwə̂k, OCB *k-wək
'State' [BI, Shi].
[T] *Sin Sukchu SR* kuj (入), *PR*, *LR* kujʔ; *MGZY* gue (入) [kuɛ]; *ONW* kuək
[<] k-prefix derivation of *yù* 域閾 (jwək) (§5.4) (Baxter / Sagart 1998: 48).

ɜɛ **yù** 域閾 (jwək) **LH** wɨk, **OCM** *wrək, OCB *wrjək
'Boundary, territory' 域 [Shi], 'threshold' 閾 [Lun], also (xjwək).

ɜɛ **xù** 閾淢 (xjwək) **LH** hwɨk, **OCM** *hwək
'Threshold' 閾 [Lun], 'city moat' 淢 [Shi].

ɜɛ **yòu** 囿 (jəu^{C}) **LH** wu^{C}, **OCM** *wəh, OCB *wjəks
'Park, garden' [Shi].

[E] *Guó* has no obvious outside cognates. It may be related to WB *kwak* 'a circle or round spot..., confined within a local area' (as rain). The occasionally cited comparandum WT *yul* 'country' seems to be related to → yōu$_{1}$ 攸.

guǒ $_1$ 果 (kuâ^B) **LH** kuɑi^B, **OCM** *kôiʔ
'Fruit > result' [Yi]. — **[E]** Etymology not clear.
[T] *Sin Sukchu SR* kwɔ (上); *MGZY* gwo (上) [kwɔ]; *ONW* kuɑ
= ? **guǒ** 餜 (kuâ^B)
PMin *kɔi^{B1} 'rice cake', also 'dried fruit', hence perhaps the same word as 果 (J. Norman, p.c.).

guǒ $_2$ 輠 → **yuán** $_5$ 員圓圜

guǒ $_3$**-luǒ** 蜾蠃 (kuâ^B-luâ^B) **LH** kuɑi^B-luɑi^B, **OCM** *kôi-rôiʔ, OCB *k(r)ōjʔ-(C)rōjʔ
'Species of small wasp' [Shi].
[E] ST, area word: PTB *k(l)wa-y ⋇ g(l)wa-y (*STC* n. 144) > WB *kwai^B* 'dammer bee'; PNorthern Naga *C-guay, Lushai *k^{h}uai^H* ~ *k^{h}ɔi^H* 'bee, wasp', Tangkhul Naga *k^{h}ui*, Thakali *koy* 'bee', Chepang *kway* 'bee'. Matisoff (1995: 64) suggests that the final *-i/-y is a ST diminutive suffix. <> Kadai: Hlai *ko:i, kuai, ka:i.* <> MK: PVM *kwe:ʔ 'bee' [Ferlus], a Chinese loan? Semai (Aslian branch of MK) *lwey* [All forms from Matisoff 1995a]. Note that none of the TB forms cited by Matisoff and in *STC* no. 157 have a medial *r* or *l* (*HST:* 41). Therefore the bisyllabic OC form is not the result of dimidiation, but simply a reduplicative compound of the common type CV-lV or *CV-rV (§2.7).

guò 過 (kuâ^C) **LH** kuɑi^C, **OCM** *kôih or *kwâih — **[T]** *ONW* kuɑ
'To pass' [Shi], 'transgress' [Lunyu], derived from *guō* next (Unger *Hao-ku* 21, 1983: 175).
⋇ **guō** 過 (kuâ) **LH** kuɑi, **OCM** *kôi or *kwâi
'To pass by' [Shu].
[E] Prob. ST although the vowels do not agree (WT *rgal* could theoretically derive from ST *gwal, but Lushai and WB forms speak against this), perh. *guò* may involve an unusual OC *a* > *o* shift: WT *rgal-ba, brgal* 'to step over, pass over, travel through, ford', Lushai *kai^H* / *kai^L* 'to cross over, go across' ? ⋇ *kal^H* 'walk, travel, proceed, pass by', WB *kai^B* 'exceed, surpass, excel'.

H

há-má 蝦蟆 (ɣa-ma) **LH** ga-ma, **OCM** *grâ-mrâ or *ga-maʔ — **[T]** *ONW* ɣä
'Frog' [Taiping yulan: Mozi] is onomatopoetic, MK has similar forms: OMon *kma(c)* 'green frog'.

hái 骸 (ɣăi) **LH** gɛɨ, **OCM** *grə̂
'Bones, skeleton' [Zuo]. Perh. related to → hé$_6$ 核 'kernel'.

hǎi$_1$ 海 (xậi^B) **LH** hə^B, **OCM** *hmə̂ʔ, OCB * hməʔ
'Ocean, sea' [BI, Shi]. The absence of MC medial *w* is unexpected.
[T] *Sin Sukchu SR* xaj (上); *MGZY* hay (上) [xaj]; *ONW* hɑi
[E] Prob. related to → huì$_7$ 晦 *hmə̂ʔ 'dark'; in numerous Zhou texts *hǎi* is described as *huì*. In OC they were (near?) homophones in spite of the difference in MC medial *w*. Semantic parallelism with → míng$_3$ 溟冥 'ocean' = → míng$_2$ 冥 'dark' supports this etymological connection.

hǎi$_2$ 醢 (xậi^B) **LH** hə^B, **OCM** *hwə̂ʔ ?
'Boneless meat sauce' [Shi], or 'meat which has been dried, minced and pickled' (*GSR* 995n). Bodman (1980: 133) compares this to WT *smig* 'purple, color of clotted blood', *smug-ma* 'stale meat, getting rotten' [Das].

hài$_1$ 亥 (ɣəi^B) **LH** gə^B, **OCM** *gə̂ʔ
The 12th of the Earthly Branches identified with the pig [OB] (the graph is the drawing of a pig), acc. to Norman (1985: 89) a loan from AA, note Viet. *gỏi* 'pig' (obsolete), Khmer *kol* (sp. *ko[r]*) 'pig' (in names of years).

hài$_2$ 害 → **gē$_3$** 割

hān$_1$ 鼾 (xân)
'To snore' [Six Dyn.].
[E] ST: WT *hal-ba* 'to pant, wheeze, snort' (*HST:* 135). Syn. → hōu 齁.

hān$_2$ 酣 → **gān$_7$** 甘

hán$_1$ 含函 (ɣậm) **LH** gəm, **OCM** *gə̂m — **[T]** *ONW* ɣɑm
'Have in the mouth' [Zuo] > 'hold back, bear resentment' 含 [Shu]; 'to hold inside, contain' (as life in grain) [Shi], (as life force *qì$_8$* 氣 in people) 函 [Hanshu] > 'cuirass' 函 [Meng] > 'envelop'.
[D] The Northern Min softened initial in 含 *ɡ̆am may indicate OC prenasalization which is confirmed by Yáo *gjɔm^2* < *ng- 'hold in the mouth' (Norman 1986: 383).

ⵣ **hàn** 含 (ɣậm^C) **LH** gəm^C, **OCM** *gə̂ms
'Put in the mouth' 含 [Zuo] > 'resent' [Zuo], 'dissatisfied' 憾 [Li].
[<] exoactive / caus. of *hán* 含函 (ɣậm) (§4.3.2).

ⵣ **hàn** 頷 (ɣậm^B) **LH** gəm^B, **OCM** *gə̂mʔ
'Jaw' [Gongyang].
[<] endoactive of *hán* 含函 (ɣậm) (§4.5) (so Bodman 1980: 110), lit. 'the thing that holds / keeps something in the mouth'. Although a regular derivation in OC, it may have been influenced by AA words for 'jaw' (Shorto 1972), see below.

[E] The final *-m* in etyma with these types of meanings is sound-symbolic (§2.9). The meanings of the OC allofams are also paralleled in some TB and AA words:

'Have / keep in the mouth':

MK: Khmer /-kam/ 'bite' ⋈ /kham/ 'clamp or cut with teeth or jaw..., bite', /kum/ 'be resentful'. <> TB-Chepang *kəmh-* be speechless'.

'Put / take into the mouth':

ST: PTB *gam (*STC:* 166; 183) > WT *'gam* 'put into the mouth', *gams, bgams* ⋈ *'kʰam-pa* 'put into the mouth', also WT *sgam* 'box', *sgam-po* 'profound'; Mru *kʰam* 'take in the mouth, suffer' ⋈ *kʰam* 'box' [Löffler 1966: 140], Miri *gam* 'seize with the teeth' (as a tiger), PTani *g(j)am 'bite'.

'Jaw':

ST: Mru *kam* 'chin', Chepang *kəm-pət* 'gills' (fish), 'gill fins'; Lepcha *kam* 'jaw'. <> PMK *tga(a)m 'jaw' (Shorto 1972): Forrest (*JAOS* 82, 1962: 334) cites Khmer *thkéam*, Stieng *gam* 'jaw', Shorto provides additional words, incl. Biat *gam* 'molar', Viet. *căm* 'chin'.

It is not clear if the following 'molar' belongs to this root (note WB *am^B*, not *gam^B*):

ST: PTB *gam (*STC* no. 50) > Chepang *magam* 'molar', Thakali *kəm-sə*, Lepcha *fo-gam* (*fo* 'tooth'), Limbu *hema* 'molar'; Garo *wa-gum* 'tooth' (*STC:* 183 n. 482; *HST:* 99), WB *am^B* 'molar'.

The notion 'keep in the mouth' is a common metaphor for emotions, therefore → $kān_2$ 堪 'endure' is prob. cognate; note also the Mru field of meaning.

Similar words are: → $xián_{11}$ 銜 'a horse's bit' (Bodman) and to → $qián_2$ 柑箝 'wooden gag'. Furthermore, Wáng Lì (1982: 605) believes it to be related to → $qiǎn_3$ 慊 'dissatisfied'; → $dàn_5$ 啖啗. These items are prob. not all genetically related, but what unites them is the phonesthemic final *-m (§2.9).

hán₂ 寒 (ɣân) **LH** gɑn, **OCM** *gân — **[T]** *ONW* ɣɑn

'Cold' (ice, a spring, season) [BI, Shi] > 'poor' [Shiji]; > *hánxīn* 寒心 'disheartened' [Shiji]. Etymology unknown.

hán₃ 函 → **hán₁** 含函

hán₄ 涵 (ɣậm) **LH** ɣəm, **OCM** *gə̂m, OCB *gom

'To soak, overflow' [Guan] belongs perh. to the wf → $chén_2$ 沈.

hǎn 闞 → **xiǎn₃, hǎn** 闞

hàn₁ 厂 → **àn₂** 岸

hàn₂ 汗 (ɣân^C) **LH** gɑn^C, **OCM** *gâns — **[D]** PMin *gan^C2

'Sweat' [Yi]. TB has similar looking words, note PKiranti *gʰàl 'sweat' (Starostin acc. to van Driem 1995: 254), or Lushai *tʰlan^L* 'sweat' [Weidert 1975: 19].

hàn₃ 扞閈 → **gān₁** 干

hàn₄ 旱 → **gān₉** 乾

Hàn₅ 漢 (xân^C) **LH** hɑn^C, **OCM** *hâns, OCB *xans

'Name of a river' in the ancient Chǔ area, can also mean 'river' generally as in 'Milky way' [Shi]. The right element in the graph was probably not phonetic, hence the initial did not include an *n.

hàn₆ 暵 (xân[^B/^C]) **LH** hɑn^B/C, **OCM** *hânʔ/s

'To scorch' [Shi].

⋈ **hàn** 熯 (xân^B) **LH** hɑn^B, **OCM** *hânʔ, OCB *njanʔ !

'To burn' [Guan], 'dry' [Yi].

[E] The phonology and hence etymology is not certain. Prob. not related to → $rán_1$ 然 *nan 'burn' because the phonetic element in *hàn* has originally been chosen for its meaning 'distress', not for its sound (so *GSR* 144). Baxter apparently considers 熯 a graphic loan for a word OCB *njan?. The difference in the initial consonants (*h- vs. *k-) makes cognation with the syn. → $gān_9$ 乾 unlikely.

$hàn_7$ 翰 'support' → **$gàn_1$** 幹

$hàn_8$ 含憾 → **$hán_1$** 含函

$hàn_9$ 頷 → **$hán_1$** 含函

$hàn_{10}$ 鑑 → **$làn_1$** 濫

$hàn_{11}$ 濫 → **$làn_1$** 濫

$háng_1$ 行 'row' → **$xíng_1$** 行

$háng_2$ 行 'strong' → **qiáng** 強彊

$háng_3$ 頏 (ɣâŋ) **LH** gɑŋ, **OCM** *gâŋ — **[T]** *ONW* ɣɑŋ

Occurs in Shi 28 together with *jié* 頡 (*jié...háng*); *SW* glosses both 'stretch the neck', this word is thus perh. a variant of → $xiàng_4$ 項, and derived from → $gāng_1$ 亢 (kâŋ) 'neck'. On the other hand, commentators interpret these words as 'flying up and flying down' (of birds).

$háng_4$ 航杭 (ɣâŋ) **LH** gɑŋ, **OCM** *gâŋ

'Go by boat' 杭 [Shi], 'boat' 航 [GY], 斻 [SW]. Whereas acc. to *Yìjīng* a → $zhōu_1$ 舟 'boat' was originally a hollowed tree trunk (canoe), *háng* was two boats combined into one, as canoes lashed together (so *SW*, although Liú Yǐ-gāng *YYYJ* 1986.1: 169 thinks a *háng* was probably constructed of boards). Acc. to *FY*, *háng* is used for *zhōu* 舟 in central and eastern China.

⋈ **huáng** 艎 (ɣwâŋ) and **bàng** 艕 (pwâŋ^C)

'Ancient Wú words for boat' [Yupian] are variants acc. to Mahdi (1994: 456). Egerod (*CAAAL* 6, 1976: 58) believes that this is the same etymon as → $xíng_1$ 行 'to go to', but it prob. has an AN origin (via AA?) *qaBaŋ 'two boats lashed together' (Mahdi 1999: 147f). → $fāng_2$ 方 is prob. the same etymon. Syn. → $chuán_1$ 船.

$hāo_1$ 撓 → **nǎo** 撓

$hāo_2$ 薅茠 (xâu) **LH** hou, **OCM** *hû (< *hwû ?)

'To clear away weeds with a hoe' 薅 [Shi], 茠 [SW: Shi].

[E] ST: Chepang *hu?-* 'to weed (around plants), pull out weeds'. Unrelated to the synonym → nòu 耨, but perh. connected with → $yún_4$ 耘 *wən < *wun (?) 'to weed'.

háo 號 (ɣâu) **LH** ɣɑu, **OCM** *ɦâu — **[T]** *ONW* ɣɑu

'To shout, cry out' [Shi].

⋈ **hào** 號 (ɣâu^C) **LH** ɣɑu^C, **OCM** *ɦâuh

'A request' [Shi, YiZhoushu], 'title, appellation' [Zuo]; 'name' [Zhouli].

[T] *Sin Sukchu SR* ɣaw (去); *MGZY* Xaw (去) [ɣaw]; *ONW* ɣɑu

[<] exopass. derivation (§4.4), lit. 'what is called'. The extension of the meaning 'shout, call' to 'ask, request' is parallel to → $hū_2$ 呼.

⋈ **huān** 讙 (xuân, xjwɐn) **LH** xuɑn, xyɑn, **OCM** *hwan / *hwân, *hon / *hôn

'To shout, joyous' [Li].

[E] ST: PTB *gaw ~ *kaw > Kanauri *ku*, Nung *go*, Lushai *ko^L / ko?^L*, JP *gau^33*, WB *k^ho* 'call' (*HST*: 51).

hǎo 好 (xâu^B) **LH** hou^B, **OCM** *hûʔ, OCB *xūʔ
'Be good, fine' [BI, Shi].
[T] *Sin Sukchu SR* xaw (上); *MGZY* haw (上) [xaw]; *ONW* hɑu

ꭗ **hào** 好 (xâu^C) **LH** hou^C, **OCM** *hûh
'To love' [Shi].
[<] exoactive / putative (§4.3.2), lit. 'consider good'

[E] Perh. ST and related to → chù$_4$, xù 畜 'rear, raise'; Baxter (acc. to Matisoff *HPTB:* 58) connects the TB words cited there to *hǎo*.

hào$_1$ 號 → **háo** 號

hào$_2$ 皓 (ɣâu^B) **LH** gou^B, **OCM** *gûʔ
'Bright, white' [Lü]. For *hào* 顥 [Lü], 昊 [Shi] / ɣâu^B, see under → hào$_3$ 浩.
[E] Related to S. *k^haau^{A1}* 'white', PHlai *kʰaːu¹ 'white' [Matisoff 1988c no. 294].

ꭗ **gǎo** 皓皋 (kâu^B) **LH** kou^B, **OCM** *kûʔ
'Be brilliant' 皋 [Shi]; 'pure, bright' 皓 [Shi]. This is prob. the s. w. as → gǎo$_1$ 暠 (kâu^B).

hào$_3$ 浩 (ɣâu^B) **LH** gou^B, **OCM** *gûʔ — **[T]** *ONW* ɣɑu
'Vast' of rising waters [Shi]. The etymology of the homophone *hào* 顥 [Lü], 昊 [Shi] (ɣâu^B) is ambiguous because it can mean 'bright, splendid' (of Heaven) and then be the s. w. as → hào$_2$ 皓.
[E] A TB cognate is perh. WB *ko^B* 'rise up, swell, bulge' ꭗ *ko* 'lift out of place, prize up', Lushai *ko^H* 'raised ground, mound, rise suddenly' (waters), 'surge' (waves). *Hào* may be an allofam of → gāo$_1$ 高 'high', although the vowels do not agree.

hào$_4$ 顥 [Lü], 昊 → **hào$_3$** 浩

hē 喝欱 (xập) **LH** həp, **OCM** *hə̂p
'To drink' 欱 [Ban Gu, Han dyn.] is cognate to, or a popular variant of, **xī** 噏 LH *xɨəp* 'to drink' [Hou Hanshu] (Baxter, p. c.) and perh. also to → xiá$_1$ 呷. It may be of ST origin: Lushai *hup^L* 'to drink from the hands, suck (water) from hand'.

hé$_1$ 禾 (ɣuâ) **LH** ɣuɑi or guɑi, **OCM** *(g)wâi
'Plant' (of grains), 'foxtail millet' [OB, Shi] (Qiu Xigui 2000: 176).
[D] PWMin *wɔi^{A2}, SMin *g-: Zhāngpíng *gue^{A2}* 'rice plant'
[E] ? -> Tai: S. *k^haa^{A2}* < *ɣ- 'straw, thatch grain' (Li F. 1976: 42).

hé$_2$ 和 (ɣuâ) **LH** ɣuɑi or guɑi, **OCM** *(g)wâi — **[T]** *ONW* ɣuɑ
'Being harmonious, concordant' [Shi].

ꭗ **hè** 和 (ɣuâ^C) **LH** ɣuɑi^C or guɑi^C, **OCM** *(g)wâih
'To harmonize, respond in singing, rime' [Shi, Zuo].
[<] exoactive of *hé* 和 (ɣuâ) (§4.3.2). An allofam is perh. → kē$_3$ 科 'class'.

hé$_3$ 何 (ɣâ) **LH** gɑi, **OCM** *gâi
'What, why, where' [Shi].
[T] *Sin Sukchu SR* ɣɔ (平), *LR* ɣɔ; *MGZY* Xo (平) [ɣɔ]; *ONW* ɣɑ
[D] Y-Guǎngzhōu *²¹hɔ^{A2}*
[<] independent pronoun derived from *hú*, see §3.3.3; Matisoff (1995: 74).

ꭗ **hú** 胡 (ɣuo) **LH** gɑ, **OCM** *gâ
'What, where' [Shi] is used adverbially (Pulleyblank 1995: 95).
[E] ST: WT *ga-na* 'where', *ga-ru* 'whither'. See also → hè$_1$ 何荷.

⋇ **xiá** 遐 (ɣa) **LH** ga, **OCM** *gâ (prob. not *grâ)
'How, why' [Shi], perh. this is simply a variant or graphic loan for *hú* 'above'.

⋇ **xī** 奚 (ɣiei) **LH** ge, **OCM** *gê — **[T]** *ONW* ɣė
'To what, whither?' [Zuo], 'how?' [Zuo, Meng]; acc. to Dobson (*LAC:* 147) a fusion of *hé yǐ* 何以. It occurs in preverbal or pre-nominal constructions (Pulleyblank 1995: 95).

⋇ **hé** 曷 (ɣât) **LH** gɑt, **OCM** *gât
'Why, how, when?' used mostly adverbially [Shi] (Pulleyblank ibid.).

⋇ **hé** 盍 (ɣâp) **LH** gɑp, **OCM** *gâp
'Why not?' [Lunyu] is a contraction of *hú bù* 胡不 (Pulleyblank ibid.).

hé₄ 河 (ɣâ) **LH** gɑi, **OCM** *gâi
'River, Yellow River' [OB, Shi].
[T] *Sin Sukchu SR* ɣɔ (平), *LR* ɣɔ; *MGZY* Xo (平) [ɣɔ]; *ONW* ɣɑ
[E] Three etymologies have been suggested for this northern word: (1) cognate to TB-WT *rgal-ba* 'to pass or ford a river' (Coblin 1986), for a parallel semantic connection of 'ford' with 'river', see → dù₂ 渡. (2) An Altaic loan, cf. Mongol *γol* 'river' (Norman). (3) Derived from *hú* 湖 (ɣuo) 'lake' (Matisoff 1995a: 71). Note also JP *kʰaʔ³¹* < *kʰak* 'water, river', but the final does not agree with OC.

hé₅ 合 (ɣập) **LH** gəp, **OCM** *gə̂p, OCB *gop
'To be together, joined, harmonious' intr. [Shi, Shu] > caus. 'to put together, match, a companion, a mate' [BI, Shi], 'harmony, concordance' [Shi, Shu]; 'agree with' [Meng], 'to answer' [Zuo]; 'close, shut' [Guoce]; later *hé* 盒 'box with a lid'. The graph shows an inverted open mouth facing down onto an opening.
[T] *Sin Sukchu SR* ɣa (入); *PR, LR* ɣɔʔ; *MGZY* Xo (入) [ɣɔ]; *ONW* ɣɑp.
[D] M-Amoy *hap^D2* 'to join, unite, shut, to fit, agree'.

= **hé** 閤 (ɣập) — **[D]** M-Amoy *kʰap^D1* < *khap* 'all'
'All together, all' (as in 'all in town know / the whole town knows...') [post-Han].

⋇ **(kʰap)** — **[D]** M-Amoy *kʰap^D1* < *khap* (< *khəp?) 蓋 'inverted' (as a bowl).

⋇ **(kap)** — **[D]** M-Amoy *kap* 'with, along with, to unite, join together'.

⋇ **gé** 閤蛤 (kập) **LH** kəp, **OCM** *kə̂p
'A small gate' 閤 [Mo] > ('two open sides fitting together':) 'oyster, mussel' 蛤 [Li].

⋇ **qià** 洽 (ɣăp) **LH** gɛp, **OCM** *grə̂p
'To accord with, unite, assemble' [Shi]; 'to sacrifice to ancestors collectively' 祫 [Li] (Karlgren 1956: 15).
[<] r-causative of *hé* *gə̂p.
[E] Alternatively, this could be a different word related to WT *'grub-pa* 'be made ready, be finished, accomplished' (Gong H. 2002b: 202).

[E] Three unrelated etyma *hé* 合 *gə̂p, → hé₈ 盍蓋 *gâp, and → huì₁ 會 *gwâts have partially converged in OC. The root *k_p* 'fit together, cover, meet' (including *kap → hé₈ 盍蓋) is widely encountered in the area:

Area etymon *kup. TB-Lushai *kʰup^L* 'to cover with anything concave side downwards, cover with an inverted vessel...', JP *kʰup³¹* 'capsize, turn over' (boat), Chepang *kʰup-* 'cover head'. The TB items agree semantically with the OC root *kap (> Mon *kɔp*), but phonologically with *kup.

PMK *kup: Khmer *gwpa* /kúuəp/ 'to join, bring together, unite', *ga'pa* /kup/ 'to join, unite, meet with, visit often', Mon inscr. *sakuip* /səkøp/ 'lid', also PVM *kəp 'to cover' [Ferlus]. Karlgren adds **xī₁** 翕 (xjəp) 'to bring / get together, concordant' [BI, Shi], but the initials are difficult to reconcile.

hé$_6$ 核 (ɣɛk) **LH** gɛk, **OCM** *grə̂k — **[D]** PMin *hut

'Kernel (of fruit)' [Shi] > 'investigate' [Shu] (< 'go to the kernel', so *GSR* no. 937a').

[E] ST: WT *rag* 'fruit stone, bead', Mikir *rak* 'fruit stone' (Bodman 1980: 86). Wáng Lì (1982: 249) relates this word to → gé$_5$ 骼 *krak 'bones' (not likely); perh. related to → hái 骸 'skeleton'.

hé$_7$ 涸 (ɣâk) **LH** gɑk, **OCM** *gâk

'To dry up' [Li] (i.e. soil, roads).

[E] Perh. related to →hè$_6$ 垎 and / or to stems under → gù$_1$ 固 (incl. Table G-1) and → jiān$_2$ 堅 (incl. Table J-1).

hé$_8$ 盍蓋 etc. (ɣâp) **LH** gɑp, **OCM** *gâp, OCB *ɦkap

('To put cover / lid on':) 'to cover (person, house), thatch' 蓋 [Zuo]; 'wooden leaf door' 闔 [Zuo], 'door leaf' 盍 [Xun], 'to shut' (mouth, door, and the like) 嗑, 闔 [Yi]. The meaning 盍 'join, unite' (actually 'close in on', as crowds of friends) [Yi] is somewhat uncertain; see Shaughnessy 1997: 90f; 301.

⋙ **gài** 蓋 (kâi^C) **LH** kɑs, **OCM** *kâts < *kâps, OCB *kats < **kaps

'A cover' (of a car) [Zhouli], 'lid' [OB, Zhoushu], 'have one's mouth shut' pass. [Shu]

[T] *Sin Sukchu SR* kai (去); *MGZY* gay (去) [kaj].

[E] Area etymon. TB-WT *'gebs-pa, bkab...* 'to cover', *sgab-pa* 'to cover', *k^{h}ebs* < *keps or *kaps 'a cover' (Bodman 1980: 49); PKiranti *kapt ~ *kap 'to thatch, cover with bed-clothes' [van Driem 1995: 252], JP *mə^{31}-kap^{31}* 'lid' ⋙ *gap^{31}* 'to cover' (house) (see also *HPTB:* 142). Perh. also WB *kap* 'join, unite, adhere', JP *kap^{55}* 'to stick, adhere to, join a group'.

PAA *kap: PMonic *p[_]kap, Nyah Kur *pəkap*, Mon *həkɔp* 'to turn sth. face down, to join an obj. face to face, face down' (this gloss reads like a description of the graph → hé$_5$ 合); Mon *gap* 'be fit for, fit to, pleasing to', Khmer *gā'pa* /koəp/, OKhmer *gap* 'to meet, strike, fit, suit, match, agree, please, be pleasing...'

The tone C derivative *gài* (LH *kɑs*, not *kuɑs* or *kos*) makes it clear that the OC rime was not *op. The three unrelated etyma → hé$_5$ 合 *gə̂p, hé$_8$ 盍蓋 *gâp, and → huì$_1$ 會 *gwâts have partially converged in OC.

hé$_9$ 盍 'why not' → **hé**$_3$ 何

hé$_{10}$ 翮 (ɣɛk) **LH** gɛk, **OCM** *grêk

'Root of a feather' [Zhouli] is perh. related to, or the s. w. as, 翱 (ɣɛk) 'wing' [SW], 'feather' [Yupian] (so Wáng Lì 1982: 251) which, however, apparently goes back to OCM *grək (not *grek).

hè$_1$ 何荷 (ɣâ^B) **LH** gɑi^B, **OCM** *gâiʔ

'To carry' (on the shoulder or back; responsibility), 'sustain' [Shi, Zuo].

⋙ **kě** 可 (k^{h}â^B) **LH** k^{h}ɑi^B, **OCM** *khâiʔ — **[D]** Y-Guǎngzhōu ^{35}*hɔ^{B1}*; K-Meixian *k^{h}ɔ^B*

'To bear, can, be able' [Shi]. The original graph is a drawing (可 without 口 'mouth') of an ax handle intended to write the word → kē$_1$ 柯 (kâ) *kâi; 口 *kǒu* has been added to indicate that 'ax handle' is only 'mouthed', i.e. is only a phonetic loan.

[T] *Sin Sukchu SR, PR, LR* k'ɔ (上); *MGZY* kho (上) [k'ɔ]; *ONW* k^{h}ɑ^B

[E] Bodman (1980: 138) compares *kě* to Chepang *k^{h}aay* 'be able'.

[E] ST: WT *'gel-ba, bkal* 'to load, lay on' ⋙ *sgal-ba* 'to load a beast of burden' ⋙ *k^{h}al* 'load, burden'. To *hè* may belong PTB *s-gal (*STC* no. 12): WT *sgal-pa* 'small of back', Garo *dźaŋ-gal* 'back', JP *kan* 'put on the back' (*STC*), Meithei *nam-gal / gan* 'back'. This etymon is distinct from PTB *m-kal 'kidney' (→ gān$_5$ 肝), and Tiddim Chin *xa:l*[3], Lushai *ṭʰaal*[L] < *kraals 'groin'; WB *kʰa*[B] 'loins'.

Perh. an old area word: PTai *ɣaan[A2] 'pole for carrying things', Saek *kʰɔɔl*[4] *(< gɔɔl*[A]) > *kʰɔɔn*[4] 'to carry on one end of a pole over the shoulder', Mak *ʔgaan*[1] (Ni Dabai in Edmondson / Solnit 1988: 91).

[C] An allofam is prob. → qí$_6$ 騎 'ride'.

hè$_2$ 鶴 (ɣâk) **LH** gɑk, **OCM** *gâuk < *glauk

'Crane' [Shi], 'glistening white' [Meng].

[E] AA: Mon *kloh* 'crane', PEKatuic *klook 'white', Khmer *kok* 'heron, egret', PVM *t-lɔ:k 'white'. Perh. related to → gǎo$_1$ 暠 'white'.

hè$_3$ 賀 → **jiā$_2$** 嘉

hè$_4$ 赫 (xɐk) **LH** hak, **OCM** *hrâk (OCB *xrak)

'Glowing red' (face), 'brilliant' > 'to manifest, fiery' (drought) [Shi], 'fiery red' [SW].

[E] The phonologically most plausible affiliation is with PTB *s-ryak > Kan. Bunan *śrag* 'ashamed', WT *šags* 'joke, jest' (at other's expense) < *rhjak. Without medial *j: PTB *s-rak ~ *k-rak: PL *s-rak[L], WB *hrak* 'be ashamed, shy', Mikir *tʰèrák < s-rak* ? 'shy, bashful'. With initial *k-*: Magari *kʰa-rak* 'be ashamed' (*STC* no. 431), WT *kʰrag* 'blood'; loaned into MK-PWa *sə[ŋ]-krak* 'red'. These forms may furthermore be related to TB ones with the root *jak: Lushai *zak*[L] */ zaʔ*[L] *< jak*, Kachin *kəjaʔ* 'be ashamed, shy' (*STC* no. 452 p. 113; pp. 106, 108). The OC form goes back to a ST stem without medial *j. These TB items have also been connected with → chì$_3$ 赤 'red' and → sè$_1$ 色 'color' (*STC* no. 431, 458). An allofam may be → xiá$_4$ 赮瑕霞騢 (ɣa) 'red'. A semantic extension of this word is perh. → hè$_5$ 赫 'be scary'.

hè$_5$ 赫 (xɐk) **LH** hak, **OCM** *hrâk, OCB *xrak

'Awe-inspiring, majestic, imposing' [Shi] vi. < 'be scary, scaring'.

ꭗ **xià, hè** 嚇 (xa[C], xɐk) **LH** hak, ha[C], **OCM** *hrâk(h)

'To scare' [Zhuang].

[<] exoact. / caus. of *hè*, lit. 'make scared' (§4.3.2).

ꭗ **xì** 虩虩 (xjɐk) **LH** hɨɑk, **OCM** *hak

'Scary' 虩 [BI, Yi], 'fear' 虩 [Zhuang].

[E] Acc. to Bodman (1980: 175) this wf is cognate to PTB *krak ~ *grak 'to fear' > WT *skrag-pa* 'afraid, terrified' ꭗ OTib *skrags* 'fear', while *HST:* 78 relates the TB item to **kè** 恪 (kʰâk) 'to respect, revere' [Shi]. *STC:* 159 n. 430 relates both *kè* and *xì* 虩虩 to the TB etymon. This wf may be a semantic extension of → hè$_4$ 赫 'red' already on the ST level: 'red' > 'red in the face' > 'angry, scary' / 'ashamed'.

hè$_6$ 垎 (ɣɐk) **LH** gak, **OCM** *grâk < *gar-k ?

'Water drying off land' [Chuci].

[E] ST: PLB *ʔkrak 'dry' [Matisoff]. For more about related and similar items, see → gù$_1$ 固 (incl. Table G-1) and → jiān$_2$ 堅 (incl. Table J-1). The source of MK-PWa *krɔh 'dry, parched' is not clear. Perh. related to → hé$_7$ 涸.

hè$_7$ 嚇 → **hè$_5$** 赫

hè$_8$ 嗃 → **náo$_3$** 撓

hè$_9$ 翯 → **gǎo$_1$** 暠

hēi 黑 (xək) **LH** hək, **OCM** *hmə̂k

'Black' [Shi]. This is a relatively late OC word which replaced → xuán$_1$ 玄 'black' during the Zhou period.

[T] *Sin Sukchu SR* xəj (入), *LR* xəjʔ; *MGZY* hiy (入) [xij]

[<] *Hēi* is perh. derived from *mò* 'ink' (it cannot be the other way around: *hm- is secondary, *m- primary) meaning originally 'to mark with ink' (as a criminal's face), 'having dark markings' (Baxter 1983); thus this word might originally have been the regular caus. of *mò* 墨 'ink, black' (§5.2.2).

ꭗ **mò** 墨 (mək) **LH** mək, **OCM** *mə̂k

'Ink' [Meng], 'black' [Zuo], 'black-branding' [Shu]. Perh. the s. w. as → mò$_{15}$ 默嘿 'silent'.

[T] *Sin Sukchu SR* məj (入), *LR* məjʔ; *MGZY* mue (入) [muɛ]

[N] Because of the WB voiceless initial in *hmaŋ* (see below) and also because 'ink' appears semantically derived from 'black' (but see the preceding paragraph), a lost prefix has been suspected in the OC word (Sagart 1999: 214).

[E] ST: WT *smag* 'dark, darkness', *mog-pa* 'dark-colored'; Limbu *mak* 'black, dark' (of color, also the color of blood) ꭗ *makt-* 'to become night', JP *maʔ^{31} < mak^{31}* black'. WB *hmaŋ* 'ink' is not a CH loan but a loan translation, it belongs to → méi$_9$ 煤 'soot' (note that WT also has a loan translation for 'ink': *snag*).

On the basis of Chinese, at least two ST roots need to be distinguished: (1) *mək 'black, dark' ? ꭗ *mə(k) 'soot, black', and (2) *mak/ŋ 'dark' (*HPTB:* 522); these have converged in PTB *mak/ŋ (in some TB languages also 'color of blood > dark red > red'). Items of the type *mak/ŋ in CH include: → mò$_8$ 莫瞙嗼 (mâk) 'obscure', → mù$_4$ 莫暮 (muo^C) 'evening', → mù$_5$ 墓 (muo^C) 'tomb'; perh. also → máng$_3$ 芒茫 'obscure', → máng$_4$ 盲 (mɐŋ) 'blind'. Etyma meaning 'silent' may belong to this complex as well, incl. *mò* 莫嗼 (mɐk), *mò* 莫寞漠 (mâk), → mò$_{15}$ 默嘿 (mək) (perh. s. w. as *mò* 墨 'ink, black' above). The word → huì$_7$ 晦 'dark' is prob. unrelated.

There are additional words with initial *m-* and almost any rime which mean 'cover, dark, blind, confused, obscure'; relations may even extend to etyma meaning 'covering vegetation: luxuriant, weeds' (→ wú$_5$ 蕪廡). An allofam is prob. → méi$_9$ 煤 'soot'.

hèn 恨 (ɣən^C) **LH** gən^C, **OCM** *gə̂ns

'To hate, quarrelsome' [Zuo].

ꭗ **hěn** 佷 (ɣən^B) **LH** gən^B, **OCM** *gə̂nʔ

'Disobedient, refractory' [Guoyu], 'hate' [Zuo].

ꭗ **gèn** 艮 (kən^C) **LH** kən^C, **OCM** *kə̂ns

'Refractory, obstinate, resist' [Yi]. The graph was prob. intended for → yǎn$_6$ 眼 'eye'.

[C] Possible allofams: **xiàn** 限 (ɣǎn^B) 'obstacle, limit' [Guoce]; **yín** 垠 (ŋjən) 'raised border, dike' [Chuci].

héng$_1$ 恒 (ɣəŋ) **LH** gəŋ, **OCM** *gə̂ŋ

'Be constant, go on' [BI, Shi], 'earlier, anciently' [Zhouli]. — Etymology not clear.

[T] *Sin Sukchu SR* ɣiŋ (平), *PR* ɣəŋ (平); *MGZY* Xing (平) [ɣiŋ]; *ONW* ɣəŋ

héng$_2$-é 姮娥 ~ 恒娥 → **é$_2$** 娥

héng$_3$, jīng 莖 → **kēng$_2$** 牼

héng$_4$ 衡 (ɣɐŋ) **LH** gaŋ, **OCM** *grâŋ

'Crosspiece, beam, yoke, steelyard, weights' [BI, Shi].

[T] *Sin Sukchu SR* ɣiŋ (平), *SR* ɣujŋ (平), *PR* ɣuŋ; *MGZY* Hÿing (平) [ɣjiŋ]

[C] See also → hóng$_5$, héng 衡橫 with which *héng* may be connected (so Karlgren 1956: 16). Possible allofam → liáng$_2$ 梁 'beam'.

ж **gěng** 哽鯁 (kɐŋ^B) **LH** kaŋ^B, **OCM** *krâŋ?
'Fishbone in throat' [Guoyu]; 'choke' [Zhuang].

hóng$_1$ 虹 (ɣuŋ) **LH** goŋ, **OCM** *gôŋ < *gloŋ
'Rainbow' [Li].
[D] Dialect forms are very irregular: PMin *ghioŋ^B, but Jiànyáng *leŋ^{Cl}*, G-Shànggāo dial. has *lan^B-luŋ^H* (Sagart 1993: 196).
[E] <> PY *kluŋ^A 'rainbow' (Haudricourt 1950: 559). Benedict (1986: 58) and Carr (*LTBA* 13.2, 1990: 105) suggest that *hóng* is related to → lóng$_3$ 龍 'dragon' and → hóng$_2$ 紅 'red'.

~ **jiàng** 虹 (kåŋ^C) **LH** kɔŋ^C, **OCM** *krôŋh
This variant survives for ex. in G-Wǔníng dial. *kɔŋ^{Cl}* (Sagart 1993: 170).

ж **dì-dōng** 蝃蝀 (tiei^C-tuŋ) **LH** tes-toŋ, **OCM** *tê(t)s-tôŋ < *-tloŋ
'Rainbow' [Shi, EY].

[E] The wide range of forms, incl. *dì-dōng* (below), speaks for a non-ST source for this etymon. <> Kam-Tai: Zhuang lgs. have *tu^2-tuŋ^2* 'rainbow' and the like, where *tu^2* is a prefix added to animals and persons. Li Xu-lian (1997) reconstructs this prefix as PT *ta, among others based on forms like Wuming *ta^6* and Bama *tiə^6*. Luó Yǒngxiàn (*MKS* 27: 1997: 272) reconstructs PTai *Druŋ: S. *ruŋ^{C2}* 'rainbow'.

hóng$_2$ 紅 (ɣuŋ) **LH** goŋ, **OCM** *gôŋ < *gloŋ, OCB *goŋ
'Pink' (Baxter 1992: 207) > 'red' [Lunyu].
[T] *Sin Sukchu SR* ɣuŋ (平); *MGZY* Xung (平) [ɣuŋ]
The following *tóng* could be a variant which is parallel to → hóng$_1$ 虹 'rainbow'; as in 'rainbow', the form with initial MC dental stop is attested earlier than the one with the guttural initial:

ж **tóng** 彤 (duoŋ) **LH** douŋ, **OCM** *lûŋ
'Red' (of ceremonial objects) [Shi], 赨 [Guan].

hóng$_3$ 訌 (ɣuŋ) **LH** goŋ, **OCM** *gôŋ
'Be disorderly, disorder, trouble' [Shi]. This word may be cognate to → hòng$_1$ 鬨 and / or be a variant of *hún* 渾 (ɣuən) (under → hùn$_1$ 混渾).

hóng$_4$ 洪 (ɣuŋ) **LH** goŋ, **OCM** *gôŋ < *gloŋ ?
'Be great, greatly' [Shi, Shu] > 'great (waters)' [Shi] is perh. cognate to → róng$_3$ 溶 (*loŋ) 'much water'. Perh. related to → hào$_3$ 浩 .

ж **hóng, jiàng** 洚 (ɣuoŋ, guŋ, gåŋ, kåŋ^C) **LH** go(u)ŋ, g/kɔŋ^C, **OCM** *g/krûŋ
'To inundate' [Meng] (Wáng Lì 1982: 379).

hóng$_5$, héng 衡橫 (ɣwɐŋ) **LH** guaŋ, **OCM** *gwrâŋ — **[T]** *ONW* ɣuëŋ
'To plow crosswise, east-west' 衡 [Shi], 橫 [Zuo]; 'transversal, horizontal' 衡 [Li], 橫 [Chuci].
[C] This word may be connected with → héng$_4$ 衡 (so Karlgren 1956: 16). A tone C derivation is 'be cross-grained, hard to deal with' [Zuo] (Downer 1959: 287).
[E] AA: Khmer *khvēṅa* /kwaaɛŋ/ 'to cross, intersect, be diagonal, crisscross' (-> Tai: S. *kwaŋ^2* 'to lie athwart, transverse, crosswise') < *vēṅa* /wɛɛŋ/ 'cut across, traverse, intersect'. The derivative *gravēṅa* /krɔwɛɛŋ/ 'turn, hurl overhead...' agrees phonologically with OC.

hóng$_6$ 鴻 'equal' → **gōng$_5$** 公

hòng$_1$ 鬨 (ɣuŋ^C, ɣåŋ^C) **LH** goŋ^C, gɔŋ^C, **OCM** *grôŋh
'Quarrel, fight' [Meng] is perh. related to → xiōng$_5$ 訩 and / or → hóng$_3$ 訌.

hòng$_2$ 戇 → **zhuàng$_3$, hòng** 戇

hōu 齁 (xəu)
'To snore' [JY]. — **[E]** ST: WT *ŋur-ba* 'to grunt' ⋈ *sŋur-ba* 'to snore'. Syn. → hān$_1$ 鼾.

hóu$_1$ 侯 (ɣəu) **LH** go, **OCM** *gô
'Target' [Shi] > 'target shooter, archer' > 'title of a feudal lord' [OB, BI, Shi] > 'border guard' [Guoyu].

⋈ **hòu** 候 (ɣəu^C) **LH** go^C, **OCM** *gôh
'To watch, be on the lookout for' [Zuo], 'aspects (of dreams)' [Lie].
[E] Acc. to Lau (1999: 44) 'watch' is the fundamental meaning from which is derived *hóu* 侯 'feudal lord, border guard, target', a tone A nominalization (§3.1); alternatively, *hòu* 'watch' may derive from 'target', hence lit. 'to target'.

[E] AA: Khmer *koḥ* /kaoh/ 'to raise (crossbow) with a view to aiming' ⋈ *kpoḥ* 'be raised up, clearly visible'; or *goḥ* /kóh/ 'to hit (squarely)'.

[C] A derivation is → guān$_7$ 觀 'to watch'. This stem is prob. distinct from → hòu$_1$ 后 'sovereign'.

hóu$_2$ 侯 (ɣəu) **LH** go, **OCM** *gô
'There is, to have', occurs only in old parts of *Shījīng*, commentators gloss it as → wéi$_2$ 惟唯隹維 'to be' or → yǒu$_2$ 有 'there is' (< 'to have').
[E] AA: PVM *kɔːʔ 'to be, have, there is' [Ferlus]; PMonic *gooʔ 'to get, possess, obtain' [Diffloth 1984: 151]. <> TB-JP *gu^{31}* 'to have'.

hóu$_3$ 侯 'root of feather' → **hòu$_1$** 后

hóu$_4$ 喉 (ɣəu) **LH** go, **OCM** *gô
'Throat' [Shi].
[E] Etymology not certain, but note TB-Chepang *guk* 'throat'. AA has similar items: PMK *kɔʔ 'neck' (Shorto 1976: 1062) > PMonic *kɔɔʔ 'neck, narrow part of a long object', PSBahn. *nəkɔː 'neck', Viet. *ko'* 'neck', Khmer *kaa* [Huffman 1975]. <> Tai S. *k^{h}ɔɔ^{A2}* < *ɣ- 'neck, throat' (Li F. 1976: 42), Saek *ɣɔɔ^{A2}*. Alternatively, this word may possibly be related to WT *mgul(-pa)* ~ *'gul* 'neck, throat' (< *'gul-ba* 'to move'), or *mgur* 'throat, neck, voice' (so Unger *Hao-ku* 35, 1986: 33). *HST* 112 connects WT *mgul* with **gěn** 頣 (kən^B) 'neck' [GY].

hóu$_5$ 猴 (ɣəu) **LH** go, **OCM** *gô — **[D]** PMin *ǧəu < *ɴgo ?
'Monkey' [Zhuang].
[E] ST: PL *ʔ-ko$^{2/1}$. The first syllable in *mǔ-hóu* 母猴 *môʔ-gô, *mù-hóu* 沐猴 *môk-gô 'macaque' may perh. be an old pre-initial (Unger *Hao-ku* 31, 1985: 308). This may be supported by the PMin form whose softened initial derives from an earlier prenasalized one acc. to Norman 1986. V. Blažek (in Pinault et al. 1997: 236f) notes LB-Akha *mjo k^{h}œ* 'monkey' which he derives from PL *mjok and suggests is the source of the CH word, which in turn, citing Lüders, might possibly have been the source of IE-PTocharian *moko. For syn. see → yóu$_8$ 猶.

hóu$_6$ 鍭 'arrow with metal tip' → **hòu$_1$** 后

hòu$_1$ 后 (ɣəu$^{B/C}$) **LH** go$^{B/C}$, **OCM** *gôʔ/h
('Head' in society:) 'sovereign, lord' [Shi], 'queen' [Zuo].

[E] Hóu$_1$ 侯 'target > archer, feudal lord' is often considered cognate (e.g. Mei Tsu-Lin in Thurgood 1985: 335f). Though possible, these two words seem to represent two different concepts and thus derive from different roots. This is supported by the consistent distinction of these near synonyms in literature. The *hòu* 后 under consideration here has the basic meaning 'head'; it is thus a ST etymon *go which is cognate to WT *go* 'headman' ⋈ *mgo* 'head'. This word is prob. a tone B derivation from the following items, lit. 'the person which is functioning as head'. This stem may perh. also be cognate to → yuán$_1$ 元 'head'.

⋈ **hóu** 鍭 (ɣəu, ɣəu^C), **LH** go, go^C, **OCM** *gô(h)

'Arrow with metal point' [Shi]. In *Shījīng* the word rimes both in *-o and in *-oh (Baxter 1992: 763).

[D] Acc. to *FY* 9,4, this is a Han period Yangtze-Huái dialect word for 'arrow'.

⋈ **hóu** 侯 (ɣəu) **LH** go, **OCM** *gô

('Head' = 'tip' of a feather:) 'root of a feather' 猴 [SW]. But Matisoff 1985a: 437 relates this word to WT *sgro* 'a large feather, quill-feather'.

hòu$_2$ 詬 → **gòu$_2$** 詬

hòu$_3$ 後 (ɣəu^B) **LH** go^B or ɣo^B, **OCM** *gôʔ or ɦôʔ

'Behind, after' [Shi], 'follow' [Zuo].

[T] *Sin Sukchu SR* ɣəw (上); *MGZY* Xiw (上) [ɣiw]; *MTang* ɣəu, *ONW* ɣou

⋈ **hòu** 後 (ɣəu^C) **LH** go^C or ɣo^C, **OCM** *gôh or *ɦôh

'Be behind, attend, support' [BI, Shi], also 候; 'to put afterward' [Zuo] (Downer 1959: 280).

[<] exoact. / tr. of *goʔ above (§4.3.2)

[E] ST: PTB *ok > WT *'og* (not *ʔog*) 'below, afterwards, later, after'; PLB *ʔok 'lower side, below' > WB *ok* 'under part, space under' (*HST:* 41); Limbu *yo* 'down, below, downhill'. For tone B in CH, see §3.2.2.

hòu$_4$ 厚 (ɣəu^B) **LH** go^B, **OCM** *gôʔ

'Thick' > 'generous' [BI, Shi].

[T] *Sin Sukchu SR* ɣəw (上); *MGZY* Xiw (上) [ɣiw]

⋈ **hòu** 厚 (ɣəu^C) **LH** go^C, **OCM** *gôh

'Thickness' [GY] (Unger *Hao-ku* 21, 1983: 183).

hòu$_5$ 候 → **hóu$_1$** 侯

hū$_1$ 乎 'in, at' → **yú$_8$** 於

hū$_2$ 呼 (xuo[^{C}]) **LH** hɑ(^{C}), **OCM** *hâ(h)

'To call, shout' [Shu] > 'to ask (request), be asked' [OB, BI]. The next word *hū* suggests that the active verb 'shout, call' had originally tone A, and that the tone C form was an exopass. derivation (§4.4), lit. 'be asked, requested'. Also in tone C is the meaning 'cry out' [Zuo] (Downer 1959: 286: restricted meaning). For a semantic parallel 'shout' > 'request', see → háo 號.

⋈ **hū** 嘑 (xuo) **LH** hɑ, **OCM** *hâ

'To shout' [Zhouli], 'abuse' [Meng].

hū$_3$ 忽 → **mén$_3$** 悶

hū$_4$ 膴 (xuo, also mju) **LH** hɑ, **OCM** *hmâ

'Dried slice of boneless meat' [SW], 'big slice of dried meat' [Liji, Zhouli], Yáng Xióng is quoted as saying 'dried bird meat'. This word makes the impression of a loan like many words which relate to everyday life and which appear first in Han period ritual books.

hū $_5$ 幠 → **wǔ** $_9$ 膴廡

hú $_1$ 胡 (ɣuo) **LH** gɑ, **OCM** *gâ

'Dewlap of an animal' (which hangs down from the chin) [Shi, SW] > 'beard' 鬍 [Han texts] (Wáng Lì 1982: 144). Acc. to Boltz (OE 35, 1992: 37); this word is cognate to *kū* 枯 'desiccated' and ultimately to → gù $_1$ 固 'solid'.

hú $_2$ 胡 (ɣuo) **LH** gɑ, **OCM** *gâ

'Steppe nomads', general term [Zhouli] (Pulleyblank *EC* 25, 2000: 20), etymology unknown.

hú $_3$ 胡 → **hé** $_3$ 何

hú $_4$**-túng** 胡同 → **xiàng** $_3$ 巷

hú $_5$ 鬍 → **hú** $_1$ 胡

hú $_6$**-dié** 胡蝶 (ɣuo-diep) **LH** gɑ-dep, **OCM** *gâ-lêp

'Butterfly' [Zhuang].

~ **jiá-dié** 蛺蝶 *kêp-lêp

'Butterfly' [Yupian] is a variant of *húdié* (Bodman). The first syllable is glossed 'butterfly' in *SW*, it survives in Y-Guǎngzhōu *kap*^{D1} 'butterfly', -> Jap. *kai* < *kapi (Bodman 1980: 146).

[E] ST: The TB forms vary: Lepcha *ha-kljóp* 'a species of butterfly, *Buprestis bicolor*', WT *p*^{h}*je-ma-leb* < *pem-a-lep*. The second syllable *lêp belongs either to the wf → dié 牒; or to PTB *lyap 'glitter, flash', see → yè$_6$ 爗. (Yan Xiuhong *ZGYW* 2, 2002: 154 has an extensive discussion of *húdié*).

hú $_7$ 湖 → **hé** $_4$ 河

hú $_8$ 弧 (ɣuo) **LH** guɑ, **OCM** *gwâ

'Bow' [Yi], 'bend, curved' [Zhouli]. Syn. → gōu $_1$ 句鉤枸區.

≍ **gū** 軱 (kuo) **LH** kuɑ, **OCM** *kwâ

'Curved bone, big bone' [Zhuang].

[E] This wf belongs to → yū $_1$ 迂紆 *ʔwa; *gū* looks like a derivation from *yū* with the nominalizing k-prefix (§5.4).

hú $_9$ 狐 (ɣuo) **LH** guɑ, **OCM** *gwâ — **[T]** *ONW* ɣo

'Fox' [Shi].

[E] PTB *gwa 'fox': OTib *ɦo* (Coblin *LTBA* 17.2, 1994: 117), Tib. dial. *gwa, WT *wa* (*STC* p. 34 n. 111), Bunan *goa-nu* ~ *gwa-nu*.

hú $_{10}$ 搰 → **kū** $_4$ 堀窟

hú $_{11}$ 壺 (ɣuo) **LH** ga, **OCM** *gâ

'Bottle-gourd, flask' [Shi], 'teapot'.

[E] <> Perh. Tai: S. *kaa*^{1} 'kettle, earthen-ware teapot'.

hǔ $_1$ 虎 (xuo^B) **LH** hɑ^B, **OCM** *hlâʔ (hl-!), OCB *hlāʔ

'Tiger' [OB, Shi]. The name of this dangerous animal is subject to taboo. It was therefore apt to be replaced by a different word, or at least undergo some modification. One way is to add a prefix or word which indicates respect, hence Mand. *lǎo-hǔ* 老虎 'old (= venerable) tiger'; the prefix *yú* < *ʔa in *yú-tù* etc. served the same purpose in the OC dialect word, see below and → ā 阿. The other method is to distort the pronunciation by using a dialect word as in *hǔ* whose phonology indicates a possible rural or vulgar origin (voiceless *lh- > MC *x*-, §5.6).

[D] The regular OC equivalent of foreign *kl- is expected to be a voiceless *lh- > MC *śj*- or *tʰ*-. Such forms are found in old dialects (Pulleyblank 1983: 427): (1) **yú-tù** 於兔 (ʔjwo-tʰuo^C) [ʔɨɑ-tʰɑh] OCM *ʔa-lhâk is a Chǔ dialect word recorded in the 5th cent. BC *Zuǒzhuàn*. The *Hòu Hànshū* has a variant **yú-shì** 於檡 (ʔjwo-śjäk) [ʔɨɑ-śiak] OCM *ʔa-lhak. The *FY* has a further graphic variant **yú-tù** 於鯱 to which Guō Pú adds that south of the Yangtze, the pronunciation of *tù* is like **gǒu-dòu** 苟竇 (kəu^B-dəu^C), i.e. a hypothetical OCM *kôʔ-lôh which comes close to AA forms.

Some modern interior Min dialects have *kʰo^B, but the stop feature is prob. secondary.

[E] PAA *kalaʔ 'tiger' > PMK *klaʔ > OKhm *klaa (> later Angkorian Khm. *khlaa*; -> Tai: S. kla²), PMonic *klaaʔ [Diffloth 1984], Munda *kula*, Kharia *ki'ṛɔʔ* (Norman a. Mei 1976: 286–288; Benedict 1976: 97; Pulleyblank 1983: 427). It is not clear if / how PVM *k-ha:lʔ, Khmer *kha:l* 'tiger' (in the name of a year) could be related. <> MK -> PTB *k-la (Matisoff 1995a: 52), PL *k-la², OBurm. *kla*, WB *kya^B* (*IST:* 334), Monpa *khai-la* looks similar to PVM.

hǔ₂-pò 琥珀 < 虎魄 (xuo^B-pʰɐk)

'Amber', lit. 'tiger's soul' [Tang dyn.: Li Bai], a loan word from a western or southern Asiatic **χarupah* 'amber' (Boodberg 1937: 359).

hǔ₃ 滸 → **àn₂** 岸

hù₁ 戶 (ɣwo^B) **LH** gɑ^B, **OCM** *gâʔ

'Door(leaf) > household' [Shi]; 'opening' [Liji].

[T] *Sin Sukchu SR* ɣu (上); *MGZY* Xu (上) [ɣu]; *ONW* ɣo

[E] ST: PTB *m-ka 'opening, mouth' (*HPTB:* 173) > PLB *ʔga¹ ⋈ *ga³ 'open, divaricate, spread' [Matisoff *D. of Lahu:* 230], WB *tam-kʰa^B* 'door', NNaga *ga^A 'door', WT *sgo* 'door' (*HST:* 66; WT *o* can derive regularly from TB *a). It is tempting to derive 戶 from → hù₃ 互梐 'barrier', yet the latter agree more closely with a different TB etymon (Lushai *kʰaar*).

hù₂ 怙 (ɣuo^B) **LH** gɑ^B, **OCM** *gâʔ

'To rely on' [Shi] is cognate to → gù₁ 固 'solid, secure, sure'.

hù₃ 互梐 (ɣou^C) **LH** gɑ^C, **OCM** *gâh

'Intertwining, crossing, barrier, a stand' (of crossing sticks) [Zhouli]; 'each other' 互; 'railings, fence' 梐 [Zhouli].

⋈ **hù** 滬 (ɣuo^B) **LH** gɑ^B, **OCM** *gâʔ

'A weir, fish stakes for catching fish' (properly written with radical 竹 instead of 水) [GY]. This could be the s. w. as **hù** 扈 'to stop, prevent' [Zuo], but is prob. unrelated to → hù₁ 戶 'door'.

⋈ **gǔ** 罟 (kuo^B) **LH** kɑ^B, **OCM** *kâʔ

'Net' [Yi] is prob. unrelated to → gū₄ 罛 'net'.

Both tone B words *hù* 滬 and *gǔ* 罟 above may be nominal derivations from *hù* 互.

[E] ST: Lushai *kʰaar^R* < *kʰaarʔ* 'a dam or weir, roughly constructed of leafy bows or bamboo lattice-work' (sometimes used for catching fish); WB *ka* 'make a barrier, cover on the side, put up fence' ⋈ *ə-ka* 'side of building, external part'; WT *dgar-ba* 'to confine, pen up' ⋈ *sgar* 'camp, encampment'. For TB final r, see §7.7.5.

The wf → gòu$_3$ 冓 agrees with *hù* in all but the vowel. Putative TB cognates seem to confirm that these are two separate roots.

hù$_4$ 沍 → **gù$_1$** 固

hù$_5$ 笏 (xuət) **LH** huət, **OCM** *hmût < *hmut
'Writing tablet' [Li]. — **[E]** <> Tai: S. *smut* 'book' (Unger *Hao-ku* 39, 1992).

hù$_6$ 護 (ɣuo^C) **LH** ɣuɑ^C, **OCM** *wâkh — **[T]** *ONW* ɣo
'Guard, protect' [Lüshi] is prob. cognate to WT *'gogs-pa* 'to prevent, avert' (*HST:* 89).

hù$_7$-hù 扈扈 (ɣuo^B) **LH** ga^B, **OCM** *gâ?
'Wide, vast' [Li] is perh. a ST word: WB *ka^B* 'be stretched apart, widen; breadth, width'.

hù$_8$ 滬 → **hù$_3$** 互枑

huā 花 (xwa)
'Flower', originally a noun (see Wáng Lì 1982: 142 for a discussion of this wf). The graph (whose OC rime should be *-ai) has been borrowed for an etymon in OC *-a).
[T] *Sin Sukchu SR* xwa (平); *MGZY* hwa (平) [xwa]; *ONW* xuä

ꕤ **huá** 華 (ɣwa) **LH** ɣua, **OCM** *(g)wrâ ? — **[T]** *ONW* ɣuä
'To be in flower' intr. > 'blossom, flower' [Shi], originally a vb. (Wáng Lì).

ꕤ **kuā** 荂 (k^{h}wa, xjwo) **LH** k^{h}ua, hyɑ, **OCM** *khrwâ, *hwa
'Flower' [Zhuang], the graph is sometimes thought to write *huā* 花.

[E] Etymology not clear. TB languages often alternate initial labial stops *p, *b with *w, also in the root for 'blossom, flower' *bar (→ pā 葩, → bàn 瓣) (Matisoff *LL* 1.2, 2000: 144–146). *Huā* may be an example of the ST *bar ~ *war variation (for the metathesis of the final *r, see §7.7.3). Alternatively, note AA-OKhmer /pkaa/ 'flower'; the complex AA initial might have been the reason for the CH development.

huá$_1$ 滑 (ɣwăt) **LH** guat, **OCM** *grût
'Slippery' [Zhouli].
[T] *Sin Sukchu SR* ɣwa (入); *MGZY* Xwa (入) [ɣwa]
[E] ST: JP *gum^{31}-rut^{31}* < *gu-mrut* 'slippery'.

huá$_2$ 華 'flower' → **huā** 花

huá$_3$ 華 'cleave' → **kū$_2$** 刳

huà$_1$ 化 → **é$_4$** 訛吪

huà$_2$ 樺 (ɣwa^C) **LH** ɣua^C, **OCM** *(g)wrâh ?
'Birch' [Yupian, JY].
[E] ST: WT *gro-ga* 'bark of birch' (Unger *Hao-ku* 33, 1986; *HPTB:* 175).

huà$_3$ 話 (ɣwai^C) **LH** guas, **OCM** *gwrâ(t)s or *grô(t)s — **[D]** PMin *ĥua^C
'Speech, lecture' [Shi].
[T] *Sin Sukchu SR* ɣwa (去); *MGZY* Xway (去) [ɣwaj]
[E] Sagart (1999: 113) derives this word from → yuē$_1$ 曰 'to say'. It is prob. cognate to WT *gros* 'speech, talk, advice' (Gong in W. Wang 1995: 47).

huà$_4$ 畫 (ɣwai^C) **LH** ɣuɛ^C, **OCM** *(g)wrekh
'Painted, with a design' adj. [BI, Shu] > 'to draw a design, depict' [Meng].
[T] *MGZY* Xway (去) [ɣwaj]; *ONW* ɣuä
[<] exopass. of *huò* 畫 (*wek) (§4.4).

ⅹ **huò** 畫 (ɣwɛk) **LH** ɣuɛk, **OCM** *(g)wrek
'To delineate, mark off, plan' [Zuo].
[T] *Sin Sukchu SR* ɣuj (入); *MGZY* Xway (入) [ɣwaj]
= **huà** 劃 (ɣwɛk) **LH** ɣuɛk, **OCM** *gwrek
'To cut' (with a knife) [SW], cut open, mark off' (Wáng Lì 1982: 270).
[E] MK: OKhmer *gur* ~ *gvar* 'to draw a line, make a drawing' [S. Lewitz, *AA Studies* 2, 1976: 742], with OC final *-k* added which caused the metathesis of the MK final *r* (§6.1): *gwer + k > *gwrek*. The vocalic discrepancy has parallels, see §11.1.3.

huà$_5$ 輠 → **huán$_1$** 桓垸

huài 壞 (kwăi^C) **LH** kuɛi^C, **OCM** *krûih, OCB *krujs
'To destroy, ruin' [Zuo] (Baxter 1992: 218).
ⅹ **huài** 壞 (ɣwăi^C) **LH** guɛi^C, **OCM** *grûih, OCB *ɦkrujs — **[T]** *ONW* ɣuëi
'To be ruined' [Shi].
[<] endopass. of *huài* 壞 (kwăi^C) (§4.6).

huān 讙 → **háo** 號

huán$_1$ 桓垸 (ɣuân) **LH** ɣuɑn, **OCM** *wân — **[T]** *ONW* ɣuɑn
'To turn around, turn back, hesitate' 桓 [Yi], 垸 [Huainan].
ⅹ **huàn** 換 (ɣuân^C) **LH** ɣuɑn^C, **OCM** *wâns
'To change' [Lie], 'exchange' 換; 'round' 輐 [Zhuang], Mand. *huǎn*!, QYS also *ŋuân*$^{B/C}$; the latter graph writes QYS *ŋuân*, Mand. *wān* 'to cut so as to round off corners' 刓 [Chuci], 园 [Zhuang].
[T] *Sin Sukchu SR* ɣwɔn (去); *MGZY* Xon (去) [ɣɔn]; *ONW* ɣuɑn
ⅹ **huà** 輠 (ɣwa^B, ɣuâi^C, ɣuân^B) **LH** guai^B, guɑi^C / S goi^C, **OCM** *grôiʔ, gôih
'To turn round' (as a wheel) [Li]. Rú Chún (3rd cent. AD), annotator of the *Hànshū*, remarks that in eastern dialects, the word 桓 was pronounced like *hé* 禾 OCB *gwaj < *goj (Baxter 1992: 296), therefore *huà* 輠 is apparently a dialect variant.
[E] This root prob. derives from ST *war or *wor: WT *'kʰor* 'circle' ⅹ *'kʰor-ba* < OTib ~ *kʰord* 'to turn around' ⅹ *sgor-mo* 'round, a circle, globe'; Lepcha *var* 'to make a circuit, go round' ⅹ *vor* 'to surround' ⅹ *van* 'turn towards'. See under → huí 回 for synonyms.

huán$_2$ 桓 (ɣuân) **LH** ɣuɑn, **OCM** *wân
'Pillar' [Li] > *huán-huán* 'pillar-like' (trees) [Shi] > 'valiant' [BI, Shi]. Perh. s. w. as → huán$_1$ 桓垸 'round'.

huán$_3$ 還 (ɣwan) **LH** ɣuan, **OCM** *wrên, OCB *wren
'To turn around, return' 還 [Shi]. Prob. the same etymon as *huán* 環鐶寰 (under → yíng$_4$ 營).
[T] *Sin S. SR* ɣwan (平); *MGZY* Xwan (平) [ɣwan]; *ONW* ɣuan
[E] AA: Khmer (*ravā'na:*) *raṅvā'na* /ruŋwoən/ 'repayment, return, recompense, fee, dues'. The AA relative explains the *r in the OC initial. See under → huí 回 for synonyms.

huán$_4$ 環鐶寰 → **yíng$_4$** 營

huán$_5$-guān 環官 'imperial palace' → **yíng$_4$** 營

huǎn$_1$ 緩 'soft' → either **xuān$_2$** 暖, or → **yuán$_8$** 爰.

huǎn$_2$ 緩 'slow' → **yuán$_8$** 爰

huǎn 輐 → **huán$_1$** 桓垸

huàn$_1$ 換 'change' → **huán**$_1$ 桓垸; → **pàn**$_1$**-huàn** 判換 'relax'

huàn$_2$ 幻 (ɣwăn^C) **LH** guɛn^C, **OCM** *(g)wrêns — **[T]** *ONW* ɣuän
'Deceit' [Shu], 'magic, illusion'. Bodman (1980: 86) compares this to WT *rol-ba* 'to practice sorcery, playfulness'.

huàn$_3$ 宦 (ɣwan^C) **LH** guan^C, **OCM** *gwrâns or *grôns
'Servant' [Guoyu] > 'officer, official' [Zuo].
[E] ST: PLB *gywan[1] > WB *kywan* 'slave, servant' (WB medial *y* can derive from earlier *r*).

huāng$_1$ 衁 (xwâŋ) **LH** huɑŋ, **OCM** *hmâŋ
'Blood' [Zuo, Xi Gong 15, quoting Yi 54, 6]. This rare word's occurrence in a traditional saying indicates that it is not part of the active vocabulary of OC, but a survival from a substrate language.
[E] AA: PNorth Bahnaric *maham, PMnong *mham, Asli *maham* (Benjamin 1976: 103), Khmu *maːm* < *mh-; without m-infix: PVM *ʔa-saːmʔ, Khmer *jham*, PMonic *chim, Katuic *ʔə(ŋ)haːm, Mundari *majɔ̃m*. The MK root was *jhaːm (Diffloth 1977: 50), or -TSɑm (Ferlus, *MKS* 7, 1978: 18). -> PMY *ntšhjaam^B (Mei 1980; Bodman 1980: 120). CH has final *-ŋ* because initial and final *m* are mutually exclusive. The OC initial was probably a voiceless *m- which can derive from, among others, a prehistoric cluster with either *h or *s.

huāng$_2$ 荒 'weed covered' → **wú**$_3$ 蕪廡

huāng$_3$ 荒 'neglect' → **wáng**$_1$ 亡

huāng$_4$ 荒 'large' → **máng**$_2$ 芒

huáng$_1$ 皇 (ɣwâŋ) **LH** ɣuɑŋ or guɑŋ, **OCM** *(g)wâŋ — **[T]** *ONW* ɣuɑŋ
'Be august, stately' [BI, Shi], 'royal, imperial'.
[E] Etymology not certain, possibly originally meaning 'royal' (derived from 'royal palace'), belonging to the AA etyma *waŋ under → yíng$_4$ 營. Tai *luaŋ* 'royal' is a loan from Khmer *(h)luːəŋ* 'king, royal'. Bodman 1980: 107 connects *huáng* with → wáng$_2$ 王 'king'. This word may early have converged with → huáng$_2$ 煌 'brilliant'.

huáng$_2$ 煌 (ɣwâŋ) **LH** ɣuɑŋ (or guɑŋ ?), **OCM** *(g)wâŋ
'Be brilliant, splendid, magnificent' 煌 > 'brown and white' (of a horse) 皇 [BI, Shi]. Perh. → huáng$_1$ 皇 is the same word; perh.related to → guāng$_1$ 光 'bright'.
[E] ? ST: WB *lwaŋ* 'glossy, shiny'.

huáng$_3$ 黃 (ɣwâŋ) **LH** ɣuɑŋ, **OCM** *wâŋ
'Be yellow, brown' [OB, Shi] is one of the ancient basic color terms (Baxter 1983).
[T] *Sin Sukchu SR* ɣwaŋ (平); *MGZY* Xong (平) [ɣɔŋ]; *ONW* ɣuɑŋ
[E] ST: WB *waŋ^B* 'brightly yellow' ⋡ *wa* 'yellow'.

huáng$_4$ 璜 (ɣwâŋ) **LH** ɣuɑŋ, **OCM** *wâŋ
'Semicircular jade insignium' [Zhouli].
[E] Prob. AA: Khmer *va'ṅa* /wuŋ/, OKhmer *vaṅ* 'ring, orbit, disc, round...', Bahnar *uāŋ*. AA -> TB-Lepcha *vyaŋ* 'ring'. Perh. related to items under → yíng$_4$ 營.

huáng$_5$ 潢 'vast' → **guǎng**$_2$ 廣

huáng$_6$ 蟥 (ɣwâŋ) **LH** ɣuɑŋ, **OCM** *wâŋ
'Leech, water leech' [SW, EY]. The first syllable → mǎ$_2$ 螞馬 in Mand. *mǎ$_3$-huáng* 馬蟥 is prob. an old prefix (Unger *Hao-ku* 31, 1985: 308; Mei Tsu-Lin).

huī₁ 灰 (xuâi) **LH** huəi, **OCM** *hwə̂
'Ashes' [Zhuang], 'charcoal' [Li].
[T] *Sin Sukchu SR* xuj (平); *MGZY* hue (平) [xuɛ]
[N] Prob. OCM *hwə̂ (not *hmə̂) because the phonetic seems to be yòu 又 *wə̂h.
[E] ST *wu: TB-Lushai *vut*[L] 'ashes, dust'.

huī₂ 煇輝暉 (xjwei) **LH** hui, **OCM** *hwəi
'Flame, brightness' 煇 [Yi]; 'light, brightness' 暉 [Yi]; 'bright' 輝 [Meng].
ℵ **wěi** 韡 (jwei[B]) **LH** wui[B], **OCM** *wəi
'Be brilliant, bright' [Shi].
[E] ST: PTB *hwa-t > WT *'od*; Matisoff (1997: 44f; *LL* 1.2, 2000: 146) sets up a large ST wf that also includes → fán₅ 燔.
Perh. **yùn** 煇 (juən[C]) **LH** wun[C], **OCM** *wəns
'Brightness' [Zhouli] (Wáng Lì 1982: 508f); 'halo' [Lü] could either be the same etymon, or be related to → yùn₂ 運暈 'revolve'.

huī₃ 徽 (xjwei) **LH** hui, **OCM** *hməi
'Rope' [Yi]. The graph writes also a different word, see under → huī₄ 麾.
This word is shared with Tai: S. *mai*[A1] < *hm- 'thread, silk'.

huī₄ 麾 (xjwie 3) **LH** hyɑi, **OCM** *hmai
'Signal flag' [Zuo], 'to signal' [Shi], i.e., something whirled about, waved.
ℵ **huī** 徽 (xjwei) **LH** hui, **OCM** *hməi
'To signal, display' [Shu], 'a flag' [Li] is apparently a vocalic variant.
[E] ST: PTB *s-mwəy (*HPTB:* 195) > WB *hmwe*[C] 'whirl about, twirl', Lushai *hmui*[R] < *hmuiʔ* 'spinning wheel'.
[E] The area word → xuè₂ 眔 'wink with eyes' has prob. influenced the CH meaning of *huī* 麾. *Huī* 麾 *hmai looks like a conflation of *huī* 撝 *hwai 'to signal' (under → wēi₂ 逶) and *huī* 徽 *hməi 'to signal'.

huī₅ 撝 'signalize' → **wēi₂** 逶

huī₆ 墮隳 (xjwie) **LH** hyɑi, **OCM** *hmai
'To destroy' 墮 [Shu], 隳 (e.g. city walls) [Lüshi].
ℵ **huǐ** 毀燬 (xjwie[B]) **LH** hyɑi[B], **OCM** *hmaiʔ ?
'To destroy, ruin' [Shi], 'perish' (people) 毀 [Hanfei]; 'destroy' (by fire), 'blazing fire' 燬 [Shi]. This word also occurs in Tai: S. *mai*[C1] < *hm- 'to burn'.
ℵ **huǐ** 焜 (xjwei[B]) **LH** hui[B], **OCM** *hməiʔ
'To burn' [SW: Shi], a phonological variant of *huǐ* above (Baxter 1992: 417).
This is also a Han-period Qí dialect word for 'fire' [FY 10: 6] (Bodman 1980: 71).
'Destroy' (by fire), 'blazing fire' 燬 may really go back to → huǒ₁ 火 'fire'.

huí 回 (ɣuậi) **LH** ɣuəi, **OCM** *wə̂i — **[T]** *ONW* ɣuai
'To revolve, swerve, deflect' [Shi], 'go around by' [Zuo]; 'go up against a stream' 洄 [Shi]. Also written 迴徊. Downer (1959: 285) reads 'go around, go by way of' in tone C which implies an 'effective' meaning.
ℵ **huí-yù** 回遹 (ɣuậi-jiwet) **LH** ɣuəi-ju(i)t, **OCM** *wə̂i-wit ?
'Be awry, crooked, perverse' [Shi].
[C] Allofams are → guī₃ 歸 'return'; → wéi₆ 違 'turn against' from which *huí* is derived.
[E] Many CH and TB words for 'round, turn' look similar. Most have initial *w- and

foreign final *-n, -l, -r*, or *-i*, and therefore they are difficult to sort out, so that Bodman, Karlgren, Wáng Lì and other investigators have connected them in different ways. The merger of earlier final *-l and *-r into either OC *-n or *-i makes it impossible at the moment to find a rational way of associating foreign with OC items:
(1) OC *-wan > MC rime *-uan, -jwɐn / -jwän* < OC *-uan, *-wan, *-on can derive from earlier ST or foreign *-wan, -war, -wal, -(w)on, -(w)or, -(w)ol*; given the latitude of sound correspondences, the vowels could in some words even have been *e* or *u*, beside *a* and *o*. See → yuán$_5$ 員圓圜, → yuán$_7$ 園, → huán$_1$ 桓垸, → huán$_3$ 還, huán 環鐶寰 (under → yíng$_4$ 營).
(2) OC *-wən or *wun MC rime *-uən / -jwən* < OC *-un / *-wən can derive from earlier ST or foreign *-un, -wun, -wən, -ul, -wul, -wəl, -ur, wur, -wər;* given *i* ~ *u* interchanges when in contact with labials, the foreign rime could also have been *-win, -wil, -wir*. See → yún$_5$ 雲, → yùn$_2$ 運暈.
(3) OC *-wəi or *-wui MC rime *-uậi / -jwei* < OC *-wəi or *-(w)ui can derive from earlier ST or foreign *-ui, -wui, -wəi, -ul, -wul, -wəl*, rarely also from *-ur, wur, -wər*. See → huí 回 (above), → wéi$_6$ 違, → guī$_3$ 歸; → wéi$_5$ 圍, → wèi$_7$ 衛.
(4) Rarer rimes can be associated with outside cognates somewhat more confidently:
OC *-weŋ See → yíng$_4$ 營, → yǒng$_7$ 禜; and → yíng$_5$ 縈, → yīng$_4$ 嬰
OC *-win See → jūn$_2$ 鈞

TB languages have additional words of this general shape and meaning, often with initial *k*. This *k* complicates the process of etymological identification even further because it may or may not have been a removable element. Such items include: (1) Lushai *kuai*^{L} / *kɔiʔ*^{L} 'bend, pull down', WB *kwe*^{B} 'bend around'. (2) Lushai *kual*^{L} 'coil', WB *kʰwe*^{B}. (3) Lushai *kul*^{H} / *kulʔ*^{L} 'be bent'. (4) Lushai *kʰɔɔr*^{R} 'double up, roll up' (→ quán$_3$ 卷拳?). (5) WT *'kʰor* 'circle, turn', Lepcha *var, vor*, note also AA-Khmer *vāra* /wíiər/ 'go around, circle, revolve'. (6) Lushai *in*^{L}*-kʰerʔ*^{L} 'twisted together'. (7) Lushai *hrual* 'roll up in the hand' ? ⋈ Lepcha *rol* 'roll'.

Furthermore, note AA: PVM *veːl 'return' ⋈ *k-veːl 'village', Bru *kəwir* 'to stir' [Huffman 1975: 13].

huǐ$_1$ 虫虺 (xjwei^B) **LH** hui^B, **OCM** *hmuiʔ ?
'Snake' 虺 [Shi], 虫 [OB, SW, Shanhaijing], 'reptile-amphibian' [Western Han] (Yates *EC* 19, 1994: 91 [apparently not 'insect']). Since 虫 is a basic graph, the word must be very old.
[E] ST: PTB *b-ruːl (*STC* no. 447) > WT *sbrul* < *s-mrulʔ*, PLB *m-r-wiy^1 [Matisoff *D. of Lahu:* 1338] > WB *mrwe* 'snake', KN *m-ruul, Lushai *ruul*^{H} < *ruul* (Shī Xiàngdōng 2000: 196), Chepang *ru* 'snake'. MC *xjwei*^{B} is a regular equivalent for TB / ST protoforms like *s-mrul, *ʔmrul or *hmrul. As to foreign initial *b-* for CH *m-*, see §5.12.2. MK-PWa *mɔy 'cobra' looks like a loan from a LB language. The syn. and ordinary word → shé$_2$ 蛇 'snake', lit. 'the winding thing', is due to taboo (see → hǔ$_1$ 虎 'tiger' for another tabooed animal).

huǐ$_2$ 毀 → **huī$_6$** 墮隳

huǐ$_3$ 燬 → **huī$_6$** 墮隳

huǐ$_4$ 焜 → **huī$_6$** 墮隳

huì$_1$ 會 (ɣwâi^C) **LH** guɑs, **OCM** *gwâts or *gôts, OCB *gots < *gops
'To join, come together' (two rivers, people) [Shi] > caus. 'to bring together, join' [BI, Shi]. → huì$_2$ 會 'lid' is a late semantic extension.

[T] *Sin Sukchu SR* ɣuj (去); *MGZY* Xue (去) [ɣuɛ]; *MTang* guɑi, *ONW* ɣuɑC
[<] endopass. of *guì* 會襘 (kuâi^C) (§4.6).

ꭗ **guì** 會襘 (kwâi^C) **LH** kuɑs, **OCM** *kwâts or *kôts
'Keep together (hair)' tr. 會 [Shi], 'bind up hair in a knot' 鬠 [Yili] (also MC *ɣuât*; also written with the phonetic of → kuò$_1$ 括); (adding up:) 'calculation, account' 會 [Li] (Karlgren 1956: 10); 'joining point of the two ends of a collar or belt' 襘 [Zuo] (Wáng Lì 1982: 487).

[E] This group is derived from → kuò$_1$ 括 *kot or *kwat (Sagart 1999: 56). The basic ST meaning seems to be: put arms / belt / band around something and connect / tie it. The three unrelated etyma → hé$_5$ 合 *gə̂p, → hé$_8$ 盍蓋 *gâp, and *huì* 會 *gwâts have partially converged in OC.

huì$_2$ 會 (ɣwâi^C) **LH** guɑs, **OCM** *gwât or *gôts — [T] *MTang* guɑi, *ONW* ɣuɑC
'Lid, cover' [Yili].
[E] This is a late [Yili] semantic extension from → huì$_1$ 會 'join, come together', formed in analogy to the common association of 'join' with 'close, lid' in the wfs → hé$_5$ 合 and → hé$_8$ 盍蓋. The former hé$_5$ 合 *gəp is related to PTB *kup (hence PCH *gup > *guəp > *gəp), the latter hé$_8$ 盍蓋 to PTB *gap (hence PCH, OC *gap). There is no ST, AA or PCH simplex *gop from which *huì* might have been derived.

huì$_3$ 會 (ɣwâi^C) **LH** guɑs, **OCM** *gwâts or *gôts
'To understand' [Tang], later 'can', aux. vb. expressing potentiality (Norman 1988: 125).

ꭗ **xiè** 解 (ɣai^B) **LH** gɛ^B, **OCM** *grêʔ
'Can', aux. vb. expressing potentiality [Tang], later replaced by the above *huì*. It is not clear if this and the above word are variants or cognates, but their similarity is suggestive. This word survives in M-Jiànyáng *hai^C*, Fúzhōu *a^{C2}*, Xiàmén *ue^{C2}*.

huì$_4$ 薈 → **wèi$_{10}$**, **yù** 蔚

huì$_5$ 賄 (xuậi^B) **LH** hwə^B, **OCM** *hmə̂ʔ
'To present, assign, valuables, dowry' [BI, Shi]. The earlier phonetic was *měi* 每 *mə̂ʔ (in BI) hence the OCM form (Schuessler 1987: 257; Baxter 1992: 352), but the word might have changed to *hwəʔ under the influence of *yòu* 侑 *wəh 'to offer' (under → yǒu$_2$ 有).

huì$_6$ 誨 (xuậi^C) **LH** hwə^C, **OCM** *hmə̂h
'To instruct' [BI, Shi] is related to → mǔ$_3$ 姆 'teacher'.
[T] *Sin Sukchu SR* xuj (去); *MGZY* hue (去) [xuɛ]
[E] ST: PL *s-ma^2 'to teach'; *CVST* 1: 26 adds WT *smo-ba, smos* 'to say'.

huì$_7$ 晦 (xuậi^C) **LH** hwə^C, **OCM** *hmə̂ʔ !, OCB *hmə(k)ʔ(s)
'Be dark, darkness' (of sky, clouds) > metaphorical 'dark' [Shi], 'night time' (vs. míng 明 'day time') [Guoyu], 'last day of the lunar month' [Chunqiu]. *Shījīng* rimes indicate tone B (Mattos 1971: 309).
[E] Prob. MK: OKhmer *kmval* /kmuuəl/ 'be cloudy, overcast, dark, beclouded, be as black as a cloud'. For the absence of final *-l in CH after a MK long vowel, see §6.9. Since the word refers primarily to meteorological and natural conditions, and seems to be related to a synonymous and (mutatis mutandis) homophonous MK etymon, it is prob. not related to ST → méi$_9$ 煤 'soot', → hēi 黑 'black', → mén$_3$ 悶 'unconsciously'. A cognate is prob. → hǎi$_1$ 海 'ocean'.

huì $_8$ 彙 (jwei^C) **LH** wus, **OCM** *wəs

'Category, class' [Yi], 'numerous' [Shi]. If related to → lèi$_2$ 類, this may perh. be a form which has treated the initial *r as a prefix and dropped it (§10.1.3). The same graph *huì* also writes → huì$_9$ 彙 'porcupine' which has possibly a similar variant in the initial.

huì $_9$ 彙 (jwei^C) **LH** wus, **OCM** *wəs (< *wus?)

'Porcupine' [SW]. Cantonese has the curious form *lœy*^{C2} (Bodman 1980: 89). The same graph also writes a word → huì$_8$ 彙 'category' which is perh. a variant of a word with initial *l-*: → lèi$_2$ 類 (§10.1.3).

[E] ST: Lushai *kuʔ*^{L} < *kus* 'porcupine, quill of a p.' In TB cognates the initial *k-* seems to be a prefix as in *ku ~ *du 'smoke'.

huì $_{10}$ 顪喙 (xjwɐi^C) **LH** hyɑs, **OCM** *hwats — **[T]** *ONW* huei^C

'Beard of chin' 顪 [Zhuang], GY also: '*jiá* 頰 jaw, cheek'; 'snout' 喙 [Zuo; *JDSW* xjwɐi^C], 'mouth' [SW] (the last graph has additional readings which prob. belong to the meaning 'to pant'). For MC *x-*, see §5.6. The meanings of these homophonous graphs slide gradually into each other ('jaw' written with 'beard'), therefore this seems to be one etymon, although 'beard' might have entered OC via KT (note the identical meanings), while 'snout' might have been inherited from ST, unless it is a TB loan. For semantics, note that a 'schnauzer' is not noted for its snout (which all dogs have), but for its striking mustache.

[E] KT: S. *nuat*^{DIL} < *hn- 'beard' which appears to have come ultimately from some Burmese-like TB lg.: WB *hnut* 'mouth, womb', used in composits for 'beard'. Since there is no hint of a nasal initial in OC, Tai is unlikely to have been the borrower. *Huì* seems to be related indirectly to → xū$_4$ 須鬚, see there for more TB cognates.

huì $_{11}$ 喙 'snout' → **huì** $_{10}$ 顪喙

huì $_{12}$ 惠 'it should be; kind' → **wéi** $_2$ 惟唯隹維

huì $_{13}$ 蟪 → **huì** $_{15}$ 嘒

huì $_{14}$ 彗篲 → **huì** $_{15}$ 嘒

huì $_{15}$ 嘒 (xiwei^C) **LH** hues, **OCM** *hwîs R!, OCB *hwets

(Go/do with small, short repetitions:) 'be twinkling' (stars) [Shi] (cf. Qiu 2000: 258).

[<] iterative devoicing §5.2.3.

⋇ **huì-huì** 嘒嘒 **OCM** *hwîs-hwîs

'To be chirping' (cicadas), 'to be jingling' (bit-bells) [Shi].

⋇ **huì** 蟪蛄 (ɣiwei^C-kuo) **LH** ɣues-kɑ, **OCM** *wîs-kâ

'A kind of cicada' (*Platypleura kaempferi*) 叀 [OB], 蟪蛄 [Zhuang], lit. 'chirping mole cricket'.

⋇ **huì** 彗篲 (zwi^C) **LH** zuis, **OCM** *s-wis

'Broom' [Li] > 'comet' [Zuo]. The old graph 習 ('bamboo'+ xí 習 'repeat') [SW 1254] confirms that 'broom' is derived from the notion of short repetetive movements, with the iterative s-prefix (§5.2.3).

hūn $_1$ 婚 (xuən) **LH** huən, **OCM** *hmə̂n — **[T]** *ONW* hon

'Relations by marriage, wife, in-laws' [BI, Shi]; 'wife's father' [EY, Zuo], 'wife's family' [SW]; *hūn-yīn* 婚姻 'relatives' [Shi], 'marriage' [Li]. Wáng Lì (1982: 508) quotes from Han-period literature: 'wedding' is called *hūn* because the ceremony takes place at dusk *hūn* 昏 (under → mén$_3$ 悶) [SW, Shiming, Baihu tong], but this looks like a folk etymology. One may speculate instead that *hūn* 'dark' signifies 'female', like its synonym → yīn_5 陰 'dark'.

$\textbf{hūn}_2$ 昏 → **$\textbf{mén}_3$** 悶

$\textbf{hūn}_3$ 閽 → **$\textbf{mén}_1$** 門

$\textbf{hūn}_4$ 葷 → **xūn** 熏燻纁焄

$\textbf{hún}_1$ 魂 (ɣuən) **LH** ɣuən, **OCM** *wûn

'Spiritual soul' [Zuo] as opposed to → pò_4 魄 'animal soul'. Since *pò* is the 'bright' soul, *hún* is the 'dark' soul and therefore cognate to → yún_5 雲 'cloud' (Carr, *CAAAL* 24, 1985: 62), perhaps in the sense of 'shadowy' because some believe that the *hún* soul will live after death in a world of shadows (Wolfram Eberhard *Guilt and Sin in ancient China*, 1967: 17).

$\textbf{hún}_2$ 渾 → **$\textbf{hùn}_1$** 混渾; → **$\textbf{hùn}_2$** 混

$\textbf{hùn}_1$ 混渾 (ɣuən^B) **LH** guən^B, **OCM** *gûnʔ

'Chaos' 混 [Lao], 'muddled, confused' 渾 [Lao] (some commentators also read LH *kuən^B* 混).

⋊ **hùn** 溷慁 (ɣuən^C) **LH** guən^C, **OCM** *gûns

'Disturbed, troubled by' [Zuo] > 'troubled, disorderly' 溷 [Chuci] > 'suffer, grief' 慁 [Guoce].

⋊ **hún** 渾 (ɣuən) **LH** guən, **OCM** *gûn

'Chaotic' [Zhuang]; also 'sound of running water' [Xun] (related?), A variant is apparently → hóng_3 訌 LH *goŋ* 'disorderly, trouble'.

⋊ **kùn** 困 (kʰuən^C) **LH** kʰuən^C, **OCM** *khûns

'Be distressed' [Shu], 'distress, exhaust' [Zuo], 'fatigue' [Li].

[T] *Sin Sukchu SR* k'un (去); *MGZY* khun (去) [k'un]; *ONW* kʰon

[E] Perh. related to Mand. *kùn* 睏 'sleepy'. Alternatively, this word may be derived from → kùn_1 困 'obstruct' [Yi], as emotions are often expressed by concrete notions, but this is not likely in light of *hùn* 溷慁 above. *HST:* 63 related this word to WT *kʰur* 'burden, load'. A further cognate may be → jiǒng_4 窘 in which case this and the doublet of *hún* point to a PCH final *-uŋ.

$\textbf{hùn}_2$ 混 (ɣuən^B) **LH** guən^B, **OCM** *gûnʔ

'Abundantly flowing' [Meng].

⋊ **hún** 渾 (ɣuən) **LH** guən, **OCM** *gûn

'Sound of running water' [Xun].

[C] This wf.may belong to → hùn_1 混渾 above. Perh. related to → hào_3 浩 *gûʔ.

$\textbf{hùn}_3$ 溷慁 → **$\textbf{hùn}_1$** 混渾

$\textbf{huó}_1$ 佸 → **$\textbf{kuò}_1$** 括

$\textbf{huó}_2$ 活 (ɣwât) **LH** guɑt, **OCM** *gwât, OCB *gʷat

'To keep alive, life' [Shi] has prob. nothing to do with 'moist' (so *GSR* 302m) because this graph with the water radical was prob. intended to write **guō** 活 (kuât) LH *kuɑt* 'to purl' (as running water) [Shi]. The etymology is possibly AA: Wa-Lawa-Bulang *gɑs 'alive' (of plants), Aslian languages *gɔs* 'to live'.

$\textbf{huǒ}_1$ 火 (xuâ^B) **LH** huɑi^B, **OCM** *hmâiʔ, OCB *hməjʔ

'Fire' [OB, Shi].

[T] *Sin Sukchu SR* xwɔ (上); *MGZY* hwo (上) [xwɔ]; *ONW* huɑ

[E] ST: PTB *mey (*STC* no. 290) > WT *me*, OTib. *smye*; Chepang *hmeʔ*; PLB *ʔmey² [Matisoff], PL *C-mi² [Bradley], WB *mi*^{B}, Lushai *mei*^{R} < *meiʔ*. The relationship with → huī$_6$ 隓隳, if any, is not clear.

huǒ$_2$ 夥 (ɣuâ^B) **LH** guɑi^B, **OCM** *gwâiʔ or *gôiʔ
'Many', an old Han-period dial. word in the outlying areas of Qí and Sòng and in the region between Chǔ and Wèi [FY 1.21]. It survives in Mǐn dialects: PMin *oi^C ~ *uai^B 'many' (Norman 1983: 204).

huò$_1$ 或 → **yǒu$_2$** 有

huò$_2$ 惑 (ɣwək) **LH** ɣuək, **OCM** *wək
'To deceive, delusion, doubt' [Lun]. Etymology not clear.

huò$_3$ 韄 (ɣwɛk) **LH** ɣuak, **OCM** *wrâk
'To bind' [Zhuang].
[E] ST: WT *'grogs-pa* 'to bind, fasten, tie, be associated with' ꭗ *grogs* 'friend, associate' (*HST* p. 42).

huò$_4$ 穫 (ɣwâk) **LH** ɣuɑk, **OCM** *wâk
'To reap, cut, harvest' [Shi], Mand. also 'capture'.

ꭗ **huò** 獲 (ɣwɛk) **LH** ɣuak, **OCM** *wak or *wrak (§9.1.4) — **[T]** *ONW* ɣuëk
'To catch, take, hit, succeed' [Shi].

ꭗ **huò** 擭 (ɣwa^C, ʔwɐk) **LH** ɣua^C, ɣuak, **OCM** *wak(h) or *wrak(h) (§9.1.4)
'A trap' [Shu] – an early general tone C derivation of the above (§3.5).
[C] This wf may be related to → jué$_{12}$ 攫.

huò$_5$ 貨 → **é$_4$** 訛吪

J

jī₁ 几 'stool' → **jǐ₁** 几机

jī₂ 飢 (kji 3) **LH** kɨ, **OCM** *kri, OCB *krjəj (Baxter 1992: 454)
'Be hungry, starve, hunger, famine' [Shi]. — **[T]** *ONW* ki — **[D]** PMin *kue

⪤ **jī** 饑 (kjei) **LH** kɨi, **OCM** *kəi — **[T]** *ONW* ki
'Famine' 饑饉 [Shi]. This word is distinct from *jī* above (Wáng Lì 1958: 550); for the difference in vowel, see §11.7.1–2.

[E] ST: WT *bkres* 'be hungry', JP *kyet³¹* 'hungry', Lepcha *krít*, Chepang *kray-* 'to hunger', Mru *krai* (Löffler 1966: 148). A possible allofam is → jìn₆ 饉殣 'famine'.

jī₃ 汲 (kjəp) **LH** kɨp, **OCM** *kəp
'To draw water' [Yi].
[E] ST: PTB *ka:p (*STC* no. 336): PLB *C-kap, WB *kʰap* 'dig up, draw water'; Garo *ko* 'draw water'; Dimasa *kʰau* 'pluck, gather, draw' (water) (*HST:* 66).

jī₄ 奇 (kje 3) **LH** kɨɑi, **OCM** *kai
'Odd (number) 奇 [Yi], 畸 [Xun]; 'unique, irregular' 奇 [Li].

⪤ **qí** 奇 (gjie 3) **LH** gɨɑi, **OCM** *gai, OCB *gaj
'Strange, extraordinary' [Zuo].
[T] *Sin Sukchu SR* gi (平); *MGZY* ki (平) [gi]

[E] This seems to be a ST etymon: WB *kʰai- < kaiᴮ* 'remarkable' (obsolete).

[C] An allofam is prob. → jǐ₃ 掎 'pull aside'. Because of the occasional *-ai ~ *-e vacillation in wfs (§11.3.3), → qǐ₅ 企跂 'stand on tiptoe' may also be related.

jī₅ 基 (kjɨ) **LH** kɨə, **OCM** *kə
'Foundation, base, settlement' [Shi].
[T] *Sin Sukchu SR* kjej (平), *PR*, *LR* ki; *MGZY* gi (平) [ki];
[N] This can hardly be related to the TB items under → jǐ 几机, nor to Lushai *keᴸ* 'foot, leg, wheel' (→ zhī₄ 支枝肢) because the vowels are different.

jī₆ 箕 (kjɨ) **LH** kɨə, **OCM** *kə
'Winnowing basket' [OB, Shi]. Unger (*Hao-ku* 38, 1992: 79) relates this word to **lí** 梩 (lji) 'basket' [Meng] and suggests a possible connection with → qǐ₂ 杞 'willow'.

jī₇ 期 'year' → **qí₈** 其

jī₈ 雞 (kiei) **LH** ke, **OCM** *kê
'Chicken, fowl' [Shi].
[T] *Sin Sukchu SR* kjej (平), *PR*, *LR* ki; *MGZY* gÿi (平) [kji]; *ONW* kėi,
[D] PMin *kei, K-Méixiàn *kaiᴬ¹*. A Han dialect form of the Chén-Chǔ-Sòng area was *zhī* 鳷 (kjie 4) [kie] *ke [FY 8, 4].
[E] Area word; since its origin is onomatopoetic, phonological correspondences are not regular: PTai *kəiᴮ¹ 'chicken' (Li F. 1976: 42), PKS *ka:i⁵, Kadai *kiᴬ. <> PMY *kai (Downer 1982) <> PVM *r-ka 'chicken' (on the vocalism, see §11.1.3).

jī₉ 積 (tsjäk) **LH** tsiek, **OCM** *tsek — **[T]** *ONW* tsiek
'To collect, accumulate' [Shi] > 'to block' [Zhuang].

⋇ **zì** 積 (tsie^C^) **LH** tsie^C^, **OCM** *tsekh
'To collect, store, wealth' [Shi] > 'provisions' [Zuo].
[<] exopass. derivation (§4.4), perh. also the verbal meanings ('be heaped'?).
[E] ST: WT *rtseg-pa* 'to put on top, pile up, stack'. Sagart (1999: 214) suggests that possibly → cè$_4$ 冊策筴 'bamboo slips > document' is related. Perh. related to → zī$_7$ 資.

jī$_{10}$ 績 (tsiek) **LH** tsek, **OCM** *tsêk
'To twist, spin' (to make thread) [Shi] > 'achievement, result' [Shu] is perh. an s-iterative of → xì$_1$ 係繫 *keh 'bind, tie up' (§5.2.3), with final *-k* (§6.1); yet PCH *s-k- is expected to yield MC k^h-.

jī$_{11}$ 隮 (tsiei[C]) **LH** tsei, **OCM** *tsə̂i, OCB *tsəi
'To ascend, rise, the mist rises' [Shi].
⋇ **jì** 霽濟 (tsiei^C^) **LH** tsei^C^, **OCM** *tsə̂ih
'To lift, disappear' (of clouds), 'clearing sky' 霽 [OB, Shu] > 'to stop' 濟 (of wind) [Zhuang], (of thoughts) [Shi].
⋇ **jì** 嚌 (dziei^C^) **LH** dzei^C^, **OCM** *dzə̂ih
'Carry a vessel to the lips' [Shu].
[C] A possible allofam could be → jì$_{16}$ 懠 'angry'.

jī$_{12}$ 幾 (kjei) **LH** kɨi, **OCM** *kəi — **[T]** *ONW* ki
'Be imminent, close to, near, at imminent risk' [Shi, Shu], 'first sign of happenings, details' 幾 [Shi, Shu]; 'auspicious, omen of good or evil' 禨 [Lie]. Karlgren (1933: 28) relates this word to → jìn$_1$ 近 'near'.

jī$_{13}$ 幾畿 (gjei) **LH** gɨi, **OCM** *gəi
'Border' (on garment) 幾 [Li], 'threshold, royal domain' 畿 [Shi]. Prob. not related to → jī$_{12}$ 幾 'close to' as Karlgren believed (1956: 10).
= **qí** 圻 (gjei) **LH** gɨi, **OCM** *gəi
'Border, a field of a certain size (1,000 sq. li)' 圻 [Zuo]. → qí$_2$ 祈 is cognate or the same word.

jī$_{14}$ 機璣 (kjei) **LH** kɨi, **OCM** *kəi — **[T]** *ONW* ki
'Mechanical device' 機 [Zhuang], 璣 [Shu]. Karlgren (1956: 5) considered this the s. w. as → jī$_{12}$ 幾 which is glossed as 'small', but *jī* 幾 really means 'be imminent, close to, first sign, detail'. Instead, *jī* is perh. cognate to → qǐ$_7$ 綮, thus meaning originally a contraption with hinges or joints, i.e. with moveable parts.

jī$_{15}$ 稽 (kiei, k^h^iei^B^) **LH** kei, k^h^ei^B^, **OCM** *kî, *khî? — **[T]** *ONW* k^h^ẹi
'Reach to' [BI, Zhuang], 'search, research, examine, comprehend' [Shu], 'calculate' [Li]; 'divine by tortoiseshell' 卟 [SW: Shu]; **zhī** 支 (tśie) [kie] 'to calculate' [Da Dai Liji] is prob. a variant if not simply a graphic loan.
⋇ **jì** 計 (kiei^C^) **LH** kei^C^, **OCM** *kîh, OCB *keps (1992: 546) — **[T]** *ONW* kẹi
'To calculate' [Zuo]. OCB is based on the assumption that *shí* 十 *gip is phonetic.
⋇ **jī** 譏 (kjei) **LH** kɨi, **OCM** *kəi
'Examine, inspect' [Meng] > 'blame' [Zuo].

jī$_{16}$ 擊 (kiek) **LH** kek, **OCM** *kêk
'Beat, strike' (a musical instrument, object) [Shi].
⋇ **jì** 轚 (kiei^C^) **LH** ke^C^, **OCM** *kêkh
'Carriages knocking against each other' [Zhouli].

⪤ **qī** 毄 (k^hiek) **LH** k^hek, **OCM** *khêk
'Beat, rub' [Zhouli].

jí₁ 及 (gjəp) **LH** gɨp, **OCM** *gəp
'To come to, reach to, together with, and' [BI, Shi].
[T] *Sin Sukchu SR* gi (入); *MGZY* ki (入) [gi]; *ONW* gip.
[D] Y-Guǎngzhōu *$^{22}k^hɐp^{D2}$*
[E] This word could be connected either with WB *k^hap* 'arrive at', JP *k^hap^{51}* to carry, reach' (*CVST* 5: 50). Or, less likely, with WT *'grub-pa, grub* 'to make ready' ⪤ *sgrub-pa, bsgrubs* 'to complete, achieve' ⪤ *grub-pa* 'complete'.
[C] Items under → jì₄ 暨 could be tone C derivations (Yú Mǐn 1948: 45; Baxter 1992: 351), but see there.

jí₂ 吉 (kjiet 4) **LH** kit, **OCM** *kit — [T] *ONW* kiit
'Auspicious, lucky, positive' [OB, BI, Shi].
[E] ST: WT *skyid-pa* 'happy' (*HST:* 87).

jí₃ 吉 (kjiet 4)
In some southern dialects this is the second syllable in the word for 'ear': Y-Dōngguǎn *$ŋɐi^{13}$-$kɐk^{44}$* 耳吉, K-Dōngguǎn *^{21}gi-^{22}kit.*

jí₄ 佶 (gjiet 4) **LH** git, **OCM** *git
'To run robustly, straight, unswerving' (of horses) [Shi].
⪤ **xié** 頡 (ɣiet) **LH** get, **OCM** *gît
'To straighten the neck' (of birds) (meaning not certain) [Shi].

jí₅ 極 (gjək) **LH** gɨk, **OCM** *gək
'Highest point, ridge of a roof, extreme, reach the end, come to, attain' [Shi].
[T] *Sin Sukchu SR* gi (入); *MGZY* ki (入) [gi]; *ONW* gik
[E] ST: PLB *kak 'expensive, intense, at its peak' (Matisoff 1972: 31; *STC:* 166 n. 444).
⪤ **jí** 亟 (kjək) **LH** kɨk, **OCM** *kək
'Be urgent' [Shi]; 'to die' [Li], 'execute, kill' 殛 [Shu]. This word is prob. not a variant of → jí₁₂ 急 (kjəp) 'be urgent'.

jí₆ 疾 (dzjet) **LH** dzit, **OCM** *dzit
'Be sick, suffering, defect, evil' [OB, Shi].
[T] *Sin Sukchu SR* dzi (入); *MGZY* tsi (入) [dzi]; *ONW* dzit
= **jí** 堲 (dzjet) **LH** dzit, **OCM** *dzit
'Detest' [Shu] (Karlgren *GSR* 923c), 'to hate' 疾 [Shu].
[E] ST *tsik: WT *ts^hig-pa* 'anger, indignation'; LB-Lahu *yɨ̂ʔ*, Motuo Monpa *ro tsik* 'angry' [*HPTB:* 344f].
⪤ **jí** 疾 (dzjet, dzi^C) **LH** dzit, dzi^C, **OCM** *dzit(s)
'Be jealous' [Chuci].
⪤ **jí** 堲 (tsjet) **LH** tsit, **OCM** *tsit, OCB *tsjit < *tsjik
'Coaled part of burning torch, to burn or scorch earth' [Guanzi].
[E] ST *tsik 'to smolder' > 'burn' / 'be ill, illness' / 'anger', PTB *m-(t)sik 'burn, angry' *[HPTB]*, WT *'ts^hig-pa* 'to burn, destroy by fire, glow; to be in rut, be inflamed, feverish' (Bodman 1980: 158); perh. Chepang *ɟik-* 'be sick, injured, hurt'. Prob. not related to *jì* 癠 'sick' (under → jǐ₅ 擠). Less likely comparanda: WT *sdig-pa* 'sin, wickedness' (Bodman 1980: 158). AA items look somewhat similar: PBahn. *ɟiʔ, Wa-Lawa-Palaung *sɨʔ 'sick'. *STC* (170 n. 455) relates this word to PTB *tsa 'hot, pain', but the vowels differ (*i* vs. *a*), see → zāi₁ 災.

jí₇ 即 (?) **LH** tsit, **OCM** *tsit
'To approach, go to, apply' > 'on the point of' [BI, Shi, Shu]; *jí-wèi* 即位 'to take one's place, seat, ascend the throne' [BI].
[T] *Sin Sukchu SR* tsi (入); *MGZY* dzi (入) [tsi]
[E] AA: Khmer *jita* /cit/, OKhmer *jit* /ɟit/ 'to be near to, to the point of, be close' ⋇ *bhjita* /pcit/ 'to bring near, draw up (a chair), to set (two things together), join, attach, to apply'.
⋇ **qiè** 切 (tsʰiet) **LH** tsʰet, **OCM** *tshît — **[T]** *MTang* tsʰiar < tsʰɨar, *ONW* tsʰėt
'Be close to' [Xun], 'eager, impatient' [Lun]. 切 also writes a homophone which is cognate to → jié₉ 節.
⋇ **nì** 昵 (ṇjet) **LH** ṇit, **OCM** *nrit — **[T]** *ONW* nit
'Familiarity' [Shu], (a ruler's) 'favorite' (person) [Shu]. The homophones → nì₂ 昵 'glue' and → nì₄ 衵 'underwear' are prob. not related.
[E] AA: Khmer *jaṃnita* /cumnit/ (i.e. etymologically *ɟ-n-it*) 'nearness, closeness, proximity, familiarity with, intimacy'. The AA nominal n-infix is taken in CH for the root initial, perh. because of the original voiced initial and the paronomastic attraction to → ěr₇ 邇 (ńźieᴮ) 'near'. The CH words *jí* and *nì* are thus allofams in an AA wf.
[C] A possible allofam could be → qīn₅ 親. Syn. are → ěr₇ 邇, → ní₁ 尼, → nì₉ 暱.

jí₈ 堲 (tsjet) **LH** tsit, **OCM** *tsit, OCB *tsjit < *tsjik
'Masonry' [Li].
[E] ST *tsik: WT *rtsig-pa* 'to wall up, a wall, masonry' (Bodman 1980: 158).

jí₉ 堲 'burn' → **jí₆** 疾

jí₁₀ 堲 'detest' → **jí₆** 疾

jí₁₁ 棘 (kjək) **LH** kɨk, **OCM** *kək, OCB *krjək
'Jujube, thorns' [Shi] is written in a *Shījīng* variant as:
~ **lì** 朸 (ljək) **LH** lɨk, **OCM** *rək, OCB *C-rjək (Baxter 1992: 474).

jí₁₂ 急 (kjəp) **LH** kɨp, **OCM** *kəp
'Be urgent, hurrying' [Shi], 'hasty, distress' [Zuo] is not a variant of *jí* 亟 (kjək) 'be urgent' (under → jí₅ 極). Etymology not clear.
[T] *Sin Sukchu SR* ki (入); *MGZY* gi (入) [ki]; *ONW* kip

jí₁₃ 集輯 (dzjəp) **LH** dzip, **OCM** *dzəp, OCB *dzjup — **[T]** *ONW* dzip
'Come together and settle (of birds), perch' [Shi] > caus. 'to collect together, unite, settle, achieve' 集 [BI, Shi], 輯 [Shi].
⋇ **zá** 雜 (dzəp) **LH** dzəp, **OCM** *dzə̂p — **[T]** *ONW* dzɑp
'Brought together, mixed' [Shi], 'variegated' [Li] (Karlgren 1956: 13).
[E] AA: Khmer *cwpa* /cùuəp/ ~ *jwpa* /cúuəp/ 'to join', intr. 'to meet, come together, encounter' ⋇ *prajcwpa* 'to meet one another'. <> The following is prob. a different etymon with the basic meaning 'close': PTB *tsup > PLB *tsup ~ *ʔtsup [Matisoff 1972: 40] > WB *cʰup* 'clench fist', Kachin *tsup* 'to gather' (as mouth of sack), 'close hands' (as in catching a ball) (*HST:* 84). KN-Lai *fuu / fuut* 'to perch' [*LTBA* 21.1: 18].
[C] This wf has perh. converged with → jì₁₀ 揖. Baxter (1992: 350) adds *cuì* 萃 (dzwiᶜ) 'collect' (under → zāo₂ 遭).

jí₁₄ 脊 (tsjäk) **LH** tsiek, **OCM** *tsek
'Spine' [Li] > 'fundamental principle, reason' [Shi].

⋈ **jí** 瘠膌 (dzjäk) **LH** dziek, **OCM** *dzek

'Emaciated' [Yi] > 'meagre, poor' (soil) [Guoce] > 'suffering' 瘠 [Shu]; 膌 [Guan] (Karlgren 1956: 10). Perh. → zì$_3$ 胔 'bones with meat on' is cognate.

jí$_{15}$ 蹐 (tsjäk) **LH** tsiek, **OCM** *tsek

'Walk with small steps' [Shi]. This may be the same etymon as → jí$_{16}$ 踖, see §11.3.2.

⋈ **jí** 脊 (dzjäk) **LH** dziek, **OCM** *dzek

'Trample, oppress' [Zhuang] (Karlgren 1956: 10).

⋈ **cǐ** 跐 (tsʰieᴮ) **LH** tsʰieᴮ, **OCM** *tsheʔ or *tshaiʔ

'To trample' [Lie].

[E] This is a vocalic variant of → jí$_{16}$ 踖 (§11.3.2). The same doublets are found in 'footprint, track' → jì$_{21}$ 蹟 which may be cognate.

jí$_{16}$ 踖 (tsjäk) **LH** tsiak, **OCM** *tsak, actually prob. *tsjak

'Walk reverently' [Lunyu]. This may be the same etymon as → jí$_{15}$ 蹐, see §11.3.2.

⋈ **jí** 踖 (dzjäk) **LH** dziak, **OCM** *dzak, actually prob. *dzjak

'To trample' [Li].

⋈ **qì**, **què** 踖 (tsʰjäk, tsʰjak) **LH** tsʰiak, **OCM** *tsʰak, actually prob. *tsʰjak

'Reverent demeanor, do with attentive movements' [Shi].

[E] ST *tsjak: WT *'čʰags-pa, bčags* 'to tread, walk, move'. Perh. also connected with AA: Semai /jak/, 'to trample', Mon /cẹ̤ak/, WrMon *jak* 'to march, travel' ('j' = dž, 'c' = tš).

The ST medial *-ia- (*-ja-) explains the *tsiak ~ *tsek doublets (→ jí$_{15}$ 蹐; §11.3.2). The same doublets are found in 'footprint, track' → jì$_{21}$ 蹟 which may be cognate.

jí$_{17}$ 藉 (dzjäk) **LH** dziak, **OCM** *dzak, prob. *tsjak

'To cultivate' (field, garden, rice) [OB, Zuo] > 'perform the plowing ceremony' [OB] > 'sacred field' 藉 [SW] (Bodde 1975: 231ff) > 'register of field revenues' 籍 [Shi] > 'a record, writing tablet' 籍 [Zuo].

[E] MK, either (1) PMK *jiik [Shorto 1976: 1049] > OMon *jik*, Spoken Mon /còik/ 'to harrow, break up for planting, to cultivate'; Khmer /cìːk/ 'to dig, dig over'. Occasionally, we find OC *a for foreign *e* or *i*, see §11.1.3. Or (2) perh. Khmer /caa/ 'to grove, plow' [Lewitz 1976: 750], with the CH final *-k* addition (§6.1).

jí$_{18}$ 籍 → **jí$_{17}$** 藉

jí$_{19}$ 楫 (tsjäp) **LH** tsiap, **OCM** *tsap

'To row' [Shi], 'oar' occurs also in JP *šap* < *tšap* 'oar' (Benedict *HJAS* 5, 1940: 111 no. 59).

jí$_{20}$ 戢濈 → **jí$_{13}$** 集輯

jí$_{21}$ 輯戢濈 → **jì$_{10}$** 揖

jǐ$_1$ 几机 (kjiᴮ 3) **LH** kɨᴮ, **OCM** *kriʔ

'Stool, small table' 几 [Shi], 机 [Zuo, Li].

[E] ST: PTB *kriy (*STC* no. 38) > PL *kre¹ > WB *kʰre* 'foot, leg' ⋈ *ə-kʰre* 'foundation, foot', WT *kʰri* 'seat, chair, throne, couch' (*HST:* 54), Lepcha *hri* 'chair'. <> AA-Khmer *grē* /krɛɛ/ 'bed, bench' could be a loan from some ST language, perh. OC (so Pou / Jenner, *J. of Oriental Studies* 11, 1973.1: 1–90).

jǐ$_2$ 己 (kjɨ) **LH** kɨəᴮ, **OCM** *kəʔ

'Self', reflexive personal pronoun [Lun]. — Etymology not clear.

[T] *Sin Sukchu SR* kjej (上), *PR*, *LR* ki; *MGZY* gi (上) [ki]

jǐ₃ 掎 (kjeᴮ 3) **LH** kɨɑiᴮ, **OCM** *kaiʔ
'Pull by one leg' [Zuo], 'pull aside' [Shi]; 'stand around close to door' 踦 [Gongyang].
※ **qī** 攲 (kʰje 3) **LH** kʰɨɑi, **OCM** *khai
'Slanting' [Xun, also MC *kjie 3*]; 'one-footed' 踦 [Guoyu]; 'one horn turning up, one down' 觭 [Yi].
[E] ST: WB *kai* 'oblique, sidewise' (Matisoff 1995a: 84). An allofam is prob. → jī₄ 奇 'odd', also possibly → jì₅ 徛 'stand', and → qǐ₅ 企跂 'stand on tiptoe' which has, however, a different OC rime (*-e).

jǐ₄ 麂 (kjiᴮ 3) **LH** kɨᴮ, **OCM** *kriʔ
'Muntjac' 麂 [post-Zhou-Han]; acc. to *GY*, 䰃 [OB] writes the same word.
[E] ST: PTB *d-kiy (*STC* no. 54): PL *kye' 'barking deer'; WB *khye, gyiᴬ* 'barking deer', JP *tʃə³³-kʰji³³* 'muntjac', *kʰyi¹-maʔ¹* 'a kind of muntjac', Lushai *saᴴ-khiᴸ* < *-kʰiʔ/h* 'barking deer'.

jǐ₅ 擠 (tsieiᴮ) **LH** tseiᴮ, **OCM** *tsîʔ or *tsə̂iʔ
'To push' [Zuo], 'urge, press, press out'.
[E] ST: PTB *tsyir ~ *tsyur 'squeeze, wring' (*HPTB*: 397): WT *'tsʰir-ba* 'to press, press out' (Unger *Hao-ku* 35, 1986: 33); Bahing *tśyur* 'wring', Kanauri *tsŭr* 'to milk'.
※ Perh. **jì** 癠 (dzieiᴮ/ᶜ]) **LH** dzei(ᴮ/ᶜ), **OCM** *dzî or *dzə̂i(ʔ/h)
'Disease' [Li], 'suffer' (Unger) < 'be pressed' ?
[E] TB-WT *gzir-ba* 'be pressed, troubled, suffer' (Unger). Prob. not related to → jí₆ 疾 'sick', but a possible allofam could be → jì₁₆ 懠.
[E] Alternatively, the OC stem may derive from earlier *st(ə)i in light of the possible allofam **dǐ** 抵 (tieiᴮ) [teiᴮ] 'push away' [Dadai Liji].

jǐ₆ 濟 (tsieiᴮ) **LH** tseiᴮ, **OCM** *tsîʔ, OCB *tsiʔ
'Many' [Shi] (Baxter 1992: 462).
※ **zǐ** 秭 (tsiᴮ) **LH** tsiᴮ, **OCM** *tsiʔ, OCB *tsjijʔ
'Large number' [Shi].

jǐ₇ 濟 'stately' → **qí₁₅** 齊

jǐ₈ 幾 (kjeiᴮ) **LH** kɨiᴮ, **OCM** *kəiʔ
'Few, how many' [Shi]. Karlgren (1956: 7) considers this cognate to → jī₁₂ 幾 which is glossed as 'small', but *jī* 幾 really means 'be imminent, close to, first sign, detail'.
[T] *Sin Sukchu SR* kjej (上), *PR*, *LR* ki; *MGZY* gi (上) [ki]; *ONW* ki
[E] PTai *kiiᶜ 'several, how many' > S. *kiiᴮ¹* (B is irregular), Saek *kii³*; prob. borrowed from CH together with the numerals.

jǐ₉ 蟣 (kjeiᴮ) **LH** kɨiᴮ, **OCM** *kəiʔ
'Louse' [Hanfei] is also an old dialect word for 'leech', still used in Mǐn (Norman 1983) which is prob. related to the old dialect words *mǎ-qí* 馬蜞 or 馬耆 'leech'. This is prob. derived from a ST etymon 'to bite', note KN *m-kei 'to bite'; for a semantic parallel, see → zhì₂ 蛭 'leech' and → dié₂ 咥 'bite'.

jì₁ 計 → **jī₁₅** 稽

jì₂ 妓 (kje 3, also gjeᴮ 3) Wei-Jin kɨe, gɨeᴮ
'A small and weak woman' [SW] (物 *wù* 'thing' in the *SW* gloss is thought to be an error for 弱 *ruò* 'weak'), perh. a euphemism for the later attested meaning 'singing girl, prostitute' [Jinshu, i.e. post-Han]. A hypothetical OC form may have been *kre.
[E] This appears to be a loan from early Vietnamese (the ancient Yuè in southern

China): MK-PVM *keːʔ 'woman' > Viet. *cái* / gái 'feminine' [Ferlus]; elsewhere in MK: PWa *krih 'girl', PNBahn. *kadrì 'female' [K. Smith 1972: 64]. Alternatively, Wáng Lì (1982: 108) following earlier commentaries relates this word to *jì* 技 (gje^B) 'skill', but this may be folk etymology. Also other foreign words for 'girl, woman' refer to someone of low standing, see → bì 嬖, → tái$_3$ 嬯臺.

jì$_3$ 既 (kjei^C) **LH** kɨs, **OCM** *kəts
'To complete, have done', mark of completed action [OB, BI, Shi, Shu].
[T] *Sin Sukchu SR* kjej (去), *PR*, *LR* ki; *MGZY* gi (去) [ki]; *ONW* ki
[<] exopass. (perfective) of *qì* 訖 (kjət) 'to finish' (§4.4); the perfect is implied in the passive meaning of tone C. Perh. cognate to → jì$_4$ 暨 'to reach', but see there.
[E] ST (?): Mru *ki* 'complete' (Löffler 1966: 129).

⋈ **qì** 訖 (kjət) **LH** kɨt, **OCM** *kət — **[T]** *ONW* kit
'To finish, cease' [Shu].

jì$_4$ 暨 (gji^C 3) **LH** gɨs, OCB *grjəts < *grjəps — **[T]** *MGZY* ki (去) [gi]
'To reach to, bring with, concur with, together with, and' [Shu].
[<] exoactive ? of → jí$_1$ 及 (gjəp) (Baxter 1992: 351). Or less likely ⋈ → qì$_3$ 迄 (xjət), → jì$_3$ 既 (kjəi^C) (the MC vowels do not agree).

jì$_5$ 徛 (gjie^B 3) **LH** gɨɑiʔ — **[T]** *ONW* ge^B
'To stand', has replaced → lì$_3$ 立 in southern dialects: Xiàmén *k^{h}ia^{C2}*, Fúzhōu *k^{h}ie^{C2}*, Jiàn'ōu *kyɛ^{B2}* (Norman 1988: 197). Perh. related to → jǐ$_3$ 掎 in the sense of 'standing around'.

jì$_6$ 寄 (kje^C) **LH** kɨɑi^C, **OCM** *kaih
'To commit to one's charge' [Lun], 'entrust to, communicate' [Li], Mand. 'send' (a letter).
[E] ? ST: perh. cognate to WB *khai^C* 'to bring', Lushai *k^{h}ai^L* 'to give a present'.

jì$_7$ 忌誋惎 (gjɨ^C) **LH** gɨə^C, **OCM** *gəh, OCB *g(r)jəʔ(s)
'To warn, detest' 惎 [Zuo], 誋 [SW] > ('be warned':) 'cautious' [Shi], 'show respect for' [Zuo], 'taboo' 忌 [Zhouli] > 'dread, hate' 忌 [Shi]. Wáng Lì (1982: 86) relates this word to → jiè$_9$ 戒誡 'guard against'.

jì$_8$ 紀 (kjɨ^B) **LH** kɨə^B, **OCM** *kəʔ, OCB *k(r)jəʔ
'Leading thread, regulate' [Shi], 'follow up, continue' [Shu]. Unger (*Hao-ku* 38, 1992: 77) relates this word to WT *'k^{h}rid-pa, bkri* 'to conduct acc. to order' [Das] ⋈ *k^{h}rid* 'row, order, serial order' [Das]; and to → lǐ$_5$ 理 (ljɨ^B) 'regulate'.

⋈ **jì** 記 (kjɨ^C) **LH** kɨə^C, **OCM** *kəh — **[T]** *ONW* kiə
'To record, remember' [Shu].

jì$_9$ 季 (kwi^C 4) **LH** kwis, **OCM** *kwis, OCB *k^{w}jits
'Youngest, young' (of persons) [BI, Shi] > 'last of a series' [Zuo], 'season, three-month period' [Tang period] — **[E]** Etymology not clear.
[D] PMin *kie^C ~ *kyi^C 'season'

jì$_{10}$ 揖 (tsjəp, tʂjəp) **LH** tsip, tʂip, **OCM** *ts(r)əp
'To cluster together, to crowd' [Shi].

= **jí** 輯戢濈 (tʂjəp) **LH** tʂip, **OCM** *tsrəp
'To gather up' 輯 [Li]; 'to fold up, gather in' (wings) 戢 [Shi]; 'be crowded together' (as horns of sheep) 濈 [Shi].

[E] ? AA: PMonic *cap, Nyah Kur '(bird) to settle on, perch', Mon *cɔp 'to adhere to, cleave to'; OKhmer /ɟap/ 'touch, join, meet, cling, adhere'.

This word has perh. converged with → jí₁₃ 集輯. Perh. → zhí₇ 蟄 (ḍjəp) 'cluster together, hibernate' belongs here.

jì₁₁ 穄 (tsjäi^C) **LH** tsias, **OCM** *tsats < *tsaps
'A kind of millet' (*Panicum miliaceum*, not glutinous).
[E] Perh. TB-WB *c^hap* 'millet' (Luce, Sagart 2002 ms: 8).

jì₁₂ 際 'connection' → **jiē₄** 接

jì₁₃ 跡 → **jì₂₁** 蹟

jì₁₄ 冀覬 (kji 3) **LH** kɨ, **OCM** *kri or *krəi ?
'To hope' 冀 [Zuo]; 'to long for' 覬 [Zuo] is prob. cognate to → xī₁₂ 希睎 (so Wáng Lì 1982: 393).
[E] Perh. ST: WT *bkri-ba* 'try to acquire, search for' (*CVST* 5: 66).

jì₁₅ 濟 (tsiei^C) **LH** tsei^C, **OCM** *tsə̂ih, OCB *tsəjs — [T] *ONW* tsėi
'To ford, to cross' (a river) vb. [Shi] > 'to help across, help over' (e.g. difficulties) [Shu] > 'to help' (people) [Lunyu], 'contribute' [Zuo], 'achieve' [Yi].

⋊ **jīn** 津 (tsjen) **LH** tsin, **OCM** *tsin
'A ford' n. [Shu].
[<] nominal n-suffix derivative from *jì* 'to ford' (§6.4.3).

[E] MK: Mon inscr. *cnis* [cnøs] > *cnih* 'a ghat, place of access to river..., landing place' < n-infix nominalization of *cis* [cøs] 'to go down, descend' vb. (e.g. down the bank to the river, also general). The Mon vowel is closer to CH than the Khmer cognate: *cuḥ* [cuh] 'go down', perh. also Viet. *xìu* [sìu] < *ž*- 'go down'. Thus both Mon and OC derived a noun from the verb with a nominalizing affix, Mon with the MK n-infix > *cnis* 'ghat', OC with the ST n-suffix *jīn* 津 'a ford'. Perh. → xī₂ 西栖 'nest, west' belongs to this wf. The ST syn. for 'ford, cross' is → dù₂ 渡.

jì₁₆ 懠 (dziei, dziei^C) **LH** dzei(^C), **OCM** *dzî(h) or *dzə̂i(h)
'Angry' [Shi]. Etymology not certain. The notion 'angry' can derive from 'rise' (cf. Mand. *qǐ* 起), hence perh. cogn. to → jī₁₁ 隮 'rise'. Or *jì* could derive from 'sick' and be related to *jì* 癠 (under → jǐ₅ 擠).

jì₁₇ 嚌 → **jī₁₁** 隮

jì₁₈ 濟 'stop' → **jī₁₁** 隮

jì₁₉ 霽 → **jī₁₁** 隮

jì₁₀ 癠 → **jǐ₅** 擠

jì₂₁ 蹟 (tsjäk) **LH** tsiek, **OCM** *tsek
'Footprint, track' [BI, Shi].

~ **jì** 跡 (tsjäk) **LH** tsiek, **OCM** *tsjak — [T] *ONW* tsiek
'Footprint, track' [Shu] (also written with radical 162).

[N] In Han and Wei-Jin poetry these two words rime in *-ek (Luo / Zhou 1958; Ting 1975), but *tsjak occurs in *Shījīng*. See §11.3.2. The root initial was OCM *j- as the phonetic of 跡 (*GSR* 800) and TB cognates indicate (§9.2); a ST medial *-ja- (*-ia-) explains the OC *-jak ~ *-ek doublets. Possible allofams are → jí₁₅ 蹐 and → jí₁₆ 踖 'walk, step', prob. as a result of paronomastic attraction.

[E] ST *C-jak: TB-Limbu *yok²* 'trace, track', Lushai *hniak^H* 'footprint, hoof-mark'.

jì $_{22}$ 繼 (kiei^C) **LH** ke^C, **OCM** *kêh
'To continue, perpetuate' [Shi] is the s. w. as *xì* 係繫 *keh (under → xì 系繫 *geh).

jiā $_{1}$ 加 (ka) **LH** kai, **OCM** *krâi — **[T]** *ONW* kä
'To add, attach, hit' [Shi].

⋇ **jià** 駕 (ka^C) **LH** kai^C, **OCM** *krâih
'To yoke' [Shi].
[<] exopass. of *jiā*: 'be attached to' (§4.4).
[E] ST *kral: WT *bkral-ba* 'to impose, place upon' (tax), 'appoint to' ⋇ *k^hral* 'tax, burden' (*HST:* 36). WB *ka^C* 'to harness, saddle' is apparently a CH loan.

jiā $_{2}$ 嘉 (ka) **LH** kai, **OCM** *krâi
'Be good, fine, excellent > consider fine, approve' [Shi], 'happy' [Zuo].

~ **jiā** 佳 (kai) **LH** kɛ, **OCM** *krê
'Be good' [Lao] appears to be a vocalic variant of the above.

⋇ **hè** 賀 (ɣâ^C) **LH** gɑi^C, **OCM** *gâih
'To congratulate' [Shi] (Karlgren 1949: 90 derives this word from *gě* next).

⋇ **gě** 哿 (kâ^B) **LH** kɑi^B, **OCM** *kâiʔ
'Be well, passable, suitable' [Shi]. Alternatively, *gě* may belong to *kě* 可 (under → hè 何荷) (so Wáng Lì 1982: 431).

[E] This wf is prob. ST, even though the rimes do not agree with TB: WT *bkra-ba* 'beautiful, blooming', *bkra-šis* 'happiness, prosperity, blessing' (*šis* 'good luck, fortune, bliss'); Lushai *t̥^ha^L / t̥^hat^L < t^hraah / t̥^hrat* 'be good, nice, virtuous, be advantageous'.

jiā $_{3}$ 夾 (kăp) **LH** kɛp, OCB *krêp — **[T]** *ONW* käp
'Be on both sides' [Shi], 'support' [Shu], 'press between' [Zuo], 'tweezers' [Zhouli].

⋇ **xiá** 狹 (ɣăp) **LH** gɛp, **OCM** *grêp, OCB *ɦkrep
[T] *ONW* ɣäp — **[D]** PMin *ɦap
'Narrow' [Li] (Karlgren 1949: 90).
[<] endopass. of *jiā* 夾 (kăp) (§4.6).

[E] Area word: PMY *nGep, PTai *g-: S. *k^hɛɛp^{D2}* (CH loans?). <> TB-JP *lə^{55}-kap^{55}* 'tweezers'. <> AA: Mon inscr. *sakep* /səkep/ 'tongs'.
[C] → xiē$_1$ 脅 (xjɐp) 'sides of body, ribs' belongs to this root, as could → jié$_1$, jiā 梜 'chopsticks'. Wáng Lì (1982: 597) proposes that synonyms under → xié$_1$ 挾協 are possibly related.

jiā $_{4}$ 挾 (tsiep) **LH** tsep, **OCM** *tsêp ?
'Grasp, hold' [Shi]; 'clasp under the arm, hold on to' [Meng], 'encompass, embrace, all round' [Shi], 浹 [Zuo].
[E] This word is prob. not related to the synonym → xié$_1$ 挾協 and the other stems listed there, because MC *ts-* rarely, if ever, derives from an earlier cluster *sk-.

jiā $_{5}$ 梜 → **jié** $_{1}$, **jiā** 梜

jiā $_{6}$ 佳 → **jiā** $_{2}$ 嘉

jiā $_{7}$ 家 (ka) **LH** ka, **OCM** *krâ
'House, household, family' [OB: *Sōrui* p. 272; Shi].
[T] *Sin Sukchu SR* kja (平); *MGZY* gya (平) [kja]; *ONW* kä
[E] ST: WT *mk^har* 'house, castle' which Beyer (1992: 114) connects with the WT items under → hù$_3$ 互桓.

⋟ **jià** 嫁 (ka^C) **LH** ka^C, **OCM** *krâh
'To give a girl in marriage' [Shi].
[<] exoactive of *jiā* (§4.3) > 'to marry' (of a woman).
[E] CH -> White Tai *xaa^B1* < *x- 'id.' (Li F. 1976: 40).

jiā$_8$ 豭 (ka) **LH** ka, **OCM** *krâ
'Male pig, boar' [Zuo, SW]; a Northeastern dialect word for → zhū$_4$ 豬 [ṭɑ] *tra 'pig' [FY]. Given the homophone *jiā* 'male deer' [SW], this may be a more general etymon for 'male' of an animal and may also be cognate to → gǔ$_7$ 羖 'ram' (so Wáng Lì 1982: 126). If *SW* is correct that 豭 is an abbreviated phonetic in → jiā$_7$ 家 *krâ 'house', then the word must be much older than *Zuǒzhuàn*, while *zhū* may be an early dialect word.

jiá$_1$ 蛺 → **hú**$_6$**-dié** 胡蝶

jiá$_2$ 莢頰鋏 → **xié**$_1$ 挾協

jiǎ$_1$ 甲 (kap) **LH** kap, **OCM** *krâp
'Shell, (finger-)nail, armour' [BI, Shi].
[T] *Sin Sukchu SR* kja (入); *MGZY* gya (入) [kja]; *ONW* käp
[D] PMin *kɑp ~ *kap
[E] ST: WT *k^hrab* 'shield, fish scales', Lepcha *hróp* (< *k^hrap) 'armour, scales' (Bodman 1980: 142). The relationship with Tai seems questionable: S. *lep^D2S* < *dl- 'finger- or toenail' (Li F. 1976: 45). *Jiǎ* is prob. not related to → jiè$_1$ 介.

⋟ Perh. **jiá** 鞈 (kǎp) **LH** kɛp, **OCM** *krə̂p
'Leather jerkin or cuirass' [Guan] (*HST:* 131).

jiǎ$_2$ 假嘏 (ka^B) **LH** ka^B, **OCM** *krâʔ — **[T]** *ONW* kä
'Be great' (of Heaven, rulers), 'abundance' [BI, Shi]. Wáng Lì (1982: 144) relates → xià$_5$, shà 廈 'building' to this wf.

⋟ **xià** 夏 (ɣa^B) **LH** ga^B, **OCM** *grâʔ — **[T]** *ONW* ɣä
'Be great' (of ruler) [Shi].

[E] Perh. related to → xián$_8$ 閑 'be large' and → jiè$_2$ 介价 'increase'. Shī Xiàngdōng 2000: 27 relates this word to WT *rgya* 'wide, broad'.

jiǎ$_3$ 假 (ka^B) **LH** ka^B, **OCM** *krâʔ
'To borrow' [Zuo] > 'simulate' [Meng] > 'deception, false' [BI, Shi, Li].
[T] *Sin Sukchu SR* kja (上); *MGZY* gya (上) [kja]; *ONW* kä
[E] ST: WT *kar-skyin* 'a loan' (Unger *Hao-ku* 35, 1986: 32). An allofam is prob. → gù$_7$ 雇.

jiǎ$_4$ 假 'come' → **gé**$_4$ 格

jià$_1$ 稼 (ka^C) **LH** ka^C, **OCM** *krâh
'Grain, to sow' [Shi].
[E] <> KT: PTai *kla^C1 'young rice plant' (Li F. 1976: 40), Saek *tlaa^3* > *traa^3* 'rice seedlings', PKS *kla^3 'rice seedling'. The medials do not agree, see §7.3.

jià$_2$ 駕 → **jiā**$_1$ 加

jià$_3$ 架 → **gé**$_3$ 格

jià$_4$ 賈價 (ka^C) **LH** ka^C, **OCM** *krâh
'Price' 賈 [Lunyu], 價 [Meng].
[T] *Sin Sukchu SR* kja (去); *MGZY* gya (去) [kja]

[E] ST: WB ə-*kya*^{C} 'price'; Lushai *k*^{h}*aar*^{R} 'to buy the whole, buy in large quantities'. <> Tai: Saek *khaa*^{5} < *gaa*^{B} 'value, price' ⪤ *khaa*^{6} < *k*^{h}*aa*^{B} 'engage in trade'. CH -> P-Miao *ɴqa^{C} [Wáng Fushi 1979] 'price' (Sagart). Perh. related to → gǔ$_{11}$ 賈.

jià$_{5}$-bù 幏布 → **bù$_{2}$** 布

jiān$_{1}$ 尖鑯 (tsjäm) **LH** tsiam, **OCM** *tsam
'Pointed, sharp' 尖 [GY], 'thin, slender, sharp-pointed' 鑯 [Zhouli].
This word is prob. cognate to *xiān* below; or it might have been influenced by words for → zān 簪 'pin'; it is possibly related to 殲 'to cut down (people)' [Shi] (Wáng Lì 1982: 616). See → yǎn$_{4}$ 剡覃 for the semantic association of 'sharp' with 'cut'.

⪤ **xiān** 銛 (sjäm) **LH** siam, **OCM** *sam
'Sharp' [Mo] has been borrowed by PTai *s-: S. *siam*^{A1} 'spade, hoe' ⪤ *siam*^{C1} 'to sharpen to a point'.

[E] ST: PTB *syam > WB *saṁ*, Gyarung *śom* 'iron', Nung *śam* 'iron, sword' (*STC:* 53). The wf → yǎn$_{4}$ 剡覃 represents a different stem (*STC:* 171 n. 457 relates *xiān* to PTB *s-ryam).

jiān$_{2}$ 堅 (kien) **LH** ken, **OCM** *kîn
'Firm' (e.g. fruit, bows), 'solid, strong' (e.g. ice) [Shi].
[T] *Sin Sukchu SR* kjen (平); *MGZY* gÿan (平) [kjɛn]; *ONW* kèn
[E] ST *kin/ŋ: WB *kyañ* 'feeling of numbness', JP *kyin* 'stiff, aching' [Matisoff 1974 no. 15], Lushai *k*^{h}*iŋ*^{F} < *k*^{h}*iŋʔ* 'dry out, get hard' (of ouside of meat etc.). For related and similar items, see → gù$_{1}$ 固 (incl. Table G-1) and Table J-1.

⪤ **qiān** 掔 (k^{h}ien, k^{h}ăn) **LH** k^{h}en, k^{h}ɛn, **OCM** *kh(r)în
'Firmly believe' tr. [Zhuang]. Aspiration as well as medial *r are unexplained, unless this is a different etymon related to AA-Mon *kriŋ* (*krɔŋ*) 'stiff, hard'.

⪤ **jié** 劼 (k^{h}ăt) **LH** k^{h}ɛt, **OCM** *khrît
'Solidly, earnestly' [Shu].

Table J-1 Hard, congeal, dry (B)

	*kreŋ ⪤	*krek	*kin	
OC	yìng 硬 (ŋɛŋ^{C}) hard		jiān 堅 *kîn hard, solid	qiān 掔 *khrin firmly believe
WT	reŋs-pa solid (not liquid)	mk^{h}regs-pa hard, firm (snow)		
Lushai			k^{h}iŋF < k^{h}iŋʔ dry out (get hard)	
JP	greŋ^{31} hard		kyin stiff	
WB			kyañ numbness	

The stems *kreŋ and *krek are e-vowel variants of *kar (under → gù 固). The stem *kin is unrelated.

jiān$_{3}$ 肩 (kien) **LH** ken, **OCM** *kên — [T] *MTang* kian < kɨan, *ONW* kèn
'Shoulder' [Shi], 'to shoulder, carry' [Shu] is shared with PKS *k-xiːn^{1} 'arm', PTai *kh- > S. *k*^{h}*ɛɛn*^{A1} 'arm'.

jiān$_{4}$ 姦 (kan) **LH** kan, **OCM** *krân
'Villain, wickedness' [Shu].

[<] perh. a k-prefix noun derived from a hypothetical root *ran (§5.4).

⋈ **shàn** 訕 (ṣan^C) **LH** ṣan^C, **OCM** *srân(s)
'To vilify, slander' [Lun].
[<] perh. an s-causative / tr. derived from a root *ran (§5.2.1).

jiān₅ 間閒 (kăn) **LH** kɛn, **OCM** *krên, OCB *kren
'To be in the middle, be inserted' [Shi], 'crevice, interstice' [Zhuang].
[T] *Sin Sukchu SR* kjan (平); *MGZY* (gÿan >) gyan (平) [kjan]; *ONW* kän

⋈ **jiàn** 間閒 (kăn^C) **LH** kɛn^C, **OCM** *krêns
'To put in between, insert, alternate, supersede' [Shi], 'to separate, differences, meddle between' [Zuo].
[<] exoactive of *jiān* 間閒 (§4.3).

[E] ST: Lushai *in^L-kaar^L* 'the space, interval, or distance between, difference' ⋈ *in^L-kaar^H-aʔ^L* 'to come between'; PLB *gra² > WB *kra^B* 'have space between, be apart' ⋈ *ə-kra^B* 'crack, opening' (-> MidMon /əkra/ 'interval, (space) between, within') ⋈ *kʰra^B* 'be between, divide, different'.

Bodman (1980: 87) relates this wf to the WT items under → chǐ₁ 拸 (*hral 'split'). → xián₅ 閑閒 'leisure' is sometimes thought to be related to *jiān*.

jiān₆ 蕳 → **lián₄** 蓮; → **lán₆** 蘭

jiān₇ 兼 (kiem[C]) **LH** kem(C), **OCM** *kêm(s) — **[T]** *ONW* kėm
'To combine, at the same time' [Shu, Yi], 'grasp, hold together, all-embracing' [Mozi].
[E] MK: PMonic *ckiəm, OMon *ckem* 'to grasp, pick up' [Diffloth 1984: 215], OMon 'handful' ⋈ *pkom* 'to collect together', Aslian *cəkam* etc. 'hold' [Benjamin 1976: 109]; PVM *gəm^A 'to hold', Khasi *kem* 'to arrest, seize, wrestle'. MK -> Lushai *kim^R* 'entire, be complete'. Perh. → qín₅ 擒 is connected.

jiān₈ 漸瀸湛 (tsjäm) **LH** tsiam, **OCM** *tsam
'To seep into, get wet, moisten, soak' 漸 [Shi, Shu]; 'to moisten, enrich, benefit' 瀸 [Lü], 'to soak' [Liji].

⋈ **jiàn** 漸 (dzjäm^B) **LH** dziam^B, **OCM** *dzamʔ
'Gradually, to advance gradually' [Shu, Yi] (< 'drop-wise', so Karlgren *GSR* 611f). *Jiān* is possibly the same etymon as → jiān₉ 熸 'extinguish'; or it might have originated in OC as a variant of *jìn* 浸 (→ chén₂ 沈, see there for further comments).

[E] AA: Khmer *jām̊* /coəm/ (darkened by water:) 'wet, soaked, permeated, steeped' (also 'dark'). Khmer ? -> Tai: S. *čom^A1* 'to sink, submerged', Saek *cɔm / cam^A1* 'to sink'.

jiān₉ 熸 (tsjäm) **LH** tsiam, **OCM** *tsam
'Extinguish' [Zuo]. This word and its derivatives may be connected with → jiān₈ 漸瀸湛; see also → chén₂ 沈 for comments.

⋈ **qián** 潛 (dzjäm) **LH** dziam, **OCM** *dzam
'Go into water, wade' [Guoyu], 'lie at bottom of water, be soaked (in pleasure)' [Shu].

⋈ **jiàn** 潛 (dzjäm^C) **LH** dziam^C, **OCM** *dzams
'To hide, secretly' [Zuo].

jiān₁₀ 鞬 (kjɐn) **LH** kɨɑn, **OCM** *kan
'Bow and arrow case' [Zuo].
[E] Perh. related to WT *rkyal-pa* 'leather sack, bag' (Unger *Hao-ku* 35, 1986: 30).

⋈ **lán** 韊 (lân) **LH** lɑn, **OCM** *rân < *C-ran
'Arrow case, quiver' [Shiji] may be related to *jiān*, but then the WT connection is doubtful.

jiān$_{11}$ 艱 → **qín**$_3$ 勤慬

jiān$_{12}$ 殲 → **jiān**$_1$ 尖鑯

jiǎn$_1$ 囝 (kjän^B 3, kjɐn^B) **LH** kɨɑn^B
'Child, son' [JY].
[E] AA: PVM *kɔːn 'son', Viet *con* [Ferlus]; Mon *kon* 'child' (Norman 1988: 231). It is a substrate word in Mǐn and other southern dialects: PMin *kiɑn^B > Jiàn'ōu *kyeŋ^{B1}*, Fúzhōu *kiaŋ^{B1}*, Xiàmén *kiã^{B1}*. According to Chén Zhōngmǐn (*LTBA* 22.2, 2000: 21ff) *jiǎn* was used instead of the northern → zǐ$_1$ 子 and → ér$_4$ 兒 as a diminutive in Mǐn and other southern dialects where occasionally it left traces only in the tone.
Syn. → zǐ$_1$ 子; → kūn$_2$ 昆.

jiǎn$_2$ 檢 (kjäm^B, kjɐm^B) **LH** kɨɑm^B, **OCM** *kamʔ — **[T]** *ONW* kam
'A measure, a control' [Xun].
⋈ **jiàn** 儉 (gjäm^B) **LH** gɨɑm^B, **OCM** *gamʔ
'Restricted, frugal, moderate' [Zuo, Meng].
[<] endopass. of *jiǎn* (§4.6).
[E] ST: Lushai *kaam^H* 'to decrease' (as water, wages, etc.) ⋈ *kiam^R* 'to lessen, to reduce, decrease, diminish'.

jiǎn$_3$ 檢 'accumulate' → **liǎn**$_1$ 斂

jiǎn$_4$ 臉 → **liǎn**$_2$ 臉

jiǎn$_5$ 錢 → **qián**$_9$ 錢

jiǎn$_6$ 蹇謇 → **yǎn**$_1$, **yàn** 衍

jiǎn$_7$ 減 (kăm^B, ɣăm^B) **LH** kɛm^B, **OCM** *krə̂mʔ ? — **[T]** *ONW* käm
'Decrease, abridge, moderate' [Li].

jiǎn$_8$ 揀 (kăn^B) **LH** kɛn^B, **OCM** *krênʔ ?
'To select' [Yi Zhou].
[E] <> Tai: S. *klan^{B1}* 'select' (as jewels) (Manomaivibool 1975: 168).

jiǎn$_9$ 搴 (kjän^B, kjɐn^B) **LH** kɨɑn^B, **OCM** *kanʔ ?
'To lift' [Zhuang].
⋈ **xiān** 掀 (xjɐn) **LH** xɨɑn, **OCM** *han
'To lift' [Zuo].
[E] This wf may be related to WT *ker-ba* 'to raise, lift', but TGTM *^{lh}re/hre: 'to raise' as well as the MC initial *xj-* indicate that the phonology is rather complex.

jiàn$_1$ 見 (kien^C) **LH** ken^C, **OCM** *kêns
'To see, visit' [OB, BI, Shi].
[T] *Sin Sukchu SR* kjen (去); *MGZY* gÿan (去) [kjɛn]; *MTang* kian < kɨan, *ONW* kėn
⋈ **xiàn** 現見 (ɣien^C) **LH** gen^C, **OCM** *gêns — **[T]** *MTang* ɣian < ɣɨan, *ONW* ɣėn
'To appear, show up' [BI, Shi].
[<] endopass. of *jiàn* 見.
⋈ **qiàn** 俔 (k^{h}ien^C, ɣien^B) **LH** k^{h}en^C, gen^B, **OCM** *khêns, *gênʔ
'To look like, look as if' [Shi].
[E] ST: PTB *m-kyen (*STC* no. 223) > WT *mk^{h}yen-pa* 'to know', PTani *ken 'know', NNaga *C-k^{h}yeŋ. The ST semantic range is similar to PIE *vid- 'to see, know'. Sometimes → xiǎn$_6$ 顯 is thought to belong to this wf.

jiàn₂ 建 (kjɐnC) **LH** kɨɑnC, **OCM** *kans
'To set up, establish' [Shi] is perh. cognate to → jiàn₃ 健.
[T] *Sin Sukchu SR* kjen (去); *MGZY* gen (去) [kɛn]

jiàn₃ 健 (gjɐnC) **LH** gɨɑnC, **OCM** *gans
'Strong' [Yi], Mand. 'healthy, strong'. Perh. endopass. of → jiàn₂ 建 (§4.6) in the sense of 'firmly established'. Not related to TB-WT *gar-ba* 'strong', see under → gù₁ 固.

jiàn₄ 楗 (gjɐnB) **LH** gɨɑnB, **OCM** *ganʔ
'Door bar, bolt' [Lao]. Syn. → guān₅ 關, → xián₇ 閑.
[E] This word could be compared to Lushai *kalʔL* 'to wrench, plait, lock' ⋈ *kalʔL-naH* 'a lock' (Unger *Hao-ku* 35, 1986: 31), but the basic meaning in Lushai is 'turn, twist'.

jiàn₅ 腱 → **jīn₅** 筋

jiàn₆ 俴 → **qiǎn₂** 淺

jiàn₇ 賤 → **qiǎn₂** 淺

jiàn₈ 劍 (kjɐmC) **LH** kɨɑmC, **OCM** *kams — **[T]** *ONW* kam
'Sword' [Zuo, under the year 650 BC].
[E] Etymology not certain. This mid Zhou period word could be derived from → yǎn₄ 剡覃 'sharp' (implied by Wulff, Geilich 1994: 110, 263), the initial *k-* would then be a nominalizing prefix (§5.4). Alternatively, swords seem to have originated in the ancient southern state of Wú (Sūzhōu area), which was famous for its sword smiths. From there the word, of unknown provenance, may have entered OC as well as PVM as *t-kɨəm [Ferlus].

jiàn₉ 儉 → **jiǎn₂** 檢

jiàn₁₀ 間閒 → **jiān₅** 間閒

jiàn₁₁ 濳 → **jiān₉** 熸

jiàn₁₂ 蔪 (dzjämB) **LH** dziamB, **OCM** *dzamʔ
'Entwine' [SW: Shu] is a ST word: WT *sdom-pa, bsdams* 'to bind, tie up'.
Perh. cogn. to → cán 蠶 'silkworm' (*HST:* 43).

jiàn₁₃ 薦 (tsienC) **LH** tsenC, **OCM** *tsə̂ns
'Grass, fodder' [Zhuang] > 'straw mat' [Chuci] > 'put on display' (loot), 'offer, present' [Shi]. Wáng Lì (1982: 289) relates this and other words to → xí₁ 席 'mat'.
[D] PMin *tsanC 'straw mattress'

⋈ **jiàn** 荐 (dzienC, dzuənC) **LH** dzenC, **OCM** *dzə̂ns
'Grass, herb' [Zuo].
[E] *STC* (p. 49; 158 n. 428) suggests that this may be cognate to WT *rtswa* 'grass'.

jiàn₁₄ 薦洊 'repeat' → **zài₄** 再

jiàn₁₅ 監鑑 (kamC) **LH** kamC, **OCM** *krâms
'To mirror' 監 [Shu], 鑑 [Shi]; 'mirror' 鑑 [Zuo].
[T] *Sin Sukchu SR* kjam (去), *PR* (kjan), *LR* kjen; *MGZY* (gÿam >) gyam (去) [kjam]
[<] exopass. of *jiān* 監 (kam), 'see oneself' (§4.4). → jìng₆ 鏡 (kjɐŋC) 'mirror' seems to be a variant. Bodman (1980: 148) adds *hàn* 鑑 (under → làn₁ 濫) to this group.

⋈ **jiān** 監 (kam[C]) **LH** kam, **OCM** *krâm
'To see, look at, inspect' [Shi]. The items under → kān₅, kàn 勘 may be variants of this word.

⋇ **lǎn** 覽 (lâmᴮ) **LH** lɑmᴮ, **OCM** *g-râmʔ — **[T]** *ONW* lɑm
'To see' [Guoce] (Bodman 1985: 159) is perh. only a col. variant of the preceding item (Zhāng Xīngyà *YWYJ* 1996.4: 11).
[E] ST: JP *mə³¹-ram⁵⁵* 'to observe, view', WB *krap* 'superintend, watch over and direct'.

jiàn₁₆ 檻 (ɣamᴮ, ɣâmᴮ) **LH** gamᴮ, **OCM** *grâmʔ
'Railing' [Chuci], 'cage' [Zhuang].
[E] ST: PLB *kram¹ 'fence, garden' > WB *kʰram* 'fence, enclosure' ⋇ *ə-ram* 'fence forming an enclosure'; prob. also WT *kʰram* 'notched wood' (*HPTB:* 253; 299).

jiāng₁ 江 (kåŋ) **LH** kɔŋ, **OCM** *krôŋ, OCB *kroŋ
'Yangtze River' [Shi], in *Shījīng* only its mid-section (Norman / Mei 1976: 283).
[E] AA: PMonic *krooŋ [Diffloth 1984: 132], LitMon *kruŋ*, Bahnar *kroŋ*, Katu *karuŋ* (Norman a. Mei 1976: 280–283; Benedict 1976: 76; Norman 1988: 18); Viet *sôŋ* 'river' < *kr-; also Malay *kroŋ*. → chuān₁ 川 and its cognates may ultimately be a variant of this etymon. For a syn. see → táng₁ 唐.

⋇ **gǎng** 港 (kåŋᴮ) **LH** kɔŋᴮ, **OCM** *krôŋʔ
'Smaller river which flows into a larger river, lake or sea' [Náncháo period, 6th c. AD].
[T] *Sin Sukchu SR* kjaŋ (上); *MGZY* gyang (上) [kjaŋ]
[D] An ancient Wú dialect word which spread into the Chǔ region; the word survives in river names in the former Wú-Chǔ area (Jiāngsū, Jiāngxī, Zhèjiāng, Anhuī, Húběi, Húnán); the Huái River marks the northern limit of this word; later > 'harbour' (Lǐ Xiǎofán / Chén Bǎoxián, *FY* 2002.3: 201–216). The irregular Mand. form originated in southern dialects where velars have not palatalized. The role of tone B is not clear.

jiāng₂ 姜 → **qiāng₁** 羌

jiāng₃ 將 (tsjaŋ) **LH** tsiɑŋ, **OCM** *tsaŋ
'Take (something or someone along), hold, support' [Shi, Shu]; perh. the meaning 'to offer, offering' (in sacrifice) [Shi] is a semantic extension (< 'take along').
[T] *Sin Sukchu SR* tsjaŋ (平); *MGZY* (dzÿang >) dzyang (平) [tsjaŋ]; *MTang* tsiaŋ < tsaŋ, *ONW* tsaŋ
[E] ST: WT *'čʰaŋ-ba* 'to hold, keep' (*HST:* 94).

⋇ **jiàng** 將 (tsjaŋᶜ) **LH** tsiɑŋᶜ, **OCM** *tsaŋh — **[T]** *MTang* tsiaŋ < tsaŋ, *ONW* tsaŋ
'To lead' [Shi, Meng] > 'leader, general' [Zuo].
[<] exoactive / caus. of *jiāng* (§4.3).

⋇ **qiāng** 將 (tsʰjaŋ) **LH** tsʰiɑŋ, **OCM** *tshaŋ
'To beg, pray, ask' (for help, gift, not to do something) [Shi].
[<] caus. aspiration of *jiāng* 將 (§5.8.2).

jiāng₄ 將 (tsjaŋ) **LH** tsiɑŋ, **OCM** *tsaŋ
'Be on the point of, about to, intend to, going to' [BI, Shi].
[E] AA: OKhmer *caṅ* /cɔŋ/, Khmer *ca'ṅa* /cɑŋ/ 'to want, desire, hope for, be willing to, about to, on the point of'.

⋇ **qiě** 且 (tsʰjaᴮ) **LH** tsʰiaᴮ, **OCM** *tshaʔ ?
'Moreover, in addition, as well' [Shi], 'about to, on the point of' [Guoce]. An allofam of jiāng₄ 將 acc. to Pulleyblank (1962: 233).
[T] *Sin Sukchu SR* ts'je (上); *MGZY* tshÿa (上) [ts'jɛ]; *ONW* tsʰia

jiāng₅-jiāng 彊 → **qiáng** 強彊

jiāng$_6$ 疆 (kjaŋ) **LH** kɨaŋ, **OCM** *kaŋ
'Limit, boundary, to delimit, territory' [BI, Shi], variant or allofam of → jìng$_6$ 竟境.

jiāng$_7$ 薑 (kjaŋ **LH** kɨaŋ, **OCM** *kaŋ — **[D]** PMin *kioŋ.
'Ginger' [Lunyu].
[E] Area word: TB-WB *kʰyaŋ*^{B} 'ginger' (*HPTB:* 302); SChin-Areng *kachiŋ* [Löffler *Anthropos* 55, 1960: 526]. <> AA: PVM *s-gəːŋ 'ginger' [Ferlus], Wa-Lawa-Bulang *s[ŋ̊]kiŋ. Note also PTai *xiŋ^{A1}: S. *kʰiŋ*^{2}, KS *siŋ* 'ginger', IN *t'aʔaŋ* 'sharp' (tasting) (Benedict *AT:* 48; 1976: 90).

jiàng$_1$ 匠 (dzjaŋ^C) **LH** dziaŋ^C, **OCM** *dzaŋh
'To fashion, cut out, make' vb. (as a sculpture, out of wood or the like) [Chuci] > 'to form, cultivate' (one's personality through education) [Huainan], *jiàng-rén* 匠人 ('woodworking man':) 'carpenter' [Meng]; 匠 'carpenter' n. [Zuo] > 'artisan' [Lunheng]; also 'stonecutter' (as a name in *Zhuāngzǐ* implies); *jiàng-rén* 匠人 'official in charge of woodworkers' [Zhouli].
[T] *Sin Sukchu SR* dzjaŋ (去); *MGZY* (tsÿang >) tsyang (去) [dzjaŋ]
[E] MK: Khmer *cāṃṅa* /caŋ/ 'to dress (wood, stone), rough out, trim...'. The verbal function in Khmer makes it unlikely that this is a loan from CH where the typical use is nominal. *Jiàng* is sometimes thought to be related to WT *byaŋ-pa* 'skilled, experienced' (→ fāng$_4$ 方) (Bodman 1980: 150), therefore the MC initial is conjectured to derive from *sb-, but this would be unusual and improbable; nor are the semantics compelling.

jiàng$_2$ 降 (kåŋ) **LH** kɔŋ, **OCM** *krûŋ — **[T]** *ONW* käŋ
'To descend, get down' [BI, Shi], e.g. cattle from hills, person from carriage; metaphorically: send down blessings, misfortune, etc.

ꭗ **xiáng** 降 (γåŋ) **LH** gɔŋ, **OCM** *grûŋ — **[T]** *ONW* γäŋ
'To submit' [BI, Shi], intr.

[E] There are no unambiguous outside cognates. Some languages have initial *l-:* Tai: S. *loŋ*^{A2} < *dl- 'to descend'. <> TB-Chepang *glyuŋh-* ~ *gruŋ-* 'to descend' ꭗ *gruŋʔ-* 'droop, drop down (object in flight), descend (in angle)'. It is not clear if / how the following may be related: TB-Lai *trùm / trúm* 'descend' ꭗ *tʰrúm / tʰrumʔ* 'to put down' [VanBik *LTBA* 25.2, 2002: 99] (KN *tr-* can derive from *kr-). Sino-Viet *xuống* [suə́ŋ] 'to descend' is an OC loan (SV *s-* < *kr-).

jiàng$_3$ 洚 → **hóng**$_4$ 洪

jiāo$_1$ 交 (kau) **LH** kau, **OCM** *krâu — **[T]** *ONW* käu
'To cross, mix with, mingle, associate with' [BI, Shi], 'exchange' [Yi], 'join' [Zuo].
[E] ST: PTB *ryaw (*STC* no. 207) > WB *ro*^{B} 'to mix, mingle', Kachin *yau* 'be mixed' ꭗ *kəjau* 'to mix, intermix'. Cf. Chepang *ljawh-ʔo* 'mixed'. <> PYao *klaau^3 'to pay'.

ꭗ **jiào** 挍 (kau^C) **LH** kau^C, **OCM** *krâuh
'To compare' [Li, Meng], 'foot-fetters, cangue' [Yi].
[<] *krau + caus. s/h-suffix (§4.3), lit. 'make cross over, cross each other'.

ꭗ **yáo** 殽 (γau) **LH** gau, **OCM** *grâu
'Mixed, confused' [Zhuang].
[<] *krau with endopass. voicing (§4.6).

ꭗ **xiào** 效 (γau^C) **LH** gau^C, **OCM** *grâuh
'Verifications, checking' (i.e. cross-checking) [Qin laws] (Yates *EC* 20, 1995: 359).
The word → jiǎo$_1$ 烄 'burn on a pyre of crossed logs' is prob. not related.

jiāo₂-méi 郊禖 → **méi₆** 媒禖

jiāo₃, yāo 呅 (kau) **LH** kau, **OCM** *krâu
'To shout' [Zhuang]. See also → yāo₄, jiāo 呅.
The OC medial *r is confirmed by WB *kro* 'shout, call out', Lahu *kù* < *kru [*STC:* 19], this word occurs also in MK languages: PNBahn. *krò 'cry' (WB loan?).

jiāo₄ 蛟 (kau) **LH** kau, **OCM** *krâu
'Scaly dragon' [Lü], 'alligator' [Li]; in later folklore *jiāo* refers to mermaids (Eberhard 1968: 378); additional definitions and etymological suggestions have been discussed by Carr (*LTBA* 13.2, 1990: 126–136). There may possibly be a connection with TB: WB k^hru^B ~ k^hyu^B 'mermaid, serpent', WT *klu* 'naga, water spirits'. However, phonologically OC and TB are far apart.

jiāo₅ 釗 → **zhāo₁** 釗

jiāo₆ 焦 (tsjäu) **LH** tsiau, **OCM** *tsau (or *tsiau)
'To roast, burn, scorch' tr. 焦 [Zuo], 燋 [Li].
[T] *Sin Sukchu SR* tsjew (平); *PR* tsjaw; *MGZY* dzÿaw (平) [tsjɛw]
[D] The graph 焦 is used for a Mǐn synonym: PMin *tau^A 'dry, scorch': Amoy ta^{A1}; this item is cognate to PVM *$traw^B$ 'dry' (Bodman 1980: 178).

ꭗ **qiáu** 樵 (dzjäu) **LH** dziau, **OCM** *dzau (or *dziau)
'Firewood' [Zuo], 'gather firewood' [Shi], 'to burn' (fuel) intr. [Gongyang].
[<] endopass. of *jiāo* tr. (§4.6), i.e. 'something that burns itself'.
[D] This is the Mǐn word for 'wood, firewood': PMin *dzʰau: Xiàmén lit. ts^hai^{A2}, col. ts^ha^{A2} 'grass and trees for fuel', Jiàn'ōu ts^hau^{A2}. This word is conventionally written → chái₁ 柴.

ꭗ **jué** 爝 (dzjak) **LH** dziɑk, **OCM** *dzauk (or *dziauk)
'A torch' [Zhuang] (Wáng Lì 1982: 219).

ꭗ **jué** 燋 (tsjak, tṣåk) **LH** tsiɑk, tṣɔk, **OCM** *tsrauk
'Torch' [Li] (Karlgren 1956: 12).
[E] ST: PTB *tsyow (*STC* no. 275) > WT *'tsʰod-pa* ~ *'tsʰo-ba* 'cook in boiling water, bake' ꭗ *btsos, rtsos* 'to roast', Kachin *tsʰu* 'boil', Lushai so^H 'boil'; Garo *so*, Dimasa *sau* 'burn'. Possible allofam → jiào₇ 僬潐醮.

jiāo₇ 膠 (kau[B]) **LH** kɔu(B), **OCM** *krû(ʔ) — **[T]** *ONW* käu
'Frost' [Chuci].
[E] MY: PWMiao *klau⁷ (P), *qḻɑk (Wáng F. S.) 'ice, snow'. For semantics, compare shuāng 霜 (under → liáng₃ 涼).

jiāo₈ 憍 → **gāo₁** 高

jiāo₉ 憍 'arrogant' → **qiáo₁** 喬

jiáo 嚼 (dzjak) **LH** dziɑk — **[D]** PMin *dzʰiak 'to eat'
'To chew' [SW], also Mand.

ꭗ **jiào** 噍 (dzjäu[C]) **LH** dziau[C], **OCM** *dzauh (or *dziauh)
'To chew' [Li].

ꭗ **jué** 爵 (tsjak) **LH** tsiɑk, **OCM** *tsauk (or *tsiauk) — **[T]** *ONW* ts(i)ak
'Status / rank in the nobility, dignity' [BI, Shi] seems to be related to the above (i.e. rank defined by agricultural revenues, i.e. food?). The semantic field 'eat ~ live off revenues' is parelleled in MK: PMon *caaʔ 'to eat', Mon 'eat, live on, by the revenues of, to govern' (under → jǔ₁ 咀).

jiǎo$_1$ 烄 (kau^B) **LH** kau^B, **OCM** *krâuʔ
'Burn on a pyre' [OB, SW], esp. in a rain ceremony.
[E] *SW* implies that *jiǎo* is related to → jiāo$_1$ 交 'cross', i.e. a pyre of crossed logs, but the semantic connection with 'crossed' may be due to the graphic element. TB cognates suggest that *jiǎo* actually means 'dry over fire, burn': WB *kro* ~ *kyo* 'to fry', JP *krau*^{33} 'dry up, overdry' ⋈ *kə*^{31}*-rau*^{33} 'dry over a fire'. *Jiǎo* may be cognate to → liào$_2$ 燎 'burn'.

jiǎo$_2$ 姣佼 (kau^B) **LH** kau^B, **OCM** *krâuʔ or *kriâuʔ
'Be beautiful, handsome' [Shi].
⋈ Perh. **liáo** 僚 (lieu[^{B}]) **LH** leu(^{B}), **OCM** *riâu(ʔ)
'Be fine, lovely' [Shi], 嫽 [GY].

jiǎo$_3$ 絞 (kau^B) **LH** kau^B, **OCM** *kriâuʔ or *krâuʔ
'To twist' [Li], 'strangle, pressing, intense' [Zuo], 'entangle'.
⋈ **liǎo** 繚 (ljäu^B, lieu^B) **LH** liau^B, leu^B, **OCM** *riauʔ
'Bind round, wrap' [Li], 'entangled'.
[C] Allofam is perh. → jiǔ$_3$ 糾 etc.

jiǎo$_4$ 皎晈皦 → **zhāo**$_3$ 昭

jiǎo$_5$ 角 (kåk) **LH** kɔk, **OCM** *krôk — **[T]** *ONW* käk — **[D]** PMin *kok 'horn; male'
'Horn' [Shi], 'sharp angle, corner'. Zhāng Xīngyà (*YWYJ* 1996.4: 9f) has collected archaistic bisyllabic dialect words for 'horn', incl. Wú-Sūzhōu, Níngbō, Shàoxìng *kɔʔlɔʔ*.
~**jué** 較 (kåk) **LH** kɔk, **OCM** *krâuk ?
'A horn-shaped bar on a carriage' [Shi] (Wáng Lì 1982: 294).
=**jiǎo-zi** 餃子
'A kind of boiled dumpling', etymologically same word as *jiǎo* 角 'horn', so named for its horn-like shape (Norman 1988: 77).
[E] ST stem *kru to which OC has added a final *-k (§6.1): PTB *kru(w) > WB *k^{h}yui, k^{h}rui* 'horn' (*STC* no. 37); the root is PTB *ru ~ *rwa as in WT *ru* ~ *rwa* 'horn'. A TB final *-ŋ variant is reflected in → gōng$_9$ 觥.
Bodman (1980: 167) compares the TB word with *qiú* 觩 (gjəu) 'long and curved, horn-like' [Shi] (under → qiú$_7$, jiū 虯 觓觩) which, however, is derived from the meaning 'twist'; *HST:* 58 relates *jiǎo* to WT *k^{h}ug* 'corner, angle' (but see → jú$_6$ 鞠鞫). Sagart (1999: 161) relates *jiǎo* to → lù$_{11}$ 鹿 'deer'; *lù* is a rare reading for 角. <> PTai *khəu^{A1} 'horn' has apparently no connection with CH.

jiǎo$_6$ 腳 (kjak) **LH** kɨak — **[T]** *MTang* kiak < kak, *ONW* kak
'Leg, foot' [Xun] is a common word in Mand. and most dialects: Yuè *kœk*^{D3}, Kèjiā *kiɔk*^{D1}. Mǐn *k^{h}au^{A1} 骹 'foot' (→ qiāo$_1$ 骹) is unrelated. Etymology not clear.

jiǎo$_7$ 蹻 (kjäu^B 3) **LH** kɨau^B, **OCM** *kauʔ
'Martial, vigorous' 蹻 [Shi]; 'energetic' 憍 [Zhuang] is perh. the same etymon as *jiǎo* 憍 'high' (under → qiáo$_1$ 喬) (so Wáng Lì 1982: 204).
⋈ **qiāo** 驕 (k^{h}jäu 3) **LH** k^{h}ɨau, **OCM** *khau
'Vigorous (horses)' [Shi].
⋈ **jué** 驕 (gjak 3) **LH** gɨak, **OCM** *gak
'Lifting the feet high, strong-looking (horses)' [Shi].
[C] These items may belong to the wf → qiáo$_1$ 喬 'high'.

jiǎo$_8$ 攪 (kau^B) **LH** kɔu^B, **OCM** *krûʔ
'To disturb' tr. [Shi]
[E] ST: WT *dkrug-pa* 'stir up' ⋈ *'kʰrug-pa* 'be disturbed, quarrel' ⋈ *sprug-pa* 'to shake, stir up'.
[C] This word could belong to the wf → xué 學 (so *HST:* 127); and / or to → lù$_{12}$ 摝.

jiào$_1$ 嶠 → **qiáo**$_1$ 喬

jiào$_2$ 覺 → **jué**$_{11}$ 覺

jiào$_3$ 叫嘂 (kieu^C) **LH** keu^C, **OCM** *kiûh
'To call out, shout' [Shi], 'clamor' [Zhouli]. Prob. s. w. as → jiào$_4$ 噭, but distinct from → zhào$_1$ 召.
[T] *Sin Sukchu SR* kjew (去); *PR* kjaw; *MGZY* gÿaw (去) [kjɛw]

jiào$_4$ 噭 (kieu^C, kiek) **LH** keu^C, kek, **OCM** *kiâuk(h)
'To shout' [Li], 'cry, weep' [Gongyang]. It is difficult to believe that *jiào* 噭 *kiâukh 'shout' and → jiào$_3$ 叫嘂 *kiûh 'shout' are not the same word in spite of their different OC rimes; at least they must have been variants. → zhào$_1$ 召 'call' is a different etymon.

jiào$_5$ 挍 → **jiāo**$_1$ 交

jiào$_6$ 教 (kau^C) **LH** kau^C, **OCM** *krâuh
'To teach, instruct, set an example' [Shi], 'allow' (to grow) [Guoyu – Harbsmeier 1981: 40].
[T] *Sin Sukchu SR* kjaw (平去); *MGZY* (gÿaw >) gyaw (平去) [kjaw]; *ONW* käu.

⋈ **xiào** 效傚 (ɣau^C) **LH** gau^C, **OCM** *grâuh
'Imitate, follow' 傚 [Shu], 效[Zuo].
[<] endopass. of *jiào* (§4.6), lit. 'be taught'.

jiào$_7$ 僬潐醮 (tsjäu^C) **LH** tsiau^C, **OCM** *tsauh
'Exhaust, finish' 醮 [Xun]; 'thoroughly understand' 潐 [Xun] > 'discern, understand' 僬 [Xun]; 'empty a cup' 釂 [Li] > 'empty a cup at a wedding ceremony' 醮 [Li].

⋈ **qiáo** 憔譙 (dzjäu) **LH** dziau, **OCM** *dzau
'Melancholy, harassed, distressed' [Zuo], 'haggard' 憔 [Guoyu]; 'deteriorate, worn out' 譙 [Shi].

⋈ Perh. **qiǎo** 悄 (tsʰjäu^B)
'Be grieved' [Shi] (the OCM initial might have been *C-s-, though, hence this word is prob. not related to the above items).

[C] Acc. to Wáng Lì (1982: 218), this wf belongs to → jiāo$_6$ 焦 'burn', but in spite of the semantic parallelism with the wf → jìn$_4$ 盡 ('exhaust, burn up') this is not certain.

jiào$_8$ 噍 → **jiáo** 嚼

jiē$_1$ 挾 → **xié**$_1$ 挾協

jiē$_2$ 皆喈 (kǎi) **LH** kɛi, **OCM** *krî, OCB *krij — **[T]** *ONW* këi
'Be together with, agree, all' [Shi]; 'be or do in unison' 喈 [Shi]. Perh. → jiē$_3$ 階 'stairs' ('harmonized steps'?) belongs to this wf. *CVST* (2: 78) relates *jiē* 'all' to WT *kʰri* '10,000' as well as to → shī$_4$ 師 'multitude'.

⋈ **xié** 偕 (kǎi) **LH** kɛi, **OCM** *krîʔ !
'Together' [Shi]. *Shījīng* rimes indicate tone B for OC (Mattos 1971: 309).

⋇ **xié** 諧 (γăi) **LH** gɛi, **OCM** *grî — **[T]** *ONW* γëi
'Be concordant, harmonious' [Shi].

jiē$_3$ 階 (kăi) **LH** kɛi, **OCM** *krî or *krə̂i ? — **[T]** *ONW* këi — **[D]** PMin *kue
'Steps, stairs' [Shi]. This may be the s. w. as → jiē$_2$ 皆喈, derived from the concepts 'together, in unison, agree'. Prob. unrelated to → gāi 陔 'stairs', but see there.

jiē$_4$ 接 (tsjäp) **LH** tsiap, **OCM** *tsap — **[T]** *ONW* tsiap
'To connect, contact' [Shi].

⋇ **jì** 際 (tsjäi^C) **LH** tsias, OCB *tsjats < *tsjaps
'Juncture, connection' [Lunyu, Zuo] (Baxter 1992: 406).
[T] *Sin Sukchu SR* tsjej (去), *PR*, *LR* tsi; *MGZY* dzi (去) [tsi]

[E] Area word: ST: WT *čʰabs* 'together'; Garo *tsap-tsap* 'adjacent'; WB *cap* 'to join, unite', Kachin *tśyap* 'adhere' (*STC:* 169 n. 452; Bodman 1980: 52). <> PAA *bcap 'id.' (?) (Shorto 1972).

jiē$_5$ 嗟 (tsja) **LH** tsia, **OCM** *tsa or *tsai ?
'Alas, oh, sigh; lamentation' [Shi]; *xū-jiē* 吁 (于) 嗟 (xju-tsja) *hwa-tsa 'alas, oh!' [Shi].

~ **jiè** 唶 (tsja^C) **LH** tsiah
'Sigh' [Hou Hanshu] which is prob. a graphic loan for 嗟. *Jiè* means also the 'sound of singing' (of birds) [Huainan]; also read *zuò* (dẓɐk) 'loud sound' (as of laughing) [SW, Shiji].

⋇ **zī** 咨 (tsi) **LH** tsi, **OCM** *tsəi or *tsi
'To sigh, moan, oh, alas!' [Shi].

jiē$_6$ 秸 (kăt) **LH** kɛt, **OCM** *krêt
'Straw' [Shu], 秸 [Li].

~ **jiē** 稭 (kăi) **LH** kɛi
'Straw' [SW, Shiji]. This graph is a variant for *jiē* 秸 (so *JY*; Wáng Lì 1982: 412).

jiē$_7$ 揭 (g/k/kʰjät 3, gjɐt) **LH** gɨat etc., **OCM** *grat etc.
'To rise, raise, lift' [Shi] is related to → jǔ$_6$ 舉 acc. to Wáng Lì (1982: 130). He also adds **qiè** 挈 (kʰiet) *khêt 'to lift' [Li].

⋇ **jiē** 揭 (kʰjäi^C) **LH** kʰɨas, **OCM** *khrats
'To lift up one's clothes' (e.g. when fording a stream) [Shi]. Syn. → kōu 摳.

jié$_1$, **jiā** 梜 (kiep, kap) **LH** kep, kap, **OCM** *kêp, *krâ/êp
'Chopsticks' [Li]. The OC form *kêp connects the word with the stem → xié$_1$ 挾協 'clasp under the arm' (Karlgren 1956: 10); OC *krâ/êp connects it with → jiā$_3$ 夾.

jié$_2$ 捷 (dzjäp) **LH** dziap, **OCM** *dzap
'Victory' [Shi], 'booty' [Zuo].

⋇ **qiè** 妾 (tsʰjäp) **LH** tsʰiap, **OCM** *tshap
'Slave woman' [Shu], 'servant girl' [Li], 'secondary wife, concubine' [BI, Zuo], prob. originally 'captive' (war booty), note the semantic range of the AA wf.

[E] MK: OKhmer *cā'pa* /cap/ 'to grasp..., seize, catch, take or seize by conquest' ⋇ Khmer *caṃṇā'pa* /cɑmnap/ 'detainee, prisoner, hostage'; Pearic *čap²* 'to catch'. MK -> Tai: S. *čiap⁴* 'to plunder, rob, steal'. The MK etymon is usually thought to belong to *zhí* 摯鷙 'to seize' (under → zhí$_5$ 執) instead; but the phonological agreement between OC and MK is perfect in the present set.

jié$_{2a}$ 睫 (tsjäp) **LH** tsiap, **OCM** *tsap
'Eyelashes' [Zhuang].
[D] Y-Guǎngzhōu *tsaap*^{7B} 'wink, blink' (R. Bauer).
[E] This word is associated with widely distributed phonesthemic etymon 'wink, blink' in East and SE Asia with the rime *-ap and various initials (see R. Bauer *LTBA* 15.2: 151–184 for an exhaustive collection). TB: WT *tsʰab-tsʰab* 'to blink'.

jié$_3$ 揭 → **jiē**$_7$ 揭

jié$_4$ 羯 (kjät 3) **LH** kɨat, **OCM** *krat — [T] *MTang* kar, *ONW* kat
'Ram', perh. 'castrated ram' [SW], is prob. cognate to → gǔ$_7$ 羖 'ram'.
[E] ST: Kanauri *kʰas*, Chitk. *kʰa, kʰəs* 'sheep'.

jié$_5$ 渴竭 (gjät 3) **LH** gɨat, **OCM** *grat — [T] *Sin Sukchu SR* gje (入)
'To dry up' (pool, swamp) [Shi, Zhouli]. For related and similar items, see → gù$_1$ 固 (incl. Table G-1) and → jiān$_2$ 堅 (incl. Table J-1).

jié$_6$ 結 (kiet) **LH** ket, **OCM** *kî̂t — [T] *MTang* kiar < kɨar, *ONW* kėt
'To tie, knot' [Shi].
⋈ **jì** 髻 (kiei^C) **LH** kes, **OCM** *kîts
'Hair-knot' [no pre-Han ex.].
[E] ST: PTB *kik (*STC* no. 484) > WT *'kʰyig-pa, bkyigs* 'to bind', WB *kyac* 'twist tight', JP *gyit*^{31} 'to tie, bind'; Kuki *d-kʰik. <> The relationship with Tai: S. *klat*^{D1}*S* < *kl-, Po'ai *čɛt* 'button, pin together' (Li 1976: 45) is unclear.

jié$_7$ 頡 → **háng**$_3$ 頏

jié$_8$ 劼 → **jiān**$_2$ 堅

jié$_9$ 節 (tsiet) **LH** tset, **OCM** *tsît — [D] PMin *tsat
('Cut' >) 'regular division' [Li], 'knots or joints on bamboo or other plants' [Shi], 'degree, rank' [Shu].
[T] *Sin Sukchu SR* tsje (入); *MGZY* dzÿa (入) [tsjɛ]; *MTang* tsiar < tsɨar, *ONW* tsėt
⋈ **qiè** 切 (tsʰiet) **LH** tsʰet, **OCM** *tshît — [T] *MTang* tsʰiar < tsʰɨar, *ONW* tsʰėt
'To cut' [Shi]. This graph also writes a homophone which is cognate to → jí$_7$ 即.
[E] ST *tsik: PTB *tsik (*STC* 64): WT *'tsʰigs* 'joint, knot, knee'; Garo *tśik*, Lepcha *tśak* 'joint'; PLB *ʔdzik > WB *cʰac* 'a joint' (Bodman 1980: 139).
Perh. not related to **jié** 截 (dziet) [dzet] *dzêt ('To cut, trim' >) 'restrain, govern' [Shi] (Unger *Hao-ku* 39, 1992) because of the different OC vowels. An allofam may be → xī$_{13}$ 膝 *sit 'knee'.

jié$_{10}$ 櫛 (tsjɛt) **LH** tṣɛt, **OCM** *tsrit
'Comb, to comb' 櫛 [Shi], 'to scrape' 楖 [Zhouli].
[E] The several words for 'comb' in CH and TB look somewhat similar, but precise phonological correspondences are elusive. *Jié* appears to be close to PTB *m-si(y) 'comb' (*STC* no. 466) > JP *pə*^{55}*-si*^{55} 'comb, rake' ⋈ *məsìt* 'to comb, rake, brush'; Mikir *iŋtʰi < msi* 'comb', Lepcha *pŭr-šit* [pər-sit] 'brush' [Bodman ICSTLL 1987: 17]. Although an additional final consonant like *-t* here is not unusual for CH, the initials are rather different. Syn. → shū$_3$ 梳.

jié$_{11}$ 楖 → **jié**$_{10}$ 櫛

jié$_{12}$ 絜 (kiet, ɣiet) **LH** ket, get, **OCM** *kêt, *gêt
'To put around and measure' (e.g. a tree) [Zhuang].

⋈ **xié** 絜 (k^hiet, ɣiet) **LH** k^het, get, **OCM** *khêt, *gêt

'Belt' [Zhuang]. Alternatively, this word could belong to → jié$_6$ 結 *kît 'to tie' (Unger *Hao-ku* no. 74, 2001, p 11), though the vowels do not agree.

[E] This wf belongs to the ST root *ke 'concave' (of body parts etc.), see → jǐng$_2$ 頸 'neck' and Table J-2 there.

ST *ket 'waist > put around the waist > belt': WT *rked-pa* 'the waist, loins, middle' (*IST:* 66), *rked-rgyan* 'belt ornament'; JP *ʃiŋ^{31}-kjit^{55}* 'waist'. CH *xié* OCM *khet, Tibetan *rket and JP *s-kit may all go back to the same ST etymon *s/r-ket. Without final *-t: Tamang *(^{1})ke:* 'belt'. Lepcha *a-rek* 'girdle' cannot be related unless it is a mangled loan from a WT word like *rked* which has undergone a metathesis of the type described in §2.8.3 (*rket > *reket > rek).

jié$_{13}$ 桀傑 (gjät 3) **LH** gɨat, **OCM** *g(r)at

'Of surpassing quality' [Shi] > 'hero' 桀 [Shi], 傑 [Meng].

⋈ **jié-jié** 桀桀 'surpassing, very tall' [Shi].

⋈ **qiè** 揭 (k^hjat 3, $k^hjɐt$) **LH** $k^hɨɑt$, **OCM** *khat

'Martial, martial-looking' [Shi].

[E] This wf is prob. cognate to TB-Lushai *hrat^F* < *hraat* 'brave, resolute'; or alternatively to WT *gyad* 'champion, athlete' (*HST:* 93).

jiě 解 ($kaɨ^B$) **LH** $kɛ^B$, **OCM** *krêʔ

'To loosen' [Meng], 'explain' [Zuo], 'divide' [Guoyu], 'cut up (an ox)' [Zhuang].

[T] *Sin Sukchu SR* kjaj (上); *PR*, *LR* kjej; *MGZY* gyay (上) [kjaj]; *ONW* këi

⋈ **xiè** 解 ($ɣaɨ^B$) **LH** $gɛ^B$, **OCM** *grêʔ — **[T]** *ONW* ɣëi

'Be slack, idle, careless' intr. [Shi]; 'understand' [Li]; syn. → huì$_3$ 會.

[<] endopass. of *jiě* 解 (§4.6).

⋈ **xiè**, **jiè** 懈 ($kaɨ^C$) **LH** $kɛ^C$, **OCM** *krêh

'Lazy, remiss' [Xiaojing]; 'be slack, idle, careless' = *ɣaɨ^B* [Shi].

⋈ **xiè-hòu** 邂逅 ($ɣaɨ^C$-$ɣəu^C$) **LH** $gɛ^C$-go^C, **OCM** *grêh-g(r)ôh

'Be carefree and happy' [Shi].

[E] ? Area stem *C-re: TB-Chepang *greh-* 'to sever, chop off, cut cleanly', perh. also PLB *priy^2 'unfasten, untie' > WB *p^{h}re* 'untie, unroll, appease' ⋈ *ə-p^{h}re* 'answer to question, key'. <> Perh. MK: Khmer *rāya* /rííəj/ 'to break up, scatter, disperse, divide up' ⋈ *srāya* /sraaj/ 'to undo (knot), untie, loosen, untangle, unravel, solve, clarify, interpret' (dream). The MK–OC vowel correspondence is regular, and a MK origin could account for the differences in initial consonants.

jiè$_1$ 介 ($kăi^C$) **LH** kɛs, **OCM** *krê(t)s

'Scale' (of animals) [Li] > 'armour' [Shi] > 'armoured men' [Shi] > 'to assist' [OB, Shi].

[E] ST: *jiè* is often thought to be cognate to → jiǎ$_1$ 甲 (so LaPolla 1994: 141; Yú Mǐn 1948: 43), but *jiè* agrees phonologically rather with TB-WB *ə-kre^B* 'scales of a fish'. <> PTai *klet^{D1}S 'fish scales' is perh. a Chinese loan. Possible allofam → jiè$_3$ 疥.

jiè$_2$ 介价 ($kăi^C$) **LH** kɛs, **OCM** *krê(t)s ?

'To increase, become great' (of army, blessings, old age, person) [Shi]. This word is prob. related to → xián$_8$ 閑 *grên 'be large', and perh. derived from → jiǎ$_2$ 假嘏 *krâʔ 'great' (but the OC vowels differ). Shī Xiàngdōng (2000: 24) relates this word to WT *rgyas-pa* 'to increase'; OC *e is the equivalent of foreign *ya/*ja (§11.3.2).

jiè$_3$ 疥 (kǎi^{C}) **LH** kɛs, **OCM** *krê(t)s ?
'Itch, scabies' [[Li] is prob. derived from, or cognate to, *jiā* 痂 (ka) *krâi 'scabies' [SW] (so Wáng Lì 1982: 432), hence < *krâi-ts. Alternatively, it could perh. be the same etymon as → jiè$_1$ 介 'scales'.

jiè$_4$ 芥 (kǎi^{C}) **LH** kɛs, **OCM** *krêts or *krâts ?
'Mustard plant' [Li].
[E] <> PTai *kat: S. *kaat^{DIL}* 'mustard plant'; Mid. Korean *kas* id. (Miyake 1997: 189).

jiè$_5$ 界 (kǎi^{C}) **LH** kɛs, **OCM** *krê(t)s
'Boundary, limit' [Shi] looks like a variant of the LH homophone → jiè$_6$ 屆 'arrive, limit' (difference in OC vowels *e vs. *i), and may be the same as → jiè$_1$ 介 'armor' in the sense of security encirclement, and thus perh. be a derivation from → jiè$_9$ 戒誡 *krə̂h 'guard against'.

jiè$_6$ 屆 (kǎi^{C}) **LH** kɛs, **OCM** *krî(t)s
'To end up, arrive, end, limit' [Shi] is prob. related to → jiè$_5$ 界 'limit'.

jiè$_7$ 借 (tsjäk) **LH** tsiak **OCM** *tsak — **[T]** *ONW* tsiek — **[D]** PMin *tsiɔk
'To borrow' [Zuo]

× **jiè** 借 (tsja^{C}) **LH** tsia^{C}, **OCM** *tsakh
'To lend' [Lunyu] (Herforth 1984, acc. to Takashima 1996 II: 130).
[<] exoactive of *jiè* 借 (tsjäk) (§4.3)

[C] This set belongs prob. to the wf → cuò$_4$ 錯, whose basic meaning is 'to cross, exchange'.

jiè$_8$ 藉 (dzja^{C}) **LH** dzia^{C}, **OCM** *dzakh
'To present' [Zuo], 'contribute, aid' [Li], 'avail oneself of, depend on' [Zuo], 'bedding or mat of straw as support for sacrifices or gifts' [Yi]. This word could either be derived from → jū$_5$ 苴 'straw' (so Wáng Lì 1982: 167), or be cognate to WT *'jags-pa* 'to give, present' (so Bodman 1980: 150).

jiè$_9$ 戒誡 (kǎi^{C}) **LH** kɛ^{C}, **OCM** *krə̂h
'To guard against, be on guard, take care, admonish' [BI, Shi], 'notify, invite' [Zuo]; 'to warn' [Yi], 'prohibit' 誡 [Xun].
[T] *Sin Sukchu SR* kjaj (去), *PR* kjej; *MGZY* gyay (上) [kjaj]; *ONW* këi

× **xiè** 駴 (ɣǎi^{B}) **LH** gɛ^{B}, **OCM** *grə̂?
'To frighten, overawe' [Zhuang].

[C] Wáng Lì (1982: 86) relates this wf to → jì$_7$ 忌誋惎 'warn'. Possible derivations may be → jiè$_1$ 介 'armour' and / or → jiè$_6$ 屆 'limit'.

jiè$_{10}$ 犗 → **gē$_3$** 割

jīn$_1$ 斤 (kjən) **LH** kɨn, **OCM** *kən — **[T]** *ONW* kin
'Ax' 斤 [BI, Zuo].
[E] ? ST: PLB *gyan² 'pick-ax' (Matisoff *LL* 1.2, 2000: 139). It may also be connected with PMY *cwI:n¹ 'ax' (Wáng FS), and / or PTai *xwaan, PKS *kwan (Matisoff).

jīn$_{1a}$ 斤 'a weight' → **jūn$_1$** 均鈞

jīn$_2$ 今 (kjəm) **LH** kɨm, **OCM** *kəm
'Today, this (day, year)' [OB, BI, Shi].
[T] *Sin Sukchu SR* kim (平), *PR*, *LR* kin; *MGZY* gim (平) [kim]; *ONW* kim.
[E] Etymology not clear. Unger (*Hao-ku* 33, 1986) suggests cognation with WT *lhem*

'now', but see → yán₂ 炎. Alternatively, the word's root may be → qí₇ 其 *gə 'this'.

jīn₃ 金 (kjəm) **LH** kɨm, **OCM** *kəm
'Metal' [BI, Shu, Shi], 'bronze, gold' [Shi].
[T] *Sin Sukchu SR* kim (平), *PR*, *LR* kin; *MGZY* gim (平) [kim]; *ONW* kim.
[D] PMin *kim 'gold'; Y-Guǎngzhōu ^{55}*kɐm*^{B1}
[E] Benedict (*HJAS* 4, 1939: 223) connects *jīn* with PTai *ɣəm^{A2} 'gold' ≍ S. *ka:m*^{B1} 'bright, striking' (used to describe rubies or pure gold), 'blood-red' (looks like a loan from Cantonese). Note the similarity with the wf → tǎn₅ 黮.

jīn₄ 津 → **jì₁₅** 濟

jīn₅ 筋 (kjən) **LH** kɨn, **OCM** *kən — **[T]** *ONW* kin
'Sinew' [Meng]. <> PTai *ʔi̯en^{A1} ~ ^{A2} 'tendon, sinew' is perh. related.

≍ **jiàn** 腱 (kjɐn, gjɐn^C) **LH** kɨɑn, gɨɑn^C, **OCM** *kan, gans
'Sinew' [Chuci].

[C] Prob. not related to → qiān₇ 牽 'pull tight' and → jiān₂ 堅 'solid, strong'.

jīn₆ 祲 (tsjəm[^{C}]) **LH** tsim(^{C}), **OCM** *tsəm(s)
'Halo around sun' [Zuo] appears to be related to WT *kʰyim* 'halo around sun' ≍ *'kʰyims-pa* 'be encircled by a halo' ≍ *'gyim-pa* 'circumference' (Bodman 1980: 58). However the initials are difficult to reconcile.

jǐn₁ 緊 (kjien^B 4) **LH** kin^B, **OCM** *kinʔ
'To bind tight' [Chuci, SW]. Acc. to *SSYP*: 211, this is the only word with a velar initial *k-* in *chóngniǔ* div. IV and is prob. a southern (note *Chuci*!) non-palatalizing dialect variant of the regular palatalized form **zhěn** 紾 (tśjen^B) 'to twist (someone's arm)' [Meng] (so Yupian; Schuessler 1996, *JCL* 24.2).
[T] *Sin Sukchu SR* kin (上); *MGZY* gyin (上) [kjin]; *ONW* kiin
[E] ST: Lushai *kʰirʔ*^{L} < *kʰirh 'to tie / bind arms behind the back; carrying cords twisted around a load', NNaga *C-kʰyin 'to tie'. Perh. also connected with WT *'khyil-ba* 'to wind, twist'. Prob. unrelated is the TB etymon WT *'gril-ba* 'be twisted, wrapped around', WB *kʰyañ* 'bind, fasten' ≍ *kʰyañ*^{B} 'thread' (< *krin) (note also *cañ*^{B} 'bind, tie together'), JP *kren*^{33} 'to tighten' (a rope). An allofam is perh. → qiān₇ 牽.

jǐn₂ 謹 → **jīng₂-jīng** 兢兢

jìn₁ 近 (gjən^B) **LH** gɨn^B, **OCM** *gənʔ
'To be near, imminent' [Shi]. Karlgren (1933: 28) relates this word to → jī₁₂ 幾 'imminent'.
[T] *Sin Sukchu SR* gin (上去); MGZ kin (上去) [gin]; *ONW* gin

≍ **jìn** 近 (gjən^C) **LH** gɨn^C, **OCM** *gəns
'To come near to, approach, keep close to' [Shi].
[<] exoactive / caus. derivation (§4.3).

[E] This etymon also occurs in PVM *t-kiɲ 'near' [Ferlus].

jìn₂ 浸 (tsjəm^C) **LH** tsim^C, **OCM** *tsəms
'To soak, overflow' [Shi].
[E] ST: WB *cim* 'steep, soak' (*HST*: 136) ≍ *cim*^{C} 'transude, ooze through'. <> Tai: *čim*^{3} 'to dip into, immerse'. This word is probably unrelated to the ones mentioned under → chén₂ 沈.

jìn₃ 禁 (kjəm^C) **LH** kɨm^C, **OCM** *krims ? — **[T]** *ONW* kim
'To prohibit' [Zuo].

[D] Y-Guǎngzhōu ^{33}*kɐm^{A1}*

[E] ST: PTB *krim (*STC* no. 379): WT *k^{h}rims* 'rule, right, law' ⋈ *'k^{h}rims* 'fear, terror, awe' (*HST:* 127), WB *krim^B* 'terrify'. In light of the WT cognates, → lǐn$_3$ 廩懔 'shake, fear' is perh. also related (so Shī Xiàngdōng 2000: 117). <> Unclear remains the relationship, if any, with MK-Khmer /praam/ 'to prohibit, forbid'.

jìn$_4$ 盡 (dzjen^B, tsjen^B) **LH** dzin^B, **OCM** *dzinʔ

'To exhaust' > 'entirely, all' [Shi].

[T] *Sin Sukchu SR* dzin (上去); *MGZY* tsin (上) [dzin]; *ONW* dzin

⋈ **jìn** 燼 (dzjen^C) **LH** dzin^C, **OCM** *dzins

'Ashes, combusted' [Shi] (Wáng Lì 1982: 540).

[T] *Sin Sukchu SR* zin (去); *MGZY* zin (平) [zin]

[<] exopass. of *jìn* 盡 (dzjen^B, tsjen^B) (§4.4), lit. 'what has been combusted'

[E] ST: WT *zin-pa* 'be finished, be at an end' (*STC:* 170 n. 455), Lushai *seeŋ^H / seen^L* 'use up, consume, spend' (money, strength), 'completely, entirely'.

jìn$_5$ 進 (tsjen^C) **LH** tsin^C, **OCM** *tsins

'To advance, enter' [Shu] > caus. 'bring / send forward' [BI, Shi, Shu]. — Etymology not clear.

[T] *Sin Sukchu SR* tsin (去); *MGZY* dzin (去) [tsin]

jìn$_6$ 饉殣 (gjen^C 3) **LH** gɨn^C, **OCM** *gəns

'Famine' 饉 [BI, Shi] > 'die of starvation' 殣 [Zuo].

This word could belong to → qín$_3$ 勤慬 (gjən) 'toil' (so Karlgren 1949: 92), but more likely it is cognate to WT *bkren ~ bgren* 'poor, hungry' and thus to → jī$_2$ 飢 'hungry' (so Karlgren 1933: 28; Bodman 1985: 151).

jìn$_7$ 墐 → **qín$_2$** 堇

jìn$_8$ 妗 (gjəm^C) — [D] PMin *ǧim^B > Amoy *kim^{C2}*, Jiàn'ōu *keŋ^{B2}*, Jiànyáng *kiŋ^{C1}*

'Aunt' [JY], fusion of *jiùmǔ* 舅母.

jìn$_9$ 紟 → **qīn$_3$** 衾

jīng$_1$ 京 (kjɐŋ) **LH** kɨaŋ, **OCM** *kraŋ — [T] *ONW* keŋ

'Mound, hill, capital city, great' [BI, Shi]. A semantic parallel is → qiū$_1$/$_2$ 丘.

[E] MK: Khmer /kraŋ/ (in toponyms:) 'steep knoll, bluff or crag overlooking a plain' < OKhmer *rāṅ* /raŋ/ 'rise up, be stiff or strong'.

⋈ **jǐng** 景 (kjɐŋ^B) **LH** kɨaŋ^B, **OCM** *kraŋʔ — [T] *ONW* keŋ

'Be great' [Shi].

⋈ **qíng** 鯨 (gjɐŋ) **LH** gɨaŋ, **OCM** *graŋ

'Whale' [Zuo] (Wáng Lì 1982: 346).

jīng$_2$-jīng 兢兢 (kjəŋ) **LH** kɨŋ, **OCM** *kəŋ

'Be fearsome, terrible' (drought) [Shi].

⋈ **jīng-jīng**, **qíng-qíng** 兢兢 (k/gjəŋ) **LH** k/gɨŋ, **OCM** *kəŋ, *gəŋ

'Be cautious' (approaching an abyss) [Shi]. This item looks like a vocalic variant of → jīng$_7$ 驚.

⋈ **jǐn** 謹 (kjən^B) **LH** kɨn^B, **OCM** *kənʔ

'Be careful, attentive, observe carefully' [Shi]. Variations in final nasals *n ~ ŋ* have parallels (§6.4.1–2), the final OC *-əŋʔ does not occur (§3.2.4).

jīng$_3$ 荊 (kjɐŋ) **LH** kɨeŋ, **OCM** *kreŋ

'Thorny shrub' [BI, Zuo], old name of the ancient state of Chǔ 楚 'briar, shrub' [SW].

[E] ? MK: Khmer *jrāṃṅa* /creəŋ/ 'to bristle' > *jajrāṃṅa* /ccreəŋ/ 'to be all bristly' [Jenner / Pou 1982: xxv] ⋇ *prēṅa* /praaɛŋ/ 'bristles' (of pig, boar, etc.), 'bristle brush'. The CH initial *k-* could be an alternate prefix, such as one forming nouns in Khmer.

jīng$_4$ 經 (kieŋ) **LH** keŋ, **OCM** *kêŋ
'To pass through' [Zuo], 'flow through, communicate' [Zhuang] > 'to take as a norm, plan, practice' [BI, Shi] > 'a warp' (in weaving) ('what is being passed through'?) [Zuo], but see next.
[T] *Sin Sukchu SR* kiŋ (平); *MGZY* gÿing (平) [kjiŋ]; *MTang* kieŋ < kɨŋ, *ONW* kėŋ
[E] ? ST: WB *ə-khyaŋB* 'diameter' (*CVST* 3: 24), WT *kyaŋ* 'straight, slender'. Wáng Lì (1982: 320) suggests that 'warp' is cognate to → gāng$_3$ 綱 'guiding rope', however *gāng* and *jīng* each belong to wfs with different semantic foci.

⋇ **jìng** 經徑逕 (kieŋC) **LH** keŋC, **OCM** *kêŋh — [T] *MTang* kieŋ < kɨŋ, *ONW* kėŋ
'A warp' 經 [Zuo] (the *JY* has this alternative tone C reading); 'small path, shortcut' [Lunyu], 'diameter' [Li], 'go, travel' 徑 [Zuo]. Karlgren suggests that 'gone far away' 逕 [Zhuang] is the s. w., but it may instead belong to the wf → jiǒng$_2$ 泂迥 'far'.
[<] exopass. of *jīng* 經 (kieŋ) (§4.4), lit. 'what is being passed through': 'a warp'.

⋇ **xíng** 陘 (ɣieŋ) **LH** geŋ, **OCM** *gêŋ
'Ravine, defile' [Zuo].
[<] endopass. of *jīng* 經, lit. 'what one passes through, is passed through'.

[C] A further allofam may be → xíng$_2$ 刑形 'law, model'.

jīng$_5$ 莖 → **xìng$_3$**, **jìng** 脛

jīng$_6$ 菁青 (tsjäŋ, tsieŋ) **LH** ts(i)eŋ, **OCM** *tseŋ, *tsêŋ
'Be luxuriant (vegetation)' [Shi] is perh. only a graphic variant of → qīng$_1$ 青 'green, blue', in spite of the difference in pronunciation (Baxter 1983).

jīng$_7$ 驚 (kjɐŋ) **LH** kɨeŋ, **OCM** *kreŋ
'Be afraid, attentive' sv. [Shi] > caus. 'to scare, alarm' [Shi].
[T] *Sin Sukchu SR* kiŋ (平); *MGZY* ging (平) [kiŋ]; *ONW* keŋ
[D] This is the word for 'to fear' in southern dialects: PMin 惊 *kiaŋ > Amoy *kiãA1*, Fúzhōu *kiaŋA1* 'be afraid'.

⋇ **jìng** 敬 (kjɐŋC) **LH** kɨeŋC, **OCM** *kreŋh — [T] *ONW* keŋ
'Be cautious, careful, respectful' sv. [Shi]; 'to warn, be careful about' [Shi].
[<] 'to warn': exoactive / caus. (§4.3).

⋇ **jǐng** 警儆 (kjɐŋB, kjäŋB) **LH** kɨeŋB, **OCM** *kreŋʔ
'To warn, admonish, be on one's guard' vt. 警 [Zuo] (儆 in addition QY *gjɐŋC*).
[<] 'be on one's guard': endoactive of *jīng* (§4.5)

[E] ? MK provides an etymological explanation: Khmer *rēṅa* /rɛɛŋ/ 'be stiff, rigid, hard' > OKhmer *krēṅa* /krɛɛŋ/ 'be stiff or rigid with fear, to fear, afraid of'. Khmer -> Tai: S. *kreeŋA1* 'to fear' (alternative: Manomaivibool 1975: 168). Löffler (1966: 141) relates *jīng* to Mru *riŋ* 'respectful'. A possible variant is → jīng$_2$ 兢.

jǐng$_1$ 井 (tsjäŋB) **LH** tsieŋB, **OCM** *tseŋʔ
'A well' [Zuo].
[T] *Sin Sukchu SR* tsiŋ (上); *MGZY* dzing (上) [tsiŋ]

⋇ **jǐng** 阱 (dzjäŋB) **LH** dzieŋB, **OCM** *dzeŋʔ
'Pitfall' 穽 [Shu], 'pit' 阱 [Li] (Karlgren 1956: 10).

[E] This last word could be related to WT *sdiŋs* 'cavity, depression' (*HST:* 118), whereas *jǐng* 'well' is prob. cognate to WT *rdziŋ* 'a pond'. Therefore, the two CH words may be unrelated.

jǐng$_2$ 頸 (kjäŋ^B, gjäŋ) **LH** kieŋ^B, gieŋ, **OCM** *keŋʔ, *geŋ
'Neck' [Zuo], unlike → lǐng 領 also figuratively 'neck' of a vessel, jug, etc.
[D] Y-Guǎngzhōu ^{35}*kɛŋ*^{B1}, Táishān ^{55}*kiaŋ*^{B1}, but Mand. *bózǐ* 脖子 'neck'.

ⅹ **jǐng** 剄 (kieŋ^B) **LH** keŋ^B, **OCM** *kêŋʔ
'Cut the throat, cut off the head' [Zuo] (Karlgren 1956: 16).

ⅹ **qiān** 顅 (k^{h}ien, kan) **LH** k^{h}en ~ kan, **OCM** *khên ~ *krên
'Long-necked' [Zhouli] is prob. connected with this wf. The alternative connection with *jiān* 肩 [ken] *ken 'shoulder' seems semantically less likely.

[E] Wáng Lì (1982: 321) considers this wf cognate to → gāng$_1$ 亢 'neck' and the allofams there. PMY *klaːŋ^A 'neck, throat' is prob. related to the latter rather than to *jǐng*. Since there is no trace of an *r in the OC initial, *jǐng* is prob. not related to → lǐng 領 'neck', but rather belongs to the ST root *ke to which also belongs → jié$_{12}$ 絜.

ST *ke(-C) 'concave' (of part of the body and the like): WT *rke-ba* 'lean' ⅹ *rked* 'waist' (Beyer 1992: 117), see → jié$_{12}$ 絜 for more; JP *keʔ*^{55} < *kek*^{55} 'concave' (of the neck, a jug) (*STC* no. 251), 'indentation, pit'; Chepang *kəyk* ~ *kek* 'neck'; NN *C-geŋ 'waist', SChin-Khami (Awa) *ken* 'waist', Chepang *keŋʔ-* and *kiŋh-* 'be constricted, narrow-waisted' ~ *kiŋʔ-* 'be constricted, narrow' (waist). See Table J-2 for synopsis.

Table J-2 for jǐng$_2$ 頸

	*ke	*ket	*kek	*keŋ
concave // lean	WT rke-ba lean		JP keʔ^{55} < kek^{55} concave	
neck	WT ske neck		Chepang kek neck	jǐng 頸 *keŋʔ neck
waist		xié 㓞 *k^{h}êt, *get belt WT rked waist JP ʃiŋ^{31}-kjit^{55} waist		NNaga *C-geŋ waist KC-Khami ken waist Chepang keŋʔ narrow-waisted

jǐng$_3$ 景 (kjɐŋ^B) **LH** kɨaŋ^B, **OCM** *kraŋʔ ? — **[T]** *ONW* keŋ
'Bright' [Zuo], 'measure by the shadow' [Shi]. The semantic association between 'light' and 'shadow' is also found in the wf → yīng$_1$ 英. A derivation is prob. → jìng$_6$ 鏡 'mirror'. Syn. → liàng 亮, → yīng$_1$ 英.

jǐng$_4$ 警儆 → **jīng$_7$** 驚

jǐng$_5$ □ 'finger' in Mǐn words: Taipei *ts^{h}iu^B-tsãi^B* 手□, *tsaŋ^B-t^{h}au^{A2}* or *tsiŋ^B-t^{h}au^{A2}* □頭 'finger'. Bauer (*CAAAL* 28, 1987: 61) compares the element *jǐng* with *ziːŋ^{A2}* 'finger' in Li lgs. on Hǎinán.

jìng$_1$ 靜靖竫 (dzjäŋ^B) **LH** dzieŋ^B, **OCM** *dzeŋʔ — **[T]** *ONW* dzieŋ
'Be quiet, tranquil, peaceful, to rest' 靖 [Shi]; 'to stop, keep qiet' 靜 [Lü]. *HST:* 55 adds *jìng* 靜 in the sense of 'pure' to this wf.
[E] Perh. MK: OKhmer *siṅ* /siŋ/ 'to stay in / at, abide, be still, contemplative...'. Note also TB-JP *sim*^{31} 'quiet, peaceful', but the difference in finals remains unexplained.

jìng$_2$ 淨 → **qīng$_2$** 清

jìng$_3$ 脛 → **xìng$_3$**, **jìng** 脛

jìng$_4$ 勁 → **qiáng** 強彊

jìng$_5$ 竟境 (kjɐŋ^B) **LH** kɨaŋ^B, **OCM** *kraŋʔ
'Boundary, limit, border' 竟 [Zuo]; 境 [Meng] is an allofam of → jiāng$_6$ 疆.

≍ **jìng** 竟 (kjɐŋ^C) **LH** kɨaŋ^C, **OCM** *kraŋh — **[T]** *ONW* keŋ
'Come to an end, entirely' [Shi].

jìng$_6$ 鏡 (kjɐŋ^C) **LH** kɨaŋ^C, **OCM** *kraŋh ?
'Mirror' [Dadai Liji].
[T] *Sin Sukchu SR* kiŋ (去); *MGZY* ging (去) [kiŋ]; *ONW* keŋ
[D] PMin *kiaŋ^C > Amoy *kiã^{C1}*, Fúzhōu *kiaŋ^{C1}*
[E] Etymology not certain. Baxter (p. c.) derives *jìng* from → liàng 亮 'light' with the nominalizing k-prefix (§5.4); alternatively, the word may be cognate to → jǐng$_3$ 景 'bright'. Perh. the late word *jìng* is a re-etymologization of the nearly identical word → jiàn$_{15}$ 監鑑 (kam^C) 'mirror'.

jìng$_7$ 敬 → **jīng$_7$** 驚

jiōng$_1$ 坰 → **jiǒng$_2$** 泂迥

jiǒng$_2$ 泂迥 (ɣiweŋ^B) **LH** ɣueŋ^B, **OCM** *wêŋʔ
'Distant' 泂 [Shi], 迥 [SW] (also read *xiòng*; *GY* also has *kiweŋ^B* for 迥).

≍ **zhēng-róng** 崢嶸 (dẓɛŋ-jwɐŋ, -ɣwɛŋ) **LH** dẓɛŋ-ɣuɛŋ, **OCM** *dzrêŋ-wrêŋ ?
'High, distant' [Chuci].

≍ **jiōng** 坰 (kiweŋ) **LH** kueŋ, OCB *kwêŋ
'Outlying parts, far from the capital' [Shi].
[<] k-prefix noun of *jiǒng* 泂迥 (ɣiweŋ^B) (§5.4) (Baxter a. Sagart 1998: 48).

≍ **xuán** 洵 (xiwen) **LH** huen, **OCM** *hwîn
'Far away' [Shi] is prob. a variant of the stem as final nasals can alternate after front vowels (§6.4.1).

[E] MK: Khmer *vēṅa* /wɛɛŋ/ 'be far, distant, long' ≍ *lveṅa* /lwéeŋ/ 'be far off, distant, remote' ≍ *chveṅa* /cwèeŋ/ 'be situated in the off side, be abnormal, queer, eccentric, unorthodox, left (hand)'. For a possible semantic parallel in OC, see → kuáng 狂. The root is perh. also encountered in PTB *wiy > WB *we^B* 'far', PL *we^2 'be far, dull'; possibly also Kanauri *rwi* 'high'. The relationship with → jiǒng$_3$ 憬 and → yǒng$_1$ 永, if any, is not clear.

jiǒng$_3$ 憬 (kjwɐŋ^B) **LH** kyaŋ^B, **OCM** *kwaŋʔ or *kwraŋʔ ?
'Be far away' [Shi]. The relationship with similar items → jiǒng$_2$ 泂迥 and → yuǎn$_1$ 遠 is not clear. Sagart (1999: 104) derives *jiǒng* from → yǒng$_1$ 永 'be long, distant'. A derivation may be → kuáng 狂, although the MC vowels do not agree.

jiǒng$_4$ 窘 (gjuen^B 3) **LH** guɨn ?, **OCM** *grun < PCH *-uŋ, OCB *grjunʔ (?)
'Be distressed, bothered' [Shi]. This word looks like a variant of → qióng$_1$ 邛 (gjwoŋ) LH gɨoŋ 'be distressed'. Otherwise, this word may belong to → hùn$_1$ 混渾.

jiǒng$_5$ 熲 → **yíng$_3$** 熒

jiū$_1$ 究 (kjəu^C) **LH** ku^C, **OCM** *kuh, OCB *k(r)jus — **[T]** *MTang* keu < kiu, *ONW* ku
'To search into, investigate' [Shi].

≍ **jiù** 救 (kjəu^C) **LH** ku^C, **OCM** *kuh, OCB *k(r)jus
'To save, help, relive' [Shi]; in this word tone C *-h appears to be the common

derivative suffix which forms exopassives (< 'having been successfully searched for'?), but the final *-h in *jiù* 究 above cannot have the same function.

[E] This word is shared with PLB *N-gu¹: WB *ku* 'help', Lahu *gu* 'prepare, practice'.

✕ qiú 求 (gjəu) **LH** gu, **OCM** *gu, OCB *grju

'To seek for, ask for' [Shi].

[T] *Sin Sukchu SR* giw (平); *MGZY* kiw (平) [giw]; *MTang* geu < giu, *ONW* gu

[E] <> PTai *gwa^{C2} 'to search for'. The Tai form points to OC *gwə. The phonetic elements in the above words (九求) may be ambiguous, they both could write words of the OC type *ku and *kwə.

Carr (*Language Studies* [Otaru Univ.] 1993.3: 34) also relates **kǎo** 考 (kʰâu^B) LH kʰouʔ *khûʔ 'to examine' [Shi] to *jiù* above.

jiū ₂ 鳩 (kjəu) **LH** ku, **OCM** *ku, OCB *k(r)ju — **[T]** *MTang* keu < kiu, *ONW* ku

'Pigeon, dove' [Shi] is today's meaning, but what bird it referred to in ancient texts is not certain.

[D] For taboo considerations, some southern dialects have an aspirated initial (A. Yue Hashimoto, p. c.): Y-Guǎngzhōu and Hongkong *kɐu^{A1}* ~ *kʰɐu^{A1}*, Fóshān, Nánhǎi et al. *kʰ-*; also M-Xiàmén *kiu^{A1}* ~ *kʰiu^{A1}*.

[E] ST: Because of *ku's onomatopoetic nature there are variant forms in ST, some with medial -r-, some without: PTB *kuw (*STC* no. 495) 'dove' > Miri *pəkü*, Meithei *kʰu-nu*, 'pigeon' (*STC:* 185; *HST* p. 118); PTB *m-krəw: PLB *N-kruw² > WB *kʰui* ~ *kʰyui* ~ *kʰrui*, Kuki *m-kʰru > Khami iŋ *məkʰru*. The Tai word looks like a loan from a Yuè dialect, yet PTai also had a medial *-r-: S. *khau^{A1}* < *khr-, *hr- 'dove'.

jiū ₃ 繆 → **jiǔ ₃** 糾

jiǔ ₁ 九 (kjəu^B) **LH** ku^B, **OCM** *kuʔ (~ kwəʔ ?), OCB *k(ʷ)juʔ

'Nine' [BI, Shi]. The graph was apparently invented for a word 'to bend' → jú₆ 鞠鞫; in WT the words for 'nine' and 'to bend' are also homophones *(dgu)*.

[T] *Sin Sukchu SR* kiw (上); *MGZY* giw (上) [kiw]; *MTang* keu < kiu, *ONW* ku

[D] PEMǐn *kəu^{B1}: M-Xiàmén, Fúzhōu *kau^B*; PWMǐn *kiu^{B1}; Y-Guǎngzhōu *^{35}kɐu^{B1}*

[E] ST: PTB *s-kwa (*HPTB:* 24) ~ *d-kəw (*HPTB:* 140): Lushai *kua^R* < *kuaʔ* (< *ʔ, not *-h < *-s) (*kɔ^L*) [*STC* no. 13] (for the rime see §10.2.3). Tamang *^{2}kuː* 'nine', WT *dgu*; PLB *guw² [Matisoff], PL *go² [Bradley]; WB *kui^B*; Garo *sku.* <> PTai *ki̯əu^{C1}: S. *kau^{C1}* 'nine' looks like a Cantonese loan.

jiǔ ₂ 久 (kjəu^B) **LH** ku^B, **OCM** *kuʔ or *kʷəʔ ?, OCB *kʷjəʔ

'Long time, long time ago' [Shi] > 'wait' [Zuo].

[T] *Sin Sukchu SR* kiw (上); *MGZY* giw (上) [kiw].

[D] M-Xiàmén *ku^B*; Y-Guǎngzhōu *^{35}kɐu^{B1}*

[E] MK: Wa-Lawa-Bulang *-[ŋ]-koʔ, it may be a CH loan.

jiǔ ₃ 糾 (kjieu^B 4) **LH** kiu^B, **OCM** *kiuʔ, OCB *k(r)jiwʔ

'To twist, plait' [Shi], 'unite' [Zuo].

✕ jiū 繆 (kjieu 4) **LH** kiu, **OCM** *kiu, OCB *k(r)jiw

'To twist' 繆 [Li], 樛 [Yili], 'down-curving (branch)' [Shi].

[D] Sagart (1999: 105) connects *jiū* to a Xīnzhōu 欣州 (Jìn) dialect word *kəʔ-liɔ* 'awkward (of a person's behavior), curved'.

[E] KT: The outside connections suggest an original *klju: PTai *kliəu^{A1} (?): S. *kliau^{A1}* 'to wind around, twist a string', Saek *tlɛɛu^{C1}*; note however PTai *kiəu^{C1} : S. *kiau^{C1}* 'to wind around, twist'.

This wf is perh. ultimately ST: TB-WT *gčud / lčud-pa, gčus / lčus, gču / lču* (< *hlju?) 'to twist, twine, plait, braid' ⋈ *gčus* 'screw', WB *kʰyu* 'twist off (fruit) with pole', Lushai *kiiu*ᴸ 'elbow' [Weidert 1975: 8].

Many variants are found under *GSR* 1064 and 1069. Baxter (1992: 513) adds → miù₁ 謬 'to lie' to this group. Allofams are → qiú₇, jiū 虯觓觩, and perh. → jiǎo₃ 絞.

jiǔ₄ 韭 (kjəuᴮ) **LH** kuᴮ, **OCM** *kuʔ — **[D]** PMin *kiuᴮ > Xiàmén *kuᴮ*
'Leek' [Shi]. Unger (*Hao-ku* 36, 1990: 48) relates *jiǔ* to WT *sko(-tse)* 'wild onion'.

jiǔ₅ 酒 (tsjəuᴮ) **LH** tsiuᴮ, **OCM** *tsju(ʔ) — **[D]** PMin *tsiuᴮ > Xiàmén, Fúzhōu *tsiuᴮ*
'Wine' 酉 [OB, BI], 酒 [Shi]. The word was also read in tone A in *Shījīng* (Mattos 1971: 309).
[T] *Sin Sukchu SR* tsiw (上); *MGZY* dziw (上) [tsiw]; *MTang* tseu < tsiu, *ONW* tsu
[N] The MC *tsj- ~ j-* alternation in 酒 ~ 酉 (*GSR* 1096) has parallels and points to an original OC root initial *j- (not *l-) in such series (see §9.2). Curiously, in its sense of 'cyclical character', *yǒu*'s 酉 Tai counterparts (Tai *rau*) and Han dynasty paronomastic glosses indicate an OC *r- initial. This has led to the identification of *(yǒu /) jiǔ* 'wine' with PTB *ru 'wine'. However, the latter belongs to → láo₃ 醪 *ru 'wine'.
[E] ST *ju: PTB *yu(w) 'wine' (*STC* no. 94), BG-Tiwa *chû* 'rice beer'.

⋈ **qiú** 酋 (dzjəu) **LH** dziu, **OCM** *dzju
'Wine-master' [Li], 'old wine' [Zhouli, SW] (Karlgren 1956: 11). This is a tone A nominalization derived from *jiǔ* (§3.1).

jiù₁ 臼 (gjəuᴮ) **LH** guᴮ, **OCM** *guʔ
'Mortar' [Yi].
[D] PMin *gʰ- > Xiàmén *kʰu*ᶜ², Fúzhōu *kʰou*ᶜ². In some Mǐn dialects the word for 'mortar' is the Mand. equivalent *jiù-kū* 臼窟 where *kū* means 'depression', then *kū* is reinterpreted as 'mortar' and *jiù* acquires the meaning 'pestle' (Branner 2000: 109).
[E] The several synonyms in the area are difficult to reconcile: PTai *grok. <> MK: PVM *t-koːlʔ > Viet. *cối* 'rice mortar' [Ferlus], PMonic *knʔɯl 'small mortar', Bahnar *tək(h)oːk* 'mortar'. Closest to OC are Bahnar or PVM (for loss of coda in OC, see §6.9), but the common Bahnaric word for 'mortar' is different: PSBahn. *ləpal ~ *nəpal, PNBahn. *apăl, also Wa-Lawa-Bulang *(m)pɑl.

jiù₂ 舅 (gjəuᴮ) **LH** guᴮ, **OCM** *guʔ
'Maternal uncle' [Shi]; 'mother's brother, husband's or wife's father'.
[D] PMin *giuᴮ > Xiàmén *ku*ᶜ², Fú'ān *kou*ᶜ²
[E] ST: PTB *kuw > WT *ʔa-kʰu ~ kʰu-bo* 'paternal uncle, husband'; WB *kui* 'honorific affix; brother' (*HST:* 154), JP *gə³¹-gu³¹* 'uncle'. *STC* (158 n. 428) relates the TB root to → kūn₁ 昆 'elder brother'. This word may be derived from → jiù₃ 舊 'old' (so Sagart 1999: 165f).

jiù₃ 舊 (gjəuᶜ) **LH** guᶜ, **OCM** *gwəʔ, OCB *gʷjɨʔ(s)
'Old (not new), ancient' [Shi]. The OC rime and tone are revealed by *Shījīng* rimes.
[T] *MTang* geu < giu, *ONW* gu — **[D]** PMin *giuᶜ
[E] This word is prob. shared with PTai *kəuᴮ 'old, ancient'.

jiù₄ 舊 (gjəuᶜ) **LH** guᶜ, **OCM** *guh
'An owl-like bird', the same as *xiū* 鵂 below' [SW], is considered related to → xiāo₃ 梟 in *HST:* 115.
[E] ST: PTB *ku ~ *gu > WB *kʰu*, Lisu *gu*; Kachin *u-kʰu*; Mikir *iŋkʰu* (*STC:* 185).

ꭗ **xiū** 鵂 (xjəu) **LH** hu, **OCM** *hu
'Owl' [Zhuang]. Because of the onomatopoetic nature of these words, exact phonological correspondences cannot be expected.

jiù$_5$ 救 → **jiū**$_1$ 究

jiù$_6$ 就 → **zào**$_2$ 造 (tsʰâu^C)

jū$_1$ 車 → **chē** 車

jū$_2$ 居 (kjwo) **LH** kɨɑ(^{C}), **OCM** *ka^A, *kaʔ, *kah
'To dwell, settlement, tranquil, comfortable' [Shi], 'sit down' [Lun]. *Shījīng* rimes indicate an early form *kaʔ; later *ka^A and *kah are equally common (Mattos 1971: 309). This may be an OC phonological variant of → chǔ$_3$ 處.
[T] *Sin Sukchu SR* ky (平); *MGZY* gÿu (平) [ky]; *MTang* ky < kø, *ONW* kø < kio (?)
[D] Y-Guǎngzhōu ^{55}*kœy*^{A1}, Táishān *kui*^{33}; M-Amoy ^{44}*ku*^{A1}

ꭗ **jù** 踞 (kjwo^C) **LH** kɨɑ^C, **OCM** *kah, OCB *k(r)jas
'To squat' 踞 [Zuo]; 'abode, dwelling, position' 居 [Shi] (Baxter 1992: 312).
[<] 'abode': exopass. of *jū* 居 (kjwo) (§4.4), lit. 'what is dwelled in'.

jū$_3$ 腒 → **gù**$_1$ 固

jū$_4$ 据 → **jù**$_6$ 據

jū$_5$ 苴 (tsʰjwo) **LH** tsʰiɑ, **OCM** *tsha
'Straw' [Shi] > 'straw as bottom in shoe' [Chuci] (also read MC *tsʰjwo, tsjwo*); 'bedding or packing of straw (for objects presented)' [Zhouli].

= **zū** 蒩 (tsuo, tsjwo, tsʰjwo) **LH** ts(ɨ)ɑ, tsʰɨɑ, **OCM** *tsa...
'Bedding or packing of straw (for objects presented)' [Zhouli].

[C] An allofam is perh. → jiè$_8$ 藉 'mat or bedding' (so Wáng Lì 1982: 167).

jū$_6$ 俱 (kju) **LH** kɨo, **OCM** *ko
'Both, all, together' [Zuo].
[E] ? ST: WT *kʰyu (-bo/-mo)* 'flock, herd, company' (so *HST:* 89; Karlgren 1956: 9).
[T] *Sin Sukchu SR* ky (平); *MGZY* gÿu (平) [ky]; *MTang* ky < kuo, *ONW* kuo

ꭗ **jù** 具 (gju^C) **LH** gɨo^C, **OCM** *goh — **[T]** *MTang* gy < guo, *ONW* guo
'Be complete, be together' [BI, Shi] > 'to provide, arrange' Zuo] > 'an implement, utensil' [BI, Zuo].

jū$_7$ 駒 (kju) **LH** kɨo, **OCM** *ko — **[T]** *ONW* kuo
'Colt, young horse' [BI, Shi].
[E] *Jū* is the same etymon as → gǒu 狗 'puppy dog' acc. to Wáng Lì (1982: 182); however, *gǒu* which comes from a non-ST language, is not a homophone of *jū*. It is more likely that *jū* is cognate to PTB *ku(r) or *kor 'horse' (*HPTB:* 385), in Monpa *kur-ta* < *ku-rta* 'horse' (*rta* <- WT 'horse'), Tani *kuu, JP *kum-ra* < *ku-mra[ŋ]* 'horse' (*mraŋ* 'horse'); Lushai *sa*^{L}*-kɔr*^{R} 'a horse, pony' (but acc. to Lorrain p. 400 this word is derived from *kɔr*^{R} 'coat'), Mru *kor-ŋa* [Löffler 1966: 123]. For the loss of final *-r, see §7.7.5. Alternatively, one may consider *jū* cognate to → qū$_4$ 驅 *kho 'to drive' (a horse), 'gallop'.

jū$_8$ 痀 → **gōu**$_1$ 句鉤枸區

jū$_9$ 拘 → **jù**$_6$ 據

jú$_1$ 局 → **qū**$_1$ 曲

jú₂ 跼 → **qū₁** 曲

jú₃ 橘 (kjuet) **LH** kuit, **OCM** *kwit, OCB *kʷjit — **[T]** *ONW* kuit
'Orange' (fruit) [Shu].
[E] <> MK-Khmer *kwic* 'tangerine'. Less likely connections are MK: Khmer *krōč* 'citrus fruit', P-Hre-Sedang *kruč* (Bodman 1980: 96) -> WB *hrok* 'citrus'.

jú₄ 掘 → **kū₄** 堀

jú₅ 鞠 (kjuk) **LH** kuk, **OCM** *kuk
'To nourish, suckle' (a child) [Shi].
This is prob. a vocalic variant of the wf → gǔ₁₄ 穀 'suckle', see Table C-2 (under → chù₄, xù 畜) for parallel stems.

jú₆ 鞠鞫 (kjuk) **LH** kuk, **OCM** *kuk
'To bow, bend' (the body) 鞠 [Lun], 'concave side of river bend' 鞫 [Shi].
[E] ST *kuk: PTB *kuk ~ *guk > WT *'gug(s)-pa, bkug, dgug* 'to bend' ⋇ *dgu* id., Bahing *kuk-* 'to bend' tr. ⋇ *guk-* 'to bend' intr., PLB *gok 'crooked, bent; return, go back', WB *kok* 'crooked, not upright' ⋇ *ə-kok* 'a crook' (Matisoff *TSR* no. 2; *STC:* 77, 125, 159; *HST:* 41–42); Kuki-Naga *m-ku:k 'knee' (*STC:* 120). The Chinese items could also be cognate to WT *'kʰyog-po ~ kʰyog-po* 'crooked, bent' ⋇ *gyog-pa* 'curved, crooked' (so Bodman 1980: 161). Prob. related to → gōu₁ 句鉤枸區. A variant with OC rime *-ok is → qū₁ 曲. Another wf with OC *o ~ *u variation is → rú₄ 懦臑.

jú₇ 鞠 'exhausted' → **qióng₂** 窮

jǔ₁ 咀 (dzjwoᴮ) **LH** dziaᴮ, **OCM** *dzaʔ
'To chew' [Guan].
[E] Area word: ST *dzaʔ > PTB *dzaʔ > Garo *chaʔ* 'eat', Chepang *jeʔ-sa* 'eat', WT *za-ba, zos / bzas* 'to eat' (*STC* p. 28) ⋇ *zas* 'food'; PL *dza² 'to eat' ⋇ *dza¹* 'food', WB *caᴮ* 'to eat, corrode, wear out' ⋇ *ca, ə-ca* 'food'. Kuki-Naga: *dza(k) 'eat' (*STC* p. 101 n. 289). <> PMK *cyaʔ (Shorto 1972): Mon *ca* 'eat', OKhmer *cya* /ciiə/ 'to eat', PSBahn. *sa: 'eat'.

⋇ **zuò** 飵 (dzâk) **LH** dzak, **OCM** *dzâk
'To eat, eat together', is a Han period Chǔ dial. word [SW; FY 1, 31] which suggests a foreign origin. Occasionally CH words have a final *-k* for a TB open syllable (§6.1).

⋇ **cān₂** 餐 (tsʰân) **LH** tsʰan, **OCM** *tshân
'To eat' [BI, Shi], 'food' [Guoce], 'meal' [Zhuang].
[T] *Sin Sukchu SR* ts'an (平); *MGZY* tshan (平) [ts'an]
[<] nominal n-suffix derivation from the ST root *dza.
[E] ST: PTB *dza 'to eat'> WT *bzan* 'food', *gzan-pa* 'to eat' (*STC:* 159 n. 428). Alternatively, *cān* could be cognate to WT *'tsʰal-ba* (< *N-tsal*) 'to eat' ⋇ *tsʰal-ma* 'breakfast' (so Unger *Hao-ku* 35, 1986: 30; *HST:* 69). Since MC *tsʰ-* = WT *gs-* (§5.9.1), the first possibility seems preferable (WT aspiration as in *tsʰal* is non-phonemic).

⋇ **càn** 粲 (tsʰânᶜ) **LH** tsʰanᶜ, **OCM** *tshâns
'Food' [Shi].
[<] exopass. of *cān*, lit. 'what is eaten' (§4.4).

jǔ₂ 筥籧 (kjwoᴮ) **LH** kɨaᴮ, **OCM** *kaʔ
'Round basket' 筥 [BI, Shi], 籧 [Li].
[E] Prob. ST: TB-PLB *kak, WB kak 'large wicker basket'; JP *kaʔ⁵⁵* 'open wicker basket'; Akha *kʰa*, Lisu *hka²-tu³* 'rough, loosely woven' (Matisoff *TSR* no. 7; *HST:* 39).

The earliest graph 筥 implies an *r in the OC initial, though. For the finals, see §3.2.2.

jǔ $_3$ 矩 (kju^B) **LH** kyɑ^B, **OCM** *kwaʔ
'Carpenter's square' [Meng], 'rule, law' [Lun]; 'troops drawn up in a square' 拒 [Zuo].
[T] *Sin Sukchu SR* ky (上); *MGZY* gÿu (上) [ky]; *MTang* ky < kuo, *ONW* kuo

⋈ **kuò** 栝 (kuât) **LH** kuɑt, **OCM** *kwât
'Carpenter's square' [Xun].
[<] nominal t-suffix (§6.2.1).

[E] Possibly related to TB-WB *kyaŋ-* 'carpenter's square' (for finals, see §3.2.4), or to WT *grwa* 'angle, corner'. Allofam → kuāng$_4$ 筐 'square basket'.

jǔ $_4$ 拒 'square' → **jǔ** $_3$ 矩

jǔ $_5$ 柜 (kju^B) **LH** kyɑ^B, **OCM** *kwaʔ
'Gutter' [Zhouli].

⋈ **qú** 渠 (gjwo) **LH** gɨɑ or gyɑ ?, **OCM** *gwa ?
'Canal' [Li] may be the s. w. as → qú$_5$ 衢 'crossroads' (note the TB / ST field of meaning below). We should expect MC *gju* which is implied by the phonetic *jù* 巨 and the cognates, but the MC rimes *-ju ~ -jwo* have merged in almost all dialects and have already mingled in some phonetic series.

⋈ **kuài** 澮 (kuâi^C) **LH** kuɑs, **OCM** *kwâts or *kôts ?
'Watering channel, drain, canal' [Shu]. For the final dental, see §6.2.1.

⋈ **què** 闕 (k^{h}jwɐt) **LH** k^{h}yɑt, **OCM** *khwat or *khot ?
'A hole' [Shi] > 'opening, breach, gate' [Li] > 'lookout tower over the gate' [Shi].
[<] aspiration for hollow objects (§5.8.6) plus t-suffix (§6.2.1) of the ST stem, therefore prob. unrelated to → jué$_9$ 撅闕 'excavate'.

[E] ST *(k)wa- 'passage through': Lushai *kua^L* 'a hole, burrow, cavity' ⋈ *kua^L / kuak^F* 'be open or clear (as way, path, road, etc.), to open (up), make way through'; WB *ə-wa^C* 'opening of door, hole'. Allofam is prob. → qú$_5$ 衢 'crossroads'.

jǔ $_6$ 舉 (kjwo^B) **LH** kɨɑ^B, **OCM** *kaʔ ? — **[T]** *MTang* ky < *ONW* kø < kio (?)
'To rise, surge, start; lift, promote' [Shi].
[E] This may be cognate to WT *'k^{h}yog-pa, k^{h}yag* 'to lift, carry' (*HST:* 103) ⋈ *skya-ba, bskyas* 'to carry'. Alternatively, Baxter / Sagart (1998: 48) relate this word to → yú$_{11}$ 舁 'to lift'.

If the root should be *ka or *kja, then → jiē$_7$ 揭 and → jiǎn$_9$ 攓 may represent forms with additional final consonants. However, a root *ka is so common that many a meaning can be associated with it, and 'lift' is also a rather broad concept.

jǔ $_7$**-jǔ** 踽踽 → **guǎ** 寡

jù$_1$ 巨距 → **kuàng**$_1$ 況

jù$_2$ 沮 (dzjwo^B) **LH** dziɑ^B, **OCM** *dzaʔ
'To leak, ooze' [Li].

⋈ Perh. **jù** 沮 (tsjwo^C) **LH** tsiɑ^C, **OCM** *tsah
'Marshy ground'.

[E] ST: WT *'dzag-pa, (g-)zags* 'to drop, drip, flow out' ⋈ *'ts^{h}ag-pa, btsags* 'to cause to trickle, strain'; PLB *ɴtsak^H 'to drop, drip' [Matisoff *TSR:* 44], WB *cak* 'fall in drops' ⋈ *ə-cak* 'a drop' (*HST:* 152; for CH tone B, see §3.2.2). Loaned into PVM: *k-ɟɔh 'to drip' [Ferlus].

jù₃ 踞 → **jū ₂** 居

jù₄-nǔ 粔籹 (gjwo^B^-ṇjwo^B^) **LH** gɨɑ^B^-ṇɑ^B^, **OCM** *ga-nraʔ ?
'Rice cake' [Chuci] could be related to WT *mna'* 'cake'; cf. Tai: S. *ka-nom* 'cake' [Unger *Hao-ku* 33, 1986].

jù₅ 懼 (gju^C^) **LH** gyɑ^C^, **OCM** *gwah
'To dread, feel apprehension' [BI, Shi].
[T] *Sin Sukchu SR* gy (去); *MGZY* kÿu (去) [gy]; *MTang* gy < guo, *ONW* guo
[E] Li F. (1976: 46) relates this word to Tai: S. *klua^A1^* < *kl-* 'to fear', and refers also to WT *'gul-ba* 'to tremble'.
⋇ **jù** 瞿 (kju^C^) **LH** kyɑ^C^, **OCM** *kwah
'Be anxious, careful' [Shi], 'frightened glance' [Li].
⋇ **yǔ-yǔ** 偊偊 (ju^B^) **LH** wɑ^B^, **OCM** *waʔ
'Be circumspect' [Liezi].
⋇ **jué** 矍戄 (xjwak) **LH** hyɑk, **OCM** *hwak
'Anxious look' 矍 [Yi] (also MC kjwak); 'scared' 戄 [Zhuang].
⋇ **kuāng** 恇 (kʰjwaŋ) **LH** kʰyɑŋ, **OCM** *khwaŋ
'To fear' 匡 [Liji], *kuāng-kuāng* 恇恇 'to fear, dread' [Hou Hanshu].
⋇ **guǎng**, **wàng** 迋 (gjwaŋ^B^ or jwaŋ^B^ ?) **LH** gyɑŋ^B^ ?, **OCM** *gwaŋ ?
'To frighten, scare' [Zuo].
[E] The root of this wf is apparently *wa- as indicated by *yǔ-yǔ*, by the QY initial *xj-* in *jué*, and by the loan graph *wàng* 迋. For the final *-ŋ* in the last two items, see §6.5.2.

jù₆ 據 (kjwo^C^) **LH** kɨɑ^C^, **OCM** *kah
'To grasp, depend on' [Shi], also later written 据. Alternatively perh. related to → jué₁₂ 攫 OC *kwak, although the rimes do not agree.
[T] *Sin Sukchu SR* ky (去); *MGZY* gÿu (去) [ky]; *MTang* ky < kø, *ONW* kø < kio (?)
⋇ **jū** 据 (kjwo) **LH** kɨɑ, **OCM** *ka in *jié-jū* 拮据 (k(j)iet-kjwo) *kit-ka
'To grasp' (a plant) [Shi].
⋇ Perh. **jū** 拘 (kju) **LH** kɨo, **OCM** *ko — [T] *ONW* kuo
'To grasp, seize' (people, horses) [BI, Shi]. The vowels differ, though (§11.1.5).

jù₇ 聚 (dzju^C^) **LH** dzio^C^, **OCM** *dzoh, OCB *dzjos
'To collect, store' [Zuo].
[T] *Sin Sukchu SR* dzy (上去); *MGZY* tsÿu (上去) [dzy]; *MTang* dzy, *ONW* dzuo
[E] ST *tso: WB *cu^C^* 'to collect, gather together', WT *'tsʰogs-pa* 'to assemble, gather, meet'. Downer (1959: 275) determined the MC reading *dzju^B^* for the verb, tone C *dzju^C^* for the nouns 'collection, stores; masses, group' [Zuo] which is an exopass. derivation (§4.4). Bodman (*BIHP* 39, 1969: 340) adds this word to *zú* 卒 (under → zāo₂ 遭).
⋇ **zú** 族 (dzuk) **LH** dzok, **OCM** *dzôk
'Clan, clansmen' [BI, Shi], a minimal segment of a lineage → zōng₁ 宗 (Chang K. C. 1976: 70) (Wáng Lì 1982: 197; *CVST* 4: 32). Affiliation with *jù* is likely in light of etymological parallels in WT (see below) and *zú* 卒 'group' (→ zāo₂ 遭).
⋇ **zuì** 最 (tsuâi^C^) **LH** tsuɑs, **OCM** *tsôts, OCB *tsots
'Collect, accumulate, highest degree' [Gongyang, Guoce] (Baxter 1992: 239). Yú Mǐn (1948: 43) relates *zuì* to → jí₁₃ 集輯 'collect'.
[T] *MTang* tsuɑi, *ONW* tsuɑC
⋇ **cóng₂** 叢 (dzuŋ) **LH** dzoŋ, **OCM** *dzôŋ
'To collect' [Shu], 'thicket' [Meng] (Wáng Lì 1982: 197). Acc. to Benedict (1976: 178)

and Bodman (*BIHP* 39, 1969: 334), this is an s-prefix derivation of → tóng$_1$ 同 'join', but see §5.7.

ж **zōng** 稯 (tsuŋ) **LH** tsoŋ, **OCM** *tsôŋ
'Sheaf, bundle' [Guoyu], 'numerous' [Zhuang].

[E] ST: WT *'dzog-pa, btsogs* 'to heap together, mix up together' ж *'tsʰogs-pa, tsʰogs* 'to assemble, meet' ж *tsʰogs* 'assemblage, crowd' ж *sogs-pa* < OTib. *stsogs-pa, bstsogs* 'to accumulate, gather together' (*HST:* 108).

juān 鐫 → **zuān** 鑽

juǎn$_1$ 卷捲 (kjwän^B 3) **LH** kyan^B, **OCM** *kron?, OCB *krjon?
'To roll, roll over, turn over' 卷 [Shi]; 'to scroll' 捲.
[T] *Sin Sukchu SR* kyen (上); *MGZY* gÿon (上) [kyɔn]
[E] ST: Lushai *hrual^H* 'roll up in the hand, twist'. Prob. an allofam of → quán$_3$ 卷拳, but see there. The Tai word is prob. a CH loan: Wuming *klian^{C1}* 'roll, scroll' (Bodman 1980: 108), Mun *gluan^{C2}* 'roll up' (Haudricourt 1950: 563).

juǎn$_2$ 臇 → **juàn$_1$** 雋

juàn$_1$ 雋 (dzjwän^B) **LH** dzyan^B, **OCM** *dzon?
'Fat' (of bird meat) [Lüshi].

ж **juǎn** 臇 (tsjwän^B) **LH** tsyan^B, **OCM** *tson?
'Fat' (of bird) [Chuci], later 'fat and rich broth'.

[E] Perh. ST, a nominal n-suffix form related to WB *cʰu* 'be fat, obese' < PTB *tsow (*STC* no. 277). This stem may be related to → sāo$_4$ 臊 'fat'.

juàn$_2$ 倦 (gjwän^C 3) **LH** gyan^C, **OCM** *gwans or *g(i)ons
'Tired' [Lunyu].
[T] *Sin Sukchu SR* gyen (去); *MGZY* kwÿan (去) [gyɛn]
[E] Bodman (1980: 150; also *HST:* 151) compares the CH word to WT *kyor-kyor* 'feeble, weak' ж *kʰyor-ba* ~ *'kʰyor-ba* 'to reel, stagger, walk as if weak'. *CVST* (5: 17) connects the next word with Lushai *kʰɔl?^{L}* 'troublesome, tiresome, harsh':

ж **guǎn** 痯 (kuân^B) **LH** kuan^B, **OCM** *kwân? or *kôn? ?
'Be exhausted' [Shi].

jué$_1$ 決 (kiwet) **LH** kuet, **OCM** *kwêt
'To cut off' [Zuo], 'bite off' [Meng], 'decide' 決 [Guoce] > 'farewell words' 訣 [Lie]. This may be the same word as → jué$_2$ 決. An allofam is → quē 缺.
[T] *Sin Sukchu SR* kye (入); *MGZY* gwÿa (入) [kyɛ]; *ONW* kuėt

jué$_2$ 決 (kiwet) **LH** kuet, **OCM** *kwêt
'To open' [Zhouli] > 'open a passage' [Shu]. This may be the same word as → jué$_1$ 決.

ж **guài** 夬 (kwai^C) **LH** kuas, **OCM** *kwrâts (or rather *kwrêts ?)
'To divide, make a breach' [Yi].
[<] perh. a double caus. formation of *jué* (tone C §4.3; and initial *r-causative §7.5)

[E] ST: WB *kyui^B* 'be broken' ж *kʰyui^B* 'to break in two' ж *kʰui^C* 'defective, wanting, incomplete' (Matisoff ICSTLL 1978: 150). Allofam → quē 缺 'break, splinter'.

jué$_3$-tí 駃騠 (kiwet-diei) **LH** kuet-dei
'A superior type of horse of the northern barbarians' [Xu Guang, Shiji; misidentified in SW] (Pulleyblank 1962: 245). The word's source is unknown, yet it shows some similarity with IE-Tocharian B *yakwe* 'horse' (< PIE *ekuos) (Pokorny 301).

jué$_4$ 映 (kiwet [GY], ɣiwet [JY]) **LH** kuet, guet, **OCM** *kwêt, *gwêt
'To wink with eyes' [GY, Liùshūgù 六書故].
[E] AA: Central Sakai *gawet, giwet*, Khasi *kʰawoit* 'beckon with hand'. See → huī$_4$ 麾 for possible variants; additional syn. → xuè$_2$ 罭.

jué$_5$ 袂 → **mèi**$_8$ 袂

jué$_6$ 厥 (kjwɐt) **LH** kyɑt, **OCM** *kot — [T] *ONW* kuat
'Stone' [Xun] acc. to commentaries; prob. related to Tai: S. *kʰot*^{D2} < *g-* 'a stone lodged in a tree' (Manomaivibool 1975: 236).

jué$_7$ 厥 (kjwɐt) **LH** kyɑt, **OCM** *kot ?
Third person pronoun 'he, she, it, they, his, her...' [BI, Shi, Shu], occasionally it also serves as possessive for the first and second persons in classical Chinese (Takashima *JAOS* 119.3, 1999: 404–431). Bodman (*JAOS* 68, 1948: 52–60; 1980: 161) relates this word to WT *kʰyod* 'you'.

jué$_8$ 蕨 (kjwɐt) **LH** kyɑt, **OCM** *kwat or *kot — [D] PMin *k̭iot 'bracken'
'Fern' (edible, *Pteridium aquilinum*) [Shi].
[E] ST: WT *skyas-ma, skyes-ma* 'fern' (Unger *Hao-ku* 39, 1992). It also occurs in PTai *kuət > *kuut^{D1} 'kind of edible fern' (*Diplazium esculentum*).

jué$_9$ 撅闕 (gjwɐt) **LH** gyɑt, **OCM** *got
'To excavate' 闕 [Zuo] > 'pull up, dig out' 撅 [Yi Zhoushu].
[E] ST: *r-ko-t (*STC* no. 420) > WT *rkod-pa* 'excavate, dig' ⋈ *rko-ba* 'to dig' (*HST:* 63); JP *got*^{31} 'dig'. This item may be related to → kū$_4$ 堀窟.

jué$_{10}$, **yù** 潏 → **xuàn**$_1$ 泫

jué$_{11}$ 覺 (kåk) **LH** kɔk, **OCM** *krûk
'To wake up' intr. [Shi], 'get insight' [Lunyu], 'grateful' [Zuo].
[T] *ONW* käk

⋈ **jiào** 覺 (kau^C) **LH** kɔu^C, **OCM** *krûkh
'To wake up' intr. [Zuo: Cheng 10, 5] is supposedly the reading of this graph in the sense of 'wake up' intr. in *Shījīng, Zuǒzhuàn,* and elsewhere, but the *Shījīng* rime requires OCM *-k, not *-kh (Baxter 1992: 611), which would agree with the intr. use. The tone C reading may therefore be a later innovation.

[E] ST: PTB *grok ~ *krok (*STC* no. 473): WT *dkrog-pa = skrog-pa* 'to stir, churn, rouse, scare'; PLB *krok 'be afraid' > WB *krok* ⋈ PLB *ʔkrok > WB *kʰrok* 'frighten'. But these TB items may belong to → jiǎo$_{12}$ 攪 instead. *HST:* 127 combines the latter with this wf.
[C] Possible additional allofam: → lù$_{12}$ 摝.

jué$_{12}$ 攫 (kjwak) **LH** kyɑk, **OCM** *kwak
'To seize' [Li], may be related to → huò$_4$ 穫, or alternatively to → jù$_6$ 據 OC *kah although the rimes do not agree.
[E] ST: WT *'gog-pa, bkog* 'snatch, seize, take away' (*HST* p. 130).

jué$_{13}$ 矍戄 → **jù**$_5$ 懼

jué$_{14}$ 驕 → **jiǎo**$_{17}$ 蹻

jué$_{15}$ 爵 → **jiáo** 嚼

jué$_{16}$ 爝燋 → **jiāo**$_6$ 焦

jué$_{17}$ 較 → **jiǎo**$_5$ 角

jué18 掘 → **kū**4 堀窟

jūn1 均鈞 (kjiuen 4) **LH** kwin, **OCM** *kwin
'Be well balanced, equal, alike' 均 [Shi] > 'weight of 30 jin' 鈞 [BI, Meng], 'soldiers' uniform' 袀 [Lü].
[<] k-prefix noun of → yún1 匀 *win 'even, uniform' (§5.4) (Baxter / Sagart 1998: 47).
[E] ST: PTB *kyi:n 'weigh' > WB *kʰyin* 'weigh, plumb, level, a balance', Lushai *ki:n* [*HPTB:* 277]. Perh. **jīn** 斤 (kjən) LH kɨn 'a weight' [Han period and later] is a popular variant.

jūn2 鈞 (kjiuen 4) **LH** kwin, **OCM** *kwin
'Potter's wheel' [Zhuang].
[<] k-prefix noun of *xún* 旬 *s-win 'all round, cycle', lit. 'the rotating thing' (§5.4).
⪤ **xún** 旬 (zjuen) **LH** zuin, **OCM** *s-win
'Everywhere, all round' [Shi] > 'ten day cycle, ten (days)' [OB, Shu], e.g. *xún yǒu wǔ rì* 旬有五日 (ten / and / five / days) '...(after) 15 days...' [Zuo: Wen 16, 6].
[T] *Sin Sukchu SR* zyn (平); *MGZY* zÿun (平) [zyn]
[<] s-iterative of a root *win 'rotate' (§5.2.3). 'Rotate' as a metaphor for cyclical time like the 'ten day cycle, week' has parallels in TB languages, e.g. Lahu *qhɔ̀* 'return' > 'year' (Matisoff *D. of Lahu:* 310). For synonyms, see under → huí 回.
⪤ **xùn** 徇殉侚 (zjuenᶜ) **LH** zuinᶜ, **OCM** *s-wins
'Go everywhere, publish throughout' 徇 [Zuo]; 'devote oneself, wholly given up to' [Zhuang] > 'accompany in death' 殉 [Zuo], 侚 [QY].
[E] This wf could equally well belong to either ST *wir (→ yún5 雲) or PAA *wil, the two may have converged in China. PAA *wil seems on balance more likely given the field of meaning in OC and AA (incl. 'go everywhere, roam, patrol'), and the prehistoric Lóngshān culture origin of the pottery wheel in eastern China (AA?). AA-Khmer /vil/ 'to turn, revolve, rotate' ⪤ /kravil/ 'ring, circle, loop' ⪤ *kravēla* /krawaaɛl/ 'to revolve, go around, go to and fro, roam, patrol, explore' ⪤ *chvēla* /cwaaɛl/ 'to turn, spin, go back and forth, come and go'; Santali *gɛrwɛl* 'ring'. This root **wil is prob. connected with → wéi5 圍 *wel.
Jūn may possibly be the same word as → jūn1 均鈞 'well balanced'. For an overview of synonyms, see under → huí 回.

jūn3 君 (kjuən) **LH** kun, **OCM** *kun
'Ruler, lord, lady' [BI, Shi] > 'treat someone like a lord' tr., 'function as ruler' intr. [Shi]; *jūn-zǐ* 君子 'son of a ruler, gentleman' (A. Waley).
[T] *Sin Sukchu SR* kyn (平); *MGZY* gÿun (平) [kyn]; *ONW* kun
[E] Etymology not certain. Perh. related to MK: Mon *kmin, kmun* /kmøn/ 'to exercise royal power, be king, reign'. Mei Tsu-Lin suggest an alternative etymology, see → yuán1 元. Baxter / Sagart (1998: 47) suggest that *jūn* is a derivation by k-prefix from → yǐn1 尹 LH winᴮ 'straight, administer', but the rimes do not agree.

jūn4 軍 (kjuən) **LH** kun, **OCM** *kun — **[T]** *ONW* kun
'Troops, army' [Shi] > 'encampment' [Zuo].
[E] Etymology not clear. Perh. ST: WT *g-yul* 'army, battle' (Unger *Hao-ku* 35, 1986, 30); since *jūn* is in a *w-initial phonetic series, *k-* may be the nominalizing prefix (§5.4), note also the prefix *g-* in WT *g-yul;* regarding WT *y-* for CH and foreign *w-, see §12.9. Alternatively, *jūn* could be a derivation from → yùn2 運暈 'be on the move'; or be related to → qún 群.

jùn₁ 郡 (gjuən) **LH** gun, **OCM** *gun
'District' [Zuo].
[E] Perh. ST: WT *kʰul* 'district, province' (Gong 1995).

jùn₂ 麴 → **qūn** 麴

jùn₃ 濬浚 (sjuen^C) **LH** suin^C, **OCM** *suns
'Be deep' > 'profound, wise' 浚 [Shi] > caus. 'to deepen' 濬 [Shu] > 'to ladle out' [Zuo], 'dig out' 浚 [Meng]. Etymology not clear.

K

kā 喀 → **kè**$_4$ 喀

kǎ 咯 → **kè**$_4$ 喀

kāi 開闓 (kʰậi) **LH** kʰəi, **OCM** *khə̂i

'To open the way, open access to, set free' [Shi, Shu], 闓 (also read MC *kʰậi*^{B}) [Guan], replaced → qǐ$_6$ 啟 'to open' because this was the Hàn emperor Jǐng's personal name (157–150 BC). Kāi could be a col. variant of *qǐ* 闓 (§9.1.1).

[T] *Sin Sukchu SR* k'aj (平); *MGZY* khay (平) [k'aj]; *ONW* kʰɑi.

[E] MY: Yao *khai*^{1} (< *kh-) 'to open' tr. ⫘ *gai*^{1} (< *ŋkh-) 'to open' intr.: 'be happy, to blossom'; these are early Chinese loans acc. to Downer (1973: 14–16; Sagart 1999: 75). <> Tai: S. *kʰai*^{A1} 'to open'.

[C] The MY wf implies that **kǎi** (kʰậi^B) *khəiʔ 'joyous, happy' 豈 [Shi], 'pleasant' 凱 [Shi] is a cognate (< 'opened up emotionally').

kǎi 豈, 凱 → **kāi** 開

kài$_1$ 欬 → **ké**$_1$ 咳欬

kài$_2$ 愾 → **qì**$_8$ 氣

kān$_1$ 刊 → **kǎn**$_2$ 砍

kān$_2$ 堪 (kʰậm) **LH** kʰəm, **OCM** *khə̂m, OCB *khum

'To endure, equal to' [Shi].

[T] *Sin Sukchu SR* k'am (平), *PR* k'an; *MGZY* kham (平) [k'am]

[D] M-Xiamen *kʰam*^{A1}

[E] ST *kəm: WB *kʰaṁ*^{A} 'receive, endure' ⫘ *ə-kʰam*^{B} 'suitable appendage'; Mru *kʰam* 'to bear, sustain' (Burmese loan?), JP *kʰam*^{31} 'endure'. *Kān*$_2$ is unrelated to the homophone → kān$_4$ 戡.

This word is prob. a ST level derivation from → hán$_1$ 含函 'have in the mouth' as this notion is a common metaphor for emotions. The CH aspirated initial may indicate causative (§5.8.2).

kān$_3$ 嵁 (kʰăm, kʰậm) **LH** kʰɛm, **OCM** *khrə̂m

'Rocky' [Zhuang].

[E] AA: Khmer /krə́əm/ 'rocky', belongs to an AA wf which includes → chán$_2$ 漸.

kān$_4$ 戡 (kʰậm) **LH** kʰəm, **OCM** *khə̂m

'To kill, execute' 戡 [Shu].

[D] Mand. 'to suppress' (a rebellion); M-Xiamen *kʰam*^{A1} 'id.'

[E] ST *kum with the core meaning 'be above, be on, on top': Lushai *kʰum*^{F} adv. 'upon, on top of, inside, against, over...', vb. 'to put on, wear' ⫘ *kʰuum*^{F} vb. 'to surpass, excel, beat, over, beyond'; WT *'gum-pa, bkum* 'to kill' ⫘ *'gum-pa, gum* 'to die' (*STC:* 175 n. 464).

This word is prob. not related to → kǎn$_3$ 砍 'chop' (tree, wood). It is also distinct from the homophone → kān$_2$ 堪 'equal to' as shown by the TB cognates. A relationship with → tān$_2$ 貪 OCM *rhə̂m 'kill' is excluded because of the difference in initial consonants. CH aspiration is associated with forceful motion §5.8.5.

kān$_5$, **kàn** 勘 (k^hậm^C) **LH** k^həm^C, **OCM** *khə̂ms
'To inspect, investigate' [Yupian, GY].
[D] M-Amoy *$k^h am^C$* 'inspect'.
[E] Perh. related to **kàn** 矙 (k^hâm^C) 'to watch' [Meng], both could be variants of *jiān* 監 *krâm(s) 'to look at, inspect' (under → jiàn 監鑑).

kǎn$_1$ 坎埳 (k^hậm^B) **LH** k^həm^B, **OCM** *khə̂mʔ
'Pit' 坎 [OB, Yi]; 'walled-in well' 埳 [Zhuang], (pitted:) 'uneven, bumpy road' [Hanshu]. For the aspirated initial which marks hollow objects, see §5.8.6.
[D] Mand. 'a pit, hole, depression; a snare, danger'. M-Xiàmén *$hɪŋ^{55/33}$-$k^h am^{51}$* 胸坎 'chest, breast'.
[E] Prob. connected with PTai *$k^h um^{A1}$: S. *$k^h um^{A1}$* 'ditch, pit, walled-in well' (Unger *Hao-ku* 76, 2002: 72), possibly also with Tai *sum^{A1}* < *$k^h r$-?* (Li 1977: 197), Ahom *k^hrūm* 'well', which could suggest that 坎 and 埳 wrote two distinct words **khə̂m 'pit' and **khrə̂m 'well' respectively (the phonetic in 埳 writes words with an OC medial *r; and medial *-r-* may disappear in Tai, first in ordinary speech, later also in writing).
[C] Similar etyma are → qǐn$_1$ 坅, → tàn$_2$ 窞, → xiàn$_3$ 陷錎; they are here tentatively grouped according to connections which emerge in Table K-1. Syn. → kēng$_1$ 坑阬.

Table K-1 for kǎn$_1$ 坎埳 'pit'

	khəm	grəm	krum	khum	lum
OC	qǐn 坅 (k^hjəm^B, ŋjəm^B) *khəmʔ hole in the earth	xiàn 陷錎 *grə̂ms small pit (as a trap)		kǎn 坎 *khə̂mʔ pit kǎn 埳 *khə̂mʔ walled-in well	kǎn-tàn 坎窞 *khə̂mʔ-lə̂mʔ ? trap pit
TB	JP mǎ^{31}-$k^h am^{55}$ pit	WB gyam^B < gram^B a trap			Lushai hum^H pitfall
Tai			Ahom k^hrūm a well	PTai *$k^h um^{A1}$ ditch, pit, walled-in well	Tai hlum pit, ditch, cavity Saek lum^{A1} < l̥- pit, hole (as trap)

kǎn$_2$ 坎 'bank of fields' → **kàn**$_2$ 磡

kǎn$_3$ 砍 (k^hậm^B)
'To sound *kham-kham*', the sound of cutting wood' 坎 [Shi]; 'to chop' (wood, a tree), 'decapitate' 砍 (*ZWDCD* 6: 1275f), a late word [e.g. Shuǐhúzhuàn].
[D] PMin *$k^h am^B$ 砍 'to fell a tree, slash, chop'
cf. **kān**$_1$ 刊 (k^hân) **LH** k^hɑn, **OCM** *khân
'To cut down' (a tree) [Shu].
[E] Words with the meaning 'chop, hew, cut' tend to have the sound-symbolic shape *k^h_N;* aspiration is associated with forceful action (§5.8.5).
ST *kəm: TB-Chepang *k^hamh-* 'fell tree'. This is possibly an area word, note MK-Khmer *khtɔ̀əm* 'to split'. Prob. not related to → kān$_4$ 戡 whose ST root is *kum.

kǎn$_4$ 歁 → **kǎn**$_6$ 顑

kǎn$_5$ 厥 → **kàn**$_2$ 磡

kǎn$_6$ 顑 (k^{h}ậm^B, xậm^C) **LH** k^{h}əm^B, həm^C, **OCM** *khə̂m?, *hə̂ms
'Emaciated' [Chuci]. For aspiration, see §5.8.1.

= **kǎn** 歁 (k^{h}ậm^B) **LH** k^{h}əm^B, **OCM** *khə̂m?
'To eat and not be satisfied' [SW], a Han period southern Chǔ, Jiāng, Xiāng dialect word for → tān$_1$ 貪 'to desire' [FY].

[E] ST: WT *skom* 'thirst', *skom-pa* 'to thirst', *skam-po* 'dry', *skem-pa, bskams* 'to make dry', *rkam-pa* 'to desire, long for' (Bodman 1980: 60; *HST*). Bodman suggests also a possible connection with → yǐn$_3$ 飲 'drink', but see there. The MC reading *xậm^C* belongs perh. to a different etymon: WT *ham-pa* 'avarice, covetousness, greed'.

kàn$_1$ 看 (k^{h}ân^C) **LH** k^{h}an^C, **OCM** *khâns
'To look' [Hanfei].
[T] *Sin Sukchu SR* k'ɔn (去), *PR, LR* k'an; *MGZY* khan (去) [k'an]
[E] ST: WT *mk^{h}an-po* 'professor, abbot' (< 'one who knows').

kàn$_2$ 磡 (k^{h}ậm^C) **LH** k^{h}əm^C, **OCM** *khə̂ms
'Cliff, bank, step' [GY].
[D] M-Amoy *k^{h}am^{C1}* 'cliff, precipice'.

ж **kǎn** 厰 (k^{h}âm^B) **LH** k^{h}am^B, **OCM** *khâm?
'Precipitous' [SW] (also other readings).
[D] In Mand. and dialects the word means 'bank along fields' 坎; in M-Amoy *k^{h}am^B* 'step, stairs'.

ж **qīn** 嶔岑 (k^{h}jəm, ŋjəm^B) **LH** k^{h}ɨm, ŋɨm^B, **OCM** *k^{h}əm
'High river bank' 岑 [Zhuang]; 'precipitous' 嶔 [Gongyang] (also MC *ts^{h}jəm*),
[D] Mand. 'side of mountain, lofty'.

[E] ST: PTB *r-ka[:]m (*STC* no. 329): WB *k^{h}am^B* (arch.), *kam^B* 'bank of river'; Lushai *k^{h}aam^L* < *k^{h}aamh* (< *-s*) 'a precipice, cliff, be precipitous' ж *kam^H* 'bank, shore, mouth' (*STC:* 183 no. 482; *HST:* 121), JP *niŋ^{55}-gam^{51}* 'river bank' ж *n^{31}-gam^{31}* 'precipice', Garo *rikam* 'bank, rim'. Loss of a ST pre-initial could be responsible for aspiration (§5.8.1).

kàn$_3$ 矙 → **kān$_5$, kàn** 勘

kāng$_1$ 康 (k^{h}âŋ) **LH** k^{h}aŋ, **OCM** *khâŋ < *khlaŋ ?, OCB *khaŋ — [T] *ONW* k^{h}aŋ
'Be at ease, have peace of mind, be prosperous, healthy' [Shi].
[E] ST *klaŋ?: Lushai *tlaŋ^R* / *tlan^L* adv. 'peaceably, quietly, calmly', vb. 'be good, kindly, peaceably, mild, calm'.

kāng$_2$ 糠 (k^{h}âŋ) **LH** k^{h}aŋ, **OCM** *khâŋ < *khlaŋ ?
'Husk of grain' [Zhuang].
[E] ST *klaŋ?: WT: *gaŋ-bu, lgaŋ-bu* 'shell, husk', perh. also Lushai *k^{h}aaŋ^R* < *k^{h}aaŋ?* 'sheath round the knot of a bamboo'. This may be an area word: AN *le(ŋ)kaŋ* 'loosening of the outer skin' (Sagart *JCL* 21.1, 1993: 34).

kàng 囥 (k^{h}âŋ^C) **LH** k^{h}aŋ^C
[D] PMin *k^{h}ɔŋ^C 'to store'
[E] Tai: S. *k^{h}aŋ^{A1}* < *k^{h}l- 'hold water, confine' (Manomaivibool *CAAAL* 6, 1976: 15).

kǎo$_1$ 考 'examine' → **jiū$_1$** 究

kǎo$_2$ 考 'beat' → **kòu$_1$** 扣叩

kǎo$_3$ 薧槁 (k^{h}âu^B) **LH** k^{h}au^B, **OCM** *khâu?
'Dried fish' [Zhouli], 'dried food' 薧 [Li]; 'dried' (tree etc.) 槁 [Li].

⪤ **kào** 犒 (k^{h}âu^C) **LH** k^{h}ɑu^C, **OCM** *khâuh
'Give food as recompense to soldiers' (< 'give dried provisions'?) [Zuo].

⪤ **gǎo** 稿 (kâu^B) **LH** kɑu^B, **OCM** *kâuʔ
'Straw' 稿 [Zuo]; 'dry straw' (in mats) 藁 [Xun].
[D] PMin *gɔ^{B1} 'rice straw'.

kào 犒 → **kǎo$_3$** 藁槁

kē$_1$ 柯 (kâ) **LH** kɑi, **OCM** *kâi — **[T]** *ONW* kɑ
'Ax handle' [Shi].
= **gē** 舸 'Mooring post for a boat'.
⪤ **kě** 軻 (k^{h}â[$^{B/C}$]) **LH** k^{h}ɑi, **OCM** *khâi — **[T]** *ONW* k^{h}ɑ
'A pair of wheels upon an axle tree' [SW].
[E] This stem refers to a strong wooden post or such to secure something, and is therefore perh. related to → gàn$_1$ 幹 'stem, support', but distinct from → gān$_4$ 竿 'pole'.

kē$_2$, kě, kè 軻 → **kē$_1$** 柯

kē$_3$ 科 (k^{h}uâ) **LH** k^{h}uɑi, **OCM** *khwâi < **k-wai ?
'Class, degree' [Lunyu]
[E] Perhaps a k-prefix noun derived from → hé$_2$ 和 'harmonious' (§5.4), hence lit. 'the things which harmonize'.

kē$_4$ 科 'cavity' → **wā$_2$** 窪

ké$_1$ 咳欬 (—) **LH** k^{h}ək
[D] Mand. 'to cough'; M-Amoy lit. *k^{h}ek^{D1}*, 'sound of coughing'.
⪤ **kài** 欬 (k^{h}ậi^C [GY]) **LH** k^{h}ə^C, **OCM** *khə̂(k)h
'To cough' 咳 [Li], 欬 [Zuo], Mand. 'asthma and coughing'.
[E] These sound-symbolic items are derivable from an OC stem *khə̂k. CH aspiration is associated with forceful outward motion (§5.8.5).
Area word. Because OC *a and *ə both correspond to foreign /a/, it is impossible to sort out which CH form, 咳欬 or → kè$_4$ 喀, is the direct cognate of the foreign words: PTB *kaːk (*STC* no. 323) (or rather *khaːk ?) > Mikir *tśiŋ k^{h}ak* 'cough up, phlegm', Lushai *k^{h}aak^H* 'eject forcibly from the throat' ⪤ *k^{h}aak^R* 'phlegm', WT *k^{h}ogs* 'cough', WB *hak* 'to hawk, raise phlegm'; Sgaw Karen *kəhaʔ* 'phlegm'. <> Tai: S. *k^{h}aak^{D1}* 'to spit out', Saek *k^{h}aak^6* 'cough up phlegm'. In some lgs. like Karen and WB, the initial is analyzed as a cluster *k + h-*, as in AA (see under → kè$_4$ 喀).

ké$_2$ 殼 (k^{h}åk) **LH** k^{h}ɔk, **OCM** *khrôk
'Shell' [Hou Hanshu], 'hollow' [Lie], i.e. 'husk', 'shell' of egg, mussel, turtle.
[D] M-Xiàmén lit. *k^{h}ok^{D1}*, col. *k^{h}ak^{D1}*, Y-Guǎngzhōu *^{33}hɔk^D*. In some modern dialects *ké* is the second syllable in the word for 'head' → tóu$_3$ 頭.
[E] In sound and meaning, this item partially overlaps with → gǔ$_{12}$, zhuó 穛 *kûk 'husk'. It makes the impression of being derived from → jiǎo$_5$ 角 *krôk 'horn' by aspiration which characterizes hollow objects (§5.8.6).

kě$_1$ 可 → **hè$_1$** 何荷

kě$_2$ 渴 (k^{h}ât) **LH** k^{h}ɑt, **OCM** *khât, OCB *khat
'Be thirsty' 渴 [Shi]; 'thirst for' 𣵻 [Guoyu]. Acc. to commentators, 'to long for' [Zuo] should be read in tone C LH *k^{h}as* (Downer 1959: 284).
[E] For related and similar items, see → gù$_1$ 固 (incl. Table G-1) and → jiān$_2$ 堅 (incl. Table J-1). <> Shared with PMY *nqhât [Downer].

kè₁ 克 (kʰək) **LH** kʰək, **OCM** *khə̂k, OCB *khək
'Be capable, predominate, conquer, vanquish, able, can, be willing' [BI, Shi]. CH aspiration is associated with forceful motion §5.8.5 as well as auxiliary verbs §5.8.4.
[E] There are no compelling etymological connections; it is adduced here to show its semantic field which is paralleled in the wf → kān₂ 堪.

kè₂ 刻 (kʰək) **LH** kʰək, **OCM** *khə̂k
'To cut, injure' [Shu], 'engrave' [Zuo] > 'intense' [Guoce]. CH aspiration is associated with forceful motion §5.8.5. — Etymology not clear.
[T] *Sin Sukchu SR* k'əj (入); *MGZY* khʰiy (入) [k'əj]; *ONW* kʰək

kè₃ 客 (kʰɐk) **LH** kʰak, **OCM** *khrâk, OCB *khrak
'Guest, visitor, stranger' [Shi], 'opponent, enemy' [Sunzi].
[T] *Sin Sukchu SR* k'əj (入), *LR* k'əjʔ; *MGZY* khyay (入) [k'jaj]
[E] Prob. ST: WT *dgra* 'enemy' (*HPTB:* 173f). *Kè* prob. belongs to a larger group → gé₄ 格 'go, come'.

kè₄ 喀 (kʰɐk) **LH** kʰak, **OCM** *khrâk
'To spit out, vomit' [Lie]. Chinese aspiration is associated with forceful outward motion §5.8.5.
[D] Mand. *kā* 喀 'noise made in coughing or vomiting' ⋈ *kǎ* 咯 'cough up phlegm', M-Amoy *kʰak*^{D2} and *keʔ*^{D1} 'clear the throat' ⋈ *kʰak*^{D1} 'expectorate, bring up phlegm'.
[E] A variant of the onomatopoetic area word for 'cough' → ké₁ 咳欬 (see there for cognates). The MC form *kʰak* could have an irregular div. II vowel for an OC *a (not *-ra-), but considering PMV *krhaːk (< *k-haːk with r-infix) 'to spit, spittle' [Ferlus], it is prob. derived from OCM *khrâk. In this case, *kè* must be a substrate survival from a MK language: PMonic *kʰaak 'to kawk, clear the throat' [Diffloth 1984: 171]; PSBahn. *haːk ~ *hɔːk 'vomit'.
[C] Perh. this word is related to → luò₁ 咯.

kè₅ 恪 → **hè₅** 赫

kěn₁ 肯 (kʰəŋᴮ) **LH** kʰəŋᴮ, **OCM** *khə̂ŋʔ
'Be willing' [Shi].
[T] *Sin Sukchu SR* k'əjŋ (上), *PR*, *LR* k'ən; *MGZY* khʰing (上) [k'əŋ]
[D] PMin *kʰeŋᴮ which is the analog to MC *kʰəŋᴮ* and *kʰieŋᴮ*
[E] Etymology not clear. Auxiliary verbs tend to have aspirated initials (§5.8.4).

kěn₂ 懇狠 (kʰənᴮ) **LH** kʰənᴮ, **OCM** *khə̂nʔ
'Sincere' 狠 [Lüshi].
~**kǔn** 悃 (kʰuənᴮ) **LH** kʰuənᴮ, **OCM** *khûnʔ
'Sincere' [Chuci]. The original syllable was prob. OC / PCH *khwənʔ which would account for the loss of rounding in one word and merger with *-un in the other.

kěn₃ 齦 (kʰənᴮ) **LH** kʰənᴮ, **OCM** *khə̂nʔ
'To gnaw, nibble' [Post-Han].
[E] Perh. ST: Lushai *kʰel*^{F} 'eat the outside of a thing, gnaw off' (Unger *Hao-ku* 35, 1986: 31).

kēng₁ 坑阬 (kʰɐŋ) **LH** kʰaŋ, **OCM** *khrâŋ
'A pit (hole)' 阬 [Zhuang], 坑 [Chuci]. A syn. is → kǎn₁ 坎埳. Aspiration is associated with the meaning 'hollow, empty' §5.8.6.
[D] Mand. 'hole, pit; to entrap'; M-Xiàmén col. *kʰĩ*^{A1} 'a ravine'. *SW* says that **gēng**

埂 (kɐŋ) is a dialect variant in the state of Qín, acc. to *Yùpiān gēng* means 'a small *kēng*' (Wáng Lì 1982: 281).

kēng $_2$ 脛 (kʰɛŋ, ɣɛŋ) **LH** kʰɛŋ, **OCM** *khrêŋ
'Shank bone of ox' [SW].
⋇ **héng, jīng** 莖 (ɣɛŋ) **LH** gɛŋ, **OCM** *grêŋ
'Stalk' [Chuci].
[E] ST: PTB *r-k(l)aŋ > WT *rkaŋ* 'marrow, leg bones, stalk'; WB *kʰraŋ-chi* < *skraŋ* 'marrow' (chi 'oil, lymph') (*STC* no. 126). These etyma *kēng* and → xìng$_3$, jìng 脛 *gêŋh as well as → tǐng$_3$ 梃, dìng 鋌 *lêŋ tend to converge. For the *a* ~ *e* variation, see §11.1.3. See Table K-2 for an overview.

Table K-2 for kēng$_2$ 脛 'leg, shank, stalk, marrow'

Lg.	*keŋ	*kraŋ ~ *kreŋ	*kliŋ
OC	xìng, jìng 脛 *gêŋh leg, shank	kēng 脛 *kʰreŋ shank bone héng, jīng 莖 *greŋ stalk	tíng 莛筳 *lêŋ stalk, stem, bamboo rod
WT		rkaŋ marrow, thighbones rkaŋ-pa foot, leg, stalk	gliŋ-bu flute
LB			*kliŋ marrow, brain
-PL			*ʔliŋ^1 ~ *hliŋ^1 flute
-WB		kʰraŋ-chi marrow	kyañ tube kyañ^B stick
Mikir	keŋ^L foot, leg		arkleŋ < r-kle/iŋ marrow
Lushai			tʰliŋR < tʰliŋʔ marrow

kōng 空 (kʰuŋ) **LH** kʰoŋ, **OCM** *khôŋ, OCB *khoŋ
'Be hollow, empty' [Shi].
[T] *Sin Sukchu SR* k'uŋ (平); *MGZY* khung (平) [k'uŋ]; *ONW* kʰoŋ
[D] M-Amoy *kʰaŋ* 'hollow, empty, a hole'.
⋇ **kòng** 空 (kʰuŋ^C) **LH** kʰoŋ^C, **OCM** *khôŋh
'To exhaust' [Shi].
[<] Exoactive / caus. of *kōng* (§5.8.2).
⋇ **kǒng** 孔 (kʰuŋ^B) **LH** kʰoŋ^B, **OCM** *khôŋʔ
'Empty' 孔 [Lao]; 'hole' 空 [Zhouli].
[<] Prob. endoactive of *kōng*, 'hole', lit. 'that which is hollow, empty' (§4.5).
[E] ST: WT *kʰuŋ* 'hole, pit, cavity; hollow'; WB *kʰoŋ^B* (*HST:* 71) 'be hollow'; WB id. 'trough, canoe' either is the same word or has merged with 'empty' (→ guān$_3$ 棺 'coffin'). CH aspiration is associated with the meaning 'hollow, empty' §5.8.6.
[C] A derivation is perh. → qiāng$_2$ 椌 'hollow wooden instrument', see there for possible MK connections. → qiōng 穹 'vault, hole' is prob. unrelated.

kǒng $_1$ 孔 → **kōng** 空

kǒng $_2$ 恐 (kʰjwoŋ^B) **LH** kʰɨoŋ^B, **OCM** *khoŋʔ
'Be afraid, fear' [BI, Shi].
[T] *Sin Sukchu SR* k'juŋ (上), *PR*, *LR* k'uŋ; *MGZY* khÿung (上) [k'juŋ]; *ONW* kʰuoŋ
[E] ST: WT *'goŋ(s)-pa, bkoŋ* 'to despond, be in fear' (*HST:* 64).

[C] Cognates might be → qióng₁ 邛 'distressed'; → gōng₁₀ 恭龔 'to respect' (Karlgren 1949: 79); → xiōng₃ 兇 'to fear' (so Wáng Lì 1982: 379).

kōu 摳 (kʰəu, kʰju) **LH** kʰo, kʰɨo, **OCM** *kho
'To pull up' (a dress) [Li].
guì 撅 (kjwäiᶜ) **LH** kyas, **OCM** *kots
'To lift' (a dress) [Li].
[E] Perh. related to PTB *ku > WB *kʰuᴮ* 'take out or up and put in dish, gather'; Yakha *kʰu* 'lift up, raise'; Bahing *ku-to* 'bring up' (*HST:* 103). Syn. under → jiē₇ 揭.

kǒu 口 (kʰəuᴮ) **LH** kʰoᴮ, **OCM** *khôʔ, OCB *kh(r)oʔ
'Mouth, opening' [OB, Shi]. Aspiration is associated with the meaning 'hollow, empty' §5.8.6.
[T] *Sin Sukchu SR* k'əw (上); *MGZY* khʰiw (上) [k'əw]; *ONW* kʰou.
[E] ST: JP *kʰu³³* 'hole, hollow'; perh. Lushai *kuaᴸ* (*kɔᴸ*) < *kuaʔ/h* 'a hollow, cavity' ⪤ *kuaᴸ* / *kuakᶠ* 'to open up' (a path). The word has been connected with PTB *ka 'mouth, opening' (*STC* no. 470) whose direct Chinese cognate is → hù₁ 戶 'door', however.

kòu₁ 扣叩 (kʰəuᴮ/ᶜ) **LH** kʰoᴮ/ᶜ, **OCM** *khôʔ/h
'To strike, attack' 叩 [[Lunyu].
⪤ **kòu** 釦敂 (kʰəuᴮ) **LH** kʰoᴮ, **OCM** *khôʔ
'To beat' 敂 [Zhouli], 'beat on some metal object, make noise' 釦 [Guoyu].
⪤ **kǔn** 捆 (kʰuənᴮ) **LH** kʰuənᴮ, **OCM** *khûnʔ
'To beat, pound' [Meng].
[E] Prob. area word. ST: WB *kʰok* < *kʰuk* 'knock, rap' (*HST:* 142). <> MK: Khmer *goḥ* /kóh/ 'to strike, hit, beat, knock' (also used in sense of striking a gong). CH aspiration is associated with forceful motion §5.8.5.
[C] Perh. cognate to → kòu₂ 寇 'rob'. Wáng Lì 1982: 185 adds to this wf: **kǎo** 考 (kâuᴮ) 'to beat' (instrument) [Shi], et al.

kòu₂ 寇 (kʰəuᶜ) **LH** kʰoᶜ, **OCM** *khôh
'To rob, robber' [Shi], 'invader, bandit' [Zuo]. This is perh. cognate to → kòu₁ 扣叩.
[E] ST: PTB *r-kuw (*STC* no. 33) > Chepang *kuʔ* 'steal', Nocte *huʔ* [Weidert 1987: 26], WT *rku-ba* 'to steal' ⪤ *rkun-ma* 'thief'; Bahing *ku*, JP *lə³¹-ku⁵⁵* 'to steal', NNaga *C/V-kə:w [French 1983: 332], WB *kʰuiᴮ* < *C-kuiᴮ*, PL *ko² 'to steal' (*HST:* 126). Loss of a ST pre-initial could be responsible for aspiration §5.8.1.

kòu₃ 鷇 'nestling' → **gǔ₁₄** 穀

kū₁ 枯 (kʰuo) **LH** kʰɑ, **OCM** *khâ
'Withered, dried' [Yi, Li].
[E] PMK: Khmer /khah/ 'to dry up or out, dry until hard, wither'.
⪤ **jū** 腒 (kjwo) **LH** kɨɑ, **OCM** *ka
'Dried meat of birds' [Li].
[E] For related and similar items, see → gù₁ 固 (incl. Table G-1) and → jiān₂ 堅 (incl. Table J-1).

kū₂ 刳 (kʰuo) **LH** kʰuɑ, **OCM** *khwâ
'Cut open, cut to pieces' [Yi]. CH aspiration is associated with forceful motion §5.8.5.
⪤ **huá** 華 (ɣwa) **LH** ɣuɑ, **OCM** *wrâ ? — [T] *ONW* ɣuä
'To cleave' [Li].

kū₃ 哭 (k^huk) **LH** k^hok, **OCM** *khôk
'To lament, weep' [Zuo].
[E] Area word. ST: Lushai *kuuk*^{H} 'shriek' (*STC:* 182 n. 479). <> PMK *kuuk 'to call (out to)' (Shorto 1976: 1064). <> AN *kuk* 'sound of sob' (Sagart *JCL* 21.1, 1993: 41). On aspiration, see §5.8.5.

kū₄ 堀窟 (k^huət) **LH** k^huət, **OCM** *khût
'Dig in the ground, underground' 堀 [Zuo]; 'cave, hole' 窟 [Zuo]. On aspiration of words with the meaning 'hollow, empty', see §5.8.6.
[E] Shared with Tai: S. *k*^{h}*ut*^{D1S}, Saek *k*^{h}*ut*^{6} < *k*^{h}*uut* 'to dig'.

⋈ **hú** 搰 (ɣuət) **LH** guət, **OCM** *gût
'To dig out' [Guoyu].

⋈ **jué** 掘 (gjuət, gjwɐt) **LH** gut, **OCM** *gut
'Dig out, dig through' (earth) [Shi]. The MC reading *gjwɐt* may have been transferred from the syn. → jué₉ 撅闕 with which it may be related.
[D] PMin *guit

kū₅ 朏 (k^huət) **LH** k^huət, **OCM** *khût
'Anus, buttocks' [Han: Yáng Xióng].
[E] ST: WT *rkub* 'buttocks', WB *lañ-kup.* CH *-t may be the result of labial dissimilation. (MK-Khmer *kù:t* n. 'bottom, behind' (anat.) is a Skt. loan and unrelated).

kǔ 苦 (k^huo^B) **LH** k^hɑ^B, **OCM** *khâʔ, OCB *khaʔ
'Be bitter' > 'distress, hardship' (of labor) [Shi], (of illness) [Zhuang].
[T] *Sin Sukchu SR* k'u (上); *MGZY* khu (上) [k'u]; *ONW* k^ho
[D] PMin *k^ho^B

⋈ **kù** 苦 (k^huo^C) **LH** k^hɑ^C, **OCM** *khâh
'Be difficult, hardship' [GY].

[E] ST *k(h)aʔ > PTB: *kaʔ (*STC* no. 8): PL *ka²; WB *kha*^{B} 'bitter' ⋈ *khak* 'difficult, hard'; WT *k*^{h}*a-ba* 'bitter' ⋈ *dka-ba* 'difficult' ⋈ *k*^{h}*ag-po* 'difficult' (*HST:* 44); Lushai *k*^{h}*a*^{L} / *k*^{h}*aak*^{F} 'be bitter' ⋈ *k*^{h}*aak*^{F} 'make bitter', Garo *kaʔ* 'bitter' [Joseph / Burling, *LTBA* 24.2, 2001: 42], NNaga *C-kha^B 'bitter' [French 1983: 296], JP *k*^{h}*a*^{55} 'bitter'.
[C] → gān₅ 肝 may be a derivation. Boltz (*OE* 35, 1992: 36ff) relates *kǔ* to → gǔ₁ 古 'old'.

kù₁ 庫 (k^huo^C) **LH** k^hɑ^C, **OCM** *khâh
'Arsenal, magazine' [Meng, Zuo] is cognate to → chē₀ 車 'carriage' acc. to Karlgren (1956: 14) (< 'storehouse for carriages').

kù₂ 苦 → **kǔ** 苦

kù₃ 褲 → **kuà** 跨

kuā₁ 荂 → **huā** 花

kuā₂ 誇 (k^hwa) **LH** k^hua, **OCM** *khwrâ
'To be boastful' [Shi].
[E] ST: WB: *krwa*^{B} 'be vain, boastful'.

kuà 跨 (k^hwa^C) **LH** k^hua^C, **OCM** *khwrâh
'To step over, pass over' [Zuo]. Wáng Lì (1982: 107) relates *kuà* to → kuǐ 跬.

⋈ **kù** 褲 (k^huo^C) **LH** k^huɑ^C, **OCM** *khwâh
'Trousers' [Mo, Li].

[E] ST *kwar ?: WB k^hwa^C 'be forked, branch' ⋈ ə-k^hra^C 'crotch, branching' ⋈ k^hwa 'separate, part, peel off', Lushai *kaar*^{F} < *kaarʔ* 'to step, pace, stride', WT *gar* 'dance'. There might have been a ST *-wa(r) ~ *-wai variation, see → kuǐ 跬 because both OC and WB have these doublets. For the OC medial *r in *kuà*, see §7.7.3.

kuài₁ 快 (k^hwai^C) **LH** k^huai^C, **OCM** *k^hwrêts
'Cheerful, happy' [Meng], 'satisfied' [Zuo]. — Etymology not clear.
[T] *Sin S. SR* k'waj (去); *MGZY* khway (去) [k'waj]; *ONW* k^huëi

kuài₂-zi 筷子 'chopsticks', → **zhù₁₄** 箸

kuài₃ 澮 → **jǔ₅** 柜

kuài₄ 塊 (k^huậi^C, k^huăi^C) **LH** k^huəih or k^huaih ?, OCM *khrûih ?
'Clod' [Zuo], 'lump' [Zhuang]. — Etymology not clear.
[T] *Sin S. SR* k'waj, k'uj (去), *LR* k'waj; *MGZY* khue (去) [k'uɛ]

kuān 寬 (k^huân) **LH** k^huɑn, **OCM** *khwân or *khôn, OCB *k^whan
'Be vast, large-minded, generous' [Shi] > 'relieve, enjoy ease' [Zuo].
[T] *Sin Sukchu SR* k'wɔn (平); *MGZY* khon (平) [k'ɔn]
[E] Perh. cognate to WT *k^hyon* 'size, extension, width...' if we assume that a root initial *w was treated in WT like an absolute initial (w- > / > y-).

⋈ **kuò** 闊 (k^huât) **LH** k^huɑt, **OCM** *khôt, OCB *khot
'Be far apart' [Shi].
[T] *Sin Sukchu SR* k'wɔ (入); *MGZY* khwo (入) [k'wɔ]

⋈ **qiè-kuò** 契闊 (k^hiat-k^huât) **LH** k^het-k^hot, **OCM** *khêt-khôt
'Be far apart' (of persons in life and death) [Shi].
[E] CH aspiration is associated with the meaning 'hollow, empty' §5.8.6.
[C] Baxter / Sagart (1998: 60) relate this wf to → guǎng₂ 廣 'wide', perh. ultimately related to the root *wa under → kuàng₁ 況.

kuǎn 窾 (k^huân^B) **LH** k^huɑn^B, **OCM** *khwânʔ or *khônʔ
'Hole' (as an opening in the flesh, between organs of a carcass) [Zhuang], 'to hollow out' (a piece of wood to make a box) [Hanshu]. Aspiration is associated with the meaning 'hollow, empty' §5.8.6.
[E] ST: PTB *kwar 'hole' (*STC* no. 350) > Lushai *k^hur*^{H} 'a hole, pit, cavity' ⋈ *k^huar*^{H} id., Tangkhul Naga *k^hur* 'hole'. This is cognate to → guàn₃ 貫 'pierce'.

kuāng₁ 匡 'crooked' → **yū₁** 迂紆

kuāng₂ 恇 → **jù₅** 懼

kuāng₃ 眶 → **qú₄**, **jù** 臞

kuāng₄ 筐 (k^hjwaŋ) **LH** k^hyɑŋ, **OCM** *khwaŋ, OCB *k^whjaŋ
'Square basket' > vb. 'put into a square basket' [Shi]; 'get boxed in' (in a military maneuver) [BI]; *kuāng-chuáng* 筐床 'bed' (which is rectangular) [Zhuang] (*chuáng* 'bed'). From the *Yìjīng* 54 line 女承筐無實 *nǚ chéng kuāng wú shí* 'the woman holds a basket, it has no fruit' (implying she is barren) derives the euphemism *chéng-kuāng* 'vagina' (Shaughnessy *JAS* 51.3, 1992: 591); this is perh. also the connotation in *Shījīng* 161.1.
[E] A final *-ŋ* derivation from the stem under → jǔ₃ 矩 'square' (§6.5.2). Alternatively, Baxter / Sagart (1998: 48) derive this word with k-prefix (§5.4) from → fāng₁ 方 'square'. If true, loss of a post-initial consonant could explain the aspiration.

kuáng 狂 (gjwaŋ) **LH** gyɑŋ^{C}, **OCM** *gwaŋ, OCB *g^{w}jaŋ
'Be foolish, crazy' [Shi]. The graph was apparently designed for 'mad dog disease, rabies'. — The etymology is not clear; possibly connected with → jiǒng$_3$ 憬.

kuàng$_1$ 況 (xjwaŋ^{C}) **LH** hyɑŋ^{C}, **OCM** *hwaŋh
'To increase, increasingly, how much the more, moreover' [Shi].
[T] *Sin Sukchu SR* xwaŋ (去), *PR* xyaŋ; *MGZY* (Hwyang >) hwyang (去) [xyaŋ].
[<] Perh. derived from *yú* below with devoicing of the initial consonant (§5.2.2), addition of *-ŋ* (§6.5.1) and tone C (§4.3), but the meanings of these elements, especially their cumulative effect, are not clear.

ⅹ **yú** 于 (ju) **LH** wɑ, **OCM** *wa — **[T]** *MTang* y < uo, *ONW* uo
'To enlarge, increase' [Shu; Li].

ⅹ **jù** 巨距 (gjwo^{B}) **LH** gɨɑʔ or gyɑʔ ?, **OCM** *gwaʔ ?
'Great' 巨 [Meng]; 'distant from' [Guoyu], 'keep at a distance' 距 [Meng]. We should expect MC *gju* which is implied by the phonetic *jù* 巨 and the cognates, but the MC rimes *-ju* ~ *-jwo* have merged in almost all modern dialects and have already been confused in some phonetic series.

[E] ST *wa 'large, wide, distant': TB-Lushai *vak^{H}* 'with force, very hard / much, exceedingly, in large numbers / quantities, (open mouth) wide'.
[C] Possibly → kuān 寬 and → guǎng$_2$ 廣 belong also to this root *wa.

kuàng$_2$ 曠 'bright' → **guāng$_1$** 光

kuàng$_3$ 曠 'desolate' → **guǎng$_2$** 廣

kuī$_1$ 刲 (k^{h}iwei) **LH** k^{h}ue, **OCM** *khwê
'To stab, slaughter' [Yi].
[D] The graph is read *ua^{A1}* in Jiāng-Huái Mand. 'stab something with a knife, slaughter'.

kuī$_2$ 巋 (k^{h}jwi[^{B}] 3) **LH** k^{h}uɨ(ʔ), **OCM** *khruiʔ / -əiʔ ?
'Isolated, alone' as a lone peak [Zhuang].
[E] Bodman (1980: 62) compared this word to WT *'k^{h}yur* 'be separated, divorced'.

kuí$_1$ 奎 → **kuǐ** 跬

kuí$_2$ 頯馗 (gjwi 3) **LH** guɨ, **OCM** *gwrə, OCB *g^{w}rju — **[T]** *ONW* gui
'Cheekbone, bones of the face' 馗 [Yi], 頯 [Zheng Xuan: Yi].
[E] Perh. related to Lepcha *tă-gryu* 'cheek' (Bodman 1980: 167).

kuí$_3$ 夔 (gjwi 3) **LH** guɨ, **OCM** *grui or *gwrə ?
A large mythical animal of various descriptions, with one foot [Guoyu], in one version 'as strong as an ox' 夔 [Shanhaijing], 'a large buffalo' in the mountains of Shǔ (Sìchuān) 犪 [Shanhaijing].
[E] Area word. Chinese *kuí* 夔 is a loan from a KT source: PTai *ɣwai^{A} 'buffalo' (Mei Tsu-Lin, AAS paper 1980); Sui *kwi^{A2}* < *gwi^{A}* 'buffalo' (Hansell 1988: 269). Note also PAN *kəbaw (Dempwolff), Tagalog *kalabao*, Malay *kĕrbao*, Fiji *karavau* (Benedict AT: 45; Mahdi 1994: 200).

ⅹ **wéi** 犩 (ŋjwi 3) **LH** ŋuɨ
'Wild buffalo' [Erya, Yupian]. This is not a pre-Han word.
[E] This is ultimately the same etymon as *kuí*, but the source might have been a TB language: PTB *lwaay 'buffalo', JP *ʔu^{33}-loi^{33}*, *ŋa^{33}-loi^{33}* (*ŋa^{33}* 'bovine'), WB *kywai* < *klway* (*STC* no. 208; Matisoff 1974 no. 262).

kuǐ 跬 (k^hjwei^B) **LH** k^hye^B, **OCM** *khweʔ

'A stride, distance covered by lifting one leg' (as opposed to → bù₄ 步 'stride of two legs) [Li].

⋈ **kuí** 奎 (k^hiwei) **LH** k^hwe, **OCM** *khwê

'Crotch of a man's leg' [Zhuang] (Karlgren 1956: 16).

[E] ST: WB *kwai^B* 'be divided, split, parted' ⋈ *k^hwai^B* 'divide, split', JP *gai^31-gai^31* 'walk with legs spread wide'. There might have been a *-wa ~ *-wai variation already on the ST level (see → kuà 跨) because both OC and WB have these doublets.

[C] This etymon may be related to → qīng₄ 傾頃 'slanting', both are connected at least in the minds of those writers who borrowed 頃 for *kuǐ* [Liji]. Wáng Lì (1982: 107) relates → kuà 跨 (k^hua^C) 'to step over, pass over' to this word family.

kuì₁ 匱 ($gjwi^C$ 3) **LH** gwɨs, **OCM** *grus ?, OCB *grjuts

'A box, coffer' [Shu]. Perhaps related to

⋈ **guǐ** 匭 ($kjwi^B$ 3) **LH** $kwɨə^B$, **OCM** *kwəʔ

'Box, chest' [Shu].

kuì₂ 餽饋 ($gjwi^C$ 3) **LH** guɨs (饋) or $guɨ^C$ (餽) ?, **OCM** *gruih

'Food' 饋 [Shi], 'to eat' [Huainanzi] > caus. 'to present food' 餽饋 [Meng].

[E] This word looks like a cognate of → yí₁₂ 遺 (jiwi 4) 'hand down, present'. However, one would expect a MC div. 4 final, not the div. 3 final which is confirmed by Mand. *kuì* (we would expect Mand. *ji* or *qi* in div. 4 syllables of this type). Also, the meanings 'food' and 'present' suggest different etyma, the meaning 'to present' for both is an accidental convergence.

kūn₁ 昆 (kuən) **LH** kuən, **OCM** *kûn, OCB *kun — **[T]** *ONW* kon

'Elder brother' [Shi].

[E] Etymology is not clear. *STC:* 158 n. 428 relates *kūn* to the same PTB root *kəw 'maternal uncle' to which belongs → jiù₂ 舅. Alternatively, note MK-MMon *ko²* / ko/ 'elder brother', CH could have added the nominal *-n* (§6.4.3).

kūn₂ 昆 (kuən) **LH** kuən, **OCM** *kûn

'Sons and grandsons, descendants' [EY, Chuci, Shiming].

[E] Perh. from the AA word for 'child': Mon *kon* 'child', PSBahn. *kɔ:n*, PNBahn. *kon 'child', Khmer dial. *kūna* /kóon/. The Southern word → jiǎn₁ 囝 is prob. a loan from PVM *kɔ:n.

kūn₃ 昆 'numerous' → **qún₀** 群

kǔn₁ 悃 a variant of → **kěn₂** 懇狠

kǔn₂ 梱 → **kùn₁** 困

kǔn₃ 捆 → **kòu₁** 扣叩

kǔn₄ 稇 → **gǔn₁** 緄

kùn₁ 困 ($k^huən^C$) **LH** $k^huən^C$, **OCM** *khûns — **[T]** *ONW* k^hon

'To obstruct' [Yi].

⋈ **kǔn** 梱 ($k^huən^B$) **LH** $k^huən^B$, **OCM** *khûnʔ

'Threshold' [Li].

[<] *Kǔn* could be an endoactive derivation from *kùn*, lit. 'the thing that obstructs' (§4.5.1); or conversely, *kùn* could be an exoactive derivation from *kǔn*, lit. 'to serve as an obstruction' (§4.3.2).

kùn$_2$ 困睏 → **hùn**$_1$ 混渾

kuō 擴 → **guǎng**$_2$ 廣

kuò$_1$ 括 (kuât) **LH** kuɑt, **OCM** *kwât or *kôt, OCB *gʷat
'Bring together' [Shi], 'to tie, bind' [Yi].
[E] ST: Lushai *kuaʔ*^{L} < *kuas* 'put arm(s) around' (tree, neck, waist, etc.). CH *-t* occasionally corresponds to TB final -s, see §3.4.

ᛯ **huó** 佸 (ɣuât, kuât) **LH** guɑt, kuɑt, **OCM** *gwât, *kwât or *gôt, *kôt
'To unite, join' [Shi] (i.e. two people coming together).
[<] endopass. of *kuò* above (§4.6).

[C] Allofam → huì$_1$ 會.

kuò$_2$ 栝 → **jǔ**$_3$ 矩

kuò$_3$ 闊 → **kuān** 寬

kuò$_4$ 鞹 (kʰwâk) **LH** kʰuɑk, **OCM** *khwâk
'Leather' [Shi].

ᛯ **guō** 郭 (kwâk) **LH** kuɑk, **OCM** *kwâk — **[T]** *ONW* kuɑk
'Outer wall of city' [Zuo] is perhaps related to *kuò*.

[E] ST: PTB *(r-)kwâk (*STC:* 74): Jiarong *werkʰwak* 'its skin'; Chaurasya *kwak-te* ~ *kok-te* 'skin' (*HST:* 134); WT *ko-ba* 'a hide, skin'. → gǔ$_{12}$, zhuó 穛 *kûk 'husk' is a somewhat similar word. See also *HPTB:* 379.

L

là$_1$ 剌 (lât) **LH** lɑt, **OCM** *rât

'To cut, hurt' [SW].

[E] ST: PTB *(g-)ra-t ⋈ *(g-)rya-t > WT *dra-ba* 'cut, clip, lop, dress, prune, pare', Lepcha *hra* 'cut', Nung *rat* 'sever', WB *hra*^{C} 'wound, slightly cut', Garo *ra* ~ *rat* 'cut, reap' (LaPolla 1994: 166). Prob. related to → liè$_1$ 列.

là$_2$ 辣 (lât) — **[D]** Mǐn: Amoy *loáh* [loaʔ^{D2}], lit. *loát* 'pungent'.

'Hot, spicy', a late word which seems to have a Tai counterpart: Saek *thaat* < *d-* 'peppers, spicy, hot', Poai *šaat*^{D2L} < *ǰ-*, 'hot, peppery', Dioi (Yay) *śat*^{I} (< *b-lat^{I}) [Maspero 1912: 87].

là$_3$ 臘 (lâp) **LH** lɑp, **OCM** *râp — **[T]** *Sin Sukchu SR* la (入); *ONW* lɑp

'Year-end sacrifice' to the spirits of the dead and the household, performed in the 12th (last) month' [BI; Zuo, year 655 BC] (Bodde 1975: 49).

[E] Zhèng Xuán comments that "*là* is a designation for the sacrifice made of animals which have been caught in a hunt *liè* 獵 (ljap)" [Shi] (Bodde ibid. 57), thus considering *là* and *liè* cognates. Boltz (*JAOS* 99, 1979: 429) relates *là* to a much later word written with the same phonetic 'to cut off, terminate' (i.e. a year) [GY].

There is a ST alternative. The wf → yè$_4$ 葉 *lap encompasses the meanings 'leaf > foliage > year > generation'. The present root *râp 'new year / change of year' seems to be a parallel etymon which also has a WT cognate *rabs* 'generation', Mikir *rap*, Rawang *rəp* 'family' [Bodman 1980: 86].

là$_4$ 蠟 (lâp)

'Wax, candle' [GY].

[E] ST: Maru *rap* 'lac insect', Nung *k'ə-rap* 'wax', WB *k*^{h}*rip* 'lac'. Viet. *sáp* 'wax' belongs to those few words which have SV *s-* (< *kr-*) for MC *l-* [Maspero 1912: 80].

lái$_1$ 來 (lậi) **LH** lə, **OCM** *rə̂k/ʔ > *rə̂, OCB *C-rə(k)

'To come' [OB, Shi].

[T] *Sin Sukchu SR* laj (平), *LR* laj; *MGZY* lay (平) [laj]; *ONW* lɑi

[N] Rimes in the oldest parts of *Shījīng* (*Dàyǎ* and *Xiǎoyǎ*) indicate a final *-k or *-ʔ for this word, but in the later *Guófēng* sections the rimes indicate an open syllable (Baxter 1992: 337).

[E] ST *rə: Kanauri *ra* 'to come', Kuki-Chin *ra: Tangkhul *ra*, 'come', Lai *raa / rat* 'to come', PLB *ra^3 'win, overcome', WB *ra*^{C}, Lahu *ǧa* 'get, obtain'; with TB final *-k: Meithei *lak*, Dulong *lǎk* (Matisoff 1995a: 49f). The range of meanings in TB (come > arrive > succeed > overcome > strength, power [Matisoff *D. of Lahu*: 1113]) connect *lái* etymologically with → lì$_1$ 力 'strength'. The ST level had apparently already doublets *lə (→ dài$_4$ 迨) ~ *rə 'arrive'.

⋈ **lài** 賚 (lậi^C) **LH** lə^C, **OCM** *rə̂(k)h

('Let come':) 'to present, reward' [Shi] (Baxter 1992: 338); 'stimulate' 勑 [SW].

[<] exoactive of *lái* 來 *rə (§4.3).

⋈ **lì** 涖 (lji^C) **LH** lɨs, **OCM** *rə(t)s

'To arrive' [Shi].

[<] *lái* 來 with final *t* or *s* (§6.3).

⋇ Perh. **lì** 戾 (liei^C) **LH** les, **OCM** *rê(t)s
'To arrive, reach, settle' [BI, Shi], a Han period Chŭ dialect word [FY 1.13].

lái₂ 來 'wheat' → **mài₄** 麥

lái₃ 鯠 (lậi) **LH** lə > lɑi
'A kind of eel' [EY, GY] is shared with Tai: S. *lai^A1* (WrSiam *hlai*) 'id.' (Manomaivibool 1975: 140).

lài₁ 瀨 (lâi^C) **LH** lɑs, **OCM** *râ(t)s
'Rapids, swift current' [Chuci; Shiji].
[D] All text occurrences of this word relate to southern China and specifically the Mǐn area (ancient Dōng Yuè 東越). It is an ancient Wú-Yuè dialect word acc. to Chén Zàn's commentary on *Hànshū*, it is still used in Mǐn dialects: PMin *l̥ɑi^C > Fúzhōu *lai^C1*, Xiàmén *lua^C2*, Jiàn'ōu *suɛ^C2* (Norman 1983: 207).
[E] ? AA: Wa-Lawa-Bulang *rah 'rapids, waterfall'. Perh. derived from an AA root 'swift', note OKhmer *rat* /rɔt/ 'to move swiftly, run'. <> PTai *hlaai^B1 'rapids in a river' [Luo Yongxian *MKS* 27, 1997: 292] is identical to the PMin form. Prob. unrelated to → lì₁₉ 厲 'a ford'.

lài₂ 賚 → **lái₁** 來

lán₁ 啉 (lậm) 'To drink' [GY, JY] is a Tang period and modern southern dialect word: M-Amoy lit. *lam^A2* 'to drink'. This is prob. the same etymon as → lín₆ □ 'drink'.

lán₂ 惏 'kill' → **tān₂** 貪

lán₃ 婪惏 'covet' → **tān₁** 貪

lán₄ 嵐 (lậm) *ONW* lɑm
'Baleful wind, wind from the mountains' was transcribing an Indic syllable in the word *vairambha*, *veramba* 'hostile wind' (Hé Yǎnán, *ZGYW* 1999.4: 317), or a Turkic word (Chén Xiùlán *ZGYW* 1999.4: 319); the 風 'wind' element was selected for semantic reasons and is not necessarily the phonetic element.

lán₅ 藍 (lâm) **LH** lɑm, **OCM** *g-râm, OCB *g-ram — **[T]** *ONW* lɑm
'Indigo' [Shi].
[E] Area word whose source may have been SE Asia: PAN *taɣum 'indigo' (Benedict *AT*: 112; *STC:* 155 n. 420, 421); PTai *gram^A2 'indigo' (Li F. 1976: 45) would be a backloan from OC (Egerod *CAAAL* 6, 1976: 56). WT *rams* 'indigo' is a CH loan (Laufer *TP* 17, 1916: 503). This word occurs also in other TB languages, note Mru *charam* 'indigo' (Löffler 1966: 140). Alternatively, Xie Caide (*YWYJ* 1999.10: 124) suggests that WT *ram(-pa)* 'quick grass' may be cognate to CH.

lán₆ 籃 (lâm) **LH** lɑm, **OCM** *g-râm, OCB *g-ram
'Basket' [GY], the Northern Mǐn initial *s-* as in Jiàn'ōu *saŋ^C1* may be due to loss of a pre-initial (Mei / Norman 1971: 99).

lán₇ 蘭 (lân) **LH** lɑn, **OCM** *g-rân, OCB *g-ran — **[T]** *ONW* lɑn
'Chinese thoroughwort' (*Eupatorium chinense*) or other plants [Shi] which had sexual significance [Zuo] and was used for perfuming bath water [Chuci] (Bodde 1975: 275; Eberhard 1968: 136); Mand. *lán-huā* 蘭花.

⋇ **jiān** 蕳 (kan) **LH** kan, **OCM** *krân
'Orchid' [Shi 95.1], a variant of the above, if not a copying error for it (Baxter 1992:

363); the same or a similar graph (written with the phonetic 閒 or 閑) also writes a variant of → lián$_4$ 蓮 'lotus seed'.

lán$_8$ 瀾 (lân) **LH** lɑn, **OCM** *g-rân
'Big wave' [Meng].
[E] Huáng Jīnguì, Shěn Xíróng (*YYWZX* 1987.8: 45) suggest that → làng 浪 is a colloquial variant. This word is phonetically too distant from Tai to be related to S. *kʰlɨɨn*^{B2} (WrSiam *glɨ:n*).

lán$_9$ 闌欄 'barrier' → **xián$_6$** 閑

lán$_{10}$ 韊 → **jiān$_{10}$** 鞬

lǎn$_1$ 懶 (lân^B) — [T] *ONW* lɑn^B — [D] PMin *diɑn^B.
'Lazy' [GY] is perh. a late popular variant of → xián$_5$ 閑閒 'leisure'.

lǎn$_2$ 濫 'join, unite' → **xián$_3$** 咸

lǎn$_3$ 覽 → **jiàn$_{15}$** 監鑑

lǎn$_4$ 攬 → **liǎn$_1$** 斂

làn$_1$ 濫 (lâm^C) **LH** lɑm^C, **OCM** *g-râms
'Overflow' [Meng], Mand. also 'flood' > 'go to excess' [Shi] > 'err' [Zuo], 'put something into water' [Guoyu], 'juicy' [Li]; also 爁 'excess, licentious' [SW: Lunyu].
⪤ **hàn** 鑑 (ɣam^C) **LH** gam^C, **OCM** *grâms
'Big bowl, basin' [Zhouli].
⪤ **hàn** 濫 (ɣâm^C) **LH** gɑm^C, **OCM** *gâms ?
'Bathtub' [Zhuang], probably an *r-less variant of *hàn* 鑑 (ɣam^C) above.
This wf is perh. connected with → lín$_3$ 淋霖 and words under → chén$_2$ 沈.

làn$_2$ 嚂 → **tān$_1$** 貪

láng$_1$ 郎 (lâŋ) **LH** lɑŋ, **OCM** *râŋ < *C-raŋ
'Veranda or corridor' (of a palace or mansion) [Hanfei] (later written 廊) > transferred to a person doing duty there, an official's title [Zhànguó and esp. Qín-Hàn] > 'young man' (term of respect) > 'husband' (Yú Lǐmíng *ZGYW* 1999.6: 445).
[T] *Sin Sukchu SR* laŋ (平); *MGZY* lang (平) [laŋ]; *ONW* lɑŋ
[D] The Northern Mǐn initial *s-* as in Jiànyáng *sɔŋ*^{A2} may be the trace of a pre-initial; the *SW* connects words with this phonetic with initial *m-* (Mei / Norman 1971: 99).
[E] PLB *laŋ^2 > WB *laŋ*^{B} 'husband' (Matisoff 1995a: 51) may be a CH loan.

láng$_2$ 廊 → **láng$_1$** 郎

láng$_3$ 筤 (lâŋ) **LH** lɑŋ, **OCM** *râŋ < *C-raŋ
'Bamboo shoot' [Yi].
[E] Tai: Po'ai *laaŋ*^{A2} < *nl/raŋ 'bamboo shoot' (*HCT*: 132) or < *raŋ (*HCT*: 142).

lǎng 朗 (lâŋ^B) **LH** lɑŋ^B, **OCM** *râŋʔ — [T] *ONW* lɑŋ
'Bright, brilliance' [Shi].
[E] Area etymon: Khmer *raṅa* /rɔɔŋ/ 'be light, bright, become clear, clarify...'; OMon *'arån* /ərɔŋ/ 'to glitter'. <> WB *roŋ* 'brightness' ⪤ *ə-roŋ* 'appearance, color, luster'. Perh. related to → liàng 亮.

làng 浪 (lâŋ^C) **LH** lɑŋ^C
[T] *Sin Sukchu SR* laŋ (去); *MGZY* lang (去) [laŋ]; *ONW* lɑŋ
[N] The basic meaning is perh. 'let go and disperse'. Through the Han period, *làng*

occurs in combination with other words: 謔浪 'ridicule' [Shi, Karlgren transl.], 波浪 'wave' [Nan-Bai chao, GY] (Huáng Jīnguì, Shěn Xíróng *YYWZX* 1987.8: 44f). Huáng and Shěn suggest that *làng* is a colloquial variant of → $lán_8$ 瀾. Prob. not related to WT *(dba'-) kloŋ* 'wave', see → $róng_3$ 溶.

$láo_1$ 牢 (lâu) **LH** lou, **OCM** *rû
'Calf' (obsolete) [OB only] > 'domestic animal' [Liji], 'pen' (for animals) [Shi].
[T] *Sin Sukchu SR* law (上); *MGZY* law (上) [law]
[E] Bodman (1980: 84) relates this word to Viet. *rào* 'enclosure with fence', an Old Sino-Viet. loan acc. to Pān Wùyún (1987: 28). This etymon may possibly be connected with → $chǒu_1$ 丑.

$láo_2$ 勞 (lâu) **LH** lɑu, **OCM** *râu
'To toil, tire' [Shi] > 'merit' [Zuo].
[T] *Sin Sukchu SR* law (平); *MGZY* law (平) [law]
ЖЖ **lào** 勞 (lâu^C^) **LH** lɑu^C^, **OCM** *râuh
'To recompense' [Shi].
[<] caus. derivation (§4.3) acc. to Downer (1959: 283).

$láo_3$ 醪 (lâu) **LH** lou, **OCM** *rû
'Spirits with sediment' [Lie].
[E] ST: WT *ru-ma* 'curdled milk', JP *ru^31^-* 'liquor' (Bodman 1980: 93). KT items may be Han or post-Han loans: PTai *xl-: S. *lɑu^C1^* 'liquor', PKS *khlaau^3^ 'rice wine'. The KT forms do not belong to → $jiǔ_5$ 酒. It is not clear if and how **zhòu** 酎 (ḍjəu^B^), LH ḍu^B^, *druʔ 'new spirits' [Liji] could be related. Viet. *ruoi* 'wine' is not connected with any of the CH items because of the final *-i;* one could speculate that it goes with **lǐ** 醴 (liei^B^) LH leiʔ 'new unclarified wine' [BI, Shi] (for the lack of medial *w* in CH, see §10.2.1).

lǎo 老 (lâu^B^) **LH** lou^B^, **OCM** *rûʔ — **[T]** *ONW* lɑu
'Be old, grow old' [BI, Shi], the Northern Mǐn initial *s-* as in Jiàn'ōu *se^C2^* may be due to loss of a pre-initial which might have been a velar considering the XS contact with *kǎo* 考 'old age' (Mei / Norman 1971: 99). Old Sino-Viet. *reu* (Pān Wùyún 1987: 28).
[E] Etymology not certain. The meanings or vowels of the following TB comparanda are not close to OC: PTB *raw (*STC* no. 268) > WT *ro* 'corpse'; Lep *hryu* 'be dry, dead' (of leaf); Lushai *ro^H^* 'be dry, dead'; WB *ro* 'very old' ЖЖ *rwat* 'old, tough', NNaga *rəw 'old' (of person).

$lào_1$ 酪 (lâk) **LH** lɑk, **OCM** *râk
Fermented thick liquid: 'a kind of acid soy made of rice or millet' [Li] (so *GSR* 766p); 'fermented milk, yogurt, sour milk, kumiss' [SW]. This is a loanword from a Central Asian language, note Mongol *ayiraɣ* < *aɣɨraɣ 'fermented milk' (Pulleyblank 1962: 250–253). This area word appears with the meaning 'milk' in Greek (*tò gála*, gen. *gálaktos*) and Latin (*lac, lactis*) (Karlgren *Deutsche Literaturzeitung* 1926). The fermented drink 'arrack' may be a different etymon, a loan from Arabic *'araq* 'fermented juice' (so Pulleyblank 1962: 250 contra Karlgren 1926).

$lào_2$ 癆 (lâu^C^) **LH** lɑu^C^
is a Northeastern (Cháoxiān 朝鮮) dialect word of the Han period for 'medicinal poison', acc. to *FY* 3 and *SW*, and in modern Xiāng dialects the col. word for 'to poison' which may be related to → $liào_3$ 療樂 'to cure'. Sagart (1995: 210) considers this word to be cognate to → dú 毒 'poison', but Starostin (*JCL* monograph 8, 1995:

402) points out that *lào* is rather cognate to TB: Lushai *ru* 'the bark, root, leaves, etc. used for fish poisoning', JP *mə-rau* 'fishing by stupefying fish by poisonous vines', Burmese *rəu* 'fish poison' etc. (Starostin's notations).

lè$_1$ 勒 (lək) **LH** lək, **OCM** *rə̂k

'Reins' [Yili]. Perh. originally 'lines' and the s. w. as *lè* 泐阞勒扐仂 'veins' (under → lǐ$_4$ 理). <> Middle Viet *mlạc* > *nhạc* (only in certain expressions) (Maspero 1912: 78).

lè$_2$ 泐阞勒扐仂 'veins' → **lǐ**$_4$ 理

lè$_3$ 樂 (lâk) **LH** lɑk, **OCM** *râuk < *C-rauk

'Joy' [BI, Shi] is thought to be cognate to → yuè$_9$ 樂 'music'.

[T] *Sin Sukchu SR* law (入), *LR* lawʔ; *MGZY* law (入) [law]; *ONW* lɑk

léi$_1$ 雷 (luậi) **LH** luəi, **OCM** *rûi

'Thunder' [Shi].

[D] Mand. Jǐnán *luei*^{32}; Y-Guǎngzhōu *løy*^{21}; K-Méixiàn *lui*^{11} [Hanyuci], PMin *l̥(u)əi: Jiàn'ōu *so*^{C1}. The Northern Mǐn initial *s-* may be due to loss of a pre-initial which might have been a velar considering modern Hénán, Héběi, and Shānxī dialect forms like *hū-léi* 呼雷, *huí-léi* 回雷; also, 'thunder' has been written as *huí* 回 in some Han period texts (Mei / Norman 1971: 99).

[E] Perh. ST: Lushai *rɔɔl*^{H} 'voice, cry (an animal), sound', WT *kʰrol* 'a sound'.

léi$_2$ 累縲 (ljwi) **LH** lui, **OCM** *rui — **[T]** *MTang* lui, *ONW* lue

'To bind' 累 [Meng], 'wind around, be attached to' 纍 [Shi] > 'string' 累 [Zhuang]; 'rope, bonds' 縲 [Lunyu]. Pulleyblank (1972: 73) connects this word with → lún$_3$ 綸, among others. OC -> Tai: S. *rɔɔi*^{C2} 'to bind together, string flowers' (Manomaivibool 1975: 138).

ж **lěi** 纍藟 (ljwi^B) **LH** lui^B, **OCM** *ruiʔ

'Creepers, lianas' 纍 [Guan]; 'a creeping plant' 藟 [Shi] (Karlgren 1956: 7).

[<] endoactive of *léi* 累縲 (ljwi), lit. 'the thing which is winding round' (§4.5.1).

[E] ST: PTB *(s-)rwey 'cane, creeper' (LaPolla 1994: 168), NNaga *rəw 'creeper, rope' [French 1983: 330], Lushai *hrui*^{R} 'a creeper, cane, rope, cord, string'; OKuki *hrui (Kom) 'rope', WB *rui*^{B}- 'kind of creeper, tree', Mru *rui* 'rope' [Löffler 1966: 132].

lěi$_1$ 耒 (ljwi^B) **LH** lui^B, **OCM** *ruiʔ

'Digging stick' (handled like a spade) [OB, Meng], originally a two-pronged fork-like spade which originated perh. in Tai cultures (W. Eberhard *Lokalkulturen II:* 224). This word looks similar to → lí$_6$ 犁 'plow'. Syn. → sì$_5$ 耜.

lěi$_2$ 磊磥 (luậi^B) **LH** luəi^B, **OCM** *rûiʔ

'Pile of rocks' 磥 [SW, JY]; 'pile of rocks, big rock' 磊 [SW, Wenxuan].

ж **lěi-luò** 磥硌 (luậi^B-lâk)

'Appearance of being strong and large' [JY, Wenxuan]; 'high' (of mountain) [Wenxuan].

ж **lěi-luǒ** 磊砢 (luậi^B-lâ^B)

'Rock-like 石[貌]' [JY, Shanhaij], 'pile of small rocks' [SW]. 砢 seems to be a variant of 硌, prob. due to graphic confusion.

[E] This may possibly have a TB connection: WT *ri* 'mountain', Kanauri *rwi* 'high'; note also WB *rui*^{B} 'ridge', all from PTB *rwi or *ruy.

lěi$_3$ 儡 → **lèi**$_4$ 累儽

lěi$_4$ 纍藟 → **léi**$_2$ 累縲

lèi$_1$ 淚 (ljwi^C) **LH** luis, **OCM** *r(i)uts
'Tears' [Chuci].
[T] *Sin Sukchu SR* luj (去); *MGZY* lue (去) [luɛ]
[E] *Lèi* is a late OC word. For phonological reasons it can hardly be related to → qì$_5$ 泣 *khrap 'weep'. The closest TB comparandum might be WB *re* < *ri 'water', JP *mə^{31}-riʔ^{55}* 'dew', if we assume a ST *rwi (with regular loss of medial *w*).
Most likely, this is a t-suffix derivation (nouns for naturally occurring things §6.2.1) of → liú$_3$ 流 *l(i)u 'to flow', hence lit. 'the things that are flowing'. TB cognates suggest a ST and PCH medial*-j-; WT *rgyun* 'the flow, current, stream'.

lèi$_2$ 類 (ljwi^C) **LH** luis, **OCM** *rus — **[T]** *ONW* lui
'Class, category' [Yi] > 'resemble, similar, equal' [Zuo] > 'be up to standards, be good' [Shi].
[E] ST: WT *rus* 'clan, lineage' (also 'bone'), Tamang *^{3}rui* 'clan', WB *rui^B* 'lineage' (also 'bone'). Perh. related to → huì$_8$ 彙.

lèi$_3$ 酹 (luâi^C) **LH** luɑs, **OCM** *g-rots
'To make a libation' [SW, Hanshu].
[E] Tai: S. *kruat^{D1}* 'to make a libation' ⋈ S. *rot^{D2}* 'to sprinkle (water) as a blessing; to water (plants)' (Manomaivibool 1975: 140f).

lèi$_4$ 累儽 (luậi^C, ljwi) **LH** luəi^C, **OCM** *rûih
'Exhausted, tired' 儽 [Lao], later 累.
[<] exopass. of *lěi* 儡 (luậi[^{B}]) (§4.4)

⋈ **lěi** 儡 (luậi[^{B}]) **LH** luəi^B, **OCM** *rûiʔ
'Damage, exhaust' [Huainan].

[E] Prob. area word: AA-Khmer /rúuj/ 'be weary, tired (out), fatigued'; TB-Lushai *rɔiʔ^L* < *rɔis* 'be weak, worn out, fade, diminish'. Alternatively the etymon could belong to the WT wf *rul-ba* 'to rot' ⋈ *brul* 'crumble' ⋈ *hrul* 'ragged' ⋈ *srul-ba* 'be corrupted', but the meanings are not as close to CH as the Khmer / Lushai ones.

lěng 冷 (lieŋ^B, lɐŋ^B) **LH** leŋ^B, **OCM** *rêŋʔ — **[D]** Yuè *laŋ^2* 'cold'
'Cold' [Zhuang] is a vocalic variant of → liáng$_3$ 涼 (§11.1.3).
[T] *Sin Sukchu SR* ləjŋ (上), *PR, LR* ləŋ; *MGZY* l^{h}ing (上) [ləŋ]
[E] ST: TB-Mikir *niŋ-kreŋ* 'cold weather, winter' (*niŋ* 'season'). CH ? -> Tai: Dioi (Yay) *śeiṅ^3* (< *b-leiŋ^3) 'cold' [Maspero 1912: 87].

lí$_1$ 狸 → **lí**$_3$ 貍

lí$_2$ 梩 → **jī**$_6$ 箕

lí$_3$ 貍 (ljɨ) **LH** liə, **OCM** (*p^{h}rə ~ *p^{h}ə-rə >) *rə ? — **[T]** *ONW* liə
Mand. 'raccoon dog', also the second syllable in Mand. *húlí* 狐狸 'fox', the latter already in *Zuǒzhuàn* and *Mèngzǐ*. But in *Shūjīng*, 狐貍 refers to two different animals where the 'cat' radical in *lí* as well as the association with → pí$_5$ 貔 (bji 4) 'leopard' imply a 'wild cat' of approximately fox size.
[D] Acc. to *FY* 8.2, *lí* is a dialect word for the region west of the Passes (Wèi valley and around Xī'ān), whereas other regions have the following forms (discussed by Sagart ICSTLL 1990: 7): **lái** 貍 (lậi) LH lə in Chén (modern Hénán) and Chǔ (modern Húběi) and between the Yangtze and Huái rivers; **pī** 豾 (p^{h}jɨ 3) LH p^{h}iə, *phrə in northern Yān (Héběi, Liáoníng) and in northern Korea; **pī-lí** 豾貍 (p^{h}jɨ 3-ljɨ) south of the Yangtze at Guō Pú's time (d. 324 AD). Zhào Zhēnfēng and Huáng Fēng suggest a connection with Miao *ple, pli* 'cat' (*YWYJ* 1998.10: 76–79). *FY* and

Guō Pú consider all these to be dialect words for → pí$_5$ 貔 which is, however, a different word. The Northern Mǐn initial *s*- in 貍 as in Jiàn'ōu *sɛ^{A2}* may be due to loss of a pre-initial labial (Mei / Norman 1971: 99).

[E] Perh. ST: Mru *pri* 'kind of leopard' (Löffler 1966: 147). If WT *ži-mi* 'cat' (also *žim-bu* ~ *žum-bu*) should derive from a hypothetical *ryi-mi, it could be cognate to *lí*. WT *bi-ši* (< *-ži* ?) 'cat' may then even be the equivalent of the CH dialectal pʰ-initial forms. In this case, the original CH word could have been a compound pí$_5$ -lí 貔貍 '(large) cat' + 'small cat'. But all this is uncertain, also because of possible Indic influence on WT words, see → pí$_5$ 貔.

lí$_4$ 釐 (ljɨ) **LH** liə, **OCM** *rə

'To control, regulate, administer' [BI, Shi] is a cognate of → lǐ$_5$ 理. Sagart (1999: 127) relates this word to → zhì$_{11}$ 治 'regulate'.

lí$_5$ 梨 (lji) **LH** li, **OCM** *ri or *rəi — **[D]** PMin *li ~ *ləi

'Pear tree, pear' [Li].

[T] *Sin Sukchu SR* ljej (平), *PR*, *LR* li; *MGZY* li (平) [li]; *ONW* li

[E] This word is also found in PMY: *rai¹ (Downer 1982). Popular belief derives the name from → lì$_7$ 利 'sharp, dysentry' (Williams 1932: 318).

lí$_6$ 犁 (liei, lji) **LH** lei, li, **OCM** *rəi ? — **[T]** *ONW* lėi — **[D]** PMin *le.

'A traction plow, to plow' [Lunyu, Guan].

[E] KT: PTai *tʰləi^{A1} 'to plow', Kam *kʰaj* 'plow' (Benedict *AT:* 38). PMY *l²ai^{3A}. Perh. related to → lěi$_1$ 耒. Syn. → sì$_5$ 耜.

lí$_7$ 犛 (ljɨ) **LH** liə, **OCM** *rə

'Yak' 犛 [Guoyu], [Zhuang].

[E] ST: prob. cognate to, if not a loan from, WT *'bri-mo* 'domesticated female yak' (Pulleyblank 1962: 137; *HST:* 162; Baxter 1985: 252).

lí$_8$ 漦 → **chí$_4$** 漦

lí$_9$ 離罹 (ljie 3) **LH** liɑi, **OCM** *rai

'To fasten in a net, get tangled, caught in a net' 離 [Shi]; 'drag into, involve, trouble, anxiety, sorrow' 罹 [Shu]. An allofam is → luó$_4$ 羅 'bird-net'.

lí$_{10}$ 離 (ljie 3) **LH** liɑi, **OCM** *rai — **[T]** *ONW* le

'To leave, depart from, be dispersed' [Shi], 'divide, distribute' [Li]. It has been suggested that **pǐ** 仳 (pʰi^B / bi^B) LH pʰiʔ / biʔ which occurs in *Shījīng* in the combination *pǐ-lí* 'be separated' represents an old pre-initial, note WT *'bral-ba* 'be separated' (under → bān$_1$ 班) (so Dǒng Wéiguāng et al. *CAAAL* 22, 1984: 112f). The Old Sino-Viet. form is *rɐi* (Pān Wùyún 1987: 28).

ӿ **lì** 離 (ljie^C 3) **LH** liɑi^C, **OCM** *raih

'To be separated from, differ from' [Li].

[<] exopass. of *lí* 離 (ljie 3) (§4.4).

[E] ST *ral: Mru *ria* < *ral* 'separated from' (Löffler 1966: 146; 134), JP *ran^{33}* 'be apart, separated, divided' ӿ *mə^{31}-ran^{31}* 'to place apart' ӿ *pə^{31}-ran^{31}* 'be separate, sort out' ӿ *gə^{31}-ran^{55}* 'to divide, distribute' ӿ *ra^{31}* 'be parted, separated' (Wolfenden 1937: 646). Another derivation from the ST stem *(C-)ral is → bān$_1$ 班 with the common ST *-l > OC *-n shift.

For an overview of similar items, see Table P-1 under → pī$_3$ 披. Some of the many similar ST roots could be related:

1. *pai 'break' → $pò_3$ 破
2. *pai 'separate, open' → $pī_3$ 披
3. *brai 'open' → $bǎi_2$ 捭, → $bò_3$ 擘
4. *trai 'open' → zhā 奓, → $zhé_6$ 磔
5. *pral 'separate' → $bān_1$ 班
6. *ral 'separate, leave' lí 離 (this entry)
7. *hral 'split' → $chǐ_1$ 拸
8. *p(r)ək 'split' → $pì_7$ 副
9. *k-hlai 'separate' → $chǐ_2$, chí 誃

Perhaps the stems in *-ai (1 to 4) form one large wf, as do perh. the forms in *-ral (5 to 7).

$lí_{11}$ 離 (ljie 3) **LH** liɑi, **OCM** *rai
'To be drooping, hanging down' (fruit on a tree etc.) [Shi], 'fall over' (like a full vessel) [Zuo].
[E] ? ST: WT *brgyal (< b-r(-)yal)* 'to sink down (senseless), faint'; the basic ST meaning may be 'to droop or fall by its / one's own weight'. Pulleyblank (1962: 215) relates the WT word to → $pí_7$ 罷疲, but the WT *b-* is prob. a pre-initial.

$lí_{12}$ 籬 (ljie 3) **LH** liɑi, **OCM** *rai
'Fence, hedge' [Chuci].
ж **lì** 厲 (ljäi^C) **LH** lias, **OCM** *rats
'Hedge' [Zhouli] is prob. related.
[E] ST: TB: Tiddim *gɔɔl^F < rɔɔls* 'fence'.

$lí_{13}$ 纚 → **$xǐ_6$** 纚屣

$lǐ_1$ 李 (ljɨ^B) **LH** liə^B, **OCM** *rəʔ — **[T]** *ONW* liə
'Plum' *(Prunus salicina)* [Shi], a fruit tree which originated in North China; the Northern Mǐn initial *s-* as in Jiàn'ōu *sɛ^{C2}* may be due to loss of a pre-initial, PMin *l̥əi^B (Mei / Norman 1971: 101).

$lǐ_2$-ěr 李耳 (ljɨ^B-ńźɨ^B) **LH** liəʔ-ńəʔ > lɨʔ-ńɨʔ
Acc. to *FY* 8.1, this is a Chǔ dialect word for 'tiger' [FY, Yijing]. Zhào Zhēnfēng and Huáng Fēng (*YWYJ* 1998.10: 76–79) suggest a connection with the Tǔjiā words *li-pa* 'male tiger' and *li-ni* 'female tiger'. The last syllable *-ni* could be related to MK-Khmer *ɲi:* 'female', unless it is a regional word for 'mother', then prob. the same etymon as → $nǎi_4$ 嬭.

$lǐ_3$ 里 (ljɨ^B) **LH** liə^B, **OCM** *rəʔ — **[T]** *ONW* liə
'Village' [Shi]
[E] Prob. ST *rwə: PTB *rwa > WB *rwa* 'town, village'; WT *ra-ba* 'fence, enclosure, wall, pen'. For the loss of ST medial *w in OC and WT, see §10.2.1. Note the Germanic semantic parallel Engl. *town* ж German *Zaun* 'fence'. The synonym PTB *gwa 'village' may belong to CH → $qiū_2$ 丘. <> Tai: S. *rua^{C2}* < *r- 'fence' (Li F. 1976: 43) may also belong to this etymon.

Alternatively, this word may belong to → $lǐ_4$ 理里 'divide into equal sections', but pre- and early-historic Chinese villages prob. were not systematically planned and platted.

$lǐ_4$ 理里 (ljɨ^B) **LH** liə^B, **OCM** *rəʔ — **[T]** *MTang* li, *ONW* liə
'Cut jade according to its veins' [Guoce], 'to divide fields into sections, boundaries' 理

[Shi]; 'a mile' 里 [Shi]. The basic meaning is 'cut in a regular way, divide into equal sections'.

ⅹ **lè** 泐阞勒扐仂 (lək) **LH** lək, **OCM** *râk — **[T]** *ONW* lək

'Vein or duct in soil; fraction' 阞 [Zhouli], 'split according to the veins' (stone) 泐 [Zhouli] > 'engrave' 勒 [Li]; 'space between fingers' 扐 [Yi] > 'a tenth' 仂 [Li]. → $lè_1$ 勒 'reins' may be the s. w.

This item and → $lǐ_5$ 理 are usually thought to be the same etymon: 'divide into sections > regulate'. Baxter (1992: 473) relates these to → $pì_7$ 副.

[E] ST: This etymon is often considered to be related to PTB *riy 'draw, paint, write, delimit' etc. (*STC* no. 429; *HST:* 66) > Lushai ri^R 'boundary, frontier, limit, line of demarcation', NNaga *rəy 'thread, boundary', and WT *'bri-ba, bris* 'to draw, write' ⅹ *ris* 'figure', WB re^B 'write, delineate, paint', Mru *pri* 'to scratch' [Löffler 1966: 133]. However, OC *ə corresponds normally to PTB *a, only rarely to *i (§11.2.2).

$lǐ_5$ 理 ($ljɨ^B$) **LH** $liə^B$, **OCM** *rəʔ

'To regulate, reason' [Yi]; 'administer' [Lüshi] is prob. related to → $lí_{10}$ 釐 'regulate', and possibly also to → $lǐ_6$ 理 'envoy'. This item and → $lǐ_4$ 理 are usually thought to be the same word, which is possible: 'divide into sections > regulate'. Middle Viet. *mlẽ, mnhẽ* 'reason' [Maspero 1912: 78] could perh. be a CH loan. A possible cognate may be → $jì_8$ 紀.

$lǐ_6$ 理 ($ljɨ^B$) **LH** $liə^B$, **OCM** *rəʔ

'An envoy' [Zuo], 'jail official' [Guanzi], 'marriage go-between' [Chuci].

This is perh. the s. w. as → $lǐ_5$ 理 'to administer' [Lüshi].

ⅹ **lì** 吏 ($ljɨ^C$) **LH** $liə^C$, **OCM** *rəh — **[T]** *MTang* li, *ONW* liə

'An official' [BI].

ⅹ **shǐ** 史使 ($ṣɨ^B$) **LH** $ṣə^B$, **OCM** *srəʔ

'To send, employ, cause' 使 [BI, Shi] > 'a secretary, scribe' 史 [BI, Shi].

[T] *Sin Sukchu SR* ṣi (上), *PR, LR* ṣɿ; *MGZY* sh^hi (上) [ṣɿ]; *MTang* ṣi, *ONW* ṣə

[<] s-caus. of *lǐ* 理 ($ljɨ^B$) (§5.2.1).

ⅹ **shì** 使 ($ṣɨ^C$) **LH** $ṣə^C$, **OCM** *srəh

'Ambassador' [Zuo] (Downer 1959: 285). The verb 'to send on a mission' [Liji] has later been derived from 'ambassador' (§3.5).

[<] exopass. of *shǐ* 史使 ($ṣɨ^B$), lit. 'one who has been sent' (§4.4).

[E] AA: OKhmer (7th cent. AD) *re /rəə ~ ree/ 'to move, change position...' has the derivative OKhmer *pre* /prəə/ 'to send' (on an errand or commission), 'to order, assign, appoint, delegate, use, make, employ' ⅹ OKhmer *paṃre* 'to serve; servant, delegate, representative, minister; service, duty'. Initial *p-* is the Khmer causative prefix, which OC has replaced with the ST / POC causative prefix *s-.

Alternatively, Unger (*Hao-ku* 36, 1990: 56) and *CVST* 2: 77 derive *shǐ* 史使 from → $lǐ_4$ 理里 ($ljɨ^B$) 'to mark, draw lines', hence lit. 'scribe'. However, though perh. cognate to WT *'bri-ba* 'to write', *lǐ* never seems to mean 'to write, record' in OC. Matisoff (*D. of Lahu:* 498) relates *shǐ* 史使 to PLB *ʔ-dziy[1] > WB *ce* 'send on business, employ'.

This wf may belong to a larger group which includes → $shì_2$ 士仕 ($dẓɨ^B$). The issue is further complicated by the question of the position of → $shì_1$ 士 ($dẓɨ^B$) in the overall picture.

$lǐ_7$ 鯉 ($ljɨ^B$) **LH** $liə^B$, **OCM** *rəʔ

'Carp' [BI, Shi] is sometimes thought to be related to Tai: S. *plaa*[1] 'fish' – unlikely.

lǐ$_8$ 禮 (liei^B) **LH** lei^B, **OCM** *rîʔ or *rə̂iʔ — **[T]** *ONW* lėi
'Rites, rituals, ceremony' [BI, Shi].
[E] Etymology not certain. Perh. related to TB-WT *že-sa < rye* 'respect' ⋈ *rje (-bo)* 'lord, nobleman' ⋈ *rjed* 'to honour, reverence'. Mru *ri* 'ritual' (Löffler 1966: 147) may perh. come from AA: OMon *reh* [reh] 'do honour to', *reh se* 'show respect'. Perh. this is an old area etymon.

lì$_1$ 力 (ljək) **LH** lɨk, **OCM** *rək, OCB *C-rjək
'Sinew, strength, force, power' [Shi, Shu].
[T] *Sin Sukchu SR* li (入); *MGZY* li (入) [li]; *ONW* lik
[N] Baxter (1992: 473) relates this word to → bī$_2$ 偪逼 'urge, press', Matisoff (1995: 52) relates it to → yì$_{22}$ 翼 'wing' because the CH graph is the drawing of a comparable extremity, an arm. However, the graph may have been intended to represent the sense 'sinew'. CH → Viet *sứ'c* 'force' [Maspero 1912: 80].
⋈ **chì** 飭 (ṭʰjək) **LH** ṭʰɨk, **OCM** *rhək ?
'To strengthen, confirm, make ready' [Shi].
[<] caus. devoicing of *lì* 力 *rək (§5.2.2).
[E] ST *rə 'strength' with the addition of a final *-k (§6.1) > PLB *(k-)ra^2 'strength, power' > PL *ra^2 'strength'. The word may possibly be related to → lái$_1$ 來 'come'.

lì$_2$ 朸 'thorns' → **jí**$_{11}$ 棘

lì$_3$ 立 (ljəp) **LH** lip, **OCM** *rəp, OCB *g-rjəp
'To stand, stand up' [BI, Shi], survives in a few dialects, but is in Mand. replaced by *zhàn* 站 (MC *ṭăm*^{C}), in southern dialects by → jì$_5$ 徛.
[T] *Sin Sukchu SR* li (入); *MGZY* li (入) [li]; *ONW* lip
[E] ST *g-rjəp: PTB *g-ryap (*STC* no. 246) 'to stand' > Bahing *rap*, Kanauri *rap*, Jiarong *ka-ryap*, Kachin *tsap < kryap*; PLB *ʔrap; PLB *ʔ-rap^L (*HPTB:* 35) > OBurm. *ryap* [*IST:* 359], WB *rap*, Mikir *arjàp < rjàp* 'to stand', perh. also WT *žabs* 'bottom, foot' (*HST:* 140).

lì$_4$ 笠 (ljəp) **LH** lip, **OCM** *rəp
'Bamboo hat' [Shi], the Northern Mǐn initial *s-* may be due to loss of a pre-initial (Mei / Norman 1971: 101) as also suggested by members of the phonetic series and the Tai word: Wuming *klop*^{D1}*S* < *kl- 'bamboo hat' (Li F. 1976: 45).

lì$_5$ 涖 → **lái**$_1$ 來

lì$_6$ 吏 → **lǐ**$_6$ 理

lì$_7$ 利 (lji^C) **LH** lis, **OCM** *rits
'Sharp' [Lunyu], 'harvest' [OB], 'be advantageous, profitable, benefit, profit' [BI, Shi]. The graph shows grain cut with a knife.
[T] *Sin Sukchu SR* ljej (去), *PR*, *LR* li; *MGZY* li (去) [li]; *ONW* li
[E] ST: PTB *ri:t 'reap, cut' (*STC* no. 371) > PLB *ri:t^L > WB *rit* 'to reap, mow, shave'; Lushai *riit*^{F} / *riʔ*^{L} 'cut, dig, or scrape with a hoe'; Mikir *rè-* 'be sharp'.

lì$_8$ 例 'arrive' → **liè**$_1$ 列

lì$_9$ 戾 (liei^C, liet) **LH** les, **OCM** *rêts, OCB *C-rets (Baxter 1992: 404)
'Cruel, misfortune' [Shi] > 'stern' [Lunyu], 'ugly' [Zhuang] > 'evil demon' [Zuo]. In *Shījīng* the graph is also borrowed for → lì$_{17}$ 厲 (Unger *Hao-ku* 75, 2002: 65).

lì$_{10}$ 戾 → **lái**$_1$ 來

lì$_{11}$ 栗 (ljet) **LH** lit, **OCM** *rit, OCB *C-rjit — **[T]** *ONW* lit
'Chestnut' [Shi] is prob. related to KS-Ten *lik^{31}* 'chestnut'.

lì$_{12}$ 栗 'dense' → **mì$_4$** 密

lì$_{13}$ 慄 (ljet) **LH** lit, **OCM** *rit
'Be apprehensive, careful, trembling' [Shi] is cognate to WT *žed-pa < ryet* 'to fear, be afraid', *bred-pa < b-ret* 'be frightened' (*HST:* 77), Lushai *ṭi^H / ṭit^L* 'timid, fearful' ⋈ *ṭiʔ^L* 'to fear, be afraid'.

lì$_{14}$ 厲 (ljäi^C) **LH** lias, **OCM** *rats
'High' [Guliang] can perh. be connected with WT *rab* 'superior, excellent' (*HST:* 94).

lì$_{15}$ 厲 (ljäi^C) **LH** lias, **OCM** *rats — **[T]** *MGZY* li (去) [li]
'To sharpen > (sharpener:) grindstone' 礪 [Shu], 'whetstone' 厲 [Shi] > 'to polish' [Xun]. 蠣 'a stinging insect' [Zhuang] is the s. w. acc. to Karlgren (1956: 4).
[C] This may be the same etymon as → lì$_{16}$ 厲 'drag something along'. A derivation is → chài 蠆 'scorpion'. An allofam is perh. → liè$_2$ 烈冽颲. Prob. not (closely) related to → lì$_7$ 利 'sharp'.
[E] ST: TB-Tani *rat, Kaman *kɹat* 'sharp-edged' (Sun *LTBA* 16.2, 1993: 184). <> PMY *rai^{1C} 'sharp'. CH -> PTai *nl/r-: S. *(lek-)nai^{A2}*, Bo'ai *lai^{A2}* 'bee's sting'.

lì$_{16}$ 厲 (ljäi^C) **LH** lias, **OCM** *rats
'Dragging something along': 'to wet clothes' (while fording a stream), 'to drag, train' (sashes) [Shi] is perh. the s. w. as → lì$_{15}$ 厲 'whetstone'. Sagart (1999: 127) relates this word to *yì* 曳 (jiäi^C) 'drag, trail' (under → yì$_{16}$ 抴).

lì$_{17}$ 厲 (ljäi^C) **LH** lias, **OCM** *rats
'Epidemic, calamity' 厲 [Shu], 勵 [Zuo], 癘 [SW]; 'destroy' 厲 [Guanzi] > perh. 'cruel' ('deadly'?) [Shi] > 'stern' [Lunyu], 'ugly' [Zhuang] > 'evil demon' [Zuo].
[E] KT: PTai *trai^A: S. *taai^{A1}* 'to die', Saek *praai^1* (Benedict in Edmondson / Solnit 1988: 330). In spite of the difficulty in reconciling PTai and OC rimes / tones, the word is of Tai origin. Karlgren (1956: 4) relates *lì* also to → lì$_{15}$ 厲 'sharp', but this is not likely in light of Tai.

lì$_{18}$ 厲 'hedge' → **lí$_{10}$** 籬

lì$_{19}$ 厲 (ljäi^C) **LH** lias, **OCM** *rats
'A ford' [Shi].
[E] ST: WT *rab(s)* 'ford'; JP *rap^{55}* 'to ford, cross a river'. Bodman (1980: 91) also relates this word to **shè** 涉 (źjäp) 'to wade, cross a stream' [Shi], but MC *źj-* is difficult to reconcile with MC *l-* < *r-. Prob. unrelated to → lài$_1$ 瀨 'rapids'.

lì$_{20}$ 勵 (ljäi^C) **LH** lias, **OCM** *rats
'To exert oneself, energetically' [Shu] is apparently related to WT *hrad-pa* 'exert oneself, push violently, stem tide'.

lì$_{21}$ 糲 (lâi^C, ljäi^C) **LH** lɑs, lias, **OCM** *rats
'Coarse husked grain' [Lie].
[E] ST: WT *'bras* 'rice' ⋈ *'bras-bu* 'fruit' (Shī Xiàngdōng 2000: 24), Lushai *raʔ^L < raʔ* or *rah* (< *-s) 'fruit'. <> AN: Malay *bĕras* 'rice' (Kuiper 1966: 61). This etymon also appears to be close to → bài$_3$ 粺 *breh (< *bre-s ?) 'fine rice' and its possible cognates.

lì$_{22}$ 歷曆 (liek) **LH** lek, **OCM** *rêk
('Make go one after the other':) 'to add up, a series, number' 歷 [BI, Shu]; 'calculate' [Shu, Zhuang], 'calendrical calculations' 曆 [Shu].
[T] *Sin Sukchu SR* li (入); *MGZY* li (入) [li]; *ONW* lėk
[E] ST: WB *re* 'to count', Kanauri *ri*, WT *rtsi-ba* < rhyi 'to count' ⋈ *rtsis-pa* 'astronomer'. For the WT initial, see §12.9; for the CH final *-k*, see §6.1.

⋈ **lì** 麗 (liei^C) **LH** le^C, **OCM** *rêkh or *rêh
'Number' [Shi].
[<] exopass. of *lì* 歷曆 (liek), lit. 'what is calculated' (§4.4).

[C] A possible allofam is → lì$_{23}$ 麗 'a pair'.

lì$_{23}$ 麗 (liei^C) **LH** le^C, **OCM** *rêh
'A pair' 麗 [Zhouli], 'mate, companion' 儷 [Zuo] > ('paired':) 'well-proportioned' [Li], 'elegant, beautiful' [BI, Chuci], 'refinement' [Shu]. This word may possibly be related to → lì$_{22}$ 歷曆. In some texts 'pair, two' is written 離 (Wáng Lì 1982: 360).
= **lí** 驪 'A pair of horses' [Hou Hanshu]. The reading *lí* belongs to 'black horse'.

lì$_{24}$-lù 轣轆 (liek-luk) **LH** lek-lok
轣轆車 'a spinning wheel' in the Han-period dialects of Zhào and Wēi [FY 5, 39]. 轆 'a pulley' (for a well rope) [Middle Chinese]. Gòng Qúnhǔ (*MZYW* 2, 2000) relates this to Tai *rɔɔk*^{8} 'pulley' (?).

lián$_1$ 連聯 (ljän) **LH** lian, **OCM** *ran or *ren
'To join, bring together' 聯 [Zhouli], 'connect, unite, in a row' 連 [Shi]; 'go one after another': 'be dripping or running (tears), rippling (waves)' 漣 [Shi].
[T] *Sin Sukchu SR* ljen (平); *MGZY* len (平) [lɛn]; *ONW* lian

⋈ **shān** 潸 (ṣan(B), ṣăn) **LH** ṣan(B) or ṣɛn, **OCM** *srân(?), or *srên
'Flowing' (of tears) [Shi].
[<] iterative of *lián* (§5.2.2).

[E] ST: PTB *ren (*STC* no. 346): *m-ren 'line up, be equal': JP *ren*^{31} 'place in a long, even row'; Mikir *ren* 'line, range, row' (*HST* p. 57). Unger (*Hao-ku* 35, 1986: 30) relates the CH word to WT *'brel-ba* 'connection, conjunction'; the final *-n* in the other TB languages could derive from *-l as well; Gong (in W. Wang 1995: 65) relates it to WT *gral* 'row, series, class'. TB items under → bìng$_2$ 並併 could possibly. belong here.

lián$_2$, liǎn 連 → **niǎn$_2$** 輦連

lián$_3$ 連 'difficult' → **miǎn$_1$** 勉

lián$_4$ 蓮 (lien [GY]) **LH** len, **OCM** *rên, OCB *g-ren — **[T]** *ONW* lėn
'Lotus fruit' [Shi, Lu version], a late character (Baxter 1992: 362). CH -> Viet *sen* 'lotus' (Maspero 1912: 80).

~ **jiān** 蕳 (kăn) **LH** kɛn, OCM *krên, OCB *kren
'Lotus fruit' [Shi 145.2], the same or a similar graph (written with the phonetic 間 or 閒) also writes a variant of → lán$_7$ 蘭 'orchid' (Baxter 1992: 363).

lián$_5$, liàn 㜻 (ljän^{A2}) **LH** lian(C) — **[D]** PMin *l̥ɑn^{C1}
'Young hen, pullet' is acc. to Guō Pú's commentary to *EY* a Jiāngdōng (Yangtze coastal region) word which is still used in southern dialects: Mǐn: Jiēyáng *nuã*^{C1}, Jiānglè *šuai*^{C1}; Kèjiā *kai*^{A1}*-lon*^{C1} (*kai*^{1} 'chicken').
[E] Etymology not clear, comparanda are scattered widely in the area: TB-Lepcha *lyeŋ* 'young' > *a-lyeŋ* 'full-grown female beast or fowl, which has not yet had young'.

<> MY: Yáo *tɕai¹-tɕaan⁵* /kjai¹-kjaan⁵/ (Norman 1983: 207), note also PKS *hŋla:ŋ⁵ 'young chicken', PTai *ɦəəŋ^B, PHlai *laŋ¹ 'chicken classifier'.

lián₆ 廉 (ljäm) **LH** liam, **OCM** *ram — **[T]** *ONW* liam
'Angle, angular' [Li] is shared with Tai: S. *liam^B1* (WSiam *hli:am* 'id.'; Manomaivibool 1975: 140).

lián₇ 廉 'modest' → **qiān₉** 謙

lián₈ 磏鎌 (ljäm) **LH** liam, **OCM** *ram (actually *riam ?) — **[T]** *ONW* liam
'Sharp, keen' (of soldier) 磏 [Hanfei]; 'sickle' 鎌 [Mo]. The graph seems to refer to a whetstone ('sharpener'). This is an allofam of → yǎn₄ 剡覃 with the earlier *r- pre-initial preserved (§9.2.1; the difference in tone is unexplained).

ж **shān** 芟摲 (ṣam) **LH** ṣam, **OCM** *srâm
'Sickle' [Guoyu], 'to mow' 芟 [Shi]; 'to cut off' 摲 (Mand. *shàn*) [Li].

[E] ST: Kuki-N. *(s-)rjam: Lushai *hriam^H* 'sharp' ж *hriam^L* 'weapon', Thado *ăhem* 'sharp' (Benedict 1976: 190). The alignment of CH with TB items suggests that → jiān₁ 尖鑯 incl. *xiān* 銛 is not related, nor is → zhǎn₂ 斬.

[C] Allofam → yán₂ 炎.

lián₉ 憐 (lien) **LH** len, **OCM** *rîn — **[T]** *ONW* lėn
'To pity, pitiful' [BI]; 'to love' in the Rǔ-Yǐng dialect of the Han period [FY 1.6] as well as in the Chǔ-Jiāng-Huái region [FY 1.17], i.e. in southern parts of China.

~ **líng** 怜 (lieŋ) **LH** leŋ ? a variant of *lián* [JY].

~ **líng** 棱 (ljəŋ) **LH** lɨŋ a Han period dialect variant of the northeast [FY 1.6].

[E] ST *rin: WT *'drin* < *ɴrin* 'kindness, favor, grace'; WB *rañ^B-* 'love' (*HST:* 119), SChin-Mro *mxien* < *mrien* 'to pity' [Hartmann ICSTLL 1999: 8]. Cognate is perh. also Lushai *riŋ^H* / *rin^F* 'to believe, trust, depend on, think'; the concept 'to love' is also derived from 'to think (of)' in the ST wf → yí₁₀ 儀宜.

liǎn₁ 斂 (ljäm^B, ljäm^C) **LH** liam^B, liam^C, **OCM** *ramʔ, rams
'To gather, accumulate' [Shi].

ж **jiǎn** 檢 (kjäm^B, kjɐm^B) **LH** kɨɑ/am^B, **OCM** *kamʔ (?)
'Accumulate' [Meng].

ж **lǎn** 攬 (lɑm^B) **LH** lɑm^B, **OCM** *lâmʔ
'To take' [Zhuang], 'pick, take' [Chuci, written with 手 underneath the phonetic]. In southern dialects: 'hold in one's arms, embrace': G-Nánchāng *lɔn^213*, K-Méixiàn *nam^31* 擜 (tone B), Y-Guǎngzhōu *lam^23* (B), M-Xiàmén *lam^51* (B).

[E] Area etymon: TB-Lushai *hrɔɔm^R* < *hrɔɔmʔ* 'grip, grasp', *hrɔɔm^R-hrɔɔm^F* 'to gather or grasp together'. <> Tai: S. *rɔɔm^A2* < *rɔm^A 'to collect, gather together' ж S. *hɔɔm^A1* < *hrɔm^A 'to gather together'. <> AA: OKhmer *rom* /room/ 'to mass, concentrate, combine' ж *jroma* /cróom/ 'to gather together into a swarm, crowd, pack...' ж *rāma* /rííəm/ 'to gather, be clustered'.

liǎn₂ 臉 (lăm^B [GY], kjäm^B) **LH** kɨam^B, **OCM** *kamʔ or *kramʔ ?
'The cheek' [JY] > Mand. 'cheeks, face' (Wáng Lì 1958: 566); the older form MC *kjäm^B* is confirmed by Tai: S. *kɛɛm^C1* 'cheek' (Li 1976: 46). Both forms prob. derive from an OC cluster. *Jiá* 頰 'cheek, face' (under → xié₁ 挾協) is prob. unrelated.

[E] ST: WT *'gram-pa* 'cheek', *'gram-rus* 'cheekbone, jawbone'.

liǎn₃ 蘞 (ljäm^A/B) **LH** liam^B, **OCM** *ramʔ
'A kind of vine' (*Ampelopsis serjaniaefolia*) [Shi].

ꭗ **liàn** 斂 (ljäm^{C}) **LH** liam^{C}, **OCM** *rams
'To dress a corpse, enshroud' [Zuo].
[E] AA, the basic meaning is 'to wrap around': OKhmer *rum* [rum] 'to wind, roll, coil, surround, encircle, wrap (a corpse)', Khmer *jram* [crum] 'be surrounded, wrapped, sheltered'; Bahnar *lôm*, Biat *n'klom* 'to wrap'. AA -> TB-Lepcha *gryóm* 'to wrap' (Forrest *JOAS* 82, 1962: 334). OC *a can reflect earlier *a and *o, the MK vowels may perh. have been /o/ or /u/.

liàn$_1$ 楝 (lien^{C}) **LH** len^{C}, **OCM** *rêns
'*Melia azederach*, a kind of tree' [SW] is shared with Tai: S. *krian^{A1}* 'id'. (Manomaivibool 1975: 140f), also Siam. *lian^{B2}* (a back-loan from CH).

liàn$_2$ 湅練鍊 (lien^{C}) **LH** len^{C}, **OCM** *rêns
'To purify' 練 [Lü] > 'refine' (metal) 鍊 [Guoce] > 'to boil silk' 湅練 [Zhouli] > 'white silk' 練 [Zuo] (Wáng Lì 1982: 569).
ꭗ Perh. **xiàn** 僩 (ɣǎn^{B}) **LH** gɛn^{B}, **OCM** *grênʔ
'Be beautiful, refined' [Shi], and
ꭗ **xián** 嫻 (ɣǎn) **LH** gɛn 'refined' [Lunheng].

liàn$_3$ 練 'to train' → **xián$_7$** 閑

liàn$_4$ 斂 'enshroud' → **liǎn$_3$** 蘞

liáng$_1$, làng 俍 (ljaŋ, lâŋ^{C}) **LH** liɑŋ, **OCM** *raŋ
'Be skillful' [Zhuang].
ꭗ **shuǎng** 爽 (ṣjaŋ^{B}) **LH** ṣɑŋ^{B}, **OCM** *sraŋʔ — **[T]** *ONW* ṣaŋ
'Be active, clever' [Zuo].
[<] intensive (?) of *liáng, làng* 俍 *raŋ (§5.2.3).

liáng$_2$ 梁 (ljaŋ) **LH** liɑŋ, **OCM** *raŋ
'Beam' [Zhuang] > 'pole, bridge, dam, weir' [Shi] is perh. related to words with the basic meaning 'crosspiece' → héng$_4$ 衡.
[D] PMin *liɔŋ 'beam' > Amoy *niũ^{A2}*, Fúzhōu *lioŋ^{A2}*
[E] ? ST: WB *k^{h}raŋ-* 'rafter, board'. Old Sino-Viet. *rɯɐŋ* (Pān Wùyún 1987: 28). Prob. AA-Wa-Lawa-Bulang *praŋ 'beam' is related, it may be a TB loan.

liáng$_3$ 涼 (ljaŋ) **LH** liɑŋ, **OCM** *raŋ
'Be chilly, cold' [Shi].
ꭗ **shuāng** 霜 (ṣjaŋ) **LH** ṣɑŋ, **OCM** *sraŋ — **[T]** *ONW* ṣaŋ
'Hoarfrost' [Shi].
[D] In some dialects also 'ice': W-Wēnzhōu *ɕyɔ$^{44/32}$-peŋ$^{44/33}$* 霜冰, M-Xiàmén *sŋ^{55}*, Cháozhōu *sɯŋ^{33}*.
[<] s-noun from *liáng* 涼 (ljaŋ) (§5.2.4).
[E] ST: PTB *graŋ (*STC* no. 120) > WT *graŋ-ba* 'be cold, become cold'; PLB *ɴkraŋ ~ *ɴkrak ~ *ʔkrak 'cold' [Matisoff 1988b]; Lushai *ṭaaŋ^{R}* < *traaŋʔ* 'dry, cold' (*STC* no. 120). This etymon seems to have a wider distribution: AA: Kharia *'raŋga* 'cold, freeze', Khmer *rɔŋa* 'cold' [Pinnow 1959: 422].
The word *cwuəŋ^{3} 'ice' in Yao lgs. (Wáng Fúshì) is a CH loan.
[C] A derivation is prob. → cāng 滄 'cold'. A vocalic variant is → lěng 冷 (§11.1.3).

liáng$_4$ 量 (ljaŋ) **LH** liɑŋ, **OCM** *raŋ
'To measure, consider' [Zuo].

[T] *Sin Sukchu SR* ljaŋ (平); *MGZY* (lÿang >) lyang (平) [ljaŋ]; *MTang* liaŋ < laŋ, *ONW* laŋ

[D] PMin *liɔŋ 'measure' > Fúzhōu *lioŋ*^{A2}

[E] ST: WT *graŋ* 'number' ⋈ *'graŋ-ba* 'to number, count' ⋈ *(b)graŋ-ba, bgraŋs* 'to count' ⋈ *sgraŋ-ba, bsgraŋs, bsgraŋ, sgroŋ* 'to enumerate' (*HST:* 108), WB *k^hraŋ* 'measure with measure of capacity'.

⋈ **liàng** 量 (ljaŋ^C) **LH** liɑŋ^C, **OCM** *raŋh

'A measure' [Lunyu].

[E] ST: WT *graŋs* 'number' (Unger *Hao-ku* 20, 1983). Possibly related to → lüè$_2$ 略.

liáng$_5$ 糧 (ljaŋ) **LH** liɑŋ, **OCM** *raŋ — [T] *MTang* liaŋ < laŋ, *ONW* laŋ

'Grain, provisions' [Shi].

⋈ **zhāng** 粻 (tjaŋ) **LH** ṭɑŋ, **OCM** *traŋ

'Provisions' [Shi] (Wáng Lì 1982: 354).

[E] ? ST: WT *'graŋ* 'satisfy with food, satiate' (*HPTB:* 303f, following Gong H.).

liǎng 兩 (ljaŋ^B) **LH** liɑŋ^B, **OCM** *raŋ?

'Two, a pair' [Shi].

[T] *Sin Sukchu SR* ljaŋ (上); *MGZY* (lÿang >) lyang (上) [ljaŋ]; *MTang* liaŋ < laŋ, *ONW* laŋ

[D] PMin *l̥ɔŋ$^{B/C}$ 'two', *liɔŋ*^{B} 'a tael' > NMin Jiànyáng *sɔŋ*^{C1} 'two', *lioŋ*^{B1} 'tael' (initial *s-* in 'two' may be due to loss of a pre-initial (Mei / Norman 1971: 101); Fúzhōu *laŋ*^{C2} 'two', *lioŋ*^{B1} 'tael'; Amoy *nŋ*^{C2} 'two', *niũ*^{B1} 'tael'.

CH -> Tai also indicates a pre-initial: Dioi *śaṅ*^{2} < *plaŋ^2 (Maspero 1912: 87).

⋈ **liàng** 輛 (ljaŋ^C) **LH** liɑŋ^C, **OCM** *raŋh

'Chariot' [Zhuang].

[<] exopass. of *liǎng* 兩 (ljaŋ^B) *raŋ?, lit. 'what is paired', i.e. a set of wheels (§4.4).

[E] Etymology not clear. (1) A loan from KT: PTai *r-: S. *raa*^{A2} 'we two (inclusive?)', Shan *ha* 'we two', Lü *hra* 'I'; PKS *hra^1 'two'. Li F. (1976: 40) associates the Tai word with CH → yú$_5$ 余 'I' for which he reconstructs OC *rag (OCM *la). (2) Cognate to PTB *s-raŋ > WT *sraŋ* 'pair of scales, weight'. (3) Finally, → shuāng$_1$ 雙 may be a derivation, but the vowels do not agree.

liàng 亮 (ljaŋ^C) **LH** liɑŋ^C, **OCM** *raŋh, OCB *C-rjaŋs

'Light' n. [Shi, Shu], of moon et al.; *liàng* refers to pale light, while → lǎng 朗 refers to brilliant light.

[E] Apparently a member of an AA wf: PEKatuic *_ieŋ: Bru *rliaŋ*, Katu *baruaŋ* 'moonlight', Khmer *-rāṃṅa* 'be light, bright' ⋈ *srāṃṅa* /sraŋ/ 'be pale, colorless'.

[C] An allofam is prob. → shuǎng$_1$ 爽, possibly also → liáng$_1$, làng 俍, → lǎng 朗, → jǐng$_3$ 景 (so Karlgren 1956: 12) and perh. → yīng$_1$ 英. Baxter relates this word to → míng$_6$ 明 OCB *mrjaŋ and → jìng$_6$ 鏡.

Items of a MKwf can be associated with individual CH words, this would explain the different OC initial consonant which seems to have no recognizable OC morphological function; note the following Khmer items:

(a) Khmer *-rāṃṅa* 'be light, bright'

liàng 亮 (ljaŋ^C) OCB *C-rjaŋs 'light'

(b) Khmer *srāṅa* /sraaŋ/ (intr., of first light of day) 'to be dim, faint, weak'

→ shuǎng$_1$ 爽 (ṣjaŋ^B) *sraŋ? 'twilight' (of dawn)

(c) Khmer *brāṅa* /príiəŋ/ intr. 'to grow light' (after dark)

→ bǐng$_1$ 炳昺邴 (bjɐŋ^B) OCB *brjaŋ? ?'bright'

(d) Khmer *paṃbrāṅa* /bampríiəŋ/ 'to shed a pale light'
→ míng$_6$ 明 (mjwɐŋ) OCB *mrjaŋ 'become bright, enlightened'

liáo$_1$ 僚 'fine' → **jiǎo$_2$** 姣佼

liáo$_2$ 膫 → **liáo$_5$** 膋

liáo$_3$ 獠 → **liào$_2$** 燎

liáo$_4$ 聊 'ringing in ears' → **liù$_3$** 翏飂

liáo$_5$ 膋 (lieu) **LH** leu, **OCM** *riâu — **[T]** *ONW* lėu
'Fat around intestines' [Shi, Li], 膫 [SW]; **zhī-liáo** 脂膫 'tallow, grease' (Giles).
[E] Etymology unknown because the following comparanda are too far removed from OC: WT *rgyu-ma* < *r-yu* 'intestines, entrails'. Alternatively, *liáo* may be connected with AA: note Semai (NW) *lʔuus* 'animal grease' [Diffloth 1976: 211], Lawa *laʔauk*, U *raʔaus* 'grease' [Diffloth id.: 218]. PTai *lau^{A2} 'pork fat, grease' (only in northern and central Tai) looks like a loan from CH *liáo*.
¤ Perh. **yú** 腴 (jiu) **LH** jo, **OCM** *jo
'Fat on belly, intestines' [Li], 'fat' [Guoce].
[C] See also → lǜ$_4$-liáo 膟膋

liáo$_6$ 瘳 → **chōu$_2$**, **liáu** 瘳

liǎo$_1$ 了 (lieu^B)
'Finish' [Tangshu], a medieval word, occurs in SE Asian lgs.: Viet *rồi* 'finished', Lang-lo *ṣoy*; Tai: S. *lew^5* (and in many Tai lgs.) [Maspero 1912: 67]. Viet initial *r-* suggests that this word existed perhaps already in OC.

liǎo$_2$ 繚 → **jiǎo$_3$** 絞

liào$_1$ 料 (lieu^C) **LH** leu^C, **OCM** *riâuh or *riûh ?
'To measure' [Guoyu], 'put hand on, stroke' [Zhuang], later 'material'.
[E] Perh. related to WT *rgyu* 'matter, substance, material'.

liào$_2$ 燎 (ljäu[^{C}], lieu^C) **LH** leu^C, **OCM** *riâuh
'To burn, make a burnt-offering' [OB, BI, Shi], 'sacrifice of burning wood' [SW], 'torch' [Shi].
[T] *Sin Sukchu SR* ljew (平上), *PR* ljaw; *MGZY* lew (上去) [lɛw]
¤ **liáo** 獠 (lieu) **LH** leu, **OCM** *riâu
'Hunt at night' (with torches) [Guan]. It appears that this was the basic form from which the verb *liàu* was derived.
[C] Perh. → jiǎo$_1$ 烄 *krâuʔ 'burn on a pyre' is related.

liào$_3$ 療藥 (ljäu^C) **LH** liau^C, **OCM** *riauh ?
'To cure' 藥 [Shi] (also MC *lâk* from OCM *riɔk?), 'treat sickness, heal' 療 [Zuo].
Allofams are → yào$_4$ 藥 (jiak) *iɔk 'to cure', and prob. also → chōu$_2$, liáo 瘳 (ṭʰjəu, lieu) *rhiu, *riû 'get cured, recover'. If *yào* should be a member of this wf, the OC initial *r- in *liào* is a former pre-initial, hence *yào* < *r-jauk, *liào* < *rjauk(h). See also → lào$_2$ 癆.
[E] ST: Mru *rok* / *tarok* 'to cure' (Löffler 1966: 152).

liè$_1$ 列 (ljät) **LH** liat, **OCM** *rat
'To divide, distribute' [Xun], 'arrange' [Zhouli], 'rank, order' [Zuo], 'degree' [Shu]. Prob. cogn. to → bié 別 (so Sagart 1999: 87), → lǚ$_1$ 旅呂, → là$_1$ 剌. Unger (*Hao-ku*

39, 1992: 88) relates *liè* to WT *gras* 'class, order, series, rank, tribe', but see → lǚ₁ 旅呂.

ꭗ **lì** 例 (ljäi^C) **LH** lias, **OCM** *rats
'Usage, rule' [Gongyang], Mand. 'example' (Sagart 1999: 133).
[<] exopass. of *liè* 列 (ljät), lit. 'what is arranged' (§4.4).

liè₂ 烈冽颲 (ljät) **LH** liat, **OCM** *rat, OCB *C-rjat
Perh. 'a sharp sensation on the skin' > 'to blaze, broil' (meat) [Shi] > (A) 'illustrious, splendid' [Shi, YiZhou] > 'brilliant deed, brilliance' [BI, Shu]; > (B) ('A burning-like sensation') > 'cool' (of a spring) 冽 [Shi]; 'violent winds' 烈風 [Shu] > 'violent, bad wind' 颲 [SW, Yupian] (Karlgren *GSR* 291). Old Sino-Viet. *rat* (Pān Wùyún 1987: 28).

ꭗ **liè-liè** 烈
'Be blazing' (of fire, heart), 'be brilliant' (person) [BI, Shi], 'be bitterly cold' (winter day) [Shi].

ꭗ **lì-liè** 栗烈 **LH** lit-liat 'bitterly cold' [Shi], a reduplicated form of *liè*.
[C] An allofam is perh. → lì₁₅ 厲 'to sharpen, whetstone'.

liè₃ 茢 (ljät) **LH** liat, **OCM** *rat or *ret ?
'Kind of rush for brooms' [Li].
[T] *Sin Sukchu* 裂 *SR* lje (入); *MGZY* 裂 lÿa (入) [ljɛ]
[E] ST: WT *dres-ma, dred-ma* 'grass for ropes and shoes' (Unger *Hao-ku* 39, 1992: 88), WB *krit* 'a kind of grass, Job's tears'.

liè₄ 劣 (ljuät) **LH** lyat, **OCM** *rot — **[T]** *ONW* luat
'Inferior' [SW].
[E] ST: PTB *ryut > JP *yut*[31] 'become worse' (illness), WB *yut* < *rut* 'inferior, mean' ꭗ *hrut* 'put down' (*STC* no. 206).

liè₅ 躐 (ljäp) **LH** liap, **OCM** *rap
'To tread, trample' [Li].
[E] ST: PTB *rap (LaPolla 1994: 166) > KN-Lushai *rap^L / raʔ^L* 'to tread (upon), trample upon', WT *skrab-pa* 'to stamp (the ground), tread' ꭗ *'kʰrab-pa* 'to strike, stump, thump'. However, the initial *k-* in the WT cognates *skrab, 'kʰrab* could theoretically derive from an earlier initial *ʔ-, note the initial *ʔr- in the putative OC cognate → yā₃ 壓 OC *ʔrap 'press down, stamp', as well as the absence of velar initials in the other TB languages; perh. also connected with **dié** 蹀 (diep) 'to trample, stamp' [Lie] (so Sagart 1999: 127), and possibly also to → niè₇ 躡 OC *nrap 'trample'.

liè₆ 獵 (ljäp) **LH** liap, **OCM** *rap or *rep?
'A kind of turtle' [Zhouli].
[E] ST: PTB *lip / *lep 'turtle' > WB *lip* (Benedict 1976: 190), Khami *lip*, Rengmitca *talip*, Mru *lip* 'tortoise' [Löffler 1966: 122]. OC and TB differences in initial and vowel have parallels, see §7.3 and §11.1.3 respectively.

liè₇ 獵 'hunt' → **là₃** 臘

liè₈ 鬣 (ljäp) **LH** liap, **OCM** *rap
'Long beard' [Zuo], 'beard, broom' [Li]. → shà 翣 'fan' may possibly be a derivate.

lín₁ 林 (ljəm) **LH** lim, **OCM** *rəm, OCB *C-rjəm
'Forest, forester' [BI, Shi].
[T] *Sin Sukchu SR* lim (平), *PR, LR* lin; *MGZY* lim (平) [lim]; *ONW* lim
[D] PMin *lam; Y-Guǎngzhōu *²¹lɐm^{A2}*

ᴥ **sēn** 森 (ʂjəm) **LH** ʂɨm, **OCM** *srəm

'Forest, dense thicket' [Han text] (Baxter 1992: 553), prob. an intensive derivative of *lín* (§5.2.3), possibly influenced by AA parallels; see below.

[T] *Sin Sukchu SR* ʂəm (平); *MGZY* shʰim (平) [ʂəm]; *ONW* ʂim.

[E] ST or area etymon: PTB *ram (*HPTB:* 299) > Northern Naga *C-ram 'forest, jungle', Lushai *ram*^{H} 'forest, jungle, country, land', Mikir *iŋrám-àw* < *m-ram* 'be woodsy, dark'. Perh. also shared with AA: Khmer *rāma* /rı́iəm/ 'to gather, be clustered > gallery forest, inundated forest...' ᴥ OKhmer /rnaam/ (i.e. r-n-aam) 'dense forest in low-lying areas...' ᴥ /samraam/ (i.e. s-m-raam) 'ground under shrub, tract of undergrowth' (note the close agreement with OC); mod. Mon *rāṃ* /rèm/ 'copse, patch of woodland'. In light of this AA etymology, the wf → lín$_2$ 林 'numerous' could possibly be related.

Other comparanda are unrelated (the vowels do not agree with OC): TB-Mru *rüm* 'forest' (Löffler 1966: 144), WB ə-rum 'cluster, clump' (of trees) ᴥ *kʰrum* ~ *kʰyum* 'cluster, clump'. The second part of Garo *bol-grim* 'forest' (*bol* 'tree') prob. means 'dark': TB-WT *rum* 'darkness, obscurity', JP *n*^{33}*-rim*^{33} 'dusk' ᴥ *rim*^{31} 'dusk' [*STC* no. 401]; also Tai: S. *khrɨm*^{A2} < *gr- 'jungle' ᴥ *khrɨm*^{C2} 'shady, lush' (Manomaivibool *CAAAL* 13, 1980: 168). PYao *k*^{2}*em*^{1} *2* 'forest' [Purnell] is not related to any of the above.

lín$_2$ 林 (ljəm) **LH** lim, **OCM** *rəm

'Numerous' [Shi 220, 2].

ᴥ **tǎn** 噴 (tʰậm^B) **LH** tʰəm^B, **OCM** *rhə̂mʔ ?

'Many, numerous' occurs only once in a *Shījīng* passage [Shi 290, 3]. SW says 'noise of many', perh. inspired by the graph (Giles: 'the sound of many people eating').

[E] Prob. AA, and if so, cognate to → lín$_1$ 林: OKhmer *rāma* /rı́iəm/ 'to gather, be clustered', PNBahn. *krǎm 'crowded'. The initials of TB-Lushai *hlɔm*^{F} 'in numbers' (Sagart 1999: 151), and MK-OMon *tuṁ* /tøm/ 'be numerous' are difficult to reconcile with OC.

lín$_3$ 淋霖 (ljəm) **LH** lim, **OCM** *rəm

'To pour (water)' 淋 [Guoce] > Mand. 'to pour, drench' > 'long rain' 霖 [Zuo].

[T] *Sin Sukchu SR* lim (平), *PR*, *LR* lin; *MGZY* lim (平) [lim]

[D] Mand. 'continuous heavy rain', Mǐn: Amoy *lam*^{A2} 'long rain'; also Amoy lit. *lim*^{A2}, col. *liam*^{A2} 'constant dripping'. In Xiāng, Kèjiā, and Yuè dialects it means 'to sprinkle, to water' (plants); Y-Guǎngzhōu ^{21}*lɐm*^{A2}.

[E] ST: JP *rim*^{33} ~ *rum*^{33} 'waterfall'. (AA: Khmer *ralɨma* /rlým/ 'drizzle, light rain' is derived from /lým/ 'dark, dim').

This may be the same etymon as → lín$_6$ □ 'drink'. Wáng Lì (1982: 612) and Sagart (1999: 127) consider *lín* cognate to → yín$_3$ 淫. For possibly related words, see → chén$_2$ 沈; → làn$_1$ 濫.

lín$_4$ 臨 (ljəm) **LH** lim, **OCM** *rəm

'To approach, look down, look upon favorably, to favor' [Shi], 'be on the brink of'.

ᴥ **lìn** 臨 (ljəm^C) **LH** lim^C, **OCM** *rəms ?

'To mourn' [Zuo], 'mourning chamber' [Li] is acc. to Downer (1959: 286) a tone C derivation with an 'effective' meaning.

[<] perh. exopass. of *lín* 臨, lit. 'be looked upon with favor / affection' ? > caus. 'mourn' (§4.4.1).

[E] ST: Lushai *rim*^{R} < *rimʔ* 'to court, make love to, inspect / make enquiries about' (a girl), WT *rim-(')gro* 'honor, homage, offerings' (*'gro* 'to walk'); perh. also JP *krem*^{33} 'to trust, to look up to' (someone).

lín₅ 鱗 (ljen) **LH** lin, **OCM** *rin
'Scale of fish or reptile' [Li]. The Northern Mǐn initial *s-* as in Jiànyáng *saiŋ*^{A2} may be due to loss of a pre-initial (Mei / Norman 1971: 101).
[E] PKS *krin⁵ 'scales'. Perh. Tai: S. *lin*^{B2} < *l-, Saek *lil*^{B2}, PKS *lin⁶ 'pangolin' (Li F. 1976: 43) is related.

lín₆ □ (ljəm ?) **LH** lim
'To drink' in southern dialects: M-Amoy *lim*$^{A1/A2}$ 'to drink' (lit. *lam*^{A2}); Taiwan *lim*^{A1} (Chén Zhāngtài, Lǐ Rúlóng 1991: 454); K-Táoyuàn *lim*^{A1} 'to drink', Méixiàn 'drink tea from the spout of a teapot' (MacIver p. 403). This is perh. the same etymon as → lán₁ 啉 (lậm) 'drink', and as → lín₃ 淋霖 'to pour'.
[E] PTai *ʔd- (or rather *ʔl- ?): S. *dɨɨm*^{B1} 'to swallow, drink' [Li 1977: 109]. Note also TB-Lushai *lem*^{F} < *lemh* 'to swallow, drink'.

lǐn₁ □ (QYS analog perh. *ljen*^{B}) is a southern dial. word for 'penis': Kèjiā *lin*^{B}, Y-Guǎngzhōu ^{35}*lɐn*^{B1}, Táishān ^{55}*lin*^{B1}; M-Taipei *lan*^{C1}*-tsiau*^{B}. Benedict (1976: 190) relates this to PTB *(m-)li 'penis', Karen *lin 'vagina', but it may simply be a survival from a Tai substratum: Tai S. *lɨŋ*^{A1} (R. Bauer [*CAAAL* 28, 1987: 61f] who, however, believes that the Tai word is a CH loan). Some Mǐn dialects have a different word: PMin *nɔi.

lǐn₂ 稟廩 (ljəmᴮ) **LH** limᴮ, **OCM** *rəmʔ < *b-rəmʔ ?
'Rations' 稟 [Li] (also read QY *pjəm*^{B}); 'granary' 廩 [BI, Shi].

ꭗ **bǐn** 稟 (pjəmᴮ) **LH** pimᴮ, **OCM** *prəmʔ ?
'To receive' [Zuo].
[T] *Sin Sukchu SR* pin (上); *MGZY* bim (上) [pim]
[E] ST: WT *'brim-pa* 'to distribute, hand out, deal out' (*STC:* 178; *HST:* 64); Nung *ərim* 'cast away' may be related, Chepang *bi-rim* n. 'container, small circular storage basket'.

lǐn₃ 廩懍 (ljəmᴮ) **LH** limᴮ, **OCM** *rəmʔ < *b-rəmʔ ?
'Shake' 廩 [Zuo] > 'full of fear, respectful' 懍 [Xun].
[D] This was a Han period Qín-Jìn (northwestern China) dialect word for 'be careful, attentive 敬' [FY 6, 28].
[E] Perh. related to → jìn₃ 禁 'forbid' (so Shī Xiàngdōng 2000: 117). But in light of a possible OC labial initial (b-rəmʔ ?), a connection with MK-Khmer /praam/ 'to prohibit, forbid' would be phonologically closer.

lìn 吝 (ljenᶜ) **LH** linᶜ, **OCM** *m-rəns ?
'Regret' [Yi], 'niggardly' [Lun].
[E] Geilich (1994: 249) compares this word with WT *sri-ba* 'be parsimonious, niggardly', Lepcha *re* 'be rare', Lushai *ren*^{H} 'to economize, be sparing with'.

líng₁ 岭 (lieŋ)
'Mountain range' [GY] may simply be a late graphic variant of → líng₆ 陵, or be cognate to TB-Kachin *kriŋ- < gliŋ-* 'hill' (*STC* p. 34 n. 109).

líng₂ 怜倰 → **lián₉** 憐

líng₃ 蛉 → **míng₅-líng** 螟蛉

líng₄ 鈴 (lieŋ) **LH** leŋ, **OCM** *rêŋ
'Small bell, banner bell' [BI, Shi] is a sound-symbolic word, it may be related to → míng₇ 鳴 OCB *mrjeŋ 'to sound' acc. to Baxter (1992: 499). Theoretically, MC could

also derive from a PCH *rin, then it may be related to WT *'dril-bu* 'bell' (Shī Xiàngdōng 2000), but this is stretching the phonology.

líng₅ 凌 → **bīng₂** 冰

líng₆ 陵 (ljəŋ) **LH** lɨŋ, **OCM** *rəŋ — **[T]** *ONW* liŋ
'Hill' [Shi], 'height' [Zuo] may be the s. w. as → líng₇ 陵泠凌 'step on / over'.
[E] ST: PTB *m-raŋ (*STC* p. 43): WB *mraŋ*[C] 'high', Trung *mraŋ* 'high, long', Kanauri *raŋ* 'mountain, high', NNaga *rəŋ 'sky, Garo *raŋ-ra* 'id.', JP *laŋ*[31] 'mountain'. Also in AA-Khasi *raŋ* and *roŋ* in expressions for 'high, above'.

líng₇ 陵泠凌 (ljəŋ) **LH** lɨŋ, **OCM** *rəŋ
('Step on/over'?:) 'Ascend' [Guoce], 'transgress' [Li], 'encroach upon, usurp, oppress, insult' 陵 [Zuo]; 'surmount' 泠 [Chuci]; 'maltreat, oppress' 凌 [Chuci].
[C] → líng₆ 陵 'hill' may be the s. w. This etymon is prob. cognate to the near homonym → píng₇ 馮憑 'walk across', just as there are doublets *líng* 凌 ~ → bīng₂ 冰 'ice'. Furthermore, this stem may be connected with → chéng₇ 徵懲 'suppress'.

líng₈ 霝零 (lieŋ) **LH** leŋ, **OCM** *rêŋ ~ rîn
'To fall' (of rain) 霝 [OB], 零 [Shi], 'drop the leaves' 蘦 [Chuci]. The graph originally consisted of 雨 'rain' with 'drops' (not 'mouths') underneath.
[T] *MTang* lieŋ < lɨŋ, *ONW* lèŋ
[E] Etymology not clear. Perh. from AA and related to the items under → píng₄ 萍 'rain master'. Or note TB-JP *mă*[31]*-raŋ*[33] 'rain', *raŋ*[31]*-ga*[31] 'violent rain' (*CVST* 2: 53). There is a remote possibility of a connection with → yǔn₂ 隕殞霣 'drop, fall, rain' if one assumes a ST root *rwe- whose initial cluster is simplified to OC *re- and *we- respectively (§10.1.3). WB *lañ*[B] < *liŋ[B] 'to fall' belongs to → diān₂ 顛傎 'fall over'.

líng₉ 靈 (lieŋ) **LH** leŋ, **OCM** *rêŋ
'Divine > felicitous, auspicious > excellent, intelligent' [BI, Shi]; 'spirit (of Heaven)' [Hanshu] > 'ghost (of a deceased)' [Hou Hanshu] > 'female shaman, shaman' [Chuci]. For semantics, cf. *mó* 魔 (< Indic Mara) both 'witch' and 'demon'.
[T] *Sin Sukchu SR* liŋ (平); *MGZY* ling (平) [liŋ]; *ONW* lèŋ
[E] MY: PMiao *qlẹŋ[A] (Wáng FS) 'ghost'. 'Ghost' and → líng₈ 霝零 'rain' are etymologically distinct, although in the meaning 'prayer for rain, rainmaster', the two converge. On the other hand, weather phenomena are divine portents, see → fēn₂ 雰氛. CH -> Viet *thiêng* (via *s-*, from *Cr-*) (Maspero 1912: 84).

lǐng 領 (ljäng[B]) **LH** lieŋ[B], **OCM** *reŋʔ, OCB *C-rěŋʔ
'Neck' [Shi], 'collar' [Li] > ('take by the neck' [Karlgren]:) 'to lead, direct' [Li].
[T] *Sin Sukchu SR* liŋ (上); *MGZY* ling (上) [liŋ]; *ONW* lieŋ
[D] 'Collar' in PMin *liaŋ[B]: Fúzhōu *liaŋ*[B1], Xiàmén *niã*[B1]
[E] ST: Lushai *riŋ*[F] 'neck'; possibly also WT *mgrin-pa* 'neck, throat'. This is prob. a variant of PTB *m-liŋ 'neck' (Matisoff 1995a: 51): WB *lañ*, Nung *liŋ*; WT *mǰiŋ-pa* ~ *'ǰiŋ-pa* < *mliŋ or *mriŋ 'neck' (*HST:* 112). Benedict connects the TB word with *(g-)liŋ 'tube' (French 1983: 525). The synonym → jǐng₂ 頸 is prob. not related.

lìng 令 (ljäŋ[C]) **LH** lieŋ(C), **OCM** *reŋ(h) ~ *rin(s)
'To order, command' [Shi].
[T] *Sin Sukchu SR* liŋ (平去); *MGZY* ling (平去) [liŋ]; *ONW* lieŋ
[N] In the OB and BI, 令 writes actually → mìng 命 'order' to which it is usually thought to be related (so Wáng Lì 1982: 329). Acc. to (Downer 1959: 286), 'to command' [Zuo] is read in tone C, 'to cause' [Zuo] in tone A.

liú$_1$ 留 (ljəu) **LH** liu, **OCM** *ru
'To stay, remain, tarry' [Shi].
[D] M-Xiàmén, Fúzhōu *lau*^{A2}. The Northern Mǐn initial *s-* as in Jiànyáng *seu*^{A2} may be due to loss of a pre-initial: PMin *l̥əu (Mei / Norman 1971: 100).

liú$_2$ 劉 (ljəu) **LH** liu, **OCM** *ru
'To slaughter, kill' [OB, Shi]; a Han period dialect word for 'to kill' in Qín, Jìn, Sòng and Wèi [FY 1, 16].
[N] In the OB, this word was written with the graph for the cyclical sign *mǎo* 卯 (mau^{B}) < *mruʔ which seems to have been intended for writing 'slaughter' as it shows perh. two pieces of meat which have been cut apart.
[T] *Sin Sukchu SR* liw (平); *MGZY* liw (平) [liw]; *MTang* leu < liu, *ONW* lu < lu
[D] The Northern Mǐn initial *s-* as in Jiànyáng *seu*^{A2} may be due to loss of a pre-initial (Mei / Norman 1971: 101).
[E] Perh. ST: KC-Tiddim *gou*^{53} / *gɔʔ*^{11} < *rouh* / *rɔʔ/h* 'to kill, slaughter'.

× **lù** 戮 (ljuk) **LH** liuk, **OCM** *ruk
'Punish by death, execute' [Shu]. Perh. this word is not related to *liú*; it could be the same word as → lù$_{17}$ 僇 'disgrace'.

liú$_3$ 流 (ljəu) **LH** liu, **OCM** *r(i)u
'To flow, float, flow away; the flow' [Shi]; 'pendants of a banner' 旒 [Shi].
[T] *Sin S. SR* liw (平); *MGZY* liw (平) [liw]; *MTang* leu < liu, *ONW* lu
[D] M-Xiàmén, Fúzhōu *lau*^{A2}
[E] This word differs from → yóu$_6$ 游遊 'float, swim' only in the initial, WT shows that they are prob. related: **r-ju > OC *ju and OC *riu, see §9.2.1. An allofam is prob. → lèi$_1$ 淚 *riuts 'tears'.

liú$_4$ 旒 → **liú**$_3$ 流

liù$_1$ 六 (ljuk) **LH** liuk, **OCM** *ruk
'Six' [OB].
[T] *Sin Sukchu SR* lu (入), *PR*, *LR* luʔ; *MGZY* lÿu (入) [ly]; *ONW* luk.
[D] PMin *l̥ok > NMin Jiànyáng *so*^{D2} (Mei / Norman 1971: 99); Y-Guǎngzhōu ^{22}*lok*^{D2}
[E] ST: PTB *d-ruk 'six': WT *drug*, Takpa *grok*; PLB *C-krok, WB *k*^{h}*rok*; JP *kruʔ*^{55}; Lepcha *tărók;* Mikir *t*^{h}*rók* < *drok*^{2}; Lushai *pa*^{L}*-ruk*^{L}. <> Tai: S. *hok*^{D1} < *hr- (MC *l-* = Tai *r-*) is a CH loan where Li's reconstructed initial may be due either to peculiarities of Tai lgs. (often *r* > *h*), or to complexity in the CH donor lg. (note PMin). <> PMY *kruk may be a loan from a TB lg.

liù$_2$ 溜 (ljəu^{C}) **LH** liu, **OCM** *r(i)u
'Gush forth' [Guan], 'a current, a stream' is shared with Tai: S. *riau*^{B2} 'rapids, vigorous, strong (current)' (Manomaivibool 1975: 139).

liù$_3$ 翏飂 (ljəu^{C}, ljeu^{C}, ljäu^{C}) **LH** liu^{C}, **OCM** *riu(k)h
'Whistling of the wind' 翏 [Zhuang], 飂 [GY]; 'wind high up in the air' 飂 [Lü].

× **liáo** 聊 (lieu) **LH** leu, **OCM** *riû
'Ringing sound in the ear' [Chuci].

lóng$_1$ 隆 (ljuŋ) **LH** liuŋ, **OCM** *ruŋ, OCB *g-rjuŋ
'Eminent' [Zuo], 'high' [Guoce].
[E] AA: Khmer *ruŋ* 'be big, tall, mighty, preeminent' × *sruŋ* 'be long enough to cover' [Jenner / Pou 1982: xli] × /sroŋ/ 'big, full'.

ꭗ **chóng** 崇 (dẓjuŋ) **LH** dẓuŋ, **OCM** *dzruŋ
'To pile on, pile high' [Shi]; 'high' (of a mountain) [SW].
[T] *Sin Sukchu SR* dẓuŋ (平); *MGZY* cung (平) [dẓuŋ]
[E] AA: Khmer /croŋ/ 'to raise up, reestablish...' ꭗ *crūṅa* /cròoŋ/ 'be upright'; Riang *tsərɔŋ*, Khasi *jrōŋ* 'high'. AA -> TB-Lepcha *kroŋ* 'high' (Forrest *JAOS* 82, 1962: 334).
An AA substrate wf would explain the odd initial interchange *r- ~ *dzr- which is unusual in a Chinese wf. A syn. or parallel stem with initial OC *l is → sōng$_2$ 崧嵩 'high' (mountain). The meaning *chóng* 'high' (of a mountain) may be due to paronomastic attraction from *sōng*, or from MK: Khmer *cuṅa* /coŋ/, OKhmer *cuṅ* /cuŋ/ 'farthest point, end, tip, top, peak...'; perh. TB-Lushai *čuŋ*^{R} (Lorrain *chung*) 'roof, top, summit, high up' is related (Khmer loan?).

lóng$_2$ 隆 (ljuŋ) **LH** liuŋ, **OCM** *ruŋ ?, OCB *g-rjuŋ
'Thundering' [Shi].
[E] ST: TB-Tamang *mu-guruŋ* 'thunder' (*mu* 'sky') (Benedict 1986: 31), JP *ruŋ*^{31} 'rumbling'. <> PYao *gluŋ^B 'rumbling of thunder' (Benedict 1976: 97).

lóng$_3$ 龍 (ljwoŋ) **LH** lioŋ, **OCM** *roŋ, OCB *C-rjoŋ
'Dragon' [OB, Shi] (discussed by Carr *LTBA* 13.2, 1990: 101 etc.).
[E] Etymology not clear. *Lóng* has been associated with TB comparanda: WT *'brug* 'thunder, dragon' may belong here or may be related to → lóng$_2$ 隆 'thundering'; Lolo *lo* 'dragon'.
Most likely is a connection with SE Asian words: AA: Viet. *rồng* 'dragon', Muong *hông* ~ *ròṅ*, Khmer *roŋ* ~ *rôŋ*, and KT: Siam. *maḥroŋ* ~ *măroŋ*. (CH -> ?) Viet *thuồng* (via *s-* from *Cr-*) (Maspero 1912: 84).
[C] A cognate may be → hóng$_1$ 虹 'rainbow' (so Carr), note for example Y-Cónghuà *loŋ*^{44} (A2) 'rainbow'.

lóng$_4$ 龍 'motley' → **máng$_7$** 尨龍

lóng$_5$ 籠 (luŋ[B]) **LH** loŋ(C), **OCM** *rôŋ(?) — [T] *ONW* luoŋ
'Bird cage' [Zhuang], 'basket' [Zhouli].
[E] AA: OKhmer /kruŋ/ 'to cover, shelter, protect, to pen (animals)' ꭗ *druṅa* /truŋ/ 'pen, cage, coop for birds and animals' < /-ruŋ/ 'to shield, screen, protect, cover'; PSBahn. *gənru:ŋ 'prison, pig pen'. MK provides an etymology and is the source of loans into area lgs.: TB > WB *khruiŋ*^{C} 'cage for birds', Garo *griŋ* (*STC* no. 389). AA -> KT: PTai *kroŋ^{B1} 'cage', PAN *kuruŋ 'cage' (Thurgood 1994: 355). Less likely is a connection with PTai *k^{h}l-: S. *k*^{h}*ɔɔŋ*^{C1} 'kind of basket'.

lóng$_6$ 聾 (luŋ) **LH** loŋ, **OCM** *rôŋ
'Deaf' [Zuo], the Northern Mǐn initial *s-* as in Jiànyáng *soŋ*^{A2} may be due to loss of a pre-initial (Mei / Norman 1971: 101). Perh. connected with → sǒng$_3$ 聳 'deaf'.

lǒng 壟隴 (ljwoŋ^B) **LH** lioŋ^B, **OCM** *roŋ?
'Mound' 壟 [Li], 隴 [Xun], a Han period dialect variant for → zhǒng$_1$ 冢塚 'mound' in the Qín-Jìn area [FY 13, 154]. It may perh. also be related to → lóu$_1$ 婁, lǒu 塿.

lòng$_1$ 弄 (luŋ[C]) **LH** loŋ^C, **OCM** *rôŋh
'To fondle, play with' [Shi].
[E] <> ? Khmer /lúuəŋ/ 'to caress, pet, stroke, soothe...' The Khmer initial consonant does not agree with OC, though; perhaps Khmer is a post-Han or recent CH loan.

lòng₂ 弄 (luŋᶜ) **LH** loŋᶜ, **OCM** *rôŋh
'Alley, lane' [Nán-Qí shū, History of the Southern Qi dyn.], in Shànghǎi for *xiàng* 巷 'lane, alley', prob. a variant (Zhāng Xīngyà *YWYJ* 1996.4: 11).

lóu₁ 婁, **lǒu** 塿 (ləuᴮ) **LH** loᴮ, **OCM** *rôʔ — **[T]** *ONW* lou
'Mound' is a Han period dialect word for 'small mound' east of the Passes (i.e. central China) [FY 13, 154]. *Lóu* is usually the 2nd syllable of a compound, see under → fù₇ 阜. A Han period dialect variant in the Qín-Jìn area is perh. *yú* 堬 (jiu) *lo [FY 13, 154]. Finally, it may be related to → lǒng 壟隴 'mound'.

lóu₂ 僂 (ləu, ljuᴮ) **LH** lo, lioᴮ, **OCM** *lô or *loʔ — **[T]** *ONW* lou
'Bend' [Xun], 'hunchbacked' [Zuo]. Although this word may possibly be a ST etymon derived from → gōu₁ 句鉤枸區: WT *rgu-re* 'bent over' ⋇ *rgur* ~ *sgur* 'crooked', it would require an unusual case of ST prefix preemption (Unger *Hao-ku* 75: 2002 discusses additional possible cases). Alternatively, *lóu* could belong to → zhǒu₁ 肘 'elbow', or even be the s. w. as → lóu₁ 婁 'mound'.

lóu₃ 髏 → **dú-lóu** 髑髏

lǒu 塿 'mound' → **lóu₁** 婁, **lǒu** 塿; → **fù₇** 阜

lòu₁ 漏 (ləuᶜ) **LH** loᶜ, **OCM** *rô(k)h
'To leak' [Shi, Zuo]. Old Sino-Viet. *rɔ* (Pān Wùyún 1987: 28).
[T] *Sin Sukchu SR* ləw (去); *MGZY* lʰiw (去) [ləw]; *MTang* ləu, *ONW* lou

⋇ **lù** 漉麗 (luk) **LH** lok, **OCM** *rôk
'To strain, drip' [Guoce], 'draw off water' (from a pond) 漉 [Li]; 'to strain, pour off' 盝 [Zhuang]; 'net' 麗 [Guoyu].
[E] Area etymon: ? ST: Lepcha *rók* 'to sift, sieve', perh. also WT *'kʰru-ba* ⋇ *'kʰrud-pa* 'to bathe' ⋇ *'kʰrus* 'bath' (Geilich 1994: 32 f). However, the Lepcha word may again be one of many AA loans, and WT may not be related. 'Net' may perh. be a different word related to TB-Mru *lok* 'net' (Löffler 1966: 142), but the initial consonants do not agree.
AA: Khmer *sroḥ* /sraoh/ 'be drained' ⋇ *samroḥ* /sɑmraoh/ 'to drain (land, pond)' < *-raḥ* /-róh/ 'to flow out, drain'.
Khmer -> Tai: S. *rua*^{B2} < *r- 'to leak' [Li F. 1976: 43]; the Tai vocalism does not agree with the OC forms, hence MK seems to be the source.

⋇ **luán** 欒 (luân) **LH** luɑn ~ lon, **OCM** *rôn
'Dripping' (water) [Guoce].

[C] A derivation is prob. → gōu₂ 溝 'a drain'.

lòu₂ 鏤 → **lù₁** 彔

lú₁ 盧壚玈 (luo) **LH** lɑ, **OCM** *râ
'Be black' 盧壚 [Shu], 玈 [Zuo] has been compared to WT *rog-po* 'black' (*HST*: 44), but the rimes do not agree.

lú₂ 廬 (ljwo) **LH** liɑ, **OCM** *ra — **[T]** *ONW* lio
'A hut, hovel, shelter' [Shi], in *Shījīng* with reference to a field hut and an archery shelter, later in *Shījīng* a hut on a tomb, a 'resting place, inn' along a highway [Zhouli]. This looks like a variant (*l > *r) of → shè₂ 舍 'resting place'.

lú₃ 蘆 (ljwo) **LH** liɑ, **OCM** *ra
'Madder plant', in *Shījīng rú-lú* 茹蘆 (ńźjwo-ljwo). Because of the compound *pú₄-lú* 蒲蘆 (buo-ljwo) it has been suggested that the OC form had a pre-initial labial whose

loss may account for the initial *s-* in Northern Mǐn forms (Mei / Norman 1971: 98).

lú₄ 顱 (luo) **LH** lɑ, **OCM** *râ
'Head', a late word [Xin Tangshu], can be compared to Tai: S. *pʰaak* < *pʰr/l- 'forehead'; see also → dú₈-lóu 髑髏.

lú₅ 臚 → **lǚ₁** 旅呂

lú₆ 艫 'boat' → **yú₁₄** 俞

lǔ₁ 鹵 (luoᴮ) **LH** lɑᴮ, **OCM** *râʔ
'Salty, rock salt' [BI, Zuo]. Li F. (1976: 45) draws attention to a possible connection with → gǔ₁₅ 鹽 'salt'.
[E] ST: PTB *s-la 'salt' > Miri *əlo*, PKaren *hla. Acc. to Matisoff (1995: 52), Baxter suggests a connection with the place name Lǔ 魯 which was a salt-marsh region in ancient times. The meaning 'rustic, coarse' [Zhuang] is sometimes thought to be connected with 'salt', but *HST:* 55 separates the two and relates 'coarse' to WT *rags-pa* 'coarse, thick, gross'.

lǔ₂ 魯 → **lǔ₁** 鹵

lǔ₃ 櫓 (luoᴮ) **LH** lɑᴮ, **OCM** *râʔ
'A large shield' [Li] has been compared to WB *hlwaᴮ* 'shield' (oblong and convex) (Unger *Hao-ku* 36, 1990: 52).

lù₁ 彔 (luk) **LH** lok, **OCM** *rôk, OCB *C-rok
'Carve wood' [SW] (Li 1977: 62, 125, 277; Baxter 1992: 504f, 543).

⋇ **lù** 錄 (ljwok) **LH** liok, **OCM** *rok
'To inscribe, record' [Gongyang; Zhouli].

⋇ **lòu** 鏤 (ləuᶜ) **LH** loᶜ, **OCM** *rô(h)
'To carve, engrave' [Shi]. The graph has an alternate reading LH *loᴬ* (Unger *Hao-ku* 1983: 20).

[E] ST: WT *'bru-ba, brus*, and *'brud-pa* 'to dig, chisel, carve, cut'; Nung *ə-ru* 'carve, write' (Benedict *HJAS* 4, 1939: 220); perh. also JP *krok⁵⁵* 'to carve' (wood) (for the CH final *-k*, see §6.1). Unger points to the morphological parallelism with WT:

鏤 OCM	*rô	<> WT	'bru < ɴ-bru
鏤 OCM	*rôh < *rôs	<> WT	brus

This wf is considered to be related to → bāo₃ 剝 'peel', but 'carve' and 'peel' are rather different activities.

lù₂ 盝 → **lòu₁** 漏

lù₃ 錄 → **lù₁** 彔

lù₄ 陸 (ljuk) **LH** liuk, **OCM** *ruk
'Land' (as opposed to water) [Shi] is perh. shared with PWa *[ʔ]rok 'dry land'.

lù₅ 路 (luoᶜ) **LH** lɑᶜ, **OCM** *râkh, OCB *g-raks
'Road, way' [Shu].
[T] *Sin Sukchu SR* lu (去), *PR, LR* lu; *MGZY* lu (去) [lu]; *ONW* lo
[D] W-Wēnzhōu *løy²¹*; M-Yǒng'ān *tiɯᶜ¹*, Jiànyáng *tiɔᶜ²*, Fúzhōu *tuoᶜ²*
[E] Unless it is related to → gé₄ 格 'go, come' (Baxter 1992: 329), it has no obvious ST etymology. It may be an AA word instead: MK-PVM *k-raːʔ 'way, path', PWa *kraʔ 'road', Pearic *kʰraː* 'road, path', and Yao *kla³*. Cognate may also be → lüè₃ 略.

lù$_6$ 路 (luo^C) **LH** lɑ^C, **OCM** *râkh — **[T]** *ONW* lo
'Grand, loud' 路 [Shi], 'big carriage, state carriage' 輅 [Shu]. The expression *lù qǐn* 路寢 *râkh tshəmʔ 'grand / royal apartment' [Shi, Chunqiu] has the variant *bó qǐn* 柏寢 (pɐk tsʰjəm^B) *prâk-tshəmʔ [Hanfei] (Unger *Hao-ku* 29, 1984: 266) which means that the reconstruction and identification of *lù* is far from certain.

lù$_7$ 簬 (luo^C) **LH** lɑ^C, **OCM** *râkh < *g-râh
'A kind of bamboo' used for making slender arrows [Shu] is listed as pre- or early-historic tribute from the Yangtze / Han River region, i.e. an area inhabited by non-Chinese people.
[E] Southern Area word: Tai: S. *kʰlaa*^{C2} (WrSiam *glaa*) 'bamboo' (Manomaivibool 1975: 141). <> PMY *l̥o^3 'bamboo'. <> MK: Bahnar *pəle*, Viet *le* 'bamboo' [Gregerson in Jenner 1976: 353]. For the difference in initials, see §7.3.

lù$_8$ 露 (luo^C) **LH** lɑ^C, **OCM** *râkh, OCB *g-raks
'Dew, to condense into droplets' (clouds) [Shi].
An OC pre-initial may explain the initial *s-* in some Northern Mǐn dialects, thus PMin *l̥o^C > Jiàn'ōu *su*^{44} (Mei / Norman 1971: 98). In a few dialects it means 'fog': W-Sūzhōu *mi*$^{24/22}$*- ləu*$^{21/44}$.
[E] Derived from → luò$_7$ 落 'to fall, drop', the AA-Khmer stem also has the semantic extension 'cover from above, drip'. An allofam is → xǔ$_1$ 湑 'to drip'.

lù$_9$ 露 (luo^C) **LH** lɑ^C, **OCM** *râkh, OCB *g-raks
'Let appear, appear' [BI, Shi] > ('let bones appear':) 'emaciated' [Zuo].
Karlgren *GSR* 766t' considers this the s. w. as → lù$_8$ 露, but it may be a separate etymon, note TB-JP *kra*^{31} 'to appear, show'.

lù$_{10}$ 鷺 (luo^C) **LH** lɑ^C, **OCM** *râkh
'Heron, egret' [Shi].
[E] AA: Khmer *kraak* 'species of heron', *k-* may be an AA prefix found in animal names [Jenner / Pou 1982: xl]. <> Tai *raa*^{C2} 'a kind of heron' (Manomaivibool 1975: 139; Unger *Hao-ku* 36, 1990: 45).

lù$_{11}$ 鹿 (luk) **LH** lok, **OCM** *rôk
'Deer, sika deer' [OB, Shi]. Sagart (1999: 161) suggests that → jiǎo$_5$ 角 'horn' is related to *lù*.
[E] The etymology is not certain; it may be ST: NNaga *gjuk* 'sambar, deer' < PTB *g-rjuk [French 1983: 188]. Benedict (acc. to French) relates the TB item to Gurung *gju* 'sheep', but this has an alternate explanation. Note also Tai: Nung *klook* 'deer' (generic term) (Benedict *AT:* 268).

lù$_{12}$ 摝 (luk) **LH** lok, **OCM** *rôk
'Shake' (as drums shake bells) [Zhouli].
[C] This word could be associated with → jué$_{11}$ 覺 or → jiǎo$_8$ 攪.

lù$_{13}$ 麓 (luk) **LH** lok, **OCM** *rôk
'Forest (in foothills)' [Shi] > 'forester' [BI, Guoyu] (also with phonetic 彔 [OB, SW]).
[E] AA: PVM *m-ru:ʔ 'forest'.

lù$_{14}$ 轆 → **lì**$_{24}$**-lù** 轣轆

lù$_{15}$ 漉 → **lòu**$_1$ 漏

lù$_{16}$ 扈 → **lòu**$_1$ 漏

lù₁₇ 僇 (ljuk) **LH** liuk, **OCM** *ruk
'Disgrace' [Lun].
[E] ST: Mru *ruk* 'shame' (Löffler 1966: 142).

lù₁₈ 戮 → **liú₃** 劉

lǘ₁ 婁 (lju) **LH** lio, **OCM** *rio < *r-jo
'To drag, trail' [Shi].
≍ **yú** 臾 (jiu) **LH** jo, **OCM** *jo
'To pull, drag' [Zhuang].

lǘ₂ 驢 (ljwo) **LH** lia, **OCM** *ra
'Donkey' [SW].
[T] *Sin Sukchu SR* ly (平); *MGZY* lÿu (平) [ly]
[N] Unger (*Hao-ku* 13, 1989) points out that the donkey must have been known in China before its first mention during the Han dynasty because 'mule' **luó** 騾 (luâ) (*Sin Sukchu SR* lɔ (平); *MGZY* lwo (平) [lwɔ]) occurs already in *Lǚshì chūnqiū*. Related are WB la^B 'mule', Tiddim $la{:}^F$ < *la:h* 'mule', but MC *l-* usually corresponds to PTB *r. Perh. the TB items are Han period or later loans.

lǚ₁ 旅呂 (ljwo^B) **LH** lia^B, **OCM** *raʔ
Anything lined up in a regular fashion: 'one after the other' [Li], 'line up in a row > set forth; troop, multitude' [OB, Shi]; 'spine' [Shi, Zhuang], 'pitchpipe' 呂 [Li] > ('spine of a roof' >) 'beam supporting rafter of a roof' 梠 [SW].
[T] *Sin Sukchu SR* ly (上); *MGZY* lÿu (上) [ly]; *ONW* lio
Perh. ≍ **lú** 臚 (ljwo) **LH** lia, **OCM** *ra
'To display, expose, arrange' [Guoyu].
[E] ST: WT *gra-ma* 'the awn, bristles, or ears of cereals; bones or skeleton of a fish, lattice, trellis, frame' (Bodman 1980: 165; *HST:* 138); Matisoff (1999: 6) adds JP n^{31}-rut^{55} n^{31}-ra^{33} 'skeleton bones' (n^{31}-rut^{55} 'bones'), Tangkhul *a-ra*, Nocte *a-ra*. Perh. also WT *gras* 'class, order, rank, tribe' (Bodman 1980: 132) which is plausible in light of WT *rus* 'bone' ~ 'clan'. Unger (*Hao-ku* 39, 1992) connects the WT word with → liè₁ 列 (ljät) 'series'.

lǚ₂ 旅 (ljwo^B) **LH** lia^B, **OCM** *raʔ
'Guest, stranger' [Zuo], 'traveler' [Yi], 'road' [Li].
Bodman (1980: 132) connects this word with WT *dgra* 'enemy' ≍ *'gras-pa* 'to hate'. Or this word may belong to a larger group which includes → gé₄ 格 'go, come'.

lǚ₃ 旅 (ljwo^B) **LH** lia^B, **OCM** *raʔ
'Lodge, lodging' [Shi]. This word has several possible etymologies: (1) cognate to → lǚ₂ 旅 'guest, traveler'. (2) An endoactive derivation (§4.5) of → lú₂ 廬 'hut'. (3) It could possibly belong to the ST stem *s-jak ~ *r-jak '24 hour day, spend the night', see → xī₁ 夕 for suggestive Lushai cognates.

lǚ₄ (?) 鋁 **OCM** *raʔ (?) The reading of this graph is conjecture.
'Material from which bronze vessels were cast' [only in Zhou BI] (Qiu Xigui 2000: 305) may be related to WT *ra-gan* 'brass', *rag-* in compounds.

lǜ₁ 律 (ljuet) **LH** luit, **OCM** *rut
('To follow':) 'to follow a model' [Li], 'law, rule' [Yi], 'row' [Shi] > 'to comb' [Xun] (Karlgren *GSR* 502c).
[T] *Sin Sukchu SR* ly (入); *MGZY* lÿu (入) [ly]; *ONW* luit
[E] Baxter (1992: 280 and 842 n. 196) derives 'rule' from the same root as → bǐ₆ 筆

'brush, writing pencil', both deriving from the notion 'draw a line, ruler'; but see *bǐ* for an alternative etymology.

ꕤ **shuài** 率帥 (ṣjuet, ṣwi^{C}) **LH** ṣuit, ṣuis, **OCM** *srut(s) — **[T]** *ONW* ṣuit

'To go along, follow, lead' 率 [Shi]; 'lead an army' 帥 [Zuo], 'obey' [Li].

[<] s-caus. of *lyǜ* 律 (ljuet) (§5.2.2).

ꕤ **shuài** 帥 (ṣwi^{C}) **LH** ṣuis, **OCM** *sruts

'Leader, officer' [Zuo].

[T] *Sin Sukchu SR* ṣuj (去), *PR*, *LR* ṣwajʔ; *MGZY* (zhway >) shway (去) [ṣwaj]

[E] ST: KN-Lushai *hruai*^{H} < *hruai* 'to lead, guide, conduct', Lai *hruaj / hruaʔj* 'to lead', NNaga *rua:y. Although this KN etymon looks suggestively similar to CH, the KN final *-uaj* is rather different from the OC final, perh. in OC some vocalic leveling had taken place after the addition of the final -t. For additional possible cognates, see → suì$_2$ 遂.

lǜ$_2$ 慮 (ljwo, ljwo^{C}) **LH** lia(^{C}), **OCM** *ra(h)

'To think of, consider' [Shi] > 'be anxious about' [Lun].

[T] *Sin Sukchu SR* ly (去); *MGZY* lÿu (去) [ly]; *ONW* lio

[E] ST *rwa- ? : WT *bgro-, bgros* 'to consider, deliberate' (Unger *Hao-ku* 20: 169), Lushai *ruat*^{F} 'to think, believe, consider'.

[C] Allofam → lüè$_2$ 略.

lǜ$_3$ 勴 → **zhù$_{12}$** 助

lǜ$_4$-liáo 膟膋 (ljuet-) **LH** luit, **OCM** *rut — **[T]** *ONW* luit-

The commentaries on the relevant passages in *Lǐjì* are ambiguous. One says 'blood and fat around intestines', another simply 'fat ar. i.' A parallel passage in *Shi* 210, 5 has 血膋 'blood and fat r. i.'; therefore the commentary to *Li* may have omitted or lost the reference to 'blood', consequently it appears that *lǜ* means 'blood' (Unger *Hao-ku* 39, 1992). If this is the case, *lǜ* would be a loan from PTai *lɨet^{D2L} (rather than PKS *pʰla:t^{7}, Kadai *plat^{D}) 'blood'. If, on the other hand, *lǜ* should be a homonym of *liáo* 'intestines', either or both could be connected with Viet-Muong: Viet. *ruột*, Muong *rɔc* 'intestines' [Pulleyblank *JCL* 22.1, 1994: 82].

lǜ$_5$ 繂率 (ljuet) **LH** luit, **OCM** *rut (or *riut ?)

'Rope' made of hemp or bamboo 繂 [SW], 'leather band' 率 [Zuo].

[E] ST: WT *rgyud < r-yut* 'string, cord' (of bow, musical instrument), 'connection' ꕤ *rgyud-pa* 'to fasten, file' (on string) (Unger *Hao-ku* 39, 1992); if WB *krui*^{B} 'thread, string, chain' should be related, the etymon needs to be analyzed differently. This is apparently a variant of → yù$_{26}$ 繘, both from PCH **rjut ~ **r-jut (§9.2.1).

luán$_1$ 欒臠 (luân) **LH** luan, **OCM** *rôn, OCB *b-ron

'Emaciated' [Shi].

[E] ST: WB *prun*^{B} 'worn away, exhausted, spent' (as property) ꕤ *pʰrun*^{B} 'wear away, exhaust, spend'.

luán$_2$ 灓 'dripping' → **lòu$_1$** 漏

luán$_3$ 鑾 (luân) **LH** luan, **OCM** *rôn, OCB *b-ron

'Bells on horse's trapping' [BI; SW 14: 6331] is related to Tai: S. *pʰruan*^{A2} < *br- 'neck bells' (for domestic animals); this is a CH loan like other words dealing with horsemanship, as Bodman (1980: 74) points out.

lüán, shuàn 孿 (ṣwan^{C}, ṣjwän^{C}) **LH** ṣuan^{C}, **OCM** *srons

'Twins' [Lü] is an ancient Zhào-Wèi (Shanxi) dialect word [FY 3.1], it may be a

doublet of → shuāng$_1$ 雙 *sroŋ (Baxter 1992: 227), but the putative ST roots would differ which speak against this (ST *zuŋ vs. *run).
[E] ST: JP *mə^{31}-run^{55}* 'twin'.

luǎn 卵 (luân^B) **LH** luɑn^B, **OCM** *rôn?, OCB *C-ron? — [T] *ONW* luɑn
'Egg' [Zuo], the Northern Mǐn initial *s-* may be due to loss of a pre-initial which might have been a velar considering Duàn Yùcái's comment that *luǎn* is read like *guān* 關 (Mei / Norman 1971: 99).
[E] ST: PTB *(s-)rwa 'nit' > WT *sro-ma* 'eggs of louse, nit', JP *tsiʔ-ru* 'louse eggs' (Benedict 1976: 190).

luàn 亂 (luân^C) **LH** luɑn^C, **OCM** *rôns, OCB *C-rons
'To rebel, disorder' [Shi].
[T] *Sin Sukchu SR* lwɔn (去); *MGZY* lon (去) [lɔn]; *ONW* luɑn
[E] Area word of AA origin: Khmer *prwla* /prùuəl/ 'be agitated, disturbed, in uproar' < *rwla* /rúuəl/ 'to boil quickly, cook, grill'; also Khmer /kaṃraaəl/ 'to run amok, get excited, agitated' < /róol/ 'to burn, blaze, roar'.
AA -> TB-WB *broŋ^B* ~ *byoŋ^B* ~ *prun^B* ~ *run^B* 'tumultuous'; WT *k^{h}ral-k^{h}rul* 'confusion, disorder' (the stem is *krul).*
CH -> Middle Vietnamese *tlọn* > *trộn* (Maspero 1912: 78). Old Sino-Viet *ron* (Pān Wùyún 1987: 28).
[C] Baxter (1992: 365) thinks it likely that this word is cognate to → biàn$_4$ 變 *prjons 'change'.

lüè$_1$ 掠略 (ljak, ljaŋ^C) **LH** liɑk, liɑŋ^C, **OCM** *rak, *raŋh.
'To rob, plunder' 掠 [Zuo], 略 [Guoyu].
[D] M-Amoy *lŋ^C* 'to beat'
[E] ST: Lushai *rɔk^L* 'to plunder, loot, raid'.

lüè$_2$ 略 (ljak) **LH** liɑk, **OCM** *rak
'To trace out, measure (area), plan' [Shu] > 'plan, method' [Zuo]; 'boundary, frontier' [Zuo].
[T] *Sin Sukchu SR* ljaw (入); *MGZY* lew (入) [lɛw]; *ONW* l(i)ak
[C] Possible allofams → lǜ$_2$ 慮; → lüè$_3$ 略; perh. also → liáng$_4$ 量.

lüè$_3$ 略 (ljak) **LH** liɑk, **OCM** *rak
'To traverse' [Zuo] > 'sketch, outline' [Meng]; 'road, way' [Zuo].
[C] This is possibly the same etymon as → lüè$_2$ 略. Perh. ⋈ → lù$_5$ 路 'road'.

lüè$_4$ 略 (ljak) **LH** liɑk, **OCM** *rak
'Be sharp' (of plows) [Shi].
[E] ? ST: PTB *mrak (*STC* no. 147): WB *mrak* 'cut keenly' ⋈ *mra^C* 'very sharp, keen', JP *ʔmyaʔ^{55}* 'torn, ragged'.

lún$_1$ 論 (ljuen, luən) **LH** luin, luən, **OCM** *run
'To discuss' [Lunyu] > 'examine' 論 [Meng]; 'principle, category' 倫 [Shi]. Acc. to Downer (1959: 277) the noun has tone C.
[T] *Sin Sukchu SR* lun (平去); *MGZY* lun (平去) [lun]; *ONW* lon
⋈ **lùn** 論 (luən^C) **LH** luən^C, **OCM** *rûns
'Theory' [Zuo].
[E] Perh. ST: Lushai *rɔɔn^H* 'to ask advice, consult' ⋈ *rɔɔn^L* < *rɔɔnh (< rɔɔns)* 'to suggest, advise'.

lún₂ 輪 (ljuen) **LH** luin, **OCM** *run — **[T]** *ONW* luin
'Wheel' [Shi]. Acc. to Robert Bauer (*Sino-Platonic Papers* 47, 1994) perh. a PIE loan whose source may ultimately be the same etymon as the one for → chē 車. Dialects have different words for 'wheel': Beijing *kú-lù* 軲轆, Y-Guǎngzhōu *tsʰɛ⁵⁵-lok⁵⁵* 車轆.

lún₃ 綸 (ljuen) **LH** luin, **OCM** *run, OCB *g-rjun
'Cord' [Li], 'to twist' [Shi], 'envelop, comprise' [Yi]. Pulleyblank (1972, 73) relates this word to → léi₂ 累縲. Acc. to Baxter (1992: 281) the following is derived from the same root:

⋇ **guān** 綸 (kwan) **LH** kuan, **OCM** *krûn ?
'Blue or green sash, kerchief' [Erya, SW].

[C] Perh. also related is → mín₃ 緡 OCB *mrjun (so Baxter).

luō 捋 (luât) **LH** luɑt, **OCM** *rôt
'Gather, pluck' [Shi]; 'to pull (up sleeves), to scrape off (sweat), milk (cows)'.
[E] PTai *ruut*^D2 'to scrape off (mud from limbs), strip off (grains from stalk)' (Manomaivibool 1975: 139). There are two possible TB cognates: Lushai *lo*^R / *lɔʔ*^L (< *lɔs) 'to pluck, pick', but the initial consonants do not agree. Or WT *'drud-pa* 'to rub, file, rub off, grind'.
[C] Allofam is perh. → guā₃ 刮 'scrape off'. Perhaps also related to → duó₄ 掇 (tuât, tjwat) 'pick, gather'.

luó₁ 蝸 → **wō**, **guā**, **luó** 蝸

luó₂ 螺 (luâ) **LH** luɑi / S loi — **[T]** *ONW* luɑ
'A spiral shell'.
[D] The initial *s-* in Northern Mǐn dialects as in Jiàn'ōu *so*^A2 may be due to the loss of a pre-initial (Mei / Norman 1971: 100).

luó₃ 騾 → **lǘ₂** 驢

luó₄ 羅 (lâ) **LH** lɑi, **OCM** *râi — **[T]** *ONW* lɑ
'Bird net' [Shi], 'gauze' [Guoce].
[D] Y-Guǎngzhōu ²¹*lɔ*^A2, K-Méixiàn *lɔ*^A2
[E] Perh. the word is related to WT *dra* 'net' (but the rimes do not agree).
[C] Allofam → lí₉ 離罹.

luó₅ 籮 (lâ) **LH** lɑi
'Hamper' [JY]; Han period dialect word for 'winnowing basket' [FY 5].
[D] Y-Guǎngzhōu ²¹*lɔ*^A2; PMin *l̥ɑi^A2: Jiānglè *šai*^D3, Fúzhōu *lai*^A2, Xiàmén *lua*^A2, lit. *lo*^A2
[E] ? ST: TB-Lushai *hrai*^R < *hraiʔ* 'a basket for measuring rice'.

luǒ₁ 砢 → **lěi₂** 磊硦

luǒ₂ 裸 (luâ^B) **LH** luɑi^B / S loi^B, **OCM** *rôiʔ — **[T]** *ONW* luɑ^B
'Bare, naked' [Zuo].
[E] ST: Lushai *ruak*^F < *ruak* 'naked'. Matisoff (1995: 64) suggests that the OC final *-i (-j) represents a ST diminutive suffix. PTai *ploi^A1 'naked' (Luo 2000: 75) seems also to be related.
[C] Prob. related to → chéng₅ 裎 'naked'.
For an overview of related and similar etyma, see Table L-1.

Table L-1 Naked, red

	ST *rojʔ ? ⋈	TB *g-roy-n ?	ST *reŋ < rojŋ?	TB *kjeŋ red
OC	luǒ 裸 *rôiʔ naked		chéng 裎 *dreŋ naked ⋈ chēng 赬 *hreŋ red (intensive)	
WT	sgre-ba naked	sgren-mo, rǰen naked		skyeŋ-ba ashamed
JP		krin^{31} bare		k^hyeŋ ~ tśeŋ red (Kachin), JP k^hye^{33}
Lushai	ruakF < ruak naked	ṭeenR < trenʔ bare (hillside)		
Mikir			-reŋ^L naked	
WB				kyaŋ red (intensive)

luò$_1$ 咯 (lâk [JY]), **LH** lɑk, **OCM** *râk
'To cough up (blood)'.
[E] Tai: S. *raak^{D2}* 'to vomit' (Manomaivibool 1975: 170). Perh. this word is cognate to → kè$_4$ 喀. The graph 咯 also writes a word *kǎ* 咯 (under → ké$_1$ 咳欬). This sound symbolic item also may be reflected in TB-Lushai *lua^L / lɔ^L, luak^F < luaʔ/h / luak* 'to vomit, be sick'.

luò$_2$ 烙 (lâk) **LH** lɑk, **OCM** *râk
'To burn' [Zhuang] also occurs in PTai *gl-: S. *k^{h}lɔɔk^{D2L}* 'to burn'.

luò$_3$ 硌 (lâk) **LH** lɑk, **OCM** *râk see → lěi$_2$ 磊磥

luò$_4$ 鞜 → **fǔ$_9$** 膚

luò$_5$ 酪 → **lào$_1$** 酪

luò$_6$ 絡 (lâk) **LH** lɑk, **OCM** *râk
'Cord, bridle' [Zhuang], 'silk thread' [Yi Zhou zhu] is perh. cognate to PLB *ʔkrak 'rope', WT *'grags-pa* 'to bind', unless WT is related to → huò$_3$ 韄.

luò$_7$ 落 (lâk) **LH** lɑk, **OCM** *râk, OCB *g-rāk
'To fall, drop, die' [Shi].
[T] *Sin Sukchu* 洛 *SR* law (入), *LR* lawʔ; *MGZY* 洛 law (入) [law]; *ONW* lɑk
[D] PMin *l̥ək 'to fall'
[E] ST: PTB *kla (*STC* 123): Lushai *tla^L / tlaak^F* 'to fall from, go down' ⋈ *t^{h}laak^F* 'throw off, drop'; WB *kya^C* 'to fall, become low' ⋈ *k^{h}ya^C* 'to throw down', Mikir *kló < kla* 'fall down', JP *k^{h}rat^{31}* 'to fall', also *mə^{31}-loʔ^{55}* 'to fall off' ⋈ *lok^{55}* describes 'falling off' (Matisoff 1995a: 46f; Bodman 1980: 145). OC has *r instead of the expected *l (TB) in the initial probably due to pronomastic attraction to AA: Khmer *gra'ka* /kruk/ (vowel /u/ instead of /a/ because of the voiced initial) 'be low, debased' < *-ra'ka* /-ruk/ 'to fall, be low, cover from above'.

Allofams with OC *r-: → xià$_1$ 下 'descend', → lù$_8$ 露 'dew'; see also → tuò$_4$ 蘀 *lhâk 'fallen leaves'.

luò$_8$ 雒 (lâk) **LH** lɑk, **OCM** *râk

'A kind of bird' [SW], this may possibly be the s. w. as *luò* 雒 (lâk) 'black horse with white mane' [Shi] and 駱 'white horse with black mane' [Shi], so called after the bird's color.

luò$_9$ 駱 → **luò$_8$** 雒

M

mā$_1$ 媽 Mand. 'mother', also in other dialects, e.g. G-Wǔníng *ma*^{A1}, but this particular dialect also has a form *maʔ*^{D1} 'mother' which is parallel to *paʔ*^{D1} 伯 'father' (Sagart 1993: 171). In some southern dialects, this etymon also means 'female' (of animals): e.g. M-Jiàn'ōu *kai*^{54}-*ma*^{22} 雞 嫲 'hen'.

ma$_2$ 嗎 Interrogative final particle in modern dialects, probably the same etymon as → wú$_4$ 無 *ma 'not' with parallels in other languages, including TB, as in Lhasa *ma*, Hakha Lai (KC) *-maa* or *-moo*.

má 麻 (ma) **LH** mai, **OCM** *mrâi — **[T]** *Sin Sukchu SR* ma (平); *ONW* mä
'Hemp' (*Cannabis sativa*), used for making linen [Shi], later also 'sesame'.
[D] PMin *mai^{A2}: Xiàmén *muã*^{A2}, Jiànyáng *moi*^{A2}, Jiàn'ōu *muɛ̃*^{C1}, Fúzhōu *muai*^{A2}
[E] Etymology not clear. A SE Asian word for 'sesame' is PKS *ʔŋra^1, MK-PMon *lŋaw, AN-Malay leŋa.

mǎ$_1$ 馬 (ma^B) **LH** ma^B, **OCM** *mrâʔ
'Horse' [OB].
[T] *Sin Sukchu SR ma* (上); *ONW mä*

ꕤ **mǎ** 禡 (ma^C) **LH** ma^C, **OCM** *mrâh
'A kind of horse sacrifice performed in the wilds' [Shi].

[E] ST: PTB *mraŋ (*STC* no. 145): > OTib. *rmaŋ*, Kan. *s-raŋ, WB *mraŋ*^{B}, JP *gum*^{31}-*ra*^{31} ~ *-raŋ*; JR *(m)bro* < *mraŋ*. For the OC ~ TB difference in finals, see §3.2.4. *STC* (p. 43 n. 139) relates PTB *mraŋ to a PTB root *raŋ 'high' (→ líng$_6$ 陵).

Horse and chariot were introduced into Shang period China around 1200 BC from the west (Shaughnessy *HJAS* 48, 1988: 189-237). Therefore this word is prob. a loan from a Central Asian language, note Mongolian *morin* 'horse'. Either the animal has been known to the ST people long before its domesticated version was introduced; or OC and TB languages borrowed the word from the same Central Asian source.

Middle Korean *mol* also goes back to the Central Asian word, as does Japanese *uma*, unless it is a loan from CH (Miyake 1997: 195). Tai *maa*^{C2} and similar SE Asian forms are CH loans.

mǎ$_2$ 螞馬 Prefix for names of insects [FY, EY] (Mei Tsu-Lin 1985: 339), as in *mǎ-yǐ* 螞蟻 'ant' (→ yǐ$_6$ 蟻), see also → huáng$_6$ 蟥.

mǎ$_3$**-huáng** 馬蟥 → **huáng**$_6$ 蟥

mà 罵 (ma$^{B/C}$) **LH** ma$^{B/C}$, **OCM** *mrâʔ/h ?
'To scold' [Zuo].
[E] Prob. ST: WT *dmod-pa* 'curse' which, however, is apparently derived from *ma* 'below' (*STC:* 189 n. 487). Note also → wǔ$_6$ 侮 *moʔ 'id.' with a different vowel. Perh. this is an areal etymon, note MK-Khmer *tmah* 'criticize in front of other, give a public dressing down'.

mǎi 買 (maɨ^B) **LH** mɛ^B, **OCM** *mrêʔ — **[T]** *ONW* mëi
'To buy' [Zuo, Zhao 26.3; Zhuang 1]. A graph similar to *mǎi* is found on OB (*Sōrui* p. 253; Lǐ Xiàodīng p. 2157), but it is not certain what word it was intended to write.
[T] *Sin Sukchu SR* maj (上); *MGZY* may (上) [maj]; *ONW* mëi

⋇ **mài** 賣 (maiᶜ) **LH** mɛᶜ, **OCM** *mrêh
'To sell' [Zhouli]. The graph was originally distinct from → yù₂₃ 賣, see SW 2679.
[<] exoactive of *mǎi* 買 (maiᴮ) (§4.3.1).
[E] ST: PTB *b-rey (*STC* no. 293 n. 207) > WT *rje-ba* < ɴ-*rje* ?) 'to barter', JP *ma³¹-ri³³* 'to buy', Garo *bre*, Dimasa *barai*. As to foreign initial *b-* for CH *m-*, see §5.12.2.
Alternative suggestions: Haudricourt a. Strecker (*TP* 77, 1991: 340) propose that *mǎi* and *mài* are loans from MY *maiᴮ* and *maiᶜ*, derived from a MY word 'to have'. Acc. to Benedict, this is a common area word, perh. of Austro-Tai origin (Benedict, *AT* *(m)baḷi).
This set is more recent than → shē₁ 賒 'trade, sell' which is parallel to PTB *ley?. Syn. → dí₆ 糴; → gǔ₁₁ 賈; → shòu₂ 售; → yù₂₃ 賣.

mài₁ 脈 (mɛk) **LH** mɛk, **OCM** *mrêk — **[D]** PMin *m̊ak ~ *mek
'Vein' [Zuo].
[E] ST: Lushai *marᴴ* < *mar* 'the pulse'. As often, CH has added a final *-k* (§6.1): The OC form is derived from *mer-k or perh. rather *mər-k, since OC *ə would agree with PTB *a (MC *-ɛk* can derive from both OC *-rək and *-rek); *mài* does not occur in early rimes which would decide the issue.

mài₂ 脈 writes Amoy *baʔᴰ¹* 'flesh'; etymology not clear, though reminiscent of → méi₅ 脢.

mài₃-mù 霢霂 (mɛk-muk) **LH** mɛk-mok, **OCM** *m(r)êk-m(r)ôk, OCB *-mok
'Drizzle, drizzling rain' n. [Shi 210, 2] may possibly be connected with the ST root under → wù₁₂ 霧.

mài₄ 麥 (mɛk) **LH** mɛk, **OCM** *mrə̂k, OCB *mrək
'Wheat' [Shi].
[D] PMin *mak > Amoy *beʔᴰ²*, Fúzhōu *maʔᴰ²*
[N] *Mài* and the alleged lái 來 (lậi) 'wheat' [Shi] are not related to → lái₁ 來 'come' (Qiu Xigui 2000: 287f), contrary to the often repeated folk etymology which is already found in *SW*. According to Pulleyblank (*EC* 25, 2000: 23), 來 is the original graph for *mài*, while 麥 (with the element 'foot') was originally intended for the more common *lái* 'come', hence *lái* 'wheat' is spurious.
[E] ST *m-rə(k) > WT *bra-bo* 'buckwheat'; cf. PLB *g-ra² 'buckwheat' [Matisoff *D. Lahu:* 1116]. For Ch. initial *m-, see §5.12.2.

mài₅ 邁勱 (maiᶜ) **LH** mas, **OCM** *mrâts
'To walk, move on, move along' (of time) 邁 [Shi] > caus. 'to encourage' 勱 [Shu].

mán 瞞 → **míng₄** 瞑

màn₁ 慢嫚 → **wàn₂** 曼

màn₂ 曼漫 → **wàn₂** 曼

màn₃ 謾 'deceive' → **wū₃** 誣

màn₄ 謾 'reckless' → **wàng₂** 妄

máng₁ 芒 (mjwaŋ, mwâŋ) **LH** m(u)ɑŋ, **OCM** *maŋ
'Beard of grain, sharp point' [Zhouli].
= **máng** 鋩 (mjwaŋ) **LH** muɑŋ, **OCM** *maŋ
'Sharp point of weapon' [Lie].
[E] Etymology not clear. Possible comparanda: (1) Perh. related to PKS *mpraːŋ¹ 'ear' (of grain), but we should expect a trace of a medial *r in MC (div. II). (2) TB-WB *ə-maŋ* 'stiff hair, bristles'.

máng₂ 芒 (mwâŋ) **LH** maŋ, **OCM** *mâŋ
'Great, extensive' [Shi].
[D] Perh. related to G-Wǔníng *maŋ*^{B} 'great' (tones do not agree) (Sagart 1993: 173).
× **huāng** 荒 (xwâŋ) **LH** huaŋ, **OCM** *hmâŋ
'Be large, too large, excessive' [Shi].
[T] *Sin Sukchu SR* xwaŋ (平); *MGZY* hwang (平) [xwaŋ]
[E] ST: WT *maŋ-po* 'much, many; having much' × *maŋ-ba* 'be much', Lushai *maŋ*^{R} 'very, much'. Perh. connected with → mèng₁ 孟, → wǔ₉ 膴廡.

máng₃ 芒茫 (mwâŋ, xwâŋ[B]) **LH** maŋ, huaŋ, **OCM** *mâŋ, *hmâŋ
'Obscure, confused' [Zhuang], perh. related to → máng₄ 盲 (mɐŋ). See under → hēi 黑 for possible wider relations.

máng₄ 盲 (mɐŋ) **LH** maŋ, **OCM** *mrâŋ — **[T]** *ONW* mëŋ
'Blind' [BI, Lao], in Mand. replaced by *xiā* 瞎.
[E] ? ST *mam (?): Lepcha *tŭr-môm* 'hazy' (of atmosphere), JP *ʔmām* (so Bodman; JP Dict.: 475 only lists *maʔ*^{31}*-maʔ*^{31}) 'dimmed, blurred of eyesight' (Bodman 1980: 121).
See under → hēi 黑 for possible wider relations; perh. also related to → máng₃ 芒茫. It is not clear if and how → méng₅ 夢矇 *môŋ 'blind' may be connected.

máng₅ 㡛 (mwâŋ) **LH** maŋ, **OCM** *mâŋ
'To soak and color silk' [Zhouli, SW]. Acc. to *SW*, the character is read like *huāng* which may indicate an OC *hmaŋ. The word is perh. related to KT: PKS *hma^{5} 'soak, pickle', Tai: S. *maa*^{B1} < *hm- 'id.'. For the final *-ŋ* in CH, see §3.2.4.

máng₆ 蘉 (mwâŋ) **LH** maŋ, **OCM** *mâŋ
'Exert oneself' [Shu] belongs possibly to *man (under → miǎn₁ 勉).

máng₇ 尨龍 (måŋ) **LH** mɔŋ, **OCM** *mrôŋ
'Parti-colored, motley' [Zuo], 'shaggy dog' 尨 [Shi]; 'parti-colored animal' 駹 [Zhouli]; 'variegated' 龍 [Zhouli]; 'mixed, disorderly' 哤 [Guoyu].
[E] ? ST. Bodman (1980: 170) compares this word to WT *mdoŋs* 'white spot on horse's forehead, eye in peacock's feather', but WT is prob. related to WB *u*^{C}*-doŋ*^{B} 'peacock' (*STC* no. 341). More likely, the OC form could instead be related to WB *kroŋ* 'be of various colors, as a tiger'.

mǎng₁ 莽 (mwâŋ^{B}) **LH** maŋ^{B}, **OCM** *mâŋʔ — **[T]** *ONW* maŋ
'Grass, weeds' [Meng], 'jungle' [Zuo]. The original graph is 茻.
[E] ST: Chepang *maŋʔ* n. 'grass'.
× **mǒ** 莽 (muo^{B}) **LH** ma^{B}, **OCM** *mâʔ
'Grass, weeds' [Chuci, GY] is an ancient dialect word for 'grass' in Chǔ and south of the Yangtze [FY 3, 8]. For the difference in finals, see §3.2.4.
[E] ST: PTB *m-lyak (*STC* no. 149): Tib.-Him. *mlyak ~ *ɴ-lyak > Kanauri *myag*, WT *'jag* < *ɴ-ljak*; PLB *mruk ~ *mrak > WB *mrak* 'grass' [*HPTB:* 80]. Unger (*Hao-ku* 51, 1995) suggests a ST form *r-mak.
[C] Possible allofams are → wú₉ 蕪廡, → xí₁ 席.

mǎng₂ 蟒 (mwâŋ^{B}) **LH** maŋ^{B}, **OCM** *mâŋʔ < *mlâŋʔ ?
'King snake' [EY], i.e. 'python' (Carr *LTBA* 13.2, 1990: 120f). It is perh. connected with Loloish *laŋ^{1} 'snake' (Zev Handel, ICSTLL 1997: 26).

māo 貓 (mau, mjäu 3) **LH** mau, **OCM** *mau
'Cat' [Shi].

[T] *Sin Sukchu SR* maw (平); *MGZY* maw, mew (平) [maw ~ mεw];
[N] The onomatopoetic nature of this word explains the MC div. II vocalism (*māo* hardly had an OC medial *r) as well as the unexpected tone A in Mandarin.

máo 毛 (mâu) **LH** mau, **OCM** *mâu
'Hair, fur' [Shi, BI].
[T] *Sin Sukchu SR* maw (平); *MGZY* maw (平) [maw]; *ONW* mau
[D] PMin *m̥âu 'hair, head hair'
[E] ST: PTB *r-maw 'hair' in Kachin *nmun nmau* 'beard' (*STC:* 192 n. 491), PLB *məwʔ 'hair' [*CVST* 1: 23).

mào$_1$ 冃帽 (mâu^C) **LH** mou^C, **OCM** *mûh — **[T]** *ONW* mau
'Head scarf, head cover' of the southern Màn-Yí people 冃 [SW], 帽 [Shiming]; 'scepter cover' 瑁 [Zhouli]; 'hat' 冒 [Hanshu].
[E] This is a late word. The *SW* allusion to a southern origin suggests that this is the same etymon as the MK → móu$_5$ 鍪 'helmet'; on the other hand, *mào* cannot be separated from the homophone ST → mào$_2$ 冒 'to cover'. Foreign 'hat' has prob. been reinterpreted as → mào$_2$ 冒 'cover' because of parallelism with the syn. → bèi$_6$ 被 'cover > headdress'.

mào$_2$ 冒 (mâu^C) **LH** mou^C, **OCM** *mûh, OCB *muks — **[T]** *ONW* mau
'To cover' (without contact, spread overhead, as sky covers the earth, a king's efforts extend over the world) [Shi]; later > 'to cover' (e.g. a corpse with cloth) [Li], (body with skin) [Hanshu]; 'hat' [Hanshu], but see → mào$_1$ 冃帽; ('cover the eyes') > 'reckless' [Zuo], 'be jealous' 媢 [Li]. In *Lǚshì chūnqiū* the word rimes apparently with *dǎo* 倒 *dâuʔ/h (no final *-k, vowels differ), *GY* has an alternate reading for 媢 in tone B (< *-ʔ), hence no OC final *-k*.
[E] ST: WB *mui^B* 'cover without contact, spread overhead, be chief' ⋈ *ə-mui^B* 'roof, a chief' (WB also *hmû* 'be chief' ⋈ *ə-hmû* 'chief'). To this root belongs also the common TB word for 'sky': WB *mui^B* (written *miugh^B*) 'sky, rain', OTib. *mu* 'sky' *(HST)*, WT *dmu, rmu, smu* 'sky' (Hoffmann 1979: 96); TGTM *^{1}hmu*, Nung *mu*; JP *lə^{31}-mu^{31}* 'sky' ⋈? *mu^{55}* 'lightning'. The syn. word for 'sky', → tiān$_1$ 天, belongs to a root 'above'.

mào$_3$ 冒 (mâu^C) **LH** mou^C, **OCM** *mûh
'To see, look' [Shu], survives in Gàn dialects: Wǔníng *mau^{C1}* 'to look at' [Sagart 1993: 173].
[E] ST *mu(ʔ) > JP *mu^{31}* 'to see', Lushai *hmùu^L / hmuʔ^L* 'to see, perceive, observe, come across, get, receive' ⋈ *hmuʔ^L* 'to show' (*CVST* 1: 43).

mào$_4$ 冒 'hat' → **mào$_1$** 冃帽

mào$_5$ 冒 'covetous' → **mò$_6$** 冒

mào$_6$ 瑁 → **mào$_1$** 冃帽

mào$_7$ 帽 → **mào$_1$** 冃帽

mào$_8$ 媢 → **mào$_2$** 冒

mào$_9$ 懋 → **wù$_{11}$** 務

mào$_{10}$ □ 'have not' in Gàn dialects (無有) → **méi$_1$** 沒

méi$_1$ 沒 (muət)
'Not have, there is no, not yet' Mand.; MC *muət* may be a col. variant of *wú* 勿 or

wèi 未, which later fused with, or was influenced by, → yǒu₂ 有 (Norman 1988: 126). This late word is not derived from → mò₄ 沒 'dive'.

méi₂ 枚 (muậi) **LH** məi, **OCM** *mə̂i
'Branch, tree trunk, board' [Shi], later 'chip, counter' > classifier for every category of noun in the Nánběicháo period, now obsolete (Lü Shūxiāng; Norman 1988: 115).
[E] AA: OKhmer *mēk* [mɛɛk] 'branch, bow, limb, twig' > 'numeral classifier for elephant tusks' (Jenner / Pou 1982: 215). After a foreign long vowel OC often drops the coda, see §6.9.

méi₃ 眉湄楣 (mji 3) **LH** mɨ, **OCM** *mrəi, OCB *mrjəj
'Edge, bank, coast, from the moment of' 湄 [BI, Shi] > 'eyebrow' 眉 ('edge / border of the eye') [Shi] (so Karlgren 1956: 5; Wáng Lì 1982: 428), 'lintel of door or window' 楣 [Yili]. For a semantic parallel 'edge' > 'rim' (of eye), see → yá₃, ái 崖涯睚.
[E] Etymology not clear. *Méi* 'eyebrow' is prob. not related to PTB *(s-)mil ~ *(s-)mul 'body hair' because it is the s. w. as 'edge, rim' – unless the semantic development should have been 'eyebrow' > 'edge, bank' (unlikely). TB has somewhat similar comparanda: WT *mu* 'border, boundary, limit, edge'; or Lushai *hmɔɔr*^{H} 'border, edge, point, end' (but see → mò₁ 末). For more words with initial *m- and the notion 'edge, lip', etc. See → wěn₁ 吻.

méi₄ 梅 (muậi) **LH** mə, **OCM** *mə̂ and *mə̂ʔ (Mattos 1971: 309)
'Japanese apricot' *(Prunus mume)*, 'plum', Mand. *méizǐ* 梅子, seems to be related to Old Japanese *ume*² 'plum' (Shibatani 1990: 120; Miyake 1997: 188). There are other tree names which have a possible Japanese connection: → sōng₁ 松 'pine'; → nài₁ 奈柰 'some kind of pear' and → zhè₁ 柘 'some kind of mulberry tree'. The source of these words is unknown.

méi₅ 脢 (muậi[C]) **LH** mə(C), **OCM** *mə̂(h), OCB *mə̂(h)
'Meat on sides of spine' [Yi] may belong to the TB items under → mí₂ 麋 'deer', but the vowels do not agree.

méi₆ 媒禖 (muậi) **LH** mə, **OCM** *mə̂ — **[D]** PMin *moi
'Marriage go-between, matchmaker' [Shi], 'god of fecundity' 禖 [Li]. A semantic extension is perh. → méi₈ 腜 'prolific'.
[E] AA: Khmer *dhmāya* [tmíiəj] 'agent, representative' > 'marriage go-between', derived from [*-dəj] 'bear, support' (→ dài₉ 戴) with the infix *-m-* which forms agental derivatives (Jenner / Pou 1982: xlvi f). The AA infix was treated like the word initial in OC (§2.6).

ᴥ **gāo-méi** 高禖 [kɑu-mə] *kau-mə̂ [Lüshi], **jiāo-méi** 郊禖 [kau-mə]
A fecundity rite which was performed at an altar outside of town *jiao* 郊 where sexual intercourse (→ jiāo₁ 交) was involved (Jensen *EC* 20, 1995: 420ff). While *gāo* merely transcribed a pre-initial, *jiāo* reflects re-etymologization.
[E] AA: Khmer *ghmāya* [kmíiəj] 'marriage broker', by alteration of the (root-) initial from [tmíiəj] above (Jenner / Pou 1982: 138). This etymon belongs to an AA wf which includes → pēi₁ 胚 'pregnant', → dài₉ 戴 'to bear'.

méi₇ 禖 → **méi₆** 媒禖

méi₈ 腜 (muậi) **LH** mə, **OCM** *mə̂
'Quickening of the fetus' [SW], perh. 'fruitful, prolific' [Shi]. This is prob. a semantic extension of → méi₆ 媒禖.

méi$_9$ 煤 (muậi) **LH** mə, **OCM** *mə̂
'Soot' [Lü].
[E] ST, but etymology not certain. (1) TB-Lahu *mū* < PLB *ʔ-mu^2 'soot / scrid' (*HPTB:* 112; 180), apparently only attested in some LB languages; if related, a merger of OCM *ə with *o must have occurred (see comment under → měi$_2$ 每).
(2) TB-Lushai *maŋ^R / man^L < maŋʔ / maŋs* 'be sooty, grimy' ⋈ *maŋ^H < maŋ* 'partially burnt wood'; rather than being a CH loan, WB *hmaŋ* 'ink' appears to be a loan translation of *mò* 墨 'ink' (made of soot) (under → hēi 黑 'black').
[C] Possible derivations are → huī$_1$ 灰 'ashes', → wén$_1$ 文 'black marks', → hēi 黑 'black' (Wáng Lì 1982: 409). Wáng Lì adds **méi** 黴 (mji 3) 'moldy, grimy' which appears in *SW* and *Chǔcí* as the first syllable of binomes (黴黧, 黴黑). Unrelated to → huì$_7$ 晦 'dark'.

měi$_1$ 美 (mji^B 3) **LH** mɨ^B, **OCM** *mrəiʔ, OCB *mrjəjʔ
'Be beautiful, handsome' [Shi: Guofeng].
[T] *Sin Sukchu SR* muj (上), *PR*, *LR* məj; *MGZY* mue (上) [muɛ]; *ONW* mi
[E] ST: PTB *moy (*STC* no. 304) > Lushai *mɔi^H*, Kachin *moi* (*HST:* 40). Note also PTB *may 'good, well' (*STC* no. 300), Mikir *mē-* 'be good', JP *tʃə^{33}-mai^{33}* 'good'.

měi$_2$ 每 (muậi^B) **LH** mə^B, **OCM** *mə̂ʔ (dialectal *moʔ ?)
'Each, every' [Shi].
[T] *Sin Sukchu SR* muj (上), *PR*, *LR* məj; *MGZY* mue (上) [muɛ]; *ONW* mɑi
[E] This may possibly be the AA word for 'one': PMK *muəy (Shorto 1976: 1054) > Khmuʔ *mooy*, OKhmer *moy* /mooj/ (-> Tai *mui*), combination form *mɔ;* PMon *muə̤* 'one' [Diffloth 1984: 141], OMon *moy;* OKhmer and OMon *mimoy* /məmooj/ 'each' < /mooj/ 'one' (Jenner / Pou 1982: 522). For the absence of final *-j* in CH after a foreign long vowel (note Khmer), see §6.9. We should expect OC *o instead of *ə which is implied by the phonetic → mǔ$_2$ 母 *moʔ; OC *Shījīng* dialectal merger of *Po with *Pə (Baxter 1992: 466) would explain the later vowel.
Chinese and Khmer associate the notion 'each, every' with 'single, one', note CH *zhī zhī yǒu wěi* 隻隻有尾 'each one has a tail' (*zhī* 隻 'single, one') (Giles p. 233 no. 1869); Mand. *yī gè yī gède* 一個一個的 'one by one, each'.

měi$_3$ 每 'covet' → **mò$_6$** 冒

mèi$_1$ 妹 (muậi^C) **LH** məs, **OCM** *mə̂s or *mîs — **[D]** PMin *ṁyai^C (or *ṁue^C)
'Younger sister' [Shi].
[T] *Sin Sukchu SR* muj (去), *PR*, *LR* məj; *MGZY* mue (去) [muɛ]
[E] ? ST: WB *ma^C* 'sister'; alternatively note Kuki *hmei* 'woman', Lushai *hmei^L* < *hmeih* 'concubine', Miju *ku-mai-*, WT *bud-med* 'woman'. For *b-* vs. *m-*, see §5.12.2.

mèi$_2$ 沬 'finish' → **mò$_1$** 末

mèi$_3$ 昧 (muậi^C) **LH** məs, **OCM** *mə̂ts — **[T]** *ONW* mɑi
'Twilight, obscure, bewildered' [BI, Shi] > 'morning twilight, dawn, earlier; dusk' [OB, BI, Shi, Shu].
⋈ **wú** 昒 (mjuət, xuət) **LH** mut, huət, **OCM** *mət, *hmə̂t < *hmət
'Dawn' [SW].
[E] Perh. connected with KS, note PKS *ɓu:t^7 'blind'.

mèi$_4$ 寐 (mi^C 4) **LH** mis, **OCM** *mi(t)s — **[T]** *MTang* mɨ, *ONW* mii
'To sleep' [Shi].
[E] ST: PTB *r-mwiy (*STC:* 174 n. 463; no. 196) > WT *rmi-ba, rmis* 'to dream', WB

mwe^{C} 'to sleep' (*HST:* 134), Magar *mis-ke*; Lushai *mu*^{H} / *mut*^{L} < *mu* / *mus* 'to lie down, sleep' is related.

mèi$_5$ 魅 (mji^{C} 3) **LH** mɨs, **OCM** *mri(t)s ?
'A kind of demon' [Zuo], 彪 [Zhouli] (discussed by Carr *LTBA* 13.2: 137); *mèi* is often combined with → chī$_4$ 魑离螭. Etymology not clear.

mèi$_6$ 昒 (muât, mai^{C}) **LH** mɑt, mas, **OCM** *mât, *mrâts
'Farsighted, dim vision' [SW] may be related to → mèi$_3$ 昧 (so Wáng Lì 1982: 465).

mèi$_7$, **huì** 痗 (muậi^{C}, xuậi^{C}) **LH** mə^{C}, huə^{C}, **OCM** *(h)mə̂h
'Be pained, to suffer' [Shi]. The relationship with → mín$_4$ 痻 'suffering' is not clear.

mèi$_8$, **jué** 袂 (mjiäi^{C} 4, kiwet) **LH** mias, kuet, **OCM** *me(t)s, *kwêt ?
'Sleeve' *jué* [Lun], *mèi* [Li]. Acc. to Baxter / Sagart (1998: 49), *jué* is a k-prefix derivation from *mèi.*

mén$_1$ 門 (muən) **LH** mən, OCM *mə̂n, OCB *mən
'Gate' [BI, Shi]. Perh. **mén** 亹 LH *mən* 'river gorge' [Shi] is the same word.
[T] *Sin Sukchu SR* mun (平); *PR*, *LR* mən; *MGZY* mun (平) [mun]; *ONW* mon < mən

ꭗ **hūn** 閽 (xuən) **LH** huən, **OCM** *hmə̂n
'Gatekeeper' [Zuo] < *mén* 門 (muən) with nominalizing devoicing (§5.2.4).

[E] ST: PTB *muːr (*STC* no. 366) > WT *mur* 'gills' ꭗ *mur-ba* 'masticate' (*HST:* 111); Limbu *mura* 'mouth, beak'; Tangkhul N. *mur* 'mouth', > Thado *mu* (< *mur) 'beak' > Lushai *hmuur*^{L} 'point, tip, prow'. Note also AA-PSBahn. *kəməːr 'fish gills' < ?; Bahn. *ɓo˙ r*, Viet *mỏ* (< p-) 'mouth' [Maspero 1912: 65]. Allofam is perhaps → wěn$_1$ 吻.

mén$_2$ 捫 (muən) **LH** mən, **OCM** *mə̂n
'To lay hands on, hold' [Shi]. *Shùn* below suggests a PCH rime *-un.

ꭗ **mín** 㨉 (mjen 3) **LH** mɨn, **OCM** *mrən ?
'To lay hands on' [Lüshi].
The following is prob. a variant of *mén* 捫 (Sagart 1999: 79):

ꭗ **shùn** 揗 (dźjuen$^{B/C}$, zjuen) **LH** źuin$^{B/C}$, zuin, **OCM** *m-lunʔ/s, *s-lun
'To lay hands on' [SW, Mo].

mén$_3$ 悶 (muən) **LH** mən, **OCM** *mə̂n
'Unconsciously' [Zhuang].

ꭗ **mèn** 悶 (muən^{C}) **LH** mən^{C}, **OCM** *mə̂ns
'Sad' [Yi], 'dull, stupid' [Lao].

ꭗ **hūn** 昏殙 (xuən) **LH** huən, **OCM** *hmə̂n
'Dusk, evening, darkness, benighted, mentally dark' 昏 [Shi]; 'blinded, confused' 殙 [Zhuang] – 殙 is also read [men^{B}, mən] (QYS *mien^{B}, muən*) which reflects prob. the common *i ~ *u variation and thus converges with *miàn* 瞑 (under → mián$_1$ 瞑眠). CH -> PMY *mwon^{4} 'evening, dusk'.

[E] ST: WT *mun-pa* 'dark' ꭗ *dmun-pa* 'darkened' ꭗ *rmun-po* 'dull, heavy, stupid'; WB *hmun*^{A} 'dim, dusky, blurred' (*STC:* 155 n. 419; *HST:* 60). Perh. also connected with AA-Khmer /-múuəl/ and /-móol/ 'be dark'.

This wf is possibly associated with → méng$_7$ 濛 'blind', → hūn$_1$ 婚, → wěn$_2$ 紊. It tends to blend into → mián$_1$ 眠, → míng$_2$ 冥. Baxter / Sagart (1998: 60) add **hū** 忽 (huət) [hut] *hmut 'careless, confused' [Shi] to this wf.

mèn 悶 → **mén**$_3$ 悶

méng_1 虻 (mɐŋ) **LH** maŋ, **OCM** *mrâŋ
'Gadfly, horsefly' [Zhuang]; also name of the plant *Fritillaria* [Shi]. Mei Tsu-Lin (1985: 338) relates this word to → yíng_6 蠅 'a fly' and PTai *ma-lɛɛŋ*^{A2}, but see → míng_5-líng 螟蛉.
[E] ST: WT *sbraŋ < s-mraŋ* ? 'a fly' (Gong 2002b: 200). For the initial *m-* ~ *b-* difference, see §5.12.2.

méng_2 氓 (mɛŋ) **LH** mɛŋ, **OCM** *mrə̂ŋ or *mrâŋ
'Population, people' 氓 [Shi], 甿 [Zhouli], 'subjects' [Meng] (commentators have suggested that *méng* refers to 'settlers from the outside', but that cannot be the meaning in *Meng* 5B, 6) > Mand. *méng* 'the common people', but *liúmáng* (!) 流氓 'hooligan' is perh. a different etymon. QYS *mɛŋ* normally goes back to OC *mrəŋ (so Li F.) or *mreŋ; the phonetic as well as the graph substitution *mèng* 孟 (mɐŋ^C) *mraŋh (Karlgren Gl. 176) favor OC *mraŋ. This word is not related to → mín_1 民 'people' as is sometimes suggested (e.g. Wáng Lì 1982: 372).
[E] ST: WT *dmaŋs* 'common people, crowd' ⋈ *'baŋs* 'subjects' (Benedict 1976: 173; *HST:* 116).

méng_3 盟 → **míng_6** 明

méng_4 萌 (mɛŋ) **LH** mɛŋ, **OCM** *mrâŋ
'Sprout' [Li].
[E] ? Area word: Lepcha *mlam* 'shoots from stump of tree', note also Viet. *mām* 'sprout, shoot' (Bodman 1980: 120).

méng_5 夢矇 (muŋ) **LH** moŋ, **OCM** *môŋ
'Blind' 矇 [Shi] > 'be blind to, unenlightened' 夢 [Shi] > 'stupidity, ignorance' 蒙 [Shu].
[E] ST: WT *mdoŋs-pa < mloŋ-s* ? 'blind'. *HST:* 61 considers this the same etymon as → méng_7 濛 'darkening'; in fact this word and → méng_7 濛, → méng_6 蒙 may be the same, in spite of *méng* here being also written with the graph 夢 which should be expected to go back to an original vowel *ə. It is not clear if and how the wf → máng_3 芒茫 may be related.

méng_6 蒙 (muŋ) **LH** moŋ, **OCM** *môŋ
'To cover' intr. (as fur, vegetation, etc.) 蒙 [Shi], 幪 [Yi Zhou] > 'filled to the brim' (of food vessels) 饛 [Shi]. See note under → méng_7 濛 'darkening'.
⋈ **měng** 幪 (muŋ^B) **LH** moŋ^B, **OCM** *môŋʔ
'Be dense, luxurious' [Shi].

méng_7 濛 (muŋ) **LH** moŋ, **OCM** *môŋ
'Darkening' (e.g. sky by rain) [Shi]. TB cognates suggest that this is not derived from the same ST etymon as → méng_5 夢矇 'blind'.
[E] ST: PTB *mu:ŋ (*STC* no. 362) > WB *hmuiŋ* 'dull, downcast' ⋈ *hmuiŋ^B* 'very dark'; JP *muŋ^{33}* 'overcast'. Alternative: WT *rmoŋ-ba* 'be obscured', WB *hmoŋ* 'very dark, darkness'.

Many words could be combined into a large wf 'cover, dark, blind': → méng_6 蒙, → méng_5 夢矇, → mén_3 悶. However, 'blind' → méng_5 夢矇 points to a medial *l, whereas there is no evidence for this in the WB words for 'dull, dark'.

měng_1 黽 (mɛŋ^B) **LH** mɛŋ^B, **OCM** *mrêŋʔ
'Toad' [Zhouli]. The character also writes a syllable *mǐn* (mjien^B 4) OCM *minʔ.

mĕng$_2$ 蠓 → **wén**$_2$ 蚊

mĕng$_3$ 懞 → **méng**$_6$ 蒙 'cover'

mèng$_1$ 孟 (mɐŋ^C) **LH** maŋ^C, **OCM** *mrâŋh ? — **[T]** *ONW* mëŋ
'Eldest' (of siblings) [Shi], 'eldest' [Shu], 'first' (of three months) [Li].
[E] ? ST: PTB *maŋ 'older' (of persons) > Trung *dəmaŋ* 'big' (of persons), 'older', WB *u^B-maŋ^B* 'uncle' (*STC:* 189). *HST:* 42 relates CH to TB words listed under → máng$_2$ 芒.

mèng$_2$ 夢 (mjuŋ^C) **LH** muŋ$^{(C)}$, **OCM** *məŋ (tone A!)
'Dream' [Shi]. *Shījīng* rimes indicate tone A for OC (Mattos 1971: 309).
[T] *Sin Sukchu SR* muŋ (去); *MGZY* wung (去) [vuŋ]; *MTang* moŋ, *ONW* muŋ
[E] ST *məŋ: WT *rmaŋ-lam* 'dream' (*lam* 'path'); Chepang *maŋʔ* 'dream', Boro *simaŋʔ* [Weidert 1987: 21], Tamang *^{3}maŋ*; PLB *s-mak ~ *s-maŋ 'dream' > WB *hmaŋ-* 'dream', *mak* 'dream'; JP *ʔmaŋ^{33}* 'to dream', Lushai *maŋ^R / man^L* 'to dream'. Perh. also related to → méng$_5$ 夢矇.

mí$_1$ 迷 (miei) **LH** mei, **OCM** *mî — **[T]** *ONW* mėi
'To go astray' [Shi].

⤫ **mí** 謎 (miei^C) **LH** mei^C, **OCM** *mîh
'Mysterious words' [GY] (Wáng Lì 1982: 430).

⤫ **mĭ** 眯 (miei^B) **LH** mei^B, **OCM** *mîʔ
'Get something in the eye, troubled sight' [Zhuang] (Wáng Lì 1982: 430).

[E] ST: Lushai *hmaiʔ^L < hmaih* 'to overlook, miss, forget' < PTB *ma:y, WB *me^C* 'forget'; Weidert 1987: 285 sets up *'mle·* 'to forget' on the basis of Tangkhul *^{1}ke-^{1}me^{3}lai*.

mí$_2$ 麋 (mji 3) **LH** mɨ, **OCM** *mr(ə)i
'David's deer' [Zuo].
[E] ? Perh. ST: Chepaŋ *maiʔ* 'meat', Bodo *mʏiʔ* 'deer', Liangmei *ka-mî* 'meat' (Weidert 1987: 35); NNaga *me:y 'meat, flesh' > *mai* and *mei* in individual languages. A single etymon for both 'meat' and 'deer' is also found in WT: *ša* 'meat' ~ *šwa* 'deer'. Alternatively, the TB items may belong to → méi$_5$ 脢, but the vowels do not agree.

mí$_3$ 彌 (mjie 4) **LH** mie, **OCM** *me — **[T]** *MTang* mɨ, *ONW* mie
('To take time, take its time to completion, run its course to completion':) 'To complete, fulfill, long-lasting' [BI, Shi] > 'extend, increase' [Zuo] > 'still more' [Lunyu].

⤫ **mĭ** 弭敉 (mjie^B 4) **LH** mie^B, **OCM** *meʔ
'To complete, fulfill' 弭 [Shi], 敉 [Shu], 'to finish' 彌 [Zhouli]; 'to be filling, full' (river) 瀰 (also MC *mjie, miei^B*), and derived metaphors 釆 [Shi].
[T] *MTang* mi, *ONW* me (i.e. QYS div. 3).

mí$_4$ 瀰→ **mí**$_3$ 彌

mí$_5$ 麑麛 'fawn' → **ní** 麑麛

mí$_6$ 糜 (mje 3) **LH** mɨai, **OCM** *mai
'To crush' (people) [Meng] which, acc. to *GSR* 17g is derived from the meaning 'rice gruel' [Li], the reverse seems more plausible, however.
[D] PMin *m̥ue^{A2}; in Southern Min, this word 'rice gruel' is used for Mand. *zhōu* 粥.
[E] ST: WT *dmyal-ba* 'to cut up into small pieces'. Allofam ? → mĭ$_7$ 靡 'small'.

mĭ$_1$ 米 (miei^B) **LH** mei^B, **OCM** *mîʔ, OCB *mijʔ.
'Rice, husked rice' [Zuo].
[T] *Sin Sukchu SR* mjej (上); *MGZY* mi (上) [mi]

[D] PMin *m̥i^{B2} 'husked rice'.

[E] Prob. an area word, but a relative with unambiguous phonological agreement is elusive; most likely cognate: PTB *ma-y (*STC* no. 305) > Garo *mi* ⋈ *me*, Dimasa *mai* 'rice, paddy', Karen Sgaw *me* 'boiled rice'; Tangkhul Naga *ma* 'paddy', Lushai *mɔi^H* beginning to form in the bud' (rice); JP *n^{33}-moi^{33}* 'blossom' (of grain) (*HST:* 125). However, this connection presupposes an OCM *mə̂iʔ. Matisoff (1995: 66) suggests that the final *-i /-y is a ST diminutive suffix. <> Yao *m̥ai^3* (Wáng Fúshì). AN *imay* 'rice' (Benedict *AT*).

Alternatively, Li Fang Kuei (1976: 45) associates the CH word with S. *ma-let^{D2}S* < *ml- 'seed', S. *met / let* 'seed, kernel', Saek *mlɛk/t^{D2}*, and refers also to WT *'bras* < *ɴbras* 'rice' (which belongs to → lì$_{21}$ 糲, though), and to *'bru* 'grain, seed' (cognate to → wù$_5$ 物, however). Egerod 1976 cites Miao *mblei*. See also → shí$_{12}$ 實 'fruit'.

mǐ$_2$ 眯 → **mí$_1$** 迷

mǐ$_3$ 芈 (mjie^B 4) **LH** mie^B, **OCM** *meʔ

The clan name of the rulers of the ancient state of Chǔ, in CH translation Xióng 熊. *Mǐ* is a KT word for 'bear' (Yan Xuequn *CAAAL* 21, 1983: 135): PKS *mu:i^1-fi, PTai *hm-: S. *mii^{A1}*, Po-ai *muui^{A1}*; Hlai *mui^4* [Matisoff 1988c: 310] (a medial *w/u* is lost after labial and acute initials in CH); farther afield we note AN: e.g. Proto-Eastern Formosan *Cumey 'bear' [Li Jen-kuei *LL* 5.2, 2004: 368]. The graph represents a sheep and writes the sound of its bleating (?).

mǐ$_4$ 弭敉 → **mí$_3$** 彌

mǐ$_5$ 渳 (mjie^B 4) **LH** mie^B, **OCM** *meʔ

'To wash' (a corpse in preparation for burial) [Zhouli] may be related to → mì$_1$ 謐, but the vowels do not agree.

mǐ$_6$ 靡 (mje^B 3) **LH** mɨai^B, **OCM** *maiʔ

'Not have, there is no' [Shi] > ('cause to get to nothing':) 'squander' [Li], 'exhaust' [Guoyu].

[T] *Sin Sukchu SR* mi (平), mjej (上), *PR* məj (平); *MGZY* mue (平 上) [muɛ]

[N] This PCH and pre-classical word 'not have, there is no' (the more common synonym was → wáng$_1$ 亡) was replaced by → wú$_4$ 無 starting only in late WZhou, so that *mǐ* survived only as a semantic derivative 'squander, exhaust'.

[<] tone B derivation from → wú$_4$ 無 *ma (§3.3.2); Matisoff (1995: 76f) suggests that the final *-i is a suffix.

[E] Prob. ST via the root *ma, perh. *mǐ* corresponds more directly to WT *med-pa* 'not have, there is no' (from *may-t – alternatively, *med-pa* (*STC* p. 183; *HST:* 61) is thought to derive from WT *ma* or *mi* 'not' + *yod-pa* 'have'). It is not clear how the following may be related: Tai-Siam. *mai^{C1}* 'no, not'; AA-Pearic *may* 'do not'.

Alternatively, the MC form could theoretically derive from a PCH *malʔ (not *maiʔ); in this case, the TB-Dulong word *màl* 'NEG + have' [LaPolla, *LTBA* 24.2: 35 et al.] may be a direct cognate.

[C] A derivation is → miè$_2$ 蔑 'not have'. Possibly the s. w. as → mǐ$_7$ 靡 'small'.

mǐ$_7$ 靡 (mje^B 3) **LH** mɨai^B, **OCM** *maiʔ

'Small, tiny' (e.g. grass) [Yi, Li].

⋈ **mó** 麼 (mje^B 3 —tone!) **LH** mɨai^B, **OCM** *maiʔ

'Small, tiny' (e.g. insects) [Lie].

[E] Etymology not certain. Given its late Zhou occurrence, it may be a semantic extension of the earlier word → mǐ$_6$ 靡 'not have' (i.e. > 'become nothing, negligible, small'?). Acc. to *HST:* 62, it could be cogn. to → mí$_6$ 糜 'crush'. Or it could be a vocalic variant of a syn. → wéi$_8$ 微 *məi.

mì$_1$ 䀄 (mjiet 4) **LH** mit, **OCM** *mit, OCB *Npjit
'To wipe a vessel clean' [SW].
[E] ST: JP *myit*^{55} 'wash' (the face) (*CVST* 1: 24). Chang a. Chang compare *mì* 䀄 with WT *'pʰyid-pa, 'pʰyi-ba* (< ɴpit) 'to wipe, blot out' (Baxter 1992: 221); Lushai *pʰiʔ* 'wash' (the face) [Weidert 1975: 16]. For the initials, see §5.12.2. Perh. related to → mǐ$_5$ 渳.

mì$_2$ 謐 → **mò$_{15}$** 默嘿

mì$_3$ 密 (mjet 3) **LH** mɨt, **OCM** *mrit, OCB *mrjit — **[T]** *ONW* mit
'Dense' (of clouds, dwellings) [BI, Shi] is acc. to Baxter (1992: 436) possibly cognate to the following (unless it is the s. w. as → mì$_4$ 密 'near'):
⋊ **lì** 栗 (ljet) **LH** lit, **OCM** *rit, OCB *C-rjit — **[T]** *ONW* lit
'Dense, compact' (of kernels, heaped grain) [Shi].

mì$_4$ 密 (mjet 3) **LH** mɨt, **OCM** *mrit ?
'To be near, close' [Zuo].
[E] AA: Khmer *piata* /bìəət/ 'be near, close, come close to, bring near, press upon...' ⋊ *paṃpiata* /bɑmbìəət/ 'to squeeze or hold tight, pin between...'. For the initials, see §5.12.2; Khmer *-ia-* corresponds often to an OC high front vowel. Alternatively, this may be the same word as → mì$_3$ 密 'dense'.

mì$_5$ 密 'silent'→ **mò$_{15}$** 默嘿

mì$_6$ 蜜 (mjiet 4) **LH** mit, **OCM** *mit
'Honey' [Chuci].
[T] *MTang* mir < mɨr, *ONW* miit — **[D]** PMin *mit
[E] Thought to be borrowed from IE-Tocharian B *mit* 'honey' < PTokharian *mjət (Behr *Oriens* 1999 / 2000: 36).

mì$_7$ 冪冥 (miek) **LH** mek, **OCM** *mêk
'To cover' 冥 [Zhouli], 冪 [Yili]; 'cover' (consisting of skin or mats) 冪 [BI], 'covering on carriage' 幦 [Li], 'floor carpet in carriage' 幎 [Zhouli].
⋊ **miè** 幭 (miet) **LH** met, **OCM** *mêt
'Cover' [Shi] reflects dialect confusion *-ek ~ *et (Baxter 1992: 300; 484).
Acc. to Baxter (1992: 300), this is perh. cognate to **bì** 辟 (biek) [bek] *bêk, OCB *ɴ-pek 'inner coffin' [Zuo]. Karlgren (1956: 18) considers *mì* an allofam of → míng$_2$ 冥 'dark'.

mì$_8$ 覓 (miek) **LH** mek, **OCM** *mêk — **[T]** *MTang* mɨk, *ONW* mėk
'To search, look for' [BI, Yùpiān, Sānguózhì, Jìnshū] has a stop initial in Mǐn dialects: Quánzhōu *baʔ*^{D2}, Amoy *ba*^{C2}, *bai*^{D2}, lit. *bek*^{D2}.

mián$_1$ 瞑眠 (mien) **LH** men, 瞑 prob. OCM *mên
'Sleep' 瞑 [Zhuang]. The graph 眠 is encountered only late in Han period texts [Shanhaijing] and since for 瞑; it thus does not reflect the OC phonetic parameters of the phonetic series *GSR* 457 民 (*min ~ *mən). *Mián* is distinct from → míng$_4$ 瞑 'close eyes'.
[T] *MTang* mian < mɨan, *ONW* mėn
[E] ST: PTB *myel [*STC* no. 197] > Chepang *mel-* 'close, shut eyes', Bahing *mjel*

'sleepy', WB *myañ*^{B} 'be sleepy, sleep'; JP *mjen*^{31}*-mjen*^{31} 'to sleep soundly' ⋈ *mjet*^{31} 'sleep a while' (*HST:* 134).

mián₂ 綿棉 (mjiän 4) **LH** mian
'Cotton' 棉 [Bái Jū-yì, Tang period]; 'wool' in *mián yáng* 綿羊 'sheep' (lit. 'wool goat') [Sungshi]. This is a late word, unless *mián-mán* 綿蠻 'tiny, delicate' in *Shījīng* is derived from 'wool'.
[E] ? ST: WT *bal* 'wool'; for the initials, see §5.12.2. However, the WT word could belong to → pán₂ 蟠 'curl' instead.

miǎn₁ 勉 (mjän^B 3) **LH** mɨan^B, **OCM** *mranʔ — **[T]** *ONW* man
'To strive, insist, make effort' [Shi]. Wáng Lì (1982: 410) relates this word to items under → mín₄ 痻 'suffering'.
⋈ **mǐn-miǎn** 黽勉 (mjen^B 3 -mjän^B 3) **LH** mɨn^B-mɨan^B, **OCM** *mrənʔ-mranʔ
'To make an effort' [Shi]. The first part LH *min*^{B} may be a reduplication syllable.
⋈ **lián** 連 (ljän) **LH** lian, **OCM** *ran
'To be toilsome, difficult, slow' [Yi].
[E] Perh. AA: OKhmer *ryān* [riiən] 'to exert oneself, apply one's mind to, study...'.
[C] Perh. related to → máng₆ 薆 'exert oneself'.

miǎn₂ 娩 (mjän^B 3) **LH** mɨan^B, **OCM** *mranʔ — **[T]** *ONW* man
'To give birth' [OB (acc. to Guo Moruo), Guóyǔ: Yuèyǔ; Wénxuǎn, GY], *GY* adds some other readings; a Qí 齊 (Shandong) dialect word acc. to a commentary to *Wénxuǎn* (Wáng Lì 1982: 585).
[E] This word appears to form a ST-like *mra/enʔ ~ *sre/anʔ pair with → chǎn₃ 產 *sre/anʔ 'produce' (§2.4.3), hence *miǎn* seems to be a ST etymon. Nevertheless, *miǎn* and *chǎn* could equally well belong to MK: Khmer *samrāla* /sɑmraal/ (s-m-raal) 'to give birth to, deliver' < *rāla* /rííəl/ 'to increase, ... distribute, propagate'. Perhaps AA has been the source of OC *mranʔ which then coincided with the ST *s-* ~ *m-* pattern.

miǎn₃ 冕 (mjän^B 3) **LH** mɨan^B, **OCM** *mranʔ
'Ceremonial cap' [BI, Shu] could be related either to → biàn₁ 弁 [bɨɑn^C] 'a cap' (so Wáng Lì 1982: 582), or to → mì₇ 冪冥 'cover'; both proposals present phonological problems.

miǎn₄ 偭 → **miàn₁** 面

miǎn₅ 湎 (mjiän^B 4) **LH** mian^B, **OCM** *menʔ
'To steep (in wine), get drunk' [Shi].
Unger (*Hao-ku* 36, 1990: 50) suggests cognation with WT *smyon-pa* 'insane, frantic, mad'.

miàn₁ 面 (mjiän^C 4) **LH** mian^C, **OCM** *mens
'Face, to face, face to face' [Shi].
[T] *Sin Sukchu SR* mjen (去); *MGZY* men (去) [mɛn]; *ONW* mian
[D] This is still the word for 'face' in southern dialects: M-Xiàmén *bĩ*^{C2}, Y-Guǎngzhōu *min*^{C}, K-Méixiàn *mian*^{C}
⋈ **miǎn** 偭 (mjiän^B 4) **LH** mian^B, **OCM** *menʔ
'To turn from, abandon' [Chuci] is cognate to the above acc. to Wáng Lì (1982: 586).
[<] perhaps endoactive of *miàn* 面 (mjiän^C 4) (§4.5).
[E] ST: PTB *s-mel (Benedict *LTBA* 1976: 180) > Lushai *hmeel*^{H} 'face' ~ *hmai*^{R} < *hmaiʔ*, JP *man*^{33} 'face', Lepcha *mlem* (< *mel-m; -m* is a common suffix in Lepcha).

miàn₂ 瞑 → **míng₄** 瞑

miǎo 眇杪 (mjiäu^B 4) **LH** miau^B, **OCM** *miauʔ
'Small, insignificant' [Shu], 'minute' [Zhuang], 'exhaust, to the utmost' [Xun], 杪 [Li].

⋈ **miào** 妙 (mjiäu^C 4) **LH** miau^C, **OCM** *miauh — **[T]** *ONW* miau
'Mysterious' [Lao] (Karlgren 1956: 9).

miào₁ 妙 → **miǎo** 眇杪

miào₂ 廟 (mjäu^C 3) **LH** mɨau^C, **OCM** *mrauh
'Ancestral temple' [BI, Shi].
[E] Perh. related to PMY *prau² 'house' (Downer 1982); a semantic parallel 'building' > 'temple' is → zōng₁ 宗. The phonetic is → zhāo₄ 朝 'morning' whose Siamese relative has a labial cluster *br-. Thus Tai 'morning' and MY 'house' happen to be near homophones. As to foreign initial *b-* for CH *m-*, see §5.12.2.

miē 乜 → **xuè₂** 受

miè₁ 滅 (mjiät 4) **LH** miat, **OCM** *met, OCB *mjet — **[T]** *ONW* miat
'To drown' [Yi], 'extinguish, destroy' [Shi].

~ **miè₂** 蔑 (miet)
'Destroy' (OB: by water) [OB]. It seems that this graph wrote the preceding word 'destroy' in the inscriptions.

⋈ **xuè** 威 (xjwät 3) **LH** hyat, **OCM** *hmet, OCB *hmjet
'To cause destruction' tr. [Shi].

[E] ST: PTB *mit (*STC* no. 374) > Chepang *hmit-* 'disappear, become extinct', *hmat-* '(almost) disappear'; Abor-Miri *mit* 'destroy', Lushai *mit^L / miʔ^L < mit / miʔ/h < mits* 'to go out, die out, be extinguished' ⋈ *ti^L-mit^L/ ti^L-miʔ^L* caus. 'to extinguish, destroy', Mikir *met < mit* 'destroy', JP *myit^{55}* 'be destroyed'.

The problem with this set is the vocalic discrepancy OC *et vs. PTB *it (an OC syllable of the type *mit does occur; §11.3.4). Perh. reanalysis as derivation from → huī₆ 隳隳 *hmai 'destroy' is responsible (*hmai + t > hmet). The direct phonological counterpart of PTB *mit may be → mò₄ 沒 *mut 'disappear, die; perish in water or fire', but see there (for *mit ~ *mut variation, see §11.5.1).

miè₂ 蔑 (miet) **LH** met, **OCM** *mêt — **[T]** *ONW* mėt
'Not have' [Shu, Shi], a negative particle [Zuo] (Pulleyblank 1995: 110) > putative ('consider nothing':) 'despise' (the old people) [Hanfei], 懱 [SW: Shu] (§6.2.2; §2.10).
[E] This word is derived from → mǐ₆ 靡 'not have' (see there for TB connections).

miè₃ 衊 (miet) **LH** met
'Blood' [SW]. The meaning 'to sully, soil, besmirch' (reputation of an ancestral house) 衊 [Hanshu] > 'sore eye, troubled eyesight' 瞡 [Lüshi], 'blood shot' (eye) [Shiming] could be a semantic extension of either → miè₂ 蔑 'not have'. The *Hànshū* phrase *wū miè* 汚衊 has prob. led to the *SW* (2145b) gloss *wū xuě* 汚血 'sully with blood' which implies a meaning 'blood' for *miè* and which has been copied into later dictionaries as 'blood'. Nevertheless, the notion 'blood' seems closely associated with this word; note also the expression *xuě-miè* 血衊 'to stain with blood'; Sagart (1999: 153) relates *miè* to TB-Tujia *mie^{53}* 'blood' [Huáng Bùfán, *TB Lexicon* no. 129].

miè₄ 幭 → **mì₇** 幂

mín$_1$ 民 (mjien 4) **LH** min, **OCM** *min
'People' [BI, Shi].
[T] *Sin Sukchu SR* min (平); *MGZY* min (平) [min]; *MTang* min < mɨn, *ONW* miin
[E] ST *mi: PTB *r-mi(y) > WT *mi* 'man, human being', Gyarung *tərmi* (i.e. *tə-rmi*) (*STC:* 158 n. 428). For the CH nominal n-suffix, see §6.4.3.

mín$_2$ 泯 'confused' → **mín**$_4$ 痻

mín$_3$ 緡 (mjen 3) **LH** mɨn, **OCM** *mrən^A!, OCB *mrjun (Baxter 1992: 434)
'String, (fishing) line' [Shi].
[E] The MC rime can also derive from *-in, *-un, or *-iŋ in which case this word may be a variant of → shéng 繩 OCM *m-ləŋ (so Mei Tsu-Lin 1985). On the basis of a *Shījīng* rime Baxter (1992: 281) suggests that *mín* is derived from the same root as the synonym → lún$_3$ 綸 OCB *g-rjun.

mín$_4$ 痻 (mjen 3) **LH** mɨn, **OCM** *mrən, OCB *mrjən (1992: 433)
'Suffering' [Shi].
~ **mǐn** 愍憫 (mjen^B 3) **LH** mɨn(^{B}), **OCM** *mrən, OCB *mrjən (p. 434, tone A!)
'Be distressed' [Shi] > 'grieved, commiserating' 愍 [Zuo], 憫 [Meng], 'sorry, melancholy' 暋 [Zhuang], a late tone B variant of mín 痻 (Baxter 1992: 433–434).
~ **mín** 泯 (mjen(^{B}) 3) **LH** mɨn(^{B})
'Be confused, disorderly, trouble' [Shu].
[E] This wf is homophonous with → mǐn$_1$ 閔 'exert oneself'; they may be the same etyma ('be pained' ~ 'take pains'). The relationship with → mèi$_7$, huì 痗 'pained' is not clear.

mín$_5$ 捪 → **mén**$_2$ 捫

mín$_6$ 忞旻 → **mǐn**$_1$ 閔

mǐn$_1$ 閔 (mjen^B 3) **LH** mɨn^B, **OCM** *mrən, OCB *mrjən (p. 434, tone A!)
'Exert oneself' [Shi].
= **mín** 忞 (mjen 3) **LH** mɨn, **OCM** *mrən
'Violent' 忞 [SW: Shu]; 'austere, stern' 旻 [Shi].
ж **mǐn** 暋敃 (mjen^B 3) **LH** mɨn^B, **OCM** *mrən?
'Be forceful' 暋 [Shu]; 'strong' 敃 [SW].
ж **mǐn** 敏 (mjen^B 3) **LH** mɨ^B, mɨn^B, **OCM** *mrə?
'Exert oneself, diligent' [BI, Shi]. A form in final *-n* begins to emerge only in the Han period (Luó and Zhōu 1958: 18).
ж **mín** 泯 (mjen[^{B}] 3) **LH** mɨn(^{B}), **OCM** *mrən(?)
'To destroy, ruin' [Zuo].
[E] ? AA: Khmer *riana* [ríiən] 'to exert oneself, endeavor...'. <> Tai: S. *man^{B1}* < *hm- 'diligent' (Manomaivibool 1975: 239) is perh. a CH loan.
[E] This wf and the homophonous → mín$_4$ 痻 may be the same etymon ('be pained' ~ 'take pains'). Allofams may be → wěi$_6$ 亹眉 'be vigorous' (so Wáng Lì 1982: 410); Wáng also adds → miǎn$_1$ 勉 'make an effort'; see there also for *mǐn-miǎn* 黽勉.

mǐn$_2$, **mín** 閩 (mjen 3 tone! [GY]) **LH** mɨn
Name of today's Fújiàn area, its major river, and the non-Han people who used to live there [Zhouli]. *Mǐn* does not mean 'snake' (Zev Handel, p. c.), the 'snake' radical [SW] is sometimes used in the names of barbarians. Acc. to *JDSW* (and following it, *JY*), the graph has other readings: *wén,* and *mán;* the composition of the graph 閩 indicates that the *Zhōulǐ* and Han time reading was not *mán.*

mǐn₃ 敏暋敃 → **mǐn₁** 閔

mǐn₄ 愍惽暋泯 'suffering' → **mín₄** 痻

mǐn₅ 皿 (mjwɐŋ^B) **LH** mɨaŋ^B, **OCM** *maŋʔ ?
'Vessel, dish, bowel' [Zuo], the word is much older than *Zuǒzhuàn* because its graph prob. goes back to the beginning of writing. Bodman (1980: 121) compares this to Viet. *mâm*, PVM *ʔbəm^A 'food tray' [Thompson]. Initial and final *m* are incompatible in CH, hence final *-ŋ*.

míng₁ 名 (mjiäŋ 4) **LH** mieŋ, **OCM** *min ~ *meŋ
'Name' [BI, Shi].
[T] *Sin Sukchu SR miŋ* (平); *MGZY ming* (平) [miŋ]; *ONW mieŋ*
[D] PMin *m̊iaŋ
[E] ST: PTB *r-miŋ > WT *miŋ*, OTib *myiŋ* 'name', Jiarong *termi*, Chepang *məyŋ* 'name', PLB *ʔ-miŋ^{1/3}; WB *mañ* 'be named' ⋈ *ə-mañ* 'name' ⋈ *hmañ^C* 'to name'; JP *myiŋ^33*; Mikir *-mén*, Lushai *hmiŋ^H* 'name' (*HST:* 111), Mru *miŋ*.
[C] Related to → mìng 命 'to name'.

⋈ **mìng** 命 (mjɐŋ^C) **LH** mieŋ^C, **OCM** *mrin ~ *mreŋ > *mreŋh (OCB *mrjiŋ[s])
'To name, give a name (to a person)' [Zuo: Min 2, 5], 'to order, command; order, decree > fate, lot > life' 令 [OB, BI], 命 [Shi]. The word was read in tone A in *Shījīng* (Mattos 1971: 309). In the OB and BI (except late WZhou BI) only the graph 令 'order' occurs, while the received texts write 命, i.e. 令 with *kǒu* 口 'mouth' added to indicate that 令 is a phonetic or semantic loan. Because *mìng* is the ordinary word for 'to order', and because the break between 令 (early inscriptions) and 命 (later texts) is quite abrupt, 令 must have stood for 命 in all Shang and Western Zou inscriptions.
[T] *Sin Sukchu SR* miŋ (去); *MGZY* ming (去) [miŋ]; *ONW* meŋ
[D] PMin *miaŋ^C 'life' > Amoy *miã^{C2}*, Fúzhōu *miaŋ^{C2}*
[<] Possibly an r-causative / trans. derivation from the noun *míng* 名 *min ~ *meŋ 'name' (§7.5); later an exoactive *-s / -h was added (§4.3.2).
[E] If related (so Wáng Lì 1982: 329), → lìng 令 'order' may have preserved a ST or PCH pre-initial *r-, hence *mreŋ < *r-miŋ which makes it a homophone of PTB *r-miŋ 'name' (so *STC:* 155 n. 419; Granet 1948: 292). WB *min^C* 'command' (a CH loan?) is prob. also related.

míng₁ₐ 銘 (mieŋ) **LH** meŋ, **OCM** *mêŋ — **[T]** *MTang* mieŋ < mɨŋ, *ONW* mėŋ
'Inscription' [BI, Liji].
[E] *Míng* 銘 is commonly thought to be related to → míng₁ 名, but the semantic link is not compelling. Phonologically, this word agrees with WT *byaŋ-ma / -bu* 'inscription, direction, label, tablet' (on which an inscription is written); for OC *m- = WT *b-*, see §5.12.2; for OC *-e- = WT *-ya-*, see §11.3.2. If related, the WT item must be a very old CH loan because there was no writing on the ST level.

míng₂ 冥 (mieŋ[B]) **LH** meŋ(B), **OCM** *mêŋ
'Be dark' (not light, no sunlight) [SW, Shi], 'night' [Shi] > 'dark of night, dark night' [Chuci]. As 'night' also written 瞑 [Yupian].
[T] *MTang* mieŋ < mɨŋ, *ONW* mėŋ — **[D]** PMin *maŋ^{A2} 'night'
[E] Area word for 'night': in Mǐn dialects *maŋ; in PMY *mhwaaN̥^{1C} [Purnell] or *m̥wɐŋ^{C1} [Wáng Fúshì 20/140] 'evening, night'. MK: PNBahn. *măŋ* 'night'. The nature of the relationship between ST *me/iŋ 'dark' and SEAsian *maŋ 'night' is not clear (loans from southern CH dialects?). <> PTB *miŋ > WB *mañ^B* ~ *mai^B* 'dark, black'.

WT *mdaŋ(s)* 'last night' may belong to this etymon, but the WT *d* remains unexplained.

[C] Allofams acc. to Karlgren 1956: 5 are → $mì_7$ 冪冥 (miek) 'to cover' (1956: 18), → $míng_4$ 瞑 'close the eyes'.

$míng_3$ 溟冥 (mieŋ) **LH** meŋ, **OCM** *mêŋ

'Ocean' [Zhuang, Lie], as in *běi míng* 北冥 'northern ocean', *nán míng* 南冥 'southern ocean'.

[E] Commentators explain that *míng* 'ocean' is the s. w. as → $míng_2$ 冥 'dark, black' (of water) (likely in light of parallelism with the unrelated → $hǎi_1$ 海). There is an outside chance, though, that the etymon is instead connected with PTB *mlik > OBurm. *mlac* 'river', WB *-mrac*, Arakanese *mreik* 'sea', SChin-Daai *mlik (tui)* 'big water, river, sea' (*tui* 'water').

$míng_4$ 瞑 (mieŋ) **LH** meŋ, **OCM** *mêŋ

'Close the eyes' [Zuo]. Karlgren relates *míng* to → $míng_2$ 冥 'dark'.

[E] *GY* makes a phonetic distinction between → $mián_1$ 瞑 'sleep' (< ST *mel) and *míng* 瞑 'close eyes' and treats these as two separate words. This is not an example of an occasional *-ŋ ~ *-n variation because ST *-l is not known to show up as CH *-ŋ*. Also, WB distinguishes *hmin*^{B} 'have the eyes shut' and *myañ*^{B} 'to sleep' < *mel. Here and in the next two items the etyma *míng* 'dark', *míng* 'close eyes' and *mián* 'sleep' have bled into each other so that they are difficult to separate out:

ꭗ **miàn** 瞑 (mien^C) **LH** men^C, **OCM** *mêns

'Dizzy, confused' [Meng]. For the near homophone *hūn* 殙, see → $mén_3$ 悶.

ꭗ **mán** 瞞 (muân) **LH** man, **OCM** *mân

'Shut the eyes, deluded' [Xun] is perhaps a vocalic variant of the a ~ e type (§11.1.3).

$míng_5$-líng 螟蛉 (mieŋ-lieŋ) **LH** meŋ-leŋ, **OCM** *mêŋ-rêŋ

'Insect on mulberry leaves' [Shi], reduplicated from *mliŋ acc. to Li Fang Kuei.

[E] Tai: S. *ma-lɛɛŋ*^{A2} < *ml/r- 'insect' (Li F. 1976: 44).

$míng_6$ 明 (mjɐŋ) **LH** mɨaŋ, **OCM** *mraŋ, OCB *mrjaŋ

'Become light, bright, enlighten' > 'morning' before sunrise > 'morrow' [OB, BI, Shi], 'next' (day, year etc.) [Zuo].

[T] *Sin Sukchu SR* miŋ (平); *MGZY* ming (平) [miŋ]; *ONW* meŋ

[D] PMin *maŋ. This is perh. the same word as

= **méng** 盟 (mjɐŋ) **LH** mɨaŋ, **OCM** *mraŋ, OCB *mrjaŋ

'Covenant, sworn agreement' [Shi] which may be derived from a meaning like 明 'make clear' (a command).

[E] AA, see under → liàng 亮 which is prob. cognate (so Baxter 1992: 491). Bodman (1980: 171) connects *míng* with WT *mdaŋs* 'color of face, appearance, brightness'.

$míng_7$ 鳴 (mjɐŋ) **LH** mieŋ, **OCM** *mreŋ, OCB *mrjeŋ

'To sound, to call' (of animals, birds, musical instruments) vb. [Shi].

[E] ST: WB *mrañ* 'to sound'; Mikir *marèŋ* 'make noise, cry', Lushai *riŋ*^{H} / *rin*^{F} 'be loud', Lepcha *r-ríŋ* 'voice, sound'. Baxter (1992: 499) suggests that one or both of the following may be related: → $líng_4$ 鈴 *C-reŋ 'small bell'; → $shēng_4$ 笙 *sreŋ 'reed-organ'.

mìng 命 → **$míng_1$** 名

miù₁ 謬 (mjeu^C) **LH** miu^C, **OCM** *mriuh, OCB *mrjiws

'Lie, error' [Zhuang] is prob. a derivation and metaphorical extension of → jiǔ₃ 糾 'twist' (Baxter 1992: 513).

[T] *Sin Sukchu SR* miw (去); *MGZY* miw (去) [miw]

miù₂ 繆 → **zhōu₃** 周

mó₁ 麼 → **mǐ₇** 靡

mó₂ 摩磨 (muâ) **LH** mai, **OCM** *mâi

'Rub, polish' [Zuo], 'touch' [Li], 'rub' (things rubbing against each other) 摩 [Zhuang]; 'grind, polish, grindstone' 磨 [Shi].

[T] *Sin Sukchu SR* mwɔ (平); *MGZY* mwo (平) [mwɔ]; *ONW* ma

[D] PMin *muai

ꭗ **mò** 塺 (muâ^C) **LH** mai^C, **OCM** *mâih

'Dust' [Chuci].

[<] exopass. of *mó* 摩磨 (muâ) (§4.4) lit. 'what has been rubbed off'.

[E] This wf appears to be cognate to WB *hmwa^C* 'pulverize' ꭗ *hmwat* 'be fine, smooth', and / or to Lushai *mee^R* < *mee?* 'be sandy and gritty' (of soil), et al. and hence also to WT *bye-ma* 'sand' (for *m-* ~ *b-* initials, see §5.12.2). OC ? -> Tai: S. *ma-laai^{A2}* 'to damage, destroy' (for the Tai /l/ see §2.7).

mó₃ 謨 (muo) **LH** ma, **OCM** *mâ? (! tone) — **[T]** *ONW* mo

'Plan, counsel' [Shi]; mò 莫 (mâk) 'to plan' [Shi] may be a graphic loan for *mó*.

ꭗ **wú** 譕 (mju) **LH** mua, **OCM** *ma

'Induce, advise' [Guan].

[E] This could possibly derive from a ST etymon meaning 'ahead, in front' which is reflected in Lushai *hma^H* 'the front, space in front of, be early, beforehand', *hma^H ŋai^H* 'to scheme, plan' (lit. *ŋai^H* 'to think' + *hma^H* 'ahead').

mò₁ 末 (muât) **LH** mat, **OCM** *mât — **[T]** *ONW* mat

'The tip' [Liji], 'end of' (branch, extremities, legs) [Zuo], 'end, final, last' [Shu] > 'to diminish' [Zuo].

ꭗ **mèi** 沫 (muâi^C) **LH** mas, **OCM** *mâts

'To finish' [Chuci].

[<] exoactive of *mò*, i.e. tr. vb. derived from 'end' (§4.3.2).

[E] The etymology is not certain. Most likely, *mò* is derived from → wú₄ 無 [mua] *ma 'not have, there is no', thus meaning something like 'the thing which comes to nothing', with the nominalizing suffix *-t* (§6.2.1). Perh. AA: PMonic *mɔh, Mon *moh, mah* 'tip, end, edge' had some paronomastic influence on the creation of the CH word, if *mò* is not an outright substrate word. Or note TB-Lushai *hmɔɔr^H* 'edge, border, end, tip' (but see → méi₃ 眉湄楣).

mò₂ 末 (muât) **LH** mat, **OCM** *mât

A negative particle [Lunyu] which is a final *-t form derived from → wú₄ 無 'not have' (§6.2.2). Its function is similar to → miè₂ 蔑 (Pulleyblank 1995).

mò₃-lì 茉莉 (muât-li^C)

'Jasmine or moly' is a loan from Skt. *mallikā* (Norman 1988: 19); -> Greek *moûly*.

mò₄ 沒 (muət) **LH** muət, **OCM** *mə̂t

'To exhaust, come to an end' [Shi], 'disappear, die' [Zuo]; 'perish in water or fire' [Xun]; 'dive' [Zhuang].

[T] *Sin Sukchu SR* mu (入); *MGZY* mu (入) [mu]; *ONW* mot

[E] Two etyma have apparently converged: (1) ST > PTB *mit 'extinguish, destroy by water or fire'. The *i ~ u* alternation is a common ST phenomenon (§11.5.1). (2) An etymon 'to dive': WB *mrup* 'to dive', which is acc. to Shorto 1972 a loan from PMK *(b)ləp ~ *b(b)lup 'immerse oneself'. CH -> Tai: S. mut^{D2} 'to dive'.

This word is unrelated to the later → $méi_1$ 沒 'not have, there is no'.

$mò_5$ 沒 'covet' → **$mò_6$** 冒

$mò_6$ 冒 (mək) **LH** mək, **OCM** *mə̂k

'Be covetous' [Shu, Zuo].

⋇ **měi** 每 (muậi[B]) **LH** mə[B], **OCM** *mə̂ʔ — **[T]** *ONW* mɑi

'Covetous' [Zhuang].

⋇ **mò** 沒 (muət) **LH** muət, **OCM** *mə̂t — **[T]** *ONW* mot

'To covet' [Guoyu], Karlgren *GSR* 492b derived the meaning 'covet' from 'dive, disappear, come to an end, have a final goal' – somewhat forced.

[E] ST: WT *mod-pa, mos-pa* 'be pleased, wish', *smon-pa* 'to wish, desire' ⋇ *mos-pa* 'to wish, be pleased'. Perh. also found in MK-Pearic *mos* 'want, love' [Headley 1977].

$mò_7$ 莫 → **$wú_4$** 無

$mò_8$ 莫瞙嗼 (mâk) **LH** mɑk, **OCM** *mâk — **[T]** *ONW* mɑk

'Obscure' 莫 [Xun], 嗼 [JY]; 'eyesight dimmed' 瞙 [GY]; this is not a common word. Possible derivation → $mù_5$ 墓 'tomb'. See under → hēi 黑 for possible wider relations.

$mò_9$-mò 莫莫 'luxuriant' → **$wǔ_9$** 膴膴

$mò_{10}$ 膜 → **$gé_2$** 隔

$mò_{11}$ 貊 貉 膜 漠 → **$mù_3$** 牧

$mò_{12}$ 塺 'dust' → **$mó_2$** 摩磨

$mò_{13}$ 墨 → **hēi** 黑

$mò_{14}$ 纆 (mək) **LH** mək, **OCM** *mə̂k

'Rope' (made of three strands) [Yi].

[E] <> AA: PWa *ʔmoʔ or *hmoʔ 'rope' [Diffloth 1980: 106].

$mò_{15}$ 默嘿 (mək) **LH** mək, **OCM** *mə̂k

'Silent' [Zuo] is thought to be cognate to 'black' → hēi 黑 (Karlgren *GSR* 904d), also *mò* 莫寞漠 'tranquil' (below) has a homophone → $mò_8$ 莫瞙嗼 'obscure', as does the TB-Lushai form below. See under → hēi 黑 for possible wider relations.

This sound-symbolic notion includes many synonyms with initial *m-:

• **mò** 莫嗼 (mɐk) **LH** mak, **OCM** *mrâk

'Be reverently quiet, settled' (of a population) [Shi]

• **mò** 莫寞漠 (mâk) **LH** mɑk, **OCM** *mâk

'Tranquil' (of population) 莫 [Shi], 'quiet, still' 寞漠 [Zhuang]. Is this merely a graphic variant of 莫嗼 (mɐk)?

• **mì** 密 (mjet 3) **LH** mɨt, **OCM** *mrit

'Silent, quiet' [Shi], 'secret' [Yi]. <> Tai: Saek *mit* 'quiet'.

• **mì** 謐 (mjiet 4) **LH** mit, **OCM** *mit

'Gentle, mild' [Shu, Hou Han].

[E] ST: Lushai $muuk^F$ 'quiet, reserved, serious; dull' (of colors), Lepcha *myak* 'be silent' (Geilich 1994: 139; 159; she includes in this wf the TB items under → $wàn_2$ 曼);

also AA-PSBahn. *mɔʔ ~ *mɔk 'silent'. For the common *i* ~ *u* alternation, see §11.5.1.

móu$_1$ 牟 'to love' → **mù$_6$** 慕

móu$_2$ 侔 (mjəu, məu) **LH** mu, mo, **OCM** *mu or *mô
'Be alike, uniform' [Zhouli]. Etymology not clear. MK may be a possible source: Mon *smoh* 'be equal, alike, conform to a norm'; however, *smoh* could derive from Indic *sama* 'same'.

móu$_3$ 眸 (mjəu) **LH** mu, **OCM** *mu
'Pupil of the eye' [Meng]. Wáng Lì (1982: 312) relates *móu* to → mù$_2$ 目 'eye'.

móu$_4$ 謀 (mjəu) **LH** mu, **OCM** *mo
'To plan, counsel' [BI, Shi].
[T] *Sin Sukchu SR* məw (平); *MGZY* (khuw >) wuw (平) [vuw]
[E] Perh. related to → mó$_3$ 謨 (so Wáng Lì 1982: 105). Alternatively, this word could be cognate to TB: WT *mo* 'lot', *mo-pa* 'soothsayer' (i.e. consultant) -> Daofu *mu-pa*, WB *hmo* 'magical power' ⋈ WB *hmo^B-sa-ra^B* 'wizard, sorcerer' [ZM92 no. 191].

móu$_5$ 鍪 (mjəu) **LH** mu, **OCM** *mu
'Helmet' [Guoce].
[E] AA: MidMon /kəmhok/ 'wide-brimmed conical hat or helmet' (-> WB *k^{h}a-mok*), Spoken Mon *həmok* 'Shan hat', Palaung *hmoʔ* 'woman's cap', Wa-Lawa-Bulang *hmok 'straw hat'; Khmer *mùək* 'hat' (-> Tai: S. *muak^{D1}* < *hm- 'hat, cap' [for the traditional etymology, see Li F. 1976: 41]), Bahn.-Stieng *muk*, Biat *mo:k*, PEKatuic *muak (<- Khmer?). For its loss of *-k*, see §6.9. The source of WT *rmog* 'helmet' is not clear (also AA?).
[C] → mào$_1$ 冒帽 'hat' may perh. be related, → mào$_2$ 冒 'cover'. The earlier syn. was → zhòu$_3$ 冑.

móu$_6$ 繆 → **jiǔ$_3$** 糾

mǒu$_1$ 牡 → **mǔ$_1$** 牡

mǒu$_2$ 某 (məu^B) **LH** mo^B, **OCM** *môʔ
'Someone, a certain, so and so' [Shu].
[T] *Sin Sukchu SR* məw, mu (上), *LR* mu; *MGZY* muw (上) [muw]; *ONW* mou^B
[E] This may possibly be of AA origin: Mon *mu, moʔ* /mɯʔ/ 'what, why', in cognate languages the etymon also means 'who, what'. Note the semantic connection between interrogative and indefinite pronouns in many lgs., incl. Mandarin, e.g. 沒甚麼 'it is nothing'.

mòu 瞀 (måk, məu^C) **LH** mɔk, mo^C, **OCM** *mrôk(h)
'Troubled eyesight' [Zhuang].
[E] ST: WT *rmogs-pa* 'eyes heavy with sleep, inert, languish'. *Mòu* may be cognate to → wù$_{12}$ 霧 (so *HST:* 82), but TB keeps the two roots distinct.

mǔ$_1$ 牡 (məu^B) **LH** mo^B, **OCM** *mûʔ, OCB *m(r)juʔ
'Male' (of quadrupeds) [OB, Shi], opposite → pìn, bì 牝 'female'.
[E] AA: OKhm *jmol* [cmọọl] 'male of animals', Aslian lgs. (Malay Penins.) *lemol, remol, limo, simo,* etc. 'male'; OMon *jmur, kmur* 'male' (elephant), MMon *jmu* / *həmù* 'strong, male', PWa *kəmɔy 'ox, wild buffalo', Jarai *təno, təmo* 'male animal' (Lewitz 1976: 768); PVM *mɔl^B 'person, people'. For the absence of a coda in CH after a foreign long vowel, see §6.9. The OB graph for this word shows a vertical stick on a horizontal ground (inverted T). The explanation may be that it was intended for

an obsolete homophone, a cognate of PVM *c-mɔːlʔ 'digging stick'. 'Male' and 'digging stick' are derivatives from a stem represented in OKhmer *cval* /cuuəl/ 'to enter, penetrate, (of animals) copulate', Khmu *cmɔɔl* 'planter du riz au plantoir' ⋇ *crmɔɔl* 'plantoir' [Ferlus *MKS* 7, 1978: 20–22]; from 'digging stick' to 'plowing' to 'acre' are simple steps, hence *mǔ* 'male' and → $mǔ_5$ 畝 'field', though not homophones in OC, may well go back to the same AA etymon.

$mǔ_2$ 母 (məu^B) < from *môʔ ≠ **LH** mə^B, **OCM** *mə̂ʔ
'Mother' [OB, Shi].
[T] *Sin Sukchu SR* mu, məw (上), *LR* mu; *MGZY* muw (上) [muw]; *ONW* mou^B
[E] This word has two possible TB cognates. (1) *Mǔ* is either derived from a hypothetical ST *məʔ: PTB *ma 'mother' > WT *ʔa-ma*, Chepang *ma* (*məʔ) (so *HST:* 110). Or (2) OC *môʔ is cognate to PTB *mow 'woman, bride' (*STC* no. 297) > WT *-mo* 'female suffix', Chepang *mo* 'wife', Lushai *moo^H* 'bride, daughter-in-law' (so Bodman 1980: 136; Baxter 1992: 469). In languages of the area words for 'mother, woman, female, daughter' have initial *m- followed by almost any vowel: OC *môʔ 'mother', WT *mo, ma* 'female', *ma* generally 'mother', LB *ma* 'female, girl, woman', WB *ma^C* 'sister', OC *mə̂s ? 'younger sister', LB *mi²* 'female' ⋇ *mi^C* 'mother, madam, daughter'; AA-MMon *mi*, OKhmer *me* 'mother'. See also → $hóu_5$ 猴.

$mǔ_3$ 姆 (məu^B) **LH** mo^B, **OCM** *môʔ
'Female teacher in harem' [Zuo] is cognate to → $huì_6$ 誨 'to instruct'; we should expect OCM *mə̂ʔ, but the word has coalesced with → $mǔ_2$ 母 'mother' due to paronomastic attraction.

$mǔ_4$ 拇 (məu^B) **LH** mo^B, **OCM** *môʔ
'Thumb' [Guoyu], 'big toe' [Yi].
[E] ST: PL: *C-ma³ 'thumb' (in composites for 'thumb' and 'big toe'). The vowels do not agree, we should expect OC *mə̂ʔ for PTB *ma; *moʔ may be due to association with → $mǔ_2$ 母 *môʔ 'mother', just as the PL word may be related to *ma* 'mother'.

$mǔ_5$ 畝 (məu^B) **LH** mə^B ~ mo^B, **OCM** *mə̂ʔ ~ *môʔ, OCB *mo/əʔ
'An acre' [BI, Shi].
[T] *Sin Sukchu SR* mu, məw (上); *MGZY* muw (上) [muw]
[D] In many dialects, including some Mandarin ones, 'acre' is not a homophone of *mǔ* 母 'mother': W-Sūzhōu col. *m^{C2}*, Wēnzhōu *mɛ^{B2}*; X-Chángshā *mɤu^B;* G-Nánchāng *mɛu^B;* Y-Guǎngzhōu *mau^{B2};* M-Xiàmén *bɔ^B*. However, 'acre' and 'mother' are homophones in most Mand. dial. and sporadically elsewhere.
[E] ? ST: WT *rmo-ba, rmos* 'to plow' (Bodman 1980: 136) ⋇ *rmod* 'the plowing' ⋇ *rmon-pa* 'plow ox', Mikir *-mò* classifier for strips of fields. However, if this word should go back to an AA root (see → $mǔ_1$ 牡), then the nature of the CH–TB relationship is not clear.

$mù_1$ 木 (muk) **LH** mok, **OCM** *môk
'Tree, wood' [OB, Shi].
[T] *Sin Sukchu SR* mu (入); *MGZY* mu (入) [mu]; *ONW* mok
[E] *Mù* has no known cognate, unless one wishes to compare it with PLB *ʔmuk 'stump' (of a tree).

$mù_2$ 目 (mjuk) **LH** muk, **OCM** *muk
'Eye' [OB, Shi].
[T] *Sin Sukchu SR* mu (入); *MGZY* wu (入) [vu]; *ONW* muk
[D] *Mù* has been replaced by *yǎn* 眼, already in Han times (acc. to *SW, GY*), in all

dialects except Mǐn: PMin *m̥ok^{D2}, but the NEMin forms go back to *mit ~ *met (Norman *CLAO* 13.2, 1984: 175ff).

[E] ST: PTB *mik ~ *myak (*STC* no. 402) > WT *dmig* 'eye', and *mik in almost every TB language, including JP *myiʔ^{31}*, Mikir *mék;* a variant is PLB *(s-)myak > WB *myak* (*HST:* 76).

The OC vowel is not certain since *mù* is not a rime word in *Shījīng*. If OC *muk, the word would be directly related to the PTB form *mik by way of the ST *u ~ *i alternation (§11.5.1). If OC *miək, the word would be directly related to the PLB form *myak.

[C] → móu$_3$ 眸 'pupil of the eye' is sometimes thought to be related to *mù* (so Wáng Lì 1982: 312).

mù$_3$ 牧 (mjuk) **LH** muk, **OCM** *mək, OCB *mjək

'Pasture, herdsman, to tend' (animals) [BI, Shi].

[T] *Sin Sukchu SR* mu (入); *MGZY* wu (入) [vu]; ONW muk

[E] ST *m/brək ?: WT *'brog-pa* < *ɴbrak* 'summer pasture, solitude, wilderness, nomad'. As to foreign initial *b-* for CH *m-*, see §5.12.2.

mù$_4$ 莫暮 (muo^C) **LH** mɑ^C, **OCM** *mâkh — **[T]** *ONW* mo

'Late' (in a season, year') 莫 [Shi], 'evening' 暮 [Meng].

[E] Two possible etymologies: (1) the original meaning is 'late'. (2) Or this word is related to 'dark, cover' → mò$_8$ 莫瞙暯 'obscure'. See under → hēi 黑 for possible wider relations. Since TB roots are inconclusive as to their ST source, Limbu *makt-* 'to become night' may either be a direct cognate of *mù* 莫暮 (not very likely given the frequent semantic connection 'dark' ~ 'night' – not 'late' ~ 'night'), or ⋇ Limbu *mak* 'black, dark' (which may equally well be a cognate of → hēi 黑). Related may also be Lepcha *ma* 'be secret, concealed, disappear'.

mù$_5$ 墓 (muo^C) **LH** mɑ^C, **OCM** *mâkh.

'Tomb, graveyard' [BI, Shi]. In most other modern dialects, the word for 'grave' is → fén$_4$ 墳.

[T] *Sin Sukchu SR* mu (去); *MGZY* mu (去) [mu]; *ONW* mo — **[D]** PMin *ṁio^C

[E] Etymology not certain. Prob. connected with AA: PVM *-mah 'tomb' [Ferlus], PSBahn. *kəhmo:c 'tomb, corpse', Wa-Lawa-Bulang *rəmɨc 'grave'. MK -> Tai: S. *hmok* 'to hide, bury' (Unger *Hao-ku* 51, 1995).

But if 'tomb' should be a Chinese derivate, one source could be → mò$_8$ 莫瞙暯 'obscure'; see there and under → hēi 黑 for possible wider relations. Alternatively, the root could be → wú 無 'not' from which is derived → wáng$_1$ 亡.

mù$_6$ 慕 (muo^C) **LH** mɑ^C, **OCM** *mâkh — **[T]** *ONW* mo

'Be loving, beloved' [BI], 'think of lovingly' [Meng].

[E] ST, perh. two parallel stems are involved: (1) *mlak: TB-KN-Khyang *amlak*, Khami-Awa *(h)la'* 'to love', SChin Daai *mhlä* 'to like, love' [Hartmann ICSTLL 1999: 2]. <> Tai: S. *mak, ma-lak* 'to love, cherish', Saek *mak^{D2}* 'to like, be fond of'.

(2) ST *mak: Lepcha *mák* 'long for', WB *mak* 'covet, wish to enjoy', JP *mak^{31}* 'desire to eat' (*HST:* 105; Unger *Hao-ku* 51, 1995).

⋇ **wǔ** 憮 (mju^B) **LH** muɑ^B, **OCM** *maʔ — **[T]** *ONW* muo^B

'To love' is a Han period southern dialect word for 'to pity' [FY 1.7], also in the east [FY 1.17].

[E] ? ST *maŋ: WB *maŋ^A* 'to like, love' (MC tone B sometimes corresponds to a foreign *-ŋ*, §3.2.4), also PKS *maŋ^4 'to like'.

⋊ **mǔ** 㷬 (muo^B [GY]) is prob. a variant of the above.

⋊ **móu** 牟 (mjəu) **LH** mu

'To love', a Han period Sòng-Lǔ dialect word [FY 1.6].

[E] Wáng Lì (1982: 176) relates this wf to → fǔ$_{10}$ 撫 'lay hands on, soothe' (unlikely). Forms like *rak* 'love' in Tai and AA lgs. derive from Indic *rāga* 'passion'.

mù$_7$ 霂 → **mài$_3$-mù** 霢霂

N

nà$_1$ 吶訥 → **nuò**$_1$, **nà** 吶訥

nà$_2$ 納 → **rù**$_1$ 入

nà$_3$ 那 (nâ^C)

'That' Mand. (Norman 1988: 119).

[T] *Sin S. SR* nɔ (去), *PR*, *LR* na; *MGZY* no (去) [nɔ]; *ONW* na

⋇ **ruò** 若 (ńźjak ~ ńźja^B) **LH** ńak, **OCM** *nak — *ONW* ńak ~ ńa

'That' [Lunheng].

⋇ **ěr** 爾 (ńźje^B) *ONW* ńe

'That' [post-Han].

[E] *Nà* prob. belongs to demonstratives in non-ST languages, note especially PAA *na 'this' which is a "very frequent type" in AA [Pinnow 1965: 33]: Khmuʔ *naa* '3rd person pronoun', Khmer *nai* (nāi) 'there', Munda *na, naa* 'this'; also Viet *nọ* 'this' [Maspero 1912: 63]. KT forms are not as close to CH: Tai: S. *nii*^{C2} < *n- 'this', S. *nan*^{C2} < *n- 'that'; Nung *nay*^{C2}, Wuming *nai*^{C2}, etc. 'this' (HCT: 113). Mand. *nà* corresponds to an OC *naih > nâ^C. The OC pronominal n-suffix (§6.4.5) is probably derived from one of these forms.

nà$_4$ 㾊 (ṇa^C, i.e. prob. na^C)

'Sick' [JY], a medieval word.

[E] Prob. a loan from PTB *na > WT *na-ba* 'sick', PL *C-na[1] 'ill', WB *na* 'be ill' (Benedict *HJAS* 4, 1939: 228). See also → nuó 儺.

nǎi$_1$ 乃 (nậi^B) **LH** nə^B, **OCM** *nə̂ʔ

'Then, now' [BI, Shi].

[T] *Sin Sukchu SR* naj (上); *MGZY* nay (上) [naj]; *ONW* nai^B

[E] *HST:* 147 relates this word to the WT post-position *na* which follows temporal clauses.

nǎi$_2$ 乃 'your' → **rǔ**$_2$ 汝

nǎi$_3$ 奶 → **nǎi**$_4$ 嬭

nǎi$_4$ 嬭 (niei^B) **LH** nei^B, **OCM** *nêʔ

'Mother' [BI, QY, Guangya], a Chǔ dialect word [GY], also *nǐ* 妳; the modern col. form is *nǎi* 奶 'breasts, milk, suckle' (Unger *Hao-ku* 5, 1982).

[D] Mǐn: Xiàmén lit. *lãi*^{B}, col. *lẽ*^{B}

[E] Etymology is not clear, but PMY *niaʔ^{2D} 'mother' could be related. Similar words in the area are WT *a-ne, ne-ne* 'paternal aunt' (*HST:* 164); or MK-Khmer *ɲi:* 'female', see → lǐ$_2$-ěr 李耳 'female tiger'.

nài$_1$ 奈柰 (nâi^C) **LH** nas

'Some kind of pear' (3rd cent. AD). Japanese *(kara)nashi* 梨 could be the analogue to OC *nas and thus be related (Unger *Hao-ku* 22, 1983). See comment under → méi$_4$ 梅.

nài$_2$ 奈 (nâi^C) **LH** nas, **OCM** *nâs

A late classical col. variant of → rú$_1$ 如 (or prob. rather MC *ńźjwo*^{C}) in the classical expression *rú hé* 如何 = *nài hé* 奈何 (occurrence of *nài* in *Shūjīng* is spurious, a later gloss) (Unger *Hao-ku* 22, 1983). Pulleyblank (*BIHP* 59.2, 1988: 339ff) derives *nài hé* from *ruò zhī hé* 若之何. See → rú$_1$ 如 for allofams.

nài$_3$ 奈 → **rú$_1$** 如

nài$_4$ 鼐 (nậi$^{B/C}$) **LH** nə$^{B/C}$, **OCM** *nə̂ʔ/h

'A large → dǐng$_3$ 鼎 ceremonial cauldron', or 'large' of a vessel [BI, Shi] is perh. a MK etymon: OMon *naʔ* 'ritual or ceremonial vessel'.

nán$_1$ 南 (nậm) **LH** nəm, **OCM** *nə̂m

'South' [BI, Shi]. The OB graph depicts something that looks like a house; in light of this it is interesting to note PMK *nəm 'house'.

[T] *Sin Sukchu SR* nam (平); PR, *LR* nan; *MGZY* nam (平) [nam]; *ONW* nɑm

[E] Etymology not certain. Benedict (ICSTLL 1989: 7) relates this to PTB *nam (his *nəm) 'sun, day, sky' > PTib. *g-nam 'sky' ꭗ *nam* 'night', also 'rain, god' in other TB languages. This etymology finds support in the old CH tradition which associates the south with the sunny side → yáng$_9$ 陽, the north with → yīn$_5$ 陰 'the dark side', → míng$_2$ 冥 'darkness, night', *shuò* 朔 (ṣåk) 'new moon, north' (under → nì$_6$ 逆), hence *nán* could originally have been the counterpart to the dark north.

nán$_2$ 男 (nậm) **LH** nəm, **OCM** *nə̂m

'Man, male' (as in *nán-nǚ* 男女 'boys and girls, men and women') > 'a low feudal title' [BI, Shi].

[E] Prob. area word, but the etymology is not certain: (1) TB-PKiranti *nam 'man' (*CVSTL* 2: 48). <> PMonic *k()ɲoom 'young child' [Diffloth 1984: 114], PWa **h/ʔn[o]m 'young man'. <> (2) PTai *hn-: S. *num^{B1}* 'young man, young'. <> Yao *nam^2* 'son'. Syn. → shì$_1$ 士.

nán$_3$ 難 (nân) **LH** nɑn, **OCM** *nân

'Be difficult' [Shi].

[T] *Sin Sukchu SR* nan (平); *MGZY* nan (平) [nan]; *ONW* nɑn

ꭗ **nàn** 難 (nân^C) **LH** nɑn^C, **OCM** *nâns

'Difficulty' [Shi].

[E] Prob. ST, but etymology not certain. This is either related to WT *mnar-ba* 'to suffer, be tormented' (so *HST:* 63); or to PTB *na 'ill' (*STC:* 159 n. 428): WT *na-ba*, *nan-te* 'be ill' ꭗ *nad* 'illness'. It is sometimes thought that WT *na* and *nar* are related as well. PTB *na may also be related to → shǔ$_2$ 癙, → nuó 儺.

nǎn$_1$ 赧 (ṇan^B) **LH** ṇan^B, **OCM** *nrânʔ — **[T]** *ONW* ṇän < nän

'To blush' [Meng] is perh. related to TB-Karen *ńa* 'red' (*STC:* 159).

nǎn$_2$ 揇 (nậm^B) **LH** nəm^B, **OCM** *nə̂mʔ

'To reach for' [Tangyun] is perh. related to PVM *nəm 'to take'.

náng 囊 (nâŋ) **LH** nɑŋ, **OCM** *nâŋ — **[T]** *ONW* nɑŋ

'A sack, bag', including a skin used as a bag [Shi] is perh. a ST word: WB *hnwaŋ* 'skin, peel off'.

nǎng 曩 (nâŋ^B) **LH** nɑŋ^B, **OCM** *nâŋʔ

'In the past, formerly' [Zuo] is related to WT *gna'-bo* 'ancient, in old times', Tangut *no* 'ancient' (*CVST* 2: 26; Gong in W. Wang 1995: 56).

náo$_1$ 呶怓 → **náo$_3$** 撓

náo$_2$ 猱獶夒夔 (nâu) **LH** nou, **OCM** *nû
'Monkey' 猱 [Shi], 獶 [Li], 夒 [OB, SW], 夔 [SW] (*ZWDCD* 2: 1359; 6: 260).
[E] Etymology is elusive, the closest fit is AA: PMon *knuuy 'macaque, general term', Mon *[k]hnu̲i 'monkey'. This word is unique to Monic and may be a derivation by n-infix (Diffloth 1984: 67). The loss of foreign final -y/-i in OC has parallels (§6.9). However, the Mon word could be a Pali loan instead: *khanoi* (Shorto).
Alternatively, the word may be connected with KD: Be *ma³-lu²* 'monkey', PHlai *nok* [Matisoff 1988c: 311]; cf. PTB *mruk, PLB *myok (several Loloish dialects have *n-*) [Matisoff]. Syn. → yù$_9$ 禺 'monkey'; → hóu$_5$ 猴; → yóu$_8$ 猶.

náo$_3$ 撓 (ṇau^B !, xâu) **LH** ṇau^B, hɑu, **OCM** *nrâuʔ, *hnâu ?
'To trouble, disturb' (e.g. a dragon, stir up people) [Zuo].
ⅹ **nào** 淖 (ṇau^C) **LH** ṇau^C, **OCM** *nrâuh
'Mud' [Zuo].
[<] exopass., lit. 'what has been stirred up' (§4.4).
ⅹ **hè** 嗃 (xau^C) **LH** hau^C, **OCM** hnrâuh ?
'Be clamouring' [Shi].
ⅹ **náo** 呶怓 (ṇau) **LH** ṇau, **OCM** *nrâu
'Disorderly, clamouring' [Shi].
ⅹ **rǎo** 擾 (ńźjäu^B) **LH** ńau^B, **OCM** *nauʔ
'To disturb' [Zuo].
ⅹ **nǎo** 惱 (nâu^B) **LH** nɑu^B — **[T]** *ONW* nɑu
'To anger, irritate' [SW], a Han and post-Han word, perh. the same etymon as *náo* 撓.
ⅹ **nuán** 奻 (nwan[^{C}]) **LH** nuan(^{C}) < nrâu-n(s)
'To quarrel' [SW].
[E] ST: WT *rñog-pa* 'to trouble, rub; troubled, thick, turbid, dirty'; WB *nok* 'dirty, foul, turbid' ⅹ *hnok* 'to stir up, make turbid, agitate, molest' (Unger *Hao-ku* 36, 1990: 51) ⅹ *hnoŋ^C* 'annoy, molest, thwart'. For the final consonants, see §6.4.4.

nǎo$_1$ 惱 → **náo**$_3$ 撓

nǎo$_2$ 腦 (nâu^B) **LH** nɑu^B ? or nou^B ?, **OCM** *nâuʔ or *nûʔ ?
'Brain' [Li].
[T] *Sin Sukchu SR* naw (上); *MGZY* naw (上) [naw]
[N] The OC rime of *nǎo* is not certain. Among others, the word *nǎo* 惱 'to anger, irritate' is written with the same phonetic and is cognate to a wf in OC *-au (→ náo$_3$ 撓), but 惱 is late [SW] and cannot help identify the OC and LH vowel of 腦.
[E] ST: PTB *nuk > PLB *nok ~ *ʔnok ~ *nuw 'brains' (Matisoff 1972: 62), WB *u^B-hnok* 'brain', JP *nuʔ^{55} < nuk* 'brain'. For the final consonants, see §3.2.2.

nào 淖 → **náo**$_3$ 撓

něi 餒 (nuậi^B) **LH** nuəi^B, **OCM** *nûiʔ
'Hungry' [Lunyu].
ⅹ Perh. **nì** 惄 (niek) **LH** nek, **OCM** *niûk
'Be hungry, desirous' [Shi]. Wáng Lì (1982: 308) relates this word to *nì* 愵 (niek) *-iɔk 'grieved' [Han].
[E] ST: WT *gñog-pa* 'to desire' ⅹ *sñog-pa* ~ *sñeg-pa* 'wish earnestly, crave' (*CVST* 2: 36). This is a parallel stem of → è$_{10}$ 餓 'hungry' (§5.12.1). A similar vocalic metathesis obtained prob. in → shuāi 衰.

nèi 內 → **rù**$_1$ 入

nèn, **nùn** 嫩 (nuən^C) *ONW* don (!)
'Tender, delicate', a late word [GY, JY].
[E] Etymology is not clear. Perh. a variant of → ruǎn 耎軟 (ńźjwän^B). Alternatively, it may be ST, related to WB *nun^B* 'weak, exhausted from illness', but this meaning barely overlaps with *nèn* 'soft to touch'. <> PMY *-on, individual lgs. have forms like *lun^5*, *gun^5*, *ɳtʃoŋ^5* (Wáng Fúshì). Finally, *nèn* is reminiscent of AA items: PMonic *lʔun 'be flexible, soft to touch' (of body part etc.), and / or PVM *k-rn-ɔːn 'young, tender' > Viet. *non* (acc. to Ferlus, an infix derivation from *kɔːn 'son').

néng$_1$ 能 (nəŋ) **LH** nə(ŋ) , **OCM** *nə̂ !
'A kind of bear' [Guoyu] apparently an area word of AA origin: Kharia *bɔnɔi* 'bear' (*-i* is suffix), Santali *bana* 'Indian black bear' -> TB-Lepcha *să-na* 'bear'.

néng$_2$ 能 (nəŋ) **LH** nə(ŋ), **OCM** *nə̂ŋ, *nə̂ʔ
'Be capable, have ability, can' [Shi]. *Shījīng* rimes indicate OCM *nəʔ. Prob. cognate to → nìng$_1$ 佞 'capable'.
[T] *Sin Sukchu SR* nəjŋ (平), *PR*, *LR* nəŋ; *MGZY* n^h ing (平) [nəŋ]; *ONW* nəŋ
[E] ? ST: WT *nus-pa* 'be able'; WB *nuiŋ* 'prevail, conquer; verb affix: potential', Mru *nöŋ* 'be able' (Löffler 1966: 142).

⋇ **tài** 態 (t^hậi^C) **LH** t^hə^C, **OCM** *nhə̂h
'Apparition, bearing, manner' [Guoce].
[E] ? ST: WT *mt^hu < m-nhu* ? 'ability, power'.

[E] The OC ~ WT difference in the vowel is unusual (§11.10.5).

ní$_1$ 尼 (ṇi) **LH** ṇi, **OCM** *nri or *ni ?
'Near, close' [Shizi], a relatively late word.
[T] *Sin Sukchu SR* njej (平), *PR* ni; *MGZY* ñi (平) [ṇi]; *ONW* ni
[E] Etymology not certain. This stem could simply be a variant of → ěr$_7$ 邇 'near', just as Mand. *nǐ* 'you' is a col. variant of *ěr* 'you'. Or it could be a conflation of → ěr$_7$ 邇 and *nì* 昵衵 *nrit (under → jí$_7$ 即). Finally, there is a possible TB cognate: KN-Khimi *kă-ni*, Haka *hni* 'petticoat' [*IST:* 207], the meaning of these items agrees with 昵衵, though. Syn. is also → jí$_7$ 即, → nì$_9$ 暱.

ní$_2$ 泥 (niei) **LH** nei, **OCM** *nə̂i or *nî
'Mud, mire' [Shu], 'muddy' (of water).
[T] *Sin Sukchu SR* njej (平), *PR* ni; *MGZY* ni (平) [ni]; *ONW* nėi
[D] In many dialects, the word means 'earth' *tǔ* 土, e.g. K-Méixiàn *nɐi^11* 'soil, earth'.

⋇ **nìng** 濘 (nieŋ^C) **LH** neŋ^C, **OCM** *nêŋh
'Mud' [Zuo].

[E] ST: KN-Lai *noj* 'muddy' (of water); a ST medial rounded (semi-) vowel regularly disappears in CH after accute initials (§10.2.1). TB shows that → niè$_4$ 涅 'black sediment in muddy water' is unrelated.

ní$_3$ 怩 (ṇi) **LH** ṇi, **OCM** *nri
'Ashamed' [Meng].
[E] ST: PTB *(r-)ni : JR *kəwurni < g-rni* 'red', *tərni* 'gold', Qiang *ńhi* 'red'; WB *ni* 'red' (*STC:* 46; 91), Lahu *ní ~ ni* 'red, bare, naked'. Pulleyblank (1973: 121) relates *ní* to words with initial *n- meaning 'shame', see → xiū$_3$ 羞.

ní$_4$ 倪 → **ér**$_4$ 兒

ní$_5$ 麑麛 (ŋiei, miei, mjie) **LH** ŋe, m(i)e, **OCM** *ŋê, *me ?
'Fawn' QYS *ŋiei, miei, mjie* 麑 [Lunyu], QYS *miei* 麛 [Li]. Wáng Lì (1982: 112) and

Sagart 1999 relate this to → ér$_4$ 兒 'child', Sagart also to WB *ŋai* 'kind of small deer, river deer'.

nǐ$_1$ 你 (nɨ^B) (LH, OC same as → ěr$_5$ 爾)
'You' [Tang], Mand. colloquialism for → ěr$_5$ 爾 (Demiéville 1950: 6), acc. to *GY* a NW dialect word. For allofams, see under → rǔ$_2$ 汝.
[T] *Sin Sukchu SR* njej (上), *PR*, *LR* ni; *MGZY* ñi (上) [ɲi]; STang nɨ^B > ni^B, *ONW* nii

nǐ$_2$ 妳 → **nǎi$_4$** 嬭

nì$_1$ 泥 'obstructed' → **niè$_5$** 敜

nì$_2$ 昵 (ṇjet) **LH** ṇit, **OCM** *nrit
'Glue' [Guoce, Zhouli], 'adhere to' 黏 [SW: Zuo].
[E] Prob. <- MK: Khmu *klɲaʔ* 'resin', the prefix *kl-* derives from *kə̄l* 'tree'. The OC final *-t* marks natural objects (§6.2.1); for the vocalism, see §11.5.2; a MC retroflex initial does not necessarily reflect an PCH *r (§7.4). This word is prob. not related to the wf → jí$_7$ 即 in light of the above MK etymology.

nì$_3$ 昵 'familiar' → **jí$_7$** 即

nì$_4$ 衵 (ṇjet) **LH** ṇit, **OCM** *nrit — **[T]** *ONW* nit
'Lady's clothes closest to the body', i.e. 'underwear' [Zuo].
[E] ST: KN-Khimi *kă-ni*, Haka *hni* 'petticoat' [*IST:* 207] (or are these CH loans?). The OC form has prob. adjusted to *nì* 昵 *nrit 'familiarity' (→ jí$_7$ 即) to which it may be related, but the TB cognates suggest a distinct etymon. The meaning has been transferred to *xiè* 褻 (under → ěr$_7$ 邇).

nì$_5$ 黏 → **nì$_2$** 昵 'glue'

nì$_6$ 逆 (ŋjɐk) **LH** ŋɨak, **OCM** *ŋrak, OCB *ŋrjak
'Go to meet, go against' [Shu], 'rebellious' [Shi], 'receive' [Yili], 'anticipate' [Lunyu].
[T] *Sin Sukchu SR* i (入), *PR* ŋi; *MGZY* ngi (入) [ŋi]; *ONW* ŋek
[<] This is the final *-k* counterpart to the cognate → yíng$_1$ 迎, or the div. 3 counterpart to the cognate → yà$_2$ 御迓訝 (if one assumes an OC medial *r like Baxter; otherwise it is derived from → yù$_{17}$ 禦).

ⵣ **shuò** 朔 (ṣåk) **LH** ṣak ? / ṣɔk, **OCM** *sŋrâk ? / *srôk
'First day of the new moon' [Shi, SW] > 'beginning' [Li]; (dark side >) 'North' [Shu, EY] (opposite of → nán$_1$ 南).
[T] *Sin Sukchu SR* ʂaw (入), *PR* ʂwawʔ; *MGZY* shwaw (入) [ʂwaw]

[E] The word LH *ṣak* is derived from *nì* 逆 'go to meet' (above), i.e. on that day the moon turns and moves toward the full moon (Matisoff, ICSTLL 1978: 13–14: Boltz, Diss.). This is an iterative s-prefix form (§5.2.3), hence lit. 'turn again toward to meet'. The puzzling MC reading *ṣåk* < *srok ? is attested already in *Lùnyǔ* where the graph is borrowed for *shuò* 數 (ṣåk) 'account' (under → shǔ$_4$ 數).

Alternatively, *shuò* 'north' may be related to TB-NNaga *swər 'night', Bodo-Garo *war, Mru *war* (with final CH *-k with the metathesis of final *r, see §6.1, resulting in OC *srak ~ *srok from *sruak) and thus be the opposite of → nán$_1$ 南 'south' < ST 'day, sun'. Possibly, distinct etyma for 'north' and 'new moon' have merged.

nì$_7$ 惄 → **něi** 餒

nì$_8$ 匿 → **tè$_5$** 慝

nì$_9$ 暱 (ṇjək) **LH** ṇək, **OCM** *nrək
'Be near, familiar with' [Shi].
[E] ST: TB-KN-Lai *neek* 'be very familiar, disrespect...' [T. Yamashita Smith *LTBA* 21.1, 1998: 29]. Syn. or cognates are → ěr$_7$ 邇, → jí$_7$ 即, → ní$_1$ 尼.

nì$_{10}$ 溺 (niek) **LH** nek < neuk, **OCM** *niâuk
'To sink, go under' [Shi].
[T] *Sin Sukchu SR* ni (入); *MGZY* ni (入) [ni]
[E] Several TB etymological connections may be possible: perh. related to WB *nac* < *nik 'sink into, be immersed' ꭗ *hnac* 'make to sink, immerse' (*STC:* 180), but the vowels do not agree. Alternatively, *nì* could be connected with WB *hnuik* 'penetrate, dive into' (with hand).

nì$_{11}$ 愵 'grieved' → **něi** 餒

nián 年 (nien) **LH** nen), **OCM** *nîn
'Harvest, crop, year' [OB, Shi].
[T] *Sin Sukchu SR* njen (平); *MGZY* nen (平) [nɛn]; *MTang* nian < nɨan, *ONW* nėn
[E] ST: PTB *s-niŋ 'year' (*STC* no. 368) > WT *na-niŋ* 'last year', Tsangla *niŋ* 'year', Mikir *niŋ*, JP *niŋ*^{33} 'year', WB *ə-hnik*, Mru *niŋ*. Syn. → rěn$_3$ 稔.

niǎn$_1$ 反 (ṇiän^B) **LH** ṇɑn^B, **OCM** *nranʔ (or *nrenʔ ?)
'To work leather to make it smooth' [SW], 'soft' [GY]; this word occurs in Southern Mǐn as 'to soften': Xiàmén *nũã*^{51} (tone B).
[E] ST: WT *mñel-ba, gñel-ba* 'to tan or dress hide', *ñer-ba* 'to tan, dress, soften' (*HST:* 146) ꭗ *mñen-pa* 'flexible, subtle', Lushai *nel*^{H} < *nel* 'be flexible' ꭗ *nel*^{L} < *nelʔ/h* 'soft' (skin), Lepcha *nŭl-lă-nól-lă* 'soft, tender' (Bodman 1980: 77).

niǎn$_2$ 輦連 (ljän^B) **LH** lian^B, **OCM** *ranʔ ?
'Cart drawn by two men' 輦 [Shi], 連 [Zhouli].
[T] *Sin Sukchu SR* ljen (上); *MGZY* len (上) [lɛn]; *ONW* (l)ian
[E] This word is perh. related to WB *hlañ* 'cart' ꭗ *ə-hlañ* 'a cartful' (Unger *Hao-ku* 36, 1990: 52), but MC *l-* usually corresponds to TB r- (§7.3).

niǎn$_3$, **rěn** 涊 (ńźjen^B) **LH** ńɨn^B, **OCM** *nənʔ
'To sweat' [Wenxuan, GY]. Unger (*Hao-ku* 36, 1990: 54) relates this word to WT *rŋul* 'sweat'. <> Note Tai: S. *hŋɨa*^{B} ~ *hɨa*^{B} 'sweat'.

niǎn$_4$ 跈踬 → **niè**$_7$ 躡

niàn$_1$ 念 (niem^C) **LH** nem, **OCM** *nə̂ms or *nêms ?, OCB *nims
'To think of, remember, remind' [BI, Shi].
[T] *Sin Sukchu SR* njem (去); *MGZY* nem (去) [nɛm]; *ONW* nėm
[N] In the phrase *wú niàn* 無念 *ma-nêms [in Shi 325] 'to think of', *wú* is thought to represent a syllabified prefix (Sagart 1999: 82), note the Khmer form below.

ꭗ **rèn** 恁 (ńźjəm^B) **LH** ńim^B, **OCM** *nəmʔ
'To think' [Shi].
[E] ST: WT *ñam(s)* 'soul, mind, thought' ꭗ *sñam-pa* 'to think, mind' (*STC:* 175 n. 465), Mikir *nióm* 'faith, religion'. This may be an area word: AA-Khmer *cɔmnam* 'remembrance, remembering, habit'; AN *nemnem* 'to think' (Sagart *JCL* 21.1, 1993: 48).

niàn$_2$ 晛 (nien^C) **LH** nėn^C, **OCM** *nêns or *nîns ?
'Sunlight' (which melts snow) [Shi]. Karlgren *GSR* 1250e considers this word cognate to → rán$_1$ 然 'burn' LH *ńian*, but the OC vowels do not agree. It may possibly be

related to → rì 日 'sun' instead. The reading *xiàn* 晛 (ɣien^{B}) LH *gen^{B}* has prob. been transferred from the graphic element 見 LH *gen^{C}*, or from *xiàn* 晛 (ɣien^{B}) LH *gen^{B}*.

niáng 孃娘 (ṇiaŋ)
'Lady' [only Tang and later].
[T] *Sin Sukchu SR* njaŋ (平); *MGZY* ñang (平) [ṇaŋ]; *ONW* naŋ ?
[E] This is possibly a fusion of *nǚ-láng* 女郎 'lady' (Coblin 1994: 389). This word is also found in Tai: S. *naaŋ^{A2}* < *n- 'lady, woman'.

niǎo 鳥 (tieu^{B}) **LH** teu^{B}, **OCM** *tiûʔ
'Bird' [Shi].
[T] *Sin Sukchu SR* njew (上); *MGZY* dÿaw (上) [tjɛw]
[N] *Niǎo* is a late pronunciation (or word?) which came into use because of a taboo. Nevertheless, the word *niǎo* does not come out of thin air; it could be connected with the KT word for 'bird': Tai: S. *nuk^{D2}S* < *nl/rok; PKS *mluk^{8}. For Chinese tone B for foreign final *-k*, see §3.2.2. The old form survives in some dialects as 'penis', e.g. Mand.-Jǐnán *tiɔ^{55}* = tone B, Y-Guǎngzhōu *tiu$^{35/A1}$*.
[E] ST *t(j)oʔ ? *STC* (192 n. 491) connects MC *tieu^{B}* with Garo *doʔ [Joseph / Burling, *LTBA* 24.2, 2001: 45], Karen *to 'bird', note also KN *m-tow 'to fly' (for CH medial *i*, see §9.1.3).

niào 尿溺 (nieu^{C}) **LH** neu^{C}, **OCM** *niâukh
'To urinate' [Zhuang].
[T] *Sin Sukchu SR* njew (去); *PR* njaw
[E] PTai *ň- ~ n-: S. *jiau^{B2}* 'to urinate', Saek *ɲuu^{B2}*.

niē 捻 (niep) **LH** nep, **OCM** *nêp or *nîp
'To pinch, nip with fingers' [SW Xīnfù, JY].
[E] ST: PLB: *nip ~ *ʔnip ~ *ʔnyit 'to squeeze, press'. CH -> Tai: S. *niip^{D1}* (WrSiam *hni:ʔb*) 'grasp (with pincers), pinch between' (Manomaivibool 1975: 163). This ST root *nip is distinct from *njap (→ shè$_{10}$ 攝 'grasp'), although they may ultimately be related as their TB cognates seem to be: PTB *nip 'press, pinch' ~ *nyap 'to press, squeeze' (*HPTB:* 112; 339).

niè$_{1}$ 㚔 'frightening' → **shè$_{9}$** 懾慹

niè$_{2}$ 臬 (ŋjät 3) **LH** ŋɨat, **OCM** *ŋrat
'Target' [Zhouli].
[E] ST: KN-Lai *ŋiat* 'to aim at', middle voice 'spy, watch'.

niè$_{3}$ 闑 'door post' → **niè$_{12}$** 齧

niè$_{4}$ 涅 (niet) **LH** net, **OCM** *nît — **[T]** *MTang* niar < nɨar, *ONW* nėt
'Black sediment in muddy water' [Lunyu].
[E] ST *nik: WB *ə-nañ ~ ə-nac* < *nik 'sediment, dregs', WT *sñigs-pa* 'impure sediment' (Shī Xiàngdōng 2000: 38; see §6.4.1 for the final cons.). The TB cognate shows that *niè* and *niè* 涅 'fill up' (under → niè$_{5}$ 敜) are not related to → ní$_{2}$ 泥 'mud'.

niè$_{5}$ 敜 (niep) **LH** nep, **OCM** *nêp or *nîp
'To fill up, stop up' (e.g. pitfalls) [Shu].
[E] ST: WT *sñobs* = *sñoms-pa*, *bsñoms* 'make equal with ground, destroy'.
~ **niè** 涅 (niet) **LH** net (neit), **OCM** *nît — **[T]** *MTang* niar < nɨar, *ONW* nėt
'To block, stop up' [Yili]. Since final *-p* tends to be somewhat unstable, this word is prob. a variant, while → niè$_{4}$ 涅 'black sediment' is prob. a different etymon.

⋇ **nì** 泥 (nieiC) **LH** neiC, **OCM** *nîh (or *nîts ?) — **[T]** *ONW* nėi
'Impeded, obstructed' [Lunyu].
[<] exopass. of *niè* 敜 (niep) or *niè₄* 涅 (niet) (§4.4).

niè₆ 踂 → **dié₆** 輒

niè₇ 躡 (ṇjäp) **LH** ṇap, **OCM** *nrap
'To trample' [Guoce].
[E] Chinese has an additional word for 'trample' with initial *n-*: → róu 蹂 (nźjəu[B/C]); *zhǎn* 蹍, *niǎn* 跈 (njän). It also may possibly be related to → liè₅ 躐 OC *rap 'trample'. Note a similar item in PLB *(s-)nak ~ *naŋ 'step on'.

niè₈ 鑷 → **shè₁₀** 攝

niè₉ 孽 (ŋjät 3) **LH** ŋɨat, **OCM** *ŋrat or *ŋret, OCB *ŋrjat — **[T]** *ONW* ŋat
'Calamity' *(GSR)*, perh. 'retribution, punishment' [OB, Shu], 'inauspicious, unhappy' 蠥 [Chuci].
[E] ST *ŋja(t) ~ *ŋe(t): WT *ñes-pa* 'evil, calamity, damage, moral fault, offense, crime', Kachin *nye* 'punish, cause woe' (*STC* no. 252).

niè₁₀ 糵 (ŋjät 3) **LH** ŋɨat, **OCM** *ŋrat
'Malt' [Li] (not 'yeast', so Unger *Hao-ku* 39, 1992). *Shìmíng* explains: 'soak wheat and let it sprout'). Acc. to Unger, the basic meaning of this stem is 'sprout', hence the items below are the s. w. Unger suggests a derivation from *yá* 芽 'sprout' which, however, is the s. w. as → yá₁ 牙 'tooth'. If true, 'tooth' would then be the ultimate origin of this wf.
[E] ST: Lushai *ŋaan*^{H} < *ŋaan* 'malt' (Unger).
= **niè** 櫱 'sprouts, shoots' (e.g. from tree trunk, family) [Shi], also MC *ŋât*.
= **niè** 孽 'concubine's son' [Meng].
⋇ **è** 枿櫱櫱 (ŋât) **LH** ŋɑt, **OCM** *ŋât
'Stump of tree, shoots from stump of tree' [SW].

niè₁₁ 槷 'pole' → **niè₁₂** 齧

niè₁₂ 齧 (ŋiet) **LH** ŋet, **OCM** *ŋêt
'To gnaw, crunch in the teeth' [Li]; 'vertical post' (in the middle of a gate) 闑 [Liji] > 'a pole' 槷 [Zhouli]. This root refers to a situation in which an object is caught or found between jaws, doors, or the like.

níng₁ 寧 (nieŋ) **LH** neŋ, **OCM** *nêŋ — **[T]** *ONW* nėŋ
'Be tranquil, at ease, favor' [BI, Shi] (*HST:* 92) > 'rather' [Zuo]. This is prob. related to WB *hñaŋ*^{B} 'soft, gentle, quiet', although it has been connected with PTB *niŋ 'heart', see → rén₂ 仁.

níng₂ 凝 → **yìng₃** 硬

nìng₁ 佞 (nieŋC) **LH** neŋC, **OCM** *nêŋh
'Capable' [Chunqiu], 'clever, artful, eloquent' [Shu, Lunyu], *bù-nìng* 不佞 'incapable', acc. to Carr (ms. 'Re-examining the hunchback and dwarf enigma'). This word is perh. related to → néng₂ 能 (nəŋ) 'be able'.

nìng₂ 濘 → **ní₂** 泥

niú 牛 (ŋjəu) **LH** ŋu, **OCM** *ŋwə, OCB *ŋʷjə
'Bovine, ox, cow' [OB, Shi].

[T] *Sin Sukchu SR* ŋiw, iw (平); *PR*, *LR* niw; *MGZY* ngiw (平) [ŋiw]; *ONW* ŋu
[D] M-Xiàmén *gu*^{A2}, Fúzhōu *ŋu*^{A2}
[E] ST *ŋwə > *nwa is shared with eastern TB and southern and western Tai languages (Weidert 1987: 129): PTB *ŋwa (*STC* no. 215) > PL *ŋja^{2}, JP *ŋa*^{33}, *wə*^{33}-; Nung *ŋwa* ~ *ŋa* ~ *nwa*, Dulong *nuŋ*^{55}-*ŋua*^{53}, WB *nwa*^{B} 'bull, ox, cow', SChin Daai (KC) *mna* 'buffalo' [Hartmann ICSTLL 1999: 2]; perh. WT *ba* (< *ŋba* < *ŋwa*?) 'cow' in light of Lepcha *sŭŋ-vo* (< *sə-ŋvo?) (so Bodman 1980: 153). A parallel stem (§2.5) may be WT: *nor* 'wealth, cattle', Lepcha *a-nór* 'herd, flock, troop, numbers, quantities' (§5.12.2). <> Tai: S. *ŋua*^{A2} < *ŋwue ? 'ox'. Because of the restricted geographic distribution, *STC* suspects CH *niú* to be a Tai loan, also Li Fang Kuei (1976: 42) concludes the Tai item is not a CH loan because it is not found in northern Tai dialects.

niǔ$_{1}$ 狃丑 (ṇjəu^{B}) **LH** ṇu^{B}, **OCM** *nriuʔ
'Finger, toe', perh. originally also 'claw, nail' (the OB graph shows a hand with prominent nails); rad. 114 QY *ṇjəu*^{B} (also *nźjəu*^{B} which is perh. spurious, deriving from a paronomastic gloss in SW) 'finger, claws' [Erya] (Unger *Hao-ku* 46, 1995).
[E] Area word: TB-PLB *s-nyuw^{1,2} 'digit, finger' > WB *lak-hñui*^{B} 'forefinger' (*STC:* 77 n. 234). <> PTai *niu^{C2} 'finger', Shan *niw* 'finger, toe, fingernail, toenail'. For the OC medial *r, see §7.6.2.

niǔ$_{2}$ 紐 (ṇjəu^{B}) **LH** ṇu^{B}, **OCM** *nr(i)uʔ, OCB *nrjuʔ
'A knot' (that can be opened) [SW], 'knot' (on a sash) [Liji] > 'button' 鈕 > any type of button or knob by which, for example, a ring can be fastened. The basic meaning could be some kind of fastener that can be easily undone. Conversely, 'button' could also have been the original meaning from which the others derived, in which case this word may be the same as → niǔ$_{1}$ 狃丑 'fingernail' > 'fingernail-shaped' > 'button'.
[T] *Sin Sukchu SR* niw (上); *MGZY* ñiw (上) [ṇiw]; *ONW* nu

niǔ$_{3}$ 鈕 → **niǔ$_{2}$** 紐

niǔ$_{4}$ 忸 → **xiū$_{3}$** 羞

niù 糅 (ṇjəu^{C}) **LH** ṇu^{C}, **OCM** *nruh
'Mixed' [Yili]; MC readings in other tones are dubious (Unger *Hao-ku* 35, 1986: 33; 36, 1990: 52).
[E] ST: WT *snor-ba* 'to confound, mingle, mix, disturb', WB *hno*^{B} 'to mix, mingle' (Unger, op. cit. p. 42, n. 67). For the metathesis of the *r, see §7.7.3.

nóng$_{1}$ 農 (nuoŋ) **LH** nouŋ, **OCM** *nûŋ
'Agriculture, peasant, to cultivate' [Shi].
[T] *Sin Sukchu SR* nuŋ (平); *MGZY* ñung (平) [ṇuŋ]; *MTang* noŋ, *ONW* nauŋ
[E] Prob. ST and cognate to → nòu 耨 'to weed' (TB-Lushai *hnu*^{F} 'work finished, weeded or harvested area'). The final *-ŋ in *nóng* could be the terminative suffix (§6.5.1): *nòu* 'to weed, hoe' > *nóng* 'get a field hoed', i.e. 'cultivated'.
[C] → nóng$_{2}$ 儂 'person, I' (< 'peasant') may be the same word; a possible allofam may be → nóng$_{3}$ 穠 'thick vegetation'.

nóng$_{2}$ 儂 (nuoŋ)
'Person, I, me' in southeastern dialects: Coastal Mǐn *noŋ, Fúzhōu *nøiŋ*^{A2}, *nøiŋ*^{A2}-*ka*^{A1} 儂家 'I, myself'; Xiàmén *laŋ*^{A2} 'person'; Wú: *ā-nóng* 阿儂 'I'. Xiàmén *lan*^{B} 'we' (inclusive) is *laŋ*^{A2} + a pronominal suffix *-n* which in turn is derived from *nóng;* Fúzhōu *i*^{A1}-*nøiŋ* 'they'. Acc. to Norman (1983: 208), the semantic development is

'peasant' (→ nóng$_1$ 農) > 'person' > pronoun 'I, me'. Alternatively, since a syllable *noŋ* occurs in some Zhuang (Tai) dialects in forms for the first person pronoun, Pān Wùyún and Chén Zhōngmǐn (*JCL* 23.2, 1995) suggest that *nóng* is a substrate word from the earlier 'Hundred Yuè' 百越 where *nóng* was a clan name and ethnonym, then > 'person' > 'I, me'.

nóng$_3$ 濃醲 膿 (ŋ̣jwoŋ, nuŋ) **LH** ŋ̣oŋ, nouŋ, **OCM** *nroŋ, *nôŋ
'Thick, rich (dew)' [Shi]; 'thick, strong (drink)' 醲 [Hanfei]; 'pus' (< 'thick matter') 膿 (only MC *nuoŋ*) [Hanfei]. This item may be related to → nóng$_4$ 穠 'thick growth' (so Wáng Lì 1982: 610).
[T] *MTang* noŋ, *ONW* nauŋ — **[D]** PMin *ŋ̣əŋ(C)
[E] CH -> Tai: PTai *hn- > S. *nɔɔŋ^{A1}* 'pus'.
ꭗ **rú** 醹 (ńźju[B]) **LH** ńo(B), **OCM** *no(ʔ)
'Strong (of spirits)' [Shi]. If tone B should be original, it would be another instance of a *-ŋ ~ -ʔ* variation.
[E] ST: WT *rno-ba, rnon-po* 'sharp, acute' (of taste, intellect); KN-Lushai *nu^H / nut^L* 'muddy' (of liquids); however, the Lushai item may instead be connected to → ní$_2$ 泥.
[C] Allofam is perh. → rú$_5$ 濡.

nóng$_4$ 穠 (ŋ̣jwoŋ, ńźjwoŋ) **LH** ŋ̣oŋ, ńoŋ, **OCM** *nroŋ, *noŋ
'Gorgeous' (of blossoms) [Shi], 'thick growth' is perh. related to → nóng$_1$ 農 'agriculture'.
ꭗ **rǒng** 氄 (ńźjwoŋ^B) **LH** ńoŋ^B, **OCM** *noŋʔ
'Bushy' (hair) [Shu]
~ **róng** 茸 (ńźjwoŋ) **LH** ńoŋ 'id.' [Zuo]
~ **róng** 茙 (nźjuŋ) **LH** ńuŋ, **OCM** *nuŋ 'luxuriant, bushy' [Lie].

nòu 耨 (nuok, nəu^C) **LH** nouk, no^C, **OCM** *nûk, *nôkh — **[T]** *ONW* nouk or nauk?
'To weed with a hoe' [Zhuang, Meng]; 'a hoe' 耨 [SW].
[E] ST: Lushai *hnu^F < hnuʔ* (< *-ʔ) 'work finished, weeded or harvested area'.
[C] Allofam → nóng$_4$ 農 'cultivate, agriculture'. This word is unrelated to the syn. → hāo$_2$ 薅茠.

nú$_1$ 奴 (nuo) **LH** na, **OCM** *nâ
'Slave' [Lun].
[T] *Sin Sukchu SR* nu (平); *MGZY* nu (平) [nu]; *ONW* no
[E] Etymology not certain. Perh. cognate to TB-Mru *nar* 'servant', SChin-Awa *tana* [Löffler, *Anthropos* 55, 1960: 530]. Ferlus (*LTBA* 22.2, 1999: 5) relates this word to → nǚ$_1$ 女 'woman'; this has semantic parallels, especially among foreign loans. Unger (*Hao-ku* 36, 1990: 44) relates it to a wf with the basic meaning 'tense' (incl. → nǔ$_1$ 弩, → nǔ$_2$ 努), hence 'press into service'.

nú$_2$ 奴 → **ā-nú** 阿奴

nú$_3$ 孥 → **nǚ$_1$** 女

nǔ$_1$ 弩 (nuo^B) **LH** na^B, **OCM** *nâʔ
'Crossbow' [Zhouli].
[T] *Sin Sukchu SR* nu (上); *MGZY* nu (上) [nu]; *ONW* no
[E] AA (Norman and Mei *MS* 32, 1976: 293–295; Benedict *AT* 1975: 110; 1976: 89): PViet-Muong *s-naːʔ 'bow, crossbow' [Ferlus], PMnong *so'na, Khmer *snaa*, PSBahn.

*sənaː 'crossbow', Pearic t^{h}ənaː 'crossbow'. Unrelated are PMonic and OMon *tŋaaʔ, Mon *hŋaʔ 'crossbow' (Diffloth 1984: 119).

The word is widely distributed in E and SE Asia: TB-Rawang (Nung) *thəna*, Dulong *tānā*, Moso (LB) *tǎna*. <> PTai *hnaa^{C}: S. *naa^{C1}* (*-mai^{C2}*) 'crossbow' (Li F. 1976: 43); in NTai *naa^{B1}* 'arrow' (particularly of a crossbow) (Manomaivibool 1975: 138), Sui *hna*; note also S. *sa-nao* 'crossbow' (<- Khmer?). <> PMY *nha^{B} 'crossbow'. <> PAN *panaq 'bow, arrow' (Sagart *JCL* 21.1, 1993: 23), *panah 'shooting weapon'.

Alternatively, Unger (*Hao-ku* 36, 1990: 44) suggests that *nǔ* is related to → nǔ$_2$ 努 which basically means 'to tense'. Gernet (acc. to Ferlus *LTBA* 22.2, 1999: 17) suggests that the homophone *nǔ* 砮 'stone used for arrowheads' has been extended to 'crossbow'.

nǔ$_2$ 努 (nuo^{B}) **LH** nɑ^{B}, **OCM** *nâʔ — **[T]** *ONW* no

努力 'to exert one's strength' [Han commentators], 怒臂 'tense / stem one's arms' [Zhuang].

⋇ **nù** 怒 (nuo^{C}) **LH** nɑ^{C}, **OCM** *nâh

'Angry' [Shi] belongs to this wf acc. to Unger (*Hao-ku* 36, 1990: 44) who analyzes this word as 'tense'.

[E] ST *nwar: TB: Lushai *nɔr^{F}* < *nɔɔrʔ* 'press, push' ⋇ Lushai *nuar^{H}* / *nɔrʔ^{L}* < *nuar* < *nɔrʔ/h* 'be displeased, disgruntled' (Unger *Hao-ku* 36, 1990: 44), Khami *nuar 'get angry' [R. Shafer *ZDMG* 102, 1952: 275]. For the OC final, see §7.7.7.

nù 怒 → **nǔ$_2$** 努

nǔ$_1$ 女 (n̥jwo^{B}) **LH** n̥ɑ^{B}, **OCM** *nraʔ < *C/r-naʔ ?

'Woman, wife, girl, daughter, female' [BI, Shi], opposite → shì$_1$ 士, → nán$_2$ 男. See also → niáng 孃娘.

[T] *Sin Sukchu SR* ny (上); *MGZY* ñÿu (上) [ɲy]; *ONW* nø < nio

[D] *nǚ -ér* 女兒 'girl, daughter', in Wú dialects *nø^{13}* (Mand. *nān*) 囡 'small child, girl, daughter', also *nø^{13}- ŋ^{13}* 囡五; 'female' of animals in Yuè dialects, e.g. Guǎngzhōu *ma^{13}-na^{35}* 馬 [乜+母] 'female horse'.

⋇ **nǜ** 女 (n̥jwo^{C}) **LH** n̥ɑ^{C}, **OCM** *nrah

'To give someone a wife' [Shu].

[<] exoactive of *nǚ* 女 (§4.3.1).

⋇ **nú** 孥 (nuo) **LH** nɑ, **OCM** *nâ

'Wife and children' [Shi, Shu]. <> Tai: S. *nɔɔŋ^{C2}* 'younger sibling' (Li F. 1976: 40), S. *naa^{C2}* 'mother's younger sibling'.

[E] Perh. ST *na: WT *mna'(-ma)* 'daughter-in-law' (Unger *Hao-ku* 33, 1986), *ña-mo* 'mistress of the house, housewife' (*HPTB:* 173f), and / or the marginal West Tib. *ñag(-mo)* 'woman' (Simon acc. to Bodman 1980: 133), for tone B in CH, see §3.3.1; JP *ʔna^{33}* 'older sister, sister-in-law' (wife of brother), address for older woman by a younger one; WB *hna^{C}-ma* 'sister' (*STC:* 187 n. 487), NNaga *ʔ-ɲa^{A} 'elder sister' [French 1983: 271]. However, the fundamental meaning of the TB items is 'sister', not 'woman, girl'.

Alternatively, Ferlus (*LTBA* 22.2, 1999: 5) connects the word with AA: Khmu *kmbraʔ* 'wife' < *kmraʔ*, OC from *k-N-raʔ*. He adds → nú$_1$ 奴 'slave' to this wf. There is a similar MK etymon, see → tái$_3$ 嬯臺.

nǚ$_2$ 籹 → **jù$_4$-nǚ** 粔籹

nuán 奻 'quarrel' → **náo$_3$** 撓

nuǎn 煖 (nuânB) **LH** nuanB, **OCM** *nônʔ — **[T]** *ONW* nuan

'Warm' 煖 [Li], 暖 [Chuci]. This word is unrelated to xuān 煖 (under → $xù_4$ 旭).

ᵹ **nuǎn** 渜 (nuânB/C) **LH** nuanB/C, **OCM** *nônʔ/s

'Hot water' [Yili].

[E] The stem of this etymon is *no(n) and apparently related to → $ruò_6$ 爇 *not 'hot'.

nuàn 偄 → **ruǎn** 耎軟

$nuè_1$ 虐 (ŋjak) **LH** ŋɨak, **OCM** *ŋauk

'To coerce, oppress, be violent' [BI, Shi] is related by Bodman (1980: 70) to *xuè, nuè* 謔 (xjak) 'to ridicule, jest' [Shi].

= **nuè** 瘧 (ŋjak) **LH** ŋɨak, **OCM** *ŋauk

'Ague' [Li].

[E] <> Tai: S. *ŋăk-ŋăk* 'shivering' ᵹ *hŋăk-hŋăk* 'shivering' (as from ague) (Unger *Hao-ku* 36, 1990: 53).

$nuè_2$ 謔 → **$nuè_1$** 虐

nuó 儺 (nâ) **LH** na, **OCM** *nâi

'To expel demons of illness' [Lunyu, GY].

[E] Etymology not certain. *Nuó* is perh. related to → $nán_3$ 難 'difficult' (so Karlgren 1956: 18; Boltz *JAOS* 99.3, 1979: 430). But it also, or instead, belongs to PTB *na ~ *nat 'ill': WB *na* 'be ill, be in pain' ᵹ *nat* 'demon, spirit' < PLB *nat (Benedict *HJAS* 4, 1939: 228). Perh. this is not a cognate but a TB loan because there is no obvious OC word with the meaning 'illness' from which *nuó* could have been derived (→ $nà_4$ 瘆 'sick' is a medieval word, and the etymology of → $shǔ_2$ 癙 'painful' is not certain); the OC rime *-ai creates difficulties for a genetic relationship as well.

$nuò_1$, **nà** 吶訥 (nuət, ńźjwät) **LH** nuət, ńuat, **OCM** *nût, *not

'Slow of speech' 訥 [Lunyu], 'speak slowly or cautiously' (Giles); 'blurt out' 吶 (Giles). Bodman (1980) links this word with Lepcha *a-nót* 'undecided' (in speech), *njot-tă* 'incessantly babbling', but on the other hand there is Tai: S. *nəəp*D2 'slow (of speech)'.

$nuò_2$ 諾 → **$ruò_1$** 若

$nuò_3$ 懦 → **$róu_1$** 柔

$nuò_4$ 糯 (nuâC [Jiyun])

'Glutinous rice' (*Oryza sativa* var. *glutinosa*) is found in all dialects (except Mǐn) as well as SEAsian languages, such as Tai *khâu nua* (Savina, *khâu* 'rice'); it is perh. connected with AA: Khmuic *lɔʔ 'glutinous rice', Viet. *lúa* 'paddy' (Ferlus 31st ICSTLL, 1998: 90), but see → $dào_4$ 稻.

O

ōu 甌 → **wǎn** $_4$ 碗

ǒu $_1$ 嘔 → **yuē** $_3$ 噦

ǒu $_2$ 偶 (ŋəu[B]) **LH** ŋo[B], **OCM** *ŋôʔ

'One of a pair, mate, counterpart' [Shu] > 'pair, double' [Li], 'two plowers working together' 耦 [Shi], 'a statue' 偶 [Huainan] > 'match, vis-à-vis' 偶 [Zuo].

ⵞ **yù** 遇 (ŋju[C]) **LH** ŋɨo[C], **OCM** *ŋoh

'To meet with, encounter' [BI, Shi] (Karlgren 1956: 13).

[T] *Sin Sukchu SR* ŋy (去); *MGZY* xÿu (去) [ɦy]

ⵞ **yú, yóng** 喁 (ŋju, ŋəu[B], ŋjuŋ) **LH** ŋɨo, ŋɨoŋ, **OCM** *ŋo(ŋ)

'Respond in singing' [Zhuang] (the QYS reading *ŋəu[B]* and / or *ŋju* may be the result of interference from other words in the phonetic series).

òu 漚 (ʔəu[C]) **LH** ʔo[C], **OCM** *ʔôh

'To soak' [Shi].

[T] *Sin S.* 歐 *SR* ʔəw (平); *MGZY* 歐 'hiw (平) [ʔəw]; *ONW* ʔou

ⵞ **wò** 渥 (ʔåk) **LH** ʔɔk, **OCM** *ʔrôk

'To moisten, smear'.

P

pā 葩 (p^{h}a)

'Flowers, blossoms' [post-Han].

[E] ST: PTB *baːr (*STC* no. 1): Lepcha *bor* 'to bloom', *a-bor* 'blossom' (Unger *Hao-ku* 35, 1986: 36); Lushai *paar*^{H} 'flower, blossom' ⋇ *parʔ*^{L} 'to open' (as flower) ⋇ *p*^{h}*arʔ*^{L} 'to open' (as hand, flower), KN-Khami *par* 'flower' (Löffler 1966: 146); WB *pan*^{B} 'flower' [Matisoff 1974: no. 149]; JP ^{1}*nam*-^{2}*pan* [Weidert 1987: 132], WT *'bar-ba* 'to blossom, to burn, catch fire, beam, radiate'. This etymon is prob. related to 'burn' → fán$_5$ 燔. WT also shows the relationship between 'burn, fire' and 'flower': *me-t*^{h}*og* 'flower' means lit. 'fire-top'.

[C] This word is perh. the same etymon as → bàn$_4$ 瓣 'petals of a flower'.

pá$_1$ 爬 (a late word, not in GY, JY, the MC form would be *ba*)

'To crawl' [Xin Fangyan], 'to climb', a col. archaism of the next item:

=pú-fú 匍匐 (buo/ bju-bjuk/ bək) **LH** bɑ-bək or bɨɑ-buk, **OCM** *ba-bək

'To crawl' [Shi and in subseq. Zhou lit.].

[T] *ONW* bo-buk

[E] The first syllable is reduplication (Norman 1988: 87). *SW* separates the two syllables: (1) *pú* (OCM *ba) '手行也', i.e. 'to crawl' [SW], *pú* = *pú-fú* [GY]; (2) *fú* = 伏 (bjuk) 'to lie on the ground' (*ZWDCD* 2: 89, 91). Thus *pú* ~ *pá* (above) follows *pú-fú* as an independent word, while *fú*, taken for a mere variant graph of 伏, becomes obsolete. <> This is perh. a ST item: Chepang *bah-sa* 'to crawl'.

pá$_2$, **bá** 耙杷 (ba[^{C}]) **LH** ba(^{C}), **OCM** *brâ(h) — **[T]** *ONW* bä

'A harrow' (Mand. *bà*), 'a rake' 杷 (Mand. *pá*) [Zhuang].

[E] Etymology not certain. This word may be derived from → bǎ 把 'handful, grasp', hence a claw-like instrument. Alternatively, *pá* could be MK: Khmer *pāra* /baar/ 'to scrape, scuff, rake...' (for the r-metathesis, see §7.7.3). In light of these possibilities, cognation with PTB *pra (*STC* no. 132) is less likely: Kanauri *bra* 'forked' (road) ⋇ *pra* 'spread, stretch', WB *pra*^{B} 'divided into several parts', JP *braʔ*^{55} < *brak*^{55} 'be forked' (*CVST* 1: 58).

pà 怕 (p^{h}a^C) *Sin Sukchu SR* p'a (去); *MGZY* pha (去) [p'a]; *SuiTang* pä^C

'To be afraid' [(Tang) Han Yu]. The graph occurs first in *SW*, but with a different meaning (Wáng Lì 1958: 576). Perh. an archaic colloquialism of the next item (so Wáng Lì 1982: 176):

⋇ **pù** 怖 (p^{h}uo^C) **LH** p^{h}ɑ^C, **OCM** *phâh — **[T]** *ONW* p^{h}o^C

'To fear' [Zhuang].

[E] Note Lushai *p*^{h}*ɔɔk*^{F} (Lorrain *phâwk*) 'to startle, frighten'; perh. also PMon *phiic 'be afraid' (for the vowels, see §11.1.3).

pái 箄 and other characters (baɨ) **LH** bɛ, **OCM** *brê

'Raft' [EY, Hou Hanshu]. — **[E]** <> PTai *bɛ^{A2} 'raft'.

pān 潘 (p^{h}uân) **LH** p^{h}ɑn, **OCM** *phân — **[D]** PEMin *p^{h}on^{A1}; CDC *phon*^{1}

'Water in which rice has been washed' [Li]. Etymology not clear.

pán₁ 般 (buân) **LH** bɑn, **OCM** *bân
'To turn around' [Li].
[T] *Sin S.* 盤 *SR* bwɔn (平), *PR*, *LR* bɔn; *MGZY* 盤 pon (平) [bɔn]
[E] ? ST: Perh. cognate to WB *pran* 'return, repeat' (*HST:* 153), Mru *plan* 'turn' (Löffler 1966: 140). Prob. cognate to → fǎn 反 'return'.

pán₂ 蟠 (buân) **LH** bɑn, **OCM** *bân
'To curl' (of a dragon) [Shàngshū dàzhuǎn] > 'to circulate' [Li].
[E] ST: PTB *boy (*STC* n. 308): WB *bhwe* 'curl in hair of animal'; Kachin *boi* 'have a cowlick'. Perh. WT *bal* 'wool' could belong here instead of to → mián₂ 綿棉 'cotton'.

pàn₁-huàn 判換 (pʰuânC-xuânC) **LH** pʰɑnC-huɑnC, **OCM** *phâns-huâns
'Be relaxed, slack' [Shi].
[E] Etymology not certain, possibly AA: Khmer *paṅ'ara* /baŋʔɑɑr/ 'be glad or rejoice..., please, delight...'. A connection of the second syllable with PTB *o:l (*STC* no. 111) > Magari *ol* 'to finish', Garo *ol* 'lax, loose, relax' may also be possible.

pàn₂ 判片 → **bàn₁** 半

pàn₃ 畔 → **bàn₁** 半

páng 旁傍 (bwâŋ) **LH** bɑŋ, **OCM** *bâŋ
'Side' [Zuo] > 'everywhere' 旁 [Shu]; 'at the side' [Zhouli], 'assist' 傍 [Liji] (傍 is also read MC *bwâŋC*).

ꭗ **bàng** 旁傍 (bwâŋC) **LH** bɑŋC, **OCM** *bâŋh
'Be or go beside' 旁 [Zuo], 傍 [Zhouli].

[E] ST: PTB *paŋ: Lushai *paŋL* 'side of body, side, flank'; PLB *paŋ: Lahu *phô* 'side, region', Akha *paw* 'side of something' ꭗ PLB *ʔpak ~ *ʔbak 'side, half, one of a pair'; note also WT *pʰyogs* 'side, direction'. It has been suggested that → kuāng₄ 筐 'square basket' is a derivation. Probably related to → fāng₁ 方.

pàng₁, pán 胖 (buân) **LH** bɑn, **OCM** *bân
'Fat, corpulent' [Li].
[E] ST: PTB *bwam (*STC* no. 172) > WT *sbom* 'thick, stout'; PLB *C-pwam: WB *pʰwamC* 'fat, plump' (applied to young of animals); JP *bom³¹* 'fat'; Lushai *puamH* 'swell, be swollen'; Peiros and Starostin (1996: I no. 223) connect the TB etyma with → péng₁ 芃 'densely growing'.

pàng₂ □ 'Hollow' in Min dialects: PMin *pʰaŋC ~ *pʰoŋC. <> Tai: Saek *phooŋC2* 'hollow, hole' (in a tree, bamboo); AA-PSBahn. *pɔ:ŋ 'hollow, flattened'. Words with the notion 'hollow' tend to be aspirated (§5.8.6).

páo 匏 (bau) **LH** bɔu, **OCM** *brû — **[T]** *MGZY* 庖 paw (平) [baw]
'Gourd' [Shi]
[E] ST: WB *bʰuB* 'gourd', Lushai *buurH* 'gourd' (Löffler 1966: 152; Unger *Hao-ku* 35, 1986: 36). Löffler relates → bāo₂ 胞 'womb' to 'gourd'. For the metathesis of the *r*, see §7.7.3.

pǎo 跑 'To run' is a recent word, but there are comparanda in other languages: TB-PL *pawˡ 'to flee'; Miao has forms like *plauCl* 'to flee'. Syn. → zǒu₀ 走.

pēi₁ 胚 (pʰuậi) **LH** pʰə, **OCM** *phə̂
'One month pregnant' [SW].
[E] AA: OKhmer /pdəj/ 'burden' > 'pregnancy' > 'vaulted' (surface of earth), 'stomach, abdomen' (Jenner / Pou 1982: 156). The word belongs to an AA wf which

includes → méi$_6$ 媒禖 'matchmaker' and → dài$_9$ 戴 'to bear'. Wáng Lì (1982: 105) already connected this word with méi$_6$. Alternative: PTB *pa:y 'pregnant' [*HPTB:* 210], but the finals do not agree.

pēi$_2$ 垺 → **fù$_8$** 阜

péi 陪培 → **bèi$_4$** 倍

pèi 沛 'uprooted' → **bá$_1$** 犮

pēn 噴歕 (pʰən[C]) **LH** pʰən(C), **OCM** *phə̂n(s)
'To blow out, spit out' 歕 [Mu Tianzi], 'to spurt' 噴 [Zhuang].
[E] ST: TB-Lushai *pʰuʔ*[L] 'to blow out of the mouth' (water, smoke), 'squirt'; WT *pʰu-ba, spun-pa* 'puff of breath'. CH aspiration is associated with forceful ejection §5.8.5.

pēng 伻 (pʰɛŋ) **LH** pʰɛŋ, **OCM** *phrêŋ
'To send, cause' acc. to commentators [Shi, Shu, EY], 'envoy' [Shu]. GY reads *pʰɛŋ*, aspirated, but also unaspirated forms are cited.
[E] ? ST: TB-WT *spriŋ-ba, spriŋs* 'to send a message, give information' ⪤ *pʰrin* 'news, message' (Geilich 1994: 64). Aspiration could be due either to loss of a ST pre-initial (§5.8.1), or to outward motion (§5.8.5).

péng$_1$ 芃 (buŋ, bjuŋ) **LH** boŋ, buŋ, **OCM** *bə̂m, *bəm
'Densely growing (trees, plants), thick-furred (fox)' [Shi].
[E] ST *pum, for cognates and parallel stems, see §2.5.1.

péng$_2$ 朋 (bəŋ) **LH** bəŋ, **OCM** *bə̂ŋ — **[T]** Pre-ONW bəŋ
'A pair, set of two' [Shi] > 'string of cowries' (consisting of two strands) [BI, Shi]; 'friend' (with whom one forms a set of two) [BI, Shi] (Bodman 1980: 149).

⪤ **bēng** 綳 (pɛŋ) **LH** pɛŋ, **OCM** *prə̂ŋ
'To bind round' [Mo] (Bodman); the OC medial *r could be the causative morpheme (§7.5), but see next.

[E] Bodman compares this wf with WT *(')pʰreŋ* 'string on which things are filed, strung' ⪤ *'pʰreŋ-ba* 'string of beads, rosary' ⪤ *'breŋ-ba* 'strap, rope', also WT *'pʰreŋ* 'to love, be fond of, greatly attached to'. However, MC ə usually corresponds to TB *a*, not *e*.

péng$_3$ 鵬 → **fèng$_3$** 鳳

péng$_4$ 蓬 (buŋ) **LH** boŋ, **OCM** *bôŋ
'Luxuriant' (of foliage) [Shi].

⪤ **běng** 菶 (puŋ[B], buŋ[B]) **LH** poŋ[B], boŋ[B], **OCM** *pôŋʔ, *bôŋʔ
'Densely growing' [Shi].

⪤ **fēng** 丰 (pʰjwoŋ) **LH** pʰuoŋ, **OCM** *phoŋ
'Flourishing, elegant' [Shi].

[E] ST *poŋ, for cognates and parallel stems, see §2.5.1. Additional allofam: → fēng$_6$ 豐.

péng$_5$-lái 蓬萊 (buŋ-lậi) **LH** boŋ-lə > boŋ-ləi (?)
A legendary island of the immortals (*xiān* 仙) in the eastern sea [Shānhǎijīng, Shǐjì], usually identified as the Bohai Sea. Etymology not clear. However, resemblance to a SE Asian word for 'sea, ocean' is striking: TB-WB *paŋ-lai* 'ocean', JP *paŋ*[33]*-lai*[33] id. This etymon looks like a loan, possibly from MK: Khmer *dhle* /tlé/ 'expanse of water' ⪤ OKhmer *danle(y)* /dənlee/ 'lake, sea' (with nasal infix) (Jenner / Pou 1982: 323); Khmer -> Pearic *thəle:* 'sea' -> Thai *tʰalee* id. Occasionally, an AA nasal infix (as in /dənlee/) is reinterpreted as the root initial which can lead to a change in the initial

consonant such as *d* > *b*. For an illustration for such reinterpretation and initial consonant substitution in AA, see §2.6.2.

péng$_6$ 篷 → **fán**$_2$ 帆

pèng 碰 (bɐŋ^C [Zìhuì]), bâŋ^C [Duan Yucai].

Mand. 'To hit, run into / meet unexpectedly' is prob. a recent col. form of → féng$_1$ 逢 夆 (Wáng Lì 1982: 390).

pī$_1$ 匹 → **pǐ**$_1$ 匹

pī$_2$ 鴄 → **pǐ**$_3$ 鴄

pī$_3$ 披 (p^{h}je 3) **LH** p^{h}ɨai, **OCM** *phai

'Divide, separate, disperse' [Zuo].

[E] ST *pai: PL *bay^1 'to separate'; WT *dbye-ba* 'parting, division, section, part' ⋈ *dbyen-pa* 'difference, discord' ⋈ *'bye-ba* 'to separate, open' (intr.) (WT medial *y* is secondary before *e*); JP *bjek*^{31} 'to divide'. Lushai *p*^{h}*el*^{H} 'split, break' may belong to → bàn$_2$, biàn 釆. For an overview of similar items, see Table P-1; for possible allofams, see → lí$_{10}$ 離.

Table P-1 Separate, open, split, break

-ai	-ak	p-ai, -e	p-ek
zhā 奓 *trai open	zhé 磔 *trak rip open	pò 破 *phâih break WB pai^C broken off Lushai peʔ^L < peh to break JP p^{h}jai^{33} break	AA-Khm. pek, pāk to split JP p^{h}jaʔ^{55} < p^{h}jak^{55} split open JP bjak^{31} break JP p^{h}jeʔ^{55} break
		pī 披 *phai divide WT dbye-ba divide PL *bay^1 separate	pī 劈 *phêk split JP bjek^{31} divide
chǐ 拸 *rhaiʔ cleave WT hral-ba to rent, tear up	chè 坼 *thrak split PTai *t^{h}r-: S. hak^{D1S} be broken	WT 'bye-ba open Lush p^{h}en^R < p^{h}enʔ to open	pì 闢 *bek < *bai-k open
WT 'dral-ba to tear		bǎi 捭 *breʔ open WB prai^B to gape	bò 擘 *prek cleave PTai *pr-: S tɛɛk^{D1L} break, tear
lí 離 *rai to separate JP ran^{33} separated Mru ria < ral id.		bān 班 *pran distribute JP pǎ^{31}-ran^{31} to separate WT 'bral-ba separated WB pra^B be divided	

Notes on Table P-1: In the linguistic area, words with meanings 'split, crack' tend to end in a sound-symbolic *-k* and have a labial initial, with almost any vowel and medial (note → bó$_7$ 鎛, → bò 擘, → bǔ$_1$ 卜, → pī$_3$ 披, → pī$_4$ 劈, → pì$_6$ 闢, → pì$_7$ 副, → pò$_2$ 膊). Therefore exact cognate correspondences are elusive, and where perfect matches occur, they may be accidental. Additional words in the area include: TB-Lepcha *bĭk* 'to split' (Forrest *JAOS* 82, 1962: 334), Chepang *pək-* 'break, shatter, crack, split' ⋈ *pəkəʔ-* 'break open' (fruit). <> Tai: S. *pliik*^{4} 'divide into small pieces, evade'. For possible allofams, see → lí$_{10}$ 離.

pī$_4$ 劈 (p^h^iek) **LH** p^h^ek, **OCM** *phêk

'To split' (wood) [SW]. *SW* glosses it with *pò* 破 *phâih; Duàn Yùcái, Wáng Lì (1982: 102f) associate this word with → pì$_7$ 副 'split'.

[E] ST: JP *p^h^jaʔ^55^* < *p^h^jak^55^* 'split open'. Also, or alternatively, this could be an 'abrupt end' final *-k derivation (§6.1.2) from either → pī$_3$ 披 *phai or → pò$_3$ 破 *phâih. For an overview over similar items, see Table P-1; for possible allofams, see → lí$_{10}$ 離.

pí$_1$ 皮 (bje 3) **LH** bɨai, **OCM** *bai

'Hide, fur, animal skin (with hair or feathers)' [Shi, SW], also hide worn as clothing [Shu].

[T] *Sin Sukchu SR* bi (平); *MGZY* pue (平) [buɛ]; *ONW* be — **[D]** PMin *p^h^ue^A2^

[E] Wáng Lì (1982: 446), following *Shìmíng*, relates this word to → bèi$_6$ 被 'cover, wear' which is plausible, see there for the ST etymology. Shafer (*IST:* 62) relates *pí* to Kachin *p^h^yi* 'skin, bark' as well as WT *p^h^yi* 'outside', but this is doubtful, see → bǐ$_1$ 比. Syn. → fū$_9$ 膚.

pí$_2$**-fú** 蚍蜉 → **fú**$_{17}$ 蜉

pí$_3$ 膍 (biei, bi 4) **LH** bei, bi, **OCM** *bî, *bi — *ONW* bėi

'Navel, stomach of an ox' [Zhuang], perhaps a variant of, or s. w. as, next:

⋇ **pí** 毘 (bi 4) **LH** bi, **OCM** *bi

'Navel' [SW].

[E] KT: PKS *lwa^1^ 'navel', Mak *ʔdaai^6^*, PT *ʔbl/r-: S. *sa-dɨɨ^A1^*. Possibly also related to → qí$_{16}$ 臍.

pí$_4$ 膍毗 (bi 4) **LH** bi, **OCM** *bi

'Abundant, large' 膍 [Shi]; 'to strengthen' (a ruler) 毗 [Shi].

[E] ST: WT *'p^h^el-ba, p^h^el* (OTib p^h^eld) 'to increase, augment, enlarge, improve, develop'.

pí$_5$ 貔 (bi 4) **LH** bi, **OCM** *bi

Prob. 'leopard, panther' [Shi, SW]. Acc. to FY 8.2 and Guō Pú, *pí* had ancient dialect variants which are discussed under → lí$_3$ 貍. In old texts *pí* refers to a large panther-like cat, whereas lí$_3$ 貍 and its dialect variants refer to a small cat-like animal. Apparently these two animals were confused by Han and esp. the commentator Guō Pú's time (d. 324 AD) due to lack of familiarity with wildlife.

[E] Prob. ST: WT *dbyi* 'lynx' (*IST:* 59). WT *byi* in *byi-la* ~ *bi-la, bi-ši* 'cat' seems to be cognate, but it may derive from Indic instead: Hindi *billā* 'cat' (Jaeschke: 376), Nepali *billi* <- Skt *biḍālaḥ* which comes in turn prob. from a non-Aryan source (Buck 1949 no. 3.62), note Kharia *blileg*, Dravidian *billi* etc. (Mei / Norman 1971: 100). On the other hand, *bi-ši* (*ši* < *ži* 'cat' ?) may suggest that *byi* is a native morpheme after all.

pí$_6$ 脾 (bjie 4) **LH** bie, **OCM** *be — **[T]** ONW bie

'Spleen, bile' [Li].

[E] ST: PTB *r-pay 'spleen': JP *pāi*, Mru *pai* [Löffler 1966: 148], but Angami Naga *ú-prì*, Mikir *pli-ha* < *-i (Matisoff 1995a: 43; also Matisoff 1978: 217: *pay ~ *play), Garo *pilai*, Chepang *leh* (Weidert 1987: 29). Note also PTai *ʔbl/ri^A1^ (Luo 2000: 85).

pí$_7$ 罷疲 (bje 3) **LH** bɨai, **OCM** *bai — **[T]** ONW be

'Weary, exhausted' 疲 [Zuo], 'emaciated' [Guan]; 'to wear out, exhaust' 罷 [Zuo].

[E] ST: PTB *bal (*STC* no. 29) > Bahing *bal* 'tired, weary'; WB *pan^B^* 'tired' (*HST:* 150) ⋇ *p^h^a^B^* 'fatigued' (as horses), JP *ba^55^* 'tired' ⋇ *ban^31^* 'tired. WT *brgyal* is prob.

unrelated, see → lí$_{11}$ 離. <> The relationship with Tai is not clear: S. *p^hlia^{A2}* < *b- 'weary, exhausted' ⋈ *plia^{C1}* < *p- 'to wear out, exhaust' (Manomaivibool 1975: 127f; 206). Allofam → bì$_{10}$ 敝弊斃 (Pulleyblank 1962: 215). For additional comments, see → fèi$_6$ 廢.

pǐ$_1$ 匹 (pʰjiet 4) **LH** pʰit, **OCM** *phit
'A pair, a set of male and female' (as husband and wife; as *pǐ-niǎo* 匹鳥 'mandarin ducks') [Shi] > 'one of a pair, peer' [BI, Shi, EY], 'a mate' [Liji], 'a single one' [Meng], 'opponent' [Zuo] > measure word for horses [BI, Shu]; 'to match' [Shi, Shu].
[E] Etymology not certain. There is a remote possibility that *pǐ* may be related to an AA word for 'two', *bar, but in Khmer which has similarities with OC, it is *pì:(r)* 'two'. The final AA *-r* would be lost in OC after a long vowel (§6.9), the OC final *-t* may represent the nominalizing suffix (§6.2.1). Alternatively, the Lushai word cited under → bì$_{24}$ 畢 'fork' could belong here instead.

pǐ$_2$ 匹 (pʰjiet 4) **LH** pʰit, **OCM** *phit
'A unit for measuring cloth, equal to four *zhàng* 丈' [SW].
[E] Etymology not clear, possibly a special application of → pǐ$_1$. On the other hand, the word is reminiscent of the TB word for 'four' *bli(s/t).

pǐ$_3$ 鳴 (pʰjiet 4) **LH** pʰit, **OCM** *phit
'Duck' 匹 [Liji].
[E] Area word. Tai: S. and Tai lgs. in general *pet^{D1}* 'duck' (Manomaivibool 1975: 331). <> AA: Viet. *vit*, NBahn. *pĕt*, but Bahnar *bip*, Sedang *pèap* 'duck' [K. Smith, *LTBA* 2.1 (n.d.): 8]. <> TB: Lolo-Zaiwa et al. *pje̱t^{55}* 'duck', Geman Deng *kɹai^{35}-pit^{55}*, perh. also JP *k^hai^{33}-pjek^{55}*, WB *b^hai^B* 'duck'. The source is prob. AA. Some of these forms show that this is not the same word as → pǐ$_1$ 匹 'a pair'.

pǐ$_4$ 庀 (pʰiᴮ 4, pʰjieᴮ 4) **LH** pʰiᴮ, pʰieᴮ, **OCM** *phiʔ, *pheʔ
'Complete, prepare' [Zuo]. Acc to *HST:* 97 cognate to → pí$_4$ 膍毗.
[E] ST: Lushai *peiʔ^L* 'to finish, complete, be ready, prepared'.

pǐ$_5$ 疕 → **bǐ$_4$** 疕

pǐ$_6$ 仳 → **lí$_{10}$** 離

pì$_1$ 屁 (pʰiᶜ 4) **LH** pʰiᶜ, **OCM** *phih
'To pass gas' [GY], a word which understandably appears late in the literature.
[E] ST: PTB *pwe ?: Limbu *p^he-ma*, Mikir *kep^hé*, Naga *b-woy³, Chin *woy-s⁴, Lushai *voiʔ* [Weidert 1987: 50; 199].

pì$_2$ 僻 → **bēi$_2$**, **bī** 陂

pì$_3$ 澼 → **pì$_4$** 擗

pì$_4$ 擗 (bjiäk 4) **LH** biek, **OCM** *bek
'Beat the breast' [Shi]. Perh. **bì** 拯 (bjet), LH *bit* 'to beat' [Lie] is a variant.
Perh. related is **pì** 澼 (pʰiek), *Sin Sukchu SR* p'i (入); *MGZY* phi (入) [p'i]; LH *p^hek* 'beat silk in water' (to make it white) [Zhuang], with iterative aspiration (§5.8.3).
⋈ **píng** 泙 (bieŋ) LH beŋ 'to beat (silk to make it white)' [Zhuang].

pì$_5$ 譬 (pʰjieᶜ 4) **LH** pʰieᶜ, **OCM** *phekh — **[T]** *ONW* pʰie
'Example, to give an example' [Shi]. This could be derived from → bǐ$_1$ 比 'compare' with the addition of a final *-k (§6.1.1).
[E] ST: WT *dpe* 'pattern, model' (*HST:* 74).

pì$_6$ 闢 (bjiäk 4) **LH** biek, **OCM** *bek < *bai-k
'To open, open up, enlarge' tr. [BI, Shi].
[E] ST *pe: WT *'byed-pa, pʰyes, dbye* 'to open' (*HST:* 114); Lushai *pʰenᴿ < pʰenʔ* 'to open'; perh. related to Thakali *pʰle 'lɔ* 'to open up'. Also, or alternatively, this could be an 'abrupt end' ('open up') final *-k* derivation (§6.1.2) of → pī$_3$ 披 'divide'.
[C] Allofam → bī$_1$ 屄. TB cognates indicate that → bǎi$_2$ 捭 'to open' may not be related. For an overview over similar items, see Table P-1 under → pī$_3$ 披; for possible allofams, see → lí$_{10}$ 離.

pì$_7$ 副 (pjək, pʰjək) **LH** pɨk, pʰɨk, **OCM** *p(h)rək ?, OCB *p(h)rjək ?
'To rend, split' (while giving birth), 'cleave, divide' [Shi, SW].
~ **pì** 疈 (pʰjək)
'Split, cut open' (e.g. fruit) [Shi, Zhouli]. The additional QYS reading *pɛk* has prob. been transferred from the syn. → bò$_3$ 擘. CH aspiration is associated with forceful motion (§5.8.5).
[E] Perh. AA and area word: Khmer /réh/ (i.e. = réʔ) 'separate, detach' ⋈ /prèh/ 'to crack, split'. <> TB-Chepang *brəʔ-* 'break' (pot) ⋈ *brəkəʔ-* 'open abdomen, gut animal'. WT *pʰrag* 'intermediate space' belongs to the ST root *par under → bàn$_1$ 半.
[C] Baxter (1992: 473) relates this to lè 泐阞勒扐仂 (under → lǐ$_4$ 里理). An allofam is perh. → pōu 剖. For an overview over similar items, see Table P-1 under → pī$_3$ 披; for possible allofams, see → lí$_{10}$ 離.

piān$_1$ 偏 (pʰjiän 4) **LH** pʰian, **OCM** *phen — **[T]** *ONW* pʰian
'Oblique, awry, side' [BI, Shi], 'side, border' [Zuo]
⋈ **pián** 諞 (bjiän(ᴮ) 4) **LH** bian(ᴮ), **OCM** *ben(ʔ)
'Be glib-tongued, insincere' [Shi].
⋈ **piàn** 片 (pʰienᶜ) **LH** pʰenᶜ, **OCM** *phêns
'Partial, one-sided' [Lunyu].
[C] This wf could be cognate to → bēi$_2$, bī 陂, belonging to the root *pai 'oblique, slope' (so Wáng Lì 1982: 445), hence *pen < *pai-n. An additional cognate is → biān$_4$ 邊.

piān$_2$ 篇 → **biǎn$_1$** 扁

pián$_1$-bì 便嬖 (bjiän-pieiᶜ) **LH** bian-peᶜ, **OCM** *ben-pêkh
'Male and female servants' [Meng, Xun]. Perh. the same etymon underlies the Yuè syllable Canton *mɐnᴬ¹* in *sɐi³³-mɐn⁵⁵-tsɐi³⁵* 細蚊仔 'child'. The Tai and Yuè nasal initial may be due to a preglottalized stop (Chén Zhōngmǐn, *MZYW* 1995.5: 1–11).
[E] KT: PKS *mpaanᴬ, PHlai *-maanᴬ 'male person' + PKS *ɓjaak 'woman, girl', PT *ʔb-: Boai *bikᴰ¹S* 'girl'.

pián$_2$ 駢 → **bìng$_2$** 並併

pián$_3$ 諞 → **piān$_1$** 偏

piàn 片 → **piān$_1$** 偏

piāo$_1$ 剽 'tip, end' → **biāo$_3$** 標

piāo$_2$ 漂 (pʰjiäu 4) **LH** pʰiau, **OCM** *phiau — **[T]** *ONW* pʰiau
'To float' (in the air), 'be tossed about' [Shi], 'to blow down' (roof tiles) 飄 [Zhuang].
⋈ **piāo** 飄 (bjiäu, pjiäu 4) **LH** biau, piau, **OCM** *biau, *piau
'To whirl, whirlwind' [Shi].
[E] ST: PTB *pyaw (*STC* no. 176) > WT *'pʰyo-ba* 'swim, soar, float'. PTai *pliuᴬ¹ 'float in

the air' may be related (so Bodman 1980: 168), but the Tai medial /l/ presents a phonological problem.

piāo₃ 薸 (bjiäu 4) **LH** biau, **OCM** *biau
'Duckweed, algae' is acc. to Guō Pú a Jiāngdōng (lower Yangtze) word, it has survived in southern dialects: Mǐn: Fúzhōu p^hiu^{A2}, Jiàn'ōu p^hiau^{C1}; Kèjiā p^hiau^{A2}, Guǎngzhōu p^hiu^{A2}. The word is a loan from MK: Viet *bèo* 'duckweed', WMon *bew* 'to ride low on the water' (Norman 1983: 206).

pín₁ 嬪 → **bīn₁** 賓

pín₂ 頻 → **bīn₂** 濱; → **fén₄** 墳

pín₃ 貧 (bjen 3) **LH** bɨn, **OCM** *brən, OCB *brjən — **[T]** *ONW* bin
'Be poor' [Shi]. — **[E]** ST: WT *dbul* 'poor' (*HST:* 120).

pǐn 品 ($p^hjəm^B$) **LH** p^him^B, **OCM** *phrəmʔ
'A kind, class, piece' [BI, Shu], 'degree' [Li].
[T] *Sin Sukchu SR* p'in (上); *MGZY* phim (上) [p'im]
[E] ST: WT *rim-pa* 'series, succession, order, method'. Perh. also connected with AA: OKhmer *braṃ* [βrɔɔm] '...go well with, suit, match, harmonize...' ⋈ *rama* [rɔɔm] 'to follow in order after...'

pìn, bì 牝 (bi^B 4, $bjien^B$ 4) **LH** bi^B, bin^B, **OCM** *bi(n)ʔ — **[T]** *ONW* biin
'Female of animals' [Shi], opposite → mǔ₁ 牡 'male' (of quadrupeds).
[E] ST: PTB *pwi(y) 'female' (*STC* no. 171) > Lushai pui^R < *puiʔ* 'a grown female' (suffix or particle) (Matisoff *LL* 1.2, 2000: 172).

píng₁ 平坪 (bjɐŋ) **LH** bieŋ, **OCM** *breŋ — **[T]** *ONW* beŋ
'Be level, even, just, peaceful, a plain' [Shi] > 'a level piece of ground' 坪 [SW] > 'a smooth board, to plain' 枰 [SW].
[D] PCoastal Mǐn *baŋ: Amoy $p\tilde{ı}^{A2}$ < *baŋ 'even, flat' ⋈ $p^h\tilde{ı}^{A2}$ < b^haŋ 'to flatten' (Bodman 1980: 56); Fúzhōu $paŋ^{A2}$; PNMin *piaŋ 'level' 平, 'yard' 坪.
[E] ST: PTB *pleŋ 'flat surface' (*STC* no. 138) > Tamang *pleŋ* 'big flat stone', JP *byen³¹-dup³¹* 'wooden plank' ~ Kachin *bren* 'flat and wide', WB *prañ* 'be full'; Nung *šiŋ-bjen* 'plank' (*šin* 'wood'); Mikir *kapleŋ* 'plank', Garo *bol-pleŋ* (*bol* 'wood'). Matisoff (1988) combines *píng* with → yíng₂ 盈嬴 'full', → zhèng₁ 正政 'straight' and → tǐng₂ 挺. Perh. → píng₃ 評 'criticize' is the s. w. (so Wáng Lì 1982: 338).

píng₂ 泙 → **pì₄** 擗

píng₃ 評 (bjɐŋ) **LH** bieŋ, **OCM** *breŋ
'To comment on, criticize' [SW] is thought to be the s. w. as → píng₁ 平坪 'level' (Wáng Lì 1982: 338).

píng₄ 萍 ($bieŋ^C$) **LH** beŋ, **OCM** *bêŋ
'Rain master' [Zhouli, Chuci (there written with 并 instead of 平); other texts borrow different graphs].
[E] AA: Khmer *bhlieŋ* 'rain', PNB *plı̰ñ 'sky', Pearic *phliŋ* 'sky' [Pinnow 1959: 405]. The connection with PMY *mblɒəŋ⁶ (Wáng FS) 'rain' (Huáng Shùxiān *YYYJ* 1989.2: 113) is only indirect. Syn. and semantics, see → fēn₂ 雰氛; → dōng₃ 涷.

píng₅ 瓶缾 (bieŋ) **LH** beŋ, **OCM** *bêŋ
'Water jug' (for drawing water) [Yáng Xióng, Later Han], 'water jug with small mouth and bulbous belly' [SW], 'bottle, jug' [Li].

[E] AA: Khmer *bīṅa* /piiŋ/ 'swollen, potbellied, earthen water pot' (part of a large wf 'swollen' in Khmer).

píng₆ 屏軿 (bieŋ) **LH** beŋ, **OCM** *bêŋ
'A protecting wall, screen, protection' [Shi], 'to protect' 屏 [Zuo]; 'curtain carriage' 軿 [SW]. Perh. related to → bì₁₂ 蔽 'screen'; acc. to Karlgren (1956: 16) related to → bìng₃ 屏 'remove'.

píng₇ 馮憑 (bjəŋ) **LH** bɨŋ, **OCM** *brəŋ ?
('Step on / over'?:) 'Ascend' [Zhouli], 'walk across' (a river) [Shi], 'maltreat' [Zuo], 'encroach upon' 馮 [Zhouli]; 'lean on, rely on' 馮 [Shi], 憑 [Shu], 凭 [SW: Shu] (also read MC *bjəŋ^C*).
[T] *Sin Sukchu SR* biŋ (平); *MGZY* ping (平) [biŋ]
[E] Karlgren (*GSR* 899d) suggests 'tread' as the basic meaning of this word. This etymon is prob. cognate to → líng₇ 陵泠凌 'transgress', just as there are doublets *líng* 凌 ~ → bīng₂ 冰 'ice'.

pìng 聘 → **fǎng₂** 訪

pō 頗坡 → **bēi₂**, **bī** 陂

pó₁ 浡 (buət) **LH** bət, **OCM** *bə̂t
'Burst forth' (as plants, fountain) [Meng].
[E] Perh. cognate to WT *'bu-ba, 'bus* 'to open, unfold' (flower), 'be lighted, kindled'.

pó₂ 婆 (buâ) *ONW* bɑ
'Old woman' [post-Han].
[E] ST: PTB *ba ~ pa (*STC:* 174 n. 463 *pwa) > PLB *bwa > WB *ə-bʰwa^B ~ ə-pʰwa^B* 'grandmother'.

pó₃ 皤 (buâ, puâ) **LH** bɑi, **OCM** *bâi
'Be white' 皤 [Yi] > 'white-haired' 番 [Shu].
[E] ST: PTB *pwaːr, note also NNaga *poj 'white' [French 1983: 318]. Allofam of → bái₁ 白 (Wáng Lì 1982: 292).

pò₁ 破 (pʰuâ^C) **LH** pʰɑi^C, **OCM** *phâih
'To break' [Shi], in southern dialects it is a synonym of → pī₄ 劈 'split wood'.
[T] *Sin Sukchu SR* p'wɔ (去); *MGZY* phwo (去) [p'wɔ]; *ONW* pʰɑ
[<] exoactive of → pī₃ 披 *phai 'separate' (§4.3.2). CH aspiration is associated with forceful motion §5.8.5.
[E] ST: WB *pai^C* 'broken off, chipped, hare-lipped' ⋊ *pʰai^C* break off in small pieces' (Matisoff 1995a: 85); Dhimal *bai* 'break', Lushai *peʔ^L < pes* 'to break, be broken' [*STC* no. 254], JP *pʰjai^33* 'break' ⋊ *pʰjeʔ^55 < pʰjek^55* 'break', also JP *bjak^31* 'break'. The rime may in fact have been PTB *ol, if Tamang *^lpʰol* 'break up lumps of soil' [Mazaudon 1973: 130], Lepcha *pʰol-pʰol* 'brittle, frangible' (of earth) ⋊ *pʰyol-pʰyol* 'crumbling, falling to pieces' [Sun *LTBA* 16.2: 148] should be related.
Late Han -> Tai: S. *pʰaa^B1* < *pʰ- 'to split, cut' (Li F. 1976: 41) (a pre-Han loan would have the Tai final *-ai).
For an overview of similar items, see Table P-1 under → pī₃ 披; for possible allofams, see → lí₁₀ 離.

pò₂ 膊 (pʰâk) **LH** pʰɑk, **OCM** *phâk
'Dismember' [Zuo]. CH aspiration is associated with forceful motion (§5.8.5).

[E] Sound-symbolic area word: TB-PLB *pak ~ *ʔpak [Matisoff *TSR:* 40] > Lahu *phâʔ* 'unfasten, dismantle' ⋈ *pâʔ* 'collapse, come undone'; Akha *pa*^{HS} 'break, split' (*HST:* 64). <> AA-PMon *tbaak 'to slash' (flesh, vegetable with a sharp blade), *pāk* 'to split'; Khmer *-pāka* /-baak/ 'to split' ⋈ OKhmer *pak* /ɓak/ 'to break, come or fall apart, separate, give way'; Bahnar *păk*, Mon *pāk*; Stieng bêk, băk 'split'.

pò₃ 膊, 胉 'shoulder blade' → **bó₄** 膊

pò₄ 魄 (pʰɐk) **LH** pʰak, **OCM** *phrâk

'Vegetative or animal soul' of a person [Zuo] which accounts for growth and physiological functions, for 'life'; as opposed to → hún₁ 魂 'spiritual soul' which makes a human personality.

[E] *Pò* 'soul' is the same word as → pò₅ 霸魄 'aspect of the moon'. With the first development of a fetus grows the vegetative soul *jì shēng pò* 既生魄 [Zuo: Zhao 7], the same phrase is used for phases of the moon. *Pò*, the soul responsible for growth, is the same as *pò* the waxing and waning of the moon (Ying-shi Yü *JAS* 41, 1981: 83). The meaning 'soul' has probably been transferred from the moon since men must have been aware of lunar phases long before they had developed theories on the soul. This is supported by the etymology 'bright', and by the inverted word order which can only have originated with meteorological expressions, see → pò₅ 霸魄. The association with the moon explains perh. why the *pò* soul is classified as Yin (see for example Matisoff 1978: 268) in spite of the etymology 'bright' (which should be Yang), *hún's* Yang classification may be due to the association with clouds and by extension sky, even though the word invokes 'dark'. 'Soul' and 'moon' are related in other cultures, by cognation or convergence, as in TB: PLB *s/ʔ-la³ 'moon, soul, spirit' (*HPTB:* 39), WT *bla* 'soul' ⋈ *zla* 'moon', PMY *bl̥a$^{A/C}$ 'spirit, soul, moon' (Benedict ICSTLL 1989: 8).

Pò is related to → bái₁ 白 'white' (Carr *CAAAL* 24, 1985: 62).

The connection, if any, with MK comparanda is not clear: Khmer *braḥ* 'devil, spirit', Stieng *brah*, Chrau *m'brãh*; AA -> TB-Lepcha *blyak* 'devil, spirit' (Forrest *JAOS* 82, 1962: 333).

pò₅ 霸魄 (pʰɐk) **LH** pʰak, **OCM** *phrâk

'An aspect of the moon', prob. originally 'brightness': *jì shēng pò* 既生霸 'after the brightness *pò* has grown' = 'second quarter of the lunar month', and *jì sǐ pò* 既死霸 'after the brightness has died' (i.e. prob. 'has started to die') = 'last quarter of the lunar month' [BI] (Shaughnessy 1991: 136ff). In this phrase, the subject *pò* follows the verb as in meteorological phenomena (note *xià yǔ* 下雨 'rain falls', see von der Gabelentz, 1881, p. 144).

[E] This is the same word as → pò₄ 魄 and cognate to → bái₁ 白 'white' (Ying-shi Yü *JAS* 41, 1981: 83; Shaughnessy; Matisoff 'Stars, moon, spirit', ICSTLL 1978); TB languages also associate 'moon' with 'white' [French 1983: 578f].

pò₆ 霸霍 'hide soaked in rain' → **fǔ₉** 膚

pōu 剖 (pʰəu^B) **LH** pʰo^B, **OCM** *phôʔ

'To cleave, cut open' [Zuo]. Wáng Lì (1982: 102) relates this word to → pì₇ 副.

póu 裒 → **bèi₄** 倍

pǒu 培 → **fù₇** 阜

pū 鋪 → **bù₃** 布

pú₁ 僕 (buk, buok) **LH** bok, **OCM** *bôk, OCB *bok — **[T]** *ONW* bok
'Servant, groom, male slave' [BI, Shi] is perh. related to WT *bu* 'son, boy' (*HST:* 164). Alternatively, *CVST* 1: 57 relates *pú* to WT *pʰrug* 'child'.

pú₂ 樸 (pʰåk) **LH** pʰɔk, **OCM** *phrôk
'To trim wood' [Shu] is perh. an aspirated iterative derivation (§5.8.3) from → bāo₃ 剝. Alternatively, it could belong to the homophonous etymon with the basic meaning 'in a natural state, unworked', as in *pú* 朴 'in a natural state', 璞 'unworked precious stone'. CH aspiration is associated with forceful motion §5.8.5.

pú₃-táo 葡萄 (buo-dâu) **LH** bɑ-dɑu
'Grape' is borrowed from Iranian *budāwa or *bādāwa (Laufer 1919: 225; Norman 1988: 19), introduced from Bactria ca. 130 BC.

pú₄ 蒲 (buo) **LH** bɑ, **OCM** *bâ
'Cattail' or some kind of rush [Shi]; see also → lú₃ 蘆.

pú₅-fú 匍匐 → **pá₁** 爬

pǔ₁ 浦 (pʰuoᴮ) **LH** pʰɑᴮ, **OCM** *phâʔ
(The Huái) 'river bank' [Shi]; '(bank) on a cove, inlet' (along the Yangtze River) [Guoce, Yuèjuè shū]. In OC, this is only a regional word restricted to the east and south of the Huai River, it is to this day found in place names in the same area, i.e. in the ancient Wú, Yuè, and Chǔ lands. Guō Pú (d. 324 AD) confirms that *pǔ* 'bay, cove, inlet' is a Jiāngnán (i.e. a southern dialect) word (Norman 1983: 206).
[E] MK: Viet *phá* < *pʰaʔ* 'inlet, cove' (Norman). This word is prob. indirectly related to PKS *pwaŋᴮ 'bank, shore', Tai: Saek *viaŋ*ᶜ¹ 'bank of a river' by way of the *-ʔ ~ *-ŋ alternation (§3.2.4). Less likely, KT may belong to → fáng₁ 坊防 'dike'. *Pǔ* is unrelated to *pō* 頗坡 (under → bēi₂, bī 陂).

pǔ₂ 溥 'wide' → **bù₃** 布

pù₁ 怖 → **pà** 怕

pù₂ 暴 (buk) **LH** bok, **OCM** *bôk
'To expose to the sun, to dry, exhibit' [Meng].
[E] ST: TB-Lushai *pʰoᴴ* 'to dry or air in sunshine'. The relationship to Tai: S. *taak* < *prak 'to expose to the sun, dry' (Li F. 1976: 45) is not clear.

Q

qī₁ 七 (tsʰjet) **LH** tsʰit, **OCM** *tshit < PCH *snhit ?
'Seven' [OB].
[T] *Sin Sukchu SR* ts'i (入); *MGZY* tshi (入) [ts'i]; *ONW* tsʰit.
[D] PMin *tsʰit.
[N] Pulleyblank (1962: 134) suggests that in light of the TB cognates the initial derives from an OC reprefixed form *snh- (§5.9.2; for examples of reprefixation in TB numerals, see Matisoff 1997a). The graph originally wrote *qiè* 切 which never had a nasal in the initial, hence prob. no *n in *qī*.
[E] ST: PTB *snis > Himalayan lgs. *snis; Jiarong *kĕsnĕs*; PLB *snit > PBurm *ʔnit > WB *kʰu-hnac*, PLolo *ɴ-šit ~ *ši; JP *să³¹-nit³¹*; Trung *snit* (*HST:* 131). CH -> Tai: S. *četᴰ¹S* 'seven' (we should expect an /n/ in the initial if the relationship was genetic).

qī₂ 咠 (ts(ʰ)jəp) **LH** ts(ʰ)ip, **OCM** *ts(h)əp < *k-səp
'To whisper' [SW: Shi].
⋈ **sà** 颯 (sập) **LH** səp, **OCM** *sə̂p
'The whistling or soughing of wind' [Chuci].
[E] Sound-symbolic area word: PTB *syip ~ *syup (*HPTB:* 356) > WT *šub-pa ~ šib-pa* 'to whisper', from a root *syup ~ *syip (*STC:* 170; *HST:* 160). But the CH item more closely resembles AA with its pre-initial: PMonic *k[-r-]sap 'to whisper' [Diffloth 1984: 214], Khmer *khsɨpa* /ksỳp/ 'to whisper, murmur' ⋈ /rsỳp/ 'be whispered, audible only as low murmur'. MK -> Tai: S. *krasípᴰ²-krasâapᴰ²*.
[C] Perh. qī 緝 'to babble' [Shi] is the same word.

qī₃ 妻 (tsʰiei) **LH** tsʰei, **OCM** *tshə̂i < *k-sə̂i, OCB *tshəj
'Consort, wife' [BI, Shi].
[T] *Sin Sukchu SR* ts'jej (平), *PR* ts'i; *MGZY* tshi (平) [ts'i]; *ONW* tsʰėi
⋈ **qì** 妻 (tsʰieiᶜ) **LH** tsʰeiᶜ, **OCM** *tshə̂ih
'Give a wife to, give as a wife' tr. [Shu].
[<] exoactive / trans. of *qī* (§4.3.1).
[E] AA: Khmer *-sai: *khsai* /ksaj/ 'be female' ⋈ Mid. Khmer *kansai* /kənsay/ 'wife' (Lewitz 1976: 769), MK -> PWMiao *ntshaiᴰ 'daughter, girl, wife'. MK *ka-, kan-* is a female marker, PEKatuic *kan 'woman'. For the initial correspondance MC *tsʰ-* < *k-s-, see §5.9.1. The word → tái₃ 嬯臺 may belong to an AA parallel stem.
Sometimes → qí₁₅ 齊 'equal' is thought to be cognate (so *SW*; Karlgren 1956: 14) thus taking *qī* to mean originally 'an equal' (to her husband), but this is unlikely given the realities of ancient societies.

qī₄ 淒悽 (tsʰiei) **LH** tsʰei, **OCM** *tshə̂i < *k-sə̂i
'Feel cold, be cold, chilly' 淒 [Shi] > 'sad, grieved' 悽 [Li]. For semantics, note → hán₂ 寒 'cold' > *hánxīn* 寒心 'disheartened'.
[E] Prob. a ST word, related to either of these two TB etyma: (1) WT *bsil-ba* 'cool' (*CVST* 4: 29), JP *gă³¹-tsi³³* 'cold', Lushai *sikᴸ* < *tsik* 'cold', perh. related to, or the same etymon as, 'to wash' → xǐ₁ 洗洒. (2) WT *(b)ser, gser-bu* 'a fresh, cold breeze, feeling cold', WB *chiᴮ* (< *-e) 'frost, hoarfrost'.

qī$_5$ 漆 (tsʰjet) **LH** tsʰit, **OCM** *tshit

'Lacquer tree, lacquer, varnish' [Shi]. Note also **zī** 滋 (tsɨ) '(plant-) juice' [Li] (Unger *Hao-ku* 39, 1992). The final *-t* marks nouns for natural objects (§6.2.1).

[E] ST: PTB *tsiy (*STC* no. 65) > WT *tsʰi-ba* 'tough, sticky matter'; PLB *dziy² 'sap, juice' > WB *ce*^{B} 'sticky, adhesive' ⋈ *che*^{B} 'paint' (*STC:* 157).

The etymology of the apparent WT cognate *rtsi* 'juice, lacquer' is ambiguous, though, as that word could also derive from *rhji* < *rhi* (§12.9 (1)) and thus be cognate to Lushai *tʰal*^{R}*-hrit*^{L} 'lac, sealing wax' (mentioned by Unger ibid.) and ultimately derive from PTB *ri 'water' > WB *re* 'water' (Gong *BIHP* 51.3, 1980).

qī$_6$ 倛僛欺諆 (kʰjɨ) **LH** kʰɨə, **OCM** *khə

'To deceive, cheat' [Lunyu], 'insult' 欺 [Zuo], 諆 [SW] > 'mask' 倛 [Xun], 'animal mask' 魌 (of bear skin, used in ceremonies) (Childs-Johnson *EC* 20, 1995: 89); perh. 'grimacing dreadfully' 僛僛 [Shi]. Etymology not clear.

[T] *Sin Sukchu SR* k'jej (平), *PR* k'i; *MGZY* khi (平) [k'i]; *MTang* kʰi, *ONW* kʰiə

qī$_7$ 谿 → **xī$_{10}$** 溪

qí$_1$ 祁 (gji 3) **LH** gɨ, **OCM** *gri ? — **[T]** *ONW* tśi, dźi?, gi?

'Great, large, numerous' [Shi]. Bodman (1980: 188) compares *qí* to WB *kri*^{B} 'great, big', PLB *k-ri² [Matisoff *TSR* no. 175].

qí$_2$ 祈 (gjei) **LH** gɨi, **OCM** *gəi — **[T]** *ONW* gi

'To pray for' (rain etc.) [Shi]. Since the *qí* 祈 prayer and sacrifice was performed outside of town *qí* 圻 (gjei) (syn. *jiāo* 郊), Jensen (*EC* 20, 1995: 422) believes that the words are cognate (see under → jī$_{13}$ 幾畿).

qí$_3$ 旂 (gjei) **LH** gɨi, **OCM** *gəi

'A banner with dragon design and bells' [Shi, SW], ⋈ → qí$_9$ 旗 acc. to Wáng Lì.

qí$_4$ 歧岐 → **zhī$_4$** 支枝肢

qí$_5$ 奇 → **jī$_4$** 奇

qí$_6$ 騎 (gjie 3) **LH** gɨɑi, **OCM** *gai — **[T]** Sui-Tang gi < *ONW* ge

'To ride' (a horse) [Zhuang].

⋈ **jì** 騎 (gjie^C 3) **LH** gɨɑi^C, **OCM** *gaih

'Rider' [Li].

[<] a LOC general purpose derivation from *qí* (§3.5).

[E] The word is prob. related to → hè$_1$ 何荷 'carry' (on the back, including on a beast of burden), hence endopass. (§4.6) 'let oneself be carried' (on the back of an animal). Alternatively, the word may be connected with the wf → zhī$_4$ 支枝肢 'branch', hence 'spreading one's legs', although the OC rimes are different (*-e).

This word has been widely borrowed by languages in the area: WB *tsi*^{B} < *ki (*STC:* 184 n. 484), MK-OKhmer /ɟih/ etc.

qí$_7$ 其 (gjɨ) **LH** gɨə, **OCM** *gə

Pronoun 'this' [Shi, Shu] (Dobson, *Songs:* 168); third person possessive pron. 'his, her, its, their, my, our' [BI, Shi, Shu].

[T] *Sin Sukchu SR* gi (平); *MGZY* ki (平) [gi]; *ONW* giə

[N] Third person possessive is the most common use of *qí.* In Early Zhou texts it also serves occasionally as a genitive particle, syn. of → zhī$_1$ 之.

[D] *Qí* has survived as a third person pron. in Wú dialects: Dānyáng, Hángzhōu, Shàoxīng *kəʔ*^{D1} or *keʔ*^{D1}, Sūzh *ke*^{A1}, Wēnzhōu *ki*^{D1} (Norman 1988: 118, 203).

[E] The origin of *qí* is not certain because in the linguistic area pronouns tend to be of the shape KV (K = velar stop). *Qí* may be ST: Lushai *kʰiF* < *kʰiiʔ* 'that', WT genitive suffix *-kyi, -gyi, -'i* (Bodman 1980: 185), but we should expect a TB /a/ in this set. Alternatively, PAA *ki/ke ~ *ku/ko 'third person pronoun' whose earliest form is perh. *kɨ [Pinnow 1965: 38] appears to be phonologically closest to the OC word.

This word looks like an unstressed ə-vowel form of → qú₂ 渠 'he' (§11.2.1), but outside cognates as well as its non-clitic use make this unlikely.

qí₈ 其 (gjɨ) **LH** gɨə, **OCM** *gə — [T] *ONW* giə
A modal particle, in OB 'be expected, should, probably, likely' (Serruys 1982: 342). Acc. to Serruys this is prob. cognate to:

=**qí** 期 (gjɨ) **LH** gɨə, **OCM** *gə
'Stipulated time, time, limit' [BI, Shi].

⋇ **jī** 期 (kjɨ) **LH** kɨə, **OCM** *kə — [T] *ONW* kiə
'Year' 朞 [Shu], 期 [Yi].

qí₉ 旗 (gjɨ) **LH** an gɨə, **OCM** *gə
'Flag with bear or tiger design' [Zuo, SW]. Wáng Lì (1982: 85) considers *qí* 旗 and → qí₃ 旂 'banner' to be cognate.

qí₁₀ 期 → **qí₇** 其

qí₁₁ 萁 → **qǐ₂** 杞

qí₁₂ 耆 (gji 3) **LH** gɨ, **OCM** *gri — [T] *ONW* gi
'Be old, aged' [Shi 300, 5].
[E] ST: WT *bgre-ba* 'to grow old'.

qí₁₃ 耆 'bring about' → **zhǐ₇** 厎底

qí₁₄ 鰭鬐 (gji 3) **LH** gɨ, **OCM** *gri
'Dorsal fin of a fish' 鰭 [Li], 鬐 [Yili].
[E] Phonologically, the OC form agrees with PTB *g-rəy (i.e. *gri ?) > WT *gri* 'knife', WB *kreB* 'copper', JP *mə³¹-gri³³* 'brass' [Matisoff *LL* 1.2, 2000: 139]. It is semantically more likely, though, that the TB items belong to → zhì₄ 銍 'sickle'.

qí₁₅ 齊 (dziei) **LH** dzei, **OCM** *dzêi, OCB *fitshəj
'Be the same, equal, in line' [Shi], 'regulate' [Yi]. As a caus. it is read in tone C [dzeiC] 'to put in equal proportions' [Zuo, Li] (Downer 1959: 282). → qī₃ 妻 'wife' is not related.
[T] *Sin S. SR* dzjej (平), *PR* dzi; *MGZY* tsi (平) [dzi]; *ONW* dzėi
[D] PMin *dze

⋇ **zī** 齊 (tsi) **LH** tsi, **OCM** *tsi
'Hemmed lower edge of garment' [Lunyu] (Karlgren 1956: 16).

⋇ **jǐ** 濟 (tsieiB) **LH** tseiB, **OCM** *tsə̂iʔ, OCB *tsəiʔ
'Stately, even' [Shi] (Baxter 1992: 462).

[E] *CVST* 4: 58 compares this etymon with TB-Lushai *čelʔL* 'equal, come up to, endure'. Phonologically more likely is cognation with WT *tsʰir* 'order, course, succession, turn'; the WT final *-r* would also explain the retroflex initial in the likely cognate → chái₂ 儕 (dẓäi) 'class, category, equals' (so Karlgren).

qí₁₆ 臍 (dziei) **LH** dzei, **OCM** *dzə̂i (< *dz(l)əi < *s-d(l)əiʔ) — [D] PMin *dzəi ~ *dzʰəi.
'Navel' [Zuo].
[E] Perh. related to PTB *lay ~ *s-tay > JP *dai³¹*, *ʃǎ³¹-dai³³* 'navel', Garo *ste* 'abdomen',

WT *lte-ba* < *ɴḷe* 'navel' (*STC:* 65), Mru *dai* 'navel'. Prob. unrelated to the synonym → pí₃ 膍.

qí₁₇ 蟣 (gjei) **LH** gɨi, **OCM** *gəi
'Water leech' is acc. to Guō Pú's commentary to *EY* a Jiāngdōng (lower Yangtze) dialect word; it still is used in southern dialects: PMin *gʰi > Fúzhōu *ma^A2-kʰi^A2*, Xiàmén *gɔ^A2-kʰi^A2*; Y-Guǎngzhōu *kʰei^A2-na^B* (Norman 1983: 207).

qǐ₁ 乞 (kʰjət) **LH** kʰɨt, **OCM** *khət — **[T]** *ONW* khit
'To ask for, beg' [Lunyu, Hanfei].
⪤ **qì** 乞 (kʰjəi^C) **LH** kʰɨs
'To give' [Hanshu] (Takashima 1996 II: 130: Herforth 1984).
[<] exoactive (extrovert, ditrans.) of *qǐ* 乞 (kʰjət) (§4.3.1).
[E] ? ST: perh. Limbu *kɛt-* 'arrive', *-kɛtt-* 'to convey, deliver'; Kanauri *ket*, Thebor *kʰet* 'to give' [*IST:* 133].

qǐ₂ 杞 (kʰjɨ^B) **LH** kʰɨə^B, **OCM** *khəʔ
'Willow' [Shi], *Lycium chinense*, a kind of creeper [Shi].
[E] Unger (*Hao-ku* 38, 1992: 76) relates this word to WT *kʰri-šiŋ* 'a creeper', lit. 'winding wood' < *'kʰri-ba* 'to wind around'; he adds qí 萁 (gjɨ) 'stalks of pulse' [Huainan], i.e. 'runner, climber', and suggests a possible connection with → jī₆ 箕 'basket'.

qǐ₃ 芑 (kʰjɨ^B) **LH** kʰɨə^B, **OCM** *khəʔ
'A kind of millet, coix' [Shi]. Unger (*Hao-ku* 38, 1992: 76) relates this word to WT *kʰre* 'millet'. Baxter a. Sagart (1998: 52) relate it to → chì₆ 饎糦 'sacrif. millet'.

qǐ₄ 起 (kʰjɨ^B) **LH** kʰɨə^B, **OCM** *khəʔ
'To rise' [Shi].
[T] *Sin S. SR* k'jej (上), *PR* k'i; *MGZY* khi (上) [k'i]; *ONW* kʰiə
[E] Unger (*Hao-ku* 38, 1992: 76) relates this word to Gurung *ri* 'to rise; WT *kye-re* (also *kyer* ?) 'upright', also PLB *kyi² 'lift up, raise' > WB *kʰyi* 'lift, raise, begin'.

qǐ₅ 企跂 (kʰjie^B/C 4) **LH** kʰie^B/C, **OCM** *kheʔ/h
'Stand on tiptoe' 跂 [Shi], 企 [Lao].
[T] *Sin Sukchu SR* k'jej (上), *PR* k'i; *MGZY* khÿi (上去) [k'ji]; Sui-Tang kʰɨ, *ONW* kʰie
⪤ **qì** 㩻 (kʰjie^C 4) **LH** kʰie^C, **OCM** *kheh
'Slanting' [SW: Shi].
[E] ST: JP *kʰyè* [Matisoff *TSR* no. 98], *n^31-kʰyeŋ^31* 'oblique, slanting'. This wf is prob. connected with → jī₄ 奇 'odd' and → jǐ₃ 掎 'pull aside'.

qǐ₆ 啟 → **qǐ₇** 綮

qǐ₇ 綮 (kʰiei^B ~ kʰieŋ^B) **LH** kʰei^B ~ kʰeŋ^B, **OCM** *khîʔ ~ *kheŋʔ
'Joint' (in the body) [Zhuang].
⪤ **qǐ** 啟 (kʰiei^B) **LH** kʰei^B, **OCM** *khîʔ, OCB *khijʔ — **[T]** *ONW* kʰėi
'To open, open up, start, enlighten' [BI, Shi], 'clear (of the sky)' [OB]; 'to kneel' [Shi] (< 'bend in the joint'); 'to bow down (the head) to the ground' 稽 [Zhouli]. The fundamental meaning was 'bend / open' (something hinged, something with a joint like a door).
The word *qǐ* 啟 'open' was tabooed after the death of Emperor Jǐng Dì 景帝 in 140 BC and was replaced by → kāi 開, acc. to *JDSW* (Sagart 1999: 76).
[C] A possible allofam is → jī₁₄ 機璣 'mechanism'.

[E] Prob. related to MK-Khmer *kēka* /kaaɛk/ 'to bend out at midpoint' (horns, arms) ⋈ *kēṅa* /kaaɛŋ/ 'form or present a sharp angle, bent sharply'; Khmer has no syllable of the type *kiik*; for the absence of final *-k in OC, see §6.9.

qǐ₈ 稽 → **qǐ₇** 綮

qì₁ 契 (kʰăt) **LH** kʰɛt, **OCM** *kʰrêt
'Skillful engraving' [SW], prob. cognate to → qì₂ 契, and / or → gè₅ 擖.

qì₂ 契 (kʰieiᶜ) **LH** kʰes, **OCM** *khêts — [T] *ONW* kʰėi
'Script notches' [Yi] (Karlgren 1956: 11).
[<] exopass. of *qiè* 鍥 (kʰiet) (§4.4), lit. 'what has been cut'.
⋈ **qiè** 鍥 (kʰiet) **LH** kʰet, **OCM** *khêt
'To cut' [Xun], 'cut through' [Zuo].
[C] An allofam is prob. → qì₁ 契 'engraving'; perh. also to → gè₅ 擖.

qì₃ 迄 (xjət) **LH** hɨt, **OCM** *hət
'To reach to' (the four seas), 'attain' (wealth), 'come to the point that' [Shi, Shu].
⋈ **xì** 氣餼 (xjəiᶜ) **LH** hɨs, **OCM** *həts
'To present' food [SW: Zuo], grain [Guoyu], or live animals [Lun] > 'animals' [Zuo].
[<] exoactive (extrovert, ditrans.) of *qì* 迄 (§4.3.1), lit. 'cause someone to attain food'.
[E] Etymology not certain: *qì* could be related to → jì₄ 暨 (gjiᶜ 3), but see there for a more likely affiliation, also the MC fricative initial *x-* usually does not alternate with a velar stop (*g-*) in a wf. Alternatively, perh. related to *yì* 詣 (ŋieiᶜ) 'come to' (under → yí₁₁ 儀).

qì₄ 訖 → **jì₃** 既

qì₅ 泣 (kʰjəp) **LH** kʰɨp, **OCM** *khəp — [T] *ONW* kʰip
'To weep' [Shi].
[E] ST: PTB *krap 'to weep' > Kanauri *krap* 'to weep', WT *kʰrab-kʰrab* 'a weeper', JP *kʰrap³¹* (Bodman 1980: 163), Chepang *kryap* 'to cry, weep', Lepcha *hryóp* (< *kʰryap). CH aspiration is associated with exhaling and outward gesture §5.8.5.

qì₆ 湇 → **zhī₃** 汁

qì₇ 葺 (tsʰjəp) **LH** tsʰip, **OCM** *tshəp or *tship (< *s-ʔip)
'To thatch a roof, cover, repair' [Zuo, Zhouli].
[<] *ʔip + ST caus. s-prefix (§5.9.1).
[E] ST: WT *skyibs* (< *s-ʔips) 'a shelter from above' (from rain etc.); prob. also cognate to NNaga *ciup 'roof'. One of the sources of WT *sk-* has been shown to be *s-ʔ-; the etymon is therefore derived from ST *ʔip: WT *yib* 'eaves, shed' ⋈ *yib-pa* 'to hide oneself, place of concealment', Lushai *uupᶠ* 'be sheltered from wind, free from draughts'. For the *up ~ *ip alternations, see §11.5.1. Prob. related to → yì₂ 邑 'settlement'.

qì₈ 氣 (kʰjeiᶜ) **LH** kɨs, **OCM** *kə(t)s
'Air' [Lie], 'breath, disposition' [Lunyu], 'vapor' [Zuo], 'vital principle' [Li].
[T] *Sin S. SR* k'jej (去), *PR* k'i; *MGZY* khi (去) [k'i]; *ONW* kʰiᶜ
⋈ **kài** 愾 (kʰậiᶜ) **LH** kʰəs, **OCM** *khə̂(t)s — [T] *ONW* kʰɑiᶜ
'Be angry' [Zuo]. This is a semantically narrower, more vernacular j-less variant of the above (§9.1.1).
[E] AA: Kharia *kʰis* 'anger', Sora *kissa* 'move with great effort', Khm *kʰɛs* 's'efforcer' ('strive after, endeavor'). It is also found in TB-JR *khɐs* 'anger' (cited by Ostapirat *LTBA* 21.1, 1998: 239). CH aspiration is associated with exhaling §5.8.5.

qià₁ 洽 → **hé** 合

qià₂ 祫 → **hé** 合

qiān₁ 千 (tsʰien) **LH** tsʰen, **OCM** *tshîn < *s-nhîn, OCB *snin
'Thousand' [OB].
[T] *Sin Sukchu SR* ts'jen (平); *MGZY* tshÿan (平) [ts'jɛn]
[N] Phonetic is → rén₁ 人 (ńźjen) 'human being' (Pulleyblank 1962: 133; Baxter 1992: 223), the initial is parallel to → qī₁ 七. Alternatively, the *tsʰ-* initial may anticipate a development which is commonly found in Mǐn dialects, see → xū₄ 須鬚 < *sn- for an example.
[E] Etymology not clear. MK has a similar-looking word, but the initial and final nasals do not agree with OC: Viet *nghìn*, Mon *l-ṅim* 'thousand' [Maspero 1912: 63].

qiān₂ 掔 → **jiān₂** 堅

qiān₃ 鉛 (jiwän) **LH** jyan, **OCM** *lon or *jon
'Lead' n. [Shu].
[T] *Sin Sukchu SR* jen (平); *MGZY* ywÿan (平) [jyɛn]
[D] Most Mand. and Wú dialects derive the word from an aspirated velar initial, e.g. W-Wēnzhōu *kʰa⁴⁴* because re-etymologization (§2.8) may have connected it with *qiān* 掔 'solid, hard' (under → jiān₂ 堅). In southern dialects, the initial agrees with the QY reading: M-Xiàmén *iɛn³⁵*, Xiāng-Shuāngfēng *uĩ¹³*.

qiān₄ 愆 → **yǎn₁**, **yàn** 衍

qiān₅ 搴 (kjänᴮ 3) **LH** kɨanᴮ, **OCM** *kranʔ
'To take, pluck' [Chuci] is perh. cognate to WT *'kʰyer-ba* 'to take, bring, carry' (*HST*: 117), although one should expect MC div. IV vocalism (< *ia, *e).

qiān₆ 騫 → **yǎn₁**, **yàn** 衍

qiān₇ 牽 (kʰien) **LH** kʰen, **OCM** *khîn
'To pull / lead by a rope' (cattle) [BI, Shu], 'attach' [Lü], *qiān niú* 牽牛 'herd-boy'.
[D] Xiāng-Shuāngfēng *kʰĩ ⁵⁵*, K-Méixiàn *kʰian⁵⁵*, Y-Guǎngzhōu *hin⁵³* 'to pull by a rope'; M-Amoy *kʰanᴬ¹* (lit. *kʰien*) 'to lead by the hand, drag along, stretch out or tighten a rope'.

※ **xián** 弦 (ɣien) **LH** gen, **OCM** *gîn
'Bowstring' [Yili], 'string of a musical instrument' [Lunyu].
[T] *ONW* ɣėn.
[<] endopass. of *qiān* 牽 (kʰien) (§4.6), lit. 'something pulled tight'.

[C] Allofam is perh. → jǐn₁ 緊.

qiān₈ 僉 (tsʰjäm) **LH** tsʰiam, **OCM** *tsʰam < *k-sam ?
'All' (the people present) [Shu].
[E] ? MK: Mon *com* 'entirely, all, solely'.

qiān₉ 謙 (kʰiem) **LH** kʰem, **OCM** *khêm
'Modest' [Yi].

※ **qiǎn** 歉 (kʰămᴮ/ᶜ) **LH** kʰɛmᴮ/ᶜ, **OCM** *khrəmʔ/s
'Deficient, modest' [Xun]; also read (kʰiemᴮ) LH kʰemᴮ, OCM *khemʔ

※ **lián** 廉 (ljäm) **LH** liam, **OCM** *rem
'Modest', integrity' [Lunyu].

[E] ST: WT *kʰram-pa* 'modest' (Geilich 1994: 262).

qiān$_{10}$ 顧 → **jǐng**$_{2}$ 頸

qián$_{1}$ 拑鉗 (gjäm 3) **LH** gɨɑm, **OCM** *gam — **[D]** PMin *gʰiam 'pincers'.
'To pinch' 拑 [Guoce], 'pinched together' 鉗 [Zhuang].

qián$_{2}$ 柑箝 (gjäm 3) **LH** gɨɑm, **OCM** *gam
'A wooden gag' 柑 [Gongyang], 箝 [Xun] is prob. an allofam of → xián$_{11}$ 銜 'horse's bit' and of → hán$_{1}$ 含函 'have in the mouth'.

qián$_{3}$ 前 (dzien) **LH** dzen (dzein), **OCM** *dzên
'Be in front of, before, former' [Shi], 'advance' [Li]. — Etymology not clear.
[T] *Sin Sukchu SR* dzjen (平); *MGZY* tsen (平) [dzɛn]; *ONW* dzėn

qián$_{4}$ 乾 (gjän 3) **LH** gɨan, **OCM** *gran — **[T]** *ONW* gan
'Heavenly' [Yi].
[E] ST: PTB *m-ka-n (*STC:* 157 n. 428; *HPTB:* 450) > WT *mkʰa* 'heaven', Limbu *kʰa* 'sky' (in expressions), Magari *nam-kʰan* 'sun', Southern Kuki *kʰa:n-* 'sky' (*LTBA* 11.2, 1988: 110).
Acc. to Benedict, these forms belong to the PTB root *ka ~ *ga 'open / opening' > 'wide', also > 'mouth, door', etc. Karlgren (1956: 13) relates this word to → gān$_{9}$ 乾 'dry' (not likely).

qián$_{5}$ 黔 (gjəm, gjäm 3) **LH** gɨəm, gɨam, **OCM** *gəm, *grəm ?
'Black' [Zuo], *qián-shǒu* 黔首 ('black heads':) 'common people' [Shiji].
[E] Perh. area word related to PTai *kʰəm⁵ 'dark', MK-PEKatuic *koŏm 'black'. See → tǎn$_{5}$ 黮 for further items.

qián$_{6}$ 潛 → **jiān**$_{9}$ 熸

qián$_{7}$ 鬵 → **xín** 尋爓

qián$_{8}$, **tán** 燂 → **xián**$_{12}$ 燅

qián$_{9}$ 錢 (dzjän) **LH** dzian, **OCM** *dzan
'Coin' [Guoyu].
[T] *Sin Sukchu SR* dzjen (平); *MGZY* tsen (平) [dzɛn]; *ONW* dzian

✕ **jiǎn** 錢 (tsjänᴮ) **LH** tsianᴮ, **OCM** *tsanʔ
'Hoe, weeder' [Shi 276].
[E] Early coins had the shapes of spades and knives; therefore *qián* is a derivation from *jiǎn* (Qiu Xigui 2000: 259). Alternatively Boltz (1994: 100) explains *qián* as 'a fragment, token'; Wáng Shèngměi (Song Dyn.) considers *qián* derived from → qiǎn$_{2}$ 淺 'shallow' > 'thin' (Qiu Xigui 2000: 258f).
Qián is loaned into PMY as *dzɪɴᴬ (Purnell 1970) 'money', and OJapanese as *zeni* (Miyake 1997: 186).

qiǎn$_{1}$ 遣 (kʰjiänᴮ 4) **LH** kʰianᴮ, **OCM** *khenʔ — **[T]** *ONW* kʰian
'To send to, send away' [BI, Shi], 'let go' [Zuo].
✕ **qiàn** 遣 (kʰjiänᶜ) **LH** khianᶜ, **OCM** *khens
'To convey (sacrificial meat) to the grave' [Li].
[E] ST: WT *skyel-ba* 'to send' (Unger *Hao-ku* 35, 1986: 30). Loss of a ST pre-initial could be responsible for aspiration §5.8.1.

qiǎn$_{2}$ 淺 (tsʰjänᴮ) **LH** tsʰianᴮ, **OCM** *tshanʔ — **[D]** PMin *tsʰiemᴮ
'Be shallow (water), thin (hair)' [Shi].

⋇ **jiàn** 俴 (dzjän^B) **LH** dzian^B, **OCM** *dzanʔ
'Be shallow, small' [Shi].

⋇ **jiàn** 諓 (dzjän$^{B/C}$) **LH** dzian$^{B/C}$, **OCM** *dzanʔ/s
'Insincere, artful' [Guoyu] (Karlgren *GSR* 155m < 'shallow words').

⋇ **jiàn** 賤 (dzjän^C) **LH** dzian^C, **OCM** *dzans — **[T]** *ONW* dzian
'Cheap' [Zuo], 'low, mean' [Lunyu].

qiǎn$_3$ 慊 (k^{h}iem^B) **LH** k^{h}em^B, **OCM** *khêmʔ < *khlemʔ
'Dissatisfied' [Li]. The OCM medial *l is suggested by the phonetic series (*GSR* 627).

⋇ **qiè** 慊愜 (k^{h}iep) **LH** k^{h}ep, **OCM** *khêp < *khlep
'Satisfied' 慊 [Meng], 愜 [Guoce]. Holding something in the mouth can be a metaphor for an emotional state, therefore these words may be derived from

⋇ **qiǎn** 嗛 (k^{h}iem^B, ɣiem^B) **LH** k^{h}em^B, gem^B, **OCM** *khêmʔ, *gêmʔ < *kh/glemʔ
'To hold in the mouth' [Dadai Liji].

[E] There is prob. no connection with → hán$_1$ 含函 (so Wáng Lì 1982: 605). On the other hand, this wf may belong to → jiān$_7$ 兼 in the sense of 'holding the jaws together'. However, note TB-Lushai *k^{h}am^R < k^{h}amʔ* (< *-ʔ) 'be satisfied, satiated; be tired of, stiff' (without medial *-l-*).

qiǎn$_4$ 歉 → **qiān**$_9$ 謙

qiàn$_1$ 欠 (k^{h}jɐm^C) **LH** k^{h}ɨɑm^C, **OCM** *khams
'To yawn' [Liji].
[T] *Sin Sukchu SR* k'jem (去), *PR*, *LR* k'jen; *MGZY* khem (去) [k'ɛm].
[D] The Cantonese initial in *haam^{C1}* 'to yawn' is a regular reflex of earlier *k^h-*.
[E] ST *k-ham: (1) PTB *kam: Chepang *kamh* 'to yawn', JP *gǎ^{31}-k^{h}am^{31}* 'yawn' [Weidert 1987: 29]. (2) PTB *ham: Lepcha *hóm* (< *k^{h}am) 'to gape, yawn' ⋇ *hyóm* (< *k^{h}jam) 'to gasp' (Bodman 1980: 160); Lushai *haam^L / ham^F* (< *haams / haamʔ*) 'to gape, yawn, to have a gap'. CH aspiration is associated with the meaning 'hollow, empty' §5.8.6 and with exhaling §5.8.5.

qiàn$_2$ 俔 → **jiàn**$_1$ 見

qiàn$_3$ 倩綪 (ts^{h}ien^C) **LH** ts^{h}en^C, **OCM** tshêns < *k-sêns ?, OCK *ts^{h}iən
'Red' 倩 [Shi], 'dark red' 綪 [Zuo].

⋇ **xīng** 騂 (sjäŋ) **LH** sieŋ, **OCM** *seŋ
'Red' [Zhouli], 'reddish brown: red horse, red sacrificial animal' [Shi].
The reason for the different final nasals is not clear (provided these words are cognates). It is tempting to relate this wf to Lushai *sen^H* 'red', Tiddim *san* (so *CVST* 4: 22); however, the TB etymon derives from PTB *tyan (*STC:* 15–16 n. 63).

qiāng$_1$ 羌 (k^{h}jaŋ) **LH** k^{h}ɨɑŋ, **OCM** *khaŋ or *khiaŋ ?
Name of different western TB tribes from Shang OB down to the present. The graph implies that these people raised sheep. Pulleyblank (1983: 418f) suggests that the name is derived from → yáng 羊 'sheep' which is also phonetic, although the *SW* states that the graph is a semantic compound. However, the name Qiāng may be a foreign word which brings to mind WT *skyoŋ-ba, bskyaŋs* 'to guard, keep, tend' (animals), PTB *kyoŋ (*STC* no. 161), Qiāng means then 'herders'. The Tib. word is cognate to → yǎng$_2$ 養 'nourish, feed, rear'.

The clan name **Jiāng** 姜 (kjaŋ) *MTang* kiaŋ < kaŋ, *ONW* kaŋ (of Rong / Zhou provenance) is not necessarily connected to Qiāng, *SW* says that *yáng* 'sheep' is only phonetic (Pulleyblank *EC* 25, 2000: 16).

qiāng₂ 椌 (kʰåŋ) **LH** kʰɔŋ, **OCM** *khrôŋ
'A hollow wooden beaten instrument of music' [Li].

ꭗ **qiàng** 椌 (kʰåŋᶜ) **LH** kʰɔŋᶜ, **OCM** *khrôŋh
'To beat' [Zhuang].

[E] Etymology not certain, perh. related to TB-Mru *kʰoŋ* 'wooden drum' (Löffler 1966: 142). The OC word may be a derivation with caus. *r (§7.5) from → kōng 空 'hollow', lit. 'a thing made empty'. Alternatively, note MK-Khmer /khòoŋ/ 'be sunken, hollow, concave' ꭗ /krɑhòoŋ/ 'hollow, hole, rut' (Jenner / Pou 1982: 397). CH aspiration is associated with the meaning 'hollow, empty' §5.8.6.

qiāng₃ 將 'beg' → **jiāng₃** 將

qiáng 強彊 (gjaŋ) **LH** gɨɑŋ, **OCM** *gaŋ
'Be strong' [Shi]; 強 [Meng].
[T] *Sin Sukchu SR* gjaŋ (平); *MGZY* (kÿang >) kyang (平) [gjaŋ]; *MTang* giaŋ < gaŋ, *ONW* gaŋ
[D] M-Xiàmén col. *kiũ*ᴬ², lit. *kioŋ*ᴬ²

ꭗ **háng** 行 (ɣâŋ[ᶜ]) **LH** gɑŋ(ᶜ), **OCM** *gâŋ(h)
'Strong, vigorous' [Lunyu] is perh. a variant of *qiáng.*

ꭗ **qiǎng** 彊 (gjaŋᴮ) **LH** gɨɑŋᴮ, **OCM** *gaŋʔ
'Make an effort, compel' 彊 [Meng]; 強 [Zuo] is a verbal derivative of *qiáng;* the meaning 'hard (soil)' prob. goes with → gāng₄ 剛鋼.

ꭗ **jiāng-jiāng** 彊彊 (kjaŋ) **LH** kɨɑŋ, **OCM** *kaŋ
'Fierce' [Shi].

ꭗ Perh. **jìng** 勁 (kjäŋᶜ) **LH** kɨeŋᶜ, **OCM** *keŋh
'Strong' [Zuo] (Wáng Lì 1982: 341).

ꭗ **gěng** 梗 (kɐŋᴮ) **LH** kaŋᴮ, **OCM** *krâŋʔ
'Strong' [Chuci].

ꭗ **qíng** 勍 (gjɐŋ) **LH** gɨaŋ, **OCM** *graŋ
'Strong, powerful' [Zuo].

[E] ST: Lepcha *kraŋ* 'be strong on legs', Lushai *ṭaŋᴴ / ṭanᴸ < ṭanh* (< *traŋs*) 'put forth all one's strength'.

Wáng Lì (1982: 341) includes many additional words. This wf 'strong' and → gāng₄ 剛鋼 'hard' with its relatives bleed into each other.

qiǎng₁ 繈襁 (kjaŋᴮ) **LH** kiɑŋᴮ, **OCM** *kaŋʔ
'String, cord' [Li], 'band' (by which infants are held on the back) [Lun], see → bǎo₁ 保. Possibly related to → gāng₃ 綱 'guiding rope (of a net)'.

qiǎng₂ 彊 'effort' → **qiáng** 強彊; 'hard' → **gāng₄** 剛鋼

qiāo₁ 骹 (kʰau) **LH** kʰau, **OCM** *khrâu
'Tibia, spoke of a wheel' [Zhouli]; 'foot' in Mǐn dialects: PMin *kʰauᴬ¹ > Amoy kʰaᴬ¹. Superficially, the Southern Mǐn and Tai forms look identical: PTai *kʰaᴬ 'leg, thigh'; Zhuang *kʰa*ᴬ 'foot' (Yue-Hashimoto *CAAAL* 6, 1976: 1), PKS *kwa¹ 'leg', but the rimes do not agree with CH. More likely, the KT item is related to → gǔ₆ 股 'thigh, leg', considering that old loans do not closely agree in the voicing and in tones.

qiāo₂ 驕 → **jiǎo₁₇** 蹻

qiāo₃ 磽墝 (kʰau, kʰieuᴮ) **LH** kʰau, kʰeuᴮ, **OCM** *khriâu(ʔ) ?
'Stony soil' 磽 [Meng], 墝 [Xun]. Perh. related to PMY *ʔrau¹ 'stone' (Downer 1982).

qiāo$_4$ 皢 'bleached white' → **zhāo$_3$** 昭

qiáo$_1$ 喬 (gjäu 3) **LH** gɨau, **OCM** *gau
'Be tall' 喬 [Shi], 僑 [Zuo]; 'cauldron with high feet' 鐈 [BI].
※ **jiāo** 憍 (kjäu 3) **LH** kɨau, **OCM** *kau
'High, lift the head' [Zhuang]; 'proud, arrogant, high' [Shi].
※ **jiǎo** 憍 (kjäu^B 3) **LH** kɨau^B, **OCM** *kauʔ — **[T]** *ONW* kau
'Lift, elevated, high' [Xun]. Perh. → jiǎo$_{17}$ 蹻 'martial' is the same etymon (so Wáng Lì 1982: 204).
※ **jiào** 嶠 (gjäu^C 3) **LH** gɨau^C, **OCM** *gauh
'Peak' [Lie]. <> Tai: S. *gook* 'hill'.
[C] Allofams could be → gāo$_1$ 高, → jiǎo$_{17}$ 蹻. This wf is prob. not (closely) related to **qiáo** 翹 (gjiäu 4) 'be precariously high' [Shi], 'lift' [Zhuang] because of the difference in OC vocalism (*-iau, not *-au). NNaga *gyaw 'high' may be cognate to the latter.

qiáo$_2$ 橋 (gjäu 3) **LH** gɨau, **OCM** *gau
'Cross-bar, cross-piece' [Yili] > 'bridge' [Zuo].
※ **jiào** 橋 (kjäu^C 3) **LH** kɨau^C, **OCM** *kauh
'A well-sweep' [Li] (Karlgren 1956: 11).

qiáo$_3$ 僑, 翹 → **qiáo$_1$** 喬

qiáo$_4$ 樵 → **jiāo$_6$** 焦

qiáo$_5$ 翹 → **qiáo$_1$** 喬

qiào$_1$ 殼 → **ké$_2$** 殼

qiào$_2$ 竅 (k^{h}ieu^C) **LH** k^{h}eu^C, **OCM** *khiâuh
'Hole, opening' [Li] is prob. a ST word: WB *k^{h}yok* 'chasm, gulf' (*HST:* 95). Alternatively or in addition, this word may be a k-prefix concrete noun derivation from → tiǎo 窕 *liâuʔ (or *jâuʔ) 'to bore a hole' (§5.4). CH aspiration is associated with the meaning 'hollow, empty' §5.8.6.

qié 茄 (gjâ) *Sin Sukchu SR* kje (平).
'Eggplant'. The MC rime is unique.
[D] Y-Guǎngzhōu *k^{h}ɛ^{A2}*, Táishān *k^{h}iɛ^{A2}*; K-Méixiàn *kj^{h}io^{A2}*; PMin *giɔ
[E] <> PTai *k^{h}ɨe^{A1} > S. *k^{h}ɨa^{A1}* 'eggplant'.

qiě 且 → **jiāng$_4$** 將

qiè$_1$ 切 → **jié$_9$** 節

qiè$_2$ 妾 → **jié$_2$** 捷

qiè$_3$ 朅 (k^{h}jat, k^{h}jɐt) **LH** k^{h}ɨat, **OCM** *khat
'Go away' [Shi] is cognate to → qù$_1$ 去 (k^{h}jwo^C) 'go away' (so Pulleyblank in Rosemont 1991: 30). CH aspiration is associated with outward motion §5.8.5.

qiè$_4$ 朅 'martial' → **jié$_{13}$** 桀傑

qiè$_5$ 竊 (ts^{h}iet) **LH** ts^{h}et, **OCM** *tshêt
'To steal' [Shu]. Bodman (ICSTLL 1988) relates this to JR *ka-sk^{h}iEt* 'to take'.

qiè$_6$-kuò 契闊 → **kuān** 寬

qiè$_7$ 鍥 → **qì$_1$** 契

qiè$_8$ 挈 → **jiē$_7$** 揭

qiè$_9$ 慊愜 → **qiǎn**$_3$ 慊

qīn$_1$ 侵 (tsʰjəm) **LH** tsʰim, **OCM** *tshəm < *k-səm ?
'Invade, encroach upon' [Shi].
[T] *Sin Sukchu SR* ts'im (平), *PR, LR* ts'in; *MGZY* tshim (平) [ts'im]; *ONW* tsʰim
[E] Two ST etymologies are possible: (1) WT *stim-pa, bstims* 'enter, penetrate' ⋈ *tʰim-pa* ~ *'tʰim-pa* 'be absorbed, disappear' (so Bodman 1980: 57). The WT items do agree just as well with → jìn$_2$ 浸 'soak' with which *qīn* may be related. (2) The CH graph shows a broom, hence perh. cognate to TB-Nung *šim* 'to sweep', Miri *səm-pek* 'broom' (*pek* 'to sweep'), Maru *šam* < *sim 'to sweep' (Benedict *HJAS* 4, 1939: 226f; *STC:* 170; *HPTB:* 305).

qīn$_2$ 綅 (tsʰjəm) **LH** tsʰim, **OCM** *tshəm, OCB *tshjəm
'Thread' [Shi], also MC *tsjəm* and *sjäm;* the reading *sjäm* may have been influenced by → xiàn$_6$ 線 (sjän) 'thread' or → xiān$_7$ 纖 (sjäm) 'fine-textured silk'.
[E] ? ST: JP *ă^{31}-tsam^{31}* 'string', WT *'tsʰem-pa* 'to sew' (*CVST* 4: 22).

qīn$_3$ 衾 (kʰjəm) **LH** kʰɨm, **OCM** *khəm
'A blanket, coverlet' [Shi].
[E] Etymology not clear. (1) The word could perh. be a k-prefix concrete noun derived from → yīn$_5$ 陰 'overcast', i.e. 'covered' (§5.9.4; §5.4). Comparanda may include: (2) WB *kʰrum* ~ *kʰyum* 'cover, overspread' (by plants), WT *grum-če* 'thick woolen blanket' (*CVST* 5: 109). (3) WT *kʰyim* 'house' (i.e. 'shelter, cover') which is derived from TB *im; but see → yì$_8$ 邑.

⋈ **jìn** 紟 (gjəmᶜ) **LH** gɨmᶜ, **OCM** *gəms
'A single shroud' [Yili].

qīn$_4$ 嶔岑 → **kàn**$_2$ 磡

qīn$_5$ 親 (tsʰjen) **LH** tsʰin, **OCM** *tshin, OCB *tshjin
'A close person, parents, affectionate' [Shi, Shu], 'oneself, personally' [Shi, Shu, BI], 'to love' (such as parents, siblings, children) [Meng].
[T] *Sin Sukchu SR* ts'in (平); *MGZY* tshin (平) [ts'in]; *ONW* tsʰin
[E] Etymology not certain. One early commentator remarks that anciently *qīn* sounded like *qiān* 千 *tshîn < *snhîn by which he may, or may not, have referred an n-initial (§5.9.1.1). Thus Boodberg (1937: 362) related *qīn* to → rén$_2$ 仁, note the overlapping meanings 'to love'.

However, the meaning 'oneself' is hardly an extension of the inter-personal notion 'to love'. Therefore *qīn* prob. belongs to a stem meaning 'near, close'. WT provides a semantic paradigm which may in fact be cognate: *gñen* 'a kinsman, relative' < *ñe-ba* 'be near, approach'. Most plausably, *qīn* is related to the AA stem → jí$_7$ 即 'approach > be close' with the nominalizing n-final (§6.4.3), then lit. 'persons close to oneself, close ones'; the words agree vocalically, and no post-initial *-n- needs to be postulated which would have been rather odd in the phonetic series 辛 in any case.

qín$_1$ 秦 (dzjen) **LH** dzin, **OCM** *dzin — [T] *ONW* dzin
The western state of Qín and the dynasty. Qín is often thought to be the source of ancient European words for 'China': Lat. 'Sina' etc., modern Western languages 'China'. Also the word for 'silk' may ultimately be derived from this name: Gr. *sērikón*, i.e. 'the Chinese one, (the stuff) from China'. These ancient loans suggest that the original final was *-r, not *-n (Pulleyblank 1962: 229–230). The graph was originally intended for *zhēn* (tṣjen) 'hazel'.

qín$_2$ 堇 (gjen 3) **LH** gɨn, **OCM** *grən
'Clay' [SW].

¾ **jìn** 墐 (gjen^C 3) **LH** gɨn^C, **OCM** *grəns
'To plaster, inter' [Shi].

qín$_3$ 勤懄 (gjən) **LH** gɨn, **OCM** *gən
'To toil, labor, be zealous' 勤 [BI, Shu]; 'sincere, energetic' [Lie] > 'sad' 懄 [Gongyang].

¾ **jiān** 艱 (kăn) **LH** kɛn, **OCM** *krən — **[T]** *ONW* kän
'Distress, difficulty, hardship' [OB, BI, Shi], 艱食 'foods of hardship / toil', i.e. cultivated foods [Shu].

[C] Perhaps cognate to → jìn$_6$ 饉殣 (gjen^C 3), but see there.

qín$_4$ 禽 (gjəm) **LH** gɨm, **OCM** *gəm — **[T]** *ONW* gim
'Game bird, bird, fowl' (opposite of → shòu 獸 'quadruped') [Zuo, EY], 'game' (animal) [Yi].
[E] Etymology not certain. It appears to be the same word as → qín$_5$ 擒 'catch' (animals etc.) and would thus be parallel to *shòu* 狩 'to hunt' ~ → shòu$_3$ 獸 'wild animal'. However, the similarity with the common AA word for 'bird' is striking:
AA: PVM *-ci:m* 'bird' [Ferlus] (the initial of Viet. *căm* [kəm^L] 'bird' could be the result of interference from a prefix or from OC); PMon *kɲciəm 'bird' (general term), Kyanzittha OMon (12th cent. AD) *kiñcem*, Mon *həcem, LitMon *gacem̀, gacem*; Nyah Kur *kəɲciam, some dialects have *ŋkyiam* and the like [Diffloth 1984: 71]; Wa-Lawa *sem; Chong (Pearic) *chiiʔm* [Huffman 1985]. <> Note also AN: PEastern Formosan *qayam 'bird' [Li Jen-kuei *LL* 5.2, 2004: 369].
These MK items cannot be late loans from Mandarin. It is also unlikely that a language family would borrow a marginal OC word (the CH word for 'bird' has been (mutatis mutandis) the equivalent of Mand. → niǎo 鳥 throughout the ages). Therefore early PMK *kcəm is the source for OC (there are more OC animal names of AA origin). The voiced velar initial may have won out in OC because of the semantic association of 'game bird' with *qín* 'catch', so that the two words converged. If *qín* 'catch' should go back to some early MK word, the two items might have been nearly identical: note OMon *ckem* 'grasp' (under → jiān$_7$ 兼) vs. a hypothetical *kcem 'bird'.

qín$_5$ 擒 (gjəm) **LH** gɨm, **OCM** *gəm ? — **[T]** *ONW* gim
'To catch, capture' (animals, people, booty) [BI, Guoyu].
[E] Etymology not certain. TB-WT *sgrim-pa* 'to hold fast, force / twist together, squeeze in' (Gong in W. Wang 1995: 86) is semantically rather removed from *qín*; PTamang *kim 'to take' [S. Georg 1996: 309] should correspond to a MC palatal initial. The word may, however, derive from an AA variant of → jiān$_7$ 兼 *kêm 'grasp'. See also → qín$_4$ 禽 'bird'.

(**qín**$_6$) □ PMin *dzim^A
'A type of crab': Fúzhōu *siŋ^{A2}*, Amoy *tsim^{A2}*, is borrowed from MK 'king crab' Bahnar *kɤtam*, WrMon *khatam* (Norman / Mei 1976: 298).

qǐn$_1$ 坅 (kʰjəm^B, ŋjəm^B) **LH** kʰɨm^B, **OCM** *khəmʔ
'Hole in the earth' [Yili]. Aspiration is associated with 'hollow, empty' §5.8.6.
[E] ST: TB-JP *mă^{31}-kʰam^{55}* 'pit'. Similar CH and foreign comparanda are here tentatively sorted out according to connections which emerge in Table K-1 under →

kǎn₁ 坎埳. <> CH loans are perh. Tai: Po'ai *kam*^{C1} < *k- 'cave', PKS *ka:m^1 'cave'; but these items could belong to → kǎn₁ 坎埳 instead.

qǐn₂-yǐn 螼蚓 → **yǐn₄** 螾蚓

qǐn₃-tiǎn 堅蚕 → **yǐn₄** 螾蚓 'earthworm'

qǐn₄ 寢 (tsʰjəm^B) **LH** tsʰim^B, **OCM** *tshəmʔ < *k-səmʔ

'To sleep' [Shi], 'sleeping apartments in a palace' [Li].

[E] ST: WT *gzim-pa* 'fall asleep, sleep' ⋈ *gzim-gzim, tsʰim-tsʰim* 'eyes dazzled' (*STC:* 170 n. 455); Manchati *im* 'sleep', Adi *im-maŋ* 'dream'; PLB *yip > WB *ʔip* 'sleep', ⋈ *sip* 'put to sleep', perh. ⋈ *ə-sim*^{B} 'concubine'; Tsangla *ip*, Ao Naga *jip*, JP id.; Mru *chim* 'put to sleep' < *s-* [Löffler 1966: 122]. Most TB forms are phonologically difficult to reconcile with the CH and WT etymon (*HST:* 134); perh. they derive from a ST *(s-)im.

qīng₁ 青 (tsʰieŋ) **LH** tsʰeŋ, **OCM** *tshêŋ < *k-sêŋ ?

'Green, blue' [Shi].

[D] PMin *tsʰaŋ 'raw' (Norman identifies the PMin form with 青, Nakajima with 生).

[E] ST *siŋ: WT *gsiŋ-ma* < *k-siŋ 'pastureland, meadow', Mikir *reŋ-seŋ* < *-se/iŋ 'green', Rawang *məsëŋ* 'green', *măšiŋ* 'blue'. This root *siŋ is identical to the ST root *siŋ 'tree, wood' (→ xīn₄ 新) and its CH homophone *xīn* 新 'new, renew', so that these items may also be part of this large wf. CH -> PVM: Sách *sɛŋ*, Viet *xanh* 'blue-green'.

A parallel stem is *saŋ, see → cāng₃ 蒼 *tshâŋ 'green'. For an overview of the *sriŋ ~ *sraŋ contrasts (§11.1.3), see Table S-1 after → shēng₂ 生; for an overview of the

Table Q-1 Live, fresh, green (B): *sriŋ ~ *siŋ

	*sriŋ live	⋈ *sriŋ green	*(k)-siŋ green	⋈ *sɪŋ
OC	shēng 生 *sreŋ live		qīng 青 *tsheŋ < *k-seŋ ? green	xìng 性 *seŋ nature, 姓 offspring, family
WT			gsiŋ-ma pastureland	
Kanauri	sriŋ live			
Mikir	reŋ^L < re/iŋ^L live		reŋ-seŋ green	
Lushai	hriŋ^H / hrinR bear, beget	hrɪŋ^H / hrin^L fresh, green		
NNaga	*C-riŋ alive	*C/V-criŋ raw, grass		
Rawang			məsëŋ green ~ măšiŋ blue	
JP		tsiŋ^{33} < rjiŋ^{33} ? grass, green		? (n^{55}-teŋ^{51} name)

sriŋ ~ siŋ contrasts, see Table Q-1. Most, but not all, ST words meaning 'live' belong to a stem with initial *sr-, while 'fresh, green' tends to belong to the stem with simple initial *s-.

[C] The graph 菁 'luxuriant' [Shi], though pronounced *jīng* (tsieŋ, tsjäŋ), may simply write *qīng* (Baxter 1983). The syn. → cāng₃ 蒼 is cognate (Wáng Lì 1982: 335) and belongs to a parallel a-vowel stem, see under → shēng$_2$ 生. Additional allofams → jīng$_6$ 菁, → xìng$_2$ 性姓, perh. → qíng$_1$ 情.

qīng$_2$ 清 (tsʰjäŋ) **LH** tsʰieŋ, **OCM** *tsheŋ < *k-seŋ ?
'Be pure, clear' (of water, sound, and also generally) [Shi].
[T] *Sin Sukchu SR* ts'iŋ (平); *MGZY* tshing (平) [ts'iŋ]; *ONW* tsʰieŋ

꞉ **jìng** 淨 (dzjäŋ^C) **LH** dzieŋ^C, **OCM** *dzeŋh — **[T]** *ONW* dzieŋ
'Clean, cleanse' [Guoyu].

꞉ **xǐng** 醒 (sieŋ, sieŋ$^{B/C}$) **LH** seŋ($^{B/C}$), **OCM** *sêŋ(ʔ/h)
'Wake up, become sober' [Zuo] (*HST:* 55).
[T] *Sin Sukchu SR* siŋ (上), *LR* siŋ; *MGZY* sing (上) [siŋ] — **[D]** PMin *tsʰaŋ^B

[E] ST *seŋ: WT *seŋ-po ~ bseŋ-po* 'clear, white, airy, pale' ꞉ *gseŋ-po* 'clear and sharp' (sound), JP *seŋ^{33}* 'clean'; Lushai *tʰiaŋ^H / thian^L* 'be clear, clean'. JP *tʃă^{55}-griŋ^{55}* 'sober' is unrelated. <> This is perh. an area word, note MK-Khmer: *cĕ̄na* /caaɛŋ/ 'be clear, bright... make clear...'

~ ST *saŋ: WT *saŋ-ba, saŋs* 'cleanse', *bzi-saŋs-te* 'having become sober again after intoxication' (*bzi* 'intoxication') ꞉ *'tsʰaŋ-ba, tsʰaŋs* 'to remove, make clean' (Unger *Hao-ku* 36, 1990: 61); WB *tsaŋ* 'clear, pure'.

Allofams are perh. → xīng$_2$ 星 'star' (*HST:* 55) and *qíng* 星 'clear sky'; → jìng$_1$ 靜靖 竫 may also be related.

For an overview of the different ST stems, see the following Table Q-2 'Clean'.

Table Q-2 Clean, clear

	*seŋ	*k-seŋ	*-saŋ
OC	xǐng 醒 *sêŋ sober	qīng 清 *tsheŋ or *k-seŋ ? pure, clear	
WT	seŋ-po ~ bseŋ-po clear, white, airy	gseŋ-po clear and sharp	saŋ-ba, saŋs cleanse, sober 'tsʰaŋ-ba, tsʰaŋs to remove, make clean
Lushai	tʰiaŋ^H / thian^L be clear, clean		
JP	seŋ^{33} clean		
WB			caŋ clear, pure

qīng$_3$ 輕 (kʰjäŋ) **LH** kʰieŋ, **OCM** *kheŋ — **[T]** *ONW* kʰieŋ
'Light' (weight) [Shi, Guoce].
[E] ST *C-jaŋ (*C-iaŋ): PTB *r-ya:ŋ ~ *gya:ŋ (*STC* no. 328; French 1983: 512): WT *yaŋ* 'light', Tamang *^{2}iaŋ*, Lushai *zaaŋ^R / zaan^L < jaaŋʔ / jaans* 'be light'; NNaga *gyaŋ, Lepcha *kyaŋ* 'be light'. For the OC vowel, see §11.3.2.

꞉ **qīng** 輕 (kʰjäŋ^C) **LH** kʰieŋ^C, **OCM** *kheŋh
'Be careless' [Zuo] (Downer 1959: 286).
[<] exoactive / putative of *qīng* (§4.3.2), lit. 'consider light, treat lightly'.

qīng$_4$ 傾頃 (kʰjwäŋ) **LH** kʰyeŋ, **OCM** *khweŋ — **[T]** *ONW* kʰueŋ
'Be slanting' > caus. 'overturn, overthrow' (wall, mandate) 傾頃 [Shi]; 'incline' (the head) 傾 [Li]. The graph 傾 is also read MC *kʰjäŋ* without medial *w* (§10.2.1).
[E] AA-PMon *kʔiəŋ / *kʔeeŋ 'to lean, be slanted > listen', Khmer *'iaṅa* /ʔiiəŋ/ 'to slant, slope, tilt, incline...'; this item also occurs in TB-JP *n^{31}-kʰjeŋ^{31}* 'slanted' (*CVST*

5: 104). The CH aspiration may stem from the AA post-initial glottal stop (§5.9.4).

qíng$_1$ 情 (dzjäŋ) **LH** dzieŋ, **OCM** *dzeŋ — **[T]** *ONW* dzieŋ
'Feelings' [Shi, Zuo], 'proper nature, circumstances' [Meng], or more fundamentally 'quality, attribute, feature' (Boltz *JAOS* 120.2, 2000: 225ff). The meaning 'feelings' has led to attempts to connect the word with ST *s-niŋ 'heart' (Benedict 1976: 170 n. 8), but the meaning 'proper nature' suggests that this word is rather cognate to → shēng$_2$ 生 'live, life' (Boltz), although the initials are difficult to reconcile.

qíng$_2$ 晴 → **xīng$_2$** 星

qíng$_3$ 勍 → **qiáng** 強彊

qíng$_4$ 鯨 → **jīng$_1$** 京

qǐng 請 (ts^{h}jäŋ^B, dzjäŋ) **LH** ts^{h}ieŋ^B, **OCM** *tsheŋ?
'To ask' [Zuo], 'request' [Lun].
[T] *Sin Sukchu SR* ts'iŋ (上); *MGZY* tshing (上) [ts'iŋ]; *ONW* ts^{h}ieŋ
[E] ST: TB-PKiranti *sìŋ 'ask' [van Driem 1995: 254: Starostin], Garo *siŋ?* 'to inquire, question, ask'.

qìng$_1$ 凊 (ts^{h}jäŋ^C) **LH** ts^{h}ieŋ^C, **OCM** *tsheŋh
'Cold' [Li]. Perh. related to → cāng$_2$ 滄.

qìng$_2$ 慶 (k^{h}jɐŋ^C) **LH** k^{h}ɨaŋ^C, **OCM** *khaŋ (or *khiaŋh (?) — **[T]** *ONW* k^{h}eŋ
'Be happy, happiness, good fortune' [BI, Shi].
[E] Etymology not certain. The word may be cognate to WT *g-yaŋ* 'happiness, blessing, prosperity'. Bodman (1980: 95) relates the WT word to → xiáng$_1$ 庠祥.

qìng$_3$ 磬 (k^{h}ieŋ^C) **LH** k^{h}eŋ^C, **OCM** *khêŋh
'To suspend' [Li] > 'musical stone' [BI, Shi]. Since OCM medial *-w- is sometimes lost before high front vowels (§10.2.1), this word may be related to → xuán$_4$ 縣懸 'suspend'. <> Or perh. connectd with PMiao *klaaŋ^1* [Purnell] 'to hang, dangle'.

qiōng 穹 (k^{h}juŋ) **LH** k^{h}uŋ, **OCM** *khuŋ
'Vault > hole' [Shi].
[<] 'hollow' aspiration of → gōng$_2$ 弓 'bow' (§5.8.6) (Karlgren 1956: 14).

qióng$_1$ 邛 (gjwoŋ) **LH** gɨoŋ, **OCM** *goŋ
'Be distressed' [Shi]. This word looks like a variant of → jiǒng$_4$ 窘 (gjuen^B 3) LH *guɨn* (?) 'be distressed'. If so, both could go back to a PCH final *-uŋ. For possible further connections see → kǒng$_2$ 恐 'be afraid' and items listed there; → qióng$_2$ 窮 may be a vocalic variant.
[E] ST: WT *gyoŋ* 'want, need, indigence'.

qióng$_2$ 窮 (gjuŋ) **LH** guŋ, **OCM** *guŋ
'Extreme, the utmost' [Zuo] > 'destitute, poverty' [Shi].
[T] *Sin Sukchu SR* gjuŋ (平); *MGZY* kÿung (平) [gjuŋ]
[C] → qióng$_1$ 邛 may be a variant.

⌘ **jú** 鞠 (kjuk) **LH** kuk, **OCM** *kuk
'Be exhausted, exhaustive > entirely' [Shi].

qióng$_3$ 惸嬛睘 (gjwäŋ) **LH** gyeŋ, **OCM** *gweŋ
'Alone and helpless' [Shi].
[E] Perh. MK: Khmer *ēna* /ʔaaɛŋ/ 'to be alone, all by oneself, solitary', but the discrepancy in the initials is unexplained.

qiū $_1$ 丘 ($k^hjəu$) **LH** k^hu, **OCM** *khwə, OCB *$k^whjə$ — **[T]** *MTang* k^heu < k^hiu, *ONW* k^hu
'Hill, mound' [Shi], 'small hill' [SW], 'waste, ruins' [Chuci]. This is prob. be the s. w. as → qiū$_2$ 丘 'village'. → qū$_5$ 虛墟 (k^hjwo) [$k^hɑ$] 'hill, mound, ruins, waste' is prob. not cognate (contra general assumptions, e.g. Wáng Lì 1982: 85).

qiū $_2$ 丘 ($k^hjəu$) **LH** k^hu, **OCM** *khwə, OCB *$k^whjə$
'Village, district' [Meng], 丘商 'the city Shang' [OB] (Keightley 2000: 57), 商丘 [Zhushu jinian].
[D] M-Xiàmén, Fúzhōu *k^hu^A* 邱 'plot of land'.
[E] ST: TB-Phön *kəwa*, Lushai *k^hua^H* 'village, town', Lai *k^hua* 'cosmos, village' [Van-Bik, *LTBA* 21.1, 1998: 221]. The TB words are often associated with those under → qú$_5$ 衢.
The homophone → qiū$_1$ 丘 'hill, mound, ruins' is prob. the same word since settlements were often built on elevated ground; a semantic parallel is → jīng$_1$ 京 'city, hill'.

qiū $_3$**-yǐn** 蚯蚓 → **yǐn** $_4$ 螾蚓

qiū $_4$ 秋 ($ts^hjəu$) **LH** ts^hiu, **OCM** *tshiu, OCB *tshjiw < PCH *C-nh(i)u.
'Autumn' [OB, Shi], perh. 'fall-winter' in OB; 'crop' [Shu].
[D] M-Xiàmén, Fúzhōu *ts^hiu^{A1}*
[E] Etymology not clear. *Qiū* might be cognate to → shōu 收 *(n)hiu 'to gather, harvest', the QYS initial *tsh-* can in some instances derive from a complex preliterate initial with a voiceless *n, as in → qī$_1$ 七 *tshit 'seven' (§5.9.1.1). Alternatively, *qiū* might be related to the wf → zú$_1$ 卒 'to end' since vegetation dies in the fall (note that *zú* also refers to dead vegetation in winter).

qiú$_1$ 求 → **jiū** $_1$ 究

qiú$_2$ 俅 (gjəu) **LH** gu, **OCM** *gu
'Gem-adorned' [Shi]. Bodman (1980: 167) relates this to WT *gru* 'luster of gems'.

qiú$_3$ 球 (gjəu) **LH** gu, **OCM** *gu, OCB *grju — **[D]** PMin *ǧiu.
'Ball', earlier some 'kind of jade' [Shi, Shu].
[E] <> Tai: Wu-ming *$klau^{A2}$* 'ball' (Bodman 1980: 108).

qiú$_4$ 逑仇 (gjəu) **LH** gu, **OCM** *gu, OCB *g(r)ju
'To assemble' (e.g. friends) [BI, Shi] > 'accumulate' (e.g. merits) 逑 [Shi] > 'mate, companion, partner, antagonist' 仇 [Shi].
[E] ? ST: Chepang *gu*, Bodo *lʏgʏ* 'friend' [Weidert 1987: 18]. <> Tai: S. *k^huu^{B2}* < *g- 'pair' (Li F. 1976: 42). Li suggests a connection with CH *yǒu* 友 'friend' (but see under → yòu$_2$ 右) and with WT *grogs* 'friend' (but see → kè$_3$ 客).

qiú$_5$ 裘 (gjəu) **LH** gu, **OCM** *gwə, OCB *$g^wjə$ (*Shījīng* rimes)
'Fur' [BI, Shi]. Bodman (1980: 166) compares this to WT *gru* 'boat' (of inflated hides). Tamang *^1kuri* 'skin' looks similar.

qiú$_6$ 泅 (zjəu) **LH** ziu, **OCM** *s-ju or *s-lu — **[D]** M-Xiàmén, Fúzhōu *siu^{A2}* 'to swim'.
'To swim' [Lie].
[E] Since this word is late, it may simply be a dialect variant of → yóu$_6$ 游遊, as in some dialects original *j- becomes a fricative (note Mǐn above). Bodman (1980: 179) draws attention to a Lushai word *hlew* 'swim'.

qiú$_7$, jiū 虯觓觩 (gjieu, kjieu) **LH** giu, kiu, **OCM** *giu, *kiu, OCB *g(r)jiw (?)
'Horned dragon' 虯 [Chuci]; 'horn-shaped, long and curved' 觓 [Guliang], 觩 [Shi]. *HST:* 130 compares 'horned dragon' with WT *klu* 'Nagas, serpent spirits', but see → jiāo$_4$ 蛟. The most likely etymology is 'twisting, wriggling' (Carr *LTBA* 13.2: 151ff), note → jiǔ$_3$ 糾 (kjeu^B) 'to twist, plait'.

qiú$_8$ 酋 → **zú** 卒

qiú$_9$ 遒 → **zāo** 遭

qū$_1$ 曲 (k^{h}jwok) **LH** k^{h}ɨok, **OCM** *khok, OCB *kh(r)jok
'To bend, bent' [Shi], 'crooked, unjust' [Zuo].
[T] *Sin Sukchu SR* k'y (入); *MGZY* khÿu (入) [k'y]; *ONW* k^{h}uok

⪤ **jú** 局 (gjwok) **LH** gɨok, **OCM** *gok, OCB *ɦkh(r)jok — **[T]** *ONW* guok
'Bent, curved' (body) [Shi], 跼 'bend the body' [Shiwen].

[E] PMK *gɔk 'be crooked, bent, lame' (Shorto 1972: 15).

[C] This wf is cognate to items under → gōu$_1$ 句鉤枸區; it may also be connected with → jú$_6$ 鞠鞫 'bend'.

qū$_2$ 屈 (k^{h}juət) **LH** k^{h}ut, **OCM** *khuṭ
'To bend' [Zuo], 'subdue' [Shi]; the graph shows a squatting (i.e. bent) person with the phonetic underneath.
[T] *Sin Sukchu SR* k'y (入); *MGZY* khÿu (入) [k'y]
[<] a final -t derivation of → jú$_6$ 鞠鞫 'bend'.
[E] Perh. ST (but the final consonants differ): WT *dgur* 'crooked, bend down' ⪤ *'k^{h}ur-ba* 'carry' (a heavy load), Lushai *kuur^H* 'to bend down, droop' ⪤ *kuur^L* 'be bowed down, burdened'. CH -> PTai *gu̯ot^{D2} 'bent'.
[C] Cognates are perh. → gōu$_1$ 句鉤枸區, → qū$_1$ 曲.

qū$_3$ 軀 (k^{h}ju[^{C}]) **LH** k^{h}ɨo, **OCM** *kho, OCB *kh(r)jo
'Body, person' [Meng].
[T] *MTang* k^{h}y < k^{h}uo, *ONW* k^{h}uo
[E] ST: PTB *(s-)kuw > WT *sku*, WB *kui* 'body' (of an animal) (*HST:* 46), Mru *kö* [Löffler 1966: 130]. Shorto (1972: 18) suggests a connection with PMK *[j]k[oo]? 'body' > OMon *jirku.* Loss of a ST pre-initial could be responsible for aspiration §5.8.1.

qū$_4$ 驅 (k^{h}ju[^{C}]) **LH** k^{h}ɨo(^{C}), **OCM** *kho(h) ?
'To drive (animals), gallop, drive out / away' [BI, Shi].
[E] ST: WT *'k^{h}yug-pa* 'to run, dart, hasten' ⪤ *'k^{h}yu-ba, k^{h}yus* 'to run' ⪤ *dkyu-ba* 'a race' ⪤ *'gyu-ba, 'gyus* 'to move quickly' (*HST:* 128). CH aspiration is associated with forceful motion §5.8.5. An allofam may be → jū$_7$ 駒 'colt'.

qū$_5$ 虛墟 (k^{h}jwo) **LH** k^{h}ɨɑ, **OCM** *kha
'Ruin-mound' 虛 [Shi], 'ruins' 墟 [Guoyu, Li], 'hill, mound, site' 虛 [Zuo], 'a large mound' [SW]. This may be a nominal derivation by k-prefix (§5.4) from → xū$_2$ 虛 'empty' (Karlgren 1956: 18). Note Lushai *ko^H* 'a mound, bank, raised ground...' which may be related. *Qū* is probably not related to → qiū$_1$ 丘.

qū$_6$ 趨 → **zōu$_2$** 騶

qú$_1$ 渠 'canal' → **jǔ$_5$** 柜

qú₂ 渠佢 (gjwo) **LH** gɨɑ, **OCM** *ga — **[T]** *ONW* gio (?) > gø
'He, she, it, they' third person pron., appears in 4th ~ 5th cent. AD, survives in many central and southern dialects: G-Línchuān *ke*^{B1}, Jīxī *ke*^{A2}; X-Qíyáng *ki*^{A1} (Norman 1988: 118 etc.), also Yuè *k*^{h}*øy*^{13} 'he'.
This pron. may be related to → qí₇ 其 through the OC *a ~ *ə alternation (§11.1.2), also the AA pronoun *kɨ has a secondary form *ka > Khmer *ge* /ke/ 'third person singular'.

qú₃ 朐軥 → **gōu₁** 句鉤枸區

qú₄, jù 臞 (gju[C]) **LH** gyɑ(C), **OCM** *gwa(h)
'Lean, emaciated' [Guoce].
[E] ST: WB *k*^{h}*wak* 'concave' (as a cup), 'sunken' (face). For the WB final *-k*, see §6.9.
ꭗ **wāng** 尪 (ʔwâŋ) **LH** ʔwɑŋ, **OCM** *ʔwâŋ
'Emaciated; deformed person' (often burnt to alleviate drought) [Zuo] (Qiu Xigui *EC* 9–10, 1983–1985: 291). For final *-ŋ,* see §6.5.2.
ꭗ **kuāng** 眶 (kʰjwaŋ) **LH** kʰyɑŋ, **OCM** *khwaŋ
'Eyesocket' [Liezi].
[<] nominalizing k-prefix derivation from *wāng* (§5.4).
[E] These words may be unrelated, but they can be phonologically reconciled if we assume a root initial *w- or *ʔw-. Perh. related to → yú₃ 盂.

qú₅ 衢 (gju) **LH** gyɑ, **OCM** *gwa
'Crossroads' [Zuo, Lüshi] is prob. not related to *qú* 躍 'to go' [Chuci], thought in turn to be a cognate of → yú₁ 于 'to go to'. It may belong to the wf → jǔ₃ 矩 'carpenter's square' in the sense of (roads intersecting at) 'right angles', but this is speculation. Most likely, it is related to → jǔ₅ 柜 'gutter' as its TB cognates there imply.

qǔ 取 (tsʰjuB) **LH** tsʰioB, **OCM** *tshoʔ
'To take, accept' [BI, Shi].
[T] *Sin Sukchu SR* ts'y (上); *MGZY* tshÿu (上) [ts'y]; *MTang* tsʰy < tsʰuo, *ONW* tsʰuo
ꭗ **qù** 娶 (tsʰjuC) **LH** tsʰioC, **OCM** *tshoh
'To take / marry a wife' [late Shi, Shu, but perh. also in OB].
[<] exoactive of *qǔ* 取 (§4.3.1).
[C] This wf is occasionally thought to be related to items under → jù₇ 聚.

qù₁ 去 (kʰjwoC) **LH** kʰɨɑC, **OCM** *khah
'To go away' intr., 'to leave' tr. [Shi]; already in early OC *qù* took over the function of *qǔ*, hence 'to eliminate, do away with' tr. [Zuo].
[T] *Sin Sukchu SR* k'y (去); *MGZY* khÿu (去) [k'y]; *MTang* kʰy, *NW corridor* kʰi, *ONW* kʰø < kʰio (?)
[N] The OB graph shows a man with a hole marked in his crotch, hence the inventors of writing had perhaps 'anus' in mind (cf. the TB cognates).
[<] exopass. (reflexive) of *qǔ* 去 (kʰjwoB), lit. 'remove oneself' (§4.4).
ꭗ **qǔ** 去 (kʰjwoB) **LH** kʰɨɑB, **OCM** *khaʔ
'To put away, eliminate, get rid of' (noxious influence, drought) [Shi]; early on, this word was superceded by *qù* (Wáng Lì 1958: 555).
[E] ST: The basic ST meaning is 'to get rid of': WT *skyag-pa, bskyags* 'to spend, lay out, expend' ꭗ *skyag ~ rkyag* 'dirt, excrement'; WB *kya*^{C} 'fall, become low, expand' ꭗ *k*^{h}*ya*^{C} 'throw down, put down' (? ꭗ *kyaŋ* 'excrement'); KC-Tiddim *kia*^{F} 'to fall' ꭗ *xia*^{F} (< *kh-) 'to let fall, fell', *kiat*^{R} ꭗ *xiat*^{R} (< *kh-) 'id.' (Geilich 1994: 171). For the final consonants, see §3.2.2. Loss of a ST pre-initial could be responsible for aspiration §5.8.1.

[C] Allofam → qiè$_3$ 朅 (k^hjät) 'go away'.

qù$_2$ 趣 → **zǒu** 走

quān 棬 → **quán$_3$** 卷拳

quán$_1$ 全牷 (dzjwän) **LH** dzyan, **OCM** *dzon
'Complete' [Meng] > 'preserve' 全 [Zhuang] > 'single-colored sacrificial animal' 牷 [Zuozhuan].
[T] *Sin Sukchu SR* dzyen (平); *MGZY* tswÿan (平) [dzyɛn]

⋈ **quán** 痊 (ts^hjwän) **LH** ts^hyan, **OCM** *tshon
'Become cured (illness)' [Zhuang] (Karlgren 1956: 13).

quán$_2$ 泉 (dzjwän) **LH** dzyan, **OCM** *dzwan (!), OCB *Sg^wjan
'Spring' (of water) [OB, Shi].
[T] *Sin Sukchu SR* dzyen (平); *MGZY* tswÿan (平) [dzyɛn]
[N] This word rimes in *Shījīng* in *-an* (Pulleyblank 1963: 209) and is therefore to be reconstructed with a labiovelar initial (Baxter 1992: 176; 232). The word could possibly be a CH n-suffix nominalization (§6.4.3) which is cognate to a PTB root *tso 'bubble, boil': WT *'tshod-ba, btsos* 'cook in boiling water'; WB *tshu* 'to boil, bubble'.

quán$_3$ 卷拳 (gjwän 3) **LH** gyɑn, **OCM** *gwan or *gon, OCB *g^wrjen 'handsome'
'Be bent, curved, curling' 卷 [Shi] > 'fist, strength' 拳 [Shi] > 'force, forceful' 捲 [Zhuang], 'power' 權 [Guoce] (? CH -> WB *khwan-* 'strength'); 'curly hair' 鬈 (also quān) [Liji] (Karlgren 1949: 90), 'wriggle' (as snake) 蜷 [Chuci].

⋈ **quān** 棬 (k^hjwän 3) **LH** k^hyɑn, **OCM** *khwan or *khon
'Crooked wood' [Guoce] > 'bowl' made thereof [Meng].
Baxter reconstructs an OC medial r in all the words of *GSR* 226.

[E] Since OC final *-n can have several sources (ST *-l, *-r, *-n, suffix *-n), a TB cognate is difficult to identify: (1) Bodman (1980: 150) relates this wf to WT *khyor* 'a handful' ⋈ *'khyor* 'to warp', or WT *'khor* 'circle. (2) Or note Lushai $k^hɔɔr^R$ 'double up, roll up'. (3) Or Lushai $kual^L$ 'to coil'. (4) Or perh. cognate to Lushai $hrual^H$ 'roll up in the hand'. (5) These could be n-suffixed forms of → gōu$_1$ 句鉤枸區. An allofam is prob. → quán$_4$ 踡.

quán$_4$ 踡 (gjwän 3) **LH** gyɑn, **OCM** *gon ?
'Walk with bent body' [SW], this could be cognate to → quán$_3$ 卷拳 and / or to → gōu$_1$ 句鉤枸區.

quán$_5$ 權 → **quán$_3$** 卷拳

quǎn$_1$ 犬 (k^hiwen^B) **LH** k^huen^B, **OCM** *khwîn?
'Dog' [BI, Shi] > 'official in charge of dogs' [OB].
[T] *Sin Sukchu SR* k'yen (上); *MGZY* khwÿan (上) [k'yEn]
[D] This word survives in Mǐn dialects (Xiàmén k^hian^{B1}), but has been replaced by → gǒu 狗 in most of the others.
[N] A rime MC -iwen cannot derive from OC *-wən (so GSR) or *-un, only from OC *-wên or *-wîn, hence OCM *khwîn?. This is also what we should expect on comparative grounds (so Starostin 1995: 229 *kh^wīn).
[E] ST *kwi? with the addition of the nominal final *-n* in Chinese (§6.4.3; *STC:* 158 n. 428): PTB *kwi? > PTib. *ki* > WT *khyi*, Kanauri *kui 'dog', Chepang *kuy?*; JP gui^{31}; PL *kwe^2 > WB k^hwe^B.

quǎn$_2$ 畎甽 → **xuàn$_1$** 泫

quē 缺 (k^hiwet, k^hjwät) **LH** k^huet, k^hyat, **OCM** *khwet
'To break, splinter' [Shi].
[<] iterative aspiration of → jué$_1$ 決 'cut' (§5.8.3), hence lit. 'cut / break repeatedly > splinter' (Karlgren 1956: 14).

què$_1$ 殼 → **ké** 殼

què$_2$ 闕 → **jŭ$_5$** 柜

qūn 皴 (ts^hjuen, tsjuen^C) **LH** ts(^{h})uin, **OCM** *tsiun
'Hare' [Guoce]; 'marmot' in Sichuan (*GYSX:* 896b) [GY].
[E] ST: PTB *yu(w) ~ *yun > Lushai *sa^L-zu^F* 'rat', *sa^L-zu^L-pui^R* 'hare' (lit. 'big rat'); JP *yu^{55} ~ yun^{33}* 'rat, mouse', WB *yun* 'rabbit' (*STC* no. 93; p. 99 n. 284; p. 158 n. 428); note WT *byi-ba* 'rat, mouse, rabbit' which may also belong. In a few phonetic series and wfs OC *j- and *ts- co-occur (§9.2). Phonologically, the TB etymon is identical to → yòu$_9$ 鼬 'weasel'.

qún 群 (gjuən) **LH** gun, **OCM** *gun
'Be a group, herd' vb. > 'herd, crowd, all' [Shi, Shu].
[T] *Sin Sukchu* 裙 *SR* gyn (平); *MGZY* 裙 kÿun (平) [gyn]; *ONW* gun

※ Perh. **kūn** 昆 (kuən) **LH** kuən, **OCM** kûn
'Numerous, swarming' (insects) [Li].

[E] ST: PTB *m-kul '20' ~ *kun 'all' (*STC* no. 10; 397) > WT *kun* 'all' (so *HST:* 89). → jūn$_4$ 軍 'army' may be related.

R

rán$_1$ 然 (ńźjän) **LH** ńan, **OCM** *nan, OCB *njan
'To burn' 然 [Meng], 燃 [Mo].
[T] *Sin Sukchu SR* rjen (平); *MGZY* Zhen (平) [rɛn]; *ONW* ńan
[D] M-Dōngān *nã*^{A2} 'to take fire accidentally' ⋈ Amoy *nã*$^{C1/C2}$ 'to singe or burn slightly', *hiã*^{A2} 'to burn'.

⋈ **shàn** 煽 (śjän^{C}) **LH** śan^{C}, **OCM** *nhans
'Blaze' > 'splendid' [Shi].
[E] ST: JP *ʃa*^{33}*-nan*^{33} 'torch' (*CVST* 2: 24). An allofam may possibly be → rè 熱 'hot'. Prob. not related to → hàn$_6$ 暵.

rán$_2$ 然 (ńźjän) **LH** ńan, **OCM** *nan — **[T]** *ONW* ńan
'To be like that' [Shi], 'affirm, approve' [Lun]. *Rán* is a fusion of → rú$_1$ 如 with an element *-n which has a demonstrative meaning (§6.4.5), cf. the later → nà$_3$ 那 'that' (Norman 1988: 86). See → rú$_1$ 如 for allofams.

rán$_3$ 呥 → **rèn**$_2$ 荏任

rǎn$_1$ 染 (ńźjäm$^{B/C}$) **LH** ńam$^{B/C}$, **OCM** *namʔ/s
'To dye' [Zhouli], 'to dip' [Zuo]. Acc. to Downer (1959: 277), the tone B form is the verb, tone C a noun 'kind of cloth' [Liji].
[T] *Sin S. SR* rjem (上去); *MGZY* 'em [> rem] (上去) [rɛm]; *ONW* ńam
[E] <> Tai: PTai *ńuɔm^{C2} 'to dye'; Old Sino-Viet. *nhuom* (Pān Wùyún 1987: 31). *HST:* 140 relates this word to WT *ñams-pa* 'be spoiled, stained, tarnished'.

rǎn$_2$ 染 'soft' → **rèn**$_2$ 荏任

ráng 瀼穰 (ńźjaŋ) **LH** ńɑŋ, **OCM** *naŋ
'Rich with dew' > 'rich with grain kernels' 瀼 [Shi]; 'rich in grain, rich' 穰 [Shi].
[E] ST: WB *hnaŋ*^{B} 'dew, fog, mist' (*HST:* 62), Lushai *hnaaŋ*^{R} / *hnaan*^{L} 'thick' (fluid), and / or Lushai *hnɔɔŋ*^{H} / *hnɔɔn*^{L} 'be damp, moist, fat' (Geilich 1994: 254).

rǎng 壤 (ńźjaŋ^{B}) **LH** ńɑŋ^{B}, **OCM** *naŋʔ
'Mould, cultivated soil' [Shu], 'territory' [Meng].
[E] KT: S. *daaŋ*^{B1} < *ʔd- (< *ʔn- ?) 'potash, lye', Li Ngam *ʔnăŋ*^{B1}.

ràng 讓 (ńźjaŋ^{C}) **LH** ńɑŋ^{C}, **OCM** *naŋh
'To concede, yield' [Shi].
[<] exopass. of *ráng*, lit. 'remove oneself' (§4.4).

⋈ **ráng** 攘禳 (ńźjaŋ) **LH** ńɑŋ, **OCM** *naŋ
'To remove, steal, thief' 攘 [Shi] > causative 'to expel, sacrifice to expel evil influence' 禳 [Zuo].

⋈ **xiāng** 襄 (sjaŋ) **LH** siɑŋ, **OCM** *snaŋ
'To remove, expel' [Shi].
[<] causative s-prefix with *ráng* (§5.2.2; Baxter / Sagart 1998: 53).
[E] ST: WT *gnaŋ, gnaŋs* 'to concede'; WB *hnaŋ*^{B} 'to give, deliver over' ⋈ WB *hnaŋ* 'drive away, drive along' (*HST:* 86), Lepcha *nóŋ* 'to go away, go forth, proceed'.

ráo₁ 橈 (ńźjäu) **LH** ńau (from earlier *niau or *nau)
'Oar' [Chuci].
[E] MK: Khmer *thnaol* 'punting pole' < nominal n-infix derivation from *daol* 'to punt'. In CH, the *n-* often survives as a perceived initial (§2.6). For the loss of the coda in CH, see §6.9.

ráo₂ 蕘 (ńźjäu) **LH** ńau, **OCM** *ŋiau or *n(i)au ?
'Herbs for fuel' [Meng], 'fuel gatherer' [Shi].

≍ **shāo** 燒 (śjäu) **LH** śau, tśʰau, **OCM** *ŋhiau or *nh(i)au ?
'To burn' [Li].
[T] *Sin Sukchu SR* ʂjew (平), *PR* ʂjew; *MGZY* shew (平) [ʂɛw];
[D] PWMin *tšʰiau, PEMin *šiau 'roast'.
[<] *ŋiau + caus. devoicing (§5.2.2).

rǎo 擾 → **náo₃** 撓

rè 熱 (ńźjät) **LH** ńat, **OCM** *ŋet or *net OCB *ŋjet (i.e. OCM ŋet)
'Hot' [Shi].
[T] *Sin Sukchu SR* rje (入); *MGZY* Zhÿa (入) [rje]; *ONW* ńat
[D] PMin *niɑt ~ *jiat
[E] The relationship with → ruò₆ 爇, if any, is not clear because of the difference in vowels, although these words are often considered cognate (so Karlgren 1956: 16). CH -> Tai: S. *ɗiat*[DIL] 'to boil (a liquid), be boiling (mad)' (Li F. 1976: 42). *Rè* has the same initial in Tai as the loan *rì* 'sun'.

rén₁ 人 (ńźjen) **LH** ńin, **OCM** *nin
'Human being, person, man' [OB, Shi] > 'other persons, someone' [Shi]. *Rén* tends to refer to a member of a clan, i.e. upper class (Gassmann *JAOS* 120.3, 2000: 348ff).
[T] *Sin Sukchu SR* rin (平); *MGZY* Zhin (平) [rin]; *ONW* ńin
[E] Etymology not certain. The TB root *mi 'human being' occurs in → mín₁ 民 'people'. There are several possible etymologies for *rén:*

(1) It may possibly be the same etymon as → rén₂ 仁 (≍ PTB *niŋ 'heart, mind'), thus literally 'having a mind'; for a semantic parallel note Tib. *sems-čan* 'having a mind, living creature' (also Latin *animal* < *animus* 'breath, spirit'). But this is rather speculative.

(2) More likely, *rén* is related to PMK *ɲah, LitMon *ñaḥ* 'people' (of either sex) [Diffloth 1984: 13f], Mod. Khmer *neǝ̌ʔ* 'specifier for ordinary persons', with fronted vowel in OC (§11.5.2) and the addition of the nominal n-suffix (§6.4.3), just as in *mín* 民. The Shang dynasty fought wars against eastern AA enemies who are called *rén* 人. It is tempting to consider this their auto-ethnonym ('human beings') (Sagart 1999: 163 who relates *rén* to WT *ñe-n* 'kinsman', though).

rén₂ 仁 (ńźjen) **LH** ńin, **OCM** *nin
'Be kind, good' [Shi, Shu], '*qīn* 親 to love' [*SWJZGL* 3471], 'kind, gentle, humane' (A. Waley) and similar translations [Lunyu, Meng]; 'pit' (i.e. 'heart'), e.g. of an apricot *xìng-rén* 杏仁 [Běncǎo; Yánshì jiāxùn, 6th cent. AD] (Baxter p.c.).
[E] The word's old graph 忎 (*qiān* 千 *tshîn < *snhîn as phonetic; Boodberg 1937: 338; in the Guōdiàn texts written with *shēn* 身 instead of *qiān* above *xīn* 心 'heart'), and its *SW* gloss *qīn*, suggest that its association with → rén₁ 人 'human being' is relatively late (Mengzi) (Pulleyblank 1995: 183; Baxter p. c. 2001); later it acquired the usual interpretation as lit. 'act like a human being' (Gassmann *JAOS* 120.3, 2000: 357).

[E] ST: PTB *s-niŋ (*STC* no. 367) > PTib. *s-niŋ > WT *sñiŋ* 'heart, mind', *sñiŋ-rje* 'kindness, mercy, compassion', *sñiŋ-po* 'chief part, main substance, quintessence' (e.g. of cream of milk, soft part of a loaf, wick of a lamp) ꭗ *ñiŋ* 'pith, essence' (W. Baxter, p. c. 2001); Kanauri *sniŋ > *stiŋ* 'heart'; PLB *s-nik ~ *s-niŋ ꭗ *s-ni 'heart' > WB *hnac-lum*^{B}, Limbu *niŋ* 'mind' (*HST;* Shī Xiàngdōng 2000: 205).

Possible allofams are → shēn$_2$ 身 'body', → qīn$_5$ 親 'to love, relative', but see there. The TB items are sometimes thought cognate to → níng$_1$ 寧 'be at peace'.

rén$_3$ 仁 'pit' → **rén$_2$** 仁

rén$_4$ 任 (ńźjəm) **LH** ńim, **OCM** *nəm

'Carry on the shoulder, to load' [Shi] > 'sustain, endure' [Zuo].

ꭗ **rèn** 任 (ńźjəm^C) **LH** ńim^C, **OCM** *nəms

'Burden (of office)' > 'charge, office' [Shu]; 'be burdened, pregnant' 妊 [SW]; 'be burdened, entrust' 任 [Zuo].

[<] exopass. of *rén*, lit. 'being loaded, be burdened' (Wáng Lì 1982: 611) > 'entrust, pregnant'. 'Pregnant' is hardly cogn. to its syn. → yùn$_1$ 孕 'pregnant'; a semantic parallel 'bear' > 'pregnant' is → pēi$_1$ 胚, also found in many other languages, including English.

[T] *Sin Sukchu SR* rim (去), *PR*, *LR* rin; *MGZY* Zhim (去) [rim]

[E] ST: WT *snom-pa, bsnams* 'to take, seize, hold, put on'. This etymon may have enjoyed wider distribution, note PKS *ṇam^1 'to hold', and AA-OKhmer *nāṃ* [nam] 'to carry, convey, transport'. See also comment under → rěn$_3$ 稔.

rén$_5$ 紝 (ńźjəm, ṇjəm) **LH** ńim, ṇim, **OCM** *nim, nrim ?

'To weave' [Zuo].

[E] KT, AN: PKS *tam^3 'to weave', PTai *tam^{B1}; AN *anem*, IN *añam* 'plait' (Benedict *AT:* 98; Sagart *JCL* 21.1, 1993: 48). Curiously, the CH word is phonetically closest to AN which is farthest afield (this also is the case with 'needle' → zān 簪).

rěn$_1$ 忍 (ńźjen^B) **LH** ńɨn^B, **OCM** *nənʔ.

'To endure' [Guoyu].

[T] *ONW* ńin — [D] PMin *niun^B ~ nin^B

[E] ST: WT *ñan-pa* 'to be able, (not) be able'.

rěn$_2$ 忍 (ńźjen^B) **LH** ńɨn^B, **OCM** *nənʔ.

'Be cruel' [Shi]. — [E] ST: WT *gñan-pa* 'cruel, fierce, severe'.

rěn$_3$ 稔 (ńźjəm^B) **LH** ńim^B, **OCM** *nəmʔ

'Year' [Zuo]. Later 'ripe' (of cereal etc.) [SW], 'harvest' [Hanshu].

[E] AA: PMonic *cnaam 'year', Mon *hnam*, Khmer *cnam*, PVM *c-n-əm 'year' [Ferlus], PNBahn. *hanăm*, PSBahn. *sənam, Pear *nim*, Wa-Lawa-Bulang *nɤm (Benedict *MKS* 18–19, 1992: 9). The AA word is perh. derived from a root 'to (trans-)plant' (Ferlus, Diffloth). AA -> TB-JP *lə^{33}-nam^{33}* 'rainy season' (*CVST* 2: 31), Lepcha *nam* 'year'. AA -> Saek (Tai lg.) *ɲaam^4* (A1) 'season'.

The word's earliest occurrences in *Zuǒzhuàn* in stock expressions like 'not lasting (more than) five years' give the impression of a relict from a substrate, rather than being part of the active language (similar to AA → huāng$_1$ 㠩 'blood'). The AA sources do not mean 'harvest' or 'ripe'; therefore it seems that AA 'year' and → rén$_4$ 任 *nəm (basic notion: 'burden, carry, bear') have converged during the Han period (ears of grain 'bearing' > 'ripe, harvest') [SW, Hanshu], perh. with additional interference from → rèn$_2$ 荏任 'soft' > 'cooked' and → nián 年 'year, harvest'. *Rěn* has perh.

tone B because it was felt to be an endoactive derivation (§4.5.1) from 'soft / heavy'.

rěn₄ 腍 → **rèn₂** 荏任

rěn₅ 涊 → **niǎn₃**, **rěn** 涊

rèn₁, rěn 荏 (ńźjəm^B) **LH** ńim^B, **OCM** *nəmʔ
'A kind of big bean' [Shi].
[E] ST: WB *ñam* 'leguminous plant'. On the other hand, Bodman and Wáng Lì (1982: 611) believe that the following is a variant, both from an original *num (a nearly identical pair also means 'great'):

ꭓ **róng** 茙 (ńźjuŋ) **LH** ńuŋ, **OCM** *nuŋ
'A kind of bean' [Lie].

rèn₂ 荏任 (ńźjəm^B) **LH** ńim^B, **OCM** *nəmʔ
'Soft' [Shi] > 'flexible, insinuating, artful' [Shu]; 'cooked' 腍 [Li], 'overcooked' 飪 [Lun].

ꭓ **rǎn** 染 (ńźjäm^B/C) **LH** ńam^B/C, **OCM** *namʔ/s — **[T]** *ONW* ńam
'Soft, flexible' [Shi].

ꭓ **rán** 呥 (ńźjäm) **LH** ńam, **OCM** *nam
'To chew' [Xun] is perh. related (< 'make soft').

[E] ST, area word: PTB *nyam (*HPTB:* 299) > WB *ńam^C* 'soft, fine, delicate'; Lushai *neem^H < neem* 'soft, yielding, weak' ꭓ *hneem^L / hnem^F < hneemh (< hneems) / hneemʔ* 'to comfort, soften, soothe' (*HST:* 136; *CVST* 2: 32); Garo *nomʔ* 'soft' [Joseph / Burling, *LTBA* 24.2: 47]. The vowel of Mru *nüm* 'soft' (Löffler 1966: 144) seems aberrant. Note also AA: Khmu *hɲjim*, PPal. *jəm*, Riang *kcəm* 'soft'; Khmer *'andāṃ* /ʔɑntoəm/ 'to chew' ꭓ OKhmer *dāṃ* [dam] 'to pound, batter...'. <> Tai: S. *nim³* 'plump, supple, pliant', *num³* 'soft, flabby, springy'. Syn. → róu₁ 柔 and other words with OC initial *n-.

rèn₃ 恁 → **niàn₁** 念

rèn₄ 妊任 → **rén₄** 任

rèn₅ 飪 → **rèn₂** 荏任

rèn₆ 腍 → **rèn₂** 荏任

rèn₇ 認 (ńźjen^C) **LH** ńɨn^C, **OCM** *nəns, i.e. perh. *niəm
'To know' [Guanyin].
[T] *Sin Sukchu SR* rin (去); *MGZY* Zhin (去) [rin] — **[D]** PMin *nin^C
[E] ST: JP *non⁵⁵* '認為, 以為 to think, consider' (*CVST* 2: 116), WT *gñan-pa* 'to listen'.

réng 仍 (ńźjəŋ) **LH** ńɨŋ, **OCM** *nəŋ
'Be done repeatedly, as before' [Shi, Lunyu].
[<] terminative derivation from → èr₁ 二 *nis 'two' (§6.5.1), lit. 'gotten to be done twice / again'. Alternatively, the word could be related to PTB *(s-)naŋ 'follow' (*STC* no. 334; p. 160 n. 432).

rì 日 (ńźjet) **LH** ńit, **OCM** *nit
'Sun' > 'day' (not night), '24 hr. period' [BI, Shi] > 'sun as spirit' [OB]; also MC *ńźi^C* (Unger *Hao-ku* 39, 1992: 88).
[T] *Sin Sukchu SR* ri (入); *MGZY* Zhi (入) [ri]; *ONW* ńit
[D] Y-Guǎngzhōu *jit^D2-tɐu^A2* 熱頭, Táishān *ŋgit^D2-heu^A2* 日頭 'sun'; PMin *nit 'sun'; in most Mand. dialects replaced by *tàiyáng* 太陽.

[E] ST: TB *nyiy > OTib. *gñi*, WT *ñi-ma* 'sun', *ñin (-mo)* 'day'; WB *ne* 'sun', *ne*^{C} 'day', PL *(?-) ne^1 'sun', (?-)ne^3 'day'; Lushai *ni*^{H} < *nii* 'sun, day'. CH -> Tai: S. *dɛɛt*^{DIL} 'sunlight' (Li F. 1976: 42).

róng$_1$ 容 (jiwoŋ) **LH** joŋ, **OCM** *loŋ
'Be generous, indulge' [Shi, Shu], 'at ease, easy' [Lunyu], 'pleased' [Meng].
[T] *Sin Sukchu SR* juŋ (平); *MGZY* yÿung (平) [juŋ]; *ONW* iuoŋ
[E] ST: WT *loŋ* 'leisure, free time' (Coblin 1986: 102), it also occurs in Tai: S. *loŋ*^{B2} ~ *looŋ*^{B2} 'feel at ease'. This word is perh. a ST-level allofam of → yú$_{17}$ 愉: *lo + ŋ (§6.5.2).

róng$_2$ 容 (jiwoŋ) **LH** joŋ, **OCM** *loŋ (or *joŋ ?) — [T] *ONW* iuoŋ
'To contain, hold' [Shi] is prob. related to WT *luŋ* ('a holder':) 'a strap, handle' and may belong to → yǒng$_3$ 甬 'suspension ring'.

róng$_3$ 溶 (jiwoŋ) **LH** joŋ, **OCM** *loŋ
'Much water' [Chuci].

ꭗ **yǒng** 涌湧 (jiwoŋ^B) **LH** joŋ^B, **OCM** *loŋʔ — [D] M-Amoy col. *yiŋ*^{B} 'wave'
'To bubble up, gush forth' (as spring) 涌 [Gongyang], 湧 [Lü].

ꭗ **xiōng** 洶 (xjwoŋ[^{B}]) **LH** hɨoŋ(^{B}), **OCM** *-oŋ(ʔ)
'To rush (as water)' [Chuci]. — Related?

[E] Area etymon. ST: WT *loŋ-pa, loŋs* 'rise up' (of water), *loŋ-loŋ* 'uprising in waves, bulging out' (Bodman 1980: 101; *HST:* 126) ꭗ *kloŋ* 'wave' (WT prob. is not related to → làng 浪 'wave'). <> AA: Khmer /rlóoŋ/ 'to rise, mount, well up' (of water, tears) ꭗ *ghloṅa* /klóoŋ/ 'rising movements of waves', acc. to Jenner / Pou (1982: 332) derivatives from the root under → sōng$_2$ 崧嵩 'high'.

This wf is prob. connected with → hóng$_4$ 洪 'great (waters)'. It may ultimately belong to → yǒng$_4$ 踊 'to jump, leap'.

róng$_4$ 融 (jiuŋ) **LH** juŋ, **OCM** *luŋ — [T] *ONW* iuŋ
'Hot air, steam, heat' [Zuo].
[E] ST: PL *ʔ-loŋ^1 'hot', WB *loŋ* 'burn, scald', *ə-loŋ* 'the burning of fire'. Possibly, this word may be a variant of the ST root *lum → xín 燖尋 (so Bodman 1980: 124).

ꭗ **chóng** 蟲 (ḍjuŋ, duoŋ) **LH** ḍuŋ, douŋ, **OCM** *d-luŋ, *lûŋ
'Hot weather' [Shi].

róng$_5$ 戎 (ńźjuŋ) **LH** ńuŋ, **OCM** *nuŋ
'You' [Shi].
[T] *Sin Sukchu SR* rjuŋ (平); *PR* ruŋ; *MGZY* Zhÿung (平) [rjuŋ]; *ONW* ńuŋ
[E] The etymology is obscure. One possibility would be to invoke the rare (and doubtful) equation PTB *a = OC *u and thus connect *róng* with PTB *naːŋ 'you' (so *STC:* 160 n. 432; see under → rǔ$_2$ 汝) (§11.9.3). Alternatively, this pronoun could be related to → nóng 農 'farmer', just as *nóng* functions as the first person pronoun in Mǐn dialects. But these are speculations.

róng$_6$ 茙 → **rèn$_1$, rěn** 荏

róng$_7$ 嶸 → **jiǒng$_2$** 泂迥

róng$_8$ 榮 → **yíng$_3$** 熒

róng$_9$-guàn 榮觀 'imperial palace' → **yíng$_4$** 營

rǒng 氄 → **nóng$_4$** 穠

róu₁ 柔 (ńźjəu) **LH** ńu, **OCM** *nu
'Flexible, soft, mild, gentle' [Shi].

⋙ **ròu** 揉 (ńźjəu^C) **LH** ńu^C, **OCM** *nuh — **[T]** *ONW* ńu
'To make pliable, subdue, tranquilize' [Shi].
[<] exoactive / caus. of *róu* 柔 (§4.3.2).

[E] ST: JP *nu*^33 'relaxed, slack' (e.g. rope) ⋙ *nu*^31 'relax' (effort, attention); perh. also WT *ñug-pa* 'to rub, stroke, caress, besmear' (*HST:* 136), Lushai *nɔɔk*^H 'rub against, loll against'. This stem OCM *nu is prob. a ST variant of the synonymous stem OCM *no (→ rú₄ 懦臑).

[C] An allofam is → ròu₁ 肉 'flesh, meat'.
Pulleyblank (1973: 121) has pointed out that there are many words with initial *n but different rimes which mean 'soft, weak', including: → rú₄ 懦臑, → rù₃ 茹, → ruǎn 耎軟, → ruò₅ 弱; in addition to Pullayblank: → rèn₂ 荏任. Syn. → xuān₂ 暖.

róu₂ 蹂 (nźjəu[^B/^C]) **LH** ńu(^B/^C), **OCM** *nu(ʔ/h)
'Tread, trample' [Shi].
[E] Perh. ST: TB-Lushai *hnu*^F < *hnuuʔ* 'footprint' (*CVST* 2: 43). For a semantic parallel trample ~ footprint, see → jí₁₅ 蹐; → niè₇ 躡.

ròu₁ 肉 (ńźjuk) **LH** ńuk, **OCM** *nuk
'Flesh, meat' [Yi].
[T] *Sin Sukchu SR* ru (入), *LR* ruʔ; *MGZY* Zhÿu (入) [ry]; *ONW* ńuk

⋙ **rù** 肉 (ńźjəu^C) **LH** ńu^C, **OCM** *nukh
(Fleshy:) 'rich' (of music) [Li] (Downer 1959: 281).
[<] a late general purpose tone C derivation (§3.5).
[E] Wáng Lì (1982: 236) includes 肉 in the wf → róu₁ 柔 'soft' which is the most likely etymology. Other languages have an etymon *na: Tai: S. *nɨa*^C2 < *n- 'flesh, meat' (cogn. acc. to Li F. 1976: 42), also KN-Khami *na* 'meat, flesh'. Possibly *ròu* is the result of convergence and re-etymologization. See → róu₁ 柔 for possible additional allofams.

ròu₂ 揉 → **róu₁** 柔

rú₁ 如 (ńźjwo, ńźjwo^C [GY]) **LH** ńɑ(^C), **OCM** *na(h)
'Be like, as if' [Shi]. The alternate MC reading *ńźjwo^C* is not only reported in *GY*, but is also required by *Shījīng* rimes (Unger *Hao-ku* 22, 1983). Acc. to Downer (1959: 287), the tone C reading belongs to the meaning 'be as good as' [Zuo].
[T] *Sin Sukchu SR* ry (平); *MGZY* Zhÿu (平) [ry]; *ONW* ńo > ńø
[E] ST: Mru *na* 'be so', KN-Khami *na* (Awa) 'be so', in Lushai in the expression *na naa naa* 'it being so, since'. The word has perh. a wider distribution: AA-OMon *ñaṅ* /ɲɔŋ/ 'resembling, be like' (loan from TB?).
[C] Allofams: → ér₂ 而, → ěr₄ 爾, → nài₂ 奈, → nuò₂ 諾, → rán₂ 然, → ruò₁ 若.

rú₂ 如 (ńźjwo) **LH** ńɑ, **OCM** *na
'To go to, proceed to' [Zuo] may belong to the area root meaning 'facing, toward' → xiàng₁ 向嚮卿.

rú₃ 茹 (ńźjwo^B/^C) **LH** ńɑ^B/^C, **OCM** *naʔ/h
'To swallow' [Shi, EY].
[D] Acc. to FY 7.27 a Wú-Yuè (i.e. ancient Zhèjiāng-Fújiàn) dialect word for 'to eat', still current in M-Xiàmén *lu*^A2 'to eat'.
[E] AA: PVM *s-ɲaːʔ 'to chew, masticate' [Ferlus]; Kharia *ɲoʔ* 'to eat'. AA -> PMY:

*naʔ[7] 'to swallow'. The AA etymon seems to have been absorbed through MY.

A similar-looking word is → xiū$_4$ 羞 'nourish'. Related may be the items under → xiǎng$_2$ 饟餉. The graph 茹 writes additional words *rù*.

rú$_4$ 懦臑 (ńźju) **LH** ńo, **OCM** *no

'Weak, timid' 懦 [Xun]; 'pliant, soft' 臑 [Xun].

[E] ST: PTB *now 'tender, soft' (*STC* no. 274) > PL *C-nu², WB *nu^C* < *no^C* 'young, tender' ※ *nu^B* 'be made soft' ※ *hnu^B* 'make soft, mollify', Lushai *no^R* < *nooʔ* 'young, tender, soft, young of animals'. This stem OCM *no is prob. a variant of the synonymous stem OCM *nu (→ róu$_1$ 柔).

※ **rú** 孺 (ńźju^C) **LH** ńo^C, **OCM** *noh — **[T]** *ONW* ńuo

'Child' [Shu]. *Rú* has an unexpected Mand. tone, Pulleyblank (1991: 268) sets up competing variants in tone A and C for the Yuan period. In the meaning 'child', *rú* occurs in OC usually (always?) as an adjective to *zǐ* 子 'child', hence the phrase means literally 'weak child', therefore *rú* is a derivation from *rú* 懦 above, perh. even the same word.

In late Zhanguo texts [Hanfei, Li] *rú-rén* 孺人 and *rú-zǐ* 孺子 is the term for the 'wife' of a low nobleman (大夫).

[C] Cognates are → xū$_4$ 須需 'wait, tarry', → ruǎn 耎軟 'soft'; perh. also → rǔ$_3$ 乳 'female breast', → ruò$_5$ 弱 'weak', → rú$_5$ 濡 'moisten'.

rú$_5$ 濡 (ńźju) **LH** ńo, **OCM** *no

'To moisten, wet, glossy' [Shi], 'soak' [Zuo].

※ **rǔ**, **ruán** 擩 (ńźjwät) **LH** ńuat, **OCM** *not

'Dip, soak' [Yili] (Pulleyblank *JCL* 21.2, 1994: 367) < *rú* 濡 (ńźju) + final t (§6.2.2).

※ **rù** 溽 (ńźjwok) **LH** ńok, **OCM** *nok

'Moist' (soil), 'rich-tasting' [Li].

[<] *rú* 濡 (ńźju) + final *-k* (§6.1).

[C] Perh. related to → rú$_4$ 懦臑 'soft', originally 'soften by soaking'; → nóng$_3$ 濃醲.

rú$_6$ 孺 → **rú$_4$** 懦臑

rú$_7$-ér 嚅唲, 儒兒 → **ér$_5$** 唲

rú$_8$ 醹 → **nóng$_3$** 濃醲

rǔ$_1$ 汝 (ńźjwo^B) **LH** ńɑ^B, **OCM** *naʔ — **[T]** *ONW* ńo^B > ńø^B

Rǔ is the name of at least two rivers, one a northern tributary of the Huái in southern Henan, the other of the Hàn river. Both were once in the non-Chinese sphere of the ancient state of Chǔ and its neighbors. The Chǔ ruling clan Xióng 熊 ('bear') had the name *mǐ* 芈 'bear' which points to a KT presence (KT *mui* 'bear'). It may therefore possibly be more than a coincidence that the KS word for 'water' is *ʔnja^A or *k-nja^A.

rǔ$_2$ 汝 (ńźjwo^B) **LH** ńɑ^B, **OCM** *naʔ

'You' [BI, Shi], an independent pronoun (§3.3.3). This word survives in col. coastal Mǐn: Xiàmén *li^B*, Fúzhōu *ny^B* (Norman 1988: 234), while most dialects have forms which go back to → ěr$_5$ 爾. G-Wǔníng *ŋjɛ^{A2}* 'you' (Sagart 1993: 173) does not agree in tone.

[E] ST: PTB *na ~ *naŋ 'you' (*STC* no. 407) > Chepang *naŋ* 'you' (sing.), PL *naŋ, WB *naŋ* 'you', *naŋ^C* 'you, your'; JP *naʔ^{55}* 'your', *naŋ^{33}* 'you' (*HST:* 163), Lushai *naŋ^R* < *naŋʔ*. For the finals, see §3.2.4.

ⱬ **nǎi** 乃 (nậiB) **LH** nəB, **OCM** *nə̂ʔ — **[T]** *ONW* nɑiB
'Your' possessive [BI, Shi] is a proclitic (unstressed) form of *rǔ* 汝 'you' (see §3.3.3). Allofam may be → ruò₂ 若; parallel stems or synonyms → ér₃ 而, → ěr₅ 爾 and its col. variant → nǐ₁ 你 'you'; → róng₅ 戎.

rǔ₃ 乳 (ńźjuB) **LH** ńoB, **OCM** *noʔ
'Nipple, breast' [Zhouli], 'milk, suckle' [Zuo] > 'breed, raise' [Lü] > 'hatch' [Li].
[T] *Sin Sukchu SR* ry (上); *MGZY* Zhÿu (上) [ry]; *ONW* ńuoB
[E] The OC vowel *o, as in *noʔ, often corresponds to foreign *u in open syllables (§11.9.1). On the other hand, *noʔ also looks like a regular endoactive derivation (§4.5.1) from → rú₄ 懦臑 *no 'soft', lit. 'the thing that is soft', a possible re-etymologization of the area word.

ⱬ **nòu, gòu** 穀 (nəuC) **LH** noC, **OCM** *nôh
'To suckle' [Zuo] is a Chǔ dial. word acc. to *Zuǒzhuàn*. The reading *nòu* is either simply a derivation from rǔ *noʔ (Pulleyblank 1983: 427); or more directly from an AA source where the etymon means 'drink, suckle' (see below).

[E] ST: PTB *nuw ~ *now (*STC* no. 419) > WT *nu-ma* 'breast' ⱬ *nu-ba* 'to suck' ⱬ *nud-pa* 'to suckle', Tsangla *nu* 'milk', Lushai *hnuL-teR* < *hnuʔ/h* 'breast, milk' ⱬ *nuF* < *nuuʔ* 'mother, married woman', PLB *no³, WB *nuiC*; JP *nu⁵¹* 'mother, mother's sister', etc. (*CVST* 2:38), JP *gə³¹-nu³¹* 'mother'. <> Perh. an area word: AA-Kharia, Mundari *nunu* 'female breast' ⱬ Mundari *nu* 'to drink', Wa-Lawa-Bulang *ɲɨʔ, PVM *ɲuːʔ 'drink'. AA may be the ultimate source of this word because it is the common word for 'drink' whereas the meanings in ST are specialized. Some TB languages indicate that the protoform was prob. *nuwʔ.
[C] Perh. cognate to → xū₆ 媭 *sno 'elder sister'; → ā-nú 阿奴 'younger brother'.

rǔ₄ 擩 → **rú₅** 濡

rǔ, rù 辱 → **xiū₃** 羞

rù₁ 入 (ńźjəp) **LH** ńip, **OCM** *nəp < *nup
'To enter, to set' (e.g. sun) [OB, Shi].
[T] *Sin S. SR* ri (入), *PR*, *LR* ryʔ; *MGZY* Zhi (入) [ri]; *ONW* ńip
[D] The expected Mand. reading *rì* is avoided for taboo reasons. PMin *nip

ⱬ **nèi** 内 (nuậiC) **LH** nuəs (> nuəis), **OCM** *nûts < PCH *nups, OCB *nups
'Inside' [BI, Shi].
[T] *Sin Sukchu SR* nuj (去), *LR* nuj; *MGZY* nue (去) [nuɛ]; *ONW* nuɑi
[<] exopass. of *nà* 納 below (§4.4)

ⱬ **nà** 納 (nập) **LH** nəp, **OCM** *nəp < *nûp — **[T]** *Sin Sukchu SR* na (入); *ONW* nɑp
'To bring inside, put into' [BI, Shi].

[E] ST: PTB *nup (*STC* no. 400) > WT *nub-pa* 'to fall, sink, set' (e.g. sun) ⱬ *nub* 'west' ⱬ *snub-pa* 'cause to perish, suppress'; Garo *nap*, Bodo *hap* < *hnup* (< **sn-?) 'to enter, set (sun), sink, drown' (Bodman 1980: 52).

rù₂ 茹 (ńźjwoC) **LH** ńɑC, **OCM** *nah
'To examine, scrutinize' [Shi].
[E] ST: WT *mno-ba* 'to think, imagine, think upon, consider'; JP *na⁵⁵* 'to feel, be aware, conscious of' (*CVST* 2: 18).

rù₃ 茹 (ńźjwoB) **LH** ńɑB, **OCM** *naʔ
'Soft' [Chuci] looks like a Chǔ dialect variant of *ròu* 揉 (under → róu₁ 柔). Alterna-

tively, it may actually belong to → rú$_3$ 茹 'swallow, eat' as 'eat' > 'chew' and 'soft' are closely related notions, see → rèn$_2$ 荏任. For potential allofams, see → róu$_1$ 柔.

rù$_4$ 洳 (ńźjwo[C]) **LH** ńɑ(C), **OCM** *na(h)
'Marsh' [Shi].
[E] ST: WT *na* 'meadow' (*HST:* 107), *na-k^{h}a* 'upland moor' in NE Tibet (Albert Tafel, *Meine Tibetreise*, Stuttgart etc. 1914: 210). Prob. an area word: MK-PWa *ʔnɐŋ 'marsh' (for finals see §3.2.4 – CH loan?). <> PAN *-na 'low-lying / easily flooded ground'; Tai-Kadai *na* 'wet rice field' -> TB-JP *na^{31}* 'wet field' (Peiros / Starostin *CAAAL* 22, 1984: 125; Sagart ms. 2002: 14).

rù$_5$ 辱 → **xiū$_3$** 羞

rù$_6$ 溽 → **rú$_5$** 濡

ruán 擩 → **rú$_5$** 濡

ruǎn 耎軟 (ńźjwän^B) **LH** ńuan^B, **OCM** *nonʔ
'Soft, weak' [Guoce], 'weak, timid' 懦 [Zuo].
[T] *Sin Sukchu SR* ryen (上); *MGZY* Zhwÿan (上) [ryɛn]
[E] ST: WB *nwai* 'stretch along' ⋈ *nwai^C* 'bend flexibly' ⋈ *hnwai^C* 'bend flexibly' ⋈ *hnwai^B* 'procrastinate', Lushai *nuai^H* 'rub'. WB final *-i* and MC *nuâ^C* ~ *nuân^C* can be reconciled if we assume an original ST *nwal. -> Old Sino-Viet. *nhuyen* (Pān Wùyún 1987: 30).

⋈ **nuàn** 偄 (nuân^C) **LH** nuɑn^C, **OCM** *nôns
'Weak' [Xun], 'weak, timid' 懦 [Zuo]. A variant reading MC *nuâ^C* points to an earlier final *l.

[C] Cognate to → rú$_4$ 懦臑; possibly also to → róu$_1$ 柔, → nèn, nùn 嫩.

ruí 蕤緌 → **ruǐ** 縈蕊

ruǐ 縈蕊 (ńźwie^B, ńźnwi^B) **LH** ńuai^B, ńui^B, **OCM** *noiʔ, *nuiʔ
'Hang down' (as jade pendent from belt) 縈 [Zuo], 'ovary of flower, fruit' 蕊 [Chuci].

⋈ **ruí** 蕤緌 (ńźwi) **LH** ńui, **OCM** *nui
'Hanging bands' (of a cap) 蕤 [Li], 'tassel' 緌 [SW: Shi], 'pennon' 緌 [Li].

[E] ST: WB *nwai* 'stretch along, as a creeper'; JP *nói* 'suspend, hang' ⋈ *ʔənōi* 'hang onto' [notations of *HPTB:* 215]; possibly WT *nar-mo* 'oblong' ⋈ *bsnar-ba* 'to extend in length, pull out' from TB *nwar could belong here. Perh. also connected with AA: OMon *jnor* ~ *jnow* 'hanging banner' with the nominalizing n-infix. *HPTB* considers the TB items under → chuí$_1$ 垂 cognate; further comparanda are → duǒ$_2$ 朵, → wěi$_2$ 委.

ruì 枘 (ńźjwäi^C) **LH** ńuai^C, **OCM** *nots
'Peg, pin, tenon' [Zhuang].
[E] AA: Khmer *tnota* /tnaaot/ 'impaling pole, skewer, spit' < *ṭota* /daaot/ 'to impale, run into...'

rùn 閏 (ńźjuen^C) **LH** ńuin^C, **OCM** *nuns (*mnuns ?)
'Intercalary month' [Shu]. — Etymology unknown.

ruò$_1$ 若 (ńźjak, GY also ńźja^B) **LH** ńɑk, **OCM** *nak
(Perhaps: 'Of all possible cases, the one like this':) 'like this, such, if' [BI, Shu] > as a full vb. 'to agree, approve' [OB, BI, Shu].
[T] *Sin Sukchu SR* rjaw (入), *LR* rjawʔ; *MGZY* Zhew (入) [rɛw]; *ONW* ńak, ńa
[<] *ruò* is derived from *rú* 如 with the distributive suffix *-k (see §6.1.2).

✱ **nuò** 諾 (nâk) **LH** nɑk, **OCM** *nâk — **[T]** *ONW* nɑk
'To agree, say yes' [Shi]. For the MC div. I, see §9.1.1.
[C] See → $rú_1$ 如 for allofams.

$ruò_2$ 若 (ńźjak) **LH** ńɑk, **OCM** *nak
'You' [Yili]. Acc. to *GY* the reading for this graph with the meaning 'you' is with final *-k, not tone B which is an alternate reading, a homophone of *rŭ* 汝 'you'. Since tone B belongs to the root and goes back to ST, the final *-k* may here be a phonological variant (§3.2.2), perh. inspired by the distributive k-suffix in the homophone → $ruò_2$ 若. Allofams are listed under → $rŭ_2$ 汝.

$ruò_3$ 若 'that' → **$nà_3$** 那

$ruò_4$ 箬 (ńźjak) **LH** ńɑk
A Han period Chŭ dialect word meaning 'bamboo skin' [SW], today *ruò-lì* 箬笠 'hat made of bamboo leaves'; the basic meaning seems to have been 'leaf' which is still current in Mĭn dialects: PMin *ṇiɔk (Norman 1983: 205).
[E] ST: PTB *s-nas (*HPTB:* 432) > Tiddim Chin *naʔ* 'leaf', Lushai *hnaʔ*[L].

$ruò_5$ 弱 (ńźjak) **LH** ńɑk, **OCM** *n(i)auk ?
'Weak > consider weak, despise' [Shu], 'young, tender' [Zuo].
[T] *Sin Sukchu SR* rjaw (入), *LR* rjawʔ; *MGZY* Zhew (入) [rɛw]; *ONW* ńak
[E] ST: WT *ñog-ñoŋ* 'soft, tender, weak'. For possible allofams, see → $róu_1$ 柔.

$ruò_6$ 爇 (ńźjwät) **LH** ńuat, **OCM** *ŋiot or *not ?
'To burn' 爇 [Zuo], 'hot, burn' 焫 [Li] (also MC *ńźjwäi*[C]).
[E] Most likely, this is a final *-t* derivation (§6.2.2) from a ST root *nwe: WB *nwe*[B], *hnwe*[B] 'warm', Lai *nwê* 'be warm' [Van Bik *LTBA* 25.2, 2002: 107]; or, less likely, from → $ráo_2$ 蕘 'fuel'. There are parallels for the medial-vowel metathesis, see → něi 餒, → shuāi 衰. For the *n-* ~ *ŋ-* vacilation in the initial, see §5.12.1. Since *ruò* is apparently related to → nuăn 煖 *non 'warm', its relationship to → rè 熱 *ŋet or *net (?) 'hot', if any, is not clear. Wáng Lì (1982: 494) relates *ruò* to → $rán_1$ 然 'burn'.

S

sā, **sǎ** 撒 → **sǎn**$_1$ 散

sǎ$_1$, **shǎi** 洒 → **shāi**, **shī** 篩

sǎ$_2$ 灑 → **shī**$_{12}$ 釃

sà 颯 → **qī**$_2$ 咠

sāi 思 (sɨ, sậi) 'bearded' or 'white-haired' [Zuo] is an allofam of → ér$_1$ 而 'whiskers' acc. to Pulleyblank. *Sāi* 腮 'jaw' is perh. the same word.

sài, **sāi**, **sè** 塞 (sək, sậi^{C}) **LH** sək, sə^{C}, **OCM** *sə̂k(h) — **[T]** *ONW* sək, sɑi
'To stop up, block; a mountain pass' [Shi]. Downer (1959: 275) determined that the verb had the reading MC *sək*, the noun tone C MC *sậi*^{C} in *Zuǒzhuàn.*
[E] Etymology not clear; prob. connected with AA-Khmer *suka* /sok/ 'to stop up, block, cram...' ꭗ *cuka* /cok/ 'to stop up, plug, block, obstruct...', but the vowels do not agree (§11.10.5). Based on his theories on OC phonology, Pulleyblank (*EC* 16, 1991: 50) believes that *sài* is cognate to WT *sub-pa* 'to stop up'.

sān 三 (sâm) **LH** sɑm, **OCM** *sə̂m
'Three' [OB, Shi]. The LH, MC vowels are irregular, one should expect MC ậ.
[T] *Sin S. SR* sam (平), *PR* san; *MGZY* sam (平) [sam]; *ONW* sɑm.
[D] PMin *sam; Y-Guǎngzhōu ^{55}*sam*^{A1}
[E] ST: PTB *sum > WT *sum* 'three' (in compositions); JP *mə*^{31}*-sum*^{33}, WB *sum*^{C}, Lushai *t*^{h}*um*^{H}. <> Tai: S. *saam*^{A1} is obviously a CH loan (Tai would have preserved an original vowel *u).

ꭗ **sān** 慘 → **sōu**$_5$ 慘

ꭗ **sàn** 三 (sâm^{C}) **LH** sɑm^{C}, **OCM** *sə̂ms
'Thrice' [Lunyu].
[<] *səm + s-suffix, adverbial derivation §3.5.1.

ꭗ **cān** 參驂 (ts^{h}ậm) **LH** ts^{h}əm, **OCM** *tshə̂m < *k-sə̂m
'Be a unit of three, be threefold' 參 [BI, Shi]; 'three horses of a team' 驂 [Shi]. Perh. 'to accumulate' [Shu] is the s. w. (so Sagart 1999: 151; he also connects the word to → shěn$_3$ 審).
[T] *Sin Sukchu SR* ts'am (平), *PR* ts'an; *MGZY* tsham (平) [ts'am].
[E] ST *səm + a ST *k-prefix (§5.9.1) > PTB *g-sum > WT *gsum* 'three', PL *C-sum^{2}, WB *sum*^{B}; Garo *git*^{h}*am*, Digaro *kəsaŋ*. Bodman (1980: 72) proposes OC *Ksəm.

ꭗ **shēn** 參 (ṣjəm) **LH** ṣəm, **OCM** *srəm
'Three stars in the Orion belt' [Shi] is thought to be related to *sān* (Baxter 1992: 550).
[<] *səm + other element (pre-initial / prefix *r?).

sǎn$_1$ 散 (sân^{B}) **LH** sɑn^{B}, **OCM** *sân? — **[T]** *ONW* sɑn
'Come loose, fall apart, scatter' [Shi].

ꭗ **sàn** 散 (sân^{C}) **LH** sɑn^{C}, **OCM** *sâns
'Disperse' [Shi].
[<] exopass. of *sǎn* 散 *san? (§4.4), lit. 'be scattered'.
[E] ST: PLB *šan 'sow, broadcast (as mustard seeds), scatter seeds' > WB *swan*^{B} 'pour upon, cast out by pouring' ꭗ *swan* 'pour out, spill, shed'.

※ **sā**, **să** 撒 (sât) **LH** sɑt, **OCM** *sât
'Cast, let go' [Zhanguozhi; JY]; *SW*, *GY* write the graph with *shā* 殺 as phonetic. This is apparently a late OC word.
[E] ST: PLB *šat 'pour, spill', Limbu *sɛs-* 'scatter, be split' ※ *sɛnt-* 'split up, disperse, break up', *sɛs-* 'scatter, spill' [Matisoff 1999: 5].

săn₂ 糝 (sậm^B) **LH** səm^B, **OCM** *səm? — **[T]** *ONW* sɑm
'Rice gruel with meat' 糝 [Zhouli], 糂 [Xun].
[E] Perh. ST: WT *rtsam-pa* < *r-tsam or *r-sam ? 'roast-flour' to be mixed with water or tea for a pap. Alternatively, Sagart (1999: 151) relates the WT word to **tǎn** (dàn) 糯 (dậm) 'rice gruel with meat', but this word is only known from *SW* and *GY*.

sàn 散 → **săn₁** 散

sāng₁ 喪 (sâŋ) **LH** sɑŋ, **OCM** *sâŋ
'Mourning, burial' [Shi], 'corpse' [Shǐjì]. For a semantic parallel 'grave' ~ 'corpse', see → mù₅ 墓. This word is prob. not related to *sàng* 喪 'lose, destroy' (under → wáng₁ 亡 'lose'), although these two words share the same graph due to similar sound and mental semantic association.
[T] *Sin Sukchu SR* saŋ (平); *MGZY* sang (平) [saŋ]
[<] prob. → zàng₁ 葬 'to bury' + nominal ST s-prefix (§5.2.4), hence *s-tsaŋ.
[E] ST: WB *saŋ-* 'grave'.

sāng₂ 桑 (sâŋ) **LH** sɑŋ, **OCM** *sâŋ
'Mulberry tree' [BI, Shi]. Etymology not clear. In early literature and folklore, this tree was associated with wild places beyond ordered civilization (Boileau *BSOAS* 65.2, 2002: 350ff).

săng 顙 (sâŋ^B) **LH** sɑŋ^B, **OCM** *sâŋ? < *smaŋ? ? — **[T]** *ONW* sɑŋ
'Forehead' [Zuo; SW 3915]; FY 10, 34 says this is an eastern Qí dialect word for central Chinese *é* 額 'forehead'; it is, however, a common pre-Han word.
[E] Etymology not clear. Since this word's source is Qí in Shandong which is believed to have been inhabited by AA speakers down to early historic times (Pulleyblank), it may be an AA word: Kharia *sɔmɔŋ*, Munda *samaŋ* 'forehead', possibly connected with the root OKhmer *saṅ* /sɔŋ/ 'to raise', since other words for 'forehead' are derived from the notion 'lift, high'.
[C] Syn. → dìng₂ 定顁, *é* 額 and *yán* 顏 (both under → yà₂ 御迓訝), → yáng₈ 揚鍚

sàng 喪 → **wáng₁** 亡

sāo₁ 搔 (sâu) **LH** sou, **OCM** *sû
'To scratch' [Shi].
[E] ST: TB-Chepang *saw-* 'itch' ※ *sos-* 'itch, scratch', Bodo *su-* 'to itch'.

※ **săo** 掃埽 (sâu^B/C) **LH** sou^B/C, **OCM** *sû?/h
'To brush, sweep' 埽 [Shi], 掃 [Li].

[C] It is often assumed that **zhǒu** 帚 (tśjəu^B) [tu?] 'broom' [Li] (M-Xiàmén *tsʰiu^B*, Fúzhōu *siu^B*) is cognate (so Wáng Lì 1982: 234), but the similarity is prob. only graphic and semantic. Perh. related to → zǎo₂ 蚤 'flea'. An allofam is → xù₃ 卹 'rub'.

sāo₂ 騷 (sâu) **LH** sou, **OCM** *sû
'To move, disturb, be shaken' [Shi], 'hastily' [Li] is perh. a vocalic variant of → sōu₃, sǒu 搜 'move'.

sāo₃ 騷 (sâu) **LH** sou, **OCM** *sû
'Sad, worried' [Guoyu: Chuyu], 'grief' [Chuci].
[E] AA: OKhmer *sok* /sook/ 'sorrow, affliction, pain, grief, be sad..., to grieve, mourn'. Loss of OC coda is due to a long vowel (§6.9).

꙳ **chóu** 愁 (dẓjəu) **LH** dẓu, **OCM** *dzru ?
'Grieved' [Chuci]. Retroflex MC *dẓ-* is unexplained, but note Tai *śraw²* -> Viet *xạu* 'sad' [Ferlus *MKS* 7, 1978: 16].

꙳ **cǎo** 草慅 (tsʰâuᴮ) **LH** tsʰouᴮ, **OCM** *tshûʔ < *C-sûʔ ?
'Troubled, grieved' [Shī] (慅 also read *sāo*) (typically of *láo* 勞 'toiling' people etc.).

꙳ **cǎo** 懆 (tsʰâuᴮ) **LH** tsʰɑuᴮ, **OCM** *tshâuʔ < *C-sâuʔ [Shi] is prob. a vocalic or graphic variant of *cǎo* above.

꙳ **cù** 踧 (tsjuk) **LH** tsiuk, **OCM** *tsuk
'Grieved' [Meng]. Occasionally final *-k* is irregularly retained.

[E] All the variations prob. reflect some AA morphological differences.

sāo₄ 臊 (sâu) **LH** sɑu, **OCM** *sâu — [T] *ONW* sɑu — [D] Min-Amoy *tsʰo⁵⁵*
'Fat of swine or dog' [Li].
[E] ST: PTB *saːw (*STC* no. 272) > Chepang *cʰəwʔ*, Garo *tʰo*, Dimasa *tʰau* 'oil'; Lushai *tʰauᴸ < sauh* (< *-s) 'fat, grease'; JP *sau³³* 'fat', *sau⁵⁵* 'oil'; WT *tsʰo-ba* 'fat, greasy'. This may be the same word as → sāo₅ 鱢. Also → juàn₁ 雋 'fat' may be related.

sāo₅ 鱢 (sâu) **LH** sɑu, S tsʰɑu, **OCM** *sâu ~ *C-sâu ?
'Putrid smell' [Yanzi].
[D] PMin *tsʰɑu 'rank, fishy'
[E] ST: PTB *saw (cf. *STC:* 54) ~ *su > Garo *so*, Dimasa *sau* 'rot, decay', Proto-Bodo *sau 'rotten'; Lushai *tʰuᶠ < suʔ* 'dried, rotten', Mikir *tʰu* 'rot, decay' [Hanson] < Kuki-Naga *su.

Wáng Lì (1982: 220) believes that this is the same word as → sāo₄ 臊 'fat' which would be parallel with → xīng₄ 腥 (sieŋ) 'raw meat, offensive smell'.

sǎo₁ 掃埽 → **sāo₁** 搔

sǎo₂ 嫂 → **sǒu₁** 叟瞍

sè₁ 色 (ṣjək) **LH** ṣɨk, S ṣək, **OCM** *srək, OCB *srjək
'Color' [Shi] (as opposed to → cǎi₂ 采 'pigment') > 'color of face' [Zuo] > 'appearance, countenance, mien' [Shi] > 'looks'.
[T] *Sin S. SR* ʂəj (入), *LR* ʂəjʔ; *MGZY* shʰiy (入) [ʂəj]; *ONW* ṣik
[E] ST: Lushai *saarᴴ* < *saar* 'prismatic colors' ꙳ *saarᴿ / sarhᴿ* 'healthy looking, rosy, ruddy'. The Lushai and CH words both refer also specifically to the healthy attractive color of the face. The OC word derives therefore from an earlier *sər-k. Alternatively, *sè* has been connected with TB items under → hè₄ 赫. → chì₃ 赤 'red' may possibly also be connected, but this is doubtful. Note also AA: OMon *sāk, sek* /saik/ 'color', Khmer *sāk* 'resemblance, pattern'.

The twist towards 'good looks / charms of women' as in *hào sè* 好色 'be fond of women' [Lunyu, Mengzi] > 'sex' may be due to an AA substrate, note Khmer /srèek/ 'thirst or lust after' < /réek/ 'enjoy oneself'.

sè₂ 澀 (ṣjəp) **LH** ṣip, **OCM** *srəp — [T] *ONW* ṣip
'Rough, astringent' [SW] (Pulleyblank *EC* 16, 1991: 50). Etymology not clear.

sè₃ 穡嗇 (ṣjək) **LH** ṣɨk, S ṣək, **OCM** *srək, OCB *srjək — [T] *ONW* ṣik
'Farming, to reap, to harvest' 嗇 [Shi], 'harvest' 嗇 [BI, Yili].

[E] Etymology not certain. Perh. related to TB-PLB *C-šak 'pluck, pick' (fruit etc.). Or to AA-Khmer *crūta* /cròot/ 'to reap, harvest' [Jenner / Pou 1982: 254], Khmer *sro:v* 'harvest the paddy'. Baxter (1992: 205) implies that this word is cog. to → cǎi$_1$ 采 (tsʰậi^B) OCB *srɨ(k)ʔ 'to gather, pluck'.

sēn 森 → **lín$_1$** 林

shā$_1$ 沙 (ṣa) **LH** ṣai, **OCM** *srâi — **[T]** *Sin Sukchu SR* ṣa (平); *ONW* ṣä
'Sand' [Shi]; 'sandfish, mudfish' 鯊 [Shi].
[E] Etymology not certain, but a TB etymon is similar: PTB *z(l)a-y < *s(l)a-y (with diminutive *-i/-y acc. to Matisoff 1995a: 68) > WB *sai^B* ~ *səlai^B* 'sand', PL *say^2, JP *dzai^{31}*- (in compounds) 'sand'. <> ? PTai *zaay: S. *saai* 'sand', Written S. *drai* may in fact reflect an earlier cluster (Maspero 1912: 86), therefore OC may be closer to Tai than to TB forms.

shā$_2$ 殺 (ṣăt) **LH** ṣa/ɛt, **OCM** *srât, OCB *srjet < *srjat
'To kill' [OB, Shu].
[T] *Sin Sukchu SR* ṣa (入); *ONW* ṣät
[E] ST: PTB *g-sat 'to kill' > WT *gsod-pa, bsad*, Chepang *sat-sa*, WB *sat*, PL *C-sat, JP *sat^{31}* 'to kill' (*STC* no. 58) ⋈ *gə^{31}-sat^{55}* 'attack' (with a weapon). AA-PMonic *k-r-cət 'to kill' (< *kcət* 'to die') appears phonologically also close to CH.

shà$_1$ 歃 (ṣăp, ṣjäp) **LH** ṣɛp, ṣap, **OCM** *srap ?
'To smear the mouth with victim's blood' (at covenant) [Zuo].
[E] AA: Khmer *sropa* /sraaop/ 'to cover with plaster or with thin slabs, plates, or gold leaf' (< *-ropa* /-róop/ 'cover'). Han-CH (?) -> Tai: S. *čap^4* 'to smear over, paint'. Perh. PLB *sap^H 'rub, stroke' is connected (*HPTB:* 337).

shà$_2$ 廈 → **xià$_5$, shà** 廈

shà 翣 (ṣap) **LH** ṣap, **OCM** *srâp
'Plume-fan' [Zuo].
[E] This word belongs to a widespread SE Asian assemblage of etyma for 'wink, blink', incl. PAN *sap* 'winnow'; K-Méixiàn *sap^7* 'wink', Y-Hongkong *saap^7* 'id'. For an exhaustive collection and treatment, see R. Bauer *LTBA* 15.2: 151–184. This word also may be an iterative derivation from → liè$_8$ 鬣 'beard, broom' (§5.2.3) due to paronomastic attraction.

shāi, shī 篩 (ṣi) **LH** ṣi, **OCM** *sri
'To sieve, screen' [Hanshu], 'a sieve' [GY].
[T] *Sin Sukchu SR* ṣi, ṣaj (平), *PR* ṣɿ; *MGZY* 簁 shʰi (平) [ṣɿ]
[D] In SMin this word has a curious stop initial: Amoy *thai^{A1}*; this is similar to → chú$_3$ 鋤.

⋈ **sǎ, shǎi** 洒 (ṣăi^B) **LH** ṣɛi^B, **OCM** *srîʔ
'To sprinkle' [Shi].
[E] ST *sri: Lushai *hri^L / hrik^F < hriih / hriik* 'to sift, screen' (*CVST* 4: 106). This cognate shows that *sǎ* is unrelated to → xǐ$_1$ 洗洒 'wash' (as suggested by Karlgren 1956: 16). There are also forms with TB initial *l which may be cognate: WB *hle^C* 'winnow', Lushai *tʰliʰ / tʰlit^L < slii / slit* 'to strain, pour off, winnow'.

This etymon has nearly converged with → shī$_{12}$ 釃 *sre, but the Lushai cognates suggest separate etymologies.

shǎi 洒 → **shāi, shī** 篩

shài$_1$, **shì** 曬 (ʂjeC) **LH** ʂeC, **OCM** *sreh
'To dry something in the sun' [SW].
[E] <> AA: PMonic *cay* 'to spread in the sun to dry'.

shài$_2$ 殺 → **shuāi** 衰

shān$_1$ 山 (ʂan, ʂăn) **LH** ʂan, ʂɛn, **OCM** *srân, OCB *srjan
'Mountain' [OB, Shi]. Etymology not clear.
[T] *Sin Sukchu SR* ʂan (平); *MGZY* (zhan >) shan (平) [ʂan] — **[D]** PMin *šan

shān$_2$ 髟彡 (ʂam) **LH** ʂam, **OCM** *srâm
'Long hair' [SW]. The graph is also used for a syn. → biāo$_1$ 髟. The TB cognates show that the MC retroflex prob. does not derive from an earlier *sr- cluster (§7.4).
[T] *Sin S.* 衫 *SR* ʂam (平), *PR* ʂan; *MGZY* 衫 sham (平) [ʂam]
[E] ST: PTB *(C-)sam (*STC* *tsâm ~ *sâm) > WT *ʔag-tsʰom* 'beard of the chin' (*ʔag* 'mouth'), Garo *miksam* 'eyebrow' (*mik* 'eye'); WB *tsʰam* 'head hair', PL *ʔ-tsam¹, JP *sam⁵⁵*, Lushai *samR < tsamʔ*.

shān$_3$ 芟摲 → **lián**$_8$ 磏鎌

shān$_4$ 潸 → **lián**$_1$ 連聯

shǎn 閃覢 → **yán**$_2$ 炎

shàn$_1$ 訕 → **jiān**$_4$ 姦

shàn$_2$ 扇 (śjänC) **LH** śanC, **OCM** *nhans ?
'Wicker door, leaf door' [Li] > 'fan'. Since shàn$_3$ 煽 'blaze' (with 扇 as phonetic) is probably related to → rán$_1$ 然 *nan 'burn', this word's OC initial was prob. also a nasal. Etymology not clear.
[T] *Sin Sukchu SR* ʂjen (去); *MGZY* (zhÿan >) shÿan (去) [ʂjɛn]; *ONW* śan

shàn$_3$ 煽 → **rán**$_1$ 然

shàn$_4$ 墠 → **tǎn** 坦

shàn$_5$ 禪 → **chǎn**$_2$ 嘽幝繟

shàn$_6$ 善 (źjänB) **LH** dźanB, **OCM** *danʔ
'Be good, good at, do well' [Shi] > put. 'approve' [Meng] > caus. 'make good' [Lunyu].
[T] *Sin Sukchu SR* ʐjen (上), *LR* ʐjen (上); *MGZY* zhen (上) [ʐɛn]; *ONW* dźan

⋙ **shàn** 膳繕 (zjänC) **LH** dźanC, **OCM** *dans
[T] *Sin Sukchu SR* ʐjen (去); *ONW* dźan
(1) **[<]** exopass. of *dan (§4.4): 'cooked food' [Shi] > 'eat' 膳 [Li], lit. 'what has been made good / ready'.
(2) **[<]** exoact. of *dan (§4.3): 'repair, put in order' 繕 [Zuo] (Wáng Lì 1982: 573).
[E] Etymology not certain. Perh. ST: Chepang *dyanh-* 'be good'; and / or AA-Khmer *cɔmnaːn* (i.e., *c-mn-aːn*) 'be good at'.

shàn$_7$ 蟺 (źjänB) **LH** dźanB, **OCM** *danʔ
'Earthworm' [Xun] is compared in *CVST* 2: 156 with Lushai *taalR < taalʔ* 'to struggle, wriggle, writhe' which may also be related to → wēi$_1$-tuó 委佗 'be winding'.

shāng$_1$ 傷 → **yáng**$_4$ 痒瘍

shāng$_2$ 湯 → **yáng**$_7$ 揚

shāng$_3$ 商 'trade' → **shē**$_1$ 賒

shǎng 賞 → **shě**$_1$ 舍

shàng$_1$ 上 (źjaŋ^B) **LH** dźɑŋ^B, **OCM** *daŋʔ or *djaŋʔ ?
'To rise' [Shi]. *Shījīng* rimes indicate occasional tone A.
[T] *Sin Sukchu SR* ʐjaŋ (上去); *MGZY* zhang (上去) [ʐaŋ]; *MTang* źaŋ, *ONW* dźaŋ
[D] The PMin 'softened' initial *d̥žioŋ^B points to PCH *m-daŋʔ or rather *m-jaŋʔ.
[E] ST *ja 'above' + ST terminative *-ŋ (§6.5.1).

ꭗ **shàng** 上 (źjaŋ^C) **LH** dźɑŋ^C, **OCM** *daŋh or *djaŋh ?
'Upper part, above' [BI, Shi].
[D] PMin *džiɔŋ^C
[<] exopass. of *d(j)aŋʔ (§4.4), lit. 'what has been raised'.

[E] ST: WT *yaŋ* as in *yaŋ-rtse* 'highest point, summit', and in *yaŋ-mes-po* 'great-grandfather' ꭗ *ya* 'above, up' (Bodman 1980: 79), Lushai *zo^H* < *jo* 'be high', *zaʔ^L* < *jas* 'to respect, reverence'. TB initial *y- sometimes corresponds to MC *źj-* < OC *dj- (§9.3). In light of the TB cognates, an allofam is prob. → shǔ$_7$ 曙 'sunrise', related to WT ꭗ *ya* 'above, up ꭗ *yar* 'up, upward' > *'čʰar-ba, šar* < *s-yar* 'ro rise' (of sun, moon).

shàng$_2$ 尚 → **cháng**$_2$ 常

shāo$_1$ 梢 (ṣau) **LH** ṣau, **OCM** *sr(i)âu
'Branch, staff' [Han: Yang Xiong et al.].

ꭗ **shào** 稍 (ṣau^C) **LH** ṣau^C, **OCM** *sr(i)âuh
'Little, few' [Zuo], 'rations' (to soldiers) [Zhouli].

ꭗ **shuò** 槊 (ṣåk, ṣau, sieu) **LH** ṣɔk, ṣau, seu, **OCM** *sriâu(k) ?
'Drawn out to a point, pointed' [Zhouli].

[E] This wf implies something which is getting smaller or thinner, tapering. It is not obvious if or how this wf may be related to → xiǎo$_1$ 小 'small'.

shāo$_2$ 燒 → **ráo**$_2$ 蕘

sháo 杓汋 → **zhuó**$_2$ 汋

shǎo 少 (śjäu^B) **LH** śau^B, **OCM** *hjauʔ ?, OCB *h(l)jewʔ — **[T]** *ONW* śau
'Be few, little, junior' [Shi].
[D] M-Amoy *tsio^{53}*

ꭗ **shào** 少 (śjäu^C) **LH** śau^C, **OCM** *hjauh ?
'Young, junior' [Lunyu], second, sub-' [Zuo].
[T] *Sin Sukchu SR* ʂjew (上), *PR* ʂjaw; *MGZY* shew (上) [ʂɛw]; *ONW* śau

[E] This etymon is often thought to be cognate to → xiǎo$_1$ 小 (sjäu^B) [siauʔ] 'small', but the alternation MC *s-* and *ś-* is exceptional if not impossible in wfs (a parallel 'set' of unrelated words is → sǐ 死 'to die' and *shī* 尸 'corpse' under → yí$_5$ 夷侇).

shào 稍 → **shāo**$_1$ 梢

shē$_1$ 賒 (śja) **LH** śa, **OCM** *lha — **[T]** *ONW* śa
'Trade on credit' [Zhouli] (Wáng Lì 1982: 164).
[E] <> ? Tai: S. *laak^3* 'to trade, exchange, barter'.

ꭗ **shì** 貰 (śjäi^C, (d)źja^C) **LH** śas, (d)źa^C, **OCM** *lhas, *m-las
'Lend, borrow' [Zhouli], 'remit' [Guoyu].
[<] *lha + s/h-suffix extrovert (§4.3.1).

ꭗ **shāng** 商 (śjaŋ) **LH** śɑŋ, **OCM** *lhaŋ
'To trade' [OB?, Zuo], 'to sell' [Hanfei] > 'debate' [Li].
[<] *lha + terminative -ŋ (§6.5.1).

[E] The word *shāng* appears earlier than the synonym → mǎi 買. A possible connection with one or another TB etymon remains speculative: PTB *lay 'change, exchange' (*STC* p. 64–66), → yí₈ 移 'change'. Or PTB *b-ley 'barter' (*STC* no. 283): Lushai *lei*^{R} 'buy, barter', Tiddim *lei*^{L} / *lei*^{H} < *leiʔ* / *leih* 'to buy', Chepang *leʔ-sa* 'to buy'. If related to the latter *ley, the CH vocalism might have been influenced by superficially similar words like → shě₁ 舍 'bestow, give'. Alternatively, Bodman (1980: 80) compares this group with WT *g-yar* 'borrow, lend, hire'.

shē₂ 畬 → **yú₇** 畬

shé₁ 舌 → **shì₁₆** 舐

shé₂ 蛇 (dźja) **LH** źa, **OCM** *m-lai

'Snake' [OB, Shi]. The OB graph seems to depict a cobra.

[T] *Sin Sukchu SR* zje (平); *ONW* ia (~ źa ?) — **[D]** PMin *dẓiɑi

[E] The etymology is not certain. Some languages have synonyms which look similar: KD-PHlai *ljʔa²: Baoding *za²*, Qiandui *ɬa²* 'snake'; on the Malay peninsula AN-Radê etc. *ala* 'snake'; or TB: Lushai *ruul*^{H}*-hlai*^{R} 'sp. of snake' (*ruul*^{H} 'snake'), JP *pə³³-lai³³* 'a sp. of iguana' (*CVST* 3: 6). However, the KD forms could be loans from CH, and the cited TB forms appear to be unrelated.

Most likely, *shé* is to be associated with an area root: MK-Khmer /-lée/ as in /rlée/ 'to snake, move sinuously' (as through water). In OC, this root also provides the second syllable in → wēi₁-tuó 委佗, *wēi-yí* 委佗 'winding, compliant, graceful'. *Shé* 'the winding thing' is then a euphemism for → huǐ₁ 虫虺 'snake' < ST *(s)mrul in order to avoid the name of a dangerous creature (for a similar taboo, see → hǔ₁ 虎 'tiger').

shě₁ 舍 (śjaᴮ) **LH** śaᴮ, **OCM** *lhaʔ

'To bestow, grant' [BI, Shi], 'give, bestow' [Zuo].

[E] Prob. AA: MMon *salah* 'to give away, disburse'.

⋇ **shè** 舍 (śjaᶜ) **LH** śaᶜ, **OCM** *lhah — **[T]** *ONW* śa

'Put down, deposit' [Zuo].

[<] *lhaʔ + s/h-suffix, perh. exoactive (§4.3).

⋇ **shǎng** 賞 (śjaŋᴮ) **LH** śɑŋᴮ, **OCM** *lhaŋʔ — **[T]** *ONW* śaŋ

'To award, reward, bestow' [BI, Shu].

[<] *lhaʔ + terminative *-ŋ* (§6.5.1), i.e. a reward is given for a completed action and is therefore itself a final, concluding act.

[E] ST: Bodman (1980: 102) compares *shǎng* to WT *sloŋ-mo* 'alms'.

[E] A superior person giving something to an inferior is the basic meaning of this wf, whereas the root from which it is prob. derived, → yǔ₉ 與, means 'to give' in general. The etyma *lhaʔ ~ *lhai (→ shī₉ 施) are prob. variants. A similar triplet of stems is found with the group 'to give up' (→ shě₂ 舍捨). The latter and this set 'bestow' tend to coalesce, may even derive from the same root (give something < let go of something?).

shě₂ 舍捨 (śjaᴮ) **LH** śaᴮ, **OCM** *lhaʔ

'To let off' [BI, Shi], 'set aside, leave' [Shi]; 'give up, let go' 捨 [Guoyu], 'shoot' [Shi].

[T] *Sin Sukchu SR* ʂje (上); *MGZY* shÿa (上) [ʂjɛ]; *ONW* śa

⋇ **shè** 舍 (śjaᶜ) **LH** śaᶜ, **OCM** *lhah

'Let go' [Shi], 'let off, liberate' [Zuo], 'pardon' [Shu].

[<] *lhaʔ + s/h-suffix, perh. exopass. 'be let go' (§4.4).

[E] Area word, prob. of AA origin: TB-KN-Lushai *thlaʔ*^{L} (< *slas) tr. 'to let go, release, set free, acquit, quit' (*CVST* 3: 53). <> AA: PMonic *blah* 'be released, go free' (Nyah

Kur), 'escape, be free from' (Mon) ⋇ *b[_]lah > Nyah Kur *phəlạh 'to release' (Nyah Kur), > Mon *həlẹạh 'let go, free from, send for'. OKhmer *lā* /laa/ 'to (de)part, leave, quit (doing), cease' ⋇ *ghlā* /klíiə/ 'part, leave, quit...' <> MK ? -> Tai: S. *sa-⁴-la⁴* 'let go'.

This wf is parallel to → yì₃₅ 繹 in CH as well as AA, the difference being OC final *-ʔ vs. OC final *-k. As a result, *shè* 舍 [śah] and *shè* 赦 [śah] 'let go, pardon' seem to be the same word written with different graphs. However, the graph 舍 implies OC *lhah (< *lhaʔ+h) and is derived from *shě* 舍捨 *lhaʔ, whereas the graph *shè* 赦 implies OC *lhakh. The roots *lhaʔ ~ *lhak ~ *lhaiʔ (→ shǐ₄ 弛) are prob. variants with parallel morphological and semantic developments. A similar triplet of stems is found with the homophone group 'to give, bestow' (→ shě₁ 舍). The latter and this set 'let go' tend to coalesce, may even derive from the same root (give something = let something go?).

shè₁ 社 (źjaᴮ) **LH** dźaᴮ, **OCM** *daʔ ? — **[T]** *ONW* dźa
'Altar to the spirit of the soil' [Shi], 'spirit of the soil' [SW], is assumed to be cognate to → tǔ₁ 土 'land, soil' (Karlgren *GSR* 62j; Wáng Lì 1982: 146).

shè₂ 舍 (śjaᶜ) **LH** śaᶜ, **OCM** *lhah
'To rest in, stop' (overnight on a trip) [Shi], 'to halt, resting place, a day's stage' [Zuo], 'lodging house' [Zhouli]. An R-variant is perh. → lú₂ 廬 'resting place'.

⋇ **shuì** 説 (śjwäiᶜ) **LH** śuɑs, **OCM** *lho(t)s (< *lhua(t)s ?)
'To halt, rest overnight' [Shi].

[E] Apparently shared with PKS: *s-lwaᴮ 'to rest'. The PCH root must have been *s-lwas, identical to the KS one, with the later regular OC initial *sl- > *lh-; KT tone B is the regular counterpart of MC tone C (< *-s). Both CH forms reflect a PCH final *s, *shè* as suffix, *shuì* as part of the root. The erstwhile PCH medial *w after acute initials survives perh. in syllables in final *-t* and *-(t)s*, as in *shuì;* however, in open syllables like *shè,* the OC (? at least MC) phonological structure does not allow a medial *w (§10.2.1). The ambivalence in the forms, as in the finals in these two words, is typical for loan words.

shè₃ 舍 'put down' → **shě₁** 舍

shè₄ 舍 'let go' → **shě₂** 舍捨

shè₅ 赦 → **yì₃₅** 繹; also → **shě₂** 舍捨

shè₆ 涉 (źjäp) **LH** dźap, **OCM** *dap — **[T]** *ONW* dźap
'To wade (through a river), cross a river' [Shi], 'to cross a river' (by boat) [Zuo].
[E] Perh. related to PTB *lip 'dive, sink, drown' (*STC* no. 375), WT *lčeb-pa* 'seek death' (by drowning), but the initials do not agree.

shè₇ 射 → **shí₉** 射

shè₈ 設 → **yì₂₈** 藝.

shè₉ 懾慹 (tśjäp) **LH** tśap, **OCM** *tep or *tap ?
'Despondent, to fear' 懾 [Li]; *zhé* 慴 'to fear' [Zhuang]; 'scared stiff, stupefied' 慹 (Mand. *zhí*), also MC *tśjəp, niep* [Zhuang].

⋇ **shè** 懾 (śjäp) **LH** śap, **OCM** *nhep or *nhap ?
'To scare, frighten' tr. *(JDSW)* [Zuo, Xiāng 11].
[E] Perh. directly related to Khmer *snap* (see below) with an intensive (?) s-prefix, except that OC has reinterpreted the devoiced initial < *s- as a trans. / caus. prefix.

⋇ **niè** 幸 (ṇjäp) **LH** ṇap ?, **OCM** *nrep
'That by which you frighten people' n. [SW] (Karlgren *GSR* no. 638d; Baxter and Sagart 1998: 52).

[E] AA: OKhmer *ñyāp* /ɲap/ 'to tremble, fear' ⋇ /sɲap/ intr. 'to shake, tremble, be frightened, terrified'. The un-ST co-occurrence of MC initial *tśj-*, *śj-* and *ṇj-* within a wf prob. reflect fragments of AA morphology, especially the initial *n-* suggests an AA infix.

shè$_{10}$ 攝 (śjäp) **LH** śap, **OCM** *nhep < *s-nep, OCB *hnjep — **[T]** *ONW* śap
'To pinch between' [Lunyu] > 'to grasp, gather up' (skirts), 'combine' (two offices) [Lunyu] > 'assist' [Shi].

⋇ **niè** 鑷 (ṇjäp) **LH** ṇap, **OCM** *nrep — **[T]** *ONW* nap
'Pincers, tweezers' [*Shìmíng* , GY].

[E] The OC pair derives from a ST doublet *s-njap ~ *r-njap: PTB *s/r-nyap 'pinch, squeeze' (*HPTB:* 339) > WT *rñab-rñab-pa* 'to seize or snatch together', Chepang *nep-* 'press together uniformly...', Mikir *nép* 'to catch'; PLB *(s-)nyap > WB *ñap* 'be pinched, squeezed between' ⋇ *hñap* 'to squeeze, press between two objects', in Lolo lgs. also 'shoes' (*HST:* 118). CH -> Tai: S. *nεεp*^{DIL} < *hn- 'pincers, to hold' (with pincers). This ST root *njap is distinct from the parallel stem *nip (→ niē$_0$ 捻 'pinch').

shè$_{11}$ 麝 (dźja^C) **LH** źa^C, **OCM** *m-lah — **[T]** *ONW* ia
'Musk deer' [EY, SW].
[E] ST: WT *gla-ba* 'musk deer' [Jaeschke] or 'river deer' [Zang-Mian 1992 no. 315–316] (*CVST* 3: 4); Loloish lgs.: *la* etc.

shéi, shuí 誰 (źwi) **LH** dźui, **OCM** *dui
'Who?' [Shi].
[<] *du + final *-i is the independent form of the pronoun (§3.3.3).

⋇ **chóu**$_7$ 疇 (ḍjəu) **LH** ḍu, **OCM** *dru (?)
'Who' [only in Shu].
[E] ST: TB-Kuki-Naga *tuʔ/h 'who': Lushai *tu*^{L}; Chepang *doh* 'what, something'.

⋇ **shú** 孰 (źjuk) **LH** dźuk, **OCM** *duk — **[T]** *ONW* dźuk
'Which one, who?' [Lun].
[<] *du + distributive k-suffix (§6.1.2).

shēn$_1$ 申伸呻 → **yǐn**$_2$ 引

shēn$_2$ 身 (śjen) **LH** śin, **OCM** *lhin ? or nhin ?, OCB *hniŋ
'Body, person, self' [BI, Shi]; 'belly' [Yijing 52] (acc. to Qiu Xigui 2000: 182 [quoting Yú Fān]; Shaughnessy 1997: 54 translates 'body', but since *shēn* contrasts with 'flesh on the spine', 'belly' may be more to the point).
[T] *Sin Sukchu SR* ʂin (平); *MGZY* shin (平) [ʂin]; *ONW* śin
[N] The alleged meaning 'pregnant' (Wáng Lì 1982: 538, based on the ancient commentator Yú Fān) is not warranted: *yǒu shēn* 有身 'pregnant' [Shijing] means lit. 'with body' (cf. Engl. 'with child'; note also the synonymous expressions *shuāng shēn* 雙身, *chóng shēn* 重身); or 'belly' is a euphemism for 'pregnant'. Therefore, *shēn* is not related to → zhèn, shēn 娠 'pregnant'. The meaning 'pregnant' may have been reinforced by the near homophone *shèng* 賸 'pregnant' (under → yùn$_1$ 孕).
[E] Etymology not certain. Geilich (1994: 274–277) suggests that *shēn* 身 'body' is related to *shēn* 申伸呻 'stretch out' (→ yǐn$_2$ 引), then lit. = 'the stretched one', also related to *shī* 尸 'corpse' (under → yí$_5$ 夷侇) which also means 'stretch out'. *Shēn* would then be a nominal n-derivation from the root in question (§6.4.3). Alternatively, Baxter (p. c. 2001) conjectures that *shēn* was OCB *hniŋ and cognate to → rén$_2$ 仁 and the TB items there, because, among other considerations, in the Guōdiàn texts → rén$_2$ 仁 is written with *shēn* 身 above *xīn* 心 'heart'.

shēn₃ 深 (śjəm^A) **LH** śim, tśʰim, **OCM** *nhəm ? — **[T]** *ONW* śim, BTD śim
'Deep' [Shi].
[D] PMin *tšʰim; Y-Guǎngzhōu ⁵⁵*sɐm^A1*
≍ **shèn** 深 (śjəm^C) **LH** śim^C, **OCM** *nhəms ?
'Depth' [Zhouli].
[<] *shēn* + s-suffix to form nouns (§3.5.2).
≍ **shěn** 淰 (śjəm^B) **LH** śim^B, **OCM** *nhəmʔ ?
'Be startled and flee' (of fish), i.e. 'go down into the deep' [Liyun] (Unger).
[<] *shēn* + tone B endoactive (§4.5).
[E] The OC initial *n- has been suggested by Unger (*Hao-ku* 47, 1995) because of *shěn* and possible cognation with → nǎn₂ 揇. If the OC initial was indeed *n-, then the following TB items are related: PTB *nem (*STC* no. 348): WB *nim* 'be low' ≍ *nim* 'be kept low, below'; Lushai *hniam^R* 'be low, sink into' (land) ≍ *hnim^H* 'dip into' tr.; Tankhul Naga *kʰənim* 'be humble', WT *nems* 'sink a little, give way' (a floor).
An alternative connection: PKiranti *gʰlàm 'deep' (van Driem 1995: 254: Starostin); or Chepang *ǰjumh-ʔo* 'deep'. See → chén₂ 沈 for syn. and further comments. → tān₃ 探 may be cognate.

shēn₄ 莘詵 (ṣjɛn) **LH** ṣɨn, **OCM** *srən
'Numerous' [Shi].
≍ **zhēn** 溱蓁 (tṣjɛn) **LH** tṣɨn, **OCM** *tsrən
'Be full of (leaves), lots of (descendants)' [Shi] (Wáng Lì 1982: 538).

shēn₅ 參 → **sān** 三

shén₁-mo 甚麼
'What' Mand. is derived from *shí wú* 十物 (źiəp mjuət) ('ten things':) 'vessels, household utensils' (Zhāng Huìyīng, see Norman 1988: 119f).

shén₂ 神 (dźjen) **LH** źin, **OCM** *m-lin
'Spirit' [BI, Shi].
[T] *Sin Sukchu SR* ẓin (平); *MGZY* cin (平) [dẓin]
[E] Perh. ST: Chepang *gliŋh* 'spirit of humans'.

shěn₁ 矧哂 (śjen^B) **LH** śin^B, **OCM** *nhinʔ
'The gums' 矧 [Li] > (show the gums:) 'smile' 哂 [Lun] (Geilich 1994: 235).
[E] ST: PTB *s-nil (*STC* no. 3; p. 177) > WT *rñil* ~ *sñil* 'gums', Kan *stil* < *snil*, Lepcha *fo-nyăl* (*fo* 'teeth'), Chepang *nəl*, Dimasa *ha-rni* (*ha* 'teeth'), Lushai *ha^H-hni^R* < *-hniʔ* (we should expect Lushai final *-l*, hence a loan?).

shěn₂ 淰 → **shēn₃** 深

shěn₃ 審 (śjəm^B) **LH** śim^B, **OCM** *-əmʔ
'To investigate, discriminate' [Lunyu], 'minutely, really' [Shu].
[E] Etymology not clear. This word could belong to → shēn₃ 深 'deep'. Karlgren *GSR* 647a considers this to be the same word as *cān* 參 'thrice' (under → sān 三), Sagart (1999: 151) relates it to **cān** 參 (tsʰậm) [tsʰəm] 'examine' [Xun], but reconciliation of the initials presents problems.

shěn₄ 瀋沈 → **chěn₂** 瀋沈

shèn₁ 腎 (źjen^B) **LH** gin^B, **OCM** *ginʔ
'Kidney' [Shu].

[E] ? ST: Perh. related to PTB *m-glun 'kidney' (*HPTB:* 73); for the vowels, see §11.5.1.

shèn₂ 蜃 (źjenC) **LH** dźinC, **OCM** *dəns
'Clam, oyster' [OB, Li]; 'some kind of dragon' [Hànshū, Tiānwén zhì], → chén₃ 辰.

shèn₃ 甚 → **zhēn₂** 斟

shèn₄ 葚 (dźjəmB, źjemB) **LH** źimB (or dźimB ?), **OCM** *(m-)dəm? ?
'Mulberry fruit' (which is dark purple or black) [Shi].
[E] Area word: AA-Khmer *dum̩* /tum/ 'be ripe, dark', PNB *qdùm 'red' seems to belong to this group. <> TB-Lushai *dum*^{H} 'black, blue' (like sky, sea), 'purple' (like distant mountains), 'dark' (in color). See → tǎn₅ 黮 for further items.

shēng₁ 升昇 → **chéng₃** 乘

shēng₂ 生 (ṣɐŋ) **LH** ṣɛŋ, **OCM** *srêŋ
'To live, be alive, fresh' [OB, BI, Shi] > ('cause to live') 'give birth to, create' [Shi]; 'a (live) sacrificial animal' 牲 [BI] > 'domestic animal' (as beast of burden).
[T] *Sin Sukchu SR* ṣəjŋ (平), *PR, LR* ṣəŋ; *MGZY* sh^{h}ing (平) [ṣəŋ]; *ONW* ṣëŋ

Table S-1 Live, fresh, green (A): *s(r)iŋ ~ *s(r)aŋ

S-1	ST *sriŋ	⌘ *sraŋ live	*(k-)siŋ green	⌘ *k-saŋ green
OC	shēng 生 *srêŋ live		qīng 青 *tshêŋ < *k-seŋ ? green	cāng 蒼 *tshâŋ < *k-saŋ ? green
WT			gsiŋ-ma pasture-land	
Kanauri	sriŋ live			
Garo		(t^{h}aŋ live) (1)		gat^{h}aŋ green
Dimasa				gat^{h}aŋ alive, green, unripe
Mikir	reŋ^L < re/iŋ^L live		reŋ-seŋ < -se/iŋ green	
Lushai	hriŋ^H / hrinR bear, beget hriŋ^H / hrin^L fresh, green			
NNaga	*C-riŋ alive *C/V-criŋ raw, grass			
Rawang			məsëŋ green ~ măšiŋ blue	
JP	tsiŋ^{33} < rjiŋ^{33} ? grass, green			
WB		hraŋ live, alive		

Note on Table S-1: (1) Garo *t^{h}aŋ < saŋ* (instead of *sraŋ or *sriŋ) is prob. formed in analogy to *gat^{h}aŋ*.

[E] ST terminative final *-ŋ derivation (§6.5.1) from ST *sri 'to be, exist', hence lit. 'come into existence > give birth > live': PTB *s-riŋ (*śriŋ) (*STC* no. 404) > Manchati *sriŋ* 'to live, alive'; Lushai *hriŋ*^{H} / *hrin*^{L} 'fresh, green' ⋈ *hriŋ*^{H} / *hrin*^{R} 'bear, beget', NNaga *C-riŋ 'alive'; Chepang *sriŋ-* 'open out' (begin to open, of buds), begin to blossom', Mikir *reŋ*^{L} 'live, come to life'; JP *tsiŋ*^{33} < *rjiŋ* 'weeds, rank grass' (*STC:* 85; *HST:* 104), NNaga *C/V-criŋ 'raw, grass' [French 1983: 351]. With vowel *a: WB *hraŋ* 'live, alive'.

ST *sri survives prob. as → tǐ 體 in CH (§7.1.2). The initial *s in *sriŋ belongs to the ST stem, but in some languages it has been reinterpreted as the caus. prefix, which explains perhaps the survival of the *s- in OC *sriŋ where the alleged caus. function was felt to be transparent, but was lost in *tǐ* as part of the stem.

ST has several parallel stems, prob. ultimately related, for the notion 'live, fresh, green':

ST *sriŋ	→	shēng 生 'live'
~ ST *sraŋ	→	WB hraŋ 'live'
~ ST *siŋ	→	xìng 性姓 'nature', qīng 青 'green'
~ ST *saŋ	→	cāng 蒼 'blue', Garo tʰaŋ 'live'

For an overview of the *s(r)iŋ ~ *s(r)aŋ contrasts (§11.1.3), see Table S-1; for an overview of the *sriŋ* ~ *siŋ* contrasts, see Table Q-1 after → qīng 青 'green'. For synonyms, see → chù$_{4}$, xù 畜.

shēng$_{3}$ 甥 (ṣɐŋ) **LH** ṣɛŋ, **OCM** *srêŋ
'Sister's son ' [Shi], (daughter's husband:) 'son-in-law' [Meng], 'father's sister's son, mother's brother's son, wife's brother, sister's husband' (K. C. Chang 1976: 89).
[E] ST: Western TB languages: WT *sriŋ-mo* 'sister' (of a male), Zangskar *ṛiŋmo;* Lower Kanauri *riŋs.*

shēng$_{4}$ 笙 (ṣɐŋ) **LH** ṣɛŋ, **OCM** *srêŋ — [T] *ONW* ṣëŋ
'Reed-organ' [Shi] may be related to → míng$_{7}$ 鳴 OCB *mrjeŋ 'to sound' acc. to Baxter (1992: 499).

shēng$_{5}$ 聲 (śjäŋ) **LH** śeŋ, **OCM** *hjeŋ ?
'Sound' (especially with respect to volume), 'note, fame' [Shi].
[T] *Sin Sukchu SR* ṣiŋ (平); *MGZY* shing (平) [ṣiŋ]; *ONW* śeŋ
[D] PMin *šiaŋ > Xiàmén col. *siã*^{A1}, Fúzhōu *siaŋ*^{44}, K-Méixiàn *saŋ*^{44}; PMin * ~ *tsʰiaŋ > Jiànyáng *tshiaŋ*^{A1}
[E] Perh. ST, note a similar-looking Lushai word with identical meaning: *tʰaŋ*^{H} / *tʰan*^{L} < *saŋ* 'become known, be renowned; to sound or travel (as sound), resound'. However, foreign initial *s-* is impossible to reconcile with MC *śj-* which goes back to an OC voiceless continuant, perh. *hj-, unless we assume *he/iŋ ~ *saŋ parallel stems of the kind which have been suggested for 'odor, smell', see under → xiāng 香. <> Tai: S. *siaŋ*^{A1} 'sound' looks like a loan from a southern CH dialect.
[C] A derivation is perh. → shèng$_{1}$ 聖 'wise'.

shēng$_{6}$ 勝 (śjəŋ) **LH** śɨŋ, **OCM** *lhəŋ ?
'Equal to, capable of, be worthy of' [BI, Shi, Lunyu].

⋈ **shèng** 勝 (śjəŋ^{C}) **LH** śɨŋ^{C}, **OCM** *lhəŋh ? — [T] *ONW* śiŋ
'To vanquish, conquer, overcome' [Shi], 'surpass' [Lunyu]
[<] *lhəŋ + s/h-suffix – perh. an exoactive / extrovert derivation of *shēng* (§4.3.1). Downer (1959: 288) considers this a pass. or neuter derivation.

[C] This wf is perh. cognate to → chéng$_{3}$ 乘.

shéng 繩 (dźjəŋ) **LH** źɨŋ, **OCM** *m-ləŋ
'String, cord; continue' [Shi].

[T] *Sin Sukchu SR* ʐiŋ (平); *MGZY* cing (平) [dʐiŋ]
[E] ST: PTB *bliŋ 'string, cord' (*HPTB*: 307): Metu (Nungish) *ambriŋ* 'cord', et al., perh. also WB *ə-hmyaŋ*ᴮ 'string, thread, fiber, nerve'; Mei Tsu-Lin (1985: 338, 342) adds WT *'pʰreŋ < ɴpreŋ*, and suggests it is a variant of → mín₃ 緡. For the *m- ~ *b- difference, see §5.12.2.

shèng₁ 聖 (śjäŋᶜ) **LH** śeŋᶜ, **OCM** *hjeŋh ? or *lheŋh ?
'Be wise' [Shi], 'a wise, knowledgeable person' [Hanfei].
[T] *Sin Sukchu SR* ʂiŋ (去); *MGZY* shing (去) [ʂiŋ]; *ONW* śeŋ
[E] This word is often related to → tīng₂ 聽 'hear' (Boltz 1994: 116) in which case OCM would be *lheŋh. Formally, it looks like a derivation from → shēng₅ 聲 'sound', in which case it would be OCM *hjeŋh and literally mean 'be renowned, one who is renowned' (for his wisdom).

shèng₂ 乘 → **chéng₃** 乘

shèng₃ 勝 → **shēng₆** 勝

shèng₄ 䞉 'pregnant' → **yùn₁** 孕

shèng₅ 盛 → **chéng₁** 成盛城

shī₁ 尸 → **yí₅** 夷侇

shī₂ 失 (śjet) **LH** śit, **OCM** *lhit — [T] *ONW* śit
'To lose, fail, neglect' [Shi], 'let go, err' [Zuo] (Unger *Hao-ku* 36, 1990: 56). Perh. the wf → yì₁₃ 泆溢 is a semantic extension of this group.
ꭗ **yì** 佚逸 (jiet) **LH** jit, **OCM** *lit — [T] *ONW* it
'To escape' [Li], 'retire' [Meng], 'neglect' 佚 [Shu]; prob. also 'to relax, be at ease, lazy, idle' 逸 [Shi].
[E] <> Note Tai: S. *let*ᴰ²*-lɔɔt*ᴰ² 'escape artfully or adroitly' (Manomaivibool 1975: 181).

shī₃ 虱 (ʂjɛt) **LH** ṣit, **OCM** *srit — [D] PMin *šət.
'Louse' [Zhuang].
[E] ST: PTB *s-rik > WT *šig < hryik* 'louse', Bunan *śrig*, Kanauri *rig*, Chepang *srəyk* 'head louse', Lushai *hrik*ᴸ, Mikir *rek*. PTB *k-rik > JP *krat*⁵⁵. CH ? -> Tai: S. *rɨat*ᴰ²ᴸ < *dr- 'bed bug' (Li F. 1976: 45) may be a CH loan (MC ṣ- = Tai *dr- is not unique).

shī₄ 師 (ṣi) **LH** ṣi, **OCM** *sri
'Multitude, army' [OB, BI, Shi] > 'captain' (of an army) [BI, Shi] > 'master'. *CVST* (2: 78) relates this word to → jiē₂ 皆喈 'all'.
[T] *Sin Sukchu SR* ʂi (平), *PR, LR* ʂʅ; *MGZY* shʰi (平) [ʂʅ]

shī₅-zǐ 獅子 (ṣi-tsɨᴮ) **LH** ṣi-tsiəʔ
'Lion' [Hanshu]
[E] <- IE-Tocharian A *śiśäk*, B *ṣecake* 'lion' (Pulleyblank *JIES* 23.3/4, 1995: 427f).

shī₆ 篩 → **shāi**, **shī** 篩

shī₇ 溼 (śjəp) **LH** śip, S tśʰip, **OCM** *lhəp — [T] *ONW* śip — [D] PMin *tšʰiap or *tšʰiep
'Damp, wet' (of soil) [BI, Yi].
ꭗ **xí** 隰 (zjəp) **LH** zip, **OCM** *s-ləp
'Low wet ground, swamp' [Shi] (Wáng Lì 1982: 593).
[E] The initials of the two words can be reconciled if we assume an OC *l-. There is prob. no connection with WT *sib-pa* 'to evaporate, to soak in, be imbibed' (of fluids) since MC *śj-* normally does not derive from *s + j.

shī₈ 詩 (śɨ) **LH** śə, **OCM** *lhə ?
'Song, ode, poem' [Shi].
[E] ST: Bodman (1980: 181) compares this to Lushai *hlaa*^R 'song, poem, poetry'.

shī₉ 施 (śje) **LH** śɑi, **OCM** *lhai
'To bestow, apply (color, the law), place' [Shi, Shu].
[T] *Sin Sukchu SR* ṣi (平), *PR, LR* ʂʅ; *MGZY* shʰi (平) [ʂʅ]; *ONW* śe

⚹ **shì** 施 (śje^C) **LH** śɑi^C, **OCM** *lhaih
'To give, bestow' [Shi], 'to bestow alms' [Li].
[<] *lhai + exoactive / caus. s/h-suffix (§4.3.2) (Downer 1959: 285).

[E] This is a final *i variant of the synonym → shě₂ 舍捨 (root *lhaʔ). A cognate is → cì₄ 賜錫 (sje^C) (root *slek) with final -*k* (§6.1).

shī₁₀ 施 'expand' → **chǐ₃** 侈哆移

shī₁₁ 施 'dodge' → **yí₆** 迤迆

shī₁₂ 釃 (ṣje) **LH** ṣe, **OCM** *sre
'To strain off' (wine) [Shi]. The graph also writes the synonym → xǔ₁ 湑 *sra 'strain off' which has a different etymology, though.
[<] *lai + s-prefix: This etymon is derived from → yí₆ 迤迆 'slant, deflect' ST *lai + iterative s-prefix (§5.2.3). For *ai ~ *e variation, see §11.3.3. The change from *l to *r is due either to Rural influence (§7.3), or to convergence with → shāi, shī 篩 *sri.
[E] ST *s-lai: Lushai *tʰlei*^R *< sleʔ* 'to sift' (by side to side motion) ⚹ *tʰle*^L */ tʰleek*^F *< slees / sleek* 'to sway / lean to one side'; see under → yí₆ 迤迆 for more Lushai cognates. Bodman (1980: 179) relates this word to Viet. *rây* 'to strain, sift, sieve'.

⚹ **sǎ** 灑 (ṣai^{B/C}, ṣje^{B/C}) **LH** ṣɛ^{B/C}, **OCM** *sreʔ/h — **[T]** *ONW* ṣä
'To sprinkle' > 'distribute' [Li].

[E] This item has nearly converged with → shāi, shī 篩 *sre, the putative Lushai cognates suggest separate etymologies.

shí₁ 十 (źjəp) **LH** dźip < gip, **OCM** *gip
'Ten' [OB, Shi].
[T] *Sin Sukchu SR* ʐi (入); *MGZY* zhi (入) [ʐi]; *ONW* dźip
[D] PMin *džep: Xiàmén col. *tsap*^{D2}, lit. *sip*^{D2}; K-Méixiàn *səp*^{D2}; Y-Guǎngzhōu ^{22}*ʃap*^{D2}
[E] ST: PTB *gip (*STC* no. 16) > WB *kyip*, Mikir *kep < kip* (Matisoff 1997a: 25). <> PMiao *ge̱u^D 'ten' is a loan either from TB or from OC. <> PTai *sip: S. *sip*^{D1S} is a CH loan, prob. from a southern dialect.

shí₂ 石 (źjäk) **LH** dźak, S dźɑk, **OCM** *dak
'Stone' [Shi]. The homophone *shí* 鼫 'marmot' [Shi] is prob. the s. w. (< 'stone rat').
[T] *Sin Sukchu SR* ʐi (入); *MGZY* zhi (入) [ʐi]; *MTang* źek < dźek, *ONW* dźek
[D] PMin *džiɔk ~ *žiak: Amoy *sioʔ*^{D2}, *siaʔ*^{D2}, Jiānglè šo^{D2}; Y-Guǎngzhōu ^{22}*sɛk*^{D2}
[E] Etymology not certain. *Shí* is prob. related to MK: PVM *l-taːʔ 'stone, rock', Khmer *ṭā* /daa/ 'rock mass..., (any) rock or boulder', to which CH would have added the familiar final -*k* (§6.1). In some MK languages, the word has an m-infix.

shí₃ 拾 (źjəp) **LH** gip, **OCM** *gip
'To pick, gather' [Zuo] is shared with PTai *kjəp (Xíng Kǎi, *MZYW* 2000: 2).

shí$_4$ 食 (dźjək) **LH** źɨk, **OCM** *m-lək
'To eat' [Shi] > ('eating of sun, moon' by a celestial monster:) 'eclipse' 食 [Shi], 蝕 [Lüshi chunqiu].
[T] *Sin Sukchu SR* ẓi (入); *MGZY* ci (入) [dẓi]; *ONW* źik
[D] This is still the word for 'eat' in southern dialects: Y-Guǎngzhōu ^{22}*sek*^{D2}, K-Méixiàn *set;* PMin *žit/k 'eclipse'.
[E] ST *ljək + pre-initial *m- (§8.1.3): PTB *m-lyak 'lick' (*STC* no. 211) > PLB *m-lyak 'to lick', WB *lyak*; WT *ljags* < ɴlyaks 'tongue', *ldag-pa* < ɴlak 'to lick'; Limbu *lak-* 'to lick'; JP *mə*^{31}*-taʔ*^{55}; Lepcha *lyak* 'taste, try', Nung *la* ~ *lɛ*, Miri *jak*, KN *m-liak > Lushai *liak*^{R} / *liaʔ*^{L}, Tangkhul *k*^{h}*əmələk* 'to lick' [*IST:* 27], Liangmei *ma-li̯ak* [Weidert 1987: 257]. *STC:* 64 considers JP *śiŋlet* 'tongue' to belong to this root, see → shì$_{16}$ 舐, also WB *hlya* 'tongue' appears to have been influenced by it. Matisoff (1995: 71) connects this wf with → shì$_{16}$ 舐 and → tián$_4$ 甜.

⋈ **(shì)** (QYS *dźɨ^{C})
[D] PMin *dž^{h}i^{C} 'raise livestock' is an exoactive / caus. derivation from an equivalent of *shí* 'eat'. Independently also in TB: Limbu *laŋma* < *laks-* 'to feed'.

⋈ **sì** 飼食 (zɨ^{C}) **LH** ziə^{C}, **OCM** *s-ləkh
'To give food to, feed' [Shi].
[T] *ONW* ziə.
[E] ST *liək + ST causative s-prefix (§5.2; §8.1.2; Pulleyblank 1973: 117), + OC exoactive / causative s/h-suffix (§4.3.2). PTB *s-lyak > PLB *ʔljak 'to feed an animal'; Garo *srak* 'lick'.

⋈ **tāi** 胎 (t^{h}ậi) **LH** t^{h}ə, **OCM** *lhə̂
'To nourish' [FY 1.5], a Han period dialect word (incl. in the ancient state Sòng) which could also have derived from earlier *s-lə(k).

shí$_5$ 蝕 → **shí**$_4$ 食

shí$_6$, **shì**, **duò** 㚆 (źje, źje^{B}, tâ^{B}) **LH** dźɑi(^{B}), tai^{B}, **OCM** *dai(ʔ) ~ *tâiʔ
'Wife's parents' (in *fù-shí* 父㚆, *mǔ-shí* 母㚆) [FY] is a Han period dialect word from Southern Chǔ, a Tai word:
[E] PTai *tai 'maternal grandmother', or PTai *ta 'maternal grandfather' (Mei Tsu-Lin AAS paper 1980).

shí$_7$ 時 'this' → **zhī**$_1$ 之

shí$_8$ 時 'time' → **zhī**$_2$ 之

shí$_9$ 射 (dźjäk) **LH** źak, S źɑk, **OCM** *m-lak — **[D]** PMin žiɔk ~ *žiak 'shoot'
'To hit with arrow' [Lunyu].

⋈ **shè** 射 (dźja^{C}) **LH** źa^{C}, **OCM** *m-lakh — **[T]** *ONW* ia — **[D]** PMin žia^{C}
'To shoot' [BI, Shi].
[<] exopass. of *shí* 射 (dźjäk), lit. (cause) 'to be hit by arrow' (§4.4.1).

⋈ **xiè** 榭 (zja^{C}) **LH** zia^{C}, **OCM** *s-lakh
'Archery hall' [Chunqiu].
[<] *-liakh + s-prefix (§8.1.2).

[E] ST: JP *ʃiŋ*^{31}*-teʔ*^{55} 'to shoot' (< *sm-lhek ?; JP *t* for TB *l*, see §12.2 JP) (*CVST* 3: 2). OC and JP prob. go ultimately back to PTB *b-la [Matisoff 1995a: 41, 67] or *mla 'arrow' > WT *mda'*, Bahing *bla*, Dimasa *bala*, Tangkhul *məla*, OBurm. *mla* [*IST:* 334], WB *hmra*^{B} (Matisoff: aspiration from earlier prefix *g-), Akha *mjà* (*STC:* 188 n. 487). Alternatively, Bodman (1980: 94) relates the wf to WT *rgyag-pa* 'to throw', but see → qù$_1$ 去.

[C] Sagart (in W. Wang *Ancestry of the Chinese Language* 1995: 369) considers this group to be part of → yì$_{35}$ 繹.

shí$_{10}$ 寔 (źjək) **LH** dźɨk, **OCM** *dək — **[T]** (ONW śik ?)
'Really' [Shi, Shu].
[E] ST: PLB *dyak 'truly, very, intensive', WB *tyak-tyak* 'very' (*HST:* 122), Lushai *tak*^{L} 'real, true'.

※ **shí** 實 (dźjet) **LH** źit (or dźit ?), **OCM** *dit ? — **[T]** *ONW* źit
'Be solid, true, really' [Shi] > 'to verify' [Shu]; perh. > 'be rich' [Shi] > 'enrich' [Shu]. This may be a mere phonetic variant of *shí* 寔.

shí$_{11}$ 寔 'this' → **shí$_{13}$** 實

shí$_{12}$ 實 (dźjet) **LH** źit, **OCM** *m-lit ?
'Fruit' [Shi], also fruit as seat of life, hence 'seed' [Shi 290, 291].
[T] *Sin Sukchu SR* ʂi (入); *MGZY* ci (入) [dʐi]; *ONW* źit
[E] Etymology not certain. Most likely, *shí* is related to a ST or area etymon: Unger (*Hao-ku* 85, 1992: 93f) relates it to TB-Lepcha *lí, lí-m* 'be ripe', *lí, a-lí* 'seed'; Mikir *lík* 'pick, pluck'. This may possibly be connected with MK: PVM *p-leːʔ > pleːʔ > tleːʔ 'fruit' [Ferlus], Khmuʔ *pleʔ,* PWa *pliʔ, Pear *phli,* PSBahn. *pəlaj, Khmer *phlaɛ. Shí* could be equally close to the AA or the TB items because the OC final *-t is a nominalizing suffix for natural objects (§6.2.1), and OC *m- for foreign *b-* has parallels (§5.12.2).
Alternatively, Baxter / Sagart (1998: 52) relate this word to → zhì$_{18}$ 質 'essential' and note a possible relationship with PTai *mlet or *mret 'grain, seed' [Li F. 1977: 93]; the Tai word could, however, also be connected with → mǐ$_{1}$ 米 'rice'.

shí$_{13}$ 實 (dźjet) **LH** źit, **OCM** *m-dit ?
'This', resumptive pronoun [Shi]. Since the word is derived from → shì$_{14}$ 是 (Pulleyblank 1995: 89) and the graph a loan application, its earlier initial was probably *d-, i.e. different from → shí$_{12}$ 實 'fruit'.
[T] *Sin Sukchu SR* ʂi (入); *MGZY* ci (入) [dʐi]; *ONW* źit

※ **shí** 寔 (źjək) **LH** dźɨk, **OCM** *dək — **[T]** *ONW* śik ?
'This', resumptive pronoun [Zuo], is considered a dialect variant of the above (Pulleyblank).

shí$_{14}$ 實 'solid, rich' → **shí$_{10}$** 寔

shǐ$_{1}$ 矢 (śiᴮ) **LH** śiᴮ, **OCM** *lhiʔ — **[T]** *ONW* śi
'Arrow' [Shi].
[E] This is prob. a ST etymon, considering that on occasion the meanings of 'arrow' and 'bow' can merge or be interchanged: PTB *d-liy 'bow' [*STC* no. 463] > Bahing *li,* Limbu *li* 'bow', Lepcha *să-lí,* Nung *tʰəli,* WB *le*ᴮ (Bodman *LTBA* 11.1, 1988), PLB *s-liy² > Lahu *hɔ̂* 'slingshot'.

shǐ$_{2}$ 矢 'display' → **yí$_{5}$** 夷侇

shǐ$_{3}$ 矢 (śiᴮ) **LH** śiᴮ, **OCM** *lhiʔ
'To swear, make a solemn declaration' [Shi]. This may be the same word as *shǐ$_{2}$* 矢 (under → yí$_{5}$ 夷侇); acc. to Qiu Xigui (2000: 397f), 矢 'swear' started out perh. as a short form of a longer phrase.

shǐ$_{4}$ 弛 (śjeᴮ) **LH** śɑiᴮ, **OCM** *lhaiʔ
'Unstring, slacken' (a bow) [Li], 'release' [Li], 'remove' [Zuo].

This is a final *i variant of the synonym → shě₂ 舍捨 (root *lhaʔ). The CH voiceless initial could be the result of a lost *k-, note the PWMiao relation *klaɨ⁷ 'release, forgive'.

shǐ₅ 弛 'extend' → **chǐ₃** 侈哆移

shǐ₆ 弛 'destroy' → **zhì₇** 阤, 陊

shǐ₇ 豕 (śjeᴮ) **LH** śeᴮ or śaiᴮ, **OCM** *lheʔ or *lhaiʔ
'Pig' (wild or domestic) [BI, Shi], 'boar' [Zuo].
[E] This is possibly of MK origin: PMonic *cliik, Mon *klot, kloik* 'pig', PWa *lik 'pig', Katuic *alic* (K. Smith *LTBA* 2.1 [n.d.]: 9) (for finals see §3.2.2). A Rural variant (§1.3.1) is prob. → xǐ₅ 狶 'swine'.

shǐ₈ 使 → **lǐ₆** 理

shǐ₉ 屎 (śiᴮ) **LH** śiᴮ, **OCM** *lhiʔ — **[T]** *Sin Sukchu SR* ʂi (上); *PR* ʂɿ
'Excrement, dung' [OB, Zhuang]; in some dialects it means other body excretions such as 'earwax, tear' (e.g. M-Xiàmén).
[E] ST *kliʔ: PTB *kliy(ʔ) 'excrement, dung' (*STC* no. 125 p. 39) > Chepang *-kliʔ* 'any kind of excrement, incl. snot, ear wax, tears etc.', WT *lči < lhyi*, Kanauri *kli*; Thulung, Bahing *kʰli*, PTamang *kli; OBurm. *kʰliy* [*IST:* 336], WB *kʰyeᴮ*, PL *ʔ/k(l)e² 'feces'; JP *kʰyi⁵⁵* (*HST:* 74), Garo *kiʔ*. CH -> PTai *xeiᶜ¹ 'excrement' could be related, in some dialects the tone points to PTai *ɣ.

shì₁ 士 (dẓɨᴮ) **LH** dẓəᴮ, **OCM** *dzrəʔ
'Male person' [Shi], 'masculine' [Yi], as in *shì-nǚ* 士女 'men and women' [BI] (syn. of the classical → nán₂ 男), or *shì fū* 士夫 ('masculine':) 'young husband' (for an older wife 老婦) [Yi]; from 'male person' derives > 'man' as in *liáng shì* 良士 'a good gentleman' [Shi]. The original notion of 'man, male, masculine' is also suggested by the graph which serves as an element in → mǔ₁ 牡 'male' (of animals).
[T] *Sin Sukchu SR* zɿ (上去), *PR* zɿ; *MGZY* cʰi (上) [dzɿ]; *MTang* dẓi (?), *ONW* dẓə (?)
[E] This word is reminiscent of AA synonyms: OKhmer *si* 'male', MK languages on the Malay Peninsula have forms like *ʔŋsiil, ensir, kəsəy* 'male, man' (Lewitz 1976: 769). Foreign final *-r* (note *ensir*) sometimes leaves a trace in the OC initial complex (§7.7.3).

shì₂ 士仕 (dẓɨᴮ) **LH** dẓəᴮ, **OCM** *dzrəʔ — **[T]** *MTang* dẓi (?), *ONW* dẓə (?)
('To give or carry out an assignment':) 'to take office, give an office, serve' 仕士 [Shi]; 'retainer, knight' (A. Waley), 'retainers' [BI, Shi] > 'servant, officer' [BI, Shi] 'officer' 士 [BI, Shi]; later 'scholar'.

It is natural to assume that *shì₁* 士 and *shì₂* 士 are the same word with the semantic development 'male > man > servant > to serve'. However, the ancient derivation *shì* 事 (below) and TB counterparts show no association with the notion 'man, maleness', while 'male' hardly derives from 'affair, serve'. Therefore it seems necessary to separate the present *shì₂* 士 'serve' from *shì₁* 士 'male'. MK relations of *shì₁* 士, if valid, would support this distinction.

ℜ **shì** 事 (dẓɨᶜ) **LH** dẓəᶜ, **OCM** *dzrəʔ, rarely *dzrəh
'Assignment, affair, thing' > 'carry out an assignment, serve' [BI, Shi]. Mostly tone B reading in *Shījīng* (Mattos 1971: 309), hence a homophone of, and perh. the s. w. as, shì₂士仕.
[T] *Sin S. SR* zɿ (去), *PR, LR* zɿ; *MGZY* cʰi (去) [dzɿ]; *MTang* dẓi (?), *ONW* dẓə (?)
[<] exopass. of *shì₂* 士仕 (§4.4), lit. 'what has been assigned'.

[E] These forms derive from the root → lǐ$_3$ 理 and are therefore ultimately AA. The MC initial *dẓ-* normally does not co-occur with MC *l-* and *ṣ-* in a ST wf, which could confirms a non-ST provenance. Possibly, MC dẓ- could here go back to an OC configuration *s-r- (≠ MC ṣ- < *sr-). <> AA or OC -> PTB *ʔ-dzəy[1] 'send on an errant' (*HPTB:* 199) > WB *ca* 'a thing' (Gong Hwang-cherng 1999), WT *rdzas* 'thing, matter, object'. TB cognates of this etymon and of → suǒ$_1$ 所 are difficult to distinguish.

shì$_3$ 仕 → **shì$_2$** 士仕

shì$_4$ 氏 (źie^B) **LH** gie^B, **OCM** *geʔ ?

An honorific which is suffixed to place names (fiefs, e.g. 夏氏 'the Lord of Xia'), kinship terms (舅氏 'the uncle'), feudal and official titles (仲氏任 'Lady Zhōng Rèn'): 'lord, lady' [BI, Shi, Shu] > 'clan' [Lun]. — **[E]** The etymology is not clear.

shì$_5$ 市 (źɨ^B) **LH** dźiə^B, **OCM** *dəʔ — **[T]** *MTang* źi < dźi, *ONW* dźə

'Market' [BI, Shi] is also found in PTai *ǰɨ^{C2} 'to buy', in Ahom 'come to terms, consent'.

shì$_6$ 柿 (dẓɨ^B) **LH** dẓə^B, **OCM** *-əʔ

'Persimmon' has an unexpected PMin form *g^{h}i^B.

shì$_7$ 世 → **yè$_4$** 葉

shì$_8$ 貰 → **shē$_1$** 賒

shì$_9$ 式 (śjək) **LH** śɨk, **OCM** *lhək — **[T]** *ONW* śik

'To use, make use of, use as model or norm' [BI, Shi].

⋈ **shì** 試 (śɨ^C) **LH** śə^C, **OCM** *lhəkh — **[T]** *MTang* śi, *ONW* śə

'Apply, make use of' > 'test, try' [Shi].

[<] *lhək + exoactive > caus. s/h-suffix (§4.3.2).

[C] This wf is perhaps connected with → yǐ$_2$ 以 'take, use'.

shì$_{10}$ 試 → **shì$_9$** 式

shì$_{11}$ 使 → **lǐ$_6$** 理

shì$_{12}$ 事 → **shì$_2$** 士仕

shì$_{13}$ 室 (śjet) **LH** śit, **OCM** *lhit ?

'House, hall' [Shi] > 'family' (as in 王室 'royal house /family/clan') [Shu].

[T] *Sin Sukchu SR* ṣi (入); *MGZY* shi (入) [ṣi]; *ONW* śit

[E] ST *k-li(s) > WT *gži < glyi* 'ground, foundation, cause; residence, abode', *sa-gži* 'earth' (as opposed to sky) ⋈ *gžis* 'native place', *yul-gžis* 'house, estate, property', *gžis sgril-ba* 'to change one's abode, move to another place' (Unger *Hao-ku* 39, 1992). These forms are cognate to PTB *mliy [*STC* no. 152] (see → dì$_1$ 地) > Lepcha *lí* 'house'; WB *mre* 'earth, ground', Mikir *mili* 'bare ground', Nung *məli* 'ground, mountain', Dulong *mǎlì* 'place' [LaPolla *LTBA* 24.2: 33]. For the OC initial of *shì* 室, see §8.1.5.

shì$_{14}$ 是 (źie^B) **LH** dźe^B, **OCM** *deʔ

'This' [Shi], an independent pronoun (§3.3.3) > 'be right, correct, so' (§6.2.2), opposite → fēi$_1$ 非.

[T] *Sin Sukchu SR* ẓɿ (上), *PR* ẓɿ; *MGZY* zhi (上) [ẓi]; *ONW* dźe

[E] ST: PTB *day (*STC* no. 21): WT *de* 'that'; JP *n^{55}-deʔ^{55}* 'this, there', *n^{55}-de^{51}* 'so (many...), thus', but Kachin *dai* 'this, that'. A derivation is → shí$_{13}$ 實.

shì$_{15}$ 恃 (źɨ^B) **LH** dźə^B, **OCM** *dəʔ — **[T]** *MTang* źi < dźi, *ONW* dźə
'To depend on, rely on' [Shi]

※ **shì** 侍 (źɨ^C) **LH** dźə^C, **OCM** *dəh
'To accompany, wait upon, attend upon' [Shi].

[C] Karlgren (1956: 17) adds *dài* 待 'wait' to this wf (under → děng$_1$ 等).

shì$_{16}$ 舐 (dźie^B) **LH** źe^B, **OCM** *m-leʔ, OCB *m-lajʔ — **[T]** *ONW* źe^B
'To lick' [Zhuang].
[D] In some dialects, this etymon means 'tongue'.

※ **shé** 舌 (dźjät) **LH** źat, **OCM** *m-lat !, OCB *mlăt
'Tongue' [Shi].
[T] *Sin Sukchu SR* zje (入); *ONW* źat
[<] *shì* 舐 *m-leʔ 'to lick' + nominal t-suffix for natural objects (§6.2.1), lit. 'licker'.

[D] Some southern dialects have preserved the OC initial *l- in this sound symbolic etymon. The equivalents of *shì* and *shé* mean variously 'tongue' or 'to lick':
(1) *Shì:* Y-Guǎngzhōu *³¹lai^B¹* 'lick', Guǎngzhōu *lei^C²* 'tongue'; K-Dànshuǐ *li^C-ma^A²* 'tongue' where *ma^A²* represents perh. the KS morpheme *ma^A²* 'tongue' (R. Bauer, *CAAAL* 28, 1987: 60).
(2) *Shé:* The 'softened' initial in PMin *d̑žiat 'tongue' may indicate prenasalization, hence OCM *m-l-, which is supported by the MY borrowing *nbret (< *mlet ?) (Norman 1986: 383). SMin Dōngshāndǎo *tsiʔ^D²* 'to lick', Fúzhōu *liak^D¹* 'to lick'.

[E] ST, the stem *m/s-lei means 'to lick' or ('licker':) 'tongue': PTB *m/s-lei (*STC* no. 281): > Kokborok (Bodo-Garo) *šlày* [Joseph / Burling *LTBA* 24.2, 2001: 52], WT *lče* < *lhye*, Kanauri-Manchati *hle*, Gurung *le'*, Dimasa *salai*, WB *hlya* (*STC* p. 64); JR *temeli*; Kuki *m-lei > Lushai *lei^H*, SChin Daai *mlei* 'tongue' [Hartmann ICSTLL 1999: 2]; Dulong *pəlaì* 'tongue' [LaPolla, *LTBA* 24.2: 26]. Benedict (*LTBA* 5.1, 1979: 21) suggests that TB 'penis', e.g. WT *mje*, is the same etymon ('body-tongue').

Since only few TB languages have forms with final *-t like CH *shé*, the t-suffix has prob. not been inherited from ST: Magari *milet* (or *me-let*), *let*, Newari *meč* 'tongue', JP *ʃiŋ³¹-let³¹*.

Initial *l- is a near-universal sound symbolic feature for 'lick / tongue', hence similar words in other languages are not likely to be related, such as MK-PVM *laːs 'tongue' [Ferlus]; Kam-Tai: S. *lia^A²* < *dl- 'to lick', PKS *lja² ? [Thurgood].

[C] Matisoff (1995: 71) connects this wf with → shí$_4$ 食 'eat' (whose TB cognates mean 'lick'), and → tián$_3$ 甜 'sweet', all of which have the phonesthemic OC initial *l-.

shì$_{17}$ 視 (źi^B, źi^C) **LH** gi^B, (gi^C?), **OCM** *giʔ
'To look at' [Shi], 'to look after, watch' (e.g. the people, of a supervisor) [Shu 26.4]. The tone C variant reading has prob. been transferred from the next item.
[T] *Sin Sukchu SR* zi (去), *PR* zɿ; *MGZY* zhi (上去) [zi]; *MTang* dźi > źi, *ONW* dźi

※ **shì** 示 (dźi^C) **LH** gi^C, **OCM** *gih
'To show' [Shi] > ('what shows, is shown', i.e. set up to be seen:) 'ancestral tablet' [OB], 'portent, sign' (from heaven) [SW]. Medieval transcriptional materials indicate that 示 had the same initial as 視 (Coblin 1991: 20–21), but later material agrees with the QYS.
[T] *Sin Sukchu SR* zi (去), *PR* zɿ; *MGZY* ci (去) [dzi]; *ONW* dźi
[<] < *giʔ + caus. s/h-suffix (§4.3.2).

※ **zhǐ** 指 (tśi^B) **LH** ki^B, **OCM** *kiʔ
'To point to' [Shi], 'aim' [Shu] > ('pointer':) 'finger' [Zuo]. Tone B is apparently part of the stem, therefore *zhǐ* is not an endoactive derivation.

[T] *Sin Sukchu SR* tʂi (上), *PR*, *LR* tʂʅ; *MGZY* ji (上) [tʂi]; *ONW* tśi

⪤ **chén**$_1$ 臣 (źjen) **LH** gin, **OCM** *gin

'Epískopos', one who 'watches' and looks after things / people on behalf of higher authority; an echo of the etymology is a phrase like *chén zuò zhèn...ěr mù* 臣作朕 ... 耳目 'the *chén* function as my (the ruler's)...ears and eyes' [Shu 5, 12]. The graph, a drawing of an 'eye', also connects the word with the notion 'to watch'. Hence on the one hand the meanings: 'a subject, servant', on the other 'minister, person in charge', 'be subject to, function as a subject of' [OB, BI], *xiǎo-chén* 小臣 'junior minister' [OB, BI]; with lesser rank 'retainers', *hǔ-chén* 虎臣 some kind of bodyguard; with low rank 'servant, subject' [BI, Shi], *chén-qiè* 臣妾 'servants and maids' [BI, Shu] (Keightley 1969: 191ff); 'servant' > 'I' (when speaking to a superior).

[T] *Sin Sukchu SR* dʐin (平); *MGZY* zhin (平) [dʐin]; *ONW* dźin

[N] OC initial *g- is supported by *GSR* 368 which includes *qiān* 掔 (kʰien), where *chén* (*GSR* 377) is phonetic.

[<] nominal *-n derivation from → shì$_{17}$ 視 *giʔ 'to watch, look after' (§6.4.3), lit. 'a watcher, supervisor'.

[E] Bodman (1980: 158) relates *chén* to WT *'gyiŋ-ba* 'look down upon, despise' (for the difference in finals, see §6.4.1), but see next:

[E] Prob. ST in light of TB-Lushai *kʰiin*^{L} 'a seer'. Additional comparanda may include MK-PWa *kɛr 'to look, watch', PMon *ŋgiir 'look for', PSBahn. *keːr 'look, aim' (for finals see §7.7.5), but the phonological distance from the OC form is rather large.

shì$_{18}$ 逝 → **chè**$_2$ 徹撤

shì$_{19}$ 誓 (źjäi^C) **LH** dźas, **OCM** *dats

'A formal statement, oath, make an oath' [BI, Shi, Shu]. Perh. the homophone **shì** 筮 'divine with milfoil oracle' [BI, Shi] is the same word (< 'make clear'). This etymon may belong to → zhé$_3$ 晢 'clear, perspicacious'.

shì$_{20}$ 嗜 → **zhǐ**$_4$ 旨

shì$_{21}$ 奭 → **chì**$_3$ 赤

shì$_{22}$ 筮 → **shì**$_{19}$ 誓

shì$_{23}$ 噬 (źjäi^C) **LH** dźas, **OCM** *dats

'To bite' [Shi, Zuo] may be cognate to WT *ldad-pa, bldad* 'to chew' ~ *blad-pa* 'to chew' (*HST:* 43), but the initial consonants do not agree. A syn. is → dié$_2$ 咥.

shì$_{24}$ 施 'give' → **shī**$_9$ 施

shì$_{25}$ 勢 → **yì**$_{28}$ 藝

shì$_{26}$ 釋 (śjäk) **LH** śak, S tśʰɑk, **OCM** *lhak — [T] *ONW* śek — [D] M-Amoy *tsʰioʔ*^{A1}

'To put into water, moisten' [Li], 'wash' (rice) [Shi], also 釋.

⪤ **xī** 淅 (siek) **LH** sek, **OCM** *sêk < *slek

'To wash rice'; for vocalic alternations, see §11.1.3.

[E] PKS *s-lak (Edm. / Yang) / *ʔlak^7 (Thurgood) 'to wash clothes'; perh. connected with PTai *zək 'wash clothes'. This etymon may possibly be ST instead and be derived from → yè$_2$ 液 'fluid'.

shì$_{27}$ 澤 'lay open the ground' → **yì**$_{35}$ 繹

shì$_{28}$ 釋 → **yì**$_{35}$ 繹

shì$_{29}$ 適 'go to' → **chè**$_2$ 徹撤

shì$_{30}$ 適 'scared' → **tì**$_4$ 惕

shì$_{31}$ 啻 (śje^C) **LH** śe^C, **OCM** *lhekh ?
'Only' 啻 [Shu], 適 (*lhek ?) [Meng]. The phonetic series has a T-like initial. The phonological differences make a relationship with → zhī$_{9a}$ 衹 *ke 'only' very doubtful.

shì$_{32}$ 識 (śjək) **LH** śɨk, **OCM** *-ək
'To know' [BI, Shi].
[T] *Sin Sukchu SR* ʂi (入); *MGZY* shi (入) [ʂi]; *ONW* śik
[C] caus. in tone C [śiə^C] 'to show, mark' [Zuo, Li] (Downer 1959: 282).

⋈ **zhì** 識 (tśɨ^C) **LH** tśə^C, **OCM** *təkh ?
'To remember, record' [OB, Shi].
The alternation of the MC initials *śj-* and *tś-* in a wf is very unusual, casting doubt on the relationship.

[E] Etymology not clear, but note some TB comparanda (OC ə = TB *i* is rare; see §11.2.2): Chepang *təyh-sa* 'to know', JP *²tše* [Weidert 1987: 28].

shì$_{33}$ 翨 → **chì**$_4$ 翅

shōu 收 (śjəu) **LH** śu, **OCM** *nhiu ?, OCB *xjiw
'To gather up, collect, take possession, remove, retire' [Shi], 'harvest' [Zuo].
[T] *Sin Sukchu SR* ʂiw (平); *MGZY* shiw (平) [ʂiw]; *ONW* śu

⋈ **shōu** 收 (śjəu^C) **LH** śu^C, **OCM** *nhiuh ?
'Harvest'.
[<] exopass. of OCM *nhiu? (§4.4), lit. 'what has been harvested' (Downer 1959: 276).

⋈ **shú** 叔 (śjuk) **LH** śuk, **OCM** *nhiuk
'To harvest' [Shi].

[E] Etymology not certain, the above connections are established on the assumption of a voiceless *nh- in the stem (based on *shú*). Alternatively, the initial might have been *hj- (Baxter), then compare TB-Lushai *zo^H < joo* 'reap benefit'. <> Tai: S. *kiau^{B1} 'to cut with a sickle, reap' is not related, see → zhāo$_1$, jiāo 釗鉊.
[C] An allofam is prob. → qiū$_4$ 秋 *tshiu 'autumn, harvest'.

shóu 熟 → **shú**$_5$, **shóu** 熟

shǒu$_1$ 手 (śjəu^B) **LH** śu^B, S tś^{h}u^B, **OCM** *nhuʔ ?, or OCB *hjuʔ ?
'Hand' [Shi].
[T] *Sin Sukchu SR* ʂiw (上); *MGZY* shiw (上) [ʂiw]; *ONW* śu
[D] PMin *tš^{h}iu^{B1} > Xiàmén *ts^{h}iu^B*, PWMin *ʃiu^{B1}.
[E] The OC form and etymology are a matter of conjecture: (1) Unger (*Hao-ku* 46, 1995: 133f) reconstructs this word with an OC nasal initial; he bases this on the *Shìmíng* (a Han period sound gloss dictionary) gloss *xū* 須 < *sn-, and the *GY* graph 杻 for QYS *ṇjəu^B ~ ṭ^{h}jəu^B* 杻 (also Wáng Lì 1982: 231). He suggests that *shǒu* is cogn. to → niǔ$_1$ 狃丑 'finger'. (2) Alternatively, *shǒu* may be derived from → shōu 收 'take, gather', tone B would then be the endoactive morpheme: 'hand' < lit. 'the thing that is doing the taking' (§4.5.1).

shǒu$_2$ 守 (śjəu^B) **LH** śu^B, **OCM** *-uʔ
'To keep, guard' [BI, Shi], 'fief' [Zuo].

⋈ **shòu** 守 (śjəu^C) **LH** śu^C, **OCM** *-uh
'Fief' [Shu, Zuo] > 'governor' 守 [Zuo] (Downer 1959: 276).
[<] -uʔ + s/h-suffix exopass. (§4.4) 'what is kept, guarded' (Lau 1999: 43), then transferred to a person: 'governor'.

shǒu $_3$ 首 (śjəu^B) **LH** śu^B, **OCM** *lhuʔ — **[T]** *ONW* śu

'Head' [BI, Shi] may already have become a homophone of *shǒu* 手 'hand' in a WZhou BI (*Yù guǐ* 遹簋); *shǒu* was replaced by → tóu$_3$ 頭 'head' by the Zhànguó period (Unger *Hao-ku* 46, 1995: 133). A tone C derivation is 'to point the head towards' [Liji] (Downer 1959: 280).

[E] ST: PTB *lu 'head': Lushai *lu^H < luu* 'head' (Unger *Hao-ku* 46, 1995: 133; *CVST* 3: 43). Less plausible would be a connection with the TB word for 'brain'; although a foreign final *-k* can regularly correspond to CH tone B (§3.2.2), it is phonologically and semantically not close: Lushai *thluak^H* (< *khl- or *sl-), WT *glod* 'brain'. There are also similarities with words outside ST: PTai *kləu^{C1} 'head, knot of hair on top of the head', PKS *kru^3-f. 'head'; PVM *k-lo:k / *k-lok 'head', but a relationship with CH is unlikely.

shòu$_1$ 受 (źjəu^B) **LH** dźu^B, **OCM** *duʔ

'Receive, accept' [BI, Shi].

[T] *Sin Sukchu SR* ʐiw (上); *MGZY* zhiw (上) [ʐiw]; *ONW* dźu

ⅹ **shòu** 授 (źjəu^C) **LH** dźu^C, **OCM** *duh — **[T]** *ONW* dźu

'To give, to hand' [BI, Shi], 'hand over' [Zuo]. → shòu$_2$ 售 'sell' is prob. the same word.

[<] *duʔ + s/h-suffix extrovert (§4.3).

[E] *CVST* (2: 3) compares this wf with WT *'tʰu-ba* 'to gather', but see → zú$_1$ 卒.

shòu$_2$ 售 (źjəu^C) **LH** dźu^C, **OCM** *duh

'To sell' [Shi 35, 5]. This is perh. a semantic extension of *shòu* 授 'give' (under → shòu$_1$ 受); or possibly also connected with MK: Khmer *ṭūra* /dòor/, OKhmer *tor ~ tvar* 'to barter, trade, exchange' (see §6.9 for the open syllable in CH). Syn. → dí$_6$ 糴; → gǔ$_{11}$ 賈; → mǎi 買; → yù$_{23}$ 賣.

shòu$_3$ 獸 (śjəu^C) **LH** śu^C, **OCM** *-uh

'Wild animal, animal' (i.e. quadruped) [Shi]. Opposite → chù$_4$, xù 畜 'domestic animal', lit. 'what is raised'.

[T] *Sin Sukchu SR* ʂiw (去); *MGZY* shiw (去) [ʂiw]

[<] exopass. of *shòu* 狩 *-uʔ 'what is hunted' (§4.4) (Wáng Lì 1982: 237). Benedict relates *shòu* to the widespread TB etymon *sya 'flesh, animal' (*STC:* 168 n. 452); however, PTB *a for OC *u (or *o) is unusual (e.g. → ròu 肉 'meat'), and a foreign *sj-* never seems to relate to a MC palatal *śj-*.

ⅹ **shòu** 狩 (śjəu^C) **LH** śu^C, **OCM** *-uʔ !, OCB *stjus

'To hunt' [BI, Shi]. *Shījīng* rimes indicate tone B (Mattos 1971: 309). The possible notional parallel with → qín$_4$ 禽 and → qín$_5$ 擒 ('bird, game bird' ~ 'catch birds') may support cognation with → shòu$_3$ 獸.

[E] Outside CH, WT *'čʰor-ba, (b)šor* 'to hunt' could theoretically be reconciled with MC if we assume a voiceless palatalized initial *rhj-, *lhj-, or *hj-, and loss of ST final *-r which has occurred in a few other words. But this is rather speculative.

shū$_1$ 殊 (źju) **LH** dźo, **OCM** *do

'To cut off' [Zuo] (Karlgren 1956: 17) > 'kill' > pass. 'to die' [Zhuang].

[T] *Sin Sukchu SR* ʐy (平); *MGZY* zhÿu (平) [ʐy]

ⅹ **zhū** 誅 (ṭju) **LH** ṭo, **OCM** *tro

'To punish, kill' [Zuo], 'to reprove' [Lunyu].

[E] ST *do(k): JP *doʔ^{31} < tok^{31}* 'cut off'. For ST cognates and / or parallel stems, see Table C-1 under → chù$_1$ 觸.

shū $_2$ 樞 (tśʰju) **LH** tśʰo, **OCM** *k-hlo ?
'Pivot' [Yi]; the graph originally wrote a word 'thorny elm'. In some Yuè and Kèjiā dialects, 'pivot' has a velar initial: Yuè HK-NT *kʰy^{A1}*, Cónghuà *kʰy^{55}*, etc.; K-Huìzhōu *ky^{33}*, Dōngguǎn *kʰi^{33}*.

shū $_3$ 梳 (ṣjwo) **LH** ṣɑ, this form would correspond to an OCM *srâ
'Comb' [SW]. Acc. to *Shìmíng*, the comb is named *shū* because its teeth are 'spaced apart' *shū* 疏, but this pun may be folk etymology.
[E] ST *Crja(t): PTB *hryat 'to comb': KN-Lai *hriat / hriaʔ* 'to comb' [*LTBA* 21.1, 1998: 16], WT *gšod-pa, (g)šad-pa* 'to comb' < *(g-)rhyat. This connection would imply a medial *-j-* in PCH while the TB final *-t* would be an innovation. For an overview of similar etyma, see Table S-2 under → shuā 刷. Syn. → jié$_{10}$ 櫛.

shū $_4$ 書 (śjwo) **LH** śɑ, **OCM** *lha ?
'Writing > book' [BI, Shi]. Etymology is not clear.
[T] *Sin Sukchu SR* ṣy (平); *MGZY* shÿu (平) [ṣy]

shū $_5$ 抒 → **chú$_2$** 除

shū $_6$ 紓 → **yù$_{25}$** 豫

shū $_7$ 舒 → **yù$_{25}$** 豫

shū $_8$ 輸 → **yú$_{18}$** 踰逾

shú$_1$ 秫 (dźjuet) **LH** źuit, **OCM** *m-lut ? — **[T]** *ONW* źuit
'Glutinous millet' [Li].
[D] PEMin *tsut^{D2}, PWMin *tsʰut^{D2} (PMin *tʃhut?) 'glutinous (rice)'.
[E] Area word: PMY *nblut 'glutinous, sticky', AN *pulut* 'sticky substance' (Sagart *JCL* 1993, 21.1: 52).

shú$_2$ 叔 'harvest' → **shōu** 收

shú$_3$ 菽 (śjuk) **LH** śuk, **OCM** *nhuk
'Bean' [Shi]
[E] ST *nhuk or *snuk: PLB *(s-)nok 'bean' > WB *nok* [Matisoff *TSR* no. 140] (*HST*: 39), JP *noʔ^{31}-* 'red bean' (*CVST* 2: 36). For the vowels, see §11.10.1.

shú$_4$ 孰 'who' → **shéi, shuí** 誰

shú$_5$, shóu 熟 (źjuk) **LH** dźuk, **OCM** *duk
'Be ripe, fruitful, productive' [Shu].
[T] *Sin Sukchu SR* ẓu (入), *PR, LR* ẓuʔ; *MGZY* zhÿu (入) [ẓy]; *ONW* dźuk
[E] ST: PKiranti *tʰok ~ tʰuk 'ripen, cooked' (van Driem 1995: 254: Starostin).
CH -> Tai: S. *suk^{D1}S* < *s- 'ripe', northern Tai dialects have a voiced initial (Li F. 1976: 44). The sibilant indicates that Tai has borrowed this word from post-Han CH.

shú$_6$ 贖 (d)źjwok) **LH** źok, **OCM** *m-lok
'To ransom, redeem' [Shi].
[E] Area etymon. ST: WT *blu-ba, blus* 'to buy off, ransom' ⋇ *blud-pa* 'release, ransom'. For initial *m-* vs. *b-*, see §5.12.2. <> MK: Khmer lùəh 'to ransom,redeem'. <> PTai *lu^{B2} 'to redeem, tribute', *dl/ru^{B2} 'to donate, ransom' [Luo Yongxian *MKS* 27, 1997: 280; 293]. *Shú* looks like a cognate of → yù$_{23}$ 賣 *luk 'sell' (Sagart 1999: 82), but see comment there.

shǔ $_1$ 鼠 (śjwo^B) **LH** śɑ^B ~ tśʰɑ^B, **OCM** *nhaʔ ?, OCB *hjaʔ (?)
'Rat' [Shi].

[T] *Sin Sukchu SR* ʂy (上); *MGZY* shÿu (上) [ʂy]; *ONW* śo > śø
[D] Southern and NW dialects have variants with affricate initial: PMin *tšʰy^B: Xiàmén *tsʰu^B*, Fúzhōu *tsʰy^B*; Kèjiā *tšʰu^B1: Méixiàn *tsʰu^B*; W-Wēnzhōu *tɕʰi^45* (Běidà *tsʰei^B*). NW-Xīníng *tʂʰy^53*, Dūnhuáng *-tʂʰu^42*, Lánzhōu *pfʰu^33*.
[E] Etymology not clear. Note AA-PMon *[c/s]naaʔ in Nyah Kur 'shrew' (a shrew is hard to distinguish from a mouse), in Mon 'squirrel'; the PMon word for 'rat, mouse' is *kniiʔ, PNBahnaric *kane 'rat' which is an alternate candidate as a source for *shǔ* if we assume the occasional shift from front vowel to OC *a (§11.1.3). <> PKS *kʰ-no^C 'rat' (Edmondson / Yang 1988) may be related. The case for OCM *n- in *shǔ* is suggested by → shǔ₂ 癙 *nhaʔ. The TB word for 'rat, mouse' *yu had acquired the meaning 'weasel' in Old Chinese (→ yòu₉ 鼬).

shǔ₂ 癙 (śjwo^B) **LH** śɑ^B, **OCM** *nhaʔ ?
'Painful, suffering' [Shi].
[E] Perh. related to the common PTB *na > WT *na-ba* 'be ill, ache' ≍ *nad* 'disease, malady, sickness' ≍ *snad-pa* 'to hurt, harm, injure'; WB *na* 'be ill, be in pain' ≍ *nat* 'demon, spirit'; Mikir *no* 'bad, evil, wrong'; Lushai *naa^H / nat^L*, Thado *nat* 'be ill' (Benedict *HJAS* 4, 1939: 227). If this item is indeed OCM *nhaʔ, it is prob. related to → nuó 儺, → nán₃ 難 'difficult'.

shǔ₃ 黍 (śjwo^B) **LH** śɑ^B, perh. **OCM** *nhaʔ ? or OCB *hjaʔ — **[T]** *ONW* śo > śø
'Millet', prob. 'glutinous millet' [OB, BI, Shi] can perh. be compared with WT *nas* 'barley'. Both millet and barley were the staple cereals grown in ancient Northern China and Tibet respectively.

shǔ₄ 數 (ʂju^B) **LH** ʂo^B, **OCM** *sroʔ
'To calculate, count' [Shi].
[T] *Sin Sukchu SR* ʂu (上); *MGZY* (zhu >) shu (上) [ʂu]; *ONW* ʂuo

≍ **shù** 數 (ʂju^C) **LH** ʂo^C, **OCM** *sroh
'Number' [Yi] > 'some, several' [Lunyu]; 'method, art' [Meng].
[<] *sroʔ + pass. s/h-suffix (§4.4), lit. 'what is counted'.

≍ **shuò** 數 (ʂåk) **LH** ʂɔk, **OCM** *srôk
'Number of times, frequently' [Lunyu, Li]; (business) 'account' 朔 [Lunyu].
[<] sroʔ + perh. distributive k-suffix (§6.1.2) (Baxter 1992: 848 n. 242).
[E] <> ? AA: Mon *ruih* [røh], hypoth. *sruih* 'to count', *lros* id.

shǔ₅ 曙 (źjwo^C) **LH** dźɑ^C, **OCM** *dah or *djah?
'Sunrise' [Guanzi, Huainan] > later also 'moon rise'. This word belongs prob. to a larger wf 'rise', see → shàng₁ 上.

shǔ₆ 屬 → **zhǔ₈** 屬

shǔ₇ 樹 (źju^B) **LH** dźo^B, **OCM** *doʔ
'To plant, place upright' [Shi], 'establish' 樹 [Zuo]; 'to stand' [Hou Hanshu], 'be in attendance' [OB], (someone standing by:) 'attendant' 豎 [Zuo].
[T] *Sin Sukchu SR* ʐy (上); *MGZY* zhÿu (上) [ʐy]

≍ **shù** 樹 (źju^C) **LH** dźo^C, **OCM** *doh
(1) 'Tree' [Zuo]. See comment below.
[T] *Sin Sukchu SR* ʐy (去); *MGZY* zhÿu (去) [ʐy]; *ONW* dźuo
[<] exopass. of *shǔ* 樹 (źju^B) (§4.4), lit. 'what is planted'.
(2) 'To raise, put up' 尌 [Han].
[<] exoact. > caus. of *shǔ* 樹 (źju^B) (§4.3), lit. 'cause to stand'.

ꭗ **zhù** 壴 (tju^C) **LH** ṭo^C, **OCM** *troh
'Post or stand for musical instruments' [OB].
[E] Area word: TB-Lushai *tuʔ^L < tus* 'to plant' (a seed) (for the vowels, see §11.9.1). <> AA: Khmer *ṭuh* /doh/ 'to grow, sprout...' ꭗ caus. /pdoh/ 'to plant, grow' (crops).

The development to the CH meaning *shù* 樹 'tree' may have been encouraged through interference from AA: PSouthern MK *jhuuʔ or *perh. *jhɨɨʔ 'wood' (substance, general) [Diffloth *MKS* 16–17, 1990: 4] > OKhmer *jhe* [Jenner / Pou], *jhö* [Diffloth] 'tree, wood', also 'fuel' in Khamuk [Shorto 1971: 117] (Khmer *jhe* is perh. more directly reflected in → chái₁ 柴). *Shù* is not a loan because PAA *j, *c normally do not correspond to an OC dental stop initial.

It is not clear if / how the following candidates for cognation are connected: WT *bžugs-pa* (< *b-dyuk-s?) 'to sit, dwell' (so *HST:* 68f), or PTB *dzu[:]k (*STC* no. 360) > WT *'dzug-pa ~ zug-pa* 'prick or stick into, plant, erect'. Syn. → zhì₂₂ 置.

shù₁ 戍 (śju^C) **LH** śo^C, tśʰo^C, **OCM** *-oh — **[T]** *ONW* śuo
'Be stationed at a military outpost' [BI, Shi], 'to guard' (the frontier) [Zuo]. Acc. to Norman 1984, this has become the word for 'house' in some Southern dialects: PMin *tšʰio^C; Y-Guǎngzhōu *³³tsʰy^CD*, Táishān *tsʰui²¹* 'house'.

shù₂ 束 (śjwok) **LH** śok, **OCM** *lhok ?
'To bind, tie together, a bundle' [Shi].
[E] Perh. ST: WB *hluiŋ^B* 'bind into a bundle'.

shù₃, shuò 欶 (ṣåk) **LH** ṣɔk, **OCM** *srôk ? < *C-sok ?
'Suck, inhale' [SW], in southern dialects (written 嗍): G-Chángshā *so³³*, Y-Guǎngzhōu *ʃɔk³³* (lower D1 tone), M-Xiàmén *suʔ³²* (D1).
[E] ST: WB *sok* 'drink, smoke'. This is prob. a sound-symbolic area word, note Khmer *ja'ka* /cuk/ 'to suck'. Perh. OC is a conflation of ST with PMK *sro:p (~ *sru[u]p) 'absorb, suck up' (Shorto 1972: 13f).

shù₄ 述術鉥 (dźjuet) **LH** źuit, **OCM** *m-lut ?
'To follow' [Li], 'proceed, pass on, then' 述 [BI, Shi] > 'road, path' (in a town) 術 [Li, SW] > 'procedure, device, art' 術 [BI, Zuo]; 'to lead' (as needle) 鉥 [Guoyu] > 'needle' [Guanzi].
[T] *Sin Sukchu SR* ʐy (入); *MGZY* cÿu (入) [dʐy]; *ONW* źuit
[<] *lut + ST m-prerfix (§8.1.3).

ꭗ **xù** 訹 (sjuet) **LH** suit, **OCM** *sut < slut ?
'To entice' [Guoce].
[<] *lut + ST caus. s-prefix (§8.1.2).

ꭗ **yǒu** 誘 (jiəu^B) **LH** ju^B, **OCM** *luʔ (or *juʔ ? — then unrelated)
'To entice, seduce, guide' [Shi].
[E] ST: WT *slu-ba, bslus* 'to entice, seduce, deceive' (Unger *Hao-ku* 36, 1990: 66). Note also PTai *l-: S. *lɔɔ^B2* 'to lure, deceive' which is prob. a CH loan. *Shù* and *xù* form a ST *s- ~ m-* set. Bodman (1980: 96) has set up a wf which combines all the items in final *-t here with → lǜ₁ 律. For additional possible comparanda, see under → suì₂ 遂.

shù₅ 署 'to place' → **zhù₁₃** 著

shù₆ 曙 → **shǔ₅** 曙

shù₇ 數 → **shǔ₄** 數

shù₈ 樹 → **shǔ₇** 樹

shuā 刷 (ṣjwät, ṣwat) **LH** ṣuat, **OCM** *srot
'Scrape clear, brush' [Zhouli].
[T] *Sin Sukchu SR* ṣwa (入); *MGZY* (zhwa >) shwa (入) [ṣwa]
[E] ST roots for 'brush' show some variaty; some of the following TB items may belong to → fú$_9$ 拂 or → bǐ$_6$ 筆 instead: Mru *charüt* 'comb' (Löffler 1966: 144); Lushai *hru / hruuk* 'to rub (off), wipe (off)', JP *brut*[2] 'a brush' *(shuāzi)* ⋇ *lə*[55]*-rut*[55] 'a brush' (shuāzi), WT *šud-pa, bšud* < *rhyut 'to rub, get scratched'. Perh. also related to Spilo-Kanauri *šwartma* 'to comb' [Bodman].
[C] A cognate is prob. → guā$_3$ 刮 *krot 'scrape'; *shuā* is not related to → shū$_3$ 梳 'comb'. Table S-2 'Brush, comb, scrape' provides an overview over similar etyma.

Table S-2 Brush, comb, scrape

	*prut brush ⋇	*C-rut / hrut	*srot	*srja(t) comb
OC	bǐ 筆 *p(r)ə/ut writing brush fú 拂 *phə/ut < * sprut ? brush off (1)	guā 刮 *krot scrape (2)	shuā 刷 *srot cleaning brush	shū 梳 *sra comb
WT		šud-pa, bšud < *rhyut to rub, get scratched (3)		gšod-pa, (g)šad-pa < *rhyat to comb
Kanauri			šwartma comb	
Lushai		hru / hruuk to rub / wipe (off)		hriat / hriaʔ to comb
Mru			charüt comb	
JP	brut[2] cleaning brush	lă[55]-rut[55] a cleaning brush		

Notes on Table S-2: (1) See under fú$_9$ 拂 for alternate etymology. (2) The OC rime *ot (instead of the expected *ut) in *guā* is perh. due to analogy with *shuā*. (3) The palatalization (Proto-Tib. medial *y) in *šud* is perh. due to influence from *gšod*.

shuāi 衰 (ṣwi) **LH** ṣui, **OCM** *srui
'To diminish, decline, decay' [Lun].
[T] *Sin Sukchu SR* ṣuj (平), *PR* ṣwaj; *MGZY* (zhway >) shway (平) [ṣwaj]

⋇ **chuī** 衰 (tṣʰwie) **LH** tṣʰuɑi, **OCM** *k-sroi
'To reduce, graduate' [Zuo].
[<] *shuāi* 衰 (ṣwi) *srui (or sroi?) with initial *k (§5.9.1).

⋇ **shài** 殺 (ṣăi^C) **LH** ṣɛs, **OCM** *srêts
'To diminish, reduce' [Zuo], 'of a smaller degree' [Li].
[<] *shuāi* 衰 (ṣwi) *srui (or *sroi?) with final -t (§6.2.2). Karlgren (1956: 11) adds this word to → shā$_2$ 殺 'kill' (unlikely). For loss of medial w, see §10.2.1.

[E] AA has a similar-looking word: Khmer /rı́iəw/ 'diminish, decrease, taper (off), slim slender...' ⋇ /srı̀iəw/ 'be small-boned and slender', but the diphthong is the reverse of CH; perh. a metathesis from *-iu to *-ui took place in OC (a parallel case may be → něi 餒 'hungry'). An alternative comparandum may be TB-Lushai *zuai*^{F} < *juaiʔ* 'decline' (in diligence, enthusiasm), but Lushai initial *z-* usually derives from PTB *y-, and the semantic agreement is not as close.

shuài₁ 率 'all' → **sōu₂** 搜

shuài₂ 率帥 → **lǜ₁** 律

shuài₃ 繂率 → **lǜ₅** 繂率

shuàn, luán 孿 'twins' → **shuāng₁** 雙

shuāng₁ 雙 (ṣåŋ) **LH** ṣɔŋ, **OCM** *srôŋ, OCB *sCr(j)oŋ) < PCH *sruŋ
'A pair' (e.g. cap pendants) [Shi].
[T] *Sin Sukchu SR* ṣaŋ (平), *PR* ṣwaŋ; *MGZY* shʰang (平) [ṣAŋ]
[E] Most likely, [ṣɔŋ] is cognate to WT *zuŋ* 'a pair, single' (*HST:* 115), Mru *choŋ* 'pair' (Löffler 1966: 142), but in this case a ST *C-zuŋ must be assumed (for initials, see §7.4). Alternatively, *shuāng* could be a doublet of → lüán, shuàn 孿 'twins'. Tai may have borrowed *shuāng* as *soŋ* 'two'.

shuāng₂ 霜 → **liáng₃** 涼

shuǎng₁ 爽 (ṣjaŋᴮ) **LH** ṣɑŋᴮ, **OCM** *sraŋʔ — **[T]** *ONW* ṣaŋ
'Twilight' (of dawn) [BI, Shu].
[E] AA: Khmer *srāṅa* /sraaŋ/ (intr., of first light of day:) 'to be dim, faint, weak' < *-rāṅa* /ríiəŋ/ 'be light, bright' ⋇ *brāṅa* /príiəŋ/ 'to grow light' (after dark). Also in TB: Trung *śraŋ* 'morning'. Some TB items under → fāng₃ 方 meaning 'morning' may belong here as well. Prob. related to → liàng 亮 'light'.

shuǎng₂ 爽 → **liáng₁, làng** 俍

shuǐ 水 (świᴮ) **LH** śuiᴮ, S tśuiᴮ, **OCM** *lhuiʔ, OCB *[l]huiʔ ?
'Water, river' [OB, Shi].
[T] *Sin Sukchu SR* ṣuj, ṣi (上), *PR* ṣi, *LR* ṣuj; *MGZY* shue (上) [ṣuɛ]; *ONW* śui
[D] PMin *tšuiᴮ
[E] ST: PTB *lwi(y) [*STC* no. 210] > JP *lui³³* 'to flow' (as water), Lushai *luiᴸ* < *luih*, Tiddim *luuiᶠ* < *luuih* 'stream, river' (*HST:* 158). Perh. this is an area etymon, note possible MK connections: OMon *lwuy*; Khmer /luj/ 'float, drift'; Viet. *lọy* 'swim', Wa-Lawa-Bulang *l[o]y 'swim'. MK -> PTai *hlwəiᴬ¹ 'to flow' > S. *laiᴬ¹* (Li 1977:137; 286); Khmer -> PTai *lɔiᴬ² > S. *lɔɔiᴬ²* 'to float' (Li 1977: 134, 288), Saek *tlooyᴬ¹* 'to flow'. Given the occasional alternation between *l* and *r,* the following may also be connected or be parallel etyma: PKS *kru:i³ 'stream', PTai *xruəiᶜ (?) > S. *huaiᶜ¹* 'mountain stream', Saek *rii³* < *hriiᶜ¹* 'id.', perh. also Tai: S. *huui³* 'a stream, creek'. Similar-looking MK etyma are prob. not connected: PNBahn. *hayŭh*, P-Hrê-Sedang *riùh* 'stream' [Smith 1972: 52], also PMonic *hiiw 'to flow, drift'.

Tone B prob. marks the word as an endoactive derivation from a ST root, lit. 'what is flowing' (§4.5.1). The voiceless initial may go back to an earlier nominalizing prefix, either *k- (§5.4) or *s- which is found in old ST nouns which relate to naturally occurring things (§5.2.4). Another derivation from the ST root may be → xuàn₁ 泫 *wînʔ 'to flow'.

shuì₁ 睡 (źwieᶜ) **LH** dźuaiᶜ, **OCM** *doih or *djoih ? — **[T]** *ONW* dźue
'To sleep' [Guoce].
[E] Since both CH and WT have a word for 'sleep' which is nearly homophonous with one for 'droop', it is probable that *shuì* is derived from → chuí₁ 垂 *doi 'droop'. The WT cognate seems to be *yur-ba* 'to slumber' ⋇ *g-yur* 'sleep' (Bodman 1980: 80) ⋇ *g-yur-ba* 'droop, hang or sink down' (of fading flowers etc.), but phonologically, the OC items are closer to a parallel stem in rime *-ol, see → chuí₁ 垂.

shuì$_2$ 稅 (śjuäi^C) **LH** śuas, **OCM** *lhots — **[T]** *ONW* śuei
'To present, give, donate' [Liji] > 'tax' [Chunqiu]. Boltz (1994: 101) relates this word to the wf → yú$_{17}$ 愉; then 'tax' means lit. 'something peeled off the top'. Alternatively, *shuì* may be derived from *shū* 輸 'to transport, convey to' (under → yú$_{18}$ 踰逾).

shuì$_3$ 挩 → **tuō$_3$** 脫

shuì$_4$ 說 → **shuō** 說

shǔn$_1$ 吮 (dźjuen^B) **LH** źuin^B, **OCM** *m-lunʔ ? — **[D]** PMin *d̯zion^B < *Ndź-
'To suck' [Hanfei].
[E] ST has several stems from a single root (for TB, see also *HPTB:* 81, 84, 481):
(1) *mlyu-n: PTB *m-lyun > Kanauri *myun 'to swallow', JP *mə^{31}-run^{31}* 'suck'.
(2) *mlyu-k: PTB *m-lyu:k > Lushai *zu^L / zuuk^F < juʔ/s / juuk* 'to drink' (by sucking a tube), 'to bite' (as leech), Ao-Naga *^{3}mɯ^{3}yuk* (*m-yuk) 'to swallow' [Weidert 1987: 457], JP *mə^{31}-yuʔ^{31}* 'throat, swallow' ⋇ *luʔ^{31} < luk* 'to drink, suck', Chepang *yok-sa* 'to swallow'.
(3) PTB *mlyuw: PLB *myuw > WB *myui* (inscr. *mlyui*) 'swallow' [Matisoff 1978: 29], Angami Naga *me-zu < m-ju* 'id.', SChin Daai *mjo* 'swallow' [Hatmann ICSTLL 1999: 2], Karen Sgaw *ju* (*STC* no. 153; p. 147f).
The complex proto-initial is prob. responsible for three different reflexes in JP: *mə^{31}-run^{31}* 'suck', *mə^{31}-yuʔ^{31}* 'throat, swallow', *luʔ^{31} < luk* 'to drink, suck'. WT *ldud-pa, blud < ɴlut* 'give to drink, to water' belongs to the same root.

shǔn$_2$ 盾楯 → **dùn$_1$**, **shǔn** 盾楯

shùn$_1$ 順 (dźjuen^C) **LH** źuin^C, **OCM** *m-luns
'To follow, agree, be agreeable' [BI, Shi].
[T] *Sin Sukchu SR* ʐyn (去); *MGZY* cÿun (去) [dʐyn]; *ONW* źuin
[<] *lun + ST m-prefix (§8.1.3).

⋇ **xún** 循馴 (zjuen) **LH** zuin, **OCM** *s-lun
'To follow, inspection tour' [Shu], 'obey' 循 [Zuo]; 'docile' 馴 [Lie] (Wáng Lì *Cíyuán zìdiǎn* 1982: 518).
[<] *lun + ST s-prefix (§8.1.2).

[E] ST: WT *'čʰun-pa* 'be tamed, subdued' ⋇ *'ǰun-pa, bčun, gžun* 'subdue, punish, soften' (*HST:* 146). OC *m- ~ *s- is parallel to the TB root for 'follow' which Matisoff (*LTBA* 15.1, 1992: 163) has set up for 'Kamarupan', see → suì$_2$ 遂 for additional possible cognates.

shùn$_2$ 揗 → **mén$_2$** 捫

shùn$_3$ 瞬 (śjuen^C) **LH** śuin^C, **OCM** *hwins
'To move the eyes, wink' [Zhuang], 'give a signal with the eyes' [Shiji], 'blink' [Lie].
[T] *Sin Sukchu SR* ʂyn (去); *MGZY* shÿun (去) [ʂyn]

⋇ **xuàn**, **shùn** 眴 (xiwen^C) **LH** hwen^C, **OCM** *hwîns
'Flutter the eyes, scared' [Zhuang].

⋇ **xún** 眴 (sjuen) **LH** suin, **OCM** *swin
'Troubled eyesight, deluded' [Zhuang].

[E] The stem of this wf is *win with the meaning 'move the eyes'. The wf overlaps with → yíng$_3$ 熒 whose stem is *weŋ with the basic meaning 'bright, dazzle, confuse'.

shuō 說 (śjwät) **LH** śuat, **OCM** *lhot
'Explain, excuse' [Lun], 'speak' [Shi].
[T] *Sin Sukchu SR* ʂye (入); *MGZY* shwÿe (入) [ʂyɛ]; *ONW* śuat

[<] caus. devoicing of *yuè* 悦閲 *lot 'relax' (under → yú$_{17}$ 愉) (§5.2.2).

⋇ **shuì** 説 (śjwäi^C) **LH** śuas, **OCM** *lhots
'To exhort' [Meng].
[<] exoactive (?) of *shuō* 説 (śjwät) *lhot (§4.3).

[C] This wf is derived from → yú$_{17}$ 愉; see there for allofams.

shuò$_1$ 朔 → **nì$_6$** 逆

shuò$_2$ 欶 → **shù$_3$**, **shuò** 欶

shuò$_3$ 蟀 → **xī$_{15}$-shuò** 蟋蟀

shuò$_4$ 掣 → **shāo$_1$** 梢

shuò$_5$ 數 → **shǔ$_4$** 數

shuò$_6$ 爍鑠 (śjak) **LH** śɑk, **OCM** *lhiauk — [T] *ONW* śak
'To melt, fuse' 爍 [Zhouli], 鑠 [Guoyu].

⋇ **yuè** 爚瀹 (jiak) **LH** jɑk, **OCM** *liauk
'To melt, disperse' 爚 [BI, Zhuang]; 'to drain off, clear the course' (of a river) [Meng], 'purify' (the heart) [Zhuang], 'to moisten, soak' 瀹 [Yili]. This may be the same etymon as → yào$_4$ 藥 'cure'.

[E] Perh. related to TB-Chepang *yu-* 'dissolve, melt'.

[C] This wf may belong to → yào$_4$ 藥 'cure'. The relationship with → xiāo$_2$ 消銷 (sjäu) 'melt' is not clear, because initial MC *śj-* < *hl- normally does not co-occur with *sj-*.

shuò$_7$ 爍 (śjak) **LH** śɑk, **OCM** *lhiauk
'To shine' [Lü], perh. s. w. as 'beautiful, fine' 鑠 [Shi].

⋇ **yuè** 爚瀹 (jiak) **LH** jɑk, **OCM** *liauk
'To shine' 爚 [Lü].

⋇ **yào** 曜耀燿 (jiäu^C) **LH** jau^C, **OCM** *liaukh, OCB *lja/ewk
'Be brilliant, shiny' 曜燿 [Shi]; 耀燿 [Zuo].

[E] This group prob. belongs to the wf → zhuó$_{11}$ 濯. *CVST* and Gong 1995 connect this etymon to WT *glog* '(flash of) lightning'.

sī$_1$ 司 (sɨ) **LH** siə, **OCM** *sə — [T] *ONW* siə
'Be in charge, manage' > 'regulation, supervisor' [BI, Shu].
[E] ST *zə: WT *mdzad-pa, mdzod* < *m-za-t* 'to do, act' ⋇ *bzo* 'work, labor', Kuhish *ca*, Mru *caŋ* 'to do, make' (Löffler 1966: 140). For an alternative affiliation of the TB items, see → zuò$_3$ 作. Unger (*Hao-ku* 30, 1984: 294) sees a possible relationship with WT *rdzi-bo* 'herdsman, shepherd, keeper' instead.
The semantic fields of similar etyma suggest that *sī* 司 'act' and → sī$_3$ 思 'think' are the same word.

sī$_2$ 私 (si^B) **LH** si^B, **OCM** *siʔ
'Private' [Shi], 'egotistic' [Li].
[T] *Sin Sukchu SR* sɿ (平); *MGZY* s^{h}i (平) [sɿ]; *ONW* si
[E] This may be related to Lushai *teei^L* < *teeis* 'myself, thyself...' since a Lushai *t-* could possibly correspond to *s-* elsewhere (§12.3). Alternatively, *STC* no. 284 connects the Lushai word with PTB *s-tay 'navel'.

sī$_3$ 思 (sɨ, sɨ^C) **LH** siə, **OCM** *sə
'To think, think of, long for' [Shi], originally 'to observe outside things, fix attention' acc. to A. Waley. The graph is also read → sāi 思 'beard'.

[T] *Sin Sukchu SR* sɿ (平); *MGZY* sʰi (平) [sɿ]; *ONW* siə
[E] The semantic fields of similar etyma suggest that → sī₁ 司 'act' and *sī₃* 思 'think' are the same word, see §6.2.2 for further comment.

⋇ **sì** 思 (sɨC) **LH** siəC, **OCM** *səh
'To brood' [Shi], 'thought' n. [Li, Yue-zao] (Unger *Hao-ku* 21, 1983: 182).

sī₄ 絲 (sɨ) **LH** siə, **OCM** *sə
'Silk' [BI, Shi] is often said to be the source of European words for 'silk', Gr. *sērikón*. The Western /r/ is then taken as proof that the OC form ended in some kind of consonant. However, it is simpler to derive Western words from → Qín₁ 秦.

sī₅ 斯 (sje) **LH** sie, **OCM** *se — [T] *MTang* si, *ONW* se
'Cleave, lop off' [Shi].
[E] ST *ser: WT *ser-ka* 'cleft, split', Chepang *ser-* 'divide, split cleanly'. TB cognates show that this is prob. not related to → xī₄ 析 *sêk 'cleave' (however, if so, see §7.7.5 for the loss of *r in OC). This word does not belong to any of the stems listed under → lí₁₀ 離.

sī₆, chī 颸 (tṣʰɨ) **LH** tṣʰə, **OCM** *tshrə ?
'Cold wind' [SW, Chuci], 'wind' [Guǎngyǎ].
[E] Etymology not clear. WT *rdzi* 'wind' which *sī* resembles (Unger *Hao-ku* 30, 1984: 294) belongs to PTB *g-li(y) 'wind' (*STC* no. 454): WB *le* 'air, wind', Tani *rji* 'wind'. WT prob. derives from earlier *ryi. More promising may be a link with PWMiao *tc-C (*tcuaC1* etc.) 'wind', especially since the CH word's first textual occurrence is in *Chǔcí*.

sí 訾 → **zǐ₅** 訾

sǐ 死 (siB) **LH** siB, **OCM** *siʔ
'To die' [OB, BI, Shi]. Tone B is prob. the result of reinterpretation as an endoactive verb (§4.5).
[T] *Sin Sukchu SR* sɿ (上); *MGZY* sʰi (上) [sɿ]; *ONW* si
[E] ST: PTB *siy 'to die' (*STC* no. 232) > WT *'čʰi-ba* < *Nsi, ši* ⋇ *gšin-po* 'dead man' ⋇ *gšid* 'funeral'; Kanauri *śi*, Chepang *si-sa*, Garo *si*, PL *ʃe²; WB *se* 'die, be extinguished'; JP *si³³* 'to die' (*HST:* 62); Lushai *tʰiH / tʰiʔL < tʰii / tʰiʔ* 'to die'. Unrelated to *shī* 尸 'corpse' (under → yí₅ 夷侇).

sì₁ 四肆 (siC) **LH** siC, **OCM** *sis?, OCB *spl(j)its
'Four' [OB]. Note the Sui-Tang form in final *-t* which parallels *bí* 鼻 'nose' (Pulleyblank *JAOS* 118.2, 1998: 205). An OC *l in the initial is suggested by the variant graph; the initial *s- may be due to interference from sān 三 'three' (Coblin 1986: 83).
[T] *Sin Sukchu SR* sɿ (去); *MGZY* sʰi (去) [sɿ]; *Sui-Tang* siC, sit?, *ONW* siC
[D] PMin *siC; Y-Guǎngzhōu *³³seiC1*, Yángshān *sɐi³⁵*
[E] ST: In spite of phonological difficulties, *sì* is prob. a ST word because of the suspected earlier *l- in CH: PTB *b-ləy 'four' [Matisoff 1995a: 52; *STC:* 94] > WT *bži* < *bli, Magari *buli*, PL *b-le², WB *leB*, Lushai *paL-liH < pa-lii*; PKaren *lis (Benedict *LTBA* 5.1, 1979: 13). <> Tai: S. *siiB1* is obviously a CH loan (no *l in the initial).

sì₂ 泗 (siC) **LH** siC, **OCM** *sih or *sis?
'Snivel' [Shi]. The etymology is uncertain; Wáng Lì (1982: 418) relates *sì* to → tì₁ 涕 'tears, mucus from nose', but see there.

sì₃ 似 (zɨB) **LH** ziəB, **OCM** *s-ləʔ or *s-jəʔ

sì₃ 似 (zɨ^B) **LH** ziə^B, **OCM** *s-ləʔ or *s-jəʔ
'To imitate, resemble' [Shi].
[T] *Sin Sukchu SR* zɿ (上); *MGZY* z^hi (上) [zɿ]
[E] This is reminiscent of TB-Lushai *zir^H < jir* 'to learn, copy, imitate', but the cognation requires the assumption of a ST root *ji(r). The TB items under → xiàng₇ 像象 could perh. belong to this etymon instead.

sì₄ 兕 (zi^B) **LH** zi^B, **OCM** *s-jəiʔ
'Wild water buffalo' [OB, Shi, EY] (Lefeuvre *MS* 39, 1990–1991: 131–157). This word was sometimes mistakenly thought to be a variant of → xī₁₁ 犀 'rhinoceros'.
[E] Area word. ST *sjəl ~ *s-jəl: TB-Lushai *sial^H < sial* 'domestic buffalo' *se^H-le^H* 'wild gayal (buffalo)' (*se-* is the contracted form of *sial^H*). <> NTai *ǰɨə^A/C (Li 1977) or *ǰɨa^A (Gedney ICSTLL 1981) 'ox, cow', the OC and PTai initials are the same as in → xiàng₅ 象 'elephant'. <> The ultimate source of this word may be AA; note Munda *sahil, saili* 'wild buffalo', Gutob (Munda) *saail* 'wild buffalo, deer' [Pinnow 1959: 423]. However, the contact with OC would be so remote that a regular phonological history is elusive.

sì₅ 耜 (zɨ^B) **LH** ziə^B, **OCM** *s-ləʔ
The usual gloss is 'plowshare, to plow' [Shi]; however this implement consisted of a blade-like spade which was attached to a → lěi₁ 耒 digging stick which thus became its handle (Bodde 1975: 233ff), hence 'spade, to cultivate with a spade'. It originated perh. in the Yao culture (W. Eberhard *Lokalkulturen II:* 224). Syn. → lí₆ 犁.

sì₆ 肆 'lax' → **yí₄** 夷

sì₇ 肆 'arrange' → **yí₅** 夷俟

sì₈ 食 → **shí₄** 食

sì₉ 賜 → **cì₄** 賜錫

sì₁₀ 嗣 → **yí₂** 貽詒

sōng₁ 松 (zjwoŋ) **LH** zioŋ, **OCM** *s-loŋ — **[T]** *ONW* zuoŋ
'Pine' (the tree) [Shi].
[D] M-Xiàmén lit. *sioŋ^A2*, col. *tsiŋ^A2*
[E] This word has been associated with Old Japanese *sugi²* 杉 *'cryptomeria'* (Miyake 1997: 197). See comment under → méi₄ 梅. It also has superficial similarity with Tai: S. *son²* 'a pine'.

sōng₂ 崧嵩 (sjuŋ) **LH** siuŋ, **OCM** *suŋ < *sluŋ ?
'High' (of mountains) 崧 [Shi], 嵩 [Li]
[D] M-Xiàmén lit. *sioŋ^A1*, col. *siŋ^A1*
[N] The phonetic implies an OC medial *l in the initial. *Sōng* is the name of several mountains in Henan, Shandong, Hunan, Jiangxi, Fujian, including the name of the sacred mountain, the axis mundi (D. Pankenier *EC* 20, 1995: 139), in Henan near Luòyáng which was already venerated during the Xia dynasty.

ⅹ **sǒng** 聳竦 (sjwoŋ^B) **LH** sioŋ^B, S ts^h(i)oŋ^C, **OCM** *soŋʔ, *C-soŋh
'To lift up, raise' 竦 [Guoyu], 'rise up high, rise sharply (of mountain)' [GY].
[D] M-Xiàmén lit. *sioŋ^B1*, col. *ts^haŋ^C1*

[E] PMK *sluuŋ (Shorto 1976: 1052) > PMonic *slooŋ 'be high up, high, tall' (person, mountain), OMon *s-lūŋ* 'be high' ⅹ *s-m-loŋ 'top' (of something) ⅹ /clɔŋ/ 'highest point, apex, spire' ⅹ PMK *s-r-luuŋ (Shorto) > OMon *sirluŋ* 'height'; Khmer /-lóoŋ/ 'high, lofty';

Palaung *hløøŋ* 'long', PWa *hloŋ 'high' ⋈ *ʔm̥-loŋ 'hill'; Kharia *j̃halɔŋ* 'high' ⋈ *sɛløŋ* 'deep'.

AA -> TB-SChin Daai *msuuŋ* 'mountain' [Hartmann ICSTLL 1999: 2]. Perh. also -> Tai: S. *hləŋ* 'rise high' ⋈ tʰa-ləŋ 'to rise, climb' (Unger *Hao-ku* 36, 1990: 53), note also S. *sa⁴-laŋ³* 'lofty, straight, tall' (tree). Tai: S. *suuŋ^{A1}* < *s- 'high' (Li F. 1976: 42) looks like a Chinese loan. A syn. or parallel stem with initial *r- is → lóng$_1$ 隆.

sōng$_3$ 鬆 (suoŋ, tsʰjwoŋ)
'Loose, slack' [GY].
[D] M-Xiàmén lit. *soŋ^{A1}*, col. *saŋ^{A1}*

⋈ **zòng** 縱 (tsjwoŋ^C) **LH** tsioŋ^C, **OCM** *tsoŋh
'To release, let off, indulgent; granted that, even though' [BI, Shi].

sǒng$_1$ 聳慫悚 (sjwoŋ^B) **LH** sioŋ^B, **OCM** *soŋʔ
'To scare, fear' 聳 [Zuo], 悚 [Hanfei]; 'be careful about' 聳 [Guoyu], 慫 [GY]; Mand. 聳 'to alarm, be sensational'.
[C] This word may possibly be related to → xiōng$_3$ 兇 'fear'.

sǒng$_2$ 慫聳 駷 (sjwoŋ^B ~ səu^B) **LH** sioŋ^B, **OCM** *soŋʔ
'To incite, encourage' 聳 [Guoyu], 慫 [GY] (QYS only *sjwoŋ^B*) > 'to shake the bit of a horse to make him run' 駷 [Gongyang] (also QYS *səu^B*); Mand. 慫 'to instigate, incite'.
[D] M-Xiàmén (lit.) *sioŋ^{B1}*

⋈ **zǒng** 縱 (tsuŋ^B) **LH** tsoŋ^B, **OCM** *tsôŋʔ
'Quickly' [Li].
[E] ST: WB *cuiŋ^B* 'drive or ride fast'.
[C] These items are related to → sù$_6$ 速 and → zǒu 走, and are ultimately derived from the root → sōu$_3$, sǒu 搜.

sǒng$_3$ 聳 (sjwoŋ^B) **LH** sioŋ^B, **OCM** *soŋʔ
'Be born deaf' [SW], a Han period dialect word from the eastern Huái-Yangtze region, in Chǔ and Chén [FY 6, 2]. This word has the same meaning and OC rime as → lóng$_6$ 聾 *rôŋ 'deaf'. The *JY* gives a variant reading *shuǎng* (ṣåŋ^B) < *sroŋʔ which makes this word look like a s-prefix allofam of *lóng*, but this reading is late and might have been prompted by a gloss 'deaf on "both" *shuāng* 雙 (ṣåŋ) ears' [FY 6].

sǒng$_4$ 聳竦 'high' → **sōng$_2$** 崧嵩

sòng$_1$ 送 (suŋ^C) **LH** soŋ^C, **OCM** *sôŋh.
'To escort, follow after, go along' [Shi], 'to send' [Zuo], 'to present' [Li].
[T] *Sin Sukchu SR* suŋ (去); *MGZY* sung (去) [suŋ]; *ONW* soŋ
[D] M-Xiàmén lit. *soŋ^{C1}*, col. *saŋ^{C1}*
[E] Etymology not certain. Note AA-PSBahn. *sɔːŋ 'hand over', and / or OKhmer *jon* /ɟoon/ 'to urge, persuade, invite, ...drive, ...accompany, escort, ...bring to, offer, present' (-> Thai *chuən* 'to urge, persuade...ask, invite...'). Association with WT *stoŋs-pa, bstaŋs* 'to accompany' (Bodman 1980: 44), or with WT *rdzoŋ-ba, (b)rdzaŋ(s)* 'to send, expedite, dismiss' are problematic because the WT vowel *a* does not agree with OC *o.
[C] It is not clear if there is an etymological connection with → cóng$_1$ 從 'follow'.

sòng$_2$ 訟 (zjwoŋ) **LH** zioŋ, **OCM** *s-loŋ
'Litigate'.

⋈ **sòng** 訟誦 (zjwoŋ^C) **LH** zioŋ^C, **OCM** *s-loŋh
'To quarrel, litigate, sue' 訟 [Shi]; 'admonish' 誦 [Lunyu].
[T] *Sin Sukchu SR* zjuŋ (去), *PR* suŋ; *MGZY* zÿung (去) [zjuŋ]; *ONW* zuoŋ
[D] M-Xiàmén (lit.) *sioŋ*^{C2}
[E] This wf could be ST and related to WT *luŋ* 'exhortation, admonition, instruction' (*HST:* 36). Alternatively, it may be connected with WT *gsuŋs* (pf. of *gsuŋ*) 'to speak' (resp.) (Unger *Hao-ku*), but the initials do not agree.
[C] → xiōng$_5$ 訩 is probably unrelated.

sōu$_1$ 搜 (ṣjəu) **LH** ṣu, **OCM** *sro/u ?
'To search' [Zhuang].
[E] Perh. AA: OKhmer *rok* /rɔɔk/ 'to seak, look for...' For loss of the AA final consonant in CH, see §6.9.

sōu$_2$ 搜 (ṣjəu) **LH** ṣu, **OCM** *sro or *sru ?
'Be many, numerous' [Shi].
⋈ **shuài** 率 (ṣjuət, ṣwi^C) **LH** ṣuit, ṣuis, **OCM** *srut(s)
'All' adj. and adv. [OB, BI, Shi].

sōu$_3$, **sǒu** 搜 (səu^B) **LH** so^B, **OCM** *sôʔ
'To move' [JY], Zhèng Xuán 'vigorous and rapid' (Karlgren Gl. 1154).
[E] ST: PTB *m-sow 'awake' > Dimasa *masau*, Lushai *t^{h}o^R / t^{h}ɔʔ^L < soʔ / sɔs*, Lai *su* 'be awake' ⋈ *džə-su* 'awaken' [VanBik *LTBA* 25.2, 2002: 106], Lakher *pət^{h}eu*, Khami *ənt^{h}au*, Ao Naga *meso* 'arise, awake' (*STC:* 65 no. 295; p. 118); Tamang *^{2}so* 'live'; WT *gson-pa* 'be alive, to wake, rouse, urge on'; WB *(ə-)c^{h}o^B* 'be quick' ⋈ *c^{h}o* 'to rouse, urge on', *so^C* 'quick, rapid'.

This root 'to rouse, move, make move, quicken, quick' has spawned a prolific wf; as on other occasions, CH etymological connections become clear by way of the larger ST picture. Note also the parallelism with the wf → zhèn$_2$ 振震 'shake / pregnant / morning'.

Related words and stems are:
→ **sù**$_6$ 速 'quick' > caus. 'urge on'
→ **sù**$_7$ 蔌 'vegetables' <> WT *'tsho-ba, sos* 'to live, revive, last; feed, graze' ⋈ *gson-pa* 'be alive, to wake, rouse, urge on'
→ **sù**$_3$ 夙 ('time when one wakes up':) 'early morning; pregnant' <> PLB: *C-sok ~ *V-sok 'morning, morrow'
→ **zǒu** 走 'run, make run, urge on' <> WB *(ə-)c^{h}o^B* 'be quick' ⋈ *c^{h}o* 'to rouse, urge on'
→ **sǒng**$_2$ 慫聳 駷 'incite, make run' <> WB *cuiŋ^B* 'drive or ride fast'
→ **xùn**$_5$ 迿 'rapid'
→ **sāo**$_2$ 騷 'move, be shaken, hastily'

sōu$_4$ 獀 (ṣjəu) **LH** ṣu, **OCM** *ṣo ? – *Leibian* səu^B < *sôʔ
'Dog'; acc. to SW *náo-sōu* 獿獀 [nɑu-ṣu] is a Southern Yuè word (Mei / Norman 1976: 279). The role of the presyllable *náo* 'monkey' is not clear.
[E] AA: Khmuʔ, Palaung-Wa *sɔʔ; PSBahn. *sɔ:, but PNBahn. *chó*, PVM *ʔa-cɔ:ʔ > Viet. *chó*, Khmer *ckae*, PEKatuic *ʔaco. If available MK forms are any guide, the underlying word with its fricative /s/ (not affricate /c/) does, contrary to *SW*, not seem to belong to the Yuè (Viet) branch of MK. For the initials, see §5.10.2. This word also appears in TB languages: Limbu *kotco* 'dog'.

sōu $_5$ 犙 (sjəu, ṣjeu) **LH** ṣu, **OCM** *sru
'Three-year-old bovine' [SW] (Baxter 1977: 287). The additional reading MC *sâm* is obviously that of the phonetic.
[E] KD: PHlai *sr-: Baoding *fu³*, Zhong-shan *tshu³* 'three' [Matisoff 1988c: 297], note also AN: PEastern Formosan *teluH 'three' [Li Jen-kuei *LL* 5.2, 2004: 370].

sǒu $_1$ 叟瞍 (səuᴮ) **LH** soᴮ, **OCM** *sô
'Old man' 叟 [Meng, Zuo], 'blind' 瞍 [Shi]. Wáng Lì (1982: 241) believes that **sǎo** 嫂 (sâuᴮ) 'elder brother's wife' [Li] was originally the same etymon. However, old age and blindness are not necessarily defining features of an elder brother's wife.

sǒu $_2$ 藪 (səuᴮ) **LH** soᴮ, **OCM** *sôʔ — **[T]** *ONW* sou
'Grassy marshland' 藪 [Shi], 棷 [Li] is perh. related to OTib. *sog* 'grassland' (Zhol inscr.) (*HST:* 88).
[E] ? AA: PSBahn. *su:h* 'wet, humid'. Alternatively, the word may be connected with **sǒu** 溲 (ṣjəuᴮ) [ṣuʔ] 'soak' [Shi].

sòu $_1$ 嗽 (səuᶜ) **LH** soᶜ, **OCM** *sôh
'To cough' [Zhouli].
[E] ST: PTB *su(w) (*STC* no. 423) > Magari *su*, Garo, Dimasa *gu-su*, WT *sud-pa* 'cough' (*HST:* 58).

sòu $_2$ 漱 → **xiǔ** $_2$ 糔溲

sū $_1$ 蘇 (suo) **LH** sɑ, **OCM** *sŋâ, OCB *sŋa (Baxter 1992: 225) — **[T]** *ONW* so
'Grass, plant', a Han period Chǔ, Huái, Jiāng dialect word [FY 3, 8].
[E] This may be the same etymon as *sù* 蘇 'revive' and belong to the wf → wù$_6$ 悟寤. The concepts 'live' ~ 'fresh, green' ~ 'plant' are often connected. Although the OC graph needs to be set up with an *sŋ-cluster, an alternative association with WT *rtswa* (prob. orthographic for *r-tsa < *r-sa) 'grass, plants' is also possible. By mid to late Han when this word appeared first in writing, an OC *sŋ- had simplified to *s- which made the graph then suitable for writing a word *sa. The item is not related to WT *sŋo-ba* 'be green' ⋇ *sŋo* 'plant, vegetable, greens'; see → yuè$_1$ 月.

sū $_2$ 蘇 'fear' → **è** $_6$ 愕鄂噩

sū $_3$ 縮 → **sù** $_8$ 肅鱐

sú 俗 (zjwok) **LH** ziok, **OCM** *s-lok
'Rustic, vulgar, custom, popular usage' [Meng, Li].
[T] *Sin Sukchu SR* zy (入); *MGZY* zy̌u (入) [zy]; *ONW* zuok
[D] M-Xiàmén lit. *siokᴰ²*, col. *sioʔᴰ²*
[E] This is prob. a ST word: WT *lugs* 'custom, way, manner' (*HST:* 60). MK-Khmer *jw* /cúuə/ 'be low, base, mean, common, vulgar' (with additon of the CH *-k*, see §6.1) looks similar, but the initials do not agree.

sù $_1$ 泝愬訴 → **yù** $_{17}$ 禦

sù $_2$ 素 (suoᶜ) **LH** sɑᶜ, **OCM** *sâh, OCB *sŋa (Baxter 1992: 225)
'Be white, colorless, plain' (also figuratively) [BI, Shi].

⋇ **suǒ** 索 (sâk) **LH** sɑk, **OCM** *sâk
'To search, inquire into, demand' [Zuo]. The Khmer forms below show the semantic connection between 'white' and 'search'.

[E] AA: Khmer /sɑɑ/ 'be white, colorless' > 'pure' > 'purify, clarify' > 'inquire into, probe, examine' ⋈ /samnaa/ 'the white metals' (this form suggests that a nasal might in fact have been present in OC, note OCB).

sù₃ 夙 (sjuk) **LH** siuk, **OCM** *suk — **[D]** M-Xiàmén lit. *siok*^{DI}
'Early morning, early, soon' [Shi].
[E] ST: PLB *C-sok ~ *V-sok 'morning, morrow' [Matisoff *TSR* no. 125], Lushai *tuuk*^{F} 'early morning' (< *suuk*?). WB *sok-kra* 'Venus' is a loan from Mon /suk/ and ultimately from Skt *śukrá* 'bright, Venus' (Shorto 1971: 379).
= **sù** 夙 (sjuk) **LH** siuk, **OCM** *suk
'To quicken' > 'become pregnant' [Shi] (Shaughnessy 1991: 103f) is prob. the same word as 'early morning' which is semantically derived from the notion 'rouse, quicken'. Shaughnessy has concluded that in OB and a BI (early Zhou, Wǔ wáng) *sù* occasionally means 'to rout' (an enemy). This is supported by the semantic range of this wf, but it is not certain if *sù* was the actual word intended by the graph, rather than a semantically closer cognate under → $sù_6$ 速.
[E] ST *so(w) 'move' (under → $sōu_3$, sǒu 搜), PTB *m-sow 'to stir, waken, move'; *sù* is 'the time when one wakes up and gets moving'. The OC final *-k in this word has been inherited from ST: *so + ST *-k of uncertain function (§6.1).

sù₄ 宿 (sjuk) **LH** siuk, **OCM** *suk — **[T]** *ONW* suk
'To stay overnight, lodge' [Shi].
[D] M-Xiàmén lit. *siok*^{DI}, col. *sik*^{DI}
⋈ **xiù** 宿 (sjəu^{C}) **LH** siu^{C}, **OCM** *sukh — **[T]** *ONW* su
('The sun's lodging stations':) 'mansion, group of constellations, part of the zodiac' [Zuo, Li] (Karlgren 1956: 12; Downer 1959: 276).
[<] exopass. of *sù* 宿 (sjuk) *suk (§4.4), lit. 'what is lodged in'.
[E] Prob. AA: OKhmer /sruk/ Proto-Khmer 'shelter, place of security as opposed to forest, settlement, homeland' ⋈ Khmer *jruka* /cruk/ 'shelter, refuge, asylum' < derivatives of /ruk/ 'go down into, take shelter' [Jenner / Pou 1982: 249]. We should expect a retroflex initial in MC, yet retroflection is occasionally lost, see for ex. → $sù_8$ 肅鱐. *STC* (155 n. 419; p. 171 n. 457) relates this word to the TB items noted under → $yè_1$ 夜, but the OC vowel *u as well as the initial are difficult to reconcile with TB.

sù₅ 粟 (sjwok) **LH** siok, S tsʰok, **OCM** *sok
'Foxtail millet' [Shi], etymology is not clear.
[D] PEMin *tsʰuok^{DI}, PWMin *ʃuok^{DI} 'unhusked rice'

sù₆ 速 (suk) **LH** sok, **OCM** *sôk
'Rapid, quick' [Lunyu], 'urge on, invite' [Shi].
[T] *Sin Sukchu SR* su (入); *MGZY* su (入) [su]; *ONW* sok
[D] M-Xiàmén lit. *sok*^{DI}, col. *sak*^{DI}
⋈ **cù** 促 (tsʰjwok) **LH** tsʰiok, **OCM** *tshok — **[T]** *ONW* tsʰuok
'To urge, press' [Zhuang].
⋈ **xù** 勗 (xjwok) **LH** hɨok, **OCM** *hok
'Urge, stimulate' [Shi], 'exert oneself' [Shu] may be a variant of *cù* 促 (tsʰjwok) above with loss of the initial.
[E] This group is part of a large wf, see under → $sōu_3$, sǒu 搜. The final *-k is the familiar CH innovation (§6.1). Spin-offs from this particular group are → zǒu 走, → $sǒng_2$ 慫聳 竦, → $xùn_5$ 遜.

sù₇ 蔌 (suk) **LH** sok, **OCM** *sôk — **[D]** M-Xiàmén *sok*^{DI}
'Vegetables' [Shi 261,3].

[E] ST: WT *'tsho-ba, sos* 'to live, revive, last; feed, graze' ⋈ *'tsho* 'life; livelihood, sustenance, nourishment, entertainment' ⋈ *gso-ba* 'to feed, nourish, rear, cure, stir up again (fire), refresh' ⋈ *gson-pa* 'be alive, to wake, rouse, urge on'; also JP n^{31}*-soi*^{33} = *niŋ*^{31}*-soi*^{33} 'life' may be related.

[<] OC has added *-k* to the ST root *so(w) (see → sōu$_3$, sǒu 搜, see there for more allofams) (§6.1). A semantic parallel is → shēng$_2$ 生 ('live' > 'fresh food').

sù$_8$ 肅鱐 (sjuk) **LH** siuk, **OCM** *siuk — **[T]** *ONW* suk

'Shrivel' [Shi], 'contract, shut' (as flowers) 肅 [Li]; 'slice of dried fish' 鱐 [Li], also QY *ṣjəu*, see below.

~ **suō** 縮 (ṣjuk) **LH** ṣuk, **OCM** *sruk — **[T]** *ONW* ṣuk

'To draw back, shrink' [Huainan].

⋈ **xiū** 修 (sjəu) **LH** siu, **OCM** *siu — **[T]** *ONW* su

'Dry up' (of plants), 'shrink' [Shi], 'dried meat' [Lunyu].

[E] ST: Lushai *tʰuᶠ* < *suuʔ* 'dried' (as fish), 'dried and rotten'; perh. ultimately connected with AA: Khmer *khsoḥ* /ksaoh/ 'be dried up / out' > 'tasteless'.

~ **sù** 鱐 (ṣjəu) **LH** ṣu, **OCM** *sr(i)u — **[T]** *ONW* ṣu

'Slice of dried fish' [Li], also read QY *sjuk*, see above.

[E] Two etyma seem to have converged in CH: (1) an old *su(k) attested in *Shījīng* from a ST (and area?) word; see under *xiū*. (2) Late Zhanguo / Han variants with medial *r, perhaps influenced by an area word AA-Khmer /rhùuət/ > /rumhùuət/ 'dried up / out, evaporation' ⋈ /hùuət/ id. <> MK -> PTai *hrụot^{D1}S 'to shrink, contract'; Be *sut*^{33} 'shrink'.

[C] An allofam is prob. → zhōu$_6$ 皺.

sù$_9$ 鱐 → **sù$_8$** 肅鱐

suān 酸 (suân) **LH** suɑn, **OCM** *sôn

'Sour' [Shu].

[E] ST and area word: PTB *su:r ~ *swa:r 'sour' (*STC* no. 42) > Kan. *sur-k*, Lushai *tʰuur*^{R} < *tʰuurʔ*, Mikir *tʰor* 'sour'; AA-Khmer [cuur], OKhmer *jūr* 'sour' is perh. connected.

suàn$_1$ 蒜 (suân^{C}) **LH** suɑn^{C}, **OCM** *sôns

'Garlic' [Dadai Liji].

[E] ST *swa-n (*HPTB:* 177): PL *swan$^{1/2}$ 'onion', WB *krak-swan*.

suàn$_2$ 算 (suân^{B}, suan^{C}) **LH** suɑn$^{B/C}$, **OCM** *sônʔ/s

'To calculate, count' [Yili] > 'reckon, take into account' [Lunyu].

[T] *Sin Sukchu SR* swɔn (去); *MGZY* son (去) [sɔn]; *ONW* suɑn

[E] Etymology is not clear. A connection with WT *'čʰor-ba, šor* 'to count' has been suggested (Gong Hwang-cherng 1991); but WT *š-* would derive from earlier *sy-.

suī 綏 (swi) **LH** sui, **OCM** *snui, OCB *snjuj — **[T]** *ONW* sui

'To pacify, comfort' [Shi], 'tranquil' [Shu], 'walk slowly' [Shi].

⋈ **tuǒ** 妥 (tʰuâ^{B}) **LH** tʰoi^{B}, **OCM** *nhôiʔ, OCB *nhojʔ

'Peaceful' [SW: syn. 安], 'to stop' [Erya] (Baxter 1992: 417).

[E] ST has *ŋ(w)al ~ *nwal parallel stems (§5.12.1) for this etymon:

(1) *C-nwal > 綏 *snui, WT *rnal* 'rest, tranquility of mind' ⋈ *mnal* 'sleep', perh. also ⋈ *ñal-ba, ñol* 'lie down, sleep' ⋈ *mñel-ba* 'get tired' ⋈ *ñel-ba* 'be ill' ⋈ *mñald-po* 'fall ill' (Bodman 1980: 70; *HST:* 124); KN-Lai *nuar / noʔr* 'be slow' [*LTBA* 20.2: 112].

(2) A ST parallel stem *ŋwal is represented by → wò$_2$ 臥 (§5.12.1).

suí 隨 → **suì**$_2$ 遂

suǐ$_1$ 髓 (swie^B) **LH** syɑi^B, S tsʰyɑi^B, **OCM** *soiʔ (< *swaiʔ?). — **[T]** *ONW* sue
'Marrow' [Kuoce].
[D] M-Xiàmén col. *tsʰe^B1*
[E] ST *swai is prob. related to ST *s(-)wi 'blood', see → xuè$_1$ 血 'blood' (Matisoff *LTBA* 15.1, 1992: 168–177). Some TB languages have a cognate of *xuě* as well as of *suǐ*, one meaning 'blood', the other 'marrow', but not always the same ones: NNaga-Chang *si* 'blood' (⋊ xuě), *hai* 'marrow' (⋊ suǐ); JP *sai^31* 'blood', *lə^33-sui^33* 'marrow' (Matisoff op. cit. p. 169).

suǐ$_2$ □ A Min word: Xiàmén *sui^B1* 'pretty, beautiful, lovely'. Norman (p. c.) suggests that this word may perh. be the same as Mand. *shuǐ* 水 'water' which is found in the sense of 'pretty' ('pretty much') in certain expressions. But note also Tai: Siam *suui^A1* 'beautiful'.

suì$_1$ 歲 (sjwäi^C) **LH** syas, **OCM** *swats
'Year' [OB, BI, Shi], 'planet Jupiter' [Zuo] (Shaughnessy 1991: 99), 'year' (of age) [Meng]. *Shānhǎijīng* implies that 'Jupiter' was already named *suì* at the beginning of the Zhou dynasty.
[T] *Sin Sukchu SR* suj (去); *MGZY* sue (去) [suɛ]; *ONW* suei
[D] PMin *hue^C 'year' (of age) does not agree with the rest of Chinese dialects; perh. there is a Tai connection.
[<] Prob. derived from → yuè$_4$ 越 'pass over' (Mei Tsu-Lin *Tsing Hua Journal of Chinese Studies* 12.1, 1979: 117–132) with the iterative s-prefix, lit. 'pass on again' (§5.2.3); the original sense was either 'traveling = passing planet' = 'Jupiter' > 'Jovian cycle' > 'year' (Takashima 1996 II: 131), or 'passing time period' = 'year' > 'year star, Jupiter' (Mei). Alternatively, *suì* may be derived from a word like → yuán$_5$ 員圓圜 *wan < ST *val 'circle', then lit. 'start the circle again'. In CH and many TB languages temporal units are seen as recurrent cycles; note *zhōu* 周 'circle' > 'week'.
[E] Mei Tsu-Lin relates *suì* further to WT *skyod* 'to go, walk; go down, set', but see → yuè$_4$ 越. The connection with PTai *xuap > S. *kʰuap^D1L* 'year' (of age of children) is not clear. Acc. to Bodman (1980: 66) Tai could be a loan from Chinese (OC *-ts from *-ts or *-ps). Note the Mǐn form which seems closer to Tai.

suì$_2$ 遂 (zwi^C) **LH** zuis, **OCM** *s-wis ~ *s-jus, OCB *zjuts — **[T]** *ONW* zue
'To advance, accomplish, achieve' [BI, Shi].
⋊ **suí** 隨 (zwie) **LH** zyɑi, **OCM** *s-wa/oi ? — **[T]** *ONW* zue
'To follow, go along' [BI, Shi]. This is prob. cognate to the preceding word (so Matisoff *LTBA* 15.1, 1992), but the rimes do not agree.
⋊ **yù** 遹 (jiuet) **LH** wit, **OCM** *wit
'To follow, come to, to the point of, thereupon' [BI, Shi, Shu].
[E] ST: PLB *s-yuy has a grammaticalized function; 'Kamarupan' *s-yuy ~ *m-yuy 'to follow' (Matisoff), Kuki-Naga *jwi 'follow' > Lushai *zui^F*, Siyin *jui*.
[C] An allofam may possibly be → duì$_7$ 隊 (so Sagart 1999: 85). This wf *wi(t) is distinct from others which all share a root *lu ~ *ju: → lǜ$_1$ 律, → yóu$_2$ 由, → shùn$_1$ 順.

suì$_3$ 穗 (zwi^C) **LH** zuis, **OCM** *s-wis
'Ear of grain' [Shi], 穟 [Shi].
[E] ST: Lushai *vui^L /vuiʔ^L < vuis* 'to ear' (of grain, grass), 'come into ear', Kuki-Chin languages *vui.

sūn $_1$ 孫 (suən) **LH** suən, **OCM** *sûn — **[T]** *ONW* son
'Grandchild' [BI, Shi].
[E] ? ST: PTB *śu(w) (so *STC:* 158) > Mikir, Meithei, Dimasa, etc. *su*, Bodo *sou*, JP *ʃu*[51] 'grandchild', Lushai *tu*[F] 'id.' (for the initial, see §12.3). The MK synonyms may be look-alikes: PMK *cuuʔ 'grandchild' (Shorto 1976: 1062) > OMon *cow*, Khmer /cav/, Palaung *su* 'grandchild' < *cu (*c- > s- is a Palaungic innovation).

sūn $_2$ 飧 (suən) **LH** suən, **OCM** *sûn
'Cooked rice' [Shi], '(warm) evening meal' [Meng] may perh. be a variant of → xín$_0$ 尋燖 [sim] *s-ləm (PTB *slum) 'to heat' (food) with labial dissimilation of the final nasal *-m* rather than vocalic dissimilation (§6.7), but this is not likely.

sǔn 損 (suən^B) **LH** suən^B, **OCM** *sûnʔ
'Diminish, subtract' [Yi], 'damage' [Lunyu].
[E] Sagart (1999: 70) derives this word from → yǔn$_2$ 隕殞霣 *winʔ 'fall, drop'. There is no MC syllable like *siwen* in div. 4, therefore a front vowel *i* might have been lost early in OC *sûnʔ (from *suinʔ ?).

꞉ **sùn, xùn** 遜巽 (suən^C) **LH** suən^C, **OCM** *sûns
'To withdraw, yield, be compliant' 遜 [Shu] (Mand. *xùn*); 'humble' 巽 [Yi] (Mandarin *sùn*).
[E] ST: TB cognates are perh. WT *sun-pa* 'be tired of, weary, renounce, resign', WB *sun* 'fail, fall behind, turn away' ꞉ *sun^B* 'spent, expended'.
[C] Sagart (1999: 82) suggests that this word family may be related to xún 循馴 (under → shùn$_1$ 順).

sùn, xùn 遜巽 → **sǔn** 損

suō $_1$ 縮 (ṣjuk) **LH** ṣuk, **OCM** *sruk
'To be straight, upright' [Meng], 'vertical, longitudinal' [Li].
[E] AA: OMon: *crok* /crɔk/ 'to set / plant upright' (flags, umbrellas, etc.); perh. related to Khmer *jara* /cɔɔr/ 'be straight' ꞉ *jhara* /chɔɔr/ 'to stand, be standing, upright, erect, straight, vertical', in which case the OC form would be the result of metathesis of the r before a final *-k*, i.e. < *sur-k (§6.1).

suō $_2$ 縮 'shrink' → **sù** $_8$ 肅

suǒ $_1$ 所 (ṣjwo^B) **LH** ṣɑ^B, **OCM** *sraʔ
'Place, position, situation' [BI, Shi]. The function as an indefinite substitute for the post-verbal element (Dobson, LAC: 157), as in *yǒu suǒ guī* 有所歸 'have a place to return to', or *suǒ qù* 所去 'what [the subject] rejects', is derived from the noun 'place' (Pulleyblank 1995: 68). → yōu$_1$ 攸 provides an exact semantic parallel.
[T] *Sin Sukchu SR* ṣu (上), *LR* ṣwɔ; *MGZY* (zhu >) shu (上) [ṣu]; *ONW* ṣø < ṣo
[E] ST *sra > PTB *sra (*HPTB:* 78): JP *ʃə*[31]*-ra*[31] 'place' (< *s-ra; Matisoff in *STC:* 171 n. 457), WB *ra* 'place, situation, thing, subject', Mru *ra* 'place' [Löffler 1966: 146], Dulong *sǎɹà* 'thing' [LaPolla *LTBA* 24.2, 2001: 2]. TB cognates to this word and to *shì* 事 'affair, thing' (→ shì$_2$ 士仕) are difficult to distinguish. It is not clear if and how WT *sa* 'place, earth' and / or Zhangzhung *slas* 'earth' are related; WT *sa* is also often associated with → shā$_1$ 沙 *srai 'sand' — not likely.

suǒ $_2$ 索 (sâk) **LH** sɑk, **OCM** *sâk
'Rope' [BI, Shi].
[T] *Sin Sukchu SR* saw (入), *PR, LR* sawʔ; *MGZY* saw (入) [saw]; *ONW* sɑk
[E] AA: PVM *ɟa:k 'rope' [Ferlus], PMonic *ɟook 'creeper, vine, rope' > Mon 'string,

cord'. AA -> Tai: S. *čʰïak*^{D2L} < PTai * ǰ- 'rope', Saek *saak*^{D2} < *z*- 'vines, rope'. In Mǐn and other southern dialects, this is the common word for 'rope' (as opposed to → shéng 繩 in the north). OC must have borrowed this word because foreign / ST *z- > OC s-, whereas OC *s- is not expected to become a voiced initial elsewhere. For a possible parallel development, see → xiāo$_2$ 消銷. Also the narrowed CH meaning 'rope' speaks in favor of a foreign origin.

suǒ$_3$ 索 'search' → **sù**$_2$ 素

suǒ$_4$ 索 'fear' → **è**$_6$ 愕鄂噩

suǒ$_5$ 瑣 (suâ^B) **LH** suɑi^B, **OCM** *sôiʔ ?

'Small' (birds), 'petty' [Shi]; 'fragments' [DuànYùcái], Mand. 'trivial, petty'.

[T] *Sin Sukchu SR* swɔ (上); *MGZY* swo (上) [swɔ]

[E] ST: JP *soi*^{31} 'small, weak, paltry', WB *swai* 'slender and tapering'. Alternatively, the word may be related to TB-Lushai *nɔi*^{R} < *nɔiʔ* 'small pieces, fragments' ⋈ *nɔi*^{H} < *nɔi* 'odd bits and pieces left over'. Pulleyblank (*JCL* 21.2, 1994: 367) suggests that *suǒ* is derived from → xiǎo$_1$ 小 'small' – very speculative.

⋈ **cuǒ** 脞硂 (tsʰuâ^B) **LH** tsʰuɑi^B, **OCM** *tshôiʔ < *C-sôiʔ ?

'Small, trifling' 脞 [Shu]; 'rubble' 硂 [GY].

T

tā 他 (t^{h}â)
Mand. 'he' 他, 'she' 她, 'it' 它.
[T] *Sin Sukchu SR* t'ɔ (平), *PR* t'a; *MGZY* tho (平) [t'ɔ]
[D] A col. word derived from → tuō$_1$ 他 'other', southern dialects: Y-Guǎngzhōu ^{55}*t^{h}a^{A1}*, K-Méixiàn *t^{h}a^{A1}*. Some Mand. dialects have the expected *t^{h}ɔ^{A1}*.

tà$_1$ 誻沓 (dâp) **LH** dəp, **OCM** *lâp — **[T]** *ONW* dɑp
'Babble' 沓 [Shi], 'babble, garrulous' 誻 [Guoyu].
[E] ST: WT *lab-pa* 'to tell' ⋈ *lo* 'talk, rumor' < *lop* (*HST:* 145); or alternatively related to WT *dob-dob-pa* ~ *čab-čob* 'talk nonsense'.
⋈ Perh. **yì** 詍 (jiäi^C) **LH** jas, **OCM** *lats < *laps (?)
'Garrulous' [Xun].

tà$_2$ 遝沓 (dâp) **LH** dəp, **OCM** *lâp — **[T]** *ONW* dɑp
'To touch, reach to' [BI], 'together with, and' 遝 [BI]; 'join, unite' 沓 [Chuci].
[E] Etymology not certain. MC *d-* can derive from an OC T-like or L-like initial, most likely from the latter: Baxter (1992; also *CVST* 3:18) relates *tà* to TB-WT *sleb-pa*, *(b)slebs* 'to arrive, reach, extend'; he also relates it to → dài$_8$ 逮.
Alternatively, a T-like initial would connect the word to AA: Khmer *ṭāpa* /daap/ 'to follow closely, close in on, be close (together)...'.

tāi$_1$ 台 (t^{h}âi) **LH** t^{h}ə, **OCM** *lhə̂
('Globe-fish like':) 'rounded' person's back in old age [Shi] (so Karlgren) brings to mind WT *ldir-ba* 'be distended, inflated'.

tāi$_2$ 胎 'nourish' → **shí**$_4$ 食

tái$_1$ 治 (dâi)
'To kill' in Mǐn: PMin *d^{h}ai^{A2}, *d^{h}i.
[E] Area word: Tai: S. *taai^{A1}*, Zhuang *t^{h}ai$^{A1/2}$* 'to die' (< PTai *trai, *prai); PMY *təjH < **pə-təjH 'to kill' ⋈ *dəjH < **mətəjH 'to die' (M. Ratliff, p. c.).

tái$_2$ 苔 (dâi) **LH** də, **OCM** *lə̂ — **[D]** PMin *d^{h}əi, *d^{h}i.
'Moss' [GY]. — **[E]** <> PTai *glai^{A2} 'moss' (Li 1977: 200).

tái$_3$ 嬯臺 (tâi) **LH** tə, **OCM** *tə̂
'Servant or slave women' 嬯 [BI], the lowest kind of servant 臺 [Zuo].
[E] AA: OKhmer *tai* /təj/ 'woman, wife' ⋈ *tai* /ɗəj/ 'female human, female slave' ⋈ OKhmer *kantai* 'female, wife', Khasi *kynthei* 'girl' (-> TB-Mikir *-kint^{h}áj*); Aslian lgs. on the Malay Peninsula: *kəndeh, kəneh, kənah* 'wife', *kenaʔ* 'females of animals', *kanʔ, kena* 'woman', *knaʔ* 'girl', *kəneh, knih*, etc. 'wife' [S. Lewitz 1976: 761–771]. Some of these items are reminiscent of → nǚ$_1$ 女, but they are prob. unrelated. MK *kn-, *k- is a female marker (see → qī$_3$ 妻).

tài$_1$ 鈦軑 → **zhī**$_8$ 桎

tài$_2$ 態 → **néng**$_2$ 能

tān$_1$ 貪 (t^{h}âm) **LH** t^{h}əm, **OCM** *rhə̂m
'Be covetous, greedy' [Shi].

[T] *Sin Sukchu SR* t'am (平), *PR* t'an; *MGZY* tham (平) [t'am]; *ONW* tʰɑm

⋇ **lán** 婪惏 (lậm) **LH** ləm, **OCM** *rə̂m < *g-rəm

'Covetous' 婪 [Chuci]; 'covetous, rapacious' 惏 [Zuo].

⋇ **làn** 嚂 (lâm^C) **LH** lɑm^C, **OCM** *râms < *g-rams

'To stuff (one's face), be gluttonous' [Huainan] may belong here.

[E] ST: PTB *d-rum (*STC* no. 457) > WT *drum-pa* 'to long, desire', WB *krum* 'be lean, pine away' ⋇ *kʰyum* 'to pine away', JP *mə³¹-rim³³* 'to crave to eat'. *HST* alternatively suggests WT *ham-pa* 'avarice, covetousness, greed' as a cognate, but see → kǎn$_6$ 顑.

tān$_2$ 貪 (tʰậm) **LH** tʰəm, **OCM** *rhə̂m — [T] *ONW* tʰɑm

'To kill' is a Han-period Chǔ dialect word [FY 1, 16], cognate to **lán** 惏(lậm) which was a Chén-Chǔ dialect word for 'kill' [FY 2, 19]. It is doubtful that this root is connected with → kān$_4$ 戡 'kill' (a southern Chǔ-Xiāng dialect word), or with **cǎn** 慘 (tsʰậm^B) 'to kill' [FY 1, 5], though it could theoretically be possible (so Sagart 1999: 151). The word may be cognate to WB *hrum^B* 'fail, be defeated'.

tān$_3$ 探 (tʰậm) **LH** tʰəm, **OCM** *nhə̂m ?

'To reach into with the hand, investigate' [Lunyu, Yi, Shu]. The initial of the phonet. series is not certain; the word may be related to → shēn$_3$ 深 'deep' (provided the initial was OCM *nh-; so Unger *Hao-ku* 47, 1995). Alternatively, the word agrees with TB-Lushai *tʰam^R* 'to feel' (especially with the hand).

tān$_4$, jiān 湛 'soak' → **jiān$_8$** 漸瀸湛

tān$_5$ 嘽 → **dān$_3$** 癉憚

tān$_6$ 灘 (tʰân) **LH** tʰɑn

'To dry up' (of a river) [SW], later 'beach'. The graph suggests an OC initial *nh-. Yet *tān* could be compared to PTB *tan > WT *tʰan-pa* 'dry weather, heat, drought', WB *tʰan^C-tʰan^C* 'nearly dry' (*STC:* 190 n.; *HPTB:* 301), if we assume that the word was written with this phonetic only during the Han period (note its first attestation in *SW*) when OC *nh- and *th- had merged into *tʰ-*. Syn. → tǎn$_2$ 坦.

tán$_1$ 覃 (dậm) **LH** dəm, **OCM** *lə̂m

'Extend, spread' [Shi].

⋇ **diàn** 簟 (diem^B) **LH** dem^B, **OCM** *lêmʔ

'Bamboo mat' [Shi] (Karlgren 1956: 16).

[E] <> MK: PWa *dɐm 'spread out a mat'.

tán$_2$ 覃 for **yǎn** 'sharp' → **yǎn$_4$** 剡覃

tán$_3$ 潭 (dậm) **LH** dəm, **OCM** *lə̂m

'A pond, pool' [Chu].

[E] This late OC southern word *(Chǔcí)* is prob. a foreign loan: PKS *tʰlam¹ (but many KS lgs. have initial *d*) <- Malay *kolam* 'pond, well, pool' <- Tamil *kulam* 'pond, tank' (Thurgood 1988: 199). Perh. → táng$_2$ 塘 is a variant of this word. Alternatively, *tán* which is glossed as a 'deep pond' could be the same word as **tán** 潭 'deep water, abyss' [Chuci], and possibly related to → shēn$_1$ 深 'deep'. TB-WB *thum^B* 'pond, lake' differs in initial and vowel.

tán$_4$ 譚 → **tán$_8$** 談

tán$_5$ 彈 (dân) **LH** dɑn, **OCM** *dân — [T] *ONW* dɑn

'Shoot pellets at' [Zuo], 'pluck, play a stringed instrument' [Li].

[D] PMin *d̥ɑn ~ *dɑn^C 'to pluck' (a lute)

ꭗ **dàn** 彈 (dân^C) **LH** dɑn^C, **OCM** *dâns — **[T]** *ONW* dɑn

'Bow for shooting pellets' [Guoce, SW]; *dàn-wán* 彈丸 'pellet' [Hanfei], later *dàn* also 'pellet'.

[<] general derivation of *tán* (§3.5).

[E] This etymon is prob. related to PTB *m-dan (*STC:* 190) or rather *tal > JP *n^{31}-dan^{33}* 'crossbow', Tiddim *t^{h}al^R* < *t^{h}alʔ* 'a bow', Lushai *t^{h}al^R* < *t^{h}alʔ* 'arrow, dart'.

tán$_6$ 彈 'shake' → **dàn$_7$** 憚

tán$_7$ 炎惔 (dâm) **LH** dɑm, **OCM** *lâm

'Brilliant, magnificent' [Zhuang], 'aflame, burning' (of sensation) [Shi]. This is an allofam of the wf under → yán$_2$ 炎.

tán$_8$ 談 (dâm) **LH** dɑm, **OCM** *lâm

'To speak' [Shi].

[T] *Sin Sukchu SR* dam (平), *PR* dan; *MGZY* tam (平) [dam]

ꭗ Perh. **zhān** 詹 (tśjäm) **LH** tśam, **OCM** *tam

'Talkative' [Zhuang]; 'to speak' 噡 [Xun]. The initial does not agree with the other items.

ꭗ **tán** 譚 (dậm) **LH** dəm, **OCM** *lə̂m

'To speak' [Zhuang] (Pulleyblank 1973: 120; he also includes → dào$_2$ 道 'to talk about' in this wf).

[E] ST: WT *gtam* < *g-lham* 'talk, discourse' ꭗ *gtom-pa* 'to speak' ꭗ WT *gdam-pa* < *glam* 'to advise, give counsel', Mikir *-lám* 'word, speech, language' [Grüßner] (*STC* 69, 191), Lushai *lam^R* < *lamʔ* 'say, pronounce, ask for' (*HST:* 137).

tán$_9$ 檀 → **zhān$_4$-tán** 栴檀

(**tán$_{10}$**) □ (dậm)

A Mǐn dial. word for 'wet': PMin *dɑm > Fú'ān, Amoy *tam^{A1}*. Loan from AA: Viet. *ăm, ãm* 'wet, moist' (Norman / Mei 1976: 298). This etymon occurs also in Tai lgs.: Lóngmíng *tom^{A2}* 'wet', Lóngzhōu *tum^{A2}* < *d- (Yue Hashimoto *CAAAL* 6, 1976: 1).

tǎn$_1$ 袒襢 (dân^B) **LH** dɑn^B, **OCM** *dânʔ — **[T]** *ONW* dɑn

'To bare (to the waist)' 襢 [Shi], 袒 [Zuo].

ꭗ **zhǎn** 襢 (tjän^B) **LH** ṭan^B, **OCM** *tranʔ

'To bare, leave open, single, simple' [Li].

ꭗ **zhàn** 襢 (tjän^C) **LH** ṭan^C, **OCM** *trans

'Bare, undecorated' (robe) [Li].

[E] Etymology not certain. (1) Pulleyblank (in Rosemont 1991: 31) adds *dàn* 但 'only' (under → dān$_2$ 單 which also could be related), hence the root means 'only, bare'. (2) *tǎn* could be cognate to → dān$_1$ 丹 'red' because nakedness is associated with 'red' (Lau 1999: 118). (3) ST: WT *star-ba* 'to clean, polish', note also *t^{h}er* 'bald, bare' (so *CVST* 2: 122). An allofam may be → tú$_3$ 徒 'bare', but see there.

tǎn$_2$ 坦 (t^{h}ân^B) **LH** t^{h}ɑn^B, **OCM** *thânʔ

'Level' [Yi] (same word as 'easygoing' → tǎn$_3$ 儃坦 ?); in southern dial. 'beach' (~ tān$_6$ 灘).

ꭗ **shàn** 墠 (źjän^B) **LH** dźan^B, **OCM** *danʔ

'Leveled area' [Shi].

tǎn$_3$ 儃坦 (t^{h}ân^B) **LH** t^{h}ɑn^B, **OCM** *thânʔ

'At ease' 坦 [Lunyu] (s. w. as 'level' → tǎn$_2$ 坦?); 'easygoing' 儃 [Zhuang].

ꭗ **dàn** 澶 (dânC) **LH** dɑnC, **OCM** *dâns
'Let loose, free of care' [Zhuang].
[C] This wf could belong either to → chǎn₂ 嘽幝繟 'slow' or to → tǎn₂ 坦 'level'.

tǎn₄ 噴 → **lín₂** 林

tǎn₅ 黮 (tʰậmB, dậmB) **LH** tʰəmB, dəmB, **OCM** *thə̂m? ~ *də̂m?
'Dark' [Zhuang].
[E] Area word: MK: Khmer *ṭaṃ* /-dɑm/ 'be dark', *daṃ* /-tum/ 'be ripe, dark', PSBahn. *dum* 'ripe, red'. <> It is not clear how the following KT items are related, especially since OC could also have had a cluster with *l in the initial: S. *damA1* < *ʔdl/r- 'dark', Saek *ramA1* 'black'; PKS *ʔnamA 'black', Be *lam13* 'black'. Acc. to Thurgood (1994: 358), the KT forms are loans from PAN *qitem 'black', Dempwolff 1938 PAN *ḍəḍəm* 'be dark' ꭗ *ləmləm* 'be gloomy' ('düster sein'); note also AA-Khmer /lým/ 'be dark, obscure, dim, unclear', Wa-Lawa-Bulang *ntɨm 'dark' (skies). <> TB-Lushai *hlimL* 'shadow, shade'.
The final *-m* is phonesthemic for 'keep in the mouth' > 'keep hidden' > 'dark', see → shèn₄ 葚, → gàn₂ 紺, → qián₅ 黔, → yīn₅ 陰 and → àn₃ 黯. Therefore it is difficult to match the disparate OC syn. with foreign items cited above and under → yīn₅ 陰.

tàn₁ 炭 (tʰânC) **LH** tʰɑnC, **OCM** *thâns
'Charcoal' [Li], 'lime' [Zuo].
[E] ST: WT *tʰal-ba* 'dust, ashes' (*STC:* 173 n. 461), Lushai *taalR* < *taal?* 'wood ashes, dust'. CH -> Tai: S. *tʰaanB1* and PMY *tʰaanC. The CH word is not related to → rán₁ 然 'burn'.

tàn₂ 窞 (dậmB) **LH** dəmB, **OCM** *lə̂m?
The earliest occurrence is in the combination *kǎn₁-tàn* 坎窞 (kʰậmB-dậmB) LH *kʰəmB-dəmB*, *khə̂m?-ʔlə̂m? ? 'trap pit' (Shaughnessy 1996) [Yi]. *SW* says "*tàn* is a small pit (*kǎn*) in a pit (*kǎn*)".
[D] In some dialects *tàn* means 'pit, puddle' as in *shuǐ-tàn* 'puddle', e.g. Y-Táishān *sui55-hem21*
[N] For the irregular aspiration of *tàn*, see §5.8.5. Except for the above *SW* entry, *tàn* occurs by itself only in post-Han texts and makes therefore the impression of an original reduplicative syllable of *khəm? with lateral initial (§2.7); but in light of the Tai connection, *tàn* has prob. been a full word in OC.
[E] *Tàn* is of KT origin or an area word (Tai /u/ precludes borrowing from CH): Tai *hlum* 'pit, ditch, cavity', Saek *lumA1* < *l̥-* 'pit, hole' (as trap), possibly also TB-Lushai *humH* 'pitfall' as trap for elephants etc. Similar CH and foreign comparanda are here tentatively sorted according to connections revealed in Table K-1 → kǎn₁ 坎埳.
The relationship with PTai *th-: S. *thamC1* 'cave', also MK-Wa *tham* (Dǒng Wéiguāng et al. *CAAAL* 22, 1984: 110) is not clear.

tāng₁ 鏜 (tʰâŋ) **LH** tʰɑŋ, **OCM** *thâŋ
'Sound of drum' [Shi].
~ **tián** 闐 (dien) **LH** den, **OCM** *dîn
'Sound of drum' [Shi some versions].

tāng₂ 湯 (tʰâŋ) **LH** tʰɑŋ, **OCM** *lhâŋ
'Hot water' for drinking [Meng], for washing oneself [Chuci]; ('hot':) 'reckless' (of feasting) [Shi].
[D] 'Warm' (of a spring) in Mǐn dialects; later 'soup'
[E] Bodman (1980: 102) relates this word to WT *rlaŋs* 'vapor, steam'.

¥ **dàng** 盪 (dâŋ^C) **LH** daŋ^C, **OCM** *lâŋh
'A basin to hold hot water for washing, wash basin' [SW] (Wáng Lì 1982: 355).

¥ **yàng** 煬 (jiaŋ^C) **LH** jaŋ^C, **OCM** *laŋh
'To heat, roast' [Zhuang] > 'cruel' [Yi Zhou shu].

táng₁ 唐 (dâŋ) **LH** daŋ, **OCM** *lâŋ
'Path in a temple' [Shi 142, 2; EY].
[T] *Sin Sukchu SR* daŋ (平); *MGZY* tang (平) [daŋ]; *ONW* daŋ
[E] AA or area word: MK: Aslian *gəløŋ*, PMonic *glɔɔŋ 'road, track, way, direction'; *g-n-lɔɔŋ 'habitual path'; OKhmer /glɔɔŋ/ 'way, path, passage > channel, canal, watercourse' (Jenner / Pou 1982: 289) (-> Tai: S. *kʰlɔɔŋ^A2* < *gl-* 'canal, watercourse'; TB-Lushai *kuaŋ^H* 'channel of a river'); Note also Viet. *đường* 'road, way, street', Muong *ta:ŋ* [Pulleyblank *JCL* 22.1, 1994: 82] (-> PTai *d-: S. *tʰaŋ^A2* 'way, road').

The PMonic form is also reminiscent of **gèng** 堩 (kəŋ^C) [kəŋ^C] *kləŋh ? 'road' [Liji], as well as of → xíng₁ 行. Wáng Lì (1982: 147) relates this word to → tú₂ 涂途塗 'path' (along the bank of a canal; paved path)'.

táng₂ 塘 (dâŋ) **LH** daŋ, **OCM** *lâŋ — **[D]** PMin *d̂oŋ 'pond'
'Dam, dike' [Guoyu]. Later 'a (round) reservoir, pond'. This could be a variant of → tán₃ 潭; the word looks like a cognate of → zhàng₄ 障 'dike, dam', but the OC initials do not agree (*t- vs. *l-).
[E] <> PYao *glaaŋ² 'pond, lake' (Bodman 1980: 112).

tāo₁ 綢 (tʰâu) **LH** tʰou, **OCM** *thû
'Envelop' [Li] prob. does not belong to → zhōu₃ 周 as we should expect MC *tʰieu*.

tāo₂ 弢 → **gāo₅** 櫜

tāo₃, táo 滔 → **yóu₁₀** 滺油

tāo₄ 滔 'reckless' → **tōu₁** 偷

tāo₅ 慆 'pleased' → **yú₁₇** 愉

tāo₆ 慆 'doubtful' → **zhòu₃** 冑

tāo₇ 韜 → **zhòu₃** 冑

táo₁ 匋陶 (dâu) **LH** dou, **OCM** *lû, OCB *b-lu
'To mold, make a mold' [Shi] > 'kiln' 匋 [SW], 陶 [Zuo] > 'pottery' [Li]. Possible cognate → yáo₁ 窯.
[T] *Sin S.* 掏 *SR* daw (平); *MGZY* 掏 taw (平) [daw]; *ONW* dau

táo₂ 桃 (dâu) **LH** dau, **OCM** *lâu, OCB *g-law
'Peach' [Shi] <- PMY *glaau^3A 'peach' (Bodman 1980: 112).

táo₃ 逃 (dâu) **LH** dau, **OCM** *lâu
'To run away' [Shi].
[E] Etymology not clear, but note MK: PVM *(kə)do 'to run (away)' [Ferlus], Bahn. *kədəw* 'run away', PNBahn. *gadăw 'run', Mon *dau* (PMon. *d-). -> Tai: Saek *theew^A2* < *d-* 'to flee, go away, leave'. However, the initials do not agree.

táo₄ 洮 (tʰâu) **LH** tʰau, **OCM** *lhâu — **[T]** *ONW* tʰau
'To pour water, wash' [Shu].
[E] PMiao *ʔleuʔ^A 'to pour'.

táo₅ 陶 'nourish' → **yù₂₂** 育毓鬻

táo₆ 萄 → **pú₃** 葡

tè₁ 貣 (tʰək, dək) **LH** tʰək, **OCM** *lhə̂k
'To beg, demand' [Xun].

ᵡ **dài, tè** 貸 (tʰə̣iᶜ) **LH** tʰəᶜ, **OCM** *lhə̂kh
'To lend' [Zuo] (Herforth 1984 acc. to Takashima 1996 II: 130).
[<] exoactive of *tè* (§4.3.1).

[E] This set is prob. related to the wf → dài₁ 代 'substitute'.

tè₂ 特 (dək) **LH** dək, **OCM** *də̂k
'Male animal, bull' [OB, Shi, Shu].
[T] *Sin S. SR* dəj (入), *LR* dəjʔ; *MGZY* tʰiy (入) [dəj]; *ONW* dək
[E] <> Tai: S. *tʰɨk*ᴰ¹*S* < *th-* (in northern dial. *d-) 'young male animal' (Li F. 1976: 43). Note also NNaga *teːk 'buffalo' [French 1983: 367].
The graph 特 appears first in a Zhanguo (late Zhou) inscription; *zhí, tè* (next) seems to be its earlier form (Baxter 1992: 338f):

= **zhí, tè** 犆 (dək) **LH** dək, **OCM** *də̂k
'Single' [Li] = 特 [Yili, Lü], but 'single' is not necessarily the same thing as 'bull', see → zhí₁ 直.

tè₃ 忒 → **dài₁** 代

tè₄ 特犆 'single' → **zhí₁** 直

tè₅ 慝 (tʰək) **LH** tʰək, **OCM** *nhə̂k
'Evil, wrong' n. (in 'do evil') [Shi].
[T] *Sin Sukchu SR* t'əj (入), *LR* t'əjʔ; *MGZY* (cʰiy > thʰiy) (入) [t'əj]
[E] ST: WT *nag* 'black, dark', also in the sense of 'criminal' ᵡ *gnag* 'black, wicked' ᵡ *snag* 'ink'; PLB *(s-)nak ᵡ *naʔ 'black' > WB *nak*; Nung *naʔ;* Trung *na* [Matisoff *TSR* no. 142], Lahu *ná* < *ʔnak* 'be deep, thick, dense, steep, hard to understand, profound' (Matisoff *D. of Lahu:* 731).

ᵡ **nì** 匿 (ṇjək) **LH** ṇɨk, **OCM** *nrək
'To conceal, what is concealed, secluded' (of plans, lands) [Shu].

téng₁ 疼 (duoŋ) **LH** douŋ
'To hurt' [GY]. *HST* keeps this late word (post-classical) in *-uŋ distinct from the one in *-oŋ (→ tōng₁ 恫).

téng₂ 騰 (dəŋ) **LH** dəŋ, **OCM** *lə̂ŋ — **[T]** *ONW* dəŋ
'To mount, rise' [Shi], 'ascend' [Li] > 'overcome, oppress' [Shi]. The phon. series *GSR* 893 implies that the OC initial was L-like which connects it with → chéng₃ 乘, but semantically and otherwise, this word appears to agree with the wf → dēng₁ 登 with an OC T-like initial.

tī₁ 梯 (tʰiei) **LH** tʰei, **OCM** *thî or *thə̂i — **[T]** *ONW* tʰėi — **[D]** PMin *tʰəi ~ *tʰuəi
'Ladder' [Guoyu].
[E] Etymology not certain. The word appears to be cognate to PTB *s-lay ᵡ *s-ley (so *HPTB:* 220): WB *hle-ka*ᴮ 'stairs, ladder', TGTM *ᴬhli, Chepang *hləyʔ* (Bodman 1980: 102; 142). <> Tai: S. *ban-dai*ᴬ¹*, kraʔ*ᴰ¹*-dai*ᴬ¹ < *ʔdl/rəiᴬ 'ladder, stairs'. CH ? -> PWMiaoA *ntai³*, PYao *tʰei¹*. However, the foreign initials do not agree with OC (T vs. L); perh. the OC item has been reinterpreted as an allofam of *dì* 第 'sequence' (under → dì₂ 弟) (Karlgren 1956: 14). – The elements WB *-ka*ᴮ ᵡ WT *skas-ka, skad* 'ladder'

and Lao k^hanC^{1}-dai^{A2} 'stairs', S. k^han^{C1} 'steps' may be related to each other (Manomaivibool 1975: 134).

tī$_2$ 剔鬄 (t^hiek) **LH** t^hek, **OCM** *lhêk

'To cut (trees)' 剔 [Shi]; 'cut off, cut to pieces' 鬄 (also read MC *t^hiei^C*) [Zhouli]; 'cut hair'. Syn. → tì$_2$ 剃.

tí$_1$ 提堤題 (diei) **LH** de, **OCM** *dê

'To raise' [Zhouli], 'to take, take up' 提 [Shi] > 'bank, dike' 堤 [Zuo] (the Mand. reading is that of 隄); 'forehead' 題 [Li].

[T] *Sin S. SR* djej (平), *PR*, *LR* di; *MGZY* ti (平) [di]; *ONW* dėi

⋊ **dī** 隄 (tiei) **LH** te, **OCM** *tê

'Bank, dike' [Li] (Karlgren 1956: 10).

[C] Possible allofams are → diān$_1$ 顛巔, → dìng$_2$ 定題 'forehead', → dìng$_3$ 町 'boundary dike', → zhěn$_3$ 畛 'id.'

tí$_2$ 禔 → **zhī$_7$** 禔

tí$_3$ 啼 (diei) **LH** de, **OCM** *dê

'To weep, howl, cry' [Zuo], later also for animal sounds (crows).

[E] ? ST: Perh. related to Lushai *ṭee^R* < *tr- 'to cry out' (in pain, fear), 'shriek', but the OC initial has no trace of an *-r-.

tí$_4$ 蹄 (diei) **LH** de, **OCM** *dê

'Hoof' [Yi] is prob. cognate to → dì$_8$ 踶 'to kick' (so *HST:* 100).

⋊ **dí** 蹢 (tiek) **LH** tek, **OCM** *têk

'Hoof' [Shi].

tǐ 體 (t^hiei^B) **LH** t^hei^B, **OCM** *rhîʔ, OCB hrijʔ — **[T]** *ONW* t^hėi

'Body, form, shape, content' [Shi].

[<] endoactive tone B derivation from the ST stem ('the thing which exists') (§4.5.1).

[E] ST *sri 'to exist' (Benedict 1976: 190) > PTB *sri(-t): WT *gšis* < *g-rhyis* (?) 'person, body, natural disposition' ⋊ WT *srid-pa* 'existence, things existing, the world, life, a single being', also 'procreate' (Stein *BSOAS* 36.2, 1973: 412ff); WB *hri^C* 'to be (in some place)'.

From the ST root is also derived → shēng$_2$ 生 'give birth, live'. It is not certain why a hypothetical ST *sr- shows up as a voiceless *rh in *tǐ* (regular development from ST? or because of a *k-sr- configuration? Note WT), but as a sr-cluster in *shēng* (*s- reanalyzed as a causative prefix ? §2.8.1).

tì$_1$ 涕 ($t^hiei^{B/C}$) **LH** t^hei^B, t^hei^C, **OCM** *thîʔ/h, OCB *thijʔ

'Tears' 涕 [Shi]; 'mucus from nose' 洟 [Li], the latter may derive from the original meaning 'tears' (so Wáng Lì 1958: 551), or both may derive directly from ST 'water'. The graph 洟 belongs to an OC initial L-phonetic series, but the graph appears late and is prob. only a loan for 涕 (in a T-series).

[E] ST: PTB *ti (STC no. 55) and PTB *tui 'water' (*STC:* 168) > Chepang *tiʔ* 'water', WT *mčʰi-ma* 'a tear' (*HST:* 146), Chepang *ma-tiʔ* 'river', Kanauri *ti 'water'. Dhimal *hna-thi* 'snot'; or Lushai *tui^R* 'water'; both roots, *ti and *tui occur in JP and Dhimal (*STC* no. 55; 168).

Wáng Lì (1982: 418) connects *tì* to → sì$_2$ 泗 'snivel' and → lèi$_1$ 淚 'tears' (unlikely). Perh. → zhì$_6$ 膣 'vagina' is a cognate.

tì₂ 剃 (tʰieiC) *ONW* tʰėi. — **[D]** PMin *tʰieC
'To cut hair' [Huainan, Yupian, JY]. This is perh. a post-Han variant of → tī₂ 鬄鬀 (tʰieiC), in OC the two forms would have been quite different, *lhêk vs. *thə̂i or *thî. It is not clear how the next item relates to these words:

⋇ **dǐ** 提 (tieiB) **LH** teB, **OCM** *têʔ
'To cut off' [Li].

tì₃ 逖 (tʰiek) **LH** tʰek, **OCM** *thêk ?
'Be distant, far away' [Shi], 'remove' [Zuo].
[E] ? PKS *kla:i¹ 'far', PTai: S. *klaiA1* 'far', but the OC initial was apparently T-like, not L-like. Prob. not related to → zhuō₂ 卓 'distant' (as proposed by Wáng Lì 1982: 211).

tì₄ 惕 (tʰiek) **LH** tʰek, **OCM** *lhêk
'Be anxious, to respect, to grieve' [Shi, Shu].

⋇ ? **shì** 適 (śjäk) **LH** śek, **OCM** *lhek ? — **[T]** *ONW* śek
'Scared' [Zhuang]. Acc. to the phonetic series, *shì* has a T-like initial, though.

tì₅ -tì 趯 → **tiào₁** 跳

tiān₁ 天 (tʰien) **LH** tʰen, **OCM** *thîn
'Sky, heaven, heavenly deity' [BI, Shi]. The graph shows a person (god) with a head in the shape of a disk like the BI character for *dīng* 丁 *têŋ 'a cyclical sign' which seems to be phonetic. The anthropomorphic graph may or may not indicate that the original meaning was 'deity', rather than 'sky'. For the *-eŋ ~ *-in variation, see §6.4.1.
[T] *Sin Sukchu SR* t'jen (平); *MGZY* then (平) [t'ɛn]; *MTang* tʰian < tʰɨan, *ONW* tʰėn
[D] Y-Guǎngzhōu *⁵³tʰinA1* 'sky', Táishān *³³henA1*; PMin *tʰien, Xiàmén *tʰĩA1*
An old NW dialect variant QY *xien*, ONW *hėn*, is also found in Tang-period Guǎngzhōu, written 祆 'Heaven' (Coblin 1994: 341). An old southern dialect form *tʰɑn survives in Mǐn-Jiānglè *tʰãiA1* 'sky' (Norman 1979: 271), which is prob. the same etymon as 坦 *tʰanB* which the *Shìmíng* records for dialects to the east of the central area (Coblin *TP* 1994: 155f).
[E] Because the deity Tiān came to prominence with the Zhou dynasty (a western state), a Central Asian origin has been suggested, note Mongolian *tengri* 'sky, heaven, heavenly deity' (Shaughnessy *Sino-Platonic Papers*, July 1989, and others, like Shirakawa Shizuka before him). Alternatively, Bodman (ICSTLL 1987) connects *tiān* with TB-Adi *taleŋ*, Lepcha *tă-lyaŋ* 'sky'. One could add JP *mə⁵⁵-len⁵¹* 'sky', yet these items could belong to → líng₆ 陵 instead.
Most likely, this word is connected with → diān₁ 顛巔 'top' (so *SW*) and its TB cognates: WT, OTib. *steŋ* 'above, upper part, that which is above' (Unger *Hao-ku* 36, 1990: 48), *steŋ-lha* 'the upper gods, gods in heaven' [Hoffmann 1979: 94]; Kachin *puŋdiŋ* 'zenith, top' (*STC*: 180); Zemi (Naga) *tiŋ* 'sky', Lushai *paL-tʰianH* 'god' (lit. 'father above') (French 1983: 157f; 374), perh. also Chepang *diŋ* '(helpful) spirits'. For a similar semantic development 'top, high' > 'sky', see → líng₆ 陵, also note the semantic parallel *shàngdì* 上帝 'god on high' (i.e. in heaven). If MC aspiration should be a reflex of an earlier *s in the initial (§5.8.1), then *tiān* would agree closely with WT *steŋ*. A common TB syn. for 'sky' belongs to the root → mào₂ 冒 'cover'.

tiān₂ 天 'brand the forehead' → **diān₁** 顛巔

tiān₃ 添 (tʰiem) **LH** tʰem
'Full' [Tangshu; JY], but PMin *diemB 'full'.

[E] <> PTai *tl- > S. tem^{A1} 'full' (Manomaivibool 1975: 133). Syn. → yíng$_2$ 盈贏.

tián$_1$ 田 (dien) **LH** den, **OCM** *lîn — **[T]** *MTang* dian < dɨan, *ONW* dėn
'Field', a general term [BI; Shi].
[D] Y-Guǎngzhōu t^hin^{A2} 'wet field'. PMin *dzʰən 'wet field' is unlikely to be related (Norman 1988: 231), but see → zēng 曾增憎橧.

⋙ **diàn** 田甸 (dien^C) **LH** den^C, **OCM** *lîns
(1) 'To cultivate, till; hunt' 田 [Shi 260, 1].
[<] exoact. of *tián* 田 *lîn (§4.3.2).
[E] ST: WT *liŋs* 'hunting or chase' (*HST:* 96).
(2) 'Demesne, royal domain, a type of fief, a feudal title' 甸 [BI; Shu].
[<] exopass. of *tián* (§4.4), lit. 'what is being / has been cultivated'.

[E] ST: WT *žiŋ* 'field' < *lyiŋ* or *ryiŋ,* Bumthang Zha ^{L}*leŋ*, Lep. *lyaŋ* 'field, land' (Forrest *JAOS* 82, 1962: 332); Cuona Monpa $leŋ^{13}$; NNaga *lji:ŋ 'grow(th)', JP $mə^{31}$-$liŋ^{33}$ 'forest', Dimasa *ha-bliŋ* 'jhum field in 2nd year of cultivation' (*ha* 'earth') [*STC* no. 378; French 1983: 254].

Some TB lgs. have forms with initial *r-* (related?): Muoto M. *ʔreŋ,* Tsangla *a-riŋ.* Kanauri *ri[ŋ]* 'field'; Lushai $riŋ^H$ 'jhom, field currently in use'.

Loaned from CH or TB into other lgs.: PMY *l̥in^A (Wang Fushi), PYao *riŋ^A (Therapan) 'wet field'; Be $leŋ^A$ (Haudricourt / Strecker *TP* 77, 1991: 337).

tián$_2$ 恬 (diem) **LH** dem, **OCM** *lîm or *lêm
'Be calm, tranquil' [Shu].
[E] ST: Lepcha *glyám* 'be calm, to calm', Lushai $thleem^R$ 'to comfort, pacify' (Geilich 1994: 267).

⋙ ? **dàn** 憺澹 (dâm$^{B/C}$) **LH** dɑm$^{B/C}$, **OCM** *dâmʔ/h or *lâmʔ/h
'Be calm' 澹 [Lao], 憺 [Chuci]. The phonetic series implies an OC T-like initial.

tián$_3$ 甜 (diem) **LH** dem, **OCM** *lîm or *lêm, OCB *lim
'Sweet' [SW].
[E] ST: PTB *lim > WT *žim-pa* < *lyim* 'sweet scented or tasting', Kanauri *im* (< *yim* < *lyim*; see Schuessler *LTBA* 22.2, 1999: 73 for the initials), Manang *lim* 'sweet, delicious', Thulung *lem* 'sweet', Limbu *limma* < *limt-* 'be sweet'; Lepcha *a-klyam;* note also WB ts^him^C.
[C] Matisoff (1995: 71) connects this wf with → shí$_4$ 食 and → shì$_{16}$ 舐. Words meaning 'sweet', 'lick', 'tongue', 'flame' often share to the same roots, see allofams → tiǎn$_1$ 忝, → tiǎn$_2$ 煔炏, → yán$_2$ 炎.

tián$_4$ 填顛 (dien) **LH** den, **OCM** *dîn
'Full, to fill, block' 填 [Guoce], 顛 [Li].

⋙ **diàn** 窴 (dien^C) **LH** den^C, **OCM** *dîns
'To stop up' [Chuci].

⋙ **tiàn** 瑱 (tʰien^C) **LH** tʰen^C, **OCM** *thîns
'Earplug or pendant of jade' [Shi] (Wáng Lì 1982: 531).

[C] Perh. cognate to → yíng$_2$ 盈贏 'full'. Syn. → tiān$_3$ 添. The graphs imply a T-like initial in OC.

tián$_5$ 闐 → **tāng$_1$** 鏜

tiǎn$_1$ 忝 (tʰiem^B) **LH** tʰem^B, **OCM** *lhîmʔ, OCB *hlimʔ
'To lick up' [Tang – Li Bai]. — **[D]** Y-Guǎngzhōu $li{:}m^{B1}$ < *limʔ* 'lick'.

[E] ST or area word: PTB *(s-)lyam > Bahing *liam,* Khambu, Yakha *lem* 'tongue', Kanauri *lem* 'lick' (*STC:* 172 n. 458). <> KS: Mulam *lja:m⁵ 'lick'.

Words meaning 'sweet', 'lick', 'tongue', 'flame' often share the same root, see allofams → tián₃ 甜, → tiǎn₂ 煔烑, → yán₂ 炎.

tiǎn₂ 煔烑 (tʰiemB/C) **LH** tʰemB/C, **OCM** *lhêmʔ/s
'Brightness of fire' [SW]. Although a dictionary word, it belongs to the wf → yán₂ 炎. Words meaning 'sweet', 'lick', 'tongue', 'flame' often share the same roots, see allofams → tiǎn₁ 舔, → tián₃ 甜.

tiàn 瑱 → **tián₂** 填顛

tiāo₁ 挑 (tʰieu) **LH** tʰeu, **OCM** *lhiâu
'Provoke' [Zuo]. — Etymology not clear.
[T] *Sin Sukchu SR* t'jew (平), *PR* t'jaw; *MGZY* thÿaw (平) [t'jɛw]

tiāo₂ 條 → **yōu₂** 悠

tiáo₁ 條 'branch' → **yōu₂** 悠

tiáo₂ 條 'orderly' → **xiū₅** 修

tiǎo 窕 (dieuB) **LH** deuB, **OCM** *liâuʔ
'To perforate, bore a hole' [Huainanzi] is perh. cognate to → qiào₂ 竅 'a hole'.

tiào₁ 跳 (dieuC) **LH** deuC, **OCM** *liâuh
'To jump' [Zhuang].

※ **chāo** 超 (ṭʰjäu) **LH** ṭʰɑu (ṭʰiau), **OCM** *t-hliau ?
'To leap onto' [Zuo], 'leap over' [Meng].

※ **tì -tì** 趯 (tʰiek-tʰiek) **LH** tʰek < tʰeuk, **OCM** *lhiâuk
'Be jumping' [Shi].

tiào₂ 糶 → **dí₆** 糴

tiē₁ 呫 (tʰiep) **LH** tʰep, **OCM** *nhêp
'To taste' [Yupian: Guliang].
[E] ST: WT *sñab-pa* 'to taste, savor' (Bodman 1980: 141).

tiē₂ 貼 → **dié₆** 輒

tiě 鐵 (tʰiet) **LH** tʰet, **OCM** *lhêt or *lhît — **[T]** *ONW* tʰét
'Iron' [Shu], defined as 'black metal' in SW. Wáng Lì (1982: 469) and Sagart (1999: 200) derive *tiě* from an etymon 'black', as found in the homophone **tiě** 驖 (tʰiet, diet) 'black horse' [Shi].
[E] Area word: WT *lčags* < *lhyaks 'iron' (*HST:* 98). Tai: S. *lekD1S* < *hl- 'iron', PKS *kʰlit⁷; PVM *khăc 'iron' (Bodman 1980: 103). This is perh. ultimately the same foreign etymon which also entered Chinese as → xí₄ 錫 'tin'.

tīng₁ 汀 → **tíng₃** 庭

tīng₂ 聽 (tʰieŋ) **LH** tʰeŋ, **OCM** *lhêŋ
'To listen, listen to' [OB, Shu].
[T] *Sin Sukchu SR* t'iŋ (平); *MGZY* thing (平) [t'iŋ]; *MTang* tʰieŋ < tʰɨŋ, *ONW* tʰéŋ
[D] In some dialects such as W-Wēnzhōu the word also means 'to smell' and is thus an analog to → wén₃ 聞 'hear, smell'.

※ **tìng, tīng** 聽 (tʰieŋC) **LH** tʰeŋC, **OCM** *lhêŋh
'To listen to' (person, advice, order) [Shi, Zuo], 'obey' [Zuo] (Downer 1959: 284).

[<] exoactive of *tīng* (§4.3). This may be a late Zhou-period derivation, commentators to some texts read all occurrences in tone A *tīng*.

[E] This etymon is often considered cognate to → shèng₁ 聖 'wise'. Outside connections are not clear; but note PHlai *ɬiːŋ¹ 'hear, say' [Matisoff 1988c, no. 295]; or AA-PNBahn. *tăŋ 'hear' ⋈ *tamăŋ 'listen', PSBahn. *kətaaŋ ~ *tɔŋ 'to hear, listen', Wa-Lawa-Bulang *hm[ɑ]ŋ 'hear, listen', PMonic *muŋ 'listen' ⋈ *grmuɯŋ 'hear', but the AA initial *t- does not agree with OC.

tíng₁ 亭 (dieŋ) **LH** deŋ, **OCM** *dêŋ
'Settle, regulate' 亭 [Lao].

= **tíng₂** 停 (dieŋ) **LH** deŋ, **OCM** *dêŋ
'To stop' [Guanyin], prob. a later meaning.

⋈ **dìng** 定 (dieŋ^C) **LH** deŋ^C, **OCM** *dêŋh
'Sit down, settle, establish, determine' [BI, Shi].
[T] *Sin Sukchu SR* diŋ (去); *MGZY* ting (去) [diŋ]; *ONW* dėŋ

[E] ST: PTB *diŋ > Lushai *diŋ^H / din^L* 'to stand, stop, halt, stand up, go straight up' (as smoke) ⋈ ? *din^F* 'to erect, build, set up' (house, image); JP *diŋ^33* 'be perfectly straight', PLB *ʔdiŋ¹ ~ *m-diŋ¹ (*HPTB:* 123) 'put, place on, set up, establish' (Lahu gloss) ⋈ *Ndiŋ¹ 'come to rest, alight' [Matisoff *Lahu D:* 642], WB *tañ* 'place in position, build', Lepcha *diŋ* 'be erect, to stand' (Bodman ICSTLL 1987).

[C] This wf could be related to → zhèng₁ 正政 'correct, govern' (Karlgren 1956: 16).

tíng₂ 停 → **tíng₁** 亭

tíng₃ 庭 (dieŋ) **LH** deŋ, **OCM** *lêŋ
'Courtyard, court of a palace, mansion, temple' [OB, BI, Shi].
[T] *MTang* dieŋ < dɨŋ, *ONW* dėŋ
[D] M-Xiàmén *tiã^A2*
[E] ST: Perh. PTB *gliŋ 'ground, land, country, region': NNaga *C/v-khliŋ 'place' (e.g. place to sit, abode) [French 1983: 532], WT *gliŋ* 'island, continent'. In a roundabout way, this etymon might have entered the language of the ancient state of Chǔ during the Han period where we find **tīng** 汀 (tʰieŋ) LH *tʰeŋ* 'island' [Chuci]; if true, the word must have been written down at a time (Han or later) when OC *hl- and *th- had merged into *tʰ-*.
[C] This is perhaps related to the wf → tǐng₂ 挺 in the sense of 'straight' > 'level'.

tíng₄ 庭 'straight' → **tǐng₂** 挺

tíng₅ 莛筳 → **tǐng₃** 梃

tǐng₁-tuǎn 町疃 → **dìng₄** 町

tǐng₂ 挺 (tʰieŋ^B) **LH** tʰeŋ^B, **OCM** *lhêŋʔ
'Straight' [Zuo].

⋈ **tíng** 庭 (dieŋ) **LH** deŋ, **OCM** *lêŋ — **[T]** *ONW* dėŋ
'Be straight, upright' (of growing grain, morals) [BI, Shi]; 'stalk, stem' 莛 [Zhuang]; 'small bamboo rods used for divination' 筳 [Chuci].

[E] ST: PTB: *bleŋ 'straight' (*STC* no. 352). The wf → zhèng₁ 正政 may belong here, but the initials point to *l- vs. *t- respectively which are difficult to reconcile. Matisoff (1988) combines this wf with → yíng₂ 盈嬴 'full', → píng₁ 平 'level' and → zhèng₁ 正政 'straight'. See also → tǐng₃ 梃.

tǐng₃ 梃, **dìng** 鋌 (dieŋ^B) **LH** deŋ^B, **OCM** *lêŋʔ
'Stick, staff' *tǐng* 梃 [Meng]; 'metal rod inserted in arrow' *dìng* 鋌 [Zhouli].

※ **tíng** 莛筳 (dieŋ) **LH** deŋ, **OCM** *lêŋ
'Stalk, stem' 莛 [Zhuang]; 'small bamboo rods used for divination' 筳 [Chuci].

[E] Perh. ST *C-liŋ (originally referring to the tibia bone, hence 'marrow' as well as the hollowed tube-like piece): PTB *r-kliŋ (*STC* no. 126) > Mikir *arkleŋ*, Lushai *tʰliŋ*^R 'marrow', Mru *kliŋ* 'id.'; WT *gliŋ-bu* 'flute' which is sometimes made of a human femur, lit. *bu* 'son' (i. e. 'derivative') of a 'gliŋ', PLB *kliŋ > PL *ʔliŋ¹ ~ *hliŋ¹ 'flute', WB *kyañ* 'tube' (Matisoff 1970 no. 98).

This etymon and the wf → kēng₂ 硜 *khreŋ as well as → xìng₃, jìng 脛 *geŋh tend to converge. For an overview, see Table K-2 under → kēng₂ 硜. Less likely, this wf may be connected with → tǐng₂ 挺 'straight'.

tōng₁ 恫 (tʰuŋ) **LH** tʰoŋ, **OCM** *thôŋ or *thôŋ ?
'Pained, grieved' [Shi].

※ **tòng** 痛 (tʰuŋ^C) **LH** tʰoŋ^C, **OCM** *lhôŋh ? or *thôŋh ? — **[T]** *ONW* tʰoŋ
'To hurt' [Zuo].
[<] *Tōng* + caus. s-suffix (§4.3.2).

[E] This wf could be related to WT *gduŋ-ba* (< *g-luŋ*?) 'to desire, long for, love, feel pain', *mtʰoŋ-ba* 'to suffer, endure pain, misfortunes' etc. (*HST:* 144). *HST:* 115 keeps this etymon distinct from the one in *-uŋ (→ téng₁ 疼). It is not clear if the OC / ST initial was of the L or T type.

tōng₂ 通 (tʰuŋ) **LH** tʰoŋ, **OCM** *lhôŋ
'Penetrate, pass through, communicate' [Shu], 'reach everywhere, clearly understand' [Lunyu].
[T] *Sin Sukchu SR* t'uŋ (平); *MGZY* thung (平) [t'uŋ]; *ONW* tʰoŋ
[E] Perh. ST, but an OC initial lateral which is implied by the phonetic series is difficult to reconcile with WT *th-*, unless the latter derives from *m-lh-: *mtʰoŋ-ba* 'to see, perceive, understand' ※ *mtʰoŋs* 'smoke hole in a roof' (*HST:* 116).

tóng₁ 同 (duŋ) **LH** doŋ, **OCM** *dôŋ
'Together, join, assemble' 同 [Shi].
[T] *Sin Sukchu SR* duŋ (平); *MGZY* tung (平) [duŋ]; *ONW* doŋ
[E] ? ST: Perh. related to TB-Lushai *in^L-tɔŋ^H / in^L-tɔn^F* 'to meet together, meet, tally, agree, occur at the same time', WT *sdoŋ-pa* 'to unite, join'. Unrelated to *cóng* 叢 (under → jù₇ 聚).

tóng₂ 銅 (duŋ) **LH** doŋ, **OCM** *lôŋ or *d(l)ôŋ ?
'Bronze, copper' 銅 [Zuo].
[E] Karlgren (1956: 5) relates this word to → tóng₁ 同 'to join' (i.e. two metals); but metals are typically associated with color, therefore the word is probably related to tóng 彤 'red' (under → hóng₂ 紅) (this idea is implied by Benedict *MKS* 18–19, 1992: 1–13). The word 'copper' occurs in some SE Asian lgs. with initial *l-*: Tai-Wuming *luːŋ²*, MK-Palaung *məlɔŋ* 'copper' (Sagart 1999: 199).

tóng₃ 筒筩 (duŋ) **LH** doŋ, **OCM** *d(l)ôŋ ?
'Tube' 筒 [Lü], 筩 [Hanfei].
[E] Area word: WT *doŋ-po* ~ *ldoŋ-po* 'tube, any hollow cylindrical vessel' (*HST:* 153), Chepang *tʰoŋ* 'tube'. <> PMK *kɗuŋ ~ *kɗiŋ 'bamboo tube' (<> Shorto (1972: 18;

Benedict *MKS* 18–19, 1992: 9). <> PTai *kl-: S. *klɔɔŋ*^{C1} 'tube, cylinder'; Li *loŋ*, IN *t'luŋ* (Benedict *AT:* 38). The initials are difficult to determine.

tóng$_4$ 彤 → **hóng**$_2$ 紅

tóng$_5$ 童僮 (duŋ) **LH** doŋ, **OCM** *dôŋ — **[T]** *MGZY* tung (平) [duŋ]
'Be young, young person, fellow; young' (of animals, i.e. without horns) 童 [Shi]; 'young person, servant' [Zuo] > 'ignorant' 僮 [Guoyu].

ꭗ **tóng** 瞳 (tʰuŋ) **LH** tʰoŋ, **OCM** *thôŋ
'Be inexperienced, ignorant' 瞳 [Zhuang], 侗 [Shi] (also MC *duŋ*). The last graph belongs to an OC L-initial series, the other clearly had initial dental stops; it is not clear how to reconcile these forms.

[E] Etymology not certain; but note TB-KN-Khami *doŋ* 'boy' (Löffler 1966: 142). <> MY: Mong *tuŋ*^{55} 'son, male' [Strecker *LTBA* 10.2, 1987: 35]. *CVST* (3: 36) relates 'stupid' to WT *blun* 'stupid, ignorant'.

tóng$_6$ 童 (duŋ) **LH** doŋ
'Sorcerer, medium, to dance' in Mǐn dialects: PMin *doŋ^A > Amoy col. *daŋ*^{A2} (lit. *doŋ*^{A2} 'boy').
[E] AA: Viet. *døong* 'to shamanize', WrMon *doŋ* 'to dance' (Norman / Mei 1976: 296).

tǒng 桶 (tʰuŋ^B) **LH** tʰoŋ^B, **OCM** *lhôŋ? or *thôŋ? ?
'Bushel, measure of capacity' [Lüshi, Shiji], later 'bucket'.
[E] Etymology not clear, note PTai *thuaŋ$^{C1/A1}$ 'bucket' (Luo Yongxian *MKS* 27, 1997: 274), a CH loan? Or perh. ST: Chepang *dʰuŋ* 'container, pot-shaped storage basket.'

tòng 痛 → **tōng**$_1$ 恫

tōu$_1$ 偷 (tʰəu) **LH** tʰo, **OCM** *lhô
'Reckless, careless' [Li] > 'rude' [Zuo] > tr. 'to slight, despise' [Zuo].
This word's meaning is rather different from the homophone 'to steal' (→ tōu$_2$ 偷) so that it is prob. directly derived from → yú$_{17}$ 愉 *lo 'pleasant' (< 'relaxed').

~ **tāo** 慆 (tʰâu) **LH** tʰou, **OCM** *lhû
'Reckless' [Shi]. This variant might have been influenced by the homophone *tāo* 滔 'overflowing' (under → yóu$_4$ 油).

ꭗ **tuō** 脱 (tʰuât, duât) **LH** tʰuɑt, duɑt, **OCM** *l(h)ôt
'Careless' [Zuo].
[T] *ONW* tʰuɑt, duɑt

[C] This group belongs to the root → yú$_{17}$ 愉 *lo 'pleasant' (< 'relaxed'), q.v.

tōu$_2$ 偷 (tʰəu) **LH** tʰo, **OCM** *lhô
'To steal' [Guan]. *CVST* (3: 42) relates this word to WB *lu*^{C} 'take by force'.

ꭗ **duó** 奪 (duât) **LH** duɑt, **OCM** *lôt
'To rob, take away' [BI, Shi]. Pulleyblank (ICSTLL 1998: 11) connects this word with **dào** 盜 (dâu^C) LH *dauh* 'thief, to rob' [Shi].

[C] This group belongs to the root → yú$_{17}$ 愉 *lo 'pleasant' (< 'relaxed'), see there for allofams.

tóu$_1$ 投 (dəu) **LH** do, **OCM** *dô — **[T]** *ONW* dou
'To throw' [Shu], 'throw out, eject, throw to, present' [Shi], 'reject' [Li].
[E] ST: WT *'dor-ba* 'to throw or cast away, throw out, eject, decline, reject' ꭗ *gtor-ba* 'to strew, scatter, throw, waste' (Unger *Hao-ku* 35, 1986: 33). For loss of ST final *-r, see §7.7.5.

tóu$_2$, yú 歈 (dəu) **LH** do, **OCM** *lô
'A kind of song' [Chuci].
[E] ST: WT *glu* 'song', Mru *klö* 'sound, melody', WB *kyu^B* 'produce melodious sound' (Löffler 1966: 130), and / or *krui^B* 'kind of song'.

tóu$_3$ 頭 (dəu) **LH** do, **OCM** *dô
'Head' [Eastern Zhou BI, Zuo], replaced earlier → shǒu$_3$ 首.
[T] *Sin Sukchu SR* dəw (平); *MGZY* tʰiw (平) [dəw]; *ONW* dou
[D] Y-Guǎngzhōu *tɐu^{A2}(-hɔk^D)* 頭(殼); K-Méixiàn *tʰɛu^{A2}-na^{A2}* 頭那, Dànshuǐ *tʰiu^{A2}-na^{A1}-hɔk^{D1}* (R. Bauer *CAAAL* 28, 1987: 60f); PMin *dʰəu^{A2}: Jiānglè *tʰəu^{D1}*, Fúzhōu *tʰau^{52}*, Xiàmén *tʰau^{A2}-kʰak;* W-Wēnzhōu *dɦeu^{21}*
[N] The initial consonant in the phonetic series 豆 could be either *d or *l, but it was prob. *d- as forms for 'skull' → dú$_8$-lóu 髑髏 show.
[E] The late appearance of *tóu* in the 6th cent BC when it began to replace → shǒu$_3$ 首 suggests that it is derived from the much earlier attested vessel → dòu$_2$ 豆 (Sagart 1999: 156), but *dòu* (tone C) looks like a derivation from *tóu* instead which may therefore originally have meant 'skull'. An allofam may be → dòu$_3$ 豈 'bean'.
The word *tóu* has two possible outside connections. (1) ST: Loloish *ʔdu^2 'head' [Matisoff LL 1.2, 2000: 168] where *u* corresponds directly to OC *o.* Or (2) MK: Khmer *-tūla* /-dool/ 'head, to bulge' which would also be a direct phonological equivalent of OC (for CH loss of final MK consonant, see §6.9). The MK word belongs to a large wf 'bulge, knoll' and would thus provide an etymology.

tóu$_4$-lú 頭顱 → **dú$_8$-lóu** 髑髏

tǒu 橢 → **duǒ$_1$** 朵

tū 突 (tʰuət, duət) **LH** tʰuət, duət, **OCM** *thût, *dût — **[T]** *ONW* dot
'To dig through, break through' [Zuo] > 'bursting forth > suddenly' [Shi].
[E] ST: PTB *tu, *du > PL *m-du^2, WB *tu^B* dig, JP *tʰu^{31}*, Nung *du* 'to dig' [*STC* no. 258], NNaga*tʰu [French 1983: 334]. Note also Lushai *tʰut^H* 'suddenly' (related?).

tú$_1$ 途 (duo) **LH** dɑ, **OCM** *lâ — **[T]** *ONW* do
'To plaster, mud, plaster' [Shi], 'to soil' [Zhuang].
[D] PMin *dʰo 'soil, earth'; for a semantic parallel 'mud' > 'earth, soil' see → ní$_2$ 泥.
[E] Tai: S. *tʰaa^{A2}* < *d- 'to smear, paint' (Li F. 1976: 40).

tú$_2$ 涂途塗 (duo) **LH** dɑ, **OCM** *lâ
'Path' (along the bank of a canal; paved path) [Zhouli]; 'road' 途 [Lie], 塗 [Lunyu].
[E] Etymology not clear. Perh. related to → táng$_2$ 塘 'dam, dike'. Wáng Lì (1982: 147) relates this word to → táng$_1$ 唐 'path in a temple', but see there. Or it may be the s. w. as → tú$_1$ 途 'mud, plaster'.

tú$_3$ 徒 (duo) **LH** dɑ, **OCM** *dâ
'Bare, naked' [Li], 'only' [Meng].
[E] ? AA: Khmer *dah*, Bahn.-Stieng *dɔh* 'to take off' (clothing) [Huffman 1975]. <> Tai: S. *taa^4* 'only, sole'. This word may have alternative etymological connections, see → tǎn$_1$ 袒襢 'to bare' and the items listed there.

tú$_4$ 圖 → **dù$_1$** 度

tǔ$_1$ 土 (tʰuo^B) **LH** tʰɑ^B, **OCM** *thâʔ — **[T]** *ONW* tʰo
'Land, soil' [Shi]. The phonetic series *GSR* 62 implies a dental stop initial.

[D] Y-Guǎngzhōu t^hou^{B1}, Táishān hu^{A2}. Some modern dialects have replaced this word with → ní$_2$ 泥.
[E] There is no obvious cognate and etymology, unless it may be related to AA-PMon *tiiʔ 'soil, ground consisting of earth, earth', Aslian *tiʔ ~ tɛʔ;* however, this would require the assumption of a shift from front vowel to OC *a (§11.1.3). Prob. related to → shè$_1$ 社.

tǔ$_2$ 吐 (tʰuoᴮ, tʰuoᶜ) **LH** tʰɑᴮ, **OCM** *thâʔ
'To spit out' [Shi].
[D] Mand. *tǔ* 'spit', *tù* 'vomit'; Y-Guǎngzhōu t^hou^{C1} (both meanings), Táishān hu^{A1}

ꭗ **tù** 吐 (tʰuoᴮ, tʰuoᶜ) **LH** tʰɑᶜ, **OCM** *thâh
'To vomit' Mand. Not all dialects have both these words.

[E] ST *twa > PTB *(m-/s-)twa > Kachin *mətʰo*, Garo *stu*, Kanauri *tʰu* 'spit'. Although *tǔ* looks like a variant of the syn. → tuò$_3$ 唾, the ST sources are quite distinct. For the lack of a Chinese medial *w*, see §10.2.1; Chinese aspiration is associated with forceful outward motion §5.8.5.

tù 兔 (tʰuoᶜ) **LH** tʰɑᶜ, **OCM** *lhâh
'Hare, rabbit' [OB, Shi]. The OC initial *lh- is revealed by the graph's use as phonetic in a word for 'tiger' in *Zuǒzhuàn* (→ hǔ$_1$ 虎).
[E] ST: TB words for 'rabbit' include Jiarong *ka-la*, Lolo lgs.: Hani t^ho^{31}-la^{33}, Lahu $t^hɔ^{54}$-la^{31} and the like [ZM 1992, nos. 292; 758]. Middle Korean *twos(ki)* 'hare' might have been borrowed from CH in connection with the animal cycle (Miyake 1997: 1988).

tuān 貒 → **tuàn** 彖

tuán$_1$ 團摶漙敦 (duân) **LH** duɑn, **OCM** *dôn
'Round, everywhere, plenty' 團 [Shiwen: Shi]; 'make round' [Li], 'collect' [Guan], 'bundle' 摶 [Zhouli]; 'rich, plentiful' (dew) 漙 [Shi]; 'plentiful' 敦 [Shi].
[T] *Sin Sukchu SR* dwɔn (平); *MGZY* ton (平) [dɔn]

ꭗ **zhuàn** 縳 (ḍjwänᴮ) **LH** ḍuɑnᴮ, **OCM** *dronʔ
'Roll and wrap up' [Zuo], 'bundle' [Zhouli].
[C] Allofam is perh. → zhuǎn$_1$ 轉 'turn around' (so Karlgren 1956: 13).

ꭗ **tuán$_2$** 剬 (duân, tśjwänᴮ) **LH** duɑn, tśuan, **OCM** *dôn, *ton
'To cut' [Li].

ꭗ **zhuǎn** 膞 (źjwänᴮ, tśjwänᴮ) **LH** dź/tśuanᴮ, **OCM** *donʔ, *tonʔ
'Cut meat, slice' [Huainan].

tuàn 彖 (tʰuânᶜ) **LH** tʰuɑnᶜ, **OCM** *thôns
'A kind of pig' [Yi, SW], variant *tuān* 貒 (tʰuânᴬ) [EY, SW, Chu]; → tún$_5$ 豚 is prob. variant of the same etymon.
[E] <> PY *duŋᴮ 'pig' (M. Ratliff, p. c.); their first textual occurrence in *Chǔcí* and Han texts suggests that these words are of MY origin.

tuī 推 (tʰuậi) **LH** tʰuəi, **OCM** *thûi, OCB *thuj
'To push away' [Shi], 'push' [Zuo], 'extend' [Meng]. CH aspiration is associated with forceful outward motion §5.8.5. Acc. to Baxter (1992: 231) perh. related to the next:

ꭗ **cuī** 催 (tsʰuậi) **LH** tsʰuəi, **OCM** *tshûi, OCB *tsʰuj (< *Sthuj ?)
'To urge, press' [SW: Shi].

ꭗ **cuī** 摧 (dzuậi) **LH** dzuəi, **OCM** *dzûi
'To repress, oppress' [Shi 258, 3].

[E] Possibly ST: Chepang *dus-* 'to push away, shove' ⋇ *dhus-* id.

tuǐ 腿 ($t^hu\hat{a}i^B$) (a hypothetical PCH form corresponding to MC might have been *thul) 'Thigh', also 'lower leg' [Tang: Han Yu; GY].
[E] MK: PMon *dɯl 'thigh'.

tuì₁ 退 ($t^hu\hat{a}i^C$) **LH** $t^hu\text{əs}$, **OCM** *thû(t)s, OCB *hnuts < *hnups (Baxter 1992: 557) 'Withdraw, retire' [Shi].
[T] *ONW* $t^hu\text{ɑi}$
[E] Etymology not clear. This may be connected with *tuì* 駾 *l(h)ots 'withdraw' (under → tuō₃ 脱). Perh. related to MK-Mon *dui'* 'to stop, keep quiet, stay put'.

tuì₂ 駾 → **tuō₃** 脱

tūn₁ 呑 ($t^h\text{ə}n$) **LH** $t^h\text{ə}n$, **OCM** *thə̂n ?
'To swallow' [Guoce].
[T] *Sin Sukchu SR* t'un (平), *PR* t'ən; *MGZY* th^hin (平) [t'ən] — **[D]** PMin $*t^hun$
[E] <> KT: PT *kl-: S. *klɨɨn*^{A1} 'to swallow', Ahom *k(l)en*, Wuming *klwan*, Saek *tlɯɯn*^{A1}; PKS *ʔdun;* cf. IN *təlun, lunlun*, Be *lun* (Benedict *AT:* 19, but withdrawn in Benedict 1976: 68). Alternatively, *CVST* 2: 10 relates this word to WT *'tʰuŋ* 'drink'.

tūn₂ 暾 ($t^hu\text{ə}n$) **LH** $t^hu\text{ə}n$, **OCM** *thûn
'The rising sun' [Chuci].
[E] This word has two possible sources, although the first appearance in *Chǔcí* favors an AA connection; perh. it is a blend of the two: (1) TB: WT *'tʰon-pa, tʰon* 'to come out, go out', WB *pɔ-tʰon*^{B} 'come out' (e. g. the sun), Monpa Cuona *⁵³tɕʰuŋ*, Motuo *tʰoŋ* 'to come out' (sun) (ZM 92 no. 1207). In ST lgs. the notion of sunrise is often associated with 'to come out, rise' (cf. WT *šar* 'to rise, east', CH *rì chū* 日出 'the sun comes out'), while 'west' → xī₂ 西棲栖 is associated with 'to go down, rest, nest'.
(2) AA: PMon *tun 'go up' (sun, water level, etc.) which is phonologically close to the OC word. In both TB and AA the word is apparently native (for PMonic, see: Diffloth 1984: 206), although their basic meanings differ (TB 'come out', vs. AA 'go up'). An allofam may be → dōng₂ 東 'east'.

tún₁ 屯 (duən) **LH** duən, **OCM** *dûn
'Hill' [Zhuang].
~ **dùn** 頓 ($tu\text{ə}n^C$) **LH** $tu\text{ə}n^C$, **OCM** *tûns
'Hill' [Shi].
[E] AA: OKhmer /duuəl/ 'knoll, hillock, mound', PVM $*dol^A$ 'hill', PSBahn. *tul ~ *nətul 'anthill'. AA -> TB-Lepcha *tʰyul* 'heap' (Forrest *JAOS* 82, 1962: 334). The relationship with → duī 堆 'mound', if any, is not clear.

tún₂ 屯 (duən) **LH** duən, **OCM** *dûn — **[T]** *Sin Sukchu* 飩 *SR* dun (平)
'Accumulate' [Yi] > 'to mass troops, put pressure on' [BI, Shi], 'garrison, station soldiers' [Zuo].
[E] ST: WT *'du-ba* 'to assemble' ⋇ *gdu-ba* 'to gather' ⋇ *'dun-sa* 'meeting place' ⋇ *'tʰun-pa* 'to gather' ⋇ *sdud-pa* 'to collect, gather' ⋇ *sdud* 'fold of garment' ⋇ *'du-ba* 'come together' ⋇ *'dus-pa* 'to unite' ⋇ *gdu-ba* 'to gather' ⋇ *'tʰu-ba* 'to gather, collect' ⋇ *(m-)dud-pa* 'knot'. Bodman (1969: 340) associates many of these WT items with *zú* 卒 (under → zāo₂ 遭). Unger (*Hao-ku* 35, 1986: 31) relates the CH word to Lepcha *tyul* 'to conglomerate, a flock'.
[C] *Tún* could possibly be related to → tún₁ 屯; and / or to → dūn₁ 敦惇.

tún₃ 純 (duən[B]) **LH** duən, **OCM** *dûn
'Tie together, envelop' [Shi].
[E] ST: WT *tʰul-pa* 'furred coat, cloak; to roll or wind up'; Nung *rədul* 'roll, wrap, enwrap', Angami Naga *rətuu* < *rtul* 'roll' (*STC* p. 110; Unger *Hao-ku* 35, 1986: 30). Perh. related to → tún₂ 屯窀 'accumulate'.

tún₄ 忳 → **chǔn** 蠢惷

tún₅ 豚 (duən) **LH** duən, **OCM** *dûn
'Young pig' [OB, Lun] (see Li Liu *EC* 21: 1996: 17). Perh. → tuàn 彖 and *tuān* 貒 are variants of this word.

tún₆ 臀 (duən) **LH** duən, **OCM** *dûn
'Buttock' [Guoyu].
[E] ST: PTB *tun > Meithei *məthun¹*, Abor-Miri *ko-dun* 'buttock', prob. also LB-Lisu *khi²¹ du²¹* [Matisoff *LTBA* 17.2, 1994: 137]. This meaning is connected with 'heel': JP *lə³¹-tʰin³³* 'heel', KN-Naga-Wancho *chi-dun* 'heel, LB-Phunoi *pi³³ tun¹¹*.
The ST etymon may have wider connections: PKS *lun² 'back, behind', Tai-Saek *tloon^A1* 'buttocks'. And / or AA items cited under → tún₁ 屯 'hill' which belong to a wf 'to bulge'. A variant is → diàn₂ 殿. A possible allofam is → dùn₄ 遯遁 'withdraw' ('go back').

tuō₁ 他 (tʰâ) **LH** tʰɑi, **OCM** *lhâi
'Other, different' [Bi, Shi], in modern dialects the word has the specialized meaning 'he, she, it, they', and is in most places pronounced → tā₁ 他. Etymology not clear. Perh. cognate to → chǐ₂, chí 誃 'to separate'; for a semantic parallel, note AA-Khmer *-dai* /-təj/ 'be other, different' ⋈ OKhmer *didai* /diidəj/ 'be different, distinct, separate'.

tuō₂, tuò 痑 → **dān₃** 癉憚

tuō₃ 脫 (tʰuât, duât) **LH** tʰuɑt, duɑt, **OCM** *l(h)ôt — **[T]** *ONW* tʰuɑt, duɑt
'Take away' 脫 [Zuo], 挩 [Lao], 'peel off' 脫 [Lie], 'take off' (clothes) [Shi, Guoyu] > 'let off, let escape' [Shi], 'escape' [Lao], 'relieve' [Gongyang].
[D] M-Amoy col. *teʔ^D2*, lit. *toat^D2*, Jiēyáng *toʔ^D2* 'take away forcibly'; Amoy col. *tʰuaʔ^D1*, lit. *tʰuat^D1* 'escape'. We would expect the tr. meanings ('take away, take off') to go with LH *tʰuat*, the intr. ('escape, careless') with LH *duat*.

⋈ **tuì** 駾 (duâi^C, tʰuâi^C) **LH** duɑs, tʰuɑs, **OCM** *l(h)ôts
'Withdraw, flee' [Shi].
[<] exopass. / reflexive of *tuō* (§4.4). We would expect the intr. use to correspond to LH *duɑs*.

⋈ **shuì** 挩 (śjwäi^C) **LH** śuat, **OCM** *lhot
'Wipe off' [Yili].

[E] ST: PTB *g-lwat (*STC* no. 209) > WT *hlod-pa* 'loose, relax' ⋈ *glod-pa* 'loosen, relax, slacken'; PLB *k-lwat > PL *k-lwat⁴ 'free', WB *hlwat* 'free, relax' ⋈ *lwat* 'be free' ⋈ *kywat* < *klwat* 'loosed, freed' ⋈ *kʰywat* < *kʰlwat* 'release, free'; Mru *lot, lon* 'loose, let out'; Lushai *tʰlɔn^L* < *thlɔns* 'to come / fall off' [Löffler 1966: 123], Lai *lot* 'free' ⋈ *še-lot* 'set free' [VanBik *LTBA* 25.2, 2002: 106], JP *lat³¹* 'to escape, get lost'. <> Tai: Shan *lɔt^D2* < *dl- 'to be free, to free' is prob. a TB loan.
[C] This group belongs to the root → yú₁₇ 愉 *lo 'pleasant' (< 'relaxed'), see there for allofams. Perh. → róng₁ 容 is related. This wf comes close to → chōu₁ 抽.

tuó₁ 佗 → **wēi₁-tuó** 委佗

tuó₂ 阤 → **zhì₇** 阤, 陊 **(duò)**

tuó₃ 鼉 (dâ, dân) **LH** dɑi, dɑn, **OCM** *dâi, *dân
'Freshwater alligator, *Alligator sinensis*' [Shi].
[E] Its mythological meanings and etymological speculations are discussed by Carr (*LTBA* 13.2, 1990: 131ff). *Tuó* is distinct from → è₅ 鱷 (ŋâk) 'aquatic reptile' [SW].
Löffler (1966: 140) relates this word tentatively to Mru *tam* 'alligator', but the final nasals do not agree. The word is also reminiscent of AA: Santali *tajan* 'broad-headed crocodile'.

tuǒ₁ 隋 (t^huâ^B) **LH** t^huɑi^B, **OCM** *lhôiʔ
'Shred sacrificial meat' [Zhouli].
[E] ST: WB *t^hwa* 'mince with a knife' is prob. unrelated since neither initial nor rime match.

tuǒ₂ 隋 (t^huâ^B) **LH** t^huɑi^B, **OCM** *lhôiʔ
'Long and narrow, oval' [Chuci].
⋈ **duò** 隋 (duâ^B) **LH** duɑi^B, **OCM** *lôiʔ
'Long and narrow' (mountain) [Shi].
[E] ST: JP *diŋ^{31}-loi^{33}* 'long and narrow' (*CVST* 3: 32).

tuǒ₃ 妥 → **suī** 綏

tuò₁ 拓 (t^hâk) **LH** t^hɑk, **OCM** *thâk
'To take up, lift' [Lie].
[T] *Sin Sukchu* 託 *SR* t'aw (入); *MGZY* 託 thaw (入) [t'aw]
[E] TB: perh. a LB loan: note PLB *ʔtak 'lift, carry'. For cognates on the ST level, see → zhì₁₅ 陟.

tuò₂ 橐 (t^hâk) **LH** t^hɑk, **OCM** *thâk
'Noise of pounding earth' [Shi].
[E] This word is onomatopoetic, but note also AA-Mon *tʌk* 'to beat', Khm *ṭɔṭɔk* 'beat (shake) a rattle' [Pinnow 1959: 318].

tuò₃ 唾 (t^huâ^C) **LH** t^huɑi^C, **OCM** *thôih
'Spittle' [SW, Hanshu], 'to spit' [Zuo].
[D] PMin *t^hoi^C; some dialects in the Yuè area have archaic rimes: Guǎngzhōu col. *t^hœ^{C1}* beside *t^hɔ^{C1}*, Zēngchéng *sœy^{C2}*, Bǎo'ān *sui^{B2}*, Enpíng *ts^{h}ui^{A2}*; K-Dōngguān *sui^B*.
[E] ST *tol > WT *t^ho-le* (i.e. *tol-e) *'debs-pa* 'to spit' (*'debs-pa* 'to throw') (*HST:* 138); WB *t^hwe^B* 'spit' (*STC:* 30 n. 95) seems to agree with the WT and CH forms. But alternatively, *STC* connects WB with PTB *twəy (= *tui) 'water'. Although *tuò* looks like a variant of the syn. → tǔ₃ 吐, the OC and the TB forms are quite distinct. CH aspiration is associated with forceful ejection §5.8.5.

tuò₄ 蘀 (t^hâk) **LH** t^hɑk, **OCM** *lhâk
'To wither, fallen leaves' [Shi].
[E] Prob. AA: Khmer *sla'ka* /slɑk/ 'to fade, wilt, dry up', from a root *-la'ka* /-lɑk/ 'to fall', acc. to Jenner / Pou 1982: 523. Alternatively, *tuò* could possibly be related to → luò₇ 落 *râk 'fall' (Unger *Hao-ku* 39, 1992: 92; Sagart 1999: 18), but then one would need to assume OCM *rhâk for *tuò* which is not supported by the phonetic series.

W

wā $_1$ 蛙 (ʔwaɨ) **LH** ʔuɛ, **OCM** *ʔwrê or *ʔwe ?
'Frog' [Zhouli].
[E] Perh. KT: PT *kw-: Boai *kwɛɛ*^{C1}, Wuming *klwe* 'small green frog'; PKS *k-wai^{C} 'small frog' (Bodman 1980: 144).

wā $_2$ 窪 (ʔwaɨ) **LH** ʔuɛ, **OCM** *ʔwrê
'Hole, hollow, concave' 窐 [Lü], 窪 [Lao].

⋇ **wā** 洼 (ʔiwei) **LH** ʔue, **OCM** *ʔwê
'Concave, puddle' [Zhuang].

⋇ **kē** 科 (kʰuâ) **LH** kʰuɑi, **OCM** *khwâi
'A hollow, cavity' [Meng], 'hollow of a tree trunk' [Yi] is perh. a nominalizing k-prefix derivation (§5.4).

wǎ 瓦 → **é**$_4$ 訛吪

wài 外 (ŋuâi^{C}) **LH** ŋuɑs, **OCM** *ŋwâts, OCB *ngʷats
'Outside, external' [OB, BI, Shi].
[T] *Sin S. SR* ŋwaj (去), *PR* ŋwaj, waj; *LR* waj; *MGZY* xue (去) [ɦuɛ]; *ONW* ŋuɑC
[N] In the OB, the graph is a vertical line with a stroke on one side ⺊, i.e. 'outside'; the graph is identical to → bǔ$_1$ 卜. 'Moon' *yuè* 月 LH *ŋyat* has been added later as phonetic. Bodman (1980: 136) connects this word with WT *ŋos* 'side, direction', see → yù$_{17}$ 禦.

wān 灣關 (ʔwan) **LH** ʔuan, **OCM** *ʔrôn
'To bend' (a bow) 關 [Meng] > later 'bent coastline, a bay' 灣. This word may be connected with → yū$_1$ 迂紆, → wēi$_1$-tuó 委佗, → wēi$_2$ 逶, or → wěi$_3$ 委.

wán 頑 → **yú**$_{23}$ 愚

wǎn$_1$ 宛 'accommodating' → **yāo**$_2$ 妖

wǎn$_2$ 婉 → **yāo**$_2$ 妖

wǎn$_3$ 苑 → **yuàn**$_1$ 苑

wǎn$_4$ 碗 (ʔuân^{B}) **LH** ʔuɑn^{B}, **OCM** *ʔônʔ
'A bowl' [Guan] (written with rad. 木).
[<] *ōu* 甌 (ʔəu) with nominalizing n-suffix (§6.4.3).

⋇ **ōu** 甌 (ʔəu) **LH** ʔo, **OCM** *ʔô
'A bowl' [Xun].

[E] ST: WB *ui*^{B} 'pot, jar, chatty'; → wèng 甕 may also be connected.

wàn$_1$ 腕 → **yū**$_1$ 迂紆

wàn$_2$ 曼 (mjwɐn^{C}) **LH** muɑn^{C}, **OCM** *mâns
'Be extending, long, wide' 曼 [Shi] > 'creeping plant' 蔓 [Shi].

⋇ **màn** 曼漫 (muân^{C}) **LH** mɑn^{C}, **OCM** *mâns — **[T]** *ONW* mɑn
'Distant, unlimited' [Zhuang] > 'free, careless' [Zhuang].

⋇ **màn** 慢嫚 (man^{C}) **LH** man^{C}, **OCM** *mrâns ?
'Be slow, negligent' [Shi] > 'indulgent' 慢 [Li] > 'to slight, be insolent' 嫚 [Zuo].

[T] *Sin Sukchu SR* man (去); *MGZY* man (去) [man]
[E] ST: Lushai *muaŋ*^{H} / *muan*^{L} 'be slow and leisurely, to linger', Lepcha *moŋ, mon* 'be quiet, silent'. (Geilich 1994: 139; 159 includes these TB items in the wf → mò$_{15}$ 默嘿 'silent').

wàn$_3$ 萬 (mjwɐn^C) **LH** muɑn^C, **OCM** *mans — **[D]** CDC *mvan*^{6}
'Ten thousand' [BI, Shi].
[T] *Sin Sukchu SR* vwan (去), *LR* vwan; *MGZY* (khan >) wan (去) [van]; *ONW* muan
[E] ST: WT *'bum* < *ɴbum* 'hundred thousand'; JP *lə*^{31}*-mun*^{31} 'ten thousand' (CH loan?). As to foreign initial *b*- for CH *m*-, see §5.12.2.
CH -> Tai: S. *hmɨn*^{B} 'ten thousand' (Unger *Hao-ku* 36, 1990: 54).

wāng$_1$ 汪 → **wū**$_1$ 汙

wāng$_2$ 尪 → **qú**$_4$, **jù** 臞

wáng$_1$ 亡 (mjwaŋ) **LH** muɑŋ, **OCM** *maŋ, OCB *mjaŋ
'To lose, disappear, flee' [BI, Shi]; 'to have none, there is not' intr. [Lunyu] (Pulleyblank 1995: 109).
[T] *Sin Sukchu SR, LR* vaŋ (平); *MGZY* wang (平) [vaŋ]; *MTang* mvuaŋ, *ONW* muaŋ
[<] ST *ma 'not' (→ wú 無) + ST terminative suffix *-ŋ* (§6.5.1).
[E] TB: Lushai *maŋ*^{F} 'to die, die out, exterminate', JP *maŋ*^{33}, Chepang *hmaŋ* 'corpse'.

⋈ **wàng** 忘 (mjwaŋ[^{C}]) **LH** muɑŋ(^{C}), **OCM** *maŋ (!)
'To forget' [BI, Shi], i.e. 'to lose' (from memory) is the s. w. as *wáng* 亡 in early OC as revealed by *Shījīng* rimes, tone C emerged later ('it has disappeared from mind, has escaped me', a perfective form in *-s / *-h of *wáng* 亡 (§3.5), acc. to Unger *Hao-ku* 20, 1983).

⋈ **wǎng** 罔 (mjwaŋ^B) **LH** muɑŋ^B, **OCM** *maŋ?
'There is no, not have' occurs in *Shūjīng* and the old parts of *Shījīng*, but is then replaced by its stem → wú$_4$ 無 in that meaning. The graph 亡 in the OB, BI may perh. write this word rather than *wáng* 亡 above.
[<] *wáng* 亡 *maŋ with the aux. vb. tone B (§3.3.2).

⋈ **huāng** 荒 (xwâŋ) **LH** huɑŋ, **OCM** *hmâŋ
'To waste' (of land, time) [BI, Shi] > 'neglect, reject' [Shu].
[<] caus. devoicing of *wáng* 亡 (mjwaŋ) (§5.2.1).

⋈ **sàng** 喪 (sâŋ^C) **LH** sɑŋ^C, **OCM** *sâŋh < *smâŋh
'To lose' (e.g. a country) [OB, Shi], 'destroy' [Shu], 'to die' [Shu, Liji] (Pulleyblank 1962: 136; Baxter 1992: 187). → sāng$_1$ 喪 'burial' is prob. unrelated.
[<] s-caus. of *wáng* 亡 *maŋ (§5.2.1) + exoactive tone C (§4.3.2).

wáng$_2$ 王 (jwaŋ) **LH** wɑŋ, **OCM** *waŋ, OCB *wjaŋ
'King' [BI, Shi].
[T] *Sin Sukchu SR* waŋ (平); *MGZY* xwang (平) [ɦwaŋ]; *ONW* uaŋ

⋈ **wàng** 王 (jwaŋ^C) **LH** wɑŋ^C, **OCM** *waŋh
'Be king, rule' [Shi 241, 4].
[<] *waŋ + s/h-suffix (§3.5).

[E] Etymology not certain. Prob. ST: WT *dbaŋ* 'might, power' ⋈ *dbaŋ-po* 'ruler', WB *aŋ* 'strength, power', NNaga *waŋ 'chief' [French 1983: 389]. The initials present difficulties, though (WT *b- vs. OC *w-), unless one assumes that occasionally WT *b*- can derive from a *w (*db*- < *dw-); the WB form seems to support this. Alternatively, *wáng* may possibly be connected with an AA homophone: OKhmer *vaṅ* ~ *vāṅ(ṅ)* 'royal palace...' (-> Tai: S.

waŋ 'palace'), cognate to *luəŋ* 'king' (-> Tai *luaŋ* 'royal'); the identification of 'king' with his palace is perh. supported by a BI where *wáng* refers not to the Zhou king but to a place (Shaughnessy 1991: 197). Thus *wáng* would belong to the complex of stems under → yíng$_4$ 營; connection with → huáng$_1$ 皇 'august' is not clear. Otherwise, speculations have related *wáng* to *wāng* 尪 (ʔwâŋ) 'emaciated' [Zuo] (under → qú$_4$, jù 臞) and → kuáng 狂 (gjwaŋ) 'mad', based on certain theories on ancient CH kingship and shamanism (see D. Keightley *JAS* 54.1, 1995: 132).

wǎng$_1$ 往 (jwaŋ^B) **LH** waŋ^B, **OCM** *waŋʔ
'To go to, gone, past' 往 [OB, BI, Shi], 迋 [Zuo].
[T] *Sin Sukchu SR* waŋ (上); *MGZY* xwang (上) [ɦwaŋ]; *ONW* uaŋ
[<] *yú* 于 *wa + ST terminative *-ŋ (§6.5.1) + endoactive (?) tone B (§4.5). Since the terminative implies an end point of the action, the meaning in some languages is 'go to' > 'arrive' > 'come'.

ꭙ **wàng** 迋 (jwaŋ^C) **LH** waŋ^C, **OCM** *waŋh
'To go' [Zuo].
[<] *waŋʔ + general purpose suffix s/h (§3.5).

[E] ST: PTB *waŋ (*STC* no. 218) > Chepang *waŋ* 'to come' (Bodman 1980: 81), Barish-Nocte *²vaŋ(ʔ)* (Chepang and Barish (= Bodo) disagree in phonation, Weidert 1987: 30), WT *'oŋ-ba* 'to come' ꭙ perhaps also WT *soŋ* < *s-waŋ* 'went', Tamang *¹waŋ* 'enter, go in, come in'; WB *waŋ* 'to enter, go or come in' ꭙ *swaŋ^B* 'to put into', PL *waŋ¹ 'to enter'; Mikir *wàŋ* 'to come' (*HST*: 86), NN *woŋ 'come'. It is not clear how Tai *luaŋ^{B2}* 'to pass time, go beyond' (Bodman 1980: 107) may relate to this ST stem.

wǎng$_2$ 枉 → **yū$_1$** 迂紆

wǎng$_3$ 罔網 (mjwaŋ^B) **LH** muaŋ^B, **OCM** *maŋʔ
'Net' 罔 [Yi], 網 [Shi]; 'to catch, snare, entangle' 罔 [Meng], 'to tie, interlace' [Chuci].
[T] *MTang* mvuaŋ, *ONW* muaŋ < maŋ
[E] Perh. KT: PTai *mɯaŋ^{A2} 'a type of fishnet' (Luo Yongxian *MKS* 27, 1997: 274), Saek *mɔɔŋ^{A2}* 'long net across the river'. This may be the s. w. as *wǎng* 罔 'deceive' (under → wū$_3$ 誣).

wǎng$_4$ 罔 'deceive' → **wū$_3$** 誣

wǎng$_5$ 罔 'not' → **wáng$_1$** 亡

wǎng$_6$-liǎng 罔兩 (mjwaŋ^B-ljaŋ^B) **LH** muaŋ^B-liaŋ^B, **OCM** *maŋʔ-raŋʔ
'Water spirit' [Zuo]. A variant is prob.:

ꭙ **wǎng-xiàng** 罔象 (mjwaŋ^B-zjaŋ^B) **LH** muaŋ^B-ziaŋ^B, late **OCM** *maŋʔ-ziaŋʔ (?)
'A water dragon which eats people' [Zhuang, Guoyu, Shiji].

[E] Perh. related to Lepcha *tə-raŋ* 'water spirit' (Geilich 1994: 290f).

wàng$_1$, guǎng 迋 'fear' → **jù$_5$** 懼

wàng$_2$ 妄 (mjwaŋ^C) **LH** muaŋ^C, **OCM** *maŋh
'Lawless, rude' [Zuo], 'reckless' [Li].

ꭙ **màn** 謾 (muân^C) **LH** man^C, **OCM** *mâns
'Excessive, reckless' [Zhuang]. For the difference in finals, see §6.4.2.

[E] This wf converges and overlaps with → wū$_3$ 誣 'deceive, false'.

wàng$_3$ 忘 → **wáng$_1$** 亡

wàng$_4$ 望 (mjwaŋ$^{A/C}$) **LH** muaŋ$^{A/C}$, **OCM** *maŋ^A
'Look toward' [Shi], 'look into the distance' [Xun], > 'hope' [Meng]. Perh. the s. w. as

→ wàng₅ 望. Tone A in older parts of *Shījīng* (Mattos 1971: 309).

[T] *Sin Sukchu SR, LR* vaŋ (去); *MGZY* wang (去) [vaŋ]; *MTang* mvuaŋ, *ONW* muaŋ < maŋ

[E] ST: PTB *mraŋ (*STC* no. 146) > Gurung (Himal.), Thakali *mraŋ* 'to see', PL *mraŋ¹ > WB *mraŋ* 'see' (*HST:* 129) ⋈ caus. PLB *s-mraŋ or *ʔmraŋ 'to show, teach' [Matisoff *D. of Lahu:* 1027], Mikir *làng* 'to see', Nung *jaŋ* (*j* = palatal glide).

wàng₅ 望 (mjwaŋ^A/C) **LH** muɑŋ, **OCM** *maŋ (tone not clear)

'Full moon' [BI, Shu] is considered to be the s. w. as → wàng₄ 望. If the OC word had the equivalent of later tone C (and the double readings in GY may be a trace of this), 'full moon' may be a regular passive derivation from the above, lit. 'the thing that is gazed at from afar' (§4.4). Alternatively, Van Auken (*JAOS* 122.3, 2002: 528) suggests that 'full moon' is cognate to → liàng 亮 'light'.

wēi₁-tuó 委佗 (ʔjwie 3-dâ) **LH** ʔyɑi-dɑi, **OCM** *ʔwai-lâi or *ʔoi-?

'Graceful, compliant' [Shi].

⋈ **wēi-yí** 委佗 (ʔjwie 3-jie) **LH** ʔyɑi-jɑi, **OCM** *ʔwai-lai or *ʔoi- ?

'Be graceful, compliant, be winding' (as road) [Shi].

⋈ **wēi-chí** 委遲 (ʔjwie 3-ḍi) **LH** ʔyɑi-ḍi, **OCM** *ʔwai-d-l(ə)i ?

'Be winding' (as road) [Shi].

[E] Qiu Xigui (2000: 374) lists over 20 graphic variants of this sound-symbolic word. The etymology is not clear. The first syllable may be related to TB-Lushai *vial^H < vial* 'to writhe', although the item could also be linked to either → wēi₃ 逶 Lushai *vai^F <vaiʔ;* or it could be an *-i final cognate of → yāo₁ 妖 or → yǎo₁ 夭殀. Lushai cognates show that this etymon is not related to → wēi₂ 逶 'fluttering'.

The second syllable *tuó / yí / chí* reflects an area etymon: TB-Chepang *kloyʔ* 'be winding' (path or stream). <> MK-Khmer /-lée/ as in /rlée/ 'to snake, move sinuously (as through water)'. AA-Khmer final /ē/ corresponds also in other words to OC *-ai.

TB languages have a similar item whose initial *t* is irreconcilable with OC *l:* Lushai *taal^R < taalʔ* 'to struggle, wriggle, writhe', or Chepang *toy-* 'to circle or spiral upward'.

[C] An allofam of the first syllable is prob. → yuān₃ 蜎肙 'worm', of the second syllable → shé₂ 蛇 'snake'.

wēi₂ 逶 (ʔjwie 3) **LH** ʔyɑi, **OCM** *ʔwai or *ʔoi ?

'Tortuous movement, fluttering' (of a flag) [Chuci]. TB (Lushai) cognates show that this etymon is not related to → wēi₁-tuó 委佗 'be winding'.

⋈ **huī** 撝 (xjwie 3) **LH** hyɑi, **OCM** *hwai

'To signalize, manifest' [Yi] is an iterative derivation (§5.2.3) from *wēi.* A variant or syn. is → huī₄ 麾.

[E] ST: PTB *wa:y (*STC* no. 90; *HPTB:* 210) > Kachin *wai* 'whirl, as a whirlpool, stir, strike out with a sweeping motion'; WB *wai^B* 'whirlpool, brandish' a sword..., 'soar around' as a bird; Lushai *vai^F < vaiʔ* 'to wave' with the hand, arm, or anything horizontally, 'brandish' (a sword) ⋈ *hui^F* 'to beckon' with hand. Acc. to Shorto 1972 likely derived from PMK *wa(a)y(-s): Palaung vay 'to wave hand, beckon', Viet. vãy 'to wave'.

[C] For an overview of synonyms for 'turn, rotate', see under → huí 回.

wēi₃ 萎 (ʔjwie 3) **LH** ʔyɑi, **OCM** *ʔoi or *ʔwai ?, OCB *ʔ(r)jojʔ

'To wither' [Shi].

⋈ **yuàn** 苑 (ʔjwɐn^B, ʔjuət) **LH** ʔyɑn^B (also ʔɨut ?), **OCM** *ʔonʔ (*ʔut ?) or *ʔwanʔ ?

'To wither' [Huainan]. For the final *-n*, see §6.4.4.

[E] ST: PTB *hwa:y (*HPTB:* 214) > Lushai *vuai^H* 'to wither, wilt, droop' ⋈ *uai^H* 'to wither, wilt, droop' ⋈ *uai*^{L} 'to hang onto, hang upon'; Tangkhul Naga *hùy* 'fade', JP *wai*^{H} ~ *woi*^{H}, Lahu *hwē 'id.'* [Matisoff *D. of Lahu:* 1111].

[D] Ancient dialect variants are cited under → yū$_2$ 菸.

wēi$_4$ 威 (ʔjwei) **LH** ʔui, **OCM** *ʔui — **[T]** *ONW* ʔui

'To overawe, intimidate' [Shu], 'imposing, majestic' [Shi], 'intimidating, majesty, dignity' [BI, Shi, Shu]. Acc. to Sagart, → guǐ$_1$ 鬼 'ghost' is a derivation.

⋈ **wèi** 畏 (ʔjwei^C) **LH** ʔui^C, **OCM** *ʔuih

'To fear, be in awe of; to respect' [Shi, Shu].

[<] *ʔui + exopass. s/h-suffix, lit. 'be intimidated' (§4.4.1).

wéi$_1$, wēi 危 (ŋjwie) **LH** ŋyɑi, **OCM** *ŋoi — **[T]** *ONW* ŋue

'High, precipitous' [Zhuang, Li, Guoyu], 'lofty' [Lunyu], 'dangerous' [Meng].

[E] ST: WB *ŋwa* 'large, high, project'. CH and WB can be reconciled if a ST final *-l is assumed. This may be a vocalic variant of → wéi$_9$ 巍 'high'.

wéi$_2$ 惟唯隹維 (jiwi) **LH** wi, **OCM** *wi

'To be' 隹 [OB, BI], 惟 [Shu], 維 [Shi]; ('it is' > 'it is only' >) 'only' 唯 [Shi and subsequent classical Chinese]; ('to consider to be' >) 'to think' [Shi and later] (*GSR* 575n; Dobson *EAC;* §2.10). Syn. of 'to be': → shì$_{14}$ 是, → yě$_1$ 也; syn. of 'only': → zhǐ$_3$ 只, *dàn* 但 (under → dān$_2$ 單).

[T] *Sin Sukchu SR* vi (平); *MGZY* ywi (平) [yi]; *ONW* iui

[E] ST: PTB *wəy > PLB *wəy 'to be' (Thurgood 1982, *CLAO* XI. 1: 65–81); Lushai *e*^{F} < *ʔeeʔ, ve*, JP *we* pres. tense particle; perh. WT *yin* 'to be' <*wi-n (?) (earlier *w disappears before *i* in WT).

[C] The negative copula → fēi$_1$ 非 incorporates this word.

⋈ **huì** 惠 (ɣiwei^C) **LH** ɣwes, **OCM** *wî(t)s

'It should be' [OB, Shu]. The OC reading is not certain. The usual meaning 'be kind, compliant' [BI, Shi] could possibly be a semantic extension ('should be' > 'to consider / treat as it should / ought to be, as expected' ?) since there is a tendency for copulas to expand to full verbs, note 'to be' > 'to think' above (Dobson *EAC;* §2.10).

[<] See §6.2.2 for the 'irrealis' role of the OC final consonants.

wéi$_3$ 為 (jwie 3) **LH** wɑi, **OCM** *wai, OCB *w(r)jaj

'To make, do, (function as:) be' [BI, Shi]. Note that often words meaning 'do, make' also develop the meaning 'function as, act as, to be'; see → yì$_6$ 役, → zuò$_3$ 作.

[T] *Sin S. SR* uj (平); *MGZY* xue (平) [ɦuɛ]; *MTang* ui, *ONW* ue

⋈ **wèi** 為 (jwie^C) **LH** wɑi^C, **OCM** *waih

'For, on behalf, because' [BI, Shi].

[E] Etymology not clear. Some lgs. have similar looking words: TB-Mikir *iŋhóy* < *m-hol* 'to do, make'. <> MK: Khm *ʔaoy* (spelled *o:y*) 'give', resultative marker; MK lgs. on the Malay peninsula 'to make, do': Semai *ʔuuy*, Jah Hut *mʔoy*, Semelai *j-ʔɔy* [Diffloth 1975]. Khmer /-wə́ə/ 'do, make' ⋈ OKhmer *thve* ~ *tve* /tβəə/ 'to do, make, perform, act, serve as, carry out function of, act as if, pretend to be...' (Jenner / Pou 1982: 349). The OC and AA vowels are rather different, though. A derivation is perh. → yì$_6$ 役.

(**wéi$_4$** 為 (jwie) **PCH** *wai or *woi ?)

'Elephant'? [Shang dyn.]. Since the element 'elephant' is puzzling in this graph for 'to do', it has been suggested that an obsolete area word for this animal had once served as phonetic, note AA-PVM *hwɔy^A, PSBahn. *ruəs, PTB *m-gwi(y) > JP *gui*^{31} 'elephant' (Matisoff *LTBA* 15.1, 1992: 169; *HPTB:* 200). For lack of initial *r in OC, see §10.1.3.

wéi₅ 圍 (jwei) **LH** wui, **OCM** *wəi — **[T]** *ONW* ui
'To surround, encircle' [Li], 'besiege' [Zuo] (Yates *EC* 19, 1994: 112) is prob. cognate to → wèi₇ 衛 even though the finals differ, prob. due to differences in the donor lgs. The basic meaning of the etymon is 'to walk around something in order to watch it'.
[E] Area etymon which is widely attested in TB and AA lgs. TB-Lushai *veel*ᶠ 'go around, surround, encircle, around, round about' ⋈ *veel*ᴿ 'to keep coming or walking near' (as those who want to steal, see what one is doing...); Siyin *vil* 'watch' [Stern *AM* X.2, 1963: 244]; WB *we*ᶜ 'to run around (an object), veer'. For additional Lushai allofams, see the cognates → wèi₇ 衛, → xiàn₁₀ 縣.
Since both WB and KN languages have MK loan words, the ultimate source of this etymon is prob. AA. PMK *wìəl basic meaning 'surround, be around, make rounds', occurs in Mon and Khmer with many prefixed derivatives (Shorto *AA Studies* 1976: 1065): PMonic *wiil 'to go around' ⋈ *tr-wiil 'to attend on, surround' [Diffloth 1984: 239]; Khmer *viala* /wíiəl/ 'to turn, move around' ⋈ /rwíiəl/ 'make one's rounds, patrol'. MK -> Tai: S. *kra⁴-ween* (McFarland: 45: *gkra⁴-wane*), Saek *vian*ᴬ² 'go around, make a circuit'. Perh. related is PVM: *veːl 'return' ⋈ *k-veːl 'village' [Ferlus]; the last word brings to mind → guī₃ 歸 'return to a place where one belongs'.

wéi₆ 違 (jwei) **LH** wui, **OCM** *wəi
'To go against, disobey, oppose; go too far, transgress' [Shi] > 'err, fault' [Zuo].
⋈ **huì** 諱 (xjweiᶜ) **LH** huiᶜ, **OCM** *hwəih
'Avoid, taboo' [Zuo].
[E] ? ST or AA: TB-Lushai *ui*ᴴ < *ʔui* 'to regret, dissuade, forbid', both OC and Lushai are perh. connected with AA: Khmer *veḥ* /wéh/ (written *viər*) 'to quit, leave, avoid, shun...', Stieng *wuir* 'avoid' (Shorto 1973: 378).
[C] Allofam is perh.. → huí 回.

wéi₇ 微 (mjwei) **LH** mui, **OCM** *məi
'It is not that, if it had not been for' [Shi] is the negative root *m- + → wéi₂ 惟 *wi 'to be' (Pulleyblank 1995: 110). It is often considered the s. w. as → wéi₈ 微 'small'.
[T] *Sin Sukchu SR* vi (平); *MGZY* wi (平) [vi]; ONW mui

wéi₈ 微 (mjwei) **LH** mui, **OCM** *məi
'Be small, eclipsed' [Shi].
[E] The etymology is not clear. It is prob. related to PTB *mwəy (*STC:* 174 n. 463) > WB *mwe*ᶜ 'fine, delicate', perh. also Chepang *mi-ʔo* ~ *məy-ʔo* 'small'. And / or it is often considered the s. w. as → wéi₇ 微 (Pulleyblank 1995: 110). Finally, it may perh. be a vocalic variant of → mǐ₇ 靡.

wéi₉ 巍 (ŋjwei) **LH** ŋui, **OCM** *ŋui
'High, majestic' [Lunyu].
⋈ **wèi** 魏 (ŋjweiᶜ) **LH** ŋuiᶜ, **OCM** *ŋuih
'High' [Zhouli].
[C] This set may be a vocalic variant of → wéi₁ 危 'high'.

wéi₁₀ 犩 → **kuí₃** 夔

wěi₁ 尾 (mjweiᴮ) **LH** muiᴮ, **OCM** *məiʔ, OCB *mjəj — **[D]** PMin *mueᴮ
'Tail' [Shi] > 'to copulate, have sexual intercourse' [Shu].
[T] *Sin Sukchu SR* vi (上); *MGZY* wi (上) [vi]; *ONW* muiᴮ
[E] ST: PTB *r-may 'tail' (*STC* no. 282) > Chepang *meʔ* 'tail', Tamang *(¹)meː*, PL *ʔ-mri²*, WB *mri*ᴮ; KN-Aimol *rəmai;* Lushai *mei*ᴿ < *meiʔ.*

wěi₂ 委 (ʔjwie^B) **LH** ʔyɑi^B, **OCM** *ʔoiʔ — **[T]** *ONW* ʔue
'To fall' [Zhuang], 'to hang down' 委 [Li]. Perh. the same word as → wěi₃ 委 ?
[E] Etymology not clear. Gong H. (in W. Wang 1995: 48) relates it to WB *lway* 'suspend from the shoulder'. The OC form is similar to words with nearly identical meaning ('hang down'): → chuí₁ 垂, → ruǐ 縈惢.

wěi₃ 委 (ʔjwie^B) **LH** ʔyɑi^B, **OCM** *ʔoiʔ
'To bend' 委 [Li], 骫 [Liezi] may be the same word as → wěi₂ 委. WB *kwe^B* 'bend, curve' ⋈ *kwe^C* 'bend around, curved' are perh. MK loans (Shorto 1972): Sre *kue* 'bent, crooked', Biat *kwɛː* (*kwac*) 'winding'. Perh. cognate to → yǎo₁ 夭殀, → yíng₅ 縈.

wěi₄ 緯 (jwei^C) **LH** wui^C, **OCM** *wəih, OCB *wjəjh ? — **[T]** *ONW* ui
'Woof' [Zuo], 'to weave' [Zhuang].

⋈ **yùn** 緷 (juən^C) **LH** wun^C, **OCM** *wəns, OCB *wjən
'Woof' [SW] (Karlgren 1933: 28).
[<] n-nominalization of *wěi* 緯 (jwei^C) (§6.4.3).

wěi₅ 韡 → **huī₂** 煇輝暉

wěi₆ 亹眉 (mjwei^B) **LH** mui^B, **OCM** *məiʔ
'Be vigorous' (of persons) [BI, Shi, EY] is cognate to items under → mín₄ 痻 'suffering' (so Wáng Lì 1982: 410). There may perh. be a connection with → wù₁₁ 務 'apply oneself, work'.

⋈ **wù** 勿 (mjuət) **LH** mut, **OCM** *mət
'Eagerly' [Li].

wèi₁ 未 (mjwəi^C) **LH** mus, **OCM** *məts (?)
'Not yet' [OB, Shi, Mand.], in contrast to → bù₁ 不, *wèi* focuses on whether an action occurred or not, without reference to the subject's intention (Norman 1988: 98). Pulleyblank (1995: 109) considers this word a fusion of the negative root *m- with the perfective particle → jì₃ 既 'already'.
[T] *Sin Sukchu SR* vi (去); *MGZY* wi (去) [vi]; *ONW* mui^C
[D] W-Wēnzhōu, Y-Guǎngzhōu *mei^C*, M-Fúzhōu *mui^C*, Xiàmén *be^C*

wèi₂ 未 (mjwei^C) **LH** mus, **OCM** *məts
The 8th of the Earthly Branches identified with the sheep / goat [OB]. Acc. to Norman (1985: 88), possibly a loan from AA: note MK: OKhmer-Lao *mamɛɛ 'goat' ⋈ Khmer *babae* ⋈ Mon *babe̤'* [Ferlus *MKS* 18–19, 1992: 56], also Atayal (AN) *miːts* 'goat'.

wèi₃ 味 (mjwei^C) **LH** mus, **OCM** *məts — **[T]** *ONW* mui
'Taste' [Yili].
[E] This word is perh. of MK origin: PMonic *[ʔ]məp 'good tasting, have a pleasant flavor, be pleasant' (the QY rime can derive from Proto-Chinese *-s, *-ts, and *-ps). Unger (*Hao-ku* 39, 1992: 89) connects *wèi* with WT *brod* 'taste'. The meaning of KN-Lushai *hmui^H* 'savory smelling', Lai *hmuj / hmuʔj* 'be fragrant' is somewhat removed from 'taste'; however, these items are phonologically close to Chinese.

Boltz (*JAOS* 99, 1979: 432) draws attention to binomes for 'taste': *zī-wèi* 嗞味 LH *tsiə-mus* [Shiji, Lie] and *cǎn-wèi* 噆味 LH *tsʰəm^B-mus* [Huainan], apparently with two different ways to write the first syllable.

wèi₄ 位 (jwi^C) **LH** wɨs, **OCM** *wrə(t)s ?, OCB *(w)rjəps
'Position, place, seat' in the center of a court or group of persons [BI, Shi].

[T] *Sin Sukchu SR* uj (去); *MGZY* xue (去) [ɦuɛ]; ONW ui

[E] Etymology not clear. Although it is often related to → lì$_3$ 立 (so Pulleyblank 1962: 233; Baxter 1992: 446), the role of 立 in the graph *wèi* is prob. semantic, not phonetic. Possibly related to WT *dbus* 'center', this word and *wèi* perh. from ST *d-wus.

wèi$_5$ 蝟 (jiwi^C 4) **LH** wi^C, **OCM** *wih
'Gadfly' [Guoyu, Chuyu].
[E] AA: PAA *ruwaj [Pinnow 1959: 268] > PVM *m-rɔːj 'a fly' [Ferlus], PMon *ruuy 'housefly' (Norman / Mei 1976: 284–285; Bodman 1980: 92), Khmer /ruj/ 'a fly' ⋇ /roj/ 'dart here and there...'. For lack of initial *r in OC, see §10.1.3.

wèi$_6$ 蜼 (jiwi^C 4, ljwi^B, jiəu^C) **LH** wi^C ~ lui^B, **OCM** *wih ~ *ruiʔ (< *r-wiʔ) OCB *lŭjs
'Kind of monkey-like animal' [Zhouli]. The form *ruiʔ is close to Wa-Lawa-Bulang *rəyol 'white-handed gibbon'; in the variant *wih, the AA initial *r- was lost, see §10.1.3,
Matisoff (1995: 71) suggests that the final *-i in *wèi* is a ST diminutive suffix added to → yóu$_8$ 猶; theoretically, the latter's initial could have been PCH *w-.

wèi$_7$ 衛 (jwäi^C 3) **LH** was (wes?), **OCM** *wets, OCB *wrjats — **[T]** *ONW* uei
'To guard, patrol' [BI, Shu]. The graph shows feet walking around an enclosure. *Wèi* is related to → wéi$_5$ 圍 'surround, encircle' even though the vowels differ and the final *-s is unusual in an etymon with ST *-l, but note the parallel word Lushai *veet^F / veʔ^L* (< *wes) 'to put round or on, cause to encircle; a single encircling' (under → wéi$_5$ 圍). For synonyms, see under → huí 回. See → wéi$_5$ 圍 for outside cognates.

wèi$_8$ 胃 (jwei^C 3) **LH** wus, **OCM** *wəts ?
'Stomach' [Li].
[E] The etymology is not clear. The OC initial is difficult to reconcile with WT *grod* 'belly, stomach'. The CH word is reminiscent of TB-PLB *ʔwik^L 'stomach', and MK-PWa *wɛk 'entrails, stomach'. However, OC is easiest to reconcile with PLB *p-wam^2 > WB *wam^B* 'stomach' (*HPTB:* 46) if we assume a PCH *wəps (*-m* ~ *-p* has parallels).

wèi$_9$ 謂 (jwei^C 3) **LH** wus, **OCM** *wəts, OCB *wjəts — **[T]** *ONW* ui
'To say, call, be called' [Shi] is thought cognate to → yún$_2$ 云 (Wáng Lì 1982: 456). Alternatively, it could possibly be a derivation from → yǒu$_2$ 有 'there is, have' (§6.2.2; §2.10).

wèi$_{10}$, yù 蔚 (ʔjwei^C, ʔjuət) **LH** ʔus, ʔut, **OCM** *ʔut(s)
'Screening' (of mist) [Shi].
[T] *Sin Sukchu* 慰 *SR* ʔuj (去); *MGZY* 慰 'ue (去) [ʔuɛ]

⋇ **yù** 鬱 (ʔjuət) **LH** ʔut, **OCM** *ʔut — **[T]** *ONW* ʔut
'Be dense' (forest) [Shi] > 'to block up' [Zuo] > 'pent up' (feelings), 'oppressed' 苑 [Shi], 'depressed' [Chuci], 'anxious' [Meng].

⋇ **huì** 薈 (ʔuâi^C) **LH** ʔuɑs, **OCM** *ʔôts
'To screen' (as mists) [Shi]. For a semantic parallel, see → yuàn$_1$ 苑.

[E] <> KT: This group could be related either to PTai *ʔu̯op^{D1}S 'to shut, cover up'; or to Tai: S. *ʔut^4* 'to compress, crowd in together' (a CH loan?).

wèi$_{11}$, yù 蔚 'artemisia, mugwort' → **yù$_{32}$** 鬱

wèi$_{12}$ 偽 → **é$_7$** 訛

wèi$_{13}$ 犩 → **kuí$_3$** 夔

wèi$_{14}$ 餧 (ʔjwei^C) **LH** ʔui^C, **OCM** *ʔuih
'To feed' (an animal)' [Liji, Chuci], Mand. 喂餵 (Wáng Lì 1982: 430).
[E] Area word: PTB *wul (*HPTB:* 416) > Lushai *vulʔ^L* 'to keep or rear' (domestic animals), 'to domesticate' ⋈ *vil^R* < *vilʔ* 'to look after, tend'; Mikir *wi^H* 'tend animals' (*STC:* 83), perh. also WB *kywe^B* 'give a meal, feed'. PMK *wiir > OMon *wir* 'keep, rear' (domestic animals) (Shorto 1972: 14); Khmer /kwíiəl/ 'to pasture animals, watch, tend'. The TB items are MK loans acc. to Shorto.

wèi$_{15}$ 魏 → **wéi**$_9$ 巍

wēn 溫 (ʔuən) **LH** ʔuən, **OCM** *ʔûn
'Warm' [Li], 'mild, gentle' [Shi].
[T] *Sin Sukchu SR* ʔun (平); *MGZY* 'un (平) [ʔun]; *ONW* ʔon
[E] ST *ur: TB-Lushai *urʔ^L* 'to burn' (in cooking), 'get smoky', *uur^H* 'to smoke, to heat, distill; to warm' ⋈ *uut^F / uʔ* 'to burn, char, scorch' ⋈ *ur^H ro^H* 'to dry' (at a fire); Mikir *ur* 'to dry over the fire' (Benedict *HJAS* 5, 1940: 122 no. 62). Prob. not (directly?) related to → yù$_{20}$, yǔ 嫗 ST *ʔo.

wén$_1$ 文 (mjuən) **LH** mun, **OCM** *mən
'Be striped, patterned' [BI, Shi], 'written character' [Zuo] > 'literature' [Lunyu] > 'refined, accomplished, cultured' [BI, Shi].
[T] *Sin S. SR* vun (平), *PR, LR* vən; *MGZY* wun (平) [vun]; *MTang* mvun, *ONW* mun
[<] Prob. a nominal n-derivation (§6.4.3) from → méi$_9$ 煤 *mə 'soot', hence lit. 'black marks, dark patterns' (as tattoos on body etc.), 'writing' (with ink). At least some of the black paints were, like ink, made from soot.

wén$_2$ 蚊 (mjuən) **LH** mun, **OCM** *mən
'Mosquito' [Zhuang].
[T] *MTang* mvun, *ONW* mun — **[D]** PMin *ṁun
[E] The identification with → wén$_1$ 文 as the insect with 'patterned markings' on its wings (Williams 1941 / 1974: 281) is prob. folk etymology. It is not clear if **měng** 蠓 (muŋ[B]) LH *moŋ* 'midge, mosquito' [Lie] is related: PMin *moŋ^B.
[E] AA 'mosquito': PSBahn., PVM *mɔːs [Ferlus], Khmer *muuh*, Stieng *mɔɔh*, Bahnaric *mɔɔs [Diffloth 1976: 223]. CH added the nominal n-suffix (§6.4.3).

wén$_3$ 聞 (mjuən) **LH** mun, **OCM** *mən, OCB *mjun
'To hear about, hear' [BI, Shi], 'to smell' [Shu]. Baxter's (1992: 352f) reconstruction *mjun 'to hear' is based on *Shījīng* rimes and an earlier form of the graph.
[T] *Sin Sukchu SR* vun (平), *PR* vən; *MGZY* wun (平) [vun]; *MTang* mvun < mun, *ONW* mun

⋈ **wèn** 問 (mjuən^C) **LH** mun^C, **OCM** *məns, OCB *mjuns
(1) 'Be heard about, renowned, fame' [Shi].
[<] *mən + passive s-suffix (§4.4).
(2) 'To ask about, inquire' [Shi].
[<] *mən + exoactive s-suffix (§4.3), lit. 'let (me) hear' (?) (cf. Baxter 1992: 431).
[E] The step from 'hear' to 'ask' is not easy to understand, but it occurs also in TB lgs., e.g. PLB *ʔna 'listen' ⋈ *na 'ask' (Matisoff *D. of Lahu:* 726f), also in Tani (J. Sun *LTBA* 16.2, 1993: 152). Perh. MK had some paronomastic influence on OC, note PMonic *smaaɲ 'inquire', Wa-Lawa-Bulang *hmaɲ 'to ask for, ask a question'. MK -> Tai: Saek *maan^{C2}* 'ask for help'.

[E] The CH word 'to smell' is prob. derived from a ST *m-nəm: PTB *m/s-nam 'smell' (*HPTB:* 250f), WT *mnam-pa* 'to smell of' ⋈ *snom-pa* (> *snum-pa*) 'smell' (Tib. -> Spilo

Kanauri *mun-* 'to smell' – recorded by N. C. Bodman); WB *nam* 'stink' ¥ *nam*$^{B/C}$ 'smell', Lushai *nam*^{H} < *nam* 'smell of', JP *mə*^{31}*-nam*^{55} 'to hear, smell'. The inversion of *n* and *m* in CH is the result of labial dissimilation or prefix-preemption.

In almost all major TB lgs. this etymon means only 'to smell'. One or other factor may help explain the application of 'to hear' in CH. The semantic affinities of hear ~ smell have a parallel in TB *na 'ear ~ nose' and hence perh. in ST, see → ěr$_1$ 耳. The CH stem may have converged with a MK etymon (cf. PMonic *smaaɲ 'inquire' above); also note WT *(m-)ñan-pa* 'to hear' which is phonologically quite close to CH. Finally, Baxter's distinct form *mjun 'hear' implies that this is a separate etymon (etymology not clear) which eventually merged phonetically with 'smell'.

wěn$_1$ 吻 (mjuən^{B}) **LH** mun^{B}, **OCM** *mən?

'Corner of the lips, shut the lips' [Zhouli].

[E] Etymology not clear. It could either be related to *mén* 門 (*HST:* 111); or to TB-Lushai *hmuui*^{L} < *hmuuih* 'the lips, upper lip' [Weidert 1987: 204], also MK-PVM *hmoy*^{A} 'lip' [Thompson]; or to TB-WB *mut* 'mouth' (in 'beard') ¥ *hmut* 'blow with the mouth', but see → fú$_8$ 弗); also MK-Khmer *mɔ̀ət* 'mouth, edge' (of water).

wěn$_2$ 紊 (mjuən^{C} - tone!) **LH** mun^{C}, **OCM** *məns

'Tangle, confused' (net) [Shu]. This word may be cognate to → mén$_3$ 悶, but the notions of 'dark > confused' and 'tangled = confused' are semantically distinct. Wáng Lì (1982: 524f) relates this word to → fēn$_4$ 紛 'mixed, confused'.

wèn 問 → **wén$_3$** 聞

wēng 翁 (ʔuŋ) **LH** ʔoŋ, **OCM** *ʔôŋ

'Old man' [FY], 'father' [SW].

[T] *Sin Sukchu SR* ʔuŋ (平); *MGZY* 'ung (平) [ʔuŋ]; ONW ʔoŋ

[E] Perh. ST: TB-Lushai *un*^{L} 'be old, elderly, venerable, ancient', WB *u*^{B} 'uncle'. Unger, (*Hao-ku* 63, 1999) connects this word with foreign items under → gōng$_4$ 公 'uncle'.

wèng 瓮甕罋 (ʔuŋ^{C}) **LH** ʔoŋ^{C}, **OCM** *ʔôŋh — **[T]** *ONW* ʔoŋ

'A bellied jar with small opening', also 'tub, vat' 瓮 [Mo], 罋 [Yili] (also QYS *ʔjwoŋ[*^{C}*]*); 'swollen' 甕 [Zhuang]. Acc. to *FY* 5, 10, this was in some parts of northern China a synonym of yīng 罌 (under → yǐng$_2$ 癭). Another similar word is → àng 盎 *ʔâŋh.

[E] Perh. ST: PL *ʔ-loŋ 'pot', WT *gžoŋ* 'tub', Lepcha *joŋ-mo* 'bucket, tub' (Unger *Hao-ku* 63, 1999). <> Tai: S. *luŋ*^{C2} < *l- 'vessel, utensil for keeping provisions'. The initial *l-* in these languages is difficult to reconcile with OC; Unger assumes a ʔ-prefix; see §5.11.

[C] Allofam → yōng$_2$ 癰 'ulcer'; → wǎn$_4$ 碗 may also be connected.

wō, guā, luó 蝸 (kwa[i]) **LH** kuai, luɑi, S kɔi, loi, **OCM** *krôi, *C-rôi

'Snail' [Li]. PMin *l̥ɔi.

[E] ST: PTB *kroy (*STC* no. 311) > WB *krwe* 'shellfish, cowry', JP *kʰoi*^{33} 'shellfish, shell' (Bodman 1980: 143). Perh. also related to PMK *gl[o]ʔ 'snail' (Shorto 1972: 16).

wǒ 我 → **wú$_2$** 吾

wò$_1$ 沃 (ʔuok) **LH** ʔouk, **OCM** *ʔâuk, OCB *ʔawk

'Be / look glossy' (of leaves) [Shi], 'sprinkle, moisten > fertile' [Zuo], 'wash' (hands) [Zhouli].

= **wù** 鋈 ... 'silvery' [Shi].

[E] This word is perh. cognate to WB u^B 'to polish, make bright', with the CH final *-k* (§6.1).

wò₂ 臥 (ŋuâ^C). **LH** ŋuɑi^C, **OCM** *ŋôih or *ŋwâih

'To lie down, sleep' [Meng].

[T] *Sin Sukchu SR ŋɔ* (去), *PR, LR ɔ; MGZY o* (去) [ɔ]; *ONW ŋua*

[E] ST has *ŋ(w)al ~ *nwal parallel stems (§5.12.1) for this etymon:

(1) *ŋwal > *ŋwaj: WT *ŋal-ba* 'to rest' ⋈ *mŋal* 'womb' (lit. resting place with body part *m-); Lushai *ŋɔi^H / ŋɔiʔ^L < ŋɔis* 'to be quiet, silent, stop, pause', NNaga *C-ŋuaj 'easy, gentle, quiet', Kachin *ŋwi* 'gentle, mild' = JP *ŋui^31* 'slow, satisfied', WB *ŋwe^C* 'gentle, moderate' (*STC* no. 315) agree phonologically with Chinese.

(2) A ST parallel stem *nwal (§5.12.1) is represented by → suī 綏.

Non-ST lgs. in the area have words which look similar: AA-PVM *t-ŋah* '(to lie) on the back', PTai *ŋai^A1* 'lie on the back looking up'.

wò₃ 幄 → **wū₄** 屋

wò₄ 渥 → **òu** 漚

wū₁ 汙 (ʔuo) **LH** ʔuɑ, **OCM** *ʔwâ

'Pool, stagnant water' 汙 [Zuo], 洿 [Meng].

[T] *Sin Sukchu SR ʔu* (平); *MGZY 'u* (平) [ʔu]; *ONW ʔo*

⋈ **wāng** 汪 (ʔwaŋ) **LH** ʔuɑŋ, **OCM** *ʔwâŋ

'Pool' [Zuo] (Pulleyblank 1962: 233).

wū₂ 巫覡 (mju) **LH** muɑ, **OCM** *ma — **[T]** *ONW* muo

'Spirit medium, shaman' [OB, Yi, Shu, Lunyu] of either sex, but eventually female [SW] when contrasted with **xí** 覡 (ɣiek) 'male shaman' [Guoyu]. *Wū* communicated with spirits, searched for the souls of the dead, rode on drums in spiritual flights, performed oracles, and were ritually killed in order to eliminate natural disasters. They harldy played a role in religion and ritual (Boileau *BSOAS* 65.2, 2002: 350ff).

[E] ST: WT *'ba-po/-mo < ɴba* 'spirit medium, shaman/ess' (*HST:* 107). As to foreign initial *b-* for CH *m-*, see §5.12.2. Another WT word for 'shaman' is *gšen* (→ xiān₂ 仙 僊). <> Tai: S. *mɔɔ^A1* < PTai *hmɔ^A 'doctor, sorcerer' is usually considered a CH loan (Li 1976: 40) and has been cited as evidence for an OC voiceless initial. MK-PWa *səmaŋ 'shaman' may also be connected.

Several alternative etymologies have been proposed: (1) Perh. → wū₃ 誣 'to deceive' is the same word. Note a WT semantic parallel 'deceive' ~ 'magical power': *sprul-ba* 'to juggle, make phantoms, miraculous power' ⋈ *'p^hrul* 'magical deception'. (2) *Wū* could be cognate to wǔ 舞 'to dance' [Shi] (Lau 1999: 87). (3) *Wū* could in addition to 'dance' be cognate to → mǔ₂ 母 'mother' as *wū* were female acc. to late Zhou and Han texts (E. Schafer, see Jensen *EC* 20, 1995: 422). (4) V. Mair (*EC* 15, 1990: 27–47) has proposed that *wū* is a loan from Iranian *maghu or *maguš 'magician', i.e. an 'able one' (specialist in ritual).

wū₃ 誣 (mju) **LH** muɑ, **OCM** *ma

'To deceive' [Lunyu], 'slander, accuse falsely' [Zuo].

[E] ST: Chepang *maʔ-* 'to lie, deceive, pretend, secretly do'.

⋈ **wǎng** 罔 (mjwaŋ^B) **LH** muɑŋ^B, **OCM** *maŋ?

'To deceive, confusion, to outwit, wits' [Shi].

[E] Tai: S. *p^hraaŋ^A2* < *br- 'to deceive, cheat'. For foreign initial *b-* for CH *m-*, see

§5.12.2. The Tai form throws doubt on the possibility that *wǎng* is the s. w. as → wǎng$_3$ 罔網 'net, to snare'.

✱ **màn** 謾 (muân[C], man^C, mjän 3) **LH** mɑ/an(^{C}), mɨan, **OCM** *mrân(s), *mân(s) 'To deceive' [Xun]. For the difference in final nasals, see §6.4.2.

[E] This wf converges and overlaps with → wàng$_2$ 妄 'reckless, false'. Perh. related to → wū$_2$ 巫 'spirit medium'.

wū$_4$ 屋 (ʔuk) **LH** ʔok, **OCM** *ʔôk

'Roof' [Shi, Zuo], 'house, room' [Shi].

[T] *Sin Sukchu SR ʔu* (入); *MGZY 'u* (入) [ʔu]; *ONW ʔok*

[E] Etymology not clear. The basic meaning of this word is apparently 'roof', yet comparanda all mean 'house'. It is sometimes associated with Tai: Po'ai *luk^{D2}S* < *dl- 'room' whose initial *l-* is difficult to reconcile with OC, see §5.11. Alternatively, note PTai *ʔj-: S. *jau^{C1}* 'home, house'. But *wū* may be closer to AA forms: PVM *k-rn-ɔʔ 'house' (with infixes and separated initial omitted in CH), and / or Kharia *oʔ,* Munda *oɽaʔ.* Wáng Lì (1982: 293) believes that *wū* was originally the same etymon as *wò* 幄 (ʔåk) 'tent'.

wū$_5$ 惡 (ʔuo) **LH** ʔɑ, **OCM** *ʔâ — **[T]** *ONW* ʔo

'How' [Lun], 'to what place, where' [Meng], also *wū hu* 惡乎. This and the following interrogatives occur before the vb, basically asking 'at / to which place' (Dobson *LAC:* 146f).

✱ **ān** 安 (ʔân) **LH** ʔɑn, **OCM** *ʔân — **[T]** *ONW* ʔɑn

'To / at what place, in what respect?' [Shi, Zuo] (Dobson). The final *-n* in this and the next item is probably the same demonstrative morpheme encountered in → rán$_2$ 然 and other grammatical words (§6.4.5).

✱ **yān** 焉 (ʔjän 3) **LH** ʔɨɑn, **OCM** *ʔan

'To what place, at which place?' [Shi] (Dobson). Probably a (sandhi?) variant of *ān* above.

[T] *Sin Sukchu SR* ʔjen, jen (平); *ONW* ʔan

wū$_6$ 烏 (ʔuo) **LH** ʔɑ, **OCM** *ʔâ

'Crow, raven' [Shi].

[T] *Sin Sukchu SR* ʔu (平); *MGZY* 'u (平) [ʔu]; *ONW* ʔo

[E] This onomatopoetic word could perh. be cognate to PL *ak^L/ a^3.

~ **yā** 鴉 (ʔa) **LH** ʔa, **OCM** *ʔa

'Crow, raven' [Zhuang], a later variant of the above which for reasons of sound symbolism preserves the earlier vowel, see §7.2.2 (Pulleyblank *AM* n.s. 9.1, 1962: 103; Unger *Hao-ku* 22, 1983).

wú$_1$ 毋 (mju) **LH** muɑ ≠ **OCM** *mə ?

'Should not, don't!' Injunctive and imperative negative [OB], already in Zhou time phonetically confused with, and read like, *wú* 無 (*DEZC:* 48, 647).

✱ **wù** 勿 (mjwət) **LH** mut, **OCM** *mət — **[T]** *ONW* mut

(1) 'Should not, don't!' Injunctive negative [OB, Shi] (*DEZC:* 48, 650; §6.2.2).

(2) 'Don't vb. him / her / it!', fusion of *wú* with *zhī* 之 [Meng et al.] (Pulleyblank 1995: 108). The OB graph is distinct from that for → wù$_5$ 物 'thing' which was therefore not a graphic loan.

✱ **méi** 沒 (muət)

沒 'not have, there is no, not yet' Mand.; MC *muət* may be a col. (j-less) variant of *wú* 勿 or *wèi* 未, which later fused with, or was contaminated by, *yǒu* 有 (Norman

1988: 126). An alternative etymology derives the meaning 'not have' from 'submerge' (e.g. Norman: Ohta). The following belong to a different stem *ma: → mǐ$_6$ 靡, → mò$_2$ 末, → wáng$_1$ 亡 (incl. *sāŋ* 喪), → wú$_4$ 無 (incl. *mò* 莫). Pulleyblank (1973: 121) combines all these words in one large wf.

wú$_2$ 吾 (ŋuo) **LH** ŋɑ, **OCM** *ŋâ

'I, my' [BI, Zuo] is a dependent pronoun and therefore functions as a subject or possessive, not the sentence-final object (§3.3.3). The BI graph is *yú* 虞 *ŋa, or with *yú* 魚 *ŋa under the 'tiger'. During the Nanbeichao and Tang periods, there is no distinction between *wǒ* and *wú*, and *wú* disappears from the col. lg. (Norman 1988: 118). *Wú* is directly cognate to the TB forms below, even though it is missing in the earliest texts.

[T] *Sin Sukchu SR* ŋu (平); *MGZY* u (平) [u]; *ONW* ŋo

[E] ST: PTB *ŋa (*STC* no. 406): WT *ŋa*; WB *ŋa* 'I' ⋈ *ŋa*^{C} obj. and poss. of *ŋa* 'I', PL *C-ŋa. Many TB languages have different etyma for this pronoun.

⋈ **wǒ** 我 (ŋâ^B) **LH** ŋɑi^B, **OCM** *ŋâiʔ

Independent pronoun 'I, we' [OB, BI, Shi], in classical texts 'I (stressed), we' (§3.3.3). Originally, the graph for *wǒ* seems to have been created to write the name of a Shang period people / country, 'sheep' 羊 was later added 義 (prob. signifying pastoralists) in order to distinguish the name from the pronoun (Sagart *TP* 81, 4–5, 1995: 328–342).

[T] *Sin S. SR* ŋɔ (上), *PR*, *LR* ɔ; *MGZY* ngo (上) [ŋɔ]; *ONW* ŋɑ

[D] Mand. *wǒ* is a col. archaism, some northern dialects have the expected *ě* (Demiéville 1950: 5; Stimson 1972: 177); some southern dialects have preserved the OC rime: Y-Fóshān ^{13}*ŋɔi*^{B2}; K-Méixiàn *ŋa*^{B}, PMin *ŋɑi^B (Norman 1988: 223).

[<] *ŋa + independent marker *-i; this final is also a suffix in TB, see below. The OC glottal element may have resulted from *ŋa + ʔi > *ŋaʔi > *ŋaiʔ. In OC, *wǒ* occurs in all sentence positions, unlike the dependent *wú* 吾, see §3.3.3 for more details.

[E] ST: PTB *ŋai (*STC* no. 285): JP *ŋai*^{33} 'I', WT *ŋed* (< *ŋai-t), Mikir *ne*, Chepang *ŋi* ~ *ni* 'we', Phom (Chang-Tangsa = Konyak) *ŋei* 'I' (Benedict 1995: 31); Lushai *ŋei*^{L} 'self', JP *ŋai*^{33} 'I'. The final *-i is a suffix (Matisoff 1995: 76f).

⋈ **áng** 卬 (ŋâŋ) **LH** ŋɑŋ, **OCM** *ŋâŋ

'I, we' is perhaps a stressed form [Shi] (Sagart 1999: 135).

[C] For possible wider connections, see → yà$_2$ 御迓訝. Syn. → yú$_5$ 予余.

wú$_3$ 吳 (ŋuo) **LH** ŋuɑ, **OCM** *ŋwâ

'To shout' [Shi].

[E] Perh. related to WT *ŋar-skad* 'roaring of a tiger' ⋈ *ŋa-ro* 'be loud'. WT does not preserve earlier medial *w (§912.9).

wú$_4$ 無 (mju) **LH** muɑ, **OCM** *ma

'There is no, not have' [later Western Zhou texts and since].

[T] *Sin Sukchu SR*, *LR* vu (平); *MGZY* wu (平) [vu]; *MTang* mvu < muo, *ONW* muo

[N] The classical meaning 'there is no, not have' emerged only later during the Western Zhou period and eventually replaced earlier forms with this meaning and grammatical function; the OB have only → wáng$_1$ 亡 for 'not have, there is no', the *Shūjīng* has both *wǎng* 罔 (under → wáng$_1$ 亡) and *wú* 無, the *Shījīng* both *wú* 無 and → mǐ$_6$ 靡. In the OB, negatives with initial *m- negate actions which are controllable by living persons (Takashima 1996: 370ff).

[D] *Wú* is the common ST negative 'not' which has survived as such in southern dialects: W-Shanghai *m*^{A2}, Y-Guǎngzhōu, Kèjiā *m*^{A2}, M-Xiàmén *m*^{C2} (Norman 1988:

199), also sporadically in Zhou texts as some investigators claim, but the instances are ambiguous.

In many dialects, this etymon fused with → yǒu 有 'to have, there is' for 'not have, there is no': G-Nánchāng, Fèngxīn *mau*^{A6}, Línchuān *mau*^{A2}; X-Chángshā *maɤ*^{C2}, Shuāngfēng *mə*^{C2}; Y-Guǎngzhōu *mou*^{B2} 冇 (Mand. *mǒu*), Táishān *mo*^{A1}; K-Méixiàn *mo*^{A2} (Norman 1988: 213 etc.).

[E] ST *ma: PTB *ma 'not', widely represented in TB languages, e.g. WT *ma* 'not', WB *ma*^{C}, PL *ma^{2} 'not'.

ꭗ **mò** 莫 (mâk) **LH** mɑk, **OCM** *mâk

'None, nothing' [Shi].

[T] *Sin Sukchu SR* maw (入), *LR* mawʔ; *MGZY* maw (入) [maw] *ONW* mɑk

[<] *ma + distributive suffix *-k (§6.1.2).

[C] Derivatives from the stem *ma are: → mǐ$_6$ 靡, → mò$_2$ 末, → wáng$_1$ 亡 (incl. *sāŋ* 喪), as well as prob. the wf under → wú$_1$ 毋; → ma 嗎 interrogative particle. Pulleyblank (1973: 121) used this large wf to show that allofams can have different rimes.

wú$_5$ 蕪廡 (mju) **LH** muɑ, **OCM** *ma

'Luxuriant' 廡 [Shu]; 'overgrown with weeds' 蕪 [Meng] > Mand. also 'mixed and disorderly'.

ꭗ **huāng** 荒 (xwâŋ) **LH** huɑŋ, **OCM** *hmâŋ

'Weed-covered' [Meng].

[C] Perh. → wǔ$_9$ 膴廡, → mǎng$_1$ 莽 are cognate; possibly also → mò$_8$ 莫瞙暯 'obscure'.

wú$_6$ 譕 → **mó$_3$** 謨

wǔ$_1$ 午 (ŋuo^{B}) **LH** ŋɑ^{B}, **OCM** *ŋâʔ

The 7th of the Earthly Branches which is associated with the horse [OB], acc. to Norman (1985: 88) a loan from MK; note Viet. *ngựa* 'horse', PVM-Pakatan *maŋəə* [Ferlus *MKS* 18–19, 1992: 57].

wǔ$_2$ 午 'go against' → **yù$_{17}$** 禦

wǔ$_3$ 五 (ŋuo^{B}) **LH** ŋɑ^{B}, **OCM** *ŋâʔ

'Be five' [Shi]. — **[T]** *Sin Sukchu SR* ŋu (上); *MGZY* u (上) [u]; *ONW* ŋo.

[D] PMin *ŋo^{B2}; Y-Guǎngzhōu ^{13}*ŋ*^{B2}

[E] ST: PTB *l-ŋa > WT *lŋa*, WB *ŋa*^{B}, PL *ŋa^{2}, Lushai *pa*^{L}-*ŋa*^{H} < *ŋaa*. CH -> KT: Tai: S. *haa*^{C1} (< hŋ-?), Sui *ŋo*^{C2}; these forms are CH loans.

wǔ$_4$ 武 (mju^{B}) **LH** muɑ^{B}, **OCM** *maʔ, OCB *Np(r)jaʔ

'Martial, military' [Shi]. — **[T]** *MTang* mvu < muo, *ONW* muo.

[E] ST: WT *dmag* 'army', PLB *mak 'war, soldier' > WB *mak* (*HST:* 107). For the finals, see §3.2.2.

wǔ$_5$ 武 (mju^{B}) **LH** muɑ^{B}, **OCM** *maʔ

'Footprint' [Shi].

[E] Etymology not clear. Cognation with TB-WT *mal* 'situation, vestige, trace' is not likely, we should also expect a trace of a foreign final *-l in CH.

wǔ$_6$ 侮 (mju^{B}) **LH** muo^{B}, **OCM** *moʔ

'To offend, insult, maltreat' [BI, Shi] may be compared to WT *dmod-pa* 'to curse, accurse, execrate', which can, however, just as well be linked to → mà 罵 'scold', especially since the WT word is prob. a derivation from *ma* 'below'.

wǔ$_7$ 憮 → **mù$_6$** 慕

wǔ $_8$ 舞
'To dance' [Shi]. — [E] ? WT *bro* 'dance' (initials, see §5.12.2). Or ⋇ → wū$_2$ 巫?

wǔ $_9$ 膴廡 (mju^B) **LH** muɑ^B, **OCM** *maʔ
'Big, important, numerous' 膴 [Shi]; 'big house' 廡 [Guan], Mand. 'hallway'. This may be the s. w. as → wǔ$_{10}$ 膴廡 and perh. be related to PTB *mra 'much, many'.
⋇ **hū** 幠 (xuo) **LH** huɑ, **OCM** *hmâ
'Great' [Shi], but this graph 幠 might have been intended to write *wǔ, hū* could be spurious.

wǔ $_{10}$ 膴廡 (mju^B) **LH** muɑ^B, **OCM** *maʔ
'Rich, beautiful' 膴 [Shi]; 'luxuriant' 廡 [Shu].
[E] Tai: S *maa*^{C1} (WrSiam *hmaa*) 'beautiful' (Manomaivibool 1975: 173).
⋇ **mò-mò** 莫莫 (mâk-mâk) **LH** mɑk, **OCM** *mâk
'Luxuriant' [Shi].
[C] This may be cognate to → máng$_2$ 芒, → wú$_5$ 蕪廡 'luxuriant'. See → mò$_8$ 莫瞙暯 'obscure' for possible additional cognates.

wǔ $_{11}$ 甒 (mju^B) **LH** muɑ^B, **OCM** *maʔ
'Jar' [Li] is perh. connected to Tai: S. *mɔɔ*^{C1} < *hm- 'cooking pot' (Unger *Hao-ku* 36, 1990: 55).

wù$_1$ 兀 (ŋuət) **LH** ŋuət, **OCM** *ŋût
'To cut the feet' [Zhuang] is perh. AA: PMonic *kuut 'to cut off, amputate' ⋇ *t-ŋ-kuut 'a segment, piece' [Diffloth 1984: 197].
⋇ **yuè** 刖 (ŋjwɐt, ŋwat) **LH** ŋyɑt, **OCM** *ŋot, *ŋrôt ?
'Cut off feet' [Shu] (so Wáng Lì 1982: 486).
[E] Mahdi (1994: 177) suggests that this word is derived from → yuè$_3$ 戉 'ax', perh. an AN loan, with the AN prefix *ŋ-.

wù$_2$ 扤 (ŋuət) **LH** ŋuət, **OCM** *ŋût
'To shake, move, endanger' [Shi] may be related to WT *'gul-ba* 'to move, shake'; in some words, Tib. has a voiced stop initial for a foreign nasal after the prefix *a-čʰuŋ* (cf. §6.7; §12.9).

wù$_3$ 勿 'not' → **wú**$_1$ 毋

wù$_4$ 勿 'eagerly' → **wěi**$_6$ 亹眉

wù$_5$ 物 (mjuət) **LH** mut, **OCM** *mət
'Variety' (of color, objects) > 'to sort, classify, class, sort' [Zuo] > 'things' [OB, Shi] (Boltz 1994: 60). The OB graph for *wù* was distinct from *wù$_3$* 勿 'don't'.
[T] *Sin S. SR* vu (入), *PR, LR* vuʔ; *MGZY* wu (入) [vu]; *MTang* mvur, *ONW* mut
[E] ST: PTB *mruw (*STC* no. 150): WT *'bru < ɴbru* 'grain, seed'; WB *myui*^{B} 'seed, seed grain' ⋇ *ə-myui*^{B} 'race, lineage, kind, class, sort', PL *C-m(y)u$^{2/3}$ 'thing' [Matisoff 1974: 312]; JP *myu*^{55} 'kind, sort', Mikir *-mū* classifier for grains, seeds, Lushai *mu*^{F} < *muuʔ* 'seed, pit, stone'. CH -> PTai *hm-: S. *muat*^{D1} 'class, sort'. As to foreign (WT) initial *b-* for CH *m-*, see §6.7.

wù$_6$ 悟寤 (ŋuo^C) **LH** ŋɑ^C, **OCM** *ŋâh
'To wake, awake' 寤 [Shi]; 'to awake, realize' 悟 [Shu].
[T] *Sin Sukchu SR* ŋu (去), *LR* wu; *MGZY* u (去) [u]; *ONW* ŋo
⋇ **sū** 蘇 (suo) **LH** sɑ, **OCM** *sŋâ — **[T]** *ONW* so
'To revive' [Yi] (Unger *Hao-ku* 36, 1990: 61).

[<] s-caus. of *wù* 悟寤 (ŋuo^C) (§5.2.1).

[E] This wf may also include → sū$_1$ 蘇 'grass'. Curiously, AA-PSBahn. has a word *rəŋal 'awaken' (cognate to Wa-Lawa-Bulang *sɑl 'awaken' tr. ?), but a final *-l* should have left a trace in MC (§6.9).

wù$_7$ 牾迕晤捂忤 → **yù$_{17}$** 禦

wù$_8$ 惡 'hate' → **è$_3$** 惡

wù$_9$ 遻 → **è$_6$** 愕鄂噩

wù$_{10}$ 蘁 → **yù$_{17}$** 禦

wù$_{11}$ 務 (mju^C) **LH** muo^C, **OCM** *moh, OCB *m(r)jos

'To apply oneself to, be intent on' [Zuo], 'occupation, task' [Yi].

[T] *MTang* mvu < mvuo, *ONW* muo

≍ **mào** 懋 (məu^C) **LH** mo^C, **OCM** *môh, OCB *m(r)jus

'To make effort, be energetic, strive' [BI, Shu].

[E] ST: PTB *mow (*STC* no. 280) > PL *mi(aw)^2 'work', Chepang *mus-* 'be competent, powerful, concentrating, specializing' ≍ *muh* 'power, influence' (esp. of shaman); Tamang *^{l}moi* 'to work'; WB *mu* 'do, perform', JP *mo^{55}* 'to do', Nung *əmu* 'labor, business'; Garo *mo* 'move', Dimasa *mau* 'move' (*HST:* 69). JP *mu^{55}* 'work, affair' 事情 has a different vowel. OC -> PTai *hm-: S. *mok^{D1}* 'apply oneself'. Syn. → wěi$_6$ 亹眉 'make effort'.

wù$_{12}$ 霧 (mju^C) **LH** muo^C, **OCM** *moh

'Fog, mist' [Shu].

[D] This word survives in almost all dialects: Y-Guǎngzhōu *mou^{22}*, M-Xiàmén *bu^{33}*, *bɔ^{24}*, Fúzhōu *muɔ^{52}*. In Y-Yángjiāng it means 'dew' *mou^{54}-ʃui^{21}* 霧水.

[E] ST: PTB *r-muw (*STC* no. 488) > WT *rmu-ba* 'fog' ≍ *rmus-pa* 'foggy'; WB *mru* 'floating dust particles'.

With final *-k: PTB *mu:k (*STC* no. 357) > WT *rmugs-pa* 'dense fog' ≍ *mug-pa* 'overcast, troubled' ≍ *smug-po* 'dark red, purple-brown'; Chepang *mus* 'cloud, fog'; Lepcha *muk* 'foggy, misty'; JP *muʔ^{31}* 'overcast'; WB *muik* 'dark, ignorant', Lushai *muuk^F* 'dull' (color). OC -> Tai S. *mɔɔk^{D1L}* < *hm- 'fog, mist' (Li F. 1976: 41), KS: Mulam *mɔk^8*.

[C] Possible allofams may be → mòu 瞀 (so *HST:* 82), → mài$_3$-mù 霢霂 'drizzle'. Words meaning 'dark, covered, obscure, dull' and the like tend to have the phonesthemic initial *m- followed by a back vowel.

wù$_{13}$ 鋈 → **wò$_1$** 沃

xī$_1$ 夕 (zjäk) **LH** ziak, **OCM** *s-jak — **[T]** *ONW* ziek

'Evening' [Shi, Zhuang]; 'evening tide' 汐 [Lèipiān], opp. *cháo* 潮 (→ zhāo$_4$ 朝).

[E] ST: PTB **s-r(y)ak* 'spend the night, full day and night, 24 hrs.' (*HPTB:* 323; *STC* p. 171; no. 203) > WT *žag < ryak* 'day' (24 hrs. from sunrise to sunrise); Kanauri *hrak* 'day', Lahul *gyag* 'day'; Lep. *ayak* 'day' (i.e., 24 hrs.); PLB *ʔrak > WB *rak, ə-rak* 'a complete day of 24 hrs.', Lahu *há* 'spend the night', *ɔ̀-há* 'night'; Lushai *riak*^{F} / *riaʔ*^{L} 'put up for the night, stay the night' (*STC* no. 203, 417; n. 487; *CVST* 2: 84); JP *yaʔ*^{55} < *yak*^{55} 'day'; Limbu *ya:kt-* 'to stay' (especially overnight). CH preinitial *s- for other lgs.' *r- and vice versa is not uncommon, see §5.3.

In the OB, the 24 hr. day started and ended some time in the evening or night. Since → rì 日 'sun' had acquired the meaning '24 hr. day' already in OC, *xī* was then restricted to the time of the day's end.

This word is thought to be cogn. to → yè$_1$ 夜 'night', but TB keeps the etyma *ryak '24 hr. day' and *ya 'night' strictly separate. → xī$_6$ 昔 is prob. related; → lǚ$_3$ 旅 'lodge' may possibly be another manifestation of this stem.

xī$_2$ 西棲栖 (siei) **LH** sei (also sen ?), **OCM** *sə̂i (or *snə̂i ?), OCB *səj

'Nest' n. [Shi] > 'to roost, rest' 棲 [Shi] 'keep still' 栖 [Lunyu]; 'west' 西 [Shi] > 'turn or go west' [Shu].

[T] *Sin S. SR* sjej (平), *PR, LR* si; *MGZY* si (平) [si]; *ONW* sėi

[E] *Xī* has several possible etymologies. (1) Because 西 appears to be the phonetic in the graph *nǎi* 迺 (nậi^B) *nə̂ʔ, some investigators assume an OC *sn- cluster. Unger (*Hao-ku* 36, 1990: 60) relates *xī* to WT *ner-ba* 'to sink, go down'; or (2) it is related instead to Chepang *nelʔ-* 'go down, set' (sun) (same etymon as WT?). (3) A MK nominal n-infix derivative from the root 'go down' as in OMon *cnis* 'ghat' < *cis* 'go down' (to the river, and generally), with PAA *tsn- > PCH *sn-, see §2.6.1. Therefore this etymon meant lit. 'the place where one goes down to' > Mon 'ghat' > OC 'nest, west'. The base form is → jì$_{15}$ 濟 'to ford' via AA. (4) *CVST* 4: 24 relates this word to WT *gze-ba* 'home, habitation, nest', which would be the simplest explanation if it were not for the possible OC medial *n.

xī$_3$ 吸 (xjəp) **LH** hɨp, **OCM** *hŋəp or *həp — **[D]** Mǐn: Xiàmén *kʰip*^{DI}

'To inhale' [Zhuang].

[E] ST: the OC initial is not clear, therefore *xī* could be cognate either to WT *rŋub-pa, brŋubs* 'to draw in (air), breathe', or, more likely, to Lushai *in*^{L}*-hip*^{H} 'draw in' (as air). An allofam may be → hē 喝欱 'drink' (Lushai *hup*^{H}); for the *u ~ *i alternations, see §11.5.1.

xī$_4$ 析 (siek) **LH** sek, **OCM** *sêk

'To cleave, split' [Shi], 'disperse' [Shu].

[E] ST *sek: Mikir *iŋsèk < m-sèk* 'to split' (Mikir *-ek* can also derive from *-ik*), JP *seʔ*^{55} < *sek* 'cut'. TB cognates show that → sī$_5$ 斯 'cleave' is prob. not (directly) related. This word does not belong to any of the stems listed under → lí$_{10}$ 離. Less likely: the meaning 'disperse' may point to a connection with MK: OKhmer /cɛɛk/ 'to divide, distribute' ≭ *chēka* /chaaɛk/ 'be divided, split, cleft, forked'. Possibly the ST and the AA etymon have coalesced. The AA word may also underlie → chā$_1$ 叉 'fork'.

xī$_5$ 淅 → **shì$_{26}$** 釋 'wash rice'

xī$_6$ 昔 (sjäk) **LH** siak, **OCM** *sak or *sjak ?
(Past time separated by at least one night:) 'Earlier, formerly, former times' [BI, Shi], 'yesterday' [Zuo]; 'night' [Zuo, Zhuang] is rare, perh. a later development, possibly derived from the implied notion 'intervening night'. Since in *Zuǒzhuàn* [Ai 4] 昔 means clearly 'night', it cannot be a graphic substitution for → xī$_1$ 夕 'evening'. **xī** 腊 [Yi] 'dried meat' (i.e. ancient meat) is the same word according to Karlgren *GSR* 798a.
[T] *Sin Sukchu SR si* (入); *MGZY si* (入) [si]
[E] This word **s(j)ak* is prob. cognate to → xī$_1$ 夕 **s-jak* 'evening' (Wáng Lì 1982: 286). They look like variants of the same PCH or ST form **s-jak* (~ **r-jak*) '24 hr. period'; in 昔 the *s- was treated like the root initial, in 夕 it was treated like a prefix; this bifurcation with doublets occurs also in roots which have initial *j- and pre-initial *r-, see §9.2.1. The development night – yesterday has parallels in TB: *ya 'night' > Chepang *yoh* 'yesterday'.
[C] This word has been connected with → yè$_1$ 夜 'night' (Wáng Lì), but see there. Sagart (1999: 67, 160) relates *xī* to → zuó 昨 'yesterday', among others.

xī$_7$ 腊 → **xī$_6$** 昔

xī$_8$ 息 (sjək) **LH** sɨk, **OCM** *sək
'To breathe' [Lunyu], 'rest' [Shi].
[T] *Sin Sukchu SR* si (入); *MGZY* si (入) [si]; *ONW* sik
[E] ST: PTB *sak (*STC* no. 485): PLB *C-sak 'breath, air, breath of life': WB ə-*sak* 'breath, life'; Mru *chak* 'heart, life' [Löffler 1966: 120]; JP *saʔ*^{31} 'to breathe' ⋉ *n*^{31}*-saʔ*^{31} 'breath, force' (*HST:* 48); Tamang *sa:* < *sak.*

xī$_9$ 奚 → **hé$_3$** 何

xī$_{10}$ 溪 (kʰiei) **LH** kʰe, **OCM** *khê — **[T]** *ONW* kʰèi
'River valley' **xī, qī** 谿 [Zuo], 'mountain stream, river' **xī** 溪 [JY]. Etymology not clear, the word looks similar to PWMiao *kle^{A1} (Purnell *gle^{1A}) 'water, river'.

xī$_{11}$ 犀 (siei) **LH** sei, **OCM** *sôi — **[T]** *ONW* sèi
'Rhinoceros' [Shi]; this word is not a variant of → sì$_4$ 兕 'wild buffalo'.
[E] ST *səj refers to a large animal: WT *bse* 'rhinoceros' (*HST:* 125); Kuki-Naga *k-saj, Lushai *saai*^{H} (Lushai *s-* is unexpected), Newari *kisii* 'elephant', Tangkhul Naga (Bhat) *səy* 'cattle', Bodo *kísi* 'deer'; perh. also PLB *dzay^2 'animal': Lahu cê-cà 'domestic animals, cattle', etc. [Matisoff 1988b]. Like other animal names, this is an area word, note MK: PMon *ksɛh,* PNB *aseh 'horse'. See also → cái$_1$ 才材財.

xī$_{12}$ 希睎 (xjei) **LH** hɨi, **OCM** *həi — **[T]** *Sin Sukchu SR* xi (平); *MGZY* hi (平) [xi]
'To hope, look for' 睎 [Lü], 希 (modern CH) is prob. cognate to → jì$_{14}$ 冀覬 (so Wáng Lì 1982: 393).

xī$_{13}$ 膝 (sjet) **LH** sit, **OCM** *sit — **[T]** *MTang* sir, *ONW* sit
'Knee' [Yili]. Unger (*Hao-ku* 39, 1992) compares this word to WT *sgyid* (< *s-yit* ?) 'bend of knee, knee joint'. Gong (*BIHP* 51.3, 1980) relates *xī* to → jié$_9$ 節 *tsît 'joint'.

xī$_{14}$ 悉 (sjet) **LH** sit, **OCM** *sit
'All, everything' [Shi], 'exhaust' [Zuo]; 'to know, comprehend'.

[E] ST: PTB *syey 'know' (*STC* no. 182) > WT *šes-pa*, Vayu *ses;* Garo *masi,* Lushai *tʰei^L / tʰeiʔ^L < sei/s* 'can, be able' [Weidert 1987: 166], PL*si², WB *si^C* [Matisoff 1974 no. 217] (*HST:* 101), Lepcha *ší* 'to look, see, appear'.

xī₁₅-shuò 蟋蟀 (sjɛt-sjuət) **LH** ṣit-ṣuit, **OCM** *srit-srut
'Cricket' [Shi]. The CH first syllable is related to the second in Tai: S. *ciŋ^{C1}-riit^{D1} ~ caŋ^{A1}-riit^{D1}* (WSiam *hri:ʔd*) 'cricket' (Manomaivibool 1975: 157).

xī₁₆ 蠵 (ɣiwei) **LH** ɣue, **OCM** *wê
'Big tortoise' [Chuci]. Etymology not clear.

xī₁₇ 櫼桸 (xjie 3) **LH** hɨɑi
'A ladle' [FY 33.6] is a Han-period dialect word in the areas of Chén, Chǔ, Sòng, and Wèi, also at Guō Pú's time (ca. 300 AD) in Jiāngdōng (lower Yangtze); today found in Mǐn: PMin *hiɑ 'ladle' (Norman 1983: 205).

xī₁₈ 翕 → **hé₅** 合

xī₁₉ 犧 → **yí₁₀** 儀宜

xī₂₀ 噏 → **hē** 喝欱

xí₁ 席 (zjäk) **LH** ziak ~ ziɑk, **OCM** *s-lak — **[T]** *ONW* ziek — **[D]** PMin *dzʰiɔk^{D2}
'Mat' for sitting or lying on [Shi].
[E] Because commentators suggest that *xí* is made of grass (薦) or rushes, and because the syn. → jiàn₁₃ 薦 means both 'grass' and 'mat', it is possible that this word is cognate to → mǎng₁ 莽 'grass, weeds' (*mlaʔ ~ mlaŋʔ). We would have here an example of the TB-like m-/s- alternation in prefixes: *mlaʔ (< *mlak?) ~ *s-lak. Wáng Lì (1982: 289) associates *xí* with other words, incl. → jiàn₁₃ 薦, *zū* 蒩 'bedding or packing of straw' (under → jū₅ 苴 — unlikely).

xí₂ 習 (zjəp) **LH** zip, **OCM** *s-ləp
'To flap' (the wings) [Lüshi], 'flutter'. *Xí₂* and *xí₃* are usually considered the same word. However, the present *xí* may instead be cognate to → yè₆ 熚 'flashing'.

xí₃ 習 (zjəp) **LH** zip, **OCM** *s-ləp
'To do repeatedly' [Shi], 'to repeat' [Shu]; 'to practice' [Lun, Li]; 'habit, custom' [Meng], 'know, be familiar with' [Guoyu]; 'additional robe over another, to cover' 襲 [Li, Zuo]. *Xí₂* and *xí₃* are usually considered the same word.
[T] *Sin Sukchu SR* zi (入); *MGZY* zi (入) [zi]; *ONW* zip
[E] Area word: TB-WT *slob-pa, slabs* 'to learn, teach' ⋊ *slobs* 'exercise, practice'. Lushai has a different vowel (MK source?): *tlip^{L1} < slip* (?) 'to repeat, do over again, to perfect'. <> MK: Khmer *dhlā'pa* /tloəp/ 'to do frequently, be used to doing, to accustom, habituate'; PMonic *[_]liəp: Nyah Kur 'skillfully', Mon *lẹp 'to know how to, be skilled at' [Diffloth 1984: 213].
[<] iterative s-prefix derivation (§5.2.3) of the following:

⋊ **yì** 肄 (i^C) **LH** jis, **OCM** *ləts < *ləps
'To exercise, practice' [Zuo]; the word may have acquired the meaning 'toil' [Shi] through convergence with → yì₁₅ 勩 *las 'toil'.

[C] This etymon partially overlaps with → dié 牒.

xí₄ 錫 (siek) **LH** sek, **OCM** *sêk < *slek — **[T]** *MTang* sɨk, *ONW* sėk
'Tin' [Shi].
[E] Area word: MK: Late OMon *slāk* /slaik/ 'bronze'. <> Tai: Longzh *hik^{D1}S*, Po'ai *liik* < *tʰr- 'tin' (reconstruction of this initial as *tʰr- is uncertain, *HCT:* 124); Nung

xlek <- Chinese. Some Tai forms for 'tin' listed in *HCT:* 124 are closer to CH forms for 'iron' (→ tiě$_0$ 鐵). Both OCM *slêk 'tin' and *lhît 'iron' prob. derive from the same foreign etymon which would have entered CH at different times. Mahdi (1994: 186) draws attention to the similarity with the AA word for 'leaf': Khasi *slak,* Khmer *slik,* Mon *slaʔ;* leaves of silver have been used as money in Java acc. to the *Sòngshǐ* (*History of the Song Dynasty*), but this is much later.

xí$_5$ 錫 'give' → **cì$_4$** 賜錫

xí$_6$ 覡 → **wū$_2$** 巫

xí$_7$ 襲 → **xí$_3$** 習

xí$_8$ 槻 'circumference' → **guī$_1$** 規

xí$_9$ 隰 → **shī$_7$** 溼

(**xí$_{10}$**) □ (ɣiei?) **LH** ge ?
A Mǐn dialect word for '(small) salted fish': PMin *ğei > Fúzhōu *kie*^{A2}, Amoy *kue*^{A2}, Jiànyáng *ai*^{B}; it is from an AA substrate: Viet. *kè* 'type of small fish' (Norman / Mei 1976: 299).

xǐ$_1$ 洗洒 (sien^B, siei^B) **LH** sei^B, **OCM** *sə̂iʔ or *sî(n)ʔ, *sə̂nʔ ? — **[T]** *ONW* sėi
'To wash' 洗 [Shi 246], 'wash clean' 洒 [Shi 43].
[E] ST *sil: PTB *(m-)sil ~ *(m-)syal 'to wash'> WT *bsil-ba* 'to wash', Lushai *sil*^{R} (*STC:* 173 n. 462; *HST:* 158), WB *tsʰe*^{B}, Mikir iŋtʰī(ʔ), JP gə^{31}-šin^{31}. Prob. not cognate to *să, shǎi* 洒 (ṣăi^B) 'to sprinkle' (under → shāi, shī 篩; so Karlgren 1956: 16). The root of this word is the same as that for 'cool' → qī$_4$ 凄悽 in CH as well as TB. Because of the OC vowel *ə, Baxter related *xǐ* to WT *sel-ba, bsal* 'to cleanse, clear, remove' (impurities etc.).

xǐ$_2$ 徙 (sje^B) **LH** sie^B, **OCM** *seʔ — **[T]** Sui-Tang si, *ONW* se
'Move toward' [BI, Lunyu], 'remove to, go to' [Zuo].
[E] Also found in WB *sai* 'carry from one place to another, remove by repeated processes'.
[C] Perh. related to → yí$_9$ 移; for similar items, see also → lí$_{10}$ 離.

xǐ$_3$ 枲 (sɨ^B) **LH** siə^B, **OCM** *səʔ
'Hemp' [Shu], the phonetic *GSR* 976 implies an OC *l in the initial, hence *CVST* 3: 4 connects this word with Lushai *la*^{L} < *laʔ/h* 'cotton', but see → zhù$_4$ 苧紵.

xǐ$_4$ 喜 (xjɨ^B) **LH** hɨə^B, **OCM** *həʔ
'To rejoice' [Shi] is prob. cognate to → xīn$_5$ 欣 (Wáng Lì 1982: 88; LaPolla 1994: 140).
[T] *Sin S. SR* xi (上); *MGZY* hi (上) [xi]; *MTang* hi, *ONW* hiə

xǐ$_5$ 狶 (xjei[^{B}]) **LH** hɨi(^{B}), **OCM** *həi(ʔ) (< *hləi(ʔ) ?)
'Swine' [Zhuang] is a Han period dialect word of S Chǔ [FY 8, 5]. This word looks like a dialect variant (*lh- > *hl > *h) of → shǐ$_7$ 豕 'pig' (§5.6).

xǐ$_6$ 纚屣縰 (ṣje^B) **LH** ṣe^B, **OCM** *sreʔ
'Band wound round the hair' 纚 [Li], also 縰 [Li]; 'sandal' 屣 [Lü], 'straw sandal' 躧 [Guoce].
⋈ **lí** 纚 (lje) **LH** lie, **OCM** *re
'Rope' [Shi].
[E] ? ST: This word is thought to be connected with WT *sle-ba, bsles ~ hle-ba, hlas* 'to

twist, plait, braid' (Bodman 1980: 71; *HST:* 47), OC *r for foreign *l has parallels (§7.3). Prob. no connection with → liè₃ 茢.

xì₁ 系繫 (ɣiei^C) **LH** ge^C, **OCM** *gêh, OCB *N-keks — **[T]** *ONW* ɣèi
'To be attached, connected' [Yi] (Baxter and Sagart 1998: 46).
[<] endopass. of *xì* 係繫 (kiei^C) (§4.6).
[D] Norman (1988: 223) suggests that this word is the source of the Kèjiā and Yuè copula 'to be': K-Méixiàn hɛ^C, Huayáng *xie^C*. The OC initial consonants in this and the following *xì* 繫 and *xī* 係 is not certain (*g- or *k-?).

ꭙ **xì** 係繫 (kiei^C) **LH** ke^C, **OCM** *kêh, OCB *keks — **[T]** *ONW* kèi
'To bind, tie up, attach' tr. 係 [OB], 繫 [Yi]; 'continue, perpetuate' 繼 [Shi] (read Mand. *jì*).

ꭙ **xī** 奚 (ɣiei) **LH** ge, **OCM** *gê
'Slave, captive, prisoner' (i.e. 'someone bound') [OB, Zhouli].
[<] tone A nominalization of *xì* 系繫 (ɣiei^C) (§3.1).
[E] Other lg. families have words which may be connected: PMY *kr-: Anc. Miao *qʰei^A 'to tie up' (Strecker 1989: 30); AA: Kharia *kɛʼɟ* 'to fasten' ꭙ *kɛkɛʼɟ* 'rope'.
[C] Perh. → jī₁₀ 績 'to twist' is an interative s-prefix derivation.

xì₂ 細 (siei^C) **LH** se^C (or sei^C), **OCM** *sêh or *sîh — **[T]** *ONW* sèi^C
'Thin, small' [Zuo].
[E] ST: PTB *ziy > West Tib. *zi* 'very small'; Limbu *ci* 'little, few'; WB *se^B* 'small, fine'; Kachin *zi* 'small' (*HST:* 135), Lushai *tee^R* / *teet^F* 'to be small'.

xì₃ 戲 (xje^C 3) **LH** hɨɑi^C, **OCM** *haih
'Joke, play' [Shi].
[T] *Sin Sukchu SR* xi (去); *MGZY* hi (去) [xi]
[E] ST: WT *'kʰyal-ba* 'joke, jest' ꭙ *(r)kyal-ka* 'joke, jest, trick' (*HST:* 99); Lushai *kʰaal^L* / *kʰalʔ^L* 'to play with' ꭙ *in^L-kʰeel^L* 'to gamble, play'.

ꭙ **xiān** 嘕 (xjän 3) **LH** hɨɑn 'laugh' [Chuci] is cogn. acc. to *HST:* 99.

xì₄ 潟 (sjäk) **LH** siak, **OCM** *sak
'Salty soil' [Zhouli] is perh. connected with → chì₁ 斥 (tśʰjäk) LH *tśʰiak* 'salty soil' (dialectal simplification?), and may belong to → gǔ₁₅ 鹽 and → lǔ₁ 鹵.

xì₅ 虩虩 → **hè₅** 赫

xì₆ 氣餼 → **qì₃** 迄

xiá₁ 呷 (xap) **LH** hap, **OCM** *hap
'To drink with a sucking movement' [SW], in some southern dialects it is the word for 'to drink': Y-Guǎngzhōu *hap^33*, W-Sūzhōu *haʔ^44*. The *QY* vocalism may be due to sound symbolism or archaistic colloquialism and not go back to OCM *-r-. This word may be related to → hē 喝欱 'drink'.
[<] Onomatopoetic area word: ST: WT *hab* 'mouthful', WB *hap* 'bite at', Lushai *hap^H* 'bite, snap' (*HST:* 43). <> AA: Santali *haʼb* 'take into the mouth', Munda *haʼb* 'bite', PMonic *haap in *caaʔ-haap* 'to eat, esp. with fingers' [Diffloth 1984: 214].

xiá₂ 祫 → **hé₅** 合

xiá₃ 狹 → **jiā₃** 夾

xiá₄ 赮瑕霞騢 (ɣa) **LH** ga, **OCM** *grâ
'Red' 赮 [SW], 'the color of dawn' [Yupian] > 'rosy dawn' 霞 [SW xinfu]; 'jade with

some red' [SW] > 'be flawed, blemished' (of a person's reputation, greatness) 瑕 [Shi]; 'horse of mixed red and white color' 騢 [Shi] (Wáng Lì 1982: 145). This word may be cognate to → hè$_4$ 赫 'red'.

xiá$_5$ 遐 'how, why' → **hé$_3$** 何

xià$_1$ 下 (ɣa^B) **LH** ga^B, **OCM** *grâʔ
'To descend, down, below' [OB, Shi].
[T] *Sin Sukchu SR* ɣja (上去); *MGZY* (Hÿa >) Hya (上去) [ɣja]; *ONW* ɣä^B

× **xià** 下 (ɣa^C) **LH** ga^C, **OCM** *grâh — **[T]** *ONW* ɣä^C
(1) 'To be put down' [Shi, old part].
[<] exopass. of *xià* 下 (ɣa^B) *graʔ (§4.4).
(2) 'To descend, fall' [Shi, late part].
[<] general tone C derivation of *xià* 下 (ɣa^B) *graʔ (§3.5).
[E] AA: Khmer *gra'ka* /kruk/ (vowel /u/ instead of /a/ because of the voiced initial) 'be low, debased'; for CH tone B, see §3.2.2, weakening of final *-k* to OC *-ʔ is perh. due to ST influence: PTB *gla × *kla 'to fall', see forms under → luò$_7$ 落.
<> Tai: S. *laa^{C1}* < *hl- 'underneath, below' seems to have a TB origin. <> CH -> PMiao *ɴGa^B 'to go down' (Wáng Fúshì 1979). — **[C]** Allofam → luò$_7$ 落 'to fall'.

xià$_2$ 暇 (ɣa^C) **LH** ga^C,**OCM** *grâh
'Be at leisure, lazy' [BI, Shi] is cogn. to → xián$_5$ 閑閒 acc. to Pulleyblank (1973: 121).

xià$_3$ 夏 'great' → **jiǎ$_2$** 假嘏

xià$_4$, hè 嚇 → **hè$_5$** 赫

xià$_5$, shà 廈 (ɣa^B) **LH** ga^B
'House, room' [Chuci] > Mand. *shà* 'tall building, mansion'. This word is prob. not related to → jiā$_7$ 家 'house'; Wáng Lì (1982: 144) relates it to → jiǎ$_2$ 假嘏 'great'.

xiān$_1$ 先 (sien) **LH** sen, **OCM** *sə̂n
'To go in front, ahead, before, former' [OB, BI, Shi, Shu].
[T] *Sin Sukchu SR* sjen (平); *MGZY* sÿan (平) [sjɛn]; *MTang* sian < sɨan, *ONW* sėn

× **xiàn** 先 (sien^C) **LH** sen^C, **OCM** *sə̂ns
'To walk before' (in order to protect) > 'take care of, attend' [Shi, Shu] is perh. a putative form, 'to put first' [Zuo] is a caus. derivation (§4.3.2) (Downer 1959: 280).
[E] ST: WT *bsel(-ba)* 'safeguard, guide' (as escorting a convoy); Chepang *syalʔ* 'lead position, former ways' × *syalʔ-* 'to lead, go, do first, open way'.

xiān$_2$ 仙僊 (sjän) **LH** sian, **OCM** *san or *sen
'An immortal' [Lie], a relatively late word. *Xiān* are men and women who attain supernatural abilities; after death they become immortals and deities who can fly through the air. For example, Lǎozi, the founder of Taoism, is called a *xiān*. *Xiān* can also refer to living persons who have unusual skills in their profession (Eberhard 1983: 287).
[N] The original graph was 僊, the simplified form 仙 has been partially inspired by the notion that *xiān* live as recluses in the mountains *shān* 山.
[E] Perh. ST: WT *gšen* < *g-syen* (?) 'shaman', one who has supernatural abilities, incl. travel through the air; Gšen-rab(s) was the founder of the ancient Tibetan Bon religion, sometimes thought to be identical with Lǎozi. – Or is WT *gšen* a CH loan?

xiān$_3$ 秈 (sjän)
'Non-glutinous rice' is a dialect word south of the Yangtze River [JY] which is shared with PTai *s-: S. *saan*^{A1} 'husked rice'.

xiān$_4$ 鮮 (sjän) **LH** sian, **OCM** *san, OCB *sjen (Baxter 1992: 296; 385)
'Be fresh' (of meat, fish) [Shu, Li], 'be fresh' [Shi].
[T] *Sin Sukchu SR* sjen (平); *MGZY* sÿan (平) [sjɛn]
[E] ST: PTB *sar > WT *gsar-ba* 'new, fresh'; WB *sa*^{C} 'make anew'; Rawang *angsar*, Trung *aksal*, Lushai *tʰar*^{H} 'new'. A possible OC vowel *e (OCB) does not agree with TB, though.

xiān$_5$ 嘕 → **xì**$_3$ 戲

xiān$_6$ 綅 → **qīn**$_2$ 綅

xiān$_7$ 纖 (sjäm) **LH** siam, **OCM** *sam or *sem ?
'Thin, slender, sharp pointed' [Zhouli] > 'fine-textured silk' [Shu].
This word has two possible etymologies: (1) ST: WT *zim-bu* 'fine, thin, slender' (*IST:* 52). (2) This could be the s. w. as *xiān* 銛 'sharp' (under → jiān$_1$ 尖).

xiān$_8$ 銛 → **jiān**$_1$ 尖

xián$_1$ 弦 → **qiān**$_7$ 牽

xián$_2$ 涎 (zjän, jiän^C) **LH** zian, jan^C, S lan^B, **OCM** *(s-)lan
'Saliva' [SW, GY].
[T] *Sin Sukchu SR* zjen (平); *MGZY* zen (平) [zɛn]
[D] The Old South variant is *lɑn^B: PMin *lɑn^B, K-Méixiàn *lan*^{A2}, Y-Zhōngshān *hɐu*^{B}*-nan*^{B} 口涎
[E] Etymology not certain. Perh. related to WT *zlan* 'moisture'. Alternatively, it may be connected with Tai: S. *(nam-) laai*^{A2} < *ml- 'saliva' (*nam* 'water'; Li F. 1976: 45).

xián$_3$ 咸 (ɣăm) **LH** gɛm, **OCM** *grə̂m
'To complete, finish, unite, completely' > 'all' (adv.) [Shi]; 'harmony' 諴 [Shu].
ꭗ **lǎn** 濫 (lâm^B) **LH** lɑm^B, **OCM** *râmʔ < *g-ramʔ ?
'To join, unite' [Liji]; or is this the s. w. as *lǎn* 攬 'take' (under → liǎn$_1$ 斂)?
[E] This word also seems to occur in Tai: S. *ruam*^{B2} < *ruam^B 'together, join together' (Manomaivibool 1975: 176).
[E] The nature of the relationship with similar words in SE Asia is not clear. AA-Khmer *brama* /prɔɔm/ OKhmer *braṃ* 'go along with, follow, be with at the same time, agree...' Khmer -> Tai: S. *pʰrɔɔm*^{C2} < *vr- 'together', Saek *phrɔɔm*^{C2} 'together, altogether' (usually thought to be related to → fán$_4$ 凡).

xián$_4$ 鹹 (ɣăm) **LH** gɛm, **OCM** *grə̂m
'Salty' [Shu].
[D] Mǐn: Xiàmén *kiam*^{A2} / *ham*^{A2} 'salted, salty'.
[E] ST: PTB *r-gyum (*STC* no. 245) > Kiranti *rum 'salt' [van Driem 1995: 249]; Kachin *dʒum*^{31} 'salt' ꭗ *ʃum*^{33} 'be salted'. CH -> Tai: S. *kʰem*^{A2} < *g- 'salty' (Li F. 1976: 46). <> Some Aslian lgs. have forms for 'salt' which look similar to OC: *garam, garɛm* [Benjamin 1976: 114], but their relationship to *xián*, if any, is not clear.
[C] This word is sometimes thought to be related to → yán$_9$ 鹽 (so Li Fang Kuei) – unlikely.

xián$_5$ 閑閒 (ɣăn) **LH** gɛn, **OCM** *grên, OCB *ɦkren — **[T]** *ONW* ? kän
'Be moving slowly, lazy' 閑 [Shi]; 'leisure' 閒 [Meng], 'peace' [Zuo].

[E] Tai: PTai *gran^{C2} 'lazy'.

Karlgren (*GSR* 191) and more recently Baxter (1992: 219) connect this word with → jiān$_5$ 間閒 'interstice time' > 'leizure', but it could well be a separate etymon; also → xià$_2$ 暇 'be at leisure' is cogn. acc. to Pulleyblank (1973: 121); perh. → lǎn$_1$ 懶 'lazy' is a popular variant.

xián$_6$ 閑 (γăn) **LH** gɛn, **OCM** *grên
'Barrier, bar' [Yi], 'obstruct, guard against' [Zuo], 'protect' [Meng]. – Syn. → guān$_5$ 關, → jiàn$_4$ 楗; possibly the s. w. as → xián$_7$ 閑.
[T] *Sin Sukchu SR* γjan (平); *MGZY* (Xÿan >) Xyan (平) [γjan]; *ONW* γän

⋟ **lán** 闌欄攔 (lân) **LH** lɑn, **OCM** *rân < *g-ran
'Barrier, to protect' 闌 [Guoce]; 'railing, pen' 欄 [Mo]; 'to obstruct' 攔 [YP, GY].
[E] ? ST: WB *ran^B* 'make a barrier on one side'. Or Lushai *k^{h}aar^R* 'to shut, close' may be cognate.

xián$_7$ 閑 (γăn) **LH** gɛn, **OCM** *grên
'To restrain, train' (horses > then general) [Shi]. This is prob. a semantic extension of → xián$_6$ 閑 'barrier'. A near-synonym → xián$_{11}$ 銜 'horse's bit', which is a near homophone, can also mean 'to train' (horses).

⋟ **liàn** 練 (lien^C) **LH** len^C, **OCM** *rêns < *g-rens — **[T]** *ONW* lėn
'To train' [Li], 'improve by training' [Mo]. Karlgren *GSR* 185i seems to consider 'improve by training' a semantic extension of → liàn$_2$ 湅練鍊 'refine'.

xián$_8$ 閑 (γăn) **LH** gɛn, **OCM** *grên — **[T]** *ONW* γän
'Be large' (of pillars and the like) [Shi] is prob. cognate to → jiè$_2$ 介价 'increase' and perh. derived from → jiǎ$_2$ 假嘏 'large'.

xián$_9$ 瞯 (γăn) **LH** grɛn, **OCM** *grên
'To spy on, watch' [Meng] is perh. related to WB *krañ^C* 'look at' (*CVST* 5: 122).

xián$_{10}$ 嫻 → **liàn$_2$** 湅練鍊

xián$_{11}$ 銜 (γam) **LH** gam, **OCM** *grâm
'To carry in the mouth, a horse's bit' [Zhuang] > 'harbor' (grief) [Shi]; later 'train' (horses). This is prob. related to → hán$_1$ 含函 'have in the mouth' (so Bodman 1980: 110) and to → qián$_2$ 柑箝 'wooden gag'.

xián$_{12}$ 燅 (zjäm) **LH** ziam, **OCM** *s-lam
'To heat, warm' 燅 [Yili]; 'to heat' [Li], 'to roast or broil soft' 燂 [Zhouli]; 'to boil' (meat) 爓 [Li]. The graphs 燂爓 are in the phonetic series in *-əm*.
[E] ST: WT *slam-pa* 'to parch'.

~ **tán, qián** 燂 (dậm, dzjäm) are additional readings for the graph.
[D] PMin *dim^C 'to reheat': Amoy *tim^{C2}*

[E] These items are derived from the stem → yán$_2$ 炎 'flame, burn' and converge semantically with → xín 爓尋 LH *zim*, OCM *s-ləm 'to heat, warm'.

xiǎn$_1$ 毨銑 (sien^B) **LH** sen^B, **OCM** *sînʔ (or *sənʔ ?)
'Glossy' (of hair) 毨 [Shu]; 'well-polished metal' 銑 [Guoyu].
[E] ST: WT *zil* 'brightness, splendor' (*HST:* 48). Gong (in W. Wang 1995: 49) connects this word to WT *gser* 'gold'.

xiǎn$_2$ 險 (xjäm^B 3, xjɐm^B) **LH** hɨam^B or hɨɑm^B, **OCM** *hŋ(r)amʔ
'Precipitous, dangerous' [Shi]. Bodman (1980: 176) relates this word to → yán$_8$ 巖.

xiǎn₃, hǎn 闞 (xǎm^B, xam^B, xâm^B) **LH** ham^B, **OCM** *h(r)âmʔ or *hrə̂mʔ ?
'Roaring, enraged' (of a tiger) [Shi].
[E] Area word: MK-PMonic *grəəm > Nyah Kur 'to growl' (of tiger or dog), Khmer *gamrāma* /kumrı́iəm/ 'to roar, shout, to cow, awe, intimidate'; Viet *sấm* (< kr-?) 'thunder' ⋇ *rấm* 'noise of thunder', Bahn. *grâm* 'thunder', Cham *gram* 'id' [Maspero 1912: 83]. Note also Mon *krṃ* 'to cheer'. <> TB-Lai *hraam* 'to growl, groan' [*LTBA* 21.1: 160]. Though onomatopoetic, these forms are probably cognates because the roaring of an animal could be expressed in many different ways, note for example TB-Limbu *u:kt-* 'to roar' (of tiger), 'thunder', or English 'roar', for that matter.

xiǎn₄ 鮮尟 (sjän^B) **LH** sian^B, **OCM** *senʔ ?, OCB *sjenʔ (Baxter 1992: 385)
'Be rare, few' 鮮 [Shi], 尟 [Yijing]. Etymology not clear.

xiǎn₅ 癬 (sjän^B) **LH** sian^B, S tsʰian^B, **OCM** *sa/enʔ ?, OCB *sjenʔ
'Scab' [Guoyu]. The OC vowel *e is suggested by the *Shìmíng*'s comment that the Shandong pronunciation was *xǐ* 徙 OCB *sjeʔ (Baxter 1992: 296).
[D] PMin *tsʰian^B ~ *sian^B

xiǎn₆ 顯 (xien^B) **LH** hen^B, **OCM** *hênʔ — **[T]** *MTang* hian < hɨan, *ONW* hėn
'Be bright, illustrious, clear, manifest' [Shi, Zuo] is sometimes thought to belong to → jiàn₁ 見 (so Wáng Lì 1982: 559), but the initials are difficult to reconcile.

xiàn₁ 見 → **jiàn₁** 見

xiàn₂ 晛 → **niàn₂** 晛

xiàn₃ 陷錎 (ɣǎm^C) **LH** gɛm^C, **OCM** *grə̂ms
'Small pit' (as a trap), 'get trapped' [OB, BI, SW]; 'fall into (a pitfall)' [Zuo] > 'throw down' 陷 [Meng], 錎 [Zhuang].
[T] *Sin S. SR* ɣjam (平), *PR* ɣjan, *LR* ɣjen; *MGZY* Hyam (平) [ɣjam]; *ONW* ɣäm.
[D] M-Amoy *ham^C2* 'fall into great calamity'; Y-Guǎngzhōu *ham^22*
[E] ST *grəm: WB *gyam^B* < *gram^B* 'a trap', perh. also JP *gyam* 'lie in wait for, hunt' [Matisoff 1974 no. 189]. Similar CH and foreign comparanda are listed in Table K-1 under → kǎn₁ 坎埳. Since OC *-əm can reflect any foreign rime other than *-am, it is difficult to relate the various CH and foreign comparanda to each other.

xiàn₄ 限 → **hèn** 恨

xiàn₅ 霰 (sien^C) **LH** sen^C, **OCM** *sêns
'Sleet' [Shi]. *SW* records an alternate character with *jiàn* 見 OCM *kênh as phonetic so that Baxter (1992: 354) reconstructs OCB *s(k)ens.
[E] ST: WT *ser-ba* 'hail', JP *sin^33* 'hail' (Bodman 1980: 173; *HST:* 135), prob. also Chepang *wer* ~ *yor* 'hail', therefore ST *swer; ST medial *w* is often lost in WT and CH (§10.2.1), in Chepang the initial cluster *sw- is apparently simplified to *w-*, note PTB *swi 'blood' > Chepang *wi*.

xiàn₆ 線 (sjän^C) **LH** sian^C, **OCM** *sans — **[D]** PMin *sian^C
'Thread' [Zhouli].
[E] The ambiguities of monosyllables is quite apparent in this etymon which can be compared to several TB items: (1) Unger (*Hao-ku* 35, 1986: 29) relates this word to WT *snal-ma* 'thread', but (2) WT *sran-bu* is a possible alternative; (3) note also Lushai *tʰil^H* < *sil* 'thread'. In addition, there is AA-Khmer *-sai* /-saj/ 'line, thread'.

xiàn₇ 羨 (zjänC, dzjänC) **LH** zianC, **OCM** *s-lans ?
'To covet, desire' [Shi] > ('what is desired':) 'affluence' [Shi]. Perh. related to → yú₆ 餘 'leftovers' (Wáng Lì 1982: 163; Geilich 1994: 247).

xiàn₈ 僩 → **liàn₂** 湅練鍊

xiàn₉ 獻憲 (xjɐnC) **LH** hɨɑnC, **OCM** *hŋans
The basic meaning seems to be 'elevate, elevated': 'to display, present' 獻 [BI, Shi] > 'eminent men' 獻 [Shu], 'illustrious' 憲 [Li] > 'exemplary, model, law' 憲 [BI, Shi].

※ **xiàn-xiàn** 憲憲 **LH** hɨɑnC, 'be elated' [Shi].

※ **yàn, yǎn** 甗 (ŋjɐnB/C) **LH** ŋɨɑnB/C, **OCM** *ŋanʔ/h
'A boiler' ('elevated' on three legs) [BI, Zuo, Zhouli, SW].

[E] A possible cognate may be WT *sŋar-ma* 'intelligent' (Gong H. *LL* 1.2, 2000: 43).

xiàn₁₀ 縣 (ɣienC) **LH** ɣ(w)enC, **OCM** *wêns
'District, county' [Zhouli]. The graph was originally intended for → xuán₄ 縣懸 'to suspend' which supports an OC *w in the initial for 'county' (for the occasional loss of *-w-, see §10.2.1).

[T] *Sin Sukchu SR* ɣjen (去); *MGZY* Xwÿan (去) [ɣyɛn]

[E] Etymology not clear. Perh. AA and related to → yíng₄ 營 because in the expression *huán nèi* 寰內 'imperial domain', huán 寰 can be read xiàn 縣; this graphic substitution also indicates that there once was a *w in the OC initial. Alternatively, *xiàn* can derive from similar looking ST words and roots, for example note TB-Lushai *veelF* 'surroundings, neighborhood, environs, suburbs' (→ wéi₅ 圍). Many of these words and wf are difficult to disentangle.

xiāng₁ 相 (sjaŋ) **LH** siɑŋ, **OCM** *saŋ
'Each other, mutually' [Shi] is classical for the preclassical allofam → xū₁ 胥 (Pulleyblank 1962: 233; 1996: 137). It is not only used when the action "is strictly reciprocal, but there is a mutual bond of some kind between subject and object" as in *xiāng cóng* 相從 '(you) follow me' [Shu], later *xiāng* functions as object pronoun (Pulleyblank 1996: 137).

[T] *Sin Sukchu SR* sjaŋ (平); *MGZY* (sÿang >) syang (平) [sjaŋ]; *MTang* siaŋ < saŋ, *ONW* saŋ

※ **xiàng** 相 (sjaŋC) **LH** siɑŋC, **OCM** *saŋh
'Look at, inspect' [Shu] > ('supervise':) 'assist, help' [Shi, Shu] > 'assistant' [Shi] > 'minister'. Boltz (*JAOS* 99.3, 1979: 431) defines *xiàng* as 'observe, vision, image, fantasy'.

[<] extrovert of *xiāng* 相 (sjaŋ) (§4.3).

※ **xiǎng₁** 想 (sjaŋB) **LH** siɑŋB, **OCM** *saŋʔ — [T] *MTang* siaŋ < saŋ, *ONW* saŋ
'To think, imagine' [Zhouli].

[<] endoactive of *xiàng* 相 'observe' (§4.5); Boltz: 'to draw up a mental image, vision' > 'to think'. This word is prob. also related to → xǔ₂ 諝 'discriminate, knowledge'.

[C] A further allofam is → xū₁ 胥 'each other' (Pulleyblank 1962: 233) which also supports the semantic connection between 'mutual' and 'help'.

xiāng₂ 香 (xjaŋ) **LH** hɨɑŋ, **OCM** *haŋ
'Fragrance, smell' [Shi] reflects the ST vocalic *haŋ counterpart to ST *hiŋ → xīng₇ 馨 'be fragrant' (Wáng Lì 1982: 323). For *a* ~ *i* variation, see §11.1.3. For an overview of related ST etyma, see Table X-1.

[T] *Sin Sukchu SR* xjaŋ (平); *MGZY* (hÿang >) hyang (平) [xjaŋ]; *MTang* hiaŋ < haŋ, *ONW* haŋ
[E] A derivation is prob. → xiǎng$_3$ 鄉饗享. Pulleyblank (1962: 140) relates this word to → fāng$_5$ 芳 'fragrant'.

Table X-1 Strong smell, odor, fragrance

Lg.	*siŋ ~	*saŋ	*hiŋ ~	*haŋ
OC	xīng 腥 *sêŋ offensive smell		xīng 馨 *hêŋ fragrant	xiāng 香 *haŋ fragrance
Lushai	(1)	t^haaŋR / t^haan^L have smell or odor like raw flesh	hiiŋ^H / hiin^L stinking	
NNaga	(1)			
JP	siŋ^{33} smell of raw food		k^hjiŋ^{33} stink	k^haŋ^{33} stink
WB		saŋ^B emit pleasant odor		

Note for Table X-1: NNaga *sriŋ 'smell', Lushai *ṭeeŋ^L / ṭeen^L < treeŋh* 'ill-smelling' seem to represent a separate root. Note also MK-Pearic *sraŋ* 'to scent'.

xiāng$_3$ 纕 (sjaŋ) **LH** siɑŋ, **OCM** *snaŋ
'Belt' [BI], 'sash' [Chuci], 'horse's belly-band' [Guoyu].
[E] AA: *camṇaṅa* /camnɑɑŋ/ 'a tie, band, strap, bond' < nominal n-infix derivative of *caṅa* /cɑɑŋ/ (OKhmer /cɔɔŋ/) 'to tie, knot, secure, attach by tying or knotting' (-> Tai /cooŋ/ 'to tie' [Jenner / Pou 1982: 52]). For the initial, see §2.6.1. It is not clear how PY *l̥ɑ:ŋ^1 ~ PM *l̥ɑ:^{5} 'rope, sash' [Wáng F.] is connected.

xiāng$_4$ 襄 → **ràng** 讓

xiāng$_5$ 卿 → **xiàng$_1$** 向嚮卿

xiáng$_1$ 庠祥 (zjaŋ) **LH** ziɑŋ, **OCM** *s-jaŋ or *s-laŋ ?
'Fortune' (good or bad) [Zuo] > 'happy omen, auspicious, lucky day' [Shi] (Wáng Lì 1958: 549). Many different etymologies are theoretically possible: *xiáng* may belong to → yù$_8$ 悆譽豫 'happy'; and / or be related to WT *g-yaŋ* 'happiness, blessing' (so Bodman 1980: 95), but see → qìng$_2$ 慶; or note Tai-Saek *laaŋ^{A1}* 'luck'.

xiáng$_2$ 庠 (zjaŋ) **LH** ziɑŋ, **OCM** *s-jaŋ or *s-laŋ ?
'School' [Meng] is perh. the same word as *xiáng* 'manage the support for the elderly' (under → yǎng$_2$ 養; s-prefix caus. of → yáng$_7$ 揚 'rise'), both imply 'make rise, raise' (then > 'educate' / 'take care of'). Alternatively, this word could also be the same etymon as → xiáng$_4$ 詳 'explain in detail'.
[C] An allofam is perh. → xù$_1$ 序 'school' (Pulleyblank 1962: 233).

xiáng$_3$ 庠 'to take care of the elderly' → **yǎng$_2$** 養

xiáng$_4$ 詳 (zjaŋ) **LH** ziɑŋ, **OCM** *s-jaŋ or *s-laŋ
'Explain in detail' [Shi, Meng], 'attention to detail, diligence' [Zuo]. This is perh. the same etymon as → xiáng$_2$ 庠 'school', and may be related to → xiàng$_6$ 象 'interpret'.

[T] *LMing: Ricci* c'iâm [ts'iaŋ]; *Sin Sukchu SR* zjaŋ (平), *LR* zjaŋ; *MGZY* (zÿang >) zyang (平) [zjaŋ]

xiáng₅ 翔 (zjaŋ) **LH** ziaŋ, **OCM** *s-jaŋ or *s-laŋ ?
'To roam back and forth' [Shi], 'fly to and fro' [Lun].
[<] iterative of *yáng* 徉 below (§5.2.3).

ж **yáng** 徉 (jiaŋ) **LH** jaŋ, **OCM** *jaŋ or *laŋ ?
'To walk irresolutely, hesitate' [Chuci].

xiáng₆ 降 → **jiàng₂** 降

xiǎng₁ 想 → **xiāng₁** 相

xiǎng₂ 饟餉 (śjaŋ^A/B/C) **LH** śaŋ^B, **OCM** *nhaŋʔ/h — [T] *ONW* śaŋ
'Bring food to' (workers in the field) 饟 [Shi], 餉 [Meng]; 'to eat' tr. [Hanfei], 'pay for soldiers' n. [Hanshu].
[E] MY: Anc. Miao *n̥on^C* [Wáng Fúshì] 'cooked rice, food', Yao: Biao Mǐn *n̥aŋ⁵*, Mien (Chiang Rai dial.) *n̥haaŋ⁵*, Dzao Men *nɔŋ⁵* [Haudricourt / Strecker, *TP* 77, 1991: 339].
[C] See also → xiǎng₃ 鄉饗享; it may be related to → rú₃ 茹.

xiǎng₃ 鄉饗享 (xjaŋ^B) **LH** hɨaŋ^B, **OCM** *haŋ^A !
'To feast' [BI]; 'enjoy the use of something' [BI, Shi], 'feast, enjoy' 享 [Zuo]. Tone A in *Shījīng* (Mattos 1971: 309); acc. to Downer (1959: 283) commentators read 'to feast, to present' [Zuo] in tone C.
[E] Etymology not certain. *SW* glosses this word as 'fragrance of grain'; the basic meaning may therefore have been to enjoy the fragrance of food; consequently, this word is perh. a tone B endoactive / introvert derivation from → xiāng₂ 香 'fragrance' (§4.5). The semantics are supported by the TB cognates: Lushai *haŋ^H / han^F (< haŋ)* 'be tasty, nice, cooked' (vegetables), PLB *haŋ² which variously means 'cooked rice, a meal, curry' in LB languages > WB *haŋ^B* 'curry' [Matisoff *D. of Lahu:* 220]. Popular perception may have connected this word with 'to face' → xiàng₁ 向嚮卿.

Semantically more plausible would be a basic meaning 'to eat' for this word, hence it may be a variant of → xiǎng₂ 饟餉; in some non-ST etyma an initial voiceless continuant shows up as a simple OC initial *h- (MC *x-*; §5.6; §1.3.1). The ultimate source would be MY.

xiǎng₄ 嚮 → **xiàng₁** 向嚮卿

xiàng₁ 向嚮卿 (xjaŋ^C) **LH** hɨaŋ^C, **OCM** *haŋh
'To face, approach' 嚮 [Shi], 'turn towards' 向 [Zhuang] > 'direction' 卿 [Hanfei], ('facing side':) 'south side, north side' 卿 = 嚮 [Shi], 'before, previously' 卿 [Meng].
[T] *Sin S. SR* xjaŋ (去); *MGZY* (hÿang >) hyang (去) [xjaŋ]; *MTang* hiaŋ < *ONW* haŋ
[D] Mǐn has an unexpected vowel: Xiàmén col. *hiã^Cl*, *ŋ^Cl*
[E] Etymology not certain, possibly an area word: ST-PLB *ʔna² 'side' > WB *ə-na^B* 'side, vicinity' ж Lahu *nā* 'forehead, brow'; Limbu *na* 'face' (also in expression 'turn the face' in a direction). <> PKS *k-na^C [Edmondson / Yang] or *ʔna^C [Thurgood 1988] 'face, in front', PTai *hna^C1 'face, front'.

Although CH has no trace of an initial *n (餉 [Meng] may only be a late graphic variant of 饟 *nhaŋh; see → xiǎng₂ 饟餉), *xiàng* agrees with a pattern of occasional loss of sonorants in devoiced initials (§5.6). Final *-ŋ* alternates with open vowels in cognate sets (§6.5.2), especially in glottalized syllables (KT tone C corresponds to CH tone B < *ʔ).

⋇ **xiāng** 鄉 (xjaŋ) **LH** hɨɑŋ, **OCM** *haŋ

'Region' [Shi] > 'village' [Lunyu], 'old home village' [Hanshu].

[<] nominalizing tone A back formation of *xiàng* (§3.1). For the semantic connection 'facing side, side' > 'region', note the parallel → fāng 方 'side' > 'area, region'.

⋇ **xiǎng** 響 (xjaŋ^{B}) **LH** hɨɑŋ^{B}, **OCM** *haŋ !

'Echo' [Zhuang, Lie].

[<] endoactive / reflexive of → xiàng$_1$ 向嚮鄉 'to face, turn toward', i.e. something that turns in (toward) itself (§4.5).

[E] Bodman (1980: 155) relates this word to Chepang *mraŋh* 'echo' ~ *mryaŋh* 'to echo', Pulleyblank (1962: 140) to WT *brag* 'echo', but the TB initials are difficult to reconcile with Chinese.

[C] An allofam may also be → rú$_2$ 如 'go to'.

xiàng$_2$ 相 → **xiāng$_1$** 相

xiàng$_3$ 巷 (ɣåŋ^{C}) **LH** gɔŋ^{C}, **OCM** *grôŋh

'Lane, street' [Shi].

[D] → lòng$_2$ 弄 'alley, lane' is a Wú dialectal variant which supports the OC initial cluster, as do forms like Jìn-Tàiyuán *xəʔ^{D2}-l-^{C}* 黑浪 (Zhāng Xīng-yà *YWYJ* 1996.4: 12). Cf. also Beijing *hú-túng* 胡同.

[E] Etymology not clear, perh. ST: WT *groŋ* 'houses, village, town', Bumthang *kroŋ* 'village' (Bodman 1980: 143; *HST:* 156); LaPolla (1994: 171) sets up PTB *g-rwa-ŋ (then perh. related to → lǐ$_3$ 里). <> PMiao *roN^{B}, PYao *raaŋ^{4} 'village' could either belong here, or it could be related to Tai → chán$_3$ 廛. <> AA is prob. unrelated: Khmer *kruṅa* /krong/, OKhmer *kuruṅ* /kruŋ/ 'to cover, shelter, protect...manage, administer, rule, realm, kingdom, royal seat, capital' (-> Tai: S. *kruŋ* 'capital city').

xiàng$_4$ 項 (ɣåŋ^{B}) **LH** gɔŋ^{B}, **OCM** *grôŋʔ — **[T]** *ONW* ɣäŋ^{B}

'Neck' [Zuo], 'stretch the neck' [Shi 191], occurs in a few Mand. dialects: Chéngdū *^{53}tɕin-^{13}xaŋ* 頸項, Yángzhōu *^{42}tɕiŋ-^{55}xaŋ* (col.).

[E] ST: Chepang *groŋ-ko* 'stretch the neck' (downward to eat, of cattle); OBurm. *k^{h}loŋ*, WB *k^{h}yoŋ^{B} ~ k^{h}roŋ^{B}* 'throat' > PWa *kroŋ 'throat'. Similar looking words are → háng$_3$ 頏 'stretch the neck', → gāng$_1$ 亢 'neck'.

xiàng$_5$ 象 (zjaŋ^{B}) **LH** ziɑŋ^{B}, **OCM** *s-jaŋʔ ? or *ziɑŋ ?, OCB *zaŋʔ

'Elephant, ivory' [OB, Shi].

[T] *MTang* ziaŋ < *ONW* zaŋ — **[D]** M-Xiàmén lit. *ts^{h}iũ^{C2}*, col. *sioŋ^{C2}*

[E] Area word (Norman 1988: 19): PTai *ǰaŋ^{C}, Saek *saaŋ^{C2} < z-* 'elephant'; MK-PMonic *ciiŋ, PSemai *ciigŋ (-ii- instead of -a- is unexpected: Diffloth 1984: 63); TB-PLB *tsaŋ 'elephant' > WB *chaŋ^{A}* (-> Haka Chin *siaŋ* 'royal, governmental' from WB *siaŋ-pahraŋ* 'elephant lord', a royal title [F. K. Lehman 1963, *The Structure of Chin Society*, Illinois Stud. in Anthrop. no. 3: 39]); Lepcha *tyaŋ-mo*, Yidu Luoba *a^{33}-taŋ^{55}* [*Zang-Mian* no. 309].

Since it is hard to believe that people all over SE Asia and as far away as the Himalayan foothills would borrow a word for an indigenous animal from Northern China, the Chinese must have been the ones who borrowed this general area word like → hǔ$_1$ 虎 'tiger' and → sì$_4$ 兕 'wild buffalo'; the latter has the same rare OC initial as *xiàng*. Under these circumstances, *xiàng* prob. did not have an OC L-like initial. Furthermore, Boodberg (1937: 363) cites variants which may confirm a sibilant / affricate: an alternative word for 'elephant' *zāng-yá* 藏牙 [tsɑŋ-ŋa] (lit. 'bury tooth'), and a place name associated with elephants *qiāng-wú* 槍吾 [ts^{h}iɑŋ-ŋɑ] (lit. 'pointed tooth'?). *Xiàng* is not cognate to → yù$_{25}$ 豫 'elephant', nor is WT *glaŋ* 'ox' related which is cognate to → gāng$_5$ 犅.

xiàng$_6$ 象 (zjaŋ^B) **LH** ziɑŋ^B, **OCM** *s-jaŋʔ ?, OCB *zaŋʔ
'To interpret, translate' (a foreign language) [Liji, Huainan], *xiàng-xū* 象胥 'interpreter' [Zhouli] (Behr 2000). This word may be cognate to → xiáng$_4$ 詳 'explain in detail', in which case *xiàng* may be an endoactive derivation of *xiáng*. Behr considers this the s. w. as → xiàng$_7$ 像象 'outline, represent'.

xiàng$_7$ 像象 (zjaŋ^B) **LH** ziɑŋ^B, **OCM** *s-jaŋʔ
'To be / look like' 象 [Zuo], 'resemble' 像 [Xun] > 'image' [Huainan], 'to delineate, outline, appearance, symbols' 象 [Shu].
[T] *Sin Sukchu SR* zjaŋ (上); *MGZY* (zÿang >) zyang (上) [zjaŋ]; *ONW* zaŋ
[E] This word is usually considered the same as → xiàng$_5$ 象 'elephant, ivory' > '(ivory) image, resemble' (so Karlgren *GSR* 728), but ivory was not the only sculpture material. Although the OC initial in 'elephant' was probably not L-like, OCB *z- and *s-l- / *s-j- might have merged in the *Zuǒzhuàn;* if so, *xiàng* 'image' may possibly derive from a ST root *la: WT *lad-mo* 'imitation, to imitate, mimic', WT *lha* 'gods, image of a deity'; Lepcha *klan* 'similar' ⋇ *klan-lǎ* 'imitation' (Geilich 1994: 55, 123); JP *sum^{31}-la^{33}* 'picture, image', *num^{31}-la^{33}* 'ghost' (for correspondence of finals, see §6.5.2). Geilich adds WT *ldem* 'statue, idol', but connects the TB items with → sì$_3$ 似.

⋇ **yáng$_3$** 佯 (jiaŋ) **LH** jɑŋ, **OCM** *jaŋ or *laŋ
'To pretend, deceive' [Hanfei] (Geilich 1994: 283).
[E] -> Tai: S. *klɛɛŋ^3* 'to pretend' (Gòng Qúnhǔ *MZYW* 2, 2000).

⋇ **yàng$_3$** 樣 (jiaŋ^C)
'Appearance, looks, kind' [Tang], a late word; Chinese commentators imply cognation with *xiàng* 像象 (*ZWDCD* 5: 403; Behr 2000).
[T] *Sin Sukchu SR* jaŋ (去); *MGZY* yang (去) [jaŋ]

xiāo$_1$ 削 → **xuē**, **xuè**, **xiāo** 削

xiāo$_2$ 消銷 (sjäu) **LH** siau, **OCM** *siau — **[T]** *ONW* siau
'To melt, dissolve' 消 [Shi], 'annihilate, disappear' [Yi]; 'melt, reduce, diminish' 銷 [Li]; 'disperse' 肖 [Zhuang]; 'sleet' (= melting snow) 霄 [SW].

⋇ **xiāo** 捎 (sieu) **LH** seu, **OCM** *siâu
'To eliminate' [Zhouli].

[E] Etymology is uncertain. Perh. (1) WT *'džu-ba ~ žu-ba* 'to melt' (*STC* p. 52); WT and OC can perh. be reconciled if we assume a ST *zjau ~ *zju. (2) Alternatively, this word may belong to the wf → xiǎo$_1$ 小 'small'. (3) Or related to PTai *ɟuak^{D2L} 'to melt, dissolve' [Luo Yongxian *MKS* 27, 1997: 285]; for loss of final *-k* in CH, see §6.9; the initial correspondence has parallels; see → suǒ$_2$ 索.
[C] → shuò$_6$ 爍鑠 (śjak) LH *śiak* < *śiauk* 'melt' may belong to this wf (so Wáng Lì 1982: 222), but the initials are difficult to reconcile (MC *śj-* < *hl- or *hj- vs. sj-).

xiāo$_3$ 梟 (kieu) **LH** keu, **OCM** *kiû
'An owl-like bird' [Shi] is perh. related to → jiù$_4$ 舊 'owl'.

xiǎo$_1$ 小 (sjäu^B) **LH** siau^B, **OCM** prob. *siauʔ rather than *sauʔ
'Be small, little, young' [OB, BI, Shi], 'belittle' [Zuo].
[T] *Sin Sukchu SR* sjew (上), *PR* sjaw; *MGZY* sÿaw (上) [sjɛw]; *ONW* siau

⋇ **xiào** 肖 (sjäu^C) **LH** siau^C, **OCM** *siauh
'To resemble' (as son his father) [Lunyu].

[<] exoactive of *xiǎo* 小 (sjäu^B) (§4.3).

⋇ **qiào** 俏 (tsʰjäu^C) **LH** tsʰiau^C, **OCM** *C-siauh ?
'Similar' [Lie], derived from *xiào* 肖 (sjäu^C) (for the initial, see §5.9.1).

[C] Similar items are → shāo₁ 梢, → shǎo 少, → suǒ₅ 瑣, → xiāo₂ 消銷.

xiǎo₂ 曉 (xieu^B) **LH** heu^B, **OCM** *hiâuʔ ?
'Clarity' [Zhuang], 'clear, understand' [Xun], 'to know' is a Han period Chǔ dialect word [FY 1, 1]; it is the word for 'to know' (in some places 'to understand') in all modern dialects from Héféi south, except in Mǐn whose word corresponds to northern *zhī* 知 (e.g. Xiàmén *ti^A1*).

[T] *Sin Sukchu SR* xjew (上), *PR* xjaw; *MGZY* hÿaw (上) [xjɛw]

[E] Area word: MY: PYao *hiu³* 'to know'; MK-Viet. *hièu* 'to know'. Kadai lgs. have a word which looks similar: Be *hu²¹* 'to know, see', PHlai *ɣweɯ¹* 'to know, recognize' [Matisoff 1988c: 306]. A KT etymon with initial *r-* could possibly be related: PTai *ruo^C2 'to know' (in many Tai dial. *r- > h-, but not in the north within China), PKS *h-ro^C 'to know (how)' (Edmondson / Yang 1988). If all these words should be related, the ultimate source might have been KT with a voiceless *r-* (*rh-*) initial > *h-*. For another word where Tai has *hr-, but OC *h-, see → xuè₄, hù 㱿 'vomit'.

xiào₁ 笑 (sjäu^C) **LH** siau^C, S tsʰiau^C, **OCM** *siauh — [D] PMin *tsʰiau^C
'To laugh, smile' [Shi]. The composition of the graph shows that the word was understood as something like *s + ʔau. Cikoski derives *xiào* from → xiǎo₁ 小 'small', hence lit. 'belittle'.

xiào₂ 校 (ɣau^C, ɣau^A/B) **LH** gau^C, **OCM** *grâuh
'An enclosure': 'enclosure for animals' [Zhouli], 'school' [Meng]; probably not related to → jiào₆ 教.

xiào₃ 效 'verification' → **jiāo₁** 交; 'imitate' → **jiào₆** 教.

xiào₄ 肖 → **xiǎo₁** 小

xiào₅ 嘯 (sieu^C) **LH** seu^C, **OCM** *siûh
'To whistle' [Li], 'to croon' [Shi].

[E] Sound-symbolic area etymon: PTB *hyu ~ *huy 'whistle' [HPTB: 65], Chepang *syu-* 'blow through' (hand etc.). <> PMK *ksiəw (Shorto 1976: 1051), PMonic *k[r]siəw 'to whisper' [Diffloth 1984: 226], Khasi *pasiaw*.

⋇ **xiāo** 箾 (sieu) **LH** seu, **OCM** *siâu
'Pipe, flute' [Zuo] (Wáng Lì 1982: 222).

xiào₆ 斅 'teach' → **xué** 學

xiē₁ 脅 (xjɐp) **LH** hɨap, **OCM** *hap ? (from **hrap ?) — [T] *ONW* hap
'Sides of the body' [Shi], 'ribs' [Zuo].

[E] ST: JP *gə³¹-rep³¹* 'rib', Kanauri *hrip, Chepang *rip*, WT *rtsib < rhyip*.
This word belongs to a complex of stems which include → jiā₃ 夾 and items under → xié₁ 挾協. Voiceless aspiration in *xiē* suggests perh. a Rural variant (§1.3.1).

xiē₂ 楔 (siet) **LH** set, **OCM** *sêt (< *snet ?), OCK *siat
'A wedge' (inserted for fastening something) [Huainan] (put between the teeth of a corpse) [Li].

[E] AA: Khmer *sniata* /snìiət/ 'peg, pin,... wedge, ...' < derivation with nominalizing n-infix from *siata* /sìiət/ '... to stick into, insert, stop or block up, plug'. The choice of the phonetic is not clear (because of → niè₁₂ 齧 'gnaw'?).

xié$_1$ 挾協 (ɣiep) **LH** gep, **OCM** *gêp ?

'Grasp, hold' [Shi]; 'clasp under the arm, hold onto' 挾 [Meng] (also read QY *tsiep*); 'in harmony, together, conform' 協 [Shu].

ꭗ **jiá** 莢頰鋏 (kiep) **LH** kep, **OCM** *kêp

'Cheek, jowl' 頰 [Yi, Zuo] > 'pod of leguminous plant' 莢 [Zhouli] > ('pod-shaped'? >) 'sword' 鋏 [Guoce]. The Mand. pronunciation would correlate with MC *kap* < *kra/ep.

[C] Allofam → jié$_1$, jiā 梜 'chopsticks'.

[E] Four etyma have blended together:

(1) → jiā$_3$ 夾 *krep 'press between'.

(2) ST *kep ~ *kiap, reflected in OCM forms *gep, *kep (*tsep?) above. PTB *gyap (*HPTB:* 338) > WT *kʰyab-pa* 'be filled with, embrace, comprise' ꭗ *skyob-pa, bskyabs* 'protect, defend, preserve', *skyabs* 'protection, help' (*HST:* 71; Bodman 1980: 64), PLB *gyap > WB *kyap* 'tight, close, crowded', Lahu *cɔ̀ʔ* 'be narrow' (of an opening).

(3) ST *(C-)rap, as reflected in OC *krap above, possibly also → xiē$_1$ 脅 'ribs'. TB-Tiddim *gaap*^{R} < *raap* 'pod'.

(4) → jiā$_4$ 挾 *tsep.

xié$_2$ 頡 → **jí**$_4$ 佶

xié$_3$, **qiè** 瀱 → **jié**$_{12}$ 絜

xié$_4$ 諧 → **jiē**$_2$ 皆喈

xiě$_1$ 寫 (sja^B) **LH** sia^B, **OCM** *saʔ — **[T]** *ONW* sia

'To pour off' (a liquid') 寫 [Li] > 'cast' (metal) 寫 [Guoyu] > 'disburden, relief' (heart, grief) [Shi].

ꭗ **xiè** 瀉 (sja^C) **LH** sia^C, **OCM** *sah

'To drain off' [Zhouli].

[<] exoactive of *xiě* 寫 (§4.3.2), lit. 'make / let pour off'. This wf is not related to → shě$_2$ 舍捨 'let off'.

xiě$_2$ 寫 (sja^B) **LH** sia^B, **OCM** *saʔ (< *slaʔ or *sjaʔ ?)

'To depict' [Guoyu], 'to write' [Shiming, Hou Hanshu].

[E] Etymology not clear. Similar-looking words in other lgs. are unrelated; Lushai *ziak*^{F} / *ziaʔ*^{L} < *jak / jaks* 'to write, draw, inscribe, engrave'; Lushai *lehk'a* (cited from Geilich 1994: 184) is a Pali loan; WB *ca* 'writing, document' (<- CH *zì* 字?), JP *tʃa*^{33} 'paint, daub, dye' [Matisoff 1974: 161]. Alternatively, one may compare the word with AA-Khmer /saak/ 'to mark, brand, duplicate, copy' ꭗ /sak/ 'to tattoo'; the semantics would be parallel to → wén$_1$ 文.

xiè$_1$ 泄洩 (sjät, jiäi^C) **LH** siat, jas, **OCM** *slat(s) ? (or *j instead of *l?)

'To leak, reduce' 洩 [Zuo], 泄 [Guanzi] > 'spread, distribute' [Liji], 'be dispersed, relieved' (suffering) 泄 [Shi].

ꭗ **yì** 洩 (jiäi^C) **LH** jas, **OCM** *lats ? (or *j instead of *l?)

'Be dispersed' 洩 [Zuo].

[E] ST: Mru *yat* 'to leak, ooze'. The phonetic implies an OC L- or J-like initial, Mru's initial *y-* seems sometimes to correspond to PTB *l- (beside *j-; it certainly corresponds to PTB *l- in ya 'easy'), therefore the root initial in this group is not certain.

xiè$_2$ 紲絏韘 (sjät) **LH** siat, **OCM** *sat or *set

'To bind' 紲 [Zhouli] > 'bridle strap' 韘 [Yili], 'leading-string' (*GSR* 339m) [Li];

'rope, fetters' [Lunyu], 'reins' 紲 [Zuo]. Sagart (1999: 73) relates 'leading-string' to → yì₁₆ 抴 'to pull'.

xiè₃ 蟹 (ɣai^B) **LH** gɛ^B, **OCM** *grêʔ — PMin *he^B.
'Crab' [Li].
[E] ST: PTB *d-ka:y (*STC* no. 51) / or Benedict acc. to French (1983: 473) *d-gra:y > NNaga *gra:n, JP *tʃə⁵⁵-kʰan⁵¹*, Mikir *čehē* 'crab', Lushai *cha^L-kai^L < -kaih* 'crab', Tangkhul *khai* 'fish'; Adi *take.*

xiè₄ 屧 (siep) **LH** sep, **OCM** *sîp < *slip
'Bottom inlay in shoe, shoe' [Lü]. Perh. related to the wf → yè₄ 葉 'leaf'.

xiè₅ 楔 → **xiē₂** 楔

xiè₆ 解 → **jiě** 解 ; → **huì₃** 會

xiè₇, jiè 懈 → **jiě** 解

xiè₈-hòu 邂逅 → **jiě** 解

xiè₉ 駴 → **jiè₉** 戒誡

xiè₁₀ 榭 → **shí₉** 射

xiè₁₁ 瀉 → **xiě₁** 寫

xiè₁₂ 褻 → **ěr₇** 邇

xīn₁ 心 (sjəm) **LH** sim, **OCM** *səm, OCB *sjəm
'Heart > mind' [Shi, Shu], 'emotions' (between people) [Shi]; > 'center' [Liji].
[T] *Sin Sukchu SR* sim (平), *PR, LR* sin; *MGZY* sim (平) [sim]; *ONW* sim.
[D] PMin *sim; Y-Guǎngzhōu ⁵⁵*sɐm^A1*
[E] ST: PTB *sam (*STC:* 51) or *səm (*STC:* 126) > Bahing *sam* 'breath, life'; Limbu *sam* 'soul'; Thakali *sam* 'heart', WT *sem(s)* 'soul, spirit, mind' ⋈ *sem(s)-pa, bsams* 'to think' ⋈ *bsams* 'thought', Lepcha *a-sŏm* 'spirit, breath', WB *ə-sam* 'sound, voice' (*STC:* 183 n. 482; *HST:* 93). A ST synonym is → rén₂ 仁.
MK has a similar word: PMK *-TSəm 'heart' [Ferlus *MKS* 7, 1978: 18], PPalaung *se:m* 'breath, heart, mind', Khmer *ŋhaəm*, Semai *ləhəm*, Wa-Lawa-Bulang *rhom 'heart, mind'. However, the *s-* may be secondary.

xīn₂ 辛 (sjen) **LH** sin, **OCM** *sin
'Bitter, pungent > painful' [Shu].
[T] *Sin Sukchu SR* sin (平); *MGZY* sin (平) [sin]; *ONW* sin.
[E] ST: PTB *m-sin (*STC* no. 234) > WT *mčʰin* 'liver', Kanauri *śin,* Chepang *sinh,* Miri *əśin,* Lushai *tʰin^L* 'liver, heart', WB *ə-sañ^B* 'liver', PL *(ʃ-)sin, JP *mə³¹-sin³¹* 'mind' (i.e. seat of thought and emotions), 'courage' (Benedict *HJAS* 4, 1939: 225; *HST:* 44), Dulong *pə̆çīn* 'heart, liver' [LaPolla, *LTBA* 24.2: 19].

xīn₃ 新 (sjen) **LH** sin, **OCM** *sin
'New, renew' [Shi].
[T] *Sin Sukchu SR* sin (平); *MGZY* sin (平) [sin]; *ONW* sin
[E] ST: PLB *C-šik or *V-šik: WB *sac* 'new'. This word may belong to the ST stem *siŋ 'alive, fresh, green' and may hence be related to → qīng₁ 青 'green' as well as → xīn₄ 薪 'wood'.

xīn₄ 薪 (sjen) **LH** sin, **OCM** *sin
'Firewood' [Shi].

[E] ST: PTB *siŋ (*STC* no. 233) > WT *šiŋ* 'tree, wood', Lepcha *śaŋ* 'firewood', Chepang *siŋʔ* 'wood, timber, tree', PLB *sik ~ *siŋ 'tree, wood' > WB *sac* (*STC* no. 233; *HST:* 161), Lushai $t^hiŋ^R$ 'tree, wood, firewood, fuel', Mru *chiŋ* 'tree' [Löffler 1966: 123]. This word may belong to the ST stem *siŋ 'alive, fresh, green' and may hence be related to → $qīng_1$ 青 'green' as well as → $xīn_3$ 新 'new, renew'.

$xīn_5$ 欣 (xjən) **LH** hɨn, **OCM** *hən
'To rejoice, make merry' [Shi] is prob. cognate to → $xǐ_4$ 喜.

xín 尋燖 (zjəm) **LH** zim, **OCM** *s-ləm — **[T]** *ONW* zim
'To warm up' 尋 [Guoyu] > 'sacrifice of boiled meat' 燖 [Li], perh. also 'large boiler' 鬵 [Shi] which is also read **qián** (QYS *dzjäm*).
[E] ST: PTB *lum^A 'warm' (*STC* no. 381) > WT *gtum-po* < *gl̥um* 'heat' (in meditation), *gtum-pa* 'ferocity, rage'; WB *lum* 'warm' ꭗ *hlum* 'warm oneself by fire' ꭗ $hlum^C$ 'heat again, warm over'; PL *lum¹; JP lum^{33} 'warm' ꭗ ma^{31}-lum^{33} 'to simmer, heat' ꭗ $ʃa^{31}$-lum^{33} 'to heat, warm' (food), Dimasa *lim* ~ *lum* 'be hot, have fever'.
Labial dissimilation of the final nasal rather than the vowel perh. took place in → $sūn_2$ 飧 'cooked rice'; this could also be the case in → $róng_4$ 融 'to heat'. Perh. → $xián_{12}$ 燅 may be related, yet TB distinguishes *-lam from *-lum.

$xìn_1$ 信 ($sjen^C$) **LH** sin^C, **OCM** *sin ! (OCB *snins)
'To believe, trust, faithfulness, truth' [Shi] > ('something written entrusted to an envoy' 書信:) 'letter' [Six Dyn.] (Wáng Lì 1958: 547). *Shījīng* rimes indicate OC tone A (Mattos 1971: 309). This is perh. the s. w. as next.
[T] *Sin Sukchu SR* sin (去); *MGZY* sin (去) [sin]; *ONW* sin
= **xùn** 訊 ($sjen^C$) **LH** sin^C 'to interrogate, question, inquire' [Shi] (< 'find the truth').
ꭗ **xún** 恂洵 (sjuen) **LH** suin, **OCM** *swin ?
'Sincere, certainly' 恂洵 [Shi] > 'to believe' 恂 [Lie].
[E] These words are prob. derived from → $yǔn_1$ 允 *win 'trust, be true, sincere'. For the loss of medial *w in *xìn*, see §10.2.1.

$xìn_2$ 信 'staying one more night' → **$yǐn_2$** 引

$xīng_1$ 狌 (sjäŋ) **LH** sieŋ, **OCM** *seŋ
'Weasel' [Zhuang].
[E] ST: PTB *sreŋ (*HPTB:* 77), WT *sre(ŋ) > *sre-moŋ, sre-mo* 'weasel', Lepcha *să-myóŋ* 'marmot', Mikir *iŋren* < *m-ren* 'mongoose', WB $hrañ^C$ 'squirrel' (*STC:* 79, 171). A different etymon is probably Lushai t^he^L-$hlei^R$ 'squirrel', Mikir $karle^H$ 'id.'. We should expect a trace of the ST *r in the MC syllable.

$xīng_2$ 星 (sieŋ) **LH** seŋ, S $ts^heŋ$, **OCM** *sêŋ — **[T]** *MTang* sieŋ < sɨŋ, *ONW* sèŋ
'Star' [OB, Shi].
[D] Y-Guǎngzhōu $^{55}sɛŋ^{A1}$, Táishān $^{33}ɬen^{A1}$, Enpíng $^{35}siaŋ^{A1}$; PMin *$ts^haŋ$ ~ *seŋ: Xiàmén col. $ts^hĩ^{A1}$ ~ san^{A1}, lit. $siŋ^{A1}$
[E] Perh. cognate to → $qīng_2$ 清 'clear'. TB-PKiranti *saŋ 'star, ray' (*CVST* 4: 99) is a derivation from a parallel ST root (see → $qīng_2$ 清).
ꭗ **qíng** 星 (dzjäŋ) **LH** dzieŋ, **OCM** *dzeŋ, OCB *ɦtshjeŋ
'Weather clearing during the night' [Shi] is perh. a derivation from 'star': < 'become starry' (so *SW*); this word is written ['night' + phonetic] as late as *SW*, but takes on the meaning of 'clearing with the sun coming out' only in post-classical literature, since then written 晴 [Yupian]. Alternatively, this word may be directly derived from → $qīng_2$ 清 'clear' (so Baxter 1992: 219).

xīng₃ 猩 (sieŋ) **LH** seŋ, **OCM** *sêŋ
'To bark' (dog) [SW]. Perhaps ST: KN-Liangmei *tʰaŋ*, Zemei *¹ke-⁵tʰaŋ* 'to bark' [Weidert 1987: 191]. For the vowels, see §11.1.3; for the initials, see §12.3 Lushai.

xīng₄ 腥 (sieŋ) **LH** seŋ, **OCM** *sêŋ — **[T]** *MTang* sieŋ < sɨŋ, *ONW* sėŋ
'Raw meat' [Lunyu], 'offensive smell' [Shu].
[E] This word belongs to a ST *saŋ ~ *s(r)iŋ set (§11.1.3) which is parallel to a ST *haŋ ~ *hiŋ pair, see Table X-1 under → xiāng₂ 香 for an overview.
ST *se/iŋ: JP *siŋ³³* 'smell, scent, odor of fresh, raw food' (Benedict 1940: 105 no. 17), Chepang *səyŋ-* 'emit smell, odor, be rotten', Lepcha *mŭŋ-šiŋ*, Rawang *pušë:ŋ* 'stench' [Bodman ICSTLL 1987: 12].
~ PTB *sriŋ: NNaga *sriŋ 'to smell', Lushai *ṭeeŋ^L / ṭeen^L < treeŋh* 'ill-smelling' seem to represent a separate root; Lushai vowel shows that this stem is unrelated to → shēng₂ 生 'fresh'.
~ PTB *saŋ: WB *saŋ^B* 'emit pleasant odor', Lushai *tʰaaŋ^R / tʰaan^L* 'have smell or odor like raw flesh' (Peiros / Starostin 1996, IV: 101), *tʰaŋ^L / tʰan^F* 'be greasy, oily'.

xīng₅ 騂 → **qiàn₃** 倩綪

xīng₆ 興 (xjəŋ) **LH** hɨŋ, **OCM** *həŋ — **[T]** *ONW* hiŋ
'To raise, start, prosper, rise' [BI, Shi]. Bodman (1980: 185) considers this a doublet of *shēng* 升 (under → chéng₃ 乘). Possibly related to Tibeto-Burman: Chepang *hiŋ-* 'stand up, set out for'.

xīng₇ 馨 (xieŋ) **LH** heŋ, **OCM** *hêŋ
'Be fragrant' (of food, spices, offerings) [Shi]. This word and → xiāng₂ 香 'fragrance' (cognate acc. to Wáng Lì 1982: 323) are ST *haŋ ~ *hiŋ variants, furthermore there is the ST *saŋ ~ *siŋ pair, see under → xiāng₂ 香 for an overview.
[E] ST *hiŋ: Lushai *hiiŋ^H / hiin^L* 'be sour, nasty smelling, stinking' (of stale food, dirty people, etc.).

xíng₁ 行 (ɣɐŋ) **LH** gaŋ, **OCM** *grâŋ
'To go, travel, act, practice, a march, road, way, manner' [BI, Shi].
[T] *Sin Sukchu SR* ɣiŋ (平); *MGZY* Hÿing (平) [ɣjiŋ]; *ONW* ɣëŋ
[D] This is still the Mǐn word for 'to go, walk': M-Xiàmén *kiã^{A2}*

ꭗ **xìng** 行 (ɣɐŋ^C) **LH** gaŋ^C, **OCM** *grâŋh
'To go on an inspection tour' [BI?, Zuo, Li], 'action' [Yi].

ꭗ **gēng** 庚 (kɐŋ) **LH** kaŋ, **OCM** *krâŋ
'Road' [Zuo]; 'to continue, succeed' (also MC *kɐŋ^C*) [Shu].

ꭗ **háng** 行 (ɣâŋ) **LH** gɑŋ, **OCM** *gâŋ
'Row, rank' [Shi] (Karlgren 1956: 12). The absence of OC medial *r is unexplained.

[E] Perh. related to AA: Khmer *raṅa* /rɔɔŋ/ 'way, line, row, or bed' (of vegetables), 'gutter'. Alternatively, perh. related to → gé₄ 格 'to go, come', → lù₅ 路 'road'. Syn. → zǒu 走.

xíng₂ 刑形 (ɣieŋ) **LH** geŋ, **OCM** *gêŋ
'Be a model, example, imitate' vb., n. [BI, Shi] > 'punishment, punish' 刑 [Shu]; > 'conform to' [Zuo] > 'form, shape' [Yi], 'appearance' [Meng], 'to appear, be manifested' 形 [Li].
[T] *Sin Sukchu SR* ɣiŋ (平); *MGZY* Hÿing (平) [ɣjiŋ]; *MTang* ɣieŋ < ɣɨŋ, *ONW* ɣėŋ
[E] Prob. ST *kriŋ: JP *kʰriŋ³¹-bo⁵⁵* 'to describe', WB *ə-kyañ^B* 'appearance', *krañ^B* 'bear, carry, conduct, perform'. However, MC has no trace of a medial *r.

xíng₃ 陘 → **jīng₄** 經

xǐng₁ 擤 (xjəŋ^C) **LH** hɨŋ^C, **OCM** *həŋh
'To blow one's nose' can be compared to Tai: S. *saŋ^B1* which has been absorbed into Yuè dialects: Guǎngzhōu *saŋ^C1* (Yue Hashimoto *CAAAL* 6, 1976: 2).

xǐng₂ 醒 → **qīng₂** 清

xìng₁ 腥 (sieŋ^C) **LH** seŋ^C, **OCM** *sêŋh — **[T]** *MTang* sieŋ < sɨŋ, *ONW* sėŋ
'Grease' [Zhouli].
[E] ST *se/aŋ: Lushai *tʰaŋ^L / tʰan^F* 'be greasy, oily'. See §11.1.3 for the vocalism.

xìng₂ 性姓 (sjäŋ^C) **LH** sieŋ^C, **OCM** *seŋ > *seŋh
('What is inborn':) 'nature' 性 [BI, Shi] > 'surname, clan name' (< 'birth') 姓 [Shi], 'offspring' [Zuo] (Pulleyblank *EC* 25, 2000: 12). 'Surname' 姓 has tone A in older parts of *Shījīng* (Mattos 1971: 309).
[T] *Sin Sukchu SR* siŋ (去); *MGZY* sing (去) [siŋ]; *ONW* sieŋ
[E] ST: this word belongs to the ST *siŋ stem of the groups listed under → shēng₂ 生 and is therefore directly related to the items under → qīng₁ 青, but only indirectly cognate to *shēng* (parallel stem ST *sriŋ). Alternatively, the medial *r of *shēng* might have been felt to be a causative infix and was thus dropped in allofams. The JP word *n^55-teŋ^51* 'name' could possibly be related, but there are phonological difficulties.

xìng₃, jìng 脛 (ɣieŋ^C) **LH** geŋ^C, **OCM** *gêŋh
'Leg, shank' [Lun].
[E] ST: PTB *keŋ ⋇ *r-kaŋ 'leg, stalk' (*HPTB:* 283) > Mikir *keŋ^L* 'foot, leg'. This etymon and the wf → kēng₂ 桱 *khreŋ as well as → tǐng₃ 梃, *dìng* 鋌 *lêŋ tend to converge. For an overview, see Table K-2 (→ kēng₂ 桱).

xiōng₁ 兄 (xjwɐŋ) **LH** hyaŋ, **OCM** *hwaŋ ?
'Older brother' [BI, Shi].
[T] *Sin Sukchu SR* xjujŋ, xjuŋ (平), *LR* xjuŋ; *MGZY* (Hÿing >) hÿing (平) [xjiŋ]
[E] Etymology not clear. A TB cognate could be PLB *ʔwyik 'elder sibling / cousin' > WB *ac* [Matisoff *D. of Lahu:* 213]. Alternatively, *STC* (p. 174 n. 463; n. 78) suggests a connection with PTB *bwaŋ 'uncle' (father's brother), but see → bó₁ 伯.

xiōng₂ 凶 'inauspicious' → **xiōng₃** 兇

xiōng₃ 兇 (xjwoŋ) **LH** hɨoŋ, **OCM** *hoŋ — **[T]** *ONW* huoŋ
'To fear' 兇 [Zuo], 凶 [Guoyu]. This word may be the same as **xiōng** 凶 'be inauspicious, baleful, bad' [BI, Shi] (< 'frightening'?). Some words have a similar rime: → kǒng₂ 恐 'to fear'; → sǒng₁ 聳慫悚.

xiōng₄ 匈 (xjwoŋ) **LH** hɨoŋ, **OCM** *hoŋ ?
'Breast', 'chest' [Meng].
[E] Etymology not clear. MC *x-* can occasionally derive from a voiceless *r (§5.6), hence it is possibly an AA word: MK-Khmer /truuŋ/, OKhmer /drooŋ/ 'ribcage, chest, breast' < derivative of /-ruuŋ/ 'to shield, protect', related to → lóng₅ 籠 'cage'. Perh. TB-Chepang *ruŋ?* 'breastbone, center of chest' could be connected. Khmer -> Tai: S. *drŏṅ*, pronounced *suaŋ^1* 'breast, chest' [Maspero 1912: 86].

xiōng₅ 訩 (xjwoŋ) **LH** hɨoŋ, **OCM** *hoŋ
'Litigate, discord' [Shi]; 'shout, bawl' 匈 [Xun].
[E] ? ST: perh. cognate to WT *gšuŋ-ba* 'to rebuke, reproach'; both WT and CH may derive from a hypothetical *hjuŋ.

[C] Perh. related to → hòng₁ 鬨; prob. unrelated to → sòng₂ 訟.

xiōng₆ 洶 → **róng₃** 溶

xióng₁ 雄 (juŋ 3) **LH** wuŋ, **OCM** *wəŋ

'Male' of birds and small animals [Shi], later also larger animals; opposite → cī 雌 'female'. Etymology not clear.

xióng₂ 熊 (juŋ) **LH** wəm, **OCM** *wəm

'A bear' [Shi]. Acc. to *SW*, *yán* 炎 OCM *wam is phonetic; if true, *yán* would confirm the final *-m in *xióng*, and *xióng* the initial *w- in *yán*.

[T] *Sin Sukchu SR* ɣjuŋ (平); *MGZY* Hÿung (平) [ɣjuŋ]; *ONW* ɣuəm?? > ɣuŋ (?) > huŋ

[D] The OC final *-m is preserved in Mǐn dialects: Amoy *him*^{A2}, Fú'ān *hem*^{A2}, Yǒng'ān *ham*^{A2} 'bear'.

[E] ST: PTB *d-wam > WT *dom* 'bear', Tebor *hom*, Jiarong *twŏm*; PL *k-d-wam, WB *(wak-) wam*; Bahing *wam*; Digaro *təham ~ təhum* (*HST:* 40); Kuki-Naga *d-wam, Lushai *sa*^{L}-*vɔm*^{H}; Mru *tom*. Other lgs. in East Asia have words which look similar: Middle Korean *kwom*, Old Japanese *kuma* (Miyake 1997: 197), Ainu *kamuy* 'bear'; on Taiwan AN languages include *cumai / cumay*. Note also AA: PMonic *kmum 'Himalayan black bear'.

xiǒng 煦 → **xù₄** 旭

xiòng 迥 → **jiǒng₂** 泂迥

xiū₁ 休 (xjəu) **LH** xu, **OCM** *hu

'To rest' [Shi].

= **xiū** 'Shade of a tree' 庥 [EY], 茠 [Huainan], 休 [Hanshu] > 'protection' (e.g. 'Heaven's protection') 休 [Shi].

[E] The original meaning may have been 'shade' > 'to shade oneself', i.e. 'rest in the shade' > 'rest' (Wáng Lì 1982: 230; Qiu Xigui 2000: 210).

xiū₂ 庥茠 → **xiū₁** 休

xiū₃ 羞 (sjəu) **LH** siu, **OCM** *snu

'Shame' [Shu], 'diffidence' [Zuo], Mand. 'shy, bashful'.

ꭗ **niǔ** 忸 (ṇjuk) **LH** ṇuk, **OCM** *nruk <*r-nuk ?

'Disgrace, ashamed' [Meng], Mand. 'blushing, bashful'.

ꭗ **rǔ, rù** 辱 (ńźjwok) **LH** ńok, **OCM** *nok

'Disgrace' [Shi], 'condescend' [Zuo].

[E] The vacillation between pre-initial *s- and *r- is also observed in TB wfs (§5.3). The role of the final *-k in *niǔ* is not clear; alternatively, *xiū* may be a tone A derivation from a root in final *-k to form a noun (§3.1). Pulleyblank (1973: 121) relates this wf to other words meaning 'shame' with initial *n- but different rimes: → chǐ₅ 恥; → ní₃ 怩 (which, however, is prob. unrelated). Eberhard (1967: 12) derives the notion 'shame' from 'dirty'.

xiū₄ 羞 (sjəu) **LH** siu, **OCM** *snu

'To nourish' [Shu], 'viands' [Zuo].

[E] Prob. related to TB-JP *noʔ*^{31} < *nok*^{31} 'to eat'; WT *ñod-pa* 'food' (lex.); cf. → rú₃ 茹 'to swallow', in dialects 'eat'. Syn. → yù₂₂ 育毓鬻 → chù₄, xù 畜.

xiū₅ 修 (sjəu) **LH** siu, **OCM** *su or *siu? < *sliu? — [T] *ONW* su

'To repair, cultivate, put in order' [Shi], 'adorn' [Li].

[<] s-caus. of *lju (§5.2.1).

⨳ **tiáo** 修 (dieu) **LH** deu, **OCM** *liû — **[T]** *MTang* diau, *ONW* dèu
'Orderly' [Shu], 'paragraph' [Guoce] (Sagart 1999: 70).

xiū$_6$ 脩 'long' → **yōu**$_2$ 悠

xiū$_7$ 脩 'dried' → **sù**$_8$ 肅鱐

xiū$_8$ 溲 → **xiǔ**$_2$ 糔溲

xiǔ$_1$ 朽 → **chǒu**$_2$ 醜

xiǔ$_2$ 糔溲 (ṣjəu^B) **LH** ṣu^B, **OCM** *sruʔ
'To wash' 糔 [Li]; 'moisten, wash, soak' 溲 [Li].

~ **xiǔ** 滫 (sjəu^B) **LH** siu^B, **OCM** *suʔ
'Wash rice' [Li], 'urinate' 滫 [Xun]. <> Tai: S. *saau*^{A2} < *zau^A 'to wash and clean' (rice). Alternatively, this word without OC medial *r may be a s-causative derivation from → yóu$_{10}$ 滺油 'flow', hence lit. 'let water flow over' > 'wash', 'let water flow' > 'urinate'.

⨳ **xiū** 溲 (ṣjəu) **LH** ṣu, **OCM** *sru
'To urinate' [Guoyu] is perh. a euphemism.

⨳ **sòu** 漱 (səu^C, ṣjəu^C) **LH** ṣu^C, **OCM** *srukh ?
'To wash' 漱 [Li].

[E] AA: Khmer *sroc* /srooc/ 'to water, irrigate, sprinkle, bathe, shower'; PNBahnaric *_raw 'wash', *rŭh 'wash clothes', P-Hrê-Sedang *srew 'wash' [K. Smith 1972: 58]. For absence of final consonant in OC, see §6.9.

xiǔ$_3$ 滫 → **xiǔ**$_2$ 糔溲

xiù$_1$ 秀 (sjəu) **LH** siu^C, **OCM** *suh (prob. < *swuh), OCB *sljus
'To flower and set ears' (grain) [Shi], 'to flower' [Lunyu], 'flourishing, beautiful' [Zuozhuan]. Sagart (1999: 72) considers this the caus. of → yòu$_7$ 褎 (jiəu^C) (§5.2.1) .
[T] *Sin Sukchu SR* siw (去); *MGZY* siw (去) [siw]
[E] ST: TB-Chepang *syu-* 'to prosper, flourish', Lushai vuul^H 'be in full bloom' (as flowers); the MC lack of a trace of a ST final *-l is unexplained; cf. §7.7.5. An alternative connection with MK: Khmer *lɔ̆ah* 'to blossom', PVM *m-loh 'to blossom' may also be possible, but a plausible ST etymology is preferable.

xiù$_2$ 袖 → **zhòu**$_3$ 冑

xiù$_3$ 嗅 → **chōu**$_3$ 犨

xiù$_4$ 褎 'sleeve' → **zhòu**$_3$ 冑

xū$_1$ 胥 (sjwo) **LH** sia, **OCM** *sa
'Together, mutually, each other' [Shi] is pre-classical for the classical allofam → xiāng$_1$ 相 (Pulleyblank 1962: 233; 1995: 137) > 'to aid, assist' [BI, Guan] > ? 'foreman' in charge of ten men [BI].
[E] Acc. to FY 6, *xū* is a Wú-Yuè dial. word for 'assist', which is prob. derived from 'mutual' as in the parallel and cognate wf → xiāng$_1$ 相 (Pulleyblank 1962: 233). The Han period (FY) association with the language of Wú and Yuè (Viet) seems to strengthen the possibility that this is originally a MK etymon: Pearic *sa:* 'each other'. However, *xū* is well attested as a CH word already in *Shījīng*.
[C] A derivation is perh. → xǔ$_2$ 諝.

xū$_2$ 虛 (xjwo) **LH** hɨa, **OCM** *ha
'Empty, modest' [Li]. In Wú dialects: Wēnlíng lit. ^{51}*xy*^{A} ~ col. ^{33}*he*^{A} (Lǐ Róng *FY*

1980: 140). Perh. related is → $qū_5$ 虛墟 in the sense of 'empty area, wasteland, ruin-mound' (so Karlgren 1956: 18).
[T] *Sin Sukchu SR* xy (平); *MGZY* hÿu (平) [xy]; *MTang* hy, *ONW* hø < hio ?

$xū_3$ 墟 (xjwo)
A Yuè dialect word: Guǎngzhōu ^{55}*hœy*^{A1}, Táishān *hui*^{21} 'seasonal market'. This word occurs also in some Tai lgs., e.g., Yay (Dioi) *hɯ*^{A1} 'market' (Luo Yongxian *MKS* 27, 1997: 284).

$xū_4$ 須鬚 (sju) **LH** sio, S tsʰio, **OCM** *sno.
'Beard of chin' 須 [Yi], 鬚 [Zuo]. This word survives in Yuè and Mǐn dialects, elsewhere it has been replaced by húzi 鬍子.
[T] *Sin S. SR* sy (平); *MGZY* sÿu (平) [sy]; *MTang* sy, *ONW* suo
[D] PMin *tsʰiu^{A1} ~ *siu^{A1}
[E] This word appears to be ST *sno 'mouth' with a semantic shift from 'mouth' to its defining edge and surrounding area: PTB *sno(w) ~ *sno(t) (Benedict *LTBA* 1976: 16) (perh. 'a cavernous opening') > WT *snod* 'vessel', *bu-snod* 'womb', Motuo Monpa *no-waŋ* 'mouth', Kanauri *sto* 'face', Lepcha (a-)so 'vessel for body-fluid' [*HPTB:* 107], WB *hnut* (see → $huì_{10}$ 顪喙) 'mouth, womb'; Pwo, Sgaw Karen *noʔ* 'mouth' (*STC:* 144f); Achang *n̥ot*^{55}*-mui*^{31} 'beard' ('mouth hair'), Leqi *nuat*^{55}*-mə*^{33}; Jiarong *tə ʃnos* 'lips'. In light of the ST etymology, *xū* has prob. no connection with PAA *ʃnu* 'hair': MK- Khasi *ʃɲuʔ* 'hair' (*ɲ* is infix), Khmer /s-ʔ/, Palaungic *s- > h-: Lawa *haɨk* 'hair'.
[C] *Xū* is prob. distantly related to → $huì_{10}$ 顪喙, perh. also to → $xǔ_4$ 盨. Pulleyblank (*EC* 16, 1991: 43) relates it to → $ér_1$ 而 'whiskers'.

$xū_5$ 須需 (sju) **LH** sio, S tsʰio, **OCM** *sno
'To wait' 須 [Shi], 'tarry' 需 [Zuo] is prob. a causative derivation from → $rú_4$ 懦臑, lit. 'make (time) pliant = stretch (time)', the semantic development is parallel to WB *nwai* (under → ruǎn 耎軟).

$xū_6$ 嬃 (sju) **LH** sio, **OCM** *sno
'Elder sister' [Chuci] may belong to the TB words for 'mother, woman' (cited under → $rǔ_3$ 乳 'breast, milk') (so *CVST* 2: 38). *Xū* would be difficult to reconcile phonologically with WT *sru-mo* 'mother's sister' (as in *STC:* 171 n. 457; *HST:* 38).

xú 徐 → **$yù_{25}$** 豫

$xǔ_1$ 湑 (sjwo$^{A/B}$) **LH** ṣɑ$^{(B)}$?, **OCM** *sra(ʔ) ?
'Be dripping' (dew), 'flowing, to strain' (spirits) (also read *shū* 釃 QY *ṣjwo*^{A} = *GSR* 878h) [Shi], 'abundant, luxuriant' [Shi], 'grain ripe so as to drop its kernels' 稰 [Li]; ('ripe grain' [?]:) 'sacrificial grain' 糈 [Chuci] (also read *shǔ* QYS *ṣjwo*^{B}).
[E] AA: Khmer *sra'ka* /srɑk/ intr. 'to drop, drip, trickle'; for CH tone B, see §3.2.2. This looks like the iterative s-prefix form (§5.2.3) of the next item whose late appearance, as well as the etymology of *xǔ*, suggest a back formation:
⋇ **lǜ** 濾 (ljwo^{C}) **LH** liɑ^{C} 'to drip' [Yupian], a late character (Wáng Lì 1982: 152). Allofam → $lù_8$ 露 'dew', ultimately → $luò_7$ 落 'fall'. Unrelated to → $shī_{12}$ 釃 (ṣie).

$xǔ_2$ 諝 (sjwo^{B}) **LH** siɑ^{B}, **OCM** *saʔ
'To discriminate, knowledge' (so Zhèng Xuán) [Huainan, Zhouli].
[E] Perh. derived from → $xū_1$ 胥 'assist' (Behr 2000) with endoactive tone B, perh. under the influence of, and parallel to, xiǎng 想 'think' in the wf → $xiāng_1$ 相.

$xǔ_3$ 煦 → **$xù_4$** 旭

xǔ$_4$ 盨 (sju^B) **LH** sio^B, **OCM** *snoʔ (perh. < **snotʔ).
'A kind of ritual vessel' [BI], an object which appears only during the Mid-Western Zhou period as a hybrid of two earlier forms (the *guǐ* 簋 and the lidded *fāngdǐng* 方鼎) (Fitzgerald-Huber 2003, The X Gong Xu, Dartmouth College, NH: 37).
[E] ? ST: TB-Lushai *no^H*, Mru *no* 'cup' [Löffler 1966: 130], note also WT *snod* 'vessel' which would connect xǔ with → xū$_4$ 須鬚 'beard'.

xù$_1$ 序 (zjwo^B) **LH** ziɑ^B, **OCM** *s-laʔ
'School' [Meng] has two possible etymologies: (1) it is the same word as 'north-south (east-west) running walls at sides of a hall, space or galleries close to such walls' [Shi] (under → xù$_2$ 序敘緒) (Wáng Lì 1982: 170). (2) It is an allofam of → xiáng$_2$ 庠 'school' (Pulleyblank 1962: 233) which is perh. derived from → yáng$_7$ 揚 'rise, raise'. In fact, *xù* may be parallel to *xiáng* in being derived from → yú$_{11}$ 舁譽 'to lift'. It must be pure coincidence that Modern Khmer 'school' *səlaa* is nearly identical to OC.

xù$_2$ 序敘緒 (zjwo^B) **LH** ziɑ^B, **OCM** *s-laʔ
'Continue, remains' 緒 [Zhuang]; 'arrange in order, continue, succeed' [Shi], 'north-south (or east-west) running walls at sides of a hall, space or galleries close to such walls' [Shi], 'order, sequence' 序 [Mand.]; 敍 [Shi, Shu] > 'line of work, work' (which is continued) 緒 [Shi]; perh. → xù$_1$ 序 'school' is the same word, i.e. place along the galleries. (*SW* and the Chinese commentaries say 'east-west running walls', Karlgren in *GSR* 83h says 'north-south running walls').
Based on his theories, Pulleyblank (1973: 120) finds cognates of *xù* in different directions: *sì* 嗣 (zɨ^C) 'continue, succeed, inherit' (under → yí$_2$ 貽詒), and **xù** 續 (zjwok) *ONW* zuok, LH *ziok* 'continue' [Shi].
[C] A paronym is → yì$_{35}$ 繹 [jak ~ jɑk] *lak.

xù$_3$ 卹 (sjuet) **LH** suit, **OCM** *sut ?
'To rub, brush' [Li]. The phonetic → xuè$_1$ 血 implies an OC *swit, but the likely cognate → sāo$_1$ 搔 *su 'to scratch' as well as the TB cognate require an OC *sut. Since *Lǐjì* is a relatively late text, OC *swit and *sut may already have merged into *suit and have made the phonetic suitable for this word.
[E] ST: PLB *sut 'wipe, sweep' [Matisoff, *Variational Semantics*] > WB *sut* 'wipe', Lahu *šìʔ* < *sit.

xù$_4$ 旭 belongs to a root *ho
'Brilliance of the rising sun' [Shi] has several readings, hence the etymology is not clear: (1) It seems to write the word also written *xǔ* 煦昫 [hɨo$^{B/C}$] 'to warm' (as the rising sun). (2) The reading (xjwok) [hɨok] goes with a meaning 'noisy' as in *xióng-xióng xù-xù* 洶洶旭旭 LH *hɨoŋ-hɨoŋ hɨok-hɨok* [Han: Yáng Xióng], from there the reading may have extended to the graph in general, including 'rising sun'. (3) The reading LH *hu^B*, glossed in *SW* as *hǎo* 好 [hou^B] < *hûʔ, is possibly inspired by the phonetic *jiǔ* 九 [ku^B] *kuʔ.

ⳤ **xǔ** 煦 (xju$^{B/C}$) **LH** hɨo$^{B/C}$, **OCM** *hoʔ/h
'To warm' (with breath or air, e.g. Heaven's warm breeze to make things grow) tr. [Liji] which is what *SW* apparently means by *zhēng* 烝 'to steam'; also *xù* 昫 'incubate eggs'. See also → xù$_4$ 旭.

ⳤ **xiǒng** 煦 (xjwoŋ^B) **LH** hɨoŋ^B, **OCM** *hoŋʔ
'Become warm, balmy' (of the rising sun) [Shi], also read *xǔ* 煦 (xju$^{B/C}$); the reading *xiǒng* is listed in the late *JY*, but final *-ŋ* agrees with the semantics:

[<] terminative *-ŋ* of *xǔ* 煦 (xju$^{B/C}$) (§6.5.1), 'become' warm thanks to the rising sun.

ж **xuǎn** 烜 (xjwɐn^{B}) **LH** hyɑn^{B}, **OCM** *hwanʔ or *honʔ ?

'To sun, dry in the sun' [Yi], 'sunlight' [Zhouli]. The *QY* reading *xjwie^{B}* 'sunlight' prob. belongs to the syn. → huī$_2$ 煇輝暉.

ж **xuān** 煖 (xjwɐn) **LH** hyɑn, **OCM** *hwan

'Warm' [Li]. This word is not related to → nuǎn 煖.

[E] All the above items prob. belong to the same root *ho or perh. *hwo 'warm in the sun'; the latter would logically result in the OC / MC forms above; *hwon would have to dissimilate to OC *hwan. This wf coalesces partially with → yù$_{20}$, yǔ 嫗, perh. together they belong to a single wf.

xù$_5$ 頊 (xjwok) **LH** hɨok, **OCM** *hŋok — **[T]** *ONW* huok

'Disconcerted' [Zhuang].

[E] ST: WT *sŋog-pa, bsŋogs* 'to vex, annoy' (*HST:* 37).

xù$_6$ 畜 → **chù$_4$, xù** 畜

xù$_7$ 婿 (—) **LH** siɑ^{C}, **OCM** *sah

'Son-in-law' [Zuo]. Mand. *xù* [ɕy^{C}], G-Nánchāng *ɕy^{A}*.

~ (siei^{C}) Col. Shāzhōu *siei* (si?), LH *se(i)h*

[D] Southern dialects typically have this latter form: PSMin *sai^{C} (Bodman 1980: 178): M-Xiàmén col. *sai^{C}*, lit. *se^{C}*, Cháozhōu *sai^{C}*, Fúzhōu *sa^{C}*; W-Wēnzhōu *sei^{C}*, K-Méixiàn *sɛ^{C}*, Guǎngzhōu *ʃai^{C2}*. The word is reminiscent of AA: PSBahn. *sa:j 'marry, spouse'.

xù$_8$ 酗 → **yù$_{21}$** 饇

xù$_9$ 勗 → **sù$_6$** 速

xù$_{10}$ 訹 → **shù$_4$** 述術鉥

xù$_{11}$ 續 → **xù$_2$** 序敘緒

xù$_{12}$ 閾淢 → **guó** 國

xuān$_1$ 宣 (sjwän) **LH** syan, **OCM** *swan, OCB *swjan

'To spread, diffuse, proclaim, display' [Shi].

[E] ST: PLB *swan² > Lahu *šē* 'sow, broadcast', WB *swan^{B}* 'pour upon, cast by pouring'.

xuān$_2$ 暖 (xjwɐn[^{B}]) **LH** hyɑn(^{B}), **OCM** *hwan(ʔ)

'Soft, mild' [Zhuang] is perh. related to WT *hol-hol* 'soft, loose, light' (*HST:* 136).

ж **huǎn** 緩 (ɣuân^{B}) **LH** ɣuɑn^{B}, **OCM** *gwânʔ

'Slack, indulgent' [Zuo], 'soft' [Lü] is perh. related (*HST:* 136); but this word could instead belong to → yuán$_8$ 爰 'slow'. Syn. → róu$_1$ 柔.

xuān$_3$ 煖 → **xù$_4$** 旭

xuán$_1$ 玄 (ɣiwen) **LH** ɣuen, **OCM** *wîn, OCB *gwin

'Black, dark' [BI, Shi] is the oldest basic color term for 'black' which is later replaced by → hēi 黑 (Baxter 1983).

xuán$_2$ 洵 'far' → **jiǒng$_2$** 泂迥

xuán$_3$ 還旋 → **yuán$_5$** 員圓圜

xuán$_4$ 縣懸 (ɣiwen) **LH** guen, **OCM** *gwîn — **[T]** *MTang* ɣuian(?), *ONW* ɣuėn

'To suspend, hang up' 縣 [Shi], 懸 [Meng] is today the word for 'high' in Mǐn: PMin *guen > Fúzhōu $keiŋ^{A2}$ 'high' ≍ $heiŋ^{A2}$ 'hanging down' (Norman 1979: 271). Tai has borrowed the word 'suspend': S. $k^hw\varepsilon\varepsilon n^{A1}$ < *xw- (Manomaivibool *CAAAL* 6, 1976: 16). Prob. related to → guà 挂 'suspend' (for final -n, see §6.4.4), perh. also to → qìng₃ 磬 'id'.

xuǎn 烜 → **xù₄** 旭

xuàn₁ 泫 (ɣiwen^B) **LH** ɣuen^B, **OCM** *wîn?
'To flow' [Lun] may derive from the same ST root *lwi 'to flow' as → shuǐ 水 'water'; earlier *r- and *l- often leave no trace in MC before initial *j- and *w-.

≍ **quǎn** 甽畎 (kiwen^B) **LH** kuen^B, **OCM** *kwîn?
'Watering channels in fields' 甽 [Zhouli], 畎 [Shu].
[<] nominalizing k-prefix derivation from *xuàn* (§5.4). The aspirated Mand. reading is probably an analogy to 犬 'dog'. *JY* gives additional readings: *xún* (MC *zjwən* and *zhùn*, $tśjuen^C$). Mǐn: Gùtiān $kyeŋ^{C1}$ (Branner 1995: 268) is similar to the MC form $kiwen^B$; Xiàmén $tsun^{C1}$ < MC $tśjuen^C$ (?).

≍ **yuán** 湲 (jwän) **LH** wan or wen, **OCM** *wan or *wen ?
'To flow' [Chuci] may be a Chǔ dialect variant of *xuàn*.

≍ **jué, yù** 潏 (kiwet, juet) **LH** kuet, juit, **OCM** *kwît ~ *wit
'To flow' 潏 [Chuci], 汩 [Chuci] (*yù* only). The graph 汩 indicates that the rime was *-wit or *-wat, but Old Sino-Viet. *lut* 'flow' could also point to OC *lut.

xuàn₂ 眩炫 → **yíng₃** 熒

xuàn₃, shùn 眴 → **shùn₃** 瞬

xuē, xuè, xiāo 削 (sjak, sjäu^C) **LH** siɑk, siau^C, **OCM** *siauk(h)?
'To scrape, pare, cut, destroy' [Shi].
[E] ST: PLB *sök 'to scrape' [Matisoff *TSR:* 54]. Downer (1959: 275) reserves the reading MC $sjäu^C$ for the noun 'dagger' [Liji].

xué 學 (ɣåk) **LH** gɔk, **OCM** *grûk
'To learn' [Shi].
[T] *Sin S. SR* ɣjaw (入), *LR* ɣjaw?; *MGZY* (Hÿaw >) Hyaw (入) [ɣjaw]; *ONW* ɣäk
[<] This word may be endopass. of → jué₁₁ 覺 'to awake, get insight', see §4.6.

≍ **xiào** 斆 (ɣau^C) **LH** gɔu^C, **OCM** *grûkh
'To teach' [Shu].
[<] exoactive of *xué* 學 (ɣåk) (§4.3.2). Perh. this wf belongs to → jué₁₁ 覺.

xuě 雪 (sjwät) **LH** syat, **OCM** *sot < *snot ?, OCB *sjot — *ONW* suat
'Snow' [OB, Shi].
[D] In some dialects it also can mean 'ice': Y-Guǎngzhōu $ʃyt^{33}$.
[E] <> KT: Tai-Po'ai $nwai^{A1}$ < *hn- 'snow'; PKS *ʔnu:i¹ (Thurgood) / *k-nui⁴ (Edmondson / Yang 1988) 'snow'.

xuè₁ 血 (xiwet) **LH** huet, **OCM** *hwît, OCB *wit — *ONW* huėt
'Blood' [Shi].
[D] PMin *huet: Xiàmén $huiʔ^{D1}$; K-Méixiàn $šiæt^B$; Yuè-Guǎngzhōu hyt^{C1}; Gàn-Nánchāng *ɕyɔt*
[E] ST *s-wiʔ ~ *swiʔ: PTB *s-hywəy (*STC* no. 222), or rather *s(-)wiʔ > Kanauri *šui*, PL *swiy², WB swe^B 'blood, disposition, spirit' [Matisoff *Var. Sem.; STC* no. 222]; Bodo-Garo *si? [Joseph / Burling *LTBA* 24.2, 2001: 42], Lushai *thiiʔ, Tiddim *siiʔ;* Chepang *wəyʔ ~ huy* 'blood', Magari *hyu < hwi* (-> Chepang *huyʔ-sa* 'to bleed'), Vayu

vi, WT *yi* in *yi(d)-dam* 'oath' ⋇ *yid* 'soul, mind' (*STC* no. 222). In some TB lgs., this etymon means 'marrow', see → suǐ$_{11}$ 髓 'marrow'. The Tai word for 'blood' S. *l̶at*^{D2L} < *l- is unrelated, see → lǚ$_4$-liáo 膟膋.

xuè$_2$ 䀏 (xjwät 3) **LH** hyat, **OCM** *hmat or *hmet
'To wink at, give signal with the eyes' [SW].

⋇ **miē** 乜
'To squint, glance (sideways)' is a more recent cognate (dialects have forms in tone C or D; Giles (*A Chinese–English Dictionary* p. 975) lists among others Canton *mêt*, Hakka *mak*, Ningpo *mi*^{C}, Peking *miè*.

[E] Area etymon *Cmit or *Cmet 'wink / signal with eyes or finger': TB-WB *hmit* 'to wink', Lahu *mèʔ*. <> AA-Khmer /mic/ ~ /meec/ 'to wink' (by way of signaling) ⋇ /tmeec/ 'shut the eyes'. <> AN: Malay *gamit* 'beckoning with the fingers' (Kuiper 1966: 61). → jué$_4$ 眣 looks like a further variant of this foreign loan. → huī$_4$ 麾 *hmai may have been influenced by *xuè*.

xuè$_3$, xiāo 削 → **xuē**, **xuè**, **xiāo** 削

xuè$_4$, hù 㱿 (xåk, xuk) **LH** hɔk, hok, **OCM** *hrok
'Vomit' [Zuo].
[E] PTai *r̯uak^{D2}, PKS *trwak^7 'vomit'.

xuè$_5$ 烕 'destroy' → **miè$_1$** 滅

xuè$_6$, nuè 謔 → **nuè$_1$** 虐

xūn 熏燻焄 (xjuən) **LH** hun, **OCM** *hwən < *C-un ? — **[T]** *ONW* hun
'To make smoke, befumed' 熏 [Shi], 燻 [Hanfei]; 'vapor, odor' 焄 [Li], 'be pungent' [Yi] > 'strong smelling vegetables' 葷 [Li] (Mand. *hūn*), 'a fragrant herb' 薰 [Zuo].
[E] This word is prob. ST, but its TB counterpart is difficult to pinpoint: perh. *(C-)wu 'smoke' (*STC:* 159 n. 429: *kəw; *HPTB:* 451), in CH with the addition of the nominal final *-n* (§6.4.3): Dulong *mɯ*^{31}*-ɯ*^{55} < *-u (?) 'smoke' (*mɯ*^{31} 'sky'), WT *du-ba* ⋇ *dud-pa* 'smoke' (a few other words have WT *d-* for a velar initial elsewhere, note → liù$_1$ 六 – Matisoff 1974: 195 n. 119), WB *k*^{h}*ui*^{B}, Bahing *kuni*, Sunwar *kun*. Alternatively, or in addition, *xūn* may belong with Kanauri *wən* 'steam'. *CVST* 5: 180 relates *xūn* to Lushai *hu*^{L} *< huh (< hus)* 'vapor, gas' and by implication to WT *hus* 'moisture, humidity'.

⋇ **yún** 芸 (juən) **LH** wun
'Fragrant plant' [Li] > 'ample, numerous' (flowers > people) [Shi] (also MC *juən*^{C}).

xún$_1$ 旬 → **jūn$_2$** 鈞

xún$_2$ 洵 'drip' → **yǔn$_2$** 隕殞霣

xún$_3$ 恂洵 'sincerely' → **xìn$_1$** 信

xún$_4$ 眴 → **shùn$_3$** 瞬

xún$_5$ 尋 (zjəm) **LH** zim, **OCM** *s-ləm
'A measure' (8 *chi*) [Shi].
[T] *Sin Sukchu SR* zim (平), *PR, LR* zin; *MGZY* zim (平) [zim]; *ONW* zim
[E] ST: PTB *la:m (*HPTB:* 298) > Lushai *hlam*^{H} *< hlam* 'measure with arms extended', WB *lam* id. ⋇ *hlam*^{B} 'reach out, stretch out' (Gong Hwang-cherng 1999: 12), JP *lə*^{31}*-lam*^{55} 'a fathom' ⋇ *lə*^{31}*-lam*^{33} 'to measure' (Bodman 1980: 106), WT *'dom* 'fathom'.

xún$_6$ 尋 'warm up' → **xín** 尋爓

xún$_7$ 循 → **shùn$_1$** 順

xùn$_1$ 訓 (xjuən^C) **LH** hun^C, **OCM** *huns
'Instruct, comply' [Shi, Shu]. Perh. ST: WT *'kʰul-ba* 'to subdue, subject' ⋈ *skul-ba, bskul* 'to exhort, admonish' (so *HST:* 143).

xùn$_2$ 徇殉侚 → **jūn$_2$** 鈞

xùn$_3$ 訊 → **xìn$_1$** 信

xùn$_4$ 遜 → **sǔn** 損

xùn$_5$ 逡 (sjuen^C) **LH** suin^C, **OCM** *suns ?
'Rapid' [Li] is related to → sù$_6$ 速 and belongs to the wf → sōu$_3$, sǒu 搜.

Y

yā$_{1}$ 押 → **yā**$_{3}$ 壓

yā$_{2}$ 鴉 → **wū**$_{6}$ 烏

yā$_{3}$ 壓 (ʔap) **LH** ʔap, **OCM** *ʔrâp or *ʔâp ?
'To press down, press upon' 壓 [Zuo]; 'stamp, seal' 押 [Hanfei].
[T] *Sin Sukchu SR* ʔja (入) — **[D]** M-Xiàmén col. *aʔ*^{D1}, *aʔ*^{D2}, lit. *ap*^{D1}
[E] A derivation is prob. → chā$_{3}$ 臿 'to stamp', with the iterative s-prefix (§5.2.3).

yá$_{1}$ 牙 (ŋa) **LH** ŋa, **OCM** *ŋrâ, OCB *ngra.
'Tusk, tooth' [Shi] > 'sprout' 芽 [Liji].
[T] *Sin Sukchu SR* ŋja (平), *PR, LR* ja; *ONW* ŋä
[D] M-Xiàmén col. *ge*^{A2}, *gia*^{A2}, lit. *ga*^{A2}
[E] AA (Norman / Mei (1976: 288–292; Norman 1988: 19): Viet *ngà*, Bahnar *ŋəla* 'tusk, ivory', Mon *ŋek*. <> PTai *ŋa^{A2}; PWMiao *ŋha^{A}. <> TB: Lushai *ŋho*^{L} 'tusk'. Pulleyblank (1983: 439) believes that OC is the donor.

yá$_{2}$ 芽 → **yá**$_{1}$ 牙; → **niè**$_{10}$ 櫱

yá$_{3}$, **ái** 崖涯睚 (ŋai) **LH** ŋaɨ, **OCM** *ŋrê
'Riverbank' 涯 [Shu], 'cliff' 崖 [Zuo], 'limit' [Zhuang], 'rim' (of the eye) 睚 [Guoce], later also 'margin, edge' (of the world).
[T] *Sin Sukchu SR* ŋja, jaj (平), *PR, LR* ja; *MGZY* yay (平) [jaj]
[E] This word looks similar to the ST stem *ŋra ~ *ŋa, but is unrelated (the basic meaning of *yá* is 'edge, limit'); for an overview of similar words, see under → yà$_{2}$ 御迓訝.

yǎ$_{1}$ 啞 (ʔa^{B}) **LH** ʔa^{B}, **OCM** *ʔâʔ ? — **[D]** M-Xiàmén col. *e*^{B1}, lit. *a*^{B1}
'Mute' [Guoce]. This onomatopoetic root represents throaty sounds. The MC div. II vocalism is unlikely to be due to an OC medial *r (Pulleyblank *JAOS* 118.2, 1998: 212), but is probably due to sound symbolism.

ⅹ **yā**, **yà** 剄 (ʔa [GY]) **LH** ʔa, **OCM** *ʔâ ?
'To cut one's throat' [Guoyu].

ⅹ **è** 啞 (ʔak) **LH** ʔak, **OCM** *ʔâk ?
'Laugh' [Yi].

[E] ST: PTB *(m-)a 'mute' (*STC* 192) > PL *ʔa$^{2/3}$, WB *a*^{C}, Kachin, Nung *məa* 'be dumb' (*HST:* 68).

yǎ$_{2}$ 雅 (ŋa^{B}) **LH** ŋa^{B}, **OCM** *ŋrâʔ — **[T]** *Sin Sukchu SR* ŋja (上), *PR* ja; *ONW* ŋä
'Proper, refined, a kind of song' [Shi].
[E] Etymology is unknown; it has been suggested that *yǎ* is connected with Xià 夏 [gaʔ] 'Xia dynasty, Chinese'.

yà$_{1}$ 亞 (ʔa^{C}) **LH** ʔa^{C}, **OCM** *ʔah or *ʔrâh ?
'Next in line, second, inferior' [BI, Shi].
Karlgren relates *yà* to → è$_{3}$ 惡 'evil', but this seems semantically forced. Bodman (1980: 87; *HST:* 97) suggests cognation with WT *rag(-pa)* 'to depend on' ⅹ *rag*

'subject, subservient, dependent'; the WT forms are cognate to Lushai ra^{R} < raaʔ 'be bad, poor'.

yà$_{2}$ 御迓訝 (ŋa^{C}) **LH** ŋa^{C}, **OCM** *ŋrâh

'To meet, welcome, provide against, receive' 御 [Shi], 迓 [Shu], 訝 [Yili], 輅 [Zuo].

[E] ST: PTB *ŋra (*STC* no. 154) > WB *ŋra^{B}* 'meet with, find', JP *nya*^{55} 'to meet, conflict, clash, frolic' (*HST:* 109).

⪤ **yán** 顏 (ŋan) **LH** ŋan, **OCM** *ŋrân, OCB *ngran

'The appearance of a face, face, countenance, color' [Shi]. Perhaps under the influence of the synonym → sè$_{1}$ 色 'color', *yán* acquired later the connotation 'sex' (Eberhard 1967: 12).

[D] From northern Chǔ eastward to the Huái region it was a Han period dialect word for 'forehead' [FY 10, 34].

[E] This noun is either derived with the nominalizing n-suffix from *yà* 御迓訝 (above), and / or it could be related to WT *ŋar* 'front-side', in the expression 'go against, instigate' (so *IST:* 37).

⪤ **é** 詻 (ŋɐk) **LH** ŋak, **OCM** *ŋrâk

'Dispute, contest' [Mo], 'insisting' [Li], 'attack' 詻 [Zhuang]; 'defiant' 額 [Shu].

[T] *Sin Sukchu SR* əj (入), *PR* ŋəjʔ; *MGZY* yay (入) [jaj]

Table Y-1 Meet, against for yà$_{2}$ 御迓訝

	ŋa	ŋak	sŋak	ŋaŋ	ŋan
ŋa-	yǔ 禦 *ŋaʔ defend wù 悟迕晤捂 *ŋâh go against	wù 蘁 *ŋâk(h) resist, oppose	sù 泝愬訴 *sŋâkh go up against		àn 岸 *ŋâns riverbank
	WT ŋo face, look				
hŋa-	hǔ 滸 *hŋâʔ riverbank WT dŋo shore, bank				hàn 厂 *hŋâns cliff, riverbank
ŋra-	ŋra	ŋrak	sŋrak	ŋraŋ	ŋran
	yà 御迓訝 *ŋrâh meet, go against WB ŋra^{B} meet with, find JP nya^{55} meet, conflict	é 詻 *ŋrâk dispute 額 forehead nì 逆 *ŋ(r)ak go to meet	shuò 朔 *sŋrakh new moon	yíng 迎 *ŋ(r)aŋ go to meet WB ŋraŋ^{B} contradict, deny	yán 顏 *ŋrân face
	WT ŋar front-side ?<-->?			Nung ŋjeŋ deny	WT ŋar front-side
ŋre	yá 崖涯 *ŋrê shore				

Notes for Table Y-1:
Two parallel stems comprise this wf, one with, one without ST / OC medial *r (§2.5).
Open vowel and final *ŋ forms are inherited from ST.
The nouns in final *-n* are CH innovations (§6.4.3). The form *yán* 顏 *ŋrân 'face' is ambiguous because it could either be *ŋra + n, or be directly related to WT *ŋar as TB final *-r can on occasion correspond to a MC div. II syllable with final *n* (§7.7.2). The forms in final *-k* are CH innovations (§6.1).
'Outside' → wài 外 does not belong to these stems.

= **é** 額 (ŋɐk) **LH** ŋak, **OCM** *ŋrâk
'Forehead' is only attested during Han and later [SW, Shiming, FY, Hou Hanshu]; it is a semantic extension of the homophone 詻 'to face' (lit. 'confront').
[D] PMin *ŋ̥iak: Xiàmén *giaʔ*^{D2}, *hiaʔ*^{D2}, lit. *gik*^{D2}
[E] ST, indirectly related to TB items: Tamang-Gurung, Thakali *ŋoh* 'forehead'. The connection with AA-Khmer *thŋa:h* 'forehead' is not clear. Wáng Lì (1982: 280) and LaPolla (1994: 141) have pointed to cognation with *yán* 顏 (above). Syn. → dìng$_2$ 定顁, → sǎng 顙, → yáng$_8$ 揚鍚.
[C] For a synopsis of related words, see Table Y-1 and notes. Cognates are → àn$_2$ 岸 'riverbank', → nì$_6$ 逆 'go against', → yíng$_1$ 迎 'go to meet', → yù$_{17}$ 禦 'defend'. Prob. unrelated is → yá$_3$, ái 崖涯睚 'riverbank'. Benedict (1995: 33) includes in this wf *wǒ* 我 'I' via 'self' (under → wú$_2$ 吾), as well as WT *dŋos* 'reality'; see however → yí$_{10}$ 儀宜 'proper'.

yān$_1$ 咽 (ʔien) **LH** ʔen (ʔein), **OCM** *ʔîn
'Gullet' [Guoce]. Wáng Lì (1982: 268) relates this wf to → yì$_{18}$ 嗌 (ʔjäk) 'throat'.
ꭗ **yàn** 咽嚥 (ʔien^C) **LH** ʔen^C (ʔein^C), **OCM** *ʔîns
'To swallow' 咽 [Meng], 嚥 [Hanfei]. The second graph 嚥 should go back to OCM *ʔêns, but since *Hánfēizǐ* is a relatively late text, the two forms may already have merged.
[<] exoactive of *yān* 咽 *ʔîn (§4.3).

yān$_2$ 焉 interrogative → **wū$_5$** 惡; 'there' → **yú$_8$** 於

yān$_3$ 淹 → **yǎn$_2$** 奄

yān$_4$ 猒 (ʔjiäm[^{C}] 4) **LH** ʔiam, **OCM** *ʔem — **[T]** *ONW* ʔiam
'Be content, satisfied, tranquil' [BI, Shi], 'to satiate, satisfy' 猒 [Guoyu], 饜 [Zuo].
ꭗ **yàn** 猒 (ʔjiäm^C 4) **LH** ʔiam^C, **OCM** *ʔems
'Be full of, satiated > abundant' [Shu, Shi]; 'fed up, tired' [Shi].
[<] exopass. of *yān* 猒饜 *ʔem 'have been filled / contented' (§4.4).
[E] This wf may belong to → yǎn$_2$ 奄. Note PTai *ʔim^{B1} 'full, satiated'.

yán$_1$ 沿 (jiwän) **LH** juan, **OCM** *lon ? or *jon ?
'Go along a river' [Shu], 'follow, imitate' [Li].
= **yuán** 緣 (jiwän) **LH** juan, **OCM** *lon ?
'Go along, follow' [Zhuang].
ꭗ **yuàn** 緣 (jiwän^C) **LH** juan^C, **OCM** *lons ?
'A hem, border on garment' [Liji].
[T] *Sin Sukchu SR*, *LR* yen (平); *MGZY* ywÿan (平) [jyɛn]
[<] exopass. of *yán* 沿 (§4.4), lit. 'what is followed / follows'.
[E] Etymology not clear. There are several possible etymologies, but the MC rounded element does not agree with the first two: (1) Tai: S. *lian*^{A2} 'imitate, follow' (Manomaivibool 1975: 235). (2) ST: Lushai *zeel*^{L} < *jeel* 'a road or path along the side of a hill or range, to walk along' (such a road); JP *mə*^{31}*-jan*^{33} '(flow) along a cliff'. (3) Or it could be derived from → yóu$_2$ 由 'go along, follow'.

yán$_2$ 炎 (jiäm 4 [JY]) **LH** jam, **OCM** *lam, prob. *liam — **[T]** *ONW* iam
'To blaze, burn' [Shi]. The graph 炎 had two different ancient readings, LH *jam* and *wam* → yán$_3$ 炎. Both forms are supported by outside connections; *yán$_2$* 炎 transcribes

Indic *yāma*. The same doublet *l- ~ *w- (Tai *w-, PTB *l-) is found in → yè$_6$ 爗 which could perh. be related.

[E] ST and area word: PTB *(s-)lyam > Tamang *me-lahm* 'flame' (*me* 'fire'), Lepcha *lim* 'to flame up' ⋈ *ă-lim* 'flame'; JP *lam^{31}* 'to flash, as bright as steel' ⋈ *gə^{31}-lam^{31}* 'flutter' ⋈ *pə^{55}-lam^{51}-laʔ^{55}* 'butterfly' ⋈ *pram^{31}* 'flashing'; WT *lčam-me-ba < lhyam* 'shining, dazzling' ⋈ *p^{h}yam-p^{h}yam-pa* 'glittering'; WB *ə-hlyam* 'coruscation of flame' ⋈ *p^{h}ə-lam* 'moth'. The first syllable in the WT *p^{h}yi-ma-leb < pyim-a-lep* 'butterfly' may be related, hence lit. the 'glittering flat thing'. <> Also AA: Khmer *lāma* /líiəm/ 'to flare, flame' ⋈ *bhlāma* /plíiəm/ 'move like a flash, immediately, next moment' ⋈ *babhlāma* /pplíiəm/ 'to gleam, glitter, glisten'.

⋈ **yàn** 燄焰 (jiäm^B) **LH** jam^B, **OCM** *lamʔ ?

'Be flaming up, blazing up (of fire)' 燄 [Shu] (also MC *jiäm^C*); 'rising' [Li], 'brilliant' 焰 [Chuci].

[<] endoactive of *yán$_2$* 炎 (jiäm 4) *lam (§4.5).

⋈ **shǎn** 閃覢 (śjäm^B) **LH** śam^B, **OCM** *lhamʔ

'To twinkle' 煔 [SW]; 'time of a short glance, moment' 覢閃 [SW: Gongyang], in modern dialects 'lightning': Mand. *shǎn diàn* 閃電. The basic meaning is apparently 'to flicker'.

[T] *Sin Sukchu SR* ʂjem (上); *MGZY* shem (上去) [ʂɛm]; *ONW* śam

[<] iterative devoicing of *yàn* 燄焰 (jiäm^B) §5.2.3.

[E] ST *l(j)am (§5.2.3): WT *lhem* 'now, at present'; note also *lhams* 'at once'.

[C] Allofams are → tán$_7$ 炎惔, → tiǎn$_2$ 煔烑, → xián$_{12}$ 燅, → yè$_6$ 爗. Words meaning 'flame', 'tongue, lick' (→ tiǎn$_1$ 舔) and 'sharp' (→ yǎn$_4$ 剡覃) are near homophones and may derive from the same root.

yán$_3$ 炎 (jäm 3 [GY]) **LH** wam, **OCM** *wam — [N] Early MC *wiam* (Pulleyblank 1991)

'To blaze, burn' [Shi]. The graph 炎 had two different ancient readings, LH *wam* and LH *jam* → yán$_2$ 炎. The same doublet *l- ~ *w- is found in the cognate → yè$_6$ 爗. Acc. to *SW*, yán 炎 < OC *wam is phonetic in *xióng* 熊 *wəm 'the bear'; if true, *yán* would confirm the final *-m in *xióng*, and *xióng* the initial *w- in *yán*.

[E] ST: JP *(g)ə^{31}-wam^{31}* 'sway up and down' (e.g., bridge) ⋈ *wam^{31}* 'a flash', Lushai *vaam^L* / *vam^F* 'red-hot glowing' of fire, iron, etc. OC -> Tai: S. *wɛɛm^{A2}* in *wɔɔm^{A2}-wɛɛm^{A2}* 'brilliant, glowing (of fire)' (Manomaivibool 1975: 180). Tai / OC -> Sino-Vietn. *viêm* [Maspero 1912: 68, n. 1].

yán$_4$ 言 → **yǔ$_6$** 語

yán$_5$ 延筵 (jiän) **LH** jan, **OCM** *lan — [T] *ONW* ian

'To extend, prolong' [Shu], 'continue' [Zuo], 'stretch' (neck) [Lunyu]; 'bamboo mat' 筵 [Shi]. The OC initial is uncertain; Viet. and Tai relations suggest *l, TB comparanda *j.

CH -> Old Sino-Viet. *lan* (Pān Wùyún 1987: 29), Tai: S. *łan^{B2}* 'delay, extend, postpone' (Karlgren 1956: 14).

⋈ **chān** 梴 (ṭʰjän) **LH** ṭʰan, **OCM** *t-hlan ?

'Long' (of beams) [Shi].

⋈ **dàn** 誕 (dân^B) **LH** dɑn^B, **OCM** *lânʔ

'Far-reaching' (of creepers), 'extending' [Shi] > 'great, vastly' [Shu] > 'boast' [Guoyu].

[E] ST: TB-WB *lhan^B* 'spread out, lay in the sun'.

Unrelated are prob. TB items with initial *y- (Shorto 1972: 17), they may have converged in OC: PTB *yaːr 'to spread out, extend, sail' (*STC:* 138) > WT *g-yor-mo* 'sail',

Lushai *zaar*[H] 'spread' (wings, a sail), JP *yan*[31] 'to unroll, spread'. 'Sail' may ultimately be connected with an AN word (Shorto), e.g. Proto-Eastern Formosan *layaR 'sail' [Li Jen-kuei *LL* 5.2, 2004: 370].

yán₆ 研 (ŋien) **LH** ŋen, **OCM** *ŋên, OCB *ŋen
'To grind' [SW] > 'examine' [Yi]. Perh. there is a connection with WT *gñer* 'take pains'.

ж **yàn** 硯 (ŋien^C) **LH** ŋen^C, **OCM** *ŋêns — **[D]** PMin *ŋ̊ian^C
'Inkstone' [SW, Shìmíng].
[<] *ŋen + general purpose s-suffix (§3.5).

yán₇ 顏 → yà₂ 御迓訝

yán₈ 巖 (ŋam) **LH** ŋam, **OCM** *ŋrâm — **[T]** *ONW* ŋäm
'Be high, lofty' (of mountains) [Shi], 'precipitous, dangerous' [Zuo].

ж **yán** 嚴 (ŋjɐm) **LH** ŋɨɑm, **OCM** *ŋam, OCB *ng(r)jam
'Majestic, stern, grave' [Shi], 'severely, strict' [Shu].
[T] *Sin Sukchu SR* jem (平), *PR, LR* jen; *MGZY* ngem (平) [ŋɛm]

ж **yǎn** 儼 (ŋjɐm^B) **LH** ŋɨɑm^B, **OCM** *ŋamʔ, OCB *ng(r)jomʔ (?)
'Dignified' [Shi].

[E] ST: WT *rŋams-pa* 'height' ж *rŋam-pa* 'splendor, majesty', perh. also WB *ŋram*^B 'scaffold, gallows'.

[C] An allofam with a stop final is → yè₈ 業. Bodman (1980: 176) adds → xiǎn₂ 險 to this wf. Note **yǎn** 巘 (ŋjɐn^B, ŋjan^B 3) *ŋran (?) 'hill-top' [Shi] which may be a variant.

yán₉ 鹽 (jiäm) **LH** jam, **OCM** *jam < *r-jam
'Salt' [Shu]. The phonetic implies an initial *r- which is supported by the WT form.
[T] *Sin Sukchu SR* jem (平), *PR, LR* jen; *MGZY* yem (平) [jɛm]; *ONW* iam
[D] Proto-Min *ziem 'a white encrustation formed from saltwater or brine' (Norman 1983: 203).

ж **yàn** 鹽 (jiäm^C) **LH** jam^C, **OCM** *jams
'To salt, pickle' [Liji] (Downer 1959: 281).
[<] *jam + exoactive / caus. s-suffix (§4.3), lit. 'make salty'; the word survives in Mǐn dialects: PMin *ziem^C2.

[E] ST *-yam: PTB *hyam (*HPTB:* 299) > Karenic-Sgaw *hɔ*, Pwo *ɣa* 'salty'; WB *yam*^B 'saltpeter' (*HST:* 128); WT *rgyam-tsʰwa < r-yam* 'a kind of salt' (Li F. 1976: 46); this ancient WT medicinal word has been considered a loan from CH (Benedict *STC:* 57 n. 186). *Yán* is sometimes thought to be related to → xián₄ 鹹 (so Li F.) – unlikely. CH -> Tai *gem. For the phonesthemic final -m, see §2.9.

yǎn₁, **yàn** 衍 (jiän^B/C) **LH** jan^B/C, **OCM** *janʔ/s, OCB *ranʔ/s
'Be overflowing > abundant, extensive' [Shi], ('floodplain':) 'lowland' [Zuo].
[E] ST: WT *yar-ba* 'to disperse, ramble, stray'.

ж **yǎn** 演 (jiän^B) **LH** jan^B, **OCM** *janʔ — **[T]** *ONW* ian
'To flow out, extend' [Guoyu]. Karlgren (1956: 15) adds

ж **qiān** 愆 (kʰjän 3) **LH** kʰɨan, **OCM** *khrian ?
'To exceed, err, fail, lack' 愆 [Shi] > 'be defective, injured' 騫 [Shi].
[E] ST: WT *'kʰyar-ba* 'to err, go astray, deviate'. QYS div. III points to an earlier *r in the syllable, it may reflect an original final *-r (§7.7.2).

ж **jiǎn** 蹇謇 (kjän^B 3, kjɐn^B) **LH** kɨɑn^B, **OCM** *krian, *kanʔ ?
('Defective':) 'lame' 蹇 [Zhuang], 'speak with difficulty' 謇 [Chuci].

yǎn$_2$ 奄 (ʔjämᴮ 3) **LH** ʔɨamᴮ, **OCM** *ʔramʔ — **[T]** *ONW* ʔam
'Be spreading over, covering, extensively' 奄 [Shi]; 弇 also QY *kəm*ᴮ 'cover' [Mu tianzi], 'narrow pass' [Zuo]; 'to cover, shut' (nose, ears) 揜 [Li].

= **yǎn** 掩 (ʔjämᴮ 3, ʔjɐmᴮ) **LH** ʔɨamᴮ, **OCM** *ʔramʔ
'To cover' [Meng] > 'thickening, gathering (clouds)' [Shi].

⋙ **yǎn** 厭 (ʔămᴮ) **LH** ʔɛmᴮ, **OCM** *ʔrə̂mʔ ?
'Cover' [Li].

⋙ **yān** 淹 (ʔjäm 3) **LH** ʔɨam, **OCM** *ʔram
'Submerge, soak' [Li].

[E] <> KT: S. *hom*ᴮ¹ (< PTai *h-), Po'ai *hɔm*ᴮ¹ 'to cover up' ⋙ Po'ai *hɔm*ᴬ¹ 'to bury'; PHlai *kom¹ 'bury, cover'. MY: Mun (Yao) *hə̣m*³³ 'to cover' (Strecker 1989: 21). It is not clear if and how PVM *ʔəmᶜ 'moist, humid' [Thomas] is related.

[C] The wf under → yān$_4$ 猒 may belong here, also → yè$_5$ 帢 'kerchief'.

yǎn$_3$ 掩厭弇揜 → **yǎn**$_2$ 奄

yǎn$_4$ 剡覃 (jiämᴮ) **LH** jamᴮ, **OCM** *jamʔ
'Pointed, sharp' (of plowshare) 覃 [Shi]; 'sharp, pierce' 剡 [Li], 'cut' [Xun]; 'jade tablet with pointed top' 琰 [Shu].

[E] ST *r-jam 'sharp'. The word *yǎn* has lost the ST initial *r- (§9.2.1) which has been preserved in → lián$_8$ 磏鎌 'sharp' (see there for cognates); in *yǎn* the ST *r- was treated as a pre-initial, in *lián* as the word initial.

yǎn$_5$ 偃 (ʔjɐnᴮ) **LH** ʔɨɑnᴮ, **OCM** *ʔanʔ
'To lie down' (on bed, trees toppled by storm) [Shi, Shu] > 'low-lying land' [Zuo].

⋙ **yǎn** 匽 (ʔjɐnᴮ/ᶜ) **LH** ʔɨɑnᴮ/ᶜ, **OCM** *ʔanʔ/s
'Gutter, latrine' (< 'lowered place, depression') [Zhouli].

[E] ? ST: Lushai *zaal*ᴴ < *jaal* 'to lie down, recline ⋙ *zalʔ*ᴸ < *jalʔ/h* 'lay on the back'. The TB initial *j- is expected to correspond to MC div. IV (ʔjiänᴮ), not III. This casts doubt on the genetic relationship. On the other hand there are no syllables of the corresponding div. IV type in MC, hence they might have merged with div. III, perh. under the influence of the similar etymon → ān$_1$ 安 'press down'.

yǎn$_6$ 眼 (ŋănᴮ) **LH** ŋɛn, **OCM** *ŋrə̂n
'Eyeballs, eyes' [Yi] > 'eyes' [Han period].

[T] *Sin Sukchu SR* ŋjan (上), *PR* jan, *LR* jen; *MGZY* yan (上) [jan]; *ONW* ŋän

[D] This word replaces mù 目 in all modern dialects except Mǐn. Acc. to Sagart (1999: 154) derived from

⋙ **ěn** 眼 (ŋənᴮ) **LH** ŋənᴮ, **OCM** *ŋə̂nʔ
'Knob, bulge' [Zhouli].

yǎn$_7$ 酓 (ʔjiämᴮ 4) **LH** ʔiamᴮ, **OCM** *ʔemʔ
'Bitter wine' [SW].

[E] PMY *ʔiːmᴬ 'bitter' [Wáng F.].

yǎn$_8$ 儼 → **yán**$_8$ 巖

yǎn$_9$ 巘 'hilltop' → **yán**$_8$ 巖

yǎn$_{10}$ 黶 (ʔjiämᴮ 4) **LH** ʔiamᴮ, **OCM** *ʔemʔ
'Black mark on face' (面有黑字) [GY]; 檿 'wild mulberry tree' (*GY*: 'mountain mulberry') [Shi].

= **ǎn** 晻 (ʔjämB 3, ʔậmB) **LH** ʔɨamB, ʔəmB, **OCM** *ʔamʔ ?
'Dark' [Xun].

yàn₁ 宴燕 (ʔienC) **LH** ʔenC, **OCM** *ʔêns, OCB *ʔens — **[T]** *ONW* ʔèn
'To be at ease, rest, feast' 燕 [BI, Shi]; 'be pleasant' (e.g. with a lamb skin; laughing) 晏 [Shi].

⋇ **yàn** 晏 (ʔienC, ʔanC) **LH** ʔenC, ʔanC, **OCM** *ʔêns, ʔrêns ?
'Be peaceful, mild' [Shi]; 'peace, at rest' [Li].

[E] A Tai word may be related: S. *len*B2 'have pleasure, play' (Manomaivibool 1975: 357), but the initial *l*- is unexplained (§5.11). A parallel stem is → ān₁ 安 (§2.5).

yàn₂ 雁 (ŋanC) **LH** ŋanC, **OCM** *ŋrâns ? — **[T]** *ONW* ŋän
'Wild goose' [Shi].

[E] *Yàn* appears to derive from → é₃ 鵝 'goose' with the noun suffix *-n (§6.4.3), but the TB connections make that doubtful: WT *ŋaŋ-pa* 'goose', WB *ŋan*B (*STC* p. 99 n. 284; *HST*: 87) where the difference in final nasals, i.e. CH / WB *-n* for WT *-ŋ*, is odd, but not unique (§6.4.1–2). CH -> PTai *hanB1 < *hŋ- 'goose' (Li F. 1976: 46). Alternatively, *yàn* and *é* may both reflect an earlier final *-l (or *-r?).

yàn₃ 鴳鷃 (ʔanC) **LH** ʔanC, **OCM** *ʔrâns
'A quail-like game bird' 鴳 [Guoyu], 鷃 [Liji].

[E] ST: KN-Lushai *ʔaar*H 'fowl', Tiddim *ʔaak*M 'fowl' < *ʔaar. AA-Bahnaric lgs. have words for 'chicken' which look similar: *ĭĕr, iăr, ial*, etc. The MC div. II vocalism (thought to derive from OC medial *r) occurs occasionally in words whose TB cognates have a final *r, see §7.7.2.

yàn₄ 燕 (ʔienC) **LH** ʔenC (~ ʔenB), **OCM** *ʔêns
'The swallow' [Shi].

[D] Some dialects have tone B: X-Chángshā *iɛn*B, W-Wēnzhōu *i*B.

[E] <> Tai: Saek *ʔeen*C2 ~ *ʔɛɛn*C2 'swallow', S. *ʔɛɛn*B1. This word is thought to be connected with → yān₁ 咽 'to swallow', but this is doubtful (note that the two English homophones are etymologically unrelated as well).

yàn₅ 嚥 → **yān₁** 咽

yàn₆ 燄焱 → **yán₂** 炎

yàn₇ 咽 → **yān₁** 咽

yàn₈ 唁諺 → **yǔ₆** 語

yàn₉ 甗 → **xiàn₉** 獻憲

yàn₁₀ 豔 (jiämC) **LH** jamC, **OCM** *jams < *r-jams (?)
'Beautiful' [Shi].

[E] Tai: S. *riam*B2 'beautiful' (Manomaivibool 1975: 221).

yāng₁ 央 → **yú₈** 於

yāng₂ 秧 (ʔjaŋ) **LH** ʔɨɑŋ, **OCM** *ʔaŋ — **[D]** PMin *ɔŋA1
'Sprout, rice seedling' [SW].

[E] This word is closely related to PMiao *ʔʑonA [Wáng Fúshì – but most Miao lgs. have the final nasal *-ŋ*] 'young rice plant' (Haudricourt / Strecker, *TP* 77, 1991: 338). It is not clear if and how the following TB words are related because of the differing initials (see §5.11): WT *lǰaŋ-ba* < *lj- 'shoots, sprouts' ⋇ *lǰaŋ-bu* 'rice seedlings', *lǰaŋ-kʰu /-gu* 'green', Lepcha *tă-lyoŋ* 'young blades...of corn, rice' (Bodman 1980: 177; *HST*: 139).

yāng₃ 殃 (ʔjaŋ) **LH** ʔɨɑŋ, **OCM** *ʔaŋ
'Calamity' [Zuo], 'damage, destroy' [Meng]. Unger (*Hao-ku* 33, 34, 1986) connects this word with → yáng₄ 痒瘍.

yáng₁ 羊 (jiaŋ) **LH** jɑŋ, **OCM** *jaŋ or *laŋ, OCB *(l)jang
'Goat, sheep' [OB].
[T] *Sin Sukchu SR* jaŋ (平); *MGZY* yang (平) [jaŋ]; *ONW* iaŋ
[E] Perh. ST: Lushai *sa^L-za^F* < *-jaaʔ* 'a wild goat', JP *ja^55* 'blue sheep', Matisoff adds WT *g-yak* 'yak' (*HPTB*: 304). It is not clear if / how PTai *l-: S. *liaŋ^A2 -pʰaa^A1* 'goat, antelope' is related, see → yǎng₂ 養. Sagart (1999: 194) raises the possibility that it is related to → yǎng₂ 養 'nourish, feed, rear', meaning lit. 'livestock', which would be semantically parallel to → chù₄, xù 畜 'nourish, rear, domestic animal'.

yáng₂ 羊 (jiaŋ) **LH** jɑŋ, **OCM** *jaŋ or *laŋ
'A fly', an eastern Qí (i.e. Shandong) Han period dialect variant for → yíng₆ 蠅 [FY 11, 12] (Mei Tsu-Lin 1985: 338); it survives in Mǐn dialects: PMin *ziɔŋ^A2 (Norman 1983: 203), and occurs in Old Sino-Viet. as *lAŋ* (Pān Wùyún 1987: 29).

yáng₃ 佯 → **xiàng₇** 像象

yáng₄ 痒瘍 (jiaŋ) **LH** jɑŋ, **OCM** *jaŋ or *laŋ
'Be sick, suffering' 痒 [Shi] (also LH *ziaŋ*); 'sore, ulcer' 瘍 [Zuo] (also LH *jaŋ^B* [Zhouli] — a late text, hence the incongruous phonetic).

ж **yàng** 恙 (jiaŋ^C) **LH** jɑŋ^C, **OCM** *jaŋh or *laŋh
'Sickness' [Chuci], 'defect, shortcoming' [Guoce].
[<] *yáng* + s/h-suffix (§3.5).

ж **shāng** 傷 (śjaŋ) **LH** śɑŋ, **OCM** *hjaŋ or *lhaŋ
'Be pained, injure, hurt' [Shi], 'to mourn' [Guanzi]. Acc. to Downer (1959: 288) 'to mourn' [Liji] is a tone C derivation (Unger *Hao-ku* 33, 1986: 34).
[<] causative of *yáng* 痒瘍 (§5.2.2). This iand the next itrems may possibly represent a different root *laŋ, not *jaŋ).

ж **qiāng** 戕 (tsʰjaŋ) **LH** tsʰiɑŋ, **OCM** *s-hjaŋ or *s-lhaŋ
'To hurt' [SW], also = *shāng* 傷.
[<] s-caus. reprefixation of *shāng* 傷 (§5.2.2).

[E] Note Tai: S. *laaŋ^A2* 'destroy', *sa-lɛɛŋ* 'harmful, unhealthy'. Unger (*Hao-ku* 33, 1986: 34) adds some other items to form a wf which includes → bìng₅ 病, → yāng₃ 殃.

yáng₅ 佯 → **xiáng₅** 翔

yáng₆ 洋 (jiaŋ) **LH** jɑŋ, **OCM** *jaŋ or *laŋ, OCB *ljang
'Much' [EY, Hanshu].

ж **yáng-yáng** 洋洋
'Vast, wide, large' (expanse of water, land), 'ample' (flowing), 'grand' (dance) [Shi]; 'much' [EY, Hanshu].

[E] ST *jaŋ: WT *yaŋs-pa* 'wide, broad, large', Lepcha *yóŋ* 'id.' (Geilich 1994: 254). Alternatively, this etymon may be related to → yáng₇ 揚.

yáng₇ 揚 (jiaŋ) **LH** jɑŋ, **OCM** *laŋ, OCB *ljang
'To rise, raise, extol, make known' 揚 [BI, Shi]; 'tossed up by the wind' 颺 [Chuci]; Bodman (1980: 102) believes that *yáŋ* 陽 'be elated' [Shi] is the same word.

ж **shāng-shāng** 湯湯 (śjaŋ) **LH** śɑŋ, **OCM** *lhaŋ
'Voluminous' (flow of water, i.e. rising river) [Shi].
[<] iterative / intensive derivation from *yáng* (§5.2.3).
[E] ST: WT *laŋ-ba* 'to rise, arise' ж *ldaŋ-ba* 'to rise, get up' ж *slaŋ-ba* ~ *sloŋ-ba* 'cause to rise' (Pulleyblank 1962: 233; *HST:* 125); Lushai *laaŋ*^{H} / *laan*^{L} 'to float, go up'. Note also Tai: S *lɯɯaŋ*^{6}, *lɯaŋ*^{6} (Gòng Qúnhǔ *MZYW* 2, 2000).
[C] Further derivations may be → yǎng$_{2}$ 養 'to raise' and items mentioned there. Allofams are → yáng$_{8}$ 揚錫; → yú$_{11}$ 舁譽 'lift, extol' also has WT cognates.

yáng$_{8}$ 揚錫 (jiaŋ) **LH** jɑŋ, **OCM** *laŋ
'Forehead' 揚 [Shi 47]; (horse's) 'metal frontlet' 錫 [BI, Shi 261, 2].
This word could be the same as → yáng$_{7}$ 揚 'lift', hence 'rising part' > 'forehead'.
[E] ST: Cuona Monpa *lʌŋ*^{55}*-pɛʔ*^{53}, Darang Deng *ma*^{31}*-plaŋ*^{35} 'forehead'. For syn. see → dìng$_{2}$ 定顁.

yáng$_{9}$ 陽暘 (jiaŋ) **LH** jɑŋ, **OCM** *laŋ, OCB *ljang — **[T]** *ONW* iaŋ
'Sunshine' 陽 [Shi], 暘 [Shu], 'be shining, shiny' 陽 [Shi] > 'sunny side, south side, north slope' (of a valley) 陽 [Shi] > 'outside (fake) appearance (of a person)' [Guoce] (in contrast to → yīn$_{5}$ 陰 'the inside reality' [Hou Hanshu]) > 'the bright, dry, male, etc. principle' (as opposed to *yīn* 陰).
[E] ST or area word: TB-Lepcha *a-lóŋ* 'reflecting light', WB *laŋ*^{B} 'be bright' ж *ə-laŋ*^{B} 'light'. <> Tai: S. *plaŋ*^{A1} 'bright' (Unger *Hao-ku* 33, 1986). See also → chāng 昌, → bǐng$_{1}$ 炳昺.

yáng$_{10}$ 楊 (jiaŋ) **LH** jɑŋ, **OCM** *laŋ, OCB *ljang
'Poplar' [Shi].
[E] ST: WT *lčaŋ-ma* < *lhyaŋ* 'willow' (*Salix viminalis*), in the Golok dialect *ɣtɕaŋ-mæ* 'willow', but *rtɕaŋ-mæ* 'poplar'. The uncommon WT *glaŋ-ma* 'a large kind of alpine willow' (Gong 2002b: 206) may be a variant or a loan from Cuona Monpa *klʌŋ*^{13}*-mʌʔ*^{53} or *klaŋ*^{33}*-ɕeŋ*^{55} 'willow' (*ɕeŋ* 'tree').

yǎng$_{1}$ 仰 (ŋjaŋ^{B}) **LH** ŋɨɑŋ^{B}, **OCM** *ŋaŋʔ, OCB *ngjangʔ
'To lift the face, look up' [Shi].
[T] *Sin Sukchu SR* ŋaŋ (上), *PR* jaŋ, ŋjaŋ, *LR* jaŋ; *MGZY* (ngÿang >) ngyang (上) [ŋjaŋ]; *ONW* ŋaŋ
[D] In southern dialects: 'to tend livestock': PMin *ɔŋ^{C} > Amoy *ŋ*^{C1}, Fúzhōu *auŋ*^{C1}; G-Ruìjīn *ɲiaŋ*^{C} *ɲiu*^{A2} 仰牛.

ж **áng** 卬昂 (ŋâŋ) **LH** ŋɑŋ, **OCM** *ŋâŋ
'Be high' 卬 [Shi], 'lift high' 昂 [Chuci].
[E] Perh. related to MK: PMonic *[_]-ŋaak 'to look upward', Viet. *ngúa*, Muong *ŋa* 'face up' (Pulleyblank *JCL* 22.1, 1994: 82). Note also Tai: S. *hŋaan*^{2} 'to turn the face upward, look up'.

yǎng$_{2}$ 養 (jiaŋ^{B}) **LH** jɑŋ^{B}, **OCM** *jaŋʔ or *laŋʔ ?, OCB *(l)jangʔ — **[T]** *ONW* iaŋ
'To nourish, feed, rear' [Shi].
[<] perh. *laŋ + endoactive tone B derivation from → yáng$_{7}$ 揚 'raise' (§4.5).

ж **yàng** 養 (jiaŋ^{C}) **LH** jɑŋ^{C}, **OCM** *jaŋh or *laŋh ?
'To keep, support' [Shu].
[<] *laŋ + the generic tone C derivation from *yǎng* (§3.5).
[N] In earlier times, 'to manage the support for the elderly' was called *xiáng* 庠 (zjaŋ)

(during the Yin dyn. acc. to SW, the Zhou dyn. acc. to Mengzi) – a PCH caus. s-prefix derivation from *laŋ (→ yáng$_7$ 揚).

[E] Two genetic connections are possible: (1) OC *jaŋʔ, PTB *s-gyoŋ (*HPTB:* 294): WB *kyoŋ*^{B} 'feed, tend cattle'; the vowel *o does not agree with OC, but WT *skyoŋ-ba, bskyaŋs* 'to guard, keep, tend' (cattle) has the vowel *a. The TB etymon is also reflected in the ethnic name → Qiāng$_1$ 羌 and the clan name Jiāng 姜. This is the preferred affiliation because it is with a genetically related TB language, and the phonetic series implies OC *j- rather than *l-. (2) Or OC *l(j)aŋʔ <> Tai: S. *liaŋ*^{C2} 'feed, nourish', Ahom *liŋ*^{C2} (Bodman 1980: 106), see also → yáng$_1$ 羊. WT and Tai could be reconciled by assuming an earlier *lj-. → yáng$_1$ 羊 'goat, sheep' is perh. also related.

yǎng$_3$ 癢 (jiaŋ^B) **LH** jɑŋ^B, **OCM** *jaŋʔ — **[D]** PMin *d̑ziɔŋ^B

'To itch' [Li].

[E] ST: open vowel finals and final *-ŋ* do occasionally alternate within a wf (§6.5.2): WT *g-ya-ba* 'to itch', Kachin *kəja,* WB *ya*^{B}, *ya*^{B}*-yam* 'itch' (*STC* no. 451), Lushai *za*^{R} < *jaʔ*, also WT *za-ba* 'to itch' must be related; Lepcha *yak* 'itch', PLB *ʔzak [Matisoff *D. of Lahu:* 1252], Lepcha *ǰak* [zyak] 'tickle' [Bodman ICSTLL 1987: 15].

yàng$_1$ 恙 → **yáng$_4$** 痒瘍

yàng$_2$ 煬 → **tāng$_2$** 湯

yàng$_3$ 樣 → **xiàng$_7$** 像象

yāo$_1$ 么 'small' → **yòu$_4$** 幼

yāo$_2$ 妖 (ʔjäu 3) **LH** ʔɨɑu, **OCM** *ʔau — **[T]** *ONW* ʔau

'Be delicate, slender' [Shi], 'good-natured' [Meng]; 'beautiful, charming' 妖 [Zhuang] > 'remarkable, supernatural, ominous' 妖 [Zuo] > 'inauspicious, unlucky' 祅 [Guoyu], 訞 [Dadai Liji]. 'Small' [SW] is prob. the same word.

ꕤ **wǎn** 婉 (ʔjwen^B) **LH** ʔyɑn^B, **OCM** *ʔonʔ (< *ʔau-nʔ ?)

'Be lovely' 婉 [Shi], 'obliging, polite' 宛 [Shi], 'accommodating' 宛 [Zhuang], 'gentle, docile' 婉 [Zuo]. 'Small' (bird) 宛 [Shi] is prob. the same word.

yāo$_3$ 祅訞 → **yāo$_2$** 妖

yāo$_4$, jiāo 咬 (ʔau) **LH** ʔau, **OCM** *ʔrâu ?

'To shout' [Zhuang]. Div. II vocalism is perh. due to sound symbolism, not to OC medial *r.

[E] ST: PTB *aːw 'cry out' (*STC* no. 273, p. 63). See also → jiāo$_3$, yāo 咬.

yāo$_5$ 腰要 (ʔjiäu 4) **LH** ʔiau, **OCM** *ʔiau, OCB *ʔjiew (i.e. *ʔjew?) — **[T]** *ONW* ʔiau

'Waist' 腰 [Guoce], 要 [Li]; 'waistband' 要 [Shi].

[E] <> PTai *ʔeu (Luo Yongxian *MKS* 27, 1997: 275), S. *sa-ʔeew* 'waist' where *sa-* is a Tai addition (Unger *Hao-ku* 36, 1990: 66), PHlai *hŋʔau*^{1} or *hj-: Baoding *hjaŭ*^{1}*-hja*^{2} [Matisoff 1988c no. 319]. PMiao *qlau^B 'waist, lower back' [Wáng F.]. Note also PLB *gjok ~ *džok 'waist' [Matisoff 1972 no. 6]. About *l* in the initial, see §5.11.

yáo$_1$ 窯 (jiäu, jiəu [QY]) **LH** jau, **OCM** *jau

'Kiln' 窯 [Mo] > 'pottery' [SW].

This is usually thought to be cognate to → táo$_1$ 匋陶 (so Wáng Lì 1982: 231).

yáo$_2$ 搖媱 (jiäu) **LH** jau, **OCM** *jau, OCB *ljaw

'To shake, be agitated' 搖 [Shi]; 'to caper, be merry' 媱 [Chuci].

[T] *Sin Sukchu SR* jew (平); *MGZY* yew (平) [jɛw]; *ONW* iau

[E] ST: WT *g-yo-ba* 'to move, shake, change place', *skyod-pa* (< *sʔjot < *s-jot ?) 'to move, agitate, shake'.

ꭗ Perh. **diào** 掉 (dieu$^{B/C}$) **LH** deu$^{B/C}$, **OCM** *diâuʔ/h
'To shake, move, arrange' [Zuo] (so Wáng Lì 1982: 214), but the two words are difficult to reconcile phonologically.

yǎo$_1$ 夭殀 (ʔjäu^B 3) **LH** ʔɨɑu^B, **OCM** *ʔauʔ — **[T]** *ONW* ʔau
'Bend' [Zuo] (the graph shows a person with tilted head) > 'break, cut off' [Zhuang] > 'kill prematurely' 夭 [Shi], 'premature death' 殀 [Meng]. For a semantic parallel, see → zhé$_2$ 折.
[E] Prob. ST, but the medials do not agree (we should expect MC div. IV *ʔjiäu*): WT *g-yo-ba, g-yos* 'to bend, incline, tilt' ꭗ *yo-ba* 'oblique, slanting', Lushai *eu*^{R} < *ʔeuʔ* to bend backward'. Perh. related to → wěi$_3$ 委.

yǎo$_2$ 咬 (ŋau^B) **LH** ŋau^B, **OCM** *ŋrâuʔ
'To bite, gnaw'.
[D] PMin ǧau^B > Amoy *ka*^{C2}, Jiānglè *hau*^{9} is reminiscent of Tai *khiau*^{C2} < *g- 'chew'.
[E] Perh. ST: TB-Chepang *ŋaawh* 'to bite' (Bodman 1980: 59).

yǎo$_3$ 舀 → **yú$_{16}$** 揄

yǎo$_4$ 杳窅 → **yōu$_4$** 幽

yǎo$_5$-jiǎo 窈糾 → **yǎo$_6$-tiǎo** 窈窕

yǎo$_6$-tiǎo 窈窕 (ʔieu^B-dieu^B) **LH** ʔeu^B-deu^B, **OCM** *ʔiûʔ-liûʔ
'Be beautiful' (of a woman) [Shi].

ꭗ **yǎo-jiǎo** 窈糾 (ʔieu^B-gjäu^B 3, -kjäu^B 3) **LH** ʔeu^B-kɨau^B, **OCM** *ʔiûʔ-kauʔ
'Be elegant, beautiful' [Shi]. The phonetic of *jiǎo* suggests that originally this syllable might have rimed with *yǎo*, i.e. OCM *kiuʔ.
Liú Yùqìng (*ZGYW* 2, 2002: 156f) concludes that the term *yǎo-jiǎo* was originally referring to something cave-like, 'dark, deep' [*SW*] of the interior of a house, then also in a metaphorical sense, finally of the beauty of a woman. The first syllable is prob. cognate to → yōu$_4$ 幽 'dark'.

yào$_1$ 窔穾 → **yōu$_4$** 幽

yào$_2$ 要 (ʔjiäu^C 4) *Sin Sukchu SR* ʔjew (平); *MGZY* Yÿaw (平) [ʔjɛw]
'Must, have to, want, will' [Tang: Du Fu (*Gǔdài Hànyǔ cídiǎn:* 1826)] col. Mand. for → yù$_5$ 欲 [Gao Ming-kai 1957: 222].

yào$_3$ 要 'if' → **ruò$_1$** 若

yào$_4$ 藥 (jiak) **LH** jɑk, **OCM** *jauk < *r-jauk, OCB *rawk — **[T]** *ONW* iak
'To cure' [Shi], 'medicinal plant' [Zhouli], 'medicine' [Zuo]. *Yào* is prob. cognate to → liào$_3$ 療樂. In addition, *yào* (and *liào*) may belong to the group of wfs 'cleanse, drain, melt, shine' mentioned under → shuò$_6$ 爍鑠 'melt'. In fact, *yào* may be the same etymon as *yuè* 瀹 'to drain off, clear the course (of a river), purify (the heart)', hence 藥 'to cure, heal' < 'drain away, purify, cleanse'. On the other hand, the word may be connected with Lushai *hlo* 'a weed, drug, medicine'.

yào$_5$ 曜耀燿 → **shuò$_7$** 爍

yē 噎 (ʔiet) **LH** ʔet (ʔeit), **OCM** *ʔît — **[T]** *ONW* ʔėt
'To choke' intr. [Shi]. This wf may be related to → yì$_{18}$ 嗌 (ʔiei^C) LH *ʔeh* 'strangle', in which case the Proto-CH stem would have been *ʔik (not *ʔit).

ⅹ **yì** 饐 (ʔieiᶜ) **LH** ʔes (ʔeis), **OCM** *ʔîts
'To choke' [Lü].

ⅹ **yì** 殪 (ʔiᶜ) **LH** ʔis, **OCM** *ʔits
'To kill' (animal; a dynasty) [Shi].

yě $_1$ 也 (jiaᴮ) **LH** jaᴮ, **OCM** *laʔ ?
[T] *Sin Sukchu SR* je (上); *ONW* ia
A phrase or sentence final particle which occurs first late in *Shījīng* [Guofeng], 'a particle of noun predication' (Pulleyblank 1995: 16), i.e. *yě* is used like the copula 'to be'; it replaces the early copula → wéi 惟.
[E] Etymology not clear. The similarity with MK-Mon *ra* is interesting: *ra* "especially at closing sentence, marking unqualified character of assertion," perh. originally the weak form of *das* 'to be' (Shorto 1971). Alternatively, *yě* may be of ST origin, being connected with the WT suffix *-la* which usually marks the dative case, but is also used as a topicalizer like *ni* 'as for...' (Beyer 1992: 278).

yě $_2$ 冶 (jiaᴮ) **LH** jaᴮ, **OCM** *laʔ — **[T]** *ONW* ia
'To smelt, fuse, cast' [Meng] occurs also in Tai: S. *hlɔɔᴮ* 'cast' (metal) (Unger *Hao-ku* 36, 1990: 55).

yě $_3$ 野 (jiaᴮ) **LH** jaᴮ, **OCM** *laʔ, OCB *ljAʔ — **[T]** *ONW* ia
'Uncultivated land, grassland' 野 [Shi], 埜 [Lü] > 'rustic, wild' 野 [Lunyu], 'open country' [Chuci]. GY has an additional reading: QYS *źjwoᴮ*, LH *dźiaʔ* 'fields, open country', 墅 'field hut, detached residence, villa' [GY], 'field' [QY ms.] (Coblin *AO* 1986: 107). It is not clear if this is cognate to *yě*.
[E] The word *yě* may have one of two possible etymological connections. (1) ST: In Tibet and the Himalayas exists a common word *la which originally might have referred to an area far from settlements, i.e. 'wilderness': WT *la* 'mountain pass, hillside, mountain slope'; SWTib.: Dzongkha, Gloskad *laᴸ* 'mountain'; Western Tib.: Zangskar *la* 'border, frontier'; Kanauri: Pat. *lha*, Kaike *la* 'mountain'; Tamang *lah²¹* 'hill'. Or (2) the word belongs to the same AA root to which also belongs → yì$_{35}$ 繹: OKhmer *lā* [laa] 'to open, unfold, extend...' ⅹ *dalā* [dlaa] 'to be open, extensive, broad' (of space); PMonic *lah > OMon 'to extend' > Mod. Mon 'be level, flat, extensive'.

yè $_1$ 夜 (jiaᶜ) **LH** jaᶜ, **OCM** *jah > jakh OCB *(l)jAks
'Night' [OB, Shi].
[T] *Sin Sukchu SR* je (去); *ONW* ia < ja
[N] OC initial *j- is likely in the phonetic series 亦. The final OC *-k is not certain. In the oldest parts of *Shījīng* (*Dàyǎ* 278; 255.5, and in 124.4) the rime words had no *-k (Baxter 1992: 311f). In later parts it rimes with words in *-akh (OCB *-aks) (Shi 17.1; 100.3); in one older ode (*Xiǎoyǎ* 194.2) *yè* rimes with words in *-ak. This distribution suggests that in early Zhou times one strain of OC was lacking the *-k. In any case, OC often adds a final *-k to words which in TB have open vowels (§6.1), therefore this is the ST etymon for 'night':
[E] ST: PTB *ya 'night' (*STC* no. 417) > Chepang *yaʔ-diŋ* 'night', *yoh* 'yesterday', *yoh-dyah-may* 'last night'; WB *ñaᶜ* 'evening' < *ne-ja* 'sun–night', JP *naʔ⁵⁵* < *nak⁵⁵* 'evening'; Dulong *ɟaʔ* 'night', Karen *hja* (*STC* p. 188). Lushai *zaanᴸ* ~ *zanᶠ* < *jaŋ* (?) 'night', *niᶠ-zaanᴸ* < *jaanh* < *jaans* 'last night', Areng (Khami/Kuki-Chin) *jaŋ* 'yesterday' (Löffler *Anthropos* 55, 1960: 553); Limbu *ya:n* 'day' (24 hrs.) (quantifier suffix). → xī$_1$ 夕 is usually thought to be cognate, but TB keeps the etyma ST *rjak '24

hrs., day, night', and *ja 'night' strictly separate, and there is no reason why this should not be done in OC.

yè₂ 液 (jiäk) **LH** jak, **OCM** *jak < *r-jak
'Fluid, moisture' [Zhuang], 'to moisten' [Zhouli].
[E] ST: PTB *ryak (*STC* no. 204) > WT *žag < ryak* 'grease' (in liquid state); WB *pan-rak* 'juice of flowers' ⋈ *ə-rak* 'liquor'; NNaga *rja:k 'oil', Lush *sa^{L}-hriak^{F}* 'grease, oil' (*HST:* 81).

yè₃ 饁 (jäp 3) **LH** jɑp (or wɑp ?), **OCM** *wap (or *jap ?)
'To carry food to' (workers in the field) [Shi] survives in PMin *jiap (or *jiat ?) 'to eat' (J. Norman's Mǐn reconstruction).

yè₄ 葉 (jiäp) **LH** jɑp, **OCM** *lap, OCB *ljap — **[T]** *ONW* iap
'Leaf, foliage, generation' [Shi]. LH *jɑp* rather than *jap* is suggested by Mǐn forms.
[D] In some southern dialects *yè* also seems to be the word for 'wing': W-Wēnzhōu *iɛ^{D2}* 'leaf', *^{2}iɛ-^{45}p^{h}ɔ* (written 翼膀) 'wing'; PMin *ziap > Yǒngān *siɔ^{B2}*, Fúān *siɛp^{D2}*, Zhèyáng *siat* 'wing'; Northern Mǐn *ziaʔ^{D2} 'fin' (J. Norman, p. c.). Perh. a substratum had some influence on this semantic development, note Tai: S. *sa^{B1}-laap^{D1L}* <- Khmer /slaap/ 'wing, feathers, hair' (*sa-* is a pre-syllable).
[E] ST: PTB *lap 'leaf' (*STC* no. 321) > Kanauri *lab* 'leaf', Nung *śelap* 'leaves for packing food'; WB *lyap* 'very thin'; Limbu *lap* 'wing', JP *lap^{31}* 'leaf', WT *lo-ma < lop*, West Tib. *lob-ma* 'leaf' ⋈ *lo < lop* 'year' ⋈ *dab-ma < ɴlap* 'leaf, wing' [J. Sun acc. to Matisoff 1995a: 67].

⋈ **shì** 世 (śjäi^{C}) **LH** śas, **OCM** *lhats < *-ps
'Generation, epoch' [Shi] > 'world' [Li] (Pulleyblank 1962: 234).
[T] *Sin Sukchu SR* ṣi (去); *MGZY* shi (去) [ṣi]; *ONW* śei
[<] iterative devoicing of *lap (§5.2.3), + s/h-suffix (§4.2), meaning successive foliages of a tree > generations.
[E] The relationship with WT *rabs* 'lineage, succession of families, generation' is not clear because the initial correspondence is unusual (OC *l = WT r).

⋈ **yì** 裔 (jiäi^{C}) **LH** jas, **OCM** *lats < *laps ?
'Posterity, descendants' [Zuo].
[<] perh. this word is a back formation (voicing) from *shì*.
[E] ? ST: Perh. WT *rabs* 'lineage, successions of families'. For the initials, see §12.9 Written Tibetan (6). However, see → là₃ 臘.

[C] Allofams are perh. → dié 牒, → xiè₄ 屧.

yè₅ 帢 (ʔjɐp) **LH** ʔɨɑp, **OCM** *ʔap
'Kerchief' is acc. to *FY* (4) a Han period dialect word current north of the Yellow River. This word belongs perh. to → yǎn₂ 奄 and has TB cognates:
[E] ST: WT *yab-pa ~ g-yab-pa < g-ʔyap* 'to lock, cover over', *yab-yab-pa* 'hide, conceal' ⋈ *skyob-pa, (b)skyabs* 'to protect, defend, preserve', *skyob(s)* 'help, assistance', *skyabs* 'protection, defense'.

yè₆ 爗 (jäp 3, also jiəp) **LH** either jap or wap, or both, **OCM** *lap, *wap
'Gleaming' [Shi].
[E] A widely distributed phonaesthetic etymon in East and SE Asia, incl. AN, with the rime *-ap and initial *r-, *l-,*w-,*j-, etc., often with pre-syllables (see R. Bauer *LTBA* 15.2: 151–184). The L-initial variant is widely encountered in the area: PTB *s-lyap (*HPTB:* 338), WT *lhab-lhab-pa, lhab-se-lhabs* 'to flutter to and fro, to glimmer, glisten', Lepcha *lyóp* [ljɔ:p] 'flap', Adi *lip-lop* 'to flash' [Bodman ICSTLL 1987: 10];

WB *lyap-lyap* 'wavingly (as flag)' ⋈ *hlyap* 'lightning'; Lushai *in*^{L}*-hlap*^{H} 'to flick, flap' (someone with cloth etc.), JP *prap*^{55} 'a flash'. <> KT: Siam. *lɛɛp*^{D2L} ~ *ma-lɛɛp* 'to flash' (as lightning); PHlai *ɬjip*^{7} 'lightning'.

The W-initial variant also occurs in Tai: S. *wɛɛp*^{D2}*-wap*^{D2} 'glittering, flashing' (Manomaivibool 1975: 180). The Tai form looks like the equivalent of a hypothetical CH compound *yè-yì* 燁熠 *wap-wəp.

A Y-initial variant is common in TB: *ya:p 'wave, fan, paddle' (*HPTB:* 339) > Lushai *zaap*, Garo *tśo*, Tangkhul Naga *k*^{h}*əyap* 'fan', WB *yap;* WT *(g-)yab-mo* 'the act of fanning' ⋈ *g-yob-pa* 'to move about, swing, brandish'.

A variant is → yì$_{27}$ 熠 'be flashing'; perh. related to 'butterfly' → hú$_{6}$-dié 胡蝶. This etymon is perh. cognate to → yán$_{2}$ ~ → yán$_{3}$ 炎 where we also find the *w- ~ *l-doublets.

yè$_{7}$ 業 (ŋjɐp) **LH** ŋɨɑp, **OCM** *ŋap, OCB *ng(r)jap — **[T]** *ONW* ŋap
'Work, deed, achievement' [BI, Shu]. — Etymology not clear.
[T] *Sin Sukchu SR* ŋje (入); *ONW* ŋap

yè$_{8}$ 業 (ŋjɐp) **LH** ŋɨɑp, **OCM** *ŋap
'Be awe-inspiring, terrifying, terrific' [Shi] belongs to the wf → yán$_{8}$ 巖.

yī$_{1}$ 一 (ʔjet) **LH** ʔit, **OCM** *ʔit
'Be one, single, whole' [OB, Shi].
[T] *Sin S. SR* ʔi (入); *MGZY* Yi (入) [ʔji]; *MTang* ʔir, *ONW* ʔiit
[D] M-Xiàmén lit. *it*^{DI}; Fúzhōu *eiʔ*^{DI}; K-Méixiàn *jit*^{DI}; Y-Guǎngzhōu *jat*^{DI}
[E] ST: PTB *ʔit (*STC:* 94): Chepang *yat* 'one', Kanauri *ʔit* 'one', and WB *ac* 'unit, one' (*HST:* 114), Lushai *zet*^{H} 'first, previous'. This word is found only at the periphery of the ST area and must therefore be old. <> Tai *ʔet* occurs only in compounds and is clearly a CH loan, the native Tai word for 'one' is *nɨŋ*$^{A2/BI}$.

yī$_{2}$ 伊 (ʔi 4) **LH** ʔi, **OCM** *ʔi
'This' [Shi], starting in the 4th ~ 5th cent. AD 'he, she, it', survives as a 3rd person pron. in Wú dialects (Norman 1988: 118).
[T] *Sin Sukchu SR* ʔi (平); *MGZY* Yi (平) [ʔji]; *STC*A ʔɨ, *ONW* ʔii
[E] ST: Lushai *ʔi*^{L} 'this, that', Chepang *ʔiʔ* 'he', WB *i* 'this'. Perh. this is a widespread sound-symbolic area word, note the AA demonstrative *i / e [Pinnow 1965: 32].

yī$_{3}$ 衣 (ʔjei) **LH** ʔɨi, **OCM** *ʔəi (?), OCB *ʔjəj
'Garment, clothes' [Shi].
[T] *Sin Sukchu SR* ʔi (平); *MGZY* ʔi (平) [ʔi]; *ONW* ʔi
[D] PMin *ʔəi 'afterbirth' is the analog to a MC div. I *ʔậi*

⋈ **yì** 衣 (ʔjəi^{C}) **LH** ʔɨi^{C}, **OCM** *ʔəih, OCB *ʔjəjs
'To wear' [Shi].
[<] exoactive of *yī* 衣 (§4.3.2).
[N] This character writes on occasion the dynastic name Yīn 殷 LH *ʔɨn* (OCB *ʔjən) which points therefore to denasalization of a final consonant that seems to have originated in an early dialect such as Shandong (Baxter 1992: 295). Consequently, the family name Yī may be derived from an original Yīn.

[E] *Yī* 'clothes' may belong to a wf whose basic meaning is 'to envelop, conceal' and hence is cognate to → yī$_{5}$ 翳, *yǐn* 隱 (Karlgren 1933: 28; Lau 1999: 69).

Prob. ST: PTB *wit ⋈ *w(y)at 'wear clothes' [*HPTB:* 333, 508] > PLB *wit ~ *ʔwit 'wear clothes, cause to wear' [Matisoff 2002 no. 181]: open vowel forms of etyma alternate often with closed syllables in ST lgs. (§6.1); ST medial *w* often disappears in CH (§10.2.1), thus the ST proto-form might have been *ʔwəi(k/t).

yī₄ 依 (ʔjei) **LH** ʔɨi, **OCM** *ʔəi
'To lean on, rely on, depend on' [Shi] is thought to be cognate to → yǐ₃ 倚 (Wáng Lì).
ꭗ **yìn** 隱 (ʔjənᶜ [GY]), **LH** ʔɨnᶜ, **OCM** *ʔəns
'To lean on' [Meng].
[C] Perh. → yīn₁ 因 is an allofam (Pulleyblank in Rosemont 1991: 32), but the vowels do not agree. This is perh. a ST word: WB *inᶜ* 'roll over and over obliquely, to lean'.

yī₅ 翳 (ʔiei[ᶜ]) **LH** ʔei(h), **OCM** *ʔə̂i(h) or *ʔî(h)
'Screen, shade, cover' [Guoyu] is prob. cognate to → yī₃ 衣 (Karlgren 1933: 28).
ꭗ **yǐ** 扆 (ʔjeiᴮ) **LH** ʔɨiᴮ, **OCM** *ʔəiʔ
'A screen' (with ax patterns) [Shu].
ꭗ **yǐn** 隱 (ʔjənᴮ) **LH** ʔɨnᴮ, **OCM** *ʔənʔ
'To conceal' [Lunyu], 'low wall' [Zuo] (Karlgren 1933: 28).
ꭗ **ài** 薆 (ʔậiᶜ) **LH** ʔəs, **OCM** *ʔə̂s
'To screen, conceal' [Chuci] (Wáng Lì 1982: 449).

yī₆ 醫 (ʔɨ) **LH** ʔɨə, **OCM** *ʔə
'Potion' [Zhouli], 'physician' [Zuo].
[E] <> KT: PHlai *ja¹* 'medicine', PKS *gja² 'medicine, to cure', PTai *ʔɨaᴬ¹ 'medicine'.

yí₁ 台 'I, my' → **yú₅** 余 'I, we'

yí₂ 貽詒 (jiɨ) **LH** jə, **OCM** *lə — **[T]** *ONW* iə
'To transmit, bequeath, hand down, give' [Shi]. This word appears to form an introvert / extrovert pair with → yǐ₂ 以 'take', like 'buy / sell', 'borrow / lend'; however, the extrovert form ought to have tone C. Here, *yí* 'give' appears to be primary while *yǐ* would be a tone B derivation. The two are prob. not cognate after all, because of what would be an unusual morphology.
ꭗ **sì** 嗣 (zɨᶜ) **LH** ziəᶜ, **OCM** *s-ləh
'Continue, succeed, inherit' [Shi].
[<] iterative / caus. of *yí* 貽詒 *lə (§5.2.3–2). Pulleyblank (1973: 120) relates this word to → xù₂ 序敘緒.
[E] ST: Lushai *tʰlaʔᴸ < tʰlaʔ/h < s-laʔ/h* (?) 'descendant, offspring, posterity' (*CVST* 3: 5), WT *slas* 'retinue, train, attendants' ꭗ *slar < sla-ru* 'afterwards, hereafter, again', the WT root *sla means 'late, later, after' (Geilich 1994: 48).
ꭗ **yìn** 胤 (jienᶜ) **LH** jinᶜ, **OCM** *ləns
'Be a follower, successor, heir, posterity' [Shi, Shu].
[<] noun from *yí* 貽詒 *lə (§6.4.3) + general purpose tone C (§3.5).
ꭗ **yìng** 媵 (jiəŋᶜ) **LH** ʔɨŋᶜ, **OCM** *ləŋh
'To make a present, exchange presents, to present (someone) to serve, concubine' [BI]; 'concubine' 媵 [Zuo].
[<] terminative of *yí* 貽詒 *lə (§6.5.1) + exoactive (§4.3). A gloss for this word includes 'a girl who follows the principal wife to her husband and becomes his concubine' (*GSR* 893k); this implies a goal with finality, hence perhaps the terminative morpheme.

yí₃ 夷 (ji) **LH** ji, **OCM** *l(ə)i, OCB ljəj — **[T]** *ONW* i < ji
The name of non-Chinese tribes, prob. Austroasiatic, to the east and southeast of the

central plain (Shandong, Huái River basin), since the Spring and Autumn period also a general word for 'barbarian' (Pulleyblank 1983: 440). Since the ancient Yuè (= Viet) word for 'sea' is said to have been *yí* [Yuè juè shū 3.8], the people's name might have originated as referring to people living by the sea (as can be observed elsewhere, e.g. the 'Morini' in Caesar's Gaul, or 'Pomerania' along the Baltic coast in Poland, cf. Lat. *mare*, Russian *morie* 'sea'). The Yuè word *yí* *l(ə)i 'sea' can be connected with AA-Khmer *dhle* /tlé/ 'expanse of water' ⋡ OKhmer *danle(y)* /dənlee/ 'lake, sea'. <> Miao lgs. have forms like *tḷi, tḷe* 'river' which, however, can instead (or also) be associated with → xī_{10} 溪.

yí_4 夷 (ji) **LH** ji, **OCM** *l(ə)i, OCB ljəj

'Be level' (road), (make level:) 'pacify, at ease' [Shi]; 'rule, norm' [BI, Shi] > 'normally' 彝 [BI]. This word 'level' is unrelated to → yì_9 易 'easy'.

⋡ **sì** 肆 (si^C) **LH** si^C, **OCM** *sih < *slih ?

'To be lax' [Shu], 'unrestrained' [Lun] > caus. 'to relax, pardon' [Shu].

[<] caus. of *yí* 夷 (ji) *li 'easy' (§5.2.2; §4.3). The meaning may have evolved under the influence of *shè* 舍 (under → shě_2 舍捨); at any rate *shě* demonstrates semantic parallelism between 'easy, relax' and 'let go'.

[C] This is prob. the same etymon as → yí_5 夷侇 'set out, spread'.

yí_5 夷侇 (ji) **LH** ji, **OCM** *li

'Extend, expose, display' 夷 [Li]; 'set out, spread out' 侇 [Yili].

⋡ **shī** 尸 (śi) **LH** śi, **OCM** *lhi — **[T]** *ONW* śi

'To spread out, lie down flat' (in order to sleep) [Lun] (Geilich 1994: 277); 'motionless, to set forth' (sacrificial dishes) [Shi] > 'personator of a dead ancestor' [Shi] > 'corpse' (Carr, *CAAAL* 24, 1985: 1ff).

[N] In Old Korean 尸 is used to transcribe what is prob. a lateral like *l* (Vovin 1999).

[E] The common assumption that *shī* is cognate to → sǐ 死 (si^B) LH si^B, *siʔ 'to die' must be rejected because MC initial *ś-* (< *lh-, *nh-, *hj-) never derives from an *s-, except when they share an initial *l or *n (such a case is *sì* below). Perh. cognate to → shēn_2 身 'body' (Geilich 1994: 277).

⋡ **shǐ** 矢 (śi^B) **LH** śi^B, **OCM** *lhiʔ — **[T]** *ONW* śi

'To line up, marshal, display, arrange' [Shi]. Perh. → shǐ_3 矢 'swear' is the same word.

⋡ **sì** 肆 (si^C) **LH** si^C, **OCM** *sih < *slih ?

'To spread, set forth, arrange' [Shi] > 'a set, row' (of ancestral vessels) [BI], (of bells) [Zhouli] > 'shop, market' [Lun, Zuo].

[<] *lhi + caus. s-prefix (§5.2.2) + s-suffix (§4.3).

[E] This is prob. the same etymon as → yí_4 夷 'level', also related to items under → yǐn_2 引 (Geilich 1994: 277).

yí_6 迤迆 (jie) **LH** jɑi, **OCM** *lai

'To slant, deflect' 迆 [Zhouli]; 'turn aside' (of a river's course) 迤 [OB, Shu].

[E] ST: Lushai lei^H 'to be on one side, be awry, leaning to one side, rock and roll' (as a boat) ⋡ $leiʔ^L$ < *leis* 'to pour out, upon, water plants'. For more CH and Lushai cognates, see → shī_{12} 釃.

⋡ **shī** 施 (śjie) **LH** śɑi, **OCM** *lhai

'Dodgingly' (of walking) [Meng].

[<] *lai + iterative (?) devoicing (§5.2.3).

⋡ **zhì** 阤 (ḍje^B) **LH** ḍɑi^B, **OCM** *d-laiʔ

'Slope' [Zhouli].

yí$_7$ 迻移䄬 → **chǐ$_1$** 拸

yí$_8$ 移 (jie) **LH** jɑi, **OCM** *lai, OCB *ljaj — **[T]** Sui-Tang i, *ONW* ie,
'To change, alter' (one's character) [Meng].
[E] ST *laj: PTB *laay 'change, exchange' (Matisoff 1995a: 42) > Chepang *hles* 'change condition' (for better), WB *lai*^{B} 'change, exchange; empty' (contents of one vessel into another, also hlai^B) ⋇ *hlai*^{B}*-p*^{h}*ai* 'exchange'; JP *lai*^{33} 'to change' ⋇ *gə*^{31}*-lai*^{33} 'change, exch.' ⋇ *mə*^{31}*-lai*^{55} 'change, substitute'; Tiddim Chin *laiʔ*^{L} (< *laih* < -*s*) 'change', Dimasa *salai* 'alter, change, exch.', Garo *sre* 'change, exchange' (*STC* p. 64). This etymon is distinct from → yí$_9$ 移 as Tiddim Chin shows.

⋇ **yì** 易 (jiäk) **LH** jek, **OCM** *lek
'To change' [OB, Shi]. The original OB graph shows the content of one vessel being changed over into another (K. Takashima, p. c.).
[<] *lai + k-extension (§6.1).
[E] ST: TB-Lushai *leet*^{F} / *leʔ*^{L} < *leet* / *leh* 'to alter, change'. CH -> Tai: S. *lɛɛk*^{D2L} < *dl- 'to change, exchange'; PKS *hlik^7 'exchange'.
Sagart (1999: 71) adds → cì$_4$ 賜錫 'be given' to this item. This root is distinct from PTB *ley 'barter' (*STC* no. 283, 293), see → shē$_1$ 賒.

[E] Shorto 1972 relates the TB items to PMK *kla(a)y > Mon *klai* 'translate', Khmer *khla:y* 'change, dissolve'. -> PTai *klai^{A1} 'to pass by, change into'. The connection with → gǎi 改 'change' if any is not clear.

yí$_9$ 移 (jie) **LH** jɑi, **OCM** *lai, OCB *ljaj
'To transfer, move' (population) [Shu], 迻 [Chuci].
[E] ST: Tiddim Chin *lal*^{R} / *lal*^{F} 'to migrate', perh. also Tamang ^{4}*le:* 'displace'. Tiddim Chin shows that this etymon is distinct from → yí$_8$ 移. A cognate may be → xǐ$_2$ 徙. <> Tai: S. *ree*^{B2} 'wander about, move, changeable' is unrelated and prob. a MK loan: OKhmer *re /ree ~ rəə/ 'to move, stir, change course or direction, come and go...'

yí$_{10}$ 儀宜 (ŋje 3) **LH** ŋɨɑi, **OCM** *ŋai
'Be proper, correct, suitable' 宜 [Shi], 儀 [BI]; 'proper conduct, demeanor, manner, dignity' 儀 [BI, Shi].
[T] *Sin S. SR* i, (ŋi)* (平), *LR* ŋi, i; *MGZY* ngi (平) [ŋi]; *ONW* ŋe

⋇ **yì** 義議 (ŋje^C 3) **LH** ŋɨɑi^C, **OCM** *ŋaih
'Be right, righteous, proper' [BI, Shi]; 'true sense, meaning' [Li]; (putative: 'consider to be right':) 'to plan, criticize' 議 [Shi]. A philosophical term like this is difficult to translate; in his *Mòzǐ* translation, Yi-pao Mei renders 義 by English 'notion, idea, view, purpose, standard'; these overlap with the KN semantic field. – The role of tone C is not clear (§4.2).

⋇ **xī** 犧 (xje 3) **LH** hɨɑi, **OCM** *hŋai
'Sacrificial animal, pure victim' > 'sacrificial' (vessel) [Shi] is prob. a derivation from the present root, the voiceless initial goes perh. back to an earlier k- or s-prefix which forms nouns (§5.4).

[E] ST *ŋaj: PTB *ŋa:y > KN-Lushai *ŋai*^{H} / *ŋaiʔ*^{L} < *ŋais* 'to think, consider, be necessary, have need to, be customary'; KN-Khami *ŋài'* 'to wish, need'; Lai *ŋaaj* / *ŋaʔj* 'to yearn, long for'; in KN this is the word for 'to love': Tiddim *ŋa:i*^{2} < *ŋa:i* / *ŋaiʔ*. Also note WT *dŋos* 'reality, real, proper, true' which may be related.

[C] Benedict (1995: 33) connects this group with wǒ 我 'I' (under → wú$_2$ 吾) and yán 顔 'face' (under → yà$_2$ 御迓訝); Matisoff (*BSOAS* 63.3, 2000: 364f) with → ài$_2$ 愛 'love'.

yí₁₁ 儀 (ŋje 3) **LH** ŋɨɑi, **OCM** *ŋai — **[T]** *ONW* ŋe
'To come' [Shu acc. to *GSR*].
[E] ST *ŋaj: JP *ŋai³³* 'to come, arrive', NNaga *ŋoj [French 1983: 318].
[D] Acc. to *FY* (2.14) an ancient Chén-Yǐng dialect word for → lái 來 'come'.

ꕤ **yì** 詣 (ŋiei^C) **LH** ŋei^C, **OCM** *ŋîh or *ŋə̂ih
'Come to' [Mo].

yí₁₂ 遺 (jiwi) **LH** wi, **OCM** *wi
'To leave, hand down' > (leave alone:) 'reject, throw away, neglect' [BI, Shi].
[T] *Sin Sukchu SR* i (平); *MGZY* ywi (平) [yi]
[E] This word is perh. related to TB: Lushai *vui^R* 'to be offended, displeased'.

ꕤ **yì** 遺 (jiwi^C) **LH** wih, **OCM** *wih
'To present' [Meng].
This etymon is prob. not related to → kuì₂ 餽饋.

yí₁₃ 疑 (ŋjɨ) **LH** ŋɨə, **OCM** *ŋə
'To doubt' [Lunyu], 'suspect, hesitate' [Li] > 'to fear' [Li] is perh. related to → ài₅ 礙 'obstruct'.
[T] *MTang* ŋi [ŋgi], *ONW* ŋiə

yí₁₄ 彝 → **yí₄** 夷

yǐ₁ 已 (jiɨ^B) **LH** jə^B, **OCM** *ləʔ
'To cease, end, finish, already' [Shi]. — Etymology is not clear.
[T] *Sin Sukchu SR* i (上); *MGZY* yi (上) [ji]; *MTang* i *ONW* iə

yǐ₂ 以 (jiɨ^B) **LH** jə^B, **OCM** *ləʔ
'To take' (e.g. prisoners) [OB], 'use, employ, in order to' tr. [BI, Shi].
[T] *Sin Sukchu SR* i (上); *MGZY* yi (上) [ji]; *MTang* i *ONW* iə
[E] ST *lə: Lushai *la^L / laak < laah* 'to take, get', Tiddim *laa^R / laak^R < laaʔ / laak* 'to take', Newari *laa-* (Unger; Geilich 1994: 137). But the TB items have also been associated with CH → yǔ₉ 與 'give'. Prob. related to → shì₉ 式 'use'; a possible derivation may be → yì₁ 弋; see also → yí₂ 貽詒.

yǐ₃ 倚 (ʔje^B) **LH** ʔɨɑi^B, **OCM** *ʔaiʔ — **[T]** *Sin Sukchu* 椅 *SR* ʔi (上)
'To lean against, pull aside, lead astray' [Shi], 'rely upon' [Guoce] is thought to be cognate to → yī₄ 依 (e.g. Wáng Lì 1982: 392).

yǐ₄ 猗 (ʔje^B) **LH** ʔɨɑi^B, **OCM** *ʔaiʔ
'Luxuriant' (leaves) [Shi] may be related to → yuàn₁ 苑 'trees with rich foliage'.

yǐ₅ 扆 → **yī₅** 翳

yǐ₆ 蟻 (ŋje^B 3) **LH** ŋɨɑi^B, **OCM** *ŋaiʔ
'Ant' [Li] > 'ant-colored' [Shu]. The first syllable in Mand. *mǎ-yǐ* 馬蟻 is prob. an old prefix which occurs also with other animal names (Unger *Hao-ku* 31, 1985: 308).
[T] *Sin Sukchu SR* i (上); *MGZY* ngi (上) [ŋi] — **[D]** PMin *ŋ̊iɑ(i)^B

~ **yǐ** 螘 (ŋjei^B) **LH** ŋɨi^B, **OCM** *ŋəiʔ
'Ant' [Chuci], a phonological variant of the above (Baxter 1992: 417; §11.1.2).
[E] ST: KN-Lai *hŋeʔr-tee* 'ant' (*tee* 'small'). This implies that both forms show the change of ST *-r > OC *-i (§7.7.4). Folk etymology derives *yí* 蟻 from 義 'orderly'.

yì₁ 弋 (jiək) **LH** jək, **OCM** *lək
('To take / seize birds':) 'to shoot (birds) with stringed arrow' [Shi], ('taker / seizer' of

birds etc.:) 'bird of prey' [Dadai Liji]. The word is supposed to mean 'take' in a *Shūjīng* passage which would be the obvious semantic communality with 'arrow' and 'eagle'. It may then be a derivation from → yǐ$_2$ 以 'take'.

[E] If this etymology holds, *yì* would not be related to WT *mda'* etc. (mentioned under → shí$_9$ 射 'shoot'). However, it could still be related to WT *glag* 'eagle, vulture' (*CVST* 3: 8).

yì$_2$ 艾刈 (ŋjɐi^C) **LH** ŋɨɑs, **OCM** *ŋa(t)s

'To mow, cut, reap' 艾刈 [Shi]; 'regulate, govern, orderly' 艾 [Shi].

[E] ST: WT *rŋa-ba, brŋas* 'to mow, cut, reap', West Tib. col. *rŋab-pa* (*HST:* 111). The origin of the meanings 'regulate' is ambiguous, it could be derived from 'to cut' (> 'trim' etc.?), or it could be derived from → yù$_{16}$ 禦.

yì$_3$ 亦 (jiäk) **LH** jak, **OCM** *jak — [T] *ONW* iek

'Also, furthermore, then' [OB, Shi].

[E] ST *wiak ?: Lushai *ve^L < veʔ/h* 'also' ⋈ *vek^R < vek* 'again, over again'. For TB *wia-* (< *we-, wia-*) = OC *ja-, see §10.1.

yì$_4$ 腋掖亦 (jiäk) **LH** jak, **OCM** *jak

'Armpit' 亦 [OB], 腋 [Zhuang], 掖 [Li], 'lift under the arms' [Zuo].

[E] ST and area word: TB-Mru *yak* 'armpit' (Löffler 1966: 119), Lushai *zak^L < jak* 'armpit'; Newari *ja:k-wa* 'armpit', Lepcha *yak* 'tickle' (L. Hayes *LTBA* 15.2, 1992: 186); JR *təjǎk* 'hand'; PTB *(g-)yak > WB *gyak-kali* 'armpit' (*STC:* 167; 170), PLB *ʔjak 'tickle', and *ʔgjak 'cubit' (i.e. 'arm'). *STC:* 34 interprets the WB form as 'arm' (PTB *(g-)yak); Shī Xiàngdōng (2000: 127) related this word to PTB *lak 'hand, arm'. <> PKS *k^{h}ja:k^7 'armpit' (Thurgood), *h-jak^D (Edmondson / Yang 1988). Tai: S. *rak^{D2}* 'the armpits' is perh. connected (Manomaivibool 1975: 252). The syn. → gē$_4$ 胳 may represent a different root.

yì$_5$ 衣 → **yī$_3$** 衣

yì$_6$ 役 (jiwäk) **LH** wek, **OCM** *wek < *wai-k

'To do service, do labor, corvée' [Shi, Shu] > 'to serve' [Meng], 'to toil' [Zhuang], 'affair, matter' [Guoyu]; > 'to function as, to be' [Guoyu]. Often words meaning 'do, make' also develop the meaning 'function as, act as, to be', see → wéi$_3$ 為, → zuò$_3$ 作.

[T] *Sin Sukchu SR* ŋyj (入); *MGZY* ywi (入) [yi]

[E] The word could be derived from wéi 為 *wai 'to do' + k-extension (§6.1) and have spread to neighboring SE Asian lgs. because Chinese and other populations were required by CH governments to perform military or other service *yì* 役: MK and Tai lgs.: Viet. *việc*, Muong [wiək] 'work, job' (Pulleyblank *JCL* 22.1, 1994: 83). <> Tai: Saek *viak^{D2L}* 'work', S. *wiek^3* [Maspero 1912: 73]. Perh. LB forms like Lahu *vêʔ < s-wat* 'work, toil, a job' (archaic) may also be connected (Benedict *LTBA* 14.2, 1991: 149).

yì$_7$ 曳泄 'drag' → **yì$_{16}$** 抴

yì$_8$ 邑 (ʔjəp) **LH** ʔip, **OCM** *ʔəp, OCB *ʔ(r)jup

'Settlement, town' [OB, BI, Shi], 'to take up residence' [Shi]; a general term for a place where people dwell, i.e. no implied reference to wall, market, administrative function, and the like.

[E] Etymology not certain, but prob. ST and related to the root *ʔip 'shelter' which is cited under → qì$_7$ 葺 'thatch' with which *yì* is prob. related. Alternatively, *yì* could be connected with PTB *ʔim 'house as a home': Magar *im ~ jum*, WB *im*, Lushai *ʔin^R* <

ʔinʔ 'dwelling house, home', TGTM *ᴮdim, Kaike *jim,* WT *kʰyim* 'house, dwelling place, home, residence'.

yì₉ 易 (jieᶜ) **LH** jeᶜ, **OCM** *lekh, OCB *ljeks
'Be easy, at ease, neglect' [Shi]. 易 was borrowed to write → yì₆ 役 (jiwäk) LH *wiek* in some pre-Han texts as if there might still have been a *w element in the initial as in the TB cognate.
[T] *Sin Sukchu SR* i (去); *MGZY* yi (去) [ji]; *Sui-Tang* i, *ONW* ie
[E] ST: PTB *lway 'easy' (*STC* no. 302): WB *lwai* 'easy, yielding', JP *loi³¹* 'easy'; WT *legs* 'good, happy, comfortable' is phonologically / morphologically identical with OC; note also WT *yag-po* ~ *'jag-po* 'good' (*STC:* 54). This word is sometimes thought to be related to *yì* 易 'change' (under → yí₈ 移), i.e. < 'changeable' (so Karlgren 1956: 12), but the TB cognates show that these are different etyma.

yì₁₀ 易 'change' → **yí₈** 移

yì₁₁ 佚 → **shī₂** 失

yì₁₂ 軼 → **yì₁₃** 泆溢

yì₁₃ 泆溢 (jiet) **LH** jit, **OCM** *lit
'To rush forth' 泆 [Shu]; 'overflow' 溢 [Xiaojing], 'inundate' [Li], 'overwhelm' [Shi].
[D] In M-Xiàmén the graph writes a different word *joʔᴬ¹* 'to wave, shake'. Perh. this wf is merely a semantic extension of the wf under → shī₂ 失.
[E] ST: Lepcha *lyit / lít* 'to overflow' (Unger *Hao-ku* 36, 1990: 56).

ᛤ **yì** 泆軼 (jiet, diet) **LH** jit, det, **OCM** *lit, *lît
'To gush forth' 泆 [Zhuang]; 'rush past, overtake' 軼 [Zuo].

ᛤ **dié** 迭跌 (diet) **LH** det, **OCM** *lît — **[T]** *MTang* diar < dɨar, *ONW* dėt
'To rush' 跌 [Mo]; 'rush into' 迭 [Zuo].

yì₁₄ 泄洩 → **xiè₁** 泄洩

yì₁₅ 勩 (jiäiᶜ) **LH** jas, **OCM** *las
'Toil, fatigue' [Shi].
[E] ST: WT *las*, OTib. and dial. *blas* 'work, toil', TGTM *gjat < *gl- (*HST:* 162). The ancient Wú dialect word *lì* 厲 (ljäiᶜ) 'to do' [FY 6; EY] could be related. Alternatively, *lì* 厲 may be connected with → lì₂₀ 勵 'energetically'. *Yì* 肄 'toil' (under → xí₃ 習) may possibly be a vocalic variant.

yì₁₆ 抴 (jiäiᶜ, jiät) **LH** jas, jat, **OCM** *lat(s)
'To pull' [Xun], 'oar' [Chuci, also 枻].
[E] Sagart (1999: 73) relates this word to 'leading string' → xiè₂ 紲絏緤. Another possible allofam is **yì** 曳 (jiäiᶜ) 'drag, trail' [Shi], 'dragging, slow moving' 泄 [Shi].

yì₁₇ 益 (ʔjiäk 4) **LH** ʔiek, **OCM** *ʔek — **[T]** *ONW* ʔiek
'To add, increase, profit' [Shi], 'more, advantage' [Lunyu]. Acc. to Bodman (1980: 66) this word is related to WT *skye(d)* 'growth, increase, profit, benefit' ᛤ *skye-ba* 'be born' ᛤ *skyed-pa, bskyed* 'to generate, procreate, produce'; the WT forms should then derive from an earlier *s-ʔe. For the CH final *-k,* see §6.1.

yì₁₈ 嗌 (ʔjäk) **LH** ʔiek, **OCM** *ʔek
'Throat' [Zhuang] > 'flesh on the neck' 膉 [Yili].

ᛤ **yì** 縊 (ʔieiᶜ) **LH** ʔeᶜ, **OCM** *ʔîth < **ʔîkh
'To strangle' [Zuo].

[E] ST: PTB *ʔik (*STC* no. 112) > Nung *i* < *ik* 'strangle'; WB *ac* 'squeeze, throttle' (*HST:* 142). WT *ske* 'neck, throat' could either derive from *s-ʔe and then belong to this wf; or it could belong to → jǐng$_2$ 頸 'neck'.

[C] This wf is prob. related to → è$_1$ 厄軛 'narrow passage', and / or to → yān$_1$ 咽 'gullet' (so Wáng Lì 1982: 268); or to → yē 噎 'choke' (Wáng Lì).

yì$_{19}$ 縊 → **yì$_{18}$** 嗌

yì$_{20}$ 膉 → **yì$_{18}$** 嗌

yì$_{21}$ 溢 → **yì$_{13}$** 泆溢

yì$_{22}$ 翼 (jiək) **LH** jək, **OCM** *lək, OCB *ljək — **[T]** *ONW* ik
'Wing' [Shi].
[D] PMin *zit 'wing': Xiàmén *sit*^{D2}
[E] ? ST: This is perh. related to PTB *g-lak 'hand' (Matisoff 1995a: 51f) > WT *lag-pa* 'hand, arm'; PLB *lak > WB *lak* 'hand' (*STC:* 171; *HST:* 37). Matisoff suggests that → lì$_1$ 力 (ljək) OCB *C-rə̆k 'strength' may be cognate to the TB items instead (the CH graph pictures an arm). Syn. CMin *ziɑp 'wing' see → yè$_4$ 葉.

yì$_{23}$ 意 → **yì$_{24}$** 憶臆

yì$_{24}$ 憶臆 (ʔjək) **LH** ʔɨək, **OCM** *ʔək, OCB *ʔ(r)jək — **[T]** *ONW* ʔik
'One's breast, thoughts' 臆 [Lie] > ('keep in one's breast / thoughts'?:) 'to remember' 憶 [Li]; ('feeling in one's breast' ?:) 'satisfied, tranquil' 憶 [Zuo].

ж **yì** 意 (ʔɨ^C) **LH** ʔɨə^C, **OCM** *ʔəkh, OCB *ʔ(r)jəks
'To think' [Shi], 'thought, intention, will' [Li].
[T] *Sin Sukchu SR* ʔi (去); *MGZY* 'i (去) [ʔi]; *MTang* ʔi, *ONW* ʔiə
[<] exoactive (?) of *yì* 憶臆 *ʔək (§4.3).

[E] In contrast to → yīng$_3$ 膺 which signifies the outside aspect of the 'breast, chest', *yì* refers to the internal aspect. Wáng Lì (1982: 312) relates this word to → yīng$_3$ 膺. Prob. not related to WT *yid* 'mind', see → xuè$_1$ 血.

yì$_{25}$ 臆 → **yì$_{24}$** 憶臆

yì$_{26}$ 肄 → **xí$_3$** 習

yì$_{27}$ 熠 (jiəp, jəp) **LH** jəp, wəp, **OCM** *wəp
'Be flashing' [Shi]. Variant of → yè$_6$ 燁.

yì$_{28}$ 藝 (ŋjiäi^C 4) **LH** ŋias, **OCM** *ŋets, OCB *ŋJets
('To establish':) 'to plant, cultivate' (a crop, land) 埶蓺[Shi], 藝 [Shu] > 'accomplished, skill' 藝 [Shu], 'art, method, rule, regular' 藝 [Zuo], 臬 [Zhuang].
[T] *Sin Sukchu SR* i (去); *MGZY* yi (去) [ji]; *ONW* ŋiei,
[E] CH -> Tai: S. *kra*^{4}*-net*^{4} 'tactics, methods, strategy'.

ж **shè** 設 (śjät) **LH** śat, **OCM** *nhet < *ŋhet, OCB *h(l)jet — **[T]** *ONW* śat
'To set up, establish' [Shi]. The OC initial is assumed on the basis of its relationship with *yì* 藝. MC *śj-* from *hŋi/e- via *hńi- is a regular development.
[<] valence increase devoicing of *yì* 藝 (§5.2.2).
[E] ST: Lushai *ŋhet*^{L} / *ŋheʔ*^{L} < *ŋhets* 'be firm, establish' ж *ŋheet*^{F} intr. 'to settle or get firm' (as earth, cooked rice). It is not clear if or how WT *gñod* 'strength, durability' (< *g-nyot* or *g-ŋyot* ?) may be related.

⋇ **shì** 勢 (śjäi^C) **LH** śas, **OCM** *nhets < *ŋhets — **[T]** *ONW* śei
('What is established, is a given, a reality':) 'force of circumstance, conditions' 勢 [Meng], 'influence' 埶 [Li].
[<] exopass. of *shè* 設 (§4.4).
[E] ST *ŋəls ?: The basic meaning of the ST root is 'certain, firm, make firm > establish': PTB *ŋeis > WT *ŋes-pa* 'certain, true, firm', Lushai *ŋei^L < ŋeih < ŋes* 'really, truly, verily', Tiddim *ŋɛːi^F < ŋɛːih < ŋɛːis* 'certainly, be sure'; Limbu *nɛma < nɛss-* 'to lie' (including of geographical features, fields, etc.). The CH meaning 'to cultivate' is therefore derived.

yì₂₉ 豙 (ŋjei^C) **LH** ŋɨs or ŋɨi^C ?, **OCM** *ŋəs ? or *ŋəih (< *ŋəls) ?
'Enraged boar' 豙 [SW] > 'bold, resolute' 毅 [Shu], note the Lushai parallel for this semantic extension.
[T] *Sin Sukchu SR* i (去); *MGZY* ngi (去) [ŋi]
[E] ST: KN: Lushai *(sa^L-)ŋhal^L < ŋhalh < ŋhals* 'wild pig' ⋇ *ŋhal^R < ŋhalʔ* 'ill-behaved, unruly, over-bold'; Paangkhua *maŋàl ~ raŋàl* 'wild boar', Tiddim Chin *ŋal^F < ŋalh < ŋals* 'wild pig'.

yì₃₀ 毅 → **yì₂₉** 豙

yì₃₁ 裔 (jiäi^C) **LH** jas, **OCM** *lats
'Border' [Zuo] can be compared to WT *ldebs* 'side, enclosure, fence' (*HST:* 47).

yì₃₂ 裔 'posterity' → **yè₄** 葉

yì₃₃ 逸 → **shī₂** 失

yì₃₄ 詣 → **yí₁₁** 儀

yì₃₅ 繹 (jiäk) **LH** jak ~ jɑk, **OCM** *lak
'Unfold, draw out' (a thread); 'long-drawn' > 'in line > repeatedly' [Lun]; 'continue' [Shi], 'in a line, succession' 繹 [Lunyu] (paronym of → xù₂ 序敍緒); 'post horses, relay station' 驛 [SW]; 'interpret, translate' 譯 [Li]; 'be relaxed, pleased, delighted' 懌 [Shi] (paronym of → yù₈ 悆譽豫); 'be tired of, weary' 斁 [BI, Shi] (< 'relax').
[T] *Sin Sukchu SR* iʔ (入); *MGZY* yi (入) [ji]

⋇ **shì** 釋 (śjäk) **LH** śak, **OCM** *lhak
'Unloose' [Yili], 'dissolve' [Li], 'let go, detach, unravel, explain' 釋 [Zuo] > 'interpret, translate'; 'put away, do away' [Shi], 'to lay open' (ground by plowing) 澤 [Shi].
[T] *Sin Sukchu SR* ʂi (入); *MGZY* shi (入) [ʂi]; *ONW* śek
[<] causative devoicing of *yì* 繹 (jiäk) (§5.2.2).

⋇ **shè** 赦 (śja^C) **LH** śa^C, **OCM** *lhakh
'Let go' [Shi], 'let off, liberate' [Zuo], 'pardon' [Shu] (paronym of *shè* 舍 under → shě₂ 舍捨). The phonetic element implies an OC final *-kh, thus the word is formally different from the homonym *shè* 舍 (under → shě₂ 舍捨).
[<] exoactive (caus.) of *shì* 釋 *lhak (§4.4).

⋇ **cì** 赤 (tsʰjäk) **LH** tsʰiak, **OCM** *s-lhak ?
'To expel' [Zhouli], lit. 'cause to let go, make go away'.
[<] caus. of *shè* 赦 *lhakh (§5.2.2).
Three different valence-increasing morphemes are added to the root *lak: (1) causative devoicing *lhak, (2) final s/h: *lhakh, (3) s-prefix: *s-lhak. A similar profusion of forms is seen in the wf → yù₂₅ 豫.

[E] Apparently this wf has expanded as a result of convergence with several paronyms, i.e.

nearly homophonous synonyms which feel somehow related: → shě$_2$ 舍捨 *lhaʔ 'let go > pardon'; (2) *la → yù$_8$ 悆譽豫 'happy'; (3) *la → xù$_2$ 序敍緒 'a line, succession'. A further derivation from the same AA root may be → yě$_3$ 野. Sagart (in *Ancestry of the CH Lg.* 1995: 369) considers → shí$_9$ 射 'shoot' to belong to this group.

This root is shared with AA: OKhmer *lā* [laa] 'to open, unfold, extend...' ⋈ *dalā* [dlaa] 'to be open, extensive, broad' (of space); PMonic *lah > OMon 'to extend'. CH has added a final *-k (§6.1).

yì$_{36}$ 譯驛懌斁 → **yì$_{35}$** 繹

yì$_{37}$ 義 → **yí$_{10}$** 儀宜

yì$_{38}$ 議 → **yí$_{10}$** 儀宜

yì$_{39}$ 殪 → **yē** 噎

yì$_{40}$ 饐 → **yē** 噎

yīn$_1$ 因 (ʔjien 4) **LH** ʔin, **OCM** *ʔin

'Rely on, depend on, follow, therefore' [BI, Shi].

[T] *Sin Sukchu SR* ʔin (平); *MGZY* Yin (平) [ʔjin]; *ONW* ʔiin

[N] This is prob. the s. w. as **yīn** 茵 (ʔjien) 'floormat' [Shi] (Karlgren *GSR* 370a). Perh. the homophone **yīn** 姻 *ʔin 'relative by marriage' [Shi] is the s. w., lit. 'dependent(s)'. → yī$_3$ 依 could be an allofam (Pulleyblank in Rosemont 1991: 32), but the vowels do not agree.

yīn$_2$ 姻 → **yīn$_1$** 因

yīn$_3$ 茵 → **yīn$_1$** 因

yīn$_4$ 湮堙闉 (ʔjien 4) **LH** ʔin, **OCM** *ʔin

'To dam up, obstruct' (floods) 陻 [Shu]; 'curved piece of wall for protection of city gate' [Shi] > 'crooked' 闉 [Zhuang]; 'block' 湮, 'stop up' 堙, 'obstruct' 湮 [Zuo]. This word is prob. not related to → yùn$_4$ 蘊薀 LH *ʔun^C* 'block, hoard'.

yīn$_5$ 陰 (ʔjəm) **LH** ʔim, **OCM** *ʔəm, OCB *ʔ(r)jum — **[T]** *ONW* ʔim

'Overcast, cloudy, dark' [BI, Shi].

⋈ **yìn** 陰蔭 (ʔjəm^C) **LH** ʔim^C, **OCM** *ʔəms

'To shelter' 陰 [Shi], 'shade' 蔭 [Zuo].

[<] exoactive of *yīn* 陰 *ʔəm 'cause to cover' (§4.3.2).

[E] ST: WB *ʔuṁ^C* 'overcast, cloudy'; Adi *muk-jum* 'shade', Lepcha *so'yŭm* 'shade'. Different TB and foreign etyma with the sound-symbolic final *-m* for 'dark' have been associated with *yīn*, although none seem to be cognate (see also → tǎn$_5$ 黮): (1) PL *c-dim^1, WB *tim* 'cloud'. (2) Bodman (1980: 87) suggests PTB *rum ~ *rim (*STC* no. 401) > WT *rum* 'darkness, obscurity', JP *rim^{31}* 'be dusk, dark' ⋈ *n^{33}-rim^{33}* 'evening'. (3) Lushai *hlim^L* 'shadow, shade, be shady'. (4) Tai: S. *klum^{C2}* 'dark, cloudy'. Wáng Lì (1982: 602) considers *yǐn* 隱 (ʔjən^B) LH *ʔɨn^B* 'conceal' to be related (under → yī$_5$ 翳), but the difference in final nasals remains unexplained.

[C] A probable allofam is → àn$_3$ 黯. A derivation is perh. → qīn$_3$ 衾 'a blanket'.

yín$_1$ 冘 (jiəm) **LH** jim, **OCM** *ləm

'To walk' [SW, Hanshu].

[E] ST: The basic meaning of the PTB root *lam 'to trample' raises the possibility that this is its OC cognate: Tiddim Chin *laam^M* / *laam^F* 'to dance' ⋈ *lam^R* 'way, road', Lai *laam / laʔm* 'to trample, dance'; WT *'čʰam-pa < ɴ-lhyam* 'to dance' ⋇ *lam* 'path, road'. The latter 'path, road' is derivable from the meaning 'to trample'.

yín₂ 垠 → **hèn** 恨

yín₃ 淫 (jiəm) **LH** jim, **OCM** *ləm (liəm ?)
'To soak' [Zhouli], 'excess, licentious, liberate, let loose' [Shu]; Mand. 'excessive' (rain), 霪 [Huainanzi, GY].
[T] *Sin Sukchu SR* im (平), *PR, LR* in; *MGZY* yim (平) [jim]
[C] Wáng Lì (1982: 612; also Sagart 1999: 127) considers this cognate to → lín₃ 淋霖. Allofam prob. → chěn₂ 瀋沈 'a liquid', → chén₂ 沈.

yín₄ 銀 (ŋjen 3) **LH** ŋɨn, **OCM** *ŋrən — **[D]** PMin *ŋyn ~ *ŋuin
'Silver' [Shu].
[T] *Sin S. SR ŋin* (平), *PR, LR in*; *MGZY ngin* (平) [ŋin]; *ONW ŋin*
[E] ST: WT *dŋul* 'silver', WT variant and Western Tib. dialects *mŋul;* WB *ŋwe*, PL *C-ŋwe¹* (*HST:* 133).

yǐn₁ 尹 (jiuenᴮ) **LH** juinᴮ, **OCM** *winʔ or *j/lunʔ
'Straight' [Shi]; 'to straighten out, arrange, administer' [BI, Shu]; 'administrator' [OB]. Acc. to Baxter / Sagart (1998: 47) → jūn₃ 君 is derived from this word, but this is phonologically problematic.
[T] *MTang* iun < iuin, *ONW* iuin

yǐn₂ 引 (jienᴮ) **LH** jinᴮ, **OCM** *linʔ (?)
'Pull, draw' [Zuo] > 'draw the bow' [Meng] > 'to pull, lead on, encourage, prolong' [Shi] > 'stretch' [Lunyu].
[T] *Sin Sukchu SR* in (上); *MGZY* yin (上) [jin]; *ONW* in
[E] The word *yǐn* is sometimes compared with WB *ə-hrañ* 'length' (recently Pān 2000: 73), WT *riŋ* 'long', but the initials do not agree.

⋇ **yìn** 靷 (jienᶜ) **LH** jinᶜ, **OCM** *lins (?)
'Pulling-strap for carriage' [Shi].
[<] *linʔ + s-suffix, prob. exopass. 'what is pulled with' (§4.4).

⋇ **zhèn** 紖絼 (ḍjenᴮ) **LH** ḍinᴮ, **OCM** *d-linʔ
'Rope by which cattle are led' 絼 [Zhouli], 紖 [Li].
[<] *linʔ + unknown initial element.

⋇ **shēn** 申伸呻 (śjen) **LH** śin, **OCM** *lhin
'Stretch, prolong' > 'continue, repeat' [Shi], 'extend' 伸 [Li] > 'straighten' 信 [Meng], 伸 [Yili] > 'chant, drone' 呻 [Li].
[<] *lin + devoicing caus. / iterative (§5.2.3-2).

⋇ **xìn** 信 (sjenᶜ) **LH** sinᶜ, **OCM** *sins (irreg. from *slins?)
'Be staying one more night, staying two nights' [Shi] (Karlgren *GSR* 384).
[<] *lin + iterative s-prefix (§5.2.2) + s-suffix (§4.3).

yǐn₃ 飲 (ʔjəmᴮ) **LH** ʔimᴮ, **OCM** *ʔəmʔ
'To drink' [BI, Shi].
[D] PMin *əmᴮ¹ 'rice water' (i.e. the water of half-cooked rice); Y-Guǎngzhōu ³⁵*(j)iɐmᴮ¹* 'rice water; to drink'.

⋇ **yìn** 飲 (ʔjəmᶜ) **LH** ʔimᶜ, **OCM** *ʔəms, OCB *ʔ(r)jum(ʔ)s
'To give to drink' [BI, Shi].
[<] *ʔəmʔ + exoactive / causative s-suffix (§4.3).

[E] ? ST: Perh. related to Lushai *ʔinᴴ* 'to drink, imbibe', Kukish *im* 'drink' (Löffler 1966:

141) (Lushai has on occasion final *-n* for TB *-m*). Alternative connection: PTB *am (*STC* no. 481) > Nung *am* 'eat', Dhimal *am* 'drink' (*STC* p. 143). Bodman (1980: 60) suggests also a possible link with → kǎn$_6$ 顑 and WT *skyem-pa* 'be thirsty' (resp.) ⋈ *skyems* 'thirst, a drink' (respect expression). Note also → lín$_6$ □ 'to drink', and the Hlai form *ʔjo:m*^{2} 'to swallow' (Matisoff in Edmondson 1988: 298). A final *-m* in words with these meanings is natural sound symbolism.

yǐn$_4$ 螾蚓 (jien^B) **LH** jɨn^B, **OCM** *lə/inʔ or *jə/inʔ — **[D]** Mǐn *un^B
'Earthworm' 螾 [Xun], 蚓 [Meng]. The Mǐn form derives from an earlier rime *-ən (螾); the following bisyllabic variants point to an OC rime *-in (蚓): *qiū-yǐn* 蚯蚓 (kʰjəu-) [Liji, Yuè-lìng] = *qǐn-yǐn* 螼蚓 (kʰjien^B 4-) [EY] = *qǐn-tiǎn* 蜸蚕 (kʰien^B-tʰien^B) [EY] (Bodman 1980: 77).
[E] Tai and TB words look similar and are sometimes considered related, but the initials are difficult to reconcile: Tai: S. *dɨan*^{A1} < *ʔdl/r- 'earthworm' (Li 1976: 45). *STC* (p. 37 n. 121; p. 171 n. 457; also *HPTB:* 78) relates *yǐn* to PTB *zril ~ *zrin > WT *srin* 'worm', Kuki-Chin *til (*CVST* 2: 160). Theoretically, the MC form could derive from a PCH *r-jil > jil (§9.2.1).

yǐn$_5$ 隱 → **yī$_5$** 翳

yìn$_1$ 喑 → **ān$_4$** 喑

yìn$_2$ 隱 → **yī$_4$** 依

yìn$_3$ 靷 → **yǐn$_2$** 引

yìn$_4$ 胤 → **yí$_2$** 貽詒

yīng$_1$ 英 (ʔjɐŋ) **LH** ʔɨaŋ, **OCM** *ʔraŋ ?, OCB *ʔrjaŋ
'Brilliant' > 'ornament; flower, blossom' [Shi].
[T] *Sin Sukchu SR* ʔiŋ (平); *MGZY* 'ing (平) [ʔiŋ]; *ONW* ʔeŋ (ʔæŋ?)
[E] Etymology not certain. Most likely is a ST connection: TB-Lushai *aaŋ*^{H} / *aan*^{L} 'to open (mouth), gape with open mouth' ⋈ *aan*^{L} tr. 'to open the mouth to receive food, to open to' (as flowers to the sun, dew, etc.); hence *yīng* may derive from the notion of an open flower. Alternatively, note an AA word: PSBahn. *ʔa:ŋ 'bright light', Bahn. *ʔa:ŋ* 'shine'. Or Lushai *eeŋ*^{R} 'light' n. ⋈ *eeŋ*^{R} / *een*^{L} 'to shine, give light, bright, brilliant'. These last items may perhaps belong to → yǐng$_1$ 影 'shadow' instead, which could also be related.

yīng$_2$ 鷹 (ʔjəŋ) **LH** ʔɨŋ, **OCM** *ʔəŋ — **[T]** *ONW* ʔiŋ
'Eagle, falcon' [Shi].
[E] ST: This etymon agrees phonologically with WT *skyiŋ-ser* 'eagle, vulture' (Benedict *MKS* 18–19, 1992: 8), if one assumes derivation from *s-ʔyiŋ. Alternatively, in spite of the difference in the initials, *yīng* is widely held to be related to a ubiquitous area word: PMK *knleeŋ 'hawk' or *k(a)laaŋ 'bird of prey, hawk, eagle' [Diffloth 1980] > Khm *klɛŋ* [Haudricourt 1950: 566], PMonic *liŋ-liəŋ 'hawk' (in Nyah Kur), Mon *kəniəŋ* 'kite' [Diffloth 1984: 69]. PTB *g-laŋ (*STC* no. 333) > WB *laŋ*^{B}*-ta*^{C} 'vulture', Kachin *laŋ* 'bird of the falcon family'; Garo *do-reŋ* 'falcon, kite', Bodo *dau-laŋ-a* 'eagle', Dimasa *dau-liŋ* 'kite' (*HST:* 76) *(do ~ dau* 'bird'). PPMY *klâŋ^2 (Downer 1982). The initial *l-* in these lgs. is difficult to reconcile with OC, see §5.11.

yīng$_3$ 膺 (ʔjəŋ) **LH** ʔɨŋ, **OCM** *ʔəŋ
'Breast, chest, breastplate, belt across breast of a horse' [BI, Shi]; 'to resist' [Shi]. In contrast to the root *yì* 臆 'one's breast, thoughts' (i.e. the inside of the chest; under →

yì$_{24}$ 憶臆), *yīng* and its cognates represent the exterior aspect of the 'chest, breast'. Wáng Lì (1982: 312) relates this word *yì* 意 (→ yì$_{24}$ 憶臆).

[E] ST: Prob. related to Lushai *eŋ^{H}* 'the breast'.

ж **yìng** 應 (ʔjəŋ^{C}) **LH** ʔɨŋ^{C}, **OCM** *ʔəŋh — **[T]** *ONW* ʔiŋ

('To turn one's chest to' >) 'to face, respond' [Shi], 'correspond, agree' [Yi, Guoyu].

[<] exoactive of *yīng* 膺 (ʔjəŋ) (§4.3).

ж **yīng** 應 (ʔjəŋ) **LH** ʔɨŋ, **OCM** *ʔəŋ

'Ought, of right' [Zuo] is perh. a back formation of *yìng* 應 (ʔjəŋ^{C}) 'respond'.

yīng$_{4}$ 嬰 (ʔjiäŋ 4) **LH** ʔieŋ, **OCM** *ʔeŋ

'Necklace' [Xun], 'surround' [Guoce] is prob. related to, or the same word as, → yíng$_{5}$ 縈 (ʔjiwäŋ 4) 'entwine'. For the absence of MC medial *w*, see §10.2.1.

yīng$_{5}$ 膺 → **bǐng$_{2}$** 秉

yíng$_{1}$ 迎 (ŋjɐŋ) **LH** ŋɨaŋ, **OCM** *ŋraŋ — **[T]** *ONW* ŋeŋ

'To meet' [Zuo]; Mand. 'go to meet, greet, welcome, receive'.

[D] PMin *ŋiaŋ > Jiànyáng *ŋiaŋ^{A1}*; Xiàmén col. *ŋiã^{A2}* / *giã*, lit. *geŋ^{A2}* / *giŋ* 'to receive ceremoniously'.

ж **yìng** 迎 (ŋjɐŋ^{C}) **LH** ŋɨaŋ^{C}, **OCM** *ŋraŋh

'Go to meet, receive' [Shi].

[E] ST *ŋraŋ: PTB *ŋraŋ (*STC* no. 155) > WB *ŋraŋ^{B}* 'contradict, deny', Nung *ŋjeŋ* 'deny'. Cognate is ST *ŋra^{B}; see under → yà$_{2}$ 御迓訝 for an overview over this large wf; the alternation between open syllable and final *-ŋ* is common in Sino-Tibetan lgs. (§6.5.2).

yíng$_{2}$ 盈嬴 (jiäŋ) **LH** jeŋ, **OCM** *leŋ, OCB *(l)jeng

'To fill, satisfy' 盈 [Shi]; 'surplus' [Shi], 'profit' 嬴 [Zuo].

[E] ST: PTB *bliŋ, *pliŋ 'fill' > TGTM *^{l}pliŋ, Bumthang Zha *bleŋ*, Chepang *bliŋh-ʔo* 'full' ж *leŋʔ-* 'be full', PL-B *m-bliŋ^{3} > OBurm plañ [*IST*: 351], WB *prañ^{C}* 'full' ж *p^{h}rañ^{C}* 'to fill' (*STC*: 176). Matisoff (1988b) combines this etymon with → píng$_{1}$ 平坪 'level', → tǐng$_{2}$ 挺 'straight' and → zhèng$_{1}$ 正政 'straight'. – Syn. → tiān$_{3}$ 添.

[C] An allofam is perh. → yùn$_{1}$ 孕 'pregnant', as well as → tián$_{4}$ 填顛.

yíng$_{3}$ 熒 (ɣiweŋ[$^{A/B/C}$]) **LH** ɣueŋ, **OCM** *wêŋ

'The light' (of a lamp, fire) 熒 [SW] > 'glowworm' 螢 [Li] > 'dazzle, confuse, delude' 熒 [Zhuang].

~ **xuàn** 眩 (ɣiwen[^{C}]) **LH** ɣuen(^{C}), **OCM** *wîn(s) ?

'Troubled sight, delude, deceive' [Meng].

~ **xuàn** 炫 (ɣien^{C}) **LH** ɣ(u)en^{C}, **OCM** *wîns

'Bright' [Guoce], 'dazzle, show off' [Zhan'guoce]. For loss of medial *w*, see §10.2.1.

ж **jiǒng** 熲 (kiweŋ^{B}) **LH** kueŋ^{B}, **OCM** *kwêŋʔ

'The light' [Shi].

[<] yíng 熒 *wêŋ + nominal k-prefix (§5.4).

ж **yíng** 瑩 (jwɐŋ) **LH** waŋ, **OCM** *wreŋ ?, OCB *wrjeng

'Bright, color of jade' [SW] > 'kind of beautiful stone' [Shi].

= **róng** 榮 (jwɐŋ) **LH** waŋ, **OCM** *wreŋ ? — **[T]** *ONW* ueŋ

'Flower' [Li] > 'flowering, prosperity' [Shi] > 'glory' [Zuo].

[E] This wf's stem is *weŋ 'bright, dazzle'; it converges with → shùn$_{3}$ 瞬 *win 'move the eyes'. For the difference in finals, see §6.4.1. Perh. this wf could be ST and be related to Lushai *veŋ^{H}* / *ven^{L}* 'be open, unobstructed by trees, clouds, be clear, be bright (weather)'.

yíng₄ 營 (jiwäŋ 4) **LH** weŋ, **OCM** *weŋ
'To lay out, plan, build' [BI, Shi], 'to encamp' [Zuo], 'to surround' [Gongyang].
[T] *Sin Sukchu SR* jujŋ (平), *PR* juŋ, iŋ, *LR* iŋ; *MGZY* yÿung (平) [juŋ]; *ONW* iueŋ

= **yíng** 塋 (jiwäŋ 4) **LH** weŋ, **OCM** *weŋ
'Grave area' [Li], i.e. a special area set aside.

ꭗ **róng-guàn** 榮觀 (jweŋ-) OCB *wrjeŋ-kʷans [Laozi ch. 26],

~ **huán-guān** 環官 (ɣwan-) OCB *wren-kʷan [Mawangdui version]
'Imperial palace' (Zhōu Zǔmó acc. to Baxter 1992: 383), the term is the equivalent of MK 'enclosure (環 or rather 寰) around official building' (官) > 'royal palace', see below. The received version seems to be a reinterpretation of the original words which are preserved in the Mawangdui ms.

ꭗ **huán** 環鐶寰 (ɣwan) **LH** ɣuan, **OCM** *wrên, OCB *wren
'Ring' [Shi], 'encircle' 環 [Meng]; 'metal ring' 鐶 [Guoce]; 'royal domain' [Guliang], 'enclosing wall around the imperial palace' 寰 (Giles). For the *-ŋ ~ -n* alternation, see §6.4.1.
[T] *Sin Sukchu SR* ɣwan (平); *MGZY* Xwan (平) [ɣwan]; *ONW* ɣuan

[E] This is a prolific AA or area etymon with vocalic variants (Shorto 1971: 345; 1973):
(1) *wiŋ: OMon *wiṅ* [wøŋ] 'surrounding, round about', *tuṁwīṅ* /təmwiŋ/ 'enclosure, enclosing hedge', Lit. Mon *wuiŋ* -> WB *wuiŋ*^{B} 'surround, circle of people, do by joint effort' ꭗ *ə-wuiŋ*^{B} 'circle, anything round'. The source of Chepang *wiŋh* 'around' (Bodman 1980: 60) is not clear, but may also be AA, note Khasi *rwiŋ* 'to go and return the same day'.
(2) *weŋ: Khmer *viaṅa* /wíiəŋ/ (OKhmer *vyaṅ*) 'be enclosed, encircled, walled town, enceinte'. MK -> Tai: Shan *vēŋ* (*vɛ̄ŋ*), S. *wiəŋ* 'town'. AA -> TB-Limbu *wɛŋ-* 'to enlarge in a circle, to amass land'; Lushai *veeŋ*^{H} 'village, hamlet'.
(3) *waŋ: Mon /waŋ/ 'enclosure around official building', Khmer *vāṃṅa* /weəŋ/ (OKhmer *vaṅ ~ vāṅ*(*ṅ*]) 'to encircle...enclose...encircling wall, walled citadel, royal palace, walled town' (-> Tai: S. *waŋ*, Shan *vāŋ* 'palace'), Bahn.-Sre *waaŋ* 'cattle yard, pound', PVM *wɔŋ*^{A} circle' (Thompson). <> PTB *hwaŋ (*STC* no. 217) > WB *waŋ* 'fence'; Lushai *huaŋ*^{H} 'yard, enclosure' ꭗ *huan*^{ll} 'a garden, yard'; JP *waŋ*^{33} 'surround, encircle, enclosure', Kiranti *waŋ-waŋ* 'circular'.

[C] Possible allofam → yǒng₇ 禜, → xiàn₁₀ 縣, → yuán₅ 員圓圜, → guī₁ 規; → huáng₁ 皇, → wáng₂ 王. Many of these words and wf 'round, turn' are difficult to disentangle.

yíng₅ 縈 (ʔjiwäŋ 4) **LH** ʔyeŋ, **OCM** *ʔweŋ
'To entwine' (as creeping plants) [Shi] may be the terminative form (§6.5.1) of → wěi₃ 委 'bend'.
[E] ST: TB: Lushai *veŋ*^{R} / *ven*^{L} < *veŋʔ* / *veŋs* 'to gird / wear round the waist' which prob. is related to this word rather than to → yíng₄ 營. Allofam → yīng₄ 嬰 'necklace'.

yíng₆ 蠅 (jiəŋ) **LH** jɨŋ, **OCM** *jəŋ or *ləŋ ?
'A fly' [Shi].
[E] ST: PTB *yaŋ^A 'a fly' (*STC*: 167) > Chepang *yaŋ* 'insect, fly', WB *yaŋ* 'a fly, insect', Kanauri *yaŋ* 'a bee, a fly' (*HST*: 82), West Tib. *bu-yaŋ* 'bumblebee'. → yáng₂ 羊 is perh. a dialect variant.

yǐng₁ 影 (ʔjɐŋ^B) **LH** ʔɨaŋ^B, **OCM** *ʔraŋʔ (?)
'Shadow' [Zhouli].

[D] Coastal Mǐn *ʔɔŋ^B > Fúzhōu *ouŋ^{B1}*, Amoy *ŋ^{B1};* Jiàn'ōu, Jiànyáng *ioŋ^{B1}* (< *ʔioŋ^B), Southern Mǐn *iã^{B1}*

[E] This word may be a cognate of → yīng₁ 英 'bright', or rather the AA items mentioned there; the semantic association of 'shadow' with 'light' is paralleled in the wf → jǐng₃ 景. Alternatively, *yǐng* may be connected with → yuàn₁ 苑 'shady'.

yǐng₂ 癭 (ʔjiäŋ^B 4) **LH** ʔieŋ^B, **OCM** *ʔeŋʔ
'Tumor, swelling' [Zhuang], Mand. 'goiter' is related to → yōng₂ 癰 LH *ʔɨoŋ* 'ulcer' by the *e ~ *o ablaut relationship (§11.3.5). An allofam is prob. **yīng** 罌 (ʔɛŋ) and other MC readings, 'bellied jar with small opening and one handle'. [SW; Mu Tianzizhuan].

yìng₁ 迎 → **yíng₁** 迎

yìng₂ 應 'respond' → **yīng₃** 膺 'breast, chest'.

yìng₃ 硬 (ŋɛŋ^C) — [T] *Sin Sukchu SR* ŋiŋ (去); *MGZY* ying (去) [jiŋ]
'Hard' [Tang: Han Yu].
⋈ **níng** 凝 (ŋjəŋ) **LH** ŋɨəŋ, **OCM** *ŋəŋ
('To become hard' >) 'to freeze, consolidate' [Shi, Shu].
[E] This etymon is reminiscent of items cited under → jiān₂ 堅 and → gāng₄ 剛鋼.

yìng₄ 繩 'full' → **yùn₁** 孕

yìng₅ 賸 媵 → **yí₂** 貽詒

yōng₁ 邕 (ʔjwoŋ) **LH** ʔɨoŋ, **OCM** *ʔoŋ < PCH *ʔuŋ
'City moat' [Shi].
⋈ **yǒng, yòng** 雍壅 (ʔjwoŋ$^{A/B/C}$) **LH** ʔɨoŋ$^{B/C}$, **OCM** *ʔoŋ(ʔ/h) ? < PCH *ʔuŋ
'Obstruct, dam up' 雍 [Zhouli], 'stop up' 壅 [Zuo].
[E] ST: WB *uiŋ* 'pond, lake' (~ *aŋ^B* 'pond, pool'?), Mru *öŋ* 'id.' (Löffler 1966: 142), JP *ʔuŋ^{33}* 'fill' (as a lake). Bodman (1980: 87) suggests WT *roŋ* 'defile, ravine, valley', but the initials are difficult to reconcile. Prob. related to → yùn₄ 蘊薀 ('stopped-up water'?).

yōng₂ 癰 (ʔjwoŋ) **LH** ʔɨoŋ, **OCM** *ʔoŋ
'Ulcer' [Meng] (< 'swelling') is cognate to → wèng 瓮甕罋 'jar, swollen'. → yǐng₂ 癭 LH *ʔieŋ^B* 'tumor' is related to *yōng* by the OC *e ~ *o ablaut relationship (§11.3.5).
[E] ST: WB *uiŋ^C* 'bulge of anything' ⋈ *uiŋ^B* 'collection of humors' (boil). Perh. the PTB form *um is a variant (for the final, see §6.7): WB *uṁ* 'protuberance, bulge', Mru *um* 'female breast, protuberance', Lushai *um^{55}* < *uum* 'swell, become prominent' (fem. breast). Another etymon 'swollen' has the same rime: → zhǒng₃ 腫踵.

yōng₃ 饔 → **yù₂₁** 飫

yóng₁ 庸 (jiwoŋ) **LH** joŋ, **OCM** *loŋ
'To use, employ, need' [Shi, BI].
⋈ **yòng** 用 (jiwoŋ^C) **LH** joŋ^C, **OCM** *loŋh
'To use; obey' (a decree) [Shi], ('use' for a sacrificial ceremony:) 'to sacrifice' tr. [OB, Yi Zhoushu].
[T] *Sin Sukchu SR* juŋ (去); *MGZY* yÿung (去) [juŋ]; *ONW* iuoŋ
[E] ST: WT *loŋs* 'the use or enjoyment of something' (e.g. wealth).

yóng₂ 喁 → **oǔ** 偶

yǒng₁ 永 (jwɐŋ^B) **LH** waŋ^B, **OCM** *wraŋʔ ?, OCB *wrjaŋʔ
'Long time, eternal' [BI, Shi]. This is the original graph for → yǒng₂ 泳 'swim'.
[T] *Sin Sukchu SR* jujŋ (上), *PR, LR* juŋ; *MGZY* xÿung (上) [ɦjuŋ]; *ONW* ueŋ

⋇ **yǒng** 詠 (jwɐŋ^C) **LH** waŋ^C, **OCM** *wraŋh ?
'To chant' [Shu] (Karlgren 1956: 8).
[<] exoactive of *yǒng* 永, lit. 'make long' (§4.3).
[E] An outside cognate is difficult to identify. Bodman (1980: 88) suggests TB-WT *rgyoŋ-ba* 'extend, stretch' ⋇ *rgyaŋ-ma* 'distance', Lepcha *hryăn* 'length, distance', all from a hypothetical ST *wrjaŋ (with WT metathesis of the *r* and regular loss of medial *w*). The connection with WT *riŋ* 'long, tall' (of space, time), Tamang *^{l}reŋ-pa* 'long', WB *hre* < *hrañ* 'be long', *hre^B* 'former time', PL *s/m-riŋ^1 'be long, length', *s/m-riŋ^2* 'long' adv. [TB: *STC* no. 433], or with → jiǒng$_2$ 泂 'distant', if any, is not clear. Bodman associates the last TB items with Kanauri *rwi* 'high'. However, phonetically less complicated and semantically closer to OC is MK-Khmer /vɛːɲ/ (< -ŋ) 'long' ⋇ *ɓɒŋvaɛŋ* 'to prolong'.

yǒng$_2$ 泳 (jwɐŋ^B) **LH** waŋ^B, **OCM** *wraŋʔ ?
'To wade, swim' [Shi].
[E] This word may be connected with Tai: PT *hwai^{C1} > S. *waai^{B2}* 'to swim' (tone B2 is spurious, Li 1977: 82), occasionally words with open finals in a tone which is suspected to go back to a final glottal stop (tone C in Tai lgs.) alternate with final *-ŋ* (§3.2.4).

yǒng$_3$ 甬 (jiwoŋ^B) **LH** joŋ^B, **OCM** *loŋʔ
'Suspension ring at the top of a bell' [Zhouli] is prob. related to WT *ʔa-loŋ* ~ *ʔa-luŋ* 'a ring' (*HST:* 125) and may belong to → róng$_2$ 容 'hold', hence *yǒng* 'a holder'.

yǒng$_4$ 踊 (jiwoŋ^B) **LH** joŋ^B, **OCM** *loŋʔ
'To jump' [Shi] (as in 'jump and bounce').
[E] ? AA: Khmer *ploṅa* /plaaoŋ/ 'to leap over' (high barrier, a height). Perh. related to the wf → yú$_{18}$ 踰逾, and possibly also to → róng$_3$ 溶.

yǒng$_5$ 涌湧 → **róng$_3$** 溶

yǒng$_6$, yòng 雍壅 → **yōng$_1$** 邕

yǒng$_7$ 禜 (jwɐŋ[^{C}]) **LH** waŋ(^{C}), **OCM** *wreŋ(h) ?
'Sacrifice to heavenly bodies and spirits of rivers and mountains to avert a natural calamity' [Zuo].
[E] Prob. PMK *wiəŋ (Shorto 1973: 375ff; 1976: 1050) > Khmer *vāṅa* /wíiəŋ/ 'to turn, twist' also means 'to turn aside from > to dodge, evasion, avoidance', OMon *weṅ* /weŋ/ 'go elsewhere, avoid'; the derivative *ravāṅa* /rwíiəŋ/ ('space, interval') looks formally like the OC word. <> TB-Lushai *veeŋ^H* / *veen^L* 'to watch, look after, protect, guard from, ward off'. Lepcha *vuŋ* 'to twist' (Forrest *JAOS* 82, 1962: 334).

yòng 用 → **yóng$_1$** 庸

yōu$_1$ 攸 (jiəu) **LH** ju, **OCM** *ju
'Place' [Shi]. The function as an indefinite substitute for the post-verbal element (Dobson's term, *LAC:* 157), as in *fēi tiān yōu ruò* 非天攸若 'this is not what Heaven approves of', is derived from the meaning 'place' (Pulleyblank 1995: 68); → suǒ$_1$ 所 is a semantic parallel.
[E] Prob. ST: WT *yul* 'place', but the loss of ST *-l in CH is unexplained (dissimilation from *juj?).

yōu$_2$ 悠 (jiəu) **LH** ju, **OCM** *liu, OCB *ljiw
'Long-trailing, longing, depressing, persistent, far away, distant' [Shi].

=**yóu** 由 (jiəu) **LH** ju, **OCM** *liu
'To prolong; a shoot from a tree' [Shu].

ꭗ **tiáo** 條 (dieu) **LH** deu, **OCM** *liû, OCB *liw — **[T]** *ONW* dėu
'Branch, to be extending branches, extend, long' [Shi] > measure for long, slender objects [starting in Han]; since documents were written on slender wooden or bamboo strips, *tiáo* became a measure for 'matters, items of business, affairs' (Norman 1988: 116).

ꭗ **tiāo** 條 (t^hieu) **LH** t^heu, **OCM** *lhiû
'Pull leaves off branches' [Shi].
[<] perhaps causative (tr.?) of *tiáo* 條 (§5.8.2).

ꭗ **xiū** 脩 (sjəu) **LH** siu, **OCM** *siu or *sliu, OCB *sljiw
'Long' (of an animal) [Shi].

yōu$_3$ 呦 (ʔjieu 4) **LH** ʔiu, **OCM** *ʔiu
'Cry of deer' [Shi]. Though sound symbolic, this word has apparently a TB parallel: Lushai *euʔ^L* (i.e. *ʔeuʔ*) 'to bark or call' (as sambhur deer).

yōu$_4$ 幽 (ʔjieu 4) **LH** ʔiu, **OCM** *ʔiu — **[T]** *ONW* ʔiu
'Dark' [Shi] > solitary, secluded, obscure, difficult to understand' [Yi], 'to confine' [Zuozhuan].

ꭗ **yǒu** 黝 (ʔjieu^B 4) **LH** ʔiu^B, **OCM** *ʔiuʔ
'Black' [Li].

ꭗ **yǎo** 杳窅 (ʔieu^B) **LH** ʔeu^B, **OCM** *ʔiûʔ or *ʔiâuʔ ?
'Dark' 杳 [Guan] > 'retired, despondent' 窅 [Zhuang].

ꭗ **yào** 窔穾 (ʔieu^C) **LH** ʔeu^C, **OCM** *ʔiâuh
'Obscure, secluded' 窔 [Yili]; 'obscure, deeply hidden' 穾 [Zhuang] (also MC ʔieu[^{B}]).

[E] ST: Mru *iu* (i.e. *ʔiu*) 'dark' (Löffler 1966: 151), perh. also related to WT *g-yog-pa* 'to cover' ꭗ *g-yogs* 'cover, lid'. Allofam is prob. → yǎo$_6$-tiǎo 窈窕.

yōu$_5$ 櫌耰 (ʔjəu) **LH** ʔu, **OCM** *ʔu
'To cover seeds with earth' [Lun, Meng].
[E] ST: Lushai *vuur^F* 'to fill' (as grave, hole), 'fill up' (with earth), 'cover'. For absence of final consonant in CH, see §7.7.5.

yóu$_1$ 尤 (jəu) **LH** wu, **OCM** *wə — **[T]** *ONW* iu
'Guilt, fault, blame' [BI, Shi].
[E] ST: WT *yus* 'blame, charge, accusation' (for the WT initial, see §12.9 (2]).

yóu$_2$ 由 (jiəu) **LH** ju, **OCM** *liu or *ju (from *wu ?)
'Proceed from' [Shi], 'go along' [Li], 'follow' [Shi].
[T] *Sin Sukchu SR* iw (平); *MGZY* yiw (平) [jiw]; *ONW* iu

ꭗ **dí** 迪 (diek) **LH** dek < deuk, **OCM** *liûk
'To advance, promote' [Shi], 'go along, follow, lead, walk, conduct' [Shu].

ꭗ **zhòu** 胄 (ḍjəu^C) **LH** ḍu^C, **OCM** *d-liuh
'Descendant', i.e. eldest son of the principal wife [Shu] (< 'the outcome, follower') (Karlgren 1956: 14). This word may belong to → yù$_{22}$ 育毓鬻 'give birth' instead. For additional possible cognates, see under → suì$_2$ 遂.

yóu$_3$ 由 'prolong' → **yōu$_2$** 悠

yóu$_4$ 油 (jiəu) **LH** ju, **OCM** *lu
'Overflowing, abundant' [Meng], prob. unrelated to → yóu$_{10}$ 滺油 and → yóu$_6$ 游遊.

[T] *Sin Sukchu SR* iw (平); *MGZY* yiw (平) [jiw]

꞉꞉ **tāo** 滔 (tʰâu) **LH** tʰou, **OCM** *lhû

'Be swelling up' (river) [Shi] > 'to assemble, to crowd' [Zhuang]. 'Reckless' may be a semantic extension, but see → tōu$_1$ 偷.

[<] *lu + caus. / intensive devoicing (§5.2.3-2).

꞉꞉ **táo** 滔 (dâu) **LH** dou, **OCM** *lû

'To assemble, to crowd' [Zhuang].

yóu$_5$ 斿 → **yóu$_6$** 游遊

yóu$_6$ 游遊 (jiəu) **LH** ju, **OCM** *ju, OCB *ju.

'Float, swim, wander' 游 [Shi]; 'to wander about' 遊 [Shi], 'leisure' [Li], 'freely, unrestrained' 逌 [Lie]; 'pendants of a banner' 斿 [Zhouli].

[T] *Sin Sukchu SR* iw (平); *MGZY* yiw (平) [jiw]; *ONW* iu — [D] PMin *ziu

[E] ST: WT *rgyu-ba* < *r-yu* 'to go, walk, move, wander, range' (of men, animals, etc.), Lepcha *yŭ*, Rawang *yɨ* 'to flow' [Bodman ICSTLL 1987: 13]. For the pre-initial *r-, see §9.2.1. Cognates are → liú$_3$ 流 (so Sagart 1999: 127), → qiú$_6$ 泅; prob. unrelated to → yóu$_4$ 油 and → yóu$_{10}$ 滺油.

yóu$_7$, yǎo 舀 → **yú$_{16}$** 揄

yóu$_8$ 猶 (jiəu) **LH** ju, **OCM** *ju < PCH *wu ?, OCB *lŭ or *jŭ

'Kind of monkey' [Shizi].

[T] *Sin Sukchu SR* iw (平); *MGZY* yiw (平) [jiw]; *ONW* iu

[E] Several other Chinese and TB words for one or another kind of monkey look similar, but direct phonological equivalence is elusive. These items include:

- PTB *myuk or *mruk [*STC:* 112, n. 314]: WB *myok* (*myuk*), Mru *yuk* 'monkey' could possibly be reconciled with *yóu* 猶 which may represent the bare root of this etymon, but see → hóu$_5$ 猴.
- Yuè dialects have a form which is reminiscent of TB: Guǎngzhōu *ma^{B2}-lɐu^{A1}* 馬騮 'monkey'.
- PL *C-lwaj^2 'monkey, gibbon' > WB *hlwai^B* (Matisoff *LL* 1.2, 2000: 169).
- MK: PNBahn. *hwa 'gibbon', Wa-Lawa-Bulang *hwaʔ 'leaf-monkey'.
- Additional words for 'monkey' are → yuán$_6$ 猿, → wèi$_6$ 蜼, → yù$_9$ 禺, → náo$_2$ 猱, → hóu$_5$ 猴.

yóu$_9$ 猶 (jiəu) **LH** ju, **OCM** *ju ?

'To laugh' [Zhuang]. *STC:* 172 n. 458 compares this to TB items under → chěn$_1$ 辴.

yóu$_{10}$ 滺油 (jiəu) **LH** ju, **OCM** *liu, 滺 OCB *ljiw

'To be flowing' 滺滺 [Shi], 油油 [Chuci].

[T] *Sin Sukchu SR* iw (平); *MGZY* yiw (平) [jiw]

[N] This word seems to be distinct from → yóu$_6$ 游遊 *ju 'to float' (not 'flow') which is suspected to have had OC initial *j-. It is also distinct from → yóu$_4$ 油 *lu 'overflowing' which had apparently no medial *-i-. By the time of the *Chǔcí,* OCM *liu and *lu had prob. merged. → dí$_7$ 滌 could possibly be related.

yǒu$_1$ 友 → **yǒu$_2$** 右

yǒu$_2$ 有 (jəu^B) **LH** wu^B, **OCM** *wəʔ — [D] M-Xiàmén *u^{C2}*

'Have, there is, some' ("definite existential quantifier" – Harbsmeier 1981: 88) [OB, Shi] > 'to possess, take possession' [BI, Shi] > 'rich' [Shi] (Karlgren *GSR* 995o).

[T] *Sin Sukchu SR* iw (上); *MGZY* ngiw (上) [ŋiw]; *MTang* eu < u, *ONW* u

[N] The element 'meat' in the graph has occasioned much speculation; perh. the graph was originally intended for the word **hǎi** 醢 (xậi^B) LH *həʔ* 'dried meat' [Shi] which also has the 又 element as phonetic.
[E] ? ST: Possibly cognate to WT *yod-pa* 'to be, to have' (for the WT initial, see §12.9 [2]); WT *o* can derive from ST *a, ə, o,* even *u,* as well as *wa* and *wə;* WT final *-d* has its counterpart in CH tone B in a few grammatical words: WT *ŋed* 'I' ⋇ *wǒ* 我 *ŋâiʔ, WT *med* 'not have' ⋇ *mǐ* 靡 *maiʔ, hence WT *yod* 'be, have' could be the equivalent of *wəʔ 'have'.

⋇ **yòu** 侑 (jəu^C) **LH** wu^C, **OCM** *wəh
'To offer, sacrifice' 有侑 [OB] > 'offer a drink, encourage to drink' 侑 [BI, Shi].
[<] exoactive of *yǒu* 有, lit. 'cause to have' (Takashima 1996: 316) (§4.3). The homophone *yòu* 右佑祐侑宥 (under → yòu$_2$ 右) is prob. a different word.
[E] ST *wəC: WT *yon* 'gift' (to priests etc.), 'offering'. For the WT initial, see §12.9 (2]); for the WT (ST) nominalizing final *-n*, see §6.4.3.

⋇ **huò** 或 (ɣwək) **LH** ɣuək, **OCM** *wə̂k
'Someone, some' ("indefinite existential quantifier" – Harbsmeier 1981: 88) [Shi].
[T] *Sin Sukchu SR* ɣuj (入), *LR* xujʔ; *MGZY* Xue (入) [ɣuɛ]; *ONW* ɣuək
[<] distributive suffix *-k added to *yǒu* 有 'there is' (§6.1.2).
[C] Possible allofam → yòu$_1$ 又.

yǒu$_3$ 酉 (jiəu^B) **LH** ju^B, **OCM** *juʔ
The 10th of the Earthly Branches, identified with the chicken [OB].
[E] ? MK: Acc. to Norman (1985: 88) this is possibly a loan from MK: Ruc *rəka,* Arem *lak*, however PVM *r-ka: 'chicken' > Viet. *gà*. In Tai, the initial is *r-*, e.g. Ahom *rao*^{C2} (Li Fang Kuei *HJAS* 8, 1945: 336), also the *Shìmíng* associates the initial with a lateral (*lǎo* 老). The graph was apparently originally intended to write 'wine' [OB, BI], presumably → jiǔ$_5$ 酒, but see there.

yǒu$_4$ 庮 (jiəu[^{B}]) **LH** ju(^{B}), **OCM** *juʔ
'To rot, decay' [Li].
[E] Prob. a ST word (*ju ?): Kuki-Naga *m-hew 'spoiled, wasted' > Lushai *heu*^{H} 'be decreased', Lakher *pəhua* 'waste away'. Alternatively, *STC* (p. 169) compares the Chinese word with PTB *zya:w ~ *zyu(w) 'to rot, decay, digest' > Kuki-Naga *su 'to rot, decay' > Lush. *t^{h}u*, Dimasa *sau*, perh. also WT *'ju-ba, bžus, bžu* 'to digest, melt'.

yǒu$_5$ 黝 → **yōu$_4$** 幽

yǒu$_6$ 誘 → **shù$_4$** 述術銶

yǒu$_7$ 莠 → **yún$_4$** 耘

yòu$_1$ 又 (jəu^C) **LH** wu^C, **OCM** *wəh
'To repeat, again, still, also' [BI, Shi].
[T] *Sin Sukchu SR* iw (去); *MGZY* ngiw (去) [ŋiw]
[<] adverbial derivation (§3.5.1) of → yǒu$_2$ 有 acc. to Downer (1959: 289); in fact, in a phrase like *shí yǒu èr yuè* 十有二月 (ten / have / two / month) 'in the 12th month' (lit. ten having two) *yǒu* is synonymous with *yòu.* Alternatively, the word may derive from ST *wə-: WT *yaŋ* 'again, also, once more', but see → cháng$_2$ 常. For the WT initial, see §12.9 (2]); for the finals, see §6.5.2.

yòu$_2$ 右 (jəu^B, jəu^C) **LH** wu^B, wu^C, **OCM** *wəʔ, wəh
'Right (side), be to the right' [OB]. The OB graph is a drawing of the right hand of

oneself, from one's own perspective to which 'mouth' was later added to distinguish it from *yòu* 又 which was commonly used to write 'repeat, again'.
[T] *Sin Sukchu SR* iw (去); *MGZY* ngiw (去) [ŋiw]; *MTang* eu < u, *ONW* u
[E] ST *wəs > WT *g-yas* 'right' (side) (for the WT initial, see §12.9 (2]; *HPTB:* 46). <> PTai *kʰwa^{A1} 'right side', PNTai *gwa^{A2}; PKS *h-wa^{A} 'right'.

The semantics in this wf are parallel to → zuǒ 左. 'Right' and 'left' are metaphors for two different concepts in OC: (1) 'to be on the right and left side of a person' > 'aid, help, support'; (2) 'left' > 'unfavorable', 'right' > 'favorable'; note the similar notion implied by Mǐn-Xiàménen 正手 *tsĩ ɳ$^{11/51}$-tsʰiu^{51}* 'right hand', lit. 'correct hand' vs. 倒手 *to$^{212/53}$-tsʰiu$^{53/21}$* 'left hand', lit. 'upside down / wrong hand'. This second metaphor explains the OB meaning 'left' > ('consider or treat as left = unfavorable' >) 'not approve, to oppose'. If this interpretation of 'left' is valid, then 'right' should also have meanings which are derivable from 'consider or treat favorably' (Takashima 1996: 314ff), like the following word:

× **yǒu** 友 (jəu^{B}) **LH** wu^{B}, **OCM** *wəʔ, OCB *wjəʔ
'Be friendly' > 'friend, companion' [BI, Shi] (< 'consider right' = 'favorably').
[<] endoactive of *yòu* 右 (jəu^{B}, jəu^{C}) (§4.5). Li Fang Kuei relates *yǒu* to → qiú$_4$ 逑仇.
[E] ST *wə: WT *ya* 'associate, companion, assistant' (for the WT initial, see §12.9 [2]).

× **yòu** 右佑祐侑宥 (jəu^{C}) **LH** wu^{C}, **OCM** *wəh
'To aid, support, assist, wait, honor, appreciate' 右佑 (< 'be to one's right') [OB, BI, Shi]; 'help, blessing' 祐 [Yi]; ('to consider or treat favorably' >) 'to forgive' 侑[Guan], 'to pardon, mitigate, magnanimous' 宥 [Shi, Shu].
[<] exoactive of *yòu* 右 (§4.3).

yòu$_3$ 囿 → **guó** 國

yòu$_4$ 幼 (ʔjieu^{C}) **LH** ʔiu^{C}, **OCM** *ʔiuh
'Be young' [Shu, Meng]. Shī Xiàngdōng (2000: 33) relates this word to WT *yu-bo* 'without horns' (of animals).
[T] *Sin Sukchu SR* ʔiw (去); *MGZY* Yiw (去) [ʔjiw]

× **yāo** 么 (ʔieu) **LH** ʔeu, **OCM** *ʔiû
'Small' [SW, EY].

yòu$_5$ 誘 → **shù$_4$** 述術鉥

yòu$_6$ 褎 'sleeve' → **zhòu$_3$** 胄

yoù$_7$ 褎 (jiəu^{C}) **LH** ju^{C}, **OCM** *juh < *wuh (?)
'Big, tall' (of grain) [Shi].
[E] ST: Lushai *vu^{R}* 'be ripe and yellow' (as standing rice), 'show up / be conspicuous' (as flowers). Sagart (1999: 72) relates this word to → xiù$_1$ 秀.

yòu$_8$ 蓲 'brood' → **yù$_{20}$**, **yǔ** 嫗

yòu$_9$ 鼬 (jiəu^{C}) **LH** ju^{C}, **OCM** *juh
'Weasel' [Dadai Liji] is phonologically identical with the widely attested TB word for 'rodent, small animal': PTB *yu or*b-yəw 'rat' (*STC* no. 93) > Chepang *yuʔ* 'animal, rodent', Mru *yu* 'weasel' (Löffler 1966: 151), WT *yos* 'hare' (in year name). The word → qūn 鵔 'hare' is perh. an allofam, see there for TB cognates.

yū$_1$ 迂紆 (ʔju) **LH** ʔya, **OCM** *ʔwa
'To bend, deflect' 迂 [Shu] (also QYS *ju*, LH *wa*); 'bent, crooked' 紆 [Zhouli] >

'astray, far away from' [Lunyu]. *HST* (41f) considers this word cog. to the WT words which are found under → yǎo₁ 夭殀.

※ **wàn** 腕 (ʔuân^C) **LH** ʔuɑn^C, **OCM** *ʔwâns

'Wrist' [Zuo, Guoce].

[<] *ʔwa + the nominalizing n-suffix (§6.4.3), lit. 'the thing that bends'; for a semantic parallel, see → zhǒu₁ 肘 'wrist, elbow'. It is not clear if Naga-Khoirao *wan* 'hand', Lotha *ewon* 'arm' are related (so Matisoff 1985a: 434).

There are words with similar meaning and initial, but different final consonants which may perh. be related:

※ **wǎng** 枉 (ʔjwaŋ^B) **LH** ʔyɑŋ^B, **OCM** *ʔwaŋʔ

'Bent, crooked' [Li], 'unjust' [Lunyu].

※ **kuāng** 匡 (k^{h}jwaŋ) **LH** k^{h}yɑŋ, **OCM** *khwaŋ

'Crooked' [Zhouli].

[E] ? ST: WB *kwaŋ^B* 'bend into a ring, go round' ※ *k^{h}waŋ* 'be bent, curved'.

※ **yuān** 冤 (ʔjwɐn) **LH** ʔyɑn, **OCM** *ʔwan (or *ʔon ?)

'Injustice' [Chuci].

[T] *Sin Sukchu SR* ʔyen (平); *MGZY* 'wÿan (平) [ʔyɛn]

[C] Allofam is → hú₈ 弧; perh. also → wěi₃ 委 'bend', → yǎo₁ 夭殀 'bend'. Syn. → gōu₁ 句鉤枸區.

yū₂ 菸 (ʔjwo) **LH** ʔɨɑ, **OCM** *ʔa

'Withered' [Chuci] is said to be an ancient Guānxī (NW) dialect word.

※ **yān** 蔫 (ʔjän 3) **LH** ʔɨɑn, **OCM** *ʔan

'Withered' [SW] is said to be an ancient Shandong (eastern) dialect word (Unger *Hao-ku* 33, 1986) which Pulleyblank (*JCL* 22.1: 95) relates to Viet. *uon* 'languid, listless'. These etyma could be ancient dialect variants of → wēi₃ 萎 'wither'.

yú₁ 于 (ju) **LH** wɑ, **OCM** *wa

'Go to (a place / do something), in, at, on, to', general locative link vb. or 'preposition' [OB, BI, Shi], indicating motion to, or inceptive action ('go flying') (Pulleyblank 1995: 53). This etymon is distinct from → yú₈ 於.

[T] *Sin Sukchu SR* y (平); *MTang* y < uo, *ONW* uo

[E] ST: PTB *wa, *s-wa: Newari *wa* 'to come', JP *wa^{31}* 'to go back'; Chepang *wah-ʔo* 'moving', *wah-sa* 'walk'; WB *swa* 'to go', Magari, Chepang *hwa* 'to walk' (*HST:* 86).

※ **yuán** 爰 (jwɐn) **LH** wɑn, **OCM** *wan

'There' [Shi] stands for the ungrammatical *于之 and is a fusion of *yú* 于 *wa plus an *-n with a demonstrative meaning, see §6.4.5 (Norman 1988: 86).

[C] Additional cognates: → wǎng₁ 往, → qú₅ 衢.

yú₂ 于 'enlarge' → **kuàng₁** 況

yú₃ 盂 (ju) **LH** wɑ, **OCM** *wa

'Bowl' [BI, Hanfei]. Prob. ST *wa: WB *k^{h}wak* 'a cup'. Perh. the s. w. as 'concave', see under → qú₄, jù 臞.

yú₄ 雩 → **yǔ₃** 雨

yú₅ 余 (jiwo) **LH** jɑ, **OCM** *la (or *ja?)

'I, we' 余 [OB, BI]. *Chǔcí* has both 予 and 余 where the former is used mostly in a post-verbal position (Pulleyblank 1995: 76), this suggests that 予 was perh. read LH *jaʔ;* see §3.3.3.

⋇ **yú** 予 (jiwo) **LH** ja^B, **OCM** *laʔ (or *jaʔ ?)
'I, we' 予 [Shi] is usually considered a graphic variant of 余 (Qiu Xigui 2000: 392), but *Shījīng* rimes indicate that this graph was read in tone B (Mattos 1971: 309).

⋇ **yí** 台 (jiɨ) **LH** jə, **OCM** *lə
'I, my' [Shu].
[<] Unstressed derivation from *yú* 予余 'I, we' (Pulleyblank 1995: 76), see §3.3.3.

[E] The etymology of *yú* is obscure. Li F. (1976: 40) who reconstructs OC *rag, relates *yú* to PTai *r-: S. *raa*^{A2} 'we two' (inclusive?), Shan *ha* 'we two', Lü *hra* 'I'. However, the Tai etymon prob. belongs to CH → liǎng 兩 'two'. Syn. → wú$_2$ 吾.

yú$_6$ 餘 (jiwo) **LH** jɑ, **OCM** *la
'Remains, leftover, surplus, superfluous' [Shi].
[T] *MTang* iy < iø < *ONW* io
[E] KT: Tai: S. *lia*^{A1} < *hl- 'to be left over' (Li F. 1976: 43); PKS *kla^1 'leftover'. In CH, a possible earlier initial consonant was treated as a pre-initial and lost. Perh. related to → xù$_2$ 序敍緒 'continue, remains'; possibly also related to→ xiàn$_7$ 羨.

yú$_7$ 畬 (jiwo) **LH** jɑ, **OCM** *la (or *ja ?)
'Field in 2nd or 3rd yr. of cultivation' [Shi 276; SW 6188], i.e. a swidden (dry) field after the slash-and-burn clearing in the first year which is called → zī$_8$ 菑.
[E] Perh. ST: if OC was *ja, *yú* would be related to *shē* and its TB cognates. Because of the different vowel, TB *low cannot be cognate.

cf. **shē** 畬 (śja) < OCM **hja ?
'Slash-and-burn field, swidden' [Tang Dynasty writers, GY], a late word.
[E] Prob. ST: PTB *hya^1 'swidden' [HPTB: 56] > PLB *hja^1 'id.', WB *ya*.

yú$_8$ 於 (ʔjwo) **LH** ʔɨɑ, **OCM** *ʔa
'Be in, at, on, to...', general locative link vb. or 'preposition' [Shi]. *Yú* 於 begins to appear occasionally in *Shījīng*, but over time gradually replaces, the older *yú* 于. The irreg. Mand. tone 2 has been transferred from → yú$_1$ 于 (*QY* would predict tone 1).
[T] *Sin Sukchu SR* ʔy (平); *MGZY* 'ÿu (平) [ʔy]; *MTang* ʔy < ʔø, *ONW* ʔio (?) > ʔø
[E] ? ST: PTB *ʔay 'to go, directional particle' [*HPTB:* 209; *-y* may be a suffix], Lushai locative, ablative, etc. suffix *a / aʔ*^{L} 'in, into, on, to...'. Alternatively, note the similarity with MK: PMonic *ʔa(a)r 'to go', post-verb after verbs of motion and vbs. with ingressive force [Diffloth 1984: 227], PVM *ʔë^C 'at, located'.

⋇ **hū** 乎 (ɣwo) **LH** ɣɑ, **OCM** *ɦâ
'In, at, on, to', general locative particle [Shi], an attrited or unstressed form of *yú* 於 (Pulleyblank 1995: 56).
[T] *Sin Sukchu SR* ɣu (平); *MGZY* Xu (平) [ɣu]; *ONW* ɣo,
[D] The irreg. Mand. tone 1 instead of the expected tone 2 comes from another reading for this graph, MC *xwo*. Because *hū* is always placed between the vb. and the n. which it modifies (N *hū* V, V *hū* N), it can function as a postposition.

⋇ **yān** 焉 (jän 3 -irregular) **LH** ʔɑn, -ɑn, **OCM** *ʔan > an — **[T]** *ONW* ʔan, -an
'In it, on it, there' [Shi] stands for *於之 which is a fusion of *yú* 於 with an element *-n with a demonstrative meaning; see §6.4.5 (Norman 1988: 86; Pulleyblank 1995: 80). The Mand. tone 1 derives from MC *ʔjan.* This word's initial div. III *j-* is exceptional. The word is parallel to *yuán* 爰 (under → yú$_1$ 于).

⋇ **yāng** 央 (ʔjaŋ) **LH** ʔɨɑŋ, **OCM** *ʔaŋ
'To hit the center' (of a target), get into the middle (of a stream, of the night) vb. > middle, center' [Shi] (Pulleyblank 1995: 171).

[T] *Sin Sukchu SR* ʔjaʔ (平); *MGZY* ('ÿang >) 'yang (平) [ʔjaŋ]

[<] *ʔa + terminative *-ŋ (§6.5.1) hence lit. 'to get to be in the middle'. This etymology is phonologically more straightforward than the traditional association with PTai *klaŋ^{A1} 'middle'.

[N] The near-synonyms / homophones 於 *ʔa and → yú$_1$ 于 *wa are distinct etyma (Pulleyblank 1995: 53f), and their derivations with the terminative suffix *-ŋ result in quite different words which cannot be phonological variants.

yú$_9$ 於 prefix → **ā** 阿

yú$_{10}$-tù 於兔, **yú-shì** 於檡 → **hǔ$_1$** 虎

yú$_{11}$ 舁譽 (jiwo) **LH** jɑ, **OCM** *la — **[T]** *MTang* iy < iø < *ONW* io

'To lift' 舁 [Han]; 'to praise' 譽 [Shi].

ꭗ **yù** 譽 (jiwo^C) **LH** jɑ^C, **OCM** *lah

'Praise, renown' [Meng].

[E] ST: WT *bla* ~ *rla* 'above, over, upper' (*HST:* 154). This wf is an allofam of → yáng$_7$ 揚 with its WT cognates; prob. cognate to → yú$_{27}$ 輿, and perh. also to → jǔ$_6$ 舉 'to rise, lift'.

yú$_{12}$ 臾 → **lǚ$_1$** 婁 'drag, trail'

yú$_{13}$ 腴 → **liáo$_5$** 膋

yú$_{14}$ 俞 (jiu) **LH** jo, **OCM** *lo

'Make a boat by hollowing the log' [SW], 窬木 'hollowed tree, canoe'; **lú** 艫 (luo) 'boat' [Xin Tangshu] is perhaps a variant of this word.

[E] This is an ancient area word: TB-WB *hlo-* 'boat'. <> PKS *lwa^A 'boat' (Edmondson / Yang 1988: 157 *s-lwa(n) on the basis of Ai-Cham *zu:n*^{2}), PTai *drɨo^{A2}, Be *lua*^{55}. The ancient (Han time) Yuè language's word for 'boat' *xū-lù* 須慮 [sio-liɑh] [Yuèjuèshū] belongs to an AA etymon *chalā*.

The meaning of this wf is 'to hollow out, make hollow' (Huáng Jīn-guì and Shěn Xí-róng *YYWZX* 1987.8: 41ff). Allofams are → dú$_4$ 櫝韇 'container', perh. also → yú$_{19}$ 窬俞 'hole', → dú$_3$ 瀆 'drain', → yú$_{16}$ 揄 'scoop'. → chuán$_1$ 船 'boat' may also be remotely related (see there for cognates), → zhōu$_1$ 舟 'boat' is not.

yú$_{15}$ 俞 (jiu) **LH** jo, **OCM** *lo

'Say yes, agree' [Shu].

[E] ST: WB *lyo* 'suit, agree with, be proper'.

yú$_{16}$ 揄 (jiu, dəu^B) **LH** jo, do^B, **OCM** *lo, *lôʔ

'To scoop out (as a mortar), pull toward oneself' [Shi, Karlgren: faulty verse?].

~ **yóu** ~ **yǎo** 舀 (jiəu, jiäu^B) **LH** ju, jau^B, **OCM** *lu ~ lauʔ

'To scoop hulled grain from a mortar' [SW: Shi]. This ordinary agricultural term shows dialectal (?) variations in the rime *-o ~ *-u ~ *-au.

[E] Area etymon: TB-Lushai *lɔɔk*^{F} / *lɔʔ*^{L} 'to scoop up'. <> MK: PMonic *[g]lɔk 'to scoop out with hand, take out with hand...'. We should expect a CH final *-k*, perh. it was weakened to *-ʔ. Perhaps related to → yú$_{14}$ 俞.

yú$_{17}$ 愉 (jiu) **LH** jo, **OCM** *lo

'Pleasant, enjoy' [Shi].

[E] ST: WB *lyo*^{C} 'loose, slack, subside' ꭗ *hlyo*^{C} 'loosen, make lax, lessen, diminish'. Syn. → yù$_8$ 悆譽豫.

ж **tāo** 慆 (tʰâu) **LH** tʰou, **OCM** *lhû
'To please' [Zuo]. Vocalic variants *o ~ *u occur elsewhere, see → yú$_{16}$ 揄.

ж **yuè** 悅閱 (jiwät) **LH** jyat, **OCM** *lot — **[T]** *ONW* iuat
'Be delighted, pleased, glad' 悅 [Shi]; 'be liked' [Shi], 'satisfied' 閱 [Shu].

ж **duì** 兌 (duâi^{C}) **LH** duɑs, **OCM** *lôts
'Glad' [Zhuang].

[C] OCM *lo is the apparent root of a large wf whose basic meaning is 'loosen, relax':

'Relax, loosen' > 'explain' → shuō 說 *lhot
'Relax' > 'careless' → tōu$_{1}$ 偷 *lhô
'Relax, loosen' > 'take off / away' → tuō$_{3}$ 脫 *lhôt
'Take away, rob' → tōu$_{2}$ 偷 *lhô

yú$_{18}$ 踰逾 (jiu) **LH** jo, **OCM** *lo (or *jo ?)
'To leap or pass over, transgress' 逾 [Shu], 踰 [Shi].
[T] *Sin Sukchu SR* y (平); *MGZY* yÿu (平) [jy]

ж **yù** 愈瘉 (jiu^{B}) **LH** jo^{B}, **OCM** *loʔ (or *joʔ ?)
'Be increasing' (grief), 'be pressing' (burden) 愈 [Shi]; 'be suffering' 瘉 [Shi]; 'surpass' [Lun], 'convalesce' 愈 [Meng].
[<] *lo + tone B: endoactive (§4.5).

ж **shū** 輸 (śju) **LH** śo, **OCM** *lho (or *hjo ?) — **[T]** *MTang* śu < śuo, *ONW* śuo
'To transport, convey' [Zuo], 'transmit' [Shu] (Huáng Jīn-guì, Shěn Xí-róng *YYWZX* 1987.8: 46f).
[<] *lo + caus. devoicing (§5.2.2).

[E] Etymology not clear. Comparanda are: (1) TB-JP *joʔ^{55}* 'to jump'; if related, the OC words should have initial*j-, not *l-. (2) AA: Khmer *lota* /lóot/ 'to jump, leap, spring', for absence of final *-t* in CH, see §6.9. Old Sino-Viet. *lɔ* (Pān Wùyún 1987: 29). Perh. related to → yǒng$_{4}$ 踊 'jump'; → shuì$_{2}$ 稅 'to present' may also be a derivation.

yú$_{19}$ 窬俞 (jiu, dəu) **LH** jo, do, **OCM** *lo, *lô
'Opening, small gate' [Lunyu].

ж **yuè** 閱 (jiuät) **LH** jyɑt, **OCM** *lot
'Hole' [Shi].

ж **duì** 兌 (duâi^{C}, tʰuâi^{C}) **LH** duɑs, **OCM** *lôts
'Open a passage through' [Shi], 'opening' [Lao] has been loaned into Tai: S. *lɔɔt^{D2L}* < *dl- 'to slip through a hole or tunnel'.

ж **duì** 奪 (duâi^{C}) **LH** duɑs, **OCM** *lôts
'Narrow passage' [Liji].

ж **dòu** 竇 (dəu^{C}, duk) **LH** do^{C}, dok, **OCM** *lôk(h) — **[T]** *MGZY* tʰiw (去) [dəw]
'Hole' [Li], 'drain' [Zuo] (Wáng Lì 1982: 295: 瀆 ж 竇 ж 窬).

[E] MK: Old Sino-Viet. *lo* 'small hole' (Pān Wùyún 1987: 29), Loven *luh* 'hole', Khmer /tluh/ 'perforate' ж /luh/ 'pass through, pierce, perforate...'. Possible allofam → yú$_{14}$ 俞.

yú$_{20}$ 揄 → **dú$_{6}$** 犢

yú$_{21}$ 覦 → **yù$_{5}$** 欲

yú$_{22}$ 魚 (ŋjwo) **LH** ŋɨɑ, **OCM** *ŋa
'Fish' n. 魚 [OB, Shi], 'to fish' 漁 [Zuo].
[T] *Sin Sukchu SR* ŋy (平); *MGZY* xÿu (平) [ɦy]; *ONW* ŋio (?) > ŋø
[E] ST: PTB *ŋyaʔ > WT *ña;* PLB *ŋa^{2} > WB *ŋa^{B};* JP *ŋa^{55}, wə^{31}-* 'fish', Lushai *ŋha^{F}*, Tiddim *ŋaa^{R} < ŋaaʔ*, KN-Khami *ŋ(y)a* (Löffler 1966: 146), Chepang *ŋaʔ* 'fish'

(Matisoff 1995a: 40; *STC* no. 189), Garo *naʔ*, Tiwa *ŋá* [Joseph / Burling *LTBA* 24.2, 2001: 43]. The TB branch has a form *ŋ(y)aʔ, the Sinitic branch *ŋ(j)a without final *ʔ*.

yú₂₃ 隅嵎 (ŋju) **LH** ŋɨo, **OCM** *ŋo
'Angle, corner' 隅 [Shi], 'corner or bend of a hill' 嵎 [Meng].
[E] Etymology not clear. WT *ŋos* 'side, margin, edge' ⋈ *dŋo* 'shore, bank, edge' (of knife) is more likely to be related to → àn₂ 岸. Theoretically possible could be cognation with WT *gru* 'corner, angle' (for the initials, §5.12.2; for the vowels, see §11.8), but see → zhǒu₁ 肘.

yú₂₄, yóng 喁 → oǔ 偶

yú₂₅ 愚 (ŋju) **LH** ŋɨo, **OCM** *ŋo — **[T]** *MTang* ŋy < ŋuo, *ONW* ŋuo
'Stupid, ignorant' 遇 [Shi], 愚 [Lunyu] occurs also in Tai: PTai *ʔŋua^B2/C2 'stupid, idiot, ignorant' (Luo Yongxian *MKS* 27, 1997: 291), S. *ŋoo^C1* 'stupid'. <> Khmer *lŋỳ:* 'stupid', *lŋùəŋ* 'ignorant'.
⋈ **wán** 頑 (ŋwan, ŋwăn) **LH** ŋuan, **OCM** *ŋrôn
'Be stupid, foolish' [Shu].

yú₂₆ 與歟 (jiwo) **LH** jɑ, **OCM** *la, OCB *la
'Interrogative particle' [Lü], fusion of 也乎 (Pulleyblank 1995: 9).
[T] *Sin Sukchu SR* y (平); *MGZY* yÿu (平) [jy]; *MTang* iy < iø < *ONW* io
⋈ **yé** 邪 (jia) **LH** ja, **OCM** *la ? — **[T]** *ONW* ia
'Id.', a later col. variant of the above (Unger *Hao-ku* 22, 1983; Pulleyblank 1995: 9).
[E] Because these items are fusions and hence secondary in OC, there is probably no connection with PLB *la² 'interrogative particle' (Matisoff 1995a: 73f) > WB *la^B*.

yú₂₇ 輿 (jiwo) **LH** jɑ, **OCM** *la — **[T]** *MTang* iy < iø < *ONW* io
'Carriage box, carriage' [Yi], 'carrier, carry on the shoulders' [Zuo].
[E] Tai: S. *lɔɔ^B* 'car, carriage' (Unger *Hao-ku* 36, 1990: 67), but Gòng Qúnhǔ (*MZYW* 2, 2000) compares this to Tai *raa²* 'car' instead (與 misprint for 輿?).
This is prob. the same etymon as → yú₁₁ 舁譽 'lift'. Baxter and Sagart (1998: 48) suggest that *yú* is also related to → chē 車 and → jǔ₆ 舉.

yǔ₁ 羽 (ju^B) **LH** wɑ^B, **OCM** *waʔ
'Feather, wing' [Shi].
[T] *Sin Sukchu SR* y (上); *MGZY* xÿu (上) [ɦy]
[E] Possibly a ST item, note PTB *wa = *(b)wa 'bird' (Matisoff *LL* 1.2, 2000: 142f). It also appears to be connected with PKS *pwa^B1 'wing' (Matisoff 1985a: 445: Benedict).

yǔ₂ 宇 (ju^B) **LH** wɑ^B, **OCM** *waʔ
'Eaves > abode, estate, territory' [BI, Shi].
[E] Etymology not clear. Perh. the s. w. as → yǔ₁ 羽 'wings' (i.e. 'wings' of a house?); or related to the stem *wa 'enlarge' under → kuàng₁ 況?

yǔ₃ 雨 (ju^B) **LH** wɑ^B, **OCM** *waʔ
'Precipitation, rain' [OB, Shi].
[T] *Sin Sukchu SR* y (上); *MGZY* xÿu (上) [ɦy]; *MTang* y < uo, *ONW* uo
⋈ **yǔ** 雨 (ju^C) **LH** wɑ^C, **OCM** *wah
'To rain (something), fall' (rain, snow) [Shi].
[<] exoactive *yǔ* (§4.3.2), i.e. 'transitive vb.' (Baxter and Sagart 1998: 58).
⋈ **yú** 雩 (ju) **LH** wɑ, **OCM** *wa
'Sacrifice with prayer for rain' [Lun] (Wáng Lì 1982: 146).

[<] a tone A noun derived from *yǔ* (§3.1).

[E] ST *waʔ > PTB *r-wa > Khambu *kəwa*, Bahing *rja-wa;* Chepang *waʔ-ʔo;* PL *r-jwa/we¹, WB *rwa*, Lushai *ruaʔ*^{L} (*HST:* 122). A rare ST parallel stem *(r)we is represented in CH by the wf → yǔn$_2$ 隕殞霣. It is not clear if or how PT *xr-: S. *haa*^{B1} 'shower', classifier for rain etc. could be related. Syn. → dōng$_3$ 涷, → fēn$_2$ 雰氛, → líng$_8$ 霝零.

yǔ$_4$ 禹 (juᴮ) **LH** wɑᴮ, **OCM** *waʔ — **[T]** *MTang* y < uo, *ONW* uo

'Insect, reptile' [SW] has been compared to PTB *was 'bee, honey' (*STC* p. 17 n. 62). However, MK-PWa *wak 'insect' is semantically closer (for the finals, see §3.2.2).

yǔ$_5$-yǔ 偊偊 → **jù$_5$** 懼

yǔ$_6$ 語 (ŋjwoᴮ) **LH** ŋɨɑᴮ, **OCM** *ŋaʔ

'Speak' [Shi].

[T] *Sin Sukchu SR* ŋy (上); *MGZY* xÿu (上) [ɦy]; *MTang* ŋy < ŋø < *ONW* ŋio (?)

ꭗ **yù** 語 (ŋjwoᶜ) **LH** ŋɨɑᶜ, **OCM** *ŋah

'To tell' [Zuo].

[<] exoact. §4.3.2. Acc. to Downer (1959: 284), tone C has an 'effective' connotation.

[E] ST: WT *ŋag, dŋags* 'speech, talk, word' ꭗ *sŋag-pa, bsŋags* 'to praise, extol, recommend' ꭗ *sŋags* 'incantation'; PLB *s-ŋak 'bird' > WB *hŋak*; JP *ŋa*^{33} 'to say'.

ꭗ **yán** 言 (ŋjɐn) **LH** ŋɨɑn, **OCM** *ŋan

'To speak, speech, talk' [Shi].

[T] *Sin Sukchu SR* jen (平); *MGZY* ngen (平) [ŋɛn]; *ONW* ŋan

[<] *ŋaʔ + nominal n-suffix (§6.4.3).

ꭗ Perh. **yàn** 唁諺 (ŋjänᶜ 3) **LH** ŋɨanᶜ, **OCM** *ŋans

'To console' 唁[Shi]; 'saying, proverb' 諺 [Zuo] are cognates of *yán* acc. to Wáng Lì (1982: 138). Although the two words look identical in most dialects except for the tone, including LH, the QYS makes a fine vocalic distinction.

yǔ$_7$ 圉圄 (ŋjwoᴮ) **LH** ŋɨɑᴮ, **OCM** *ŋaʔ

'Prison' 圄 [Li], 圉 [YiZhoushu]; 'to imprison, keep horses, groom' [Zuo], 'border, contain' [BI, Shi], 'restrain, embarrass' 圉 [Meng].

ꭗ **àn** 犴 (ŋânᶜ) **LH** ŋɑnᶜ, **OCM** *ŋâns

'Prison' 岸 [Shi], 犴 [Xun].

[<] *ŋaʔ + nominal n-suffix (§6.4.3).

[C] An allofam is → yù$_{16}$ 禦 'manage' (i.e. 'control'). PMY *ŋo¹ 'prison' is prob. a Chinese loan.

yǔ$_8$ 與 (jiwoᴮ) **LH** jɑᴮ, **OCM** *laʔ

'To be with, join company, associate with, with, and' [Shi, SW] > 'help' [Meng]. The meanings make it unlikely that this is the same word as → yú$_{11}$ 舁譽 'to lift'. SW makes a graphic distinction between this *yǔ$_8$* and *yǔ$_9$*.

[T] *Sin Sukchu SR* y (上); *MGZY* yÿu (上) [jy]; *MTang* iy < iø, *ONW* io

ꭗ **yù** 與 (jiwoᶜ) **LH** jɑᶜ, **OCM** *lah (or *jah ?) — **[T]** *MTang* iy < iø, *ONW* io

'To participate' [Zuo]. Acc. to Downer (1959: 285), tone C implies an 'effective' meaning.

yǔ$_9$ 與与 (jiwoᴮ) **LH** jɑᴮ, **OCM** *laʔ — **[T]** *MTang* iy < iø, *ONW* io

'To give' 與 [Shi, Shu], 与 [SW]; 'to present, give' 予 [Shi].

[E] The wf → shě$_1$ 舍 is prob. derived from this word, *yǔ* is hence related to foreign etyma mentioned there. *CVST* (3: 3) connects the word with the TB items under → yǐ$_2$

以 'take, use'; but note WT *gla* 'pay, wages, fee' (*HPTB*:173f), Lakher *hla* 'to present, offer (sacrifice), give'; or alternatively JP *ja* 'to give'.

yǔ $_{10}$ 傴 → **gōu** $_1$ 句鉤枸區

yù $_1$ 芋 (ju^C) **LH** wɑ^C, **OCM** *wah
'Taro' [Yili].
[E] Area word: PMY *vəu^{B2} (Wáng FS 12/263), WB *wa^C* 'kind of potato'.

yù $_2$ 汩 → **xuàn** $_1$ 泫

yù $_3$ 谷 'nourish' → **yù** $_{22}$ 育毓鬻

yù $_4$ 浴 (jiwok) **LH** jok, **OCM** *lok
'To bathe, wash' [Lunyu].
[T] *Sin Sukchu SR* y (入); *MGZY* yÿu (入) [jy]
[E] Area word. Chinese and WT share a final *-k, the other TB lgs. have open syllables: WT *ldug(s)-pa, ldugs < ɴluk* 'to pour' (water into vessel, on hands) > 'cast, found' (*STC:* 110). Also AA-Pearic *klu:k* 'to pour'. <> PTB *(r-)lu(w) ~ *(m-)lu(w) > Angami Naga *rəlu* 'bathe', NNaga *C/V-ru [French 1983: 334]. Mikir *iŋlu < m-lu*, Dimasa *lu* 'to pour', Karen *lu* 'to pour'. Also Mru *lu,* WB *k^{h}yui^B* 'wash, bathe' [Löffler 1966: 130]. There is a similar but unrelated item *zhù* 鑄 'to cast, pour' (under → zhù$_5$ 注) whose initial is a dental stop. The relationship with → yě$_2$ 冶 'smelt, cast', if any, is not clear.

yù $_5$ 欲 (jiwok) **LH** jok, **OCM** *lok — **[T]** *ONW* iuok
'To want, wish' [Shi]; 'desire, passion' 慾 [Lun]. The colloquial Mand. form is thought to be → yào$_2$ 要.
⪤ **yú** 覦 (jiu[^{C}]) **LH** jo(^{C}), **OCM** *lo or *loh
'To look for, desire' [Zuo].
[<] perh. exoact. (§4.3).
[E] ST: WB *lui* 'desire, wish for; be lacking, wanted' ⪤ *ə-lui* 'desire, need'. Alternatively, one could set up OC *jok and relate the etymon to PTB *ryu: WT *žu-ba, žus* 'to request; a request, wish, question', WHim *ru-* 'ask', Mikir *arǰu < r-ju* 'to ask, to hear', NNaga *ryəw 'ask for' [French 1983: 330], Lushai *zot^F < jot* 'ask, inquire'.

yù $_6$ 慾 → **yù** $_5$ 欲

yù $_7$ 裕 (jiu^C) **LH** jo^C, **OCM** *lokh
'Be indulgent, abundant, opulent' [Shi, Shu] can be compared with WT *lhug-po* 'wide, diffuse, luxurious' ⪤ *lhug-par* 'amply, copiously, plentifully'. *CVST* (3: 32) relates *yù* to WB *lok* 'enough, sufficient'.

yù $_8$ 悆譽豫 (jiwo^C) **LH** jɑ^C, **OCM** *lah — **[T]** *MTang* iy < iø, *ONW* io
'Pleased' 悆 [SW: Shu]; 'joy' 豫譽 [Shi]; 'happy' 豫 [Shu], 'amusement, recreation' [Meng].
[C] This is prob. the same word as → yù$_{25}$ 豫 'slow' (< 'relaxed'). A derivation may be → xiáng$_1$ 庠祥 'happy omen'. A cognate and paronym is → yì$_{35}$ 繹 'pleased'.
[E] The related AA root under the cognate → yì$_{35}$ 繹 'pleased' also has the semantic range 'open up' > 'carefree, happy': OKhmer *lā* [laa] 'to open, unfold, extend...' ⪤ *klā* [klaa] 'be free of restraint, be lively, merry, gay'. Gòng Qúnhǔ (*MZYW* 2, 2000) compares this word to Tai *raa^{B2}* 'happy'.

yù $_9$ 禺 (ŋju^C) **LH** ŋɨo^C, **OCM** *ŋoh
'Monkey' [Li, N. Pr.].

[E] ST: Kuki-Naga branch of PTB: *ŋa:w 'ape' > Lushai *ŋau^{H}* < *ŋau* 'grey monkey' (*STC:* 192 n. 491). Note also → náo$_{2}$ 猱獿 *nu 'monkey'; if related, inter-lingual borrowing is probably responsible for the variants. For other similar-looking words for 'monkey', see → yóu$_{8}$ 猶.

yù$_{10}$ 遇 → **oǔ** 偶

yù$_{11}$ 菀 'pent up' → **wèi**$_{10}$, **yù** 蔚

yù$_{12}$ 飫 → **yù**$_{21}$ 饇

yù$_{13}$ 域 → **guó** 國

yù$_{14}$ 閾 → **guó** 國

yù$_{15}$ 御 → **yù**$_{16}$ 禦 'control'

yù$_{16}$ 禦 (ŋjwo^{B}) **LH** ŋɨɑ^{B}, **OCM** *ŋaʔ
('To control':) 'to secure' (an area 方) [BI, YiZhou], 'to curb' [Zhuang], 'hinder, prevent' [Meng] (*yù*$_{16}$ and *yù*$_{17}$ blend into each other).
[E] ST: WT *mŋa'* 'might, dominion', *mŋa'-ba* 'having, owning, to be'; the fundamental ST meaning might have been 'be in control'.

⋈ **yù** 御 (ŋjwo^{C}) **LH** ŋɨɑ^{C}, **OCM** *ŋah — **[T]** *MTang* ŋy < ŋø < *ONW* ŋio (?)
'To drive (a chariot), to direct, manage' [BI, Shi]; ('drive' >) 'drive out, exorcise' [OB].
[E] ST: WB *moŋ^{B}* 'threaten, drive away' ⋈ *ə-moŋ^{B}* 'driving' (§2.8.3).

[C] Allofam is → yǔ$_{7}$ 圉圄 'prison, restrain'. See also → yì$_{2}$ 艾刈.

yù$_{17}$ 禦 (ŋjwo^{B}) **LH** ŋɨɑ^{B}, **OCM** *ŋaʔ — **[T]** *MTang* ŋy < ŋø, *ONW* ŋø < ŋio
'To defend, object, oppose, prevent' [BI, Shi] (*yù*$_{16}$ and *yù*$_{17}$ blend into each other).

⋈ **wù** 啎迕晤捂 (ŋuo^{C}) **LH** ŋɑ^{C}, **OCM** *ŋâh
'To go against' 啎 [Lü], 迕 [Lie]; 'encounter' 啎迕 [Chuci]; 'face to face' 晤 [Shi]; 'to turn against' 捂 [Yili]; 'oppose' 忤 [Hanfei]; 'resist' [Li] (Qiu Xigui 2000: 335).

⋈ **wù** 蘁 (ŋâk, ŋuo^{C}) **LH** ŋɑk, ŋɑ^{C}, **OCM** *ŋâk(h)
'Resist, oppose' [Zhuang].

⋈ **sù** 泝愬訴 (suo^{C}) **LH** sɑ^{C}, **OCM** *sŋâkh
'Go upward against' 泝 [Shi]; 'go up against current' 泝 [Zuo]; 'complain' 愬 [Shi], 'accuse, inform' 訴 [Zuo].
[<] perh. intensive of *wù* 蘁 *ŋâk(h) (§5.2.3) (Baxter and Sagart 1998: 53).

[E] ST: WT *ŋo* 'face, countenance, air, look'. WT *ŋos* 'side, direction' belongs to CH → wài 外 'outside' (so Bodman 1980: 136). For an overview of related words, see under → yà$_{2}$ 御迓訝.

yù$_{18}$ 喻諭 (jiu^{C}) **LH** jo^{C}, **OCM** *joh or *loh ?
'To understand, instruct' [Lun] > 'example' 喻 [Meng]; 'proclaim, understand' 諭 [Li, Guoce].
[E] ? ST: WT *blo* 'mind, intellect'.

yù$_{19}$ 愈瘉 → **yú**$_{18}$ 踰逾

yù$_{20}$, **yǔ** 嫗 (ʔju^{B}) **LH** ʔɨo^{B}, **OCM** *ʔoʔ
(Of birds:) 'to sit on eggs, incubate' 嫗伏 [Liji] > 'to warm with body' (as mother a child, or the earth all things to make them grow) [Liji].
[E] ST *ʔo: PLB *ʔu^{3} > WB u^{B} (i.e. /ʔu^{B}/) 'lay an egg' ⋈ *ə-u^{B}* 'egg' (*HPTB:* 180).

⋈ **yù** 嫗 (ʔju^{C}) **LH** ʔɨo^{C}, **OCM** *ʔoh
'Mother' [SW] > 'Mrs.' [Shiji] > '(old) woman' [Guangya].

[<] a late general purpose tone C derivation of *yù, yǔ* 嫗 (§3.5), lit. 'the one who is breeding, mothering'.

⋈ **yòu** 蓲 (ʔjəu^C) **LH** ʔu^C
'To brood, hatch (eggs)' is acc. to Guō Pú's commentary to FY 8, 4 a Jiāngdōng (lower Yangtze) dialect word; it survives today in Mǐn dialects: Jiàn'ōu *iu^{Cl}*, Chóngān *ieu^{Cl}* (Norman 1983: 206).

⋈ **yù** 燠 (ʔjuk) **LH** ʔuk
'Warm' (of season, house, clothing) [Shi].
[E] ST: WB *uik* (i.e. *ʔuik*) 'feel warm, close'.

[C] This wf coalesces partially with → xù$_4$ 旭, perh. they together form a single wf. → wēn 溫 'warm' could be an allofam, but it prob. belongs to a ST root *ʔur, while the above items belong to ST *ʔo.

yù$_{21}$ 饇 (ʔju^C, k^hju) **LH** ʔɨo^C, k^hɨo, **OCM** *ʔoh, kho (?)
'To be satiated, full' (of food, wine) [Shi].
[E] ? ST: Perh. WT *myo-ba, myos ~ smyo-ba, smyos* 'insane, mad, drunk', if Tib. *m-* is a prefix.

~ **yù** 飫 (ʔjwo^C) **LH** ʔɨɑ^C, **OCM** *ʔah
'To satiate, nourished' 於 [Shu], 飫 [Shi] seems to be a vocalic variant of the preceding word.

⋈ **xù** 酗 (xju^C) **LH** hɨo^C, **OCM** *hoh
'Drunk, mad' (with wine) [BI, Shu].
[<] *ʔoh + initial MC *x-* which may represent 'intensive' 'devoicing' (§5.2.3).

⋈ **yōng** 饔 (ʔjwoŋ) **LH** ʔɨoŋ, **OCM** *ʔoŋ
'Cooked meal' (for sacrifice to the dead) [Shi], (for banquet) [Meng].
[<] *ʔoh + terminative *-ŋ* (§6.5.1), lit. '(something for) getting to be full'.

yù$_{22}$ 育毓鬻 (jiuk) **LH** juk, **OCM** *luk
'To give birth, to rear, breed, nourish' 育 [Shi, Shu]; 'produce' 毓 [OB, BI, Zhouli]; 'nourish' [Zhouli], 'young' 鬻 [Shi]. Baxter and Sagart (1998: 52) derive → zhōu$_5$ 粥鬻 'rice gruel' from this word.
[E] ST: JP *lu^{31}* 'give birth' (to a child).

⋈ **dú** 毒 (duok) **LH** douk, **OCM** *dûk < *lûk ? — [T] *ONW* douk
'To nourish' [Lao]. The graph 毒 was used in this late Zhou text when *C-l- and *d- had apparently already merged. Or was this graph simply borrowed for *yù*?

⋈ **táo** 陶 (dâu) **LH** dou, **OCM** *lû
'To nourish' [FY 1.5] a Han period Qín dialect word.

⋈ **yù** 谷 (juk) **LH** jok, **OCM** *lok
'To nourish' [Lao] a vocalic variant.

[C] Table C-2 (under → chù$_4$, xù 畜) shows the phonological and semantic connections among similar looking words. This etymon is not related to any of the other stems in that table, nor to → xiū$_4$ 羞. Perh. connected with *chōu* 抽 (under → yóu$_2$ 由).

yù$_{23}$ 賣 (jiuk) **LH** juk, **OCM** *luk
'To sell' [BI]. Originally, this graph was distinct from the one for *mài* 'sell', see *SW* 2776.
[E] MK: OKhmer /lɔk/, Khmer /luk/ ~ /ruk/ 'to sell, to fine'. *Yù* looks like a cognate of → shú$_6$ 贖 *m-lok 'ransom' (Sagart 1999: 82), but the vowels should be identical in a closely related introvert / extrovert pair; also, simultaneous close connections with

both TB-WT (→ shú$_{6}$ 贖) as well as MK are difficult to explain, therefore these words may not be related. Syn. → dí$_{6}$ 糴; → gǔ$_{11}$ 賈; → mǎi 買; → shòu$_{2}$ 售.

yù$_{24}$ 豫 (jiwo^{C})
Supposedly 'large elephant' [*SWJZGL* 4277] (Karlgren *GSR* 83e). There is prob. no such word. (1) There is no early text in which this word means 'elephant'; (2) the ancient graph (*gǔwén* 古文) did not have *xiàng* 象 'elephant' as a graphic element. *SW* was guessing at the original meaning of the graph (cf. *shè* 射 'to shoot', §1.4.2).

yù$_{25}$ 豫 (jiwo^{C}) **LH** jɑ^{C}, **OCM** *lah — **[T]** *MTang* iy < iø < *ONW* io
'Slow and deliberate' [Lao], 'think beforehand' [Li], 'anticipate' [Zuo].
[E] Karlgren *GSR* 83e derives this word from the homophone 'elephant' → yù$_{24}$ 豫 [SW] (< 'elephant-like') which is unlikely. This is prob. the s. w. as → yù$_{8}$ 悆譽豫 'pleased' (both from < 'relaxed') (so Wáng Lì 1982: 162). A semantic parallel is → yú$_{17}$ 愉.

⋈ **shū** 舒 (śjwo) **LH** śɑ, **OCM** *lha
'Relax, slowly, leisurely, easy' [Shi], 'lazy' [Shu].
[<] *la + devoicing (meaning?) (§5.1)
[E] ST: WT *sla-ba* 'easy' (*CVST* 3: 1).

= **shū** 紓 (śjwo, dźjwo) **LH** śɑ, źɑ ?, **OCM** *lha ~ *mla ?
'Be remiss' [Shi], 'relax, alleviate, delay' [Zuo]. If the reading MC *dźjwo* can be trusted, the initial *m- is prob. inherited from ST.

⋈ **xú** 徐 (zjwo) **LH** ziɑ, **OCM** *s-la
'Walk slowly, gently' [Meng], 'slow, by and by' [Zuo], 'quiet' [Zhuang].
[<] *la + s-prefix (meaning?) (§5.2).

[E] Three different valence-increasing morphemes are added to the root *la: (1) final s/h: *la-h, (2) causative devoicing *lha, (3) s-prefix: *s-la. A similar profusion of forms is seen in the wf → yì$_{35}$ 繹.

yù$_{26}$ 繘 (kjuet, jiuet) **LH** kiut (kuit), juit, late **OCM** (k-)ju(i)t ?
'Well rope' [Li] occurs also in WT: *rgyud* < *r-yut* 'string, cord'. This could possibly be a variant of → lǜ$_{5}$ 繂率, both from PCH *rjut ~ *r-jut (§9.2.1), provided the late OCM form (Liji) was already *-uit* and had merged with the reflex of *-wit*.

yù$_{27}$ 遹 → **suì$_{2}$** 遂

yù$_{28}$ 潏 → **xuàn$_{1}$** 泫

yù$_{29}$ 譽 → **yú$_{11}$** 舁譽

yù$_{30}$ 語 → **yǔ$_{6}$** 語

yù$_{31}$ 燠 → **yù$_{20}$**, **yǔ** 嫗

yù$_{32}$ 鬱 (ʔjuət) **LH** ʔut, **OCM** *ʔut — **[T]** *ONW* ʔut
'A fragrant herb' [Li]. Unger (*Hao-ku* 39, 1992) suggests that this is the s. w. as → wèi$_{10}$, yù 蔚 'a kind of artemisia'.

yù$_{33}$ 鬱 'dense' → **wèi$_{10}$**, **yù** 蔚

yuān$_{1}$ 鳶 (jiwän) **LH** juan, **OCM** *jon ?
'Hawk, kite' [Shi] is shared with TB-PL: *(k-)dzwan^{1} 'hawk'.

yuān$_{2}$ 冤 → **yū$_{1}$** 迂紆

yuān$_3$ 蜎肙 (ʔiwen, ʔjwän[B]) **LH** ʔuen(B), **OCM** *ʔwên, *ʔwen(ʔ)
'Small worm' 肙 [SW] > 'be bending, crawling' (as a caterpillar) 蜎 [Shi]
[<] *-n nominalization (§6.4.3) of a ST etymon: → wēi$_1$(-tuó) 委佗, TB-Lushai *vial* 'writhe'.

yuán$_1$ 元 (ŋjwɐn) **LH** ŋyɑn, **OCM** *ŋon or *ŋwan
'Head' [Zuo, Xi 33] (Unger *Hao-ku* 28, 1984: 251; Mei 1985: 335), 'to be at the head, first, eldest, principal, great' [BI, Shi].
[T] *Sin Sukchu SR* ŋyen (平); *MGZY* xwÿan (平) [ɦyɛn]; *ONW* ŋuan
[E] *Yuán* is perh. related to PTB *m-gaw ~ *(s-)gaw (*STC* no. 490) > WT *go* 'headman, beginning, source' ⋈ *mgo* 'head, summit, beginning' ⋈ *mgon-po* 'protector, master, lord'. WT *mg-*, *mb-* = CH *ŋ-*, *m-* does occur elsewhere, but is rare. Alternatively, the WT etyma could also be related to → gāo$_1$ 高 (kâu) (so *HST:* 93), yet *yuán*'s semantic agreement with WT is significant. Mei Tsu-Lin (in Thurgood etc. 1985: 335f) considers both *yuán* and → *jūn*$_3$ 君 (kjuən) 'lord, prince' variants which he relates to WT *mgon*.
[C] → yuán$_{12}$ 黿 may be the same word. Allofams are perh. → hòu$_1$ 后, → yuán$_3$ 原.

yuán$_2$ 㕣 (jiwänB) **LH** juanB, **OCM** *lonʔ
'Marsh between mountains' [SW] has perh. a Tai connection: S. *leen*A2 'marsh, mire' (Manomaivibool 1975: 235).

yuán$_3$ 原 (ŋjwɐn) **LH** ŋyɑn, **OCM** *ŋwan, OCB *ŋwjan
'A plain, highland' [Shi], 'spring, source' [Meng] is perh. the s. w. as → yuán$_1$ 元 'head' (Qiu Xigui 2000: 275).

yuán$_4$ 謜 (ŋjwɐn) **LH** ŋyɑn, **OCM** *ŋon or *ŋwan
'Quiet talk' [SW: Meng] is perhaps related to PTB *ŋoj 'mild, quiet'.

yuán$_5$ 員圓圜 (jwän) **LH** wen, **OCM** *wen, OCB *wjən
'Circle' 員 [Shi]; 'round' 圜 [Yi], 員 [Meng], 圓 [Hanfei]; 'return' 員 [Shu]; *yuán* 'circle' is symbolic for 'sky, heaven', *fāng* 方 'square' for 'earth' [Huainan].
[T] *Sin Sukchu SR* yen (平); *MGZY* xwÿan (平) [ɦyɛn]; *ONW* uan

⋈ **yuàn** 院瑗 (jwänC) **LH** wenC, **OCM** *wens (?)
'Wall around a courtyard' 院 [Mo]; 'ring-shaped jade insignium' 瑗 [Xun], also MC *jwɐnC;* Downer (1959: 280) adds caus. 'encircle oneself > put on' (a buff coat) 擐 [Zuozhuan].

⋈ **xuán** 還旋 (zjwän) **LH** zyan, **OCM** *s-wen, OCB *-en
'To turn around, to wheel' 旋 [Zuo], 'to turn around, return' 還旋 [Shi], 'turn away, all round' 旋 [Shi, Yi] > (turning this way and that:) 'agile' 還 [Shi]; 'ring' 旋 [Zhouli].
[<] caus. of *yuán* 員圓圜 (jwän) (§5.2.2), lit. 'make go around'.

[E] Area word: PMK *wial 'turn around' (Shorto 1972: 4; 1973: 380) ⋈ *wal 'bend, return, halo'. <> ST *w(i)al: PTB *wal (*STC* no. 91) > WB *wan*B 'circular', Kachin *wan*, Lushai *val*R 'be in the form of a ring or circle' (*HST:* 55) ⋈ *hual*L 'to surround, encircle'. CH -> Tai: S. *wian*A2 'revolve, encircle, circle' (Manomaivibool 1975: 179). MC *-jä-* suggests that the OC vocalism was not /a/ but frontish (e, ia?), therefore prob. not (directly?) related to → huán$_1$ 桓垸. Or this CH wf, or some of its members, belong to → yíng$_4$ 營. Most likely, the area roots *weŋ ~ *wen and *wial ~ *wel have converged in OC. For synonyms, see → huí 回.

yuán$_6$ 猿 (jwɐn) **LH** wɑn, **OCM** *wan
'Monkey' [Zhuang, Guoce].

[E] ST etymon with the OC nominal final *-n (§6.4.3): PTB *woy ~ *(b)woy (*STC* no. 314), JP *woi*[33]. Alternatively, the root could be AA: PMK *swaaʔ 'monkey' (Shorto 1976: 1062), PNBahn. *hwa 'gibbon', Wa-Lawa-Bulang *hwaʔ 'leaf monkey'. For synonyms for 'monkey', including possible variants, see → yóu$_8$ 猶.

yuán$_7$ 園 (jwɐn) **LH** wɑn, **OCM** *wan, OCB *wjan — **[T]** *ONW* uan
'Garden, park' [Shi].
[E] This word is prob. derived from one or other root *wan 'round, encircle' (see → huí 回), semantically like *yuàn* 院瑗 'wall around a courtyard' (→ yuán$_5$ 員圓圜), see → yíng$_4$ 營. Therefore, the following are unrelated: TB-KN-Kom *ra-hụn* 'garden'; AA-Khmer *swna* /sùuən/ 'care for, look after > flower / pleasure garden' (Jenner / Pou 1982: 373) -> KT *swjaan (Li acc. to Benedict *AT:* 37; 1976: 90) > S. *suan*^{A1} 'garden'. <> PMY *weŋ² 'garden' agrees phonologically with CH (M. Ratliff, p. c.).

yuán$_8$ 爰 (jwɐn) **LH** wɑn, **OCM** *wan
'Be slow' [Shi]. Acc. to Karlgren (1956: 14), the following is related:
ꭗ **huǎn** 緩 (ɣuânᴮ) **LH** ɣuɑnᴮ, **OCM** *wanʔ
'Slow, delay' [Meng] > 'slack, indulgent' [Zuo] > 'negligent' [Yi], but this word could instead belong to → xuān$_2$ 暖 'soft, mild'. Gong (1995) relates *huǎn* to WT *'gor-ba* 'to tarry, linger, loiter'.

yuán$_9$ 湲 → **xuàn$_1$** 泫

yuán$_{10}$ 爰 → **yú$_1$** 于

yuán$_{11}$ 緣 → **yán$_1$** 沿

yuán$_{12}$ 黿 (ŋjwɐn) **LH** ŋyɑn, **OCM** *ŋon or *ŋwan
'Large turtle' [Zuo] is perh. the same word as → yuán$_1$ 元 (Unger *Hao-ku* 28, 1984: 251, 260). On the other hand, this word may be related to
ꭗ **áo** 鼇 (ŋâu) **LH** ŋɑu, **OCM** *ŋâu
'Turtle' [Liezi]. If *yuán* should be the original form, the final nasal has been lost in the process of back formation.

yuǎn$_1$ 遠 (jwɐnᴮ) **LH** wɑnᴮ, **OCM** *wanʔ
'Far away, distant, far-reaching, extending' [Shi].
[T] *Sin Sukchu SR* yen (上); *MGZY* xwÿan (上) [ɦyɛn]; *ONW* uan
ꭗ **yuàn** 遠 (jwɐnᶜ) **LH** wɑnᶜ, **OCM** *wans
'Keep at a distance, keep away' [Shi].
[<] *wanʔ + exoactive > caus. s-suffix (§4.3.2).
[E] This item has no apparent TB cognate, but may be an unexplained rime *-an variant of the wf → jiǒng$_2$ 泂迥 *weŋʔ 'distant'. Allofam is perh. → jiǒng$_3$ 憬 *kwaŋʔ which represents a transitional rime. Baxter and Sagart (1998: 60) relate this etymon to → yuè$_4$ 越 'pass over'.

yuǎn$_2$ 裷 (ʔjwɐnᴮ) **LH** ʔyɑnᴮ, **OCM** *ʔwanʔ or *ʔonʔ
'Sleeve' is an ancient Jiāngdōng (lower Yangtze) dialect word acc. to Guō Pú's commentary to *FY* 29.32. It still survives in Mǐn dialects: PMin *ʔyonᴮ > Fú'ān *un*^{B1}, Fúzhōu *uoŋ*^{B1}, Xiàménen *ŋ*^{B}, Jiànyáng *yeŋ*^{B1} (Norman 1983: 206). 'Sleeve' is perh. connected with wàn 腕 'wrist' (under → yū$_1$ 迂紆).

yuàn$_1$ 苑 (ʔjwɐnᴮ) **LH** ʔyɑnᴮ, **OCM** *ʔonʔ, OCB *ʔjonʔ
'Trees with rich foliage, umbrageous' [Guoyu] > 'pent up' (feelings) [Shi]. For a semantic parallel, see → wèi$_{10}$, yù 蔚.

[T] *Sin Sukchu SR* ʔyen (上); *MGZY* 'wÿan (上) [ʔyɛn]

ꭗ **yuàn** 怨 (ʔjwɐn^{C}) **LH** ʔyɑn^{C}, **OCM** *ʔons, OCB *ʔjons

(1) ('Pent up':) 'resent, bear resentment' [Shi].

[<] perhaps exoactive of *yuàn* 苑 (ʔjwɐn^{B}) (§4.3).

(2) ('Who is resented':) 'enemy' (also read with tone A).

[<] exopass. of *yuàn* 苑 (ʔjwɐn^{B}) (§4.4).

[C] An allofam may be → yǐ$_4$ 猗 'luxuriant foliage'.

yuàn$_2$ 苑 'wither' → **wēi$_3$** 萎

yuàn$_3$ 怨 → **yuàn$_1$** 苑

yuàn$_4$ 院瑗 → **yuán$_5$** 員圓圜

yuàn$_5$ 緣 → **yán$_1$** 沿

yuàn$_6$ 願 (ŋjwɐn^{C}) **LH** ŋyɑn^{C}, **OCM** *ŋons, OCB *ŋjons — [T] *ONW* ŋuan

'To wish' [Shi]. Prob. not related to Lushai *ŋiat^{F}* 'to demand, wish for'.

yuē$_1$ 曰 (jwɐt) **LH** wɑt, **OCM** *wat

'To say' (usually introducing direct discourse), 'to be called' [OB, BI, Shi].

[E] Etymology not clear. This word is cognate to → huà$_3$ 話 acc. to Sagart (1999: 113). Syn. → yún$_2$ 云.

[T] *Sin Sukchu SR* ŋye (入); *MGZY* xwÿa (入) [ɦyɛ]; *MTang* uar, *ONW* uat < wat

yuē$_2$ 約 (ʔjak) **LH** ʔɨɑk, **OCM** *ʔiauk

'To bind' [Shi], 'cord' [Zuo] > 'restrain, restrict' [Lunyu] > 'abbreviate, condensed, essential' [Li, Meng].

ꭗ **yào** 約 (ʔjiäu^{C} 4) **LH** ʔiau^{C}, **OCM** *ʔiaukh ?

'Bond, contract, agreement' [Zuo].

[E] ST: WB *yok* 'wind around, as thread'.

yuē$_3$ 噦 (ʔjwɐt, ʔjwät) **LH** ʔyɑt, **OCM** *ʔwat or *ʔot

'Sound of vomiting' [Li].

ꭗ **ǒu** 嘔 (ʔəu^{B}) **LH** ʔo^{B}, **OCM** *ʔôʔ

'To vomit' [Zuo].

[E] This is an onomatopoetic expression, other lgs. in the area have similar words: PTB *ʔaw 'vomit' (*HPTB:* 227), PLB *ut 'to belch'; Lushai *uak^{R};* PMonic *tl-ʔɔɔʔ, Mon *həʔɔʔ* 'to vomit, regurgitate' [Diffloth 1984: 151]; also WB *an* 'vomit'; WT *skyug-pa* (< *s-ʔyuk* ?) 'vomit, eject'.

yuè$_1$ 月 (ŋjwɐt) **LH** ŋyɑt, S ŋɨot, **OCM** *ŋwat, OCB *ŋʷjat

'Moon > month' [OB, Shi].

[T] *Sin Sukchu SR* ŋye (入); *MGZY* xwÿa (入) [ɦyɛ]; *MTang* ŋuar, *ONW* ŋuat,

[D] Mand. *yuè* 'month', *yuè-liáng* 月亮 'moon'; Gàn *ŋyœʔ^{D2}-kwɔŋ^{A1}* 月光 'moon' (in Mand. 'moonlight'); Y-Guǎngzhōu *jyt^{D2}-kuɔŋ^{A1}* 月光 'moon', Táishān *ŋgut^{D2}-kɔŋ^{A1};* PMin *ŋyot: Xiàmén col. *geʔ^{D2}*, lit. *guat^{D2}*

[E] ST: Unger (*Hao-ku* 39, 1992) proposes as cognate WT *ŋo(s)* 'waxing and waning moon, half moon', Lepcha *ñóm*. These belong to PTB *ŋow (*STC* no. 296) > WT *sŋo* 'blue-green', Lushai *ŋo^{H}* 'white, fair', Thado *ŋou* 'clean', Lepcha *ta-ŋot* 'white hair, old' ꭗ *ŋo* 'old' (Bodman 1980: 136). The widespread semantic association of 'moon' with 'white' would support this etymology; see → bái$_1$ 白, → pò$_4$ 魄, → pò$_5$ 霸魄 for a parallel. There may possibly be a connection with → ài$_1$ 艾 'white-haired', but that is phonologically problematic. Matisoff sets up PTB *s-ŋʷ(y)at 'moon, star' (*HPTB:* 85) or PTB *s-ŋwa-t 'star / moon' (*HPTB* (24; 26). <> Tai *ŋuat*[D2] 'recurring period' (Manomaivibool 1975: 330) would be a CH loan if the ST etymology is correct.

yuè₂ 刖 → **wù₁** 兀

yuè₃ 戉鉞 (jwɐt) **LH** wat, **OCM** *wat
'Battle-ax' [BI, Shu, Shi]. Mahdi (1994: 177) points out that the *yuè* type ax has been found in archeological sites south of the Yangtze and in the Austronesian speaking areas (Chang Kwang-chih 1963; Chén Zhōngmǐn *LTBA* 22.2: 42) where the word for 'iron', in places 'ax', is reconstructed PAN *bari > *basi, in some lgs. *wasi* and the like. Yuè < *wat could therefore perh. be an AN loan. The etymon also occurs in AA: PWa *wac 'knife, sickle, sword', OMon *rwas* /rwɔs/ 'weapon', perh. -> TB-JP *n³¹-waʔ⁵⁵ < n³¹-wak⁵⁵* notched knife.
Curiously, some Taiwanese tribes have the tradition that they originally came from 'Vasai' across the Taiwan straits on the mainland, i.e. the area which has been known as Yuè 越 < *wat since mid-Zhou times.

yuè₄ 越 (jwɐt) **LH** wat, **OCM** *wat — **[T]** *ONW* wat
'To go on, go beyond, transgress' [Shi, Shu] > 'furthermore, and now, later on' [BI, Shi, Shu], 'far away' [Guoyu].
[<] *yuè* may be derived from → yú₁ 于 'to go' with a t-suffix of unknown function.
[C] A derivation is prob. → suì₁ 歲 'year'. Baxter and Sagart (1998: 60) relate *yuè* to → yuǎn₁ 遠 'far away'; Matisoff (ICSTLL 1978: 16) relates *kuò* 闊 'far apart' (under → kuān 寬) to this word.

yuè₅ 越 (jwɐt) **LH** wat, **OCM** *wat
The ancient state of Yuè, earlier Yú-yuè 於越 *ʔa-wat; see → yuè₃ 戉鉞.

yuè₆ 岳嶽 (ŋåk) **LH** ŋɔk, **OCM** *ŋrôk — **[T]** *ONW* ŋäk
'Mountain, peak' 嶽 [Shi], 岳 [Shu].
[E] ? AA: PNBahn. *ŋŏk 'mountain'. Note also PHlai *hŋwʔo³ 'mountain'. Perh. also connected with WB *ŋok, ŋok-ŋak* < PLB *ʔŋokᴸ 'project, stick up or out' and WB *ŋroŋ*ᶜ 'any sharp thing sticking out, sharp stump or thorn', WT *rŋog* 'hump' (of an animal); for a semantic parallel, note Khmer *kóok* 'knoll, hillock' ⋇ Lao 'hump, bump' (of ox).

yuè₇ 悅閱 → **yú₁₇** 愉

yuè₈ 閱 'gate' → **yú₁₉** 窬俞

yuè₉ 樂 (ŋåk) **LH** ŋɔk, **OCM** *ŋrâuk — **[T]** *ONW* ŋäk
'Music' [Shi].
[E] The etymological relationship with → lè₃ 樂 'joy' has been much debated, extensively by K. Wulff (*Det Kgl. Danske Videnskabernes Selskab, historisk-filologiske meddelelser* XXI, 2, 1935, København), more recently by Unger (*Hao-ku* 19, 1983) who suggests something like OCM *grâuk 'joy' from which is derived *ɴ-grâuk 'music'. For the semantics Unger draws attention to WT *rol-ba* 'to enjoy' vs. *rol-mo* 'music'. On the other hand, there is no other example of QY initial *ŋ- ~ l-* in a wf. In the popular mind, the concept 'music' can easily be connected with 'joy', hence perh. the same graph for these near homophones. The graph 樂 originally wrote 'oak' *lì* 櫟 (liek), OCM *riâuk which is therefore the actual phonetic.

yuè$_{10}$ 籥 (jiak) **LH** jɑk, **OCM** *liauk ?, OCB *ljewk
'Bamboo flute' [Shi]. Baxter (1992: 535) suggests that the following item is from the same root:

⪤ **dí** 笛篴 (diek) **LH** dek < deuk, **OCM** *liûk, OCB *liwk
'Flute' [SW, Fengsu tong].
[T] *Sin Sukchu SR* di (入); *MGZY* ti (入) [di]

yuè$_{11}$ 爚瀹 'melt' → **shuò**$_{6}$ 爍鑠

yuè$_{12}$ 爚 'shine' → **shuò**$_{7}$ 爍

yún$_{1}$ 匀 (jiuen) **LH** win, **OCM** *win
'Even, uniform' [JY] is cognate to → jūn$_{1}$ 均鈞.

yún$_{2}$ 云 (jwən) **LH** wun, **OCM** *wən — **[T]** *ONW* un
'To say it' [Lunyu], 'is called', 'to speak' intr. (Pulleyblank 1995: 81f; see §6.4.5).
[C] Perh. cognate to → wèi$_{9}$ 謂 (so Wáng Lì 1982: 456).
Syn. → yuē$_{1}$ 曰.

yún$_{3}$ 芸 → **xūn**$_{1}$ 熏燻纁焄

yún$_{4}$ 耘 (jwən) **LH** wun, **OCM** *wən (< *wun ?)
'To weed' [Shi].
[E] ST: WT *yur-ma* 'the act of weeding', for the initial correspondence, see §12.9 WT. Note also **yǒu** 莠 (jiəu^{B}) **LH** ju^{B} **OCM** *juʔ (< *wuʔ ?) 'weeds' [Shi] which may be connected.

yún$_{5}$ 雲 (jwən) **LH** wun, **OCM** *wən
'Cloud' [OB, Shi].
[T] *Sin Sukchu SR* yn (平); *MGZY* xwin (平) [ɦwin]
[D] PMin *hiun, W-Wēnzhōu *ɦyoŋ*^{A2}, Guǎngzhōu *wan*^{A2}
[E] This word has no obvious outside connection, except possibly TB-Mikir *iŋhùn* < *m-hùn* 'clouds'; or alternatively KN *vaan* > Lushai *vaan*^{L} < *vaanh* 'sky' (in some lgs., 'sky' and 'cloud' are the same word).

However, 'cloud' is possibly cognate to → yùn$_{2}$ 運暈 'revolve', thus *yún* was lit. a 'whorl' or 'swirl' in the sky (the OB graph for *yún* shows a whorl). Therefore one or other of the numerous synonymous and similar-looking roots in the area (see under → huí 回) is probably represented here. Closest is perh. AA-Khmer /wul/ 'to turn (around), revolve, rotate, spin, whirl, eddy, swirl'. From *wul to *wun is only one phonological step; an equally appropriate root PTB *wir would instead require two steps, in addition to *-r* > *-n* also the change *u* > *i* (§11.5.1): TB-Lushai *vir*^{R} < *virʔ* 'rotate, revolve, spin' ⪤ *vir*^{L} < *virh* (< *-s*) 'a whorl', Mru *wir* 'rotate, spin', WT *'k*^{h}*yir-ba* 'to turn around in a circular course', JP-Hkauri *kə-wīn* 'rotate' [Matisoff 1974: 166]; WB *ə-k*^{h}*yin* 'a time period, season' (for semantics, note *xún* 旬 under → jūn$_{2}$ 鈞).

yǔn$_{1}$ 允 (jiuen^{B}) **LH** juin^{B}, **OCM** *junʔ or *winʔ
'To trust, be true, sincere' [Shi] seems to be related to → xìn$_{1}$ 信 'believe, trust'; if so, OC should be expected to be *winʔ (not *junʔ). On the other hand, the word may be related to TB-WB *yum* 'believe, trust' (for the final nasal, see §6.7).
[T] *Sin Sukchu SR* yn (上); *MGZY* yŷun (上) [jyn]

yǔn₂ 隕殞賈 (jiwen^B) **LH** win^B, **OCM** *w(r)ən(ʔ) or *win(ʔ) ?, OCB *wrjɨn(ʔ)
'To drop, fall' 隕 [Shi]; 'fall to the ground' [Zuo], 'to rain, fall down like rain' 賈 [Gongyang]; 'to drop, lose' (one's life) 殞 [Guoyu]; 'lose' 隕 [Zuo] > caus. 'to overthrow' 隕 [Zuo], 'destroy' 殞 [Xun].

≈ **xún** 洵 (sjuen) **LH** suin, **OCM** *swin
'To drip, tears falling' [Guoyu].
[<] iterative derivation of *yǔn* (§5.2.3).

[E] ST *(r)we is a rare parallel stem of ST *(r)wa 'rain' (→ yǔ₃ 雨): TB-Mikir *arwè ~ ruwè* < *r-we^L* 'rain', also in Lolo lgs. *we (?) (but *HPTB:* 128 derives these forms from *r-wa). For CH final *-n,* see §6.4.4. Syn. include → yǔ₃ 雨, → líng₈ 霝零 'rain, fall'.

yùn₁ 孕 (jiəŋ^C) **LH** jɨŋ^C, **OCM** *ləŋh — **[T]** *ONW* iŋ
'Pregnant' [Zuo, GY] is prob. the s. w. as **yìng** 繩 'full' (of ears of grain) [Zhouli].
[D] Medieval dictionaries and non-Mandarin modern dialects reflect a reading which is the equivalent of QY *jiəŋ^C:* W-Wēnzhōu *ɦiaŋ^{C2},* M-Xiàmén lit. *jiŋ^{C2},* Fúzhōu *eiŋ^{C2},* Cháozhōu *eŋ^A*. Occasional forms with the equivalent of QYS rime *-jen* prob. represent secondary developments: Guǎngzhōu *jan^{C2}* (but northern Yuè dialects point to *-jəŋ*), M-Xiàmén col. *jin^{C2}*. Mand. dialects have forms riming in *-un* which may possibly reflect the ancient (LH and OC) form *jun*. Many modern dialects have replaced this word with other expressions.

≈ **shèng** 䞍 (dźjəŋ^C) **LH** źɨŋ^C, **OCM** *m-ləŋh
'Pregnant' [Guanzi; GY] (GY 432; *GYSX:* 884).

[C] This etymon is perh. related to → yíng₂ 盈贏 (jiäŋ) 'full' because the two words differ only in the vowels (as can occasionally be observed within wfs), and because the phrase 孕育 'to conceive and give birth' is rendered as 贏育 (*-eŋ) in *Guǎnzǐ*. More tenuous would be identification with the WT dictionary word *liŋs-pa* 'quite round or globular'.

yùn₂ 運暈 (juən^C) **LH** wun^C, **OCM** *wəns
'Revolve, turn around' [Yi], 'move' [Zhuang], 'longitudinal' 運 [Guoyu]; 'bring supply of food to' [Zuo]; 'vapor, halo' 暈 [Lü].
[T] *Sin Sukchu SR* yn (去); *MGZY* xwin (去) [ɦwin]; *ONW* un
[E] → yún₅ 雲 'cloud' is prob. related. Karlgren (1933: 28) relates this etymon to → wéi₅ 圍, Wáng Lì (1982: 398) to → huí 回, but see there.

yùn₃ 緷 → **wěi₄** 緯

yùn₄ 蘊薀 (ʔjuən^{B/C}) **LH** ʔun^{B/C}, **OCM** *ʔunʔ/s — **[T]** *ONW* ʔun
'To block, accumulate' (pent-up feelings) 蘊 [Shi] > 'to hoard, accumulate' 薀 [Zuo].

≈ **yùn** 韞 (ʔjuən^B) **LH** ʔun^B, **OCM** *ʔunʔ
'To pack, store up' [Lunyu].

≈ **yùn** 慍 (ʔjuən^C) **LH** ʔun^C, **OCM** *ʔunh
'To hate' [Shi] (note 蘊薀 'pent-up feelings'), 'grieved' [Li].

[E] This wf may perh. be related to → yōng₁ 邕; for the difference in final nasal, see §6.4.2. The wf → yīn₄ 湮堙闉 'to obstruct' is probably not related. We have prob. these developments:

PCH *ʔuŋ	> LH ʔoŋ	(→ yōng₁ 邕)
	> LH ʔun	(yùn 蘊薀)

Z

zá$_1$ 噆 (tsập) **LH** tsəp, **OCM** *tsə̂p

'To bite, sting and suck' (as a mosquito) [Zhuang].

[E] Sound symbolic area word: PTB *dzo:p (*STC* no. 69) > PLB *ʔcup ~ ʔɟup ~ *C-cup 'suck, milk'; Thado *tsop,* Siyin *tuop,* Dimasa *dźop;* Lushai *fɔɔp^F* (Lorrain fâwp) / *fɔʔ^L* 'to kiss, suck'; WT *'jo-ba, bžos* 'to milk' derives from a form with medial *j (PTib. *-op > WT *-o, see §12.9); JP *mə^{31}-sup^{31}* 'to suck', *tʃup^{31}* 'suck'. *HPTB:* 382 lists many TB variants. Note also AA: Kharia *jo'b* 'to suck', Munda *cɛpɔ'd,* Khmer *-jāpa* /-cíiəp/ 'to take in, suck'.

Foreign words with the rime *-op, -up* usually become MC *-əp* (via earlier *-wəp*, with the medial *w* lost due to dissimilation); occasionally, such words appear in OC as *-ot, *-ut, thus → chuò$_2$ 啜歠 'drink' may be related. Karlgren (1956: 18) relates this word to → cǎn 噆 'hold in the mouth'.

zá$_2$ 雜 → **jí$_{13}$** 集輯

zāi$_1$ 災 (tsậi) **LH** tsə, **OCM** *tsə̂ — **[T]** *ONW* tsɑi

'Natural disaster' (fire, drought, flood, locusts, eclipse, pestilence, etc.), 'accident, injury' 災 [OB, Shi], 烖 [Li], 'conflagration' [Zuo, SW, Hanshu].

[E] ? ST *tsə > TB: JP *tsa^{31}* 'be damaged' ⋈ *ʃə^{31}-tsa^{31}* 'to destroy'. This root blends into a homophone meaning 'warm, heat, fever, pain': PTB *tsa 'be hot' (*STC* no. 62) > WT *tsʰa-ba* 'hot, heat, sharp (spices), illness' ⋈ *tsʰad-pa* 'heat, fever' ⋈ *tsʰan-ma* 'hot, warm'; TGTM *¹tshawa 'fever', *²tsha* 'be in pain'; Chepang *ca* 'sore, wound' ⋈ *ca-* 'have sores', Mikir *sò-* 'hot, excessive, be ill, sore'; NNaga *dzat* 'suffer' [French 1983: 223], Garo *sa* 'ache, pain'; WB *ə-cha* 'hunger, something faulty or hurtful', Lahu *cha* 'to shine, be bright' (of the sun). *STC* (170 n. 455) relates PTB *tsa 'hot, pain' to → jí$_6$ 疾, but see there.

[C] Prob. cognate to → zī$_8$ 菑 'slash and burn', and possibly to → zéi 賊.

zāi$_2$ 栽哉 (tsậi) **LH** tsə, **OCM** *tsə̂

'To plant' 栽 [Li]; 'to begin' 哉 [Shu].

[T] *Sin Sukchu SR* tsaj (平); *MGZY* dzay (平) [tsaj]; *ONW* tsɑi

⋈ **zài$_3$** 載 (tsậi^C) **LH** tsə^C, **OCM** *tsə̂h — **[T]** *ONW* tsɑi^C

'To initiate, start work, undertaking, achievement; at first' [Shi, Shu].

⋈ **zài** 栽 (dzậi^C) **LH** dzə^C, **OCM** *dzə̂h

'To board, erect building frames' [Shi, Zuo].

[E] The basic meaning of this wf is 'to be at a place > to put at a place > put into place > plant / initiate'. The word → zài$_1$ 在 'to be in, at' is prob. related; this wf belongs perh. to ST *tsə 'come forth' from which → zǐ$_1$ 子 (tsɨ^B) is derived.

zǎi 載 → **zài$_4$** 再

zài$_1$ 在 (dzậi^B) **LH** dzə^B, **OCM** *dzə̂ʔ

'Be in, at, to exist' [OB, BI, Shi] appears to be the endoactive form of the items under → zāi$_2$ 栽哉 (§4.5). On the other hand, Matisoff (ICSTLL, Bangkok 2000: 8) compares *zài* to Lahu *chɛ̂* ⋈ *jɛ̂* 'stop, cease, come to rest' *N-dzay² (JAM) or *cya² ⋈ *jya² (Bradley 1979). Allofam → cún 存.

[T] *Sin S. SR* dzaj (上去); *MGZY* tsay (上去) [dzaj]; *ONW* dzɑi

zài$_2$ 載 (tsậi^C) **LH** tsə^C, **OCM** *tsə̂h
'To load, carry, pour, fill, conveyance' [Shi].

ꭗ **zài** 載 (dzậi^C) **LH** dzə^C, **OCM** *dzə̂h
'To load, a load' [Shi]

ꭗ **zī** 仔 (tsɨ[^{B}]) **LH** tsiə(^{B}), **OCM** *tsə(ʔ)
'A burden' [Shi].

[E] This wf could possibly be part of → zāi$_2$ 栽哉, here in the sense of 'to put into place > put on, place onto, load'.

zài$_3$ 載 'start' → **zāi**$_2$ 栽哉

zài$_4$ 再 (tsậi^C) **LH** tsə^C, **OCM** *tsə̂h
'Twice, again and again' [Shi].
[T] *Sin Sukchu SR* tsaj (去); *MGZY* dzay (去) [tsaj]; *ONW* tsɑi^C

ꭗ **zǎi** 載 (tsậi^B) **LH** tsə^B, **OCM** *tsə̂ʔ
'A turn' (as in: 'it is his turn to...'), 'a year' [Shu].
[<] endoactive / tr. of *zài*.

ꭗ **zī** 茲 (tsɨ) **LH** tsɨ, **OCM** *tsə
'Year' [Guoce], as in *jīn zī* 今茲 'this year', *lái zī* 來茲 'next year'.

ꭗ **jiàn** 薦洊 (dzien^C) **LH** dzen^C, **OCM** *dzə̂ns
'Repeat, repeatedly' 薦 [Shi], 'repeat, a second time' 洊 [Yi], 'repeat, increase' 荐 [Zuozhuan].

zān 簪 (tsậm, tṣjəm) **LH** tsəm, tṣəm, **OCM** *tsrəm
'Hairpin' [Xun].
[D] PMin *t̑sam (> Jiānglè *tsoŋ^{A1}*, Fúzhōu *tsaŋ^{A1}*) ~ *tsem (> Amoy *tsiam^{A1}*); Y-Guǎngzhōu *^{55}tsam^{A1}*

ꭗ **zèn** 譖 (tṣjəm^C) **LH** tṣəm^C, **OCM** *tsrəms
'To slander' tr. [Shi]. For semantics, see → zhēn$_8$ 箴鍼, → cì$_2$ 朿.

[E] Area word *C-rum ~ *C-rim 'needle'; the OC word is phonetically closest to lgs. which are farthest afield (this is also the case with 'weave' → rén$_5$ 紝): AN-PCham *jurŭm, IN *daɣum* 'needle' (Benedict *AT:* 113); AA-PNBahn. *jarŭm,* PSBahn. *ɟərum,* Sre *jurum* -> TB-Lepcha *ryŭm*, Mikir *iŋprìm* 'needle'; *IST:* 237 lists *prum ~ prim > ṭim* for Kuki-Chin lgs. OC can be derived from a form *jrum or *crum. Cf. also PKS *tsʰom^A 'needle'.

zāng 臧 (tsâŋ) **LH** tsɑŋ, **OCM** *tsâŋ
'Be good' (of quality of persons, horses, state) [Shi].
[E] ST: WT *bzaŋ-po* 'good' (*HST:* 87).

zàng$_1$ 葬 (tsâŋ^C) **LH** tsɑŋ^C, **OCM** *tsâŋh
'To bury' (a corpse) [Lunyu]. Old texts seem to confirm what the graph suggests, that the dead were once wrapped in straw or grass, i.e. literally 'concealed'; therefore *zàng* may possibly be related to → cáng 藏.
[C] An allofamis is prob. → sāŋ 喪 'burial'.

zàng$_2$ 藏 → **cáng** 藏

zāo$_1$ 傮 → **zú**$_1$ 卒

zāo$_2$ 遭 (tsâu) **LH** tsou, **OCM** *tsû — **[T]** *ONW* tsɑu
'Meet, encounter' [Shi].

ꭗ **cáo** 曹 (dzâu) **LH** dzou, **OCM** *dzû
'Come together' [Guoyu], 'crowd' [Zuo].

[T] *MGZY tsaw* (平) [dzaw]; *Sin Sukchu SR dzaw* (平)
[<] endopass. / intr. of *zāo* 遭 (tsâu) (§4.6).

ж **qiú** 遒 (dzjəu) **LH** dziu, **OCM** *dzu
'To collect, bring together' (blessings, states) [Shi].

ж **zòng** 綜 (tsuoŋ^C) **LH** tsuŋ^C, **OCM** *tsûŋh
'Bring together, collect, sum up' [Yi].
[E] ST: WB *cuiŋ* 'cohere'; Lushai *čhuŋ^H* (Lorrain *chhung*) 'family, household'.

ж **zú** 卒 (tsuət) **LH** tsuət, **OCM** *tsût, OCB *Stut
'Group' (of men, families, states) [Li], 'soldier, army' [Zuo].
[T] *MTang* tsur < tsuir, *ONW* tsuit
[<] derived from *zāo* 遭 above with the nominal t-suffix (§6.2.1).
[C] Karlgren (1956: 13) considers this word a cognate of → zú$_1$ 卒 'to die' (unlikely).

ж **cuì**$_1$ 萃 (dzwi^C) **LH** dzuis, **OCM** *dzuts, OCB *dzjuts < *dzjups ?
'To collect, assemble' [Shi], 'assemblage, crowd' [Meng]. Bodman links this word to → zú$_1$ 卒; Baxter (1992: 350) considers this word a tone C derivation from → jí$_{13}$ 集輯 (dzjəp) 'collect'.

[E] Bodman (1969) combines *zú* 卒, *cuì* 萃 with → tún$_2$ 屯窀, *zuì* 最 (under → jù$_7$ 聚) and other items into a large ST wf 'to collect, accumulate'.

zǎo$_1$ 早 (tsâu^B) **LH** tsou^B, **OCM** *tsû?
'Early' [Shu]. Acc. to Norman (1986: 382) the Northern Mǐn 'softened initial' *ṱs- indicates OC prenasalization which is supported by Yao *dzjou^3* < *ntz- 'early'.
[T] *Sin Sukchu SR* tsaw (上); *MGZY* dzaw (上) [tsaw]; *ONW* tsɑu
[E] *Zǎo* is prob. derived from → zào$_3$ 造 'do, make, begin' and thus semantically similar to other words for 'morning' (→ chén$_5$ 晨, → sù$_3$ 夙). WB *co^B* 'early, premature' ж *c^{h}o^C* 'be early' (as rains), JP *tʃau^{33}* are prob. Tai loans (Matisoff 1974: 178): PTai *zau^{B2} 'time of cock crowing' (Luo Yongxian *MKS* 27, 1997: 293) or *ɟau^{C2} [Li Fang Kuei].

zǎo$_2$ 蚤 (tsâu^B) **LH** tsou^B, **OCM** *tsû?
'Flea' [Zhuang]. Unger (*Hao-ku* 39, 1992) suggests cognation with → sāo$_1$ 搔 'scratch', hence lit. 'itcher'.

zǎo$_3$ 澡 (tsâu^B) **LH** tsɑu^B, **OCM** *tsâu?
'To wash' [Li].
[E] PMY *nts^{l}aau$^{3\ B/C}$ 'to wash (bathe)'. Note also TB-Lushai *su^L / suuk^F < tsu?/h* 'to wash', but the vocalism does not agree with OC.

zào$_1$ 皂 (dzâu^B) **LH** dzou^B, **OCM** *dzû?
'An acorn, black-dying fruit' [Zhouli]. *CVST* (4: 13) relates this word to WT *ts^{h}os* 'paint, dye' which, however, could phonologically also agree with → cǎi$_2$ 采 *tshə? 'full of color, color' [Shi].

zào$_2$ 造 (ts^{h}âu^C) **LH** ts^{h}ou^C, **OCM** *tshûh
'To proceed to' [Shi, Meng], 'reach to' (mountains the sky) [Hou Hanshu].

ж **jiù** 就 (dzjəu^C) **LH** dziu^C, **OCM** *dzuh
'To proceed, achieve' [Shi] (Wáng Lì 1982: 311).
[T] *Sin Sukchu SR* dziw (去); *MGZY* tsiw (去) [dziw]; *MTang* dzeu < dziu, *ONW* dzu
[N] This wf is perh. related to → zào$_3$ 造, → zú$_1$ 卒.

zào$_3$ 造 (dzâu^B) **LH** dzou^B, **OCM** *dzû? — **[T]** *ONW* dzɑu
'To do, make, build' (boats, bridges), 'be active, begin' [Shi]; 'to achieve' [Shi].

[N] The element → gào$_0$ 告 'report' with initial *k-* is not phonetic, it was part of the original word 造 *tshûh 'to go and offer' (a sacrifice), 'go and appear in court' which usually would involve some announcement or report. Therefore, there is no need to postulate an *sk-like initial.
[E] ST: PTB *tsuk > WT *'tsʰugs-pa* 'go into, commence, take root' ⋇ *'dzugs-pa ~ zug-pa* 'to stick into, set, erect, put down, begin' ⋇ *'tsʰud-pa* 'be put into, enter', PLB *tsuk^H 'build' (a house). An allofam is prob. → zǎo$_1$ 早 'early'. This wf is perh. related to → zào$_2$ 造, → zú$_1$ 卒.

zé$_1$ 則 (tsək) **LH** tsək, **OCM** *tsə̂k
'Consequently, thereupon, otherwise' [BI, Shi].
[T] *Sin S. SR* tsəj (入), *LR* tsəjʔ; *MGZY* dzʰiy (入) [tsəj]; *ONW* tsək
[E] Etymology not certain. Unger (see Geilich 1994: 289) suggests that this is **zī** 茲 LH *tziə*, *tsə 'this' [Shi] with the distributive k-suffix (§6.1.2). If true, the meaning 'a norm' [BI, Shi] would prob. represent a different word.

zé$_2$ 責 (tṣɛk) **LH** tṣɛk, **OCM** *tsrêk, OCB *tsr(j)ek (< *Strek?)
'Request, reprove, hold responsible' [Shu].
⋇ **zhài** 債 (tṣai^C) **LH** tṣai^C, **OCM** *tsrêkh
'Debt' [Shu]. Acc. to Baxter (1992: 231). → zhé$_8$ 謫 is possibly related.

zé$_3$ 擇 (ḍɐk) **LH** ḍak, **OCM** *d-lak
'To choose' [Shi].
[T] *Sin Sukchu SR* dẓəj (入); *MGZY* cay (入) [dẓaj]; *MTang* ḍëk, *ONW* dëk
[E] KT: PKS *la:i^6 'to pick, select', Tai: S. *lɨak^{D2}* 'to choose'. QY div. II *ḍɐk* results from the same OC L-like initial which with all other rimes has yielded QY div. III initial *ḍj-*. Final *-k* added to *-ai yields *-ak in a few other words as well.

zé$_4$ 柞 → **chá$_2$** 槎

zé$_5$ 笮 (tṣɐk) **LH** tṣak, **OCM** *tsrâk
'A quiver' [Yili].
[E] AA: Khmer /craak/ 'insert, introduce, shove into...'

zé$_6$ 矠 (dẓɛk) **LH** dẓɛk, **OCM** *dzrêk
'To spear' (fish) [Guoyu].
[E] This word is a variant of → chuō 擉 and → cè$_5$ 簎 whose OC vowel may be due to interference from either → chā$_1$ 叉 *tshrai 'fork' (incl. 'tree fork for spearing fish') or *cì* 刺 (tsʰjäk) [tsʰiek] *tshek 'stab' (under → cì$_2$ 朿), semantically parallel to → cè$_5$ 簎.

zè 仄昃 → **cè$_1$** 側

zéi 賊 (dzək) **LH** dzək, **OCM** *dzə̂k — **[T]** *ONW* dzək
'To injure, damage; robber' [BI, Shi] may possibly be related to → zāi$_1$ 災 'disaster, injury'.
[E] ? ST: WT *ǰag* < ? 'robbery' (*HST:* 127) looks like a cognate, but a WT palatalized initial usually does not correspond to an unpalatalized one in Chinese. On the other hand, a MK palatal initial may; note Khmer /chak/ 'to snatch' ⋇ /cmak/ 'thief' [Jenner / Pou 1982: xlvii].

zèn 譖 → **zān** 簪

zēng 曾增憎橧 (tsəŋ) **LH** tsəŋ, **OCM** *tsə̂ŋ
'To add' [Meng] > 'to double, to rise high' 曾 [Chuci]; 'increase, numerous' 增 [Shi];

'bundles of branches' 橧 [Li] > 'to hate' 憎 [BI, Shi] may be the same word (i.e. emotional increase, accumulation).

[T] *Sin Sukchu SR* tsəjŋ (平), *PR* tsəŋ; *MGZY* dzʰing (平) [tsəŋ]; *ONW* tsəŋ

⋈ **céng** 層 (dzəŋ, tsəŋ) **LH** dzəŋ, **OCM** *dzə̂ŋ

'In two stories, double' [Chuci].

[T] *Sin Sukchu SR* dzəjŋ (平), *PR, LR* dzəŋ; *MGZY* tsʰing (平) [dzəŋ]

[D] Perh. this (i.e. MC *dzəŋ*) is the s. w. as PMin *tsʰən^{A2} 'wet rice field' (J. Norman, p. c.); note also *zěng* 矰 (tsəŋ^{B}) 'wet field' [JY], but initial and tone don't agree with PMin. Chen and Li (1991: 24) identify the Mǐn word with *chéng* 塍 (dźjəŋ) 'raised path between fields' [SW].

[<] endopass. of *zēng* (tsəŋ) (§4.6), lit. 'what is increased, raised'.

[E] Prob. ST: WT *'tsʰeŋ-ba* 'increase, improve' (*CVST* 4: 4), WB *chaŋ*^{C} 'to place one uopn another, step, grade'. Alternatively, this group may be an iterative s-prefix derivation (§5.7) from → dēng$_1$ 登 (*HST:* 126), but *ts-* from *st- is doubtful.

zèng 甑 → **zhēng**$_4$ 烝

zhā 奓 (ṭa) **LH** ṭai, **OCM** *trâi

'To open' (a door) [Zhuang], the graph shows a person with the legs opened.

This word's final *-k* variant is → zhé$_6$ 磔. OC rimes *-e and *-ai do occasionally mix in wfs, the initial OC *tr- could derive from some consonant + medial *r* as is also seen in the allofam → bò$_3$ 擘 and its Tai cognates. Therefore this word may be cognate to → bǎi$_2$ 捭 OC *breʔ 'to open'. For an overview of similar items, see Table P-1 under → pī$_3$ 披. For a listing of similar words and possible allofams, see → lí$_{10}$ 離.

zhá 札 (tṣăt) **LH** tṣɛt, **OCM** *tsrêt

'To die prematurely' [Zuo], 'pestilence' [Zhouli].

⋈ **zhài** 瘵 (tṣăi^{C}) **LH** tṣɛs, **OCM** *tsrêts, OCB *tsr(j)êts

'To suffer, hurt' [Shi].

[E] AA: Zhèng Xuán (commentary to *Zhōulǐ*) says that *zhá* means 'to die' in the ancient Yuè (Viet) lg. (Pulleyblank 1983: 438), which however does not necessarily mean that *zhá* is a loan from PVM; it could have come from other AA branches: PVM *k-ce:t > Viet. *chêt* 'to die' (Norman / Mei 1976: 277); PSBahn. *kəsit ~ *kəsət 'to die, dead', Katuic *cɛ:t 'dead' ⋈ *k/gəcɛ:t 'to kill'; PMonic *kcət* 'to die' ⋈ k-r-cet 'to kill'; Khmer /sə̀t/ 'to die' ⋈ /bɑnsìiət/ 'to kill' (*ban-* is caus. prefix). For the initials, see §10.5.2.

zhà 籗 → **chuō** 擉

zhái 宅 (ḍɐk) **LH** ḍak, **OCM** *drâk

'To inhabit, reside, dwell, settle, residence' [Shi, Shu], 'homestead, farmstead' [Meng]; Mand. 'residence, house'.

[T] *Sin Sukchu SR* dẓəj (入), *LR* dẓəjʔ; *MGZY* cay (入) [dẓaj]; *MTang* ḍěk, *ONW* děk

[E] MK: Khmer *dak* 'put down, settle, lodge...' ⋈ *dəmnak* (i.e. *d-mn-ak*) 'residence'. As in many words, OC has an assumed *r in the initial which is absent in other lgs. (§7.6.2). Alternatively, it has been suggested that *zhái* may be connected with Tai: S. *rɨak*^{D2} (perh. 'field'?) (Manomaivibool 1975: 150–153).

zhài$_1$ 債 → **zé**$_2$ 責

zhài$_2$ 廌 → **zhì**$_{25}$, **zhài** 廌

zhài$_3$ 瘵 → **zhá** 札

zhān$_1$ 占 (tśjäm) **LH** tśam, **OCM** *tem, OCB 占 *tjem (Baxter 1992: 541)
('To look at, gaze, look at omens, dreams':) 'prognosticate, interpret' [OB, BI, Shi].

~ **zhān** 瞻 (tśjäm) **LH** tśam, **OCM** *tam (actually *tiam), *tjam (Baxter 1992: 539)
'To look at, gaze' [Shi]. The OC vacillation between *-em and *-am points to an actual *-iam (§11.3.2).
[T] *ONW* tśam

ⅹ **chān** 佔覘 (ṭʰjäm) **LH** ṭʰam ?, **OCM** *threm
'To look, observe' 佔 [Li] > 'to spy' 覘 (also read ṭʰjämᶜ) [Zuo].

[E] ? AA: OKhmer /cam/ 'to watch over, watch for, keep in mind' [Jenner / Pou 1982: 67], Viet *xem* [sem] < *tśʰj- (and also *ṭʰj-?) 'to see, look at, watch'. The initial correspondance is not clear, though.

zhān$_2$ 沾霑 (tjäm) **LH** ṭam, **OCM** *tram or *trem ? — **[T]** *MTang* ṭam, *ONW* tam
'To moisten, soak through' 霑 [Shi], 沾 [Chuci]. Perh. cognate to → jiān$_8$ 漸瀸湛 (so Karlgren 1949: 80).
[E] AA: Khmer /tram/ 'to soak, steep' ⅹ /tɑmram/ 'soaking, immersion, anything soaked in water / brine' ⅹ OKhmer *jrāṃ*, Khmer /croəm/ 'mud, foul-smelling mud'. PNBahn. *trăm, PSBahn. *təram 'soak', *kəram 'sink'; Katuic *tərh[ə/a]m 'soak'.

zhān$_3$ 呫 'taste' → **tiē**$_2$ 呫

zhān$_4$**-tán** 栴檀 (tśjän-dân) **LH** tśan-dɑn, **OCM** *dân
'Sandalwood' <- Indic: Skt. *candana*. The earlier word consists of just the second syllable [Shi] where the connection with Skt. is doubtful.

zhān$_5$ 旃 → **dān**$_1$ 丹

zhān$_6$ 詹 → **tán**$_8$ 談

zhǎn$_1$ 展 (tjänᴮ) **LH** ṭɑnᴮ, **OCM** *tranʔ
'Roll over' 輾 [Shi], 'unfold, open' 展 [Yili] > 'develop, set forth' [Zuozhuan] > 'examine' [Liji].

ⅹ **zhàn** 展 (tjänᶜ) **LH** ṭɑnᶜ, **OCM** *trans
'A ritual robe' [Shi] is perhaps a derivation (i.e. 'rolled = draped around'?).
[E] ST: WT *rdal-ba, brdal* 'to spread, unfold, extend over' (*HST:* 139), WB *tanᴮ* 'extend in a line, stretch out straight' ⅹ *ə-tanᴮ* 'line, row, duration, length'.

zhǎn$_2$ 斬 (tṣămᴮ) **LH** tṣɛmᴮ, **OCM** *tsrêmʔ ?, OCB *tsrjamʔ
'To cut off, cut down' [Shi].

ⅹ **chán**, **zhàn** 鑱 (dẓam[ᶜ]), **LH** dẓam(ᶜ), **OCM** *dzrâm(s)
'Sharp' [Mo].
[<] endopass. of *zhǎn* (§4.6), lit. 'be cutting' intr.

ⅹ **chán** 讒 (dẓăm, dẓam[ᶜ]) **LH** dẓɛm or dẓam(ᶜ), **OCM** *dzrâm(s) ?, OCB *tzrjom
'To slander' [Zuo]. For semantics, compare items under → zān 簪, from which *zèn* 譖 (tṣjəmᶜ) 'slander' is derived.

[E] AA: PVM *cɛmᴮ 'to chop' [Thompson]; Khmer *cram* 'to hack' (a learned r-infix from a col. form without, Khmer *càm* 'cop up, cut'; a CH loan acc. to Pou / Jenner *J. of Oriental Studies* 11, 1973: 1–90; however, OC already had this medial*-r-). <> PTai *thr-: S. *hamᶜ¹* 'chop, hack' (Luo Yongxian ICSTLL 2002).

zhǎn$_3$ 蹍 → **niè**$_7$ 躡

zhǎn$_4$ 襢 → **tǎn**$_1$ 袒襢

zhàn$_1$ 湛 (ḍăm^B) **LH** ḍɛm^B, **OCM** *drə̂m? ?
'Be soaking' (as dew) [Shi]; 'deep' [Chuci].
[E] PYao *rjɛm 'to water, soak' [Purnell]. Prob. related to → chén$_2$ 沈.

zhàn$_2$ 戰 (tśjän^C) **LH** tśan^C, **OCM** *tans
'War, battle' [Lunyu].
[T] *Sin Sukchu SR* tʂjen (去); *MGZY* jÿan (去) [tʂjɛn]; *ONW* tśan
[E] This word is commonly thought to be cognate to WT *ral* 'fight, war' (so *STC:* 155 n. 419; p. 173 n. 461), Lushai *raal*^{H} 'enemy', or to *rgyal* 'victory, victorious'. However, TB initial *r for OC *t- is unlikely.
As in many lgs., the word for 'war, battle' *zhàn* may be a semantic extension *zhàn* 戰 'tremble, fear' (under → dàn$_7$ 憚) (Geilich 1994: 238). The semantics are identical to Greek *pólemos* 'war' which is derived from a root 'tremble, fear' (Buck 1949; §20.13). The TB word *ra:l belongs to the root 'separate' which is cognate to CH → lí$_{10}$ 離 'depart from, divide' which has a semantic parallel in Skt. *vigraha*- 'strife, war' (Buck ibid.).

zhàn$_3$ 戰 'tremble, fear' → **dàn**$_7$ 憚

zhàn$_4$ 棧 (dẓăn$^{B/C}$, dẓan^B) **LH** dẓan^B (or dẓɛn$^{B/C}$?), **OCM** *dzrân? ?
'A shed made of intertwined branches' [Zhuang], 'carriage box made of lath or bamboo' [Shi].
[E] Manomaivibool (1975: 157) relates *zhàn* to Tai: S. *raan*^{C2} 'machan, booth, stall, shop'. For the initials, see §7.1.5.

zhàn$_5$ 站 → **lì**$_3$ 立

zhàn$_6$ 鑱 → **zhăn**$_2$ 斬

zhàn$_7$ 顫 → **dàn**$_7$ 憚

zhāng$_1$ 張 (tjaŋ) **LH** ṭaŋ, **OCM** *traŋ
'Make long, to string a bow' [*Shījīng*], 'string an instrument' [Guoce], 'stretch, extend' [Laozi].

※ **zhàng** 張帳 (tjaŋ^C) **LH** ṭaŋ^C, **OCM** *traŋh
'Be swollen, conceited; wanting to go to stool' 張 [Zuo]; 'a tent' (< 'something stretched') 帳 [Shiji], 'a curtain' [Chuci].
[<] exopass. of *traŋ (§4.4), lit. 'be stretched'.

※ **zhăng** 長 (tjaŋ^B) **LH** ṭaŋ^B, **OCM** *traŋ?, OCB *trjaŋ?
'To grow tall' [Meng], 'increase, elder' [Shi].
[T] *Sin Sukchu SR* tʂjaŋ (上); *MGZY* jang (上) [tʂaŋ] — **[D]** PMin *tɔŋ^B
[<] endoactive of *traŋ 張 (§4.5).

※ **cháng** 長 (ḍjaŋ) **LH** ḍaŋ, **OCM** *draŋ, OCB *ɦtrjaŋ — **[T]** *MTang* ḍaŋ, *ONW* daŋ
'Be long, tall, long-lasting' [BI, Shi].
[D] PMin *d̯ɔŋ
[<] endopass. (§4.6) of *traŋ 張, lit. 'be extended, stretched' (intr. voicing; Baxter and Sagart 1998: 46). The lack of TB cognates indicates that this word is a CH innovation.

※ **zhàng**$_5$ 長 (ḍjaŋ^C) **LH** ḍaŋ^C, **OCM** *draŋh
'Length, measure of length' [Li].
[<] LOC general derivation *draŋ (§3.5.2) (Baxter and Sagart 1998: 55: a noun derived from a 'gradable adjective').

[E] ST: WT *'dren-ba, draŋ(s)* 'to draw, drag, pull, draw tight' (a rope), PLB *raŋ 'draw, pull, drag'; Lushai *ṭaŋ*^{H} / *ṭan*^{L} 'be distended' (as breasts w. milk), *ṭʰaŋ*^{H} / *ṭʰan*^{L} 'to grow', perh. also WB *kraŋ^C* 'tense, tight' (see §12.9 WT (5) for the TB initial correspondences).

Several lgs. have a syn. with simple initial *t*-, perh. of AA origin: Khmer /-daaŋ/ ⋈ /trɑdaaŋ/ 'stretch out, extend' ⋈ /taaŋ/ 'draw out, prolong, lengthen'; Mon *dāŋ*, Bahnar *tăŋ* 'stretch out'. AA -> TB-Lepcha *daŋ* (Forrest *JAOS* 82, 1962: 334); WB *taŋ^B* 'tighten, become tense, stiff' (from *tr-?); WT *t^haŋ-po* 'hardy, strong, tense' (*HST:* 150). Table Z-1 provides an overview of the ST items.

Table Z-1 Tight, tense for zhāng₁ 張

	*kraŋ	*Craŋ	*taŋ
OC		zhāng 張 *traŋ pull tight	
WT		'dren-ba, draŋs pull tight	tʰaŋ-po tight
KC	*kraŋ		
-Lushai	kr- > tr -->	ṭaŋ^H / ṭan^L < traŋ / tranh be distended (as breasts w. milk)	
-Tiddim	kaŋ^33 / kan^53 < kaŋ / kanh stretch		
Mikir	iŋkaŋ^L <m-kaŋ tense		
JP	kren^33 pull tight kaŋ^33 pulled tight		
WB	kraŋ^C tense, tight		taŋ^B tighten

zhāng₂ 粻 → **liáng₅** 糧

zhāng₃ 章 (tśjaŋ) **LH** tśɑŋ, **OCM** *taŋ

'Be distinguishing, distinction' [Shi, Shu], 'to display' [Shu] > 'emblem, insignium, jade tablet' [Shi, Shu].

[E] ST: KC-Tiddim *ta:ŋ^M / ta:n^F* 'be bright, shining' ⋈ *ta:n^F* ⋈ *ta:t* 'to illuminate'.

zhāng₄ 獐 (tśjaŋ) **LH** tśɑŋ, **OCM** *taŋ (or *kiaŋ ?)

'River deer' [Lü].

[D] In Mǐn the word has initial *k-:* Xiàmén *kiũ^{A1}*, hence perh. OCM *kiaŋ?

zhǎng 長 → **zhāng₁** 張

zhàng₁ 丈 (ḍjaŋ^B) **LH** ḍɑŋ^B, **OCM** *draŋ?

'Old man' 丈 [Lunyu], 杖 [Yi].

[T] *Sin Sukchu SR* dʑjaŋ (上); *MGZY* cang (上) [dʑaŋ]; *MTang* ḍaŋ, *ONW* daŋ

[E] ST: PTB *źraŋ (*STC* no. 205) (or rather *ryaŋ ?) > WT *žaŋ* an honorific: *žaŋ-žaŋ* 'chief uncle', WB *ə-hraŋ* 'master, lord', Kuki *r(j)aŋ ~ *traŋ 'father's sister's husband', Mru *taraŋ* 'uncle' (Löffler 1966: 140). This may be an old area word: PAN *guDaŋ* 'adult, grown up' (Sagart *JCL* 21.1, 1993: 32 associates AN with items under → zhāng₁ 張). This word is sometimes thought to be the same as → zhàng₃ 杖 'staff', i.e. someone who walks with, or leans on, a staff (unlikely).

zhàng₂ 丈 (ḍjaŋ^B) **LH** ḍɑŋ^B, **OCM** *draŋ? — **[T]** *MTang* ḍaŋ, *ONW* daŋ

'A length measure of ten *chǐ* [Zuo].

[D] PMin *dɔŋ^B

[E] ST: Lushai *ṭaaŋ^H-kai^H* a measure as much as the distance from the tip of the middle finger to...breast bone...'.

zhàng₃ 杖 (ḍjaŋ^B) **LH** ḍaŋ^B, **OCM** *draŋʔ — **[D]** PMin *dʰioŋ^B
'Stick, staff' [Lunyu].
[T] *Sin Sukchu SR* dʐjaŋ (上); *MGZY* cang (上) [dʐaŋ]; *MTang* ḍaŋ, *ONW* daŋ
[D] PMin *dʰɔŋ^B

ⅹ **zhàng** 杖 (ḍjaŋ^C) **LH** ḍaŋ^C, **OCM** *draŋh
'To lean on' [Zuo].
[E] Area word: TB-Lushai: *tiaŋ^R* 'a walking stick, a staff'. <> Benedict (1976: 171) relates *zhàng* to a Proto-Austro-Tai *(n)ti(y)aŋ 'stick, handle, post, tree': Javanese *tiyaŋ*, Malay *tiaŋ* 'post', Fiji *ndia* 'stick, handle'. <> PTai *deeŋ ~ *tʰeeŋ 'stick, bar'. <> MK: Khmer *ṭaṅa* /daaŋ/ OKhmer *toŋ* /ɗɔɔŋ/ 'shaft, stock, shank' ⅹ *-toṅa* /-taaoŋ/ 'stock, stem, stick'.

zhàng₄ 障 (tśjaŋ[C]) **LH** tśaŋ^C, **OCM** taŋh
'Dike, dam up' [Zuo], 'obstacle' [Li]; Mand. 'hinder, obstruct, barrier, block'. The word looks like a cognate of → táng₂ 塘, but the OC initials do not agree (*t- vs. *l-).

zhàng₅ 張帳 → **zhāng₁** 張

zhāo₁, jiāo 鉊釗 (tśjäu, kieu) **LH** tśau, keu < kiau, **OCM** *kiau
'To cut' 釗 [SW]; 'a big sickle' 鉊 (MC *tśjäu* only) [Guan]; 鉊 is a Han period dialect word from the eastern Huái-Yangtze region, in Chǔ and Chén [FY 5, 30].
[E] KT: Prob. a Tai word: Lao *kiau^B1* 'to reap, sickle', S. *kiau^B1* 'to cut with a sickle' ⅹ *khiau^A2* < *g- 'a sickle' (Li 1976: 47).

zhāo₂ 招 → **zhào₁** 召

zhāo₃ 昭 (tśjäu) **LH** tśau or kiau ?, **OCM** *kiau
'Be bright, illustrious, glorious, enlighten' [Shi, Shu].
Acc. to *SW zhāo* 釗 (tśjäu, kieu) is a loan graph for 昭, therefore the OC stem in this wf was prob. *kiau (not *tiau); note also the allofams *jiǎo* 皎皦 and *qiāo* below.

ⅹ **zhào₄** 炤照 (tśjäu^C) **LH** tśau^C or kiau^C, **OCM** *kiauh
'To shine, be brilliant, visible' 炤 [BI, Shi]; 'shine, shine on' (of sun, moon) 照 [Shi].
[T] *Sin Sukchu SR* tʂjew (去); *MGZY* jew (去) [tʂɛw]; *ONW* tśau
[<] exoactive / tr. of *zhāo* 昭 (tśjäu) (§4.3).

ⅹ **zhǎo-zhǎo** 昭昭 (tśjäu^B) **LH** tśau^B or kiau^B, **OCM** *kiauʔ
'Glorious' [Shi].

ⅹ **jiǎo** 皎皦 (kieu^B) **LH** keu^B (i.e. keiau^B), **OCM** *kiâuʔ
'Bright' 皎皦 [Shi], 皎 [Chuci]; 'distinct' 皦 [Lunyu].
[D] Amoy *kiau^A1* col. 'bright and decided' / lit. 'beautiful'.

ⅹ **qiāo** 髐 (kʰieu) **LH** kʰeu, **OCM** *khiâu
'Bleached white (of bones)' [Zhuang].
[<] Probably a tone A noun of *jiǎo* 皎皦 (§3.1).

zhāo₄ 朝 (ṭjäu) **LH** ṭau, **OCM** *trau, OCB *trjaw — **[T]** *ONW* tau
'Morning' [BI, Shi]. A labial initial may be assumed for OC because *zhāo* serves as phonetic for → miào₂ 廟 'temple', note also Tai. See also §7.1.4.
[E] <> Tai: S. *pʰrau^A2* < *br- 'morning' (Manomaivibool 1975: 302).

ⅹ **cháo** 朝潮 (ḍjäu) **LH** ḍau, **OCM** *drau, OCB *ɦtrjaw — **[T]** *ONW* dau
('Perform the morning ceremony':) 'go / come to court, to an audience' intr. 朝 [Shi]; 'morning tide' 潮 [Chuci], opp. 'evening tide' → xī₁ 夕汐.

zhǎo$_1$ 爪 (tṣau^B) **LH** tṣɔu^B, **OCM** *tsrûʔ — **[D]** M-Xiàmén col. *liãõ^{B1}* (< ?).
'Claw' 爪 [Shi], 叉 [SW]. This is the s. w. as, or cognate to, → zhuā 抓 'grasp'; it may perh. also be related to → sāo$_1$ 搔 'scratch'.

zhǎo$_2$ 找
'To search for'. The word first appears in the Ming dynasty, etymology unknown (Norman 1988: 76).

zhǎo$_3$ 昭 → **zhāo**$_3$ 昭

zhào$_1$ 召 (ḍjäu^C) **LH** ḍɑu^C, **OCM** *drauh
'To call, summon' [BI, Shi].
[E] Prob. related to Tai: S. *rɨak^{A2}* 'summon, call' (Manomaivibool 1975: 152), for the initials see §7.1.4, for the finals §6.9.

ж **zhāo** 招 (tśjäu) **LH** tśau, **OCM** *tau — **[T]** *ONW* tśau
'To beckon, summon' [Shi] > 'signalize' [Guoyu].

ж **zhào** 詔 (tśjäu^C) **LH** tśau^C, **OCM** *tauh
'To tell, declare' [BI, Shu] is perh. related.

zhào$_2$ 詔 → **zhào**$_1$ 召

zhào$_3$ 炤照 → **zhāo**$_3$ 昭

zhào$_4$ 兆 (ḍjäu^B) **LH** ḍɑu^B, **OCM** *d-lauʔ
'To prognosticate omen, symptom' [Zuo].
[E] Perh. ST: Chepang *hrawʔ-* 'forebode, portend ill fortune, be ill'.

zhào$_5$ 濯 → **zhuó**$_{11}$ 濯

zhē 著 (tjak, ḍjak)
[T] *Sin Sukchu SR* tṣjaw, dzjaw (入), *LR* tṣjawʔ; *MGZY* jew, cew (入) [tṣɛw ~ dẓɛw]
A Mand. progressive suffix, first appears in the 9th cent. AD; in Wú dial.: *tsɨ* (< Southern MC *tjɤ*), it has now also assumed the function of the perfective aspect marker (Mei Tsu-Lin *CAAAL* 9, 1978: 39ff.).

zhé$_1$ 耴 (tjäp) **LH** ṭɑp, **OCM** *trap
'Hanging ears' [Zuo, N. Pr.], also **dā** 耷 (tâp) LH *tap* 'ears long and hanging down' [GY] is acc. to *JY* the common graph for *zhé*.
[E] Perh. connected with Tai *tuːp 'hanging ears' (of dog) (*STC*: 181 n. 479).

zhé$_2$ 折 (tśjät) **LH** tśat, **OCM** *tet, OCB *tjet (1998) — **[T]** *ONW* tśat
'To break off' tr. [Shi], 'destroy' [Yi], 'decide' [Shu].

ж **shé** 折 (źjät) **LH** dźat, **OCM** *det, OCB *N-tjet (1998) — **[T]** *ONW* dźat
'To bend' intr. [Li], 'be cut off, broken off > to die prematurely' [Shu].
[<] endopass. of *zhé* 折 (tśjät) (§4.6) (Baxter and Sagart 1998: 43). For a semantic parallel, see → yǎo$_1$ 夭殀.

[E] ST *tet ~ *tjat (for the vowels, see §11.3.2): Chepang *tet-* 'break or snap a rope, tear cloth'. PTB *tsyat (*STC* no. 185), or rather *tyat (Baxter and Sagart 1998: 43f): PLB *tsat ~ *C-tsat 'break in two, cut through, conclude'; WT *'čhad-pa, čhad* 'to cut, explain' ж *gčod-pa, bčad* 'to cut'. Lushai *čat^L / čaʔ^L* (Lorr. *chat*) 'to break or snap' (as rope, string), 'asunder, apart' ж *čhat^L / čhaʔ^L* 'to fetch or cut' (long pieces of cane etc.).
[C] Karlgren 1956: 16 relates → zhé$_3$ 哲 'wise' (< 'penetrating') to this wf.

zhé₃ 哲 (tjät) **LH** ṭat, **OCM** *trat — **[T]** *ONW* tat
'Be intelligent, wise, clever' sv [Shi]; a Han period Qí-Sòng (eastern) dialect word for 'know' [FY 1.1].

⋊ **chè** 徹 (ḍjät, ṭʰjät) **LH** ḍat, ṭʰat, **OCM** *drat, *thrat, OCB *ɦthrjet, *thrjet
'To understand' tr. [BI, Shi].
[T] *ONW tʰat*
[<] The form LH *ḍat* is perh. endopass. of *zhé* (§4.6); LH *ṭʰiat* may reflect a transitive / caus. form (§5.8.2).

[E] Several etymological suggestions have been made: Karlgren (1956: 16) relates 哲 to → zhé₂ 折 'break, decide' (hence 哲 'penetrating'). Or it may be connected with → zhī₅ 知 'to know' (so Pulleyblank in Rosemont 1991: 32).

However, the most likely connection is with TB, although the OC initial seems more complex: WB *tat* 'to know, be skilled in', JP *mə³¹-tat³¹* 'to listen', Tani *tas 'to listen / hear' (also 'to ask') (Sun *LTBA* 16.2, 1993: 180), WT *tʰos-pa* 'to hear'.

zhé₄ 晢 (tśjät, tśjäiᶜ) **LH** tśat, tśas, **OCM** *tat(s), OCB *tjats
'Be bright, shining' [Shi], 'perspicacious' [Shu].

⋊ **chè** 澈 (ḍjät) **LH** ḍat, **OCM** *drat
'Be clear, limpid' (water) [Yi].

[C] An allofam may be → shì₁₉ 誓.

zhé₅ 蜇 'sting' → **chài** 蠆

zhé₆ 磔 (ṭɐk) **LH** ṭak, **OCM** *trâk
'To rip open' (a victim) [Zhuang].
[<] Final *-k* variant of → zhā 奓 (§6.1.1), perh. also connected with **duó** 剫 (dâk) LH *dak* 'to cleave' [Zuo / Guō Pú]. This may be part of a larger group, see → bò₃ 擘 and → lí₁₀ 離. For an overview over similar items, see Table P-1 under → pī₃ 披.

zhé₇ 摺 (tśjäp) **LH** tśap, **OCM** *tap — **[T]** *ONW* tśap
'To fold' [GY; Nánshǐ], not an OC word.
[E] ST: WB *tʰap* 'to place one on the other, add to, repeat, do again', *ə-tʰap* 'layer' (*HST:* 124); JP *tʰap³¹-tʰap³¹* 'layer upon layer', *dapᶠ* 'to line something with something flat'. CH <> Tai: S. *tʰapᴰ²S* < *dap 'to overlay, superimpose'. Note also Tai: S. *tʰopᴰ²S* < *dop 'to fold' (is the source of the Tai word a SE Asian TB lg.?).
[C] This word does not belong to the syn. → dié 牒.

zhé₈ 讁 (ṭɛk, ḍɛk) **LH** ṭɛk, ḍɛk, **OCM** *trêk, *drêk, OCB *trek
'To blame, punish' 適 [Shi], 讁 [Zuo]. Possibly related to → zé₂ 責 'hold responsible'.

zhé₉ 轍 蹴 (ḍjät) **LH** ḍat, **OCM** *drat
'Track' of wheel 轍 [Zuo], also 'footprint' as the graph 蹴 (*GSR* 286f) suggests.
[E] ST: WT *rjes* < *ryes* 'trace, track' (Unger *Hao-ku* 39, 1992). For the complex initials, see §7.1.4.

zhé₁₀ 慴 → **shè₉** 慴慹

zhě 赭 (tśjaᴮ) **LH** tśaᴮ, **OCM** *taʔ
'Red paint' [Shi].
[E] ST: PTB *t(y)a (*STC:* 159 n. 429): WB *tya* 'very red', *ta* 'very red, flaming' (*HST:* 129). *STC* links *zhě* to other CH words for 'red'.
[C] → zhū₁ 朱 may perh. be related.

zhè₁ 柘 (tśjaC) **LH** tśaC, **OCM** *takh — **[T]** *ONW* tśa
'A kind of thorny tree whose leaves can be used in place of mulberry leaves in feeding silkworms' [Shi].
[E] This word has been compared to Middle Korean *tak* 'mulberry tree' (Miyake 1997: 197, 203). See comment under → méi₄ 梅.

zhè₂ 宅 → **zhái** 宅

zhè₃ 炙 → **zhì₁₄** 炙

zhēn₁ 珍 (tjen) **LH** ṭin, **OCM** *trən
'Precious' [Zuo].
[E] ? ST: WT *rin* 'price, value' (Geilich 1994: 249).

zhēn₂ 斟 (tśjəm) **LH** tśim, **OCM** *təm — **[T]** *ONW* tśim
'To pour in, ladle out, serve' (< 'to fill up'?) [Chuci].
≭ Perh. **shèn** 甚 (źjəmB/C) **LH** dźimB/C, **OCM** *dəmʔ/s
'Excessive, much' [Li].
[T] *Sin Sukchu SR* ʐim (上去); *LR* ʐim (上); *MGZY* zhim (上) [ʐim]; *ONW* dźimB/C
[E] ? ST: PTB *tyam ~ *dyam 'full', KN-Tiddim dim 'be full' (*STC* no. 226).

zhēn₃ 椹 (tjəm) **LH** ṭim, **OCM** *trəm
'Chopping block' [Zhouli]. Baxter (1992: 551) relates this word to → zhěn₁ 枕.

zhēn₄ 貞 (tjäŋ) **LH** ṭeŋ, **OCM** *treŋ — **[T]** *MTang* ṭeŋ, *ONW* teŋ
'To test, try out, correct, verify' [OB].
≭ **zhēn, zhēng** 偵 (tjäŋ, ṭʰjäŋ[C]) **LH** ṭeŋ, ṭʰeŋ, **OCM** *t(h)reŋ
'To test, verify' [Li].
[E] Tai: S. *tʰlɛɛŋA1* 'id.' (Manomaivibool 1975: 149). Perh. related to → zhèng₂ 證.

zhēn₅ 真 (tśjen) **LH** tśin, **OCM** *tin
'To be true, real' [Zhuang].
[T] *Sin Sukchu SR* tʂin (平); *MGZY* jin (平) [tʂin]
[E] ST: WT *bden-pa* 'true'. Perh. connected with → zhēn₄ 貞,

zhēn₆ 振 → **zhèn₂** 振震

zhēn₇ 桭 (tśjen) **LH** tśin, **OCM** *tən
'Be numerous, in a flock' (birds, sons) [Shi].
≭ **zhēng** 烝 (tśjəŋ) **LH** tśɨŋ, **OCM** *təŋ
'Be many, numerous' (people, animals) [Shi] is apparently a variant of the above.

zhēn₈ 箴鍼 (tśjəm) **LH** kim, **OCM** *kim — **[T]** *ONW* tśim — **[D]** PMin *tšim ~ *tšem
'Needle' 鍼 [Zuozhuan], 箴 [Liji] > 'to criticize' 箴 [Zuozhuan]. For a semantic parallel, see → zān 簪, → cì₂ 朿.
[E] Etymology not clear. OC -> Viet. *kim* 'needle' (Bodman 1980: 183). -> Tai: Saek *kimA1* 'needle'; PTai *khi̯emA1 'needle' is perh. to be connected with 鍼 (gjiäm 4) [GY]. <> PYao *si:mA1 'needle', PMiao *kɐəŋA1 [Wáng FS]. <> MK: Khmu *skam* 'needle' (related?) (Benedict *MKS* 18–19, 1992: 4). *HPTB:* 198 compares the CH word with PTB **kap* 'needle', both may go back to ST *kəm ~ *kəp.

zhēn₉ 溱蓁 → **shēn₄** 莘詵

zhěn₁ 枕 (tśjəmB) **LH** tśimB, **OCM** *kimʔ, OCB *Kjumʔ — **[T]** *ONW* tśim
'Headrest, pillow' [Shi]. A tone C verb 'to pillow oneself on' [Zuo] (Downer 1959: 280) is an exoactive / caus. derivation (§4.3).

[E] ST *kum ~ *kim: PTB *mkum (*STC* no. 482) > WB k^hum 'block, bench, table', PL *m-gum[2]; Lushai k^hum^L 'bedstead'; JP k^hum^{55} 'headrest, pillow', Lepcha *kam* 'block', *buŋ-kʰum* 'pillow' (Bodman 1980: 183; *HST:* 118); Nung *məkʰim* (*HPTB:* 503). For the *i* ~ *u* variations, see §11.5.1.

zhěn₂ 疹 (ṭʰjenᶜ) **LH** ṭʰinᶜ, **OCM** *thrəns or *rhəns
'Fever' [Shi], 'suffer' [Shi] is perh. a MK word: Khmer *krùn* vb. 'have a fever', the OC vowel *ə after an initial with *r could correspond to foreign *u as in → chén₆ 塵 'dust'.

zhěn₃ 畛 (tśjen[ᴮ]) **LH** tśinᴮ, **OCM** *tənʔ, OCB *tjənʔ
'Path between fields' [BI, Shi], 'boundary dikes' [Zhuang] is perh. cognate to the synonymous → dìng₃ 町.

zhěn₄ 紾 → **jǐn₁** 緊

zhèn₁ 朕 (ḍjəmᴮ) **LH** ḍimᴮ, **OCM** *drəmʔ, *drəŋʔ
'My, our' [BI, Shi, Shu], etymology not clear.

zhèn₂ 振震 (tśjenᶜ) **LH** tśinᶜ, **OCM** *təns — *ONW* tśin
('To stir, be stirring':) 'to shake, rouse, quake' 振 [Shi] > 'to alarm, fear' 震 [OB, Shi], 'scared' 振 [Guoce]; 'thunder' 震 [Shi]; > 'move' [Li], 'lift' 振 [Guoyu] > 'save, help' 振 [Yi], 'endow, succor' 賑 [Mo].
[D] M-Xiàmén col. *tĭn*ᴮˡ, lit. *tsin*ᴮˡ 'to shake' (*tĭn*ᴮˡ does not agree with the QYS).

= **zhèn₃, shēn** 娠 (tśjenᶜ, śjen) **LH** tśin, **OCM** *təns
'Pregnant' 娠 [Zuo], 'become pregnant' 震 [Shi]. The reading *shēn* has prob. been transferred from → shēn₂ 身 'body' with which it is unrelated. 'Pregnant' is derived from 'to shake, rouse, excite' (e.g. a grasshopper from hibernation, i.e. coming to life), hence lit. 'start stirring, moving' (of an embryo).

⋇ **zhēn₅** 振 (tśjen) **LH** tśin, **OCM** *tən
'Majestic' [Shi] is prob. related because of the frequent semantic connection between 'shake' and 'fear, fearsome'.

[E] Prob. ST even though the TB vowel does not agree: PTB *tur 'tremble, shake, pulse' [HPTB: 369] > WB *tun* 'tremble, shake'; cf. also Chepang *dhər-* 'to shake, vibrate'. The semantic field of this wf is parallel to → sōu₃, sǒu 搜: 'move / stir > pregnant, morning'.
[C] A closely related etymon is → chén₅ 晨 'morning'.

zhèn₃, shēn 娠 → **zhèn₂** 振震; → **zhèn₄** 侲娠

zhèn₄ 侲娠 (tśjenᶜ) **LH** tśin, **OCM** *təns
'Child, boy or girl' [Han texts]; in the ancient Yān-Qí region (NE and Eastern China) the word meant 'someone who raises horses' (stable boy / girl?), 娠 also refers to a 'maid' of an official's wife [FY 3, 3]. Perh. related to → zhèn₂ 振震, i.e. someone moving about, being busy?

zhèn₅ 酖鴆 → **chén₂** 沈

zhèn₆ 紖; 絼 'rope' → **yǐn₂** 引

zhèn₇ 陳 → **chén₇** 陳

zhēng₁ 正征 → **zhèng₁** 正政

zhēng₂ 爭 (tṣɛŋ) **LH** tṣɛŋ, **OCM** *tsrêŋ
'To fight, quarrel' [Shi].

[T] *Sin Sukchu SR* tʂəjŋ (平), *PR, LR* tʂəŋ; *MGZY* jʰing (平) [tʂəŋ]; *ONW* tʂëŋ
[E] ST: WT *'dziŋ-ba* 'quarrel, contend, fight' (*HST:* 122), WB *cac* 'war, battle'.

zhēng₃-róng 崢嶸 → **jiǒng₂** 泂迥

zhēng₄ 烝 (tśjəŋ) **LH** tśɨŋ, **OCM** *təŋ
'To steam' (food) [Shi]. Sagart (1999: 73) derived the following from this word:

⋇ **zèng** 甑 (tsjəŋ) **LH** tsɨŋ, **OCM** *tsəŋ
'Boiler, earthenware pot for steaming rice' [Meng].

zhēng₅ 烝 'many' → **zhēn₇** 振

zhēng₆ 蒸 (tśjəŋ) **LH** tśɨŋ, **OCM** *təŋ — **[T]** *ONW* tśiŋ
'Brushwood' (as firewood) [Shi].
[E] ST: PTB *taŋ (*STC* no. 320) > WT *tʰaŋ* 'pine, fir, evergreen tree', WB *tʰaŋ^B* 'fuel, firewood', in compounds also 'pine, fir' (*HST:* 79).

zhēng₇ 蒸 'to offer' → **chéng₂** 丞承

zhēng₈ 徵 → **zhèng₂** 證

zhēng₉ □
'Elbow, heel' occurs in southern dialects: PMin *taŋ ~ *tiaŋ: Yǒng'ān *tĩ^A1*, Jiàn'ōu *tiaŋ^A1*, Fúzhōu *taŋ^A1*, Fú'ān *naŋ^A1*, Amoy *tĩ^A1*, Jiēyáng *tẽ^A1*; Y-Guǎngzhōu *sau^B1-tsaaŋ^A1* 'elbow', *kœk^D1m?-tsaaŋ^A1* 'heel'. Etymology not clear.

zhěng₁ 拯 → **chéng₂** 丞承

zhěng₂ 整 → **zhèng₁** 正政

zhèng₁ 正政 (tśjäŋ^C) **LH** tśeŋ^C, **OCM** *teŋh
'Be straight, correct > govern, determine' 正 [Shi, Shu]; 'to govern, government' 政 [BI, Shi, Shu], 'remonstrate' 証 [Guoce].
[T] *Sin Sukchu SR* tʂiŋ (去); *MGZY* jing (去) [tʂiŋ]; *ONW* tśeŋ
[<] exoact. / tr. derivation of *zhēng* (§4.3.2).

⋇ **zhēng** 正征 (tśjäŋ) **LH** tśeŋ, **OCM** *teŋ
'Center of target; first (month)' [BI, Shi] > ('to target, make straight for':) 'to march on / against, campaign' 征 [BI, Shi]. Contrary to traditional belief (*GSR* 833o), the basic meaning is not 'to correct' > 'punish by military expedition', although the (royal, imperial) attacker likes to see his action thus morally justified.

⋇ **zhěng₂** 整 (tśjäŋ^B) **LH** tśeŋ^B, **OCM** *teŋ?
'Be orderly' [Zuo], caus. 'arrange, dispose' (troops) [Shi] (Unger *Hao-ku* 36, 1990: 50)
[<] endoactive of *zhēng* 正征 (tśjäŋ) (§4.5).

[E] ST or area word: TB-Lushai *diiŋ^F* 'to go straight or direct, go straight through without breaking the journey', etc.; Chepang *dʰeŋ-* 'be straight'; JP *teŋ^31* 'right, correct', Lepcha *atʰáŋ* 'right, correct', WB *tañ^C* 'straightforward, direct'. <> AA: Khmer *diaṅa* /tíiəŋ/ 'be true, accurate, correct, right'.

This wf could be related to → tíng₁ 亭 (so Karlgren 1956: 16), but prob. not to → tǐng₂ 挺 because the initials are different (*l- vs. *t-). Matisoff (1988) combines this wf with → yíng₂ 盈贏 'full', → píng₁ 平 'level', → tǐng₂ 挺 'straight'.

zhèng₂ 證 (tśjəŋ^C) **LH** tśɨŋ^C, **OCM** *təŋh
'Testify, prove' [Lunyu]. Perh. related to → zhēn₄ 貞, and / or → zhēn₅ 真.
[T] *Sin Sukchu SR* tʂiŋ (去); *MGZY* jing (去) [tʂiŋ]; *ONW* tśiŋ

ꭗ **zhēng** 徵 (tjəŋ) **LH** ṭiŋ, **OCM** *trəŋ ? — **[T]** *MTang* ṭiŋ, *ONW* tiŋ
'To examine, verify, summon' [Shu], 'test, testify, prove' [Zuo].
[E] MK-Khmer *diaṅa* /tíiəŋ/ 'be true, accurate, correct' ꭗ *phdiaṅa* /ptíiəŋ/ 'to correct, verify, confirm' (or are these CH loans?). Perh. related to → zhēn$_4$ 貞.

zhī$_1$ 之 (tśɨ) **LH** tśə, **OCM** *tə
[T] *Sin S. SR* tʂi (平), *PR, LR* tʂʅ; *MGZY* ji (平) [tʂi]; *ONW* tśə
(1) Demonstrative pronoun 'this, he, she, it'. As a subject it is common in OB, sporadic in *Shījīng* and subsequent classical texts, but it is everywhere the normal object pronoun 'him, her, it'. Placed after the negatives *bù* 不 and *wú* 毋, the obj. pronoun is reduced to its initial *t-* and fused with the preceding negatives yielding *fú* 弗 (pjuət) 'not it' and *wù* 勿 (mjuət) 'don't...it', see under → bù$_1$ 不 and → wú$_1$ 毋.
(2) Derived from the pronoun is the use as the common genitive marker. A medieval colloquial genitive marker was written → dǐ$_2$ 底; subsequently → de$_3$ 的 appears for the first time in a Song document (Coblin p. c.) and later in a Yuan inscription of 1238 (Mei Tsu-Lin *BIHP* 59.1, 1988). However, these forms may be unrelated to *zhī* because they imply a final *-k*.

ꭗ **shí** 時 (zɨ) **LH** dźə, **OCM** *də
Demonstrative pronoun 'this, now, then' [Shi]. Pulleyblank (1995: 89) considers *shí* a relatively unemphatic form of → shì$_{14}$ 是. See also §3.3.3.
[T] *Sin S. SR* ʐi (平), *PR, LR* ʐʅ; *MGZY* zhi (平) [ʐi]; *ONW* dźə
[E] ST: WT *da* 'there'.

zhī$_2$ 之 (tśɨ) **LH** tśə, **OCM** *tə (= *tiə ?)
'To go, proceed' [Shi].
[T] *Sin S. SR* tʂi (平), *PR, LR* tʂʅ; *MGZY* ji (平) [tʂi]; *ONW* tśə
[E] ST *tjə ?: WT *čʰa-ba* 'to go, become, be going to'; WB *ca^C* 'begin, at first' ꭗ *ə-ca^C* 'beginning'. These TB items do not belong to → chū$_3$ 初 as has been suggested.

ꭗ **shí** 時旹 (źɨ) **LH** dźə, **OCM** *dəʔ (tone!)
'Time, season' [BI, Shi]. OC -> Tai: S. *tii^1* < *d-* 'time, favorable occasion'.
[<] *tə + endopassive devoicing (§4.6) + endoactive tone B (§4.5) forming an introvert noun, 'what is proceeding'.

ꭗ **zhì** 志 (tśɨ^C) **LH** tśə^C, **OCM** *təh
'Goal, purpose, will, wish' [Shu] > 'spirit, mind, record, treatise' [Zuo]. Note the semantic proximity with the root in the phrase 不如我所之 '[My thoughts] are not equal to (where I am going:) my purpose' [Shi 54, 5].
[<] *tə + exopass. s/h-suffix (§4.4), lit. 'what is being proceeded to'. This word is unrelated to → shì$_{32}$ 識 (suggested by Wáng Lì 1982: 95).

ꭗ **zhǐ** 止趾 (tśɨ^B) **LH** tśə^B, **OCM** *təʔ
'Foot > heel' [BI, Shi]; > 'to settle, stop' 止 [Shi].
[<] *tə + endoactive tone B noun derivation (§4.5). This word is not related to the TB items under → jǐ$_1$ 几机.

ꭗ **chén** 辰 (źjen) **LH** dźin, **OCM** *dən — **[T]** *ONW* dźin
'Date, time, season' [BI, Shi].
[<] *dəʔ 時 + the nominal n-suffix (§6.4.3), lit. 'what is proceeding'. *Chén* partially converges with → chén$_5$ 晨辰. It replaces its simplex *shí* 時 in southern dialects as the word for 'time': M-Fúzhōu *seiŋ^{A2}-ŋau^{C2}* 辰候, Y-Guǎngzhōu *si^{A2}-sɐn^{A2}* 時辰 (for Mand. *shí-hòu* 時候).

zhī₃ 汁 (tśjəp) **LH** kip, **OCM** *kip — **[T]** *ONW* tśip
'Juice, sap, melting snow' [Li].
[D] PMin *tšep
⋈ **qì** 湆 (kʰjəp) **LH** kʰɨp
'Juice' [Yili] is perh. a cognate of *zhī* (Unger *Hao-ku* 47, 1995: 141); the dialect word from East of the Passes *xié* 協 (ɣiep) [gep] [FY 3, 7] is prob. related.
[E] Etymology not certain. Perh. related is PLB *ʔgrip 'lac, pine resin': WB *kʰrip, kʰyip* [*STC:* 38] (*CVST* 5: 65); or to Kachin *məgyep* 'liquor' (*STC:* 38); or *HST:* 99 relates *zhī* to WT *čʰab* 'water', but initial velars do not palatalize in WT. Prob. not related to → chěn₂ 瀋沈 'a liquid'.

zhī₄ 支枝肢 (tśje) **LH** tśe < kie, **OCM** *ke — **[T]** *ONW* tśe (kie?) — **[D]** PMin *ki
'Limb, branch' 支枝 [Shi, Yi], 'body limb' 肢 [Meng]; 'to separate' 支, 'go astray' 枝 [Xun] (OC -> Tai: S. *kee*ᴬ¹ 'go astray').
= **chì** 翅 (śjeᶜ) // **LH** kie, **OCM** *ke
'Wing' [Guoce] (< 'limb'). The reading *chì* (śjeᶜ) has been transferred from an unrelated synonym, see → chì₄ 翅.
⋈ **qí** 跂岐 (gjie 4) **LH** gie, **OCM** *ge — **[T]** *ONW* gie
'Bifurcating, forked (road)' 跂 [Lie]; 'to stride' 岐 [Shi] (*HST* p. 65).
[E] ST: Chepang *gweʔ* 'finger' ⋈ *keŋ* 'twig, branch', *hluŋ keŋ-* 'be distracted' (*hluŋ* 'mind'), Lushai *ke*ᴸ 'leg' [Weidert 1975: 28], Tani *ke(ŋ) 'finger'; WT *'gyed-pa, bgyes, bkye* 'to divide' (Bodman 1980: 182). → qí₆ 騎 'to ride' may be related.

zhī₅ 知 (tje) **LH** ṭe, **OCM** *tre
'To know, understand' [Shi].
[T] *Sin Sukchu SR* tʂi (平); *MGZY* ji (平) [tʂi]; *ONW* te
⋈ **zhì** 智 (tjeᶜ) **LH** ṭeᶜ, **OCM** *treh
'Knowledge, wisdom' [BI, Shu, Meng] > 'be wise' [Zuo] (Downer 1959: 287).
[<] exopass. of *zhī* 知 (tje) *tre, lit. 'what is known' (§4.4).
[E] Prob. ST: Lushai *hria*ᴿ / *hre*ᴴ / *hriat*ᶠ 'to know' (*CVST* 2: 73), JP *tʃe*³³ < *rje*³³ 'to know', perh. WT *rig-pa* 'to know'.

zhī₆ 隻 (tśjäk) **LH** tśek, **OCM** *tek — **[T]** *ONW* tśek — **[D]** PMin *dziɔk ~ *dzit
'Single' [Gongyang], measure word for individual birds, animals, and things that occur naturally in pairs, eventually extended to include other objects (Norman 1988: 116).
[E] ST *tjak: PTB *tyik ~ *tyak (*STC* p. 94; *HPTB:* 346) > PLB *C-tikᴸ, *ti² 'one' > WB *tac* ⋈ PLB *ʔdik 'only' (Matisoff 1997a: 81) > Lahu *tí* 'only'; Limbu *thik* 'a little, only'; WT *gčig* 'one'; JR *kətiag* (Beyer 1992: 83). Vowel *e* as in OC (from *-ja-): Bumthang *t(h)ek*, Cuona Monpa *tʰeʔ*⁵⁴ (Matisoff 1997a: 20; *HPTB:* 507). ⋈ PLB *day² ⋈ *tí* 'only' > WB *tʰi*ᴮ 'single, alone' (Matisoff 1997a: 21), JP *tai*³³ 'single'. For the vowels, see §11.3.2.

zhī₇ 禔 (diei, tśje, źje) **LH** tśe, **OCM** *te, *de
'Peace, happiness' [SW: Yi].
[E] ST: WT *bde-ba* 'happy' (*HST:* 91).

zhī₈ 桎 (tśjet) **LH** tśit, **OCM** *tit — **[T]** *ONW* tśit
'Foot fetters' [Zhouli]. The final *t is prob. a nominal suffix (§6.2.1).
[E] ST: WB *tʰit* 'stocks for confinement'.
⋈ **tài, dì** 鈦軑 (dieiᶜ, dâi) **LH** des, dɑs, **OCM** *dês, *dâs
'Foot shackle for criminals' 鈦 [Guan]; ('shackle for axle':) 'wheel-axle cap' 軑

[Chuci] (Unger *Hao-ku* 39, 1992). The vowel correspondence is unusual, perh. these two CH words are unrelated.

zhī$_{9a}$ 祇 (tśje) **LH** tśe < kie, **OCM** *ke
'Only' [Shi].

≍ **zhǐ$_{3}$** 只 (tśje^{B}) **LH** tśe^{B} < kie^{B}, **OCM** *keʔ — **[T]** *ONW* kie ~ tśe ?
'Only' [Post-Han]. The LHan and earlier readings belong to an OC particle [Shi]. This seems to be the s. w. as zhī 祇 above, but the difference in tone is unexplained (has tone B been transferred from the particle?). This wf is prob. not related to → shì$_{31}$ 啻 'only', nor to zhī$_{6}$ 隻 'single'.

[E] Prob. ST: TB *kya(-) 'one' as in Kamarupan lgs. *ke*, *k^{h}e*, perh. these are cognate to WT *rkyaŋ-pa*, WB *k^{h}yaŋ^{B}* 'single' [Matisoff 1997a: 18]. For the connections 'one' - 'single' - 'only', note Engl. 'only' (< one-ly) and the items under zhī$_{6}$ 隻. For the vowels, see §11.3.2.

zhī$_{9b}$ 祗 (tśi) **LH** tśi, **OCM** *ti
'Be reverent, revere, respect' [BI, Shu]. *CVST* (2: 126) relates this word to WT *sti-ba* 'honor, respect, reverence'.

zhī$_{10}$ 脂 (tśi) **LH** tśi, **OCM** *ki ? — **[T]** *ONW* tśi
'Grease' (for lubrication) [Shi]. *SW* says that *zhī* belongs to animals with horns, → gāo$_{3}$ 膏 'grease, fat' to animals without horns (e.g. pigs). The OC initial is not certain, the phonetic implies an OC *k-, but palatalization of 旨 may have occurred so early in the Zhou period that it could also be used for words with original dental initials.
[E] The TB area has words for 'grease, fat' with the final *-il*, but with initial consonants which are difficult to reconcile with the CH word: PTB *tsil (*STC:* 168f.) > WT *ts^{h}il* 'fat' n.; Kanauri *tsil* 'marrow'; PL *tsi^{1} 'fat', WB *c^{h}i* 'oil', *k^{h}raŋ-c^{h}i* 'marrow' [Matisoff 1978: 183f] (*STC:* 169 n. 452). Also, note AA: Santali *itil* 'be fat', Khmer *kɔn-ṭul.*

zhī$_{11}$ 遲 (ḍi) **LH** ḍi, **OCM** *dri — **[T]** *ONW* di
'To tarry, slow' [Shi].
[E] <> ? AA: Semai /kərdiʔ/, Temiar /kədɨʔ/ 'to cease from activity, wait', Mon /tə̤ʔ/, WMon *dui'* 'to stop, keep quiet, stay put'.

≍ **zhì** 遲 (ḍi^{C}) **LH** ḍi^{C}, **OCM** *drih
'To wait' 遲 [Xun]; 'to sow late, unripe' 稺穉 [Shi].

zhī$_{12}$ 織 (tśjək) **LH** tśɨk, **OCM** *tək — **[T]** *ONW* tśik
'To weave' vb. [Shi].
[E] ST: PTB *tak (*STC* no. 17) > WT *'t^{h}ag-pa* 'to weave' ≍ *t^{h}ags* 'texture, web'; PLB *tak / *dak 'weave, spin'.

≍ **zhì** 織 (tśɨ^{C}) **LH** tśə^{C}, **OCM** *təkh — **[T]** *ONW* tśə^{C}
'Woven cloth, be woven' [Shi].
[<] exopass. of *zhī* 織 (tśjək) (§4.4), lit. 'what is woven'.
[E] ST: WT *btags* pf. of *'t^{h}ag-* 'woven' ≍ *t^{h}ags* 'texture, web', JP *daʔ^{31} < dak^{31}* 'woven material'.

[E] Some TB lgs. have a variant, or different etymon, with initial *r: PLB *rak, *k-rak, also Mutwang (Rawang - Nung) *raʔ* 'weave' [Matisoff *TSR:* 70]; Lushai *ṭah^{L} < traʔ* or *trah* 'to weave, woven'. There is another word with *t- ~ *r- variants: PTB *ti ~ *ri 'water' (PTB *tap 'fireplace' and *rap 'shelf over fireplace' (*STC:* 19) are apparently different words). Tibetan and Chinese (where applicable) have the T-variant, Burmese the R-variant.

zhí$_1$ 直 (dj̣ək) **LH** ḍɨk, **OCM** *drək
'Simply, only' [Meng]. Karlgren *GSR* 919a believes that the homophone 'straight, right' [Shi] is the same word (see under → zhì$_{22}$ 置).
[T] *Sin Sukchu SR* dẓi (入); *MGZY* ci (入) [dẓi]; *ONW* dik

× **zhí** 職 (tśjək) **LH** tśɨk, **OCM** *tək
'Simple, only' [Shi].

× **tè** 特犆 (dək) **LH** dək, **OCM** *dək — **[T]** *ONW* dək
'Single' 犆 [Li], 'single, an only one' 特 [Yili], 'only' [Lü]; 'a mate, a match for' 特 [Shi]. The meaning 'male animal, bull' 特 (see → tè$_2$ 特) could be derived from the meaning 'a mate, match', but this is speculation.

[E] ? ST: *tak* 'one' in several Western Himalayan lgs., e.g. Darmiya *taku* 'one'.

zhí$_2$ 直 (dj̣ək) **LH** ḍɨk, **OCM** *drək
'Straight, right' [Shi] could either belong to → zhì$_{22}$ 置 'set up', or to → zhí$_1$ 直 'single' (so Karlgren *GSR* 919a). Probable allofam → dé$_2$ 德.
[E] ST: PLB *N-d(y)ak^L 'truly, very', WB *tyak-tyak* 'very'; Lushai *tak*^{L} 'real, true, genuine, very'. It is not clear if / how the following may be related: Lushai *dik*^{L} 'right, accurate, true, proper, correct'; JP *tik*^{55} 'always 一直'.

zhí$_3$ 值殖植稙 → **zhì**$_{22}$ 置

zhí$_4$ 姪 (diet, dj̣et) **LH** det, ḍet, **OCM** *lît or *d-lit ?, OCB *dīt — **[T]** *ONW* dėt
'Nephew, niece' [Zuo].
[E] ST: PTB *b-ləy 'nephew, grandchild' (*STC* no. 448; Matisoff 1995a: 52), OBurm. *mliy*, WB *mre*^{B} 'grandchild' [*IST:* 337]. For the initials, see §8.1.1; §8.1.5; for the final *-t, see §6.2.

zhí$_5$ 執 (tśjəp) **LH** tśip, **OCM** *təp — **[T]** *ONW* tśip
'To hold, seize, take' [BI, Shi]. → zhí$_6$ 縶馽 'bind' etc. is perh. cognate.

× **zhì** 摯鷙 (tśi^C) **LH** tśi^C, **OCM** *təps ?
'To catch, seize' 摯 [Shujing]; 'bird of prey' 鷙 [Chuci], 'seize a prey' [Li] (Baxter and Sagart 1998: 57); 'ceremonial gift' 贄 [Shujing] is thought to be cognate (Wáng Lì 1982: 591f).
[E] ? ST: Perh. WT *čʰab* 'power, authority' (*HST:* 120). AA: Khmer and OKhmer /cap/ 'hold, grasp' is thought to be related, but the initials and vowels do not match very closely, see → jié$_2$ 捷.

zhí$_6$ 縶馽 (tjəp) **LH** ṭip, **OCM** *trəp ? — **[T]** *ONW* tip
'Rope, tether' [Shi], 'to bind' 縶 [Zuo]; 'to hobble, bind the front feet of a horse' 馽 [Zhuang].
[E] Note Lushai *čep*^{L} / *čeʔ*^{L} (Lorrain *chep, cheh*) 'to nip, clip, clamp, fasten, bind, pinch', to which the CH word may be related. Perh. cognate to → zhí$_5$ 執 'hold'.

zhí$_7$ 蟄 (dj̣əp) **LH** ḍip, **OCM** *drəp
'Be hibernating, clustering' (of insects, snakes) [Shi, Yi] may belong to → jì$_{10}$ 揖.

zhí$_8$ 職 (tśjək) **LH** tśɨk, **OCM** *tək
'Duty, attend to, manage' [Zuo], 'duties of office' [Shi]. This word could belong to the wf → zhì$_{22}$ 置.

zhí$_9$ 職 'simple' → **zhí**$_1$ 直

zhí$_{10}$, **dé** 樴 → **zhì**$_{22}$ 置

zhí$_{11}$ 慹 → **shè**$_9$ 慴慹

zhǐ$_1$ 止趾 → **zhī**$_2$ 之

zhǐ$_2$ 沚 → **zhōu**$_2$ 洲

zhǐ$_3$ 只 'only' → **zhī**$_{9a}$ 祇

zhǐ$_4$ 旨 (tśi^B) **LH** ki^B, **OCM** *kiʔ, OCB *kjijʔ

'Be fine tasting, excellent' [Shi] > (flavor:) 'basic idea' [Yi] (so Karlgren *GSR* 552a).

[T] *Sin S. SR* tʂi (上), *PR, LR* tʂʅ; *MGZY* ji (上) [tʂi]; *ONW* tśi

⋇ **shì** 嗜 (źi^C) **LH** gi^C, **OCM** *gih, OCB *gjijs — **[T]** *ONW* dźi^C

'Enjoy' (food) [Shi] > 'enjoy, like very much' [Chu].

[E] ST: *dgyes-pa* 'rejoice' ⋇ *dge-ba* 'happiness, virtue' (Bodman 1980: 182; *HST:* 73).

zhǐ$_5$ 耆 'bring about' → **zhǐ**$_7$ 厎底

zhǐ$_6$ 指 → **shì**$_{17}$ 視

zhǐ$_7$ 厎底 → **zhì**$_1$ 至

zhǐ$_8$ 紙 (tśje^B) MHan tśɑiʔ or kiɑiʔ ? — **[T]** *ONW* tśe

'Paper' [Hou Hanshu].

[E] Bodman (1980: 184) relates this to Viet. *giấy*, PVM *k-cajʔ [Ferlus] 'paper' which, like the PMin form *tšiɑi^B, presupposes an OC rime *-ai rather than the QY's *-e. When this word was committed to writing, the rimes OC *-ai and *e had already merged in some dialects, a process which is observed already in late Zhou texts (Pulleyblank 1962: 216).

zhǐ$_9$ 黹 (ṭi^B) **LH** ṭi^B, **OCM** *triʔ

'Embroidery' [BI, Zhouli].

⋇ **chī** 絺 (ṭʰi) **LH** ṭʰi, **OCM** *thri

'Embroidered cloth, fine cloth' [Shi].

[<] Tone A noun of *zhǐ* 黹 (ṭi^B) (§3.1).

⋇ **zhì** 紩 (ḍjet) **LH** ḍit, **OCM** *drit

'To sew' [GY].

⋇ **zhì** 緻 (ḍi^C) **LH** ḍis, **OCM** *drits — **[T]** *ONW* di

'To mend (old clothes)' [Yupian] was a Han period Qín dialect word for *zhì* 紩 'to sew' (above) [FY 4].

[E] Etymology not certain. Possibly from ST *C-rwi: Lushai *ṭʰui^H* 'to sew', JP *ri^{31}* 'thread'; for absence of the medial *w* in CH, see §10.2.1. Alternatively, this wf could be related to MK: Khmer *tir* 'to sew clothes or tree leaves' [S. Lewitz *AA Studies* 2, 1976: 742]; the metathesis of the MK final *-r may have been occasioned by the final consonant forms in this wf (*-irt* > *-rit*), but can also occur in words with simple final *-r, see §7.7.3 and §6.1.

zhì$_1$ 至 (tśi^C) **LH** tśis, **OCM** *tits

'To come to, get to, arrive at, reach to' [BI, Shi]. See §8.1.5 on *GSR* 413.

[T] *Sin S. SR* tʂi (去), *PR, LR* tʂʅ; *MGZY* ji (去) [tʂi]; *ONW* tśi

[E] ST: WT *mčʰis-pa* (to have arrived): 'to be, be there, exist'.

⋇ **zhì** 致 (ṭi^C) **LH** ṭis, **OCM** *trits

'To bring, bring about, effect' [BI, Shi].

[E] caus. of *zhì* 至 by *r in the initial (Pulleyblank 1973: 118; §7.5).

[T] *Sin S. SR* tʂi (去), *PR, LR* tʂʅ; *MGZY* ji (去) [tʂi]; *ONW* ti

⋇ **zhǐ** 厎底 (tśi^B) **LH** tśi^B, **OCM** *tiʔ

'To come to, bring about, effect, accomplish, achieve' [Shi]; 'come to' [Chuci]; 'to bring about, establish, settle' 耆 [Shi]. The root initial is a dental, the graph 耆 which had an OC velar initial was perh. borrowed after palatalization.

[E] ST: WT *mčʰi-ba* 'come, go, say'.

[E] ST: WT *mčʰi-ba* ⋇ *mčʰis-pa*, see above; Tiddim *cì* 'to say', Bodo *mitiʔ*, Garo *maʔ-si-a* (Weidert 1987: 25). Lushai *tiᴸ / tiʔᴸ < tiih / tiʔ/h* 'to do, perform, treat, think, say' ⋇ *tiʔ* 'cause to be, cause, make', WB *te* 'make something and do something with it', Lahu *te*.

zhì₂ 蛭 (tśjet, ṭjet, tiet, ṭjäiᶜ) **LH** tet ? tśit ? ṭit ?, **OCM** *tit..., OCB *tr̆t, tīt, PCH *m-lhit ?
'Water leech' [SW, GY].
[E] ST etymon, although the correspondence of the initial consonants is unusual (§8.1.5): PTB *m/s-li:t 'water leech' (*STC* no. 396; *HPTB:* 350), but KN *m-hliit (*IST:* 27) Lushai *hliit < C-lit*; Lepcha *hlet-bŭ*, Karen Pho *səli, Chepang *lit*. TB cognates to words in *GSR* 413 have pre-initial *m- (§8.1.5). The unrelated Mand. word for 'leech' also has the *m-prefix: *mă-huáng* 螞蟥, so do old dialect words *mă-qí* 馬蜞, *mă-qí* 馬耆. Alternatively, *CVST* 2: 129 connects *zhì* with WT *sdig* 'scorpion'.
[C] The word may possibly be related to → dié₂ 咥 *lit 'to bite'.

zhì₃ 輊 (ṭiᶜ) **LH** ṭis, **OCM** *trits, OCB *tr̆ts — **[T]** *ONW* tiᶜ
'Be weighed down' [Shi].
[E] ST: PTB *s-ləy-t ~ *s-rəy-t 'heavy' (*HPTB:* 49) > WT *lči-ba < lhyi, lǰi-ba < lyi;* Kanauri *li-ko* 'heavy', Lepcha *lí, lím*, PL *C-li² > WB *leᴮ*, JP *li³³;* KN *rit > Lushai *ritᴸ / riʔᴸ < rit / rih* 'be heavy'. 'Leech' → zhì₂ 蛭 with the same phonetic points to an initial *l (§8.1.5); Qiang-Queyu *qa⁵⁵-rlə⁵⁵* 'heavy' may or may not support an original initial *rl- for OC and KN; a prefix OC *r- for PTB *s- would not be unusual; see §5.3.

zhì₄ 銍 (ṭjet) **LH** ṭit, **OCM** *trit
'Sickle, cut with a sickle' [Shi] > 'ears of grain' [Shu].
[E] Perh. ST: WT *gri* 'knife', WB *kreᴮ* 'copper', JP *mə³¹-gri³³* 'brass', Lushai *hreiᴸ < hreih* 'ax, hatchet'; for the initial correspondence see §7.1.4; §8.1.5; for final *-t see §6.2.1. Alternatively, Luo Yongxian (ICSTLL 2002) suggests that *zhì* is related to Tai: Po-ai *liipᴰ¹ᴸ* < *tʰr- 'small knife used to cut or reap glutinous rice', Wu-ming *rep*, Yay (Dioi) *tʰep*, but the Tai and CH final consonants do not agree. Alternatively, the TB items may belong to → qí₁₄ 鰭鬐 'fin' (semantically less likely).

zhì₅ 窒 (ṭjet, tiet) **LH** ṭit, **OCM** *trit — **[T]** *ONW* tit
'To stop up' [Shi], 'blockheaded [Lunyu].
[E] ST: WT *'dig-pa* 'to stop up' ⋇ *'dig* 'a stopper' (*HST:* 142).

zhì₆ 膣 (ṭjet, tiet) [Yupian, 6th cent. AD] (the reading may simply be that of the phonetic)
'Vagina' (ZWDCD), 'vulva' (Sino-Japanese acc. to Benedict); the meaning is only later attested (Benedict *LTBA* 14.1, 1991: 143).
[E] ST *tey (Benedict): PTB *teyᴮ, PKaren *ʔteᴮ (Benedict *LTBA* 5.1, 1979: 22). The CH form goes back to a hypothetical OC *tit which brings it close to the TB / ST etymon *ti 'water' as in → tì₁ 涕 *thiʔ/h 'tears': JP *mə³¹-di³³* 'be moist, be wet' ⋇ *mə³¹-dit³¹* 'to moisten, be wet'; PLoloish *Ntit 'soak in water' ⋇ *ʔtit 'to immerse' (or *Ntik ⋇ ʔtik) ⋇ Lahu *dì* (< *Ndi) 'ejaculate' (of a man), 'moisten due to sexual excitement' (of a woman) (Matisoff 1978: 33; 2002: 53 no. 109). Apparently *zhì* has the nominal t-suffix for natural objects, lit. 'the moist thing' (§6.2.1). The etymon is also reminiscent of MK-PVM *k-cɛ:ʔ 'vagina'. Syn. → bī₁ 屄.

zhì$_7$ 阤, 陊 (duò) (Mand. *tuó*), 陊 (Mand. *duò*) (ḍje^B) **LH** ḍɑi^B, **OCM** *d-laiʔ
'To fall down' 陊 [SW]; 'fall down, collapse' 阤 [Guoyu].

⋈ **shǐ** 弛 (śje^B) **LH** śɑi^B, **OCM** *lhaiʔ
'To destroy' (e.g. a house) [Guoyu].
[E] ST: WB *lai^B* 'fall down from an erect posture' (< *lañ*) ⋈ *hlai^B* 'throw down from an erect posture' (< *hlañ^B*). Note also PKS *lai^4 'to fall'.

zhì$_8$ 阤 'slope' → **yí** $_6$ 迤地

zhì$_9$ 杝, 扡 → **chǐ**$_1$ 拸

zhì$_{10}$ 忮 (tśje^C) **LH** kie^C, **OCM** *keh
'Wicked, malignant' [Shi].
[E] Tai: S. *keek^{D1}* 'wicked, perverted' (Manomaivibool 1975: 160).

zhì$_{11}$ 治 (ḍɨ[^{C}]) **LH** ḍə^C, **OCM** *d-ləh
'To work, make, regulate, govern' [Shi] > 'well-governed, in good order' [Yi], 'punish' [Zuo]. Downer (1959: 287) reads 'well-governed' [Liji] in tone C, the other meanings in tone A. Sagart (1999: 127) relates this word to → lí$_4$ 釐 'regulate'. If related, *zhì* may possibly belong to an AA wf; see → lǐ$_5$ 理.
[T] *Sin S. SR* dʐi (去); *MGZY* ci (去) [dʐi]; *MTang* ḍi, *ONW* diə

zhì$_{12}$ 志 → **zhī**$_2$ 之

zhì$_{13}$ 痣 (tśɨ^C) **LH** tśə^C or kiə^C ?
'Black mole' [Shiji 誌, GY].
[D] A commentary to *Shǐjì* says that *zhì* 誌 is the ordinary word for 'black mole' in the southern Wú and Chǔ dialects. PMin *ki^C.

zhì$_{14}$ 炙 (tśjäk) **LH** tśak, **OCM** *tak ?
'To roast' [Shi].

⋈ **zhè** 炙 (tśja^C) **LH** tśa^C, **OCM** *takh ?
'Be roasted' [Shi], 'a roast meat' [Zuo] (Downer 1959: 274).
[<] *tak + pass. (§4.4) < 'what has been roasted'.
[E] ? ST: PLB *kyik > Lahu *chîʔ* 'be hot (enough to burn)', WB *k^{h}yac* 'be burnt' (as food); if related the OC form was probably *k(i)ek or *kiak.

zhì$_{15}$ 陟 (tjək) **LH** ṭɨk, **OCM** *trək — **[T]** *ONW* tik
'To ascend, die' [Shi], 'promote' [Shu].
[E] ST: PLB *ɴtak 'ascend' > WB *tak* 'go up, ascend, advance, increase', ~ *ʔtak 'lift, carry', ~ *tak 'upper part, top surface': WB *ə-t^{h}ak* 'upper part, prior time' [Matisoff *TSR:* 48]; WT *ltag-pa* 'the upper part / place', and / or *t^{h}eg-pa* 'lift, raise' (so *HST:* 110), JP (*lə^{31}-*) *t^{h}aʔ^{31}* 'above'. *HST:* 154 associates WT *ltag-pa* with → tuò$_1$ 拓 (t^{h}âk) 'to take up, lift' [Lie] which may perh. be a loan from a TB lg. Wáng Lì (1982: 253) and Matisoff (*BSOAS* 63.3, 2000: 363) relate this word to → dēng$_1$ 登 'ascend'.

zhì$_{16}$ 疐 (ṭi^C) **LH** ṭis, **OCM** *trits
'To slip, trip' [Shi]. This etymon is apparently parallel to, but distinct from, the syn. → dié$_3$ 跌, see there for more.

⋈ **zhì** 躓 (ṭi^C) **LH** ṭis (ṭɨs ?), **OCM** *trəts ?
'To stumble' [Zuo] which writes prob. the s. w. as 疐 above (so Duàn Yùcái).
[E] ST: WT *'dred-pa* 'to slip, slide, glide'; Kanauri *bret (*HST:* 135). This etymon occurs also in AA-PMon *t[-r-]lɯt -> Tai: Saek *thlɤɤt^{D2L}* < *d-*.

zhì$_{17}$ 懥懫 (tśi^C, ṭʰi^C) **LH** tśis, ṭʰis, **OCM** *tits, *thrits ?
'Be angry' 懥 [Shi], 懫 [Shu]. As in → zhì$_{16}$ 疐, the two graphs for this word are MC homophones but placed in different OC rime categories.

zhì$_{18}$ 質 (tśjet) **LH** tśit, **OCM** *tət — **[T]** *ONW* tśit
'Natural qualities' [Li], 'substance' [Yi], 'essential' [Lunyu].
[E] Etymology not clear. Unger (*Hao-ku* 39, 1992: 88) relates this word to WT *gšis* 'nature, temper, natural disposition' (the correspondence of the initials is unusual), while Baxter and Sagart (1998: 52) derive this word by t-prefix from → shí$_{12}$ 實 'fruit, solid, really'. Karlgren (1956: 16) connects this word with **zhì** 質 (ṭi^C) LH *ṭis*, *trəts 'pledge, security give, hostage' [Zuozhuan].

zhì$_{19}$ 躓 → **zhì**$_{16}$ 疐

zhì$_{20}$ 值 → **zhì**$_{22}$ 置

zhì$_{21}$ 植 (źjək, ḍɨ^C) **LH** dźɨk or ḍə^C, **OCM** *dək or *drəkh — **[T]** *ONW* dźik
'Aim, will' [Chuci] could belong either to → zhì$_{22}$ 置, or to → zhī$_2$ 之.

zhì$_{22}$ 置 (ṭɨ^C) **LH** ṭə^C, **OCM** *trəkh — **[T]** *MTang* ṭi, *ONW* tiə
'To set, place, arrange' [Shi].
[E] ST: WT *'jog-pa, bžag* 'to put, place, arrange'.
⋇ **zhí** 稙 (tjək) **LH** ṭɨk, **OCM** *trək — **[T]** *ONW* tik
'To sow or plant early' [Shi].
⋇ **zhí** 值植 (ḍɨ^C) **LH** ḍə^C, **OCM** *drəkh
'Hold upright' 值 [Shi], 植 [Shu], 'a pole' 植 [Li] (植 has also the MC reading *źjək*).
⋇ **zhí** 殖植 (źjək) **LH** dźɨk, **OCM** *dək — **[T]** *ONW* dźik
'To plant, cultivate' 殖 [Shu], 植 [Zhouli], 'raise, establish' 殖 [Guoyu], 植 [Zhouli]; 'to place' 植 [Lun]; 'grow, flourish' 植 [Huainan] (has also the MC reading *ḍɨ*^{C}).
⋇ **zhí, dé** 樴 (tśjək) **LH** tśɨk, **OCM** *tək
'A pole' [Zhouli].
[C] Possible allofams: → zhí$_8$ 職 'duty', → zhì$_{21}$ 植 'aim, will'. Syn. → shǔ$_7$ 樹.

zhì$_{23}$ 紩 → **zhǐ**$_9$ 黹

zhì$_{24}$ 彘 (ḍjäi^C) **LH** ḍas, **OCM** *d-lats
'Wild boar, pig' [OB, Li].
[E] KT: PKS *ʔdlaai^B 'wild pig', PHlai *lat 'wild boar'.

zhì$_{25}$, **zhài** 廌 (ḍje^B, ḍai^B) **LH** ḍɛ^B ?, **OCM** *dreʔ
'Some kind of small deer' [OB, SW]. When hunting, Shang dynasty kings would often kill this animal by the hundreds [OB], but later its identity was mostly forgotten. *SW* has the variant **xiè-zhì** 解廌 or 解豸 LH *gɛʔ-ḍɛʔ*. This riming binome makes it likely that the LH reading was *ḍɛʔ* rather than *ḍieʔ*. Curiously, in a passage in *Zuǒzhuàn* (Xuan 17) 豸 is supposedly a graphic loan for 解 'understand' which raises the suspicion that the latter ended up as a pre-syllable in the animal name due to a misunderstood gloss. Be that as it may, the element *xiè* 解 'distinguish, understand' may be responsible for the belief that this animal could tell straight from crooked, right from wrong.
[E] PMK *draay (Shorto 1976: 1048) > OMon *dray 'hog deer' (-> WB *darai* 'hog deer'), Biat *ɗraai* 'swamp deer', PVM *k-ɗeː 'deer' [Ferlus], Khm. *triəy* 'stag'. <> PYao *djai^2 'deer' [Purnell].

zhì₂₆ 雉 (ḍi^B) **LH** ḍi^B, **OCM** *driʔ
'Pheasant' [Shi].
[E] ST: WB *rac* 'pheasant', WT *sreg-pa* 'partridge', Lushai *va^L-hrit^L*, SChin-Areng *tari'* (Löffler *Anthropos* 55, 1960: 529), Mru *rik*, Garo *grit* 'pheasant' (*STC* no. 403; *HPTB:* 507), perh. also Chepang *rut-waʔ*. OC *-ʔ for PTB *-k is regular, see §3.2.2; for the initials, see §7.1.4.

zhì₂₇ 摯鷙 → **zhí₃** 執

zhì₂₈ 贄 → **zhí₃** 執

zhì₂₉ 遲 → **zhī₁₁** 遲

zhì₃₀ 制製 (tśjäi^C) **LH** tśas, **OCM** *ta(t)s or *kia(t)s ?
'To cut out' (as clothes) 制 [Shi], 製 [Zuo] > 'robe, cloak' 製 [Zuo] > 'regulate > institution, law' 制 [Zuo], sometimes thought to be related to → zhé₂ 折 (tśjät).
[T] *Sin Sukchu SR* tʂi (去); *MGZY* ji (去) [tʂi]; *ONW* tśei

zhì₃₁ 滯 → **chè₂** 徹撤

zhì₃₂ 緻 → **zhǐ₉** 黹

zhì₃₃ 織 → **zhī₁₂** 織

zhì₃₄ 識 → **shì₃₂** 識

zhōng₁ 中 (ṭjuŋ) **LH** ṭuŋ, **OCM** *truŋ, OCB *k-ljuŋ
'Be in the middle, middle, inside' 中 [BI, Shi]; 'inner garment, middle, medium' 衷 [Zuo]. Baxter (1992: 233) reconstructs *k-l- on the basis of a Han sound gloss (Coblin 1983: 156) and WT. This may be the same word as → zhōng₂ 忠 'sincere'.
[T] *Sin S. SR* tʂjuŋ (平), *PR, LR* tʂuŋ; *MGZY* jung (平) [tʂuŋ]; *MTang* ṭuŋ, *ONW* tuŋ

⋈ **zhòng** 中 (ṭjuŋ^C) **LH** ṭuŋ^C, **OCM** *truŋh
'Hit the center, hit, attain' [Zuo].
[<] exoactive of *zhōng* 中 *truŋ (§4.3).
[E] OC -> Tai: S. *troŋ^A1* 'hit the point' (<> Manomaivibool 1975: 148).

⋈ **zhòng** 仲 (ḍjuŋ^C) **LH** ḍuŋ^C, **OCM** *druŋh
'The 2nd (middle) of three or more brothers' [Shi], 'second of the month' [Shu].

[E] The etymology is not certain. PMiao *ntrɔŋ^A 'middle' is close to the OC form. Perh. related to TB-WT *gžuŋ* < *glyuŋ* or *gryuŋ* (?) 'middle' (<> *HST:* 53). But other etyma may be related instead: *STC:* (182 n. 479) relates *zhōng* to PTB *tuːŋ 'inside' (*STC* no. 390) > Manchati *toŋ(-riŋ)* 'inside', Chepang *duŋ* 'inside' (esp. of a dwelling) ⋈ *duŋʔ-* 'push to the center'; WB *ə-twaŋ^B* 'inside, inner part of a thing', Lushai *čʰuŋ^H* 'inside of anything' (<> *CVST* 2: 3); Rawang *ǎ-duŋ* 'middle' (*IST:* 55). The basic meaning of both these TB etyma is 'inside', not 'middle', however. Finally, there is yet another root meaning 'inside' < 'excavate' in AA, see under → chuán₁ 船 'boat'.

zhōng₂ 忠 (ṭjuŋ) **LH** ṭuŋ, **OCM** *truŋ
'Sincere, loyal, integrity' [Lunyu]. Perh. this is the s. w. as → zhōng₁ 中.
[E] ST: WT *gžuŋ* 'to attend to, sincere' (<> Bodman 1980: 123; *HST:* 107). CH -> Tai: S. *troŋ^A1* 'faithful, loyal' (Manomaivibool 1975: 148).

zhōng₃ 妐 (tśjuŋ) **LH** tśuŋ, **OCM** *tuŋ (= *C-juŋ ?)
'Father-in-law' [Lüshi].
[E] ST: Lepcha *(a-)jóŋ* 'uncle', Stod *əjəŋ* 'maternal uncle, father-in-law' (Unger *Hao-ku* 63, 1999: 246). The root initial was probably *j-, see §9.3.

zhōng$_4$ 終 (tśjuŋ) **LH** tśuŋ, **OCM** *tuŋ
'To end, terminate, complete, completely' [Shi]. Wáng Lì (1982: 608) derives → dōng$_1$ 冬 'winter' from this word.
[T] *Sin Sukchu SR* tʂjuŋ (平), *PR, LR* tʂuŋ; *MGZY* jung (平) [tʂuŋ]; *ONW* tśuŋ
[E] ST: Chepang *doŋʔ-* 'to end, cease' (period of time, spell of weather, speech), KN-Lai *doŋ / doʔŋ* 'to end' [*LTBA* 21.1: 210]. The connection with the following is not clear (for the difference in final consonants, see §6.7): WB *tum^C* ? 'be ended' (season) (*CVST* 2: 4), JP *t^{h}um^{31}* 'be ended, terminated', Lushai *č^{h}um^F* < *č^{h}umʔ* 'finish reaping', also Lai *t^{h}um* 'be ended' ⋇ *džə-t^{h}um* 'end something' [Van Bik *LTBA* 25.2, 2002: 106].

zhōng$_5$ 螽 (tśjuŋ) **LH** tśuŋ, **OCM** *tuŋ (= *C-juŋ ?), OCB *tjuŋ
'Locust, grasshopper' [Shi].
[E] ST: WB *kjuiŋ^B ~ gjuiŋ^B* 'locust' (*HST:* 104). The root initial was prob. *j-, see §9.3.

zhǒng$_1$ 冢塚 (tjwoŋ^B) **LH** ṭoŋ^B, **OCM** *troŋʔ
'A mound, peak; be great' 冢 [Shi]; 'a mound, tomb' 塚. This is still the word for 'tomb' in some dialects, e.g. Mǐn-Jiàn'ōu *tœyŋ^{21};* in most modern dialects, the word for 'tomb' is → fén$_4$ 墳. A possible Han period dialect variant is → lǒng 壟隴.
[E] ST: PTB *m/r-duŋ (*HPTB:* 310) > WT *rduŋ* 'a small mound, hillock', WB *toŋ* 'hill, mountain'. Note also PMY *tr^{2}ɔŋ^1 'mountain' [Purnell].

zhǒng$_2$ 種 (tśjwoŋ^B) **LH** tśoŋ^B, **OCM** *toŋʔ — **[T]** *ONW* tśuoŋ
'Seeds, cereals' [Shi] > 'descendants' [Guoce].
[E] <> AA-PVM *k-co:ŋʔ 'seed' [Ferlus].

⋇ **zhòng** 種 (tśjwoŋ^C) **LH** tśoŋ^C, **OCM** *toŋh
'To sow' [Shi], later also 'to plant' (a tree).
[<] exoactive of *zhǒng* 種 (tśjwoŋ^B) (§4.3).
[E] This may possibly be the same word as → zhǒng$_3$ 腫踵 'to swell', a seed then being something that first swells before growing sprouts.

[E] ST: Chepang *tuŋʔ-* 'to plant' ⋇ *duŋ* 'shoot, sprout' (growing) ⋇ *duŋ-* 'to sprout, grow' (esp. plant), Tangsa (Barish) *^{l}toŋ(ʔ)* (Weidert 1987: 22).

zhǒng$_3$ 腫踵 (tśjwoŋ^B) **LH** tśoŋ^B, **OCM** *toŋʔ
'Swell, swollen' 腫 [Zuo] > 'tumor' 腫 [Zhouli] > 'heel' [Li] > 'follow in the footsteps of' 踵 [Zuo]. For the semantic link between 'swollen' and 'heel' (< * 'swelling'), see Matisoff (*LTBA* 17.2, 1994: 144). There are other etyma for 'swollen' with the same rime: → yōng$_2$ 癰 and → wèng 瓮甕罋 'jar, swollen'.
[T] *Sin Sukchu SR* tʂjuŋ (上); *MGZY* jung (上) [tʂuŋ]

⋇ **zhòng** 尰 (źjwoŋ^B) **LH** dźoŋ^B, **OCM** *doŋʔ
'Be swollen, inflated' [Shi].
[<] endopass. of *zhǒng* 腫踵 (tśjwoŋ^B) (§4.6).

[E] ST: Limbu *thɔŋt-* 'to swell'.

zhòng$_1$ 重 (ḍjwoŋ^B) **LH** ḍoŋ^B, **OCM** *droŋʔ — **[T]** *ONW* duoŋ
'Heavy' [Shi] > 'important' [BI, Zuo], 'increase, to honor' [Zuo].

⋇ **chóng** 重 (ḍjwoŋ) **LH** ḍoŋ, **OCM** *droŋ
'Double, two, accumulate' [Shi] > 'twice, repeat' [Zuo].
[<] exoactive of *zhòng* 重 (ḍjwoŋ^B) (§4.3).
[T] *Sin Sukchu SR* dzjuŋ (平), *PR* dʐuŋ; *MGZY* cÿung (平) [dzjuŋ]; *ONW* duoŋ

[E] Etymology not certain, but note TB-WB *cum* 'double, form a pair' (for the final nasal, see §6.7).

zhòng₂ 湩 (ṭjwoŋ^C, tuŋ^C) **LH** ṭoŋ^C, toŋ^C, **OCM** *troŋh, *tôŋh
'Milk (of cows and mares)' [Mu tianzi zhuan], 'milk-like fluid' [SW] is a loan from some ancient Central Asian lg. (Pulleyblank 1962: 250ff). LH was probably *toŋ^C* because it is the simpler reading and MC *ṭioŋ^C* is the reading of the phonetic element.

zhòng₃ 尰 → **zhǒng₃** 腫踵

zhòng₄ 眾 (tśjuŋ^C) **LH** tśuŋ, **OCM** *tuŋh (*tjuŋh ?)
'Be numerous, all, the multitude (i.e. common people) [OB, BI, Shi].
[T] *Sin Sukchu SR* tʂjuŋ (去), *PR, LR* tʂuŋ; *MGZY* jung (去) [tʂuŋ]; *ONW* tśuŋ
[E] Prob. ST: WT *yoŋs* 'all, whole' (incl. multitude of people) ⋈ OTib. *yoŋ* 'in all, at all times, ever before'; for the initials, see §9.3.

zhōu₁ 舟 (tśjəu) **LH** tśu, **OCM** *tu
'Boat' [OB, Shi]. Acc. to the *Yìjīng,* a *zhōu* was originally a hollowed tree trunk (canoe) (Huáng Jīnguì, Shěn Xíróng *YYWZX* 1987.8: 41ff) like → yú₁₄ 俞.
⋈ **zhōu** 輈 (ṭjəu) **LH** ṭu, **OCM** *tru
'Carriage pole' [Shi] may perh. be cognate ('trunk' > 'pole' / 'canoe'?).
[E] AA: Khmer *du:k*, Bahn. *du:k 'boat', PVM *ɗo:k -> Tai-S. *tu:k^{D1}* 'boat' (Manomaivibool 1975: 159). For the lack of final consonant in CH, see §6.9. Syn. → chuán₁ 船.

zhōu₂ 洲 (tśjəu) **LH** tśu, **OCM** *tu
'Island in a river' [BI, Shi].
[T] *Sin Sukchu SR* tʂiw (平); *MGZY* jiw (平) [tʂiw]
Several synonyms with different vowels may be related:
⋈ **zhǔ** 渚 (tśjwo^B) **LH** tśɑ^B, **OCM** *taʔ
'Islet' [Shi], smaller than *zhōu* [EY 12.2].
⋈ **zhǐ** 沚 (tśɨ^B) **LH** tśə^B, **OCM** *təʔ
'Islet' [Shi], smaller than *zhǔ* [EY 12.2].
⋈ **chí** 坻 (ḍi) **LH** ḍi, **OCM** *dri (?)
'Islet' [Shi], smaller than *zhǐ* [EY 12.2].

zhōu₃ 周 (tśjəu) **LH** tśu, **OCM** *tiu — [T] *ONW* tśu
'To surround, encircle, circle, everywhere, curve (in the road)' [Shi].
⋈ **chóu** 綢 (ḍjəu) **LH** ḍu, **OCM** *driu — [T] *MTang* ḍeu < ḍu, *ONW* du
'To be wrapped around, pressed tightly together, dense' [BI, Shi], 'bind around' [Shi]; 'nightgown' 裯 [Shi] (Karlgren 1956: 17).
⋈ **chóu-móu** 綢繆 (ḍjəu-mjeu) **LH** -miu, **OCM** *driu-mriu, OCB *drjiw-mrjiw
'Be tied around' [Shi] (Baxter 1992: 513).
[E] Etymology not certain. Perh. connected with TB-WT *gču-ba* ~ *lču-ba* 'screw' ⋈ *gčud-pa* ~ *lčud-pa* 'to turn, twist, plait, braid'. Alternative: Tai: S. *diw³* 'strips of rattan or bamboo bent in a circle to which ribs of a cage are fastened' (McFarland: 330). Other alternative: note AA: Khmer *jwta* /cúuət/ 'to encircle or wrap (the head) in a length of cloth', the final *-t* would be lost in OC after a long vowel (§6.9); the initials could be reconciled if the source had *tj-* or *tšj-* (as opposed to *ts-*); a parallel case may be → zhōu₄ 周. A doubtful comparandum is → tāo₁ 綢.

zhōu₄ 周 (tśjəu) **LH** tśu, **OCM** *tiu
'To have aid, help' [Shi], 'relieve, succor' 賙 [Zhouli].
[E] Etymology not clear. Perh. the s. w. as → zhōu₃ 周 'surround' as words for 'help,

aid' are often derived from the notion 'next to, or around, a person' (see under → zuǒ 左 and → yòu$_2$ 右). Alternatively, note AA: Khmer *jwya* [ɟuuj] /cúuəj/ 'to aid, help, succor, rescue, save', the final *-j* would be lost in OC after the long vowel (§6.9). For the initials, see the comment under → zhōu$_3$ 周.

zhōu$_5$ 粥鬻 (tśjuk) **LH** tśuk, **OCM** *tuk — **[T]** *ONW* tśuk — **[D]** PMin *tšyk
'Rice gruel' [Zuo, Li].
[E] ST: Association with WT *t^hug-pa* 'soup, broth' (Bodman 1980: 172; *HST:* 137) is more straightforward than Karlgren's (1956: 17) derivation from → yù$_{22}$ 育毓鬻 'produce'.

zhōu$_6$ 皺 (tṣjəu) **LH** tṣu, **OCM** *tsru
'Wrinkles, furrows; to frown' [Tang: Han Yu] (Unger *Hao-ku* 35, 1986: 34).
⋇ **zhòu** 縐 (tṣjəu^C) **LH** tṣu^C, **OCM** *tsruh
'To crinkle, crepe' [Shi].
[<] exoactive of *zhōu* 皺 (tṣjəu) (§4.4).
[E] ? ST: Lepcha *a-sŭr* 'wrinkle'. Prob. related to → sù$_8$ 肅鱐 'shrivel, contract'.

zhǒu$_1$ 肘 (tjəu^B) **LH** ṭu^B, **OCM** *truʔ
'Wrist, elbow' [OB, Zuo].
[<] This is a tone B endoactive body part derivation (§3.3.2) from a root *tru which also underlies → chù$_2$ 絀, hence lit. 'the thing that is bending'. The phonetic in the latter may indicate some sort of velar in the complex initial, hence the word may be related to TB-WB *krui^C* 'bow down, stoop', and perh. also to WT *gru-mo* 'elbow' (*HST:* 70), which lit. means 'corner, angle', however. Note also PTai *x-: S. *k^hɔɔ^{C1}* (loan?). The Lushai word for 'elbow' *kiu^L* < *kiuʔ/h* may belong to the root → jiǔ$_3$ 糾. For a semantic parallel, see *wàn* 腕 (under → yū$_1$ 迂紆).

zhǒu$_2$ 帚 → **sāo$_1$** 搔

zhòu$_1$ 祝 → **zhù$_{10}$** 祝

zhòu$_2$ 晝 (tjəu^C) **LH** ṭu^C, **OCM** *tru(k)h ? — **[T]** *ONW* tu
'Time of daylight, daytime, morning, day' [BI, Shi].
[D] PMin *təu^C > Xiàmén, Fú'ān *tau^C* 'afternoon'.
[E] ST: WT *gdugs* elegant sp. 'midday, noon' (Bodman 1980: 172; *HST:* 61).
OC -> Tai: S. *truu^{B1}* 'early morning' (Manomaivibool 1975: 148).

zhòu$_3$ 冑 (ḍjəu^C) **LH** ḍu^C, **OCM** *d-luh or *d-juh ?
'Helmet' [Shi].
⋇ **yòu** 褎 (jiəu^C) **LH** ju^C, **OCM** *luh or *juh ?
'Full dress' [Shi].
⋇ **xiù** 袖褎 (zjəu^C) **LH** ziu^C, **OCM** *s-luh or *s-juh ?, OCB *zjus
'Sleeve' 褎 [Shi], 袖 [Zuo]. The role of *s- is not clear, perhaps iterative because sleeves come in pairs.
⋇ **tāo** 韜慆 (t^hâu) **LH** t^hou, **OCM** *lhû
'To wrap, cover' 韜 [Yili]; 'conceal, doubtful' 慆 [Zuo]. This word may be unrelated. This wf refers to any kind of 'cover' one slips over something.

zhòu$_4$ 冑 'descendant' → **yóu$_2$** 由

zhòu$_5$ 酎 → **láo$_3$** 醪

zhòu$_6$ 啄味 → **zhǔ$_7$** 斸

zhòu$_7$ 縐 → **zhōu**$_6$ 皺

zhū$_1$ 朱 (tśju) **LH** tśo, **OCM** *to — **[T]** *ONW* tśuo
'Be red, scarlet' [BI, Shi] may be an old basic word for 'red', rivaling → chì$_3$ 赤 (Baxter 1983).
[E] MK: PVM *tɔh 'red' [Ferlus]. → zhě 赭 may perh. be cognate.

zhū$_2$ 株 (tju) **LH** ṭo, **OCM** *tro or *trio ?
'Tree trunk' [Yi; Hanfei].
[E] Perh. AA: PMonic *chuuʔ 'wood'; in Mon also 'tree' (§5.10.4).

zhū$_3$ 誅 → **shū**$_1$ 殊

zhū$_4$ 豬 (tjwo) **LH** ṭɑ, **OCM** *tra
'Pig' [Zuo].
[T] *Sin Sukchu SR* tʂy (平); *MGZY* jÿu (平) [tʂy]
[D] CDC *cie*^{A1}; more archaic forms are preserved in southern dialects: M-Fúzhōu *ty*^{A1}, Cháozhōu *tɯ*^{A1}, Xiàmén *ti*^{A1}; X-Chángshā *ty*^{A1}; W-Kāihuà *tɑ*^{A1}
[E] Perh. a ST word: Mru *tia* '(wild) pig' (Löffler 1966: 146). Alternatively, → jiā$_8$ 豭 is said to be a dialect form of *zhū* [FY]; but since *jiā* appears to be much older than *zhū*, the latter could have developed *Cr- > tr- > ṭ which seems to be associated with rural words (§1.3.1; §7.1.4).

zhū$_5$ 諸 'all' → **duō** 多

zhú$_1$ 竹 (tjuk) **LH** ṭuk, **OCM** *truk
'Bamboo' [Shi].
[T] *Sin Sukchu SR* tʂy (入), *PR* tʂuʔ; *MGZY* jÿu (入) [tʂy]; *ONW* tuk
[E] PTai: S. *tɔɔk*^{D1L} < *prɔɔk, PKS *tʰruk 'bamboo strip'; or PTai *ʔdrok 'a kind of bamboo' (Luo Yongxian *MKS* 27, 1997: 293). <> PMiao *ɖəu^D.

zhú$_2$ 逐 (ḍjuk) **LH** ḍuk, **OCM** *d-luk
'To pursue' (animals, not men) [OB, Shu] (Schuessler 1987: 851; Qiu Xigui 2000: 213). See → zhuī$_2$ 追 for a near synonym which may be related in spite of the difference in finals.

zhú$_3$ 燭 (tśjwok) **LH** tśok, **OCM** *tok — **[T]** *ONW* tśuok
'Torch' [Li]. Note the syn. → zhuó$_3$ 灼 and the comment there.
[E] ST: PLB *duk 'burn, be blazing' ※ *ʔduk 'kindle, set on fire' [Matisoff *TSR:* 39] > WB *tok* 'blaze, flame, shine, glitter'; WT *dugs-pa* 'to make warm, to light, kindle'; Lushai *duk*^{L} 'be glowing with heat' (like ashes) (*HST:* 151). This word may have a wider distribution, note MK: Bahnar *tōk*, Stieng *dúk* 'to burn'.

zhú$_4$ 躅 (ḍjwok) **LH** ḍok, **OCM** *drok
'To check the foot, stop walking' [Yi], 'stamp the foot' [Xun].

※ **zhù** 住 (ḍju^C) **LH** ḍo^C, **OCM** *dro(k)h
'To stop' [Lie] > 'dwell' in a place [Nan Qishu].

※ **dòu** 逗 (dəu^C) **LH** do^C
'To stop, dwell, stay' [Hou Hanshu], perhaps a variant of *zhù* 住 (ḍju^C).

[E] ST: WT *'dug-pa* 'to sit, dwell, stay, remain' (*HST:* 141); or WT *rdog-pa* 'step, kick, walk'; JP *tʰoŋ*^{31} 'stop'.

zhú$_5$ 築 (tjuk) **LH** ṭuk, **OCM** *truk
'To stamp earth, earth up' (earth into walls) > 'build' [Shi]; 'beat, strike' [Zhouli].
[E] ST *truk: WT *rdug-pa* 'to strike against, to stumble at'; WB *tuik* 'strike against,

engage in combat'. For more ST cognates and / or parallel stems, see under → chù$_1$ 觸.

zhŭ $_1$ 主 (tśju^{B}) **LH** tśo^{B}, **OCM** *toʔ
'Master' [Shi].
[T] *Sin Sukchu SR* tʂy (上); *MGZY* jÿu (上) [tʂy]; *ONW* tśuo^{B}
[E] Etymology not clear; note these comparanda: (1) ST: WT *jo-bo* 'elder brother, lord, nobleman' ⋈ *jo-mo* 'mistress, lady, goddess'. (2) WT *t^{h}u* 'chief' (Peiros and Starostin *CAAAL* 22, 1984: 125). (3) MK: PMon *[d]ndooʔ Nyah Kur 'headman', Mon 'to teach, instruct'. (4) Tai: S. *čok^{4}* 'a leader, chief' (for final *-k*, see §3.2.2).

zhŭ $_2$ 拄 → **zhù** $_9$ 柱

zhŭ $_3$ 麈 (tśju^{B}) **LH** tśo^{B}, **OCM** *toʔ
'A large deer living in the mountains' [Yi Zhoushu]; its tail was used as a duster.
[E] This word is perh. connected to MK: PMonic *-truus 'boy, man', OKhmer *trus 'strong male of animals'; Kha Boloven *truy* 'male of deer', but we should expect an *r in the OC initial.

zhŭ $_4$ 煮 (tśjwo^{B}) **LH** tśɑ^{B}, **OCM** *taʔ ?
'To boil, cook' [Li].
[T] *Sin Sukchu SR* tʂy (上); *MGZY* jÿu (上) [tʂy] — **[D]** PMin *tšy^{B}
[E] Bodman (1980: 134) compares this word with WB *kyak*, Lushai *tlak^{L} < klak* 'to boil' (vegetables). If related, an OC *kiaʔ needs to be assumed which had palatalized by the time of the *Lǐjì*, but this would leave Lushai still unexplained.

zhŭ $_5$ 渚 → **zhōu** $_2$ 洲

zhŭ $_6$ 貯褚 (ṭjwo^{B}) **LH** ṭɑ^{B}, **OCM** *traʔ
'To store away, bag for clothes' 褚 [Zuo] (Mand. *chŭ*); 'to store, supplies, storehouse, ownership' [BI], 'to heap' 貯 [Guliang].
⋈ **chú** 儲 (ḍjwo) **LH** ḍɑ, **OCM** *dra
'To collect, store up' [Guiyu]. Karlgren (1956: 17) connects this word with *zhū* 諸 'all' (under → duō 多).

zhŭ $_7$ 斸 (ṭjwok) **LH** ṭok, **OCM** *trok
'To cut' 斸 [Guoyu], 'cut out, eradicate' 钃 (zhuó) [Xun].
⋈ **zhuó** 斲 (ṭåk) **LH** ṭɔk, **OCM** *trôk
'To hew, chop, carve' (trees, wood) 斲 [Shi], 'to carve, chisel' 琢 [Shi], 'break open' 斲 [Zuo]; 'to castrate' 斀 [SW: Shu], 'to beat, strike' 椓 [Shi].
[D] In some Yuè dialects this is the word for 'to chop, cut' (written → duò$_4$ 剁): HK col. *tœk^{D}*, Jiāngmén *tiœk^{B1}*, Dòumén (Zhen) *tiɔk^{D1}*, Băo'ān *tiɔ^{B2}*. The late word Mand. **duò** 剁 (tuâ^{B}) [GY] 'chop, cut' may be related.
[E] ST *trok: Mikir *artòk < r-tò/uk* 'chop off'.
= **zhuó** 啄 (ṭåk, tuk) **LH** ṭɔk, tok, **OCM** *trôk.
[D] Mĭn: Amoy col. *teʔ^{D1}*, lit. *tok^{D1}*, Zhāngzhōu *tøʔ*
'To peck up' [Shi].
⋈ **zhòu** 啄咮 (təu^{C}, ṭjəu^{C}) **LH** to^{C}, ṭu^{C}, **OCM** (*tô(k)s, i.e. prob.:) *tôh, *troh
'Beak' 咮 [Shi], 啄 [Han texts]. In MC, there is no div. II in the QY rime *-əu*.
[E] ST *trok: PLB *tok 'peck, strike with a curved instrument, hook onto', WB *tok-hra* 'woodpecker'.
[E] TB parallel stem: Lushai *tśu^{L} / tśuk^{L}* (Lorr. *chu*) 'to bite' (as snake), 'peck, strike with

a pecking motion, knock against, injure', WT *mčʰu* 'lip, bill or beak of birds' (the WT word is not related to → chún₁ 脣漘).

[C] For ST cognate and / or parallel stems, see under → chù₁ 觸 for an overview.

zhǔ₈ 屬 (tśjwok) **LH** tśok, **OCM** *tok
'To attach, connect' [Li], 'copulate' [Mozi], 'touch' [Zuo], 'to apply' (e.g. ear to wall) [Shijing].

× **shǔ** 屬 (źjwok) **LH** dźok, **OCM** *dok — **[T]** *ONW* dźuok
'Be connected, attached to' [Shi], 'belong to' [Shu]; ('fit': 'socket' and related items:) 'vulva, penis, to copulate' (the *SW* radical of *shǔ* is 'tail' – *GSR* 1224s).
[<] endopass. voicing of *zhǔ* 屬 (§4.6).

~ **zhuó** 豚 (tjuk)
'Vulva, penis' [GY], lit. 'socket' acc. to Mei Tsu-Lin 1979.
[E] ST: PTB *s-tu 'vagina' (*HPTB:* 247), WT *stu*, Chepang *tuʔ* 'female genitals', perh. also Lushai *ču*^{L} (Lorrain *chhu*) as in *ču*^{L}*-hmul*^{R} 'female pubic hair' (*hmul*^{R} 'hair').

× **zhù** 祝 (tśjuk) **LH** tśuk, **OCM** *tuk
'To bind, attach' [Shi]. Rather than being cognate to *zhǔ,* this word may perh. instead be the base for → zhù₁₀ 祝 'prayer', i.e. 'binder'.
[T] *Sin Sukchu SR* tʂy (入); *MGZY* jÿu (入) [tʂy]

[E] ST ?: Perh. WT *gtogs-pa* 'to belong to, be part of' × *tʰog-pa* 'to gather' (*HST:* 52), *rdogs-pa* 'to bind, fasten, tie'. <> Li F. (1976: 41) associates Tai-S. *tʰuuk*^{DIL} < *tʰ- 'right, cheap, to touch' with → chù₁ 觸, but the S. word is only in its last sense a loan from ST, while 'right, cheap' belongs with WB *tʰuik* 'be worth, have a certain value, be worthy, be fit' and with Mon *tʰɔik* 'be good, right'.

TB has a parallel stem *dzo:k, *tso:k (*STC* note 178): Chang *su:k* 'vulva', JP *məcóʔ* 'socket, vagina', PLB *ɟok > WB *cok.* With final *ʔ: Chepang *tuʔ* 'vagina' (Weidert 1987: 27), Lushai *čʰu*^{F} (Lorr. *chhu*) < *čʰuuʔ* 'vulva' (Benedict *LTBA* 5.1, 1979); Benedict also adds WT *stu* 'vulva'.

[C] This stem may be related to → zhù₇ 注 'touch'. For alternatives, see → dào₁ 倒.

zhù₁, chú 宁 (ḍjwo(ᴮ)) **LH** ḍɑ(ᴮ), **OCM** *dra(ʔ)
'Space between gate and gate-screen' [Liji]. Perh. related to → cháng₅ 場 [ḍaŋ].

zhù₂ 佇 → **zhù₁₃** 著

zhù₃ 羜 (ḍjwoᴮ) **LH** ḍɑᴮ, **OCM** *draʔ
'Lamb' [Shi] (syn. **tà** 羍 (tʰât) LH *tʰɑt* 'lamb' [OB, SW]).
[E] Etymology not certain; perh. ST: WT *ra-ma* 'goat', Kanauri *la.* For the initial correspondence, see §7.1.4; §12.9 WT (6).

zhù₄ 苧紵 (ḍjwoᴮ) **LH** ḍɑᴮ, **OCM** *draʔ — **[T]** *ONW* døᴮ
'Ramie' 苧, 紵 [Shi], 'cloth' or 'rope' made thereof [Hanshu], 苧 [Shiji].
[D] M-Xiàmén *tɯ*^{B2}*;* Zhōngbǎo *kyʔ*^{D2} (common in Kè-Mǐn, Branner 1995: 268).
[E] ? ST: WT *ras* 'cotton cloth'; Lushai *la*^{L} < *laʔ/h* 'cotton'. For the initial correspondence, see §7.1.4; §12.9 WT (6). <> PMiao *ndoᶜ 'hemp' (discussed by Strecker *LTBA* 10.2, 1987: 49).

zhù₅ 注 (tśjuᶜ, tjuᶜ) **LH** tśoᶜ, ṭoᶜ, **OCM** *toh, *troh
'To pour' [Shi].

= **zhù** 鑄 (tśjuᶜ) **LH** tśoᶜ, **OCM** *toh
'To cast' (metal) [BI, Zuo].

⋈ **zhǔ** 斗 (tśju^B) **LH** tśo^B, **OCM** *toʔ

'Ladle' [Zhouli] is a tone B noun derived from *zhù,* lit. 'the thing which does the pouring'.

⋈ **dǒu** 斗 (təu^B) **LH** to^B, **OCM** *tôʔ

'Bushel, ladle, name of a constellation' [Shi].

[E] Bodman (1980: 172) compares WT *čʰu* 'water' ⋈ *'čʰu-ba, bčus* 'to ladle or scoop water, irrigate' and also includes *dǒu* in this wf. TB *lu 'to pour, cast' has initial *l and belongs to → yù$_4$ 浴 'to pour, bathe'.

zhù$_6$ 注 (tśju^C, ṭju^C) **LH** tśo^C, ṭo^C, **OCM** *toh, *troh

'To flow into, join, meet' intr. (as a river flows into another / the ocean) [Meng 3A, 4; Shanhaijing 5]. 'To conduct water' [Shi] may be this word or belong to → zhù$_5$ 注 'to pour'.

[E] Etymology not certain. On the one hand, this word seems to be the cognate of WT *mdo* 'point where two valleys / rivers meet', i.e. 'confluence, lower part of valley'; it could be the s. w. as → zhù$_7$ 注 'be touched'. On the other hand, this may be the same word as → zhù$_5$ 注 'to pour' which, however, has a different WT cognate.

zhù$_7$ 注 (tśju^C, ṭju^C) **LH** tśo^C, ṭo^C, **OCM** *toh, *troh

'To apply' [Zuo], 'be touched' [Zhuang], 'bring together' [Zhouli].

⋈ **dòu** 鬭 (təu^C) **LH** to^C, **OCM** *tôh

'To come in contact with, meet, next following day' [OB].

[E] ST: WB *tui^C* 'touch lightly', Lushai *tuuk^F* 'to touch' (as in a game). This stem may be related to → zhǔ$_8$ 屬 'attach, connect'.

zhù$_8$ 住 → **zhú$_4$** 躅

zhù$_9$ 柱 (ḍju^B) **LH** ḍo^B, **OCM** *droʔ

'Pillar' [Yili].

[T] *Sin Sukchu SR* dẓy (上); *MGZY* cÿu (上) [dẓy]

⋈ **zhǔ** 拄 (ṭju^B) **LH** ṭo^B, **OCM** *troʔ

'To prop up, support' [Guoce] (Karlgren 1956: 9).

[E] ST: TB-WB *tuiŋ* 'post, column'; SChin Daai *ktuŋ* 'post' [Hartmann ICSTLL 1999: 6], JP *toʔ^31 < tok^31* ⋈ *ʃə^55-to^55* 'pillar'. For the TB final *-ŋ*, see §3.2.4). Perh. related to → zhuó$_9$ 棁.

zhù$_{10}$ 祝 (tśjuk) **LH** tśuk, **OCM** *tuk

'Prayer; invoker' [BI, Shi], 'to pray' [Zuo]. This word may perh. be the same etymon as 'to bind, attach' (i.e. 'a binder'), see → zhǔ$_7$ 屬.

[T] *Sin Sukchu SR* tṣy (入); *MGZY* jÿu (入) [tṣy]

⋈ **zhòu** 祝 (tśjəu^C) **LH** tśu^C, **OCM** *tukh

'To curse' [Shi] (Karlgren 1956: 12).

[<] perh. extrovert (§4.3).

⋈ **dǎo** 禱裯 (tâu^B/C) **LH** tou^B, tou^C, **OCM** *tûʔ/h

'To pray' 禱 [Shi]; 'a horse sacrifice consisting of a prayer 裯 promising a sacrificial animal offering' [SW; *Zhōulǐ*] (Sterckx *EC* 21, 1996: 64).

[E] There is no outside etymological connection, similarity with AA-Pearic *tro:* 'to pray' is prob. coincidence.

zhù$_{11}$ 祝 (tśjuk) **LH** tśuk, **OCM** *tuk

'Cut off' [Gongyang].

[E] ST *tu(k): Lushai *tuk*^{L} 'cut, chop', JP *t*^{h}*u*^{33} 'cut'. For ST cognate and / or parallel stems, see under → chù$_1$ 觸 for an overview.

zhù$_{12}$ 助 (dẓjwo^C) **LH** dẓɑ^C, **OCM** *dzrah
'Aid, help' (in a cooperative endeavor) [Shi], almost certainly a semantic generalization of → chú$_3$ 鋤耡. — [T] *Sin Sukchu SR* dẓu (上); *MGZY* cu (上) [dẓu]

ꭗ **lǜ** 勴 (ljwo^C) **LH** liɑ^C, **OCM** *rah
'To help' [SW] (Gong Hwang-cherng 1999: 9).

zhù$_{13}$ 著 (ṭjwo^C) **LH** ṭɑ^C, **OCM** *trakh
'To place, order of place, position' [Zuo].
[E] ST: PTB *ta (*STC* no. 19) > WT *sta-gon* 'preparation' ꭗ *stad-pa* 'to put on, lay on', Tsangla *t*^{h}*a* 'to put, place', Kanauri *ta* 'place, set, appoint', Kachin *da* 'put, place', PLB *ta^2, WB *tha*^{B} < *ʔta*^{2} 'put, place', Lushai *daʔ*^{L} 'to put, place, set, put aside' (*Comparative Vocabulary of Five ST Languages* 2: 5).

ꭗ **zhuó** 著 (ṭjak) **LH** ṭɑk, **OCM** *trak — [T] *ONW* tak
'To place, put, apply' [Li].

ꭗ **zhuó** 著 (ḍjak) **LH** ḍɑk, **OCM** *drak — [T] *MTang* ḍak, *ONW* dak
'To attach, come in contact with' [Li], 'be attached to' [Guangyun] (Baxter and Sagart 1998: 46)
[<] endopass. voicing of *zhuó* 著 (§4.6).

ꭗ **shù** 署 (źjwo^C) **LH** dźɑ^C, **OCM** *da(k)h
'To place, position' [Guoyu].

ꭗ **zhù** 佇竚 (ḍjwo^B) **LH** ḍɑ^B, **OCM** *draʔ
'To stand in attendance' 佇 [Shi]; 'to stand' 竚 [Chuci].

zhù$_{14}$ 箸 (ḍjwo^C) **LH** ḍɑ^C, **OCM** *drah
'Chopsticks' [Li]. Norman (1988: 76): "Acc. to a Mǐng work by Lù Róng, the word *zhù* was tabooed on boats because it was homophonous with *zhù* 住 'stop'; it was replaced by a word of opposite meaning *kuài* 快 '(go) fast'," hence *kuàizi* 筷子.

zhù$_{15}$ 壴 → **shù**$_7$ 樹

zhù$_{16}$ 鑄 → **zhù**$_5$ 注

zhuā 抓 (tṣau$^{A/B/C}$), **LH** tṣɔu^B/h ?, **OCM** *tsrûʔ/h ? — [D] M-Xiàmén *tsua*^{A1}
'To grasp' [Zhuang].
[E] This word is cognate to → zhǎo$_1$ 爪 [tṣauʔ] *tsrûʔ 'claw', may even be the s. w. Derivations and cognates are perh. → cháo$_2$ 巢 [dẓau] *dzrâu 'nest', and → chāo$_2$ 剿勦 'snatch', in spite of different OC vowels. <> This word is prob. related to Tai: S. *cau*^{B1} '(of a bird) grasp, perch, sit' (Manomaivibool 1975: 155), Hlai *tsau*^{3} 'perch' [Matisoff 1988c: 300].

zhuān 專 (tśjwän) **LH** tśuan, **OCM** *ton
'Alone' [Lun], 'entirely, exclusively' [Meng], 'have sole power, make sole object' [Zuo].
[E] MK: Khmer *-tola* /-taaol/ 'be alone, single', Mod. Khmer *tò:l*.

zhuǎn$_1$ 轉 (ṭjwän^B) **LH** ṭuan^B, **OCM** *tron — [T] *MTang* ṭuan, *ONW* tuan
'To turn around, turn away' [Shi]. Acc. to Norman (1986: 382) the Northern Mǐn 'softened initial' *t̬- points to OC prenasalization which is supported by Yao *dzwon*^{5} < *ndz- 'return'.

ꭗ **chuán** 傳 (ḍjwän) **LH** ḍuan, **OCM** *dron
'To transmit' [Lunyu], 'remove' [Li].

[T] *Sin Sukchu SR* dʐyen (平); *MGZY* cwÿan (平) [dʐyɛn]; *MTang* ḍuan, *ONW* duan

⋇ **zhuàn** 傳 (ḍjwän^C) **LH** ḍuan^C, **OCM** *drons

'A record' [Zuo].

[<] exopass. of *chuán* 傳 (ḍjwän) (§4.4), lit. 'what has been transmitted'.

⋇ **zhuàn** 傳 (ṭjwän^C) **LH** ṭuan^C, **OCM** *trons

'Relay' (of post etc.) [Zuo].

[E] ST: Old Tib. *'drul* 'to transmit, communicate' [Li / Coblin 1987: 415]. An allofam is perh. → tuán$_1$ 團摶漙敦 'round' (so Karlgren 1956: 13).

zhuǎn$_2$ 腨 'cut meat' → **tuán$_1$** 團摶漙敦

zhuàn$_1$ 傳 → **zhuǎn$_1$** 轉

zhuàn$_2$ 縳 → **tuán$_1$** 團摶漙敦

zhuàng$_1$ 狀 (dʐjaŋ^C) **LH** dʐɑŋ^C, **OCM** *dzraŋh

'Form, shape' [Guoyu], 'depict, describe' [Zhuang], 'appearance, record of merits' [Zuozhuan].

[T] *Sin Sukchu SR* dʐaŋ (去), *PR* dʐwaŋ; *MGZY* c^hang (去) [dʐAŋ]; *ONW* dẓaŋ (?)

[E] AA: Khmer *rāṅa* /rííəŋ/ 'body build, form, figure, shape, cut, seize, dimension, height, stature, bearing'. Khmer -> Tai: S. *raaŋ*^{B2} 'form, shape' (Manomaivibool 1975: 157), and perh. also to WB *caŋ* 'frame, stage', consequently 狀 is prob. also cognate to → chuáng$_1$ 床 'bed'. Perh. connected with → fāng$_4$ 方. For the initials, see §7.1.5.

zhuàng$_2$, chòng 揰 → **chuáng$_2$** 揰

zhuàng$_3$, hòng 戇 (xuŋ^C, ṭåŋ^C) **LH** hoŋ^C, ṭɔŋ^C, **OCM** *hôŋh ~ trôŋh

'Stupid' [Xun].

[E] AA: PMonic *trɔɔʔ 'foolish, insane' (for finals, see §6.5.2).

zhuī$_1$ 隹鵻騅 (tświ) **LH** tśui, **OCM** *tui

'Bird with a short tail' [SW]; 'a kind of bird' ('turtle dove'?) 鵻 [Shi]; (horse of that bird's color? >) 'horse of mixed gray and white color' 騅 [Shi].

[E] Perh. ST *twil (?): WT *mčʰil-ba* 'a little bird'.

zhuī$_2$ 追 (ṭwi) **LH** ṭui, **OCM** *trui

'To pursue' (men, enemy troops, not animals) [OB, Shi] > 'to escort, recollect, be mindful' (Schuessler 1987: 855; Qiu Xigui 2000: 213).

[E] Perh. related to TB-Lushai *čʰui*^{H} (Lorr. *chhui*) < *chui* 'to track, trace, follow up, follow a trail', Chepang *dyul-* 'follow a trail...'. However, if related to Chepang we should expect a Lushai final *-l;* the role of the *r in the OC initial is not clear. See → zhú$_2$ 逐 for a near synonym which may be related in spite of the difference in finals.

zhuì$_1$ 墜 (ḍwi^C) **LH** ḍus, **OCM** *drus

'To fall' [Lun], 'fall down' [Zhouli], 'throw down' [Shu].

[E] AA: Khmer OKhmer *ruḥ* /ruh/ 'to fall, drop' ⋇ *jruḥ* /cruh/ 'to fall, drop, come off...' intr. ⋇ *jamruḥ* /cumruh/ 'to let fall, knock down...' tr.; PNBahn. *ruh 'waterfall', PVM *ruh 'to fall' intr. AA final *-h* can derive from *-s,* but that seems not to be the case here. For the initials, see §7.1.4. Alternatively, the word may instead belong to AA-OKhmer *tol,* Khmer *ṭwla* /dùuəl/ 'to fall down, drop'.

zhuì$_2$ 硾 → **chuí$_1$** 垂

zhuì$_3$ 贅 → **zhuó$_{10}$, zhuì** 綴

zhūn$_1$ 淳 → **chún$_2$** 淳

zhūn₂ 惇 → **dūn₁** 敦惇

zhūn₃ 肫 'sincere' → **dūn₁** 敦惇

zhuō₁ 穛 → **gǔ₁₂**, **zhuō** 穛

zhuō₂ 卓 (ṭåk) **LH** ṭɔk, **OCM** *trâuk
'Distant' [Chuci], 'high' [Lunyu].
[T] *Sin Sukchu SR* tʂwaw, *LR* tʂwawʔ; *MGZY* jwaw (入) [tʂwaw]; *ONW* täk

⋟ **chuò** 逴 (ṭʰåk) **LH** ṭʰɔk, **OCM** *thrâuk
'Far, distant' [Chuci].

[C] → tì₃ 逖 is prob. unrelated.

zhuó₁ 勺酌 → **zhuó₂** 汋

zhuó₂ 汋 (tśjak, źjak, jiak) **LH** tśɑk, jɑk, **OCM** *kiauk ?, *jauk
'Ladle' [Zhuang], 'ladle out, pour out' [Guliang].

⋟ **zhuó** 勺酌 (tśjak) **LH** tśɑk, **OCM** *kiauk ?
'To pour into a cup, draw water' 酌 [Shi], 'to ladle, serve wine' 勺 [Li], 'ladle out, pour out' 汋 [Guliang].
[E] CH -> Tai: S. *tak*^{D1S} < *t- 'to dip up water' (Li F. 1976: 41) has been borrowed after palatalization of the initial velar.

⋟ **sháo** 勺杓 (źjak) **LH** dźɑk, **OCM** *diauk or *C-jauk
'Ladle 杓 [Li], 汋 [Zhuang], 'ladle, cup' 勺 [Zhouli]. If we follow the first possible etymology below, the QY initial could be explained as a palatalized earlier *kiok.

[E] ST: Two TB etyma 'ladle' could be related to CH:
(1): PTB *s-kyok 'ladle' (Benedict 1976: 184; Bodman 1980: 128) > WT *skyogs-pa* 'scoop, ladle', WB *yok* 'ladle', JP *tʃo*^{31} 'ladle'.
(2): Lepcha *lăk* 'to pour (out)' (liquid, not metal) (Unger *Hao-ku* 33, 1986), Chepang *lhayk* 'ladle' (Bodman 1980: 128), PL *ʔ-ljuk^{L} 'ladle'. These items may possibly belong to → yú₁₆ 揄 'scoop out' instead.

zhuó₃ 灼 (tśjak) **LH** tśɑk, **OCM** *tiauk ?
'To burn, illuminate, brightly, clearly' [Shu], 'brilliant' [Shi].

⋟ **dì** 的 (tiek) **LH** tek, **OCM** *tiâuk
'Bright, brilliant' [Li], 'mark in target'.

[E] Prob. not related to → zhú₃ 燭.

zhuó₄ 斫 (tśjak) **LH** tśɑk, **OCM** *tauk ? — **[T]** *ONW* tśak
'To cut, hack' [Mo].
[E] ST: PTB *tuk (*STC* no. 387) > PLB *ɴtök ~ *ʔtök 'to cut by a blow, hack away at' [Matisoff *TSR:* 49], WB *tok* 'fillip, cut by a single light blow, gnaw', JP *tok*^{55} 'cut into pieces'; Garo *dok* ~ *dak* 'knock, pound'. For alternative comparanda and / or parallel stems, see under → chù₁ 觸 for an overview.

zhuó₅ 斱 → **chá₂** 槎

zhuó₆ 椓 → **zhǔ₇** 斸

zhuó₇ 啄 → **zhǔ₇** 斸

zhuó₈ 豚 → **zhǔ₈** 屬

zhuó₉ 梲 (tśjwät) **LH** tśuɑt or tśyat, **OCM** *tot
'Short pillars supporting rafters' [Lunyu].
[E] ST: WT *rtod-pa* 'a post' (Unger *Hao-ku* 39, 1992). Perh. related to → zhù₉ 柱.

zhuó$_{10}$, **zhuì** 綴 (tjwät, tjwäi^C) **LH** ṭuat, ṭuas, **OCM** *trot(s)
'To sew, stitch, connect' [Shi, Shu]; only MC *tjwäi^C*: 'needles used as tallies' 錣 [Guan].

ﬠ **zhuì** 贅 (tśjwäi^C) **LH** tśuas or tśyas, **OCM** *tots
'To unite, together' [Shi].
[E] ST: WT: *gtod-pa, btod-pa* 'to tether, tie up, stake' ﬠ *rtod-pa* 'to tether, a stake or peg' (Bodman 1980: 175; *HST:* 150). Bodman adds **zhuó** 錣 (ṭwat) LH *ṭuat* ~ *ṭiot* 'sharp point at end of whip'.

zhuó$_{11}$ 濯 (ḍåk) **LH** ḍɔk, **OCM** *d-liauk, OCB *lrewk
'Be clean, brilliant, bright, glossy; to moisten, wash' [Shi] (Baxter 1992: 522).

ﬠ **zhào** 濯 (ḍau^C) **LH** ḍau^C, **OCM** *d-liaukh
'To wash clothes' [Li].
[<] exoactive / caus. of *zhuó* 濯 (ḍåk) (§4.3), lit. 'make bright'.

ﬠ **dí** 翟 (diek) **LH** dek, **OCM** *liâuk, OCB *lewk
A long-tailed pheasant which lives in the mountains [Shi, SW], 'feather' of such a pheasant [Shi]. This animal is possibly related to the above words because if it had no striking shiny feathers, it would have been of no interest. For a semantic parallel (shiny ~ bird), see → hè$_2$ 鶴 'crane'. In this phonetic series 翟, MC *ḍ-* seems to derive from some OC L-like initial. Perh. → shuò$_7$ 爍 and → dí$_7$ 滌 'to clean' are related.
[E] ? ST: WB *hlyo* (i.e. *-au*) 'wash' (hair, clothes).

zhuó$_{12}$ 穛 → **gǔ**$_{12}$, **zhuó** 穛

zhuó$_{13}$ 斲 → **zhǔ**$_7$ 斸

zhuó$_{14}$ 著 → **zhù**$_{13}$ 著

zī$_1$ 仔 → **zài**$_2$ 載

zī$_2$ 滋 → **qī**$_5$ 漆

zī$_3$ 玆 'black' → **zī**$_8$ 菑

zī$_4$ 玆 'year' → **zài**$_4$ 再

zī$_5$ 嗞 → **wèi**$_3$ 味

zī$_6$ 咨 'sigh' → **jiē**$_5$ 嗟

zī$_7$ 資 (tsi) **LH** tsi, **OCM** *tsəi or *tsi, OCB *tsjij — **[T]** *ONW* tsi
'Property, resources' [Shi], 'provisions, materials' [Zuo], 'possess, rely on' [Meng], 'furnish, give' [Guoce]; Mand. 'money, capital'.

ﬠ **zī** 穦 (dzi) **LH** dzi, **OCM** *dzəi or *dzi
'Provisions, store of grain' [SW: Shi]. Perh. related to → jī$_9$ 積.
[E] ST *tsəj: PTB *(t)sa:y ﬠ *(d)za:y 'property, livestock, talent'. For the vowel correspondence, see §11.6. Matisoff (1995: 42f) connects the TB etymon with → cái$_1$ 才材財, but the rimes do not agree; some of the TB words there are here associated with → xī$_{11}$ 犀 'rhinoceros'.

zī$_8$ 菑 (tṣɨ) **LH** tṣə, **OCM** *tsrə
A field cleared by slash and burn (Wáng Lì 1982: 96): 'to break the soil, recently broken field, field under cultivation for one year' [Shi].
[<] r-caus. of *zāi* 災 'conflagration' (§7.5).

※ **zī**, **zì** 菑椔 (tṣɨ^C) **LH** tṣə^C, **OCM** *tsrəh
('Cleared by burning':) 'dead tree stumps' 菑 [Shi], 椔 [EY] (Wáng Lì).

※ **zī** 緇 (tṣɨ) **LH** tṣə, **OCM** *tsrə
'Black' (< color of burnt soil?) [Shi] is perh. the s. w. as *zī* 菑 above.

※ **zī** 玆 (tsɨ) **LH** tsiə, **OCM** *tsə — **[T]** *ONW* tsiə
'Black' [SW: Zuo] may be a mere variant of *zī* 緇 above.

zī₉ 緇 → **zī₈** 菑

zǐ₁ 子 (tsɨ^B) **LH** tsiə^B, **OCM** *tsəʔ, OCB *tsjəʔ
'Offspring' (Sagart 1999: 164): Child, son' [OB, Shi], 'young of animals' [Shi], 'plant seeds, eggs'. Syn. → ér₄ 兒, → jiǎn₁ 囝.
[T] *Sin Sukchu SR tsɿ* (上); *MGZY dzʰi* (上) [tsɿ]; *ONW tsiə*
[D] In Mand. suffixed to nouns as diminutive marker, to persons, animals, things in general (Norman 1988: 114). Acc. to *FY* 10.4, *zǎi* 崽 is a southern dialect form of the Han period, still used today (§9.1.1).
[<] endoactive noun (§4.5.1), lit. 'one who has come forth' (i.e. offspring).
[E] ST *tsə 'to come forth' (as child at birth). In this ST root the 'offsping, child' is the agent, note WT *čʰuŋ-ma-la bu btsas* 'a son (*bu* [subj.]) has come forth (*btsas*) for (*-la*) the wife (*čʰuŋ-ma*)', i.e. 'the wife has given birth to a son' (Jaeschke p. 434). By contrast, with the verb → shēng₂ 生 'give birth', the woman is the agent.
ST: PTB *tsa (*STC* no. 59) > WT *tsʰa-bo* 'grandchild', Atsi *tso*, Maru *tsō*, PBurm. *tsa^B; Lushai *fa^F* 'child, son, daughter', JP *gə^31-ʃa^31* 'child'.

※ **zì** 子 (tsɨ^C) **LH** tsiə^C, **OCM** *tsəh
'To treat as a child' [Shu].
[E] exoactive / putative of *zǐ* 子 (tsɨ^B) (§4.3).

※ **cí** 慈 (dzɨ) **LH** dziə, **OCM** *dzə
'To be loving, kind' [Zuo].
[<] endopass. of the active root *tsə (§4.6; see comment above)
[E] ST: WT *mdza'-ba* 'to love' (as friends, kinsmen), WB *ca* 'to have tender regard for, feel for' (*STC* no. 67).

※ **zì** 孳字 (dzɨ^C) **LH** dziə^C, **OCM** *dzəh
'To breed' 孳 [Shu], 字 [Yi]; 'nurture, love' 字 [Shi]; 字 ('progeny':) 'compound character of script consisting of two or more elements' as opposed to *wén* 文 'graph consisting of a single element' [SW] (W. Boltz in M. Loewe, ed. 1993: 431).
[T] *Sin Sukchu SR dzɿ* (去); *MGZY tsʰi* (去) [dzɿ]; *ONW dziə*
[<] exoactive (tr.) of *cí* 慈 (dzɨ) (§4.3).
[E] The 'softened initial' of Northern Mǐn dialects *d̯z- may suggest OC prenasalization which is supported by the Yao loan *dzaaŋ⁶* < *ndz- (Norman 1986: 383). This would agree with WT *mdza'-ba* (see *cí* above). <> WB *ca* 'writing, letter' is apparently a CH loan (Sagart 1999: 211).

[E] ST *tsə: WT *btsa'-ba, btsas* 'to come forth' (as child at birth).
[C] To the same root may belong the wfs → zāi₂ 栽哉 'to plant', → cái₁ 才材財 'be well endowed, ability, talent'; possibly also → cǎi₁ 采 'harvest'.

zǐ₂ 秄 → **zì₄** 剚

zǐ₃ 姊 (tsi^B) **LH** tsi^B, **OCM** *tsiʔ, OCB *tsjijʔ
'Elder sister' [Shi].
[E] MK: PMonic *kmciiʔ 'sister' (in Old Mon). OC and MK agree exactly (*tsiʔ / ciiʔ, the configuration Mon *km- precedes also other terms for humans). Phonetically less

direct is the connection with PTB *dzar (*STC* no. 68) from a hypothetical ST *dzər ~ *tsər (*STC:* 170 n. 455).

zǐ₄ 秭 → **jǐ₆** 濟

zǐ₅ 訾 (tsje[B]) **LH** tsie[B], **OCM** *tseʔ

'Defame, slander' [Shi].

⋇ **cí** 疵 (dzje) **LH** dzie, **OCM** *dze

'Flaw' [Shi], 'defect' [Zuo].

⋇ **sí** 訾 (zje) **LH** zie, **OCM** *?

'Fault' [Li]. However, the MC initial *z-* derives from OCM *s-l- or *s-j- and hence does not agree with the other words.

zì₁ 自 (dzi[C]) **LH** dzi[C], **OCM** *dzih ?

'Self' [OB, Shi] is used adverbially, the near syn. *jǐ* 己 is a personal pronoun (Pulleyblank 1995: 83). The original graph is identical with → bí 鼻 'nose' (*SW*), the drawing of a nose. This has occasioned much speculation about a possible phonetic and etymological relationship of *zì* with *bí* (e.g. MC *dzi*[C] < OC *sb-?, note also WT *sbrid-pa* 'sneeze'), but phonologically these two syllables are difficult to reconcile; in fact, Xǔ Shèn (*SW*) says nothing about the sounds, he prob. only pointed out that the *graphs* are the same. Perh. there was originally a mental association between graph and meaning as one customarily points to one's nose when pointing to oneself.

[T] *Sin Sukchu SR* dzɿ (去); *MGZY* tsʰi (去) [dzɿ]; *ONW* dzi

[E] The homophone *zì* 自 'from' [OB, Shi] is written with the same graph; perh. 'from' and the adverbial 'self' are the same word, 'self' is the source location from where the action originates. (Note German 'er hat das *von sich aus* gemacht' [lit. 'he did this *out from* self'] = 'er hat das *selbst* gemacht' ['he did it *himself*']).

zì₂ 字孳 → **zǐ₁** 子

zì₃ 胔 (dzje[C]) **LH** dzie(C), **OCM** *dze(h)

'Bones with meat on' 骴 [Zhouli], 髊 [Lü], 'carcass, bones of an animal' 胔 [Li] is perh. cognate to → jí₁₄ 脊 'spine'. This word is distinct from → cí₂ 胔.

zì₄ 剚 (tṣɨ[C]) **LH** tṣə[C], **OCM** *tsrəh

'Pick, hoe' [Guanzi].

⋇ Perh. **zǐ** 耔 (tsɨ[B]) **LH** tsiə[B], **OCM** *tsəʔ ?

'To hoe up earth around a plant' [Shi].

[E] This wf is perh. related to WT *tsʰi-ba* 'furrow' (in a plowed field).

zì₅ 積 → **jī₉** 積

zì₆ 菑椔 → **zī₈** 菑

zōng₁ 宗 (tsuoŋ) **LH** tsouŋ, **OCM** *tsuŋ

'Ancestral temple, ancestral, lineage' (which performs ancestor worship), 'royal clan; to venerate, honor' [OB, BI, Shi].

[T] *Sin Sukchu SR* tsuŋ (平); *MGZY* dzung (平) [tsuŋ]; *ONW* tsouŋ

[E] ST: WT *rdzoŋ(s)* 'castle, fortress' as administrative center, WB *(ə-)cʰoŋ* 'a building'. A Chinese temple is conceived and designed as an abode for deities or ancestors, from a simple structure to a palace (L. Thompson 1996: 60). "To govern the [*zōng* 'lineage temple'] was to govern the town" (Chang K.C. 1976: 70).

zōng₂ 稯 → **jù₇** 聚

zǒng 縱 → **sǒng**$_2$ 慫聳駷 (2)

zòng$_1$ 從 → **cóng**$_1$ 從

zòng$_2$ 縱 → **sōng**$_3$ 鬆

zòng$_3$ 綜 → **zāo**$_2$ 遭

zōu$_1$ 陬 (tsəu, tsju) **LH** tso, tsio, **OCM** *tso
'Angle, corner' [Guoce].
[E] ST: WT *zur* 'edge, corner, side, aside' ⋈ *'dzur-ba* 'to give or make way, evade'; Lepcha *sur* 'angle, corner' (Unger *Hao-ku* 35, 1986: 33).

zōu$_2$ 騶 (tṣjəu) **LH** tṣu, **OCM** *tsro — **[D]** Mǐn: Xiàmén (lit.) *tsɔ*^{A1}
'Groom' [Shi].
⋈ **cǒu-mǎ** (**qū-mǎ**) 趨馬 (tsʰəu^B-ma^B) **LH** tsʰo^B-ma^B, **OCM** *tshôʔ
'Manager of horses' [Shi].
[E] The words are derived from → chú$_4$ 芻 'hay, fodder > feed / raise' (horses, cattle), but *cǒu-mǎ* may have been influenced by items under → zǒu 走 'to run'.

zǒu 走 (tsəu^B) **LH** tso^B, **OCM** *tsôʔ.
'To run' [BI, Shi, classical CH] > 'to go' [Yili].
[T] *Sin Sukchu SR* tsəw (上); *MGZY* dzʰiw (上) [tsəw]; *ONW* tsou^B
[D] Mand. 'to walk' where 'run' is replaced by → pǎo 跑; southern dialects use *xíng* 行 for 'walk' (Norman 1988: 197). M-Xiàmén lit. *tsɔ*^{B1}, col. *tsao*^{B1} 'to run'.
⋈ **zòu** 奏 (tsəu^C) **LH** tso^C, **OCM** *tsôh
'To hasten forward, bring forward, offer, make a report, play music' [BI, Shi].
[<] exoactive of *zǒu* 走 (tsəu^B) (§4.3).
⋈ **qù** 趣 (tsʰju^C) **LH** tsʰio^C, **OCM** *tshoh
'Hasten to' [Shi].
[T] *Sin Sukchu SR* ts'y (去); *MGZY* tshÿu (去) [ts'y]; *MTang* tsʰy, *ONW* tsʰuo
⋈ **qū** 趨 (tṣʰju) **LH** tṣʰo, **OCM** *tshro
'To hasten, run to' [Shi], 'strive for, aim' [Meng].
[T] *Sin Sukchu SR* ts'y (平); *MGZY* tshÿu (平) [ts'y]
⋈ **zòu** 驟騶 (dẓjəu^C) **LH** dẓu^C, **OCM** *dzroh, OCB *dzrjos
'Fast-running' (horse) [Shi], 'quickly, suddenly' [Zuo], 騶 [Li].
[E] This group belongs to a large ST wf whose root and core meaning is represented by → sōu$_3$, sǒu 搜 'to rouse'. It is more immediately related to → sù$_6$ 速 'quick'.

zòu$_1$ 奏 → **zǒu** 走

zòu$_2$ 驟騶 → **zǒu** 走

zū 蒩 → **jū**$_5$ 苴

zú$_1$ 卒 (tsjuet) **LH** tsuit, **OCM** *tsut, OCB *Stjut
'To finish, end, die' [Shi, Zuo] (esp. of a ruler, of vegetation in winter [Zuo]); 'finally, in the end' [Zuo]; 'exhaust > entirely, utterly' [Shi]. Caus. 'bring to an end, accomplish' [Shi]. For the final *-t, see §6.2.2.
[E] ST: Limbu *cu:tma* (*cu:t-*) 'be finished, be completed'. Bodman (1969: 327) relates this word to WT *sdud-pa* 'to close, conclude, terminate'.
⋈ **cuì** 瘁悴 (dzwi^C) **LH** dzuis, **OCM** *dzuts
'To be exhausted, suffering' 瘁 [Shi], 'distressed' 悴 [Meng].

⋇ **qiú** 酋 (dzjəu) **LH** dzu, **OCM** *dzu
'To end' (one's life naturally) [Shi].

⋇ **zāo** 傮 (tsâu) **LH** tsou, **OCM** *tsû
'Complete, end' [Xun].

[C] This wf is perh. related to → zào$_2$ 造 and → zào$_3$ 造; possible allofam → qiū$_4$ 秋.

zú$_2$ 卒 → **zāo$_2$** 遭

zú$_3$ 足 (tsjwok) **LH** tsiok, **OCM** *tsok
'Lower leg with foot, leg, foot' (of person, bed, vessel) [OB, Shi], also of hills (foothills).
[E] Etymology not certain. *Zú* agrees with a MK etymon except for the final consonants: PMonic *juŋ 'lower limb, leg, foot, base' (in Mon), also 'foot of a hill' (Nyah Kur); Wa-Lawa-Bulang *joŋ 'foot', Semai /jugŋ/, Temiar /juk/ (from -ŋ).

zú$_4$ 足 (tsjwok) **LH** tsiok, **OCM** *tsok
'Enough, sufficient' [OB, Shi]; caus. in tone C LH *tsio*^{C} 'to complete, form' [Zuo] (Downer 1959: 282).
[T] *Sin Sukchu SR* tsy (入), *PR, LR* tsuʔ; *MGZY* dzÿu (入) [tsy]; *ONW* tsuok
[E] Prob. ST: WT *čʰog-pa* 'be sufficient' (*HST:* 144).

zú$_5$ 族 → **jù$_7$** 聚

zǔ 祖 (tsuo^B) **LH** tsɑ^B, **OCM** *tsâʔ — **[T]** *ONW* tso
'Deceased grandfather, ancestor' [BI, Shu], 'sacrifice to the spirits of the road' [Shi]. Both meanings are derived from the basic notion 'move on'.
[<] endoactive noun of a root *tsa (§4.5.1), lit. 'the one who is gone'.

⋇ **cú** 徂殂 (dzuo) **LH** dzɑ, **OCM** *dzâ
'To go, go away, march' 徂 [Shi] > 'to pass away, die' 殂 [BI, Shu]; a Han period dialect word for 'to marry' (of a woman) in Qí [FY 1, 14].
[<] ? endopass. of a root *tsa (§4.6), perh. lit. 'to get to be gone'.

zuān 鑽 (tsuân) **LH** tsuɑn, **OCM** *tsôn
'To bore, perforate' [Zhuang] > 'penetrate' [Lunyu].

⋇ **juān** 鐫 (tsjwän) **LH** tsyan, **OCM** *tson
'Chisel, sharp point' [Mo].

[E] ST: PTB *tsow 'thorn' (*STC* no. 276; *HST:* 46) > Chepang *cuʔ*, Bodo *suʔ* (Weidert 1987: 26); Mikir *arsō* < *r-sō* 'sharpen' ⋇ *iŋsō* < *m-sō* 'cutting edge', WB *chu*^{B} 'thorn' ⋇ *cu*^{B} 'prick, pierce' < PLB *tsu^2. WT *mtsʰon* 'any pointed or cutting instrument'.
[C] The word → zuò$_6$ 鑿 (dzâk) 'to bore, chisel out' may be related.

zuǐ 嘴 (tswie^B ?)
'Mouth, beak, snout' [JY], a late word (Wáng Lì 1982: 116) which is prob. the s. w. as
= **zuǐ, zī** 觜 (tswie^B, tsie) **LH** tsye^B ?, tsie ?, **OCM** *tsoiʔ ?, *tse or *tsai?
'Beak' [Li].
[E] This word is perh. related to WT *mtsʰul-pa* 'lower part of face, muzzle, beak'.

zuì$_1$ 醉 (tswi^C) **LH** tsuis, **OCM** *tsuts — **[T]** *ONW* tsui
'Drunk' [Shi].

⋇ **cuì** 啐 (tsʰuậi^C) **LH** tsʰuəs, **OCM** *tsʰûts
'To taste, drink' 啐 [Liji].

[E] ST: WB *cut* 'suck, imbibe, absorb'.
[C] This wf belongs perh. to the same root as → cuì 淬 'dip into' because of the common

notion that one 'soaks' in vices, note → yín$_3$ 淫; *cuì* 啐 and 淬 may be the same word. Alternatively perh. connected with WT *bzi* 'intoxication' (Unger *Hao-ku* 36, 1990: 62).

zuì$_2$ 最 → **jù$_7$** 聚

zuì$_3$ 罪 (dzuậi^B) **LH** dzuəi^B, **OCM** *dzûiʔ — **[T]** *ONW* dzuɑi
'Crime, offense, guilt' [BI, Shi]. The original graph for *zuì* looks similar to *huáng* 皇 so that Qín Shǐ Huángdì 秦始皇帝 replaced it with 罪 which was the original graph for 'fish trap' [SW] (Wáng Lì 1982: 406); the element *fēi* 非 is therefore not phonetic. The etymology is not clear, unless it is a ST word cognate to Lushai *sual^R* 'bad, wicked, evil, wrong, to misbehave, sin' ⋈ *sual^H* 'to rape' (a woman).

zūn 尊 (tsuən) **LH** tsuən, **OCM** *tsûn
'To honor, perform (a sacrifice)' > 'ritual vessel' [OB, BI, Shi].
[T] *Sin Sukchu SR* tsun (平); *MGZY* dzun (平) [tsun]; *ONW* tson,
[E] ST: WT *btsun-pa* 'noble, honorable' ⋈ *mts^{h}un* ~ *btsun* 'household gods, soul of ancestors' (*HST:* 95).

zǔn 撙 (tsuən^B) **LH** tsuən^B, **OCM** *tsûnʔ
'Regulated, to regulate' [Li, Guoce].
[E] ST: WT *ts^{h}ul* 'way of acting, conduct, right way, orderly' (*HST:* 123).

zuó 昨 (dzâk) **LH** dzɑk, **OCM** *dzâk
'Yesterday' [Zhuang]. Sagart (1999: 67, 160) relates *zuó* to → xī$_6$ 昔 (sjäk) 'previously, yesterday', among others.
[T] *Sin Sukchu SR* dzaw (入), *LR* dzawʔ; *MGZY* tsaw (入) [dzaw]

zuǒ 左 (tsâ^B) **LH** tsɑi^B, **OCM** *tsâiʔ.
'Left (side)' [BI, Shi] > ('consider or treat as left' = 'unfavorable' >) 'not approve, to oppose' [OB] (Takashima *EC* 5, 1979–1980: 54), 'disagree' *xiāng-zuǒ* 相左 [Zuo]; 'crooked' (road) [Hanshu].
[T] *Sin Sukchu SR* tsɔ (上), *LR* tsɔ; *MGZY* dzo (上) [tsɔ]; *ONW* tsɑ
[D] Y-Guǎngzhōu ^{35}*tsɔ^{B1}*, K-Méixiàn *tsɔ^B*
[N] For the meanings, see comments under → yòu$_2$ 右. The OB graph is a drawing of the left hand of oneself, from one's own perspective, just as *yòu$_2$* 右 'right' (side) shows the right hand in this fashion, to which 'mouth' (= 'phonetic loan') was later added to distinguish it from *yòu$_1$* 又 which was commonly used to write 'and, furthermore'. Since 'mouth' was already used for 'right', another mark had to be found for the graphic differentiation of 'left', but the choice of *gōng* 工 'work' has occasioned much speculation.
[E] <> This word also occurs in PTai *zai^{C2} 'left'.

⋈ **zuǒ** 左佐 (tsâ^C) **LH** tsɑi^C, **OCM** *tsâih
'To help, assist, aid' (< be to one's (left) side) [BI, Shi]. The semantics are the mirror image of → yòu$_2$ 右.

zuò$_1$ 佐 → **zuǒ** 左

zuò$_2$ 坐 (dzuâ^B) **LH** dzuɑi^B, **OCM** *dzôiʔ
'To sit' [Shi].
[T] *Sin Sukchu SR* dzwɔ (上); *MGZY* tswo (上) [dzwɔ]; *ONW* dzuɑ
[D] PMin *dzoi^B

⋈ **zuò** 坐 (dzuâ^C) **LH** dzuɑi^C, **OCM** *dzôih
'Seat' [Zuo] (Downer 1959: 275).

[<] exopass. derivation (§4.4), lit. 'what is sat on'.

[E] Bodman (1980: 134) compares *zuò* to WT *sdod-pa* 'to sit', but this raises many phonological difficulties (for the initials, see §5.7). This word is shared with PKS *dzuːi[6] 'to sit'.

zuò$_3$ 作 (tsâk) **LH** tsɑk, **OCM** *tsâk

'To get up' (in the morning) [Lunyu] > 'to start, start work' [Shu], 'to sprout' [Shi] > 'to do, perform, work, set up, build' [OB, BI, Shi] > 'act as, be' [Shu]; intr. 'to be active' [Shi]. Some OB forms of the graph suggest a hand, palm facing up, holding a small plant or stick. Also other words meaning 'do, make' develop the meaning 'function as, act as, to be', see → wéi$_3$ 為, → yì$_6$ 役.

[T] *Sin Sukchu SR* tsaw (入), tsɔ (去), tsu (去), *PR* tsɔ, *LR* tsawʔ; *MGZY* dzaw (入) [tsaw], dzu (去) [tsu]

ꭗ **cuò** 措 (tsʰuoᶜ) **LH** tsʰɑᶜ, **OCM** *tshâkh

'To establish' [Yi], 'to place' [Lunyu], 'lay aside, cease' [Li].

[E] This etymon may perh. be related to WT *mdzad-pa* 'to do, act', Kukish *ca*, Mru *caŋ* 'to do, make' (Löffler 1966: 140), yet there are phonological and semantic difficulties, therefore the TB items are more likely related to → sī$_1$ 司.

zuò$_4$ 飵 → **jǔ$_1$** 咀

zuò$_5$ 酢醋祚胙 → **cuò$_4$** 錯

zuò$_6$, záo 鑿 (dzâk) **LH** dzɑk, **OCM** *dzâuk

'To bore, chisel out' [Shi]; 'a borer' [Lunheng].

[E] <> TB-WB *chok* 'chisel'.

ꭗ **zào** 鑿 (dzâuᶜ) **LH** dzɑuᶜ

'A hole' [Zhouli] (Downer 1959: 275).

[<] exopass. of *zuò, záo* 鑿 *dzâuk (§4.4), lit. 'what has been bored'.

[C] An allofam is prob. → zuān 鑽 'to bore'. Note also AA-OKhmer *coḥ* /coh/ 'to bore, pierce' (-> Tai: S. /cɔ̀q/ 'to make a hole' [Jenner / Pou 1982: 67]); this may possibly be an area etymon.

ENGLISH INDEX

CORRIGENDA

p. 6 — 4th line from bottom, change "we find the interrogative xī..." to "we find occasionally the interrogative xī..."

p. 19 — 'Fire' huǒ ... *hmə̂iʔ (not *hməiʔ)
'Lose' sàng ... *smâŋh (not *smaŋh)
'Neglect' huāng ... *hmâŋ (not *hmaŋ)

p. 68 — middle: 'You' should be "ɜɛ rǔ 汝", not "ɜɛ rú 如"

p. 154 — **bǎi**$_2$ change "(baɨ^{B}) LH bɛ^{B}, OCM brêʔ" to "(paɨ^{B}) LH pɛ^{B}, OCM prêʔ"

p. 168 — **bǐng**$_1$ change "(bjɐŋ^{B}) LH bɨaŋ^{B}, OCM *braŋʔ" to "(pjɐŋ^{B}) LH pɨaŋ^{B}, OCM *praŋʔ"

p. 177 — change "**cǎo**$_2$ 操 (tsʰâu^{B}) **LH** tsʰɑu^{B}, **OCM** *tshâuʔ" to "**cāo** 操 (tsʰâu) **LH** tsʰɑu, **OCM** *tshâu"
Change: "**[<]** exopass. of *cǎo* 操 (tsʰâu^{B})" to "**[<]** exopass. of *cāo* 操 (tsʰâu)."

p. 256 — **gōng**$_8$ last line of entry: change "MK → Tai" to "Khmer → Tai."

p. 347 — 5th line from top under **lèi** 淚 'tear': change "泣 *khrap" to "泣 *khrəp".

p. 361 — Second to last line: change "Acc. to (Downer 1959" to "Acc.to Downer (1959"

p. 415 — **píng**$_4$ should be MC "(bieŋ)", not "(bieŋ^{C})"

p. 423 — **qì**$_8$ 氣 should read "LH kʰɨs, OCM *khə(t)s", not "LH kɨs, OCM *kə(t)s"

p. 462 — sǎ under **shī**$_{12}$: OCM should be *srêʔ/h, not *sreʔ/h

p. 488 — **tái**$_3$ 嬯臺 should be "(dậi), LH də, OCM *də̂", not "(tậi) LH tə, OCM *tə̂"

p. 518 — middle (line 23 from top): should read "Méixiàn *ŋai*^{B}", not "Méixiàn *ŋa*^{B}"

ABOUT THE AUTHOR

Axel Schuessler studied Classical Chinese, Tibetan, and other Asian languages, as well as Indo-European linguistics and Sanskrit at the Universität München, where he received his Ph.D. in Chinese philology in 1966. He is now professor emeritus of Wartburg College in Iowa, where he taught until 1996. He has written articles mostly on Old Chinese phonology and has compiled an inventory of the Early Zhou Chinese lexicon (*Dictionary of Early Zhou Chinese,* University of Hawai'i Press, 1987).